New Zealand (Aotearoa)

Bay of Islands & Northland
(p139)

Auckland Region
(p76)

Waikato & Coromandel Peninsula
(p181)

Rotorua & the Bay of Plenty
(p291)

Taupo & the Ruapehu Region
(p264)

Taranaki & Whanganui
(p231)

The East Coast
(p332)

Marlborough & Nelson
(p402)

Wellington Region
(p366)

The West Coast
(p446)

Christchurch & Canterbury
(p479)

Queenstown & Wanaka
(p572)

Dunedin & Otago
(p537)

Fiordland & Southland
(p608)

D0103884

Charles Rawlings-Way
Brett Atkinson, Andrew Bain, Peter Dragicevich,
Samantha Forge, Anita Isalska, Sofia Levin

Contents

WHITE-WATER RAFTING P63

JONATHAN NODEN-WILKINSON/SHUTTERSTOCK ©

MARCONI COUTO DE JESUS/SHUTTERSTOCK ©

STANISLAV FOSENBAUER/SHUTTERSTOCK ©

WAITANGI DAY P160

MILFORD SOUND P619

Contents

Contents

ON THE ROAD

ABEL TASMAN NATIONAL PARK P435

TRAM IN CHRISTCHURCH P482

Contents

Welcome to New Zealand

Get ready for mammoth national parks, dynamic Māori culture, and world-class surfing and skiing. New Zealand can be mellow or action-packed, but it's always epic.

Walk on the Wild Side

There are just 4.8 million New Zealanders, scattered across 268,021 sq km: bigger than the UK with one-fourteenth of the population. Filling in the gaps are the sublime forests, mountains, lakes, beaches and fiords that have made NZ one of the best hiking (locals call it 'tramping') destinations on the planet. Tackle one of the epic 'Great Walks' – you might've heard of the Heaphy and Milford Tracks – or spend a few hours wandering along a beach, paddling a canoe or mountain biking through some easily accessible wilderness.

Food, Wine & Beer

British-influenced classics like fish and chips aren't going anywhere, but NZ gastronomy has come a long way, baby. Chefs in Auckland, Wellington and Napier borrow influences from as far afield as South Pacific islands and western Europe for creative takes on locally sourced lamb and seafood like abalone, oysters and scallops. Meanwhile, the vegetarian and vegan food scenes grow evermore prominent and inventive. Wash it all down with coffee culture, an edgy craft-beer scene and legendary cool-climate wines (like sublime sauvignon blanc and pinot noir).

Māori Culture

New Zealand's all-conquering All Blacks would never have become back-to-back rugby world champions without their unstoppable Māori players. But this is just one example of how Māori culture impresses itself on contemporary Kiwi life: across NZ you can hear Māori language, watch Māori TV, join in a *hāngi* (Māori feast) or catch a cultural performance with song, dance and a blood-curdling *haka* (war dance). Māori design continues to find expression in *tā moko*, Māori tattooing (often applied to the face) and the delicate artistry of bone, shell and *pounamu* (greenstone) sculpture.

The Real 'Big Easy'

New Zealand isn't a place where you encounter many on-the-road frustrations: buses and trains generally run on time; main roads are in good nick; ATMs proliferate; pickpockets, scam merchants and bedbug-ridden hostels are few and far between; and the food is unlikely to send you running for the nearest public toilets (usually clean and stocked with the requisite paper). And there are no snakes, and only one poisonous spider – the endangered katipo. This decent nation is a place where you can relax and enjoy (rather than endure) your travels.

By Anita Isalska, Writer

New Zealand lives up to the hype – not easy, in a country that wins lavish praise from millions of visitors. This land is more magical than its movie sets: volcanoes smoulder, fiords are pinch-yourself pretty and beaches have dreamy surf. But it's NZ's understated charms that reeled me in, like New Zealanders' disarming honesty and humour, and the pioneer spirit that endures in remote areas. Tolerant and eco-conscious NZ feels like a sanctuary in a turbulent world. I'd hide out here forever.

For more about our writers, see p704

Above: Routeburn Track (p592)

New Zealand

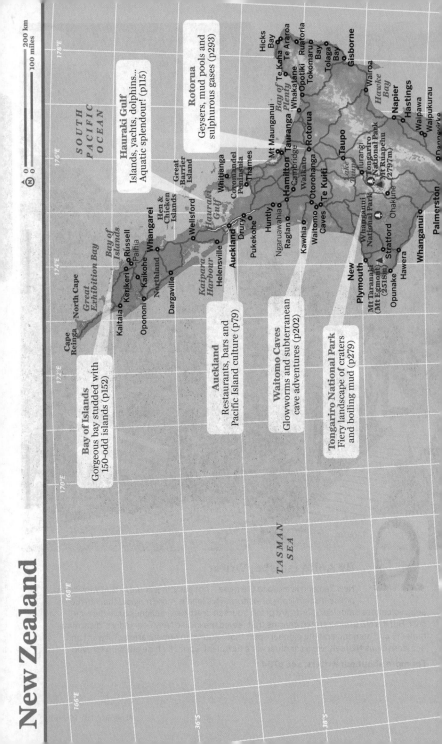

Bay of Islands
Gorgeous bay studded with
150-odd islands (p152)

Auckland
Restaurants, bars and
Pacific Island culture (p79)

Waitomo Caves
Glowworms and subterranean
cave adventures (p202)

Tongariro National Park
Fiery landscape of craters
and boiling mud (p279)

Hauraki Gulf
Islands, yachts, dolphins...
Aquatic splendour! (p115)

Rotorua
Geysers, mud pools and
sulphurous gases (p293)

0   100 miles
0   200 km

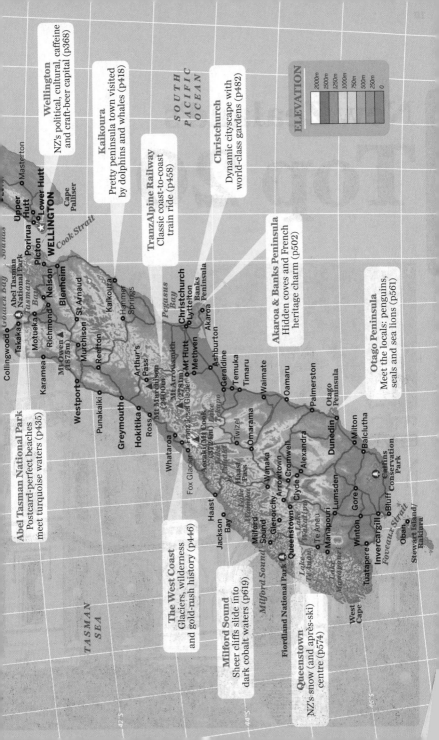

Wellington
NZ's political, cultural, caffeine and craft-beer capital (p368)

Kaikoura
Pretty peninsula town visited by dolphins and whales (p418)

TranzAlpine Railway
Classic coast-to-coast train ride (p458)

Christchurch
Dynamic cityscape with world-class gardens (p482)

SOUTH PACIFIC OCEAN

ELEVATION

2000m
1500m
1250m
1000m
750m
500m
250m
0

Abel Tasman National Park
Postcard-perfect beaches meet turquoise waters (p435)

Akaroa & Banks Peninsula
Hidden coves and French heritage charm (p502)

Otago Peninsula
Meet the locals: penguins, seals and sea lions (p561)

The West Coast
Glaciers, wilderness and gold-rush history (p446)

TASMAN SEA

Milford Sound
Sheer cliffs slide into dark cobalt waters (p619)

Queenstown
NZ's snow (and après-ski) centre (p574)

Collingwood ○ *Golden Bay*
Takaka ○ Abel Tasman National Park
Motueka ○ *Tasman Bay*
Karamea ○ Richmond ○ Nelson ○ Blenheim
Mt Owen ▲ (1875m) ○ St Arnaud
Westport ○ Murchison ○ Reefton
Punakaiki ○ Mt Murchison ▲ ○ Arthur's Pass
Greymouth ○ (2400m) ○ Mt Arrowsmith ▲
Hokitika ○ (2781m) ○ Mt Hutt ○ Methven
Ross ○ Whataroa ○
Fox Glacier ○ Franz Josef Glacier
Aoraki/Mt Cook ▲ (3724m) *Lake Tekapo*
Haast ○ *Lake Pukaki* Twizel ○
Jackson Bay ○ *Haast Pass* Omarama ○
Milford Sound ○ Wanaka ○ Cromwell ○
Milford ○ Glenorchy ○ Arrowtown ○ Clyde ○ Alexandra
Fiordland National Park ○ Queenstown ○ *Lake Wakatipu*
Lake Te Anau Te Anau ○ Lumsden ○
Lake Manapouri Manapouri ○ Gore ○
West Cape ○ Tuatapere ○ Winton ○ Invercargill ○
Foveaux Strait Oban ○
Stewart Island/ Rakiura

Hamner Springs ○
Kaikoura ○
Pegasus Bay
Christchurch ○ Banks Peninsula
Lyttelton ○ Akaroa ○
Ashburton ○
Geraldine ○ Temuka ○ Timaru ○
Waimate ○
Oamaru ○
Palmerston ○
Otago Peninsula
Milton ○ Dunedin ○
Balclutha ○
Catlins Conservation Park
Bluff Conservation Park

Cape Palliser
Upper Hutt ○ ● Lower Hutt
Porirua ○ ● Picton
Porirua ● WELLINGTON
Cook Strait
Masterton ○

New Zealand's
Top 20

Wellington

1 One of the coolest little capitals in the world, windy Wellington (p368) lives up to the hype. It's long famed for a vibrant arts-and-music scene, fuelled by excellent espresso, a host of craft-beer bars, and more cafes and restaurants per head than New York. Edgy yet sociable, colourful yet often dressed in black, Wellington is big on the unexpected and unconventional. Erratic weather only adds zest to the experience...though it plays havoc with all those hip haircuts. Parliamentary Library, New Zealand Parliament (p368)

Tongariro National Park

2 At the centre of the North Island, Tongariro National Park (p279) presents an eye-popping landscape of alpine desert punctuated by three smouldering volcanoes. Often rated as one of the world's best single-day wilderness walks, the challenging Tongariro Alpine Crossing skirts the base of two of the mountains and provides views of craters, brightly coloured lakes and the vast Central Plateau. The crossing's popularity has skyrocketed, causing the DOC to step in and limit visitor numbers. Fortunately, there are numerous other ways to explore this alien landscape. Blue Lake, Tongariro Northern Circuit (p282)

Waiheke Island & the Hauraki Gulf

3 A yachtie's paradise, the island-studded Hauraki Gulf (p115) is Auckland's aquatic playground, sheltering its harbour and east-coast bays and providing ample excuse for the City of Sails' pleasure fleet to breeze into action. Despite the busy maritime traffic, the gulf has its own resident pods of whales and dolphins. Rangitoto Island is an icon of the city, its near-perfect volcanic cone providing the backdrop for many a tourist snapshot. Yet it's Waiheke, with its beautiful beaches, acclaimed wineries and upmarket eateries, that is Auckland's most popular island escape.

Waiheke Island (p117)

Urban Auckland

4 Held in the embrace of two harbours and built on the remnants of long-extinct volcanoes, Auckland (p76) isn't your average metropolis. It's regularly rated one of the world's most liveable cities, and while it's never going to challenge NYC or London in the excitement stakes, it's blessed with good beaches, wine regions and a thriving dining, drinking and live-music scene. Cultural festivals are celebrated with gusto in ethnically diverse Auckland, which has the biggest Polynesian population of any city in the world.

Kaikoura

5 First settled by Maōri with their taste for seafood, Kaikoura (p418; meaning 'to eat crayfish') is NZ's best spot for both consuming and communing with marine life. Feast on crayfish, go on a fishing excursion, or take a boat tour or flight to see whales, dolphins, seals and marine bird life. In NZ, marine mammal tour operators adhere to strict guidelines developed and monitored by the country's DOC. Following a severe earthquake in November 2016, Kaikoura has also rebounded to become a fascinating destination to observe the profound impact of seismic activity.

Seal at Kaikoura

Bay of Islands

6 Turquoise waters lapping pretty bays, dolphins frolicking at the bows of boats, pods of orcas gliding gracefully by: chances are these are the kinds of images that drew you to NZ in the first place, and these are exactly the kinds of experiences that the Bay of Islands (p152) delivers so well. Whether you're a hardened sea dog or a confirmed landlubber, there are myriad options to tempt you out on the water to explore the 150-odd islands that dot this beautiful bay. Dolphins in the Bay of Islands

Milford Sound

7 Whatever the weather, Milford Sound (p619) will dazzle you with its collage of waterfalls, forbidding cliffs and dark cobalt waters, with the iconic profile of Mitre Peak rising above. Fiordland's waterfalls are even more spectacular when fed by rain, but blue-sky days set rainbows sparkling from their mist. Either way, keep your eyes peeled for seals, dolphins and the elusive Fiordland crested penguin, especially if you're exploring NZ's most famous fiord by kayak.

Queenstown

8 Queenstown (p574) may be world-renowned as the birth-place of bungy jumping, but there's more to NZ's adventure hub than leaping off a bridge attached to a giant rubber band. The Remarkables mountain range provides a jagged indigo backdrop to days spent skiing, hiking or mountain biking, before dining in cosmopolitan restaurants or party-ing in some of NZ's best bars. Keep the adrenaline flowing with hang gliding, kayaking or river rafting, or ease into your NZ travels with more sedate detours to Glenorchy or historic Arrowtown.

Rotorua

9 The first thing you'll notice about Rotorua (p293) is the sulphur smell – this geothermal hotspot whiffs like rotten eggs. But as the locals point out, volcanic by-products are what everyone is here to see: gushing geysers, bubbling mud, steaming cracks in the ground, boiling pools of mineral-rich water... Rotorua is unique: a fact exploited by some fairly commercial local businesses. But you don't have to spend a fortune – there are plenty of affordable (and free) volcanic encounters to be had in parks, Māori villages or just along the roadside. Champagne Pool, Wai-O-Tapu Thermal Wonderland (p307)

Māori Culture

10 New Zealand's indigenous Māori culture (p658) is accessible and engaging: join in a *haka* (war dance); chow down at a traditional *hāngi* (Māori feast cooked in the ground); carve a pendant from bone or *pounamu* (jade); learn some Māori language; or check out an authentic cultural performance with song, dance, legends, arts and crafts. Big-city and regional museums around NZ are crammed with Māori artefacts and historical items, but this is truly a living culture: vibrant, potent and contemporary.

9

The West Coast

11 A remote, end-of-the-road vibe defines the West Coast (p446). Road trips along SH6, from isolated wildlife haven Haast to tramping outpost Karamea, thread together an alluring combination of sights: must-see Franz Josef and Fox Glaciers, Hokitika's greenstone galleries and geological wonders like Pancake Rocks. There are countless detours to mountainbiking and tramping trails, many of which follow the footsteps of early pioneers. Primeval wilderness is often only a short journey away by foot (or helicopter, or jetboat...). Fox Glacier (p473)

Heaphy Track

12 Beloved of NZ trampers (and, in winter, mountain bikers), the four- to six-day Heaphy Track (p443) is the jewel of Kahurangi National Park, the great wilderness spanning the South Island's northwest corner. Highlights include the mystical Gouland Downs and surreal nikau palm coast, while the townships at either end – at Golden Bay and Karamea – will bring you back down to earth with the most laid-back of landings.

©RADIUS IMAGES/GETTY IMAGE

Central Otago

13 Here's your chance to balance virtue and vice. Take to two wheels to negotiate the easygoing Otago Central Rail Trail, cycling through some of NZ's most beautiful landscapes (p563) and the heritage streetscapes of former gold-mining towns. All the while, snack on the summer stone fruit for which the region is famous. Balance the ledger with well-earned beers at one of the numerous historic pubs. Alternatively, taste your way to viticultural ecstasy in the vineyards of one of the country's most acclaimed wine regions. Bannockburn, near Cromwell (p570)

Rugby

14 Rugby Union is NZ's national game and governing preoccupation. If your timing's good, you might catch the revered national team (and reigning back-to-back world champions), the All Blacks, in action. The 'ABs' are resident gods: drop any of their names into a conversation and you'll win friends for life. Visit the New Zealand Rugby Museum (p259) in Palmerston North, watch some kids running around a suburban field on a Saturday morning, or yell along with the locals in a small-town pub as the big men collide on screen.

Abel Tasman National Park

15 Here's nature at its most seductive: lush green hills fringed with golden sandy coves, slipping gently into warm shallows before meeting a crystal-clear sea. Abel Tasman National Park (p435) is a postcard-perfect paradise where you can put yourself in the picture, assuming an endless number of poses – tramping, kayaking, swimming, sunbathing – before finally setting up tent by cerulean shores.

Waitomo Caves

16 Waitomo (p202) is a must-see: an astonishing maze of subterranean caves, canyons and rivers perforating the northern King Country limestone. Black-water rafting is the big lure here (like white-water rafting but through a dark cave), plus glowworm grottoes, underground abseiling and more stalactites and stalagmites than you'll ever see in one place again. Above ground, Waitomo township is a quaint collaboration of businesses: a swish restaurant, craft brewery, pub and some more-than-decent accommodation. But don't linger in the sunlight – it's party time downstairs!

LUKAS BISCHOFF PHOTOGRAPHY/SHUTTERSTOCK ©

Skiing & Snowboarding

17 New Zealand is studded with massive mountains, and you're almost guaranteed to find decent snow right through the winter season (June to October). Most of the famous slopes are on the South Island: hip Queenstown and hippie Wanaka (p599) are where you want to be, with iconic ski runs like Coronet Peak, the Remarkables and Treble Cone close at hand. There are also dedicated snowboarding and cross-country (Nordic) snow parks here. And on the North Island, Mt Ruapehu offers the chance to ski down a volcano. Snowboarding on Mt Ruapehu (p283), Tongariro National Park

Akaroa & Banks Peninsula

18 Infused with Gallic ambience, Akaroa (p505) bends languidly around one of the prettiest harbours on Banks Peninsula. These clear waters, perfect for kayaking and sailing, are inhabited by the world's rarest dolphin. Elsewhere on the peninsula, the Summit Rd snakes around the rim of an ancient volcano while winding side roads descend to hidden bays and coves. Spend your days discovering the peninsula's many surprises: whimsical gardens, sea-kayaking safaris and colonies of rare, white-flippered penguins. Akaroa (p505)

IVANGRIGORYEV/SHUTTERSTOCK ©

TranzAlpine Railway

19 One of the world's most scenic train journeys, the TranzAlpine (p458) cuts clear across the country from the Pacific Ocean to the Tasman Sea in less than five hours. Yes, there's a dirty great mountain range in the way – that's where the scenic part comes in. Leaving the Canterbury Plains, a cavalcade of tunnels and viaducts takes you up through the Southern Alps to Arthur's Pass, where the 8.5km Otira tunnel burrows through the bedrock of NZ's alpine spine. Then it's downhill (only literally) to workaday Greymouth...a jumping-off point to adventures aplenty. View from TranzAlpine of Waimakariki River Valley en route to Arthur's Pass (p514)

Otago Peninsula

20 Along with a constant backdrop of coastal vistas, the Otago Peninsula (p561) offers some of the best opportunities for wildlife-spotting in the country. Dozens of little penguins achieve peak cuteness in their nightly beachside waddle, while their much rarer yellow-eyed cousin, the hoiho, can be glimpsed standing sentinel on deserted coves. Sea lions and seals laze around on the rocks while albatrosses from the world's only mainland colony swoop and soar above.

Need to Know

For more information, see Survival Guide (p671)

Currency
New Zealand dollar ($)

Language
English, Māori

Visas
Citizens of 60 countries, including Australia, the UK, the US and most EU countries, don't need visas for NZ (length-of-stay allowances vary). See www.immigration.govt.nz.

Money
Credit cards are used for most purchases in NZ, and are accepted in most hotels and restaurants. ATMs are widely available in cities and larger towns.

Mobile Phones
European phones should work on NZ's network, but most American or Japanese phones will not. It's straightforward to buy a local SIM card and prepaid account at outlets in airports and large towns (provided your mobile is unlocked).

Time
New Zealand time (GMT/UTC plus 12 hours)

When to Go

Auckland
GO Feb–Apr

Rotorua
GO Oct–Dec

Wellington
GO Dec–Feb

Christchurch
GO Jan–Mar

Queenstown
GO Jun–Aug

High Season
(Dec–Feb)

➡ Summer brings busy beaches, gorgeous tramping weather, festivals and sporting events.

➡ Accommodation prices rise in most destinations – book ahead.

➡ High season in ski towns is winter (June to August).

Shoulder
(Mar–Apr)

➡ Prime travelling time: fine weather, autumn colours, warm(ish) ocean and long evenings.

➡ Shorter queues, and popular road-trip routes are clear, especially after Easter.

➡ Spring (September to November) means the end of snow season, and lambs.

Low Season
(May–Aug)

➡ Brilliant southern-hemisphere skiing and snowboarding from mid-June.

➡ Outside ski resorts, get accommodation deals and a seat in any restaurant.

➡ Warm-weather beach towns may be half asleep so reserve accommodation ahead.

Useful Websites

100% Pure New Zealand
(www.newzealand.com) Comprehensive official tourism site.

Department of Conservation
(www.doc.govt.nz) DOC parks, trail conditions and camping info.

Lonely Planet (www.lonely planet.com/new-zealand) Destination information, hotel bookings, traveller forum and more.

Destination New Zealand
(www.destination-nz.com) Event listings and info from NZ history to fashion.

Te Ara (www.teara.govt.nz) Online encyclopedia of NZ.

Important Numbers

Regular NZ phone numbers have a two-digit area code followed by a seven-digit number. When dialling within a region, the area code is still required. Drop the initial 0 if dialling from abroad. If you're calling the police but don't speak English well, ask for Language Line, which may be able to hook you up with a translator.

NZ country code	64
International access code from NZ	00
Emergency (Ambulance, Fire, Police)	111
Directory Assistance (charges apply)	018

Exchange Rates

Australia	A$1	NZ$1.10
Canada	C$1	NZ$1.14
China	Y10	NZ$2.21
Euro zone	€1	NZ$1.72
Japan	¥100	NZ$1.29
Singapore	S$1	NZ$1.08
UK	UK£1	NZ$1.97
US	US$1	NZ$1.46

For current exchange rates, see www.xe.com.

Daily Costs

Budget: Less than $150

➡ Dorm beds or campsites: $25–40 per night

➡ Main course in a budget eatery: less than $15

➡ InterCity or Naked Bus pass: 15 hours or five trips $125–159

Midrange: $150–250

➡ Double room in a midrange hotel/motel: $110–200

➡ Main course in a midrange restaurant: $15–32

➡ Car rental: from $40 per day

Top End: More than $250

➡ Double room in an upmarket hotel: from $200

➡ Three-course meal in a classy restaurant: $80

➡ Domestic flight Auckland to Christchurch: from $100

Opening Hours

Opening hours vary seasonally depending on where you are. Most places close on Christmas Day and Good Friday. See Directory (p679) for more information.

Arriving in New Zealand

Auckland Airport Airbus Express buses run into the city every 10 to 30 minutes, 24 hours. Door-to-door shuttle buses run 24 hours (from $35). A taxi into the city costs $80 to $90 (45 minutes).

Wellington Airport Airport Flyer buses ($9) run into the city every 10 to 20 minutes from around 7am to 9pm. Door-to-door shuttle buses run 24 hours (from $20). A taxi into the city costs around $30 (20 minutes).

Christchurch Airport Christchurch Metro Purple Line runs into the city regularly from around 7am to 11pm. Door-to-door shuttles run 24 hours (from $23). A taxi into the city costs around $45 to $65 (20 minutes).

Safe Travel

New Zealand is no more dangerous than other developed countries, but take normal safety precautions, especially after dark on city streets and in remote areas. See Safe Travel (p679) for info on a few driving and environmental concerns to be aware of.

First Time New Zealand

For more information, see Survival Guide (p671)

Checklist

➡ Ensure your passport is valid for at least three months past your intended return date from New Zealand

➡ Book rental cars, campervans and train tickets well in advance, particularly for travel during summer

➡ Got travel insurance? Does it cover your planned activities, like winter sports?

➡ Read up on Māori culture and learn a few words

What to Pack

➡ Sturdy walking shoes – visiting NZ without doing at least some tramping (hiking) is a crime!

➡ A small day pack

➡ NZ electrical adaptor

➡ Sunglasses for bright southern days

➡ A beanie (woolly hat) for unexpectedly chilly evenings

➡ Reusable water bottle

➡ Earplugs for hostel dorms

Top Tips for Your Trip

➡ Allow more driving time than you think you need. Outside cities, roads are narrow and winding, and there are often mountains or hills to navigate. Save time with internal flights, and don't try to see the whole country in two weeks.

➡ Be aware that booked activities are often cancelled for weather reasons. If you have your heart set on a helicopter ride or wildlife walk that could be rained off, build extra time into your itinerary in case your tour is bumped to the following day.

➡ Dress for NZ's famously fickle weather with layers you can add or remove as the weather decides what it wants to do.

➡ Don't expect wi-fi to be fast or free outside cities. It's common for hotels and cafes to offer vouchers for a limited amount of data, and connections are often slow.

What to Wear

Given the locals' propensity to tramp off into the wilderness at any given moment, dress norms in NZ are generally fairly practical and versatile. Sure, dress to the nines for a night out on the town in Auckland, Wellington or Christchurch – but elsewhere the key to comfort and commodity is to layer up. The weather here can change in a blink: you'll be best equipped to adapt if you can quickly add or remove clothes to keep pace with the temperature.

Sleeping

Book beds well in advance in peak tourist seasons: November through March (particularly summer holidays from Christmas to late January), at Easter, and during winter (June to September) in snowy resort towns like Queenstown and Wanaka.

Motels & Pubs Most towns have low-rise, midrange motels. Even small towns usually have a pub with rooms.

Holiday Parks Ideal if you're camping or touring in a campervan. Choose from unpowered tent sites, simple cabins and en-suite units.

Hostels Backpacker hostels include beery, party-prone joints and family-friendly 'flashpackers'.

Hotels Choices range from small-town pubs to slick global-chain operations – with commensurate prices.

Language

The majority of New Zealanders speak English (with a delightfully mangled accent), but Māori (te reo Māori, officially) is NZ's other official language. Many Māori words cross over into daily English parlance: at the very least, you'll hear *kia ora* (hello) regularly. Online, www.maoridictionary.co.nz has a handy translator.

Bargaining

Haggling and bargaining aren't traditionally part of commercial culture in NZ. The only circumstances where you might have some luck are farmers markets (chipping a couple of dollars off the price of a big bag of kiwifruit at the end of the day) or large private purchases (buying a local guy's car for a knock-down price).

Tipping

Tipping is completely optional in NZ.

Guides Your kayaking guide or tour group leader will happily accept tips; up to $10 is fine.

Restaurants The total on your bill is all you need to pay (though sometimes a service charge is factored in). If you like, reward good service with 5% to 10%.

Taxis If you round up your fare, don't be surprised if the driver hands back your change.

TIM90/SHUTTERSTOCK ©

Etiquette

New Zealanders are a laid-back, modest bunch as a whole – exercising the usual good manners will help endear you to the locals.

Greetings Shake hands when meeting someone for the first time, and look people in the eye.

Attitude Brash, self-satisfied, arrogant attitudes really annoy people (note: this is how they perceive Australians to be and not what Kiwis are like!).

Māori Customs Adhere to strict Māori protocols (p662) if visiting *marae* (meeting-house complexes). Otherwise respectful behaviour goes a long way.

Invitations If you're invited to dinner or a barbecue at someone's house, bring some wine, beer, meat or a bunch of flowers.

What's New

Stargazing on Great Barrier Island

Following its 2017 recognition as a Dark Sky Sanctuary, Great Barrier – the first island in the world to be awarded this status – now offers the opportunity for stargazing tours. (p124)

Wildwire Wanaka

The Italians have been climbing via ferrata routes for decades and they've arrived in NZ big time, with the world's highest waterfall via ferrata on the Treble Cone slopes. (p601)

Pike29 Memorial Track

From 2019 trampers and mountain bikers can embark on NZ's latest 'Great Walk', a 45km route between Blackball and Punakaiki commemorating lives lost in 2010's Pike River Mine disaster. (p461)

Napier's Dining Scene

Recent openings have given Napier the most exciting restaurant scene in provincial NZ. Bistronomy, Greek National Cafe and Hapi are highlights. (p338)

Canterbury Earthquake National Memorial

Unveiled on the sixth anniversary of the 22 February 2011 earthquake that claimed 185 lives in Christchurch, this memorial provides a place for Cantabrians to reflect and remember. (p487)

Suter Art Gallery

Following a two-year makeover, Nelson's historic Suter Art Gallery has reopened as a modern 21st-century institution featuring fascinating NZ art and the bonus of a wonderful riverside cafe. (p425)

He Tohu

A new space at the National Library in Wellington houses three of NZ's most precious sets of political documents: the 1835 Declaration of Independence of the United Tribes of New Zealand; the 1840 Treaty of Waitangi; and the 1893 Women's Suffrage Petition. (p373)

Whitestone City

Opened in 2017, this new interactive museum celebrates Oamaru's Victorian heritage with quirky attractions, including a penny-farthing carousel and a replica streetscape. (p546)

Ziplining at Driving Creek Railway

Following an 18-minute journey on this narrow-gauge mountain railway, it's now possible to travel back down the forest-covered hill on an exciting series of eight zip lines. (p215)

Toi Art

At Te Papa, NZ's amazing national museum on the Wellington waterfront, the new Toi Art gallery is now open, showcasing iconic works from the national collection alongside challenging contemporary pieces. Spread over two levels, it's free and very family-friendly. (p368)

For more recommendations and reviews, see lonelyplanet.com/new-zealand

If You Like...

Cities

Auckland Sydney for beginners? We prefer 'Seattle minus the rain', infused with vibrant Pacific Islander culture. (p76)

Wellington All the lures you'd expect in a capital city, packed into a compact CBD and hillsides dotted with Victorian architecture. (p368)

Christchurch Re-emerging post-earthquakes with energy and verve, largely due to the determination and resilience of proud locals. (p482)

Dunedin Exuding artsy, boozy ambience (so many students!) and close to superb wildlife-viewing opportunities on the Otago Peninsula. (p549)

Napier Art deco and Spanish Mission architecture, complemented by new restaurant openings and a relaunched museum and gallery complex. (p350)

New Plymouth The perfect urban hub, with fab galleries, cool cafes and bars, and accessible wilderness. (p234)

Beaches

Karekare Spellbinding black-sand beach, an hour's drive west of Auckland, with wild surf (Eddie Vedder nearly drowned here!). (p129)

Hahei Iconic Kiwi beach experience on the Coromandel Peninsula, with mandatory side trip to Cathedral Cove. (p223)

Wharariki No car park, no ice-cream vans... This isolated stretch near Farewell Spit is for wanderers and ponderers. (p442)

Manu Bay New Zealand's most famous surf break (seen *Endless Summer*?); there's not much sand, but the point break is what you're here for. (p194)

Abel Tasman Coast Track No need to Photoshop this postcard paradise – these golden beaches, blue bays and verdant hills are for real. (p435)

Wainui On the North Island's East Coast: surfing, sandcastles, sunshine... The quintessential beach-bum beach. (p340)

Curio Bay Sure, it gets chilly on the South Island – but bodacious waves keep surf bunnies flocking to this arc of golden sand. (p629)

Extreme Activities

Queenstown bungy Strap yourself into the astonishing Shotover Canyon Swing or Nevis Bungy, and propel yourself into the void. (p577)

Abel Tasman Canyons Swim, slide, abseil and leap down the Torrent River torrents. (p437)

Waitomo black-water rafting Don a wet suit, a life vest and a helmet with a headlamp, and rampage along an underground river. (p203)

Skydive Franz Get an eyeful of glacier from 19,000ft, NZ's highest jump (you'll see Aoraki/Mt Cook, too). (p470)

Extreme Auckland Check out SkyWalk and SkyJump at the Sky Tower, and EcoZip Adventures – adventurous thrills with views. (p91)

Canyonz Negotiate cliffs, waterfalls and streams as you climb and abseil through pristine NZ bush near Thames. (p213)

Rafting the Buller River A classic rafting experience served by excellent operators based in Murchison. (p448)

Wine Regions

Marlborough The country's biggest wine region just keeps on turning out superb sauvignon blanc (and other varieties). (p416)

Martinborough A small-but-sweet wine region a day trip from Wellington: easy cycling and easy-drinking pinot noir. (p397)

Waiheke Island Auckland's favourite weekend playground has a hot, dry microclimate: perfect for Bordeaux-style reds and rosés. (p117)

Central Otago Responsible for much of the country's best pinot noir and riesling; drink some. (p563)

PLAN YOUR TRIP IF YOU LIKE...

Waipara Valley A short hop north of Christchurch are some spectacular vineyards producing equally spectacular riesling. (p512)

Hawke's Bay Warm days shift into chardonnay nights on the sunstroked East Coast. (p357)

Foodie Experiences

Eating in Auckland New restaurants, ethnic culinary enclaves and a growing food-truck scene all make Auckland NZ's eating capital. (p103)

Central Otago vineyard restaurants Eye-popping scenery combined with the best of NZ food and wine. (p563)

Christchurch city scene The big southern CBD restaurant and bar scene is burgeoning (again). (p495)

Bluff oysters Guzzle silky, salty oysters between March and August; time your visit for May's oyster festival. (p627)

Wellington Night Market Foodie fun after work on Friday, then again after your lazy Saturday. (p390)

West Coast whitebait Whitebait fritters, bound in egg, are a South Island obsession. Try them on pizza, too. (p466)

NZ lamb Carnivores won't want to miss NZ's best-loved meat; Queenstown's local-minded Public Kitchen & Bar is a good place to start. (p586)

Coromandel seafood Fresh succulent seafood...make a day of it at September's Whitianga Scallop Festival. (p220)

Tramping

Milford Track A justifiably famous 'Great Walk', Milford features 54km of gorgeous fiords, sounds, peaks and raindrops. (p612)

Top: White-water rafting on the Kaituna River (p309), Rotorua Lakes.

Bottom: Cheese on display at Gibbston Valley winery (p582)

Routeburn Track Those with plenty of 'Great Walk' kilometres in their boots rate the Routeburn as the best of the bunch. (p592)

Tongariro Alpine Crossing Be dazzled by ultramarine crater lakes and marvel at steam-huffing volcanic vents on this challenging trail. (p282)

Mt Taranaki short walks Hardened trampers can scale the summit but strolling its photogenic flanks is equally rewarding. (p241)

Banks Peninsula Track Rolling hills and picturesque bays along 29km of volcanic coast...unleash your inner geologist. (p503)

Lake Angelus Track Yes, the zigzag up Pinchgut Track is a bit of a rude awakening, but the views along Mt Robert Ridge last all day. (p444)

Old Ghost Road Bike it or hike it, this engaging West Coast trail oozes history. (p451)

Queen Charlotte Track The joys of camping (sea breezes, lapping waves, starry nights) or luxurious lodges. Either way, you win. (p409)

Māori Culture

Rotorua Catch a cultural performance featuring a *haka* (war dance) and a *hāngi* (Māori feast), with traditional song, dance and storytelling. (p306)

Footprints Waipoua Explore the staggeringly beautiful Waipoua kauri forest on Northland's west coast with a Māori guide. (p176)

Te Ana Māori Rock Art Centre Learn about traditional Māori rock art in Timaru before exploring remote sites around South Canterbury. (p519)

Hokitika The primary source of NZ *pounamu* (greenstone), home to master carvers of stone, bone and paua in traditional Māori designs. (p462)

Toi Hauāuru Studio Visit this Raglan studio for contemporary Māori carving, visual arts and *tā moko* (tattooing). (p193)

Okains Bay Māori & Colonial Museum This nationally significant collection includes a replica *wharenui* (meeting house), *waka* (canoes) and more. (p503)

Off-The-Beaten-Track Experiences

Stewart Island The end of the line! Catch the ferry to Oban and get lost for a few days. (p633)

Karamea Lesser-trodden marvels like the Oparara Arch and secluded Scotts Beach reward tramps on the northern West Coast. (p453)

East Cape Take a few days to detour around this very untouristy corner of the North Island. (p333)

Whanganui River Road Drive alongside the Whanganui River past Māori towns and stands of trees, remnants of failed Pākehā (European New Zealander) farms. (p253)

Forgotten World Highway A lonesome, forested 150km between Taumaranui and Stratford (or the other way around). (p244)

Opononi & Omapere Clear waters, tranquil settlements, the North Island's northwestern coast is seriously understaffed – just how we like it. (p176)

Molesworth New Zealand's largest cattle farm traverses some seriously remote terrain – take a Molesworth tour. (p512)

Haast Chat to fishermen and drive to lonely Jackson Bay on the South Island's land of no phone signal. (p476)

Pubs, Bars & Beer

Wellington Garage Project and Golding's Free Dive, just two of 20-something craft-beer dens in the capital (thirsty politicians?). (p386)

Queenstown The only place in NZ where you can head out for a big Monday or Tuesday night and not be the only one there. (p587)

Auckland The country's biggest city is developing as a hoppy hub: head to Galbraith's Alehouse, Hallertau or Brothers Beer. (p107)

Nelson Home of NZ hops, Nelson boasts its own craft-beer trail featuring a host of breweries and legendary inns. (p429)

Dunedin Glug at Speight's and Emerson's breweries and brilliant bars in NZ's best university town. (p558)

Hamilton Local craft beers are hugely popular around Hood St nightlife precinct; try Craft, Wonder Horse and Little George. (p188)

Mike's Taranaki's finest craft brews a short jaunt from New Plymouth. (p240)

Pomeroy's Old Brewery Inn The best pub in Christchurch. (p497)

Skiing

Treble Cone Everything from challenging downhill terrain to snowboard half-pipes, within striking distance of Wanaka. (p599)

Coronet Peak The Queenstown area's oldest ski field, just 18km from town; night skiing on Friday and Saturday. (p580)

Cardrona More skiing in the Wanaka area, with slopes to suit all levels of experience. (p606)

Whakapapa & Turoa The North Island's biggest and best ski fields wind down Mt Ruapehu in Tongariro National Park, easily accessible from Taupo. (p283)

Canterbury From Mt Hutt and Methven's après-ski buzz, to smaller fields like Ohau, Round Hill, Porters and Broken River. (p55)

Arrowtown (p595) in autumn

Markets

Otago Farmers Market
Organic fruit and veg, robust coffee and homemade pies in Dunedin; stock up for life on the road. (p557)

Nelson Market A big, busy weekly market featuring everything from bratwurst to vegan cheese. (p429)

River Traders Market Whanganui's riverside market is a Saturday-morning fixture with up to 100 stalls. (p252)

Harbourside Market The ulterior motive for visiting this weekly fruit-and-veg market is the multi-ethnic food stalls and adjacent artisan City Market. (p390)

Otara Flea Market A taste of the South Pacific in Auckland. (p112)

Rotorua Night Market Thursday night hoedown in downtown Rotorua. Food, drink, buskers... it's all good. (p305)

Hastings Farmers Market One of the original, and still one of the best, farmers markets in NZ. (p358)

Christchurch Farmers Market Local cheeses, organic fruit and craft beer beside historic Riccarton House. (p496)

History

Waitangi Treaty Grounds In the Bay of Islands, where Māori chiefs and the British Crown signed the contentious Treaty of Waitangi. (p158)

Arrowtown Gold rush–era town crammed with heritage buildings and the remains of one of NZ's earliest Chinese settlements. (p595)

Oamaru Victorian Precinct Beautifully restored whitestone buildings and warehouses, now housing eclectic galleries, restaurants and artisan workshops. (p544)

Te Papa Wellington's vibrant treasure-trove museum, where history – both Māori and Pākehā – speaks, sparkles and shakes. (p368)

Waiuta South of Reefton on the South Island, explore the rusty relics of a ghost town, abandoned to nature in 1951. (p449)

Shantytown Embrace gold-rush nostalgia at this authentic recreation of an 1860s mining town, south of Greymouth on the West Coast. (p458)

Toitū Otago Settlers Museum Human settlement on the South Island, told through interactive displays and a 100,000-object collection. (p550)

Month by Month

January

New Zealand peels its eyes open after New Year's Eve, gathers its wits and gets set for another year. Great weather, cricket season in full swing and happy holidays for the locals.

🎆 Festival of Lights

New Plymouth's Pukekura Park is regularly plastered with adjectives like 'jewel' and 'gem', but the gardens really sparkle during the Festival of Lights. Pathways glow and trees shine with thousands of lights and there's live music, dance and kids' performances. Sometimes twinkles until early February. (p237)

☆ World Buskers Festival

Christchurch hosts a gaggle of jugglers, musos, tricksters, puppeteers, mime artists and dancers throughout the 10-day summertime World Buskers Festival. Shoulder into the crowd, see who's making a scene in the middle and maybe leave a few dollars. Avoid if you're scared of audience participation... (p492)

February

The sun is shining, the kids are back at school and the sauv blanc is chillin' in the fridge: this is prime party time across NZ. Book your festival tickets (and beds) in advance.

🎆 Waitangi Day

On 6 February 1840 the Treaty of Waitangi was first signed between Māori and the British Crown. Waitangi Day remains a public holiday across NZ, but in Waitangi itself (the Bay of Islands) there's a lot happening: guided tours, concerts, market stalls and family entertainment. (p160)

☆ Fringe

Wellington simmers with music, theatre, comedy, dance, visual arts...but not the mainstream acts gracing the stage at the New Zealand Festival. Fringe shines the spotlight on unusual, emerging, controversial, low-budget and/or downright weird acts. In other words, the best stuff. (p377)

☆ Hamilton Sevens

It's not rugby season, but early February/late January sees the world's seven-a-side rugby teams crack heads in Hamilton as part of the HSBC Sevens World Series: everyone from stalwarts Australia, NZ and South Africa to minnows like Kenya and Canada. Great excuse to party. (p186)

🍷 Marlborough Wine & Food Festival

New Zealand's biggest and best wine festival features tastings from more than 40 Marlborough wineries, plus fine food and entertainment. The mandatory over-indulgence usually happens on a Saturday early in the month. Keep quiet if you don't like sauvignon blanc... (p414)

☆ New Zealand Festival

Feeling artsy? This month-long spectacular happens in Wellington in February to March every even-numbered year, and is sure to spark your imagination. New Zealand's cultural capital exudes artistic enthusiasm with theatre, dance, music, writing and visual arts. International acts aplenty. (p377)

⚑ Art Deco Weekend

Napier, levelled by an earthquake in 1931 and rebuilt in high art-deco style, celebrates its architectural heritage with this high-steppin' fiesta, featuring music, food, wine, vintage cars and costumes over a long weekend in mid-February. (p354)

March

March brings a hint of autumn, harvest time in the vineyards and orchards (great if you're looking for work), long dusky evenings and plenty of festivals plumping out the calendar. Locals unwind post–tourist season.

⚑ Pasifika Festival

With upwards of 140,000 Māori and notable communities of Tongans, Samoans, Cook Islanders, Niueans, Fijians and other South Pacific Islanders, Auckland has the largest Polynesian community in the world. These vibrant island cultures come together at this annual fiesta at Western Springs Park. (p96)

☆ WOMAD

Local and international music, arts and dance performances fill New Plymouth's Bowl of Brooklands to overflowing at WOMAD. An evolution of the original world-music festival dreamed up by rock and art aficionados including Peter Gabriel, who launched the inaugural UK concert in 1982. Perfect for families. (p236)

⚑ Artists Open Studios & Festival of Glass

Whanganui has earned its artistic stripes as a centre for gorgeous glass, myriad local artists and workshops gearing up for this classy glassy fest in March. Expect lots of 'how-to' demonstrations, exhibitions and open studios. (p250)

☆ Auckland City Limits

Get yer rocks off! Auckland City Limits is an international indie-rock festival loosely modelled on Austin City Limits in the US – the NZ version occupying four stages at Western Springs Stadium for a day in March every two years (next event in 2020). (p96)

⚑ Te Matatini National Kapa Haka Festival

This engrossing Māori *haka* (war dance) competition (www.tematatini.co.nz) happens in early March/late February in odd-numbered years: much gesticulation, eye-bulging and tongue extension. Venues vary: it's in Wellington for 2019. And it's not just the *haka*: expect traditional song, dance, storytelling and other performing arts.

✕ Wildfoods Festival

Eat worms, baby octopi and 'mountain oysters' at Hokitika's comfort-zone-challenging food fest. Local classics like whitebait patties are represented too, if you aren't hungry for pork-blood casserole. Tip: avail yourself of quality NZ brews and wines to wash down taste-bud offenders. (p463)

April

April is when canny travellers hit NZ: the ocean is still swimmable and the weather still mild, with nary a tourist or queue in sight (...other than during Easter, when there's pricey accommodation everywhere).

☆ National Jazz Festival

Every Easter, Tauranga hosts the longest-running jazz fest in the southern hemisphere. There's a dedicated Māori jazz stage, a New Orleans–style village and plenty of fine NZ food and wine to accompany the finger-snappin' za-bah-de-dah sonics. (p313)

✕ Clyde Wine & Food Festival

Easter is harvest time around little Clyde in Central Otago, where the historic main street fills with more than 40 tables and trestles hocking the best of regional food and wine... don't leave without a swig of its pinot noir. (p569)

May

Party nights are over and a chilly winter beckons. Thank goodness for the Comedy Festival! Last chance to explore Fiordland and Southland in reasonable weather (though some trails are already off limits). Farmers markets overflow.

✕ Bluff Oyster & Food Festival

Truck down to the deep south for some slippery, salty specimens at this unpretentious event. It's chilly in May, but live music and oyster eating/opening competitions warm everybody up. Non-guzzlers of bivalves can enjoy their pick of gourmet burgers, cheese rolls, chowders and more. (p627)

☆ New Zealand International Comedy Festival

Three-week laugh-fest (www.comedyfestival.co.nz) with venues across Auckland, Wellington and various regional centres: Whangarei to Invercargill with all the midsized cities in between. International gag-merchants (Arj Barker, Danny Bhoy, Bill Bailey) line up next to home-grown talent.

June

Time to head south: it's ski season! Queenstown and Wanaka hit their stride. For everyone else, head north: the Bay of Plenty is always sunny, and is it just us, or is Northland underrated?

✷ Matariki

Māori New Year (www.teara.govt.nz/en/matariki-maori-new-year) is heralded by the rise of Matariki (aka Pleiades star cluster) in May and the sighting of June's new moon. Three days of remembrance, education, music, film, community days and tree planting take place, mainly around Auckland, Wellington and Northland.

☆ New Zealand Gold Guitar Awards

These awards in chilly Gore – NZ's country and western capital, if you didn't know – cap off a week of ever-lovin' country twang and boot-scootin' good times, with plenty of concerts and buskers. (p628)

July

Ski season slides on, reaching its peak with Queenstown's Winter Festival. If you want to avoid crowds, hit Mt Ruapehu on the North Island. Alternatively, stay cosy at NZ's international film festival.

✷ Queenstown Winter Festival

This southern snow-fest has been running since 1975, and now attracts more than 45,000 snow bunnies. It's a four-day party, with fireworks, live music, comedy, a community carnival, masquerade ball, and wacky ski and snowboard activities on the mountain slopes. Sometimes starts in late June. (p582)

☆ New Zealand International Film Festival

After separate film festivals (www.nzff.co.nz) in Wellington, Auckland, Dunedin and Christchurch, discover which regional towns are brimming with film buffs when a selection of flicks hits the road from July to November (Gore and Masterton, we're looking at you).

✦ Russell Birdman

Birdman rallies are so '80s, but they sure are fun to watch. This one in Russell features a cast of costumed contenders propelling themselves off a jetty in pursuit of weightlessness. Discos, cake-decoration and spaghetti-eating contests for kids round out a satisfying, family-friendly fest. (p156)

August

Land a good deal on accommodation pretty much anywhere except the ski towns. Winter is almost spent, but tramping season's a long way off. Music and art are your saviours...or cosy up in a pub to watch some rugby!

🍺 Beervana

Attain beery nirvana at this annual craft-beer guzzle fest in Wellington (it's freezing outside – what else is there to do?). Sample the best of NZ's booming beer scene. Not loving beer is heresy, but yes, it also has cider and wine. (p378)

☆ Bay of Islands Jazz & Blues Festival

You might think that the Bay of Islands is all about sunning yourself on a yacht while dolphins splash you with saltwater. And you'd be right. But in winter, this jazzy three-day festival provides a toe-tapping alternative, showcasing over 45 acts from around NZ. (p154)

September

Spring is sprung. The amazing and surprising World of WearableArt is always a hit. And will someone please beat Canterbury in the annual ITM rugby cup final?

⚜ World of WearableArt

A bizarre (in the best possible way) two-week Wellington event featuring amazing hand-crafted garments. Entries from the show are displayed at the World of WearableArt & Classic Cars Museum in Nelson after the event (Cadillacs and corsetry?). Sometimes spills over into October. (p378)

October

Post-rugby and pre-cricket, sports fans twiddle their thumbs: a trip to Kaikoura, perhaps? Around the rest of NZ October is 'shoulder season' – reasonable accommodation rates, minimal crowds and no competition for the good campsites.

⚔ Kaikoura Seafest

Kaikoura is a town built on crayfish. Well, not literally, but there sure are plenty of crustaceans, many of which find themselves on plates during Seafest. Also a great excuse to raise a few toasts and dance around to live music. (p422)

⚜ Nelson Arts Festival

We know, Nelson is distractingly sunny. But it's worth stepping inside for two weeks of comedy, cabaret, dance and rock opera at Nelson Arts Festival. (p427)

November

Across Northland, the Coromandel Peninsula, the Bay of Plenty and the East Coast, NZ's iconic pohutukawa trees bloom, the weather picks up and tourists start to arrive. Lock in your trail bookings early, trampers.

⚜ NZ Tattoo & Art Festival

Australasia's biggest tattoo culture festival attracts thousands of tatt fans to New Plymouth every November. It's hugely popular with ink aficionados and their admirers (not necessarily family viewing). Enquire ahead if you're hoping to get inked by one of many international tattooists in attendance. (p237)

🍷 Toast Martinborough

Swirl a wine glass, inhale deeply, pretend you can detect hints of berry and oak...it's time to practise your wine connoisseur face in upmarket Martinborough. The Wairarapa region produces some seriously good pinot noir, and it's every wine lover's duty to sample some. (p396)

⚜ Oamaru Victorian Heritage Celebrations

The good old days... When Queen Vic sat dourly on the throne, when hems were low and collars were high. Old Oamaru thoroughly enjoys this tongue-in-cheek historic homage: dress-ups, penny-farthing races, choirs, guided tours and more. (p546)

🏃 Lake Taupo Cycle Challenge

Feeling fit? Try cycling 160km around Lake Taupo in NZ's largest cycling event, and then come and talk to us. Held on the last Saturday in November for more than 40 years, Lake Taupo Cycle Challenge is open to individuals and teams. (p273)

December

Summertime! The crack of leather on willow resounds across the nation's cricket pitches, and office workers surge towards the finish line. Everyone gears up for Christmas and shopping centres are packed out.

⚜ Rhythm & Vines

Wine, music and song (all the good things) in sunny east-coast Gisborne on New Year's Eve. Top DJs, hip-hop acts, bands and singer-songwriters compete for your attention at Rhythm & Vines. Or maybe you'd rather drink some chardonnay and kiss someone on the beach. (p341)

Itineraries

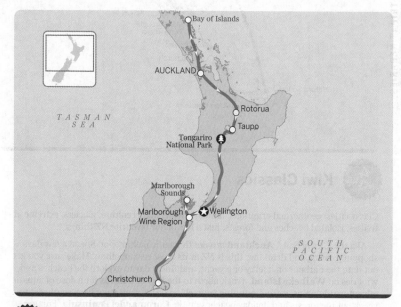

2 WEEKS North & South

From the top of the north to halfway down the south, here's a quick-fire taste of New Zealand's best.

Kick things off in **Auckland**: it's NZ's biggest city, with awesome restaurants and bars, galleries and boutiques, beaches and bays. Not an urbanite? Hoof it a few hours north to the salt-licked **Bay of Islands** for a couple of days of R&R.

Set your bearings southwards to **Rotorua**, a unique geothermal hotspot: geysers, mud pools, volcanic vents and Māori culture make for an experience that fires all the senses. Further south, invigorating **Taupo** has the ragged craters and Emerald Lakes of **Tongariro National Park** nearby. Get into some tramping, mountain biking or skydiving, then boot it down to **Wellington**, a hip little city with an irrepressible arts scene.

Across Cook Strait, see what all the fuss is about in the world-famous **Marlborough Wine Region**. If you're not a wine fan, the hypnotically hushed inlets, ranges and waterways of the **Marlborough Sounds** are nearby. Swinging further south, cruise into **Christchurch** to enjoy southern hospitality in a city of rapid reinvention.

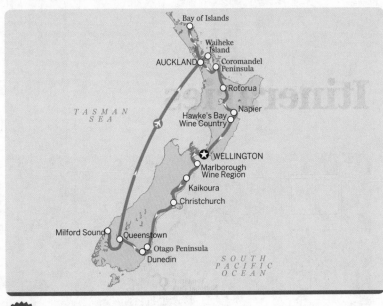

Kiwi Classics

Classy cities, geothermal eruptions, fantastic wine, Māori culture, glaciers, extreme activities, isolated beaches and forests: just a few of our favourite NZ things.

Aka the 'City of Sails', **Auckland** is a South Pacific melting pot. Spend a few days shopping, eating and drinking: this is NZ at its most cosmopolitan. Make sure you get out onto the harbour on a ferry or a yacht, and find a day to explore the beaches and wineries on **Waiheke Island**. Truck north to the **Bay of Islands** for a dose of aquatic adventure (dolphins, sailing, sunning yourself on deck), then scoot back southeast to check out the forests and holiday beaches on the **Coromandel Peninsula**. Further south in **Rotorua**, get a nose full of eggy gas, confront a 10m geyser, giggle at volcanic mud bubbles and experience a Māori cultural performance.

Meander down to **Napier** on the East Coast, NZ's attractive art-deco city. While you're here, don't miss the bottled offerings of the **Hawke's Bay Wine Country** (*...ohh, the chardonnay*). Down in **Wellington**, the coffee's hot, the beer's cold and wind from the politicians generates its own low-pressure system. This is NZ's arts capital: catch a live band, buskers, a gallery opening or some theatre.

Swan over to the South Island for a couple of weeks to experience the best the south has to offer. Start with a tour through the sauvignon blanc heartland of the **Marlborough Wine Region**, then chill for a few days between the mountains and the whales offshore in laid-back **Kaikoura**. Next stop is the southern capital **Christchurch**, swiftly rebuilding after the earthquakes. Follow the coast road south to the wildlife-rich **Otago Peninsula**, jutting abstractly away from the Victorian facades of Scottish-flavoured and student-filled **Dunedin**. Catch some live music while you're in town.

Head inland via SH8 to bungy- and ski-obsessed **Queenstown**. Don't miss a detour over to Fiordland for a jaw-dropping road trip and boat cruise around **Milford Sound**, before returning to Queenstown for your flight back to Auckland.

10 DAYS Auckland Encounter

Is there another 1.4-million-strong city with access to *two* oceans and vibrant Polynesian culture? Immerse yourself in city and seaside, then swing north and south of Auckland to majestic forests and caves.

Allow at least three days in **Auckland** for its stellar bars, restaurants, museums and beaches. Admire Māori and South Pacific Islander exhibits at Auckland Museum, then wander across to K Rd for lunch. Visit Auckland Art Gallery and the iconic Sky Tower, then Ponsonby for dinner and drinks.

Ferry over to **Rangitoto Island's tramping trails**, then chug into Devonport for a meal. Admire tall timber in **Waitakere Ranges Regional Park** and wild surf at **Karekare** and **Piha**, then hit the Britomart restaurants. Breakfast in Mt Eden, climb Maungawhau, then ferry-hop to **Waiheke Island** for wineries and beaches.

For your final few days, take your pick of activities beyond the big smoke. Driving a northerly loop out of Auckland takes you snorkelling at **Goat Island Marine Reserve**, sailing the **Bay of Islands**, ocean gazing at **Cape Reinga** and ogling kauri trees at **Waipoua Forest**. Leave a couple of days to delve south to **Waitomo Caves**, surf at **Raglan** or beach yourself at **Whitianga**.

2 WEEKS Northern Exposure

Three-quarters of New Zealanders live on the North Island – time to find out why!

Begin in **Auckland**, NZ's biggest city. Eat streets abound: try Ponsonby Rd in Ponsonby, K Rd in Newton and New North Rd in Kingsland. Hike up One Tree Hill (Maungakiekie) to burn off resultant calories, and don't miss the Auckland Art Gallery and Auckland Museum.

Venture south through geothermal **Rotorua** – home to some truly amazing volcanic sights – then cruise over to the sunny **East Coast**. By the seaside and encircled by the chardonnay vines of **Hawke's Bay Wine Country**, art-deco **Napier** is a hit with architecture buffs. Heading south, follow SH2 into the sheepy/winey region of **Wairarapa**, before driving over the Rimutaka Range into hip, art-obsessed **Wellington**.

Looping back northwest to Auckland, pick and choose your pit stops: the New Zealand Rugby Museum in **Palmerston North**, some crafty glass in **Whanganui** or the epic **Mt Taranaki**, rising like Olympus behind New Plymouth. Go underground at **Waitomo Caves** or surf the point breaks near **Raglan**.

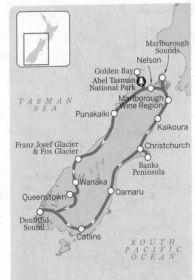

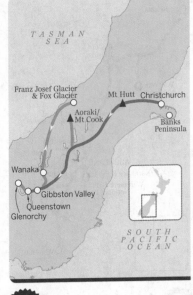

Southern Circuit
3 WEEKS

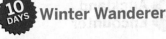

Winter Wanderer
10 DAYS

Loop around the best of the South Island.

Wing into **Christchurch** to find a vibrant city rebuilding post-earthquakes. Grab a coffee and check out the Canterbury Museum.

City saturated? Visit the geologically/culturally eccentric **Banks Peninsula**, then head north for a wildlife encounter in **Kaikoura**. Continue through to the famous **Marlborough Wine Region**, and lose a day on the whisper-still waterways of the **Marlborough Sounds**.

Detour west through artsy **Nelson** to **Abel Tasman National Park** and ecofriendly **Golden Bay** (more paintbrushes than people). Dawdle south along the West Coast; allow time to gape at the Pancake Rocks at **Punakaiki** and embark on a guided tramp or helihike at **Franz Josef Glacier** or **Fox Glacier**. From here, track inland through to hip/hippie **Wanaka** and adventure sport and ski hub **Queenstown**. From here, venture southwest to Manapouri for a mesmerising day cruise to **Doubtful Sound** before wending east to the overgrown deep-south **Catlins** for a couple of days of waterfalls, wave-lashed coves and penguin-spotting.

Back up the east coast, wheel through Dunedin to surprisingly hip **Oamaru**, before rolling back into Christchurch.

We know, a whole bunch of you are here for one thing only: South Island snow!

Fly into **Christchurch** and spend a day acclimatising at lively bars and restaurants. Intermediate skier or better? Your next stop is **Mt Hutt** for 365 skiable hectares. As you push south, detour to admire views of snowy **Aoraki/Mt Cook** before continuing to **Queenstown**, offering world-class skiing, great restaurants and a kickin' nocturnal scene. Coronet Peak is the area's oldest ski field, with excellent skiing for all levels (great for snowboarders, too). The visually remarkable Remarkables are more family friendly.

Need a break from snow? Drive around Lake Wakatipu to gorgeous **Glenorchy**; or get lost in the wineries of **Gibbston Valley**. Alternatively, Queenstown's extreme activities are still on offer in winter: bungy jumping, jetboating, mountain biking and more.

Get back on the slopes in **Wanaka** (Queenstown's low-key little brother). Nearby ski fields include Treble Cone, Cardrona and Snow Farm New Zealand, NZ's only commercial Nordic (cross-country) ski area.

From Wanaka, take an overnight trip to the West Coast to helihike or ice climb **Franz Josef Glacier** and **Fox Glacier**. Backtrack to Queenstown for your next flight.

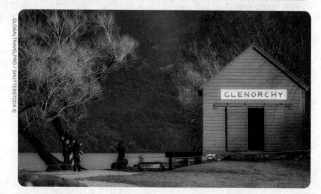

Top: Franz Josef
Glacier (p468)

Bottom: Glenorchy
(p590)

GLOBALTRAVELPRO / SHUTTERSTOCK ©

Getting Around New Zealand

For more information, see Transport (p683)

Travelling by Car

New Zealand is long and skinny, and many roads are two-lane country by-ways: getting from A to B requires a bit of planning (and usually takes longer than you think it might). But with your own car (or campervan – a hugely popular way of getting around NZ) you can travel at your own tempo, explore remote areas and visit regions with no public transport.

Car Hire

Car hire is available in all major towns; rates from the big international companies (Avis, Budget, Hertz, Europcar, Thrifty et al) start at around $40 per day. You'll get a better rate from a local NZ firm – from around $30 per day – but vehicles may be older and service levels perhaps not as slick.

For campervans, daily rates for a two-/four-/six-berth van booked well in advance start at around $120/150/230. New Zealand is brilliantly set up for campervans, with a network of excellent holiday parks around the country. A powered site at a holiday park will generally set you back about $35 per night.

Top tip: make sure your contract includes unlimited kilometres, so you can travel as far and as wide as necessary.

RESOURCES

Automobile Associations

New Zealand's **Automobile Association** (AA; ☑0800 500 444; www.aa.co.nz/travel) is a handy resource for maps, insurance and accommodation listings, and provides emergency breakdown assistance for members of many affiliated overseas organisations (bring your membership card).

Road Conditions

New Zealand's weather, particularly in mountainous regions, can change from sunny to stormy in a matter of minutes. Road washouts and closures are common. To check road conditions see www.nzta.govt.nz/traffic or call 0800 444 449.

Insurance

New Zealand's no-fault Accident Compensation Corporation (www.acc.co.nz) scheme covers personal injury, but make sure you also have third-party insurance, covering damage to other vehicles if an accident is your fault. Try the Automobile Association.

No Car?

Bus

There are reliable, frequent bus services to most destinations around the country (usually cheaper than flying), though services thin out in rural areas. The main nationwide operators are **InterCity** (☎07-348 0366; www.intercity.co.nz) and **Naked Bus** (☎09-979 1616; https://nakedbus.com).

Plane

Fast-track your holiday with affordable, frequent, fast internal flights. Carbon-offset your flights if you're feeling guilty. **Air New Zealand** (☎0800 737 000; www.airnewzealand.co.nz) is the national carrier, but there are myriad smaller airlines serving regional hubs beyond the main cities.

Train

Trains across NZ offer reliable, regular and scenic services (if not fast or cheap) along specific routes on both islands.

Great Journeys of New Zealand (☎0800 872 467, 04-495 0775; www.greatjourneysofnz.co.nz) is the operator, running the **Capital Connection** between Palmerston North and Wellington, the **Coastal Pacific** between Christchurch and Picton, the **Northern Explorer** between Auckland and Wellington, and the **TranzAlpine** over the Southern Alps between Christchurch and Greymouth.

Classic Kiwi Road Trips

Milford Hwy (p617) Gasp at alpine peaks, sigh along thrilling forest-wrapped roads...the drive from Te Anau to Milford Sound is one of the world's finest.

Pacific Coast Hwy (p333) Māori historical sites and bedazzling beaches hem this road through a long-lost corner of the North Island.

The Great Coast Road (p455) Overhanging cliffs and otherworldly rock formations crop up on this route along the wild, windswept West Coast.

Forgotten World Hwy (p244) Be lulled by this lonely forest road, undulating between Stratford and Taumarunui. Don't miss a pit stop at the pub in Whangamomona.

Arthur's Pass (p515) Between Canterbury and the West Coast, the Southern Alps' highest pass is a feat of daredevil engineering. Check the snow report before you hit the road.

Southern Scenic Route (p621) Allow a week to do justice to this meandering route between Queenstown and Dunedin, through a lonesome region known as the Catlins.

DRIVING FAST FACTS

➡ Drive on the left; the steering wheel is on the right (...in case you can't find it).

➡ Give way to the right at intersections.

➡ Blood alcohol limit 0.05% (0% for drivers under 20).

➡ At single-lane bridges, give way if the smaller red arrow is pointing in your direction of travel.

➡ Highway speed limit 100km/h; 50km/h in urban areas.

ROAD DISTANCES (KM)

	Auckland	Christchurch	Napier	Queenstown
Christchurch	980			
Napier	420	760		
Queenstown	1455	480	1235	
Wellington	640	340	320	815

Routeburn Track (p592)

Plan Your Trip

Hiking in New Zealand

Hiking (aka bushwalking or tramping, as Kiwis call it) is almost a national religion in New Zealand. It's a rewarding way to delve into the country's abundant natural beauty and feast your eyes on mountain vistas, hidden waterfalls and (if you're lucky) rare wildlife. There are thousands of kilometres of tracks here – including the Department of Conservation (DOC) 'Great Walks' – plus an excellent network of huts and campgrounds.

Top NZ Hikes

Top Five Multiday Hikes

Lake Waikaremoana Track, Te Urewera

Abel Tasman Coast Track, Abel Tasman National Park

Heaphy Track, Kahurangi National Park

Routeburn Track, Fiordland/Mt Aspiring National Parks

Milford Track, Fiordland National Park

Top Five Day Hikes

Mt Robert Circuit, Nelson Lakes National Park

Key Summit, Fiordland National Park

Taranaki Falls and Tama Lakes, Tongariro National Park

Ben Lomond Walkway, Queenstown

Te Whara Track, Whangarei, Northland

Best Hikes for Beginners

Coromandel Coastal Walkway, Coromandel Peninsula

Wainui Falls Track, Golden Bay, Abel Tasman National Park

Rob Roy Track, Mt Aspiring National Park

Mt Manaia Track, Whangarei, Northland

Rangitoto Summit Track, Auckland

Planning

When to Go

Mid-December–late January Beaut weather but crowded in places. Tramping high season is typically during school summer holidays, starting a couple of weeks before Christmas – plan around them if you can.

January–March Summer weather lingers into March: wait until February if possible, when tracks are (marginally) less crowded. Most non-alpine tracks can be walked enjoyably from late October to April, but snow can hang around into summer.

May–September Winter is not the time to be out in the wild, especially in the South Island or at altitude in the North Island – some tracks close in winter because of avalanche danger and have reduced facilities and services.

What to Bring

Primary considerations: your feet and your back. Break in your footwear and practise walking with your tramping gear and rucksack before setting out.

Suitable footwear Check that your footwear is suitable for the type of trip you have planned – you can ask at outdoor stores around NZ.

Backpack and liner You'll be carrying your backpack for most of the trip, so make sure it's a comfy fit and roomy enough for your gear (without being too heavy). It's well worth buying a waterproof pack liner to keep its contents dry.

All-weather layers Warm clothing, wet-weather gear and sun protection are essential wherever and whenever you hike. Fleece, merino or polypropylene layers are useful, and don't forget sunglasses, sunscreen and a hat (whatever the season). New Zealand's weather is changeable, so expect to remove and add layers throughout the day.

Insect repellent Spray to keep sandflies away (although covering up is best).

Food prep If you're camping or staying in huts without cooking facilities (check with DOC), bring a camping stove. Don't forget your scroggin (trail mix) – a mixture of dried fruit and nuts (and sometimes chocolate) for munching en route.

Resources

Before heading into the bush, get up-to-date information from the appropriate source – usually the DOC, Mountain Safety Council or regional i-SITE visitor information centres.

Websites

DOC (www.doc.govt.nz) Track descriptions, alerts, and exhaustive flora and fauna information for all parts of the conservation estate. DOC offices supply leaflets (mostly $2 or less) detailing hundreds of NZ walking tracks.

Mountain Safety Council (www.mountainsafety.org.nz) Plenty of info and safety advice, and a handy trip-planning tool that pulls together your route with relevant safety warnings, weather forecasts and a suggested packing list.

Met Service (www.metservice.com) New Zealand's national weather forecaster issues weather warnings and has forecasts specific to outdoor areas.

New Zealand Tramper (www.tramper.co.nz) Articles, photos, lively forums and excellent track and hut information.

Te Araroa (www.teararoa.org.nz) The official website for NZ's 3000km trail from Cape Reinga to Bluff.

Freewalks (www.freewalks.nz) Descriptions, maps and photos of long and short tramps all over NZ.

Tramping New Zealand (www.trampingnz.com) Region-by-region track info with diary-style trip reports.

Maps

The NZ Topo50 topographical map series produced by Land Information New Zealand (LINZ; www.linz.govt.nz) is the most commonly used. Bookshops don't often have a good selection of these maps but many outdoor stores stock them. The LINZ website has a list of retailers, and DOC offices often sell the latest maps for local tracks. Download free maps in image format from the LINZ website (search for 'Map Chooser'). NZ Topo Map (www.topomap.co.nz) has an interactive topographic map, useful for planning.

Books

➡ *Lonely Planet's Hiking & Tramping in New Zealand* describes over 50 walks of various lengths and degrees of difficulty.

➡ *202 Great Walks: The Best Day Walks in New Zealand* by Mark Pickering is a handy guide to short, family-friendly excursions.

Kea, Aoraki/Mt Cook National Park (p531)

➡ *A Walking Guide to New Zealand's Long Trail: Te Araroa* by Geoff Chapple is the definitive book for NZ's continuous trail that runs the length of the country.

➡ *Tramping* by Shaun Barnett and Chris Maclean is a meticulously researched history of NZ's favourite outdoor pastime.

➡ *A Bunk for the Night* by Shaun Barnett, Rob Brown and Geoff Spearpoint takes a different angle – a guide to NZ's impressive network of backcountry huts.

TRACK SAFETY

Thousands of people tramp across NZ without incident, but too many meet their maker in the mountains. Many trails are only for fit, well-equipped trampers with plenty of experience – if you don't fit that description, don't attempt them. DOC visitor centres (www.doc.govt.nz) offer great advice on trips to suit all levels of experience, so just ask.

New Zealand's constantly changing weather requires trampers to prepare for all conditions. High-altitude walks are subject to snow and ice, even in summer, and rivers can rise rapidly: always check weather and track conditions before setting off, and be prepared to change your plans or sit out bad weather.

Refer to the Mountain Safety Council (www.mountainsafety.org.nz) for safety tips and a trip-planning tool that incorporates weather forecasts and DOC alerts; you can also share your trip plans with friends. Log your walk intentions online with Adventure Smart (www.adventuresmart.org.nz), and tell a friend or local.

Mt Taranaki (Egmont National Park; p240)

➡ Bird's Eye Guides from Potton & Burton Publishing have fab topographical maps, and there are countless books covering tramps and short urban walks around NZ – scan the bookshops.

Track Classifications

Tracks in NZ are classified according to various features, including level of difficulty. The widely used track classification system is as follows:

Easy Access Short Walk (Easiest) Even track up to an hour long with wheelchair and stroller access. No steps or steep bits.

Short Walk (Easy) Even track up to an hour long, constructed to 'walking shoe' standard (ie walking boots not required). Suitable for all ages and fitness levels.

Walking Track (Easy) Well-formed walks from a few minutes to a full day; walking shoes or boots recommended. Suitable for most ages and fitness levels. Mostly even, possible muddy and steep areas.

Great Walk or Easier Tramping Track (Intermediate) Well formed; major water crossings have bridges and track junctions have signs. Light hiking boots and reasonable fitness required.

Tramping Track (Advanced) Requires skill and experience; hiking boots essential. Suits moderate to high fitness levels. Water crossings may not have bridges, track will be unformed and possibly steep.

Route (Expert) Requires a high degree of skill and experience, plus navigation and outdoor survival skills. Sturdy hiking boots essential. Well-equipped, very fit trampers only.

Guided Walks

If you're new to tramping or just want a more comfortable experience than the DIY alternative, several companies can escort you through the wilds, usually staying in comfortable huts (showers!), with meals cooked and equipment carried for you.

Places on the North Island where you can sign up for a guided walk include Mt Taranaki, Lake Waikaremoana and Tongariro National Park. On the South Island try the Abel Tasman Coast Track, Queen Charlotte Track, Heaphy Track, Old Ghost Road, Routeburn Track, Milford Track or Hollyford Track. Prices for multiday guided walks start at around $1200, and rise to $2000 and beyond for more deluxe experiences.

Getting To & From Trailheads

Getting to and from trailheads isn't always straightforward, except for popular trails serviced by public and dedicated trampers' transport. And these (eg Abel Tasman Coast Track) are also the most crowded.

When it comes to one-way trails, having a vehicle only helps with getting to one end of the track (you still have to collect your car afterwards). If you aren't lucky enough to have a local friend to pick you up/drop you off, there are a good number of operators that can bus, boat or fly trampers to/from their desired trailhead (advance booking essential). You can also charter a private vehicle to drop you at one end, then pick you up at the other (unless you're walking back to your vehicle). If you intend to leave a vehicle at a trailhead, don't leave anything valuable inside – theft from cars in isolated areas is a significant problem. There may be preferable parking options at towns near the trailhead, like Te Anau's Safer Parking (p613).

The Great Walks

New Zealand's most popular tracks are its official 'Great Walks', one of which is actually a river canoe trip. A 10th Great Walk joins the party in 2019. Natural beauty abounds, but at peak times prepare yourself for crowds, especially over summer.

New Zealand's Great Walks are described in Lonely Planet's *Hiking & Tramping in New Zealand,* and are detailed in pamphlets provided by DOC visitor centres and online at www.greatwalks.co.nz.

RESPONSIBLE TRAMPING

If you went straight from the cradle into a pair of hiking boots, some of these tramping tips will seem ridiculously obvious; others you mightn't have considered. Online, Leave No Trace (www.lnt.org) is a great resource for low-impact hiking and camping, and Freedom Camping (http://freedomcamping.org) has tips on freedom camping etiquette and responsible camping. When in doubt, ask DOC or i-SITE staff.

The obvious:

➡ Time your tramp to avoid peak season: less people = less stress on the environment and fewer snorers in the huts.

➡ Carry out *all* your rubbish. Burying rubbish disturbs soil and vegetation, encouraging erosion, and animals will dig it up anyway.

➡ Don't use detergents, shampoo or toothpaste in or near lakes and waterways (even if they're biodegradable).

➡ Use lightweight kerosene, alcohol or Shellite (white gas) stoves for cooking; avoid disposable butane gas canisters.

➡ Where there's a toilet, use it. Where there isn't one, dig a hole and bury your by-product (at least 15cm deep, 100m from any waterway).

You mightn't have considered:

➡ Wash your dishes at hut or campsite facilities, or at least 50m from watercourses; use a scourer, sand or snow instead of detergent.

➡ If you *really* need to scrub your bod, use biodegradable soap and a bucket, at least 50m from any watercourse. Spread the waste water around widely to help the soil filter it.

➡ If open fires are allowed, use only dead, fallen wood in existing fireplaces. Leave any extra wood for the next happy camper.

➡ Keep food-storage bags out of reach of scavengers by stashing them in your pack.

➡ Feeding wildlife (such as inquisitive mountain kea) can lead to unbalanced populations, diseases and animals becoming dependent on handouts. Keep your dried apricots to yourself.

➡ If tracks pass through muddy patches, just plough straight on through – skirting around the outside increases the size of the quagmire.

Top: View from Roys
Peak (p600), Wanaka

Bottom: Fern in
Hollyford Valley (p592)

K IRELAND/SHUTTERSTOCK ©

Tickets & Bookings

To tramp these tracks you'll need to book online or at DOC visitor centres and some i-SITES before setting out. These track-specific tickets cover you for hut accommodation (from $22 to $70 per adult per night, depending on the track) and/or camping ($6 to $20 per adult per night). You can camp only at designated camping grounds; note there's no camping on the Milford Track.

In the off-peak season (May to September) you can use Backcountry Hut Passes or pay-as-you-go Hut Tickets on all Great Walks except for the Lake Waikaremoana Track, Heaphy Track, Abel Tasman Coast Track and Rakiura Track (advance bookings required year-round). Kids under 17 years stay in huts and camp for free on all Great Walks (bookings still required).

You can book at DOC visitor centres by phoning 0800 694 732 or 03-249 8514, using the online booking system on www. greatwalks.co.nz, or by emailing great-walksbookings@doc.govt.nz. Book as far in advance as possible, especially if you're planning on walking during summer.

Other Tracks

From short and sweet to multiday tramps, there are a lot more walks in NZ than the Great ones!

North Island

Tongariro Alpine Crossing (one day) A tricky 19km tramp through surreal Tongariro National Park.

NZ'S GREAT WALKS

WALK	DISTANCE	DURATION	DIFFICULTY	DESCRIPTION
Abel Tasman Coast Track *	60km	3-5 days	Easy to intermediate	NZ's most popular walk (or sea kayak); beaches and bays in Abel Tasman National Park (South Island)
Heaphy Track *	78km	4-6 days	Intermediate	Forests, beaches and karst landscapes in Kahurangi National Park (South Island)
Kepler Track **	60km (loop)	3-4 days	Intermediate	Lakes, rivers, gorges, glacial valleys and beech forest in Fiordland National Park (South Island)
Lake Waikare-moana Track *	46km	3-4 days	Easy to intermediate	Lake views, bush-clad ridges and swimming in Te Urewera (North Island)
Milford Track **	54km	4 days	Easy to intermediate	Rainforest, sheer valleys and peaks, and 580m-high Sutherland Falls in Fiordland National Park (South Island)
Paparoa Track and Pike29 Memorial Track *	55km	2-4 days	Intermediate	Opens in 2019. Limestone cliffs, mining history and majestic sunsets amid the Paparoa Range (South Island)
Rakiura Track *	32km (loop)	3 days	Intermediate	Bird life (kiwi!), beaches and lush bush on remote Stewart Island (Rakiura; off the South Island)
Routeburn Track **	32km	2-4 days	Intermediate	Eye-popping alpine scenery around Mt Aspiring and Fiordland National Parks (South Island)
Tongariro Northern Circuit **	43km (loop)	3-4 days	Intermediate to advanced	Through the active volcanic landscape of Tongariro National Park (North Island)
Whanganui Journey **	87km or 145km	3 or 5 days	Intermediate	Canoe or kayak down a mysterious river in Whanganui National Park (North Island)

* Bookings required year-round

** Bookings required peak season only (October to April)

Great Walks

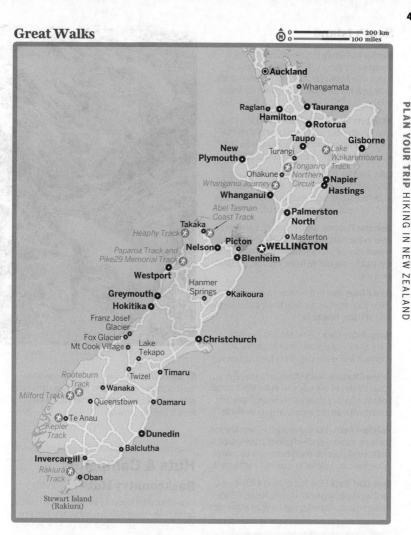

Rangitoto Island Summit (four to five hours) It's a 25-minute ferry ride (or two-hour kayak) from Auckland to the 600-year-old volcano of Rangitoto, best seen from its crater summit after a two-hour loop around the island.

Pinnacles Track (two to four hours) An easyish 4km bushwalk to Aorangi Forest Park's rock stalagmites, which played a starring role in *The Return of the King*.

Aotea Track (two to three days) This 25km track follows routes laid down by loggers who came to Great Barrier Island in a quest for kauri trees, leaving historic relics in their wake.

Pouakai Circuit (two to three days) A 25km loop passing lowland rainforest, cliffs and subalpine forest, tussock and swamp at the foot of Mt Taranaki in Egmont National Park.

Mt Holdsworth–Jumbo Circuit (three days) A 24km, medium-to-hard clamber through beech forest to the alpine tops of Tararua Forest Park, close to Masterton.

Te Paki Coastal Track (three to four days) A 48km easy beach tramp (camping only) along the rugged Northland coastline.

South Island

Mueller Hut Route (four hours ascent) Yes, it involves a hardcore 1040m climb up the Sealy Range near Aoraki/Mt Cook, but the rewards are geological wonders, fascinating plant life and an amazing hut.

Mt Robert Circuit (five hours return) Spy indigo Lake Rotoiti along this special, moderately challenging 9km circuit through ancient rocks and alpine herbs in Nelson Lakes National Park.

Lake Angelus Track (two days) On this tough 22km-return hike in Nelson Lakes National Park, a startling alpine ridge leads to a 1650m-altitude DOC hut beside a pristine cirque lake.

Welcome Flat (two days) Follow the Karangarua River in the shadow of some of NZ's loftiest peaks, reward yourself with a soak in natural hot pools, and sleep in popular Welcome Flat Hut. It's 18km each way.

Banks Track (two to three days) A crowd-free 29km walk over hills, through forest and along the cliffs of Banks Peninsula.

Hump Ridge Track (three days) An excellent 61km alpine and coastal circuit beginning and ending at Te Waewae Bay, 20km from Tuatapere.

Queen Charlotte Track (three to five days) A 70km, moderate one-way walk in the Marlborough Sounds, affording great watery views. Top-notch accommodation and water transport available.

Hollyford Track (four to five days) A 56km low-level tramping track in Fiordland follows in the optimistic footsteps of pioneers. Apple trees mark the site of Jamestown, too isolated to grow into a settlement.

Rees-Dart Track (four to five days) A 70km hard tramping loop in Mt Aspiring National Park, through glacier-fed valleys and over an alpine pass.

Aoraki/Mt Cook National Park (p531)

St James Walkway (five days) This moderately tough tramping track passes through a significant conservation area, home to some 430 species of flora. It's 66km one way.

TE ARAROA

Epic! Te Araroa (www.teararoa.org. nz) is a 3000km tramping trail from Cape Reinga in NZ's north to Bluff in the south (or the other way around). The route links up existing tracks with new sections. Built over almost 20 years, mostly by volunteers, it's one of the longest hikes in the world: check the website for maps and track notes, plus blogs and videos from hardy types who have completed the end-to-end epic.

Huts & Campsites

Backcountry Huts

In addition to Great Walk huts, DOC maintains more than 950 Backcountry Huts in NZ's national and forest parks. Hut categories are as follows:

Basic Huts Very basic enclosed shelters with little or no facilities. Free.

Standard Huts No cooking equipment and sometimes no heating, but mattresses, water supply and toilets. Fees are $5 per adult per night.

Serviced Huts Mattress-equipped bunks or sleeping platforms, water supply, heating, toilets and sometimes cooking facilities. Fees are $15 per adult per night.

Note that bookings are required for some huts (see the website for listings): book online at https://booking.doc.govt. nz or at DOC visitor centres. Kids aged 11

Mueller Hut, Sealy Tarns Track (p533), Aoraki/Mt Cook National Park

to 17 stay for half price; kids aged 10 and under stay free. For comprehensive hut details see www.doc.govt.nz/parks-and-recreation/places-to-stay.

If you do a lot of tramping, a six-month Backcountry Hut Pass ($92 per adult) might be a good idea; otherwise use pay-as-you-go Backcountry Hut Tickets ($5; you'll need to use three of these for a Serviced Hut). Date your tickets and put them in the boxes provided at huts. Accommodation is on a first-come, first-served basis. In the low season (May to September), Backcountry Hut Tickets and Passes can also be used to procure a bunk or campsite on some Great Walks.

Standard Backcountry Campsites are often nearby the huts, and usually have toilets and fresh water, and possibly picnic tables, fireplaces and/or cooking shelters. Prices vary from free to $8 per person per night.

Conservation Campsites

Aside from Great Walk campsites, DOC also manages more than 200 'Conservation Campsites' with categories as follows:

Basic Campsites Basic toilets and fresh water; free on a first-come, first-served basis.

Standard and Backcountry Campsites Toilets and water supply, and perhaps barbecues and picnic tables; $6 to $8 on a first-come, first-served basis. Standard campsites have boat or vehicle access.

Scenic Campsites High-use sites with toilets and tap water, and sometimes barbecues, fireplaces, cooking shelters, cold showers, picnic tables and rubbish bins. Fees from $13 per night.

Serviced Campsites Full facilities: flush toilets, tap water, hot showers and picnic tables. They may also have barbecues, a kitchen and a laundry; from $18 per night.

Note that bookings are necessary for all Serviced Campsites, plus some Scenic and Standard Campsites in peak season (October to April). Book online (https://booking.doc.govt.nz) or at DOC visitor centres.

DOC publishes free brochures with descriptions, and instructions to find every campsite (even GPS coordinates). Pick up copies from DOC visitor centres before you hit the road, or download them from their website.

Freedom campers, note that you'll be slapped with a $200 fine if you camp anywhere there isn't a camping sign.

Coronet Peak (p58)

Plan Your Trip

Skiing & Snowboarding

New Zealand is a premier southern-hemisphere destination for snow bunnies, where wintry pursuits span all levels: family-friendly ski areas, cross-country (Nordic) skiing, daredevil snowboarding terrain and pulse-quickening heliskiing. The NZ ski season varies between areas but it's generally mid-June through September, though it can run as late as mid-October.

Best Skiing & Snowboarding

Best for Beginners or with Kids

Mt Hutt, Central Canterbury

Cardrona, Queenstown

The Remarkables, Queenstown

Mt Dobson, South Canterbury

Roundhill, South Canterbury

Coronet Peak, Queenstown

Best Snowboarding

Mt Hutt, Central Canterbury

Treble Cone, Wanaka

Cardrona, Wanaka

Ohau, South Canterbury

Whakapapa & Turoa, Tongariro National Park

Best Après-Ski Watering Holes

Powderhorn Chateau, Ohakune

Dubliner, Methven

Cardrona Hotel, Cardrona

Lalaland, Wanaka

Rhino's Ski Shack, Queenstown

Planning

Where to Go

The variety of locations and conditions makes it difficult to rate NZ's ski fields in any particular order. Some people like to be near Queenstown's party scene or Mt Ruapehu's volcanic landscapes; others prefer the quality high-altitude runs on Mt Hutt, uncrowded Rainbow or less-stressed club skiing areas. Club areas are publicly accessible and usually less crowded and cheaper than commercial fields, even though nonmembers pay a higher fee.

Practicalities

New Zealand's commercial ski areas aren't generally set up as 'resorts' with chalets, lodges or hotels. Rather, accommodation and après-ski carousing are often in surrounding towns, connected with the slopes via daily shuttles. It's a bonus if you want to sample a few different ski areas, as you can base yourself in one town and day trip to a few different resorts. Many club areas have lodges where you can stay, subject to availability.

Visitor information centres in NZ, and Tourism New Zealand (www.newzealand.com) internationally, have info on the various ski areas and can make bookings and organise packages. Lift passes usually cost $65 to $120 per adult per day (half price for kids) but more for major resorts. Lesson-and-lift packages are available at most areas. Ski and snowboard equipment rental starts at around $50 a day (cheaper for multiday hire). Private/group lessons start at around $120/60 per hour.

Websites

www.snow.co.nz Reports, webcams and ski info across the country.

www.nzski.com Reports, employment, passes and webcams for Mt Hutt, Coronet Peak and the Remarkables.

www.skiandride.nz Good all-round online portal for South Island ski areas with road conditions, school holiday dates and other practical info.

www.chillout.co.nz Portal to info on 13 ski areas and sales of ski passes that access them all. The 'Chill Travel Pass' areas are Awakino, Broken River, Cheeseman, Craigieburn, Fox Peak, Hanmer Springs, Mt Dobson, Mt Lyford, Mt Olympus, Rainbow and Temple Basin (plus a couple of days on Treble Cone and Porters).

www.mtruapehu.com Reports, passes, courses and webcams for Mt Ruapehu's Whakapapa and Turoa ski areas.

North Island

Tongariro National Park

Whakapapa & Turoa (p283) On either side of Mt Ruapehu, these well-run twin resorts comprise NZ's largest ski area, though it comes at a cost of more exposed terrain (watch those weather

Ohau snow fields, Ruataniwha Conservation Park (p528)

reports). Whakapapa has 65 trails spread across 1050 hectares, plus cross-country skiing, a terrain park and NZ's highest cafe! Drive from Whakapapa Village (6km; free parking) or shuttle bus in from National Park Village, Taupo, Turangi or Whakapapa Village. Smaller Turoa has a beginners lift, snowboarding, downhill and cross-country skiing, and over 722m of vertical descent from the High Noon Express chairlift. There's free parking or shuttle-bus transport from Ohakune, 17km away, which has the North Island's liveliest après-ski scene.

Tukino (p284) Club-operated Tukino is on Mt Ruapehu's east, 46km south from Turangi. It's quite remote, 14km down a gravel road from the sealed Desert Rd (SH1), and you need a 4WD vehicle to get in (unless you book onto a shuttle). It's uncrowded, and has runs to suit most levels.

Taranaki

Manganui (p241) Offers volcano-slope, club-run skiing on the eastern slopes of spectacular Mt Taranaki in Egmont National Park, 22km from Stratford, 55km from New Plymouth (and a 25-minute walk from the car park). Taranaki is a surf-mad province so expect the slopes to be dominated by snowboarders. Limited lodge accommodation up the mountain.

South Island

Queenstown & Wanaka

Coronet Peak (p580) At the Queenstown region's oldest commercial ski field, snow-making systems and treeless slopes provide excellent skiing and snowboarding for all levels, with plenty of family-friendly options. There's night skiing on Fridays and Saturdays (and on Wednesdays in July). Shuttles run from Queenstown, 16km away.

The Remarkables (p580) Visually remarkable, this ski field is also near Queenstown (24km away) – shuttle buses run during ski season. It has a good smattering of intermediate, advanced and beginner runs. Kids' club offered for five- to 15-year-old snow bunnies, and childcare options for younger pups.

Treble Cone (p599) The highest and largest of the southern lakes ski areas is in a spectacular location 26km from Wanaka, with steep slopes suitable for intermediate to advanced skiers (a rather professional vibe). There are also half-pipes and a terrain park for boarders.

Cardrona (p606) Around 34km from Wanaka, with several high-capacity chairlifts, beginners tows and the southern hemisphere's biggest park and pipe playground for the freestylers. Buses run from Wa-

Snowboarder

naka and Queenstown during ski season. A friendly scene with good services for skiers with disabilities, plus an on-mountain crèche for under-fives.

Snow Farm New Zealand (p606) New Zealand's only commercial Nordic (cross-country) ski area is 33km from Wanaka on the Pisa Range, high above the Cardrona Valley. There are 55km of groomed trails, huts with facilities and thousands of hectares of open snow.

South Canterbury

Mt Dobson (p526) The 3km-wide basin here, 26km from Fairlie, has a terrain park and famously dry powder. There's a huge learners' area and plenty for intermediates (and up high, dry powder and challenging terrain to suit more experienced snowheads). On a clear day you can see Aoraki/Mt Cook and the Pacific Ocean from the summit.

Roundhill (p527) A small field with wide, gentle slopes, perfect for beginners and intermediates, with a trump card of NZ's largest vertical drop (783m). It's 32km from Lake Tekapo village.

Ohau (☏03-438 9885; www.ohau.co.nz; daily lift passes adult/child $90/36) This commercial ski area with a secluded feel is on Mt Sutton, 42km from Twizel. There are intermediate and advanced runs, excellent snowboarding, two terrain parks

and sociable Lake Ohau Lodge, overlooking glorious views.

Fox Peak (p526) An affordable, uncrowded club ski area 40km from Fairlie in the Two Thumb Range. Expect rope tows, good cross-country skiing and dorm-style accommodation.

Central Canterbury

Mt Hutt (p517) One of the highest ski areas in the southern hemisphere, as well as one of NZ's best. It's close to Methven; Christchurch is 118km to the east – ski shuttles service both towns. Road access is steep – be extremely cautious in lousy weather. The ski area is exposed to the mercy of the elements (leading locals to dub it 'Mt Shut') but the season is long. Plenty of beginner, intermediate and advanced slopes, with chairlifts, heliskiing and wide-open faces that are good for learning to snowboard. Kids aged under 10 ski free.

Porters (p514) The closest commercial ski area to Christchurch (96km away on the Arthur's Pass road). The 'Big Mama' run boasts a 680m drop, but there are wider, gentler slopes, too. There's also a terrain park, good cross-country runs along the ridge, and lodge accommodation.

Temple Basin (p514) A club field with a cult following, 4km from the Arthur's Pass township. It's a 50-minute walk uphill from the car park to the ski-area lodges. There's floodlit skiing at night and excellent backcountry runs for snowboarders. Diehard snowheads only.

Craigieburn Valley (p514) Centred on Hamilton Peak, Craigieburn Valley is no-frills backcountry heaven, 40km from Arthur's Pass. It's one of

---

HELISKIING

New Zealand's remote heights are tailor-made for heliskiing, with operators covering a wide off-piste area along the pristine slopes of the Southern Alps, including extreme skiing for the hardcore. Costs range from around $900 to $1450 for three to eight runs. Heliskiing is available at Coronet Peak, Treble Cone, Cardrona, Mt Hutt, Ohau and Hanmer Springs; independent operators include the following:

Alpine Heliski (p580)

Harris Mountains Heli-Ski (p580)

Methven Heliski (p516)

Over The Top (p581)

Southern Lakes Heliski (p580)

Winter Sports Areas

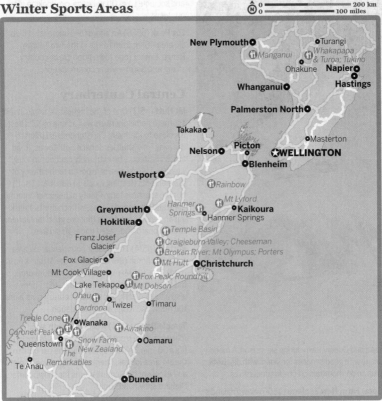

NZ's most challenging club areas, with upper intermediate and advanced runs (no beginners). Accommodation in please-do-a-chore lodges.

Broken River (p514) Not far from Craigieburn Valley, this club field is a 15- to 20-minute walk from the car park and has a real sense of isolation. Reliable snow, laid-back vibe and sheltered enough to minimise bad-weather closures. Catered or self-catered lodge accommodation available.

Cheeseman (p514) A club area in the Craigieburn Range, this smallish family-friendly operation is around 100km from Christchurch. Based on Mt Cockayne, it's a wide, sheltered basin with drive-to-the-snow road access. Lodge accommodation available.

Mt Olympus (p514) Difficult to find (but worth the search), 2096m Mt Olympus is 58km from Methven and 12km from Lake Ida. This club area has intermediate and advanced runs, and there are solid cross-country trails to other areas. Access is sometimes 4WD-only, depending on conditions. Lodge accommodation available.

Northern South Island

Hanmer Springs (p510) A friendly commercial field based on Mt St Patrick, 17km from Hanmer Springs township (linked by shuttles), with mostly intermediate and advanced runs.

Mt Lyford (p510) Around 60km from both Hanmer Springs and Kaikoura, and 4km from Mt Lyford village, this is more of a 'resort' than most NZ ski fields, with accommodation and eating options. There's a good mix of runs and a terrain park.

Rainbow (p445) Borders Nelson Lakes National Park (100km from Nelson, a similar distance from Blenheim), with varied terrain, minimal crowds and good cross-country skiing. Chains are often required. St Arnaud is the closest town (32km).

Otago

Awakino (p541) A small player in North Otago, but worth a visit for intermediate skiers. Oamaru is 45km away; Omarama is 66km inland. Weekend lodge-and-ski packages available.

Bungy jumping with Sky Jump (p91), Auckland

Plan Your Trip

Extreme New Zealand

From midair adventures to deep dives, New Zealand is pure adrenaline. Inspired by NZ's rugged landscape, even the meekest travellers muster the courage to dangle on a bungy rope, skydive above mountains or thunder down river rapids. New Zealand pioneered thrills like bungy jumping and jetboating, and locals' daredevil attitude is infectious. There's nowhere better than NZ to see what you're made of...

Best Extreme New Zealand

Best Skydive Drop Zones
Queenstown

Fox & Franz Josef Glaciers

Taupo

Bay of Islands

Top White-Water Rafting Trips
Tongariro River, Taupo

Kaituna River, Rotorua

Shotover Canyon, Queenstown

Rangitikei River, Taihape

Buller Gorge, Murchison

Top Mountain-Biking Tracks
Redwoods Whakarewarewa Forest, Rotorua

Old Ghost Road, Westport

Queen Charlotte Track, Marlborough

West Coast Wilderness Trail, Hokitika

Alps 2 Ocean, South Canterbury

On the Land

Mountain Biking & Cycle Touring

Jaw-dropping mountains interlaced with farm tracks and old railway lines...it would be hard to design better mountain-biking terrain than NZ. The New Zealand Cycle Trail (www.nzcycletrail.com), some 2500km of tracks, helped mountain biking grow from a weekend sport to a national craze. Its popularity among outdoors enthusiasts of a certain age (and the potential for gear one-upmanship) has led mountain biking to be dubbed 'the new golf'. But no age group is immune, and the variety of trails in NZ brings a choice of gentle pootles in meadows to multiday cycle tours, half-day downhill thrill rides to challenging week-long MTB adventures.

Mountain-bike parks – most with various trail grades and skills areas (and handy bike hire, usually) – are great for trying mountain biking NZ style. The most famous is Rotorua's Redwoods Whakarewarewa Forest, but among legions of others are Wellington's Makara Peak, Auckland's Woodhill Forest and Queenstown's downhill park, fed by the Skyline Gondola.

Classic trails include the 42 Traverse around Tongariro National Park, the Rameka on Takaka Hill and the trails around Christchurch's Port Hills – but this is just the tip of the iceberg. An increasing number of DOC hiking trails are being converted to dual use – such as the tricky but epic Heaphy Track and challenging, history-rich Old Ghost Road – but mountain biking is often restricted to low season due to hiker numbers. Track damage is also an issue, so check with DOC before starting out.

Your clue that there's some great biking around is the presence of bike-hire outfits. Bowl on up and pick their brains. Most likely cycle-obsessed themselves, they'll soon point you in the direction of a ride appropriate to your level. The go-to book is *Classic New Zealand Mountain Bike Rides* (from bookshops, bike shops and www. kennett.co.nz).

If cycle touring is more your pace, check out the *Pedallers' Paradise* booklets by Nigel Rushton (www.paradise-press.co.nz). Changeable weather and road conditions mean cycle touring is less of a craze but there are remarkable road journeys, such as the Southern Scenic Route in the deep south.

Rock Climbing

Time to chalk-up your fingers and don some natty little rubber shoes. On the North Island, popular rock-climbing areas include Whanganui Bay, Kinloch, Kawakawa Bay and Motuoapa near Lake Taupo; Mangatepopo Valley and Whakapapa Gorge on the Central Plateau; Humphries Castle and Warwick Castle on Mt Taranaki; and Piarere and popular Wharepapa South in the Waikato.

On the South Island, try the Port Hills area above Christchurch or Castle Hill on the road to Arthur's Pass. West of Nelson, the marble and limestone mountains of Golden Bay and Takaka Hill provide prime climbing. Other options are Long Beach (north of Dunedin), and Mihiwaka and Lovers Leap on the Otago Peninsula.

Raining? You'll find indoor climbing walls all around the country, including at Rotorua, Whangarei, Auckland, Tauranga, Taupo, Wellington, Christchurch and Hamilton.

Climb New Zealand (www.climb.co.nz) has the low-down on the gnarliest overhangs around NZ, plus access and instruction info. Needless to say, instruction is a must for all but the most seasoned climbing pros.

In the Air
Bungy Jumping

Bungy jumping was made famous by Kiwi AJ Hackett's 1987 plunge from the Eiffel Tower, after which he teamed up with champion NZ skier Henry van Asch to turn the endeavour into an accessible pursuit for anyone.

Today their original home base of Queenstown is a spiderweb of bungy cords, including the AJ Hackett's triad: the 134m Nevis Bungy (the highest in NZ); the 43m Kawarau Bungy (the original); and the Ledge Bungy (at the highest altitude – diving off a 400m-high platform). There's another scenic jump at Thrillseekers Canyon near Hanmer Springs. On the North Island, head to Taihape, Rotorua or Auckland, although the most scenic jump is over the Waikato River in Taupo. Huge rope swings offer variation on the theme; head to Queenstown's Shotover Canyon or Nevis Swing for that swooshy buzz.

Paragliding & Hang Gliding

A surprisingly gentle but still thrilling way to take to the skies, paragliding involves setting sail from a hillside or clifftop under a parachute-like wing. Hang gliding is similar but with a smaller, rigid wing. Most flights are conducted in tandem with a master pilot, although it's also possible to get lessons to go it alone. To give it a whirl, try a tandem flight in Queenstown, Wanaka, Nelson, Motueka, Hawke's Bay, Christchurch or Auckland. The New Zealand Hang Gliding and Paragliding Association (www.nzhgpa.org.nz) rules the roost.

Rock climbing in Whanganui (p248)

Skydiving

With some of the most scenic jump zones in the world, NZ is a fantastic place to take a leap. First-time skydivers can knock off this bucket-list item with a tandem jump, strapped to a qualified instructor, experiencing up to 75 seconds of free fall before the chute opens. The thrill is worth every dollar, from $249 for a 9000ft jump to $559 for NZ's highest free-fall jump (a nerve-jangling 19,000ft, on offer in Franz Josef). Extra costs apply for a DVD or photographs capturing your mid-air terror/delight. Check out the New Zealand Parachute Federation (www.nzpf.org) for more info.

On the Water
Jetboating

The jetboat was invented in NZ by an engineer from Fairlie – Bill Hamilton (1899–1978) – who wanted a boat that could navigate shallow, local rivers. He credited his eventual success to Archimedes, but

Cycling in Nelson (p425)

as most jetboat drivers will inevitably tell you, Kiwi Bill is the hero of the jetboat story.

River jetboat tours can be found throughout NZ, and while much is made of the hair-raising 360-degree spins that see passengers drenched and grinning from ear to ear, they are really just a sideshow. Just as Bill would have it, jetboat journeys take you deep into wilderness you could otherwise never see, and as such they offer one of NZ's most rewarding tour experi-ences. In Haast and Whataroa, jetboat tours plunge visitors into pristine wilder-ness, aflutter with birds.

Big ticket trips such as Queenstown's Shotover, Kawarau and Dart all live up to the hype. But the quieter achievers will blow your skirt up just as high. Check out the Buller and Wilkin in Mt Aspiring National Park, and the Whanganui – one of the most magical A-to-B jetboat trips of them all.

NGA HAERENGA

The New Zealand Cycle Trail (www.nzcycletrail.com) – known in Māori as Nga Haerenga, 'the journeys' – is a 22-strong series of off-road trails known as Great Rides. Spread from north to south they are of diverse length, terrain and difficulty, with many following history-rich old railway lines and pioneer trails, while others are freshly cut, flowing and big fun. Almost all penetrate remarkable landscapes.

There are plenty of options for beginner to intermediate cyclists, with several hardcore exceptions including the Old Ghost Road, which is growing to interna-tional renown. The majority are also well supported by handy bike hire, shuttles, and dining and accommodation options, making them a mighty desirable way to explore NZ.

Bungy jumping in Queenstown (p577)

vorce boats', present a different kind of challenge.

There are ample places to get paddling. Hotspots include Waiheke and Great Barrier Islands, the Bay of Islands and Coromandel Peninsula, Marlborough Sounds (from Picton) and Abel Tasman National Park. Kaikoura is exceptional for wildlife spotting, and Fiordland for jaw-dropping scenery. Wellington is noteworthy for offering the chance to paddle a traditional Māori *waka* (canoe). The Kiwi Association of Sea Kayakers (www.kask.org.nz) gives a good primer on paddling techniques, plus resources for kayakers with a disability.

Scuba Diving & Snorkelling

New Zealand is just as enchanting under the waves, with warm waters in the north, interesting sea life all over and some impressive shipwrecks. The flag-bearer is the Poor Knights Islands, where subtropical currents carry and encourage a vibrant mix of sea life. Also swimming with marine life is the wreck of the Greenpeace flagship *Rainbow Warrior,* which slumbers beneath the Cavalli Islands (reached from Matauri Bay).

Other notable sites for scuba and snorkelling include the Bay of Islands, Hauraki Gulf, Goat Island and Gisborne's Te Tapuwae o Rongokako Marine Reserve. In the Marlborough Sounds, the MS *Mikhail Lermontov* is one of the world's largest diveable cruise-ship wrecks. In Fiordland, experienced divers can head for Dusky Sound, Milford Sound and Doubtful Sound, which have clear conditions and the occasional friendly fur seal or dolphin. Snorkellers should check out the reefs of Taputeranga Marine Reserve (Wellington) and wildlife-rich Waiheke Island.

Expect to pay anywhere from $160 for a short, introductory, pool-based scuba course, and around $600 for a four-day, PADI-approved, ocean-dive course. One-off organised boat- and land-based dives start at around $170.

New Zealand Underwater Association (www.nzunderwater.org.nz) Clean seas and diving-safety advocates whose website has safety info, diving tips, gear maintenance advice and more.

Dive New Zealand (www.divenewzealand.com) New Zealand's only dedicated dive magazine, plus safety info and listings of dive clubs and shops.

Parasailing & Kiteboarding

Parasailing (dangling from a modified parachute over the water, while being pulled along by a speedboat) is perhaps the easiest way for humans to achieve assisted flight. There are operators in the Bay of Islands, Bay of Plenty, Taupo, Wanaka and Queenstown.

Kiteboarding (aka kitesurfing), where a mini parachute drags you across the ocean on a mini surfboard, can be attempted at Paihia, Tauranga, Mt Maunganui, Raglan, Wellington and Nelson. Karikari Peninsula near Cape Reinga on NZ's northern tip is a kiteboarding mecca.

Though it's less adrenaline-soaked, stand-up paddle boarding (SUP) is increasingly popular across NZ. The gentle waters of the Bay of Islands, Tauranga and Gisborne are ideal places for beginners.

Sea Kayaking

Sea kayaking offers a wonderful perspective of the coastline and gets you close to marine wildlife you may otherwise never see. Meanwhile tandem kayaks, aka 'di-

NICRAM SABOD/SHUTTERSTOCK ©

Top: Shotover Jet
(p578), Queenstown

Bottom: Kayaking
in Milford Sound (p619)

SURFING IN NEW ZEALAND

North Island

Raglan, Waikato New Zealand's most famous surf break with a buzzing boarder community and superb surf beaches extending south. Almost a pilgrimage spot for overseas surfers.

Surf Highway, Taranaki Take your pick from consistent Fitzroy Beach, big 'n' busy Stent Rd, experts-only Green Meadows Point (Opunake) and the heavy waves of Ohawe Beach (Hawera), all along the 'Surf Highway' (Hwy 45).

Whangamata, Coromandel Exceptional surf breaks and gear hire and surf schools aplenty.

Bay of Plenty Mt Maunganui is an all-year all-rounder, suitable for most levels and hugely popular in summer, and Matakana Island has brisk waves that suit intermediate surfers.

Gisborne, East Coast Consistent surf and some of NZ's mildest weather. The town's Midway Beach has waves with clout, while pros are fond of Sponge Bay (be careful, there are hidden rocky hazards).

Wellington Region Head to popular Lyall Bay, exposed but not too challenging Castlepoint, or (if you're a pro) Tora Point.

South Island

Marlborough & Nelson Wear a thick wet suit in the Kaikoura Peninsula, where you'll share waves with dolphins, or head to the epic surf at Mangamaunu and Hapuku's Meatworks (intermediates and up).

Canterbury Popular Taylors Mistake has some of Christchurch's best surf and North Brighton suits a range of skill levels.

Dunedin, Otago Dunedin is a good base for surfing on the South Island. Head to St Clair Beach for offshore worthy of the international surf competitions held here.

West Coast Relatively sheltered Punakaiki Beach is a good mixed-level destination while Tauranga Bay (Westport) is best for experienced surfers.

Southland Colac Bay (near Riverton) is an easy, breezy surf spot while Porridge Point (Pahia) is one for the pros.

White-Water Rafting, Kayaking & Canoeing

Epic mountain ranges and associated rainfall mean there's no shortage of great rivers to raft, nor any shortage of operators ready to get you into the rapids. Rivers are graded from I to VI (VI meaning they can't be safely rafted), with operators often running a couple of different trips to suit ability and age (rougher stretches are usually limited to rafters aged 13 or above).

Queenstown's Shotover and Kawarau Rivers are deservedly popular, but the Rangitata (Geraldine), Buller (Murchison) and the Arnold and Waiho rate just as highly. For a multiday epic, check out the Landsborough. The central North Island dishes up plenty, including the popular Tongariro, Rangitikei, Mohaka and Wairoa. There are also the Kaituna Cascades near Rotorua, the highlight of which is the 7m drop at Okere Falls.

Kayaking and canoeing are rampant, particularly on friendly lake waters, although there are still plenty of places to paddle the rapids, including some relatively easy stuff on the Whanganui 'Great Walk'.

New Zealand Rafting Association (www.nz-rafting.co.nz) River conservation nonprofit; river gradings and listings of rafting operators.

New Zealand Kayak (www.kayaknz.co.nz) Community-based kayaking magazine.

Green-lipped mussels

Eat & Drink
Like a Local

Travellers, start your appetites! Eating in New Zealand is a highlight of any visit. You can be utilitarian if money is tight, or embrace NZ's full culinary bounty, from fresh seafood and gourmet burgers to farmers market fruit-and-veg and crisp-linen fine dining. Eateries range from fish and chip shops and pub bistros to retro cafes and ritzy dining rooms. Drinking here, too, presents boundless opportunities to have a good time, with Kiwi coffee, craft beer and wine at the fore.

NE39/SHUTTERSTOCK ©

Best Eating & Drinking

Best NZ Restaurants

Kika Tapas-style Italian in Wanaka. (p604)

Noble Rot French-Kiwi medley within a chic Wellington wine bar. (p384)

Riverstone Kitchen Smashing brunch and splendid Oamaru gardens. (p547)

Pegasus Bay The pick of the Waipara Valley winery restaurants. (p513)

Cassia Sophisticated Indian in Auckland, plus craft beer and gins. (p102)

Best Pubs & Bars

Golding's Free Dive The best craft-beer bar in Wellington. (p386)

Lovebucket Auckland's best quirky cocktails and craft beer. (p110)

Emporium Napier's most civilised bar. (p356)

Smash Palace Comfort in chaos at this kooky Christchurch bar. (p497)

Mussel Inn Long-standing, unpretentious Golden Bay gastropub. (p441)

Modern NZ

Once upon a time (yet not so long ago) NZ subsisted on a modest diet of 'meat and three veg'. Though small-town country pubs still serve their unchanging menu of roasted meats and battered fish, overall NZ's culinary sophistication has evolved dramatically. In larger towns, kitchens thrive on bending conventions and absorbing gastronomic influences from around the planet, all the while keeping local produce central to the menu.

Immigration has been key to this culinary rise – particularly the post-WWII influx of migrants from Europe, Asia and the Middle East – as has an adventurous breed of local restaurant-goers and the elevation of Māori and Pacific Islander flavours and ingredients to the mainstream.

In order to wow the socks off increasingly demanding diners, restaurants must now succeed in fusing contrasting ingredients and traditions into ever more innovative fare. The phrase 'Modern NZ' has been coined to classify this unclassifiable technique: a melange of East and West, a swirl of Atlantic and Pacific Rim, and a dash of authentic French and Italian.

Traditional staples still hold sway (lamb, beef, venison, green-lipped mussels), but dishes are characterised by interesting flavours and fresh ingredients rather than fuss, clutter or snobbery. Spicing ranges from gentle to extreme, seafood is plentiful, and meats are tender and full flavoured. Enjoy!

Vegetarians & Vegans

More than 10% of New Zealanders are vegetarian (more on the North than the South Island), and numbers are rising. Most large urban centres have at least one dedicated vegetarian cafe or restaurant: see the Vegetarians New Zealand website (www.vegetarians.co.nz) for listings. Beyond this, almost all restaurants and cafes offer some vegetarian menu choices (although sometimes only one or two). Many eateries also provide gluten-free and vegan options.

LOCAL DELICACIES

Touring the menus of NZ, keep an eye out for these local delights: kina (sea urchin), paua (abalone; a type of sea snail), kumara (sweet potato, often served as chips), whitebait (tiny fish, often cooked into fritters or omelettes) and the humble kiwi fruit.

Cafes & Coffee

Somewhere between the early 2000s and now, NZ cottoned on to coffee culture in a big way. Caffeine has become a nationwide addiction: there are Italian-style espresso machines in virtually every cafe, boutique roasters are de rigueur and, in urban areas, a qualified barista (coffee maker) is the norm. Auckland, Christchurch and student-filled Dunedin have borne generations of coffee aficionados, but Wellington takes top billing as NZ's caffeine capital. The cafe and bean-roasting scene here rivals the most vibrant in the world, and is very inclusive and family friendly. Join the arty local crew and dunk yourself into it over a late-night conversation or an early-morning recovery.

Sweet Endings

Of course, New Zealanders have a sweet tooth! Inventive desserts crowd the menus in city restaurants – dessert pizzas, deconstructed lamingtons, vegan cheesecakes – but most Kiwi sugar rushes originate in childhood comfort foods. Well suited to all those road trips are tooth-gripping Pineapple Lumps, a chocolate-coated chewy sweet that dates back to the 1950s. Equally likely to rouse childhood nostalgia in Kiwis is hokeypokey ice cream (vanilla with chunks

Havana Coffee Works (p384), Wellington

of honeycomb). Some sweet treats are disputed territory: the queen of Kiwi desserts is the pavlova, a meringue base heaped with cream and berries, kiwifruit or passion fruit, often served at Christmas. Aussies also claim to have invented this cream-crowned wonder...we respectfully disagree.

TO MARKET, TO MARKET

There are more than 50 farmers markets held around NZ. Most happen on weekends and are upbeat local affairs, where visitors can meet local producers and find fresh regional produce. Mobile coffee is usually present, and tastings are offered by enterprising and innovative stallholders. Bring a carrier bag, and get there early for the best stuff! Check out www.farmersmarkets.org.nz for major market locations, and ask locally about smaller, and seasonal, markets.

Pubs, Bars & Beer

Kiwi pubs were once male bastions with dim lighting, smoky air and beer-soaked carpets – these days they're more of a family affair. Sticky floors and pie-focused menus still abound in rural parts of NZ but pubs are generally where parents take their kids for lunch, friends mingle for sav blanc and tapas, and locals of all ages congregate to roar at live sports screenings. Food has become integral to the NZ pub experience, along with the inexorable rise of craft beer in the national drinking consciousness.

Myriad small, independent breweries have popped up around the country in the

Brothers Beer (p107), Auckland

last decade. Wellington, in particular, offers dozens of dedicated craft-beer bars, with revolving beers on tap and passionate bar staff who know all there is to know about where the beers have come from, who made them and what's in them. A night on the tiles here has become less about volume and capacity, more about selectivity and virtue.

But aside from the food and the fancy beer, the NZ pub remains a place where all Kiwis can unite with a common purpose: to watch their beloved All Blacks play rugby on the big screen – a raucous experience to say the least!

Wine Regions

Like the wine industry in neighbouring Australia, the NZ version has European migrants to thank for its status and success – visionary visitors who knew good soils and good climate when they saw it, and planted the first vines. New Zealand's oldest vineyard – Mission Estate Winery (p357) in Hawke's Bay – was established by French Catholic missionaries in 1851 and is still producing top-flight wines today.

But it wasn't until the 1970s that things really got going, with traditional agricultural exports dwindling, Kiwis travelling more and the introduction of BYO ('Bring Your Own' wine) restaurant licensing conspiring to raise interest and demand for local wines.

Since then, NZ cool-climate wines have conquered the world, a clutch of key regions producing the lion's share of bottles. Organised day tours via minivan or bicycle are a great way to visit a few select wineries.

YOUR SHOUT!

At the bar, 'shouting' is a revered custom, where people take turns to pay for a round of drinks. Disappearing before it's your shout won't win you many friends. Once the drinks are distributed, a toast of 'Cheers!' is standard practice: look each other in the eye and clink glasses.

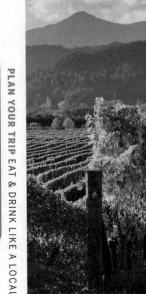

Vineyards in the Marlborough Region (p416)

Marlborough New Zealand's biggest and most widely known wine region sits at the top of the South Island, where a microclimate of warm days and cool nights is perfect for growing sauvignon blanc. You could spend many days touring the many cellar doors here (and why not?).

Hawke's Bay The North Island's sunny East Coast is the cradle of the NZ wine industry and second-largest producer – chardonnay and syrah are the mainstays. The Gisborne region a bit further north also produces terrific chardonnays, along with great pinot gris.

The Wairarapa Just an hour or two over the hills from Wellington, the Wairarapa region – centred on boutiquey Martinborough – is prime naughty-weekender territory, and produces winning pinot noir.

Central Otago Reaching from Cromwell in the north to Alexandra in the south and Gibbston near Queenstown in the west, the South Island's Central Otago region produces sublime riesling and pinot noir.

Waipara Valley Not to be left out of proceedings, Christchurch has its own nearby wine region – the Waipara Valley just north of the city – where divine riesling and pinot noir come to fruition.

Auckland & Around Vineyards established in the early 1900s unfurl across the countryside around Auckland, producing swell syrah and pinot gris to the north and chardonnay to the west. In the middle of the Hauraki Gulf, a short ferry ride from Auckland, Waiheke has a hot, dry microclimate that just happens to be brilliant for growing reds and rosés.

Plan Your Trip

Travel with Children

New Zealand's a dream for family travel: kid-centric activities, family-friendly accommodation, a moderate climate and very few critters that can bite or sting. Cuisine is chilli-free and food servers are clued up on dietary requirements. Base yourself in a sizeable town for amenities galore and excursions within a short drive.

New Zealand for Kids

Fabulous wildlife parks, beaches, parks, snowy slopes and interactive museums proliferate across NZ. There are countless attractions and amenities designed specifically for kids but families needn't stick to playgrounds and holiday parks. Kid-appropriate adventures, from glaciers to white-water rafting, are everywhere...if parents are brave enough, that is.

Children's Highlights

Beaches

Hahei Beach The classic NZ summer beach. On the Coromandel Peninsula. (p223)

Ngarunui Beach Learn to surf on gentle Waikato waves in view of lifeguards. (p194)

Mt Maunganui Sand and surf for the kids, cafes and bars for the oldies. (p317)

Hot Water Beach Dig your own hot pool in the Coromandel sand (but check the temperature). (p224)

St Kilda & St Clair Beaches Kids don't mind chilly Dunedin, parents can warm up in the saltwater pool. (p554)

Best Regions for Kids

Rotorua & the Bay of Plenty

Wow, bubbling volcanic mud, stinky gas, gushing geysers and Māori *haka* performances! Rotorua is hard to beat from a kid's perspective. And around the Bay of Plenty coast are beaut beaches and plenty of fish and chip shops.

Wellington Region

You need a compact city if you're walking around with kids. Wellington fits the bill, with a brilliant museum, a ratchety cable car, lots of cheery cafes and fab Kapiti Coast beaches less than an hour away.

Queenstown & Wanaka

New Zealand's winter sports scene suits pro snowheads (and après-ski fans) but it's just as easy to enjoy with kids...actually, it's more fun. Cardrona has kid-friendly skiing, and there's Wanaka's Puzzling World for ski-free days.

Christchurch & Canterbury

Nature parks, row boats, the International Antarctic Centre and botanic gardens in the big city, and the amazing Banks Peninsula not far away (penguins, dolphins and pretty birds).

Wildlife Encounters

Kiwi Birdlife Park, Queenstown Spot a kiwi and myriad squawking birds. (p575)

Akaroa Dolphins Watch dolphins from a catamaran, in the company of a wildlife-spotting dog. (p507)

West Coast Wildlife Centre, Franz Josef Meet the world's rarest kiwi and tuatara (pint-sized dinosaurs). (p468)

Zealandia, Wellington Twittering birds in the predator-free Wellington hills. (p368)

Royal Albatross Centre Watch little penguins waddle ashore at dusk from Pilots Beach on the Otago Peninsula. (p562)

Culture with Kids

Te Papa, Wellington Earthquakes, Māori culture and molten magma. (p368)

Auckland Museum The Auckland volcanic field and a 25m *waka taua* (war canoe). (p86)

Hobbiton, Matamata Tours of hobbit holes and a drink in the Green Dragon Inn. (p198)

Canterbury Museum, Christchurch A mummy, dinosaur bones and a cool Discovery Centre. (p487)

Puke Ariki, New Plymouth A mighty big shark plus Māori exhibits and more. (p234)

Shantytown, Greymouth All aboard a steam train for gold-panning in a recreated gold-rush town. (p458)

But We're Hungry Now...

Mt Vic Chippery, Wellington Exceptional fish and (five kinds of!) chips. (p385)

Hastings Farmers Market Fill a basket and have a picnic. (p358)

Kiwifruit, Motueka Pick up a ripe bag at harvest time at the Sunday market. (Map p432; Wallace St; ⊙8am-1pm Sun)

Sweet Alice's Fudge Kitchen, Hokitika Candies, ice cream and fudge on the West Coast. (Map p464; ☑03-755 5359; 27 Tancred St; fudge per slice $7; ⊙10am-5pm)

Gisborne Farmers Market (p339) Macadamia nuts, oranges, pastries...and all of it local.

Planning

For all-round information and advice, check out Lonely Planet's *Travel with Children*. Plan ahead by browsing Kidz Go! (www.kidzgo.co.nz) or pick up a free copy of its booklet from tourism info centres in Queenstown, Wanaka and Fiordland.

Accommodation

Many motels and holiday parks have playgrounds, games rooms and kids' DVDs, and often fenced swimming pools, trampolines and acres of grass (many have laundry facilities, too). Cots and high chairs aren't always available at budget and midrange accommodation, but top-end hotels supply them and some provide child-minding services. The bach (a basic holiday home) is a good-value option, while farmstays can be highly entertaining with the menagerie of animals on-site.

Many B&Bs promote themselves as blissfully kid-free, and most hostels focus on the backpacker demographic. But there are plenty of hostels (including YHA) that do allow kids.

Getting Around

If your kids are little, check that your car-hire company can supply the right-sized car seat for your child, and that the seat will be properly fitted. Some companies legally require you to fit car seats yourself.

Most public transport – buses, trains, ferries etc – caters for young passengers, with discounted fares and a helping hand getting your stroller/nappy bag/shopping aboard.

Consider hiring a campervan for the whole trip. These formidable beasts are everywhere in NZ, kitted out with beds, kitchens, even toilets and TVs. Hire companies proliferate in major centres, with reasonable rates once you consider the savings on accommodation (and goodbye unpacking, repacking and leaving teddy in a hotel room).

Useful Websites

Kids Friendly Travel (www.kidsfriendlytravel.com) Directs you to baby equipment hire, accommodation listings and more.

LetsGoKids (http://letsgokids.co.nz) Download the NZ edition for family travel inspiration and money-saving vouchers.

Kidspot (www.kidspot.co.nz) The 'Family Fun' section has suggestions for child-friendly activities, road trips and more.

Kids New Zealand (www.kidsnewzealand.com) Listings of family-friendly cafes and activities.

Regions at a Glance

Auckland Region

Eating & Drinking
Geology
Coastline

Restaurants, Bars & Cafes

As well as having the lion's share of the nation's best restaurants, Auckland has excellent markets, a plethora of cheap Asian eateries, a hip cafe and bar scene, and wine regions on three of its flanks. And coffee culture is booming (don't tell anyone from Wellington...).

Volcanic Viewpoints

Auckland is, quite literally, a global hotspot: over 50 separate volcanoes have formed this unique topography – and the next one could pop up at any time. Take a hike up one of the dormant cones dotting the landscape for a high, wide and handsome city panorama.

Beaches

From the calm, child-friendly bays facing the Hauraki Gulf to the black-sand surf beaches of the west coast, to the breath-taking coastline of the offshore islands, beach lovers are spoiled for choice around Auckland.

p76

Bay of Islands & Northland

Coastline
Wilderness
History

Beaches & Bays

Beautiful bays line Northland's east coast, making it a favourite destination for families, surfers and fishing fans.

Ancient Forests

Kauri forests once blanketed NZ's entire north, and in the pockets where the giants remain, particularly in the Waipoua Forest, they're an imposing sight.

Kerikeri & Waitangi

New Zealand was settled top down by both Māori and Europeans, with missionaries erecting the country's oldest surviving buildings in Kerikeri. In nearby Waitangi, the treaty that founded the modern nation was first signed.

p139

Waikato & the Coromandel Peninsula

Coastline
Towns
Caves

Beaches & Surf

Find safe swimming and world-class surf at legendary Manu Bay. Beaches on the Coromandel are extremely popular in summer, but glorious isolation can still be yours.

Small-Town Charm

Te Aroha, Cambridge, Matamata and Raglan have great pubs, cafes, restaurants and friendly locals, while Thames and Coromandel Town display their historic gold-rush roots.

Waitomo Caves

Don't miss black-water rafting (along underground rivers) at Waitomo Caves, NZ's most staggering cave site...or just float lazily through amazing grottoes of glowworms.

p181

Taranaki & Whanganui

Wilderness
Cities
Coastline

National Parks

Isolated Whanganui National Park is steeped in Māori lore. Lording over New Plymouth, Mt Taranaki (Egmont National Park) is a picture-perfect peak with fabulous tramping.

Underrated Hubs

Midsized cities New Plymouth, Whanganui and Palmerston North are usually overlooked by travellers but you'll find fantastic restaurants, hip bars, wonderful museums and friendly folk.

Surf & Sand

Hit Surf Hwy 45 south of New Plymouth for black-sand beaches and gnarly breaks. Whanganui offers remote, storm-buffered beaches, while the Horowhenua District has acres of empty brown sand.

p231

Taupo & the Ruapehu Region

Wilderness
Scenery
Outdoor Activities

Lake & Rivers

New Zealand's mightiest river (the Waikato) is born from NZ's greatest lake (Taupo): aquatic pursuits abound (kayaking, sailing, fishing) and hot springs bubble up nearby.

Dramatic Land

Three steaming, smoking, occasionally erupting volcanoes – Ruapehu, Tongariro and Ngauruhoe – are an imposing sight, and the focus of skiing in winter and tramping the rest of the year.

Extreme Taupo

Skydiving, bungy jumping, whitewater rafting, jetboating, mountain biking, wakeboarding, parasailing, skiing – you want thrills, you got 'em.

p264

Rotorua & the Bay of Plenty

Geothermal Activity
Indigenous Culture
Activities

Volcanic Hubbub

The Rotorua landscape is littered with geysers, geothermal vents and hot springs. New Zealand's only active marine volcano, Whakaari (White Island), is 48km off the coast.

Māori Culture

Engage with Māori culture in Rotorua at traditional dance and musical performances, *haka* (war dances) and *hangi* (Māori feasts).

Outdoor Sports

Paragliding, surfing, skydiving, zorbing, jetboating, blokarting, white-water rafting, mountain biking, kayaking...or just have a swim at the beach.

p291

The East Coast

Coastline
Wine
Architecture

Coastal Scenery

Follow in the footsteps of early Māori and James Cook along this stretch of coastline, home to the East Cape Lighthouse and Cape Kidnappers' gaggling gannet colony.

Wine Regions

Sip your way through Gisborne's bright chardonnays, then head to Hawke's Bay for seriously good Bordeaux-style reds and fine winery dining.

Art-Deco Napier

Napier's art-deco town centre is a magnet for architecture lovers, the keenest of whom time their visit for the annual Art Deco Weekend in February.

p332

Wellington Region

Arts
Eating & Drinking
Nightlife

Museums & Galleries

Crowbarred into the city centre are quality display spaces including the interactive Te Papa museum and internationally flavoured City Gallery Wellington.

Cafe Culture

With more than a dozen roasters and scores of hip cafes, Wellington remains the coffee capital of NZ. Start with Havana Coffee Works or Fidel's.

Bars

Between the boho bars around Cuba St and Courtenay Pl's glitzy drinking dens, you should find enough to keep you buzzed until sun up.

p366

Marlborough & Nelson

Wine
Wilderness
Nature

Marlborough Wine Region

Bobbing in Marlborough's sea of sauvignon blanc, riesling, pinot noir and bubbly are barrel loads of quality cellar-door experiences and regional food.

National Parks

Not satisfied with just one national park, the Nelson region has three: Nelson Lakes, Kahurangi and Abel Tasman. You could tramp in all three over a week.

Kaikoura Wildlife

The top of the South Island is home to a menagerie of creatures, both in the water and on the wing. Pretty little Kaikoura offers myriad wildlife tours.

p402

The West Coast

Wilderness
Outdoor Activities
History

Natural Wonders

Around 90% of its territory lies within the conservation estate. Don't miss Punakaiki's Pancake Rocks and the Oparara basin.

Tramping

Expect dramatic views along hour-long tracks and hardcore epics, like the wind-scoured, wildlife-rich Cape Foulwind Walkway.

Pioneering Heritage

The West Coast's raffish pioneering heritage comes vividly to life in places like Reefton and Shantytown (Greymouth), and in ghost towns like Waiuta.

p446

Christchurch & Canterbury

History
Outdoor Activities
Scenery

Christchurch & Akaroa

Earthquakes have damaged Christchurch's architectural heritage, but the Canterbury Museum, Botanic Gardens and New Brighton St still showcase the city's history. Nearby, Akaroa proudly celebrates its French heritage.

Tramping & Kayaking

Explore alpine valleys around Arthur's Pass, kayak on Akaroa Harbour, or visit Aoraki/Mt Cook National Park for tramping and kayaking amid glacial lakes.

Banks Peninsula & the Southern Alps

Descend from Banks Peninsula's Summit Rd to explore hidden bays and coves, and experience nature's grand scale: the river valleys, soaring peaks and glaciers of the Southern Alps.

p479

Dunedin & Otago

Wildlife
Wine
History

Birds, Seals & Sea Lions

Seals, sea lions and penguins patrol the Otago Peninsula, while rocky Taiaroa Head is the planet's only mainland breeding location for the magnificent royal albatross.

Bannockburn & Waitaki Valley

Barrel into the craggy valleys of Bannockburn for excellent vineyard restaurants or delve into the up-and-coming Waitaki Valley wine scene for riesling and pinot gris.

Victoriana

Explore the arty and storied streets of Dunedin, or escape by foot or penny-farthing bicycle into the heritage ambience of Oamaru's Victorian Precinct.

p537

Queenstown & Wanaka

Outdoor Activities
Scenery
Wine

Extreme Queenstown

Few places on earth offer so many adventurous activities: bungy jumping, river rafting, skiing and mountain biking only scratch Queenstown's adrenaline-fuelled surface.

Mountains & Lakes

Queenstown's photogenic combination of Lake Wakatipu and the soaring Remarkables is a real jaw-dropper. Or venture into prime NZ wilderness around Glenorchy and Mt Aspiring National Park.

Southern Wineries

Start with lunch at Amisfield Winery's excellent restaurant, then explore the Gibbston subregion and finish with a riesling tasting at Rippon, overlooking gorgeous Lake Wanaka.

p572

Fiordland & Southland

Scenery
Outdoor Activities
Cruises & Coast

Epic Landscapes

The star of the deep-south show is remarkable Milford Sound, but take time to explore the rugged Catlins coast or remote, end-of-the-world Stewart Island.

Tramping

Test yourself by tramping the Milford or Hump Ridge Tracks, or amble easy hour-long trails along the Milford Hwy.

Watery Thrills

Cruise or kayak around glorious Doubtful Sound, test the surf in Curio Bay or get sprayed by waterfalls in the Catlins.

p608

On the Road

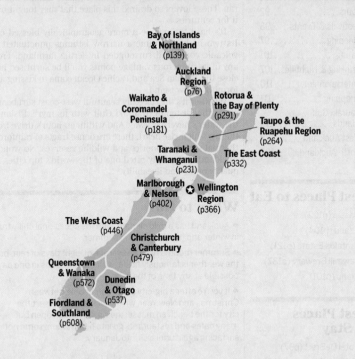

Auckland Region

Best Places to Eat

➡ Cassia (p102)

➡ Azabu (p104)

➡ Tantalus Estate (p121)

➡ Sawmill Brewery (p137)

➡ Giapo (p101)

Best Places to Stay

➡ Hotel DeBrett (p97)

➡ Waiheke Dreams (p120)

➡ XSPOT (p127)

➡ Ascot Parnell (p100)

➡ Piha Beachstay – Jandal Palace (p130)

Why Go?

Paris may be the city of love, but Auckland is the city of many lovers, according to its Māori name, Tāmaki Makaurau. Those lovers so desired this place that they fought over it for centuries.

It's hard to imagine a more geographically blessed city. Its two harbours frame a narrow isthmus punctuated by volcanic cones and surrounded by fertile farmland. From any of its numerous vantage points you'll be surprised how close the Tasman Sea and Pacific Ocean come to kissing and forming a new island.

Whether it's the ruggedly beautiful west-coast surf beaches, or the glistening Hauraki Gulf with its myriad islands, the water's never far away. And within an hour's drive from the city's high-rise heart, there are dense tracts of rainforest, thermal springs, wineries and wildlife reserves. No wonder Auckland is regularly rated one of the world's top cities for quality of life and liveability.

When to Go

➡ Auckland has a mild climate, with the occasional chilly frost in winter and high humidity in summer.

➡ Summer months have an average of eight days of rain, but the weather is famously fickle, with 'four seasons in one day' possible at any time of the year.

➡ If you're after a big-city buzz, don't come between Christmas and New Year, when Aucklanders desert the city for the beach en masse; the sights remain open but many cafes and restaurants go into hibernation, some not surfacing again until well into January.

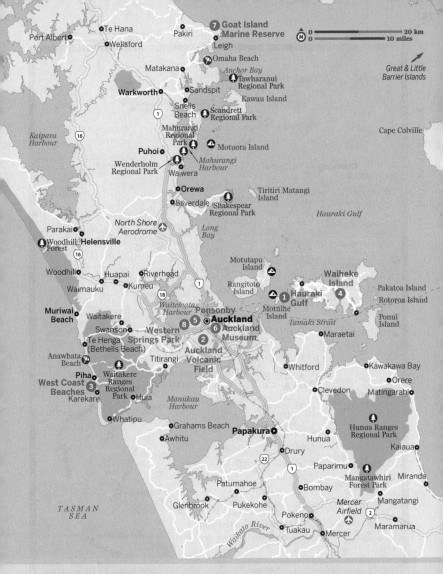

Auckland Highlights

1 **Hauraki Gulf** (p115)
Getting out on the water and visiting the island sanctuaries dotting this beautiful expanse.

2 **Auckland Volcanic Field** (p98) Exploring Auckland's fascinating volcanic mountains, lakes and islands.

3 **West Coast Beaches** (p129) Treading the mystical and treacherous black sands of Karekare and Piha.

4 **Waiheke Island** (p117)
Schlepping around world-class wineries and beaches.

5 **Ponsonby** (p108) Buzzing around the cafes, restaurants and bars of Auckland's hippest inner-city suburb.

6 **Auckland Museum** (p86) Being awed by the Māori *taonga* (treasures) and moved, literally, in the eruption

simulation and, figuratively, in the war memorial galleries.

7 **Goat Island Marine Reserve** (p138) Swimming with the fishes only a few steps from the beach at this pretty bay.

8 **Pasifika Festival** (p96) Soaking up the Polynesian vibe at this massive festival, held in March at Western Springs Park.

Auckland

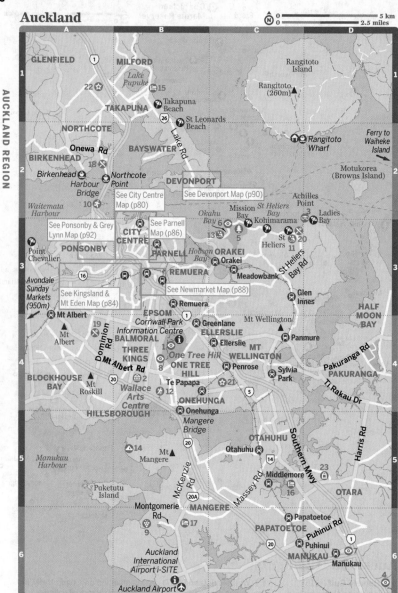

ⓘ Getting There & Away

Auckland is linked to the rest of the world with direct flights to/from Asia, North America, South America, Australia and the South Pacific. Domestic flights reach all parts of the country, and buses or trains head north and south to the Bay of Islands, Hamilton, Wellington and other provincial centres. Ferries are a vital service to reach Waiheke, Great Barrier and the other islands of the Hauraki Gulf. Auckland Transport (p115) has information on using buses, trains and ferries to get around Auckland and the surrounding region.

Auckland

AUCKLAND

📕 09 / POP 1.42 MILLION

History

Māori occupation in the Auckland area
dates back around 800 years. Initial settlements were concentrated on the Hauraki
Gulf islands, but gradually the fertile isthmus beckoned and land was cleared for
growing food.

Over hundreds of years Tamaki's many
different tribes wrestled for control of the
area, building *pā* (fortified villages) on the
numerous volcanic cones. The Ngāti Whatua *iwi* (tribe) from the Kaipara Harbour
took the upper hand in 1741, occupying the
major *pā* sites. During the Musket Wars of
the 1820s they were decimated by the northern tribe Ngāpuhi, leaving the land all but
abandoned.

At the time the Treaty of Waitangi was
signed in 1840, Governor Hobson had his
base in the Bay of Islands. When Ngāti
Whatua chief Te Kawau offered 3000 acres
of land for sale on the northern edge of
the Waitemata Harbour, Hobson decided
to create a new capital, naming it after
one of his patrons, George Eden (Earl of
Auckland).

Beginning with just a few tents on a
beach, the settlement grew quickly, and soon
the port was busy exporting the region's
produce, including kauri timber. However,
it lost its capital status to centrally located
Wellington after just 25 years.

Since the beginning of the 20th century
Auckland has been New Zealand's fastest-
growing city and its main industrial centre.
Political deals may be done in Wellington,
but Auckland is the big smoke in the land of
the long white cloud.

In 2010 the municipalities and urban
districts that made up the Auckland Region were merged into one 'super-city',
and in 2011 the newly minted metropolis was given a buff and shine to prepare
it for hosting the Rugby World Cup. The
waterfront was redeveloped, the art gallery and zoo were given a makeover, and a
swag of new restaurants and bars popped
up – leaving a more vibrant city in the
Cup's wake.

The years since then have seen Auckland maintain its impetuous growth and
increasingly multicultural make-up – it is
the preferred destination for new immigrants to NZ – and while housing prices
and traffic snarls continue to frustrate
residents, it's still thrillingly and energeti-
cally the only true international city in the
country.

◎ Sights

Auckland is a city of volcanoes, with the
ridges of lava flows forming its main thor-
oughfares and its many cones providing islands of green. As well as being by far the
largest, it's also the most multicultural of
NZ's cities. A sizeable Asian community rubs
shoulders with the biggest Polynesian population of any city in the world.

The traditional Kiwi aspiration for a
freestanding house on a quarter-acre section has resulted in a vast, sprawling city.
The CBD was long ago abandoned to commerce, and inner-city apartment living has

City Centre

AUCKLAND REGION

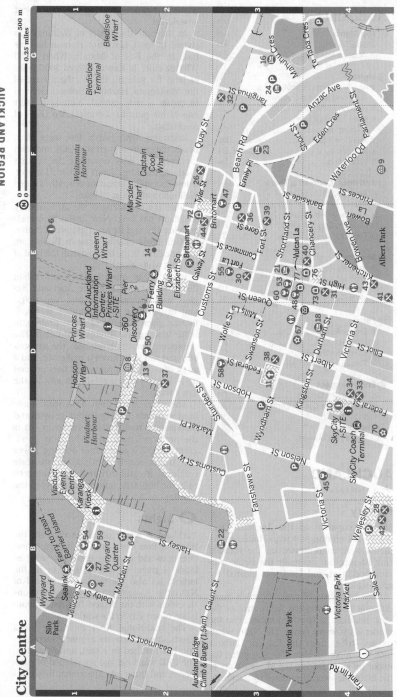

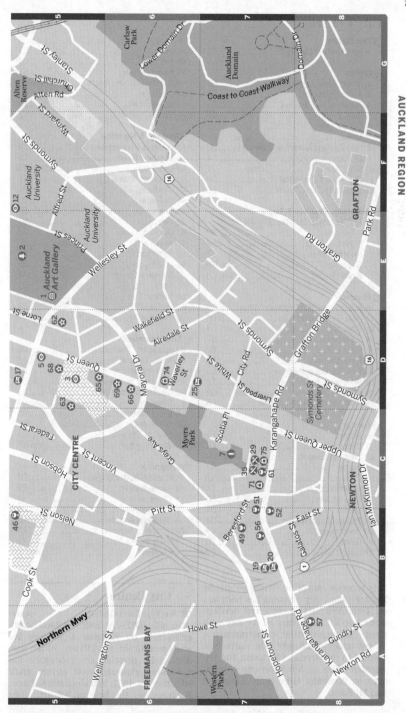

CITY CENTRE

FREEMANS BAY

NEWTON

GRAFTON

Auckland Domain

Carlaw Park

Alten Reserve

Western Park

Myers Park

Symonds St Cemetery

Coast to Coast Walkway

Lower Domain Dr

Domain Dr

Park Rd

Grafton Rd

Grafton Bridge

Stanley St

Churchill St

Alten Rd

Wynyard St

Symonds St

Alfred St

Princes St

Auckland University

Auckland University

Wellesley St

Lorne St

Wakefield St

Airedale St

Symonds St

City Rd

White St

Liverpool St

Karangahape Rd

Upper Queen St

Symonds St

Queen St

Mayoral Dr

Waverley St

Scotia Pl

Greys Ave

Federal St

Vincent St

Hobson St

Nelson St

Cook St

Pitt St

Beresford St

Galatos St

East St

Ian McKinnon Dr

Karangahape Rd

Hopetoun St

Howe St

Wellington St

Northern Mwy

Gundry St

Newton Rd

1 Auckland Art Gallery

City Centre

only recently caught on. While geography has been kind, city planning has been less so. Unbridled and ill-conceived development has left the centre of the city with plenty of architectural embarrassments. To get under Auckland's skin you're best to head to the streets of Victorian and Edwardian villas in hip inner-city suburbs such as Ponsonby, Grey Lynn, Kingsland and Mt Eden.

◎ City Centre

★ **Auckland Art Gallery** GALLERY
(Map p80; ☑09-379 1349; www.aucklandart-gallery.com; cnr Kitchener & Wellesley Sts; adult/student/child $20/17/free; ☺10am-5pm) Auckland's premier art repository has a striking glass-and-wood atrium grafted onto its 1887 French-chateau frame. It showcases the best of NZ art, along

with important works by Pieter Bruegel the Younger, Guido Reni, Picasso, Cézanne, Gauguin and Matisse. Highlights include the intimate 19th-century portraits of tattooed Māori subjects by Charles Goldie, and the starkly dramatic text-scrawled canvasses of Colin McCahon.

Free 60-minute tours depart from the foyer daily at 11.30am and 1.30pm.

Albert Park   PARK
(Map p80; Princes St) Hugging the hill on the city's eastern flank, Albert Park is a charming Victorian formal garden overrun by students from the neighbouring University of Auckland during term time. The park was once part of the Albert Barracks (1847), a fortification that enclosed 9 hectares during the New Zealand Wars. A portion of the original barracks wall survives at the centre of the university campus.

Sky Tower   TOWER
(Map p80; ☑09-363 6000; www.skycityauckland. co.nz; cnr Federal & Victoria Sts; adult/child $29/12; ☺8.30am-10.30pm Sun-Thu, to 11.30pm Fri & Sat Nov-Apr, 9am-10pm May-Oct) The impossible-to-miss Sky Tower looks like a giant hypodermic giving a fix to the heavens. Spectacular lighting renders it space age at night and the colours change for special events. At 328m it is the southern hemisphere's tallest structure. A lift takes you up to the observation decks in 40 stomach-lurching seconds; look down through the glass floor panels if you're after an extra kick. Consider visiting at sunset and having a drink in the Sky Lounge Cafe & Bar.

The Sky Tower is also home to the SkyWalk (p91) and SkyJump (p91).

Civic Theatre   THEATRE
(Map p80; ☑09-309 2677; www.aucklandlive. co.nz/venue/the-civic; cnr Queen & Wellesley Sts) The 'mighty Civic' (1929) is one of only seven 'atmospheric theatres' remaining in the world and a fine survivor from cinema's Golden Age. The auditorium has lavish Moorish decoration and a starlit southern-hemisphere night sky in the ceiling, complete with cloud projections and shooting stars. It's mainly used for touring musicals, international concerts and film-festival screenings.

Old Government House   HISTORIC BUILDING
(Map p80; Waterloo Quadrant) FREE Built in 1856, this stately building was the colony's seat of power until 1865 when Wellington became the capital. The construction is unusual in that it's actually wooden but made to look like stone. It's now used by the University of Auckland, but feel free to wander through the lush gardens.

University Clock Tower   ARCHITECTURE
(Map p80; 22 Princes St) The University Clock Tower is Auckland's architectural triumph. This stately 'ivory' tower (1926) tips its hat towards art nouveau (the incorporation of NZ flora and fauna into the decoration) and the Chicago School (the way it's rooted into the earth). It's usually open, so wander inside.

St Patrick's Cathedral   CHURCH
(Map p80; ☑09-303 4509; www.stpatricks.org.nz; 43 Wyndham St; ☺7am-7pm) Auckland's Catholic cathedral (1907) is one of the city's loveliest buildings. Polished wood and Belgian stained glass lend warmth to the interior of the majestic Gothic Revival church. There's a historical display in the old confessional on the left-hand side.

Aotea Square   SQUARE
(Map p80; Queen St) The civic heart of the city.

Moses   SCULPTURE
(Map p80; Myers Park) This reproduction of Michelangelo's *Moses* was made from marble from the same quarry as the original.

◉ Britomart, Viaduct Harbour & Wynyard Quarter
Stretching for only a small grid of blocks above the train station, Britomart is a compact enclave of historic buildings and new developments that has been transformed into one of the city's best eating, drinking and shopping precincts. Most of Auckland's

---

ESSENTIAL AUCKLAND

Eat amid the diverse and cosmopolitan scene of Ponsonby Central (p104).

Drink world-class craft beer at Hallertau (p131) or the Sawmill Brewery (p137).

Read *Under the Mountain* (1979) – Maurice Gee's teenage tale of slimy things lurking under Auckland's volcanoes.

Listen to *Melodrama* (2017) – The successful sophomore album from Devonport's very own Lorde.

Watch *The Piano* (1993) – Multiple Oscar winner filmed at Karekare Beach.

Celebrate at Pasifika (p96)

Go online www.aucklandnz.com; www. lonelyplanet.com/new-zealand/auckland

Kingsland & Mt Eden

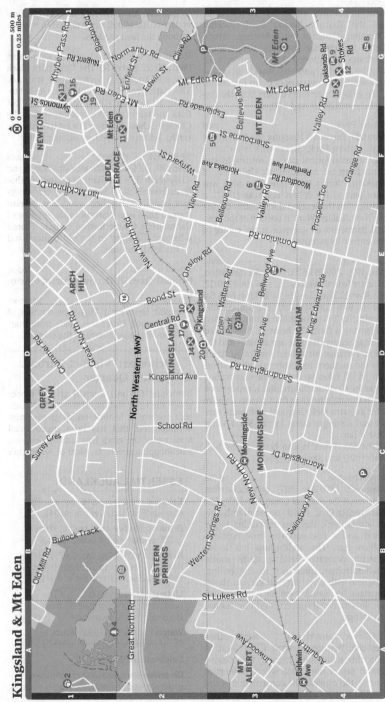

N 0 500 m
0 0.25 miles

MT EDEN
NEWTON
EDEN TERRACE
ARCH HILL
GREY LYNN
WESTERN SPRINGS
KINGSLAND
SANDRINGHAM
MORNINGSIDE
MT ALBERT

Mt Eden Rd
Boston Rd
Khyber Pass Rd
Symonds St
Nugent Rd
Normanby Rd
Clive Rd
Enfield St
Edwin St
Mt Eden Rd
Esplanade Rd
Bellevue Rd
Sherbourne St
Oaklands Rd
Stokes Rd
Valley Rd
Grange Rd
Horoeka Ave
Wyndard St
Woodford Rd
Pentland Ave
Bellevue Rd
Valley Rd
Prospect Tce
Ian McKinnon Dr
View Rd
Dominion Rd
Onslow Rd
Bellwood Ave
Bond St
Kingsland
Central Rd
Watters Rd
Eden Park
Reimers Ave
King Edward Pde
New North Rd
Great North Rd
Cummin Rd
North Western Mwy
Kingsland Ave
Sandringham Rd
School Rd
New North Rd
Morningside
Morningside Dr
Surrey Cres
Western Springs Rd
Sainsbury Rd
St Lukes Rd
Old Mill Rd
Bullock Track
Great North Rd
Linwood Ave
Asquith Ave
Baldwin Ave
Mt Eden

Kingsland & Mt Eden

top fashion designers have recently decamped to the Britomart area from further uptown in High St.

Once a busy commercial port, the Viaduct Harbour was given a major makeover for the 1999/2000 and 2003 America's Cup yachting events. It's now a fancy dining and boozing precinct, and guaranteed to have at least a slight buzz any night of the week. Historical plaques, public sculpture and the chance to gawk at millionaires' yachts make it a diverting place for a stroll.

Connected to the Viaduct by a bascule bridge, Wynyard Quarter opened in advance of another sporting tournament, 2011's Rugby World Cup. With its public plazas, waterfront eateries, events centre, fish market and children's playground, it has quickly become Auckland's favourite new place to promenade. At the Silo Park area, down the western end, free outdoor Friday night movies and weekend markets have become summertime institutions. Most of Wynyard's better restaurants are set back from the water, on Jellicoe St.

New Zealand Maritime Museum MUSEUM
(Map p80; ☑09-373 0800; www.maritime museum.co.nz; 149-159 Quay St; adult/child $50/25, incl harbour cruise $50/25; ⊙9am-5pm, free tours 10.30am & 1pm Mon-Fri) This museum traces NZ's seafaring history, from Māori voyaging canoes to the America's Cup. Recreations include a tilting 19th-century, steerage-class cabin and a 1950s beach store and bach (holiday home). 'Blue Water Black Magic' is a tribute to Sir Peter Blake, the Whitbread-Round-the-World and America's Cup-winning yachtsman who was murdered in 2001 on an environmental monitoring trip in the Amazon. Packages including an optional one-hour harbour cruise on a heritage boat are also available.

Lighthouse PUBLIC ART
(Map p80; Queens Wharf) Auckland's most recent installation of public art is this replica 'state house' – a form of public housing popular in NZ in the 1930s and 1940s – erected by artist Michael Parekōwhai at the end of Queens Wharf in early 2017. Māori-influenced *tukutuku* panels punctuate the exterior, while inside is a neon-lit, stainless-steel representation of British maritime explorer Captain James Cook. The house's idiosyncratic design is a commentary on sovereignty and colonialism. Best visited after dark.

Auckland Fish Market MARKET
(Map p80; ☑09-379 1490; www.aucklandfish market.co.nz; 22-32 Jellicoe St; ⊙7.30am-6pm) Early morning auctions combine with fish shops, cafes and restaurants, and a seafood-cooking school.

◉ Mt Eden

★Mt Eden VOLCANO
(Maungawhau; Map p84; 250 Mt Eden Rd) From the top of Auckland's highest volcanic cone (196m) the entire isthmus and both harbours are laid bare. The symmetrical crater (50m deep) is known as Te Ipu Kai a Mataaho (the Food Bowl of Mataaho, the god of things hidden in the ground) and is considered highly *tapu* (sacred). Do not enter it, but feel free to explore the remainder of the mountain. The remains of *pā* terraces and food storage pits are clearly visible.

Eden Garden GARDENS
(Map p88; ☑09-638 8395; www.edengarden.co.nz; 24 Omana Ave; adult/child $10/free; ⊙9am-4pm) On Mt Eden's rocky eastern slopes, this mature garden is noted for its camellias, rhododendrons and azaleas.

Parnell

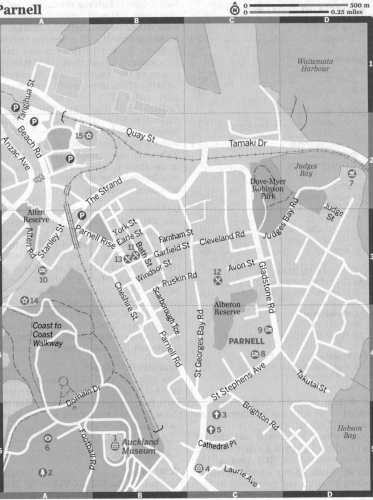

Parnell & Newmarket

Parnell is one of Auckland's oldest areas, and amid the cafes, restaurants and fancy retailers are several heritage buildings. Neighbouring Newmarket is a busy shopping precinct known for its boutiques.

★ **Auckland Museum**   MUSEUM
(☑09-309 0443; www.aucklandmuseum.com; Auckland Domain, Parnell; adult/child $25/10; ⊙10am-5pm) This imposing neoclassical temple (1929), capped with an impressive copper-and-glass dome (2007), dominates the Auckland Domain and is a prominent part of the Auckland skyline, especially when viewed from the harbour. Admission packages can be purchased, which incorporate a highlights tour and a Māori cultural performance ($45 to $55).

The displays of Pacific Island and Māori artefacts on the museum's ground floor are essential viewing. Highlights include a 25m war canoe and an extant carved meeting house (remove your shoes before entering). There's also a fascinating display on Auckland's volcanic field, including an eruption simulation, and the upper floors showcase military displays, fulfilling the building's dual role as a war memorial. Auckland's

Parnell

main Anzac commemorations take place at dawn on 25 April at the cenotaph in the museum's forecourt.

Check the website for details of interesting, one-off local and international exhibitions.

Auckland Domain PARK
(Map p86; Domain Dr, Parnell; ◷24hr) Covering about 80 hectares, this green swathe contains the Auckland Museum, sports fields, interesting sculpture, formal gardens, wild corners and the **Wintergarden** (Map p80; Wintergarden Rd, Parnell; ◷9am-5.30pm Mon-Sat, to 7.30pm Sun Nov-Mar, 9am-4.30pm Apr-Oct) **FREE**, with its fernery, tropical house, cool house, cute cat statue, coffee kiosk and neighbouring cafe. The mound in the centre of the park is all that remains of Pukekaroa, one of Auckland's volcanoes. At its humble peak, a totara tree surrounded by a palisade honours the first Māori king.

St Mary's Church CHURCH
(Map p86; Parnell Rd, Parnell; ◷10am-3pm) Next door to the **Holy Trinity Cathedral** (Map p86; ☏09-303 9500; www.holy-trinity.org.nz; cnr St Stephens Ave & Parnell Rd, Parnell; ◷10am-3pm), this wonderful wooden Gothic Revival church (1886) has a burnished interior and interesting stained-glass windows.

Kinder House HISTORIC BUILDING
(Map p86; ☏09-379 4008; www.kinder.org.nz; 2 Ayr St, Parnell; by donation; ◷noon-3pm Wed-Sun) Built of volcanic stone, this 1857 home displays the watercolours and memorabilia of the Reverend Dr John Kinder (1819–1903), headmaster of the Church of England Grammar School.

◉ Tamaki Drive

This scenic, pohutukawa-lined road heads east from the city, hugging the waterfront. In summer it's a jogging/cycling/rollerblading blur.

A succession of child-friendly, peaceful swimming beaches starts at **Ohaku Bay**. Around the headland is **Mission Bay**, a popular beach with an electric-lit, art-deco fountain, historic mission house, restaurants and bars. Safe swimming beaches **Kohimarama** and **St Heliers** follow. Further east along Cliff Rd, the **Achilles Point Lookout** (Map p78; Cliff Rd, St Heliers) offers panoramic views and Māori carvings. At its base is **Ladies Bay**, popular with nudists.

Buses 767 and 769 from behind Britomart station follow this route, while buses 745 to 757 go as far as Mission Bay.

Kelly Tarlton's Sea Life Aquarium AQUARIUM
(Map p78; ☏09-531 5065; www.kellytarltons.co.nz; 23 Tamaki Dr, Orakei; adult/child $39/22; ◷9.30am-5pm) In this topsy-turvy aquarium sharks and stingrays swim over and around you in transparent tunnels that were once stormwater tanks. You can also enter the tanks in a shark cage with a snorkel ($124), or dive straight into the tanks ($265). Other attractions include the Penguin Discovery tour (10.30am Tuesday to Sunday, $199 per person) where just four visitors per day can get up close with Antarctic penguins. For all tickets, there are significant discounts online, especially for midweek visits.

A free shark-shaped shuttle bus departs from 172 Quay St (opposite the Ferry Building (p115)) hourly on the half-hour from 9.30am to 3.30pm.

Bastion Point PARK
(Map p78; Hapimana St, Orakei) Politics, harbour views and lush lawns combine on this pretty headland with a chequered history. An elaborate cliff-top garden mausoleum honours Michael Joseph Savage (1872–1940), the country's first Labour prime minister, whose socialist reforms left him adored by

the populace. Follow the lawn to a WWII gun embankment – one of many that line the harbour.

◉ Devonport

With well-preserved Victorian and Edwardian buildings and loads of cafes, Devonport is an extremely pleasant place to visit and only a short ferry trip from the city. There are also two volcanic cones to climb and easy access to the first of the North Shore's beaches.

For a self-guided tour of historic buildings, pick up the *Old Devonport Walk* pamphlet from the Visit Devonport (p113) information centre. Bikes can be hired from the ferry terminal.

Ferries to Devonport (adult/child return $12/6.50, 12 minutes) depart from the Ferry Building at least every 30 minutes from 6.15am to 11.30pm (until 1am Fridays and Saturdays), and from 7.15am to 10pm on Sundays and public holidays. Some Waiheke Island and Rangitoto ferries also stop here.

Mt Victoria (Takarunga; Map p90; Victoria Rd, Devonport) and **North Head** (Maungauika; Map p90; Takarunga Rd, Devonport; ⊙6am-10pm) were Māori *pā* and they remain fortresses of sorts, with the navy maintaining a presence. Both have gun embankments and North Head is riddled with tunnels, dug at the end of the 19th century in response to the Russian threat, and extended during WWI and WWII. The gates are locked at night, but that's never stopped teenagers from jumping the fence for scary subterranean explorations.

Between the two, **Cambria Reserve** stands on the remains of a third volcanic cone that was largely quarried away.

Newmarket ⓝ

Torpedo Bay Navy Museum MUSEUM
(Map p90; ☑09-445 5186; www.navymuseum.mil.nz; 64 King Edward Pde, Devonport; ⊙10am-5pm) **FREE** The navy has been in Devonport since the earliest days of the colony. Its history is on display at this well-presented and often moving museum, focusing on the stories of the sailors themselves.

◉ Kingsland & Western Springs

Auckland Zoo ZOO
(Map p84; ☑09-360 3805; www.aucklandzoo.co.nz; Motions Rd; adult/child $28/12; ⊙9.30am-5pm, last entry 4.15pm) ⏺ At this modern, spacious zoo, the big foreigners tend to steal the attention from the timid natives, but if you can wrestle the kids away from the tigers and orang-utans, there's a well-presented NZ section. Called Te Wao Nui, it's divided into six ecological zones: Coast (seals, penguins), Islands (mainly lizards, including NZ's pint-sized dinosaur, the tuatara), Wetlands (ducks, herons, eels), Night (kiwi, naturally, along with frogs, native owls and weta), Forest (birds) and High Country (cheekier birds and lizards).

Frequent buses (adult/child $5.50/3) run from 99 Albert St in the city to bus stop 8124 on Great North Rd, where it is a 700m walk to the zoo's entrance.

Western Springs PARK
(Map p84; Great North Rd; ⚐) Parents bring their children to this picturesque park for the popular playground. It's a pleasant picnic spot and a good place to get acquainted with pukeko (swamp hens), ducks and pushy geese. This coastal lake was formed by a confluence of lava flows, where more than 4 million litres of spring water bubble up into the central lake daily. From the city, catch any bus heading west via Great North Rd (adult/child $5/3). By car, take the Western Springs exit from the North Western Motorway.

◉ Other Areas

★ One Tree Hill VOLCANO, PARK
(Maungakiekie; Map p78) This volcanic cone was the isthmus' key *pā* and the greatest fortress in the country. At the top (182m) there are 360-degree views and the grave of John Logan Campbell, who gifted the land to the city in 1901 and requested that a memorial be built to the Māori people on the summit. Nearby is the stump of the last 'one tree'. Allow time to explore surrounding **Cornwall Park** with its mature trees and historic Acacia Cottage (1841).

City Walk
City Centre Ramble

START ST KEVIN'S ARCADE,
KARANGAHAPE RD
END WYNYARD QUARTER
LENGTH 4.5KM; AROUND 3 HOURS

This walk aims to show you some hidden
nooks and architectural treats in Auckland's
somewhat scrappy city centre. Start among
the restaurants and vintage boutiques of
1 St Kevin's Arcade (p112) and take the
stairs down to Myers Park. Look out for the
reproduction of Michelangelo's **2 Moses**
(p83) at the bottom of the stairs. Continue
through the park, taking the stairs on the
right just before the overpass to head up to
street level.

Heading down Queen St, you'll pass the
3 Auckland Town Hall (p111) and **4 Aotea
Square** (p83), the civic heart of the city. On
the next corner is the wonderful **5 Civic
Theatre** (p83). Turn right on Wellesley St
and then left onto Lorne St. Immediately to
your right is **6 Khartoum Pl**, with tiling that
celebrates NZ women's historic victory, becoming the first in the world to win the vote.
Head up the stairs to the **7 Auckland Art
Gallery** (p82).

Behind the gallery is **8 Albert Park**
(p83). Cross through it and turn left onto
Princes St, where a row of **9 Victorian
merchant's houses** faces the **10 University
Clock Tower** (p83). Cut around behind the
clock tower to **11 Old Government House**
(p83) and then follow the diagonal path back
to Princes St. The attractive building on the
corner of Princes St and Bowen Ave was once
the city's main **12 synagogue**.

Head down Bowen Ave and cut through
the park past the **13 Chancery precinct** to
the **14 High St** shopping strip. Take a left
onto **15 Vulcan Lane**, lined with historic
pubs. Turn right onto Queen St and follow
it down to the **16 Britomart train station**
(p115), housed in the former central post office. You're now standing on reclaimed land –
the original shoreline was at Fort St. Detour
to the nearby **17 Britomart** precinct for good
bars, restaurants and fashion boutiques.

From Britomart train station, turn left on
Quay St and head to **18 Viaduct Harbour**,
bustling with bars and cafes, and then continue over the bridge to the rejuvenated
19 Wynyard Quarter.

Devonport

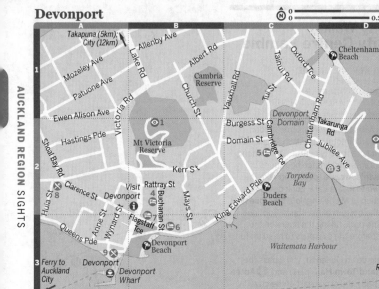

Devonport

◉ Sights

🛏 Sleeping

✖ Eating

The Cornwall Park Information Centre (p113) has fascinating interactive displays illustrating what the *pā* would have looked like when 5000 people lived here. Near the excellent children's playground, the **Stardome** (Map p78; ☑09-624 1246; www.stardome.org.nz; 670 Manukau Rd; shows adult/child from $12/10; ⊙10am-5pm Mon, to 9.30pm Tue-Thu, to 11pm Fri-Sun) FREE offers regular stargazing and planetarium shows (usually 7pm and 8pm Wednesday to Sunday, with extra shows on weekends) that aren't dependent on Auckland's fickle weather.

To get to One Tree Hill from the the city take a train to Greenlane and walk 1km along Green Lane West. By car, take the Greenlane exit off the Southern Motorway and turn right into Green Lane West.

★ **Wallace Arts Centre**   GALLERY
(Map p78; ☑09-639 2010; www.tsbbankwallace artscentre.org.nz; Pah Homestead, 72 Hillsborough Rd, Hillsborough; ⊙10am-3pm Tue-Fri, to 5pm Sat & Sun) FREE Housed in a gorgeous 1879 mansion with views to One Tree Hill (p88) and the Manukau Harbour, this arts centre is endowed with contemporary New Zealand art from an extensive private collection, which is changed every four to six weeks. Have lunch on the veranda at the excellent **Homestead Cafe** and wander among the magnificent trees in the surrounding park. The art is also very accessible, ranging from a life-size skeletal rugby ruck to a vibrant Ziggy Stardust painted on glass.

Bus 299 (Lynfield) departs every 15 minutes from Queen St, outside the Civic Theatre (p83), and heads to Hillsborough Rd ($5.50, 40 minutes).

Auckland Botanic Gardens   GARDENS
(Map p78; ☑09-267 1457; www.auckland botanicgardens.co.nz; 102 Hill Rd, Manurewa; ⊙8am-6pm Apr-Sep, to 8pm Oct-Mar) 🌿 FREE This 64-hectare park has more than 10,000 plants

(including threatened species), dozens of themed gardens and an infestation of wedding parties. By car, take the Southern Motorway, exit at Manurewa and follow the signs. Otherwise take the train to Manurewa ($9, 43 minutes) and then walk along Hill Rd (1.5km).

MOTAT
MUSEUM

(Museum of Transport & Technology; Map p84; ☑09-815 5800; www.motat.org.nz; 805 Great North Rd, Western Springs; adult/child $19/10; ☺10am-5pm) This technology boffin's paradise is spread over two sites and 19 hectares. In the Great North Rd site look out for former Prime Minister Helen Clark's Honda 50 motorbike and the pioneer village. The Meola Rd site features the Aviation Display Hall with rare military and commercial planes. The two are linked by a vintage tram (free with admission, $1 otherwise), which passes Western Springs (p88) park and the zoo (p88). It's a fun kids' ride whether you visit MOTAT or not.

🏃 Activities

Nothing gets you closer to the heart and soul of Auckland than sailing on the Hauraki Gulf. If you can't afford a yacht cruise, catch a ferry instead.

Trading on the country's action-packed reputation, Auckland has sprouted its own set of thrill-inducing activities. Look around for backpacker reductions or special offers before booking anything.

Visitor centres and public libraries stock the city council's *Auckland City's Walkways* pamphlet, which has a good selection of urban walks, including information on the Coast to Coast Walkway.

Boating & Kayaking

Auckland Sea Kayaks
KAYAKING

(Map p78; ☑0800 999 089; www.auckland seakayaks.co.nz; 384 Tamaki Dr, St Heliers) 🖉 Guided trips (including lunch) to Rangitoto ($185, 6½ hours) and Motukorea (Browns Island; $135, four hours). Multiday excursions and sunset paddles are also available.

Fergs Kayaks
KAYAKING

(Map p78; ☑09-529 2230; www.fergskayaks.co.nz; 12 Tamaki Dr, Orakei; ☺9am-5pm) Hires kayaks (per hour from $25), paddle boards ($30), bikes ($20) and inline skates ($20). Guided kayak trips head to Devonport ($100, three hours, 8km) or Rangitoto ($160, six hours, 13km).

Extreme Sports

Auckland Bridge Climb & Bungy
ADVENTURE SPORTS

(Map p78; ☑09-360 7748; www.bungy.co.nz; 105 Curran St, Westhaven; adult/child climb $125/85, bungy $160/130) 🖉 Climb up or jump off the Auckland Harbour Bridge.

SkyWalk
ADVENTURE SPORTS

(Map p80; ☑0800 759 925; www.skywalk.co.nz; Sky Tower, cnr Federal & Victoria Sts; adult/child $145/115; ☺10am-4.30pm) The SkyWalk involves circling the 192m-high, 1.2m-wide outside halo of the Sky Tower (p83) without rails or a balcony. Don't worry, it's not completely crazy – there is a safety harness.

SkyJump
ADVENTURE SPORTS

(Map p80; ☑0800 759 586; www.skyjump.co.nz; Sky Tower, cnr Federal & Victoria Sts; adult/child $225/175; ☺10am-5.15pm) This thrilling 11-second, 85km/h base wire leap from the observation deck of the Sky Tower (p83) is more like a parachute jump than a bungy. Combine it with the SkyWalk in the Look & Leap package ($290).

Other Activities

Coast to Coast Walkway
WALKING

(Map p78; www.aucklandcity.govt.nz) Heading right across the country from the Tasman to the Pacific (which is actually only 16km), this walk encompasses One Tree Hill (p88), Mt Eden (p85), the Domain (p87) and the

---

ONE TREE TO RULE THEM ALL

Looking at One Tree Hill (p88), your first thought will probably be 'Where's the bloody tree?'. Good question. Up until 2000 a Monterey pine stood at the top of the hill. This was a replacement for a sacred totara that was chopped down by British settlers in 1852. Māori activists first attacked the foreign usurper in 1994, finishing the job in 2000.

After much consultation with local Māori and tree experts, a grove of six pohutukawa and three totara trees was planted on the summit in mid-2016. In an arboreal version of the *X-Factor*, the weaker performing trees will be eliminated, with only one tree left standing by 2026.

Auckland's most beloved landmark achieved international recognition in 1987 when U2 released the song 'One Tree Hill' on their acclaimed *The Joshua Tree* album. It was only released as a single in NZ, where it went to number one for six weeks.

Ponsonby & Grey Lynn

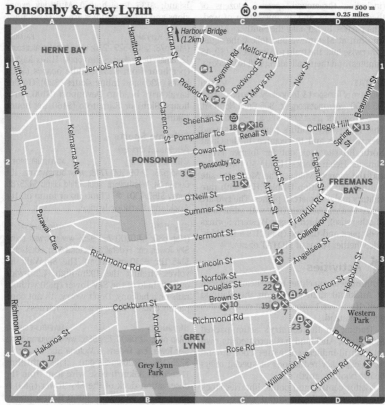

university, keeping mainly to reserves rather than city streets.

Do it in either direction: starting from the Viaduct Basin and heading south, it's marked by yellow markers and milestones; heading north from Onehunga there are blue markers. Our recommendation? Catch the train to Onehunga and finish up at the Viaduct's bars. From Onehunga station, take Onehunga Mall up to Princes St, turn left and pick up the track at the inauspicious park by the motorway.

Rapu NZ Surf'n'Snow Tours SURFING
(☑09-828 0426; www.rapuadventures.com; 1-/2-/5-/7-/14-day tour $120/199/800/1160/2154) One- or two-day surfing courses include transport, gear and two two-hour lessons each day, usually at Piha (others can tag along for the ride only for $50). Tours of five days or longer include accommodation (October to May only). Snow packages include transport to Mt Ruapehu.

Parnell Baths SWIMMING
(Map p86; ☑09-373 3561; www.parnellbaths. co.nz; Judges Bay Rd, Parnell; adult/child $6.40/ free; ⏰6am-8pm Mon-Fri, 8am-8pm Sat & Sun Nov-Easter) Outdoor saltwater pools with an awesome 1950s mural.

☞ Tours

Cultural

Tāmaki Hikoi CULTURAL
(☑021 146 9593; www.tamakihikoi.co.nz; 1/3hr $50/95) Guides from the Ngāti Whatua *iwi* (tribe) lead various Māori cultural tours, including walking and interpretation of sites such as Mt Eden (p85) and the Auckland Domain (p87).

TIME Unlimited CULTURAL
(☑09-846 3469; www.newzealandtours.travel; adult/child from $195/97.50) ✎ Cultural, walking and sightseeing tours from a Māori perspective.

Ponsonby & Grey Lynn

Food & Wine

Big Foody Food Tour   TOURS
(☑ 021 481 177, 0800 366 386; www.thebigfoody.com; per person $125-185) Small-group city tours, including visits to markets and artisan producers, and lots of tastings. A recent addition is hop-fuelled explorations of Auckland's burgeoning craft-beer scene.

Auckland Wine Trail Tours   TOURS
(☑ 09-630 1540; www.winetrailtours.co.nz) Small-group tours around west Auckland wineries and the Waitakere Ranges (half/full day $125/255); further afield to Matakana ($265); or a combo of the two ($265).

Walking

Bush & Beach   WALKING
(☑ 09-837 4130; www.bushandbeach.co.nz) 🚶 Tours including guided walks in the Waitakere Ranges and along west-coast beaches ($150 to $235); three-hour city minibus tours ($80); and food and wine tours in either Kumeu or Matakana (half/full day $235/325).

Auckland Ghost Tours   WALKING
(☑ 09-832 8047; www.aucklandghosttours.com; adult/child from $50/25; ⏱ 7pm Oct-Mar, 6pm Apr-Sep) Stories of Auckland's scary side on a two-hour walking tour of the central city. A new addition is a spooky stroll around the city's oldest cemetery.

Bus

Toru Tours   BUS
(☑ 027 457 0011; www.torutours.com; per person $79) The three-hour Express Tour will depart with just one booking – ideal for solo travellers.

Auckland Hop On, Hop Off Explorer   BUS
(Map p80; ☑ 0800 439 756; www.explorerbus.co.nz; adult/child per day $45/20) Two services – the red or blue route – take in the best of the waterfront, including attractions along Tamaki Drive (p87), or highlights including Mt Eden (p85) and the Auckland Zoo (p88). Red route buses depart from near Princes Wharf hourly from 10am to 3pm (more frequently in summer), and it's possible to link to the blue route at the Auckland Museum (p86).

Boat

Riverhead Ferry   CRUISE
(Map p80; ☑ 09-376 0819; www.riverheadferry.co.nz; Pier 3, Ferry Terminal; per cruise $35) Harbour and gulf cruises, including a 90-minute jaunt up the inner harbour to Riverhead, returning after two hours' pub time. Departure times depend on the tides. Check the website for details.

Fullers   CRUISE
(Map p80; ☑ 09-367 9111; www.fullers.co.nz; adult/child $42/21; ⏱ 10.30am & 1.30pm) Twice daily 1½-hour harbour cruises, including Rangitoto and a free return ticket to Devonport.

Other Tours

Red Carpet Tours   TOURS
(☑ 09-410 6561; www.redcarpet-tours.com) 🚶 Tours with a *Lord of the Rings/Hobbit* focus ranging from six days ($3085) to 14 days ($7250) around all of Middle Earth. Discounts available for twin-share and triple-share bookings.

FILIP FUXA/SHUTTERSTOCK ©

BOYLOSO/SHUTTERSTOCK ©

1. Piha (p130)
Piha has long been a favourite escape for Aucklanders.

2-3. Urban Auckland
New Zealand's most populous city is watched over by the architecturally triumphant University Clock Tower (p83) and Sky Tower (p83), the tallest structure in the southern hemisphere, where you can enjoy the view with a coffee at the Sky Lounge Cafe & Bar.

4. Mt Eden (p85)
Auckland's highest volcanic cone, it rises 196m above the isthmus, with a crater 50m deep in its centre..

©DENIZUNLUSU/GETTY IMAGES

✿ Festivals & Events

Auckland Tourism's website (www.auckland nz.com) has a thorough events calendar.

Laneway Festival   MUSIC
(http://auckland.lanewayfestival.com; Albert Park; ☺Jan) International indie bands in a one-day festival on Anniversary Day (the Monday following the last weekend in January).

ASB Classic   SPORTS
(www.asbclassic.co.nz; ☺Jan) Watch leading tennis players warm up for the Aussie Open; held early January at the ASB Tennis Centre (Map p80; www.tennisauckland.co.nz; 1 Tennis Lane, Parnell).

Auckland Anniversary Day Regatta   SPORTS
(www.regatta.org.nz; ☺Jan) The 'City of Sails' lives up to its name; held Monday of the last weekend in January.

Movies in Parks   FILM
(www.moviesinparks.co.nz; ☺Jan-Mar) Free movies on Friday and Saturday nights in various locations.

Music in Parks   MUSIC
(www.musicinparks.co.nz; ☺Jan-Mar) Free gigs in various locations.

Lantern Festival   CULTURAL
(www.aucklandnz.com/lantern; Albert Park; ☺Feb) Three days of Asian food, culture and elaborately constructed lantern tableaux in Albert Park to welcome the Lunar New Year (usually held in February).

Auckland Pride Festival   LGBT
(www.aucklandpridefestival.org.nz; ☺Feb) Two-week festival of music, arts, sport and culture celebrating the LGBT community. Highlights include the Pride Parade, Pride Party and the Big Gay Out.

Splore   MUSIC
(www.splore.net; Tapapakanga Regional Park; ☺mid-Feb) Three days of camping and music (generally of the dancey and soulful variety), held by the beach. Headliners include big-name international acts.

Big Gay Out   LGBT
(☺mid-Feb) Thousands pack out Coyle Park, Pt Chevalier, on a Sunday in mid-February for a giant LGBT fair day with entertainment, food stalls and bars.

Pasifika Festival   CULTURAL
(www.aucklandnz.com/pasifika; ☺Mar) Western Springs (p88) park hosts this giant Polynesian party with cultural performances, and food and craft stalls; held over a weekend in early to mid-March.

Auckland City Limits   MUSIC
(www.aucklandcitylimits.com; Western Springs Park; ☺Mar) One-day festival featuring big-name international rock, indie and hip-hop acts.

Auckland Arts Festival   PERFORMING ARTS
(www.aucklandfestival.co.nz; ☺Mar) Held over three weeks in March, this is Auckland's biggest celebration of the arts.

Auckland Cup Week   SPORTS
(www.ellerslie.co.nz; Ellerslie Racecourse; ☺early Mar) The year's biggest horse races.

AUCKLAND IN...

Two Days

Start by acquainting yourself with the inner city. Begin by walking from Karangahape Rd (K Rd) to the Wynyard Quarter (p85), stopping along the way to have at least a quick whiz around the New Zealand section of the Auckland Art Gallery (p82). Catch a ferry to Devonport (p88), head up North Head and cool down at Cheltenham Beach (weather and tide permitting), before ferrying back to the city for dinner.

On day two, head up One Tree Hill (p88), wander around Cornwall Park (p88) and then visit the Auckland Museum (p86) and Domain (p87). Take a trip along Tamaki Drive (p87), stopping at Bastion (p87) or Achilles Point (p87) to enjoy the harbour views. Spend the evening dining and bar hopping in Ponsonby (p108).

Four Days

On the third day, get out on the Hauraki Gulf (p115). Catch the ferry to Waiheke Island (p117) and divide your time between the beaches and the wineries.

For your final day, head west. Grab breakfast in Titirangi (p128) before exploring the Waitakere Ranges Regional Park (p129), Karekare (p129) and Piha (p130). Freshen up for a night on the town in Britomart (p83).

Polyfest   CULTURAL
(www.asbpolyfest.co.nz; Sports Bowl, Manukau; ☺mid-Mar) Massive Auckland secondary schools' Māori and Pacific Islands cultural festival.

Royal Easter Show   FAIR
(www.eastershow.co.nz; ASB Showgrounds, 217 Green Lane West; ☺Mar/Apr) It's supposedly agricultural but most people attend for the funfair rides.

**Auckland International Cultural
Festival**   CULTURAL
(www.facebook.com/culturalfestival; Mt Roskill War Memorial Park; ☺late Mar / early Apr) One-day festival with ethnic food stalls and cultural displays and performances.

NZ International Comedy Festival   COMEDY
(www.comedyfestival.co.nz; ☺Apr-May) Three-week laughfest with local and international comedians.

GABS   BEER
(Great Australasian Beer Spectacular; www.gabs festival.com; ASB Showgrounds; ☺late Jun) A dazzling array of craft beer, cider and street food combine at Auckland's brilliant version of one of the world's best beer festivals.

NZ International Film Festival   FILM
(www.nzff.co.nz; ☺Jul) Art-house films for two weeks from mid-July, many in the beautiful Civic Theatre (p83).

NZ Fashion Week   CULTURAL
(www.nzfashionweek.com; ☺Aug) Held at the Viaduct Events Centre.

Auckland Heritage Festival   CULTURAL
(www.heritagefestival.co.nz; ☺Sep) Two weeks of (mainly free) tours of Auckland's neighbourhoods and historic buildings; from late September.

Diwali Festival of Lights   CULTURAL
(www.aucklandnz.com/diwali; Aotea Sq; ☺mid-Oct) Music, dance and food from Auckland's Indian community in Aotea Sq.

Grey Lynn Park Festival   FAIR, MUSIC
(www.greylynnparkfestival.org; ☺Nov) Free festival of arts and crafts, food stalls and live music in one of Auckland's more interesting inner suburbs; third Saturday in late November.

Santa Parade   CHRISTMAS
(www.santaparade.co.nz; ☺late Nov) The big guy in red parades along Queen St before partying in Aotea Sq (p83); last Sunday of November.

Christmas in the Park   CHRISTMAS
(www.christmasinthepark.co.nz; ☺mid-Dec) A huge concert and party in Auckland Domain (p87).

Silo Cinema & Markets   FILM
(www.silopark.co.nz; Silo Park, Wynyard Quarter; ☺Dec-Easter) Classic movies screened outdoors on Friday nights, and markets with food trucks, DJs and craft stalls on Friday nights and Saturday and Sunday afternoons.

🛏 Sleeping

Auckland's city centre has plenty of luxury hotels, with several international chains. Any backpackers who leave with a bad impression have invariably stayed in crummy, noisy digs in the city centre. Not all of the cheap city accommodation is bad, but you'll find much better hostels in inner suburbs such as Ponsonby, Parnell, Freemans Bay and Mt Eden. Devonport has beautiful Edwardian B&Bs within a relaxing ferry ride of the city.

🛏 City Centre

Attic Backpackers   HOSTEL $
(Map p80; ☎09-973 5887; www.atticbackpackers. co.nz; 31 Wellesley St; dm $33-40, s/tw without bathroom $65/95; @🛜) Centrally located Attic Backpackers features good facilities and an even better vibe. White walls and plenty of windows keep everything bright and fresh, and there's a rooftop area conducive to meeting other travellers.

YHA Auckland International   HOSTEL $
(Map p80; ☎09-302 8200; www.yha.co.nz; 5 Turner St; dm $36-40, r with/without bathroom $120/105; 🛜) 🌿 Clean and brightly painted, this 170-bed YHA has a friendly vibe, good security, a games room and lots of lockers.

Waldorf Celestion   APARTMENT $$
(Map p80; ☎09-280 2200; www.celestion -waldorf.co.nz; 19-23 Anzac Ave; apt from $193; P@🛜) A rash of Waldorfs have opened in recent years, all presenting similar symptoms: affordable, modern apartments in city-fringe locations. We prefer this one for its stylish crimson and charcoal colour palette.

★Hotel DeBrett   BOUTIQUE HOTEL $$$
(Map p80; ☎09-925 9000; www.hoteldebrett.com; 2 High St; r from $370; 🛜) This hip historic hotel has been zhooshed up with stripy carpets and clever designer touches in every nook of the 25 extremely comfortable rooms. Prices include a continental breakfast, free unlimited wi-fi and a pre-dinner drink.

AUCKLAND VOLCANIC FIELD

Some cities think they're tough just by living in the shadow of a volcano. Auckland's built on 50 of them and, no, they're not all extinct. The last one to erupt was Rangitoto about 600 years ago and no one can predict when the next eruption will occur. Auckland's quite literally a hot spot – with a reservoir of magma 100km below, waiting to bubble to the surface. But relax: this has only happened 19 times in the last 20,000 years.

Some of Auckland's volcanoes are cones, some are filled with water and some have been completely quarried away. Moves are afoot to register the field as a World Heritage site and protect what remains. Most of the surviving cones show evidence of terracing from when they formed a formidable series of Māori pā (fortified villages). The most interesting to explore are Mt Eden (p85), One Tree Hill (p88), North Head (p88) and Rangitoto (p116), but Mt Victoria (p88), Mt Wellington (Maungarei), Mt Albert (Owaira-ka), Mt Roskill (Puketāpapa), Lake Pupuke, Mt Mangere and Mt Hobson (Remuera) are all also worth a visit.

CityLife   HOTEL $$$
(Map p80; ☑09-379 9222; www.heritagehotels. co.nz/citylife-auckland; 171 Queen St; apt from $217; P🅿🛜🏊) 🅿 A worthy tower-block hotel offering numerous apartments over dozens of floors, ranging from studios to three-bedroom suites. Facilities include a heated lap pool, gym and valet parking. The location couldn't be more central.

Waldorf Stadium   APARTMENT $$$
(Map p80; ☑09-337 5300; www.stadium -apartments-hotel.co.nz; 40 Beach Rd; apt from $213; 🛜🚹) This large newish block has spacious (if generic) family-friendly apartments with double-glazing to keep out the road noise.

Britomart, Viaduct Harbour & Wynyard Quarter

Sofitel Viaduct Harbour   HOTEL $$$
(Map p80; ☑09-909 9000; www.sofitel-auckland. com; 21 Viaduct Harbour Ave; d from $420; P🅿🛜🏊) Auckland is one of the world's great harbour cities, so it makes perfect sense to stay beside the water. In close proximity to the restaurants and bars of Viaduct Harbour and the Wynyard Quarter, the Sofitel has classy rooms and suites arrayed around a central ornamental pool. Moored yachts bob nearby, and Auckland's 'City of Sails' moniker definitely rings true.

Adina Apartment
Hotel Britomart   APARTMENT $$$
(Map p80; ☑09-393 8200; www.adinahotels.com; 2 Tapora St; d/apt from $199/269; P🅿🛜) Handily located for concerts and events at Spark Arena (p110), eating and drinking in the Britomart (p83) precinct, and for harbour transport from the Ferry Building (p115), the Adina Britomart has colourful and mod-ern suites and apartments with a touch of Scandi natural-wood style. There's a decent in-house bar and restaurant also.

Ponsonby & Grey Lynn

Ponsonby Backpackers   HOSTEL $
(Map p92; ☑09-360 1311; www.ponsonby -backpackers.co.nz; 2 Franklin Rd, Ponsonby; dm $33-35, s/d without bathroom $60/82; P🅿@🛜) This elegant two-storey turreted villa has a friendly vibe, sunny rooms and a nice gar-den area. Central Auckland is a pleasant 20-minute walk away, and the buzz of Pon-sonby Rd is right on your doorstep.

Verandahs   HOSTEL $
(Map p92; ☑09-360 4180; www.verandahs.co.nz; 6 Hopetoun St; dm $34-38, s $64, d with/without bathroom $106/88; P🅿@🛜) Ponsonby Rd, K Rd and the city are an easy walk from this grand hostel, housed in two neighbouring villas overlooking the mature trees of West-ern Park. It's definitely one of Auckland's best backpackers.

Brown Kiwi   HOSTEL $
(Map p92; ☑09-378 0191; www.brownkiwi.co.nz; 7 Prosford St, Ponsonby; dm $32-35, s/d without bathroom $70/84; @🛜) This low-key hostel is tucked away in a busy-by-day commercial strip, a stone's throw from Ponsonby's shop-ping and grazing opportunities. The garden courtyard is made for mooching.

Abaco on Jervois   MOTEL $$
(Map p92; ☑09-360 6850; www.abaco.co.nz; 57 Jervois Rd, Ponsonby; r/ste from $145/205; P🅿🛜) Well positioned for cafes and buses, this con-temporary, neutral-toned motel has stain-less-steel kitchens with dishwashers in the fancier units, and fridges and microwaves

in the studios. The darker rooms downstairs are cheaper.

Great Ponsonby Arthotel
B&B $$$

(Map p92; ☑ 09-376 5989; www.greatpons.co.nz; 30 Ponsonby Tce, Ponsonby; r $260-400; 🅿 🛜) ✒ In a quiet cul-de-sac near Ponsonby Rd, this deceptively spacious Victorian villa has gregarious hosts, impressive sustainability practices and great breakfasts. Studio apartments open onto an attractive rear courtyard. Rates include breakfast.

🛏 Newton

Haka Lodge
HOSTEL $

(Map p80; ☑ 09-379 4556; www.hakalodge.com; 373 Karangahape Rd; dm $31-41, r with/without bathroom $139/109; 🛜) ✒ The transformation of one of Auckland's dodgiest old pubs into a bright and shiny hostel is a modern miracle. Dorms have custom-made wooden bunks with privacy curtains, lockers and their own power points – making them perhaps the most comfortable bunkrooms in Auckland. Wi-fi is free and unlimited. And it couldn't be better located for the bustling K Rd scene.

Haka Hotel
HOTEL $$

(Map p80; ☑ 09-281 3097; https://hakahotels. co.nz; 2 Day St; d from $161; 🅿 🛜) Part of the burgeoning Haka empire – also including excellent hostels and tours – this new opening in a quiet lane just off bohemian Karangahape features chic and modern accommodation ranging from compact studios through to one- and two-bedroom suites. Many rooms have balconies and harbour views, and mod cons include coffee machines and Chromecast functionality on flat-screen TVs.

🛏 Mt Eden

Bamber House
HOSTEL $

(Map p84; ☑ 09-623 4267; www.bamberhouse. co.nz; 22 View Rd, Mt Eden; dm $32-36, r with/without bathroom $100/85; 🅿 @ 🛜) ✒ The original house here is a mansion of sorts, with some nicely maintained period trimmings and large grounds. The new prefab cabins have less character but come with en suites.

Oaklands Lodge
HOSTEL $

(Map p84; ☑ 09-638 6545; www.oaklandslodge. co.nz; 5a Oaklands Rd, Mt Eden; dm $30-38, s/d without bathroom $55/85; 🅿 @ 🛜) In a leafy cul-de-sac, this bright, well-kept hostel is close to Mt Eden village and city buses.

Bavaria
B&B $$

(Map p84; ☑ 09-638 9641; www.bavariabandb hotel.co.nz; 83 Valley Rd, Mt Eden; s/d from $130/180; 🅿 @ 🛜) This spacious villa offers large, airy, well-kept rooms, all of which have bathrooms, although some of them are closet sized. The communal TV lounge, dining room and deck all encourage mixing and mingling. A hot and cold buffet breakfast is included in the rates.

Eden Villa
B&B $$$

(Map p84; ☑ 09-630 1165; www.edenvilla.co.nz; 16 Poronui St, Mt Eden; r $250; 🅿) These pretty wooden villas are what Auckland's leafy inner suburbs are all about. This one has three comfortable en-suite bedrooms, a pleasantly old-fashioned ambience and charming hosts who prepare a good cooked breakfast. We prefer the room at the rear, which has the original bath-tub and views straight over the garden to Mt Eden (p85) itself.

Eden Park B&B
B&B $$$

(Map p84; ☑ 09-630 5721; www.bedandbreakfast nz.com; 20 Bellwood Ave, Mt Eden; s/d $165/250; 🅿 🛜) The hallowed turf of Auckland's legendary Eden Park (p111) rugby ground is only a block away and, while the rooms aren't overly large, they mirror the Edwardian elegance of this fine wooden villa.

🛏 Parnell & Newmarket

Quest Carlaw Park
APARTMENT $$

(Map p80; ☑ 09-304 0521; www.questcarlawpark. co.nz; 15 Nicholls Lane; apt from $189; 🅿 @ 🛜) ✒ It's in an odd spot but this set of smart, modern apartments is handy for Parnell, the city and the Domain, and if you've got a car, you're practically on the motorway.

MĀORI NZ: AUCKLAND

Evidence of Māori occupation is literally carved into Auckland's volcanic cones. The dominant *iwi* (tribe) of the isthmus was Ngāti Whatua, but these days there are Māori from almost all of NZ's *iwi* living here.

For an initial taste of Māori culture, start at Auckland Museum (p86), where there's a wonderful Māori collection and a culture show. For a more personalised experience, take a tour with TIME Unlimited (p92), Potiki Adventures (p120) or Ngāti Whatua's Tāmaki Hikoi (p92), or visit the marae (meeting house) and recreated village at Te Hana (p136).

NORTH SHORE BEACHES

Fine swimming beaches stretch from North Head (p88) to Long Bay. The gulf islands shelter them from strong surf, making them safe for supervised children. Aim for high tide unless you fancy a lengthy walk to waist-deep water. **Cheltenham Beach** is a short walk from Devonport. **Takapuna Beach**, closest to the Harbour Bridge, is Auckland's answer to Bondi and the most built up. Nearby **St Leonards Beach**, popular with gay men, requires clambering over rocks at high tide.

Quality Hotel Parnell   HOTEL **$$**
(Map p86; 09-303 3789; www.theparnell.co.nz; 10-20 Gladstone Rd; r from $167; P) More than 100 motel rooms and units are available in this renovated complex. The newer north wing has great harbour views.

★ **Ascot Parnell**   B&B **$$$**
(Map p86; 09-309 9012; www.ascotparnell. com; 32 St Stephens Ave, Parnell; r $295-375; P@) The Ascot's three luxurious bedrooms share a spacious apartment in a modern mid-rise block. You're in no danger of stumbling into the owners' private space; they have a completely separate apartment next door. The largest room grabs all of the harbour views but you can enjoy the same vista from the large terrace leading off the communal living area.

Devonport

Parituhu   B&B **$$**
(Map p90; 09-445 6559; www.parituhu.co.nz; 3 King Edward Pde; r $140-160; P) There's only one double bedroom (with its own adjoining bathroom) available in this relaxing and welcoming Edwardian waterfront bungalow. The well-travelled hosts are excellent company and know the city very well.

Grange Lodge   MOTEL **$$**
(Map p78; 09-277 8280; www.grangelodge.co.nz; cnr Grange & Great South Rds, Papatoetoe; apt $159-239; P) If you've driven up from the south, consider staying at this friendly little suburban motel that's handy for the airport. From the Southern Motorway, take the East Tamaki Rd exit, turn right and right again onto Great South Rd.

Devonport Motel   MOTEL **$$**
(Map p90; 09-445 1010; www.devonportmotel. co.nz; 11 Buchanan St, Devonport; r $150-180; P) This minimotel has two units in the tidy back garden. They're modern, clean, self-contained and in a quiet location close to Devonport's attractions.

Devonport Sea Cottage   COTTAGE **$$**
(Map p90; 09-445 7117; www.devonportsea cottagenz.com; 3a Cambridge Tce, Devonport; cottage $160; P) Head up the garden path to your own cute and cosy self-contained cottage. Weekly rates are available.

Peace & Plenty Inn   B&B **$$$**
(Map p90; 09-445 2925; www.peaceandplenty. co.nz; 6 Flagstaff Tce; r $295-385; P) Stocked with antiques, this perfectly located, five-star Victorian house has romantic and luxurious en-suite rooms with TVs, flowers, free sherry/port and local chocolates.

Other Areas

Ambury Regional Park   CAMPGROUND **$**
(Map p78; 09-366 2000; http://regionalparks. aucklandcouncil.govt.nz/ambury; 43 Ambury Rd, Mangere; sites per adult/child $15/6; P) A slice of country in suburbia, this regional park is also a working farm. Facilities are limited (a vault toilet, warm showers and not much shade) but it's handy to the airport, right on the water and dirt cheap.

Emerald Inn   MOTEL **$$**
(Map p78; 09-488 3500; www.emerald-inn. co.nz; 16 The Promenade, Takapuna; d/ste $200/285; P) Across the harbour bridge in Takapuna, the Emerald Inn is arrayed around a leafy courtyard and pool. It's just metres to Takapuna Beach, and there's plenty of good eating and drinking opportunities in the immediate area. Options range from studio units to one- and two-bedroom suites, and the friendly owners are packed with ideas of things to see and do.

Self-contained holiday villas and a cottage are just next door and enjoy views of Rangitoto Island.

Jet Park   HOTEL **$$**
(Map p78; 09-275 4100; www.jetpark.co.nz; 63 Westney Rd, Mangere; r from $199; P@) Located within the industrial area edging the airport, Jet Park has comfortable rooms and a vibe that exceeds that of the average midrange airport hotel. With departure screens in the lobby and free airport shuttles, there's no excuse for missing your flight.

✕ Eating

Because of its size and ethnic diversity, Auckland tops the country when it comes to dining options and quality. Lively eateries have sprung up to cater to the many Asian students, and offer inexpensive Japanese, Chinese and Korean staples. If you're on a budget, you'll fall in love with the city's food halls.

Aucklanders demand good coffee, so you never have to walk too far to find a decent cafe, especially in suburbs like Ponsonby, Mt Eden and Kingsland. Some double as wine bars or have gourmet aspirations, while others are content to fill their counters with fresh, reasonably priced snacks.

The city's hippest new foodie enclaves are Britomart (p83) (the blocks above the train station) and Federal St (under the Sky Tower), and recent openings have resurrected and reinforced the culinary reputation of Ponsonby (p103). The Wynyard Quarter (p85) and the former City Works Depot on the corner of Wellesley and Nelson Sts are also up-and-coming areas. Easily reached by train, Orakei Bay Village in the city's eastern suburbs is another emerging precinct.

You'll find large supermarkets in most neighbourhoods: there's a particularly handy **Countdown** (Map p80; ☑09-275 2567; www.countdown.co.nz; 76 Quay St; ⊙24hr) at the bottom of town and a **New World** (Map p92; ☑09-307 8400; www.newworld.co.nz; 2 College Hill, Freemans Bay; ⊙7am-midnight) by Victoria Park. Self-caterers should consider the Otara Flea Market (p112) and Avondale Sunday Markets (p112) for cheap, fresh vegetables, and La Cigale (p106) for fancier fare and local artisan produce.

✕ City Centre

Chuffed
CAFE $
(Map p80; ☑09-367 6801; www.chuffedcoffee.com; 43 High St; mains $6.50-18; ⊙7am-4pm Mon-Wed, 7am-10pm Thu & Fri, 9am-10pm Sat, 9am-4pm Sun) Concealed in a lightwell at the rear of a building, this hip place, liberally coated in street art, is a definite contender for the inner-city's best cafe. Grab a seat on the indoor-outdoor terrace and tuck into cooked breakfasts, Wagyu burgers, lamb shanks or surprisingly flavour-packed toasted sandwiches. From Thursday to Saturday nights, cocktails and craft beers also feature.

Best Ugly Bagels
BAKERY, CAFE $
(Map p80; ☑09-366 3926; www.bestugly.co.nz; City Works Depot, 90 Wellesley St; filled bagels $6-14; ⊙7am-3pm; ☑) Hand-rolled, boiled and wood-fired, Best Ugly's bagels are a thing of beauty. Call into its super-hip bakery in a converted heavy-vehicle workshop and order one stuffed with pastrami, bacon, smoked salmon or a variety of vegetarian fillings. Or just ask for a cinnamon bagel slathered with cream cheese and jam. The coffee is killer, too.

★ Giapo
ICE CREAM $$
(Map p80; ☑09-550 3677; www.giapo.com; 12 Gore St; ice cream $10-22; ⊙noon-10.30pm Sun-Thu, to 11.30pm Fri & Sat; ☑) 🍦 That there are queues outside this boutique ice-cream shop even in the middle of winter says a lot about the magical confections that it conjures up. Expect elaborate constructions of ice-cream art topped with all manner of goodies, as Giapo's extreme culinary creativity and experimentation combines with the science of gastronomy to produce quite possibly the planet's best ice-cream extravaganzas.

AUCKLAND FOR CHILDREN

All of the east-coast beaches (St Heliers, Kohimarama, Mission Bay, Okahu Bay, Cheltenham, Narrow Neck, Takapuna, Milford, Long Bay) are safe for supervised kids, while sights such as **Rainbow's End** (Map p78; ☑09-262 2030; www.rainbowsend.co.nz; 2 Clist Cres, Manukau; unlimited rides adult/child $57/46; ⊙10am-5pm; 🐾), Kelly Tarlton's Sea Life Aquarium (p87), Auckland Museum (p86) and Auckland Zoo (p88) are all firm favourites. Parnell Baths (p92) has a children's pool, but on wintry days, head to the thermal pools at Parakai (p132) or Waiwera (p134).

For a spot of kid-oriented theatre, and a great family restaurant and children's playground, check out what's scheduled at Whoa! Studios (p110), an easy train journey west of the city in Henderson.

Baby-changing facilities are widespread, often in shopping malls and integrated within public toilets. City buses, trains and ferries offer convenient access for prams, and pavements are generally in good condition.

Depot
MODERN NZ **$$**

(Map p80; ☑09-363 7048; www.eatatdepot.co.nz; 86 Federal St; dishes $16-38; ⊗7am-late) TV chef Al Brown's popular eatery offers first-rate comfort food in informal surrounds (communal tables, butcher tiles and a constant buzz). Dishes are designed to be shared, and a pair of clever shuckers serve up the city's freshest clams and oysters. It doesn't take bookings, so get there early or expect to wait.

Odette's
MODERN NZ **$$**

(Map p80; ☑09-309 0304; www.odettes.co.nz; Shed 5, City Works Depot, 90 Wellesley St; dishes $19-40; ⊗8am-3pm Sun & Mon, 7am-11pm Tue-Sat) Nothing about Odette's is run of the mill. Not the bubbly light fixtures or the quirky photography, and certainly not the menu. How about lamb meatballs with saffron mustard for brunch? Or wild mushrooms served with a truffle pancake and cashew cream? In the evening the more cafe-ish items are replaced with dishes for sharing. It gets hectic on weekends.

Ima
MIDDLE EASTERN **$$**

(Map p80; ☑09-377 5252; www.imacuisine.co.nz; 53 Fort St; breakfast & lunch $10-24, dinner shared dishes $17-27; ⊗7am-11pm Mon-Fri, 8.30am-10pm Sat & Sun) Named after the Hebrew word for mother, Ima's menu features an array of Israeli, Palestinian, Yemeni and Lebanese comfort food, along with meat pies and sandwiches at lunchtime. Rustle up a group for Ima's excellent shared dinners and feast on whole fish, chicken *meschan* (a whole bird slow-cooked with herbs and spices and then grilled) or slow-cooked lamb shoulder.

Inti
SOUTH AMERICAN **$$**

(Map p80; ☑09-374 0981; www.inti.nz; cnr O'Connell & Chancery Sts; shared plates $14-36; ⊗noon-3pm Tue-Fri, 5pm-late Tue-Sat; ☑) ⚑ Welcome to one of Auckland's most interesting new restaurants where modern South American dishes are served in a spacious and elegant dining room. Chef Javier Carmona harnesses ingredients as diverse as alpaca, aji chillies, almonds and ants to create contemporary interpretations of classic Latin American street food. Come along with an open mind and prepare for a sublime culinary adventure.

Federal Delicatessen
AMERICAN **$$**

(Map p80; ☑09-363 7184; www.thefed.co.nz; 86 Federal St; mains $11-26; ⊗7am-late) Celebrity chef Al Brown's take on a New York Jewish deli serves up simple stuff like bagels and sandwiches, matzo-ball soup and lots of delicious comfort food to share (turkey meatloaf, spit-roasted chicken, New York strip steak). White butcher tiles, vinyl booth seating and waitstaff in 1950s uniforms add to the illusion.

Kimchi Project
KOREAN, CAFE **$$**

(Map p80; ☑09-302 4002; www.facebook.com/pg/thekimchiprojectnz; 20 Lorne St; snacks $12-18, mains $18-35; ⊗7am-10pm Sun-Thu, to midnight Fri & Sat) Begin with a brunch of *matcha* latte and *yuzu* muesli, or escape to the palm-fringed courtyard for Asian-inspired street food including spicy pulled-pork tacos, and *bao* (steamed buns) crammed with prawns. Packed with pork belly and topped with an egg, the kimchi fried rice is simple but brilliant.

Scarecrow
CAFE **$$**

(Map p80; ☑09-377 1333; www.scarecrow.co.nz; 33 Victoria St East; mains $16-32; ⊗7am-5pm Mon, 7am-10pm Tue-Fri, 8am-5pm Sat & Sun; ☑) ⚑ Organic and vegan ingredients shine at this bustling cafe near Albert Park. Bentwood chairs add a Gallic ambience, and the menu veers towards European and Middle Eastern flavours. Try the *shakshuka* baked eggs or house-smoked fish cakes for brunch, or return at night for New Zealand lamb with *labneh* and hummus. A compact deli section sells local artisan food products.

★ Cassia
INDIAN **$$$**

(Map p80; ☑09-379 9702; www.cassiarestaurant.co.nz; 5 Fort Lane; mains $32-40; ⊗noon-3pm Wed-Fri, 5.30pm-late Tue-Sat) Occupying a moodily lit basement, Cassia serves modern Indian food with punch and panache. Start with a *pani puri,* a bite-sized crispy shell bursting with flavour, before devouring a decadently rich curry. The Delhi duck is excellent, as is the Goan-style snapper. Artisan gins and NZ craft beer are other highlights. Cassia is often judged Auckland's best restaurant.

Grove
MODERN NZ **$$$**

(Map p80; ☑09-368 4129; www.thegrove restaurant.co.nz; St Patrick's Sq, Wyndham St; 9-/12-course degustation $99/145; ⊗noon-3pm Thu & Fri, 6pm-late Mon-Sat) Romantic fine dining: the room is moodily lit, the menu encourages sensual experimentation and the service is effortless. If you can't find anything to break the ice from the extensive wine list then give it up, mate – it's never going to happen.

O'Connell Street Bistro EUROPEAN $$$
(Map p80; ☑09-377 1884; www.oconnellstbistro.
com; 3 O'Connell St; mains $38-45; ⊘11.30am-
3pm & 5-11pm Mon-Fri, 5-11pm Sat) O'Connell
Street is a grown-up treat, with smart decor
and wonderful food and wine, satisfying
lunchtime power brokers and dinnertime
daters alike. If you're dining before 7.15pm,
a fixed-price menu is available (two/three
courses $40/45).

Britomart, Viaduct Harbour & Wynyard Quarter

Baduzzi ITALIAN $$
(Map p80; ☑09-309 9339; www.baduzzi.co.nz;
cnr Jellicoe St & Fish Lane, Wynyard Quarter;
mains $16-36; ⊘11.30am-late; ☑) This smart
and sassy eatery does sophisticated spins
on meatballs – try the crayfish ones – and
other robust but elegant Italian dishes. Cosy
up in the intimate booths, grab a seat at the
bar, or soak up some Auckland sunshine
outside.

Amano ITALIAN $$
(Map p80; ☑09-394 1416; www.amano.nz; 66-68
Tyler St; mains $22-34; ⊘restaurant 7am-late,
bakery 6.30am-6pm Mon-Sat, to 4pm Sun) ✔
Rustic Italian influences underpin this
bistro-bakery in a repurposed warehouse in
Auckland's Britomart precinct, but there's
real culinary savvy evident in the open
kitchen. Many dishes harness seasonal pro-
duce and ingredients from the owners' farm
in West Auckland, and Amano effortlessly
transitions from a buzzy caffeine-fuelled
daytime cafe to a sophisticated evening
bistro featuring New Zealand wines and
craft beers.

Store CAFE $$
(Map p80; ☑09-366 1864; www.thestore
britomart.nz; 5b Gore St; mains $15-26; ⊘7am-
3pm) With tables spilling into the fairy-
light and flower-strewn space at the centre
of Britomart, this chic cafe is as fresh and
effervescent as the sparkling water that arrives unbidden when you're seated. Seasonal
vegetables and fruits feature prominently on
an interesting and enticing menu spanning
cooked breakfasts, pasta dishes, market fish
and salt-beef sandwiches.

Giraffe MODERN NZ $$$
(Map p80; ☑09-358 1093; www.girafferestaurant.
co.nz; Viaduct Harbour, 85-87 Customs St West;
shared plates $15-32; ⊘7am-late Mon-Fri, from
8am Sat & Sun) ✔ The latest opening from
Simon Gault, one of NZ's most well-known
chefs, Giraffe combines a stylish but casual
harbourside dining room with an intensely
local and seasonal menu. The restaurant
was named by Gault's then 3½-year-old
daughter, and the menu is packed with so-
phisticated and superior versions of comfort
food such as pork and prawn Wellington,
and roast chicken.

Ponsonby & Grey Lynn

Auckland's busiest restaurant-cafe-bar strip
is so damn cool it has its own website (www.
iloveponsonby.co.nz).

AUCKLAND'S MULTICULTURAL MENU

Around 30% of New Zealanders live in Auckland, and the country's biggest city is also the most ethnically diverse. With immigration – especially from Asia – has come a cosmopolitan restaurant scene, and savvy Auckland foodies (and a few of the city's top chefs) keenly explore central fringe neighbourhoods for authentic tastes of the city's multicultural present and future.

Head to Dominion Rd in Balmoral (catch bus 267 from stop 7058 near the intersection of Queen and Wellesley Sts and get off at stop 8418) to be surrounded by Auckland's best Chinese food.

A few blocks west (catch bus 249 from stop 7022 in Victoria St East to stop 8316 on Sandringham Rd) are some of the city's best Indian and Sri Lankan restaurants. Our favourite is Paradise (p106), specialising in the Mughlai cuisine you'd find on the streets of Hyderabad.

At the city's bustling night markets – held in a different suburban car park each night of the week – scores of stalls serve food from a diverse range of countries, from Argentina and Samoa, to Hungary and Turkey. Most convenient for travellers is the Thursday Henderson Night Market (p106).

If you're in town around late March or early April, the Auckland International Cultural Festival (p97) offers a very tasty peek into the city's ethnically diverse future. Online, Cheap Eats (www.cheapeats.co.nz) scours Auckland for the city's best food for under $20.

Dizengoff
CAFE $

(Map p92; ☑09-360 0108; www.facebook.com/dizengoff.ponsonby; 256 Ponsonby Rd, Ponsonby; mains $8-22; ⊙6.30am-4pm) This stylish shoebox crams in a disparate crowd of corporate and fashion types, Ponsonby denizens and travellers. There's a Jewish influence to the food, with tasty Israeli platters, chopped liver, bagels and chicken salads, along with tempting baking, heart-starting coffee and a great stack of reading material.

Bird on a Wire
FAST FOOD $

(Map p92; ☑09-378 6369; www.birdonawire.co.nz; Ponsonby Central, 136-146 Ponsonby Rd; mains $10-17; ⊙7.30am-late) Tasty sandwiches and healthy burgers, seasonal salads and rotisserie chickens to take away. Select your baste of choice – Jamaican jerk or truffle butter, perhaps – and you're sorted.

Burgerfuel
BURGERS $

(Map p92; ☑09-378 6466; www.burgerfuel.com; 114 Ponsonby Rd, Ponsonby; burgers $6-15; ⊙11am-10pm Sun-Wed, to midnight Thu, to 4am Fri & Sat; ☑) An excellent homegrown gourmet burger chain, with branches all over the city.

★ Azabu
JAPANESE, PERUVIAN $$

(Map p92; ☑09-320 5292; www.azabuponsonby.co.nz; 26 Ponsonby Rd; mains & shared plates $16-35; ⊙noon-late Wed-Sun, from 5pm Mon & Tue) Nikkei cuisine, an exciting blend of Japanese and Peruvian influences, is the focus at Azabu. Amid a dramatic interior enlivened by striking images of Tokyo, standout dishes include the tuna sashimi tostada, Japanese tacos with wasabi avocado, and king prawns with a jalapeño and ponzu dressing. Arrive early and enjoy a basil- and chilli-infused cachaca cocktail at Azabu's Roji bar.

★ Saan
THAI $$

(Map p92; ☑09-320 4237; www.saan.co.nz; 160 Ponsonby Rd, Ponsonby; dishes $14-32; ⊙4pm-late Mon & Tue, noon-late Wed-Fri, 11am-late Sat & Sun) Hot in both senses of the word, this super-fashionable restaurant focuses on the fiery cuisine of the Isaan and Lanna regions of northern Thailand. The menu is conveniently sorted from least to most spicy and split into smaller and larger dishes for sharing. Be sure to order the soft-shell crab.

Lokanta
GREEK, TURKISH $$

(Map p92; ☑09-360 6355; www.lokanta.nz; 137a Richmond Rd; meze $7-19, mains $25-33; ⊙4pm-late Tue-Sun) Featuring the cuisine of the eastern Mediterranean, unpretentious Lokanta is a laid-back alternative to the more trendy eateries along nearby Ponsonby Rd. Greek and Turkish flavours happily co-exist, and robust Greek wines partner well with hearty dishes including chargriiled octopus and roast goat with a barley risotto. The coconut and almond baklava introduces a tropical influence to the classic dessert.

Ponsonby Central
CAFE $$

(Map p92; www.ponsonbycentral.co.nz; 136-138 Ponsonby Rd, Ponsonby; mains $15-35; ⊙7am-10.30pm Sun-Wed, to midnight Thu-Sat) Restaurants, cafes, bars and gourmet food shops fill this upmarket former warehouse space offering everything from Auckland's best pizza and Argentinian barbecue to Indo-Burmese curries partnered with zingy cocktails. It's a prime eating and drinking destination and offers excellent dining options from breakfast right through to dinner. And if you're after the city's best gourmet burgers, look no further.

Siostra
ITALIAN $$

(Map p92; ☑09-360 6207; www.siostra.co.nz; 472 Richmond Rd; dishes $17-29; ⊙5-11pm Tue-Thu & Sat, noon-11pm Fri) Run by a charming pair of sisters, Siostra is the perfect little neighbourhood bistro, serving up hearty Italian fare with a modern sensibility. Highlights include the pork tortellini with *cavolo nero* (black kale) and the excellent slow-cooked lamb shoulder.

Blue Breeze Inn
CHINESE $$

(Map p92; ☑09-360 0303; www.thebluebreezeinn.co.nz; Ponsonby Central, 146 Ponsonby Rd, Ponsonby; mains $28-35; ⊙noon-late) Regional Chinese flavours combine with a funky retro Pacific ambience at this so-hip-it-hurts eatery. The waitstaff are sassy, the rum cocktails are deliciously strong, and menu standouts include pork belly and pickled cucumber steamed buns, and cumin-spiced lamb.

★ Sidart
MODERN NZ $$$

(Map p92; ☑09-360 2122; www.sidart.co.nz; Three Lamps Plaza, 283 Ponsonby Rd, Ponsonby; 5-course lunch $65, 7-course dinner $145; ⊙noon-2.30pm Fri, 6-11pm Tue-Sat) No one in Auckland produces creative degustations quite like Sid Sahrawat. It's food as art, food as science but, more importantly, food to fire up your taste buds, delight the brain, satisfy the stomach and put a smile on your face. The restaurant is a little hard to find, tucked away at the rear of what was once the Alhambra cinema.

Cocoro
JAPANESE $$$

(Map p92; ☑09-360 0927; www.cocoro.co.nz; 56a Brown St, Ponsonby; dishes $9-38, degustation menu $95-200; ⊙noon-2pm & 5.30-10pm Tue-Sat)

Japanese elegance infuses everything at this excellent restaurant, from the soft lighting and chic decor, to the delicate flavours of the artistically arranged food. At lunchtime it offers an affordable *donburi* rice bowl ($20 to $24) and a multiplate option ($39), while in the evening multicourse degustation menus showcase the chefs' skills.

Ponsonby Road Bistro MODERN NZ $$$
(Map p92; 09-360 1611; www.ponsonbyroad bistro.co.nz; 165 Ponsonby Rd, Ponsonby; mains $34-36; noon-12.30am Mon-Fri, 4pm-12.30am Sat) The service is first-rate at this modern, upmarket restaurant, which introduces Asian flavours to predominantly French- and Italian-style bistro dishes. Imported cheese and wine are a highlight, and the crispy-based pizzas make a delicious shared snack.

Newton

Karangahape Rd (K Rd) is known for its late-night clubs, but cafes and plenty of inexpensive ethnic restaurants are mixed in with the vintage clothing stores, secondhand boutiques, tattooists and adult shops.

★Gemmayze St LEBANESE $$
(Map p80; 09-600 1545; www.facebook.com/gemmayzest; St Kevins Arcade, 15/183 Karangahape Rd; meze & mains $18-34; 6-11.30pm Tue-Sat, noon-3pm Thu & Fri;) Located amid the restored heritage architecture of St Kevins Arcade, Gemmayze St presents a modern and stylish update on traditional Lebanese cuisine. Delicate mint, orange blossom and rosewater cocktails are prepared at the beaten-copper bar, while shared tables encourage lots of sociable dining on meze and expertly grilled meats. The $18 lunchtime selection of five meze is excellent value.

Bestie CAFE $$
(Map p80; www.bestiecafe.co.nz; St Kevins Arcade, Karangahape Rd; mains $12-19; 7.30am-3.30pm Mon-Fri, 9am-4pm Sat & Sun;) One of the recently opened cafes and restaurants in revitalised St Kevins Arcade, Bestie is a perfect refuelling stop after trawling the arty and vintage shops along Karangahape Rd. Try to secure a table overlooking leafy Myers Park, and partner coffee or *kombucha* with signature dishes such as Bestie's ricotta doughnuts, or flatbread with chorizo, *labneh* and a chilli fried egg.

★French Cafe FRENCH $$$
(Map p84; 09-377 1911; www.thefrenchcafe.co.nz; 210 Symonds St; 3-/4-/7 courses $110/135/160; noon-3pm Fri, 6pm-late Tue-Sat)

The legendary French Cafe has been rated as one of Auckland's top restaurants for more than 20 years and it still continues to excel. The cuisine is nominally French-influenced, but chef Simon Wright sneaks in lots of tasty Asian and Pacific Rim touches. The service is impeccable.

Kingsland

Atomic Roastery CAFE $
(Map p84; 0800 286 642; www.atomiccoffee.co.nz; 420c New North Rd, Kingsland; snacks $9-11; 8am-3pm) Java hounds should follow their noses to this, one of the country's best-known coffee roasters. Tasty accompaniments include pies served in mini-frypans, bagels, salads and cakes.

Mondays VEGETARIAN, VEGAN $$
(Map p84; 09-849 7693; www.mondays wholefoods.com; 503b New North Rd, Kingsland; shared plates & mains $15-36; 8am-3pm Mon-Fri, 9am-4pm Sat & Sun;) Mondays' humble outward appearance segues to a sunny ivy-framed courtyard that's perfect for enjoying some of Auckland's healthiest cafe fare. Brunch options include quinoa pilaf with sumac and *dukkah*, while the craft beer, cider and wine menu – with many sustainable and organic tipples – partners well with shared plates. Try the surprising pulled jackfruit tacos.

Mt Eden

Brothers Juke Joint BBQ BARBECUE $
(Map p84; 09-638 7592; www.jukejoint.co.nz; 5 Akiraho St, Mt Eden; snacks $10-15; 11.30am-10pm Tue-Sat, to 8pm Sun;) A spin-off from central Auckland's excellent Brothers Beer (p107) craft beer bar, Juke Joint BBQ serves up Southern US–style barbecue in a hip renovated warehouse. Retro 1960s furniture informs the decor and the compact kids' play area is popular with local families on weekend afternoons. Brothers' own brews are joined by the best from other Kiwi breweries on the gleaming taps.

Zool Zool RAMEN, JAPANESE $
(Map p84; 09-630 4445; www.zoolzool.co.nz; 405 Mt Eden Rd, Mt Eden; snacks $9-18, ramen $14-18; 11.30am-2pm & 5.30-10pm Tue-Sun) A co-production between two of Auckland's most respected Japanese chefs, Zool Zool is a stylish and modern take on a traditional *izakaya* (Japanese pub). Some of the city's best ramen noodle dishes are underpinned by hearty and complex broths, and dishes

made for sharing over frosty mugs of Japanese beer include tempura squid, soft-shell crab and *panko*-crumbed fried chicken.

Frasers CAFE **$$**
(Map p84; ☑ 09-630 6825; cnr Mt Eden & Stokes Rds, Mt Eden; mains $13-35; ⊙ 6am-11pm Mon-Fri, 7am-11pm Sat & Sun) One of Mt Eden's most loved cafes has been reborn after a stylish makeover. The coffee and cakes are still great – especially the baked New York cheesecake – but now wine and craft beer partner the concise menu of comfort-food classics. Try the mushrooms on sourdough for breakfast, or go for the veal schnitzel with crispy potato gratin at dinner.

✕ Parnell & Newmarket

Hansan VIETNAMESE **$**
(Map p88; ☑ 09-523 3988; www.hansan.co.nz; 55 Nuffield St, Newmarket; mains $11-17; ⊙ 11am-10pm) A branch of a small local chain serving good-value, authentic Vietnamese food.

La Cigale FRENCH, MARKET **$**
(Map p86; ☑ 09-366 9361; www.lacigale.co.nz; 69 St Georges Bay Rd, Parnell; cafe $8-19, bistro 2-/3 courses $38/50; ⊙ market 9am-1.30pm Sat & Sun, cafe 9am-4pm Mon-Fri, to 2pm Sat & Sun, bistro 5pm-late Wed) Catering to Francophile foodies, this warehouse stocks French imports and has a patisserie-laden cafe. During the weekend farmers markets, this *cigale* (cicada) really chirps, with stalls laden with local artisan produce. On occasional Thursday evenings it becomes a food-truck stop, while on Wednesdays it's converted into a quirky evening bistro serving simple rustic dishes. Check the website for what's on.

Winona Forever CAFE **$$**
(Map p86; ☑ 09-974 2796; www.facebook.com/winonaforevercafe; 100 Parnell Rd; mains $13-21; ⊙ 7am-4.30pm Mon-Fri, 8am-4pm Sat & Sun) Some of Auckland's best counter food – including stonking cream doughnuts – partners with innovative cafe culture at this always-busy eatery near good shopping and art galleries along Parnell Rd. Local residents crowd in with travellers for coffee, craft beer and wine, and one of the cafe's signature dishes – the Ladyboy, a Thai-influenced eggs Benedict with grilled prawns.

Han KOREAN **$$**
(Map p86; ☑ 09-377 0977; www.hanrestaurant.co.nz; 100 Parnell Rd, Parnell; mains $20-34; ⊙ 11am-2.30pm Tue-Sat, 5pm-late Wed-Sun) ✐ Korean flavours continue to influence Auckland's dining scene, and Han's evolution

from a food truck to a standalone restaurant is testament to the innovation of chef Min Baek. Lunch is a more informal affair – think Korean-style burgers and healthy rice bowls – but the dinner menu really shines with modern dishes including beef short rib with beetroot and asparagus.

✕ Devonport

Calliope Road Cafe CAFE **$$**
(Map p90; ☑ 09-446 1209; www.facebook.com/CalliopeRoadCafe; 33 Calliope Rd, Devonport; mains $13-28; ⊙ 8am-3pm) This Devonport cafe is set a little back from the main tourist strip, and serves a tasty mix of cafe classics and Southeast Asian dishes to locals in the know.

Devon on the Wharf TURKISH, CAFE **$$**
(Map p90; ☑ 09-445 7012; www.devononthewharf.nz; Devonport Wharf, Queens Pde; meze $10-20, mains $19-35; ⊙ 7am-11pm Mon-Fri, 8am-11pm Sat & Sun; ✐) From downtown Auckland, make the short ferry journey to Devonport to visit this laid-back cafe packed with Turkish influences. Combine harbour views with brunch options including *menemen* (baked eggs), or try a meze dinner selection of grilled haloumi, hummus and *lahmacun* (Turkish-style pizza). Levantine-inspired cocktails and a concise craft-beer selection are served at what is maybe Auckland's longest bar.

✕ Other Areas

Henderson Night Market MARKET **$**
(www.aucklandnightmarket.co.nz; Waitakere Mega Centre, under Kmart; ⊙ 5.30-11pm Thu) Of Auckland's bustling night markets, held in a different suburban car park each night of the week, the Henderson market is the most convenient for travellers to reach. Expect dozens of stalls serving food from Argentina and Samoa, to Hungary and Turkey. Catch a western-line train from Britomart to Henderson and walk 650m to underneath the Kmart department store.

Paradise INDIAN **$**
(Map p78; ☑ 09-845 1144; www.paradiseindianfood.co.nz; 591 Sandringham Rd, Sandringham; mains $12-18; ⊙ 11.30am-9.30pm; ✐) Paradise serves a delicious array of curry and biryani dishes from both its very pleasant restaurant and the attached takeaway counter. Our favourite is the *baghara baingan* (eggplant curry). There's another branch just around the corner doing a nightly Indian buffet ($17 to $20) from 6.30pm.

Engine Room
MODERN NZ **$$**
(Map p78; ✆09-480 9502; www.engineroom.
net.nz; 115 Queen St, Northcote; mains $32-35;
◔noon-3pm Fri, 5.30-11pm Tue-Sat) One of
Auckland's best restaurants, this informal
eatery serves up lighter-than-air goat's-
cheese soufflés, inventive mains and oh-my-
God chocolate truffles. It's worth booking
ahead and catching the ferry to North-
cote Point; the restaurant is a further 1km
walk away.

Takapuna Beach Cafe
CAFE **$$**
(Map p78; ✆09-484 0002; www.takapuna
beachcafe.co.nz; 22 The Promenade; mains $19-
30; ◔6.30am-6pm) Sophisticated cafe fare
combined with excellent views of Takapuna Beach ensure that this cafe constantly
buzzes. If you can't snaffle a table, grab an
award-winning ice cream – our favourite is
the salted caramel – and take a lazy stroll
along the beach.

St Heliers Bay Bistro
MODERN NZ **$$**
(Map p78; www.stheliersbaybistro.co.nz; 387
Tamaki Dr, St Heliers; brunch $16-27, dinner $27-
34; ◔7am-11pm) Head along Tamaki Dr
to this classy eatery with harbour views.
No bookings are taken, but the switched-
on crew soon find space for diners. Look
forward to upmarket takes on the classics
(pasta, burgers, fish and chips), along with
cooked breakfasts, tasty salads and lots of
Mediterranean influences. Excellent ice
cream, too – best enjoyed walking along
the beach.

🍷 Drinking & Nightlife
Auckland's nightlife is quiet during the
week – for some vital signs, head to Ponson-
by Rd, Britomart or the Viaduct. Karanga-
hape Rd (K Rd) wakes up late on Friday and
Saturday; don't even bother staggering this
way before 11pm.

🍸 City Centre

Brothers Beer
CRAFT BEER
(Map p80; ✆09-366 6100; www.brothersbeer.
co.nz; City Works Depot, 90 Wellesley St; ◔noon-
10pm) This beer bar combines quirky decor
with 18 taps crammed with Brothers' own
brews and guest beers from NZ and further
afield. Hundreds more bottled beers await
chilling in the fridges, and bar food includes
pizza. There are occasional movie and com-
edy nights, and beers are available to take
away. The adjacent City Works Depot has
other good eating options.

WORTH A TRIP

Clearly the roar of jets doesn't bother
grapes, as NZ's most awarded winery
is just 4km from the airport. The park-
like grounds of **Villa Maria** (Map p78;
✆09-255 0666; www.villamaria.co.nz; 118
Montgomerie Rd, Mangere; ◔9am-6pm
Mon-Fri, to 4pm Sat & Sun) are a green
oasis in the encircling industrial zone.
Short tours ($5) take place at 11am and
2pm. There's a charge for tastings ($5,
refundable on purchase), but lingering
over a lunch of wine and antipasto
(platters $45 to $55, lunch $28 to $38)
on the restaurant's terrace sure beats
hanging around the departure lounge.

Gin Room
BAR
(Map p80; www.ginroom.co.nz; Level 1, 12 Vulcan
Lane; ◔5pm-midnight Tue & Wed, 5pm-2am Thu,
4pm-4am Fri, 6pm-4am Sat) There's a slightly
dishevelled colonial charm to this bar, dis-
creetly tucked away above Auckland's oldest
pub, which is completely in keeping with its
latest incarnation as a gin palace. There are
at least 50 ways to ruin mother here – ask
the bar staff for advice – and that's not even
counting the juniper-sozzled cocktails.

Brewers Co-operative
CRAFT BEER
(Map p80; ✆09-309 4515; 128 Victoria St; ◔11am-
10pm) With 27 craft beers on tap, this cor-
ner bar is a good central-city option for an
interesting brew and a feed of seafood and
chips served the traditional way, in paper.
It's popular with the after-work crowd on
Friday evenings.

Jefferson
BAR
(Map p80; www.thejefferson.co.nz; basement, Impe-
rial Bldg, Fort Lane; ◔4pm-1am Mon-Thu, to 3am Fri
& Sat) Lit by the golden glow of close to 600
different whisky bottles, this subterranean
den is a sophisticated spot for a nightcap.
There's no list – talk to the knowledgable
bar staff about the kind of thing you're after
(peaty, smooth, smoky, not too damaging to
the wallet) and they'll suggest something.

Vultures' Lane
PUB
(Map p80; ✆09-300 7117; www.vultureslane.co.nz;
10 Vulcan Lane; ◔11.30am-late) With 22 taps,
more than 75 bottled beers and sports on
the TV, this pleasantly grungy historic pub
is popular with the savviest of Auckland's
craft-beer fans. Check the website for what's
currently on tap, and also for news of reg-
ular tap takeovers from some of New Zea-
land's best brewers.

Mo's BAR

(Map p80; ☑09-366 6066; www.mosbar.co.nz; cnr Wolfe & Federal Sts; ⊙2pm-late Mon-Fri, 6pm-late Sat; ☎) There's something about this tiny corner bar that makes you want to invent problems just so the bartender can solve them with soothing words and an expertly poured martini.

Cassette Nine CLUB

(Map p80; ☑09-366 0196; www.cassettenine.com; 9 Vulcan Lane; ⊙4pm-late Tue-Fri, 6pm-late Sat) Hipsters gravitate to this eccentric bar-club for music ranging from live indie to international DJ sets.

Britomart, Viaduct Harbour & Wynyard Quarter

Caretaker COCKTAIL BAR

(Map p80; www.caretaker.net.nz; Roukai Lane; ⊙5pm-3am) New York style infuses this cocktail bar concealed behind an old door inscribed with the title 'Caretaker'. The decor is equally eclectic, and a handful of tables and leather sofas means the bar always feels intimate and convivial. Choose from the very considered cocktail list, or just describe what you like and the bartenders will work their bespoke mixology magic.

Dr Rudis MICROBREWERY

(Map p80; ☑021 048 7946; www.drrudis.co.nz; Viaduct Harbour, cnr Quay & Hobson Sts; ⊙7am-4am) Viaduct Harbour's best views – usually including a bevy of visiting super-yachts – combine with Dr Rudi's very own craft beers and a menu featuring wood-fired pizza and excellent seafood and barbecue platters de-

signed to defeat even the hungriest group. There are also a couple of tenpin bowling lanes to get active on.

Jack Tar PUB

(Map p80; ☑09-303 1002; www.jacktar.co.nz; North Wharf, 34-37 Jellicoe St, Wynyard Quarter; ⊙8am-late) A top spot for a late-afternoon/early-evening beer or wine and pub grub amid the relaxed vibe of the waterfront Wynyard Quarter.

Sixteen Tun CRAFT BEER

(Map p80; ☑09-368 7712; www.16tun.co.nz; 10-26 Jellicoe St, Wynyard Quarter; tasting 4/6/8 beers $12/18/24; ⊙11.30am-late) The glister of burnished copper perfectly complements the liquid amber on offer here in the form of dozens of NZ craft beers by the bottle and a score on tap. If you can't decide, go for a good-value tasting 'crate' of 200mL serves.

Ponsonby & Grey Lynn

Along Ponsonby Rd, the line between cafe, restaurant, bar and club gets blurred. A lot of eateries also have live music or become clubs later on.

★ Freida Margolis BAR

(Map p92; ☑09-378 6625; www.facebook.com/freidamargolis; 440 Richmond Rd; ⊙4-11pm Sun-Wed, to 2am Thu-Sat) Formerly a butchers – look for the Westlynn Organic Meats sign – this corner location is now a great little neighbourhood bar with the ambience of the backstreets of Bogota. Loyal locals sit outside with their well-behaved dogs, sup-

CRAFT BEER AROUND AUCKLAND

Nelson, as the country's major hop-growing region, and bohemian Wellington both claim to be the 'craft beer capital of NZ', but while the southern centres have been debating the title over a few brews, Auckland's northern craft-beer scene has been fizzing and fermenting away to excellence. Driven by the sheer relative size of the market, there are now plenty of opportunities around Auckland for travelling beer fans to explore the diversity of the Kiwi beer scene.

In Auckland's rural hinterland both Hallertau (p131) and Sawmill Brewery (p137) offer award-winning beers with restaurant-worthy food, while across on Waiheke Island, three different craft breweries offer an alternative to the island's world-beating wines. For real island diversity, contrast rustic and relaxed Boogie Van Brewing (p121) with the stylish, brick-lined Alibi Brewing tasting room at Tantalus Estate (p121).

In the city, Brothers Beer (p107), Galbraith's Alehouse and Vultures' Lane (p107) are all essential destinations, while June's annual GABS (p97) festival is Auckland's very own version of the world-famous beer festival first launched in Melbourne, Australia.

Excellent Auckland region brewery names to look out for in restaurants and bars include 8 Wired, Behemoth, Liberty and Epic.

GAY & LESBIAN AUCKLAND

The Queen City (as it's known for completely coincidental reasons) has by far New Zealand's biggest gay population, with the bright lights attracting gays and lesbians from all over the country. However, the even brighter lights of Sydney eventually steal many of the 30- to 40-somethings, leaving a gap in the demographic. There are very few gay venues and they only really kick off on the weekends. For the latest, see the monthly magazine *Express* (available from gay venues), or online at www.gayexpress.co.nz.

The big event on the calendar is the Auckland Pride Festival (p96). Also worth watching out for are the regular parties held by Urge Events (www.facebook.com/urgebar); the only reliably fun and sexy nights out for the over 30s, they book out quickly.

Venues change with alarming regularity, but these ones were the stayers at the time of writing:

Family (Map p80; ☑09-309 0213; 270 Karangahape Rd, Newton; ☺9am-4am) Trashy, brash and extremely young, Family gets crammed on weekends, with drag hosts and dancing into the wee hours, both at the back of the ground-level bar and in the club downstairs.

Eagle (Map p80; ☑09-309 4979; www.facebook.com/the.eagle.bar; 259 Karangahape Rd, Newton; ☺4pm-1am Mon, Tue & Sun, to 2am Wed & Thu, to 4am Fri & Sat) A cosy place for a quiet drink early in the evening, getting more raucous as the night progresses. Get in quick to put your picks on the video jukebox or prepare for an entire evening of Kylie and Taylor.

Centurian (Map p80; ☑09-377 5571; www.centuriansauna.co.nz; 18 Beresford St, Newton; before/after 3pm $25/30; ☺11am-2am Sun-Thu, to 6am Fri & Sat) Gay men's sauna.

---

ping on sangria, wine and craft beer, and enjoying eclectic sounds from the owner's big vinyl collection.

Annabel's　　　　　　　　　WINE BAR
(Map p92; www.annabelswinebar.com; 277 Ponsonby Rd; ☺3-11pm) A self-described 'neighbourhood bar', Annabel's would also be right at home in the backstreets of Bordeaux or Barcelona. Cheese and charcuterie platters combine with a Eurocentric wine list, while Spanish beers and classic Negroni cocktails also help turn the South Pacific into the south of France. A thoroughly unpretentious affair; worth a stop before or after dining along Ponsonby Rd.

SPQR　　　　　　　　　　　　BAR
(Map p92; ☑09-360 1710; www.spqrnz.co.nz; 150 Ponsonby Rd, Ponsonby; ☺noon-late) Quite the best place to see and be seen on the Ponsonby strip, SPQR is a magnet for local scenesters who are quick to nab the tables on the footpath. Head inside for a more discreet assignation lit by the flattering glow of candles reflected in the burnished copper bar. The food is excellent too, especially the Roman-style thin-crust pizza.

Bedford Soda & Liquor　　COCKTAIL BAR
(Map p92; ☑09-378 7362; www.bedfordsoda liquor.co.nz; Ponsonby Central, Richmond Rd, Ponsonby; ☺noon-midnight) Candlelight and a semi-

industrial fit-out set the scene for a New York–style bar devoted to the American drinking culture. The cocktails are pricey but worth it: some come wreathed in smoke, others in the alcoholic equivalent of a snow globe, while the 'salted caramel Malteaser whisky milkshake' is exactly as decadent as it sounds.

Dida's Wine Lounge & Tapas Bar　WINE BAR
(Map p92; ☑09-376 2813; www.didas.co.nz; 54 Jervois Rd, Ponsonby; ☺noon-midnight) Great food and an even better wine list attract a grown-up crowd. There's an associated wine store, providore and cafe next door.

🍷 Newton

★Madame George　　　　　　　BAR
(Map p80; ☑09-308 9039; www.facebook.com/madamegeorgenz; 490 Karangahape Rd; ☺5pm-late Tue-Sat) Two patron saints of cool – Elvis Presley and Al Pacino – look down in this compact space along Karangahape Rd. Shoot the breeze with the friendly bar staff over a craft beer or Auckland's best cocktails, or grab a shared table out front and watch the passing theatre of K Rd.

★Galbraith's Alehouse　　　BREWERY
(Map p84; ☑09-379 3557; http://alehouse.co.nz; 2 Mt Eden Rd; ☺noon-11pm) Brewing real ales and lagers on site, this cosy English-style

pub in a grand heritage building offers bliss on tap. There are always more craft beers from around NZ and the world on the guest taps, and the food's also very good. From April to September, Galbraith's Sunday roast is one of Auckland's best.

★Lovebucket   COCKTAIL BAR, CRAFT BEER
(Map p80; ☑09-869 2469; www.lovebucket. co.nz; K'Road Food Workshop, 309 Karangahape Rd; ⊙4pm-late Tue-Sun) Lovebucket is a more sophisticated alternative to K Rd's often youthful after-dark vibe. Courtesy of shared ownership with the Hallertau Brewery in West Auckland, Lovebucket's craft-beer selection is one of Auckland's best – including barrel-aged and sour beers. Quirky cocktails and a well-informed wine list join interesting bar snacks such as cheeses, charcuterie and gourmet toasted sandwiches.

Wine Cellar   WINE BAR
(Map p80; www.facebook.com/winecellar stkevins; St Kevins Arcade, 183 Karangahape Rd, Newton; ⊙5pm-midnight Mon-Thu, to 1am Fri & Sat) Secreted downstairs in an arcade, the Wine Cellar is dark, grungy and very cool, with regular live music in the neighbouring Whammy Bar.

🍽 Kingsland

Portland Public House   BAR
(Map p84; www.facebook.com/theportlandpublic house; 463 New North Rd, Kingsland; ⊙4pm-midnight Mon-Wed, 4pm-2am Thu & Fri, noon-2am Sat, noon-midnight Sun) With mismatched furniture, cartoon-themed art, and lots of hidden nooks and crannies, the Portland Public House is like spending a few lazy hours at a hipster mate's place. It's also an excellent location for live music.

☆ Entertainment

For listings, check the *New Zealand Herald*'s *Time Out* magazine on Thursday and again in its Saturday edition. Tickets for most major events can be bought from **Ticketek** (☑0800 842 538; www.ticketek.co.nz), with an outlet at **SkyCity Theatre** (Map p80; ☑09-363 6000; www.skycity.co.nz; cnr Wellesley & Hobson Sts), and **Ticketmaster** (☑09-970 9700; www.ticketmaster.co.nz) at Spark Arena and the **Aotea Centre** (Map p80; ☑09-309 2677; www.aucklandlive.co.nz; 50 Mayoral Dr). **iTicket** (☑0508 484 253; www.iticket.co.nz) handles a lot of smaller gig and dance party tickets.

Live Music
Whammy Bar   LIVE MUSIC
(Map p80; www.facebook.com/thewhammybar; 183 Karangahape Rd, Newton; ⊙8.30pm-4am Wed-Sat) Small, but a stalwart on the live indie music scene nonetheless.

Ding Dong Lounge   LIVE MUSIC
(Map p80; ☑09-377 4712; www.dingdonglounge nz.com; 26 Wyndham St; ⊙6pm-4am Wed-Fri, 8pm-4am Sat) Rock, indie and alternative sounds from live bands and DJs, washed down with craft beer.

Power Station   LIVE MUSIC
(Map p84; www.powerstation.net.nz; 33 Mt Eden Rd, Eden Terrace) Midrange venue popular with up-and-coming overseas acts and established Kiwi bands.

Spark Arena   STADIUM
(Map p86; ☑09-358 1250; www.sparkarena.co.nz; Mahuhu Cres) Auckland's top indoor arena for major touring acts.

Cinema
Most cinemas offer cheaper rates on weekdays before 5pm; Tuesday is usually bargain day.

Academy Cinemas   CINEMA
(Map p80; ☑09-373 2761; www.academycinemas. co.nz; 44 Lorne St; tickets adult/child $16/10) Foreign and art-house films in the basement of the Central Library. Cheap $5 movies on Wednesdays.

Rialto   CINEMA
(Map p88; ☑09-369 2417; www.rialto.co.nz; 167 Broadway, Newmarket) Mainly art-house and international films, plus better mainstream fare and regular specialist film festivals.

Event Cinemas   CINEMA
(Map p80; ☑09-369 2400; www.eventcinemas. co.nz; Level 3, 297 Queen St) Blockbusters, bowling alley and food court.

Theatre, Classical Music & Comedy
Auckland's main arts and entertainment complex is grouped around Aotea Sq. Branded Auckland Live (www.aucklandlive.co.nz), it's comprised of the Town Hall, Civic Theatre and Aotea Centre, along with the Bruce Mason Centre in Takapuna. The new ASB Waterfront Theatre (p111) in Wynyard Quarter is home to the Auckland Theatre Company.

Whoa! Studios   THEATRE
(☑09-838 4553; https://whoastudios.co.nz; 8 Henderson Valley Rd, Henderson; tickets $25-30; 🏢) Exciting and educational kids' shows

are performed at this innovative theatre in Henderson – expect extreme fun and irreverence – and the whole shebang also features a brilliant kids' playground and the excellent **Grounds Eatery** (☑09-393 8448; https://whoastudios.co.nz/the-grounds; mains $20-33; ☺9am-3pm Mon-Wed, to late Thu-Sun; ☺) ✎. Check the website for what's scheduled in the theatre – usually across school holidays – but it's worth visiting just for the restaurant and playground.

Q Theatre   THEATRE
(Map p80; ☑09-309 9771; www.qtheatre.co.nz; 305 Queen St) Theatre by various companies and intimate live music. Silo Theatre (www.silotheatre.co.nz) often performs here.

ASB Waterfront Theatre   THEATRE
(Map p80; ☑ box office 0800 282 849; www.asbwaterfronttheatre.co.nz; 138 Halsey St, Wynyard Quarter) The new ASB Waterfront Theatre is used by the Auckland Theatre Company and also for occasional one-off shows and concerts. There's a good selection of bars and restaurants in close proximity.

Classic Comedy Club   COMEDY
(Map p80; ☑09-373 4321; www.comedy.co.nz; 321 Queen St; ☺6.30pm-late) Stand-up performances most nights, with legendary late-night shows during the annual Comedy Festival (p97).

Auckland Town Hall   CLASSICAL MUSIC
(Map p80; ☑09-309 2677; www.aucklandlive.co.nz; 305 Queen St) This elegant Edwardian venue (1911) hosts the NZ Symphony Orchestra (www.nzso.co.nz) and Auckland Philharmonia (www.apo.co.nz), among others.

Sport

Eden Park   SPECTATOR SPORT
(Map p84; ☑09-815 5551; www.edenpark.co.nz; Reimers Ave, Mt Eden) This stadium hosts top rugby (winter) and cricket (summer) tests by the All Blacks (www.allblacks.com) and the Black Caps (www.blackcaps.co.nz), respectively. It's also the home ground of Auckland Rugby (www.aucklandrugby.co.nz), the Blues Super Rugby team (www.theblues.co.nz) and Auckland Cricket (www.auckland cricket.co.nz). Catch the train from Britomart to Kingsland and follow the crowds.

Mt Smart Stadium   SPECTATOR SPORT
(Map p78; ☑09-366 2048; www.mtsmart stadium.co.nz; 2 Beasley Ave, Penrose) Home ground for the Warriors rugby league team

---

AUCKLAND TOP 10 PLAYLIST

Download these Auckland songs to your MP3 player:

➡ 'Me at the Museum, You in the Wintergardens' – Tiny Ruins (2014)

➡ '400 Lux' – Lorde (2013)

➡ 'Grey Lynn Park' – The Veils (2011)

➡ 'Auckland CBD Part Two' – Lawrence Arabia (2009)

➡ 'Forever Thursday' – Tim Finn (2008)

➡ 'Riverhead' – Goldenhorse (2004)

➡ 'A Brief Reflection' – Nesian Mystik (2002)

➡ 'Dominion Road' – The Mutton Birds (1992)

➡ 'Andy' – The Front Lawn (1989)

➡ 'One Tree Hill' – U2 (1987)

(www.warriors.kiwi), Auckland Football Federation (www.aucklandfootball.org.nz) and Athletics Auckland (www.athleticsauckland.co.nz). Also *really* big concerts.

North Shore Events Centre SPECTATOR SPORT
(Map p78; ☑09-443 8199; www.nseventscentre.co.nz; Argus Pl, Wairau Valley) One of the two home courts of the NZ Breakers basketball team (www.nzbreakers.co.nz) and an occasional concert venue. The other home court is at Spark Arena.

🔒 Shopping

Followers of fashion should head to the Britomart (p83) precinct, Newmarket's Teed and Nuffield Sts, and Ponsonby Rd. For vintage clothing and secondhand boutiques, try Karangahape Rd (K Rd) or Ponsonby Rd.

🔒 City Centre

★Real Groovy   MUSIC
(Map p80; ☑09-302 3940; www.realgroovy.co.nz; 369 Queen St; ☺9am-7pm) Masses of new, secondhand and rare releases in vinyl and CD format, as well as concert tickets, giant posters, DVDs, books, magazines and clothes.

★Unity Books   BOOKS
(Map p80; ☑09-307 0731; www.unitybooks.co.nz; 19 High St; ☺8.30am-7pm Mon-Sat, 10am-6pm Sun) The inner-city's best independent bookshop.

PASIFIKA IN AUCKLAND

There are nearly 195,000 Pacific Islanders (PI) living in Auckland, making it the world's principal Polynesian city. Samoans are by far the largest group, followed by Cook Islanders, Tongans, Niueans, Fijians, Tokelauans and Tuvaluans. The biggest PI communities can be found in South Auckland and pockets of West and Central Auckland.

Like the Māori renaissance of recent decades, Pasifika has become a hot commodity for Auckland hipsters. You'll find PI motifs everywhere: in art, architecture, fashion, homewares, movies and especially in music. The annual Pasifika Festival (p96) in March is a wonderful two-day celebration of Pacific culture.

Strangely Normal CLOTHING
(Map p80; ✆09-309 0600; www.strangely normal.com; 19 O'Connell St; ⊙10am-6pm Mon-Sat, 11am-4pm Sun) Quality, NZ-made men's tailored shirts straight out of *Blue Hawaii* sit alongside hipster hats, sharp shoes and cufflinks.

Pauanesia GIFTS & SOUVENIRS
(Map p80; ✆09-366 7282; www.pauanesia.co.nz; 35 High St; ⊙9.30am-6.30pm Tue-Fri, 10am-5pm Sat-Mon) Homewares and gifts with a Polynesian and Kiwiana influence.

🏠 Britomart

Zambesi CLOTHING
(Map p80; ✆09-303 1701; www.zambesi.co.nz; 56 Tyler St; ⊙10am-6pm Mon-Fri, 11am-5pm Sat & Sun) Iconic NZ label much sought after by local and international celebs. Also in **Ponsonby** (Map p92; ✆09-360 7391; www.zambesi.co.nz; 169 Ponsonby Rd, Ponsonby; ⊙10am-6pm Mon-Fri, 11am-5pm Sat & Sun) and **Newmarket** (Map p88; ✆09-523 1000; www.zambesi.co.nz; 38 Osborne St, Newmarket; ⊙10am-6pm Mon-Fri, 11am-5pm Sat & Sun).

Karen Walker CLOTHING
(Map p80; ✆09-309 6299; www.karenwalker.com; 18 Te Ara Tahuhu Walkway, Britomart; ⊙10am-6pm) Join Madonna and Kirsten Dunst in wearing Walker's cool (but pricey) threads. Also in **Ponsonby Rd** (Map p92; ✆09-361 6723; www.karenwalker.com; 128a Ponsonby Rd, Grey Lynn; ⊙10am-5.30pm Mon-Sat, 11am-4pm Sun) and

Newmarket (Map p88; ✆09-522 4286; www.karenwalker.com; 6 Balm St, Newmarket; ⊙10am-6pm).

🏠 Ponsonby & Grey Lynn

Women's Bookshop BOOKS
(Map p92; ✆09-376 4399; www.womens bookshop.co.nz; 105 Ponsonby Rd, Ponsonby; ⊙10am-6pm Mon-Fri, to 5pm Sat & Sun) Excellent independent bookshop.

🏠 Newton

⭐**St Kevins Arcade** SHOPPING CENTRE
(Map p80; www.stkevinsarcade.co.nz; 183 Karangahape Rd) Built in 1924, this historic, renovated shopping arcade has interesting stores selling vintage clothing and organic and sustainable goods. The arcade also has excellent cafes and restaurants.

Bread & Butter Letter ARTS & CRAFTS
(Map p80; ✆09-940 5065; www.breadand butterletter.co.nz; 225 Karangahape Rd; ⊙10am-6pm Mon-Fri, 10am-5pm Sat, 11am-5pm Sun) Sells an excellent selection of arts, crafts, foodstuffs and homewares from local New Zealand designers. Bread & Butter Letter also offers retro and vintage Kiwiana products for sale.

🏠 Kingsland

⭐**Royal Jewellery Studio** JEWELLERY
(Map p84; ✆09-846 0200; www.royaljewellery studio.com; 486 New North Rd, Kingsland; ⊙10am-4pm Tue-Sun) Work by local artisans, including beautiful Māori designs and authentic *pounamu* (greenstone) jewellery.

🏠 Other Areas

⭐**Otara Flea Market** MARKET
(Map p78; ✆09-274 0830; www.otarafleamarket.co.nz; Newbury St; ⊙6am-noon Sat) Held in the car park between the Manukau Polytech and the Otara town centre, this market has a palpable Polynesian atmosphere and is good for South Pacific food, music and fashion. Catch a train on the southern line to Papatoetoe and then switch to a bus to Otara.

Avondale Sunday Markets MARKET
(www.avondalesundaymarkets.co.nz; Avondale Racecourse, Ash St; ⊙5am-noon Sun) This large, popular market has a strong Asian and Polynesian atmosphere and is excellent for fresh produce. Take the train from Britomart station to Avondale.

ⓘ Information

INTERNET ACCESS

Auckland Council offers free wi-fi in parts of the city centre, Newton, Ponsonby, Kingsland, Mt Eden and Parnell. All public libraries offer free wi-fi, and a few internet cafes catering to gaming junkies are scattered about the inner city.

MEDICAL SERVICES

Auckland City Hospital (☑09-367 0000; www.adhb.govt.nz; 2 Park Rd, Grafton; ⊙24hr) The city's main hospital has a dedicated accident and emergency (A&E) service.

Starship Children's Health (☑09-307 4949; www.adhb.govt.nz; Park Rd, Grafton; ⊙24hr) Has its own A&E department.

POST

Post Office (Map p80; ☑0800 501 501; www.nzpost.co.nz; 155 Queen St; ⊙9am-5.30pm Mon-Fri)

Post Office (Map p92; ☑0800 501 501; www.nzpost.co.nz; 314 Ponsonby Rd, Ponsonby; ⊙9am-5.30pm Mon-Fri, to 1pm Sat)

TOURIST INFORMATION

Auckland International Airport i-SITE (Map p78; ☑09-365 9925; www.aucklandnz.com; International Arrivals Hall; ⊙6.30am-10.30pm)

Cornwall Park Information Centre (Map p78; ☑09-630 8485; www.cornwallpark.co.nz; Huia Lodge, Michael Horton Dr; ⊙10am-4pm)

Karanga Kiosk (Map p80; ☑09-365 1290; cnr Jellicoe & Halsey Sts, Wynyard Quarter; ⊙9.30am-4.30pm) Looking like a precariously stacked set of shipping containers, this volunteer-run centre dispenses information on goings on around the waterfront.

Princes Wharf i-SITE (☑09-365 9914; www.aucklandnz.com; Princes Wharf; ⊙9am-5pm) Auckland's main official information centre, incorporating the **DOC Auckland Visitor Centre** (Map p80; ☑09-379 6476; www.doc.govt.nz; Princes Wharf; ⊙9am-5pm Mon-Fri, extended hours Nov-Mar).

SkyCity i-SITE (Map p80; ☑09-365 9918; www.aucklandnz.com; SkyCity Atrium, cnr Victoria & Federal Sts; ⊙9am-5pm)

Visit Devonport (Map p90; www.visitdevonport.co.nz; Victoria Rd; ⊙9am-5pm Mon-Fri; 🐾)

ⓘ Getting There & Away

AIR

Auckland is the main international gateway to NZ, and a hub for domestic flights. **Auckland Airport** (AKL; Map p78; ☑09-275 0789; www.aucklandairport.co.nz; Ray Emery Dr, Mangere) is 21km south of the city centre. It has separate international and domestic terminals, a 10-minute walk apart from each other via a signposted footpath; a free shuttle service operates every 15 minutes (5am to 10.30pm). Both terminals have left-luggage facilities, eateries, ATMs and car-rental desks.

BUS

Coaches depart from 172 Quay St, opposite the Ferry Building (p115), except for InterCity services, which depart from **SkyCity Coach Terminal** (Map p80; 102 Hobson St). Many southbound services also stop at the airport.

Go Kiwi (☑0800 446 549; www.go-kiwi.co.nz) offers daily Auckland City–Auckland Airport–Thames–Tairua–Hot Water Beach–Whitianga shuttles.

InterCity (☑09-583 5780; www.intercity.co.nz) has direct services to Kerikeri (from $37, 4½ hours, three daily), Hamilton (from $16, two hours, 16 daily), New Plymouth (from $35, 6¼ hours, daily), Taupo (from $25, five hours, five daily) and Wellington (from $29, 11 hours, four daily).

Naked Bus (www.nakedbus.com) travels along SH1 as far north as Paihia ($25, four hours) and as far south as Wellington (from $25, 11 hours), as well as heading to Tauranga ($15, 3½ hours), Rotorua ($18, 3¾ hours) and Napier (from $24, 12 hours). Some services are operated by ManaBus (www.manabus.com).

CAR & CAMPERVAN

Hire

Auckland has many hire agencies around Beach Rd and Stanley St close to the city centre.

A2B (☑0800 545 000; www.a2b-car-rental.co.nz; 167 Beach Rd; ⊙7am-7pm Nov-Apr, 7.30am-5pm May-Oct) Cheap older cars with no visible hire-car branding.

Apex Car Rentals (☑09-307 1063; www.apexrentals.co.nz; 156 Beach Rd; ⊙8am-5pm)

Budget (☑09-976 2270; www.budget.co.nz; 163 Beach Rd; ⊙7am-6pm Mon-Fri, 8am-5pm Sat & Sun)

Escape (☑0800 216 171; www.escaperentals.co.nz; 61 The Strand; ⊙9am-3pm) Eccentrically painted campervans.

Go Rentals (☑09-257 5142; www.gorentals.co.nz; Bay 4-10, Cargo Central, George Bolt Memoral Dr, Mangere; ⊙6am-10pm)

Hertz (☑09-367 6350; www.hertz.co.nz; 154 Victoria St; ⊙7.30am-5.30pm)

Jucy (☑0800 399 736; www.jucy.co.nz; 2-16 The Strand; ⊙8am-5pm)

Kea, Maui & Britz (☑09-255 3910; www.maui.co.nz; 36 Richard Pearse Dr, Mangere; ⊙8am-4.30pm)

NZ Frontiers (☑09-299 6705; www.newzealandfrontiers.com; 30 Laurie Ave, Papakura)

Omega (☑ 09-377 5573; www.omegarentals. com; 75 Beach Rd; ⊙ 8am-5pm)

Quality (☑ 0800 680 123; www.quality rental.co.nz; 8 Andrew Baxter Dr, Mangere; ⊙ 8am-4pm)

Thrifty (☑ 09-309 0111; www.thrifty.co.nz; 150 Khyber Pass Rd; ⊙ 8am-5pm)

Wilderness Motorhomes (☑ 09-255 5300; www.wilderness.co.nz; 11 Pavilion Dr, Mangere; ⊙ 8am-5pm)

Purchase

Mechanical inspection services are on hand at secondhand car fairs, where sellers pay to display their cars.

Auckland Car Fair (☑ 09-529 2233; www.car fair.co.nz; Ellerslie Racecourse, Greenlane East; display fee $35; ⊙ 9am-noon Sun) Auckland's largest car fair.

Auckland City Car Fair (☑ 09-837 7817; www. aucklandcitycarfair.co.nz; 27 Alten Rd; display fee $30; ⊙ 8am-1pm Sat)

MOTORCYCLE

NZ Motorcycle Rentals (☑ 09-486 2472; www. nzbike.com; 72 Barrys Point Rd, Takapuna; per day $140-290) Guided tours of NZ also available.

TRAIN

Northern Explorer (☑ 0800 872 467; www. greatjourneysofnz.co.nz) trains leave from **Auckland Strand Station** (Ngaoho Pl) at 7.45am on Mondays, Thursdays and Saturdays and arrive in Wellington at 6.25pm. Stops include Hamilton (2½ hours), Otorohanga (three hours), Tongariro National Park (5½ hours), Ohakune (six hours), Palmerston North (8½ hours) and Paraparaumu (9¾ hours). Standard fares to Wellington range from $119 to $219.

ⓘ Getting Around

TO/FROM THE AIRPORT

Taxis usually costs $80 to $90 to the city, more if you strike traffic.

SkyBus (☑ 09-222 0084; www.skybus.co.nz; one way/return adult $18/32, child $6/12; 🛜) runs bright-red buses between the terminals and the city, every 10 to 15 minutes from 5.15am to 7pm and at least half-hourly through the night. Stops include Mt Eden Rd or Dominion Rd, Symonds St, Queen St and Britomart. Reservations are not required; buy a ticket from the driver, the airport kiosk or online. Small discount if you book online.

Super Shuttle (☑ 09-522 5100; www.super shuttle.co.nz) is a convenient door-to-door shuttle charging $35 for one person heading between the airport and a city hotel; the price increases for outlying suburbs. Save money by sharing a shuttle. A lengthier alternative is to catch the 380 bus to Onehunga ($3.50, 30 minutes, at least hourly 7am to 7.30pm), where you can catch a train to Britomart in the city centre ($5.50, 27 minutes, half-hourly 6am to 10pm).

AIR

The major domestic services flying to/from Auckland include the following:

Air New Zealand (☑ 09-357 3000; www.air newzealand.co.nz) Flies to Kerikeri, Whangarei, Tauranga, Rotorua, Taupo, Gisborne, New Plymouth, Napier, Whanganui, Palmerston North, Kapiti Coast, Wellington, Nelson, Blenheim, Christchurch, Queenstown and Dunedin.

Air Chathams (☑ 09-257 0261; www.air chathams.co.nz) Flies to Whakatane, Whanganui and the Chatham Islands.

Barrier Air (☑ 0800 900 600, 09-275 9120; www.barrierair.kiwi; adult/child from $99/94) Flies to Great Barrier Island (Claris and Okiwi) and Kaitaia.

FlyMySky (☑ 09-256 7025, 0800 222 123; www.flymysky.co.nz; adult/child one way $109/79) Flies to Claris, Great Barrier Island.

Jetstar (☑ 0800 800 995; www.jetstar.com) Flies to Wellington, Christchurch, Queenstown, Dunedin, Palmerston North, New Plymouth, Nelson and Napier.

BICYCLE

Auckland Transport publishes free cycle maps, available from public buildings such as stations, libraries and i-SITEs. Bikes can be taken on most ferries and trains for free (dependent on available space), but only folding bikes are allowed on buses.

Adventure Cycles (☑ 09-940 2453; www. adventure-auckland.co.nz; 9 Premier Ave, Western Springs; per day $30-40, per week $120-160, per month $260-350; ⊙ 7.30am-7pm Thu-Mon) hires road, mountain and touring bikes, runs a buy-back scheme and does repairs.

CAR & MOTORCYCLE

Auckland's motorways jam badly at peak times, particularly the Northern and Southern Motorways. It's best to avoid them between 7am and 9am, and from 4pm to 7pm. Things also get tight around 3pm during term time, which is the end of the school day.

Expect to pay for parking in central Auckland from 8am to 10pm. Most parking meters are pay-and-display and take coins and credit cards; display tickets inside your windscreen. City fringe parking is free on Sundays.

Prices can be steep at parking buildings. Better value are the council-run, open-air car parks near the old train station at 126 Beach Rd ($8 per day) and on Ngaoho Pl, off the Strand ($7 per day).

PUBLIC TRANSPORT

The **Auckland Transport** (☏ 09-366 6400; www.at.govt.nz) information service covers buses, trains and ferries, and has an excellent trip-planning feature.

Auckland's public transport system is run by a hodgepodge of different operators, but there is now an integrated AT HOP smartcard (www.athop.co.nz), which provides discounts of at least 20% on most buses, trains and ferries. AT HOP cards cost $10 (nonrefundable), so are really only worthwhile if you're planning an extended stay in Auckland. An AT HOP day pass costs $18 and provides a day's transport on most trains and buses and on North Shore ferries.

Bus

Bus routes spread their tentacles throughout the city and you can purchase a ticket from the driver. Some bus stops have electronic displays giving an estimate of waiting times, but be warned, they are often inaccurate.

Single-ride fares in the inner city are $3.50/2 (adult/child). If you're travelling further afield, there are fare stages from $5.50/3 to $11/6.

The most useful services are the environmentally friendly Link Buses that loop in both directions around three routes (taking in many of the major sights) from 7am to 11pm:

City Link (adult/child $1/50c, every seven to 10 minutes) Wynyard Quarter, Britomart, Queen St, Karangahape Rd.

Inner Link (adult/child $3.50/2, every 10 to 15 minutes) Queen St, SkyCity, Victoria Park, Ponsonby Rd, Karangahape Rd, Museum, Newmarket, Parnell and Britomart.

Outer Link (maximum $5.50, every 15 minutes) Art Gallery, Ponsonby, Herne Bay, Westmere, MOTAT 2, Pt Chevalier, Mt Albert, St Lukes Mall, Mt Eden, Newmarket, Museum, Parnell, University.

Ferry

Auckland's Edwardian baroque **Ferry Building** (Map p80; 99 Quay St) sits grandly at the end of Queen St. Ferry services are run by **Fullers** (☏ 09-367 9111; www.fullers.co.nz) (to Bayswater, Birkenhead (Map p78), Devonport (Map p90), Great Barrier Island, Half Moon Bay, Northcote Point (Map p78), Motuihe, Motutapu, Rangitoto and Waiheke) and **360 Discovery** (Map p80; ☏ 09-307 8005; www.fullers.co.nz) (to Coromandel, Gulf Harbour, Motuihe, Rotoroa and Tiritiri Matangi). Both leave from an adjacent pier.

Sealink (Map p80; ☏ 0800 732 546; www.sealink.co.nz) ferries to Great Barrier Island leave from Wynyard Wharf, along with some car ferries to Waiheke, but most of the Waiheke car ferries leave from Half Moon Bay in east Auckland.

Train

Auckland's train services are limited and infrequent but the trains are generally clean, cheap and on time – although any hiccup on the lines can bring down the entire network.

Impressive **Britomart train station** (Queen St) has food retailers, foreign-exchange facilities and a ticket office. Downstairs there are left-luggage lockers.

There are just four train routes. One heads west to Swanson, while the other three head south, terminating in Onehunga, Manukau and Pukekohe. Services are at least hourly from around 6am to 10pm (later on the weekends). Buy a ticket from machines or ticket offices at train stations. All trains have wheelchair ramps.

TAXI

Auckland's many taxis usually operate from ranks, but they also cruise popular areas. **Auckland Co-op Taxis** (☏ 09-300 3000; www.cooptaxi.co.nz) is one of the biggest companies. Cab companies set their own fares, so there's some variance in rates. There's a surcharge for transport to and from the airport and cruise ships, and for phone orders. Uber also operates in Auckland.

HAURAKI GULF ISLANDS

Stretching between Auckland and the Coromandel Peninsula, the Hauraki Gulf is dotted with *motu* (islands), and is as equally stunning as Northland's Bay of Islands. Some islands are only minutes from the city and make excellent day trips. Wine-soaked Waiheke and volcanic Rangitoto really shouldn't be missed. Great Barrier requires more effort (and cash) to get to, but provides an idyllic escape from modern life.

There are more than 50 islands in the Hauraki Gulf Marine Park, many administered by DOC. Some are good-sized islands, others are no more than rocks jutting out of the sea. They're loosely put into two categories: recreation and conservation. The recreation islands can easily be visited and their harbours are dotted with yachts in summer. The conservation islands, however, have restricted access. Permits are required to visit some, while others are closed refuges for the preservation of rare plants and animals, especially birds.

ⓘ Getting There & Away

Frequent passenger ferries depart from the piers by the Ferry Building on Auckland's Quay St for Waiheke and Rangitoto. Boats to

Motutapu, Motuihe, Rotoroa and Tiritiri Matangi are sporadic. Regular car ferries steam out of Wynyard Wharf heading to Waiheke and Great Barrier. Kawau also has good ferry connections, departing from Sandspit, north of Auckland.

Flights head to Great Barrier Island from Auckland Domestic Airport and North Shore Aerodrome.

Rangitoto & Motutapu Islands

POP 75

Sloping elegantly from the Hauraki Gulf, 259m-high Rangitoto (www.rangitoto.org) is the largest and youngest of Auckland's volcanic cones. As recently as 600 years ago it erupted from the sea and was active for several years before settling down. Māori living on Motutapu (Sacred Island; www.motutapu.org.nz), to which Rangitoto is joined by a causeway, certainly witnessed the eruptions, as footprints have been found embedded in ash, and oral history details several generations living here before the eruption.

In contrast to Rangitoto, Motutapu is mainly covered in grassland, which is grazed by sheep and cattle. Archaeologically, this is a very significant island, with the traces of centuries of continuous human habitation etched into its landscape.

In 2011 both islands were officially declared predator-free after an extensive eradication program. Endangered birds such as takahe and tieke (saddleback) have been released and others such as kakariki and bellbirds have returned of their own volition.

WALKING ON RANGITOTO

Rangitoto makes for a great day trip. Its harsh scoria slopes hold a surprising amount of flora (including the world's largest pohutukawa forest) and there are excellent walks, but you'll need sturdy shoes and plenty of water. Although it looks steep, up close it's shaped more like an egg sizzling in a pan. The walk to the summit only takes an hour and is rewarded with sublime views. At the top a loop walk goes around the crater's rim. A walk to lava caves branches off the summit walk and takes 30 minutes return. There's an information board with walk maps at the wharf.

The only accommodation option on the islands is a basic **DOC campsite** (www.doc.govt.nz; Home Bay, Motutapu; sites per adult/child $8/4) at Home Bay, Motutapu. It's a three-hour walk from **Rangitoto Wharf** (Map p78); otherwise Fullers runs direct ferries to Home Bay on weekends and public holidays.

ⓘ Getting There & Away

Fullers (☎09-367 9111; www.fullers.co.nz; adult/child return $33/16.50) has ferry services to Rangitoto from Auckland's Ferry Building (p115) (adult/child return $33/16.50, 25 minutes, three daily on weekdays, four on weekends) and Devonport (two daily). It also operates the **Volcanic Explorer** (☎09-367 9111; www.fullers.co.nz; adult/child incl ferry $68/34; ⊙departs Auckland 9.15am & 12.15pm), a guided tour around the island in a canopied 'road train'. 'Early Bird' ferry tickets (adult/child $20/10) departing Auckland at 7.30am are available online if you're after a good deal.

Motuihe Island

Between Rangitoto and Waiheke Islands, 176-hectare Motuihe (www.motuihe.org.nz) has a lovely white-sand beach and a fascinating history. There are three *pā* sites, last occupied by the Ngāti Pāoa tribe. The island was sold in 1840 (for a heifer, blankets, frocks, garden tools, pots and pans) and from 1872 to 1941 served as a quarantine station. During WWI the dashing swashbuckler Count von Luckner launched a daring escape from the island (where he was interned with other German and Austrian nationals), making it 1000km to the Kermadec Islands before being recaptured.

Motuihe has been rendered pest-free and is now subject to a vigorous reforestation project by enthusiastic volunteers. As a result, endangered birds have returned, including the loquacious tieke. There are no permanent residents or shops, except for a weekend kiosk in summer.

The only accommodation on the island is a standard **DOC campsite** (☎09-379 6476; www.doc.govt.nz; sites per adult/child $8/4).

ⓘ Getting There & Away

Motuihe is a yachtie's paradise, and the easiest way to get here is on your own boat. **Fullers** (☎09-367 9111; www.fullers.co.nz; adult/child return $32/16) runs sporadic ferries on a seemingly random schedule.

Waiheke Island

📍 09 / POP 9200

Close to Auckland and blessed with its own warm, dry microclimate, Waiheke Island has long been a favourite escape for city dwellers and visitors alike. On the island's landward side, emerald waters lap at rocky bays, while its ocean flank has excellent sandy beaches.

While beaches are Waiheke's biggest drawcard, wine is a close second. There are around 30 boutique wineries scattered about, many with tasting rooms, swanky restaurants and breathtaking views. The island also boasts plenty of quirky galleries and craft stores, a lasting legacy of its hippyish past.

When you've had enough of supping, dining, lazing on the sand and splashing in the surf, there are plenty of other pursuits to engage in. A network of walking trails leads through nature reserves and past the clifftop holiday homes of the Auckland elite. The kayaking is excellent and there are ziplines to whizz along and clay pigeons to shoot.

🎯 Sights

🎯 Beaches

Waiheke's two best beaches are **Onetangi**, a long stretch of white sand at the centre of the island, and **Palm Beach**, a pretty little horseshoe bay between Oneroa and Onetangi. Both have nudist sections; head west just past some rocks in both cases. **Oneroa** and neighbouring **Little Oneroa** are also excellent, but you'll be sharing the waters with moored yachts in summer. Reached by an unsealed road through farmland, **Man O' War Bay** is a compact sheltered beach that's excellent for swimming.

🎯 Wineries

⭐ **Man O' War**   WINERY
(📞 09-372 9678; www.manowarvineyards.co.nz; 725 Man O' War Bay Rd; ⏱ 11am-4pm Mon-Fri, to 6pm Sat & Sun Dec-Feb, 11am-4pm Mar-Nov) Settle in with a tapas platter and a glass of Man O' War's Valhalla Chardonnay at Waiheke's only beachfront tasting room. If the weather is good, go for a swim in beautiful Man O' War Bay.

Wild On Waiheke   WINERY, BREWERY
(📞 bookings for current week 09-372 3434, future and group bookings 09-372 4225; www.wildon waiheke.co.nz; 82 Onetangi Rd; tastings per beer or wine $2-3; ⏱ 11am-4pm Thu-Mon, daily

late Dec-Easter; 👶) This winery and microbrewery offers tastings, archery, laser clay shooting, *pétanque*, a sandpit and a giant chessboard.

Goldie Estate   WINERY
(📞 09-372 7493; www.goldieestate.co.nz; 18 Causeway Rd, Surfdale; tastings refundable with purchase $10; ⏱ noon-4pm Wed-Sun) Founded as Goldwater Estate in 1978, this is Waiheke's pioneering vineyard. The attached delicatessen sells well-stocked baskets for a picnic among the vines ($55 for two people).

Stonyridge   WINERY
(📞 09-372 8822; www.stonyridge.com; 80 Onetangi Rd; tastings per wine $4-18; ⏱ 11.30am-5pm) 🌿 Waiheke's most famous vineyard is home to world-famous reds, an atmospheric cafe and the occasional dance party. Order a bottle of wine and a gigantic deli platter and retreat to one of the cabanas in the garden.

🎯 Art, History & Culture

The *Waiheke Art Map* brochure lists galleries and craft stores.

Dead Dog Bay   GARDENS
(📞 09-372 6748; www.deaddogbay.co.nz; 100 Margaret Reeve Lane; adult/child $10/free; ⏱ 9am-5pm) Wander steep pathways through privately owned rainforest, wetlands and gardens scattered with sculpture. Cash only.

Waiheke Island Artworks   ARTS CENTRE
(2 Korora Rd, Oneroa) The Artworks complex houses the **Artworks Theatre** (📞 09-372 2941; www.artworkstheatre.org.nz), the **Waiheke Island Community Cinema** (📞 09-372 4240; www.waihekecinema.net; tickets adult/child $18/8), the attention-grabbing **Waiheke Community Art Gallery** (📞 09-372 9907; www.waihekeartgallery.org.nz; ⏱ 10am-4pm) **FREE** and **Whittaker's Musical Museum** (📞 09-372 5573; www.musical-museum.org; suggested donation $5; ⏱ 1-4pm, live shows 1.30pm Sat), a collection of antique instruments. This is also the place for free internet access, either on a terminal at the **Waiheke Library** (📞 09-374 1325; www.aucklandlibraries.govt.nz; ⏱ 9am-6pm Mon-Fri, 10.30am-4pm Sat; 🖥) or on Artworks' wi-fi network.

Waiheke Museum & Historic Village   MUSEUM
(www.waihekemuseum.org.nz; 165 Onetangi Rd; suggested donation $3; ⏱ noon-4pm Wed, Sat & Sun) Displays islander artefacts in six restored buildings.

Waiheke Island

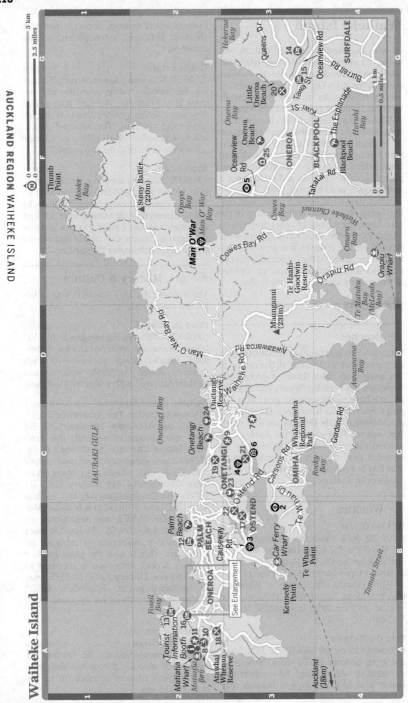

Waiheke Island

🏃 Activities

Walking

The island's beautiful coastal walks (ranging from one to three hours) include the 3km **Cross Island Walkway** (from Onetangi to Rocky Bay). Other tracks traverse **Whakanewha Regional Park**, a haven for rare coastal birds and geckos, and the Royal Forest & Bird Protection Society's three reserves: **Onetangi** (Waiheke Rd), **Te Haahi-Goodwin** (Orapiu Rd) and **Atawhai Whenua** (Ocean View Rd).

Te Ara Hura is a 100km network of connected trails taking in coastline, forests, vineyard stops and historic places. Route markers indicate the way ahead on the island, and more information and detailed maps are available online at www.aucklandcouncil.govt.nz. Search for 'Waiheke Island Walkways'.

iWalkWaiheke   WALKING
(☏021 960 690; www.iwalkwaiheke.co.nz; 11 Totara Rd, Onetangi; day walks per person $195) 🌿 Options include half- and full-day walks taking in the island's forests and beaches, and two-day/one-night walks including meals, accommodation and vineyard visits. Operator Vicki Angland has been resident on the island for more than 20 years, and walks reflect an eco policy reinforcing the island's environmental, cultural and conservation aspects.

Hike Bike Ako   WALKING, CYCLING
(☏021 465 373; www.hikebikeako.co.nz; from $129; ☺Nov-Mar) Explore the island with Māori guides on a walking or an e-biking tour, or a combination of both. Tours include pick-up from the ferry, and a large dose of Māori legend, history and culture.

Other Activities

EcoZip Adventures   ADVENTURE SPORTS
(☏09-372 5646; www.ecozipadventures.co.nz; 150 Trig Hill Rd; adult/child/family $119/79/317; ☺9am-5pm) With vineyard, native bush and ocean views, EcoZip's three separate 200m zip-lines make for an exciting ride, and there's a gentle 1.5km walk back up through the bush after the thrills. Costs include free transfers from Matiatia Wharf (p122) or Oneroa if you don't have your own transport. Bookings are essential.

Ross Adventures   KAYAKING
(☏09-372 5550; www.kayakwaiheke.co.nz; Matiatia Beach; half-/full-day trips $125/195, per 1/2/3/6hr $30/45/50/60) It's the fervently held opinion of Ross that Waiheke offers kayaking every bit as good as the legendary Abel Tasman National Park. He should know – he's been offering guided sea kayak trips for 20 years. Experienced sea kayakers can comfortably circumnavigate the island in four days, exploring coves and sand spits inaccessible by land. Paddle boards also available for hire.

☞ Tours

Waiheke Island Wine Tours TOURS
(☑09-372 2140; www.waihekeislandwinetours.co.nz) Options include Views, Vines & Wines ($125 per person, six hours with a two-hour break for lunch at a restaurant of your choice), tailor-made Platinum Private Tours ($560 per couple) and Indulgence Two-Day Tours ($1100 per person including two nights' accommodation).

Potiki Adventures CULTURAL
(☑021 422 773; www.potikiadventures.co.nz; adult/child $150/80) Day-long island tours from a Māori cultural perspective, including beaches, a bush walk, a vineyard visit and demonstrations of traditional musical instruments and weaving.

Ananda Tours TOURS
(☑09-372 7530; www.ananda.co.nz) Wine tours ($120), gourmet wine and food tours ($185), and a wine connoisseurs' tour ($295) are among the options. Small-group, informal tours can be customised, including visits to artists' studios.

Fullers TOURS
(☑09-367 9111; www.fullers.co.nz; Matiatia Wharf) Runs a Wine on Waiheke tour (adult $140, 4½ hours, departs Auckland 12.30pm) visiting three of the island's top wineries, and including a platter of nibbles. There's also the Taste of Waiheke tour (adult $150, 5½ hours, departs Auckland 10.30am), which includes three wineries plus an olive grove and light lunch. Other packages include EcoZip's (p119) zipline and olive-oil tastings.

Fullers also operates the Waiheke Island Explorer (p122), a hop-on, hop-off bus service travelling on a 90-minute loop around 15 different stops.

✵ Festivals & Events

Headland Sculpture on the Gulf ART
(www.sotg.nz; ⊙Feb) A 2.5km cliff-top sculpture walk, held for a month in February in odd-numbered years.

Waiheke Wine & Food Festival FOOD & DRINK
(http://festival.waihekewine.co.nz; ⊙Mar/Apr) Four days of wine, food and music events. Seventeen different vineyards are involved, and shuttle buses travel between the different locations.

Waiheke Island International Jazz Festival MUSIC
(www.waihekejazzfestival.co.nz; prices vary by event; ⊙Mar/Apr) Local and international acts across the island from Friday to Sunday during Easter.

🛏 Sleeping

Waiheke is so popular in the summer holidays that many locals rent out their houses and bugger off elsewhere. You'll need to book ahead and even then there are very few bargains. Prices drop considerably in winter, especially midweek. For midrange accommodation, a good option is to book a holiday home through www.bookabach.co.nz or www.holidayhouses.co.nz.

★**Fossil Bay Lodge** CABIN $
(☑09-372 8371; www.fossilbay.net; 58 Korora Rd, Oneroa; s $60, d $85-90, tent $100-120, apt $130; 🖭) Three cabins face the main building, which houses the communal toilets, kitchen and living area, and a compact self-contained upstairs apartment. 'Glamping' tents each have a proper bed and their own toilet, and one also includes a private outdoor kitchenette. Apart from the occasional squawking duck – or toddler from the adjacent Steiner kindergarten – it's a very peaceful place.

Hekerua Lodge HOSTEL $
(☑09-372 8990; www.hekerualodge.co.nz; 11 Hekerua Rd, Oneroa; campsites $20, dm $32-35, s/d/tw $60/90/90; 🖭🌊) This secluded hostel is surrounded by native bush and has a barbecue, stone-tiled pool, spa pool, sunny deck, casual lounge area and its own walking track. It's far from luxurious, but it has a laid-back and social feel.

Tawa Lodge GUESTHOUSE $$
(☑09-372 6675; www.pungalodge.co.nz; 15 Tawa St, Oneroa; r $110-120, apt $175-225; 🖭) Between the self-contained two-person cottage at the front (our pick of the lot, due to the sublimely romantic views) and the apartment and house at the rear are three reasonably priced loft rooms sharing a small kitchen and bathroom.

★**Waiheke Dreams** RENTAL HOUSE $$$
(☑09-818 7129; www.waihekedreams.co.nz; 43 Tiri Rd, Oneroa; 1-/2-bedroom house $250/350) Dream a little dream of a luxurious, modern, spacious, open-plan, two-bedroom house on the crest of a hill with unsurpassed views over Oneroa Bay and the Hauraki Gulf – then pinch yourself and wake up with a smug smile in View43. Tucked at the rear is the considerably smaller one-bedroom CityLights, which glimpses Auckland's glimmer over the back lawn.

Enclosure Bay

B&B $$$

(☑ 09-372 8882; www.enclosurebay.co.nz; 9 Great Barrier Rd; r/ste $450/600; 🐾) If you're going to shell out for a luxury B&B, you expect it to be special, and that's certainly what's offered here. Each of the three guest rooms have sumptuous views and balconies, and the owners subscribe to the nothing's-too-much-trouble school of hospitality.

✕ Eating

Waiheke has some excellent eateries and, if you're lucky, the views will be enough to distract from the hole being bored into your hip pocket. There's a supermarket in Ostend.

Te Matuku Oysters

SEAFOOD $

(☑ 09-372 8600; www.tematukuoysters.co.nz; 17 Belgium St; ⊗ 9am-5pm) 🍤 Head to this combination seafood retailer and deli selling local gourmet produce for the freshest and best-value oysters on the island. Just $20 will get you 12 freshly shucked oysters. Enjoy with lemon juice and Tabasco at the simple stand-up tables for a quintessential Waiheke experience. Mussels and clams are also for sale.

Dragonfired

PIZZA $

(☑ 021 922 289; www.dragonfired.co.nz; Little Oneroa Beach; mains $12-16; ⊗ 10am-8pm Dec-Feb, 11am-7pm Fri-Sun Mar-Nov; 🍴) Specialising in 'artisan wood-fired food', this caravan by the beach serves the three Ps: pizza, polenta plates and pocket bread. It's easily Waiheke's best place for cheap eats.

Annex

CAFE $

(☑ 09-372 9988; www.facebook.com/theannex waiheke; 10 Putiki Rd; snacks $5-12; ⊗ 9.30am-3pm Fri-Mon) 🍤 Framed by fruit trees, this 1920s-era wooden cottage makes for a perfect stop away from Waiheke's busier tourist spots. A superior range of teas and infusions are served either hot or cold in the relaxing rear courtyard, and snacks include sweet treats by the Little Tart Bakery – try its delicious cinnamon brioche – or excellent sourdough grilled-cheese sandwiches.

Shed at Te Motu

MODERN NZ $$

(☑ 09-372 6884; www.temotu.co.nz/the-shed; 76 Onetangi Rd; shared plates small $16-21, large $29-42; ⊗ 11am-5pm daily, 6pm-late Fri & Sat Nov-Apr, reduced hours May-Oct) Secure a table shaded by umbrellas in the Shed's rustic courtyard for shared plates imbued with global influences and served by the restaurant's savvy and equally international waitstaff. Highlights might include shiitake pancakes with kimchi and black garlic, or the wonderfully slow-cooked lamb shoulder partnered with a delicate biryani-spiced pilaf. Te Motu's standout wines are its stellar Bordeaux-style blends.

Casita Miro

SPANISH $$

(☑ 09-372 7854; www.casitamiro.co.nz; 3 Brown St; tapas $9-19, ración $30-35; ⊗ noon-3pm Mon-Wed, to late Thu-Sun) A wrought-iron and glass pavilion backed with a Gaudí-esque mosaic garden is the stage for a very entertaining troupe of servers who will guide you through the menu of delectable tapas and *ración* (larger dishes), designed to be shared. In summer the sides open up, but otherwise, at busy times, it can get noisy.

★ Tantalus Estate

MODERN NZ $$$

(☑ 09-372 2625; www.tantalus.co.nz; 70-72 Onetangi Rd; mains $33-37; ⊗ 11am-4pm) 🍤 Up a winding driveway framed by grapevines, Waiheke's newest vineyard restaurant and tasting room channels an Iberian ambience, but the savvy and diverse menu effortlessly covers the globe. Secure a spot under rustic chandeliers crafted from repurposed tree branches, and enjoy a leisurely lunch imbued with Asian and Mediterranean influences.

Cable Bay

MODERN NZ $$$

(☑ 09-372 5889; www.cablebay.co.nz; 12 Nick Johnstone Dr; meze $12-27, pizza $26-29, mains $42-45; ⊗ 11am-late; 🐾) Impressive ubermodern architecture, interesting sculpture and beautiful views set the scene for this acclaimed restaurant. The food is sublime, but if the budget won't stretch to a meal, stop in for a wine tasting ($10 for five wines, refundable with a purchase, 11am to 5pm daily) or platters, pizza and shared plates at the Verandah bar.

🍸 Drinking & Nightlife

Boogie Van Brewing

MICROBREWERY

(☑ 027 519 9737; www.facebook.com/BoogieVan Brewing; 29b Tahi Rd, Ostend; ⊗ noon-5pm Fri-Sun) San Francisco expat Rick Paladino is enjoying island life at this compact microbrewery. Taproom hours are limited to Friday to Sunday afternoons, when Rick and his Kiwi partner Rochelle are on hand to guide tastings of their six core beers inspired by stoner rock. Given Rick's West Coast US roots, look forward to big and bold hop forward brews.

Charlie Farley's BAR
(☑09-372 4106; www.charliefarleys.co.nz; 21 The Strand, Onetangi; ☺8.30am-late) It's easy to see why the locals love this place when you're supping on a Waiheke wine or beer under the pohutukawa on the beach-gazing deck.

🛍 Shopping

Waiheke Wine Centre WINE
(☑ 09-372 6139; www.waihekewinecentre.com; 153 Oceanview Rd, Oneroa; ☺9.30am-7.30pm Mon-Thu, to 8pm Fri & Sat, from 10am Sun) Located in Oneroa's main street, this well-stocked and authoritative store features wine from all of Waiheke's vineyards, and is a good place to pick up information on wine destinations around the island. A special sampling system allows customers to purchase concise pours of various wines.

ℹ Information

There is a convenient **tourist information booth** (Matiatia Wharf; ☺9am-4pm) open for most arrivals at the ferry terminal at Matiatia Wharf. Online see www.tourismwaiheke.co.nz, www.waiheke.co.nz and www.aucklandnz.com.

There are ATMs in Oneroa.

ℹ Getting There & Away

360 Discovery (☑09-307 8005; www.fullers. co.nz) You can pick up this tourist ferry at **Orapiu** on its limited voyages between Auckland and Coromandel Town. However, note that Orapiu is quite remote and not served by buses.

Fullers (☑ 09-367 9111; www.fullers.co.nz; return adult/child $36/12; ☺5.20am-11.45pm Mon-Fri, 6.15am-11.45pm Sat, 7am-10.30pm Sun) Frequent passenger ferries from Auckland's Ferry Building to **Matiatia Wharf** (40 minutes), some via Devonport (adding an extra 10 minutes to the journey time).

SeaLink (☑0800 732 546; www.sealink. co.nz; return adult/child/car/motorcycle $37/20/175/72; ☺6am-6pm) Runs **car ferries** to Kennedy Point, mainly from Half Moon Bay, east Auckland (45 to 60 minutes, at least hourly), but some leave from Wynyard Wharf in the city (60 to 80 minutes, three per day).

ℹ Getting Around

BICYCLE
Various bicycle routes are outlined in the *Bike Waiheke!* brochure, usually available at the Matiatia Wharf. **Waiheke Bike Hire** (☑ 09-372 7937; www.waihekebikehire.co.nz; Matiatia; per day

$35) hires mountain bikes from its base in the car park near the wharf.

Parts of Waiheke are quite hilly, so ease the load with a hybrid machine from **Onya Bikes** (☑ 022 050 2233; www.ecyclesnz.com; 124 Oceanview Rd, Oneroa; per day $60), combining pedalling with electric motors.

BUS
The island has bus services, starting from Matiatia Wharf and heading through Oneroa (adult/child $2/1, three minutes) on their way to all the main settlements, as far west as Onetangi (adult/child $5.50/3, 35 minutes). A day pass (adult/child $10/6) is available from the Fullers counter at Matiatia Wharf. Some services in the middle of the day can be as much as an hour apart, so to avoid lengthy waits at bus stops, consult a timetable from Auckland Transport (p115).

Another option is the **Waiheke Island Explorer** (www.fullers.co.nz; 1 day adult/child/family incl ferry tickets $60/30/162, 2 day $90/45/243) bus, a hop-on, hop-off service covering 15 different stops around the island. A full circuit takes 90 minutes and attractions along the route include vineyards, beaches, activities and restaurants.

CAR, MOTORCYCLE & SCOOTER
There are petrol stations in Oneroa and Onetangi.

Fun Rentals (☑ 09-372 8001; www.funrentals. co.nz; 14a Belgium St, Ostend; per day from $60) Includes free pick-ups and drop-offs to the ferries.

Island Scoot (☑ 021 062 5997; www.island scoot.nz; cnr Tui St & Mako Rd, Oneroa; per day $79; ☺9am-6pm)

Rent Me Waiheke (☑ 09-372 3339; www.rent mewaiheke.co.nz; 14 Oceanview Rd, Matiatia; per day car/scooter $79/69)

Waiheke Auto Rentals (☑ 09-372 8998; www. waihekerentals.co.nz; Matiatia Wharf; per day car/scooter from $89/69)

Waiheke Rental Cars (☑ 09-372 8635; www. waihekerentalcars.co.nz; Matiatia Wharf; per day car/4WD from $79/109)

TAXI
Island Taxis (☑ 09-372 4111; www.islandtaxis. co.nz)

Waiheke Express Taxis (☑ 0800 700 789; www.waihekeexpresstaxis.co.nz)

Rotoroa Island

From 1911 to 2005 the only people to have access to this blissful little island on the far side of Waiheke were the alcoholics and drug addicts who came (or were sentenced) here to dry out, and the Salvation Army staff who cared for them. In 2011, 82-hectare Rotoroa (www.rotoroa.org.nz; adult/child $5/3) opened to the public for the first time in a century, giving visitors access to three sandy swimming beaches and the social history and art displays in the restored buildings of the former treatment centre.

There are three well-appointed, wildly retro holiday homes for rent, sleeping four ($375) to eight ($650) people, and excellent hostel accommodation in dorms (per person $35) in the former Superintendent's House.

ⓘ Getting There & Away

360 Discovery (☑09-307 8005; www.fullers. co.nz; adult/child from Auckland $52/30, from Orapiu $23/13) From Auckland the ferry takes 75 minutes, stopping at Orapiu on Waiheke Island en route. Services are infrequent and don't run every day. Prices include the island access fee.

Tiritiri Matangi Island

This magical, 220-hectare, predator-free island (www.tiritirimatangi.org.nz) is home to the tuatara (a prehistoric lizard) and lots of endangered native birds, including the very rare and colourful takahe. Other birds that can be seen here include the bellbird, stitchbird, saddleback, whitehead, kakariki, kokako, little spotted kiwi, brown teal, New Zealand robin, fernbird and penguins; 78 different species have been sighted in total. The saddleback was once close to extinction, with just 150 left, but there are now up to 1000 on Tiritiri alone. To experience the dawn chorus in full flight, stay overnight at the **DOC bunkhouse** (☑09-425 7812; www.doc.govt.nz; adult/child $30/20); book well ahead and ensure there's room on the ferry.

The island was sold to the Crown in 1841, deforested, and farmed until the 1970s. Since 1984 hundreds of volunteers have planted 250,000 native trees and the forest cover has regenerated. An 1864 **lighthouse** stands on the eastern end of the island.

It's a good idea to book a guided walk ($5) with your ferry ticket; the guides know where all the really cool birds hang out.

ⓘ Getting There & Away

360 Discovery (☑09-307 8005; www.fullers. co.nz; ⊙Wed-Sun) Ferries depart for Tiritiri Matangi Island at 9am from Wednesday to Sunday, leaving the island at 3.30pm. The journey takes 70 minutes from Auckland's ferry terminal (adult/child return $70/40) or 20 minutes from Gulf Harbour ($55/32).

Motuora Island

Halfway between Tiritiri Matangi and Kawau, Motuora has 80 predator-free hectares and is used as a kiwi 'crèche'. There's a wharf on the west coast of the island, but you'll need your own boat to get here. The **DOC campsite** (☑09-379 6476; www. doc.govt.nz; sites per adult/child $8/4) requires bookings.

ⓘ Getting There & Away

You'll need your own boat to get here.

Kawau Island

POP 300

Kawau Island lies 50km north of Auckland off the Mahurangi Peninsula. There are few proper roads through the island – residents rely mainly on boats.

The main attraction is **Mansion House** (☑09-422 8882; www.doc.govt.nz; adult/child $4/2; ⊙noon-2pm Mon-Fri, noon-3.30pm Sat & Sun Sep-May), an impressive wooden manor. A set of short walks (10 minutes to two hours) are signposted from Mansion House, leading to beaches, the old copper mine and a lookout; download DOC's *Kawau Island Historic Reserve* map (www.doc.govt.nz).

Online, www.kawauisland.org.nz is also a good source of information, and features a list of self-contained rental accommodation.

🛏 Sleeping & Eating

Beach House   BOUTIQUE HOTEL **$$$**
(☑09-422 8850; www.kawaubeachhouse.co.nz; Vivian Bay; r/ste from $345/620) In the north of the island, on Kawau's best sandy beach, this upmarket complex has luxurious rooms facing the beach, a large paved courtyard, or in a cottage set back in the bush. It's a remote spot but it has its own restaurant (open to hotel guests only), so there's no need to go anywhere.

Mansion House Cafe   CAFE **$$**
(☑09-422 8903; www.facebook.com/mansion housenz; 5 Schoolhouse Bay Rd; lunch $16-18; ⊙hours vary) If you haven't packed a picnic, this idyllically situated eatery serves tasty lunches, Devonshire teas with freshly baked scones, and hearty dinners.

ⓘ Getting There & Away

Kawau Cruises (☎0800 111 616; www.kawau cruises.co.nz) Departing Sandspit several times daily, the Mansion House Cruise (adult/child $55/31) allows plentiful time on the island before returning via an afternoon departure back to Sandspit. Check the website as summer and non-summer departure times vary.

Another option is the Mail Run Cruise (adult/child $68/34, including barbecue lunch $95/50), which departs Sandspit at 10.30am and circles the island, delivering the post to 75 different wharves.

Great Barrier Island

POP 860

Great Barrier has unspoilt beaches, hot springs, old kauri dams, a forest sanctuary and a network of tramping tracks. Because there are no possums on the island, the native bush is lush.

Although only 88km and a 30-minute flight from Auckland, Great Barrier seems a world away. The island has no supermarket, no mains electricity supply (only private solar, wind and diesel generators) and no mains drainage (only septic tanks). Some roads are unsealed and petrol costs are high. Mobile-phone reception is improving but still limited and there are no banks, ATMs or street lights. Two-thirds of the island is publicly owned and managed by DOC.

From around mid-December to mid-January is the peak season, so make sure you book transport, accommodation and activities well in advance.

Named Aotea (Cloud) by the Māori, and Great Barrier (due to its position at the edge of the Hauraki Gulf) by James Cook, this rugged and exceptionally beautiful place falls in behind South, North and Stewart as NZ's fourth-largest island (285 sq km). It closely resembles the Coromandel Peninsula to which it was once joined, and like the Coromandel it was once a mining, logging and whaling centre (although those industries have long gone).

Tryphena is the main settlement, 4km from the ferry wharf at Shoal Bay. Strung out along several kilometres of coastal road, it consists of a few dozen houses and a handful of shops and accommodation places. From the wharf it's 3km to Mulberry Grove, and then another 1km over the headland to Pah Beach and the Stonewall Store (p127).

The airport is at **Claris**, 12km north of Tryphena, a small settlement with a general store, bottle shop, laundrette, garage, pharmacy and cafe.

Whangaparapara is an old timber town and the site of the island's 19th-century whaling activities. **Port FitzRoy** is the other main harbour on the west coast, a one-hour drive from Tryphena. These four main settlements have fuel available.

🏃 Activities

Water Sports

The beaches on the west coast are safe, but care needs to be taken on the surf-pounded eastern beaches. **Medlands Beach**, with its wide sweep of white sand, is one of the most beautiful and accessible beaches on the island. Remote **Whangapoua**, in the northeast, requires more effort to get to, while **Kaitoke**, **Awana Bay** and **Harataonga** on the east coast are also worth a visit.

Okiwi Bar has an excellent right-hand break, while Awana has both left- and right-

---

DARK SKY SANCTUARY

Designated a Dark Sky Sanctuary by the International Dark-Sky Association in 2017 – one of only three regions in the world to enjoy such status – Great Barrier is quickly becoming regarded as one of the southern hemisphere's best places to observe the night sky.

Because there is no mains electricity or street lights on the island – all businesses and residents utilise solar power and batteries – light pollution is extremely minimal, and the Barrier's 88km ocean separation from Auckland means the city's far-reaching 'light dome' has no effect either.

Also because Great Barrier is almost 60% protected conservation land, future development is legislated to be minimal, and the entire island will be able to maintain this high standard of darkness and Dark Sky Sanctuary status in the future.

Just 30 minutes' flight from the country's international airport and in easy travelling proximity for the 1.42 million residents of Auckland, Great Barrier's stellar night sky is a significant tourism asset that the island's residents are keen to enhance and protect.

hand breaks. Pohutukawa trees shelter the pretty bays around Tryphena.

Diving is excellent, with shipwrecks, pinnacles, lots of fish and more than 33m visibility at some times of the year.

Mountain Biking

With rugged scenery and relatively little traffic on the roads, mountain biking is a popular activity on the island. There's a designated 25km ride beginning on Blind Bay Rd, Okupu, winding beneath the Ahumata cliffs before crossing Whangaparapara Rd and beginning the 15km Forest Rd ride through beautiful forest to Port FitzRoy. Cycling on other DOC walking tracks is prohibited.

Walking

The island's very popular walking tracks are outlined in DOC's free *Great Barrier Island (Aotea Island)* booklet. Before setting out, make sure you're properly equipped with water and food, and be prepared for both sunny and wet weather.

The most popular easy walk is the 45-minute **Kaitoke Hot Springs Track**, starting from Whangaparapara Rd and leading to natural hot springs in a bush stream. Check the temperature before getting in and don't put your head under the water.

Windy Canyon, which is only a 15-minute walk from Aotea Rd, has spectacular rock outcrops and affords great views of the island. From Windy Canyon, an excellent trail continues for another two to three hours through scrubby forest to Hirakimata (Mt Hobson; 621m), the highest point on the island, with views across the Hauraki Gulf and Coromandel. Near the top of the mountain are lush forests and a few mature kauri trees that survived the logging days. From Hirakimata it is 40 minutes south to **Mt Heale Hut** (⌂09-379 6476; www.doc.govt.nz; dm per adult/child $15/7.50).

A more challenging tramp is the hilly **Tramline Track** (five hours), which starts on Aotea Rd and follows old logging tramlines to Whangaparapara Harbour. The initial stages of this track are not maintained and in some parts the clay becomes slippery after rain.

Of a similar length, but flatter and easier walking, is the 11km **Harataonga Coastal Walk** (five hours), which heads from Harataonga Bay to Whangapoua.

Many other trails traverse the forest, taking between 30 minutes and five hours. The **Aotea Track** combines bits of other paths into a three-day walk, overnighting in **Mt Heale** (⌂09-379 6476; www.doc.govt.nz; dm per adult/child $15/7.50) and **Kaiaraara** (⌂09-379 6476; www.doc.govt.nz; dm per adult/child $15/7.50) Huts. At the time of research, consideration was being given to making the Aotea Track one of NZ's Great Walks. Check the Department of Conservation website (www.doc.govt.nz) for the latest update and for detailed information on negotiating the Aotea Track.

Other Activities

Good Heavens OUTDOORS
(⌂09-429 0876; www.goodheavens.co.nz; group tours per person $90, minimum 2 people private tours $400) ✎ The Milky Way, constellations and other celestial attractions – sometimes including Saturn and Jupiter – are observed through telescopes and the naked eye, and Good Heavens' avid Dark Sky (p124) Ambassadors can even set up their skywatching gear conveniently at your accommodation. Booking ahead is vital, preferably for your first night on the island to allow flexibility for weather conditions.

Crazy Horse Trike Tours SCENIC DRIVE
(⌂09-429 0222, 0800 997 222; www.greatbarrier islandtourism.co.nz; per person from $75) Jump on the back of Steve Bellingham's custombuilt motorised trike and let the friendly GB local drive you around the island. Options include two-hour sightseeing tours, beach visits, kayaking, hot springs and forest walks. Steve's a very entertaining source of information on interesting local stories and island history.

🛏 Sleeping

Unless you're camping, Great Barrier isn't a cheap place to stay. At pretty much every price point you'll pay more than you would for a similar place elsewhere. In the low season, however, rates drop considerably.

Check accommodation and island information websites for packages including flights and car rental. Note that accommodation rates soar for around two weeks following Christmas and the island also gets very busy during this time. **Island Accommodation** (⌂021 138 7293; www.island accommodation.co.nz) offers a booking service, which is handy for finding self-contained houses for longer stays.

There are **DOC campsites** (⌂09-379 6476; www.doc.govt.nz; sites per adult/child $13/6.50) at Harataonga Bay, Medlands Beach, Akapoua Bay, Whangapoua, The Green and Awana Bay. All have basic facilities, including

Great Barrier Island

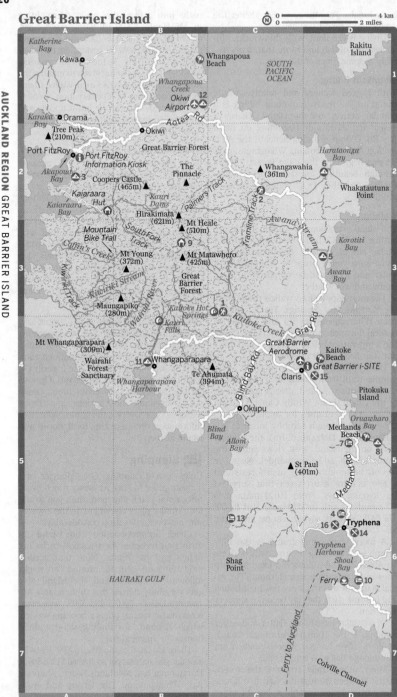

N
0 ————— 4 km
0 ————— 2 miles

Rakitu Island

Katherine Bay

Kawa

Whangapoua Creek

Whangapoua Beach

SOUTH PACIFIC OCEAN

Okiwi Airport 12

Karaka Bay

Orama

Tree Peak (210m)

Aotea Rd

Okiwi

Port FitzRoy

Port FitzRoy Information Kiosk 3

Akapoua Bay

Coopers Castle (465m)

Great Barrier Forest

The Pinnacle

Harataonga Bay

Whangawahia (361m) 6

Whakatautuna Point

Kaiaraara Hut

Kaiaraara Bay

Kauri Dams

Palmers Track

2

Hirakimata (621m)

Mt Heale (510m)

Tramline Track

Awana Stream

Korotiti Bay

5

Mountain Bike Trail

South Fork Track

9

Mt Matawhero (425m)

Mt Young (372m)

Coffin's Creek

Kiwiriki Track

Kiwiriki Stream

Wairahi River

Great Barrier Forest

Awana Bay

Maungapiko (280m)

Kaitoke Hot Springs

1

Kauri Falls

Kaitoke Creek

Gray Rd

Mt Whangaparapara (309m)

Great Barrier Aerodrome

Kaitoke Beach

Wairahi Forest Sanctuary

11 Whangaparapara

Te Ahumata (394m)

Great Barrier i-SITE

Claris 15

Pitokuku Island

Whangaparapara Harbour

Blind Bay Rd

Okupu

Blind Bay

Allom Bay

Oruawharo Bay

Medlands Beach 7

8

St Paul (401m)

Medland Rd

13

4

16 Tryphena

14

Shag Point

HAURAKI GULF

Tryphena Harbour

Shoal Bay

Ferry 10

Ferry to Auckland

Colville Channel

Great Barrier Island

water, cold showers (except for the Green), toilets and a food-preparation shelter. You need to bring your own gas cooking stove as open fires are prohibited. Book in advance online.

Medlands Beach
Backpackers & Villas HOSTEL $
(☑09-429 0320; www.staymedlands.com; 9 Mason Rd; dm/d without bathroom $35/90, units from $250; 🖥) Chill out in the garden of this house on the hill, overlooking beautiful Medlands Beach. The backpackers area is simple, with a little double chalet for romantic budgeteers at a slight remove from the rest. The self-contained houses sleep up to seven.

Aotea Lodge APARTMENT $$
(☑09-429 0628; www.aotealodge.com; 41 Medland Rd, Tryphena; apt $130-220; 🖥) A well-tended, sunny garden surrounds these reasonably priced units, perched on the hill just above Tryphena. They range from a two-bedroom house to an unusual mezzanine unit loaded with bunks, and each has its own cooking facilities. Look forward to lots of bird life in the surrounding garden.

Shoal Bay Lodge RENTAL HOUSE $$
(☑09-429 0890; www.shoalbaylodge.co.nz; 145 Shoal Bay Rd; house from $160) 🌿 Hidden among the trees, this three-bedroom house

offers sea views, birdsong and solar power. Arm yourself with a glass of wine and stake a place on the deck at sunset.

⭐ **XSPOT** APARTMENT $$$
(☑027 429 0877; www.xspot.co.nz; 21 Schooner Bay Rd, Tryphena; d $230; 🖥📶) 🌿 Great Barrier's most spectacular accommodation option is also one of its more remote. A 25-minute drive from Tryphena – rent a 4WD vehicle – XSPOT is a spacious and stylish one-bedroom apartment with expansive windows offering jaw-dropping 270-degree views of the ocean. Equipped with a full kitchen and modern bathroom, it's the kind of place to linger amid spectacular marine vistas.

Eating

In summer, most places open daily but for the rest of the year hours can be sporadic. A monthly guide to opening hours is on www.thebarrier.co.nz, but it pays to call ahead for an evening meal.

Self-caterers will find small stores in Tryphena, Claris, Whangaparapara and Port FitzRoy. Tryphena's **Stonewall Store** (☑09-429 0451; 82 Blackwell Dr; ⏱8.30am-6pm) has a good selection of wine, beer and local produce, and also operates a small market (from 10am Saturday).

Swallow BURGERS $
(☑09-429 0226; www.facebook.com/Burger ShackGBI; Main Rd, Claris; burgers $10-16; ⏱11am-7pm) Hands down the best burgers of the island with massive overflowing options including pork belly or beef, blue cheese and caramelised onions. Also wraps, seafood and Janene's Dreams icy treats handmade on the Barrier. During summer there's a couple of other food carts nearby selling juices and coffee.

Tipi & Bob's PUB FOOD $$$
(☑09-429 0550; www.waterfrontlodge.co.nz; 38 Puriri Bay Rd, Tryphena; breakfast $16-20, dinner $39-44; ⏱7.30-10am & 5-10pm) Serving simple but satisfying meals in large portions, this popular haunt has an inviting deck overlooking the harbour. The steak and seafood combos are always good. There's also a cheaper menu in the bar.

🍸 Drinking & Nightlife

⭐**Currach Irish Pub** IRISH PUB
(☑09-429 0211; www.currachirishpub.co.nz; 78 Blackwell Dr, Tryphena; mains $20-30; ⏱4pm-late Boxing Day–Easter, closed Wed Mar-Dec; 🖥♿) This excellent pub offers craft beer, seafood, steak and burgers, and is GB's main social

centre. Wood-fired pizza combines with an alfresco salad bar, and there are regular live gigs with a Gaelic and folky bent. Sunday quiz night is loads of fun, and a separate room features rotating exhibitions from local artists, all of it for sale.

Accommodation in renovated heritage rooms ($130 to $150) is available at the attached **Innkeepers Lodge**, and there's also a compact four-bed dorm ($35) with a full kitchen.

ⓘ Information

The **Great Barrier i-SITE** (Destination Great Barrier Island; ☑ 09-420 0033; www.great barrier.co.nz; ⊙ 9am-3pm Mon-Sat; 🛜) at the Great Barrier Aerodrome at Claris also has a good range of Department of Conservation (DOC) information.

Go Great Barrier Island (☑ 0800 997 222; www.greatbarrierislandtourism.co.nz) offers a personal online planning service for island visits including all transport, rental cars and accommodation. Also runs tramper shuttles to tracks and arranges island tours by van or trike.

Port FitzRoy Information Kiosk (☑ 09-429 0848; www.thebarrier.co.nz; ⊙ 9am-3pm Mon-Sat) is a privately run kiosk that publishes the *Great Barrier Island Visitor Information Guide*.

ⓘ Getting There & Away

AIR

FlyMySky (p114) flies at least three times a day between Claris' **Great Barrier Aerodrome** (Claris Airport) and Auckland. Cheaper flights are available if you travel to the island on a Sunday or leave on a Friday ($89), and there's a special return fare for flying one way and ferrying the other (adult/child $180/148).

Barrier Air (p114) departs from both Auckland Domestic Airport and North Shore Aerodrome 42 times a week for the 30-minute flight to Claris. Also occasional flights from both Auckland airports to **Okiwi**.

BOAT

SeaLink (☑ 0800 732 546, 09-300 5900; www.sealink.co.nz; adult/child/car one way $84/61/290, return $106/84/359) runs car ferries four days a week from Wynyard Wharf in Auckland to Tryphena's **Shoal Bay** (4½ hours) and once a week to Port FitzRoy (five hours). The last part of the crossing can get rough.

ⓘ Getting Around

Most roads are narrow and windy but even small hire cars can handle the unsealed sections. Many of the accommodation places will pick you up from the airport or wharf if notified in advance.

Aotea Car Rentals (☑ 0800 426 832; www. aoteacarrentals.co.nz; Mulberry Grove, Shoal Bay) Rents cars (from $60), 4WDs (from $70) and vans (from $99).

Go Great Barrier Island Can arrange rental cars and tramper shuttles to island tracks.

Great Barrier Wheels (☑ 021 226 6055, 09-429 0062; www.greatbarrierwheels.co.nz; 67 Hector Sanderson Rd, Claris; ⊙ 8am-7pm Mon-Sat) Has a diverse range of cars from $60 to $85 per day. Also operates shuttle services from Claris to Tryphena ($25), Medlands ($25), Whangaparapara ($25) and Port FitzRoy ($30, minimum four passengers), as well as trampers' shuttles.

WEST AUCKLAND

West Auckland epitomises rugged: wild black-sand beaches, bush-shrouded ranges and mullet-haired, black-T-shirt-wearing 'Westies'. This is just one of several stereotypes of the area's denizens. Others include the back-to-nature hippie, the eccentric bohemian artist and the dope-smoking surfer dude, all attracted to a simple life at the edge of the bush.

Add to the mix Croatian immigrants, earning the fertile fields at the base of the Waitakere Ranges the nickname 'Dallie Valley' after the Dalmatian coast where most hailed from. These pioneering families planted grapes and made wine, founding one of New Zealand's major industries.

ⓘ Getting There & Away

There are regular buses as far as Titirangi and Helensville but no services to the west-coast beaches. The best options for the beaches are to rent a car or join a day tour from Auckland.

Titirangi

POP 3200

This little village marks the end of Auckland's suburban sprawl and is a good place to spot all manner of Westie stereotypes over a coffee, wine or cold beer. Once home to New Zealand's greatest modern painter, Colin McCahon, there remains an artsy feel to the place. Titirangi means 'Fringe of Heaven' – an apt name for the gateway to the Waitakere Ranges. This is the last stop for petrol and ATMs on your way west.

WAITAKERE RANGES

This 160-sq-km wilderness was covered in kauri until the mid-19th century, when logging claimed most of the giant trees. A few stands of ancient kauri and other mature natives survive amid the dense bush of the regenerating rainforest, which is now protected inside the Waitakere Ranges Regional Park. Bordered to the west by wildly beautiful beaches on the Tasman Sea, the park's rugged terrain is a spectacular sight. Sadly the forest is facing a new threat, with the fungal disease kauri dieback already affecting many trees in the regional park. To prevent its further spread, the Auckland Council made the decision to close all tracks through the forested section of the park. However, you can still visit **Arataki** (☑09-817 0077; www.aucklandcouncil.govt.nz; 300 Scenic Dr; ⊙9am-5pm) **FREE**, the park's impressive visitor centre, where staff can advise on any non-forested tracks that remain open. The Māori carvings at the entrance depict the ancestors of the local Kawerau *iwi* and there are expansive views over the rainforest from its rear deck. On the ground floor, the 12-minute *Dawn to Dusk* video offers an informative overview of the Ranges.

There are no bus services through the main part of the park. If you're driving, take the northwestern motorway from central Auckland, exit at Te Atatu and continue on SH13.

⊙ Sights

Te Uru Waitakere Contemporary Gallery GALLERY
(☑09-817 8087; www.teuru.org.nz; 420 Titirangi Rd; ⊙10am-4.30pm) **FREE** This excellent art gallery is housed in a spectacular modern building on the edge of the village beside the heritage splendour of the former Hotel Titirangi. Rotating exhibitions and installations are sourced both from NZ and internationally, and the curator's remit could stretch from photography and sculpture to mixed media or video. The gallery also features a small shop selling interesting jewellery, pottery and gifts. Check the website for upcoming exhibitions.

McCahon House MUSEUM
(☑09-817 7200; www.mccahonhouse.org.nz; 67 Otitori Bay Rd, French Bay; $5; ⊙1-4pm Wed-Sun) It's a mark of the esteem in which Colin McCahon is held that the house he lived and painted in during the 1950s has been opened to the public as a mini-museum. The swish pad next door is home to the artist lucky enough to win the McCahon Arts Residency. Look for the signposts pointing down Park Rd, just before you reach Titirangi village. The house is around 2km down the hill.

✕ Eating

Deco Eatery MEDITERRANEAN **$$**
(☑09-817 2664; www.decoeatery.co.nz; Lopdell House, 418 Titirangi Rd; mains $16-30; ⊙7am-late Mon-Fri, 7.30am-late Sat & Sun; ☑) Located amid the heritage vibe of Lopdell House, Deco's decor channels a Turkish ambience, while the menu combines Anatolian classics with a broader Mediterranean focus. The restaurant is spacious and sunny, and a great stop before or after visiting the nearby surf beaches of Piha or Karekare.

ⓘ Getting There & Away

The commuter-oriented bus 209 ($7, 45 minutes) travels from bus stop 7081 at 105 Albert St in central Auckland on Monday to Friday from 3pm to 6pm. For journeys at other times and on weekends, catch a bus or train to New Lynn and transfer to a Titirangi-bound bus there.

Karekare

Few stretches of sand have more personality than Karekare. Those prone to metaphysical musings inevitably settle on descriptions such as 'spiritual' and 'brooding'. Perhaps history has left its imprint: in 1825 it was the site of a ruthless massacre of the local Kawerau *iwi* by Ngāpuhi invaders. Wild and gorgeously undeveloped, this famous beach has been the setting for on-screen moments both high- and low-brow, from Oscar winner *The Piano* to *Xena: Warrior Princess*.

From the car park the quickest route to the black-sand beach involves wading through a stream. Karekare rates as one of the most dangerous beaches in the country, with strong surf and ever-present rips, so don't even think about swimming unless the beach is being patrolled by lifeguards (usually only in summer). Pearl Jam singer Eddie Vedder nearly drowned here while visiting Neil Finn's Karekare pad.

Follow the road over the bridge and up along Lone Kauri Rd for 100m, where a short track leads to the pretty **Karekare Falls**. This leafy picnic spot is the start of several walking tracks.

ⓘ Getting There & Away

There is no public transport to Karekare. To get here, head through Blockhouse Bay and Titirangi from central Auckland, merge onto Scenic Dr, and then continue on Piha Rd until you reach the well-signposted turn-off to Karekare Rd.

Piha

📞 09 / POP 600

If you notice an Auckland surfer dude with a faraway look, chances are they're daydreaming about Piha. This beautifully rugged, iron-sand beach has long been a favourite for Aucklanders escaping from the city's stresses – whether for day trips, weekend teenage parties or family holidays.

Although Piha is popular, it's also incredibly dangerous, with wild surf and strong undercurrents, so much so that it's spawned its own popular reality TV show, *Piha Rescue*. If you don't want to inadvertently star in it, always swim between the flags, where lifeguards can provide help if you get into trouble.

Piha may be bigger and more populated than neighbouring Karekare, but there's still no supermarket, liquor shop, bank or petrol station, although there is a small general store that doubles as a cafe, takeaway shop and post office.

◎ Sights & Activities

The view of the coast as you drive down Piha Rd is spectacular. Perched on its haunches near the centre of the beach is **Lion Rock** (101m), whose 'mane' glows golden in the evening light. It's actually the eroded core of an ancient volcano and a Māori *pā* site. A path at the south end of the beach takes you to some great lookouts. At low tide you can walk south along the beach and watch the surf shooting through a ravine in another large rock known as the **Camel**. A little further along, the waves crash through the **Gap** and form a safe swimming hole. A small colony of little penguins nests at the beach's north end.

For surfboard hire, try Piha Store or **Piha Surf Shop** (📞09-812 8723; www.piha surf.co.nz; 122 Seaview Rd; ⊙8am-5pm).

🛏 Sleeping & Eating

★**Piha Beachstay –
Jandal Palace**   HOSTEL $
(📞09-812 8381; www.pihabeachstay.co.nz; 38 Glen Esk Rd; dm/s $40/79, d with/without bathroom $140/89; @⊛) ✔ Attractive and ecofriendly, this wood-and-glass lodge has extremely smart facilities. It's 1km from the beach but there's a little stream at the bottom of the property and bush walks nearby. In winter an open fire warms the large communal lounge.

Black Sands Lodge   APARTMENT $$
(📞021 969 924; www.pihabeach.co.nz; Beach Valley Rd; cabin $180, apt $240-280; ⊛) These two modern conjoined apartments with private decks match their prime location with appealing touches, such as stereos and DVD players. The cabin is kitted out in a 1950s Kiwiana-bach style and shares a bathroom with the main house. Bikes and wi-fi are free for guests, and in-room massage and lavish dinners can be arranged on request.

Piha Store   BAKERY $
(📞09-812 8844; 26 Seaview Rd; snacks $3-10; ⊙7.30am-5.30pm) Call in for pies and other baked goods, groceries and ice creams. The attached Lion Rock Surf Shop (www. lionrocksurfshop.com) rents surfboards and body boards.

Piha Cafe   CAFE $$
(📞09-812 8808; www.facebook.com/thepihacafe; 20 Seaview Rd; mains $14-28; ⊙8am-3pm Mon & Wed, to 9.30pm Thu-Sat, to 5pm Sun) ✔ Big-city standards mesh seamlessly with sand-between-toes informality at this attractive ecofriendly cafe. Cooked breakfasts and crispy pizzas provide sustenance for a hard day's surfing. After the waves, head back for a cold beverage on the deck. Black Sands craft beer from nearby West Auckland is usually on tap; the pilsner is especially refreshing.

ⓘ Getting There & Away

There's no public transport to Piha, but **Rapu** (📞021 550 546, 09-828 0426; www.rapu adventures.com; return from Auckland $50) provides shuttles from central Auckland when the surf's up. Piha is also often included in the daytrip itinerary of Bush & Beach (p93).

Te Henga (Bethells Beach)

Breathtaking Bethells Beach is reached by taking Te Henga Rd at the northern end of Scenic Dr in Auckland's western suburbs. It's a raw, black-sand beach with surf, windswept dunes and walks, such as the popular one over giant sand dunes to Lake Wainamu (starting near the bridge on the approach to the beach).

🛌 Sleeping & Eating

Wainamu Luxury Tents B&B $$$
(☑ 022 384 0500, 09-810 9387; www.facebook. com/wainamu; d $200-250; ⊙ Oct-Jun) 🌿 Inspired by safari tents from Botswana and Māori *whare* (houses), these very comfortable tents combine quiet rural locations, recycled timber construction and a luxurious 'glamping' vibe. Cooking is done on barbecues, lighting from gas lamps and candles is practical and romantic, and outdoor baths also enhance the whole experience. Free-range eggs, fresh-baked bread and muesli combine in DIY breakfast packs.

Bethells Cafe BURGERS, PIZZA $
(☑ 09-810 9387; www.facebook.com/thebethells cafe; Bethells Beach car park; mains $12-17; ⊙ 5.30-9.30pm Fri, 10am-6pm Sat & Sun Nov-May, 10am-6pm Sun Jun-Oct) Less a cafe and more a food truck with an awning, Bethells Cafe does a roaring trade in burgers (beef and vegetarian), pizza, cakes and coffee. On Friday nights it's pretty much the perfect Kiwi beach scene, with live musicians entertaining the adults while the kids surf the sand dunes.

❶ Getting There & Away

There's no public transport to Te Henga.

Kumeu & Around

West Auckland's main wine-producing area still has some vineyards owned by the original Croatian families who kick-started New Zealand's wine industry. The fancy eateries that have mushroomed in recent years have done little to dint the relaxed farmland feel to the region, but everything to encourage an afternoon's indulgence on the way back from the beach or the hot pools. Most cellars offer free tastings. Kumeu itself is a rapidly expanding dormitory suburb of West Auckland, but great wine, food and beer is nearby.

🏃 Activities

Coopers Creek WINE
(☑ 09-412 8560; www.cooperscreek.co.nz; 601 SH16, Huapai; ⊙ 10.30am-5.30pm) Buy a bottle, spread out a picnic in the attractive gardens and, from January to Easter, enjoy Sunday afternoon jazz sessions.

THE GREAT GANNET OE

After honing their flying skills, young gannets get the ultimate chance to test them – a 2000km journey to Australia. They usually hang out there for several years before returning home, never to attempt the journey again. Once back in the homeland they spend a few years waiting for a piece of waterfront property to become available in the colony, before settling down with a regular partner to nest – returning to the same patch of dirt every year. In other words, they're your typical young New Zealander on their rite-of-passage Overseas Experience (OE).

Kumeu River WINE
(☑ 09-412 8415; www.kumeuriver.co.nz; 550 SH16; ⊙ 11am-4.30pm Mon-Sat) Owned by the Brajkovich family, this winery produces one of NZ's best chardonnays, among other varietals.

🍴 Eating & Drinking

Tasting Shed TAPAS $$
(☑ 09-412 6454; www.thetastingshed.co.nz; 609 SH16, Huapai; dishes $14-29; ⊙ 4-10pm Wed & Thu, noon-11pm Fri-Sun) Complementing its rural aspect with rustic chic decor, this slick eatery conjures up delicious dishes designed to be shared. It's not strictly tapas, as the menu strays from Spain and appropriates flavours from Asia, the Middle East, Croatia, Serbia, Italy and France.

Hallertau BREWERY
(☑ 09-412 5555; www.hallertau.co.nz; 1171 Coatesville–Riverhead Hwy, Riverhead; share plates $9-24, mains $17-40; ⊙ 11am-10pm) Hallertau offers tasting paddles ($12 to $14) of its craft beers served in its spacious and sociable *biergarten*, and inside on cosy tables near the bar. Regular guest beers, good food, and occasional weekend DJs and live music make it popular with Auckland's hopheads. Our pick from the food menu are the beef *krokets*.

Riverhead PUB
(☑ 09-412 8902; www.theriverhead.co.nz; cnr Queen St & York Tce, Riverhead; ⊙ 11am-late) A blissful terrace, shaded by oak trees and overlooking the river, makes this 1857 hotel a memorable drink stop, even if the menu (mains $31 to $39) doesn't quite live up to its gastropub ambitions. Make a day of it, with a boat cruise (p93) from the city to the pub's own jetty. There's usually live music on Sundays from 1.30pm.

❶ Getting There & Away

From central Auckland, Kumeu is 25km up the Northwestern Motorway (SH16). Catch a bus to Westgate and then transfer to bus 122 or 125 to Kumeu.

Muriwai Beach

A rugged black-sand surf beach, Muriwai Beach's main claim to fame is the **Takapu Refuge gannet colony**, spread over the southern headland and outlying rock stacks. Viewing platforms get you close enough to watch (and smell) these fascinating seabirds. Every August hundreds of adult birds return to this spot to hook up with their regular partners and get busy – expect lots of outrageously cute neck-rubbing, bill-touching and general snuggling. The net result is a single chick per season; December and January are the best times to see the little ones testing their wings before embarking on an impressive odyssey (p131).

Nearby, a couple of short tracks will take you through beautiful native bush to a lookout that offers views along the 60km length of the beach.

Apart from surfing, Muriwai Beach is a popular spot for hang gliding, parapunting, kiteboarding and horse riding. There are also tennis courts, a golf course and a cafe that doubles as a takeaway chippie. Wild surf and treacherous rips mean that swimming is safe only when the beach is patrolled (swim between the flags).

❶ Getting There & Away

There is no public transport to Muriwai.

Helensville

📞 09 / POP 2600

A smattering of heritage buildings, antique shops and cafes makes village-like Helensville a good whistle-stop for those taking SH16 north.

🏃 Activities

Tree Adventures OUTDOORS
(📞 0800 827 926; www.treeadventures.co.nz; Restall Rd, Woodhill; ropes courses $19-42; ⏰ 9.30am-5.30pm) A set of high-ropes courses within Woodhill Forest, located 14km south of Helensville, consisting of swinging logs, nets, balance beams, Tarzan swings and a flying fox.

Parakai Springs SWIMMING, SPA
(📞 09-420 8998; www.parakaisprings.co.nz; 150 Parkhurst Rd; adult/child $24/12; ⏰ 10am-9pm Sun-Thu, to 10pm Fri & Sat; ♿) Aucklanders bring their bored children to Parakai, 2km northwest of Helensville, on wet wintry days as a cheaper alternative to Waiwera. It has large thermally heated swimming pools, private spas (per 30 minutes per person $5) and a couple of hydroslides.

Woodhill Mountain Bike Park MOUNTAIN BIKING
(📞 027 278 0969; www.bikeparks.co.nz; Restall Rd, Woodhill; adult/child $10/8, bike hire from $35; ⏰ 8am-5.30pm Thu-Tue, to 10pm Wed) Maintains many challenging tracks (including jumps and beams) within Woodhill Forest, 14km south of Helensville.

❶ Information

Visitor Information Centre (📞 09-420 7162; www.helensville.co.nz; 27 Commercial Rd; ⏰ 10am-3pm Mon-Fri) Housed inside the local Citizens Advice Bureau. Pick up free brochures detailing the *Helensville Heritage Trail* and *Helensville Riverside Walkway*.

❶ Getting There & Away

Bus 125x heads from 105 Albert St (bus stop 7081) in central Auckland to Helensville ($12.50, 1½ hours) from 3.20pm to 6.25pm Monday to Friday. For alternative journeys beyond this commuter-friendly service, you'll need to change buses at the Westgate shopping centre, around 20km west of central Auckland.

NORTH AUCKLAND

The Auckland supercity sprawls 90km north of the CBD to just past the point where SH16 and SH1 converge at Wellsford. The semirural area north of Auckland's suburban sprawl encompasses beautiful beaches, regional parks, tramping trails, quaint villages and wineries. Plus there are excellent opportunities for kayaking, snorkelling and diving. Consider visiting on a day trip from Auckland or as a way to break up your trip on the journey north.

Long Bay Regional Park

The northernmost of Auckland's East Coast bays, Long Bay is a popular family picnic and swimming spot, attracting more than a million visitors a year. A three-hour-return coastal walk heads north from the sandy beach to the Okura River, taking in secluded Grannys Bay and Pohutukawa Bay (which attracts nude bathers).

ⓘ Getting There & Away

Regular buses head to Long Bay from Mayoral Dr in the city (adult/child $7/4, 90 minutes). If you're driving, leave the Northern Motorway at the Oteha Valley Rd exit, head towards Browns Bay and follow the signs.

Shakespear Regional Park

Shooting out eastward just before Orewa, the Whangaparaoa Peninsula is a heavily developed spit of land with a sizeable South African expat community. At its tip is this gorgeous 376-hectare regional park, its native wildlife protected by a 1.7km pest-proof fence.

Sheep, cows, peacocks and pukeko ramble over the grassy headland, while pohutukawa-lined **Te Haruhi Bay** provides great views of the gulf islands and the city. Walking tracks take between 40 minutes and two hours, exploring native forest, WWII gun embankments, Māori sites and lookouts. If you can't bear to leave, there's an idyllic beachfront **camping ground** (☑09-366 6400; www.aucklandcouncil.govt.nz; sites per adult/child $15/6) with flush toilets and cold showers.

ⓘ Getting There & Away

It's possible to get here via a tortuous 1½-hour bus trip from central Auckland (adult/child $9/5). An alternative is to take the 50-minute **360 Discovery** (☑09-307 8005; www.fullers.co.nz; adult/child $15/8) ferry service to Gulf Harbour, a Noddy-town development of matching townhouses, a marina, country club and golf course. Enquire at the ferry office about picking up a bus or taxi from here. Alternatively, walk or cycle the remaining 3km to the park. The ferry is a good option for cyclists wanting to skip the boring road trip out of Auckland; carry-on bikes are free.

Orewa

☑09 / POP 7400

Orewa's main beach is a lovely expanse of sand; however, locals fear that the town is turning into New Zealand's equivalent of Queensland's Gold Coast. It is, indeed, very built up and high-rise apartment towers have begun to sprout, but unless they start

exporting retirees and replacing them with bikini-clad parking wardens, it's unlikely to reach the Gold Coast's extremes. Quieter and more compact **Hatfields Beach** is just 2km north over the hill.

⊙ Sights & Activities

Orewa Beach BEACH
Orewa's 3km-long stretch of sand is its main drawcard. Being in the Hauraki Gulf, it's sheltered from the surf but still patrolled by lifeguards in the peak season.

Te Ara Tahuna Estuary Cycle & Walkway CYCLING, WALKING
Starting from South Bridge this 8km route loops around the estuary and includes explanations of the area's past as a centre for Māori food gathering.

Snowplanet SNOW SPORTS
(☑09-427 0044; www.snowplanet.co.nz; 91 Small Rd, Silverdale; day pass adult/child $69/49; ⊙10am-10pm Sun-Thu, 9am-midnight Fri & Sat) Snowplanet offers indoor skiing, snowboarding and tubing throughout the year. It's just off SH1, 8km south of Orewa.

🛏 Sleeping

Orewa Motor Lodge MOTEL $$
(☑09-426 4027; www.orewamotorlodge.co.nz; 290 Hibiscus Coast Hwy; units $160-210; ☎) One of the motels lining Orewa's main road, this refurbished complex has scrupulously clean wooden units prettied up with hanging flower baskets. There's also a spa pool.

Waves
MOTEL $$$

(☑09-427 0888; www.waves.co.nz; cnr Hibiscus Coast Hwy & Kohu St; units from $185; 🐾) This complex offers spacious, self-contained apartments, and the downstairs units have gardens and spa baths. It's only a few metres from the beach.

✖ Eating & Drinking

Casablanca
MEDITERRANEAN $$

(☑09-426 6818; www.casablancacafenz.co.nz; 336 Hibiscus Coast Hwy; mains $16-29; ⊙11am-10pm Mon-Fri, 9am-10pm Sat & Sun) Turkish, North African and Mediterranean flavours feature at this buzzy cafe. Try the hearty baked Moorish eggs and you'll be set for the next chapter of your Kiwi road trip.

Coast
CRAFT BEER

(☑09-421 1016; www.coastorewa.co.nz; 342 Hibiscus Coast Hwy; ⊙11am-11pm) Craft beer, cocktails and wine combine with good meals and bar snacks – try the barbecued-duck tacos – at this Orewa outpost of Auckland's Deep Creek Brewing. Settle in for ocean views from the upper deck, and look forward to gigs from local musos most Friday and Saturday nights. Deep Creek's seasonal Lupulin Effect brews are always worth trying.

❶ Getting There & Away

Direct buses head to Orewa from central Auckland (adult/child $12/7, 1¼ hours) and Waiwera (adult/child $2.50/1.50, 12 minutes).

Waiwera

☑09 / POP 285

This pleasant river-mouth village has a great beach, but it's the *wai wera* (hot waters) that attract visitors. Warm mineral water bubbles up from 1500m below the surface to fill the 19 pools of the Waiwera Thermal Resort. Nearby, the 134-hectare Wenderholm Regional Park incorporates bird life, beaches, colonial history and walks.

⊙ Sights & Activities

Wenderholm Regional Park
PARK

(☑09-366 2000; www.aucklandcouncil.govt.nz; 37 Schischka Rd) Squeezed between the Waiwera and Puhoi Rivers, the exquisite 134-hectare Wenderholm Regional Park has a diverse ecology, abundant bird life, beaches and walks (30 minutes to 2½ hours). The Couldrey family were the original colonial settlers of the Wenderholm area, and their **homestead** (www.aucklandcouncil.govt. nz; adult/child $5/free; ⊙1-4pm Sat & Sun, daily Jan-Easter) dating from the 1860s is now a museum. The camping ground (site per adult/child $15/6) provides only tap water and toilets, and the council also rents three comfortable self-contained houses ($133 to $171).

Waiwera Thermal Resort
SWIMMING, SPA

(☑09-427 8800; www.waiwera.co.nz; 21 Waiwera Rd; adult/child $30/16; ⊙10am-8pm Fri-Sun; 🚼) As well as numerous thermal pools, there are big water slides, barbecues, private tubs ($40) and a health spa, or you can watch a flick in the movie pool. It's lots of fun for families.

❶ Getting There & Away

Bus 981 from Auckland's Fanshawe St heads to Waiwera (adult/child $12.50/7, 1¼ hours) via Orewa.

Puhoi

☑09 / POP 450

Forget dingy cafes and earnest poets – this quaint village is a slice of the real Bohemia. In 1863 around 200 German-speaking immigrants from the present-day Czech Republic settled here in what was then dense bush.

⊙ Sights & Activities

Church of Sts Peter & Paul
CHURCH

(www.holyname.org.nz; Puhoi Rd) The village's pretty Catholic church dates from 1881 and has an interesting tabernacle painting (a copy of one in Bohemia), stained glass and statues.

Bohemian Museum
MUSEUM

(☑09-422 0852; www.puhoihistoricalsociety.org. nz; Puhoi Rd; adult/child $3.50/free; ⊙noon-3pm Sat & Sun, daily Jan-Easter) Tells the story of the hardship and perseverance of the original Bohemian pioneers.

Puhoi River Canoe Hire
CANOEING, KAYAKING

(☑09-422 0891; www.puhoirivercanoes.co.nz; 84 Puhoi Rd; ⊙Sep-Jun) Hires kayaks and Canadian canoes, either by the hour (kayak/canoe $25/50) or for an excellent 8km downstream journey from the village to Wenderholm Regional Park (single/double kayak $50/100, including return transport). Bookings are essential.

✕ Eating & Drinking

Puhoi Valley CAFE $$
(☎09-422 0670; www.puhoivalley.co.nz; 275 Ahuroa Rd; mains $15-23; ☺10am-4pm; ⚑) Renowned across NZ, Puhoi Valley cheese features heavily on the menu of this upmarket cheese shop and cafe, set blissfully alongside a lake, fountain and children's playground. In the summer there's music on the lawn, perfect with a gourmet ice cream.

★Puhoi Pub PUB
(☎09-422 0812; www.puhoipub.com; 5 Saleyards Rd; ☺10am-10pm Mon-Sat, to 8pm Sun) There's character and then some in this 1879 pub, with walls completely covered in old photos, animal heads and vintage household goods.

❶ Getting There & Away

Puhoi is 1km west of SH1. The turn-off is 2km past the Johnstone Hills tunnel. There's no public transport.

Mahurangi & Scandrett Regional Parks

At the southern and eastern edges of the Mahurangi Peninsula northeast of Auckland, the Mahurangi Regional Park and Scandrett Regional Park are convenient as day trips from the city, or as a relaxing overnight stay in simple accommodation or at basic campsites. Walking tracks, coastal forests, sheltered beaches and Māori and colonial history all feature.

◉ Sights

Mahurangi Regional Park PARK
(☎09-366 2000; http://regionalparks.auckland council.govt.nz; 190 Ngarewa Dr, Mahurangi West) Straddling the head of Mahurangi Harbour, Mahurangi Regional Park is a boater's paradise incorporating areas of coastal forest, pā sites and a historic homestead and cemetery. Its sheltered beaches offer prime sandy spots for a dip or picnic and there are loop walks ranging from 1½ to 2½ hours.

The park has three distinct fingers: Mahurangi West, accessed from a turn-off 3km north of Puhoi; Scott Point on the eastern side, with road access 16km southeast of Warkworth; and isolated Mahurangi East, which can only be reached by boat. Accommodation is available in four basic campsites (per adult/child $10/4) and four baches ($111 to $171), sleeping six to eight.

Scandrett Regional Park PARK
(☎09-366 2000; http://regionalparks.auckland council.govt.nz; 114 Scandrett Rd, Mahurangi East) On the ocean side of the Mahurangi Peninsula, Scandrett Regional Park has a sandy beach, walking tracks, patches of regenerating forest, a historic homestead, pā sites and great views towards Kawau Island. Three baches (sleeping six to eight) are available for rent and there's room for campervans (per adult/child $8/4).

❶ Getting There & Away

You'll need your own transport to reach these parks. Some parts can only be reached by boat.

Warkworth

☎09 / POP 5000
River-hugging Warkworth makes a pleasant pit stop, its cutesy main street retaining a village atmosphere. Increases in Auckland's real estate prices and better motorway access have seen the town grow in popularity in recent years, but it is still a laid-back spot near good beaches and wine country.

◉ Sights & Activities

Dome Forest FOREST
(SH1) Two kilometres north of Warkworth, a track leads through this regenerating forest to the Dome summit (336m). On a fine day you can see the Sky Tower from a lookout near the top. The summit walk takes about 1½ hours return, or you can continue for a gruelling seven-hour one-way tramp through the Totora Peak Scenic Reserve, exiting on Govan Wilson Rd.

Warkworth District's Museum MUSEUM
(☎09-425 7093; www.warkworthmuseum.co.nz; Tudor Collins Dr; adult/child $7/3; ☺10am-3pm) Pioneer-era detritus is displayed at this small local museum. Of more interest is the surrounding Parry Kauri Park, which harbours a couple of giant kauri trees, including the 800-year-old McKinney kauri (girth 7.6m).

Ransom Wines WINE
(☎09-425 8862; www.ransomwines.co.nz; Valerie Close; tasting with purchase free, otherwise donation to Tawharanui Open Sanctuary $5; ☺10am-4pm Tue-Sun) Well signposted from SH1, about 3km south of Warkworth, Ransom produces great food wines and showcases them with good-value tasting platters crammed with smoked meats and local cheeses.

WORTH A TRIP

You'll see the terraces of a lot of historic *pā* (fortified village) sites etched into hillsides all around NZ, but if you want to get an idea of how these Māori villages actually looked, take a one-hour guided tour of the recreated *pā* at **Te Hana Te Ao Marama** (☑09-423 8701; www. tehana.co.nz; 307-308 SH1, Te Hana; adult/child $28.50/18.50; ⊙9am-5pm Wed-Sun). It's best to book ahead.

✕ Eating & Drinking

Chocolate Brown   CAFE $$
(☑09-422 2677; www.chocolatebrown.co.nz; 6 Mill Lane; mains $10-25; ⊙8am-4pm) Decked out with quirky NZ-themed art – mostly for sale – this cafe serves excellent coffee, robust eggy breakfasts and delicious home-style baking. Definitely leave room for a few cacao-infused goodies from the chocolate shop next door; there are also plenty of gift packs for the folks back home.

Tahi Bar   CRAFT BEER
(☑09-422 3674; www.tahibar.com; 1 Neville St; ⊙3.30pm-late Tue-Thu, noon-late Fri-Sun) Tucked down a quiet laneway, Tahi features nine ever-changing taps of New Zealand craft beer. It's an exceptionally friendly spot with decent platters and pub grub, and a rustic and sunny deck. Ask if any beers from award-winning and Warkworth-based 8 Wired Brewing are available.

🔒 Shopping

Honey Centre   FOOD
(☑09-425 8003; www.honeycentre.com; 7 Perry Rd; ⊙8.30am-5pm) About 5km south of Warkworth, the Honey Centre makes a diverting pit stop, with its cafe, free honey tasting and glass-fronted hives. The shop sells all sorts of bee-related products, from candles to mead.

ℹ Getting There & Away

InterCity (☑09-583 5780; www.intercity. co.nz) services pass through town, en route between Auckland and the Bay of Islands.

Matakana
☑09 / POP 291

Around 15 years ago, Matakana was a nondescript rural village with a handful of heritage buildings and an old-fashioned country pub. Now the locals watch bemused as Auckland's chattering classes idle away the hours in stylish wine bars and cafes.

The reason for this transformation is the area's boutique wineries, which are developing a name for pinot gris, merlot, syrah and a host of obscure varietals. Local vineyards are detailed in the free *Matakana Coast Wine Country* (www.matakanacoast.com) and *Matakana Wine Trail* (www.matakana wine.com) brochures, available from the Matakana Information Centre.

Also available at the centre is information on B&B accommodation, tours exploring the rural and coastal hinterland, and a growing array of local stores specialising in antiques and vintage furniture and homewares.

◉ Sights & Activities

Tawharanui Regional Park   BEACH
(☑09-366 2000; http://regionalparks.auckland council.govt.nz/tawharanui; 1181 Takatu Rd) A partly unsealed road leads to this 588-hectare reserve at the end of a peninsula. This special place is an open sanctuary for native birds, protected by a pest-proof fence, while the northern coast is a marine park (bring a snorkel). There are plenty of walking tracks (1½ to four hours) but the main attraction is **Anchor Bay**, one of the region's finest white-sand beaches.

Camping is allowed at two basic sites near the beach (adult/child $15/6) and there's a six-person bach for hire ($171).

Omaha Beach   BEACH
The nearest swimming beach to Matakana, Omaha has a long stretch of white sand, good surf and ritzy holiday homes. It's the kind of place you might see a former NZ prime minister on the golf course, which is set a few genteel blocks back from the beach.

Brick Bay Sculpture Trail   GARDENS
(☑09-425 4690; www.brickbaysculpture.co.nz; Arabella Lane, Snells Beach; adult/child $12/8; ⊙10am-5pm) After taking an hour-long artistic ramble through the beautiful grounds and native bush of Brick Bay Wines, recuperate with a wine tasting at the architecturally impressive cafe. Ask about the annual 'Folly' competition, where an up-and-coming New Zealand artist is funded to construct their winning design, which is subsequently installed at Brick Bay.

Blue Adventures   WATER SPORTS
(☑022 630 5705; www.blueadventures.co.nz; 331 Omaha Flats Rd, Omaha; lessons per hr from $59) Offers kitesurfing, paddle-boarding and wakeboarding lessons and rentals from Omaha and Orewa.

Matakana Bicycle Hire CYCLING
(☑09-423 0076; www.matakanabicyclehire.co.nz; Matakana Country Park, 1151 Leigh Rd; half-/full-day hire from $30/40, tours from $110) Hire a bike to explore local vineyards and beaches. Pick up a *Matakana Trails* map from the information centre detailing routes to nearby Omaha and Port Wells.

🛌 Sleeping

BeauRegard Accommodation COTTAGE $$
(☑021 803 378; www.beauregard.co.nz; 603 Matakana Rd; d incl breakfast $160-190; ✳️🛜) Sitting in rural surroundings, a 4km drive from Matakana village, these three one-bedroom self-contained cottages are the ideal stylish haven for exploring the beaches and vineyards of the surrounding area. Each of the cottages has a Gallic name – Bel-Air, Voltaire or Bastille – and the French–Kiwi hosts have plenty of ideas for tasty discoveries at local markets and restaurants.

🍴 Eating & Drinking

Matakana PUB FOOD $$
(☑09-422 7518; www.matakana.co.nz; 11 Matakana Valley Rd; mains $22-37; ⏰11.30am-1am) Matakana's heritage pub features stylish decor, local wines and craft beers, and decent bistro food, sometimes including Mahurangi oysters. An American-style smoker turns out good low 'n' slow barbecue – try the pork belly or the spicy ribs – and occasional DJs and live acts enliven the cool outdoor space. The pub quiz on Wednesdays is always a good time.

★Sawmill Brewery MICROBREWERY
(☑09-422 6555; www.sawmillbrewery.co.nz; 1004 Leigh Rd; ⏰noon-10pm) Sawmill is recognised as one of the Auckland region's best craft breweries. Relax with a tasting rack of brews amid the rustic but hip decor, and order up a storm from the share-plates menu. It's all good, but we're partial to the citrusy Double IPA with goat, hummus and cumin flatbreads.

Vintry WINE BAR
(☑09-423 0251; www.vintry.co.nz; 2 Matakana Valley Rd; ⏰3-10pm) In the Matakana Cinemas complex, this wine bar serves as a one-stop cellar door for all the local producers. Beers from local craft breweries are on tap, and the same owners operate a riverside bistro downstairs serving breakfast, lunch and dinner.

⭐ Entertainment

Matakana Cinemas CINEMA
(☑09-422 9833; www.matakanacinemas.co.nz; 2 Matakana Valley Rd) The fantastical Matakana Cinemas complex has a domed roof reminiscent of an Ottoman bathhouse. Titles tend to the art house end of the spectrum, but major Hollywood blockbusters are also screened.

🛍 Shopping

Matakana Village Farmers Market MARKET
(www.matakanavillage.co.nz; Matakana Sq, 2 Matakana Valley Rd; ⏰8am-1pm Sat) This excellent farmers market lures plenty of Aucklanders up the highway.

ℹ Information

Matakana Information Centre (☑09-422 7433; www.matakanainfo.org.nz; 2 Matakana Valley Rd; ⏰10am-late) In the foyer of the Matakana Cinemas complex. It's usually staffed from 10am to 1pm, but open late daily for maps and brochures.

ℹ Getting There & Away

Matakana village is a 10km drive northeast of Warkworth along Matakana Rd; there's no regular public transport. Ferries for Kawau Island leave from Sandspit, 8km east of Warkworth along Sandspit Rd.

Leigh
☑09 / POP 390

Appealing little Leigh (www.leighbythesea.co.nz) has a picturesque harbour dotted with fishing boats, and a decent swimming beach at **Matheson Bay**.

Apart from the extraordinary Goat Island Marine Reserve (p138) on its doorstep, Leigh's other claim to fame is the legendary live-music venue Leigh Sawmill Cafe (p138), which sometimes sees surprisingly big names drop in to play a set or two.

🔴 Sights

Goat Island Marine Discovery Centre AQUARIUM
(☑09-923 3645; www.goatislandmarine.co.nz; 160 Goat Island Rd; adult/child/family $9/7/20; ⏰10am-4pm Dec-Apr, Sat, Sun & public & school holidays May-Nov; 🚻) Staffed by marine experts and graduate students from the University of Auckland, this centre is packed with interesting exhibitions on the ecosystem of the marine reserve, and is worth visiting before venturing into Goat Island's

Only 3km from Leigh, 547-hectare **Goat Island Marine Reserve** (www.doc.govt.nz; Cape Rodney to Okakari Point Marine Reserve, Goat Island Rd) was established in 1975 as the country's first marine reserve. In less than 40 years the sea has reverted to a giant aquarium, giving an impression of what the NZ coast must have been like before humans arrived. You only need step knee-deep into the water to see snapper (the big fish with blue dots and fins), blue maomao and stripy parore swimming around.

Excellent interpretive panels explain the area's Māori significance (it was the landing place of one of the ancestral canoes) and provide pictures of the species you're likely to encounter.

There are **dive areas** all around Goat Island, which sits just offshore, or you can snorkel or dive directly from the beach. Colourful sponges, forests of seaweed, boarfish, crayfish and stingrays are common sights, and if you're very lucky you may see orcas and bottle-nosed dolphins. Visibility is claimed to be at least 10m, 75% of the time.

waters. The interactive displays and the tide pool full of marine creatures are great for children.

🏃 Activities

Goat Island Dive & Snorkel   DIVING
(☑ 09-422 6925; www.goatislanddive.co.nz; 142a Pakiri Rd; snorkel set hire adult/child $25/18, incl wetsuit $39/28) This long-standing operator offers guided snorkelling, PADI courses and dive trips in the Goat Island Marine Reserve and other key sites throughout the year. It also hires snorkelling and diving gear.

Octopus Hideaway   SNORKELLING
(☑ 021 926 212; www.theoctopushideaway.nz; 2 Seatoun Ave; ⊙ 10am-6pm Tue-Sun) This crew hires snorkelling gear (adult/child $25/18, including wetsuit $38/26), and offers guided two-hour day ($75/55) and night ($90/70) snorkel expeditions.

☞ Tours

Glass Bottom Boat Tours   BOATING
(☑ 09-422 6334; www.glassbottomboat.co.nz; Goat Island Rd; adult/child $30/15; ⊙ Sep-Apr) A glass-bottomed boat provides an opportunity to see the underwater life of Goat Island Marine Reserve while staying dry. Trips last 45 minutes and run from the beach (weather permitting). Go online or ring to check conditions and to book.

🍷 Drinking & Nightlife

Leigh Sawmill Cafe   PUB
(☑ 09-422 6019; www.sawmillcafe.co.nz; 142 Pakiri Rd; ⊙ 10am-late late Dec–mid-Feb, Thu-Sun mid-Feb–late Dec) This spunky little venue is a regular stop on the summer rock circuit, sometimes attracting surprisingly big names. The pizzas ($25) are thin and crunchy like they should be, and best enjoyed in the garden on a lazy summer's evening. It sometimes closes for private functions so it's wise to check its Facebook page before setting out.

❶ Getting There & Away

You'll need your own wheels to get here.

Pakiri
☑ 09 / POP 50
Blissful Pakiri Beach, 12km past Goat Island (4km of the road is unsealed), is an unspoilt expanse of white sand and rolling surf – a large chunk of which is protected as a regional park.

Pakiri Horse Riding (☑ 09-422 6275; www.horseride-nz.co.nz; Rahuikiri Rd) has 60 horses available for superb bush-and-beach rides ranging from one hour ($80) to multiday 'safaris'. Accommodation is provided in basic but spectacularly situated beachside cabins (dorm/cabin $40/200) or in a comfortable four-bedroom house ($500) secluded among the dunes.

❶ Getting There & Away

There's no public transport to Pakiri; you'll need your own car to get here. The last few kilometres are winding and unsealed.

Bay of Islands & Northland

Best Places to Eat

➡ Provenir (p161)
➡ Dune (p143)
➡ Sandbar (p143)
➡ Gables (p157)
➡ Cafe Bianca (p143)

Best Places to Stay

➡ Endless Summer Lodge (p173)
➡ Arcadia Lodge (p156)
➡ Old Oak (p169)
➡ Kahoe Farms Hostel (p168)
➡ Mangawhai Chalets (p143)

Why Go?

For many New Zealanders, the phrase 'up north' conjures up sepia-toned images of family fun in the sun, pohutukawa in bloom and dolphins frolicking in pretty bays. From school playgrounds to work cafeterias, owning a bach (holiday house) here is a passport to popularity.

Beaches are the main drawcard and they're here in profusion. Visitors from more crowded countries are sometimes flummoxed to wander onto beaches without a scrap of development or another human being in sight. The west coast shelters the most spectacular remnants of the ancient kauri forests that once blanketed the top of the country; the remaining giant trees are an awe-inspiring sight and one of the nation's treasures.

It's not just natural attractions that are on offer: history hangs heavily here. The site of the earliest settlements of both Māori and Europeans, Northland is unquestionably the birthplace of the nation.

When to Go

➡ Northland's beaches go crazy at New Year and remain busy throughout the January school holidays. Prices shoot up and accommodation can be in short supply.

➡ The long, lazy days of summer usually continue into February and March, making these the best months to visit.

➡ The 'winterless north' boasts a subtropical climate, most noticeable from Kerikeri upwards, which averages seven rainy days per month in summer, but 16 in winter.

➡ In winter the average highs hover around 16°C and the average lows around 7°C.

➡ Temperatures are often a degree or two warmer than Auckland, especially on the east coast.

Bay of Islands & Northland Highlights

1 Cape Reinga (p171) Watching oceans collide while souls depart.

2 Waipoua Forest (p177) Paying homage to the ancient kauri giants of this numinous forest.

3 Poor Knights Islands (p151) Diving at one of New Zealand's, if not the world's, top spots.

4 Bay of Islands (p152) Cruising northern waters and claiming your own island paradise among the many in this bay.

5 Ninety Mile Beach (p170) Surfing the giant sand dunes on this remote and seemingly endless stretch of sand.

6 Waitangi Treaty Grounds (p158) Delving into history and culture, both Māori and colonial.

7 Mangawhai Heads (p142) Soaking up the chilled-out surf-town vibe, honing your body-surfing skills and exploring the rolling dunes across the estuary.

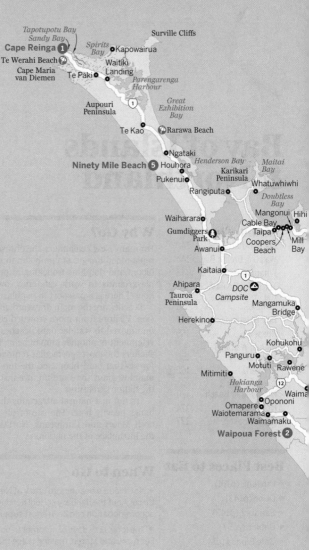

Tapotupotu Bay
Sandy Bay
Cape Reinga **1**
Te Werahi Beach
Cape Maria van Diemen
Te Paki
Spirits Bay
Waitiki Landing
Kapowairua
Surville Cliffs

Parengarenga Harbour

Aupouri Peninsula
Great Exhibition Bay
Te Kao
Rarawa Beach

Ngataki
Houhora
Ninety Mile Beach 5
Pukenui
Henderson Bay
Karikari Peninsula
Maitai Bay
Whatuwhiwhi
Rangiputa
Doubtless Bay

Waiharara
Gumdiggers Park
Awanui
Mangonui
Cable Bay
Taipa
Coopers Beach
Hihi
Mill Bay

Kaitaia
Ahipara
Tauroa Peninsula
DOC Campsite
Mangamuka Bridge
Herekino

Kohukohu
Panguru
Mitimiti
Motuti
Rawene
Hokianga Harbour
Waima
Omapere
Waiotemarama
Opononi
Waimamaku
Waipoua Forest 2

TASMAN SEA

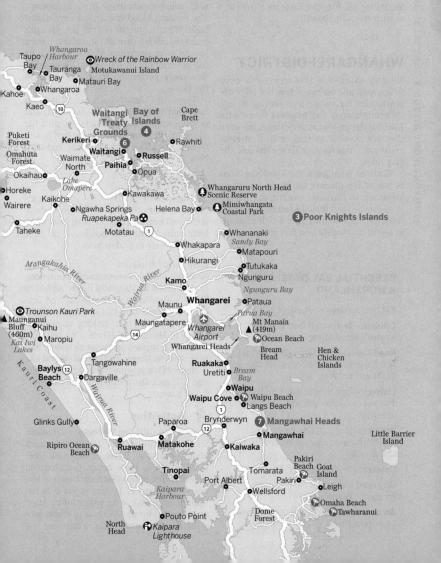

SOUTH PACIFIC OCEAN

Whangaroa
Harbour
Taupo
Bay
Tauranga
Bay
Kahoe
Whangaroa
Kaeo
10

Wreck of the Rainbow Warrior
Motukawanui Island
Matauri Bay

Puketi
Forest
Omahuta
Forest
Okaihau
Horeke
Wairere
Taheke

Kerikeri
Waitangi
Waimate
North
Lake
Omapere
Kaikohe
Ngawha Springs
Ruapekapeka Pa
Motatau

Waitangi
Treaty
Grounds
6
Paihia
Opua
Kawakawa

Bay of
Islands
4

Cape
Brett

Russell
Rawhiti

Whangaruru North Head
Scenic Reserve
Helena Bay
Mimiwhangata
Coastal Park

3 Poor Knights Islands

Mangakahia River
Wairua River

Whakapara
Hikurangi
Kamo
Whananaki
Sandy Bay
Matapouri
Tutukaka
Ngunguru
Ngunguru Bay

Trounson Kauri Park
Maunganui
Bluff
(460m)
Kai Iwi
Lakes
Kaihu
Maropiu
14

Maunu
Maungatapere

Whangarei
Whangarei
Airport
Whangarei Heads

Pataua
Parua Bay
Mt Manaia
(419m)
Ocean Beach
Bream
Head
Hen &
Chicken
Islands

Kauri Coast
Baylys
Beach
12
Tangowahine
Dargaville
Wairua River

Ruakaka
Uretiti
Bream
Bay

Waipu
Waipu Beach
Langs Beach

Glinks Gully

Paparoa
12
Brynderwyn
7 Mangawhai Heads

Waipu Cove

Little Barrier
Island

Ripiro Ocean
Beach
Ruawai
Matakohe
Kaiwaka
Mangawhai

Tinopai
Port Albert
Tomarata
Pakiri
Beach
Pakiri
Goat
Island
Leigh

Kaipara
Harbour
Wellsford
Dome
Forest
Omaha Beach
Tawharanui

North
Head
Pouto Point
Kaipara
Lighthouse

ⓘ Getting There & Away

AIR

Air New Zealand (☎ 0800 737 000; www.air newzealand.co.nz) Daily flights from Auckland to Whangarei and Kerikeri.

Barrier Air (p166) Links Kaitaia to Auckland.

BUS

InterCity (☎ 09-583 5780; www.intercity. co.nz) Buses head from Auckland to Kerikeri via Waipu, Whangarei and Paihia.

Mana Bus (☎ 09-367 9140; www.manabus. com) Services link Auckland to Paihia via Waipu and Whangarei. Note that these are offered in collaboration with Naked Bus.

WHANGAREI DISTRICT

To truly experience this area you'll need to get wet, and scores of beaches offer opportunities for swimming, surfing or just splashing about. The hotspots heave with Kiwi holidaymakers at peak times, but even then it's possible to find isolated stretches of sand where your footprints are the only ones.

North of Whangarei, the Tutukaka Coast is one of the planet's top three coastlines, according to *National Geographic Traveler* magazine, and the late Jacques Cousteau rated the neighbouring Poor Knights Islands as one of the world's best dive sites.

ESSENTIAL BAY OF ISLANDS & NORTHLAND

Eat fresh Orongo Bay oysters.

Drink Northland craft beer at Mangawhai's Wood Street Freehouse (p144).

Read *The House of Strife* (1993), Maurice Shadbolt's riveting novel set during the Northland War.

Listen to *Cape Reinga Way* (2011) by The Nukes, ukuleles heading to the afterlife.

Watch *Land of the Long White Cloud* (2009), fishing philosophers on Ninety Mile Beach.

Celebrate Waitangi Day (p160).

Go green and sing to the trees with Footprints Waipoua (p176).

Go online www.northlandnz.com; www. kauricoast.com.

Mangawhai

POP 2400

Mangawhai village sits at the base of a gorgeous horseshoe estuary, but it's the surf beach at Mangawhai Heads, 5km further on, that's the real treat.

Various Māori tribes inhabited the area before the 1660s, when Ngāti Whatua became dominant. In 1807 Ngāti Whatua defeated Ngāpuhi in a major battle, letting the survivors escape. One of them was Hongi Hika, who in 1825 returned, armed with muskets obtained from Europeans. The ensuing bloodbath all but annihilated Ngāti Whatua and the district became *tapu* (sacred, taboo). British squatters moved in and were rewarded with land titles by the government in the 1850s. Ceremonies were only performed to lift the *tapu* in the 1990s.

These days Mangawhai is benefiting from improved traffic links with Auckland, and new housing subdivisions are expanding the spread of the area. Down on the surf beach, though, it's still a quintessential laid-back New Zealand beach town.

⊙ Sights

★ **Mangawhai Heads** BEACH
(Wintle St) Mangawhai's main claim to fame is the surf beach at the northern head of its large estuary. The large beach-side car park fills up quickly in peak season.

Mangawhai Museum MUSEUM
(☎ 09-431 4645; www.mangawhai-museum.org. nz; Molesworth Dr, Mangawhai Heads; adult/child $12/3; ⊙ 10am-4pm) One of regional New Zealand's best museums, this spectacular building on the main road linking Mangawhai village to Mangawhai Heads is packed with interesting displays on the area's history and environment. Check out the roof shaped like a stingray (Mangawhai means 'stream of the rays'). There's also a sun-drenched cafe worthy of a stop.

🏃 Activities

Mangawhai Cliff Top Walkway TRAMPING
Starting at Mangawhai Heads, this track affords extensive views of sea and land. It takes two to three hours, provided you time it with a return down the beach at low tide. This is part of Te Araroa, the national walking track. Ask at the visitor information centre (p144) for the *Tracks and Walks* brochure detailing other walks in the area.

WORTH A TRIP

KAIWAKA KAI

If you're feeling peckish on the route between Auckland and Whangarei or the Kauri Coast, stop for *kai* (food) at Kaiwaka.

It's an unusual spot for a Dutch-style delicatessen, but the **Kaiwaka Cheese Shop** (☑09-431 2195; www.cheese-shop.co.nz; 1957 SH1, Kaiwaka) has long been an essential stop for travelling foodies seeking some luxury additions to their holiday provisions. Dutch dominates but you'll also find British and NZ cheese, and a good selection of wine and tasty snacks.

Another great option is **Cafe Bianca** (☑09-431 2327; 1956 SH1, Kaiwaka; mains $7-20; ⊙9am-3.30pm Thu-Tue; ☎). Beyond the rough wooden exterior is a corrugated-iron-lined speakeasy where staff dressed as flappers deliver cooked breakfasts, gourmet burgers and seafood chowder to bemused road-weary patrons seated at Edwardian tables. Try the beef burger – it's surprisingly light and exceedingly delicious.

☞ Tours

Wined About Bike Tours   CYCLING
(☑09-945 0580; www.winedabout.co.nz; per person $50) Three different self-guided tour options include all the good things in life: Art & Chocolate, Wineries & Olives or a Free-style Ride exploring Mangawhai village and nearby beaches. Pick-ups are included in the prices, both before and after riding.

ᕮ Sleeping

Mangawhai Heads
Holiday Park   HOLIDAY PARK $
(☑09-431 4675; www.mangawhaiheadsholidaypark. co.nz; 2 Mangawhai Heads Rd; sites from $18, units with/without bathroom from $105/65; ☎☎) With an absolute waterfront location on the sandy expanse of Mangawhai's estuary, this laid-back combo of campsites, units and cabins is a retro slice of Kiwiana holiday style. Visit in summer for a vibrant halo of red blooms from groves of ancient pohutukawa trees. It's a family-friendly place, with an expectation of no noise after 10.30pm.

Mangawhai Backpackers:
The Coastal Cow   HOSTEL $
(☑09-431 5246; www.facebook.com/mangawhai backpackers; 299 Molesworth Dr, Mangawhai Heads; dm $20, s $55-89, d & tw $68-95, f $102-136) The rooms at this unassuming house-style hostel have been spruced up with a splash of pale-blue paint. Bathrooms are shared and there's a pleasant barbecue area on the back deck. Family rooms sleep up to four people.

★ Mangawhai Chalets   CHALET $$
(☑09-431 5029; www.mangawhaichalets.co.nz; 252 Molesworth Dr, Mangawhai Heads; units from $130; ☎☎) There's a Cape Cod feel to the three stylishly decked out cedar chalets positioned in the lavender-filled garden behind the main house. All of the units have fridges and there's a communal kitchen with a barbecue and a stove in the open-sided 'club-house', should the cooking urge take you.

Mangawhai Lodge   B&B $$
(☑09-431 5311; www.seaviewlodge.co.nz; 4 Heather St, Mangawhai Heads; s/d $185/195, apt $185-250; ☎) ✿ This hillside lodge has smartly furnished rooms opening onto a picture-perfect wraparound veranda with terrific sea views. Choose between two classic B&B rooms and two apartments with kitchenettes.

✕ Eating & Drinking

★ Dune   CAFE $$
(☑09-431 5695; www.facebook.com/thedune mangawhai; 40 Moir St, Mangawhai village; mains $19-28; ⊙9am-9pm Wed-Sun, extended hours summer) ✿ Despite the name, Mangawhai's best eatery is nowhere near the sands. Situated in the heart of the village, Dune is half bar, half cafe – with sunny outdoor tables arrayed around both. The food is excellent, including a deliciously smoky brisket, gourmet pizza and lots of yummy vegetable side dishes. Much of the produce is sourced from the owners' family farms.

★ Sandbar   CAFE, BISTRO $$
(☑09-431 5587; www.sandbarmangawhai.co.nz; Fagan Pl, Mangawhai Heads; mains brunch $12-19, lunch $18-22, dinner $31-33; ⊙9am-3pm daily & 6-10pm Fri & Sat, extended hours summer; ☎) Polished concrete floors and a living wall set a quietly stylish scene for a daytime cafe and night-time bistro. Evening meals are sophisticated and deftly constructed, featuring the likes of fresh fish, Scotch fillet, merino lamb and wonderfully fluffy gnocchi with wild mushrooms and truffle oil.

Mangawhai Tavern PUB

(☑ 09-431 4505; www.mangawhaitavern.co.nz; 2 Moir St, Mangawhai village; ⊙11am-late) One of the country's oldest pubs – established in 1865, but twice burnt down since then – the tavern's harbourside location is a top spot for an afternoon beer. There's live music most Saturday nights and Sunday afternoons, and across the Christmas–New Year period some of NZ's top bands rock the outside stage. The meals are also very good.

Wood Street Freehouse BAR

(☑ 09-431 4051; www.woodstreetfreehouse.co.nz; 12 Wood St, Mangawhai Heads; mains $18-26, shared plates $10-12; ⊙4pm-late Mon-Fri, from noon Sat & Sun; ▣) Craft beer has arrived in Mangawhai at this buzzing bar/cafe, including a good selection from Northland brewers. Excellent food includes burgers, gourmet pizzas and shared plates – the truffle and parmesan fries are addictive. They also host regular family-friendly movie nights.

ⓘ Information

Visitor Information Centre (☑ 09-431 5090; www.mangawhai.co.nz; Molesworth Dr, Mangawhai Heads; ⊙9am-6pm daily Jan & Feb, 2-5pm Fri, 11am-5pm Sat, 11am-1pm Sun Mar-Dec) Staffed sporadically but there are information boards outside. Ask about opportunities to visit local vineyards and olive groves.

ⓘ Getting There & Away

Mangawhai is around 80 minutes by car from Auckland. There is no regular public transport.

Waipu & Bream Bay

POP 1680

Waipu is a sleepy rural town with a fascinating history, giggle-inducing name and a couple of excellent swimming beaches nearby at **Waipu Cove** and **Langs Beach**.

Waipu's original 934 British settlers came from Scotland via Nova Scotia (Canada) between 1853 and 1860. These canny Scots had the good sense to eschew frigid Otago, where so many of their kindred settled, for sunnier northern climes. Waipu celebrates its Scottish heritage with the annual Highland Games in January.

Bream Bay has miles of blissfully deserted beach, blighted only slightly by a giant oil refinery at the north end. At **Uretiti**, a stretch of beach south of a Department of Conservation (DOC) campsite is unofficially considered 'clothing optional'. Over New Year the crowd is evenly split between Kiwi families, serious European nudists and gay guys from Auckland and Northland.

⊙ Sights & Activities

There are excellent walks in the area, including the 3km **Waipu Coastal Trail**, which heads south from Waipu Cove to Ding Bay via the Pancake Rocks. The 2km **Waipu Caves Track** starts near the entrance to a large cave containing glowworms and limestone formations; bring a torch and sturdy footwear.

Waipu Museum MUSEUM

(☑09-432 0746; www.waipumuseum.co.nz; 36 The Centre, Waipu; adult/child $10/5; ⊙9.30am-4.30pm) In this fascinating little museum Waipu's Scottish heritage comes to life through holograms, a short film and interactive displays. Fun fact: church services were still being held in Scots Gaelic in Waipu right up until 1907.

✿ Festivals & Events

Waipu Highland Games SPORTS

(www.waipugames.co.nz; ⊙1 Jan) Only 10% of current residents are direct descendants of the original Scots, but there's a big get together every year, when the Highland Games, established in 1871, take place in Caledonian Park.

🛏 Sleeping

Camp Waipu Cove HOLIDAY PARK $

(☑09-432 0410; www.campwaipucove.com; 869 Cove Rd, Waipu Cove; sites/r from $38/45, units with/without bathroom from $120/70) Set beside a blissful stretch of beach with views to craggy islands, this well-kept campground has a range of simple cabins, motel-style units, bunk rooms, and tent and campervan sites. Facilities include a colourful and clean toilet block, communal kitchen, playground, giant chess set and TV room. Native birds flitter around in profusion.

DOC Uretiti Campsite CAMPGROUND $

(☑09-432 1051; www.doc.govt.nz; SH1, Uretiti; sites per adult/child $13/6.50) At Uretiti, there is a DOC campsite with hot showers and stellar beach views amid rolling sand dunes.

Waipu Wanderers Backpackers HOSTEL $

(☑09-432 0532; www.waipu-hostel.co.nz; 25 St Marys Rd, Waipu; dm/s/d $33/49/70; 🛜) There are only three rooms at this friendly backpackers in Waipu township, set behind a lovely old house lined with citrus trees; bathrooms are shared. Look forward to free cereal and toast, and fruit in season.

✕ Eating

Cove CAFE $$
(☑ 09-432 0234; www.thecovecafe.co.nz; 910 Cove Rd, Waipu Cove; breakfast $12-19, mains $22-35; ⊙ 8am-late summer, 9am-9pm Thu-Mon winter) This heritage cottage near Waipu covers all the bases, from coffee and breakfast bagels to pizza, gourmet burgers, craft beer and healthy smoothies, and the deck is a very pleasant spot to celebrate exploring NZ. The baking is particularly tempting.

McLeod's Pizza Barn PIZZA $$
(☑ 09-432 1011; www.facebook.com/mcleodspizza barn; 2 Cove Rd, Waipu; pizzas $13-29, mains $20-27; ⊙ 11.30am-9pm Wed-Sun Apr-Nov, daily Dec-Mar) The flavour combinations may seem almost as odd as a Scots-named pizzeria, but the crispy-based pizzas are delicious. Try the Gumdigger, with smoked salmon, asparagus, blue-vein cheese and pesto, and wash it down with a craft beer from Waipu's very own McLeod's Brewery. Other crowd-pleasing menu options include burgers, lamb shanks and pasta dishes.

Waipu Cafe Deli CAFE $$
(☑ 09-432 0990; www.facebook.com/waipu.cafe. deli; 29 The Centre, Waipu; mains $12-19; ⊙ 8am-3pm) Enticing salads, sandwiches, cooked breakfasts, pasta, muffins and organic fair-trade coffee are served at this attractive little cafe on Waipu's main drag.

ⓘ Getting There & Away

InterCity (p142) has three or four coaches a day to and from Auckland (from $23, 2½ hours), Whangarei (from $18, 25 minutes), Kawakawa (from $28, 1½ hours), Paihia (from $25, 1¾ hours) and Kerikeri (from $25, 2¼ hours).

Mana Bus (p142), in association with Naked Bus, has two or three daily coaches to and from Auckland (from $17, two hours), Warkworth (from $15, one hour), Whangarei ($10, 45 minutes), Kawakawa ($14, 1¾ hours) and Paihia ($14, two hours).

Waipu Cove can be reached by a particularly scenic route that heads from Mangawhai Heads through Langs Beach. Otherwise, turn off SH1 38km south of Whangarei.

Whangarei

☑ 09 / POP 56,400

Northland's only city is surrounded by natural beauty, and its compact town centre offers plenty of rainy-day diversions. There's a thriving artistic community, some good walks, and interesting cafes and bars.

◉ Sights

This attractive riverside marina is home to museums, galleries, cafes, shops, public art and an information centre. It's a great place for a stroll, with a marked **Art Walk** and **Heritage Trail**. An **artisans' fair** (www.artisans fair.org.nz) is held on Saturdays from late October to Easter under the shade of the pedestrian bridge.

Clapham's National Clock Museum MUSEUM
(☑ 09-438 3993; www.claphamsclocks.com; Lower Dent St, Town Basin; adult/child $10/4; ⊙ 9am-5pm) This charming collection of 1600 ticking, gonging and cuckooing timepieces is more interesting than you'd imagine. There are all manner of kooky and kitschy items displayed alongside the more august specimens, such as the venerable 1690 English-built grandfather clock.

AH Reed Memorial Kauri Park FOREST
(www.wdc.govt.nz; Whareora Rd) 🅿 FREE A grove of immense 500-year-old kauri trees has been preserved in this lush tract of native bush, where a cleverly designed boardwalk leads you effortlessly up into the canopy. To get here, head north on Bank St and turn right into Whareora Rd.

Abbey Caves CAVE
(Abbey Caves Rd) FREE Abbey Caves is an undeveloped network of three caverns full of glow-worms and limestone formations, 6km east of town. Grab a torch, strong shoes, a mate for safety and prepare to get wet. The surrounding reserve is a forest of crazily shaped rock extrusions. Ask at the i-SITE (p149) about an information sheet for the caves.

Whangarei Quarry Gardens GARDENS
(☑ 09-437 7210; www.whangareigardens.org.nz; 37a Russell Rd, Kensington; admission by donation; ⊙ 9am-5pm) 🅿 Green-fingered volunteers have transformed this old quarry into a blissful park with a lake, waterfalls, pungent floral aromas, wild bits, orderly bits and lots of positive energy. Plus there's a visitor centre and an excellent cafe. To get here, take Rust Ave, turn right into Western Hills Dr and then left into Russell Rd.

Whangarei Falls WATERFALL
(Otuihau; Ngunguru Rd, Glenbervie) Short walks around these 26m-high falls provide views of the water cascading over the edge of an old basalt lava flow. The falls can be reached on the Tikipunga bus ($3, no service on Sundays), leaving from Rose St in the city.

Whangarei

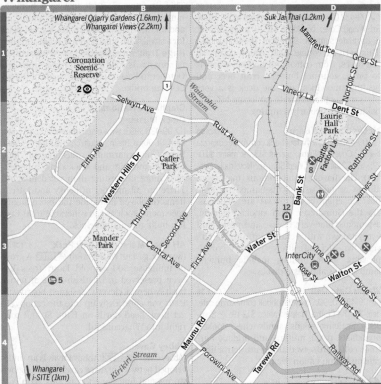

Kiwi North   MUSEUM
(☑ 09-438 9630; www.kiwinorth.co.nz; 500 SH14, Maunu; adult/child $20/5; ⊙10am-4pm) 🅿 Five kilometres west of Whangarei, this complex includes 19th-century buildings and a museum displaying Māori and colonial artefacts. A gecko and kiwi house offers a rare chance to see the country's feathery fave in a darkened nocturnal house.

Whangarei Art Museum   GALLERY
(☑09-430 4240; www.whangareiartmuseum. co.nz; The Hub, 91 Dent St, Town Basin; ⊙10am-4pm) FREE Whangarei's public gallery has an interesting permanent collection, but the two large gallery spaces usually house temporary exhibitions by local and regional artists.

🕴 Activities

The free *Hatea River Walk & Surrounds* brochure, available from the i-SITE (p149), has maps and detailed descriptions of some excellent local tracks. The **Hatea River Walk** follows the river from the Town Basin to the falls (90 minutes each way, or return on bus 303A). Longer tracks head through **Parihaka Reserve**, which is just east of the Hatea River and encompasses the remnants of a volcanic cone (241m) and a major *pā* (fortified village) site. The city is spread out for inspection from the lookout at the top, which is accessible by car. Other tracks head through **Coronation Scenic Reserve**, an expanse of bush immediately west of the centre that includes two *pā* sites and abandoned quarries.

Skydive Ballistic Blondes   SKYDIVING
(☑0800 695 867; www.skydiveballisticblondes. co.nz; 10 Domain Rd, Onerahi; skydive $199-380) Not only is this the oddest-named skydiving outfit in the country, it's also the only one licensed to land on the beach (Ocean Beach, Ruakaka or Paihia).

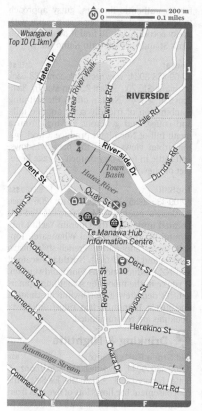

on a farm 6km from town and right next to Abbey Caves, Little Earth makes most other hostels look downright shabby in comparison. Forget dorm rooms crammed with nasty, spongy bunks: settle down in a proper cosy bed with nice linen. Resident critters include miniature horses and alpacas, and there's a free-standing cabin available.

Whangarei Falls Holiday Park & Backpackers HOSTEL, HOLIDAY PARK $
(☑09-437 0609; www.whangareifalls.co.nz; 12 Ngunguru Rd, Glenbervie; sites/dm from $25/32, s/d $60/72; 🛜🏊) Located 5km from central Whangarei, but a short walk from Whangarei Falls, this holiday park has good-value cabins, some with small kitchenettes but none with private bathrooms. It's also part of the YHA network and has a 10-bed dorm with bunks, along with smaller backpackers rooms.

Whangarei Top 10 HOLIDAY PARK $
(☑09-437 6856; www.whangareitop10.co.nz; 24 Mair St, Kensington; sites from $22, units $68-160; 🛜) 🌿 This centrally located riverside holiday park has friendly owners, a better-than-average set of units, and super-shiny stainless-steel surfaces. Mair St is off Hatea Dr, north of the city centre; a pleasant bushwalk from the back of the park follows the river to the Town Basin.

🚗 Tours

Pacific Coast Kayaks KAYAKING
(☑09-436 1947; www.nzseakayaking.co.nz; hire 4/8hr $60/80, tours $40-150) Hires kayaks and offers guided paddles to various locations in the Whangarei region. Pick-ups and drop-offs are free from the Whangarei suburb of Onerahi, and charged for locations such as Tutukaka ($50), Matapouri ($60) and Whangaroa ($130).

Pupurangi Hire & Tour CULTURAL
(☑09-438 8117; www.hirentour.co.nz; Jetty 1, Riverside Dr) Various hour-long tours of Whangarei, all with a Māori flavour, including *waka* (canoe) trips on the river ($35). Also hires kayaks (per hour $17), *waka* ($25), aquacycles ($17) and bikes ($15).

🛏 Sleeping

Little Earth Lodge HOSTEL $
(☑09-430 6562; www.littleearthlodge.co.nz; 85 Abbey Caves Rd; s/d/tr from $67/78/96; 🛜) Set

Lupton Lodge
B&B $$

(☑09-437 2989; www.luptonlodge.co.nz; 555 Ngunguru Rd, Glenbervie; s/d/ste/apt from $145/190/290/310; 🖥🌊) The rooms are spacious, luxurious and full of character in this historic homestead (1896), peacefully positioned in farmland 5km past Whangarei Falls in the direction of Tutukaka. Wander the orchard, splash around the pool or shoot some snooker in the guest lounge. Also available is a stylish apartment in a renovated barn.

Lodge Bordeaux
MOTEL $$

(☑09-438 0404; www.lodgebordeaux.co.nz; 361 Western Hills Dr; apt from $195; 🖳🖥🌊) This upmarket European-styled motel has tasteful units with stellar kitchens and bathrooms (most with spa baths), private balconies on the upstairs rooms, and access to a barbecue, small swimming pool and excellent wine.

✖ Eating

La Familia
CAFE $

(☑09-438 8404; www.lafamilia.nz; 84 Cameron St; mains $11-17, pizza $14-19; ⊙7am-4pm Tue-Sat, 9am-3pm Sun) Versatility rules at this cosy corner location. Good pastries, bagels, counter food and coffee segue in to robust mains and pizzas for lunch. There's a compact wine list and a good selection of beers.

Fat Camel
ISRAELI $$

(☑09-438 0831; 12 Quality St; mains $10-25; ⊙9am-9pm) In a pedestrian laneway lined with ethnic eateries, this little Israeli cafe stands out for its pita pockets and platters laden with falafels, salads and grilled meat. For something a little different try the *malawach*, a Yemeni flaky pastry-like pancake served with salad and dips. The coffee's good, too.

Quay
CAFE, BISTRO $$

(☑09-430 2628; www.thequaykitchen.co.nz; 31 Quayside, Town Basin; mains brunch $14-20, dinner $29-35, pizza $21-25; ⊙9am-10pm) Sit out on the wraparound veranda of this beautiful riverside villa or take a table in the stylish, hollowed-out interior. The menu shuffles from cooked breakfasts to pizza and bistro-style meals in the evening.

Suk Jai Thai
THAI $$

(☑09-437 7287; www.sukjai.co.nz; 93 Kamo Rd, Kensington; mains $17-35; ⊙11.30am-2.30pm Tue-Sat & 5-10pm daily; 🖉) It's well worth a trip to the suburbs to seek out this cheerful and relaxed restaurant, popular with Thai expats for its authentic flavours, gutsy approach to spice, and desserts such as banana with sticky coconut rice. To find it head north on Bank St and veer left onto Kamo Rd.

Nectar
CAFE $$

(☑09-438 8084; www.nectarcafe.co.nz; 88 Bank St; mains $10-20; ⊙7am-2.30pm Mon-Fri, 8am-2pm Sat; 🖉) 🍃 Nectar offers the winning combination of friendly staff, organic milk and coffee, and generous servings from a menu full of Northland produce. Check out the urban views from the back windows, and settle in for a lazy brunch of eggs Benedict or chewy bagels.

TopSail
BISTRO $$$

(☑09-436 2985; www.topsail.co.nz; 206 Beach Rd, Onerahi; mains $40-44; ⊙6pm-late Wed-Sat) Located upstairs in the Onerahi Yacht Club, around 10km from central Whangarei, TopSail serves superlative French-style bistro classics and lots of fresh Northland seafood and NZ produce such as Fiordland venison. If you're in the mood for something upmarket, it's definitely a worthwhile destination and just a 15-minute taxi ride from town. Bookings are recommended.

🍷 Drinking & Nightlife

Old Stone Butter Factory
BAR

(☑09-430 0044; www.thebutterfactory.co.nz; 8 Butter Factory Lane; ⊙11am-late Tue-Sat) This cool basement bar hosts lots of live gigs from touring Kiwi bands along with the occasional poetry night or gay mixer. As the hours dissolve, DJs kick in. Burgers and pizza are good value, and the sunny courtyard is ideal for a coffee, craft beer or wine.

Frings
PUB

(☑09-438 4664; www.frings.co.nz; 104 Dent St; ⊙11am-8pm Sun, Tue & Wed, 11am-11.45pm Thu-Sat) This popular pub brews its own beers, and has a terrace, wood-fired pizzas, and lots of live music including Thursday jam nights. Grab a seat on the deck shaped like the prow of a ship.

🔒 Shopping

You can often pick up well-priced art and craft at **Quarry Arts Centre** (☑09-438 1215; www.quarryarts.org; 21 Selwyn Ave; ⊙9.30am-4.30pm) **FREE**.

Bach
ARTS & CRAFTS

(☑09-438 2787; www.thebach.gallery; Town Basin; ⊙9.30am-4.30pm) Co-op store representing over 100 Northland artisans.

OLD RUSSELL ROAD

The quickest route to Russell takes SH1 to Opua and then crosses by ferry. If you're coming from the south, the old Russell Rd is a snaking scenic alternative that adds about half an hour to the trip.

The turn-off is easy to miss, located 6km north of Hikurangi at Whakapara (look for the sign to Oakura). After 13km stop at the **Gallery & Cafe** (☑ 09-433 9934; www.gallery helenabay.co.nz; 1392 Russell Rd, Helena Bay; mains $10-20; ☺10am-4pm), high above **Helena Bay**, for fair-trade coffee, scrummy cake, amazing views, and interesting Kiwiana art and craft.

Near Helena Bay an unsealed detour leads 8km to **Mimiwhangata Coastal Park** (☑ 09-433 6554; www.doc.govt.nz; 453 Mimiwhangata Rd, Helena Bay) FREE, which features sand dunes, pohutukawa trees, jutting headlands and picturesque beaches. Here, DOC-managed accommodation includes an eight-person lodge (per week $945), a simple but comfortable cottage (per week $630), and a beach house (per week $630), all of which sleep seven to eight people. Basic camping (per adult/child $13/6.50) is available at secluded Waikahoa Bay.

Back on Russell Rd, **The Farm** (☑ 09-433 6894; www.thefarm.co.nz; 3632 Russell Rd, Whangaruru; sites/dm $15/20, r with/without bathroom $80/60) is a rough-and-ready backpackers that rambles through various buildings, including an old woolshed. The rooms are basic and it's a popular park-up spot for campervans, but off season it's a chilled-out rustic escape. Best of all, you can arrange a horse trek ($50, two hours), dirt biking (from $50), kayaking and fishing.

At an intersection shortly after The Farm, Russell Rd branches off to the left for an unsealed, winding section traversing the **Ngaiotonga Scenic Reserve**. Unless you're planning to explore the forest (there are two short walks: the 20-minute Kauri Grove Nature Walk and the 10-minute Twin Bole Track), you're better off veering right onto the sealed Rawhiti Rd.

After 2.6km, a side road leads to the **Whangaruru North Head Scenic Reserve**, which has beaches, walking tracks and fine scenery. A loop route from DOC's sheltered **Puriri Bay Campsite** (☑ 09-433 6160; www.doc.govt.nz; Whangaruru North Rd, Whangaruru; sites per adult/child $13/6.50) leads up to a ridge, offering a remarkable coastal panorama.

If you want to head directly to Russell, continue along Rawhiti Rd for another 7km before veering left onto Manawaora Rd, which skirts a succession of tiny idyllic bays before reconnecting with Russell Rd.

Otherwise take a detour to isolated **Rawhiti**, a small Ngāpuhi settlement where life still revolves around the *marae* (traditional meeting place). Rawhiti is the starting point for the tramp to **Cape Brett**, a tiring eight-hour, 16.3km walk to the top of the peninsula, where overnight stays are possible in DOC's **Cape Brett Hut** (☑09-407 0300; www. doc.govt.nz; dm adult/child $15/7.50). The hut must be booked in advance. An access fee is charged for crossing private land (adult/child $40/20), which you can pay at the Bay of Islands i-SITE (p162). Another option is to take a water taxi to Cape Brett Lighthouse from Russell or Paihia and walk back.

A shorter one-hour walk leads through Māori land and the **Whangamumu Scenic Reserve** to Whangamumu Harbour. There are more than 40 ancient Māori sites on the peninsula and the remains of an unusual whaling station.

Tuatara Design Store   ARTS & CRAFTS
(☑09-430 0121; www.tuataradesignstore.com; 29 Bank St; ☺9.30am-5.30pm Mon-Fri, 8am-3.30pm Sat) Māori and Pasifika design, art and craft.

ⓘ Information

DOC Whangarei Office (☑ 09-470 3300; www.doc.govt.nz; 2 South End Ave, Raumanga;

☺8am-4.35pm Mon-Fri) Located just off SH1 around 2km south of central Whangarei.

Te Manawa Hub Information Centre (☑ 09-430 1188; www.whangareinz.com; 91 Dent St, Town Basin; ☺9am-5pm; ☎) Central branch of the i-SITE, in the foyer of the Whangarei Art Museum.

Whangarei i-SITE (☑09-438 1079; www. whangareinz.com; 92 Otaika Rd (SH1); ☺9am-5pm) Information, cafe, toilets and showers.

ⓘ Getting There & Away

AIR

Whangarei Airport (WRE; ☑ 09-436 0047; www.whangareiairport.co.nz; Handforth St, Onerahi; ☎) is at Onerahi, 6km southeast of the city centre. Air New Zealand (p142) flies to/from Auckland. Taxis into town cost around $25. Bus route 2 ($3) stops at the airport at least hourly until around 6.30pm on weekdays, but only until 1.30pm on Saturdays; there are no Sunday services.

BUS

Long distance coaches stop at the Hub (p149), in the Town Basin.

InterCity (p142) has three or four buses a day to/from Auckland (from $31, three hours), Waipu (from $18, 25 minutes), Paihia (from $12, 1¼ hours) and Kerikeri (from $12, 1¾ hours).

Mana Bus (p142) has two or three services a day to/from Auckland (from $20, 2¾ hours), Waipu ($10, 45 minutes) and Paihia ($12, 1¼ hours).

West Coaster (☑ 021 380 187; www.dargaville.co.nz; one way $10) links Dargaville and Whangarei twice daily on weekdays.

ⓘ Getting Around

BUS

City Link Whangarei (www.citylinkwhangarei.co.nz, cash fare per adult/child $3/2) operates buses on seven routes, all departing from Rose St. The most useful are routes 2 (to the airport), 3 (Whangarei Falls) and 6 (Kiwi North). Services are reduced on Saturdays and there are no buses on Sundays.

TAXI

A1 Cabs (☑ 09-438 3377; www.whangarei.bluebubbletaxi.co.nz)

Whangarei Heads

Whangarei Heads Rd winds 35km along the northern reaches of the harbour to the Heads' entrance, passing mangroves and picturesque pohutukawa-lined bays. There are great views from the top of **Mt Manaia** (419m), a sheer rock outcrop above McLeod Bay, but prepare for a lung- and leg-busting 1½-hour climb.

Bream Head caps off the craggy finger of land. A five-hour one-way walking track from **Urquharts Bay** to **Ocean Beach** passes through the **Bream Head Scenic Reserve** and lovely **Smugglers Bay** and **Peach Cove**.

Magnificent **Ocean Beach** stretches for miles on the other side of the head-land. There's decent surfing to be had and lifeguards patrol the beach in summer. A detour from **Parua Bay** takes you to glorious **Pataua**, a small settlement that lies on a shallow inlet linked to a surf beach by a footbridge.

🏃 Activities

Bream Head Coast Walks   TRAMPING
(☑ 09-434 0571; www.coastwalks.nz; 395 Ody Rd; 2/3 nights $435/535; ☉Oct-May) Enjoyed across two or three days, this self-guided walking network traverses farmland, public walkways and stunning coastal scenery. Accommodation is in a luxury lodge and excellent food is included. The lodge is used as a base for each night after undertaking a variety of walks in the area. Track notes are included and pick-ups from Whangarei can be arranged.

🛏 Sleeping & Eating

Kauri Villas   B&B $$
(☑ 09-436 1797; www.kaurivillas.com; 73 Owhiwa Rd, Parua Bay; apt/ste from $195/220; ☎☒) Perched on a hill with views back over the harbour to Whangarei, this pretty blue-trimmed villa has a charming old-world feel and two massive suites, each with two bedrooms and a sitting room. There's also a self-contained apartment across the lawn, sleeping up to 10 people.

Ara Roa   RENTAL HOUSE $$$
(☑ 027 320 0770; www.araroa.nz; Harambee Rd, Taiharuru; d $325-950; ☎☒) This collection of five different architecturally striking properties dotted around a coastal peninsula ranges from the two-bedroom Te Huia – with sunset views and a bush track where kiwi are often heard after dark – to the gorgeous one-bedroom Glasshouse at the very end of the peninsula. Two-bedroom Aria has its own lap pool.

Parua Bay Tavern   PUB FOOD $$
(☑ 09-436 5856; www.paruabaytavern.co.nz; 1034 Whangarei Heads Rd; mains $15-28; ☉11.30am-late Wed-Sun) A magical spot on a summer's day, this friendly pub is set on a thumb-shaped peninsula, with a sole pohutukawa blazing red against the green water. Grab a seat on the deck, a cold beverage and a decent pub meal, including good burgers and pizza.

ⓘ Getting There & Away

There's no public transport on this winding ocean-fringed drive.

Tutukaka Coast & the Poor Knights Islands

At the **Poor Knights Islands**, colourful underwater scenery combines with two decommissioned navy ships to provide a perfect playground for divers. Dive boats depart from the bustling marina at **Tutukaka**, a small fishing settlement 28km northeast of Whangarei.

From Tutukaka the road heads slightly inland, popping out 10km later at the golden sands of **Matapouri**. A blissful 20-minute coastal walk leads from here to **Whale Bay**, fringed with giant pohutukawa trees.

Continuing north from Matapouri, the wide expanse of **Sandy Bay**, one of Northland's premier surf beaches, comes into view. Long-boarding competitions are held here in summer. The road then loops back to join SH1 at Hikurangi. A branch leading off from this road doubles back north to the coast at **Whananaki**, where there are more glorious beaches and the Otamure Bay DOC campsite.

🏃 Activities

Tutukaka's dive crews cater to both first-timers and experienced divers. There are some excellent walks along the coast; ask about options at the Whangarei i-SITE (p149).

Yukon Dive   DIVING
(✆09-434 4506; www.yukon.co.nz; Marina Rd; 2 dives incl full gear $290) An owner-operator offering dive trips for a maximum of 12 people at a time. Trips for non-divers incorporating snorkelling and kayaking are also available ($190).

★ Dive! Tutukaka   DIVING
(✆0800 288 882; www.diving.co.nz; Marina Rd; 2 dives incl gear $289) ✦ Dive courses include a three-day PADI open-water course. For non-divers, the **Perfect Day Ocean Cruise** (www.aperfectday.co.nz, $189) includes lunch and snacks, snorkelling in the marine reserve, kayaking through caves and arches, paddle boarding, and sightings of dolphins (usually) and whales (occasionally). Cruises run from November to May, departing at 11am and returning at 4pm.

Tutukaka Surf   SURFING
(✆021 227 0072; www.tutukakasurf.co.nz; Marina Rd; 2hr lesson from $75; ⊙shop 9am-5pm daily Nov-Feb, 10am-5pm Fri-Mon Mar-Oct) Runs surf lessons in Sandy Bay, 10km northwest of Tutukaka, at 9.30am most days in summer and on the weekends otherwise. Private lessons can be arranged at other times. They also hire surfboards (per day $45) and stand-up paddle boards (per day $20) from their Tutukaka store.

🛏 Sleeping & Eating

DOC Otamure Bay Campsite   CAMPGROUND $
(✆09-433 8402; www.doc.govt.nz; Rockell Rd, Whananaki; sites per adult/child $13/6.50) This scenic campsite is located near a sandy beach with plenty of shade from well-established pohutukawa trees. Expect cold showers, drinking water and little else.

Pacific Rendezvous   MOTEL $$$
(✆09-434 3847; www.pacificrendezvous.co.nz; 73 Motel Rd, Tutukaka; apt from $229) Perfectly situated for spectacular views on the manicured, lawn-covered southern head of Tutukaka Harbour, this is a great choice for families and small groups. The multiroom units are all individually owned and decorated.

Schnappa Rock   CAFE $$
(✆09-434 3774; www.schnapparock.co.nz; Marina Rd, Tutukaka; mains brunch $14-23, dinner $25-36; ⊙8am-late Oct-May, closed Sun night Jun-Sep) ✦

MARINE RICHES AT THE POOR KNIGHTS

Established in 1981, the Poor Knights marine reserve is rated as one of the world's top-10 diving spots. The islands are bathed in a subtropical current from the Coral Sea, so varieties of tropical and subtropical fish not seen in other NZ waters can be observed here. The waters are clear, with no sediment or pollution problems. The 40m to 60m underwater cliffs drop steeply to the sandy bottom and are a labyrinth of archways, caves, tunnels and fissures that attract a wide variety of sponges and colourful underwater vegetation. Schooling fish, eels and rays are common (including manta rays in season).

The two main volcanic islands, Tawhiti Rahi and Aorangi, were home to the Ngāti Wai tribe, but since a raiding-party massacre in 1825 the islands have been *tapu* (forbidden). Even today the public is barred from the islands, in order to protect their pristine environment. Not only do tuatara and Buller's shearwater breed here, but there are unique species of flora, such as the Poor Knights lily.

Filled with expectant divers in the morning and those capping off their perfect day in the evening, this cafe-restaurant-bar is often buzzing. Top NZ bands sometimes play on summer weekends.

ⓘ Getting There & Away

Whangarei Coastal Commuter (☑0800 435 355; www.coastalcommuter.co.nz; one way/return per person $25/40) Whangarei Commuter Shuttles runs a daily shuttle for travellers on dive trips, leaving Whangarei in the morning and returning in the afternoon.

BAY OF ISLANDS

The Bay of Islands ranks as one of NZ's top summertime destinations. Lingering shots of its turquoise waters and 150 undeveloped islands feature heavily in the country's tourist promotions. Most of the action here is out on the water, whether that be yachting, big-game fishing, kayaking, diving or cruising around in the company of whales and dolphins.

It's also a place of enormous historical significance. Māori knew it as Pēwhairangi and settled here early in their migrations. As the site of NZ's first permanent British settlement (at Russell), it is the birthplace of European colonisation in the country. It was here that the Treaty of Waitangi was drawn up and first signed in 1840; the treaty remains the linchpin of race relations in NZ today.

TWIN COAST CYCLE TRAIL – POU HERENGA TAI

This cycle route stretches from the Bay of Islands clear across the country to the Hokianga Harbour. OK, so that's only 87km, but as far as we're concerned that still gives you boasting rights when you get home. The complete route takes two days and travels from Opua to Kawakawa, Kaikohe, Okaihau and Horeke before finishing at Mangungu Mission Station.

The most popular day ride is the 14km section from **Kaikohe** to **Okaihau**, which passes through an abandoned rail tunnel before skirting **Lake Omapere**.

The trail is well described at www.twincoastcycletrail.kiwi.nz, which includes details of bike hire and shuttle transport.

🏃 Activities

The Bay of Islands offers some fine subtropical diving, made even better by the sinking of the 113m navy frigate HMNZS *Canterbury* in Deep Water Cove near Cape Brett. Local operators also head to the wreck of the *Rainbow Warrior* off the Cavalli Islands, about an hour north of Paihia by boat. Both offer a colourful feast of pink anemones, yellow sponges and abundant fish life.

There are plenty of opportunities for kayaking, sailing or cruising around the bay, either on a guided tour or by renting and going it alone. Note that some boat companies do not operate during the winter months.

There are some good walks in the area, including an easy 5km track that follows the coast from Opua to Paihia.

Bay of Islands Kayaking   KAYAKING
(☑021 272 3353; www.bayofislandskayaking.co.nz; tours $80-150) Rents sea kayaks and organises guided expeditions to **Haruru Falls** (Haruru Falls Rd, Haruru) and the outer islands.

Great Escape Yacht Charters   BOATING
(☑09-402 7143; www.greatescape.co.nz; 4 Richardson St, Opua) Offers introductory sailing lessons (two-day course $445) and longer options.

Flying Kiwi Parasail   PARASAILING
(☑09-402 6068; www.parasailnz.com; solo $115, tandem per adult/child $95/65) Departs from both Paihia and Russell wharves for NZ's highest parasail (1200ft/366m).

ⓖ Tours

Where do you start? First by praying for good weather, as torrential rain or choppy seas could exclude some options. The Bay of Islands i-SITE (p162) and accommodation operators can book tours.

Boat

Options include sailing boats, jetboats and large launches. Boats leave from either Paihia or Russell, calling into the other town as their first stop.

One of the bay's most striking islands is **Piercy Island (Motukōkako)** off Cape Brett, at the bay's eastern edge. This steep-walled rock fortress features a vast natural arch – the famous **Hole in the Rock**. Provided the conditions are right, most boat tours will pass right through the heart of the island. En route it's likely you'll encounter bottlenose and common dolphins, and you may see orcas, other whales and penguins.

Bay of Islands

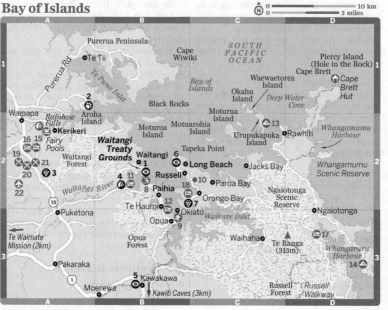

Bay of Islands

The best way to explore the bay is under sail. Either help crew the boat (no experience required), or just spend the afternoon island-hopping, sunbathing, swimming, snorkelling, kayaking and fishing.

The Rock   CRUISE
(☎ 0800 762 527; www.rocktheboat.co.nz; dm/d/f $268/650/894) 🐾 A former vehicle ferry that's now a floating hostel, the *Rock* has dorms, private rooms and a bar. The cruise departs at 5pm and includes a barbecue

and seafood dinner, then time spent island-hopping, fishing, kayaking, snorkelling and swimming the following day. It's also possible just to do the overnight portion (adult/child $208/178) or the daytime cruise ($128/98).

R Tucker Thompson
BOATING
(☎09-402 8430; www.tucker.co.nz; ☺Nov-Mar) Run by a charitable trust with an education focus, the *Tucker* is a majestic tall ship offering day sails (adult/child $149/75, including a barbecue lunch) and late-afternoon cruises (adult/child $65/33).

Phantom
BOATING
(☎0800 224 421; www.yachtphantom.com; day sail $110) A fast 50ft racing sloop, known for its wonderful food. Allows BYO (bring your own) beer and wine.

She's a Lady
BOATING
(☎0800 724 584; www.sailingbayofislands.com; day sail $97) Day sails include lunch, fishing, snorkelling and paddling a see-through-bottomed kayak.

Ecocruz
CRUISE
(☎0800 432 627; www.ecocruz.co.nz; dm/d $725/1700; ☺departs 8am Tue & Fri Oct-May) 🌿 Three-day/two-night sailing cruise aboard the 72ft ocean-going yacht *Manawanui*. Prices include accommodation, food, kayaking, sustainable fishing and snorkelling.

Gungha II
BOATING
(☎0800 478 900; www.bayofislandssailing.co.nz; day sail $110) A 65ft ocean yacht with a friendly crew, departing from both Russell and Paihia; lunch included.

Bus

It's cheaper and quicker to take trips to Cape Reinga from Ahipara, Kaitaia or Doubtless Bay, but if you're short on time, various long day trips (10 to 12 hours) leave from the Bay of Islands. They all drive one way along Ninety Mile Beach, stopping to sandboard on the dunes.

Fullers Great Sights (p160) runs regular bus tours and backpacker-oriented versions, both stopping at Puketi Forest. The standard, child-friendly version (adult/child $150/75) includes an optional lunch at Houhora. It also runs Awesome NZ (p160) tours, with louder music, more time sandboarding, and stops for a snack at Taipa and to devour fish and chips at Mangonui.

Explore NZ's (p160) Dune Rider tour (adult/child $150/110) also gives you the chance to sample Mangonui's feted fish and chips.

Transport options to the Hokianga and Waipoua Forest are limited, so a day trip makes sense if you don't have your own car or if you're time starved. Fullers' Giants & Glow Worms (adult/child $129/65) takes in Tāne Mahuta (p177) and the Kawiti Caves (p166) on an eight-hour tour with local Māori guides.

Total Tours
FOOD & DRINK
(☎0800 264 868; www.totaltours.co.nz; tours $80) Departing from Paihia, these bus or van tours head into the countryside around Kerikeri for a half-day Wine, Food and Craft tour or a half day devoted to just wine. Customised tours taking in the Kawiti Caves (p166) and Kawakawa Hundertwasser toilets can be arranged.

🎊 Festivals & Events

Bay of Islands Country
Rock Festival
MUSIC
(☎09-404 1063; www.country-rock.co.nz; festival pass $60; ☺May) Country-rock bands jangle and twang from stages in Paihia and Russell over the second weekend in May.

Bay of Islands Jazz & Blues Festival
MUSIC
(☎09-404 1063; www.jazz-blues.co.nz; festival pass $60; ☺Aug) Local and international acts take to stages in Paihia and Russell over the second weekend in August.

🛈 Getting There & Away

AIR

Bay of Islands (Kerikeri) Airport (KKE; ☎09-407 6133; www.bayofislandsairport.co.nz; 218 Wiroa Rd) is 8km southwest of Kerikeri. Air New Zealand (p142) flies here from Auckland.

Super Shuttle (☎0800 748 885; www.supershuttle.co.nz; Kerikeri Airport) provides shuttles between Kerikeri Airport and Bay of Islands destinations such as Kerikeri ($12) and Paihia ($27).

ABC Shuttles & Tours (☎022 025 0800; www.abcshuttle.co.nz; tours from $40) also provides airport transfers to Bay of Islands towns.

BUS

InterCity (p142) and **Mana Bus** (p142) both have services from Auckland to Kawakawa and Paihia. InterCity continues on to Kerikeri and as far north as Kaitaia.

Russell

📱 09 / POP 720

Although it was once known as the hell-hole of the Pacific, those coming to Russell for debauchery will be sadly disappointed: they've missed the orgies on the beach by 180 years. Instead they'll find a historic town with gift shops and B&Bs, and, in summer, you can rent kayaks and dinghies along the Strand.

History

Before it was known as a hellhole, or even as Russell, this was Kororāreka (Sweet Penguin), a fortified Ngāpuhi village. In the early 19th century the tribe permitted it to become Aotearoa's first European settlement. It quickly became a magnet for rough elements, such as fleeing convicts, whalers and drunken sailors. By the 1830s dozens of whaling ships at a time were anchored in the harbour. In 1839 Charles Darwin described it as full of 'the very refuse of society' in his book *The Voyage of the Beagle* (originally known as *Narrative of the Surveying Voyages of His Majesty's Ships* Adventure *and* Beagle).

In 1830 the settlement was the scene of the so-called Girls' War, when two pairs of Māori women were vying for the attention of a whaling captain called Brind. A chance meeting between the rivals on the beach led to verbal abuse and fighting. This minor conflict quickly escalated as family members rallied around to avenge the insult and harm done to their respective relatives. Hundreds were killed and injured over a two-week period before missionaries managed to broker a peace agreement.

After the signing of the Treaty of Waitangi in 1840, Okiato (where the car ferry now leaves from) was the residence of the governor and the temporary capital. The capital was officially moved to Auckland in 1841 and Okiato, which was by then known as Russell, was eventually abandoned. The name Russell ultimately replaced Kororāreka.

Sights

Pompallier Mission HISTORIC BUILDING
(📱09-403 9015; www.pompallier.co.nz; 5 The Strand; adult/child $10/free; ⊙10am-4pm) Built in 1842 to house the Catholic mission's printing press, this rammed-earth building is the mission's last remaining building in the western Pacific, and NZ's oldest factory. Over its seven years of operation, a staggering 40,000 books were printed here in Māori. Admission in-

Russell

⊙ **Sights**
1 Christ Church B2
2 Pompallier Mission............................ A3
3 Russell Museum A2

⊕ **Activities, Courses & Tours**
4 Russell Mini Tours............................. A2

🛏 **Sleeping**
5 Arcadia Lodge.................................... B3
6 Bellrock Lodge.................................. B2
7 Duke of Marlborough Hotel A2
8 Hananui Lodge & Apartments........... A2
9 Motel Russell B3
10 Russell Top 10.................................. B1

🍴 **Eating**
11 Gables.. A2
12 Hell Hole A2
13 Hōne's Garden................................... A2
14 Newport Chocolates......................... A2

🍷 **Drinking & Nightlife**
15 Duke of Marlborough Tavern............. A2

cludes extremely interesting hands-on tours that lead you through the entire bookmaking process, from the icky business of tanning animal hides for the covers, to setting the type and stitching together the final books.

Omata Estate
WINERY

(☑ 09-403 8007; www.omata.co.nz; 212 Aucks Rd; ⊙ 11am-6pm Oct-May, by appointment Jun-Sep) With a growing reputation for red wines – especially its old-growth syrah – Omata Estate is one of Northland's finest wineries. To complement the tastings and sea views, shared platters ($40) are available. The winery is on the road from Russell to the car ferry at Okiato.

Christ Church
CHURCH

(www.oldchurch.org.nz; Church St) English naturalist Charles Darwin made a donation towards the cost of building this, the country's oldest surviving church (1836). The graveyard's biggest memorial commemorates Tamati Waka Nene, a powerful Ngāpuhi chief from the Hokianga who sided against Hōne Heke in the Northland War. The church's wooden exterior has musket and cannonball holes dating from the 1845 battle.

Maiki
HILL

(Flagstaff Rd) Overlooking Russell, this is the hill where Hōne Heke chopped down the flagpole four times. You can drive up, but the view justifies a climb. Take the track west from the boat ramp along the beach at low tide, or head up Wellington St.

Russell Museum
MUSEUM

(☑ 09-403 7701; www.russellmuseum.org.nz; 2 York St; adult/child $10/free; ⊙ 10am-4pm) This small museum has a well-presented Māori section, a large 1:5 scale model of Captain Cook's *Endeavour,* and a 10-minute video on the town's history.

☞ Tours

Russell Nature Walks
ECOTOUR

(☑ 027 908 2334; www.russellnaturewalks.co.nz; 6080 Russell Whakapara Rd; adult/child from $55/25) *Located in privately owned native forest 2.5km south of Russell, guided day and night tours provide the opportunity to see native birds, including the weka and tui, and insects such as the weta. Glowworms softly illuminate night tours, and after dark there's the opportunity to hear (and very occasionally see) kiwi. Walks last 1½ to two hours.

Russell Mini Tours
BUS

(☑ 09-403 7866; www.russellminitours.com; cnr The Strand & Cass St; adult/child $30/15; ⊙ tours 11am, noon, 1pm & 2pm year-round, also 10am, 3pm & 4pm Oct-Apr) Minibus tour around historic Russell with commentary.

✿✿ Festivals & Events

Russell Birdman
SPORTS

(www.russellbirdman.co.nz; Russell Wharf; ⊙ Jul) Lunatics with various flying contraptions jump off Russell wharf into frigid waters.

Tall Ship Race
SAILING

(www.russellboatingclub.org.nz; ⊙ Jan) Held in Russell on the first Saturday after New Year's Day.

🛏 Sleeping

Wainui
HOSTEL $

(☑ 09-403 8278; www.wainuilodge-russell-nz.com; 92d Te Wahapu Rd; dm/s/d $29/54/68; 🛜) Hard to find but worth the effort, this modern bush retreat with direct beach access has only two rooms that share a pleasant communal space. It's 5km from Russell on the way to the car ferry; you wouldn't want to stay here without your own wheels. Take Te Wahapu Rd and then turn right into Waiaruhe Way.

Russell Top 10
HOLIDAY PARK $$

(☑ 09-403 7826; www.russelltop10.co.nz; 1 James St; sites from $25, unit with/without bathroom from $150/100; @🛜) This leafy and extremely well-maintained holiday park has a small store, good facilities, wonderful hydrangeas, tidy cabins and excellent self-contained units with decks, coffee machines and views over the bay.

Motel Russell
MOTEL $$

(☑ 09-403 7854; www.motelrussell.co.nz; 16 Matauwhi Rd; units from $120; 🛜🌊♨) Sitting amid well-tended gardens, this old-fashioned motel offers a good range of units and a kidney-shaped pool that the kids will love. The studios are a little dark, but you really can't quibble for this price in central Russell.

★ Arcadia Lodge
B&B $$$

(☑ 09-403 7756; www.arcadialodge.co.nz; 10 Florance Ave; r/ste $220/330; ⊙ Sep-Jun; 🛜) The characterful rooms of this 1890 hillside house are kitted out with interesting antiques and fine linen, while the breakfast is probably the best you'll eat in town – complemented by spectacular views from the deck. Grab a book from the library and a drink from the honesty bar, and find a quiet spot in the garden to relax in.

Bellrock Lodge
APARTMENT $$$

(☑ 09-403 7422; www.bellrocklodge.co.nz; 22 Chapel St; unit $350; ❋🛜) Each of Bellrock's four self-contained units has its own ter-

HŌNE HEKE & THE NORTHLAND WAR

Just five years after he had been the first signatory to the Treaty of Waitangi, Ngāpuhi chief Hōne Heke was so disaffected that he planned to chop down Kororāreka's flagstaff, a symbol of British authority, for the fourth time. Governor FitzRoy was determined not to let that happen and garrisoned the town with soldiers and marines.

On 11 March 1845 the Ngāpuhi staged a diversionary siege of the town. It was a great tactical success, with Chief Kawiti attacking from the south and another party attacking from Long Beach. While the troops rushed off to protect the township, Hōne Heke felled the Union Jack on Maiki for the fourth and final time. The British were forced to evacuate to ships lying at anchor. The captain of the HMS *Hazard* was wounded severely in the battle and his replacement ordered the ships' cannons to be fired on the town; most of the buildings were razed. The first of the New Zealand Wars had begun.

In the months that followed, British troops (united with Hokianga-based Ngāpuhi) fought Heke and Kawiti in several battles. During this time the modern *pā* (fortress) was born, effectively the world's first sophisticated system of trench warfare. It's worth stopping at Ruapekapeka Pā (p165), south of Kawakawa, to see how impressive these fortifications were.

Eventually Heke, Kawiti and George Grey (the new governor) made their peace, with no side the clear winner.

race offering awe-inspiring views over the bay. The rooms are pleasantly furnished but it's the outlook rather than the ambience which justifies the price. It's a short walk down to the town centre but you'll certainly work off any dinner calories on the steep climb back.

Duke of Marlborough Hotel
HISTORIC HOTEL **$$$**

(☑09-403 7829; www.theduke.co.nz; 35 The Strand; r $150-280; ☏) Holding NZ's oldest pub licence, the Duke boasts about 'refreshing rascals and reprobates since 1827', although the building has burnt down twice since then. The upstairs accommodation ranges from small, bright rooms in a 1930s extension, to snazzy, spacious doubles facing the water.

Hananui Lodge & Apartments
MOTEL **$$$**

(☑09-403 7875; www.hananui.co.nz; 4 York St; units $155-250; ☏) Choose between sparkling motel-style units in the trim waterside lodge or apartments in the newer block across the road. The pick of the bunch is the upstairs waterfront units with views straight over the beach.

✕ Eating

Hell Hole
CAFE **$**

(☑0221757847;www.facebook.com/hellholecoffee; 19 York St; snacks $6-12; ☺7am-5pm Jan & Feb, 8am-3pm Mar, Apr, Nov & Dec) Bagels, baguettes and croissants all feature with the best coffee in town at this compact spot one block back from the waterfront. Beans are locally roasted, and organic soft drinks and artisan ice blocks all combine to make Hell Hole a hugely popular place.

Newport Chocolates
CAFE **$**

(☑09-403 8888; www.newportchocolates.co.nz; 1 Cass St; chocolates around $3; ☺10am-6pm Tue-Thu, 10am-7.30pm Fri & Sat) The delicious artisan chocolates are all handmade on-site, with flavours including raspberry, lime and chilli, and, our favourite, caramel and sea salt. It's also a top spot for divinely decadent hot chocolate and refreshing frappés.

★ Gables
CONTEMPORARY **$$**

(☑09-403 7670; www.thegablesrestaurant.co.nz; 19 The Strand; mains lunch $22-28, dinner $27-35; ☺noon-3pm & 5.30-10pm Wed-Mon) Serving an imaginative take on Kiwi classics (lamb, beef, seafood), the Gables occupies an 1847 building on the waterfront built using whale vertebrae for foundations. Ask for a table by the windows for maritime views and look forward to top-notch local produce, including oysters and cheese.

Hōne's Garden
PIZZA **$$**

(☑0224663710;www.facebook.com/honesgarden; 10 York St; pizza $18-25; ☺noon-10pm Wed-Mon Nov-Apr) Head out to Hōne's pebbled courtyard for wood-fired pizza (with 11 different varieties), cold craft beer on tap and a thoroughly easy-going Kiwi vibe. An expanded menu features tasty wraps and healthy salads. Antipasto platters are good for groups and indecisive diners.

Drinking & Nightlife

Duke of Marlborough Tavern PUB
(☑09-403 7831; www.duketavern.co.nz; 19 York
St; mains $19-24; ☺noon-11pm Tue-Sat, to 6pm
Sun Mar-Nov, noon-late daily Dec-Feb) Not to be
confused with the historic hotel of the same
name on the waterfront, this cosy locals'
tavern dates only from 1976. Pub quiz on a
Tuesday night is always good fun, and there
are pool tables and well-priced pub meals.

ⓘ Information

Russell Booking & Information Centre (☑09-
403 8020; www.russellinfo.co.nz; Russell
Wharf; ☺8am-5pm, extended hours summer)

ⓘ Getting There & Away

The quickest way to reach Russell by car is
via the car ferry (car/motorcycle/passenger
$13/5.50/1), which runs every 10 minutes from
Opua (5km from Paihia) to Okiato (8km from
Russell), between 6.50am and 10pm. Buy your
tickets on board. If you're travelling from the
south, a scenic alternative is the coastal route
via Russell Rd.

On foot, the easiest way to reach Russell is
on a **passenger ferry** from Paihia (adult/child
return $12/6). They run from 7am to 9pm (until
10pm October to May), generally every 30 minutes, but hourly in the evenings. Buy your tickets
on board or at the **i-SITE** (p162) in Paihia.

Paihia, Waitangi & Haruru

☑09 / POP 2532
The birthplace of NZ (as opposed to Aotearoa), Waitangi inhabits a special but
somewhat complex place in the national
psyche – aptly demonstrated by the mixture
of celebration, commemoration, protest and
apathy that accompanies the nation's birthday (Waitangi Day, 6 February).

It was here that the long-neglected and
much-contested Treaty of Waitangi was first
signed between Māori chiefs and the British
Crown, establishing British sovereignty or
something a bit like it, depending on whether you're reading the English or Māori version of the document. If you're interested in
getting to grips with NZ's history and race
relations, this is the place to start.

Joined to Waitangi by a bridge, Paihia
would be a fairly nondescript coastal town
if it wasn't the main entry point to the Bay
of Islands. If you're not on a tight budget,
catch a ferry to Russell, which is prettier but
much quieter.

⊙ Sights

★**Waitangi Treaty Grounds** HISTORIC SITE
(☑09-402 7437; www.waitangi.org.nz; 1 Tau
Henare Dr, Waitangi; adult/child $50/free; ☺9am-
5pm) 🅿 Occupying a headland draped in
lawns and bush, this is NZ's most significant historic site. Here, on 6 February 1840,
after much discussion, the first 43 Māori
chiefs signed the Treaty of Waitangi with
the British Crown; eventually, over 500
chiefs would sign it. Admission incorporates a guided tour and spirited cultural
performance, and entry to the **Museum
of Waitangi**, the **Whare Rūnanga** (carved
meeting house) and the historic **Treaty House**.

Opened in 2016, **Te Kōngahu Museum
of Waitangi** is a modern and comprehensive showcase of the role of the treaty in the
past, present and future of Aotearoa New
Zealand. It provides a warts-and-all look at
the early interactions between Māori and
Europeans, the events leading up to the
treaty's signing, the long litany of treaty
breaches by the Crown, the wars and land
confiscations that followed, and the protest
movement that led to the current process of
redress for historic injustices. Many *taonga*
(treasures) associated with Waitangi were
previously scattered around NZ, and this
excellent museum is now a repository for a
number of key historical items. One room
is devoted to facsimiles of all the key documents, while another screens a fascinating
short film dramatising the events of the initial treaty signing.

The **Treaty House** was shipped over as
a kit-set from Australia and erected in 1834
as the four-room home of the official British
Resident James Busby. It's now preserved
as a memorial and museum containing displays about the house and the people who
lived here. Just across the lawn, the magnificently detailed **Whare Rūnanga** was
completed in 1940 to mark the centenary of
the treaty. The fine carvings represent the
major Māori tribes. It's here that the cultural performances take place, starting with a
haka pōwhiri (challenge and welcome) and
then heading inside for *waiata* (songs) and
spine-tingling *haka* (war dances).

Near the cove is the 35m, 6-tonne *waka
taua* (war canoe) **Ngātokimatawhaorua**,
also built for the centenary. A photographic exhibit details how it was fashioned from
gigantic kauri logs. There's also an excellent
gift shop selling Māori art and design, with
a carving studio attached.

Paihia

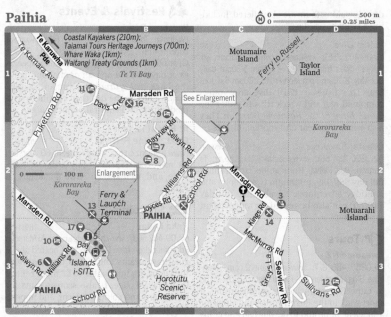

Paihia

⊙ Sights
1 St Paul's Anglican Church	C2

✪ Activities, Courses & Tours
2 Awesome NZ	B3
3 Bay Beach Hire	C2
4 Explore NZ	A3
5 Fullers Great Sights	A3
6 Paihia Dive	A3

🛏 Sleeping
7 Abri Apartments	B2
8 Allegra House	B2
9 Breakwater Motel	B1
10 Haka Lodge	A3
11 Seabeds	A1
12 Tarlton's Lodge	D3

✚ Eating
13 Charlotte's Kitchen	A2
14 El Cafe	C2
15 Legends	B2
16 Provenir	B1

⊙ Drinking & Nightlife
17 Alongside	A3
Kings Road Bar & Brasserie	(see 14)

Tours leave on the hour from 10am to 3pm. Admission is discounted to $25 for NZ residents upon presentation of a passport or driver's licence.

St Paul's Anglican Church　CHURCH
(36 Marsden Rd, Paihia) The characterful St Paul's was constructed of Kawakawa stone in 1925, and stands on the site of the original mission church, a simple *raupo* (bulrush) hut erected in 1823. Look for the native birds in the stained glass above the altar – the kotare (kingfisher) represents Jesus (the king plus 'fisher of men'), while the tui (parson bird) and kereru (wood pigeon) portray the personalities of the Williams brothers (one scholarly, one forceful), who set up the mission station here.

🏃 Activities

Bay Beach Hire　KAYAKING, BOATING
(☎ 09-402 6078; www.baybeachhire.co.nz; Marsden Rd, Paihia; ☺ 9am-5pm) Hires kayaks (from $15 per hour), sailing catamarans ($50 first hour, $40 per additional), mountain bikes ($75 per day), boogie boards ($10/25 per hour/day), stand-up paddle boards ($25 per hour), fishing rods (from $10 per day), wetsuits and snorkelling gear (both $20 per

day). Kayaking tours are also offered, including a twilight paddle ($69).

Paihia Dive
DIVING

(☑09-402 7551; www.divenz.com; 7 Williams Rd, Paihia; dives from $249; ☺7.45am-5.30pm daily Oct-May, 8.30am-5pm Mon-Fri, to 1.30pm Sat Jun-Sep) This five-star PADI dive crew offers combined reef and wreck trips to either the *Canterbury* or the *Rainbow Warrior*. They also sell fishing gear and snorkelling sets.

Coastal Kayakers
KAYAKING

(☑0800 334 661; www.coastalkayakers.co.nz; Te Karuwha Pde, Paihia) Runs guided tours (half/full day $89/139, minimum two people) and multiday adventures. Kayaks (half/full day $40/60) can also be rented for independent exploration.

👉 Tours

Awesome NZ
BUS

(☑0800 486 877; www.awesomenz.com; Maritime Bldg, Marsden Rd, Paihia; tour $130) Trips to Cape Reinga including sandboarding, a short walk in the Puketi Forest and stops for a snack at Taipa and to devour fish and chips at Mangonui.

Explore NZ
CRUISE

(☑09-402 8234; www.exploregroup.co.nz; cnr Marsden & Williams Rds, Paihia) 🥇 Explore's four-hour Discover the Bay cruise (adult/child $149/90 including barbecue lunch) heads to the Hole in the Rock and stops at Urupukapuka Island.

Fullers Great Sights
CRUISE

(☑09-402 7421; www.dolphincruises.co.nz; Maritime Bldg, Marsden Rd, Paihia) 🥇 The four-hour Hole in the Rock Cruise (adult/child $107/54) heads out to the famous sea arch and stops at Urupukapuka Island on the way back. The full-day Cream Trip (adult/child $129/65, November to April only) follows the mail route around the bay. Boats stop at Russell wharf for pick-ups on all trips.

Taiamai Tours Heritage Journeys
CULTURAL, CANOEING

(☑09-405 9990; www.taiamaitours.co.nz; 2½hr tour $135; ☺departs 9am Tue, Thu, Sat & Sun Oct-Apr) 🥇 Paddle a traditional 12m carved *waka* (canoe) from the Waitangi bridge to the Haruru Falls. The Ngāpuhi hosts wear traditional garb, and perform the proper *karakia* (incantations) and share stories. The price includes admission to the Waitangi Treaty Grounds (p158).

🎊 Festivals & Events

Waitangi Day
CULTURAL

(Waitangi Treaty Grounds; ☺6 Feb) Various ceremonial events at Waitangi Treaty Grounds on 6 February, including speeches, a naval salute and an annual outing for the huge *waka taua* (war canoe) Ngātokimatawhaorua. The day then continues with food, music and cultural performances.

It! Bay of Islands Food & Wine Festival
FOOD & DRINK

(www.paihianz.co.nz; Village Green, 60 Marsden Rd; adult/child $55/15; ☺Oct) A day of food, wine and well-known Kiwi musicians in Paihia.

🛏 Sleeping

Haka Lodge
HOSTEL $

(☑09-402 5637; www.hakalodge.com; 76 Marsden Rd, Paihia; dm/r from $29/99; 🛜) Located above good restaurants and across the road from the wharf, it's impossible to be more central than Haka Lodge. It also scores points for its modern and colourful decor, and appealing shared spaces with huge flat-screen TVs and unlimited wi-fi access. Accommodation ranges from excellent dorms to private rooms with en suites and TVs.

Seabeds
HOSTEL $

(☑09-402 5567; www.seabeds.co.nz; 46 Davis Cres, Paihia; dm/s/d $28/69/89; 🛜) Offering comfortable, friendly, stylish budget digs in a converted motel, Seabeds is one of Paihia's best hostels. Little design touches give it a stylish ambience, and it's in a quieter location than most of Paihia's more social hostels along Kings Rd. Best of all, all of the rooms have their own bathrooms.

Beachside Holiday Park
HOLIDAY PARK $

(☑09-402 7678; www.beachsideholiday.co.nz; 1290 Paihia Rd (SH11); sites from $20, units with/without bathroom from $100/75; 🛜) Wake up at the water's edge at this small, sheltered camping ground, south of Paihia township. The angular lemon cabins have 1970s charm, and there are kayaks for hire.

Abri Apartments
APARTMENT $$

(☑09-402 8003; www.abriapartments.co.nz; 10-12 Bayview Rd, Paihia; apt $165-185; 🛜) Choose between one of two free-standing pole houses, set within subtropical gardens, or a spacious one-bedroom suite under the owners' home. All three offer wonderful bay views and kitchen facilities, and there's a free guest laundry, too.

Baystay B&B
B&B $$

(☑09-402 7511; www.baystay.co.nz; 93a Yorke Rd, Haruru; r $165-185; ❄ @ ☎) Enjoy valley views from the spa pool of this slick, gay-friendly establishment. Yorke Rd is off Puketona Rd, just before the falls. Minimum stay of two nights; no children under 12 years.

Breakwater Motel
MOTEL $$

(☑09-402 7558; www.breakwatermotel.co.nz; 1 Bayview Rd, Paihia; unit $145-195; ❄ ☎) Located by the little headland that breaks up the Paihia strip, this older motel has been renovated within an inch of its life. The units are tidy and modern, and each has its own kitchen. Best of all are the Waterfront Suites, with balconies and patios facing the sea.

Allegra House
B&B $$$

(☑09-402 7932; www.allegra.co.nz; 39 Bayview Rd, Paihia; r $260-290, apt $305; ❄ ☎) Offering quite astonishing views of the bay from an eyrie high above the township, Allegra has three handsome B&B rooms and a spacious self-contained apartment. Best of all is the top room, with its large rooftop terrace. If you feel the need for a singalong, there's a guest lounge with a piano.

Tarlton's Lodge
B&B $$$

(☑09-402 6711; www.tarltonslodge.co.nz; 11 Sullivans Rd, Paihia; r $320-350; ☎) Striking architecture combines with modern decor in this hilltop B&B with expansive bay views. All three suites have their own outdoor spa, perfect for a romantic stay. Look forward to excellent breakfasts.

✖ Eating

El Cafe
LATIN AMERICAN $

(☑09-402 7637; www.facebook.com/elcafepaihia; 2 Kings Rd, Paihia; mains $11-15; ⊙8am-4pm; ☎) This excellent Chilean-owned cafe has the best coffee in town and terrific breakfast burritos, tacos and baked-egg dishes, such as spicy *huevos rancheros*. The Cuban pulled-pork sandwich is truly a wonderful thing. The fruit smoothies are also great on a warm Bay of Islands day.

Legends
PUB FOOD $$

(☑09-402 6037; www.kravecateringpaihia.co.nz; 1 Joyces Rd, Paihia; mains $16-27; ⊙5-10pm) When locals are after a substantial, old-fashioned, good-value meal (think burgers, fish and chips, fried seafood platters and a roast of the day), they head to this no-nonsense restaurant at the Paihia Ex-Servicemen's Club. Drinks can be ordered separately from the

bar, but mind that you return your plates and glasses before you leave to avoid a telling off.

Charlotte's Kitchen
CONTEMPORARY $$

(☑09-402 8296; www.charlotteskitchen.co.nz; Paihia Wharf, 69 Marsden Rd, Paihia; mains lunch $16-27, dinner $20-35; ⊙11.30am-late Mon-Fri, 8am-late Sat & Sun) Named after an escaped Australian convict who was NZ's first white female settler, this hip restaurant/bar occupies a cheeky perch on the main pier. Bits of Kiwiana decorate the walls, while the menu takes a swashbuckling journey around the world, including steamed pork buns, quesadillas, Cubano sandwiches and a particularly delicious Asian-style broth with pork dumplings.

Whare Waka
CAFE $$

(☑09-402 7437; www.waitangi.org.nz; Waitangi Treaty Grounds, 1 Tau Henare Dr, Waitangi; mains $13-19; ⊙8am-4pm) Located beside a pond studded with ducks, backed by bush and overlooking the Treaty Grounds (p158), the Whare Waka (Boathouse) is a top spot for good cafe fare during the day, and to return to for a *hāngi* (earth-oven-cooked) dinner and concert on Tuesday, Thursday and Sunday evenings from December to March.

★ Provenir
CONTEMPORARY $$$

(☑09-402 0111; www.paihiabeach.co.nz; Paihia Beach Resort, 130 Marsden Rd, Paihia; mains $30-40; ⊙8-10am & 6pm-late) A concise seasonal menu of main dishes showcases regional NZ produce and local seafood (including plump oysters from nearby Orongo Bay), underpinned by subtle Asian influences and one of Northland's best wine lists. Desserts are extraordinarily creative and well worth leaving room for.

❦ Drinking & Nightlife

Kings Road Bar & Brasserie
BAR

(☑09-402 6080; 14 Kings Rd, Paihia; ⊙11.30am-midnight; ☎) Slink into this low-lit bar for a cosy beverage on one of the couches or a crack at the free pool table.

Alongside
BAR

(☑09-402 6220; www.alongside35.co.nz; 69 Marsden Rd, Paihia; ⊙8am-10pm) Quite possibly the biggest deck in all of Northland extends over the water, and a versatile approach to entertaining begins with coffee and bagels for breakfast before the inevitable transformation of Alongside into a very enjoyable bar. There are bar snacks and meals on offer, and lots of comfy lounges ready for conversations fuelled by cocktails or cold beer.

ⓘ Information

Bay of Islands i-SITE (☎09-402 7345; www. northlandnz.com; 69 Marsden Rd, Paihia; ⊗8am-5pm Mar-Dec, to 7pm Jan & Feb) Information and bookings.

ⓘ Getting There & Away

All **buses** (Maritime Building, Paihia) serving Paihia stop at the Maritime Building by the wharf.

InterCity (p142) has three or four coaches a day to and from Auckland (from $29, four hours), Waipu (from $25, 1¾ hours), Whangarei (from $12, 1¼ hours), Kawakawa (from $15, 20 minutes) and Kerikeri (from $15, 20 minutes).

Mana Bus (p142), in association with Naked Bus, has two daily coaches to and from Auckland ($34, four hours), Warkworth ($27, three hours), Waipu ($14, two hours), Whangarei ($12, 1¼ hours) and Kawakawa (from $7, 20 minutes).

Ferries (Paihia Wharf) depart regularly for Russell, and there are seasonal services to Urupukapuka Island.

ⓘ Getting Around

For bike rental, visit Bay Beach Hire (p159).

Urupukapuka Island

The largest of the bay's islands, Urupukapuka is a tranquil place criss-crossed with walking trails and surrounded by aquamarine waters. Native birds are plentiful thanks to a conservation initiative that has rendered this and all of the neighbouring islands predator free; check that there aren't any rats, mice or ants stowing away on your boat or in your gear before leaving the mainland.

🛏 Sleeping

DOC Campsites   CAMPGROUND $
(www.doc.govt.nz; sites per adult/child $13/6.50) There are DOC campsites at Cable, Sunset and Urupukapuka Bays. They have water supplies, cold showers (except Sunset Bay) and composting toilets; bring food, a stove and fuel. Bookings are required year-round.

ⓘ Getting There & Away

Explore NZ (p160) runs ferries to Otehei Bay (adult/child $35/20) from Paihia and Russell; they're supposedly year-round, although they can be irregular in winter. Most of the scheduled bay cruises moor at Otehei Bay for a little island time.

Bay of Islands Kayaking (p152) can arrange kayaking trips and camping gear for the island. Note that it does not rent to solo kayakers, so you'll need to find a friend.

Kerikeri

☎09 / POP 6500

Kerikeri means 'dig dig', which is apt, as lots of digging goes on around the area's fertile farmland. Famous for its oranges, Kerikeri also produces kiwifruit, vegetables and wine. If you're looking for some back-breaking, poorly paid work that the locals aren't keen to do, your working holiday starts here.

A snapshot of early Māori and British interaction is offered by a cluster of historic sites centred on the picturesque river basin. In 1819 the powerful Ngāpuhi chief Hongi Hika allowed Reverend Samuel Marsden to start a mission under the shadow of his Kororipo Pā (p163). There's an ongoing campaign to have the area recognised as a Unesco World Heritage Site.

MĀORI NZ: BAY OF ISLANDS & NORTHLAND

Known to Māori as Te Tai Tokerau, this region has a long and proud Māori history and today has one of the country's highest percentages of Māori people. Along with East Cape, it's a place where you might hear Māori being spoken. In mythology the region is known as the tail of the fish of Māui.

Māori sites of particular significance include Cape Reinga (p171), the Waitangi Treaty Grounds (p158), Ruapekapeka Pā (p165) and, in the Waipoua Forest, Tāne Mahuta (p177).

Māori cultural experiences are offered by many local operators, including Footprints Waipoua (p176), Ahikaa Adventures (p172), Sand Safaris (p171) and **Rewa's Village** (☎09-407 6454; www.rewasvillage.co.nz; 1 Landing Rd; adult/child $10/5; ⊗10am-4pm). Many businesses catering to travellers are owned or run by Māori individuals or *hapū* (subtribal) groups.

○ Sights

★ Kerikeri Mission Station
HISTORIC BUILDING

(☑09-407 9236; www.historic.org.nz; 246 Kerikeri Rd; museum $8, house tour $8, combined $10; ☺10am-4pm) Two of the nation's most significant buildings nestle side by side on the banks of Kerikeri Basin. Start at the **Stone Store**, NZ's oldest stone building (1836). Upstairs there's an interesting little museum, while downstairs the shop sells Kiwiana gifts as well as the type of goods that used to be stocked here in the 19th century. Tours of neighbouring **Kemp House** depart from here. Built by the missionaries in 1822, this humble yet pretty wooden Georgian-style house is NZ's oldest building.

Kororipo Pā
HISTORIC SITE

(Kerikeri Rd) FREE Just up the hill from Kerikeri Mission Station is a marked historical walk that leads to the site of Hongi Hika's *pā* (fortress) and village. Little remains aside from the terracing that once supported wooden palisades. Huge war parties once departed from here, terrorising much of the North Island and slaughtering thousands during the Musket Wars. The role of missionaries in arming Ngāpuhi remains controversial. The walk emerges near the cute wooden St James Anglican Church (1878).

Aroha Island
WILDLIFE RESERVE

(☑09-407 5243; www.arohaisland.co.nz; 177 Rangitane Rd; ☺9.30am-5.30pm) FREE Reached via a permanent causeway through the mangroves, this 12-hectare island provides a haven for the North Island brown kiwi and other native birds, as well as a pleasant picnic spot for their nonfeathered admirers. It has a visitor centre, kayaks for rent (from $22), and you can also arrange after-dark walks to spy kiwi in the wild (adult/child $40/15) can also be arranged. You've got around a 50% chance of seeing a kiwi, and booking ahead is essential.

🏃 Activities

Kerikeri River Track
WALKING

Starting from Kerikeri Basin, this 3.5km-long track leads through beautiful native bush past **Wharepuke Falls** and the **Fairy Pools** to the **Rainbow Falls**, where even on dim days the 27m drop conjures dancing rainbows. Alternatively, you can reach Rainbow Falls from Rainbow Falls Rd.

Northland Paddleboarding
WATER SPORTS

(☑027 777 1035; www.northlandpaddleboarding.co.nz; beginner lessons per hour $60) Lessons and guided paddles departing from various locations around Kerikeri.

WORTH A TRIP

Te Waimate Mission (☑09-405 9734; www.tewaimatemission.co.nz; 344 Te Ahu Ahu Rd, Waimate North; adult/child $10/5; ☺10am-5pm Fri-Tue Nov-Apr, to 4pm Sat-Mon May-Oct) Set in verdant farmland 18km southwest of Kerikeri, this pretty little cottage holds several claims to fame. It's NZ's second-oldest house (built in 1831) and the site of the country's first European-style farm. Many of the exotic trees surrounding it are amongst the oldest of their kind in the country, and Charles Darwin stayed here in 1835. Inside, the story of the mission station and its inhabitants is outlined in displays in rooms dotted with items of original furniture.

🛏 Sleeping

Aroha Island
CAMPGROUND $

(☑09-407 5243; www.arohaisland.co.nz; 177 Rangitane Rd; sites/units from $20/125) 🖉 Kip among the kiwi on the eco island of love *(aroha)*. There's a wide range of reasonably priced options, from the peaceful campsites with basic facilities by the shelly beach, to a whole house. The entire island, indoors and out, is nonsmoking.

Wharepuke Subtropical Accommodation
CABIN $$

(☑09-407 8933; www.accommodation-bay-of-islands.co.nz; 190 Kerikeri Rd; cabins $180; 🛜) 🖉 Best known for its food and lush gardens, Wharepuke also rents five self-contained one-bedroom cottages hidden among the palms. They have the prefabricated look of holiday-park cabins, but are a step up in terms of fixtures and space.

Kauri Park
MOTEL $$

(☑09-407 7629; www.kauripark.co.nz; 512 Kerikeri Rd; units from $130; 🛜🌊) Hidden behind tall trees on the approach to Kerikeri, this well-priced motel has a mixture of units of varying layouts. The premium suites are extremely comfortable, but all options are spacious and stylishly furnished.

Pagoda Lodge
LODGE, CAMPGROUND $$

(☑09-407 8617; www.pagoda.co.nz; 81 Pa Rd; sites/safari tents/caravans from $40/120/130, units with/without bathroom from $145/110; ☺Nov-Mar; 🛜) Built in the 1930s by an oddball Scotsman with an Asian fetish, this lodge features

Kerikeri

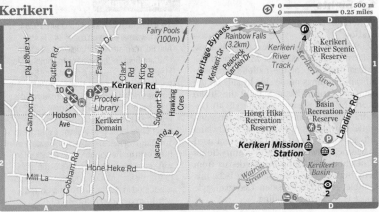

Kerikeri

◉ Top Sights
1 Kerikeri Mission Station D2

◉ Sights
2 Kororipo Pā D2
3 Rewa's Village D2
4 Wharepuke Falls D1

⊕ Activities, Courses & Tours
5 Kerikeri River Track D2

▭ Sleeping
6 Pagoda Lodge D2
7 Wharepuke Subtropical
   Accommodation C1

✕ Eating
8 Bay of Islands Farmers Market A1
9 Cafe Jerusalem B1
   Village Cafe .... (see 9)
10 Ziezo A1

◒ Drinking & Nightlife
11 La Taza Del Diablo A1

pagoda-shaped roofs grafted onto wooden cottages. The property descends to the river and is dotted with Buddhas, gypsy caravans, and safari tents with proper beds, or you can pitch your own. Take Cobham Rd, turn left into Kerikeri Inlet Rd, then left into Pa Rd.

Relax a Lodge HOMESTAY $$
(☎09-407 6989; www.relaxalodge.co.nz; 1574 Springbank Rd (SH10); s/d $55/70, cottages $120-145; ☎) Located in an orange grove, 4km out of town, this quiet rural retreat has tidy backpacker rooms in the main house (bathrooms are shared) and attractive self-contained cottages, sleeping two to four people, dotted around the property.

Moon Gate Villa B&B $$$
(☎09-929 5921; www.moongatevilla.com; 462 Kerikeri Rd; ste $339-369, cottage $299; ☎⛱) A stream-like water feature flows through the centre of this modern house, set amid tropical foliage on the approach to Kerikeri. The larger of the two suites has a huge spa bath, while the other has an extra single room attached for parties of three. There's also a compact self-contained cottage in the garden and a solar-powered swimming pool.

✕ Eating

Bay of Islands Farmers Market MARKET $
(www.bayofislandsfarmersmarket.co.nz; Hobson Ave; ⊙8.30am-noon Sun) On a Sunday morning the car park behind the post office is lined with tents selling everything from gourmet sausages to oversized carrots. Grab a coffee and graze on the free samples.

★ Rusty Tractor CAFE $$
(☎09-407 3322; www.rustytractorcafe.co.nz; 582 Kerikeri Rd; mains breakfast $17-20, lunch $20-26; ⊙8am-4pm; ☎▥) As decadent breakfasts go, Rusty Tractor's doughnuts with crème fraiche and berries take some beating. There are healthier options, too, and the coffee's up with the best in Kerikeri. Otherwise, treat yourself to a glass of wine while the kids play on the rocketship slide on the back lawn.

Ziezo BISTRO $$
(☎09-407 9511; 55 Kerikeri Rd; mains $20-29; ⊙5pm-late Thu-Sun) This stylish bistro certainly brightens up Kerikeri's retail-focused main street, and the food is equally interesting.

Ziezo is the Dutch equivalent of *voila* ('here it is!') and, alongside classic bistro dishes, a subtle Netherlander influence reveals itself in beef rendang (the classic curry from former colony Indonesia) and Dutch apple pie.

Marsden Estate CONTEMPORARY $$
(☑ 09-407 9398; www.marsdenestate.co.nz; 56 Wiroa Rd; mains breakfast $16-18, lunch $28-38; ☺ 10am-4pm; ⊕) The interior of this winery restaurant is large and featureless so opt for the covered terrace at the rear, which has wonderful views over the vines and a pretty pond. Cooked breakfasts give way to sophisticated lunches that match prime local produce with flavours from all over the world.

Cafe Jerusalem ISRAELI $$
(☑ 09-407 1001; www.cafejerusalem.co.nz; Village Mall, 85 Kerikeri Rd; mains $17-20; ☺ 10am-late Mon-Sat) Northland's best falafels, lamb shawarma (kebab) and meze platters, all served with a smile and a social vibe. Most mains come with rice, pitta bread, tabouli and a salad. Try the *shakshuka* (baked eggs in a spicy tomato sauce) for a hearty brunch.

Village Cafe CAFE $$
(☑ 09-4074062; www.facebook.com/thevillagecafe kerikeri; Village Mall, 85 Kerikeri Rd; mains $12-20; ☺ 8am-4pm Mon-Fri, 8.30am-2pm Sat & Sun) This cute little cafe is popular with locals for good coffee, freshly prepared counter food, and a relaxed menu of brunch and lunch dishes. Grab a table outside in the Northland sunshine, and order the hearty potato hash.

Ake Ake BRITISH, FRENCH $$$
(☑ 09-407 8230; www.akeakevineyard.co.nz; 165 Waimate North Rd; mains $30-36; ☺ noon-3pm & 6-9pm Mon-Sat, noon-3pm Sun, tastings 10am-4.30pm; ⊕) ✆ At this upmarket winery restaurant, the rural setting is complemented by hearty but sophisticated country fare such as lamb shanks, wild game pie, confit duck and steak. The Sunday roasts are legendary. After lunch, work off some of the calories on the 1km self-guided trail through the vineyard. Free overnight parking is available for customers with self-contained vehicles.

🍷 Drinking & Nightlife

La Taza Del Diablo BAR
(☑ 09-407 3912; www.facebook.com/eltazadel diablo; 3 Homestead Rd; ☺ 11.30am-late Wed-Sun; 📶) This Mexican-style bar is about as energetic and raffish as buttoned-down Kerikeri gets with a decent selection of tequila, Mexican beers, and, just maybe, Northland's best margaritas. Tacos, enchiladas and chimi-

changas all feature on the bar snacks menu, and occasional live gigs sometimes raise the roof in this genteel town.

ℹ Information

Procter Library (6 Cobham Rd; ☺ 8am-5pm Mon-Fri, 9am-2pm Sat; 📶) Tourist brochures and free internet access.

ℹ Getting There & Away

AIR
Bay of Islands (Kerikeri) Airport (p154) is 8km southwest of town. Air New Zealand flies from Auckland to Kerikeri. **Super Shuttle** (p154) provides shuttles between Kerikeri Airport and Bay of Islands destinations such as Kerikeri ($12) and Paihia ($27).

BUS
InterCity (p142) buses leave from a stop at 9 Cobham Rd, opposite the library. Destinations include Auckland (from $29, 4½ hours, three daily), Whangarei (from $12, 1¾ hours, daily), Paihia (from $15, 20 minutes, three daily), Mangonui ($28, one hour, daily) and Kaitaia ($37, 1¾ hours, daily).

Hokianga Link (☑ 021 405 872; www.buslink.co.nz) offers a weekly minibus service between Kerikeri and Omapere, which expands to twice weekly in summer.

Kawakawa
☑ 09 / POP 1220
Kawakawa would be just another ordinary, economically challenged Northland town if it weren't for a couple of extraordinary features in its modest town centre: an architecturally significant public toilet and a steam train that runs along the main street. There are also a pair of important Māori sites hidden within the surrounding farmland that are fascinating in their own right and well worth a detour.

◎ Sights

Ruapekapeka Pā HISTORIC SITE
(www.ruapekapeka.co.nz; Ruapekapeka Rd) FREE
For 10 days in January 1846, 1600 British troops bombarded 500 Māori warriors hunkered down in a *pā* (fortress) composed of trenches, tunnels and wooden palisades on this lonely hillside. Ruapekapeka translates as 'the bat's nest' but by the time the British broke through, the bats had already flown, leaving them (not for the first time) with an empty *pā*. This stalemate was to be the final battle of the Northland War; following this the parties made peace.

Kawiti Caves CAVE
(☎09-404 0583; www.kawiticaves.co.nz; 49 Waiomio Rd; adult/child $20/10; ☺8.30am-4pm) Explore these glowworm-illuminated limestone caverns on a 30-minute subterranean tour led by direct descendants of Ngāti Hine chief Kawiti, who fought the British at Ruapekapeka Pā during the first of the New Zealand wars.

Kawakawa Public Toilets NOTABLE BUILDING
(58 Gillies St) It's rare that public toilets are a town's claim to fame but Kawakawa's were designed by Austrian-born artist and eco-architect Friedensreich Hundertwasser, who lived near Kawakawa in an isolated house without electricity from 1973 until his death in 2000. The most photographed toilets in NZ are typical Hundertwasser – lots of organic, wavy lines decorated with ceramic mosaics and brightly coloured bottles, and with grass and plants on the roof.

Other examples of his work can be seen in Vienna and Osaka.

🏃 Activities

Bay of Islands Vintage Railway RAIL
(☎ 09-404 0684; www.bayofislandsvintagerailway.org.nz; Gilies St; adult/child $20/5; ☺10.45am, noon, 1.15pm, 2.30pm Fri-Sun, daily school holidays) Take a 50-minute spin down the main street of Kawakawa to Taumarere and back in a carriage pulled by either Gabriel the steam engine or a vintage diesel engine.

❶ Getting There & Away

InterCity (p142) coaches stop at Kawakawa junction, with three or four services daily to and from Auckland (from $37, 3¾ hours), Waipu (from $28, 1½ hours), Whangarei (from $14, 50 minutes), Paihia (from $15, 20 minutes) and Kerikeri (from $17, 50 minutes).

Mana Bus (p142), in association with Naked Bus, has two daily coaches to and from Auckland ($34, four hours), Warkworth ($27, 2¾ hours), Waipu ($14, 1¾ hours), Whangarei ($12, one hour) and Paihia (from $7, 20 minutes).

ABC Shuttles & Tours (p154) runs tours from Paihia to Kawakawa and the caves ($40 not including cave admission).

THE FAR NORTH

Here's your chance to get off the beaten track, even if that sometimes means onto unsealed roads. The far-flung Far North always plays second fiddle to the Bay of Islands for attention and funding, yet the subtropical tip of the North Island has more breathtaking coastline per square kilometre than anywhere apart from the offshore islands. While the 'winterless north' may be a popular misnomer, summers here are long and leisurely. Note that parts of the Far North are noticeably economically depressed and in places could best be described as gritty.

❶ Getting There & Away

Barrier Air (☎09-275 9120; www.barrierair.kiwi; Kaitaia Airport) flies between Auckland and Kaitaia.

InterCity (p142) operates a daily coach between Kerikeri and Kaitaia, stopping in all the main Doubtless Bay settlements along the way.

Far North Link (☎ 09-408 1092; www.buslink.co.nz) has limited weekday bus services linking Kaitaia to Mangonui, Ahipara and Pukenui.

ARTISANS OF KERIKERI

You'd be forgiven for thinking that everyone in Kerikeri is involved in some small-scale artisanal enterprise, given the bombardment of craft shops on the way into town. A little further afield, a handful of vineyards are doing their best to stake Northland's claim as a wine region. The little-known red grape chambourcin has proved particularly suited to the region's subtropical humidity, along with pinotage and syrah.

Look out for the *Art & Craft Trail* and *Wine Trail* brochures. Here are our tasty recommendations:

Ake Ake (p165) Wine tastings (usually $8) are free with lunch or a purchase of wine.

Cottle Hill (☎09-407 5203; www.cottlehill.co.nz; 28 Cottle Hill Dr; tastings $5, free with purchase; ☺10am-5pm daily Nov-Mar, Wed-Sun Apr-Oct) Wine, port, grappa and liquors.

Get Fudged & Keriblue Ceramics (☎09-407 1111; www.keriblueceramics.co.nz; 1691 SH10; ☺9am-5pm) An unusual pairing of ceramics and big, decadent slabs of fudge.

Makana Confections (☎09-407 6800; www.makana.co.nz; 504 Kerikeri Rd; ☺9am-5.30pm) Artisan chocolate factory with a cafe attached.

Marsden Estate (p165) Wine tastings and lunch on the terrace.

PUKETI & OMAHUTA FORESTS

Inland from Kerikeri, the Puketi and Omahuta Forests form a continuous expanse of native rainforest. Logging in Puketi was stopped in 1951 to protect not only the remaining kauri but also the endangered kokako bird. Keep an eye out for this rare charmer (grey with a blue wattle) on your wanders.

The forests are reached by several entrances and contain a network of walking tracks varying in length from 15 minutes (the wheelchair-accessible Manginangina Kauri Walk) to two days (the challenging Waipapa River Track); see the DOC website (www.doc.govt. nz) for other walks.

Sleeping is restricted to a **DOC campsite** (☑ 09-407 0300; www.doc.govt.nz; Waiare Rd; sites per adult/child $8/4) 🌿 and 18-bunk hut, and also B&B accommodation with Adventure Puketi. Most travellers visit from Paihia or Kerikeri.

Adventure Puketi (☑ 09-401 9095; www.forestwalks.com; 476 Puketi Rd; tours $65-155) 🌿 leads guided ecowalks through the forest, including night-time tours to seek out the nocturnal wildlife. It also offers very comfortable B&B accommodation on the edge of the forest. Check the website for packages incorporating tours and accommodation.

If you don't have your own vehicle, tour buses are the best option for reaching Cape Reinga.

Matauri & Tauranga Bays

It's a short detour from SH10, but the exceptionally scenic loop route leading inland to these awesome beaches is a world away from the glitzy face presented to tourists in the Bay of Islands.

Matauri Bay is a long, sandy surf beach, 18km off SH10, with the 17 **Cavalli Islands** scattered offshore. On top of the headland above the park is a monument to the *Rainbow Warrior;* the Greenpeace ship's underwater resting place among the nearby-islands is a popular dive site.

Back on the main road, the route heads west, passing through pleasant **Te Ngaere** village and a succession of little bays before the turn-off to **Tauranga Bay**, a smaller beach where the sand is a peachy pink colour.

🏃 Activities

Northland Sea Kayaking   KAYAKING
(☑ 09-405 0381; www.northlandseakayaking.co.nz; half-/full-day tours $90/115) Down a private road leading from Tauranga Bay, Northland Sea Kayaking leads kayak explorations of this magical coastline of coves, sea caves and islands. Accommodation is available in conjunction with tours for $35 extra per person.

🛏 Sleeping

Matauri Bay Holiday Park   HOLIDAY PARK $
(☑ 09-405 0525; www.matauribayholidaypark. co.nz; Matauri Bay Rd; sites/units from $20/60) Taking up the north end of the beach, this

holiday park has only a handful of cabins but plenty of space to pitch a tent or park a campervan. There's also a shop selling groceries, booze and petrol.

ⓘ Getting There & Away

There is no public transport to these areas.

Whangaroa Harbour

Just around the headland from Tauranga Bay is the narrow entrance to Whangaroa Harbour. The small fishing village of **Whangaroa** is 6km from SH10 and calls itself the 'Marlin Capital of NZ'.

There are plenty of charter boats for game-fishing (December to April); prices start at around $1200 a day. If you're planning to hook a monster, insist on it being released once caught – striped marlin and swordfish are among NZ's least-sustainable fishing options.

On the other side of the harbour's north head is **Taupo Bay**, a surf beach that attracts a loyal Kiwi contingent in summer. On easterly swells, there are quality right-handers to surf at the southern end of the bay, by the river mouth. It's reached by an 11km road signposted from SH10.

🏃 Activities

An excellent 20-minute hike starts from the car park at the end of Old Hospital Rd and goes up **St Paul's Rock** (213m), which dominates Whangaroa village. At the top you have to use a wire cable to pull yourself up, but the views make it worth the effort.

The **Wairakau Stream Track**, heading north to Pekapeka Bay, begins near the church hall on Campbell Rd in Totara North on the other side of the bay. It's an extremely beautiful, undeveloped stretch and you can cool off in swimming holes along the way. The two-hour (5.6km) hike passes through forest, an abandoned farm and around a steep-walled estuary before arriving at DOC's **Lane Cove Hut** (⏰09-407 0300; www. doc.govt.nz; adult/child $15/7.50) 🖉.

🛏️ Sleeping & Eating

★**Kahoe Farms Hostel**   HOSTEL $
(⏰09-405 1804; www.kahoefarms.co.nz; 1266 SH10; dm $32, r with/without bathroom from $116/86; 🛜) On SH10, 10km north of the turn-off to Whangaroa, this hostel has a deservedly great reputation – for its comfortable accommodation, bucolic setting and home-cooked Italian food, but mostly for its welcoming owners. The backpackers' cottage is great, but slightly up the hill there's an even more impressive villa with excellent-value en-suite rooms.

Marlin   PUB FOOD $$
(⏰09-405 0347; www.marlinhotel.co.nz; 578 Whangaroa Rd; mains $14-28; ⏰noon-1am Sun, 9am-1am Mon-Sat) A friendly local pub with good honest tucker served from the attached cafe. Inside there are a few impressive wall-mounted game fish that definitely didn't get away.

ℹ️ Information

Boyd Gallery (⏰09-405 0230; www.whangaroa. co.nz; 537 Whangaroa Rd; ⏰8am-7pm) General store and tourist information office.

ℹ️ Getting There & Away

There is no public transport to Whangaroa Harbour. Buses usually drop off at SH10 in nearby Kahoe, immediately west of the harbour and 15km from Whangaroa village.

Doubtless Bay

POP 1662

The bay gets its unusual name from an entry in Cook's logbook, where he wrote that the body of water was 'doubtless a bay'. No kidding, Cap'n. It's a big bay at that, with a

---

THE BOMBING OF THE RAINBOW WARRIOR

On the morning of 10 July 1985, New Zealanders awoke to news reporting that a terrorist attack had killed a man in Auckland Harbour. The Greenpeace flagship *Rainbow Warrior* had been sunk at its anchorage at Marsden Wharf, where it was preparing to sail to Mururoa atoll near Tahiti to protest against French nuclear testing.

A tip-off from a Neighbourhood Watch group eventually led to the arrest of two French foreign intelligence service (DGSE) agents, posing as tourists. The agents had detonated two mines on the boat in staggered explosions – the first designed to cause the crew to evacuate and the second to sink her. However, after the initial evacuation, some of the crew returned to the vessel to investigate and document the attack. Greenpeace photographer Fernando Pereira was drowned below decks following the second explosion.

The arrested agents pleaded guilty to manslaughter and were sentenced to 10 years' imprisonment. In response, the French government threatened to embargo NZ goods from entering the European Economic Community – which would have crippled NZ's economy. A deal was struck whereby France paid $13 million to NZ and apologised, in return for the agents being delivered into French custody on a South Pacific atoll for three years. France eventually paid over $8 million to Greenpeace in reparation – and the bombers were quietly freed before their sentence was served.

Initially French President François Mitterrand denied any government involvement in the attack, but following an inquiry he eventually sacked his Defence Minister and the head of the DGSE, Admiral Pierre Lacoste. On the 20th anniversary of the attack, *Le Monde* newspaper published a report from Lacoste dating from 1986, declaring that the president had personally authorised the operation.

The bombing left a lasting impact on NZ, and French nuclear testing at Mururoa ceased for good in 1996. The wreck of the *Rainbow Warrior* was re-sunk near Northland's Cavalli Islands, where, today, it can be explored by divers. The masts were bought by the Dargaville Museum (p179) and overlook the town. The memory of Fernando Pereira endures in a peaceful bird hide in Thames, while a memorial to the boat sits atop a Māori *pā* site at Matauri Bay, north of the Bay of Islands.

string of pretty swimming beaches heading towards the Karikari Peninsula.

The main centre, **Mangonui** (meaning 'Big Shark'), retains a fishing-port feel, despite cafes and gift shops now infesting its well-labelled line of historical waterfront buildings. They were constructed in the days when Mangonui was a centre of the whaling industry (1792–1850) and exported flax, kauri wood and gum.

The popular holiday settlements of **Coopers Beach**, **Cable Bay** and **Taipa** are restful pockets of beachside gentrification.

◉ Sights & Activities

Grab the free *Heritage Trail* brochure from the visitor information centre for a 3km self-guided walk that takes in 22 historic sites. Other walks lead to attractive **Mill Bay**, west of Mangonui, and **Rangikapiti Pā Historic Reserve**, which has ancient Māori terracing and a spectacular view of Doubtless Bay – particularly at sunrise and sunset. A walkway runs from Mill Bay to the *pā* (fortified village site), but you can also drive nearly to the top.

Butler Point Whaling Museum   MUSEUM
(☑ 09-406 0006; www.whalingmuseumbutlerpoint. com; Marchant Rd; Hihi; adult/child $25/5; ⊘ by appointment) This small private museum is set in lovely gardens at Hihi, 15km northeast of Mangonui. The centrepiece is a still-lived-in Victorian homestead built by retired whaling captain, William Butler, who settled here in 1838, had 13 children and became a trader, farmer, magistrate and Member of Parliament. Visits must be prearranged and start with a guided tour of the house, after which you're welcome to wander around the grounds for as long as you like.

⬛ Sleeping

Puketiti Lodge   GUESTHOUSE **$$**
(☑ 09-406 0369; www.puketitilodge.co.nz; 53 Puketiti Dr; r $150; ⊘ Nov-Mar; @ �🖥) You'll need a car to get here, but the views from the generously proportioned deck more than justify the distance from the water. The two spacious rooms each have a double bed and a set of bunks, and there's a communal kitchen and lounge, too. Turn inland at Midgley Rd, 6km south of Mangonui village, just after the Hihi turn-off.

Mangonui Waterfront Apartments Motel   APARTMENT **$$**
(☑ 09-406 0347; www.mangonuiwaterfront.co.nz; 88 Waterfront Dr, Mangonui; apt $120-250; �🖥) Character radiates from the kauri boards

of these apartments, which occupy a set of historic houses on the Mangonui waterfront. Each is different, ranging from a small bedsit to a two-bedroom unit with a full kitchen sleeping up to five people. Best of all is one-bedroom Tahi, with French doors opening onto the best balcony in Mangonui.

★**Old Oak**   HISTORIC HOTEL **$$$**
(☑ 09-406 1250; www.theoldoak.co.nz; 66 Waterfront Dr, Mangonui; s/d/ste from $175/225/275; ✳ 🖥) This atmospheric 1861 kauri inn is now an elegant boutique hotel with contemporary design and top-notch furnishings in its six rooms and suites. It oozes personality, not least because the building is reputedly haunted.

Ramada Resort Reia Taipa Beach   RESORT **$$$**
(☑ 09-406 0656; www.ramadataipa.co.nz; 22 Taipa Point Rd, Taipa; apt from $270; ✳ 🖥 🏊) Renovated accommodation and a warm welcome combine at this long-standing resort, which offers a choice between beachfront and poolside studio units and apartments. There's also an on-site restaurant, a tennis court and a spa pool.

✕ Eating

The Thai   THAI **$$**
(☑ 09-406 1220; www.thethaimangonui.co.nz; 80 Waterfront Dr, Mangonui; mains $21-27; ⊘ 5-11pm Tue-Sun; ✐) Northland's best Thai restaurant serves zingy dishes with intriguing names such as Angry Pig, Kiwi Chick and Mangonui Showtime, and there's also a good range of Isaan (northeastern Thai) dishes to go with a frosty Singha beer. Actually, make that one of New Zealand's best Thai restaurants.

Little Kitchen on the Bay   CAFE **$$**
(☑ 09-406 1644; www.facebook.com/littlekitchen nz; 118 Waterfront Dr, Mangonui; mains $12-20; ⊘ 8am-3pm) With a terrace facing the water and a sun-drenched interior, this cute cafe serves Mangonui's best coffee, excellent counter food and good mains. Menu options include burgers, pies, toasted sandwiches, curries, sticky pork belly and laksa.

ⓘ Information

Doubtless Bay Visitor Information Centre
(☑ 09-406 2046; www.doubtlessbay.co.nz; 118 Waterfront Dr, Mangonui; ⊘ 10am-5pm Mon-Sat Jan-Apr, to 3pm May-Dec) Excellent source of local information.

ⓘ Getting There & Away

InterCity (p142) stops here daily, en route between Kerikeri ($28, one hour) and Kaitaia ($25, 40 minutes).

Far North Link (p166) has a weekday service to Kaitaia ($5, one hour), timed around office hours.

Both buses stop outside Wilton's Garage in Mangonui, outside the sports store in Coopers Beach, opposite the shop in Cable Bay and outside the Z petrol station in Taipa.

Karikari Peninsula

The oddly shaped Karikari Peninsula bends into a near-perfect right angle. The result is beaches facing north, south, east and west in close proximity, so if the wind's annoying you or you want to catch some surf, a sunrise or a sunset, just swap beaches.

Despite its natural assets, the sun-baked peninsula has largely escaped development, with farmers well outnumbering tourist operators. There's no public transport and you won't find a lot of shops or eateries either. However change is in the air.

In 2017 plans to turn Carrington Resort into the country's biggest tourist complex were announced. Locals were concerned about the scale of the proposal but, at the time of research, plans had yet to be finalised.

⊙ Sights & Activities

Tokerau Beach is the long, sandy stretch forming the western edge of Doubtless Bay. Neighbouring **Whatuwhiwhi** is smaller and more built-up, facing back across the bay. Lovely **Maitai Bay**, with its twin coves, is a great spot for swimming – the water is sheltered enough for the kids, but with enough swell to body surf. It's located at the lonely end of the peninsula down an unsealed road.

Rangiputa faces west at the elbow of the peninsula; the pure white sand and crystal-clear sheltered waters come straight from a Pacific Island daydream. A turn-off on the road to Rangiputa takes you to remote **Puheke Beach**, a long, windswept stretch of snow-white sand dunes forming Karikari's northern edge.

Airzone Kitesurf School   KITESURFING
(📞 021 202 7949; www.kitesurfnz.com; 1-/2-/3-day course $195/380/560; ⊙ Nov-Mar) The unique set-up of Karikari Peninsula makes it one of the world's premium spots for kitesurf-

ing. Learners get to hone their skills on flat water before heading to the surf, while the more experienced can chase the wind around the peninsula.

🛏 Sleeping

Karikari Lodge   HOSTEL $
(📞 09-406 7378; www.karikarilodge.co.nz; 26 Inland Rd, Whatuwhiwhi; dm/r/cabin $35/65/80; 🐾) More like a family-run homestay than a backpackers hostel, this Pasifika-themed place has only three bedrooms, shared bathrooms and a separate cabin in the garden. Perks include free use of kayaks, boogie boards, surfboards and stand-up paddle boards. There's also a full kitchen and barbecue facilities if you get lucky while fishing.

Whatuwhiwhi Top 10
Holiday Park   HOLIDAY PARK $
(📞 09-408 7202; www.whatuwhiwhitop10.co.nz; 17 Whatuwhiwhi Rd; sites from $40, unit with/without bathroom from $100/75; 🐾🚸) Sheltered by hills and overlooking the beach, this friendly complex has a great location, good facilities, free barbecues and a playground. It also offers dive air fills and kayaks for hire.

DOC Maitai Bay Campsite   CAMPGROUND $
(www.doc.govt.nz; Maitai Bay Rd; sites per adult/child $13/6.50) 🍃 A large first-in, first-served (no bookings) camping ground at the peninsula's most beautiful beach, with flush toilets, drinking water and cold showers.

Carrington Resort   RESORT $$$
(📞 09-408 7222; www.carrington.co.nz; 109 Matai Bay Rd; r/villa from $215/315; 🐾🏊) There's something very Australian-looking about this hilltop lodge, with its wide verandas and gum trees, tempered by Māori and Pacific design in the spacious rooms and villas. The view over the golf course to the dazzling white beach is exquisite. The resort has its own upmarket restaurant along with a seasonal cafe in its vineyard across the road.

ⓘ Getting There & Away

There is no public transport to the Karikari Peninsula.

Cape Reinga & Ninety Mile Beach

Māori consider Cape Reinga (Te Rerenga Wairua) the jumping-off point for souls as they depart on the journey to their spiritual homeland. That makes the Aupouri Peninsula a giant diving board, and it even resembles one – long and thin, it reaches 108km to form NZ's northern extremity. On its west coast Ninety Mile Beach (Ninety Kilometre Beach would be more accurate) is a continuous stretch lined with high sand dunes, flanked by the Aupouri Forest.

◎ Sights

★**Cape Reinga** VIEWPOINT
(Far North Rd) State Hwy 1 terminates at this dramatic headland where the waters of the Tasman Sea and Pacific Ocean meet, breaking together into waves up to 10m high in stormy weather. Cape Reinga is the end of the road both literally and figuratively: in Māori tradition the spirits of the dead depart the world from here, making it the most sacred site in all of Aotearoa. Out of respect, you're requested to refrain from eating or drinking in the vicinity.

The actual departure point is believed to be the 800-year-old pohutukawa tree clinging to the rocks on the small promontory of Te Rerenga Wairua (Leaping Place of the Spirits) far below; to those in corporeal form, access is forbidden.

From the car park it's a rolling 1km walk to the lookout, passing the Cape Reinga Lighthouse along the way. Information boards detail the area's ecology, history and cultural significance. Little tufts of cloud sometimes cling to the ridges, giving sudden spooky chills even on hot days.

Contrary to expectation, Cape Reinga isn't actually the northernmost point of the country; that honour belongs to the inaccessible Surville Cliffs which can be spotted to the right in the distance. In fact, it's much closer to the westernmost point, Cape Maria van Diemen, immediately to the left.

★**Te Paki Giant Sand Dunes** DUNES
(www.doc.govt.nz; Te Paki Stream Rd) A large chunk of the land around Cape Reinga is part of the Te Paki Recreation Reserves managed by DOC. It's public land with free access; leave the gates as you found them and don't disturb the animals. There are 7 sq km of giant sand dunes on either side of the mouth of the Te Paki Stream. During summer, Ahikaa Adventures (p172) are on hand to rent sandboards ($15) for those wishing to clamber up and toboggan back down.

Gumdiggers Park MUSEUM
(☑09-406 7166; www.gumdiggerspark.co.nz; 171 Heath Rd, Waiharara; adult/child $13/6; ☺9am-4.30pm Nov-Apr) Kauri forests covered this area for 100,000 years, leaving ancient logs and the much-prized gum (used for making varnish and linoleum) buried beneath. Digging it out was the region's main industry from the 1870s to the 1920s. In 1900 around 7000 gumdiggers were digging holes all over Northland, including at this site. Start with the 15-minute video, and then walk on the bush tracks, leading past gumdiggers' huts, ancient kauri stumps, huge preserved logs and holes left by the diggers.

⭑ Activities

Natives OUTDOORS
(☑09-409 8482; www.natives.co.nz) The local Ngāti Kuri people, guardians of the sacred spaces around the Cape, have come up with a unique way of funding reforestation. For $35 you can assuage your carbon guilt by planting a native tree or bush of your choice, or letting the staff plant it for you.

Te Paki Coastal Track TRAMPING
From Cape Reinga, a walk along **Te Werahi Beach** to **Cape Maria van Diemen** (a five-hour loop) takes you to the westernmost point of New Zealand. This is one of many sections of the three- to four-day (48km) coastal track from Kapowairua to Te Paki Stream that can be tackled individually.

⭒ Tours

Bus tours go to Cape Reinga from Kaitaia, Ahipara, Doubtless Bay and the Bay of Islands, but there's no scheduled public transport up here.

Petricevich Cape Reinga Tours ADVENTURE
(☑09-408 2411; www.capereingatours.co.nz; adult/child $55/30) Visit Cape Reinga and the Te Paki dunes and zoom along Ninety Mile Beach in the Dune Rider bus. Sandboarding is included. Pick-up points include Mangonui, Kaitaia and Ahipara.

Far North Outback Adventures ADVENTURE
(☑09-409 4586; www.farnorthtours.co.nz; price on application) Flexible, day-long 4WD tours from Kaitaia/Ahipara, including morning tea and lunch. Options include visits to remote areas such as Great Exhibition Bay.

Sand Safaris ADVENTURE
(☑09-408 1778; www.sandsafaris.co.nz; adult/child $50/30) Coach trips from Ahipara, Kaitaia and Awanui, including sandboarding and a picnic lunch in Tapotupotu Bay.

Harrisons Cape Runner ADVENTURE

(📞0800 227 373; www.harrisonscapereingatours.
co.nz; adult/child $50/25) Day trips in a 4WD
truck-like bus along Ninety Mile Beach to
Cape Reinga that include sandboarding and
a picnic lunch in Tapotupotu Bay. They depart Kaitaia at 9am daily, returning at 5pm.

Ahikaa Adventures CULTURAL

(📞09-409 8228; www.ahikaa-adventures.co.nz;
Te Paki Stream Rd; tours $70-190) Māori culture
permeates these tours, which can include
sandboarding, kayaking, snorkelling, fishing and pigging out on traditional *kai* (food)
cooked in a *hāngi* (earth oven).

🛏 Sleeping

There are few good accommodation options
on the peninsula itself. The DOC has basic
but spectacularly positioned **sites** (www.doc.
govt.nz; sites per adult/child $8/4) 🌿 at **Rarawa
Beach, Kapowairua** and **Tapotupotu Bay**.
Only water, flush toilets and cold showers
are provided. Bring a cooker, as fires are not
allowed, and plenty of repellent to ward off
mosquitoes and sandflies. 'Freedom/Leave
No Trace' camping is allowed along the Te
Paki Coastal Track.

North Wind Lodge Backpackers HOSTEL $

(📞09-409 8515; www.northwind.co.nz; 88
Otaipango Rd, Henderson Bay; dm/s/tw/d
$30/60/66/80; ☺Sep-May) Six kilometres
down an unsealed road on the Aupouri
Peninsula's east side, this unusual turreted house offers a homey environment and
plenty of quiet spots on the lawn to sit with
a beer and a book. It's within walking distance of a beautiful beach.

ℹ Getting There & Away

Apart from numerous tours, there's no public
transport past Pukenui – and even this is limited
to Thursday-only buses from Kaitaia ($5, 45
minutes) operated by Far North Link (p166).

As well as Far North Rd (SH1), rugged vehicles can travel along Ninety Mile Beach itself.
However, cars have been known to hit soft sand
and be swallowed by the tides – look out for
unfortunate vehicles poking through the sands.
Check tide times before setting out; avoid it
2½ hours either side of high tide. Watch out for
'quicksand' at Te Paki Stream – keep moving.
Many car-rental companies prohibit driving on
the sands; if you get stuck, your insurance won't
cover you.

It's best to fill up with petrol before hitting the
Aupouri Peninsula.

Kaitaia

📞09 / POP 4890

Nobody comes to the Far North to hang
out in this provincial town, but it's a handy
stop if you're after a supermarket, a post
office or an ATM. It's also a jumping-off
point for tours to Cape Reinga and Ninety
Mile Beach.

⊙ Sights

Te Ahu Centre ARTS CENTRE

(📞09-401 5200; www.kaitaianz.co.nz; Cnr South
Rd & Matthews Ave) This civic and community centre features a cinema, theatre, tourist
information centre, gallery and the **Te Ahu
Heritage** (📞09-408 9454; www.teahuheritage.
co.nz; adult/child $7/free; ☺8.30am-5pm Mon-
Fri) exhibits of the Far North Regional Museum. Artefacts include kauri gum, carved
pounamu weapons and wood carvings dating to the 14th century. There's also a cafe,
and free wi-fi at the library. The centre's foyer is circled by a series of *pou* (carved posts)
featuring the different cultures – Māori,
British, Croatian etc – that have had a major
impact in the local area.

Each of the parts of the centre have their
own opening hours.

🛏 Sleeping & Eating

Loredo Motel MOTEL $$

(📞09-408 3200; www.loredomotel.co.nz; 25 North
Rd; units from $120; 🛜🏊) Opting for a breezy
Spanish style, this tidy motel has well-kept
units set among palm trees and lawns, with
a swimming pool.

Gecko Cafe CAFE $

(📞09-408 1160; 71 Commerce St; mains $9-18;
☺7am-3pm Mon-Fri, 8am-1.30pm Sat) Morning
queues of locals attest to the Gecko having
the best coffee in town (they roast their
own), and the food's pretty good, too. Kick
off another day on the road with mush-
rooms and chorizo, or grab a mussel-fritter
burger for lunch.

Beachcomber BISTRO $$

(📞09-408 2010; www.beachcomber.net.nz; 222
Commerce St; mains lunch $19-36, dinner $25-38;
☺11am-2.30pm Mon-Fri & 5-9pm Mon-Sat; 🚗🍴)
This Pacific-themed family restaurant is easily the best dinner option in Kaitaia, with a
wide range of seafood, meat and vegetarian
fare, and a well-stocked salad bar. Save room
for the pavlova of the day.

ℹ️ Information

DOC Kaitaia Area Office (📞09-408 6014; www.doc.govt.nz; 25 Matthews Ave; ⏰8am-4.30pm Mon-Fri) It's a regional office rather than an information centre, but the staff are happy to provide up-to-date track information and advice.

Far North i-SITE (📞09-408 9450; www.northlandnz.com; Te Ahu Centre, cnr Matthews Ave & South Rd; ⏰8.30am-5pm) An excellent information centre with advice for all of Northland.

ℹ️ Getting There & Away

AIR
Kaitaia Airport (KAT; 📞021 818 314; Quarry Rd, Awanui) is 6km north of town. **Barrier Air** (p166) flies to and from Auckland (one hour).

BUS
Far North Link (p166) has services to Ahipara ($3.50, 15 minutes) and Doubtless Bay ($5, one hour) on weekdays, and to Pukenui ($5, 45 minutes) on Thursdays.

InterCity (p142) buses depart daily from the Te Ahu Centre (p172) and head to Kerikeri ($37, 1¾ hours) via Doubtless Bay ($25, 40 minutes).

Ahipara

📞 09 / POP 1060

All good things must come to an end, and Ninety Mile Beach does at this spunky beach town. A few holiday mansions have snuck in, but mostly it's just the locals keeping it real, rubbing shoulders with visiting surfers.

The area is known for its huge sand dunes and massive kauri gumfield, where 2000 people once worked. Sandboarding and quad-bike rides are popular activities on the dunes above Ahipara and further around the Tauroa Peninsula.

👁️ Sights

Shipwreck Bay BEACH
(Te Kōhanga; Wreck Bay Rd) The best surfing is at this small cove at Ahipara's western edge, so named for shipwrecks still visible at low tide.

🏃 Activities

Ahipara Treks HORSE RIDING
(📞09-408 2532; www.taitokerauhoney.co.nz/ahipara-horse-treks; 11 Foreshore Rd; 1hr/2hr $65/85) Offers beach canters, including some farm and ocean riding (when the surf permits).

Ahipara Adventure ADVENTURE SPORTS
(📞09-409 2055; www.ahiparaadventure.co.nz; 15 Takahe Rd) Hires sand toboggans ($15 per half day), surfboards ($40 per half day), body boards ($20 per half day), stand-up paddle boards ($50 per half day), blokarts for sand yachting ($80 per hour) and quad bikes ($115 per hour).

NZ Surfbros SURFING
(📞021 252 7078; www.nzsurfbros.co.nz; 27 Kaka St; 2hr lesson $60) Rents boards and offers surfing lessons and five-day surf tours (from $599 including accommodation, meals and transport from Auckland).

🛏️ Sleeping & Eating

⭐Endless Summer Lodge HOSTEL $
(📞09-409 4181; www.endlesssummer.co.nz; 245 Foreshore Rd; dm/r from $30/86; 🛜) Across from the beach, this superb kauri villa (1880) has been beautifully restored and converted into an exceptional hostel. There's no TV, which encourages bonding around the long table and wood-fired pizza oven on the vine-covered back terrace. Body boards and sandboards can be borrowed and surfboards can be hired.

Ahipara Holiday Park HOLIDAY PARK $
(📞0800 888 988; www.ahiparaholidaypark.co.nz; 168 Takahe Rd; sites/dm/tw/d from $18/28/75/85, unit with/without bathroom from $105/75; 🛜) There's a large range of accommodation on offer at this holiday park, including cabins, motel units and a worn but perfectly presentable YHA-affiliated backpackers' lodge. The communal hall has an open fire and colourful murals.

GEMS Seaside Lodge APARTMENT $$
(📞027 820 9403; www.gemsseasidelodge.co.nz; 14 Kotare St; apt from $150; 🛜) Who cares if it's a bit bourgeois for Ahipara? These two upmarket, self-contained apartments have watery views and there's direct access to the beach. The bottom floor is a spacious studio, while the upper-floor apartment has two bedrooms and two bathrooms.

North Drift Cafe CAFE $
(📞09-4094093;www.facebook.com/northdriftcafe; 250 Ahipara Rd; mains $9-20; ⏰8am-2.30pm) Start the day with a cooked breakfast and Ahipara's best coffee on the sunny front deck of this relaxed little cafe. Come back at lunch for a burger, fish and chips, or Cajun chicken tacos. In summer, they reopen at 5pm for dinner from Thursday through to Sunday.

BAY OF ISLANDS & NORTHLAND AHIPARA

NGĀTI TARARA

As you're travelling around the north you might notice the preponderance of road names ending in '-ich'. Then there's the trilingual signage in the Kaitaia and Dargaville museums. *Haere mai, dobro došli* and welcome to one of the more peculiar ethnic conjunctions in the country.

From the end of the 19th century, men from the Dalmatian coast of what is now Croatia started arriving in NZ looking for work. Many ended up in Northland's gumfields. Anglo-NZ society wasn't particularly welcoming to the new immigrants, particularly during WWI, as they were travelling on Austrian passports. Not so the small Māori communities of the north. Here the immigrants found an echo of Dalmatian village life, with its emphasis on extended family and hospitality, not to mention a shared history of injustice at the hands of colonial powers.

The Māori jokingly named them Tarara, as their rapid conversation in their native tongue sounded like 'ta-ra-ra-ra-ra' to Māori ears. Many Croatian men married local *wahine* (women), founding clans that have left several of today's famous Māori with Croatian surnames, such as singer Margaret Urlich and former All Black Frano Botica. You'll find large Tarara communities in the Far North, Dargaville and West Auckland.

ⓘ Getting There & Away

Far North Link (p166) has a weekday bus to Kaitaia ($3.50, 15 minutes), departing Ahipara early in the morning and returning in the evening.

HOKIANGA

The Hokianga Harbour stretches out its skinny tentacles to become the fourth-biggest in the country. Its ruggedly beautiful landscape is painted in every shade of green and brown. The water itself is rendered the colour of ginger ale by the bush streams that feed it.

Of all the remote parts of Northland, this is the pocket that feels the most removed from the mainstream. Pretension has no place here. Isolated, predominantly Māori communities nestle around the harbour's many inlets, as they have done for centuries. Discovered by legendary explorer Kupe, it's been settled by Ngāpuhi since the 14th century. Hippies arrived in the late 1960s and their legacy is a thriving little artistic scene.

Many of the roads remain unsealed, and, while tourism dollars are channelled eastward to the Bay of Islands, this truly fascinating corner of the country remains remarkably undeveloped, just as many of the locals like it.

ⓘ Getting There & Away

The only public transport is a weekly Hokianga Link (p165) minibus service between Kerikeri and Omapere, which expands to twice weekly in summer.

Kohukohu

📞 09 / POP 165

Quick, someone slap a preservation order on Kohukohu before it's too late. There can be few places in NZ where a Victorian village full of interesting kauri buildings has been so completely preserved with hardly a modern monstrosity to be seen. During the height of the kauri industry it was a busy town with a sawmill, shipyard, two newspapers and banks. These days it's a very quiet backwater on the north side of Hokianga Harbour, 4km from the Rawene car ferry (p175).

⊙ Sights

Village Arts   GALLERY
(📞 09-405 5827; www.villagearts.co.nz; 1376 Kohukohu Rd; ⊙10am-3pm) A sophisticated surprise in such a small place, this gallery fills a restored heritage building with ever-changing exhibitions – mainly from Hokianga artists.

🛏 Sleeping & Eating

Tree House   HOSTEL $
(📞 09-405 5855; www.treehouse.co.nz; 168 West Coast Rd; sites/dm/s/d from $20/32/64/82; 🖝) One of the country's very best hostels, the Tree House has dorm rooms in the wood-lined main building and brightly painted little cottages set among the surrounding fruit and nut trees. Bathrooms are shared and there's a communal kitchen and dining space. This quiet retreat is 2km from the ferry terminus (turn sharp left as you come off the ferry).

Koke Cafe   CAFE $
(☑09-405 5808; 1374 Kohukohu Rd; mains $8-16;
☺8am-4pm Wed-Sun, extended in summer) Set up
on the street-side terrace of the Kohukohu
Hotel, this little cafe serves decent coffee and
food, including bagels, gourmet pies, pork
sandwiches, burgers and cooked breakfasts.

❶ Getting There & Away
There's no public transport, so you'll need your
own vehicle. Look forward to the scenic **ferry
crossing** (☑09-405 2602; www.fndc.govt.nz;
car/campervan/motorcycle $20/40/5, passen-
ger $2; ☺7.30am-8pm) across the harbour to
slightly less sleepy Rawene.

Horeke & Around
Tiny Horeke was NZ's second European settlement after Russell. A Wesleyan mission
operated here from 1828 to 1855, while in
1840, 3000 Ngāpuhi gathered here for what
was the single biggest signing of the Treaty of
Waitangi. Nowadays its an all-but-forgotten
hamlet, with pig-hunting dogs usually outnumbering people on the dusty streets.

The rustic **Horeke Hotel** (☑09-401 9133;
www.horekehotel.nz; 2118 Horeke Rd; ☺1pm-late
Wed-Sun, bistro 5.30-8pm Thu-Sun) is reputedly
New Zealand's oldest pub – the first cold
one was poured back in 1826 – and the garden bar rocks with live music on occasional
weekends during summer.

Horeke is also the western end point of
the Pou Herenga Tai Twin Coast Cycle Trail
(p152).

⊙ Sights
Wairere Boulders Nature Park   PARK
(☑09-401 9935; www.wairereboulders.co.nz; Mc-
Donnell Rd; adult/child/family $15/5/35, cash only;
☺to 5pm/7pm winter/summer) 🖉 At Wairere,
massive basalt rock formations have been
eroded into odd fluted shapes by the acid-
ity of ancient kauri forests. Allow 40 minutes for the main loop track; expect a few
dips and climbs. An additional track leads
through rainforest to a platform at the end
of the boulder valley (1½ hours). The park
is signposted from SH1 and Horeke; the last
3km are unsealed.

⨭ Sleeping
Horeke Hotel   PUB $$
(☑09-401 9133; www.horekehotel.nz; 2118 Horeke
Rd; r $130-150) Simple but clean accommoda-
tion in the local pub. All three room have en
suites and harbour views.

❶ Getting There & Away
There is no public transport, so the only way to
get here is by bike or car. The main sealed ap-
proach to town is Rangiahua Rd, heading south
from SH1. Horeke Rd, heading north from SH12,
is rough and unsealed.

Rawene
POP 471
Founded shortly after nearby Horeke,
Rawene was NZ's third European settle-
ment. A surprising number of historic build-
ings (including six churches!) remain from
a time when the harbour was considerably
busier than it is now. Information boards
outline a heritage trail of the main sights.

There's an ATM in the Four Square gro-
cery store, and you can get petrol here.

⊙ Sights
No 1 Parnell   GALLERY
(☑09-405 7520; www.no1parnell.weebly.com; 1
Parnell St; ☺9am-4.30pm) Occupying a cen-
tury-old corner building originally built as
a grocery store, this upmarket commercial
gallery exhibits interesting work by local
artists alongside some from further afield.
There's a sun-filled cafe attached.

⨭ Sleeping & Eating
Rawene Holiday Park   HOLIDAY PARK $$
(☑09-405 7720; www.raweneholidaypark.co.nz; 1
Marmon St West; sites from $18, unit with/without
bathroom $130/65; 🖥🐾) Tent sites shelter in
the bush at this nicely managed park. The
cabins range from basic units where you'll
need to bring your own linen (or pay extra to
hire a set) to fully made-up units with kitchenettes. There's only one en-suite unit.

Boatshed Cafe   CAFE $
(☑09-405 7728; www.facebook.com/boatshedcafe
rawene; 8 Clendon Esplanade; mains $8.50-15;
☺8.30am-4pm) You can eat overlooking the
water in Hokianga's best cafe, which occupies a historic boat shed near the car ferry.
It's a cute place with excellent food and a gift
shop that sells local art and crafts.

❶ Getting There & Away
A car ferry heads to the northern side of the
Hokianga, docking 4km south of Kohukohu
at least hourly. You can buy your ticket for
this 15-minute ride on board. It usually leaves
Rawene on the half-hour and the north side on
the hour.

You can request a pick-up by the Hokianga Link (p165) minivan by calling the Opononi i-SITE. Services head between Opononi (30 minutes) and Kerikeri (one hour) on Thursdays, as well as Tuesdays in summer.

Opononi & Omapere

POP 414

Although they were once separate villages, Opononi and Omapere have now merged into one continuous coastal community spread along a beautiful stretch of coast near the south head of Hokianga Harbour. The water's much clearer here and good for swimming, and views are dominated by the mountainous sand dunes across the water at North Head. If you're approaching Omapere from the south, the view of the harbour is nothing short of spectacular.

⊙ Sights & Activities

**Arai-te-uru Recreation
Reserve**   NATURE RESERVE
(Signal Station Rd, Omapere) Covering the southern headland of the Hokianga Harbour, this reserve offers magnificent views over the harbour and along the wild west coast. A short walk leads to the site of an old signal station built to assist ships making the treacherous passage into the Hokianga. It closed in 1951 due to a decline in ships entering the harbour. A track also heads down to pretty little **Martin's Bay**.

Hokianga Bone Carving Studio   COURSE
(☑09-405 8061; hokiangabonecarvingstudio@
gmail.com; 15 Akiha St, Omapere; class incl lunch $60) Book in for a day course in Jim Taranaki's ocean-facing studio and learn how to create your own Māori-inspired bone carving.

⌒ Tours

Footprints Waipoua   CULTURAL
(☑09-405 8207; www.footprintswaipoua.co.nz;
Copthorne, 334 SH12, Omapere; adult/child $95/35)
🍃 Led by Māori guides, this four-hour twilight tour into Waipoua Forest is a fantastic introduction to both the culture and the forest giants. Tribal history and stories are shared, and mesmerising *karakia* (prayers, incantations) are recited before the gargantuan trees. Daytime tours ($80) are also available, but the twilight tours amplify the sense of spirituality.

Hokianga Express   ADVENTURE
(☑021 405 872; hkexpress@xtra.co.nz; Opononi
Jetty; adult/child $27/17; 🚻) Take a boat ride across to the north side of the harbour and

attack the giant sand dunes armed with a boogie board for a swift descent; at high tide you can skim straight out over the water. The boat departs daily in summer (weather permitting) and on demand at other times, but bookings are essential regardless.

🛏 Sleeping & Eating

Globetrekkers Lodge   HOSTEL $
(☑09-405 8183; www.globetrekkerslodge.com;
281 SH12, Omapere; dm/s/d $29/54/70; 🖥) Unwind in casual style at this homey hostel with harbour views and bright dorms. Private rooms don't have their own bathrooms but there are plenty of thoughtful touches, such as writing desks, mirrors, art and fluffy towels. There's a stereo but no TV, encouraging plenty of schmoozing in the grapevine-draped barbecue area.

Kokohuia Lodge   B&B $$$
(☑021 779 927; www.kokohuialodge.co.nz; 101 Kokohuia Rd, Omapere; r $320; 🖥) 🍃 Luxury and eco-friendly practices combine at this B&B, nestled in regenerating native bush high above the silvery dune-fringed expanse of the Hokianga Harbour. Solar energy and organic and free-range produce all feature, but there's no trade-off for luxury in the modern and stylish accommodation.

Hokianga Haven   APARTMENT $$$
(☑09-405 8285; www.hokiangahaven.co.nz;
226 SH12, Omapere; r $220; 🖥) Fall asleep only steps from the beach in this spacious self-contained studio apartment tucked underneath a modern house. An additional queen room is available for friends or family travelling together. Alternative healing therapies can be arranged.

Landing Cafe   CAFE $
(☑09-405 8169; www.thelandingcafe.co.nz; 29
SH12, Opononi; mains $10-15; ⊙9am-3pm; 🖥)
Stylish Kiwiana decor combines with good coffee at this appealing place attached to the tourist office. Grab a table on the expansive deck and tuck into scrambled eggs with smoked salmon while gazing over the water. It's head and shoulders above other local eateries.

Opononi Hotel   PUB
(☑09-405 8858; www.opononihotel.com; 19 SH12;
mains $13-36) Try to score an outside table at this friendly local pub so that you can take in the improbable views of Opononi's massive sand dunes just across the harbour. There are regular live gigs in summer and it's a good place to watch the rugby.

ℹ Information

Opononi i-SITE (☎ 09-405 8869; www.
hokiangatourism.org.nz; 29 SH12; ⊙ 8.30am-
5pm) Excellent information office with a good
range of local souvenirs.

ℹ Getting There & Away

A Hokianga Link (p165) minivan heads between
Omapere and Kerikeri ($15, 1½ hours) on Thurs-
days. From December to March it also operates
on Tuesdays.

Waiotemarama & Waimamaku

The neighbouring Waiotemarama and
Waimamaku villages, nestled between the
Hokianga Harbour and the Waipoua Forest,
are the first of many tiny rural communities
scattered along this underpopulated stretch
of SH12.

🏃 Activities

Labyrinth Woodworks   OUTDOORS
(☎ 09-405 4581; www.nzanity.co.nz; 647 Waiotemarama Gorge Rd; maze adult/child $4/3; ⊙ 9am-
5pm) Crack the code in the outdoor maze by
collecting letters to form a word. The puzzle
museum and retro board games are also interesting. Nearby walks lead to a waterfall
and magnificent kauri trees.

🍴 Eating

Morrell's Cafe   CAFE $
(☎ 09-405 4545; 7235 SH12, Waimamaku; mains $11-
17; ⊙ 9am-3pm) This cafe and craft shop occupies a former cheese factory. It's the last good
eatery before Dargaville so drop in for coffee,
an eggy breakfast or a freshly baked scone.

ℹ Getting There & Away

There is no public transport to Waiotemarama
and Waimamaku.

KAURI COAST

Apart from the odd bluff and river, this
coast is basically unbroken and undeveloped for the 110km between the Hokianga
and Kaipara Harbours. The main reason for
coming here is to marvel at the kauri forests, one of the great natural highlights of
NZ. If you're a closet tree hugger you'll need
8m-long arms to get them around some of
the big boys here.

There are few stores or eateries and no
ATMs north of Dargaville, so stock up beforehand. Trampers should check DOC's website
(www.doc.govt.nz) for walks in the area.

ℹ Getting There & Away

West Coaster (p150) buses shuttle between
Dargaville and Whangarei from Monday to
Friday.
   Te Wai Ora Coachlines (☎ 027 482 2950;
www.tewaioracoachlines.com; adult/child
$50/40) has a weekly shuttle between Dar-
gaville and Auckland.

Waipoua Forest

The highlight of Northland's west coast,
this superb forest sanctuary – established
in 1952 after much public pressure – is the
largest remnant of the once-extensive kauri forests of northern NZ. The forest road
(SH12) stretches for 18km and passes some
huge trees – a kauri can reach 60m in height
and have a trunk more than 5m in diameter.
   Control of the forest has been returned to
Te Roroa, the local *iwi* (tribe), as part of a
settlement for Crown breaches of the Treaty
of Waitangi. Te Roroa runs the Waipoua Forest Visitor Centre (p178), cafe and camping
ground near the south end of the park.

⊙ Sights

⭐**Te Matua Ngahere**   LANDMARK
From the Kauri Walks car park, a 20-minute
walk leads past the **Four Sisters**, a graceful stand of four tall trees fused together at
the base, to Te Matua Ngahere (The Father
of the Forest). At 30m, he has a significant
presence. Reinforced by a substantial girth –
he's the fattest living kauri (16.4m) – the tree
presides over a clearing surrounded by mature trees resembling mere matchsticks in
comparison. It's estimated that he could be
up to 3000 years old.
   A 30-minute (one way) path leads from
near the Four Sisters to **Yakas**, the sev-
enth-largest kauri.

⭐**Tāne Mahuta**   LANDMARK
Near the north end of the park, not far
from the road, stands mighty Tāne Mahuta,
named for the Māori forest god. At 51.5m,
with a 13.8m girth and wood mass of 244.5
cubic metres, he's the largest kauri alive, and
has been holding court here for somewhere
between 1200 and 2000 years. He's easy to
find and access, with a well-labelled car park
(complete with coffee cart) on the highway.

🛌 Sleeping

Waipoua Forest Campground CAMPGROUND $
(📞09-439 6445; www.teroroa.iwi.nz/visit-waipoua;
1 Waipoua River Rd; sites/units from $15/20) Situated next to the Waipoua River and the visitor centre, this peaceful camping ground offers hot showers, flush toilets and a kitchen. The cabins are extremely spartan, with unmade squab beds (bring your own linen or hire it).

Waipoua Lodge B&B $$$
(📞09-439 0422; www.waipoualodge.co.nz; 4748 SH12; ste $625; 🐾) 🐾 This fine old villa at the southern edge of the forest has four luxurious, spacious suites, which were originally the stables, the woolshed and the calf-rearing pen. Decadent dinners ($95) are available.

ℹ️ Information

Waipoua Forest Visitor Centre (📞09-439 6445; www.teroroa.iwi.nz/visit-waipoua; 1 Waipoua River Rd; ⏰9am-2pm daily Nov-Mar, Wed-Sun Apr-Oct) Te Roroa's information centre has an interesting exhibition on the kauri forests, and a cafe. They can also arrange guided tours ($25) and cultural activities, and there's a swimming hole, picnic area and walking track nearby.

ℹ️ Getting There & Away

There is no public transport to Waipoua Forest. If you don't have a car, consider taking a tour from Omapere with Footprints Waipoua (p176) or from Paihia with Fullers Great Sights (p160).

Trounson Kauri Park

This 586-hectare stand of old-growth forest has been subject to active predator eradication since 1995 and has become an important mainland refuge for threatened native bird species. An easy half-hour (1.8km) loop walk leads from the picnic area by the road, passing through beautiful forest with streams, some fine kauri stands, a couple of fallen trees, and two pairs of trees with conjoined trunks known as the Four Sisters.

The neighbouring holiday park runs **guided night walks** (adult/child $30/20), which explain the flora and nocturnal wildlife that thrives here. You might even catch a rare glimpse of a brown kiwi in the wild.

🛌 Sleeping

**Kauri Coast Top 10
Holiday Park** HOLIDAY PARK $
(📞09-439 0621; www.kauricoasttop10.co.nz; 7 Opouteke Rd; sites from $44, units with/without bathroom from $114/90; 🐾🐾) Set beside the Kaihu River, 2km from SH12, this excellent holiday park has attractive motel units and a brace of tidy cabins, with or without their own bathrooms and kitchens. As well as their famed guided night walks, there's a swimming hole and an adventure playground with a flying fox and trampoline.

**DOC Trounson Kauri
Park Campsite** CAMPGROUND $
(www.doc.govt.nz; Trounson Park Rd; sites from $30) A step-up from most DOC campsites, this one has both powered and unpowered sites, and a communal kitchen, flush toilets and hot showers.

ℹ️ Getting There & Away

There is no public transport to Trounson Kauri Park. If you're approaching by car from the north, it's easier to take the second turn-off to the park, near Kaihu, which avoids a rough unsealed road.

Kai Iwi Lakes

These three trout-filled freshwater dune lakes nestle together near the coast, 12km off SH12. The largest, **Taharoa**, has blue water fringed with sandy patches. **Lake Waikere** (meaning 'rippling waters') is popular with waterskiers, while **Lake Kai Iwi** (Food for the Tribe) is good for kayaking and swimming, as it's off limits to motorised craft. A half-hour walk leads from the lakes to the coast and it's another two hours to reach the base of volcanic **Maunganui Bluff** (460m); the hike up and down it takes five hours.

🛌 Sleeping

Kai Iwi Lakes Campground CAMPGROUND $
(📞09-439 0986; www.kaiiwicamp.nz; Domain Rd; adult/child $15/8) The largest of the two campsites at the side of Lake Taharoa, Pine Beach has flush toilets and coin-operated hot showers ($2 for three minutes). More sites are available at Promenade Point (cold showers only).

ℹ️ Getting There & Away

There is no public transport to Kai Iwi Lakes. From SH12, it is a 12km drive to the coast.

Baylys Beach

Baylys Beach is a village of brightly coloured baches (holiday cottages) and a few new mansions, 12km from Dargaville. It lies on 100km-long Ripiro Ocean Beach, a surf-pounded stretch of coast that has been the site of many shipwrecks.

The beach is a gazetted highway: you can drive along the sand at low tide, although it is primarily for 4WDs. Despite being NZ's longest drivable beach, it's less well known and hence less travelled than Ninety Mile Beach. Ask locals about conditions and check your car-rental agreement before venturing onto the sand: you probably won't be covered by insurance and if you don't know what you're doing, you're very likely to get stuck. Quad bikes can be hired at the holiday park.

🏃 Activities

Baylys Beach Horse Treks   HORSE RIDING
(📞027 697 9610; www.baylysbeachhorsetreks. webs.com; 1hr/2hr beach ride $70/125) Offers half-hour riding lessons ($25) and horse treks along the broad expanse of Baylys Beach. The minimum age for beach rides is 14, unless the child is experienced. Younger children can take an hour-long paddock ride ($40).

🛌 Sleeping

Baylys Beach Holiday Park   HOLIDAY PARK $
(📞09-439 6349; www.baylysbeach.co.nz; 24 Seaview Rd; sites $20, units with/without bathroom from $90/80; 🌐) This midsized camping ground has attractive cream-and-green units scattered around a lawn circled by pohutukawa trees. Options range from basic cabins to a self-contained cottage sleeping six. They also rent quad bikes and take bookings for horse treks.

Sunset View Lodge   B&B $$
(📞021 231 4114; www.sunsetviewlodge.co.nz; 7 Alcemene Lane; r $175-195; ⊙Jul-May; 🌐🐕) If gin-in-hand sunset gazing is your thing, this large, modern B&B fits the bill. The upstairs rooms have terrific sea views and all of them have decks. Children are not permitted.

❶ Getting There & Away

There is no public transport to Baylys Beach. Most travellers visit from Dargaville or en route to/from the Waipoua Forest.

Dargaville

📞09 / POP 4250

When a town proclaims itself the 'kumara capital of NZ' (it produces two-thirds of the country's sweet potatoes), you should know not to expect too much. Founded in 1872 by timber merchant Joseph Dargaville, this once-important river port thrived on the export of kauri timber and gum. Once the forests were destroyed, it declined, and today it's a quiet backwater servicing the agricultural Northern Wairoa area.

◎ Sights

Dargaville Museum   MUSEUM
(📞09-439 7555; www.dargavillemuseum.co.nz; Harding Park; adult/child $15/5; ⊙9am-4pm) The hilltop Dargaville Museum is more interesting than most regional museums. There's a large gumdigging display, plus maritime, Māori and musical-instrument sections, and a neat model railway. Outside, the masts of the *Rainbow Warrior* are mounted at a lookout near a *pā* site, and there's a recreation of a gumdiggers' camp.

Kumara Box   FARM
(📞09-439 7018; www.kumarabox.co.nz; 503 Pouto Rd; kumara show $20, train ride $10; ⊙by prior booking) To learn all about kumara, book ahead for Kumara Ernie's show. It's surprisingly entertaining, usually involving a journey by home-built tractor-train through the fields to 'NZ's smallest church'. There's also an extensive shell collection, and a communal kitchen and bathroom facilities for campervanners looking for a park for the night ($12).

🛌 Sleeping & Eating

Campervans can stay at the Dargaville Museum car park for $15 per night and at Kumara Box farm for $12.

Greenhouse Backpackers   HOSTEL $
(📞09-439 6342; greenhousebackpackers@ihug. co.nz; 15 Gordon St; dm/r $30/74; @🌐) This converted 1921 schoolhouse has classrooms partitioned into a large bunk-free dorm and a communal lounge, both painted with colourful murals. Better still are the cosy units in the back garden.

Aratapu Tavern   TEX-MEX $$
(📞09-439 5923; www.aratapu.com; 701 Pouto Rd; mains $15-22; ⊙noon-late Tue-Sun; 🌐) This welcoming country pub, around 7km from Dargaville on the road to Poutu Point, is deservedly famous for its lamb shanks, but also of flavour-packed interest is the Tex-Mex food, including tacos and burritos, prepared by the bubbly Texan co-owner. There's occasional live music in the garden bar on Saturdays.

WORTH A TRIP

POUTO POINT

A narrow spit descends south of Dargaville, bordered by the Tasman Sea and Wairoa River, and comes to an abrupt halt at the entrance of NZ's biggest harbour, the Kaipara. It's an incredibly remote headland, punctuated by dozens of petite dune lakes and the lonely **Kaipara Lighthouse** (built from kauri in 1884). Less than 10km separates Kaipara Harbour's north and south heads, but if you were to drive between the two you'd cover 267km.

A 4WD can be put to its proper use on the ocean-hugging 71km stretch of beach from Glinks Gully near Dargaville. The DOC's *Pouto Hidden Treasures* is a helpful guide for motorists, with tips for protecting both your car and the fragile ecosystem. It can be downloaded at www.doc.govt.nz.

Blah, Blah, Blah... CAFE $$
(☑09-439 6300; 101 Victoria St; breakfast $10-19, lunch $10-20, dinner $22-35; ☺9am-3.30pm Sun & Mon, to 8pm Tue-Sat; ☜) The number-one eatery and best bar in central Dargaville has a garden area, hip music, deli-style snacks, and beer, wine and cocktails. The global menu includes excellent cooked breakfasts, pizza and steak.

ⓘ Information

DOC Te Tai Kauri/Kauri Coast Office (☑09-439 3450; www.doc.govt.nz; 150 Colville Rd; ☺8am-4.30pm Mon-Fri) An area office rather than a visitor centre, but a good source of Northland tramping and camping information.

Visitor Information Centre (☑09-439 4975; www.kauriinfocentre.co.nz; 4 Murdoch St; ☺9am-6pm Sep-Jun, 10am-5pm Tue-Sun Jul & Aug; ☜) Operates out of the Woodturners Kauri Gallery & Studio. Books accommodation and tours.

ⓘ Getting There & Away

Shuttle buses run by West Coaster (p150) link Dargaville with Whangarei twice daily on weekdays.

Te Wai Ora Coachlines (p177) runs shuttles linking Dargaville to Auckland (three hours) via Warkworth and Matakohe, departing Auckland on a Friday evening and returning from Dargaville on a Sunday evening.

Matakohe
♫ 09 / POP 400

Apart from its rural charms, the key reason for visiting Matakohe is the superb Kauri Museum. The museum shop stocks mementoes crafted from kauri wood and gum.

Facing the museum is the tiny kauri-built **Matakohe Pioneer Church** (1867), which served both Methodists and Anglicans, and acted as the community's hall and school. Nearby, you can wander through a historic schoolhouse (1878) and post office/telephone exchange (1909).

◎ Sights

Kauri Museum MUSEUM
(☑09-431 7417; www.kau.nz; 5 Church Rd; adult/child $25/8; ☺9am-5pm) 🕭 The giant cross-sections of trees at this superb museum are astounding in themselves, but the entire industry is brought to light through life-sized reproductions of a pioneer sawmill, boarding house, bushman's hut and Victorian home – along with photos, artefacts, and fabulous furniture and marquetry. The Gum Room holds a weird and wonderful collection of kauri gum, the amber substance that can be carved, sculpted and polished to a jewel-like quality.

🛏 Sleeping

Matakohe Holiday Park HOLIDAY PARK $
(☑09-431 6431; www.matakoheholidaypark.co.nz; 66 Church Rd; sites $38, units with/without bathroom from $120/65; ☒) 🕭 This well-kept little park has modern amenities, plenty of space, a playground and good views of Kaipara Harbour. Accommodation ranges from basic cabins without bathrooms to self-contained two-bedroom motel units.

Matakohe House B&B $$
(☑09-431 7091; matakohebnb@gmail.com; 24 Church Rd; r $170-180; ☜) This B&B inhabits a pretty villa near the Kauri Museum. The simply furnished rooms open onto a wraparound veranda and offer winning touches such as complimentary port and chocolates. There's also a small kitchen for making hot beverages and a communal lounge with a piano.

ⓘ Getting There & Away

Te Wai Ora Coachlines (p177) runs a bus to Dargaville leaving Auckland on Friday night and returning on Sunday night. This service stops at Matakohe's Kauri Museum on request.

Waikato & the Coromandel Peninsula

Best Places to Eat

➡ Hayes Common (p186)

➡ Madame Woo (p187)

➡ Refinery (p230)

➡ Rock-It Kitchen (p192)

➡ Port Road Project (p227)

Best Places to Stay

➡ Earthstead (p197)

➡ Solscape (p191)

➡ Bow St Studios (p192)

➡ Out in the Styx (p196)

➡ Aroha Mountain Lodge (p199)

Why Go?

Verdant rolling hills line New Zealand's mighty Waikato River, and adrenaline junkies can surf at Raglan, or undertake extreme underground pursuits in the extraordinary Waitomo Caves.

But this is also Tainui country. In the 1850s this powerful Māori tribal coalition elected a king to resist the loss of land and sovereignty. The fertile Waikato was forcibly taken from them, but they retained control of the rugged King Country to within a whisper of the 20th century.

To the northeast, the Coromandel Peninsula juts into the Pacific, forming the Hauraki Gulf's eastern boundary. The peninsula's east coast has some of the North Island's best white-sand beaches, and the muddy wetlands and picturesque stony bays of the west coast have long been a refuge for alternative lifestylers. Down the middle, the mountains are criss-crossed with walking tracks, allowing trampers to explore large tracts of isolated bush studded with kauri trees.

When to Go

➡ Beachy accommodation in Waihi, Whitianga, Whangamata and Raglan peaks during the summer holidays from Christmas until the end of January. New Year's Eve in particular can be very busy.

➡ Balmy February and March are much quieter around the Coromandel Peninsula with settled weather and smaller crowds. Rainfall peaks in the mountainous Coromandel region from May to September.

➡ The Waikato region can see summer droughts, but the southern area around Taumarunui is often wetter and colder.

➡ If you avoid the height of school summer holidays (Christmas to January), accommodation is plentiful in the Waikato region.

➡ Raglan's surf breaks are popular year-round.

Waikato & the Coromandel Peninsula Highlights

1 Far North Coromandel (p217) Travelling remote gravel roads under a crimson canopy of ancient pohutukawa trees.

2 Te Whanganui-A-Hei Marine Reserve (p220) Kayaking around hidden islands, caves and bays.

3 Karangahake Gorge (p229) Penetrating the mystical depths of the dense bush.

4 Hahei Beach (p223) Watching the offshore islands glow in the dying haze of a summer sunset.

5 Waitomo Caves (p202) Seeking subterranean stimulation and trying black-water rafting.

6 Raglan (p190) Hitting the surf (and then the pub) at this unhurried surf town.

7 Sanctuary Mountain Maungatautari (p196) Tramping through an inland island paradise.

8 Hobbiton Movie Set Tours (p198) Channelling your inner Bilbo or Frodo at this fascinating film set.

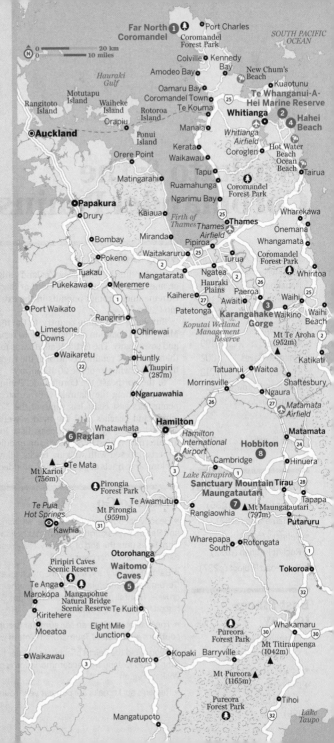

ⓘ Getting There & Away

Hamilton is the region's transport hub, with its airport (p189) servicing extensive domestic routes. Buses link the city to everywhere in the North Island. Most inland towns are also well connected on bus routes, but the remote coastal communities (apart from Mokau on SH3) are less well served.

Transport options on the Coromandel Peninsula are more limited, and the beaches and coastline of the area are most rewarding with independent transport.

WAIKATO

History

By the time Europeans started to arrive, this region – stretching as far north as Auckland's Manukau Harbour – had long been the homeland of the Waikato tribes, descended from the Tainui migration. In settling this land, the Waikato tribes displaced or absorbed tribes from earlier migrations.

Initially European contact was on Māori terms and to the advantage of the local people. Their fertile land, which was already cultivated with kumara and other crops, was well suited to the introduction of new fruits and vegetables. By the 1840s the Waikato economy was booming, with bulk quantities of produce exported to the settlers in Auckland and beyond.

Relations between the two cultures soured during the 1850s, largely due to the colonists' pressure to purchase Māori land. In response, a confederation of tribes united to elect a king to safeguard their interests, forming what became known as the Kīngitanga (King Movement).

In July 1863 Governor Grey sent a huge force to invade the Waikato and exert colonial control. After almost a year of fighting, known as the Waikato War, the Kingites retreated south to what became branded the King Country.

The war resulted in the confiscation of 3600 sq km of land, much of which was given to colonial soldiers to farm and defend. In 1995 the Waikato tribes received a full Crown apology for the wrongful invasion and confiscation of their lands, as well as a $170 million package, including the return of land that the Crown still held.

Hamilton

☏ 07 / POP 206,400

Landlocked cities in an island nation are never going to have the glamorous appeal of their coastal cousins. Rotorua compensates with boiling mud and Taupo has its lake, but Hamilton, despite the majestic Waikato River, is more prosaic.

The city definitely has an appeal, with vibrant bars and excellent restaurants and cafes around Hood and Victoria Sts. You're guaranteed to eat really well after visiting highlights like the Hamilton Gardens (p184).

The great grey-green Waikato River rolls right through town, but the city's layout largely ignores its presence: unless you're driving across a bridge you'll hardly know it's there. Thankfully, work has begun on a development to provide access from the CBD to riverside walking trails.

Most people blast along SH1 between Auckland and Hamilton in about 1½ hours, but if you're keen to meander, the upper Waikato has some interesting diversions including Ngaruawahia, where you will find **Turangawaewae Marae** (☏ 07-824 5189; 29 River Rd).

Waikato & King Country

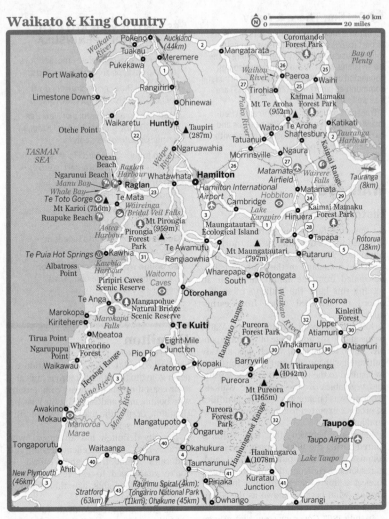

⊙ Sights

★ Waikato Museum
MUSEUM

(☑ 07-838 6606; www.waikatomuseum.co.nz; 1 Grantham St; by donation; ⊙ 10am-5pm) **FREE** The excellent Waikato Museum has several main areas: an art gallery; interactive science galleries; Tainui galleries housing Māori treasures, including the magnificently carved *waka taua* (war canoe), *Te Winikawaka;* and a Waikato River exhibition. The museum also runs a rigorous program of public events. Admission is charged for some displays, and there is a full schedule of one-off and visiting exhibitions.

★ Hamilton Gardens
GARDENS

(☑ 07-838 6782; www.hamiltongardens.co.nz; Cobham Dr; guided tour adult/child $15/8; ⊙ enclosed gardens 7.30am-5pm, info centre 9am-5pm, guided tours 11am Sep-Apr) **FREE** Spread over 50 hectares southeast of the city centre, Hamilton Gardens incorporates a large park, cafe, restaurant and extravagant themed enclosed gardens. There are separate Italian Renaissance, Chinese, Japanese, English, American and Indian gardens complete with colonnades, pagodas and a mini Taj Mahal. Equally interesting are the sustainable Productive Garden Collection, fragrant herb garden and precolonisation Māori Te Parapara garden. Look for the impressive *Nga Uri O Hinet-uparimaunga* (Earth Blanket) sculpture at the main gates.

Recent additions include a Tudor-style garden and a tropical garden with more than 200 different warm-climate species. Booking ahead for the guided tours is recommended. To get to the gardens, catch bus 29 (adult/child $3.30/2.20) from the Hamilton Transport Centre (p189).

Zealong Tea Estate PLANTATION
(☑ 0800 932 566; www.zealong.com; 495 Gordonton Rd, Gordonton; tea experience adult/child $49/25; ☺ 10am-5pm Nov-Apr, Tue-Sun May-Oct, tours 9.30am & 2.30pm) Interesting tours learning about the only tea plantation in NZ, located around 10km northeast of Hamilton. Delicious high-tea experiences offering tea-infused treats are also available (adult/child $85/60).

Waikato River RIVER, PARK
Bush-covered walkways run along both sides of the river and provide the city's green belt. Jogging paths continue to the boardwalk circling **Lake Rotoroa**, west of the centre. **Memorial Park** is closer to town and has the remains of PS *Rangiriri* – an iron-clad, steam-powered gunboat from the Waikato War – embedded in the river bank. At the time of research, improved walking access was being developed from Victoria St, Hamilton's main shopping thoroughfare.

Riff Raff MONUMENT
(www.riffraffstatue.org; Victoria St) One of Hamilton's more unusual public artworks is a life-sized statue of *Rocky Horror Picture Show* writer Richard O'Brien, aka Riff Raff, the time-warping alien from the planet Transsexual. It looks over a small park on the site of the former Embassy Theatre where O'Brien worked as a hairdresser, though it's hard to imagine 1960s Hamilton inspired the tale of bisexual alien decadence. Opposite the statue, the bright red 'Frankenfurter's Lab' actually conceals recently installed public toilets.

Classics Museum MUSEUM
(☑ 07-957-2230; www.classicsmuseum.co.nz; 11 Railside Pl, Frankton; adult/child $20/8; ☺ 7am-3pm Mon-Fri, 8am-4pm Sat & Sun) Travel in time amid this collection of more than 100 classic cars from the first half of the 20th century. Even if you're not a motorhead, you'll still be dazzled by the crazy Amphicar and the

cool Maserati and Corvette sports cars. The museum is just off SH1, northwest of central Hamilton.

Hamilton Zoo ZOO
(☑ 07-838 6720; www.hamiltonzoo.co.nz; 183 Brymer Rd; adult/child/family $23/11/66, tours extra; ☺ 9am-4.30pm, last entry 3pm) Hamilton Zoo houses 500-plus species including wily and curious chimpanzees. Guided-tour options include Eye2Eye and Face2Face opportunities to go behind the scenes to meet various animals, plus daily Meet the Keeper talks from the critters' caregivers. The zoo is 8km northwest of Hamilton city centre.

ArtsPost GALLERY
(www.waikatomuseum.co.nz/artspost; 120 Victoria St; ☺ 10am-5pm) FREE This contemporary gallery and gift shop is housed in a grand, former post office. It focuses on the best of local art: paintings, glass, prints, textiles and photography.

Taupiri MOUNTAIN
About 26km north of Hamilton on SH1 is Taupiri (287m), the sacred mountain of the Tainui people. You'll recognise it by the cemetery on its slopes and the honking of passing car horns – locals saying hi to their loved ones as they pass by. In August 2006 thousands gathered here as the much-loved Māori queen, Dame Te Atairangikaahu, was transported upriver by *waka* (canoe) to her final resting place, an unmarked grave on the summit.

🏃 Activities

Waikato River Explorer CRUISE
(☑ 0800 139 756; www.waikatoexplorer.co.nz; Hamilton Gardens Jetty; adult/child $35/18; ☺ usually Wed-Sun, daily 26 Dec-6 Feb) Scenic 1½-hour cruises along the Waikato River depart from the Hamilton Gardens (p184) jetty. Days of departure vary, especially outside of summer, so check the website for departure dates and times. Also see the website for other cruises incorporating wine-tasting.

Extreme Edge CLIMBING
(☑ 07-847 5858; www.extremeedgehamilton.co.nz; 90 Greenwood St; day pass incl harness adult/child $18.50/14; ☺ noon-9.30pm Mon-Fri, 9am-7pm Sat & Sun; ♿) Near the Frankton train station, west of town, Extreme Edge has hyper-coloured climbing walls, 14m of which are overhanging. There's a kids' climbing zone and free safety lessons.

Kiwi Balloon Company
BALLOONING

(☑ 07-843 8538, 021 912 679; www.kiwiballoon company.co.nz; per person $370) Float above lush Waikato countryside. The whole experience takes about four hours and includes a champagne breakfast and an hour's flying time.

★☆ Festivals & Events

New Zealand Rugby Sevens
SPORTS

(www.sevens.co.nz; ⊙early Feb) Held at Hamilton's Stadium Waikato across the first weekend of February, this is the New Zealand leg of the international Rugby Sevens Series. Look forward to lots of running rugby from teams representing many countries. Favourites usually include New Zealand (of course...), Fiji and South Africa, and attending the event in fancy dress is definitely encouraged.

Hamilton Gardens Arts Festival
PERFORMING ARTS

(☑ 07-859 1317; www.hgaf.co.nz; ⊙Feb) Music, comedy, theatre, dance and movies, all served up alfresco in the Hamilton Gardens (p184) during the last two weeks of February.

Balloons over Waikato
SPORTS

(☑ 07-856 7215; www.balloonsoverwaikato.co.nz; ⊙Mar) A colourful hot-air-balloon fest.

⨀ Sleeping

★ City Centre B&B
B&B $

(☑ 07-838 1671; www.citycentrebnb.co.nz; 3 Anglesea St; r $90-125; @ ⓢ ⌘) At the quiet riverside end of a central city street (just five minutes' walk to the Victoria and Hood Sts action), this sparkling self-contained apartment opens onto a swimming pool. There's also a bedroom available in a wing of the main house. Self-catering breakfast is provided. Minimum stay of two nights.

Backpackers Central
HOSTEL $

(☑ 07-839 1928; www.backpackerscentral.co.nz; 846 Victoria St; dm $30, s $49, r $82-125; @ ⓢ) Well-run hostel with dorms and singles on one floor, doubles and family rooms on another – some with en-suite bathrooms and all with access to a shared kitchen and lounge. Worth considering as an alternative to a motel room if you're travelling as a couple or in a group.

Hamilton City Holiday Park
HOLIDAY PARK $

(☑ 07-855 8255; www.hamiltoncityholidaypark. co.nz; 14 Ruakura Rd; campsites/cabins/units from $36/60/88; @ ⓢ) Simple cabins and leafy sites are the rule at this shady park. It's reasonably close to town (2km east of the centre) and very affordable.

Atrium on Ulster
MOTEL $$

(☑ 07-839 0839; www.atriumonulster.co.nz; 281 Ulster St; d $145-245; ⓢ) Our pick as the best of the motels along Hamilton's Ulster St strip slightly north of the central city. Studios and one- and two-bedroom apartments all feature stylish decor, facilities include a gym and hot tub, and the sporting attractions at Waikato Stadium are very close.

Anglesea Motel
MOTEL $$

(☑ 07-834 0010; www.angleseamotel.com; 36 Liverpool St; units from $150; @ ⓢ ⌘) Getting great feedback from travellers, the Anglesea has plenty of space, friendly managers, a pool, squash and tennis courts, and not un-stylish decor.

✕ Eating

Duck Island Ice Cream
ICE CREAM $

(☑ 07-856 5948; www.duckislandicecream.co.nz; 300 Grey St; ice cream from $4.50; ⊙11am-6pm Tue-Thu & Sun, to 9pm Fri & Sat; ⌘) A dazzling array of ever-changing flavours – how does rhubarb and Szechuan peppercorn or blackberry, sage and honey sound? – makes Duck Island one of NZ's best ice-cream parlours. The sunny corner location is infused with a hip retro vibe, and the refreshing housemade sodas and ice-cream floats are other worthy reasons to cross the river to Hamilton East.

Banh Mi Caphe
VIETNAMESE $

(☑ 07-839 1141; www.facebook.com/banhmicaphe; 198/2 Victoria St; snacks & mains $10-17; ⊙noon-late Tue-Sat) Fresh spring rolls, Vietnamese *banh mi* (sandwiches) and steaming bowls of *pho* (noodle soup) all feature at this hip spot channelling the backstreets of Hanoi.

★ Hayes Common
CAFE $$

(☑ 027 537 1853; www.hayescommon.co.nz; cnr Plunket Tce & Jellicoe Dr, Hamilton East; mains $21-34; ⊙8am-11pm Wed-Sat, to 4pm Sun & Tue; ⌘) ⌀ Journey across to Hamilton East to this bustling new opening in a former garage. Thoroughly unpretentious, Hayes Common's versatile menu stretches from *acai* bowls for breakfast through to *dukkah* fried eggs or a jerk-chicken burger for lunch. Dinner options including lamb with harissa are equally cosmopolitan, and the wine list and local craft beers on tap will ensure you linger.

A special section of the menu is dedicated to vegan options. When you're finished eating, it's a short walk to the riverside for views across to the CBD.

Hamilton

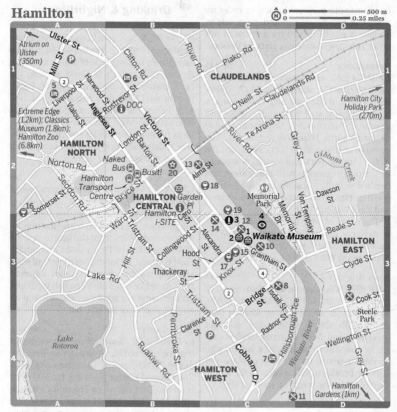

Hamilton

◎ Top Sights
1 Waikato Museum C3

◎ Sights
2 ArtsPost C3
3 Riff Raff C3
4 Waikato River C3

🛏 Sleeping
5 Anglesea Motel A1
6 Backpackers Central B1
7 City Centre B&B C4

🍴 Eating
Banh Mi Caphe .... (see 3)
8 Chim Choo Ree C3

9 Duck Island Ice Cream D3
10 Gothenburg C3
11 Hayes Common C4
12 Madame Woo C3
13 Palate B2
14 River Kitchen C3

🍷 Drinking & Nightlife
15 Craft C3
16 Good George Brewing A2
17 Little George C3
18 Local Taphouse C2
19 Wonderhorse C2

🎭 Entertainment
20 Lido Cinema B2

★ **Madame Woo**   MALYASIAN $$
(☏ 07-839 5605; www.madamwoo.co.nz/hamilton;
6 Sapper Moore-Jones Pl; mains $26-32; ☺11am-
late; ☑) 🍴 The authentic flavours of Ma-

laysian street food are served in this high-
ceilinged space just off Victoria St. Partner
Asian-inspired cocktails or craft beer with
Madame Woo's signature hawker rolls

crammed with pork or chicken, or order up a feast of punchy curries and zingy salads. Service is excellent, and it's a crime to not order Portuguese-style egg tarts for dessert.

Gothenburg
TAPAS $$

(07-834 3562; www.gothenburg.co.nz; ANZ Centre, 21 Grantham St; shared plates $8-27; ⊙9am-11pm Mon-Fri, 11.30am-late Sat) Showcasing a scenic riverside spot with high ceilings and a summer-friendly deck, Gothenburg is one of our favourite Hamilton restaurants. The menu of shared plates effortlessly spans the globe – try the pork and kimchi dumplings or the potato gnocchi with blue cheese and candied walnuts – and the beer list features rotating taps from Scandinavian breweries and local Waikato craft brewers.

The range of wine and cocktails is equally stellar – especially the orange espresso martini – and the dessert of chai and gingerbread panna cotta is a Gothenburg classic.

River Kitchen
CAFE $$

(07-839 2906; www.theriverkitchen.co.nz; 237 Victoria St; mains $14-19; ⊙7am-4pm Mon-Fri, 8am-3pm Sat & Sun; ⌨) River Kitchen does things with simple style: cakes, gourmet breakfasts and fresh seasonal lunches (angle for the salmon hash), and a barista who knows his beans. It's the kind of place you visit for breakfast, come back to for lunch, then consider for breakfast the next day.

Chim Choo Ree
MODERN NZ $$$

(07-839 4329; www.chimchooree.co.nz; 14 Bridge St; mains $36-38; ⊙11.30am-2pm Mon-Fri, 5pm-late Mon-Sat) In a heritage building beside the river, Chim Choo Ree focuses on small plates such as tuna tartare with rugby grapefruit, goat curd tortellini, and confit pork belly, plus larger, equally inventive mains using duck, lamb, venison and snapper. Local foodies wash it all down with a great wine list and flavourful NZ craft beers. A six-course tasting menu is $100.

Palate
MODERN NZ, FUSION $$$

(07-834 2921; www.palaterestaurant.co.nz; 20 Alma St; mains $34-38; ⊙11.30am-2pm Tue-Fri, 5.30pm-late Tue-Sat) Simple, sophisticated Palate has a well-deserved reputation for lifting the culinary bar across regional NZ. The innovative menu features highlights such as beef-cheek ravioli with smoked mushroom and a blue-cheese pudding. The wine selection is one of Hamilton's finest, local craft breweries are well supported with seasonal brews on offer, and a good-value express lunch is $25 for two courses.

🍷 Drinking & Nightlife

Craft
CRAFT BEER

(07-839 4531; www.facebook.com/craftbeer hamilton; 15 Hood St; ⊙3pm-late Wed-Fri, from 1pm Sat) Fifteen rotating taps of amber goodness flow at Craft, which is plenty to keep the city's craft-beer buffs coming back. Brews from around NZ make a regular appearance, with occasional surprising additions from international cult breweries. Quiz night kicks off most Wednesdays at 7pm, and decent sliders and wood-fired pizza could well see you making a night of it.

Local Taphouse
BAR

(07-834 4923; www.facebook.com/thelocal taphouse; Sky City, 346 Victoria St; ⊙11am-10pm) Part of Hamilton's Sky City eating and drinking precinct, the Local Taphouse features locally sourced beers from the nearby regions of Waikato, Bay of Plenty and Coromandel. Food is served, including hearty pots of mussels and gourmet burgers. Other adjacent Sky City options include a Spanish tapas and grill restaurant, a good daytime cafe and an elegant after-dark cocktail bar.

Little George
CRAFT BEER

(07-834 4345; www.facebook.com/littlegeorge popupbar; 15 Hood St; ⊙4pm-1am Tue-Thu, 3pm-3am Fri, 5.30pm-3am Sat) The more central sibling to Good George Brewing, Little George is an excellent bar along Hood St's nightlife strip. Beers from Good George are regularly featured, but guest taps also showcase other Kiwi craft breweries. Good bar snacks are available, and a local food truck is usually on hand from 4pm to 9pm on Thursdays. Taco Tuesdays are also good value.

Good George Brewing
BREWERY

(07-847 3223; www.goodgeorge.co.nz; 32a Somerset St, Frankton; tours incl beer $22; ⊙11am-late, tours from 6pm Tue-Thu) Channelling a cool industrial vibe, the former Church of St George is now a shrine to craft beer. Order a flight of five beers ($15), and partner the hoppy heaven with wood-fired pizzas ($22) or main meals ($25 to $34). Our favourite brews are the citrusy American Pale Ale and the zingy Drop Hop Cider. Tours must be booked ahead.

Wonderhorse
COCKTAIL BAR, CRAFT BEER

(07-839 2281; www.facebook.com/wonderhorse bar; 232 Victoria St; ⊙5pm-3am Wed-Sat) Tucked away around 20m off Victoria St, Wonderhorse regularly features craft beers from niche local brewers including Shunters Yard and Brewaucracy. Vintage vinyl is often spinning on the turntable, and sliders and Asian street eats combine with killer cocktails at one of Hamilton's best bars.

☆ Entertainment

Lido Cinema CINEMA
(📞 07-838 9010; www.lidocinema.co.nz; Level 1, Centre Place, 501 Victoria St; tickets adult/child $16/10; ⏰ 10am-late) Art-house movies with $11 Tuesday tickets.

ℹ Information

Anglesea Clinic (📞 07-858 0800; www.angleseamedical.co.nz; cnr Anglesea & Thackeray Sts; ⏰ 24hr) For accidents and urgent medical assistance.

DOC (Department of Conservation; 📞 07-858 1000; www.doc.govt.nz; Level 5, 73 Rostrevor St; ⏰ 8am-4.30pm Mon-Fri) Maps and brochures on walking tracks, campsites and DOC huts.

Hamilton i-SITE (📞 0800 242 645, 07-958 5960; www.visithamilton.co.nz; cnr Caro & Alexandra Sts; ⏰ 9am-5pm Mon-Fri, 9.30am-3.30pm Sat & Sun; 📶) Accommodation, activities and transport bookings, plus free wi-fi right across Garden Pl.

Post Office (📞 07 839 4991; www.nzpost.co.nz; Centre Place, inside Paper Plus; ⏰ 9am-5.30pm Mon-Sat, 10am-4pm Sun) The most central post office option is located in a Paper Plus store in the Centre Place mall.

Waikato Hospital (📞 07-839 8899; www.waikatodhb.govt.nz; Pembroke St; ⏰ 24hr) Main hospital for the Waikato region; around 3km south of central Hamilton.

ℹ Getting There & Away

AIR

Hamilton International Airport (HIA; 📞 07-848 9027; www.hamiltonairport.co.nz; Airport Rd) is 12km south of the city. **Air New Zealand** (📞 0800 737 000; www.airnewzealand.co.nz) has regular direct flights from Hamilton to Christchurch, Palmerston North and Wellington.

Super Shuttle (📞 0800 748 885, 07-843 7778; www.supershuttle.co.nz; one way $30) offers a door-to-door service into the city. **Aerolink Shuttles** (📞 0800 151 551; www.aerolink.nz; one way $80) also has airport services, while **Raglan Scenic Tours** (📞 021 0274 7014, 07-825 0507; www.raglanscenictours.co.nz) links the airport with Raglan. A taxi (p190) costs around $55. InterCity runs a direct bus from Hamilton to Auckland Airport.

BUS

All buses arrive at and depart from the **Hamilton Transport Centre** (📞 07-834 3457; www.hamilton.co.nz; cnr Anglesea & Bryce Sts; 📶).

Waikato Regional Council's Busit! coaches serve the region, including Ngaruawahia, Cambridge, Te Awamutu and Raglan.

InterCity (📞 09-583 5780; www.intercity.co.nz) services numerous destinations including the following:

DESTINATION	PRICE ($)	DURATION	FREQUENCY (DAILY)
Auckland	12-32	2hr	11
Cambridge	10-22	25min	9
Matamata	10-18	50min	4
Ngaruawahia	10-21	20min	9
Rotorua	14-35	1½hr	5
Te Aroha	10	1hr	2
Te Awamutu	10-15	35min	3
Wellington	30-75	5hr	3

Naked Bus (https://nakedbus.com) services run to the following destinations (among many others):

DESTINATION	PRICE ($)	DURATION	FREQUENCY (DAILY)
Auckland	17-19	2hr	5
Cambridge	15	30min	5-7
Matamata	20	1hr	1
Ngaruawahia	15	30min	5
Rotorua	10	1½hr	4-5
Wellington	25-45	9½hr	1-2

TRAIN

Hamilton is on the **Northern Explorer** (📞 0800 872 467; www.greatjourneysofnz.co.nz) route between Auckland (from $49, 2½ hours) and Wellington (from $119, 9½ hours) via Otorohanga (from $59, 45 minutes). Trains depart Auckland on Mondays, Thursdays and Saturdays and stop at Hamilton's **Frankton train station** (Fraser St), 1km west of the city centre; there are no ticket sales here – see the website for ticketing details.

ℹ Getting Around

Hamilton's **Busit!** (📞 0800 4287 5463; www.busit.co.nz; city routes adult/child $3.30/2.20) network services the city centre and suburbs daily from around 7am to 7.30pm (later on Fridays). All buses pass through Hamilton Transport Centre. Busit! also runs a free CBD shuttle looping around Victoria, Liverpool, Anglesea and Bridge Sts every 10 minutes (7am to 6pm weekdays).

Victoria St is the city's main shopping area and parking can be difficult to secure. You'll have more luck finding parking a few blocks to the west.

For a taxi, try **Hamilton Taxis** (☑07-847 7477, 0800 477 477; www.hamiltontaxis.co.nz).

Alternatively, you can rent a car from **RaD Car Hire** (☑07-839 1049; www.radcarhire.co.nz; 383 Anglesea St; ⊙7.30am-5pm Mon-Fri, 8am-noon Sat).

Raglan

☑07 / POP 2740

Laid-back Raglan may well be New Zealand's perfect surfing town. It's small enough to have escaped mass development, but big enough to exhibit signs of life including good eateries and a bar that attracts big-name bands in summer. Along with the famous surf spots to the south, the harbour just begs to be kayaked upon. There's also an excellent arts scene, with several galleries and shops worthy of perusal.

◎ Sights

Old School Arts Centre   ARTS CENTRE, GALLERY
(☑07-825 0023; www.raglanartscentre.co.nz; Stewart St; ⊙10am-2pm Mon-Fri) FREE A community hub, the Old School Arts Centre has changing exhibitions and workshops, including weaving, carving, yoga and storytelling. Movies screen here regularly during summer ($15): grab a snack and a beer to complete the experience. The hippie/artsy **Raglan Creative Market** happens out the front on the second Sunday (10am to 2pm) of the month.

HORSE RIDING AROUND RAGLAN

Tramping, surfing, paddle boarding and kayaking are all popular ways to explore the stellar blend of forest and ocean scenery around Raglan, but horse riding is also highly regarded. Two well-established operators offer excursions ranging from beach rides – even riding bareback into the shallows of the ocean – through to farm rides and negotiating forested paths. Check out **Surf & Turf** (☑027 435 2648; www.raglanhorseriding.co.nz; 3953B SH23; from $65) for the best opportunities to blend equine and ocean action, and hook up with **Wild Coast Ruapuke** (☑07-825 0059; www.wildcoast.co.nz; 1549 Whaanga Rd, Ruapuke; from $130) 🎏 for exciting combinations of bush, beach and farm scenery around Mt Karioi.

🏃 Activities

Raglan Rock   ROCK CLIMBING, CAVING
(☑0800 724 7625; www.raglanrock.com; climbing half-day $120, caving & canyoning $120) Full instruction and all equipment for climbing on the limestone cliffs of nearby Stone Valley, or the exciting Stupid Fat Hobbit climb and abseil above Raglan Harbour. Caving options include Stone Valley and the more challenging Rattlesnake. Canyoning is also available – ask about after-dark canyoning trips taking in a glowworm-illuminated waterfall. Minimum two people.

Raglan Watersports   WATER SPORTS
(☑07-825 0507; www.raglanwatersports.co.nz; 5a Bankart St; group/private paddle-boarding lessons per person $45/65) A well-run, one-stop spot for paddle-boarding lessons, hire and guided tours; kayak rental and tours; kiteboarding and surfing lessons; and board hire. Bikes can also be hired – see the website for recommendations on local rides.

Raglan Kayak & Paddleboard   KAYAKING
(☑07-825 8862; www.raglaneco.co.nz; Bow St Jetty; single/double kayaks per half day $45/65, 3hr guided harbour paddle per person $89; ⊙Nov-May) Raglan Harbour is great for kayaking. This outfit rents kayaks and runs guided tours. Learn the basics on the gentle Opotoru River, or paddle out to investigate the nooks and crannies of the pancake rocks on the harbour's northern edge. Paddle-board rental, tours and lessons are also available.

Solscape   SURFING
(☑07-825 8268; www.solscape.co.nz; 611 Wainui Rd; board & wetsuit hire per half day $35) Super Solscape offers 2½-hour surfing lessons ($85).

👉 Tours

Waihine Moe Sunset Harbour Cruise   CRUISE
(☑07-825 7873; www.raglanboatcharters.co.nz; Raglan Wharf; adult/child $49/29; ⊙Thu-Sun late Dec-Mar) Two-hour sunset cruises, including a few drinks, around Raglan Harbour on the *Wahine Moe*. Ninety-minute morning harbour cruises ($30/15 per adult/child) leaving from Raglan's Bow St jetty are also available on the smaller *Harmony* vessel. Complimentary pick-ups are included.

Raglan Scenic Tours   TOURS
(☑07-825 0507; www.raglanscenictours.co.nz; 7a Main Rd; 2½hr Raglan sightseeing tour adult/child $60/20) Sightseeing tours, including around the Raglan area and departures (adult/child

Raglan

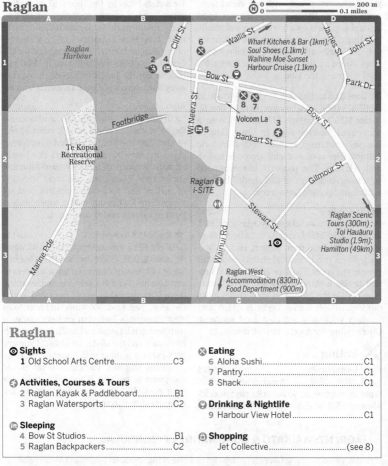

Raglan

⊙ Sights
1 Old School Arts Centre............................C3

⊕ Activities, Courses & Tours
2 Raglan Kayak & Paddleboard................B1
3 Raglan Watersports.................................C2

⊑ Sleeping
4 Bow St Studios..B1
5 Raglan Backpackers................................C2

⊗ Eating
6 Aloha Sushi..C1
7 Pantry...C1
8 Shack..C1

⊕ Drinking & Nightlife
9 Harbour View Hotel.................................C1

⊕ Shopping
Jet Collective....................................(see 8)

$48/15) to Bridal Veil Falls or Te Toto Gorge. Treks up Mt Karioi can be arranged (adult from $60).

🛏 Sleeping

Solscape　　　　　　　　　HOSTEL, CABIN $
(☎07-825 8268; www.solscape.co.nz; 611 Wainui Rd; campsites per person $20, caboose dm/d $30/80, tepees per person $40, cottage d $100-220; @🖥)
🖉 With a hilltop location fringed by native bush, Solscape's ecofriendly accommodation includes tepees, bell tents, rammed-earth domes, railway carriages and stylish eco-baches. There's room for tents and campervans, and simpler cottages are also available. Environmental impact is minimised with solar energy, and organic produce from the permaculture garden is used for guest meals in the Conscious Kitchen cafe.

Yoga, massage and surfing lessons are all available. Solscape is also YHA-affiliated.

Raglan West Accommodation　　MOTEL $
(☎07-282 0248; www.raglanwestaccommodation. com; 45 Wainui Rd; d $90; 🖥) Good-value accommodation with simple self-contained kitchenettes just a short walk – via a handy footbridge – to the cafes, restaurants and shops of Raglan. There's also a good cafe close by for a leisurely breakfast.

Raglan Backpackers　　　　　HOSTEL $
(☎07-825 0515; www.raglanbackpackers.co.nz; 6 Wi Neera St; vehicle sites per person $19, dm $29-31, s $59, tw & d $78; @) This laid-back hostel

is right on the water, with sea views from some rooms. Other rooms are arranged around a garden courtyard or in a separate building. There are free bikes and kayaks for use, and surfboards for hire, or take a yoga class, strum a guitar or drip in the sauna. No wi-fi – it 'ruins the vibe'.

★ **Bow St Studios** APARTMENT $$
(☑ 07-825 0551; www.bowstreet.co.nz; 1 Bow St; studios $155-245, cottages $175-195; ☜) With a waterfront location right in town, Bow St has self-contained studios and a historic cottage. The cool and chic decor is stylish and relaxing. The property is surrounded by a subtropical garden and shaded by well-established pohutukawa trees.

Hidden Valley COTTAGE $$
(☑07-825 5813; www.hiddenvalleyraglan.com; SH23, Te Uku; d $195-245) Located on 12 hectares of native forest 3km from Raglan, Hidden Valley features two individual chalets, both with private spa pools. The Tree Tops chalet is nestled beside a stand of kahikatea (NZ white pine), while the Mountain View chalet looks out towards Mt Karioi. Decor is stylish and modern with fully self-contained kitchens. Check online for good midweek discounts.

✖ Eating

Food Department CAFE $
(☑07-282 0248; www.facebook.com/food departmentraglanroast; 45 Wainui Rd; pizza slices $6, whole pizza $18-24; ☺8am-8.30pm Thu-Mon, to 5pm Tue & Wed) Pizza by the slice and interesting gelato – our favourite is the cinnamon and rice – reinforce the authentic Italian credentials of the Food Department. The scattering of mismatched retro furniture is good for the first coffee of the day, and comfort food like lasagna can be purchased to eat in or take away. Also a great place for a leisurely brunch.

Aloha Sushi JAPANESE $
(☑07-825 7440; www.facebook.com/AlohaSushi Raglan; 4 Wallis St; sushi $1.60-2, mains $10-23; ☺10am-8pm Wed-Mon; ☑) Rolled-to-order sushi, udon noodles and *donburi* rice bowls, all with a touch of hip Hawaiian-Japanese surfer style. Check out the great selection of surfing and rock-music posters, and set yourself up for the day with a super-healthy bowl of salmon and avocado *poke*.

★ **Rock-It Kitchen** CAFE $$
(☑07-825 8233; www.rockitraglan.co.nz; 248 Wainui Rd; mains $20-35; ☺9am-3pm Sun-Thu, to late Fri & Sat; ☑) ✿ Around 3km from town adjacent to surf beaches, Rock-It Kitchen combines rustic decor – it's housed in an old woolshed – with the area's best food. NZ wines and beer from west Auckland's Hallertau brewery combine with Scotch fillet steak and truffle potato mash for dinner, and the all-day breakfast of kumara hash cakes is popular with hungry surfers.

During summer, the outdoor tables are the place to be, and if the tide's right, it's even possible to steer a kayak way up the Wainui estuary from Raglan.

MĀORI NZ: WAIKATO & COROMANDEL PENINSULA

The Waikato and King Country region remains one of the strongest pockets of Māori influence in New Zealand. This is the heartland of the Tainui tribes, descended from those who disembarked from the Tainui *waka* (canoe) in Kawhia in the 14th century. Split into four main tribal divisions (Waikato, Hauraki, Ngāti Maniapoto and Ngāti Raukawa), Tainui are inextricably linked with the Kīngitanga (King Movement), which has its base in Ngaruawahia.

The best opportunities to interact with Māori culture are Ngaruawahia's Regatta Day and Koroneihana celebrations. Interesting *taonga* (treasures) are displayed at museums in Hamilton and Te Awamutu.

Reminders of the Waikato Land War can be found at Rangiriri, Rangiaowhia and Orakau. See www.thewaikatowar.co.nz to download maps, audio files and a smartphone app covering various locations of the fighting from 1863 to 1864.

Dozens of *marae* (meeting house) complexes are dotted around the countryside – including at Awakino, and at Kawhia, where the Tainui *waka* is buried. You won't be able to visit these without permission, but you can get decent views from the gates. Some regional tours include an element of Māori culture, including Ruakuri Cave (p202) at Waitomo.

Although it has a long and rich Māori history, the nearby Coromandel Peninsula doesn't offer many opportunities to engage with the culture. Historic *pā* (fortified village) sites are dotted around, with the most accessible being Paaku (p225). There are others at Opito Beach, Hahei and Hot Water Beach.

Shack
INTERNATIONAL $$

(☑07-825 0027; www.theshackraglan.com; 19 Bow St; mains $15-21; ⊘8am-4pm; 🛜🍴) 🍴 Brunch classics – try the chickpea-and-corn fritters – and interesting mains such as kimchi fried rice and slow-roasted lamb shoulder feature at Raglan's best cafe. A longboard strapped to the wall, wobbly old floorboards, up-tempo tunes and international staff serving Kiwi wines and craft beers complete the picture. Healthy options include an *acai* bowl crammed with fruit, granola and local coconut yoghurt.

Pantry
CAFE $$

(☑07-825 8405; 23 Bow St; mains $15-20; ⊘8am-4pm daily, 5-9pm Thu-Sat; 🍴) 🍴 Previously dubbed the Raglan Social Club, this spacious and sunny location on the main street reopened in October 2017 as the Pantry. Look forward to excellent counter food – including fresh salads prepared daily – and Thursday to Saturday dinner specials (eat in or take away), including tacos and gourmet burgers. Imported beer and cider both available on tap.

There are also plenty of vegetarian and vegan options.

🍷 Drinking & Nightlife

Wharf Kitchen & Bar
BAR, CAFE

(☑07-825-0010; www.thewharfkitchenbar.co.nz; 43 Rose St; ⊘9.30am-late) Recently opened near the town's wharf, this is the best place to combine a wine or cold beer with afternoon sunshine or a Raglan sunset. Inside, the decor mixes Raglan's heritage with a maritime vibe, and a good food menu includes plump mussels, fish tacos and snapper ceviche. Shared platters ($38 to $55) are good for groups or hungry couples.

Harbour View Hotel
PUB

(☑07-825 8010; www.harbourviewhotel.co.nz; 14 Bow St; ⊘11am-late) Classic old pub with main-street drinks on the shaded veranda. Decent pizza too and occasional live music on weekends and during summer.

🛍 Shopping

★ Toi Hauāuru Studio
ART

(☑021 174 4629, 07-825 0244; www.toihauauru.com; 4338 Main Rd; ⊘10am-5pm Wed-Sun) Run by local artist Simon Te Wheoro, this excellent gallery/shop is located 2km from Raglan on the road from Hamilton. Contemporary artwork and sculpture with a Māori influence and *pounamu* (greenstone) carvings are for sale. Simon is also skilled in the

Māori art of *ta moko* (tattoo) – if you're keen for one, get in touch via the website.

Quirky local surfwear and colourful Māori *hei tiki* (pendants) make affordable and interesting souvenirs.

Soul Shoes
SHOES

(☑07-825 8765; www.soulshoes.co.nz; Raglan Wharf, Wallis St; ⊘10am-5pm) World famous in Raglan since 1973, Soul Shoes' range of handmade leather footwear has been joined by equally cool satchels, backpacks and bags. It also has an outlet (open Thursday to Monday) on Volcom Lane in central Raglan.

Jet Collective
ARTS & CRAFTS

(☑07-825 8566; www.jetcollective.co.nz; 19a Bow St; ⊘10am-4pm Wed-Mon) Funky gallery-shop showcasing 100% Raglan artists with everything from music CDs and mixed media pieces through to retro Kiwiana-inspired work. It's also a good spot to drop in and chat with the friendly team about Raglan's growing and diverse arts scene.

❶ Information

Raglan i-SITE (☑07-825 0556; www.raglan.org.nz; 13 Wainui Rd; ⊘9am-5pm Tue-Thu, to 6.30pm Fri & Sat, to 5.30pm Sun & Mon) Department of Conservation (DOC) brochures, plus information about accommodation and activities including kitesurfing and paddle boarding. Check out the attached museum, especially the exhibition on the history of Raglan's surfing scene.

West Coast Health Centre (☑07-825 0114; 12 Wallis St; ⊘9am-5pm Mon-Fri) General medical assistance.

❶ Getting There & Away

Raglan is 48km west of Hamilton along SH23. Unsealed back roads connect Raglan to Kawhia, 50km south; they're slow, winding and prone to rockslides, but scenic and certainly off the beaten track. Head back towards Hamilton for 7km and take the Te Mata/Kawhia turn-off and follow the signs; allow at least an hour.

Waikato District Council's **Busit!** (☑0800 4287 5463; www.busit.co.nz; adult/child $9/5.60) heads between Hamilton and Raglan (one hour) four times daily on weekdays and twice daily on weekends.

Raglan Scenic Tours (p190) runs a Raglan–Hamilton shuttle bus (one way $42.50) and direct transfers to/from Auckland International Airport.

❶ Getting Around

Raglan Taxi (☑027 825 8159) Local taxi service.

South of Raglan

South of Raglan, the North Island's west coast unfurls with a series of excellent surf beaches. Whale Bay and Manu Bay draw board riders from around the world, and for non-surfers, there are scenic walking opportunities around Mt Karioi and Mt Pirongia.

◉ Sights

Mt Karioi   MOUNTAIN
(Sleeping Lady) In legend, Mt Karioi (756m), the Sleeping Lady (check out that profile), is the sister to Mt Pirongia. At its base (8km south of Whale Bay), **Te Toto Gorge** is a steep cleft in the mountainside, with a vertigo-inducing lookout perched high over the chasm. Starting from the Te Toto Gorge car park, a strenuous but scenic track goes up the western slope. It takes 2½ hours to reach a lookout point, followed by an easier hour to the summit.

From the eastern side, the **Wairake Track** is a steeper 2½-hour climb to the summit, where it meets the Te Toto Track.

Waireinga   WATERFALL
(Bridal Veil Falls) Just past Te Mata (a short drive south of the main Raglan–Hamilton road) is the turn-off to the 55m-high Waireinga, 4km from the main road. From the car park, it's an easy 10-minute walk through mossy native bush to the top of the falls (not suitable for swimming). A further 10-minute walk leads down to the bottom. Lock your car: theft is a problem here.

Mt Pirongia   MOUNTAIN
(www.mtpirongia.org.nz) The main attraction of the 170-sq-km Pirongia Forest Park is Mt Pirongia, its 959m summit clearly visible from much of the Waikato. The mountain is usually climbed from Corcoran Rd (three to five hours, one way) with tracks to other lookout points. Interestingly, NZ's tallest known kahikatea tree (66.5m) grows on the mountainside. There's a six-bunk DOC hut near the summit if you need to spend the night: maps and information are available from Hamilton DOC (p189).

🏃 Activities

The surf spots near Raglan – Indicators, Whale Bay and Manu Bay – are internationally famous for their point breaks. Bruce Brown's classic 1964 wave-chaser film *The Endless Summer* features Manu Bay.

Manu Bay   SURFING
A 2.5km journey from Ngarunui Beach will bring you to Manu Bay, a legendary surf spot said to have the longest left-hand break in the world. The elongated uniform waves are created by the angle at which the Tasman Sea swell meets the coastline (it works best in a southwesterly swell).

Whale Bay   SURFING
Whale Bay is a renowned surf spot 1km west of Manu Bay. It's usually less crowded than Manu Bay, but from the bottom of Calvert Rd you have to clamber 600m over the rocks to get to the break.

Ngarunui Beach   SURFING, SWIMMING
Less than 1km south of **Ocean Beach**, Ngarunui Beach is great for grommets learning to surf. On the cliff top is a clubhouse for the volunteer lifeguards who patrol part of the black-sand beach from late October until April. This is the only beach with lifeguards, and is the best ocean beach for swimming.

Raglan Surf School   SURFING
(📞 07-825 7873; www.raglansurfingschool.co.nz; 5b Whaanga Rd, Whale Bay; rental per hr surfboards from $20, body boards $5, wetsuits $5, 3hr lesson incl transport from Raglan $89) Raglan Surf School prides itself on getting 95% of first-timers standing during their first lesson. It's based at Karioi Lodge in Whale Bay. It also operates **Surfdames** (📞 07-825 7873; www.surfdames.co.nz; 5b Whaanga Rd, Whale Bay; surfing lessons per person $100), which offers women-only surfing experiences incorporating lessons with yoga, massage and beauty treatments.

🛏 Sleeping

Karioi Lodge   HOSTEL $
(📞 07-825 7873; www.karioilodge.co.nz; 5b Whaanga Rd, Whale Bay; dm/d $33/79; @ 🖥) 🚗 Deep in native bush, Karioi Lodge offers a sauna, mountain bikes, bush and beach walks, sustainable gardening, tree planting and the Raglan Surf School. There are no en suites, but the rooms are clean and cosy. Campervan travellers can stay for $18 per person in forested surroundings with access to Karioi's bathroom and kitchen facilities.

Sleeping Lady Lodgings   LODGE $$
(📞 07-825 7873; www.sleepinglady.co.nz; 5b Whaanga Rd; lodges $175-280) Sleeping Lady Lodgings is a collection of very comfortable self-contained houses all with ocean views.

ℹ Getting There & Away

There is no public transport. Tours are available with Raglan Scenic Tours (p190).

Te Awamutu

☑ 07 / POP 9800

Deep into dairy-farming country, Te Awamutu (which means 'The River Cut Short'; the Waikato beyond this point was unsuitable for large canoes) is a pleasant rural service centre. With a blossom-tree-lined main street and a good museum, TA (aka Rose Town) makes a decent overnighter.

◉ Sights

★ Te Awamutu Museum   MUSEUM
(☑ 07-872 0085; www.tamuseum.org.nz; 135 Roche St; by donation; ☺ 10am-4pm Mon-Fri, to 2pm Sat) Te Awamutu Museum has a superb collection of Māori *taonga* (treasures) and an excellent display on the Waikato War. The highlight is the revered *Te Uenuku* ('The Rainbow'), an ancient Māori carving estimated to be up to 600 years old. If you're a fan of the Finn brothers from Crowded House and Split Enz, videos, memorabilia and a scrapbook are available on request – Te Awamutu is their home town.

🏃 Activities

Bryce's Rockclimbing   CLIMBING
(☑ 07-872 2533; www.rockclimb.co.nz; 1424 Owairaka Valley Rd) Bryce's Rockclimbing is situated in a rural area 25km southeast of Te Awamutu, near hundreds of climbs at various crags (many of which are within walking distance). The surreal landscape provides some of the best rock climbing in the North Island, but it's an area best suited to those with at least basic climbing skills.

Friendly owner Bryce Martin can offer independent advice on accessing the different climbing locations in the region.

On site is NZ's largest retail climbing store, selling and hiring a full range of gear. Another option is the excellent online store (www.shop.rockclimb.co.nz). There's also comfortable accommodation, and all rooms have private en-suite bathrooms (dorm/double $30/76). Breakfast is available to guests by request. Accommodation is also open to hikers, cyclists, anglers and general travellers. Your own transport is required to get here.

TE AWAMUTU'S SACRED SOUND

In the opening lines of Crowded House's first single 'Mean to Me', Neil Finn single-handedly raised his sleepy home town, Te Awamutu, to international attention. It wasn't the first time it had provided inspiration – Split Enz songs 'Haul Away' and 'Kia Kaha', with big bro Tim, include similar references.

Despite New Zealand's brilliant songwriting brothers being far from the height of their fame, Finn devotees continue to make the pilgrimage to Te Awamutu. Ask at the i-SITE (p196) about Finn postcards and the interesting scrapbook focused on the brothers' achievements. For Finn completists, there's more to see at the Te Awamutu Museum by request.

🛏 Sleeping & Eating

Rosetown Motel   MOTEL $$
(☑ 0800 767 386, 07-871 5779; www.rosetownmotel. co.nz; 844 Kihikihi Rd; d $130-150; 🖥❄) The older-style units at Rosetown have kitchens, new linen and TVs, and share a spa. A solid choice if you're hankering for straight-up, small-town sleeps.

Walton St Coffee   CAFE $
(☑ 022 070 6411; www.facebook.com/waltonstreet collective; 3 Walton St; snacks & meals $6-15; ☺ 7am-3pm Tue-Fri, 8.30am-1pm Sat) 🍴 In a rustic building with exposed beams and retro furniture, this combo of cafe, gallery and performance space is Te Awamutu's top spot for coffee. The menu has a strong focus on organic and gluten-free options. Try the Buddha Bowl, a changing concoction of fresh seasonal veggies and the grain of the day, topped with a cashew and herb dressing.

Red Kitchen   CAFE $$
(☑ 07-871 8715; www.redkitchen.co.nz; 51 Mahoe St; mains $14-21; ☺ 7am-5.30pm Mon-Fri, 7.30am-2.30pm Sat) Excellent coffee, counter food, cosmopolitan brunches and lunches, and food store all feature at this sunny spot. Try the macadamia and cranberry muesli or the creamy mushrooms on ciabatta. Pick up gourmet TV dinners from Monday to Friday – actually really good – and fire up the motel microwave for your evening meal.

WORTH A TRIP

SANCTUARY MOUNTAIN MAUNGATAUTARI

Can a landlocked volcano become an island paradise? Inspired by the success of pest eradication and native species reintroduction in Auckland's Hauraki Gulf, pest-proof fencing has been installed around the three peaks of Maungatautari (797m) to create the impressive **Sanctuary Mountain Maungatautari** (07-870 5180; www.sanctuary-mountain.co.nz; 99 Tari Rd, Pukeatua; adult/child $20/8).

Hiking through the mountain's pristine native forest (around six hours) is a popular activity, and shorter guided tours are available from the visitor centre. Fauna-related attractions include two only-in-NZ species: the tuatara and the kiwi. Accommodation and trailhead transport can be provided by **Out in the Styx** (07-872 4505; www.styx.co.nz; 2117 Arapuni Rd, Pukeatua; dm/s/d $125/185/320).

ℹ Information

Te Awamutu i-SITE (07-871 3259; www.teawamutuinfo.co.nz; 1 Gorst Ave; ⊙9am-5pm Mon-Fri, to 2.30pm Sat & Sun) Has plenty of local information.

ℹ Getting There & Away

Te Awamutu is on SH3, halfway between Hamilton and Otorohanga (29km either way). The regional bus service **Busit!** (0800 4287 5463; www.busit.co.nz) is the cheapest option for Hamilton (adult/child $6.70/4.50, 50 minutes, eight daily weekdays, three daily weekends). Three daily **InterCity** (09-583 5780; www.intercity.co.nz) services connect Te Awamutu with Auckland ($23, 2½ hours) and Hamilton ($11, 30 minutes).

Cambridge

 07 / POP 15,200

The name says it all. Despite the rambunctious Waikato River looking nothing like the Cam, the good people of Cambridge have done all they can to assume an air of English gentility with village greens and tree-lined avenues.

Cambridge is famous for the breeding and training of thoroughbred horses. Equine references are rife in public sculpture, and plaques boast of past Melbourne Cup winners. It's also an emerging dining destination, with some excellent eateries worth the short drive from Hamilton.

⊙ Sights

Cambridge Museum MUSEUM
(07-827 3319; www.cambridgemuseum.org.nz; 24 Victoria St; by donation; ⊙10am-4pm Mon-Fri, to 2pm Sat & Sun) In a former courthouse, the quirky Cambridge Museum has plenty of pioneer relics, a military history room and a range of local history displays.

Jubilee Gardens GARDEN, MONUMENT
(Victoria St) Apart from its Spanish Mission town clock, Jubilee Gardens is a wholehearted tribute to the 'mother country'. A British lion guards the cenotaph, with a plaque that reads 'Tell Britain ye who mark this monument faithful to her we fell and rest content'. Across the road in leafy Victoria Sq, a farmers market is held every Saturday morning.

Lake Karapiro LAKE
(07-827 4178; www.waipadc.govt.nz; Maungatautari Rd) Eight kilometres southeast of Cambridge, Lake Karapiro is the furthest downstream of a chain of eight hydroelectric power stations on the Waikato River. It's an impressive sight, especially when driving across the top of the 1947 dam. The 21km-long lake is also a world-class rowing venue.

🏃 Activities

Te Awa CYCLING, WALKING
(The Great New Zealand River Ride; www.te-awa.org.nz) The Te Awa cycling and walking path meanders for 70km along the Waikato River, from Ngaruawahia north of Hamilton, to Horahora south of the city. It's a flat and scenic route. Highlights include riding from the Avantidrome in Cambridge – a training hub for NZ's elite cycling athletes – south to the shores of Lake Karapiro. See the website for details.

Boatshed Kayaks KAYAKING
(07-827 8286; www.theboatshed.net.nz; The Boatshed, 21 Amber Lane; single/double kayak 3hr $20/40, paddle board 2hr $40; ⊙9am-5pm Wed-Sun) Boatshed Kayaks has basic kayaks and paddle boards for hire. You can paddle to a couple of waterfalls in around an hour. There are also guided kayak trips (adult/child $110/75) at twilight to see a glowworm canyon up the nearby Pokewhaenua stream; bookings are essential.

See the website for other guided kayaking on Lake Karapiro and the Waikato River.

Waikato River Trails
CYCLING, WALKING

(www.waikatorivertrails.com) The 103km Waikato River Trails track is part of the Nga Haerenga, New Zealand Cycle Trail (www.nzcycletrail.com) project. Winding south and east from near Cambridge – beginning at the Pokaiwhenua Bridge – the trails pass Lake Karapiro (p196) and go into the South Waikato area to end at the Atiamuri Dam.

You can either walk or cycle the five combined trails (or parts thereof), with lots of history and local landscapes en route. Download the free map showing five stages from the website.

🛏 Sleeping

Cambridge Motor Park
HOLIDAY PARK $

(☑ 07-827 5649; www.cambridgemotorpark.co.nz; 32 Scott St; campsites from $36, units $70-115; 🛜) A quiet, well-maintained camping ground with lots of green, green grass. The emphasis is on tents and vans here, but the cabins and units are fine.

Cambridge Coach House
B&B, CABIN $$

(☑07-823 7922; www.cambridgecoachhouse.co.nz; 3796 Cambridge Rd, Leamington; ste from $165, cottage from $175; 🛜🐾) This farmhouse accommodation is a beaut spot to relax amid Waikato's rural splendour. There are two stylish suites and a self-contained cottage. Flat-screen TVs and heat pumps are convenient additions, and guests are welcome to fire up the barbecue in the leafy grounds. It's a couple of kilometres south of town, en route to Te Awamutu.

★ Earthstead
B&B $$$

(☑ 07-827 3771; www.earthstead.co.nz; 3635 Cambridge Rd, Monvale; d $219-419; 🛜) 🍴 In a rural setting a short drive south of Cambridge, Earthstead has two units – Earth House and Cob Cottage – constructed using ecofriendly and sustainable adobe-style architecture, and two other options with an elegant European vibe. Fresh and organic produce from Earthstead's compact farm is used for breakfast, including eggs, honey and freshly baked sourdough bread.

🍽 Eating

Cambridge Farmers Market
MARKET $

(www.waikatofarmersmarkets.co.nz; ⊘8am-noon Sat) Local flavours abound at this excellent weekly market held in the leafy surroundings of Victoria Sq.

Paddock
CAFE $

(☑07-827 4232; www.paddockcambridge.co.nz; 46a Victoria St; snacks & mains $9-18; ⊘8am-5pm Mon-Thu, to 8pm Fri & Sat, to 4pm Sun) Free-range this and organic that punctuate the menu at this cool slice of culinary style that looks like it's dropped in from Auckland or Melbourne. Distressed timber furniture and a vibrant and colourful mural enliven Paddock's corner location, and artisan sodas and healthy smoothies – try the banana, date and cinnamon – partner well with gourmet bagels and burgers.

Alpha Street Kitchen & Bar
MODERN NZ $$

(☑07-827 5596; www.alphast.co.nz; 47 Alpha St; mains $23-43; ⊘11am-late Tue-Sun; 🍴) Formerly the National Hotel, this heritage space is now one of the Waikato's best new restaurants. Sit outside for a leisurely lunch of miso smoked salmon or sophisticated spins on lamb or venison for dinner. The shared plates dishes – think tempura oyster sliders or chorizo and potato croquettes – also work very well as bar snacks.

Alpino cucina e vino
ITALIAN $$

(☑07-827 5595; www.alpino.co.nz; 43 Victoria St; pizzas $19-26, mains $29-38; ⊘11.30am-9.30pm Wed-Sun) In a heritage former post office, the stylish and elegant yet informal and approachable Alpino cucina e vino is one of the best restaurants in the Waikato region. The main menu focuses on excellent pasta, hearty Italian-style mains – try the rosemary and parmesan risotto with a confit duck leg – and top-notch wood-fired pizza that's also available for takeaway.

🍷 Drinking & Nightlife

Good Union
PUB

(☑07-834 4040; www.goodunion.co.nz; 98 Victoria St; ⊘11am-late) Hamilton's Good George Brewing (p188) empire has now spread to this Cambridge venue in a colourful and characterful former church. Secure a spot in the interesting heritage interior, or grab a place on the huge outdoor deck and partner Good George's excellent beers and ciders with pizza, tacos and hearty main dishes. Visit on a weekend afternoon for occasional live music.

ℹ Information

Cambridge i-SITE
(☑ 07-823 3456; www.cambridge.co.nz; cnr Victoria & Queen Sts; ⊘9am-5pm Mon-Fri, 10am-4pm Sat & Sun; 🛜) has free **Heritage & Tree Trail** and town maps, plus internet access.

WAIKATO & THE COROMANDEL PENINSULA CAMBRIDGE

❶ Getting There & Away

Being on SH1, 22km southeast of Hamilton, Cambridge is well connected by bus. Waikato Regional Council's **Busit!** (📞 0800 4287 5463; www.busit. co.nz) heads to Hamilton ($6.70, 40 minutes, seven daily weekdays, three daily weekends).

InterCity (📞 09-583 5780; www.intercity. co.nz) services numerous destinations including the following:

DESTINATION	PRICE ($)	DURA-TION	FREQUENCY (DAILY)
Auckland	19-47	2½hr	12
Hamilton	16	30min	8
Matamata	15-20	30min	2
Rotorua	15-36	1¼hr	5
Wellington	29-70	8½hr	3

Naked Bus (📞 09-979 1616; https://nakedbus. com) runs services to the same destinations:

DESTINATION	PRICE ($)	DURA-TION	FREQUENCY (DAILY)
Auckland	15	2½hr	6
Hamilton	13	30min	5
Matamata	25	2¼hr	1
Rotorua	15	1¼hr	4
Wellington	51	9½hr	1

Matamata

📞 07 / POP 7800

Matamata was just one of those pleasant, horsey country towns you drove through until Peter Jackson's epic film trilogy *The Lord of the Rings* put it on the map. During filming, 300 locals got work as extras (hairy feet weren't a prerequisite).

Following the subsequent filming of *The Hobbit*, the town has now ardently embraced its Middle Earth credentials, including a spooky statue of Gollum, and given the local information centre an appropriate extreme makeover.

Most tourists who come to Matamata are dedicated Hobbit-botherers. For everyone else there's a great cafe, avenues of mature trees and undulating green hills.

◉ Sights

Hobbiton Movie Set Tours   FILM LOCATION
(📞 0508 446 224 866, 07-888 1505; www.hobbiton tours.com; 501 Buckland Rd, Hinuera; adult/child tours $84/42, dinner tours $195/152.50; ⏱ tours 10am-4.30pm) Due to copyright, all the movie sets around NZ were dismantled after the filming of *The Lord of the Rings*, but Hobbiton's owners negotiated to keep their hobbit holes, which were then rebuilt for the filming of *The Hobbit*. Tours include a drink at the wonderful Green Dragon Inn. Free transfers leave from the Matamata i-SITE – check timings on the Hobbiton website. Booking ahead is strongly recommended. The popular Evening Dinner Tours on Sunday and Wednesday include a banquet dinner.

To get to Hobbiton with your own transport, head towards Cambridge from Matamata, turn right into Puketutu Rd and then left into Buckland Rd, stopping at the Shire's Rest Cafe.

Wairere Falls   WATERFALL
About 15km northeast of Matamata are the spectacular 153m Wairere Falls, the highest on the North Island. From the car park it's a 45-minute walk through native bush to the lookout or a steep 1½-hour climb to the summit.

Firth Tower   MUSEUM, HISTORIC BUILDING
(📞 07-888 8369; www.firthtower.co.nz; Tower Rd; grounds free, buildings adult/child $10/5; ⏱ grounds 10am-4pm daily, buildings 10am-4pm Thu-Mon) Firth Tower was built by Auckland businessman Josiah Firth in 1882. The 18m concrete tower was then a fashionable status symbol; now it's filled with Māori and pioneer artefacts. Ten other historic buildings are set around the tower, including a school room, church and jail. It's 3km east of town.

🏃 Activities

Opal Hot Springs   HOT SPRINGS
(📞 0800 800 198; www.opalhotsprings.co.nz; 257 Okauia Springs Rd; adult/child $8/4, 30min private spas $10/5; ⏱ 9am-9pm) Opal Hot Springs isn't nearly as glamorous as it sounds, but it does have three large thermal pools. Turn off just north of Firth Tower and follow the road for 2km. There's a holiday park here, too.

🛏 Sleeping

Matamata Backpackers   HOSTEL $
(📞 07-880 9745; www.matamatabackpackers. co.nz; 61 Firth St; dm/r $28/70; 🛜) Handily located a short walk from the bus departure point to Hobbiton, this well-run and welcoming 2017 opening offers the best value beds around town. Colourful bed linen enlivens the simply decorated dorms and private rooms, and hostel facilities include spacious shared common areas.

Broadway Motel & Miro Court Villas
MOTEL **$$**

(☑07-888 8482; www.broadwaymatamata.co.nz; 128 Broadway; d $115-185, 2-bedroom apt $290; @⛲) This sprawling family-run motel complex has spread from a well-maintained older-style block to progressively newer and flasher blocks set back from the street. The nicest are the chic apartment-style Miro Court villas.

Eating & Drinking

Workman's Cafe Bar
CAFE **$$**

(☑07-888 5498; 52 Broadway; mains $12-33; ⊙7.30am-10pm Wed-Sun) Truly eccentric (old transistor radios dangling from the ceiling, a wall full of art-deco mirrors, Johnny Cash on the stereo), this funky eatery has built itself a reputation that extends beyond Matamata. It's also a decent bar later at night.

Redoubt Bar & Eatery
PUB

(☑07-888 8585; www.redoubtbarandeatery.co.nz; 48 Broadway; ⊙11am-1am) Look forward to thin-crust pizzas named after *LOTR* characters, a winning salmon and hash stack, occasional movie nights in the adjacent laneway, and live music most weekends. It's also a mini-shrine to all things sporty and Matamata-related, and a few interesting tap beers definitely hit the spot.

Information

Matamata i-SITE (☑07-888 7260; www.matamatanz.co.nz; 45 Broadway; ⊙9am-5pm) Housed in a wonderful Hobbit gatehouse. Hobbiton tours leave from here.

Getting There & Away

Matamata is on SH27, 20km north of Tirau. **InterCity** (☑09-583 5780; www.intercity.co.nz) runs to Cambridge ($15, 40 minutes, two daily), Hamilton ($15, one hour, three daily), Rotorua ($28, one hour, two daily) and Tauranga ($25, one hour, two daily). **Naked Bus** (☑09-979 1616; https://nakedbus.com) offers similar services, plus a bus to Auckland ($17, 3½ hours, two daily).

Coromandel Adventures (p216) runs a Monday to Friday shuttle service from Coromandel Town to Rotorua, stopping at Matamata en route.

Te Aroha

☑07 / POP 3800

Te Aroha has a great vibe. You could even say that it's got 'the love', which is the literal meaning of the name. Tucked under the elbow of the bush-clad Mt Te Aroha (952m), it's a good base for tramping or 'taking the waters' in the town's therapeutic thermal springs. It's also the southern trailhead on the Hauraki Rail Trail. The sleepy main street is good for trawling for quirky antiques and vintage clothing and accessories. Many of the town's attractions are arrayed around Te Aroha's leafy hillside Domain.

◉ Sights

Te Aroha Museum
MUSEUM

(☑07-884 4427; www.tearoha-museum.com; Te Aroha Domain; adult/child $5/2; ⊙11am-4pm Nov-Mar, noon-3pm Apr-Oct) In the town's ornate former thermal sanatorium (aka the 'Treasure of Te Aroha'). Displays include quirky ceramics, old spa-water bottles, historical photos and an old printing press.

Activities

Mt Te Aroha
TRAMPING, MOUNTAIN BIKING

Trails up Mt Te Aroha start at the top of the domain. It's a 45-minute climb to Bald Spur/Whakapipi Lookout (350m), then another 2.7km (two hours) to the summit. Ask at the i-SITE (p200) about mountain-bike trails.

Te Aroha Mineral Spas
SPA

(☑07-884 8717; www.tearohamineralspas.co.nz; Boundary St, Te Aroha Domain; 30min session adult/child $19/11; ⊙10.30am-9pm Mon-Fri, to 10pm Sat & Sun) In the Edwardian Hot Springs Domain, this spa offers private tubs, massage, beauty therapies and aromatherapy. Also here is the temperamental Mokena Geyser – the world's only known soda geyser – which blows its top around every 40 minutes, shooting water 3m into the air (the most ardent eruptions are between noon and 2pm). Book ahead for spas and treatments.

Sleeping & Eating

Te Aroha Holiday Park
HOLIDAY PARK **$**

(☑07-884 9567; www.tearohaholidaypark.co.nz; 217 Stanley Rd; campsites from $20, on-site vans s/d $30/45, cabins & units $65-110; @🛜⛲) Wake up to a bird orchestra among the oaks at this site equipped with a grass tennis court, gym and hot pool, 2km southwest of town.

★Aroha Mountain Lodge
LODGE, B&B **$$**

(☑07-884 8134; www.arohamountainlodge.co.nz; 5 Boundary St; s/d/cottage $135/145/320) Spread over two lovely Edwardian villas on the hillside above town, the plush Mountain Lodge offers affordable luxury (*sooo* much nicer than a regulation motel) and optional breakfast ($20 per person). The self-contained Chocolate Box sleeps six to eight.

Domain Cottage Cafe
CAFE $

(☑ 07-884 9222; Whitaker St, Te Aroha Domain; snacks & mains $8-22; ☺ 9am-3pm Tue-Sun) Very pleasant daytime cafe in the heritage surroundings of the Te Aroha Domain. Definitely worthy of a stop for coffee and cake even if you're only passing through town. The stonking lamb sandwich is perfect after hiking or biking on nearby Mt Te Aroha (p199).

Ironique
CAFE $$

(☑ 07-884 8489; www.ironique.co.nz; 159 Whitaker St; mains $10-35; ☺ 8am-4pm Mon-Wed, to late Thu-Sun) Come for a coffee and a restorative breakfast of eggs Benedict after tackling the Hauraki Rail Trail, or pork belly or pumpkin risotto for dinner. Don't overlook venturing to the quiet courtyard out the back for a few drinks.

ⓘ Information

Te Aroha i-SITE (☑ 07-884 8052; www.tearoha nz.co.nz; 102 Whitaker St; ☺ 9.30am-5pm Mon-Fri, to 4pm Sat & Sun) Ask about walking trails on Mt Te Aroha (p199) and other local sights.

ⓘ Getting There & Away

Te Aroha is on SH26, 21km south of Paeroa and 55km northeast of Hamilton. Waikato Regional Council's **Busit!** (☑ 0800 4287 5463; www. busit.co.nz) runs to/from Hamilton (adult/child $8.40/4.20, one hour, weekdays at 5.15pm). Te Aroha is also a stop on Monday to Friday shuttle services provided by Coromandel Adventures (p216) linking Coromandel Town and Rotorua.

KING COUNTRY

Holding good claim to the title of New Zealand's rural heartland, this is the kind of no-nonsense place that raises cattle and All Blacks. A bastion of independent Māoridom, it was never conquered in the war against the King Movement. The story goes that King Tawhiao placed his hat on a large map of NZ and declared that all the land it covered would remain under his *mana* (authority), and the region was effectively off-limits to Europeans until 1883.

The Waitomo Caves are the area's major drawcard. An incredible natural phenomenon in themselves, they also feature lots of adrenaline-inducing activities.

Kawhia

☑ 07 / POP 670

Along with resisting cultural annihilation, low-key Kawhia (think mafia with a K) has avoided large-scale development, retaining its sleepy fishing-village vibe. There's not much here except for the general store, a couple of takeaways and a petrol station. Even Captain Cook blinked and missed the narrow entrance to the large harbour when he sailed past in 1770.

⊙ Sights

Maketu Marae
HISTORIC SITE

(www.kawhia.maori.nz; Kaora St) From Kawhia Wharf, a track extends along the coast to Maketu Marae, which has an impressively carved meeting house, Auaukiterangi. Two stones here – Hani and Puna – mark the burial place of the **Tainui waka** (a 14th-century ancestral canoe). You can't see a lot from the road, but the *marae* is private property and shouldn't be entered without permission. Email the Maketu Marae Committee for access.

Ocean Beach
BEACH, HOT SPRING

(Te Puia Rd) Four kilometres west of Kawhia is Ocean Beach and its high, black-sand dunes. Swimming can be dangerous, but one to two hours either side of low tide you can find the **Te Puia Hot Springs** in the sand – dig a hole for your own natural hot pool.

Kawhia Regional Museum & Gallery
MUSEUM, GALLERY

(☑ 07-871 0161; www.facebook.com/Museum Kawhia; Omimiti Reserve, Kawhia Wharf; by gold coin donation; ☺ 11am-4pm, reduced hours Mar-Nov) Kawhia's modest waterside museum has local history, nautical and Māori artefacts, and regular art exhibitions. It doubles as the visitor information centre.

🏃 Activities

Kayaks can be hired from **Kawhia Beachside S-Cape** (☑ 07-871 0727; www.kawhia beachsidescape.co.nz; 225 Pouewe St; campsites from $40, cabins $65-110, units $135-165; ☎) and Kawhia Motel.

🛏 Sleeping & Eating

Kawhia Motel
MOTEL $$

(☑ 07-871 0865; www.kawhiamotel.co.nz; cnr Jervois & Tainui Sts; d $129-159; ☎) These six perkily painted, well-kept, old-school motel units are right next to the shops. Kayaks and bikes are available for hire.

Rusty Snapper
CAFE $$

(☑ 07-871 0030; www.facebook.com/rustysnapper kawhia; 64 Jervois St; mains $12-24; ☺10am-4pm, extended hours Jan & Feb) Freshly baked scones, slices and cakes combine with the best coffee in town, and if you're after fish and chips or fresh, seasonal seafood, the Rusty Snapper's a top spot, too. Local oysters and whitebait fritters often feature.

ⓘ Information

For local information see www.kawhiaharbour.co.nz.

ⓘ Getting There & Away

Kawhia doesn't have a bus service. Take SH31 from Otorohanga (58km) or explore the scenic but rough road to Raglan (50km, 22km unsealed).

Otorohanga
☑ 07 / POP 2700

Otorohanga's main street is festooned with images of cherished Kiwiana icons: sheep, gumboots, jandals, No 8 wire, All Blacks, pavlova and the beloved Buzzy Bee children's toy. The town's Kiwi House is also well worth a visit.

⊙ Sights

Ed Hillary Walkway
MEMORIAL
As well as the Kiwiana decorating the main street, the Ed Hillary Walkway (running off Maniapoto St) has information panels on the All Blacks, Marmite and, of course, Sir Ed.

**Otorohanga Kiwi House
& Native Bird Park**
ZOO
(☑ 07-873 7391; www.kiwihouse.org.nz; 20 Alex Telfer Dr; adult/child $24/8; ☺9am-5pm, kiwi feedings 10.30am,1.30pm & 3.30pm daily) This bird barn has a nocturnal enclosure where you can see active kiwi energetically digging with their long beaks, searching for food. This is one of the only places where you can see a great spotted kiwi, the biggest of the three kiwi species. Brown kiwi are also on display, and there's a breeding program for these birds here. Other native birds on show include kaka, kea, morepork and weka.

⌂ Sleeping

Otorohanga Holiday Park
HOLIDAY PARK $
(☑ 07-873 7253; www.kiwiholidaypark.co.nz; 20 Huiputea Dr; campsites from $40, cabins & units $75-130; @ 🕏) It's not the most attractive locale, but this friendly park's tidy facilities include a fitness centre and sauna.

✕ Eating & Drinking

Ō Cafe
CAFE $$
(☑07-8738714;www.facebook.com/Cafe.Otorohanga; 35 Maniapoto St; mains $12-20; ☺7.30am-3.30pm) Otorohanga's newest and most cosmopolitan cafe is a goodie, with big shared tables, lots of natural light, and a versatile menu stretching from breakfast classics and home-style baking through to hearty lunch options. We can personally recommend the lamb burger with zingy beetroot relish. The attached gift shop sells a few eclectic examples of local arts and crafts.

Thirsty Weta
PUB, CRAFT BEER
(☑ 07-873 6699; www.theweta.co.nz; 57 Maniapoto St; ☺10am-2am; 🕏) Hearty meals including pizza, steak, burgers and quesadillas (mains $12 to $38). Later on a pub-meets-wine-bar ambience kicks off as the local musos plug in. It's one of just a handful of places you'll

---

KINGITANGA

The concept of a Māori people is a relatively new one. Until the mid-19th century, New Zealand was effectively comprised of many independent tribal nations, operating in tandem with the British from 1840.

In 1856, faced with a flood of Brits, the Kīngitanga King Movement formed to unite the tribes to better resist further loss of land and culture. A gathering of leaders elected Waikato chief Pōtatau Te Wherowhero as the first Māori king, hoping that his increased *mana* (prestige) could achieve the cohesion that the British had under their queen.

Despite the huge losses of the Waikato War and the eventual opening up of the King Country, the Kīngitanga survived – although it has no formal constitutional role. A measure of the strength of the movement was the huge outpouring of grief when Te Arikinui Dame Atairangikaahu, Pōtatau's great-great-great-granddaughter, died in 2006 after 40 years at the helm. Although it's not a hereditary monarchy (leaders of various tribes vote on a successor), Pōtatau's line continues to the present day with King Tūheitia Paki.

find craft beers on tap from the local King Country Brewing Co (p206). Our favourite is the well-balanced pale ale.

ⓘ Information

Otorohanga i-SITE (☏ 07-873 8951; www.otorohanga.co.nz; 27 Turongo St; ☺9am-5pm Mon-Fri year-round, 10am-2pm Sat Oct-Apr; 🛜) Free wi-fi and local information.

ⓘ Getting There & Away

BUS

InterCity (☏ 09-583 5780; www.intercity.co.nz) buses run from Otorohanga to Auckland ($20 to $42, 3¼ hours, three daily), Te Awamutu ($10 to $21, 30 minutes, three daily), Te Kuiti ($10 to $21, one hour, three daily) and Rotorua ($25 to $53, 2½ hours, two daily).

Naked Bus (☏ 0900 625 33; https://nakedbus.com) runs one bus daily to Waitomo Caves at 5pm ($13, 20 minutes). Other departures include Hamilton ($16, one hour) and New Plymouth ($22, 3¼ hours).

Caves Shuttle & Taxi Service (p206) is a convenient service linking Otorohanga and Waitomo with scheduled departures or on demand. Book through local information centres or accommodation providers. Transport to Auckland or Hamilton airports is also available.

TRAIN

Otorohanga is on the **Northern Explorer** (☏ 0800 872 467; www.greatjourneysofnz.co.nz) train route between Auckland (from $59, 3¼ hours) and Wellington (from $139, nine hours) via Hamilton (from $59, 50 minutes); it also stops at Palmerston North, Ohakune and National Park. Southbound trains run on Mondays, Thursdays and Saturdays, and northbound trains return from Wellington to Auckland on Tuesdays, Fridays and Sundays.

Waitomo Caves

☏ 07 / POP 500

Even if damp, dark tunnels are your idea of hell, head to Waitomo anyway. The limestone caves and glowing bugs here are one of the North Island's premier attractions.

The name Waitomo comes from *wai* (water) and *tomo* (hole or shaft): dotted across this region are numerous shafts dropping into underground cave systems and streams. There are 300-plus mapped caves in the area: the three main caves – Glowworm, Ruakuri and Aranui – have been bewitching visitors for over 100 years.

Your Waitomo experience needn't be claustrophobic: the electrically lit, ca-thedral-like Glowworm Cave is far from squeezy. But if it's tight, gut-wrenching, soaking-wet, pitch-black excitement you're after, Waitomo can oblige.

There's no petrol in town, but there's an ATM at Kiwi Paka (p205). It's best to stock up on cash, groceries and petrol in either Te Kuiti or Otorohanga though.

◉ Sights

Waitomo Caves
Visitor Centre VISITOR CENTRE
(☏ 0800 456 922; www.waitomo.com; Waitomo Caves Rd; ☺9am-5pm) The big-three Waitomo Caves are all operated by the same company, based at the spectacular Waitomo Caves Visitor Centre (near the Glowworm Cave). Various combo deals are available, including a Triple Cave Combo (adult/child $97/44), and other deals incorporate exciting underground thrills with the Legendary Black Water Rafting Company. Check the website. For the cave tours, try to avoid the large tour groups, most of which arrive between 10.30am and 2.30pm.

★ **Glowworm Cave** CAVE
(☏ 0800 456 922; www.waitomo.com/waitomo-glowworm-caves; adult/child $51/23; ☺45min tours half-hourly 9am-5pm) The guided tour of the Glowworm Cave, which is behind the visitor centre, leads past impressive stalactites and stalagmites into a large cavern known as the **Cathedral**. The highlight comes at the tour's end when you board a boat and swing off onto the river. As your eyes grow accustomed to the dark you'll see a Milky Way of little lights surrounding you – these are the glowworms. Book your tour at the visitor centre.

Ruakuri Cave CAVE
(☏ 0800 782 587, 07-878 6219; www.waitomo.com/ruakuri-cave; adult/child $74/29; ☺2hr tours 9am, 10am, 11am, 12.30pm, 1.30pm, 2.30pm & 3.30pm) Ruakuri Cave has an impressive 15m-high spiral staircase, bypassing a Māori burial site at the cave entrance. Tours lead through 1.6km of the 7.5km system, taking in caverns with glowworms, subterranean streams and waterfalls, and intricate limestone structures. Visitors have described it as spiritual – some claim it's haunted – and it's customary to wash your hands when leaving to remove the *tapu* (taboo). Book tours at the visitor centre, or at the departure point, the Legendary Black Water Rafting Company.

GLOWWORM MAGIC

Glowworms are the larvae of the fungus gnat. The larva glowworm has luminescent organs that produce a soft, greenish light. Living in a sort of hammock suspended from an overhang, it weaves sticky threads that trail down and catch unwary insects attracted by its light. When an insect flies towards the light it gets stuck in the threads – the glowworm just has to reel it in for a feed.

The larval stage lasts from six to nine months, depending on how much food the glowworm gets. When it has grown to about the size of a matchstick, it goes into a pupa stage, much like a cocoon. The adult fungus gnat emerges about two weeks later.

The adult insect doesn't live very long because it doesn't have a mouth. It emerges, mates, lays eggs and dies, all within about two or three days. The sticky eggs, laid in groups of 40 or 50, hatch in about three weeks to become larval glowworms.

Glowworms thrive in moist, dark caves but they can survive anywhere if they have the requisites of moisture, an overhang to suspend from and insects to eat. Waitomo is famous for its glowworms but you can see them in many other places around New Zealand, both in caves and outdoors.

When you come upon glowworms, don't touch their hammocks or hanging threads, try not to make loud noises and don't shine a light right on them. All of these things will cause them to dim their lights. It takes them a few hours to become bright again, during which time the grub will go hungry. The glowworms that shine most brightly are the hungriest.

Aranui Cave   CAVE
(📞 0800 456 922; www.waitomo.com/aranui-cave; adult/child $50/23; ⏰1hr tours depart 9am-4pm) Three kilometres west from the Glowworm Cave (p202) is Aranui Cave. This cave is dry (hence no glowworms) but compensates with an incredible array of limestone formations. Thousands of tiny 'straw' stalactites hang from the ceiling. Book tours at the visitor centre (p202), from where there is transport to the cave entrance. A 15-minute bush walk is also included.

Waitomo Caves Discovery Centre   MUSEUM
(📞 07-878 7640; www.waitomocaves.com; 21 Waitomo Caves Rd; adult/child $5/free; ⏰8.45am-5pm) FREE Adjoining the Waitomo i-SITE (p206), the Waitomo Caves Discovery Centre has excellent exhibits explaining how caves are formed, the flora and fauna that thrive in them, and the history of Waitomo's caves and cave exploration.

🏃 Activities

Underground

Legendary Black Water Rafting Company   CAVING
(📞 0800 782 5874; www.waitomo.com/black-water-rafting; 585 Waitomo Caves Rd) The Black Labyrinth tour ($142, three hours) involves floating in a wetsuit on an inner tube down a river through Ruakuri Cave (p202). The highlight is leaping off a small waterfall

and then floating through a long, glowworm-covered passage. The trip ends with showers, soup and bagels in the cafe. There's also the more adventurous Black Abyss tour ($246, five hours).

The latter includes a 35m abseil into Ruakuri Cave, a zipline and more glowworms and tubing.

Minimum ages apply for all tours, and there are occasional discounts if you prebook online. Check the website for combo deals also incorporating entry to the other Waitomo caves.

Spellbound   CAVING
(📞 0800 773 552, 07-878 7622; www.glowworm.co.nz; 10 Waitomo Caves Rd; adult/child $75/26; ⏰3hr tours 10am, 11am, 2pm & 3pm) Spellbound is a good option if you don't want to get wet, are more interested in glowworms than an 'action' experience, and want to avoid the big groups in the main caves. Small-group tours access parts of the heavily glowworm-dappled Mangawhitiakau cave system, 12km south of Waitomo (and you still get to ride on a raft!).

Kiwi Cave Rafting   CAVING
(📞 0800 228 372, 07-873 9149; www.blackwater raftingwaitomo.co.nz; 95 Waitomo Caves Rd) These small-group expeditions ($250, five hours) start with abseil training, followed by a 27m descent into a natural cave, and then a float along a subterranean river on an inner-tube. After some caving, a belayed rock climb up

Waitomo Caves

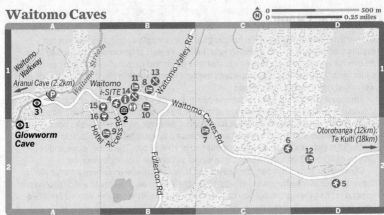

Waitomo Caves

a 20m cliff brings you to the surface. Book directly online with Kiwi Cave Rafting for a significant discount.

Glowing Adventures   CAVING
(☑ 0508 445 694, 07-878 7234; www.glowing.co.nz; 1199 Oparure Rd; per person $159) 🌱 Located on a family farm, the Waitomo region's newest subterranean option operates small-group tours (maximum eight people) through more remote and unmodified caves. Tours involve clambering over boulders, up hills and through underground streams, so a moderate level of fitness and adventure is required. Glowworms are aplenty, and you'll spend around two hours of the three-hour tour underground.

Waitomo Adventures   CAVING
(☑ 0800 924 866, 07-878 7788; www.waitomo. co.nz; 654 Waitomo Caves Rd) Waitomo Adventures offers various cave adventures, with a substantial 20% discount for advance online bookings at least 12 hours prior. The Lost World trip ($405/580, four/seven hours) combines a 100m abseil with walking, rock climbing, wading and swimming. Haggas Honking Holes ($275, four hours) includes three waterfall abseils, rock climbing and a subterranean river.

TumuTumu Toobing ($215, four hours) is a walking, climbing, swimming and tubing trip. St Benedict's Cavern ($215, three hours) includes abseiling and a subterranean flying fox.

CaveWorld   CAVING
(☑ 0800 228 338, 07-878 6577; www.caveworld. co.nz; cnr Waitomo Caves Rd & Hotel Access Rd) CaveWorld runs the Tube It black-water rafting trip ($139, two hours) through glow-worm-filled Te Anaroa. Also available is the Footwhistle Glowworm Cave Tour ($59, one

hour), incorporating a stop in a forest shelter for a mug of restorative *kawakawa* tea, a natural tonic made with leaves from an indigenous bush plant. Twilight Footwhistle tours are $65.

Walking

The Waitomo i-SITE (p206) has free pamphlets on walks in the area. The walk from Aranui Cave (p203) to Ruakuri Cave (p202) is an excellent short path. From the Waitomo Caves Visitor Centre (p202), the 5km, three-hour-return **Waitomo Walkway** takes off through farmland, following Waitomo Stream to the **Ruakuri Scenic Reserve**, where a 30-minute return walk passes by a natural limestone tunnel. There are glowworms here at night – drive to the car park and bring a torch to find your way.

Dundle Hill Walk   TRAMPING
(☑ 07-878 7640; www.dundlehillwalk.co.nz; adult/child $75/35) The self-guided privately run Dundle Hill Walk is a 27km, two-day/one-night loop walk through Waitomo's bush and farmland, including overnight bunkhouse accommodation high up in the bush.

🛏 Sleeping

Waitomo Top 10 Holiday Park   HOLIDAY PARK $
(☑ 07-878 7639, 0508 498 666; www.waitomopark.co.nz; 12 Waitomo Caves Rd; campsites from $44, cabins & units $95-190; @ 🖥 ☱ 🐾) This lovely holiday park in the heart of the village has spotless facilities, modern cabins and plenty of outdoor distractions to keep the kids busy. The cabins are a good alternative to dorm accommodation for friends travelling together, and renovated communal bathrooms are spotless.

YHA Juno Hall Waitomo   HOSTEL $
(☑ 07-878 7649; www.junowaitomo.co.nz; 600 Waitomo Caves Rd; campsites from $17, dm $30, d with/without bathroom $84/74; @ 🖥 ☱) A slick purpose-built hostel 1km from the village with a warm welcome, a warmer wood fire in the woody lounge area, and an outdoor pool and tennis court.

Kiwi Paka   HOSTEL $
(☑ 07-878 3395; www.waitomokiwipaka.co.nz; Hotel Access Rd; dm/s/d $35/65/75, chalet s/d/tw/q $95/100/110/150; @ 🖥) This purpose-built, Alpine-style hostel has four-bed dorms in the main lodge, plus separate peak-roofed chalets, the on-site Morepork Cafe and tidy facilities. Popular with big groups.

Huhu Chalet   RENTAL HOUSE $$
(www.airbnb.com; 10 Waitomo Caves Rd; d $150) Concealed in a quirky pyramid structure that was once part of an advertising sign, Huhu Chalet has a cosy mezzanine bedroom upstairs, and a vibrant (red!) and modern bathroom and living space downstairs. With its simple wooden walls and a scattering of retro furniture, there's a warm Kiwiana vibe to the chalet, and Waitomo's best restaurant is literally metres away.

Waitomo Caves Guest Lodge   B&B $$
(☑ 07-878 7641, 0800 465 762; www.waitomocavesguestlodge.co.nz; 7 Waitomo Village Rd; s/d incl breakfast $100/150; 🖥) Bag your own cosy little hillside en-suite cabin at this central operation with a sweet garden setting. The top cabins have valley views. Large continental breakfasts, friendly and helpful owners, and the on-site managerial skills of Thomas the cat are also big ticks.

Abseil Inn   B&B $$
(☑ 07-878 7815; www.abseilinn.co.nz; 709 Waitomo Caves Rd; d $140-180; 🖥) A *veeery* steep driveway takes you to this delightful B&B with four themed rooms, great breakfasts and witty hosts. The biggest room has a double bath and valley views.

🍴 Eating

Waitomo General Store   CAFE $
(☑ 07-878 8613; www.facebook.com/waitomogeneralstore; 15 Waitomo Caves Rd; snacks & mains $8-18; ⊙ 8.30am-4pm Mar-Nov, to 8.30pm Dec-Feb; 🖥) The Waitomo General Store cafe has pre- and post-caving sustenance including hearty burgers, good coffee and tap beer. Fire up the free wi-fi on the sunny deck.

★Huhu   MODERN NZ $$
(☑ 07-878 6674; www.huhucafe.co.nz; 10 Waitomo Caves Rd; mains $15-32; ⊙ noon-late; 🖥) Huhu combines expansive terrace views and contemporary NZ food. Sip a Kiwi wine or craft beer – including brews from the local King Country Brewing Co (p206) – or graze the menu of delights including slow-cooked lamb, smoked salmon and roast duck. Downstairs is a small King Country Brewing beer bar that's open mainly in summer. For lunch, try the moreish buttermilk chicken.

🍸 Drinking & Nightlife

Tomo   PUB
(☑ 07-878 8448; Hotel Access Rd; ⊙ 11am-late) The welcoming Tomo is Waitomo's pub and home turf for the King Country Brewing Co.

A frosty pale ale teamed with a fish burger, chowder or the massive pork ribs could be just the thing after a busy day underground. Served on the sunny deck, of course. Keep an eye out for the pub's very friendly resident black cat.

King Country Brewing Company BREWERY (☑ 021 498 665; www.kingcountrybrewingco.co.nz; Tomo, Hotel Access Rd; ☺ 11am-late) This craft brewery based at Tomo (p205) pub brews pilsner, IPA, pale ale, wheat beer and cider. Due to contractual issues with bigger breweries, not all the beers are on tap at the pub, but they are all available in Waitomo at Huhu (p205). You'll also find them at Thirsty Weta (p201) in Otorohanga.

❶ Information

Waitomo i-SITE (☑ 0800 474 839, 07-878 7640; www.waitomocaves.com; 21 Waitomo Caves Rd; ☺ 9am-5.30pm) Internet access, post office and booking agent.

❶ Getting There & Away

Naked Bus (☑ 0900 625 33; https://naked bus.com) runs one bus daily to Waitomo Caves village at 5pm ($13, 20 minutes). Other departures include Hamilton ($16, one hour) and New Plymouth ($22, 3¼ hours).

Caves Shuttle & Taxi Service (☑ 07-873 9083; www.cavesshuttlewaitomo.co.nz; adult/child $15/8) links Otorohanga and Waitomo with scheduled departures or on demand. Book through local information centres or accommodation providers. Shuttles depart Otorohanga at 10am and 5pm, and Waitomo at 10.30am and 6pm. Transport to Auckland or Hamilton airports is also available.

Waitomo Wanderer (☑ 0800 000 4321, 03-477 9083; www.travelheadfirst.com) operates a daily return service from Rotorua or Auckland, with optional caving, glowworm and tubing add-ons. It'll even integrate Hobbiton into the mix if you're a JRR Tolkien or Sir Peter Jackson fan.

South from Waitomo to Taranaki

This obscure route heading west of Waitomo on Te Anga Rd is a slow but fascinating alternative to SH3 if Taranaki's your goal. Only 12km of the 111km route remains unsealed, but it's nearly all winding and narrow. Allow around two hours (not including stops) and fill up with petrol.

◉ Sights

The **Mangapohue Natural Bridge Scenic Reserve**, 26km west of Waitomo, is a 5.5-hectare reserve with a giant natural limestone arch. It's a five-minute walk to the arch on a wheelchair-accessible pathway.

About 4km further west is **Piripiri Caves Scenic Reserve**, where a five-minute walk leads to a large cave containing fossils of giant oysters. Bring a torch and be prepared to get muddy after heavy rain. Steps wind down into the gloom...

The impressively tiered, 30m **Marokopa Falls** are 32km west of Waitomo. A short track (15 minutes return) from the road leads to the bottom of the falls.

Just past Te Anga you can turn north to Kawhia, 59km away, or continue southwest to **Marokopa** (population 1560), a small black-sand village on the coast. The whole Te Anga/Marokopa area is riddled with caves.

The road heads south to **Kiritehere**, through idyllic farmland into **Moeatoa** then turns right (south) into Mangatoa Rd. Now you're in serious backcountry, heading into the dense **Whareorino Forest**. For trampers, there's the 16-bunk, DOC-run **Leitch's Hut** (☑ 07-878 1050; www.doc.govt.nz; per adult $5).

At **Waikawau** take the 5km detour along the unsealed road to the coast near **Ngarupupu Point**, where a 100m walk through a dank tunnel opens out on an exquisitely isolated stretch of black-sand beach. Think twice about swimming here as there are often dangerous rips in the surf.

The road then continues through another twisty 28km, passing lush forest and the occasional farm before joining SH3 east of Awakino.

Walks in the **Tawarau Forest**, 20km west of the Waitomo Caves, are outlined in DOC's *Waitomo & King Country Tracks* booklet ($1, available from DOC in Hamilton or Te Kuiti), including a one-hour track to the Tawarau Falls from the end of Appletree Rd.

⌷ Sleeping

Marokopa Campground HOLIDAY PARK $ (☑ 07-876 7444; marokopacampground@xtra. co.nz; Rauparaha St; campsites per person from $19, dm $25, cabin d $50, cottage $130) Marokopa Campground ain't flash but it's in a nice spot, close to the coast. There's a small shop for grocery basics, and it also offers accommodation in its Sunset Hill cottage around eight minutes' walk from the beach.

ⓘ Getting There & Away

There's no public transport to Marokopa, but it's a very scenic drive here in your own vehicle.

Te Kuiti

☑07 / POP 4380

Cute Te Kuiti sits in a valley between picturesque hills. Welcome to the shearing capital of the world, especially if you visit for the annual Great New Zealand Muster. It's also the birthplace of the late Sir Colin Meads, one of NZ's most iconic All Blacks.

⊙ Sights

Sir Colin Meads Statue   STATUE
(Rora St) This statue commemorates the late Sir Colin Meads, a legendary captain of the All Blacks, and regarded as one of New Zealand's finest rugby players. Nicknamed 'Pinetree', and a lifelong resident of Te Kuiti and the King Country, Sir Colin's laconic and pragmatic demeanour means he's also fondly remembered as the quintessential Kiwi – a 'good bugger' in local parlance.

Big Shearer   LANDMARK
(Rora St) The 7m-high, 7½-tonne Big Shearer statue is at the southern end of town.

🎉 Festivals & Events

**Great New Zealand
Muster**   CULTURAL, FOOD & DRINK
(www.waitomo.govt.nz/events/the-great-nz-muster; ⊙late Mar/early Apr) The highlight of the Great New Zealand Muster is the legendary Running of the Sheep, when 2000 woolly demons stampede down Te Kuiti's main street. The festival includes sheep-shearing championships, a parade, Māori cultural performances, live music, barbecues, *hāngi* and market stalls.

🛌 Sleeping & Eating

Waitomo Lodge Motel   MOTEL $$
(☑07-878 0003; www.waitomo-lodge.co.nz; 62 Te Kumi Rd; units $130-175; 🐾) At the Waitomo end of Te Kuiti, this motel's modern rooms feature contemporary art, flat-screen TVs and little decks overlooking Mangaokewa Stream from the units at the back. A couple of resident animals include Willow the friendly terrier.

Bosco Cafe   CAFE $
(☑07-878 3633; www.boscocafe.me; 57 Te Kumi Rd; mains $10-22; ⊙8am-6pm; 🐾) This excellent industrial-chic cafe offers great coffee

and tempting food – try the bacon-wrapped meatloaf with greens or the tasty chicken wraps.

Stoked Eatery   CAFE $$
(☑07-878 8758; www.stokedeatery.co.nz; Te Kuiti Railway Station, 2 Rora St; mains $17-38; ⊙10am-late) This busy restaurant and bar in the former railway station celebrates a great location on the station platform with a relaxed ambience and a menu of hearty fare. Servings are very generous; standouts include lamb shanks or the buttermilk-fried chicken. A decent wine list and local craft beer on tap make Stoked a good option for a drink, too.

ⓘ Information

Te Kuiti DOC (Department of Conservation; ☑07-878 1050; www.doc.govt.nz; 78 Taupiri St; ⊙8am-4.30pm Mon-Fri) is the area office for the surrounding Maniapoto region.

Te Kuiti i-SITE (☑07-878 8077; www.waitomo.govt.nz; Rora St; ⊙9am-5pm Mon-Fri, 10am-2pm Sat & Sun, closed weekends May-Oct; 🐾) has internet access and visitor information.

ⓘ Getting There & Away

InterCity (☑09-583 5780; www.intercity.co.nz) buses run daily to the following destinations (among others): Auckland ($24 to $49, 3½ hours, three daily), Mokau ($14 to $29, two hours, one daily), New Plymouth ($15 to $29, 2½ hours, one daily), Otorohanga ($10 to $21, 20 minutes, three daily) and Taumarunui ($10 to $21, 1¼ hours, one daily).

Naked Bus (☑09-979 1616; https://nakedbus.com) runs to Hamilton ($16, 1½ hours, two daily), New Plymouth ($16, 2¼ hours, one daily) and Otorohanga ($11, 20 minutes, two daily).

Pio Pio, Awakino & Mokau

From Te Kuiti, SH3 runs southwest to the coast before following the rugged shoreline to New Plymouth. Detour at Pio Pio (population 400) to Hairy Feet Waitomo (p208), one of New Zealand's newest Middle Earth themed attractions.

Along this scenic route the sheep stations sprout peculiar limestone formations before giving way to lush native bush as the highway winds along the course of the Awakino River. This river spills into the Tasman at Awakino (population 60), a small settlement where boats shelter in the estuary while locals find refuge at the rustic Awakino Hotel (p209).

Five kilometres further south, as Mt Taranaki starts to emerge on the horizon,

PUREORA FOREST PARK

Fringing the western edge of Lake Taupo, the 780-sq-km Pureora Forest is home to New Zealand's tallest totara tree. Logging was stopped in the 1980s after a long campaign by conservationists, and the subsequent regeneration is impressive. Tramping routes through the park include tracks to the summits of **Mt Pureora** (1165m) and the rock pinnacle of **Mt Titiraupenga** (1042m). A 12m-high tower, a short walk from the Bismarck Rd car park, provides a canopy-level view of the forest for bird-watchers.

Cyclists can ride the spectacular **Timber Trail** from Pureora village in the north of the forest southwest for 85km to Ongarue. Two days is recommended. Accommodation and shuttle transport is available at **Pa Harakeke** (07-929 8708; www.paharakeke.co.nz; 138 Maraeroa Rd; d $150) ✎, an interesting Māori-operated initiative near Pureora village.

For shuttles and bike hire, contact Epic Cycle Adventures (p209) in Taumarunui. See www.thetimbertrail.com and www.thetimbertrail.nz for maps, shuttle and bike hire information and route planning.

Awhina Wilderness Experience (www.facebook.com/AwhinaWildernessExperience) offers five-hour walking tours with local Māori guides through virgin bush to the summit of Titiraupenga, their sacred mountain.

Accommodation includes three DOC campsites (www.doc.govt.nz; adult/child $8/4), with self-registration boxes, and a couple of interesting lodges and chalets.

To stay overnight in one of the three standard DOC huts you'll need to buy hut tickets in advance, unless you have a Backcountry Hut Pass. Hut tickets, maps and information are available from DOC.

There's also the rustic but comfortable **Black Fern Lodge** (07-894 7677; www.blackfernlodge.co.nz; Ongarue Stream Rd, Waimiha; per person from $60) at around the half-way point of the Timber Trail. It gets rave reviews for its home cooking.

There's no scheduled public transport, but Epic Cycle Adventures (p209) in Taumarunui can arrange shuttles.

is the village of Mokau (population 400). It offers a fine black-sand beach and good surfing and fishing. From August to November the Mokau River (the second-longest on the North Island) spawns whitebait and subsequent swarms of territorial whitebaiters.

⊙ Sights & Activities

A little south of Awakino the impressive **Maniaroa Marae** dominates the cliff above the highway. This important complex houses the anchor stone of the Tainui *waka*, which brought this region's original people from their Polynesian homeland. You can get a good view of the intimidatingly carved meeting house, **Te Kohaarua**, from outside the fence – don't cross into the *marae* unless someone invites you.

Hairy Feet Waitomo   FILM LOCATION
(07-877 8003; www.hairyfeetwaitomo.co.nz; 1411 Mangaotaki Rd, Pio Pio; tours adult/child $50/25; ⊙ tours 10am & 1pm) Detour at Pio Pio northwest to the Mangaotaki Valley and Hairy Feet Waitomo, one of NZ's most interesting Middle-earth–themed film location attractions. Scenes from *The Hobbit* were filmed

here with a background of towering limestone cliffs.

Mokau River Tours   BOATING
(0800 665 282; www.mokauriver.co.nz; adult/child $60/10) Mokau River Tours operates a three-hour river cruise on the MV *GlenRoyal*, including a stop upriver in an old camping ground in the forest.

🛌 Sleeping & Eating

Mokau Motel   MOTEL $$
(06-752 9725; www.mokaumotels.co.nz; SH3, Mokau; s/d/ste from $100/115/130; 🐾) Above the village, the Mokau Motel offers fishing advice, self-contained units and three luxury suites.

Whitebait Inn   CAFE $$
(06-752 9713; www.whitebaitinn.co.nz; 55 North St, Mokau; snacks & mains $12-27; ⊙7.30am-6.30pm) A great place to try the local speciality of whitebait in this classic Kiwi diner. Look for the quirky statue of the whitebait fisherman on the roof before getting stuck into tasty fritters or an omelette stuffed into a fresh slice of fluffy white bread. Add a squeeze of lemon juice and salt and pepper and you're good to go.

Awakino Hotel
PUB FOOD $$

(☎06-752 9815; www.facebook.com/AwakinoHotel; SH3, Awakino; meals $13-22; ⊙11am-10pm Sun-Thu, to midnight Fri & Sat) The Awakino River spills into the Tasman at Awakino, where boats shelter in the estuary while locals find refuge at the rustic Awakino Hotel. Look forward to hearty meals, including whitebait fritters, and a pleasant garden bar. New ownership has revived this classic Kiwi pub.

ⓘ Getting There & Away

InterCity (www.intercity.co.nz) buses run from Te Kuiti to Mokau (from $14, one hour, one daily) as part of a bus service linking Auckland to New Plymouth.

Taumarunui

☑06 / POP 5140

Taumarunui on a cold day can feel a bit miserable, but this town in the heart of the King Country has potential. The main reason to stay here is to kayak on the Whanganui River or as a cheaper base for skiing in Tongariro National Park. There are also some beaut walks and cycling tracks around town.

For details on the Forgotten World Hwy between Taumarunui and Stratford, contact Eastern Taranaki Experience (p257). Details on canoeing and kayaking on the Whanganui River can be obtained from Whanganui National Park (p255).

◉ Sights

Te Peka Lookout, across the Ongarue River on the western edge of town, is a good vantage point.

Raurimu Spiral
HISTORIC SITE

(Map p254) The Raurimu Spiral, 30km south of town, is a unique feat of railway engineering that was completed in 1908 after 10 years of work. Rail buffs can experience the spiral by catching the *Northern Explorer* train linking Auckland and Wellington to National Park township. Unfortunately as of 2012 this train no longer stops in Taumarunui.

🕏 Activities

The 3km **Riverbank Walk** along the Whanganui River runs from Cherry Grove Domain, 1km south of town, to Taumarunui Holiday Park.

Epic Cycle Adventures
MOUNTAIN BIKING

(☎022 023 7958; www.thetimbertrail.nz; 9 Rata St, Manunui; bike & shuttle from $105) Arranges bike hire and convenient shuttles if you're keen to tackle the Timber Trail. Check the website for more details on this interesting ride.

🖝 Tours

Forgotten World Adventures
TOURS

(☎080072452278; www.forgottenworldadventures. co.nz; 9 Hakiaha St; half-/1-/2-day tours from $125/230/595; ⊙booking office 9am-2pm) Ride the rails on quirky, converted former golf carts along the railway line linking Taumarunui to the tiny hamlet of Whangamomona in the Taranaki region. The most spectacular trip takes in 20 tunnels. Other options include a rail and jetboat combo and a longer two-day excursion covering the full 140km from Taumarunui to Stratford (including an overnight stay in Whangamomona).

Forgotten World Jet
ADVENTURE

(☎0800 7245 2278, 07-895 7181; www.fwj.co.nz; Cherry Grove Domain; 1/2hr from $105/205) High-octane jetboat trips on the Whanganui River. Longer eight-hour adventures take in the spectacular Bridge to Nowhere, and trips incorporating rail journeys with Forgotten World Adventures are also available.

🛏 Sleeping & Eating

Taumarunui Holiday Park
HOLIDAY PARK $

(☎07-895 9345; www.taumarunuiholidaypark. co.nz; SH4; campsites from $18, cabins & cottages $55-90; @🕏) On the banks of the Whanganui River, 4km east of town, this shady camping ground offers safe river swimming and clean facilities. The friendly owners have lots of ideas on what to see and do.

Twin Rivers Motel
MOTEL $$

(☎07-895 8063; www.twinrivers.co.nz; 23 Marae St; units $90-215; 🕏) The 12 units at Twin Rivers are spick and span. Bigger units sleep up to seven.

Copper Tree Cafe
CAFE $$

(☎07-896 7442; 75 Hakiaha St; mains $14-24; ⊙9am-4pm Mon-Wed, 9am-9pm Thu & Fri, 10am-4pm Sat & Sun) A switched-on young couple have enlivened this main-street cafe. Hearty quiche and homemade pies are served with chips and salad, while eggs Benedict partners with good coffee for brunch. At the time of research, the friendly owners were opening for dinner on Thursday and Friday nights, too.

ⓘ Information

Taumarunui i-SITE (☑07-895 7494; www.
visitruapehu.com; 116 Hakiaha St; ☺8.30am-
5.30pm) Visitor information and internet access.

ⓘ Getting There & Away

Taumarunui is on SH4, 81km south of Te Kuiti
and 41km north of National Park township. **InterCity** (☑0508 353 947; www.intercity.co.nz)
buses head to Auckland (from $30, 4½ hours)
via Te Kuiti and to Palmerston North (from $33,
4½ hours) via National Park.

Owhango

☑06 / POP 210

A pint-sized village where all the street names
start with 'O', Owhango makes a cosy base for
walkers, mountain bikers (the 42 Traverse
(p286) ends here) and skiers who don't want
to fork out to stay closer to the slopes in Tongariro National Park. Take Omaki Rd for a
two-hour loop walk through virgin forest in
Ohinetonga Scenic Reserve.

🛏 Sleeping

Blue Duck Station   LODGE, HOSTEL $
(Map p254; ☑07-895 6276; www.blueduckstation.
co.nz; RD2, Whakahoro; dm $45, d $100-195) 🖉
Overlooking the Retaruke River 36km southwest of Owhango (take the Kaitieke turn-off
1km south of town), this ecosavvy place is
actually various lodges, offering accommodation from dorms in old shearers' quarters to a
self-contained family cottage sleeping eight.
The owners are mad-keen conservationists,
restoring native-bird habitats and historic buildings. Activities include bush tours,
horse riding, kayaking and mountain biking.

Forest Lodge   LODGE $
(Map p280; ☑07-895 4854; www.forest-lodge.co.nz;
12 Omaki Rd; dm/d from $25/60, motel d $80; @🖥🖠)
A snug backpackers with comfortable, clean
rooms and good communal spaces. For privacy junkies there's a separate self-contained
motel next door. Mountain-bike rental and
bike-shuttle services for the 42 Traverse are
available too. Staff here can also arrange
dorm ($30) and private room accommoda-
tion ($60) in the nearby Owhango Hotel.

ⓘ Getting There & Away

Owhango is 14km south of Taumarunui on SH4.
All the **InterCity** (☑0508 353 947; www.inter
city.co.nz) buses that stop in Taumarunui also
stop here.

COROMANDEL PENINSULA

The Coromandel Peninsula juts into the Pacific east of Auckland, forming the eastern
boundary of the Hauraki Gulf. Although relatively close to the metropolis, the Coromandel offers easy access to splendid isolation.
Its dramatic, mountainous spine bisects it
into two very distinct parts.

The east coast has some of the North Island's best white-sand beaches. When Auckland shuts up shop for Christmas and New
Year, this is where it heads. The cutesy historic gold-mining towns on the western side
escape the worst of the influx, their muddy
wetlands and picturesque stony bays holding less appeal for the masses. This coast
has long been a refuge for alternative lifestylers. Down the middle, the mountains are
criss-crossed with walking tracks, allowing
trampers to explore large tracts of untamed
bush where kauri trees once towered and
are starting to do so again.

History

This whole area – including the peninsula,
the islands and both sides of the gulf – was
known to the Māori as Hauraki. Various *iwi*
(tribes) held claim to pockets of it, including
the Pare Hauraki branch of the Tainui *iwi*
and others descended from Te Arawa and
earlier migrations. Polynesian artefacts and
evidence of moa-hunting have been found,
pointing to around 1000 years of continuous
occupation.

The Hauraki *iwi* were some of the first to
be exposed to European traders. The region's
proximity to Auckland, safe anchorages and
ready supply of valuable timber initially led
to a booming economy. Kauri logging was
big business on the peninsula. Allied to the
timber trade was shipbuilding, which took
off in 1832 when a mill was established at
Mercury Bay. Things got tougher once the
kauri around the coast became scarce and
the loggers had to penetrate deeper into the
bush for timber. Kauri dams, which used
water power to propel the huge logs to the
coast, were built. By the 1930s virtually no
kauri remained and the industry died.

Gold was first discovered in NZ near Coromandel Town in 1852. Although this first
rush was short-lived, more gold was discovered around Thames in 1867 and later
in other places. The peninsula is also rich
in semiprecious gemstones, such as quartz,

Coromandel Peninsula

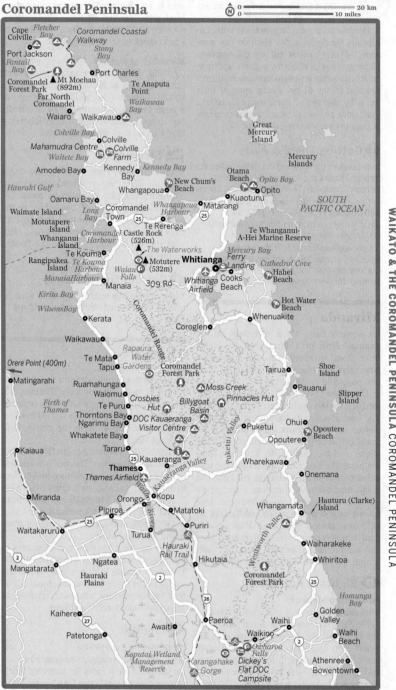

agate, amethyst and jasper. A fossick on any west-coast beach can be rewarding.

Despite successful interactions with Europeans for decades, the Hauraki *iwi* were some of the hardest hit by colonisation. Unscrupulous dealings by settlers and government to gain access to valuable resources resulted in the Māori losing most of their lands by the 1880s. Even today there is a much lower Māori presence on the peninsula than in neighbouring districts.

ⓘ Getting There & Away

Daily buses on the Auckland–Tauranga route pass through Thames and Waihi, while others loop through Coromandel Town, Whitianga and Tairua.

It's definitely worth considering the beautiful **360 Discovery** (☎ 0800 360 3472; www. 360discovery.co.nz) ferry ride from Auckland via Waiheke Island to Coromandel Town.

A convenient Monday to Friday service offered by Coromandel Adventures (p216) links Coromandel Town and Rotorua. In the height of summer, this service runs daily.

Miranda

It's a pretty name for a settlement on the swampy Firth of Thames, just an hour's drive from Auckland. The two reasons to come here are splashing around in the thermal pools and bird-watching.

This is one of the most accessible spots for studying waders or shorebirds all year round. The vast mudflat is teeming with aquatic worms and crustaceans, which attract thousands of Arctic-nesting shorebirds over the winter – 43 species of wader have been spotted here. The two main species are the bartailed godwit and the lesser or red knot, but it isn't unusual to see turnstones, sandpipers and the odd vagrant red-necked stint. One godwit tagged here was tracked making an 11,570km nonstop flight from Alaska. Short-haul travellers include the pied oystercatcher and the threatened wrybill from the South Island, and banded dotterels and pied stilts.

◉ Sights & Activities

**Pukorokoro Miranda
Shorebird Centre**   WILDLIFE RESERVE
(☎ 09-232 2781; www.miranda-shorebird.org.nz; 283 East Coast Rd; bird-watching pamphlet $2; ⊙ 9am-5pm) The Miranda Shorebird Centre has bird-life displays, hires out binoculars and sells useful bird-watching pamphlets. Nearby is a hide and several walks (30 min-

utes to two hours). The centre offers clean bunk-style accommodation (dorm beds/rooms $25/95) with a kitchen. Visit the website to check out recent sightings.

Miranda Hot Springs   HOT SPRINGS
(☎ 07-867 3055; www.mirandahotsprings.co.nz; Front Miranda Rd; adult/child $14/7, private spa extra $15; ⊙ 9am-9pm) Miranda Hot Springs has a large thermal swimming pool (reputedly the largest in the southern hemisphere), a toasty sauna pool and private spas.

🛏 Sleeping

Miranda Holiday Park   HOLIDAY PARK $
(☎ 07-867 3205; www.mirandaholidaypark.co.nz; 595 Front Miranda Rd; campsites per person $27, units $90-190; @ 🛜 ☒) 🐾 Next door to the Miranda Hot Springs, Miranda Holiday Park has excellent sparkling-clean units and facilities, its own hot-spring pool and a floodlit tennis court.

ⓘ Getting There & Away

There is no public transport to Miranda. Most travellers visit en route to/from Auckland and Thames.

Thames

☑ 07 / POP 7060

Dinky wooden buildings from the 19th-century gold rush still dominate Thames, but grizzly prospectors have long been replaced by alternative lifestylers. It's a good base for tramping or canyoning in the nearby Kauaeranga Valley.

Captain Cook arrived here in 1769, naming the Waihou River the 'Thames' 'on account of its bearing some resemblance to that river in England'; you may well think otherwise. This area belonged to Ngāti Maru, a tribe of Tainui descent. Their spectacular meeting house, Hotunui (1878), holds pride of place in the Auckland Museum.

After opening Thames to gold miners in 1867, Ngāti Maru were swamped by 10,000 European settlers within a year. When the initial boom turned to bust, a dubious system of government advances resulted in Māori debt and forced land sales.

◉ Sights

★ **Goldmine Experience**   MINE
(☎ 07-868 8514; www.goldmine-experience.co.nz; cnr Moanataiari Rd & Pollen St; adult/child $15/5; ⊙ 10am-4pm Jan-Mar, to 1pm Sat & Sun Apr, May &

Sep-Dec) Walk through a mine tunnel, watch a stamper battery crush rock, learn about the history of the Cornish miners and try your hand at panning for gold ($2 extra).

Butterfly Forest GARDENS
(☑07-868 8080; www.butterfly.co.nz; Victoria St; adult/child $15/7; ☺9.30am-4.30pm Sep-May, 10.30am-3.30pm Sat & Sun Jun-Aug) Around 3km north of town within the Dickson Holiday Park is this enclosed jungle full of hundreds of exotic flappers.

School of Mines &
Mineralogical Museum MUSEUM
(☑07-868 6227; www.historicplaces.org.nz; 101 Cochrane St; adult/child $10/free; ☺11am-3pm Jan & Feb, Wed-Sun Mar-Dec) The Historic Places Trust runs tours of these buildings, which house an extensive collection of NZ rocks, minerals and fossils. The oldest section (1868) was part of a Methodist Sunday School, situated on a Māori burial ground. The Trust has a free self-guided tour pamphlet taking in Thames' significant buildings.

🏃 Activities

Canyonz OUTDOORS
(☑0800 422 696; www.canyonz.co.nz; trips $390) All-day canyoning trips to the Sleeping God Canyon in the Kauaeranga Valley. Expect a vertical descent of over 300m, requiring abseiling, water-sliding and jumping. Trips leave from Thames at 8.30am; 7am pick-ups from Hamilton are also available. Note that Thames is only a 1½-hour drive from central Auckland, so with your own transport a day trip from Auckland is possible.

JollyBikes CYCLING
(☑07-867 9026; www.jollybikes.co.nz; 535 Pollen St; mountain bike/e-bike hire per day from $45/80; ☺9.30am-5pm Mon-Fri, to 2pm Sat) Rents out mountain bikes and e-bikes, does repairs and has plenty of information on tackling the Hauraki Rail Trail.

🛏 Sleeping

Sunkist Guesthouse B&B $
(☑07-868 8808; www.sunkistguesthouse.nz; 506 Brown St; s/d & tw $75/95; @☎) Formerly the Lady Bowen Hotel, this character-filled 1860s heritage building offers singles, twins and doubles, and a sunny garden. Breakfast is included and all rooms share bathrooms. The well-equipped kitchen is ideal for self-catering meals, and there's a pleasant outdoor barbecue area.

THE HAURAKI RAIL TRAIL

The Hauraki Rail Trail, which runs from Thames south to Paeroa, and then further south to Te Aroha, or east to Waihi, is growing in popularity due to its proximity to the bigger cities of Auckland and Hamilton. Two- and three-day itineraries are most popular, but shorter sections of the trail can be very rewarding, too. The spur from Paeroa east through the Karangahake Gorge via Waikino to Waihi is spectacular as it skirts a picturesque river valley. The key centres of Thames, Paeroa, Te Aroha and Waihi have an expanding range of related services including bike hire, shuttles and accommodation.

See www.haurakirailtrail.co.nz for detailed information including trail maps and recommendations for day rides. At the time of research, planning was underway to extend the trail west from Kopu around the Firth of Thames via Miranda to Kaiaua. Check the website for the latest.

Brunton House B&B B&B $$
(☑07-868 5160; www.bruntonhouse.co.nz; 210 Parawai Rd; r from $160; @☎☒) This impressive two-storey kauri villa (1875) has a modern kitchen and bathrooms, while staying true to the building's historic credentials (there are no en suites). Guests can relax in the grounds, by the pool, in the designated lounge or on the upstairs terrace. During summer, lawn tennis is an option on the property's own grass court.

Grafton Cottage & Chalets CHALET $$
(☑07-868 9971; www.graftoncottage.co.nz; 304 Grafton Rd; units $140-220; @☎☒) Most of these attractive wooden chalets perched on a hill have decks with awesome views. The hospitable hosts provide free internet access and breakfast, as well as use of the pool, spa and barbecue areas.

Coastal Motor Lodge MOTEL $$
(☑07-868 6843; www.stayatcoastal.co.nz; 608 Tararu Rd; units $164-169; ☎) Motel and chalet-style accommodation is provided at this smart, welcoming place, 2km north of Thames. It overlooks the sea, making it a popular choice, especially in the summer months.

WAIKATO & THE COROMANDEL PENINSULA THAMES

Thames

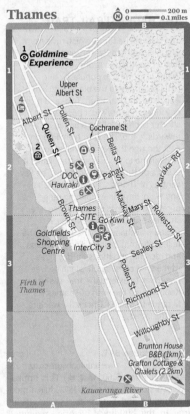

Thames

◎ Top Sights
1 Goldmine Experience A1

◎ Sights
2 School of Mines &
    Mineralogical Museum A2

◔ Activities, Courses & Tours
3 JollyBikes B3

◔ Sleeping
4 Sunkist Guesthouse............................. A1

◙ Eating
5 Cafe Melbourne.................................... A2
6 Coco Coffee Bar A2
7 Wharf Coffee House & Bar................. B4

◔ Drinking & Nightlife
8 Junction Hotel A2

◔ Shopping
9 Bounty Store... A2

✕ Eating & Drinking

Cafe Melbourne   CAFE $
(☑07-8683159;www.facebook.com/cafemelbourne
grahamstown; 715 Pollen St; mains $13-20; ☺8am-
5pm Mon-Thu, to 9pm Fri, 9am-4pm Sat & Sun)
Stylish and spacious, this cafe definitely
channels the cosmopolitan vibe of a certain
Australian city. Shared tables promote a convivial ambience, and the menu travels from
ricotta pancakes to beef sliders and fish
curry for lunch. It's in a repurposed building called the Depot where you'll also find a
juice bar and a deli with artisanal bread and
takeaway salads.

Wharf Coffee House & Bar   CAFE $
(☑07-868 6828; www.facebook.com/thewharf
coffeehouseandbar; Shortland Wharf, Queen St;
snacks & mains $10-18; ☺9am-3pm Mon & Tue,
to 7pm Wed, Sat & Sun, to 9pm Thu & Fri) Perched
beside the water, this rustic wood-lined pavilion does great fish and chips. Grab a table
outside with a beer or a wine to understand
why the Wharf is a firm local favourite. The
smoked seafood platter is especially good.

Coco Coffee Bar   CAFE $
(☑07-868 8616; 661 Pollen St; snacks from $5;
☺6.45am-2pm Mon-Sat) Occupying a corner of
an old villa, this chic little cafe serves excellent coffee and enticing pastries and cakes.

Junction Hotel   PUB
(☑07-868 6008; www.thejunction.net.nz; 700
Pollen St; ☺10am-late) Serving thirsty gold
diggers since 1869, the Junction is the archetypal slightly rough-around-the-edges,
historic, small-town pub. Live music attracts
a younger crowd on the weekends, while
families head to the corner-facing Grahamstown Bar & Diner for hearty pub grub of bar
snacks, pizza and mains ($15 to $33).

🔒 Shopping

★ Bounty Store   ARTS & CRAFTS
(☑07-868 8988; www.facebook.com/bountystore;
754 Pollen St; ☺9.30am-5pm Tue-Fri, 9.30am-2pm
& 5-6pm Sat) Excellent arts and crafts shop
with loads of local products and a quirky selection of Kiwiana NZ works. Highly recommended for distinctive souvenirs and gifts.

ℹ Information

DOC Hauraki (Department of Conservation;
☑07-867 9180; www.doc.govt.nz; cnr Pahau &
Kirkwood Sts) Offers track information.
Thames i-SITE (☑07-868 7284; www.the
coromandel.com/thames; 200 Mary St;

⊙ 9am-4pm Mon-Fri, to 1pm Sat & Sun) An excellent source of information for the entire Coromandel Peninsula.

❶ Getting There & Away

InterCity (☑ 09-583 5780; www.intercity. co.nz) has bus services to Auckland ($22, 1½ hours) and Hamilton ($25, 1¾ hours). **Go Kiwi** (☑ 0800 446 549; www.go-kiwi.co.nz) services Auckland ($49, 2¼ hours) and Whitianga ($39, 1¾ hours). A Monday to Friday shuttle from Coromandel Adventures (p216) links Coromandel Town and Rotorua with stops en route at Thames and Matamata; from December to April this service runs daily.

Coastal Route from Thames to Coromandel Town

From Thames, narrow SH25 snakes along the coast past pretty little bays and rocky beaches. Sea birds are plentiful, and you can fish, dig for shellfish and fossick for quartz, jasper and even gold-bearing rocks. The landscape turns crimson when the po-hutukawa (often referred to as the 'New Zealand Christmas tree') blooms in December.

A handful of stores, motels, B&Bs and camping grounds are scattered around the picturesque bays. At **Tapu** turn inland for a mainly sealed 6km drive to the **Rapaura Water Gardens** (☑ 07-868 4821; www.rapaurawatergardens.co.nz; 586 Tapu-Coroglen Rd; adult/child $15/6; ⊙ 9am-5pm) 🍽, combining water, greenery and sculpture.

From **Wilsons Bay** the road heads away from the coast and negotiates several hills and valleys before dropping down to Coromandel Town, 55km from Thames. The view looking towards the island-studded Coromandel Harbour is exquisite.

🍴 Eating

Waiomu Beach Cafe   CAFE $$
(☑ 07-868 2554; www.facebook.com/waiomubeachcafe; 622 Thames Coast Rd, Waiomu Bay; mains $11-25; ⊙ 7am-5pm) Just north of Te Puru, stop at the colourful Waiomu Beach Cafe for hearty breakfasts, gourmet pizza, freshly squeezed juices and healthy salads. Locally brewed craft beer from around the peninsula is also available.

❶ Getting There & Away

Driving your own vehicle is recommended around this spectacular and winding coastal road. Coromandel Adventures (p216) runs shuttles linking Thames and Coromandel Town.

Coromandel Town

☑ 07 / POP 1480

Crammed with heritage buildings, Coromandel Town is a thoroughly quaint little place. Its natty cafes, interesting art stores, excellent sleeping options and delicious smoked mussels could keep you here longer than you expected.

Gold was discovered nearby at Driving Creek in 1852. Initially the local Patukirikiri *iwi* (tribe) kept control of the land and received money from digging licences. After initial financial success the same fate befell them as the Ngāti Maru in Thames. By 1871, debt had forced them to sell all but 778 mountainous acres of their land. Today fewer than 100 people remain who identify as part of this *iwi*.

Note that Coromandel Town is just one part of the entire Coromandel Peninsula, and its location on the peninsula's west coast means it is not a good base for visiting Cathedral Cove and Hot Water Beach on the peninsula's east coast.

⊙ Sights

Many historic sites are featured in the Historic Places Trust's *Coromandel Town* pamphlet, available at the Coromandel Town Information Centre (p217).

**Coromandel Mining
& Historic Museum**   MUSEUM
(☑ 07-866 8987; 841 Rings Rd; adult/child $5/free; ⊙ 10am-4pm mid-Dec–Jan, 10am-1pm Sat & Sun Feb–mid-Dec) Small museum with glimpses of pioneer life.

🏃 Activities

★**Driving Creek Railway**   RAIL
(☑ 07-866 8703; www.dcrail.nz; 380 Driving Creek Rd; adult/child $35/13; ⊙ 10.15am, 11.30am, 12.45pm, 2pm, 3.15pm & 4.30pm, additional times summer) 🍽 A lifelong labour of love for its conservationist owner, the late Barry Brickell, this unique train runs up steep grades, across four trestle bridges, along two spirals and a double switchback, and through two tunnels, finishing at the 'Eye-full Tower'. The one-hour trip passes artworks and regenerating native forest. Booking ahead is recommended in summer.

**Coromandel Goldfield
Experience**   SCENIC DRIVE
(www.dcrail.nz) Illuminating the story of the Coromandel Goldfields, this new experience combines a journey by electric mine train

to Copeland's Stream where gold was first discovered in NZ in 1853 with a visit to a historic Stamper Battery and panning for gold. Check the website for prices and departure times.

☞ Tours

Coromandel Adventures   DRIVING
(☑0800 462 676; www.coromandeladventures. co.nz; 90 Tiki Rd; tours adult/child from $75/45) Various tours around Coromandel Town and the peninsula, plus shuttles to Whitianga. Also runs a handy shuttle service linking Coromandel Town to Rotorua via Thames, Paeroa, Te Aroha, Matamata and Tirau. The shuttle runs Monday to Friday from May to November and daily from December to April.

🛏 Sleeping

Enquire at **Coromandel Accommodation Solutions** (☑07-866 8803; www.accommodation coromandel.co.nz; 265 Kapanga Rd; units & apt $129-250; ☎) about renting a house at one of the nearby beaches.

Tui Lodge   HOSTEL $
(☑07-866 8237; www.coromandeltuilodge.co.nz; 60 Whangapoua Rd; campsite per person $20, dm $29-32, r $70-90; @☎) Pleasantly rural but still just a short walk to town, Coromandel's best backpackers has plenty of trees, free bikes, fruit (in season) and straight-up rooms. The pricier ones have en suites.

Anchor Lodge   MOTEL, HOSTEL $
(☑07-866 7992; www.anchorlodgecoromandel. co.nz; 448 Wharf Rd; dm $31, d $75, units $145-370; @☎☒) This upmarket backpacker-motel combo has its own gold mine, glowworm cave, small heated swimming pool and spa. The 2nd-floor units have harbour views.

Coromandel Motel
& Holiday Park   HOLIDAY PARK $
(☑07-866 8830; www.coromandeltop10.co.nz; 636 Rings Rd; campsites from $46, units $90-135; @☎☒) Well kept and welcoming, with nicely painted cabins, attractive units and manicured lawns – it gets busy in summer, so book ahead. Also hires bikes ($20 per day). The spotless cabins with shared bathrooms are good value for backpackers.

Hush Boutique
Accommodation   RENTAL HOUSE $$
(☑07-866 7771; www.hushaccommodation.co.nz; 425 Driving Creek Rd; cabins from $125; ☎) 🖉 Four rustic but stylish private cabins with en-suite bathrooms are scattered through-

out native bush at this easygoing spot. Natural wood creates a warm ambience. Located beside a peaceful stream, the alfresco area with a barbecue and full cooking facilities is a top spot to catch up with fellow travellers. The adjacent Hush House accommodates up to six ($355).

Green House   B&B $$
(☑07-866 7303; www.greenhousebandb.co.nz; 505 Tiki Rd; r $195; @☎) Good old-fashioned hospitality with three smartly furnished rooms on offer. The property has been refurbished, and guests enjoy sea views and a rural outlook.

Jacaranda Lodge   B&B $$
(☑07-866 8002; www.jacarandalodge.co.nz; 3195 Tiki Rd; s $90, d $155-185; ☎) 🖉 Located among 6 hectares of farmland and rose gardens, this two-storey cottage is a relaxing retreat. Look forward to excellent breakfasts from the friendly owners, Judy and Gerard, often using produce – plums, almonds, macadamia nuts and citrus fruit – from the property's spray-free orchard. Some rooms share bathrooms.

Driving Creek Villas   COTTAGE $$$
(☑07-866 7755; www.drivingcreekvillas.com; 21a Colville Rd; villas $345; ☎) This is the posh, grown-up's choice – three spacious, self-contained, modern, wooden villas with plenty of privacy. The Polynesian-influenced interior design is slick and the bush setting, complete with bubbling creek, sublime.

🍴 Eating

Driving Creek Cafe   VEGETARIAN $
(☑07-866 7066; www.drivingcreekcafe.nz; 180 Driving Creek Rd; mains $9-20; ⊙9am-5pm Tue-Sun; ☎🖉) 🖉 Vegetarian, vegan, gluten-free, organic and fair-trade delights await at this funky mudbrick cafe. The food is beautifully presented, fresh and healthy. Once sated, the kids can play in the sandpit while the adults check their email on the free wi-fi. Don't miss ordering a terrific juice or smoothie, and try the buckwheat blinis or a tasty felafel wrap.

Coromandel Oyster Company   SEAFOOD $
(☑07-866 8028; www.freshoysters.co.nz; 1611 Tiki Rd; snacks & meals $5-25; ⊙10am-5.30pm) Briny-fresh mussels, scallops, oysters and cooked fish and chips and flounder. Coming from Thames you'll find it on the hill around 7km before you reach Coromandel Town. Ask if the excellent chowder is available.

★ **Wharf Road**   CAFE, VEGETARIAN **$$**
(☑07-8667538; www.facebook.com/pg/wharfroad;
24 Wharf Rd; mains $12-18; ⊙8am-3pm; ☑) ⊘
Bringing cosmopolitan cool to Coromandel
Town, Wharf Road offers the opportunity to
ease into another day equipped with excel-
lent coffee, interesting brunch dishes such
as avocado bagels or Turkish eggs with chilli
butter, and an easygoing soundtrack of lop-
ing Kiwi reggae. Lunch amid the wood-lined
space is equally popular, with wine and craft
beer balancing super-healthy organic and
vegetarian bowls.

Coromandel Mussel Kitchen   SEAFOOD **$$**
(☑07-866 7245; www.musselkitchen.co.nz; cnr
SH25 & 309 Rd; mains $15-26; ⊙9am-3pm mid-
Sep–early Jun) This cool cafe-bar sits among
fields 3km south of town. Mussels are served
with Thai- and Mediterranean-tinged sauces
or grilled on the half-shell. In summer the
garden bar is perfect for a mussel-fritter
stack and a frosty craft beer from MK Brewing Co, the on-site microbrewery. Smoked
and chilli mussels and bottles of the beers
are all available for takeaway.

Pepper Tree   MODERN NZ **$$**
(☑07-866 8211; www.peppertreerestaurant.co.nz;
31 Kapanga Rd; mains lunch $16-28, dinner $25-
36; ⊙10am-9pm; ☎☑) Coromandel Town's
most upmarket option dishes up generously
proportioned meals with an emphasis on
local seafood. On a summer's evening, the
courtyard tables under the shady tree are
the place to be.

Y Drinking & Nightlife

Star & Garter Hotel   PUB
(☑07-866 8503; www.starandgarter.co.nz; 5
Kapanga Rd; ⊙11am-late) Making the most of
the simple kauri interior of an 1873 build-
ing, this smart pub has pool tables, decent
sounds and a roster of live music and DJs
on the weekends. The beer garden is smartly
clad in corrugated iron.

🔒 Shopping

Source   ARTS & CRAFTS
(☑07-8667345; 31 Kapanga Rd; ⊙10am-4pm) Cre-
ative showcase of more than 30 local artists.

ℹ Information

Coromandel Town Information Centre (☑07-
866 8598; www.coromandeltown.co.nz; 85
Kapanga Rd; ⊙10am-4pm; ☎) Good maps and
local information. Pick up the Historic Places
Trust's *Coromandel Town* pamphlet here.

ℹ Getting There & Away

The best way to Coromandel Town from Auckland
is on a 360 Discovery (p212) ferry (one way/
return $60/95, two hours, daily in summer, Sat-
urdays and Sundays other seasons), which makes
a stop at Orapiu on Waiheke Island en route. The
ferry docks at Hannafords Wharf, Te Kouma, from
where free buses shuttle passengers the 10km
into Coromandel Town. It's also possible to book
same-day return trips visiting Coromandel desti-
nations like the Driving Creek Railway (p215).

There's no charge for carrying your bike on a
360 Discovery ferry. Touring cyclists can avoid
Auckland's traffic fumes and treacherous roads
completely by catching the ferry at Gulf Harbour
to Auckland's ferry terminal and then leapfrog-
ging directly to Coromandel Town.

Leaving from a stop (Woollams Ave) near the
Coromandel Town Information Centre, **InterCity**
(☑09-583 5780; www.intercity.co.nz) has buses
linking Coromandel Town to Hamilton ($40, 3½
hours) and **Go Kiwi** (☑0800 446 549; www.
go-kiwi.co.nz) heads to Auckland ($59, 4½
hours). Coromandel Adventures (p216) runs
a shuttle from Coromandel Town to Rotorua
(Monday to Friday from May to November and
daily from December to April), with a key stop in
Matamata for Hobbiton (p198).

Far North Coromandel

Supremely isolated and gobsmackingly
beautiful, the rugged tip of the Coroman-
del Peninsula is well worth the effort re-
quired to reach it. The best time to visit is
summer, when the gravel roads are dry, the
pohutukawa trees are in their crimson glory
and camping's an option (there isn't much
accommodation up here).

⊙ Sights

The tiny settlement of **Colville** is a remote
rural community populated by alternative
lifestylers. There's not much here except for
the quaint **Colville General Store** (☑07-866
6805; Colville Rd, Colville; ⊙8.30am-5pm; ☑) ⊘
and the **Hereford 'n' a Pickle** (☑07-866 6937;
www.facebook.com/hereford.n.a.pickle;   Colville
Town; pies $4-6; ⊙9am-4pm, reduced hours Apr-
Oct; ☎) cafe.

Three kilometres north of Colville the
sealed road turns to gravel and splits to
straddle each side of the peninsula. Fol-
lowing the west shore, ancient pohutukawa
shade turquoise waters and stony beaches.
The small DOC-run **Fantail Bay Campsite**
(☑07-866 6685; www.doc.govt.nz; Port Jack-
son Rd; adult/child $13/6.50) is 23km north

WORTH A TRIP

COROMANDEL FOREST PARK

More than 30 walks criss-cross the Coromandel Forest Park, spread over several major blocks throughout the centre of the Coromandel Peninsula. The most popular hike is the challenging six- to eight-hour return journey up to the **Pinnacles** (759m) in the Kauaeranga Valley behind Thames. Other outstanding tramps include the Coromandel Coastal Walkway in Far North Coromandel, from Fletcher Bay to Stony Bay, and the Puketui Valley walk to abandoned gold mines.

For a guided walking adventure in the Coromandel, contact **Walking Legends** (☑ 07-312 5297, 0800 925 569; www.walkinglegends.com; 4-day trip from $1590).

The DOC **Pinnacles Hut** has 80 beds, gas cookers, heating, toilets and cold showers. The 10-bunk **Crosbies Hut** is a four- to six-hour tramp from Thames or the Kauaeranga Valley. There are also four backcountry campsites (adult/child $8/4): one near each hut and others at Moss Creek and Billygoat Basin; expect only a toilet. Eight other conservation campsites (adult/child $13/6.50) are accessible from Kauaeranga Valley Rd. Book online at www.doc.govt.nz.

The **DOC Kauaeranga Visitor Centre** (Department of Conservation; ☑ 07-867 9080; www.doc.govt.nz; Kauaeranga Valley Rd; ⊙ 8.30am-4pm) has interesting displays about the kauri forest and its history. Maps and conservation resources are available for purchase and staff dispense advice. The centre is 14km off SH25; it's a further 9km along a gravel road to the start of the trails.

There is no scheduled public transport, so having a car or arranging a shuttle is necessary. Enquire at the Thames i-SITE (p215) about shuttles.

of Colville. Another 7km brings you to the beachfront DOC **Port Jackson Campsite** (☑ 07-866 6932; www.doc.govt.nz; Port Jackson Rd; adult/child $13/6.50).

There's a spectacular **lookout** about 4km further on. **Great Barrier Island** is only 20km away, looking every part the extension of the Coromandel Peninsula that it once was. The road stops at **Fletcher Bay** – a magical land's end. Although it's only 37km from Colville, allow an hour for the drive. There's another DOC **campsite** (☑ 07-866 6685; www.doc.govt.nz; Fletcher Bay; adult/child $13/6.50) here, as well as **Fletcher Bay Backpackers** (☑ 07-866 6685; www.doc.govt. nz; Fletcher Bay; dm $26).

At **Stony Bay**, where the east coast road terminates, there's another DOC **campsite** (☑ 07-866 6822; www.doc.govt.nz; Stony Bay; adult/child $13/6.50, bach $80) and a small DOC-run bach (holiday home) that sleeps five. Heading south there are a couple of nice beaches peppered with baches on the way to the slightly larger settlement of **Port Charles**, where you'll find **Tangiaro Kiwi Retreat** (☑ 07-866 6614; www.kiwiretreat.co.nz; 1299 Port Charles Rd, Port Charles; units $220-350; ☎).

Another 8km brings you to the turn-off leading back to Colville, or you can continue south to **Waikawau Bay**, where there's a large DOC **campsite** (☑ 07-866 1106; www.doc. govt.nz; Waikawau Beach Rd, Waikawau Bay; adult/child $15/6.50) that has a summer-only store. The road then winds its way south past **Kennedy Bay** before cutting back to come out near the Driving Creek Railway (p215).

🏃 Activities

Coromandel Coastal Walkway   WALKING
This is a scenic 3½-hour, one-way hike between Fletcher Bay and Stony Bay. It's a relatively easy walk with great coastal views and an ambling section across farmland.

Coromandel Discovery   WALKING
(☑ 07-866 8175; www.coromandeldiscovery.co.nz; 39 Whangapoua Rd, Coromandel Town; adult/child $135/75) If you're not keen on walking the return leg of the Coromandel Coastal Walkway, Coromandel Discovery will drive you from Coromandel Town up to Fletcher Bay and pick you up from Stony Bay four hours later. Ask about other tours exploring Cathedral Cove and Hot Water Beach.

🛏 Sleeping

Mahamudra Centre   RETREAT $
(☑ 07-866 6851; www.mahamudra.org.nz; RD4, Main Rd, Colville; campsite/dm/s/tw $18/28/50/80) The Mahamudra Centre is a serene Tibetan Buddhist retreat with a stupa, meditation hall and regular meditation courses. It offers simple accommodation in a parklike setting.

Colville Farm LODGE $$

(☎07-866 6820; www.colvillefarmholidays.co.nz; 2140 Colville Rd; d $50-100; @ 🛜) The 1260-hectare Colville Farm has a range of interesting accommodation, including bare-basics bush lodges and self-contained houses. Guests can try their hands at farm work (including milking) or go on horse treks ($40 to $150, one to five hours).

❶ Getting There & Away

There is no public transport. The best time to visit is summer, when the gravel roads are dry.

Coromandel Town to Whitianga

There are two routes from Coromandel Town southeast to Whitianga. The main road is the slightly longer but quicker SH25, which enjoys sea views and has short detours to pristine sandy beaches. The other is the less-travelled but legendary 309 Rd, an unsealed, untamed route through deep bush.

309 Road

Starting 3km south of Coromandel Town, the 309 Rd cuts through the Coromandel Range for 21km (most of which is unsealed but well maintained), rejoining SH25 7km south of Whitianga.

Highlights include a quirky **water park** (☎07-866 7191; www.thewaterworks.co.nz; 471 309 Rd; adult/child $25/20; ⊙10am-6pm Nov-Mar, to 4pm Apr-Oct; 🖈) 🎣, and just 2km further west there's a two-minute walk through bush to the 10m-high **Waiau Falls**. A further 500m on, an easy 10-minute bush walk leads to an amazing **kauri grove**. This stand of 600-year-old giants escaped the carnage of the 19th century, giving a majestic reminder of what the peninsula once looked like. The biggest tree has a 6m circumference.

Accommodation is limited to **Wairua Lodge** (☎07-866 0304; www.wairualodge.co.nz; 251 Old Coach Rd; r $195-275), but it's only a short drive to either Coromandel Town or Whitianga at either end of the 309 Rd.

Not all of the 309 Rd is sealed, but it's an easy drive if you take it carefully. No public transport covers this route.

SH25

SH25 starts by climbing sharply to an incredible lookout before heading steeply down. The turn-off at Te Rerenga follows the harbour to **Whangapoua**. There's not much at this beach except for holiday homes and a pleasant holiday park. Walk along the rocky foreshore for 30 minutes to the remote, beautiful and often-deserted and undeveloped **New Chum's Beach**, regarded as one of the most beautiful in the country. Be ready to take your shoes off and wade through a lagoon to get there, and consult the map near the beach store in Whangapoua before you start walking.

Continuing east on SH25 you soon reach **Kuaotunu**, a more interesting holiday village on a beautiful stretch of white-sand beach, with a cafe-gallery, a store and an ancient petrol pump.

Heading off the highway at Kuaotunu takes you (via an unsealed road) to one of Coromandel's best-kept secrets. First the long stretch of **Otama Beach** comes into view – deserted but for a few houses and farms. Continuing along the narrowing road, the sealed road finally starts again and you reach **Opito**, a hidden-away enclave of 250 flash properties (too smart to be called baches), of which only 16 have permanent residents. From this magical beach, you can walk to the Ngāti Hei *pā* (fortified village) site at the far end.

🍽 Sleeping & Eating

Whangapoua Holiday Park HOLIDAY PARK $

(☎07-866 5215; www.whangapouaholidaypark. co.nz; 1266 Whangapoua Rd, Whangapoua; campsites from $20, cabins $75-105; ⊙mid-Oct–Apr) This holiday park has cosy cabins and leafy campsites with well-maintained kitchen and ablution blocks.

Leighton Lodge B&B $$

(☎07-866 0756; www.leightonlodge.co.nz; 17 Stewart Pl, Opito; s $160-190, d $200-220; @) One of the 'real' residences in Opito houses the delightful folks of Leighton Lodge. This smart B&B has chatty owners, an upstairs room with a view-hungry balcony and a self-contained flat downstairs. Say 'hi' to Fern, the owners' very friendly labrador.

★Luke's Kitchen & Cafe CAFE, PIZZA $$

(☎07-866 4420; www.lukeskitchen.co.nz; 20 Blackjack Rd, Kuaotunu; mains & pizza $15-28; ⊙cafe & gallery 8.30am-3.30pm, restaurant & bar 11am-10pm, shorter restaurant hours Apr-Oct) Luke's Kitchen & Cafe has a rustic surf-shack ambience, cold brews including local craft beer from the tiny Blue Fridge Brewery, and excellent wood-fired pizza. Occasional live music, seafood and creamy fruit smoothies make Luke's an essential stop. Adjacent is Luke's daytime cafe and gallery with very good coffee, home-baked goodies and eclectic local art for sale.

ⓘ Getting There & Away

The best way to explore the meandering roads is by car. Kuaotunu is also a stop on **Go Kiwi** (p224) shuttles linking Matarangi and Auckland.

Whitianga

📞 07 / POP 4700

Whitianga's big attractions are the sandy beaches of Mercury Bay and the diving, boating and kayaking opportunities afforded by the craggy coast and nearby **Te Whanganui-A-Hei Marine Reserve**. The pretty harbour is a renowned base for game-fishing (especially marlin and tuna between January and March).

The legendary Polynesian explorer and seafarer Kupe is believed to have landed near here sometime around AD 950. The name Whitianga is a contraction of Te Whitianga a Kupe (Crossing Place of Kupe).

◉ Sights

Buffalo Beach stretches along Mercury Bay, north of Whitianga Harbour. A five-minute **passenger ferry** (📞07-866 3462; www.whitiangaferry.co.nz; adult/child/bicycle $5/3/1.50; ⊙7.30am-7.30pm & 8.30-10.30pm) ride will take you across the harbour to **Ferry Landing**. From here you can walk to local sights like **Whitianga Rock Scenic & Historical Reserve**, a park with great views over the ocean, and the **Shakespeare Cliff Lookout**. Further afield are Hahei Beach (13km), Cathedral Cove (15km) and Hot Water Beach (18km, one hour by bike). Look forward to relatively flat terrain if you're keen on riding from Ferry Landing to these other destinations. **Cathedral Cove Shuttles** (📞027 422 5899; www.cathedralcoveshuttles.co.nz; from $15; ♿) runs a handy service.

Lost Spring SPRING
(📞07-866 0456; www.thelostspring.co.nz; 121a Cook Dr; per 90min/day $40/70; ⊙9.30am-6pm Sun-Fri, to 8pm Sat) This expensive but intriguing Disney-meets-Polynesia thermal complex comprises a series of hot pools in a lush jungle-like setting complete with an erupting volcano. It's the ideal spot to relax in tropical tranquillity, with a cocktail in hand. There's also a day spa and cafe. Children under 14 must be accompanied by an adult in the pools.

Mercury Bay Museum MUSEUM
(📞07-866 0730; www.mercurybaymuseum.co.nz; 11a The Esplanade; adult/child $7.50/2; ⊙10am-4pm) A small but interesting museum focusing on local history – especially Whitianga's most famous visitors, Kupe and Cook.

🏃 Activities

Bike Man CYCLING
(📞07-866 0745; thebikeman@xtra.co.nz; 16 Coghill St; per day $25; ⊙9am-5pm Mon-Fri, to 1pm Sat) Rent a bike to take across on the ferry and journey to Hahei and Hot Water Beach.

Windborne BOATING
(📞027 475 2411; www.windborne.co.nz; day sail $95; ⊙Dec-Apr) Day sails in a 19m 1928 schooner from December to April, and also departures to the Mercury Islands ($150) in February and March.

⌒ Tours

There are a baffling number of tours to **Te Whanganui-A-Hei Marine Reserve**, where you'll see interesting rock formations and, if you're lucky, dolphins, fur seals, penguins and orcas. Some are straight-out cruises while others offer optional swims and snorkels.

Ocean Leopard BOATING
(📞0800 843 8687; www.oceanleopardtours.co.nz; adult/child $90/50; ⊙10.30pm, 1.30pm & 4pm) Two-hour trips taking in coastal scenery, naturally including Cathedral Cove (p223). The boat has a handy canopy for sun protection. A one-hour Whirlwind Tour (adult/child $60/35) is also on offer.

Glass Bottom Boat BOATING
(📞07-867 1962; www.glassbottomboatwhitianga.co.nz; adult/child $95/50) Two-hour tours exploring the Te Whanganui-A-Hei Marine Reserve.

Whitianga Adventures BOATING
(📞0800 806 060; www.whitianga-adventures.co.nz; adult/child $75/45) A two-hour Sea Cave Adventure in an inflatable.

Cave Cruzer BOATING
(📞0800 427 893; www.cavecruzer.co.nz; adult/child 1hr $60/35, 2hr $80/45) Tours on a rigid-hull inflatable.

🎊 Festivals & Events

Scallop Festival FOOD & DRINK
(📞07-867 1510; www.scallopfestival.co.nz; ⊙Sep) One-day showcase of food, entertainment and more than a few people's favourite bivalves.

Sleeping

Turtle Cove
HOSTEL $

(☑ 07-867 1517; www.turtlecove.co.nz; 14 Bryce St; dm $29-30, d $77-198; @ 🛜) Colourful shared areas and a spacious modern kitchen make Turtle Cove one of the best hostels in the Coromandel Peninsula and Waikato area. The largest dormitories have only six beds, making Turtle Cove more like a friendly homestay than a rip-roaring party palace. The team at reception is unfailingly helpful with plenty of ideas on how to maximise your time.

On the Beach Backpackers Lodge
HOSTEL $

(☑ 07-866 5380; www.coromandelbackpackers. com; 46 Buffalo Beach Rd; dm $27, d & tw $80-115, f $160; @) Brightly painted and beachside, this large YHA-affiliate has a wide range of rooms, including some with sea views and en suites. It provides free kayaks, boogie boards and spades (for Hot Water Beach). Bikes ($20) are also available if you're keen to catch the ferry and cycle to Hahei.

Mercury Bay Holiday Park
HOLIDAY PARK $

(☑ 07-866 5579; www.mercurybayholidaypark. co.nz; 121 Albert St; campsites from $28, units $95-220; @ 🛜 🏊 🚻) Strangely planted in a suburban neighbourhood, this small holiday park is comfortable and clean, with playgrounds, trampoline, swimming pool and pool table.

Beachside Resort
MOTEL $$

(☑ 07-867 1356; www.beachsideresort.co.nz; 20 Eyre St; units $195-225; 🛜 🏊) Attached to the sprawling Oceans Resort, this modern motel has tidy units with kitchenettes and balconies on the upper level. Despite the name, it's set back from the beach but it does have a heated pool.

Within the Bays
B&B $$$

(☑ 07-866 2848; www.withinthebays.co.nz; 49 Tarapatiki Dr; r $275-325; @ 🛜) It's the combination of charming hosts and incredible views that make this B&B set on a hill overlooking Mercury Bay really worth considering. It's extremely well set up for guests with restricted mobility – there's even a wheelchair-accessible bush track on the property. Find it 5km from Whitianga town.

Eating

Coghill House
CAFE $

(☑ 07-866 0592; www.thecog.co.nz; 10 Coghill St; mains $10-18; ⊙ 8am-3pm) Get an early start on the sunny terrace of this side-street cafe, where good counter food is partnered with huge pancake stacks and plump tortilla

Whitianga

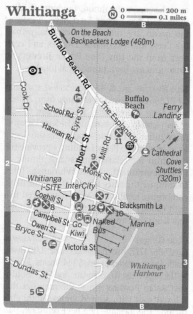

wraps. Look forward to the best coffee in town, too.

Stoked
CAFE, BAR $$

(☑ 07-866 0029; www.getstoked.co.nz; 19 The Esplanade; pizza $18-25, mains $24-32; ⊙ noon-late Fri-Sun, from 4pm Thu) With a charcoal oven as its kitchen hub, Stoked turns out dishes like manuka smoked salmon, tandoori chicken thigh and good wood-fired pizza. Views of the ocean are mandatory, especially from the deck, and Coromandel wines and craft beer from the tiny Blue Fridge Brewery in Kuaotunu are both proud local touches.

Salt Restaurant & Bar MODERN NZ, SEAFOOD **$$**
(⏹ 07-866 5818; www.salt-whitianga.co.nz; 2 Blacksmith Lane; shared plates $12-30, mains $25-39; ⏱ 4pm-late Mon-Thu, from noon Fri-Sun) Views of the Whitianga marina – including the sleepy ferry crossing to Ferry Landing – provide the backdrop for relaxed but stylish dining at this restaurant attached to Whitianga Hotel. In summer the place to be is out on the deck, combining local wines with pan-seared fish with Cloudy Bay clams or Coromandel oysters from the raw bar.

Blue Ginger SOUTHEAST ASIAN **$$**
(⏹ 07-867 1777; www.blueginger.co.nz; 1/10 Blacksmith Lane; shared plates $9-14, mains $22-28; ⏱ 11am-2pm Tue-Fri, 5pm-late Tue-Sat) Southeast Asian flavours infuse the menu at this relaxed spot with shared tables. Highlights include Indonesian-style beef rendang, pad thai noodles and a great roast-duck red curry. Beer and wine are not served.

Poivre & Sel FRENCH **$$$**
(⏹ 07-866 0053; www.poivresel.co.nz; 2 Mill Rd; 2/3 courses $58/76; ⏱ 5pm-late Tue-Sat) This Mediterranean-style villa – complete with a garden shaded by palm trees – is the most stylish eatery in town. Local Coromandel seafood and NZ produce shines with French flavours – try the bouillabaisse seafood soup – while the restaurant's bar opens at 5pm for combinations ($20 to $30) of French champagne with cheese or garlic snails. Booking for dinner from 6pm is recommended.

🍷 Drinking & Nightlife

Whitianga Hotel PUB
(⏹ 07-866 5818; www.whitiangahotel.co.nz; 1 Blacksmith Lane; ⏱ 11am-late) Good-value pub food, lots of frosty beers on tap and a relaxed garden bar equal a classic Kiwi pub experience. Challenge the locals on the pool table and return on weekend nights for DJs and cover bands playing songs you'll probably know all the words to.

❶ Information

Whitianga i-SITE (⏹ 07-866 5555; www. whitianga.co.nz; 66 Albert St; ⏱ 9am-5pm Mon-Fri, to 4pm Sat & Sun) Information and internet access. Hours are extended in summer.

❶ Getting There & Away

BOAT
A five-minute passenger ferry (p220) ride will take you across the harbour to Whitianga Rock Scenic & Historical Reserve, Flaxmill Bay, Shakespeare Cliff Lookout (p220), Captain Cook's Memorial, Lonely Bay and Cooks Bay.

BUS
InterCity (⏹ 07-348 0366; www.intercity.co.nz) links Whitianga to Thames ($25, 90 minutes, twice daily) for onward transfer to Auckland and Hamilton. Go Kiwi (p224) links Whitianga to Thames ($39, 90 minutes, one daily) and Auckland ($64, 3½ hours, one daily). This service also loops around Hot Water Beach and Hahei; check the website for timings. **Naked Bus** (https:// nakedbus.com) also services Whitianga.

Coroglen & Whenuakite

The blink-and-you'll-miss-them villages of Coroglen and Whenuakite are on SH25, south of Whitianga and west of Hot Water Beach. Along this route are a few interesting diversions, including a good craft brewery and a weekly **farmers market** (⏹ 07-866 3315; www.facebook.com/coroglenfarmersmarket; SH25, Coroglen; ⏱ 9am-1pm Sun late Oct-early Jun).

🏃 Activities

Rangihau Ranch HORSE RIDING
(⏹ 07-866 3875; www.rangihauranch.co.nz; Rangihau Rd, Coroglen; rides per hr $60) The folks at Rangihau Ranch will lead you on horseback up a historic packhorse track, through beautiful bush to spectacular views. Accommodation in a quaint rural cottage ($150) is also available.

🛏 Sleeping

Seabreeze Holiday Park HOLIDAY PARK **$**
(⏹ 07-866 3050; www.seabreezeholidaypark.co.nz; 1043 SH25, Whenuakite; campsite per person $19-25, dm $34, unit $85-170; 🛜) A friendly and grassy park with the bonus of an on-site craft brewery. What's not to like?

🍴 Eating & Drinking

Colenso CAFE **$**
(⏹ 07-866 3725; www.colensocafe.co.nz; SH25, Whenuakite; mains $10-19; ⏱ 10am-4pm) Better than your average highway stop, Colenso has excellent fair-trade coffee, scones, cakes and light snacks, as well as a shop selling homewares and gifts. Try the delicious macadamia nut brittle.

Hot Water Brewing Co
CRAFT BEER

(☑07-866 3830; www.hotwaterbrewingco.com; Seabreeze Holiday Park, 1043 SH25, Whenuakite; ⊙11am-late) Hot Water Brewing Co is a modern craft brewery with lots of outdoor seating. Standout brews include the hoppy Kauri Falls Pale Ale and the robust Walker's Porter. OK bar snacks and pizza are available.

Coroglen Tavern
PUB

(☑07-866 3809; www.coroglentavern.co.nz; 1937 SH25, Coroglen; ⊙10am-late) The legendary Coroglen Tavern is the archetypal middle-of-nowhere country pub that attracts big-name Kiwi bands in summer.

🛈 Getting There & Away

InterCity (p215) buses linking Thames to Whitianga stop at Whenuakite and Coroglen.

Hahei

☑07 / POP 270

A legendary Kiwi beach town, little Hahei balloons to 7000 people in summer but is nearly abandoned otherwise – apart from the busloads of tourists doing the obligatory stopoff at Cathedral Cove. It's a charming spot and a great place to unwind for a few days, especially in the quieter months. It takes its name from Hei, the eponymous ancestor of the Ngāti Hei people, who arrived in the 14th century on the Te Arawa canoe. Online, see www.hahei.co.nz.

⊙ Sights

Cathedral Cove
BEACH

Beautiful Cathedral Cove, with its famous gigantic stone arch and natural waterfall shower, is best enjoyed early or late in the day – avoiding the worst of the hordes. From the Cathedral Cove car park, around 2km north of Hahei, it's a rolling walk of around 30 to 40 minutes. On the way there's rocky Gemstone Bay, which has a snorkelling trail where you're likely to see big snapper, crayfish and stingrays, and sandy Stingray Bay.

If you walk from Hahei Beach directly to Cathedral Cove, it will take about 70 minutes. Another option is the 10-minute Cathedral Cove Water Taxi (☑027 919 0563; www.cathedralcovewatertaxi.co.nz; adult one way/return $15/30, child $10/20; ⊙every 30min).

If you're driving, you're best leaving your car at the Hahei Park N'Ride Car Park at the entrance to Hahei village, as over the peak summer months, the Cathedral Cove car park

(and the cove itself) can be exceptionally busy. You can either walk the 2km to the Cathedral Cove car park from Hahei, or, from 10am to 6pm, catch a Go Kiwi (p224) shuttle ($5).

Hahei Beach
BEACH

Long, lovely Hahei Beach is made more magical by the view to the craggy islands in the distance. From the southern end of Hahei Beach, it's a 15-minute walk up to Te Pare, a pā (fortified village) site with splendid coastal views.

🏃 Activities

Cathedral Cove Sea Kayaking
KAYAKING

(☑07-866 3877; www.seakayaktours.co.nz; 88 Hahei Beach Rd; half/full day $115/190; ⊙8.45am & 1.30pm, additional departures Dec & Jan) This outfit runs guided kayaking trips around the rock arches, caves and islands in the Cathedral Cove and Mercury Bay area. The Remote Coast Tour heads the other way when conditions permit, visiting caves, blowholes and a long tunnel.

Hahei Beach Bikes
CYCLING

(☑021 701 093; www.haheibeachbikes.co.nz; bike hire half/full day $35/45) Friendly owner Jonny provides maps with key points of interest and a spade for digging a spa pool at Hot Water Beach. Most times of the year bikes can be picked up from the Hahei Holiday Park (41 Harsant Ave), but Jonny can also deliver bikes to travellers arriving at Ferry Landing off the ferry from Whitianga, or to Hahei village.

👉 Tours

Hahei Explorer
ADVENTURE

(☑07-866 3910; www.haheiexplorer.co.nz; adult/child $95/50) Hour-long jetboat rides touring the coast.

🛏 Sleeping

Tatahi Lodge
HOSTEL, MOTEL $

(☑07-866 3992; www.tatahilodge.co.nz; Grange Rd; dm $33, r $84-130, units from $175; @🕏) A wonderful place where backpackers are treated with at least as much care and respect as the lush, bromeliad-filled garden. The dorm rooms and excellent communal facilities are just as attractive as the pricier motel units.

Purangi Garden Accommodation
COTTAGE $$

(☑07-866 4036; www.purangigarden.co.nz; Lees Rd; d $180-200) On a quiet cove on the Purangi River, this relaxing spot has accommodation ranging from comfortable chalets through to larger houses and a spacious, self-contained yurt. Well-established gardens and rolling lawns lead to the water – perfect for swimming and kayaking – and don't be surprised if the friendly owners drop off some organic fruit or freshly baked bread.

Hahei and Hot Water Beach are both a short drive away.

The Church COTTAGE $$
(☎07-866 3533; www.thechurchhahei.co.nz; 87 Hahei Beach Rd; cottages $150-230; 🐾) ✆ Set within a subtropical garden, these beautifully kitted out, rustic timber cottages have plenty of character. The switched-on owners are really welcoming and have loads of ideas on what to do and see around the area.

🍴 Eating & Drinking

The Church MEDITERRANEAN $$
(☎07-866 3797; www.thechurchbistro.co.nz; 87 Hahei Beach Rd; mains $30-35; ☺3pm-late, reduced hours Mar-Oct) This charming wooden church is Hahei's swankiest eatery. A concise menu of European-influenced mains includes a French-style soup crammed with local seafood, and braised chicken pot pie with pancetta and peas in a madeira sauce. Definitely leave room for excellent desserts and try to book ahead – especially over summer – as the heritage dining room is relatively compact.

★ Pour House PUB
(☎07-866 3354; www.coromandelbrewingcompany. co.nz; 7 Grange Rd; ☺5pm-late Mon-Fri, noon-late Sat & Sun May-Nov, from noon daily Dec-Apr) Home base for the Coromandel Brewing Company, this pub and bistro regularly features around five of its beers in a modern ambience. Platters of meat, cheese and local seafood combine with decent pizzas in the beer garden. Our favourite brew is the Code Red Irish Ale.

❶ Getting There & Away

In the absolute height of summer school holidays the council runs a bus service from the Cooks Beach side of Ferry Landing to Hot Water

❶ BEACH SAFETY

Hot Water Beach has dangerous rips, especially directly in front of the main thermal section. It's one of the four most dangerous beaches in New Zealand in terms of drowning numbers, although this may be skewed by the huge number of tourists that flock here. Regardless, swimming here is *not* safe if the lifeguards aren't on patrol.

Beach, stopping at Hahei. Ask at the Whitianga i-SITE (p222).

Go Kiwi (☎07-866 0336; www.go-kiwi.co.nz) runs a daily service linking Hahei and Hot Water Beach to Auckland and Whitianga.

Cathedral Cove Shuttles (p220) offers a convenient transport service from Ferry Landing to nearby beaches and attractions. Service is by request via phone or text.

From Ferry Landing to Hahei is around 10km. Bikes can be rented from Hahei Beach Bikes (p223), with pick-up at Hahei Holiday Park (p223).

Hot Water Beach

Justifiably famous, Hot Water Beach is quite extraordinary. For two hours either side of low tide, you can access an area of sand in front of a rocky outcrop at the middle of the beach where hot water oozes up from beneath the surface. Bring a spade, dig a hole and, voila, you've got a personal spa pool. Surfers stop off before the main beach to access some decent breaks. The headland between the two beaches still has traces of a Ngāti Hei *pā* (fortified village).

⊙ Sights & Activities

Moko Artspace GALLERY
(☎07-866 3367; www.moko.co.nz; 24 Pye Pl; ☺10am-5pm) Near Hot Water Beach, Moko is full of beautiful things – art, sculpture, jewellery – with a modern Pasifika/Māori bent.

Hot Water Beach Store OUTDOORS
(☎07-866 3006; Pye Pl; ☺9am-5pm) Spades ($5) can be hired from the Hot Water Beach Store, which has a cafe attached.

🛏 Sleeping & Eating

Hot Water Beach

Top 10 Holiday Park HOLIDAY PARK $
(☎07-866 3116; www.hotwaterbeachtop10.co.nz; 790 Hot Water Beach Rd; campsites from $25, dm $30, units $90-165; @🐾) ✆ Bordered by tall bamboo and gum trees, this is a very well-run holiday park with everything from grassy campsites through to a spacious and spotless backpackers lodge and stylish villas with arched ceilings crafted from NZ timber.

Hot Waves CAFE $$
(☎07-866 3887; 8 Pye Pl; mains $12-26; ☺8.30am-4pm Mon-Thu & Sun, to 8.30pm Fri & Sat) In summer everyone wants a garden table at this excellent cafe. For a lazy brunch,

PUKETUI VALLEY

Located 12km south of Tairua is the turn-off to Puketui Valley and the historic **Broken Hills Gold-Mine Workings** (www.doc.govt.nz), which are 8km from the main road along a mainly gravel road. There are short walks up to the sites of stamper batteries, but the best hike is through the 500m-long Collins Drive mine tunnel. After the tunnel, keep an eye out for the short 'lookout' side trail, which affords panoramic views. It takes about three hours return. Remember to take a torch and a jacket with you. Look for the Department of Conservation (DOC) brochure in information centres in Tairua and Whangamata.

Accommodation is limited to a DOC **campsite** (www.doc.govt.nz; adult/child $13/6.50). There is no public transport to the Puketui Valley. Most travellers visit en route between Tairua and Whangamata.

try the eggs Benedict with smoked salmon or a breakfast burrito. It also hires spades for the beach ($5). Ask about occasional Friday-night music sessions.

❶ Getting There & Away

Cathedral Cove Shuttles (📞 027 422 5899; www.cathedralcoveshuttles.co.nz; per person depending on destination $4-40; ⏰ 9am-late Dec-Feb, to 10.30pm Mar-Nov) and Go Kiwi both stop here. It's also a popular destination for cyclists leaving from Ferry Landing across the water from Whitianga. Look forward to a rolling ride of around 18km from Ferry Landing to Hot Water Beach.

Tairua & Pauanui

📞 07 / POP 1270

Tairua and its twin town Pauanui sit either side of a river estuary that's perfect for windsurfing or for little kids to splash about in. Both have excellent surf beaches (Pauanui's is probably a shade better) and both are ridiculously popular in the summertime, but that's where the similarity stops. While Tairua is a functioning residential town (with shops, ATMs and a choice of eateries), Pauanui is an upmarket refuge for Aucklanders. Friendly Tairua knows how to keep it real.

❍ Sights & Activities

Various operators offer fishing charters and sightseeing trips. Enquire at the information centre (p226).

Paaku   MOUNTAIN

Around seven million years ago Paaku was a volcanic island, but now it forms the northern head of Tairua's harbour. Ngāti Hei had a *pā* here before being invaded by Ngāti Maru in the 17th century. It's a steep 15-

minute walk to the summit from the top of Paku Dr, with the pay-off being amazing views over Tairua, Pauanui and the Alderman Islands. Plaques along the way detail Tairua's colonial history; only one is devoted to its long Māori occupation.

🛏 Sleeping & Eating

**Tairua Backpackers
& Beach Villa B&B**   HOSTEL $

(📞 07-864 8345; www.tairuabackpackers.com; 200 Main Rd; dm $30, s $74-83, d $83-93, f $117-140; @🛜) Rooms are homey and casual at this estuary-edge hostel in a converted house, and the dorm scores great views. Guests can help themselves to fishing rods, kayaks, sailboards and bikes. When we last dropped by the switched-on managers were completing a colourful top-to-toe renovation. Highly recommended.

Sunlover Retreat   B&B $$$

(📞 07-864 9024; www.sunlover.co.nz; 20 Ridge Rd; d $320-350; 🛜) Enjoy stunning views of Paaku and Tairua at this stylish B&B high above the harbour. Two of the three suites have private outdoor balconies, and huge picture windows provide plenty of light and space. Decor is chic, modern and dotted with quirky NZ art, and guests receive a warm welcome from Rover, the Sunlover Retreat labradoodle.

Manaia Kitchen & Bar   CAFE $$

(📞 07-864 9050; www.manaiakitchenbar.co.nz; 228 Main Rd; mains breakfast $12-18, lunch $17-24, dinner $24-32; ⏰ 9am-late Thu-Tue) With courtyard seating for lazy summer brunches and a burnished-copper bar to prop up later in the night, Manaia is the most cosmopolitan spot on the Tairua strip. Interesting menu options include fish tacos and calamari with spicy harissa, and Tairua's most

OFF THE BEATEN TRACK

OPOUTERE

File this one under Coromandel's best-kept secrets. Apart from a cluster of houses there's nothing for miles around. Swimming can be dangerous, especially near Hikinui Islet, which is close to the beach. On the sand spit is the **Wharekawa Wildlife Refuge**, a breeding ground for the endangered New Zealand dotterel.

On the accommodation front, **Copsefield** ($\square$ 07-865 9555; www.copse field.co.nz; 1055 SH25; r $120-200; $\widehat{\ }$) is a peaceful country-style villa set in attractive, lush gardens with a spa and riverside swimming hole. The main house has three attractive B&B rooms, while cheaper accommodation is offered in a separate bach-style cottage.

With a change in Hikuai, it's possible to catch the **Go Kiwi** ($\square$ 0800 446 549; www.go-kiwi.co.nz) Auckland–Whitianga shuttle to Opoutere.

authentic pizzas are prepared by an Italian chef. There's occasional live music and DJs on Friday nights.

Old Mill Cafe   CAFE $$
($\square$ 07-864 9390; www.theoldmillcafetairua.com; 1 The Esplanade; mains $15-25; $\otimes$ 8am-4pm Thu-Sun) With colourful walls, elegant veranda furniture and harbour views, the Old Mill Cafe serves interesting cafe fare like Spanish baked eggs for breakfast and Thai prawn curry for lunch. Quite possibly the Coromandel's best muffins, too.

ℹ Information

Tairua Information Centre ($\square$ 07-864 7575; www.thecoromandel.com/tairua; 223 Main Rd; $\otimes$ 9am-5pm) Information, maps, and accommodation and transport bookings.

ℹ Getting There & Away

InterCity (www.intercity.co.nz), Naked Bus (www.nakedbus.com) and Go Kiwi (www.go-kiwi.co.nz) all run bus services to Tairua.

Tairua and Pauanui are connected by a **passenger ferry** ($\square$ 027-497 0316; $5; $\otimes$ daily Dec & Jan), which departs around every hour from 10am to 4pm across the peak of summer and holiday weekends. In other months the ferry offers a water-taxi service.

Whangamata

$\square$ 07 / POP 3560

When Auckland's socially ambitious flock to Pauanui, the city's young and free head to Whangamata to surf, party and hook up. It can be a raucous spot over New Year, when the population swells to more than 40,000. It's a true summer-holiday town, but in the off-season there may as well be tumbleweeds rolling down the main street.

🏃 Activities

Besides fishing (game-fishing runs from January to April), other activities include snorkelling near Hauturu (Clarke) Island, and surfing, orienteering and mountain biking. There are also excellent walks.

The **Wentworth Falls** walk takes 2½ hours (return); it starts 3km south of the town and 4km down the unsealed Wentworth Valley Rd. A further 3km south of Wentworth Valley Rd is Parakiwai Quarry Rd, at the end of which is the **Wharekirauponga** walk, a sometimes muddy 10km return track (allow 3½ to four hours) to a mining camp, battery and waterfall that passes unusual hexagonal lava columns and loquacious bird life.

A popular destination for kayaking and paddle boarding is **Whenuakura** (Donut Island). Note that in an effort to boost the islands' status as wildlife sanctuaries, it's not permitted to land on them. Boating around the islands is allowed.

SurfSup   WATER SPORTS
($\square$ 021 217 1201; www.surfsup.nz; 1 Wharf Rd; half-/full-day surfboard hire $30/50, kayak from $40/60, 1/2hr paddle board $20/30) Paddle-boarding and surfing lessons are available, and kayaking and paddle-boarding tours to Whenuakura (Donut Island) run daily from December to March.

Kiwi Dundee Adventures   TRAMPING
($\square$ 07-865 8809; www.kiwidundee.co.nz) 🖉 Styling himself as a local version of Crocodile Dundee, Doug Johansen offers wilderness one- to 16-day wilderness walks and guided tours in the Coromandel Peninsula and countrywide.

🎉 Festivals & Events

Whangamata Beach Hop   CULTURAL
(www.beachhop.co.nz; $\otimes$ late Mar-early Apr) This annual celebration of retro American culture – expect hot rods, classic cars, motorbikes and rock and roll music – is a great time to be

in town. Dust off the classic white T-shirt and leather jacket combo, pile high the beehive hairdo, but definitely book accommodation if you're planning on attending.

🛏 Sleeping

Surf n Stay NZ   HOSTEL $
(📞07-865 8323; http://surfnstaynewzealand.com; 227 Beverly Tce; dm $34-36, s $60, d $120; 🛜) In a quiet street a block from the waves, this hostel owned by a friendly Kiwi-Brazilian couple has dorms and private rooms that are clean and comfortable. Cooked breakfast included. There's also the option of surfing and paddle-boarding lessons (from $70), hire of paddle boards, surfboards and kayaks (from $20), and longer surf camps, some incorporating yoga.

A nearby self-contained unit is $150.

Wentworth Valley Campsite   CAMPGROUND $
(📞07-865 7032; www.doc.govt.nz; 474 Wentworth Valley Rd; adult/child $13/6.50) 🚗 More upmarket than most DOC camping grounds, this campsite is accessed from the Wentworth Falls (p226) walk and has toilets, showers and gas barbecues.

Breakers   MOTEL $$
(📞07-865 8464; www.breakersmotel.co.nz; 324 Hetherington Rd; units $185-245; 🛜🏊) Facing the marina on the Tairua approach to Whangamata, this newish motel features an enticing swimming pool, and spa pools on the decks of the upstairs units.

🍴 Eating

Soul Burger   BURGERS $
(📞07-865 8194; www.soulburger.co.nz; 441 Port Rd; burgers $11-17; ⏱5pm-late Wed-Sun, daily Dec-Feb) Serving audacious burgers with names like Soul Blues Brother and Vegan Vibe, this hip corner joint is also licensed so you can have an ice-cold beer with your burger.

★ Port Road Project   CAFE $$
(📞07-865 7288; www.facebook.com/portroadproject; 719 Port Rd; mains $15-25; ⏱8am-3pm Thu-Mon, longer hours Dec-Feb; 🍸) 🚗 Sleek Scandi style makes the new Port Road Project a standout in sleepy Whanga. Join the locals on the sunny, shared tables and partner the all-day menu with fine coffee, Hamilton craft beer and cider, and a good wine list. Ask about occasional evening openings – especially over summer – offering innovative shared plates or feasts from the American-style barbecue.

Argo Restaurant   MODERN NZ $$
(📞07-865 7157; www.argorestaurant.co.nz; 328 Ocean Rd; mains $26-35; ⏱5-9.30pm Mon, Thu & Fri, 2-10pm Sat & Sun, daily late Dec-early Feb; 🛜) Whangamata's classiest restaurant offers a concise and evolving menu of bistro classics that might feature twice-cooked pork belly or confit duck leg. Starters to look for include sautéed scallops and prawns or fresh oysters. The airy deck is perfect for a few lazy afternoon tipples of NZ craft beer or wine. During the height of summer, hours are extended.

SixfortySix   CAFE $$
(📞07-865 6117; www.sixfortysix.co.nz; 646 Port Rd; mains $10-26; ⏱8am-4pm Sun-Fri, to 11pm Sat; 🍸) 🚗 SixfortySix does tasty counter food like baguettes crammed with hoisin pulled pork, as well as more substantial mains including a great scallop and bacon burger. NZ wine, local craft beer and freshly squeezed juices and smoothies join good coffee on the drinks menu. During summer, evening dinner hours are extended, and a pop-up Mexican cantina dispenses tacos, burritos and margaritas.

🍷 Drinking & Nightlife

Lincoln   PUB
(📞07-865 6338; www.facebook.com/thelincoln whangamata; 501 Port Rd; ⏱5pm-late Tue-Fri, 11am-late Sat) Part pub, part bistro, part cafe and all-round good times feature at this versatile spot on Whangamata's main drag. DJs kick in on summer weekends.

ℹ Information

Whangamata Info Plus (📞07-865 8340; www. thecoromandel.com/whangamata; 616 Port Rd; ⏱9am-5pm Mon-Fri, 9.30am-3.30pm Sat & Sun) Staffed by a friendly and well-informed team.

ℹ Getting There & Away

Go Kiwi (📞0800 446 549; www.go-kiwi. co.nz) has a shuttle service to Auckland ($75, 3½ hours, one daily) and to other parts of the Coromandel region.

Waihi & Waihi Beach

📞07 / POP 4527 & 1935

Gold and silver have been dragged out of Waihi's Martha Mine, New Zealand's richest, since 1878. The town formed quickly thereafter and blinged itself up with grand buildings and an avenue of impressive phoenix palms.

After closing down in 1952, open-cast mining restarted in 1988, and proposals to harness the potential of other nearby mines forecast mining to continue to around 2020. Another more low-key bonanza is also taking place, with Waihi an integral part of the excellent Hauraki Rail Trail (p213).

While Waihi is interesting for a brief visit, it's Waihi Beach where you'll want to linger. The two places are as dissimilar as surfing is from mining, separated by 11km of farmland. The long sandy beach stretches 9km to Bowentown, on the northern limits of Tauranga Harbour, where you'll find sheltered beaches such as beautiful **Anzac Bay**. There's a popular 45-minute walk north through bush to pristine **Orokawa Bay**.

◎ Sights

Waihi's main drag, Seddon St, has interesting sculptures, information panels about Waihi's golden past and roundabouts that look like squashed daleks. Opposite the visitor centre (p230), the skeleton of a derelict **Cornish Pumphouse** (1904) is the town's main landmark, atmospherically lit at night. From here the **Pit Rim Walkway** has fascinating views into the 250m-deep **Martha Mine**.

The *Historic Hauraki Gold Towns* pamphlet (free from the visitor centre) outlines walking tours of both Waihi and Paeroa.

★ Gold Discovery Centre   MUSEUM
(☑07-863 9015; www.golddiscoverycentre.co.nz; 126 Seddon St, Waihi; adult/child $25/13; ⊙9am-5pm, to 4pm Apr-Nov) Waihi's superb Gold Discovery Centre tells the area's gold-mining past, present and future through interactive displays, focusing on the personal and poignant to tell interesting stories. Holograms and short movies both feature, drawing visitors in and informing them through entertainment. Good luck in taking on the grizzled miner at 'virtual' Two-Up (a gambling game using coins).

Athenree Hot Springs   HOT SPRINGS
(☑07-863 5600; www.athenreehotsprings.co.nz; 1 Athenree Rd, Athenree; adult/child $7/5.50; ⊙10am-7pm) 🍃 In cooler months, retreat to these two small but blissful outdoor hot pools, hidden within a **holiday park** (☑07-863 5600; www.athenreehotsprings.co.nz; 1 Athenree Rd, Athenree; campsite from $54, unit $85-175; @🛜🌊) 🍃.

🏃 Activities

Waihi Bicycle Hire   CYCLING
(☑07-863 8418; www.waihibicyclehire.co.nz; 25 Seddon St, Waihi; bike hire half/full day from $30/40; ⊙8am-5pm) Bike hire and loads of

information on the Waihi end of the Hauraki Rail Trail. Fun tandems and efficient e-bikes are both available.

Goldfields Railway   RAIL
(☑07-863 8251; www.waihirail.co.nz; 30 Wrigley St, Waihi; adult/child return $20/12, bikes per route extra $2; ⊙departs Waihi 10am, 11.45am & 1.45pm Sat, Sun & public holidays) Vintage trains depart Waihi for a 7km, 30-minute scenic journey to Waikino. It's possible to take bikes on the train so they can be used to further explore the Karangahake Gorge section of the Hauraki Rail Trail. The timetable varies seasonally so check the website.

☞ Tours

Waihi Gold Mine Tours   TOURS
(☑07-863 9015; www.golddiscoverycentre.co.nz/tours; Gold Discovery Centre, 126 Seddon St, Waihi; adult/child $34/17; ⊙10am & 12.30pm, additional tours Dec-Feb) To get down into the spectacular Martha Mine, join a 1½-hour Waihi Gold Mine Tour departing from the Gold Discovery Centre.

🛏 Sleeping

Bowentown Beach
Holiday Park   HOLIDAY PARK $
(☑07-863 5381; www.bowentown.co.nz; 510 Seaforth Rd, Waihi Beach; campsites from $50, units $85-195; @🛜) Having nabbed a stunning stretch of sand, this impressively maintained holiday park makes the most of it with first-rate motel units and camping facilities.

Beachfront B&B   B&B $$
(☑07-863 5393; www.beachfrontbandb.co.nz; 3 Shaw Rd, Waihi Beach; r $140) True to its name with absolute beachfront and spectacular sea views, this comfortable downstairs flat has a TV, fridge and direct access to the surf. It's also just a short stroll to an excellent oceanfront cafe.

Waihi Beach Lodge   B&B $$$
(☑07-863 5818; www.waihibeachlodge.co.nz; 170 Seaforth Ave, Waihi Beach; d $295; 🛜) A short stroll from the beach, this accommodation features colourful and modern rooms, and a studio apartment with its own kitchenette. Legendary breakfasts are often served on the sunny deck. Ask friendly owners Greg and Ali how they're going with their homemade honey and limoncello, and look forward to sampling both. Chatty Greg is a great source of local information.

KARANGAHAKE GORGE

The road between Waihi and Paeroa, through the bush-lined ramparts of the Karangahake Gorge, is one of the best short drives in the country. Walking and biking tracks take in old Māori trails, historic mining and rail detritus, and dense bush. In Māori legend the area is said to be protected by a *taniwha* (supernatural creature). The local *iwi* managed to keep this area closed to miners until 1875, aligning themselves with the militant Te Kooti.

The very worthwhile 4.5km **Karangahake Gorge Historic Walkway** (www.doc.govt.nz) takes 1½ hours (each way) and starts from the car park 14km west of Waihi. The eastern spur of the **Hauraki Rail Trail** also passes through, and it's possible to combine a ride on the train from Waihi with a spin on the trail through the most spectacular stage of the gorge. Bikes can be rented from the **Waikino Station Cafe** (📞07-863 8640; www.facebook.com/waikinostationcafe; SH2; mains $10-20; ⊙10am-3pm Mon-Fri, 9.30am-4pm Sat & Sun). Across the river from the cafe is the **Victoria Battery Tramway & Museum** (📞027 351 8980; www.vbts.org.nz; Waikino; ⊙10am-3pm Wed, Sun & public holidays).

A few kilometres further west, Waitawheta Rd leads across the river from SH2 to **Owharoa Falls**. Opposite the falls is the **Bistro at the Falls Retreat** (📞07-863 8770; www.fallsretreat.co.nz; 25 Waitawheta Rd; pizzas $24-26, mains $30-40; ⊙11am-10pm Wed-Sun; 🚸), while adjacent is self-contained country-style **accommodation** (📞07-212 8087; www.fallsretreat.co.nz/accommodation; 25 Waitawheta Rd; d $150).

There is a range of shorter walks and loop tracks leading from the main car park at Karangahake Gorge; bring a torch as some pass through tunnels. A two-hour tramp will bring you to **Dickey's Flat** (www.doc.govt.nz; Dickey's Flat Rd; adult/child $8/4), where there's a free DOC campsite and a decent swimming hole. You'll find DOC information boards about the walks and the area's history at the main car park.

Further up the same road, **Ohinemuri Estate Winery** (📞07-862 8874; www.ohinemuri.co.nz; Moresby St; mains $16-33, shared platters $45; ⊙10am-4pm Wed-Sun) has Latvian-influenced architecture and serves excellent lunches.

Goldfields Railway trains link Waihi to Waikino from where it is an interesting and mainly flat bike ride on a very scenic spur of the Hauraki Rail Trail through the Karangahake Gorge. Otherwise this route is best driven.

Manawa Ridge LODGE $$$
(📞07-863 9400; www.manawaridge.co.nz; 267 Ngatitangata Rd, Waihi; r $950) 🌿 The views from this castle-like eco-retreat, perched on a 310m-high ridge 6km northeast of Waihi, take in the entire Bay of Plenty. Made of recycled railway timber, mudbrick and lime-plastered straw walls, the rooms marry earthiness with sheer luxury.

✕ Eating

★**Surf Shack** CAFE $$
(📞07-863 4353; www.surfshackcafe.co.nz; 123 Emerton Rd, Waihi Beach; mains $10-22; ⊙9am-2.30pm Wed-Sun; 🚸) On the outskirts of Waihi Beach, the Surf Shack is definitely worth a detour for its plate-filling salads and quite possibly the best burgers in New Zealand. Other menu highlights include snacks inspired by the street food of Mexico, Greece and Southeast Asia, and the drinks list combining NZ craft beer, *kombucha* and organic cold-press juices ticks all the boxes.

Waihi Beach Hotel BISTRO $$
(📞07-863 5402; www.waihibeachhotel.co.nz; 60 Wilson Rd, Waihi Beach; mains $20-30; ⊙7am-late Thu-Sun, extended hours Nov-Mar; 🚸) 🌿 The Beach Hotel's interesting menu includes spiced beans and chorizo with poached eggs for brunch and a terrific fish burger with hand-cut chips for dinner. Relaxed sophistication informs the service, and the drinks list includes house-made sodas and smoothies. Many ingredients are sourced from the immediate Waihi area. Check the website for regular gigs and DJs on weekends.

Flatwhite CAFE $$
(📞07-863 1346; www.flatwhitecafe.co.nz; 21 Shaw Rd, Waihi Beach; mains brunch $13-24, dinner $23-39; ⊙8am-10pm; 🚸) Funky, licensed and right by Waihi Beach, Flatwhite has a lively brunch menu, decent pizzas and flash burgers. Our favourite off the dinner menu is the *dukkah*-rubbed salmon with harissa yoghurt. The best place to sit is on the spacious

deck or oceanfront lawn as you combine a frosty beer or chilled white wine with brilliant Pacific views.

Porch Kitchen & Bar
CAFE $$

(☑07-863 1330; www.theporchwaihibeach.co.nz; 23 Wilson Rd, Waihi Beach; mains brunch $14-27, dinner $28-32; ⊗8am-3pm Sun-Thu, to 11pm Fri & Sat) In Waihi Beach township, this buzzy combo of cafe and bar serves hearty breakfasts and substantial mains. Kick off your day with its legendary eggs Benedict, or return for seafood pasta crammed with mussels and prawns. Bar snacks combine well with craft beer, and on Saturday nights from 5pm, there's happy-hour drink prices and occasional live music.

ⓘ Information

Waihi i-SITE (☑ 07-863 9015; www.waihi.org.nz; 126 Seddon St, Waihi; ⊗ 9am-5pm, to 4pm Apr-Nov) has local information and houses the interesting Gold Discovery Centre (p228), a modern and interactive showcase of the gold-flecked past, present and future of the Waihi region. There's also a good **information centre** (www.waihibeachinfo.co.nz; Wilson Rd, Waihi Beach; ⊗10am-3pm) at Waihi Beach. It's volunteer-run, so hours can be flexible.

ⓘ Getting There & Away

Waihi is serviced by **InterCity** (p189) buses, which head to Hamilton ($33, 2½ hours), Tauranga ($19, one hour) and Thames ($15, 50 minutes).

Paeroa

☑07 / POP 3980

Paeroa is the birthplace of Lemon & Paeroa (L&P), an icon of Kiwiana that markets itself as 'world famous in New Zealand'. Ironically, the fizzy drink is now owned by Coca-Cola Amatil and produced in Auckland. Still, generations of Kiwi kids have pestered their parents to take this route just to catch a glimpse of the giant L&P bottles. See www.paeroa.org.nz for the full story of this iconic Kiwi tipple. For fans of yesteryear, Paeroa's main street has a few excellent vintage and antique shops.

⊙ Sights

Historical Maritime Park
MUSEUM

(☑07-862 7121; www.historicalmaritimepark.co.nz; 6894 SH2; adult/child $5/2; ⊗10am-3pm) Around 3km northwest of Paeroa on SH2,

this excellent riverside maritime museum includes details of Captain James Cook's visit to the Firth of Thames and his explorations of the nearby Waihou River in 1769. Other exhibitions focus on the importance of river trade to the Coromandel goldfields. The museum is definitely worth a stop while travelling north or south.

Paeroa Museum
MUSEUM

(☑07-862 8942; 37 Belmont Rd; adult/child $2/1; ⊗noon-3pm Tue-Fri) This small museum has a grand selection of Royal Albert porcelain and other pioneer and Māori artefacts – look in the drawers.

🛏 Sleeping & Eating

★**Refinery**
CAFE $

(☑07-862 7678; www.the-refinery.co.nz; 5 Willoughby St; snacks $8-14; ⊗8.30am-4pm Wed-Fri, from 9am Sat & Sun) Get pleasantly lost in the Refinery, a spacious showcase of 1960s and 1970s Kiwiana style including a turntable where customers are encouraged to play the vinyl records that fill overflowing bins. Good coffee and food (especially the grilled sandwiches – try the Cuban) are best enjoyed on the retro collection of old sofas and dining room furniture filling this heritage building.

There's stylish **accommodation** (☑07-862 7678; www.the-refinery.co.nz; 5 Willoughby St; d from $99; ☞) here, too. Welcome to a true Kiwi gem and one of the country's best cafes.

L&P Cafe, Bar & Brasserie
CAFE $$

(☑07-862 6753; www.lpcafe.co.nz; SH2; mains $11-20; ⊗8am-late) At the L&P Cafe, Bar & Brasserie you can order everything from L&P-battered onion rings and fish and chips through to L&P-braised pork belly. Leave room for dessert of L&P ice cream. Of course.

ⓘ Information

Paeroa Information Centre (☑07-862 6999; www.paeroa.org.nz; Old Post Office Bldg, 101 Normanby Rd; ⊗9am-5pm Mon-Fri) Information and brochures including on how to tackle the Hauraki Rail Trail.

ⓘ Getting There & Away

InterCity (www.intercity.co.nz) runs buses to Paeroa linking to Thames ($15, 30 minutes, three daily) and Hamilton ($25, five hours, one daily).

Taranaki & Whanganui

Best Places to Eat

➡ Monica's Eatery (p238)

➡ Social Kitchen (p238)

➡ Saigon Corner (p260)

➡ Opunake Fish, Chips and More (p246)

➡ Citadel (p251)

Best Places to Stay

➡ One Burgess Hill (p237)

➡ Ducks & Drakes (p237)

➡ Ahu Ahu Beach Villas (p245)

➡ Tivoli Homestay (p238)

➡ King & Queen Hotel Suites (p238)

➡ Browns Boutique B&B (p251)

Why Go?

Halfway between Auckland and Wellington on New Zealand's underappreciated west coast, Taranaki (aka 'the 'Naki') is the country's Texas, with oil and gas streaming in from offshore rigs. But in New Plymouth free galleries, a provincial museum and dining hot spots attract young families and retirees from Auckland craving a slower pace without compromising lifestyle. Travellers are following suit.

Behind the city the stunning Mt Taranaki demands to be photographed, if not visited. The volcanic terrain is responsible for the area's black-sand beaches, lapped up by surfers and holidaymakers during summer.

Further east the history-rich Whanganui River curls its way through Whanganui National Park down to Whanganui city, a 19th-century river port ageing with grace and embracing its local arts scene. Palmerston North, the Manawatu region's main city, is a students' town courtesy of caffeinated Massey University literati. Beyond the city, the region blends rural grace with yesterday's pace.

When to Go

➡ In January and February, cruise the 105km-long Surf Hwy 45 and find your favourite black-sand beach – surf's up in summer!

➡ Powder snow and picture-perfect runs on Mt Taranaki make July the ideal time to visit.

➡ In December the crowds arrive to see the lights in Pukekura Park at the annual Festival of Lights.

Taranaki & Whanganui Highlights

1 Mt Taranaki (p240) Hiking up or around this massive cone.

2 New Zealand Rugby Museum (p259) Flexing your All Blacks spirit in Palmerston North.

3 Surf Highway 45 (p244) Riding big breaks along this surf-battered coast.

4 New Plymouth (p234) Savouring experimental art at the dazzling Len Lye Centre and bouncing from bean to bean at the city's cafes.

5 New Zealand Glassworks (p248) Watching a glass-blowing demonstration in Whanganui.

6 Whanganui National Park (p253) Redefining serenity on a Whanganui River canoe or kayak trip – or taking on an extreme jetboating adventure.

7 Whanganui River Road (p253) Traversing the road by car or bike – it's all about the journey, not how fast you get there.

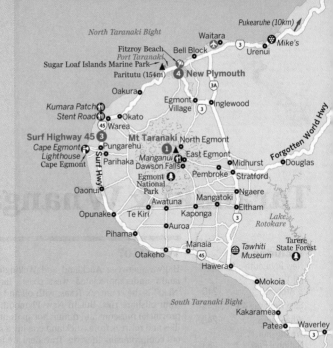

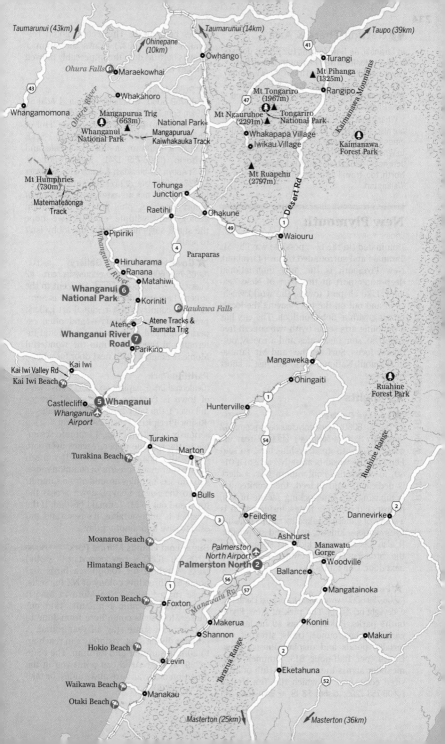

ℹ Getting There & Away

In Taranaki, Air New Zealand (p239) has domestic flights to/from New Plymouth. Naked Bus (www.nakedbus.com) and InterCity (www.intercity.co.nz) buses also service New Plymouth. Shuttle services run between Mt Taranaki and New Plymouth.

Whanganui and Palmerston North airports are also serviced by Air New Zealand, and both cities are on the radar for InterCity (no service to Whanganui with Naked Bus). KiwiRail Scenic Journeys (p262) trains stop in Palmerston North, too, travelling between Auckland and Wellington.

New Plymouth

📞 06 / POP 74,200

Dominated (in the best possible way) by Mt Taranaki and surrounded by lush farmland, New Plymouth is the only international deep-water port in this part of New Zealand. Like all port towns, the world washes in and out on the tide, leaving the locals buzzing with a global outlook. The city has a bubbling arts scene (with two superb free galleries), some fab cafes and a rootsy, outdoorsy focus. Surf beaches and Mt Taranaki (Egmont National Park) are just a short hop away.

◉ Sights

★ **Len Lye Centre**   GALLERY
(📞06-759 6060; www.lenlyefoundation.com; 42 Queen St; ⊙10am-5pm; 🅿) FREE 'Great art goes 50-50 with great architecture', so said Len Lye, the world-beating NZ artist (1901–80) to whom this contemporary-art gallery is dedicated. And indeed, the architecture is amazing: an interlocking facade of tall, mirror-clad concrete flutes, inside which is a series of galleries linked by ramps housing Lye's works – kinetic, noisy and surprising. It also has a cinema, kids' art sessions and the broader Govett-Brewster Art Gallery next door. Don't miss it.

★ **Pukekura Park**   GARDENS
(📞06-759 6060; www.pukekura.org.nz; Liardet St; ⊙daylight hr) FREE The pick of New Plymouth's parks, Pukekura has 49 hectares of gardens, playgrounds, trails, streams, waterfalls, ponds and display houses. **Rowboats** (per half-hour $15, summer only) meander across the main lake (full of arm-sized eels), next to which the **Tea House** (📞06-758 7205; dishes $8-19; ⊙9am-4pm; 🅿)

serves light meals. The technicolored Festival of Lights (p237) draws the summer crowds here, as does the impeccably mowed **cricket oval**.

★ **Puke Ariki**   MUSEUM
(📞06-759 6060; www.pukeariki.com; 1 Ariki St; ⊙9am-6pm Mon, Tue, Thu & Fri, to 9pm Wed, to 5pm Sat & Sun) FREE Translating as 'Hill of Chiefs', Puke Ariki is home to the i-SITE (p239), a museum, a library, a cafe and **Arborio** (📞06-759 1241; www.arborio.co.nz; 65 St Aubyn St; breakfast & lunch $10-26, dinner $21-38; ⊙9am-late; 🕭) restaurant. The excellent museum has an extensive collection of Māori artefacts, plus colonial, mountain geology and wildlife exhibits (we hope the shark suspended above the lobby isn't to scale).

★ **Govett-Brewster Art Gallery**   GALLERY
(📞06-759 6060; www.govettbrewster.com; 42 Queen St; ⊙10am-5pm) FREE Adjacent to the superb Len Lye Centre (p234), this is arguably the country's best regional art gallery, presenting contemporary – and often experimental and provocative – local and international shows. Pop into the wonderful Monica's Eatery (p238) next door for a bite.

Paritutu Rock   HILL
(Centennial Dr; ⊙daylight hrs) FREE Just west of town is Paritutu, a steep-sided, craggy hill over 150m tall whose name translates as 'Rising Precipice'. 'Precipice' is right – it's a seriously knee-trembling, 15-minute scramble to the top, the upper reaches over bare rock with a chain to grip on to. If you can ignore your inner screams of common sense, you can see for miles around at the summit: out to the Sugar Loaves, down across the town and out to Mt Taranaki beyond. If the weather is unfavourable, it's best (and safest!) to save it for another day.

Sugar Loaf Islands Marine Park   ISLAND
(📞06-759 0350; www.doc.govt.nz; ⊙24hr) FREE A refuge for 10,000 sea birds and home to a breeding colony of NZ fur seals, these rugged islets (Ngā Motu in Māori) are eroded volcanic remnants, 1km offshore. Most seals come here from June to October, but some stay all year round. A popular diving spot, visibility can reach up to 20m in summer and autumn. The i-Site (p239) at Puke Ariki can point you in the direction of kayak hire and guides, or take a tour (p236).

New Plymouth

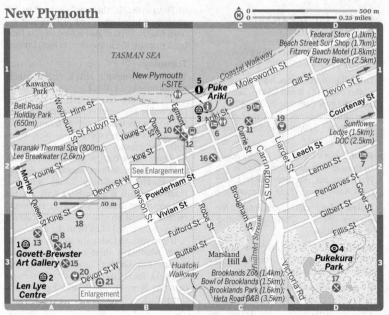

New Plymouth

Wind Wand SCULPTURE
(Puke Ariki Landing, St Aubyn St; ⊘24hr) FREE
The wonderfully eccentric Wind Wand at Puke Ariki Landing was designed by Len Lye – the artist who has put this town on the map in modern times. This 45m-high kooky kinetic sculpture is a truly beloved icon of bendy pole-ness. Look for it all lit up at night.

Brooklands Park PARK
(☑06-759 6060; www.newplymouthnz.com; Brooklands Park Dr; ⊘daylight hrs) FREE Adjoining Pukekura Park, Brooklands Park is home to the Bowl of Brooklands, a world-class outdoor sound-shell that hosts festivals such as WOMAD (p236), and old-school rockers including Fleetwood Mac. Park highlights include a 2000-year old puriri tree, a 300-variety rhododendron dell and the farmy (and free!) **Brooklands Zoo** (⊘9am-5pm; 🚻) FREE.

ESSENTIAL TARANAKI & WHANGANUI

Eat in one of Palmerston North's hip George St eateries.

Drink third-wave coffee from Ozone Coffee Roaster's **Bean Store** (Bean Store by Ozone Coffee; ☑ 06-757 5404; www.ozonecoffee.co.nz; 47a King St; dishes $5-12; ⊙ 7am-3.30pm Mon-Fri, 7am-2pm Sat, 8am-2pm Sun).

Read *Came a Hot Friday*, a 1964 novel by Ronald Hugh Morrieson, born in Hawera, about two conmen who cheat bookmakers throughout the country.

Listen to the rockin' album *Back to the Burning Wreck* by Whanganui riff-monsters The Have.

Watch *The Last Samurai* (Edward Zwick, 2003), co-starring Tom Cruise (though Mt Taranaki should get top billing).

Go green and paddle a stretch of the Whanganui River, an awe-inspiring slice of NZ wilderness.

Go online www.visit.taranaki.info, www. whanganuinz.com, www.manawatunz. co.nz

⚡ Activities

Taranaki Thermal Spa   SPA
(☑ 06-759 1666; www.pureone.co.nz/taranaki-thermal-spa.html; 8 Bonithon Ave; treatments from $13; ⊙ 10am-7.30pm Tue-Fri, 2-8pm Sat & Sun Dec-Apr, 10am-9pm Tue-Sun May-Nov) The warm mineral water filling the tanks at Taranaki Thermal Spa was discovered during the search for oil in 1906. Private baths are filled on arrival and there's a suite of massage and beauty therapies available, although not on Sundays. An absolute tonic.

Surfing

New Plymouth's black, volcanic-sand beaches are terrific for surfing. Close to the eastern edge of town are **Fitzroy Beach** and **East End Beach** (allegedly the cleanest beach in Oceania). There's also decent surf at **Back Beach**, near Paritutu (p234), at the western end of the city. Otherwise, head south along Surf Hwy 45.

Beach Street Surf Shop   SURFING
(☑ 06-758 0400; www.facebook.com/Beachstreet NZ/; 39 Beach St; 1hr lessons per person from $100; ⊙ 10am-5pm Mon-Fri, to 3pm Sat & Sun; ♠) Close

to Fitzroy Beach, this surf shop offers lessons, gear hire (surfboard/SUP/wetsuit per hour $15/25/10) and surf advice (see its Facebook page for the low-down on local breaks).

Tramping

The New Plymouth i-SITE (p239) stocks the *Taranaki: A Walker's Guide* booklet, which includes coastal, local reserve and park walks. The excellent **Coastal Walkway** (11km) from Bell Block to Port Taranaki gives you a surf-side perspective on New Plymouth and crosses the much-photographed **Te Rewa Rewa Bridge** (☑ 06-759 5150; www. visit.taranaki.info; Te Rewa Rewa Bridge; ⊙ 24hr). The **Huatoki Walkway** (5km), following Huatoki Stream, is a rambling walk into the city centre. Alternatively, the *New Plymouth Heritage Trail* brochure, taking in historic hot spots, is a real blast from the past.

If you wish to tackle the mountain (p241) itself, whether a short loop or a multiday tramp, Top Guides Taranaki (p241) and Taranaki Tours (p242) run shuttle services between New Plymouth and Egmont National Park.

↻ Tours

Chaddy's Charters   BOATING
(☑ 06-758 9133; www.chaddyscharters.co.nz; Ocean View Pde, Lee Breakwater; trips adult/child $40/15; ⊙ 8am-4pm Sep-Jun, 9am-4pm Jul & Aug; ♠) Take a trip out to visit the Sugar Loaf Islands with Chaddy: expect at least four laughs a minute during a one-hour bob around on the swell. Departs daily from Lee Breakwater, tide and weather permitting. You can also hire kayaks (single/double per hour $15/30), bikes ($10 per hour) and stand-up paddle boards ($30 per hour). Winter opening hours vary with the weather.

Canoe & Kayak Taranaki   KAYAKING
(☑ 06-751 2340; www.canoeandkayak.co.nz; 468 St Aubyn St; 1¼ hr $50) Call ahead for seasonal kayak tours or book in for a stand-up paddle board course.

✿ Festivals & Events

★ WOMAD   MUSIC, CULTURAL
(World of Music, Arts & Dance; ☑ 0800 484 253; www.womad.co.nz; ⊙ Mar) A diverse array of local and international artists perform at the **Bowl of Brooklands** (☑ 06-759 6060; www.npeventvenues.nz; Brooklands Park Dr; ⊙ performance days only) each March. Hugely popular, with music fans trucking in from across NZ. Camping sites available to purchase online.

Taranaki International Arts Festival ART
(☑ 06-759 8412; www.taft.co.nz; ⊙ Aug & Sep)
The regional big-ticket arts fest: theatre, dance, music, visual arts, parades and plenty of food and wine.

Taranaki Garden Spectacular CULTURAL
(☑ 0800 746 363; www.gardenfestnz.co.nz; ⊙ Oct-Nov) A long-running NZ flower fest: more rhododendrons than you'll ever see in one place again.

NZ Tattoo & Art Festival CULTURAL
(www.nztattooart.com; ⊙ Nov) This saucy skin fest attracts thousands of ink fans over a busy weekend in November. Get yourself a new 'badge', or check out the BMX stunt riders or the burlesque gyrators.

Festival of Lights CULTURAL
(☑ 06-759 6060; www.festivaloflights.nz; ⊙ Dec-Feb) Complete with live music, 1000 light installations and costumed characters roaming the undergrowth, this colourful display illuminates Pukekura Park (p234) from mid-December to early February.

🛌 Sleeping

★ **Ducks & Drakes** HOSTEL, HOTEL $
(☑ 06-758 0404; www.ducksanddrakes.co.nz; 48 Lemon St; hostel dm/s/d from $32/68/90, hotel r from $130; 🖥) The hostel here occupies a labyrinthine 1920s heritage building with bright feature walls and fancy timberwork brimming with character. Upstairs rooms are the pick: secluded, quiet and catching the morning sun. Next door is a pricier hotel wing with snazzy studios and one-bedroom suites, to which the owner escapes when his teenage daughter has friends over.

Belt Road Holiday Park HOLIDAY PARK $
(☑ 06-758 0228, 0800 804 204; www.beltroad. co.nz; 2 Belt Rd; campsites from $23, cabins $75-145; 🖥) ✔ Set among grassy lawns studded with pohutukawa trees, this holiday park sits atop a bluff overlooking the Tasman Sea, about a 15-minute walk from town. The half-dozen best cabins have million-dollar views and there's a play area for the kids, complete with a trampoline.

Heta Road B&B B&B $
(☑ 06-759 1205; www.lookafterme.co.nz/ accommodation/heta-homestay; 206d Heta Rd, Highlands Park; d from $85; 🅿🖥) Just 4km from town, this elevated B&B makes for a peaceful and affordable base. The hosts have a background in tourism and are happy to share tips alongside a sense of humour

(*Fawlty Towers* references abound). There are four rooms, two with en suites and all with access to a spa and cinema room.

Sunflower Lodge HOSTEL $
(☑ 06-759 0050, 0800 422 257; www.sunflowerlodge. co.nz; 33 Timandra St; dm/s/tw/d/tr from $33/64/78/78/105; @🖥) Down a steep driveway a few minutes' drive south of town, the YHA Sunflower does its best to transcend its rest-home origins and mostly succeeds. Dorms maxing out at four people, a whiteboard listing free activities and a view towards the west coast – not to mention quality mattresses and a barbecue pavilion – help the cause.

Ariki Backpackers HOSTEL $
(☑ 06-769 5020; www.arikibackpackers.com; 25 Ariki St; dm $30, d $70-90; @🖥) Upstairs at the old Royal Hotel, welcoming Ariki offers downtown hostelling with funky carpets, a roomy lounge area with well-loved couches and a fantastic roof terrace looking across the park to Puke Ariki (p234). Most rooms have their own shower and toilet. Bikes, surfboards and kayaks for hire, but cuddles with Ronnie the golden retriever are free.

The owners have the whole building, so keep an eye out for deals, DJs and late-night shenanigans at the lounge next door.

★ **One Burgess Hill** MOTEL, APARTMENTS $$
(☑ 06-757 2056; www.oneburgesshill.co.nz; 1 Burgess Hill Rd; d from $146, 1-/2-bedroom ste from $186/255; 🖥) Completely exceeding motel expectations, lovely One Burgess Hill is a complex of 15 stylish units on a green hillside, about 5km south of central New Plymouth (en route to Mt Taranaki). Slick interior design, nifty kitchens, wood heaters and private valley views offer a departure from the usual drive-in motels. Upstairs rooms have baths by the bed overlooking the Waiwhakaiho River.

Metrotel MOTEL $$
(☑ 06-222 0036; www.themetrotel.co.nz; 22 Gill St; d $130-160, 2-bedroom ste $255; 🅿🖥) Opened in 2017, there are hints of history in the original 1920s warehouse walls. Rooms are simple but slick whether boasting a pop of colour, exposed light bulbs or couches half-upholstered in animal print. Two-bedroom mezzanine rooms have high ceilings, wheelchair-accessible studios have wooden decks and two-bedroom studios a separate kitchen and lounge.

Fitzroy Beach Motel MOTEL $$
(☑ 06-757 2925, 0800 757 2925; www.fitzroybeach motel.co.nz; 25 Beach St; 1-/2-bedroom units from

$160/200, extra person $20; 📞) This quiet motel is just 200m from Fitzroy Beach and has been thoroughly redeemed with a major overhaul and extension. Highlights include a calming colour palette, quality carpets, double glazing, lovely bathrooms, big TVs and an absence of poky studio-style units (all are one- or two-bedroom). Free bikes, too.

★ King & Queen Hotel Suites
BOUTIQUE HOTEL $$$

(📋 06-757 2999, 0800 574 683; www.kingandqueen. co.nz; cnr King & Queen Sts; d from $179, ste from $219-440; P@📞) This regal hotel occupies the corner of King and Queen Sts (get it?) in the cool West End Precinct. Run by unerringly professional staff, each suite features antique Moroccan and Euro furnishings, lustrous black tiles, hip art, leather couches and touches of industrial chic. Guests can borrow free bikes, and there are chargeback facilities set up with some of New Plymouth's top cafes, bars and restaurants.

Tivoli Homestay
B&B $$$

(📋 06-751 1206; www.tivolihomestay.co.nz; 22 Scott St, Moturoa; d $229; P📞) About 5km west of the town centre and 1km from Paritutu Rock (p234) is this charismatic, three-room B&B with friendly owners. Aside from serving one of the best breakfasts in New Plymouth, the upstairs common spaces (including an outdoor deck and fairy-tale-like turret) boast views over Mt Taranaki, across the Central Plateau and out to sea.

✕ Eating

Public Catering Co.
CAFE $

(📋 06-759 7090; www.publiccatering.co.nz; White Hart courtyard, 43a Queen St; $6-10; ⊙8am-3.30pm Mon-Sat, 9am-3pm Sun) Another White Hart Precinct gem, this cafe is a front for a gourmet catering company. The cabinet flaunts doughnuts, pies and Reuben sandwiches, while hot meat rolls and the soup are winners on a cold day. There's one communal table in the textural space – all decorative concrete blocks and exposed piping – but if it's warm, opt for gelato in the courtyard.

Ms White Pizza & Beer Garden
PIZZA $

(www.mswhite.co.nz; White Hart Courtyard, 47 Queen St; pizza $13-19; ⊙4-10pm Mon & Tue, 11am-10pm Wed, Thu & Sun, to 11pm Fri & Sat; ✍) Sharing a fairy-light-draped courtyard with Snug Lounge (p239), Ms White serves traditional wood-fired Italian pizza and more than 40 varieties of craft beer from an outdoor kitchen. Choose from pizza *rosse* bases with tomato sauce and mozzarella or pizza *bianche* with olive oil in place of tomato. Look out for $10 Monday specials and be sure to use the hashtag: #pizzawillneverbreakyourheart.

★ Social Kitchen
LATIN AMERICAN $$

(📋 06-757 2711; www.social-kitchen.co.nz; 40 Powderham St; share plates $30-55; ⊙noon-late; 📞) Inside what was once the Salvation Army Citadel, this trendy restaurant is filled with neon charm and taxidermy. Hanging meat and pigs' heads are displayed like art, but you can avoid them in the courtyard strung with colourful festoon lights. Arrive hungry and share flavour-packed Spanish sausage and Waitoa free-range chicken cooked in a Mibrasa charcoal oven.

★ Monica's Eatery
MODERN NZ $$

(📋 06-759 2038; www.monicaseatery.co.nz; cnr King & Queen Sts; breakfast $13-19, lunch $15-39, dinner $23-40; ⊙6.30am-late; 📞✍) Beside the Govett-Brewster Art Gallery (p234) and Len Lye Centre (p234), this all-day diner is homey despite its contemporary interior. Perhaps it's seeing handmade pappardelle lowered into bowls through the open kitchen, or the upbeat soundtrack that swings between Bill Withers and the Supremes. It's quite possibly the staff, who advise holding onto warm house focaccia for 'sauce mopping'. Whatever it is, we feel at home here.

Federal Store
CAFE $$

(📋 06-757 8147; www.thefederalstore.com; 440 Devon St E; mains $12-19; ⊙7am-4.30pm Mon-Fri, 8.30am-4.30pm Sat & Sun; ✍🐾) Super-popular and crammed with retro furniture, Federal conjures up a 1950s corner-store vibe. Switched-on staff in dinky headscarves take your coffee requests at the counter as you queue beneath colourful bunting, keeping you buoyant until your southern fried chicken bagel, *shakshuka* or eggs Benedict arrives. Cakes, tarts and premade counter food are also available. Kid-friendly.

Kathakali
SOUTH INDIAN $$

(📋 06-758 8848; www.kathakali.co.nz; 39a Devon St E; mains $17-22; ⊙noon-2pm & 5-10pm Tue-Sun; ✍) Wander upstairs from Devon St to this local favourite where staff know regulars by name. The menu delivers all sorts of South Indian delights, from must-order *dosa* (savoury pancakes) with coconut chutney and *sambar* (lentil soup), to mixed vegetable korma with coconut and ground cashews. Somehow, Kerala doesn't seem so far away.

Bach on Breakwater
CAFE **$$**

(☑06-769 6967; www.bachonbreakwater.co.nz; Ocean View Pde, Lee Breakwater; mains $12-25; ⊗9.30am-4pm Wed-Fri, to 5pm Sat & Sun; ☑) Constructed from weighty recycled timbers, this cool cafe-bistro in the Lee Breakwater precinct looks like an old sea chest washed up after a storm. The all-day brunch menu ranges from a vegan version of a big breakfast to New Yorker french toast slathered in peanut butter. Vegans, vegetarians and gluten-free diets can follow the handy colour-coded cabinet.

Meat & Liquor
AMERICAN **$$$**

(☑06-7591 227; www.meatandliquor.co.nz; 34a Egmont St; mains $26-45; ⊗noon-2pm Thu & Fri, 5-11pm daily; ☎) Follow the glow of red neon past **Frederic's** (☑06-759 1227; www.frederics. co.nz; 34 Egmont St; plates $14-21, mains $19-30; ⊗noon-midnight; ☎) bar and up the stairs to the dining room, where tea towels replace napkins and butcher's paper sits in for tablecloths. Leave vegetarian pals at home and share 400g cuts of sustainable beef, local lamb rump and pork. We love the built-in bar and catchy slogan: 'fine cuts nice drop'.

🍷 Drinking & Nightlife

★ Snug Lounge
COCKTAIL BAR

(☑06-757 9130; www.snuglounge.co.nz; cnr Devon St W & Queen St; small plates $9-19; ⊗4pm-late Mon-Sat, noon-late Sun) Located inside the iconic former White Hart Hotel, this savvy bar on the downtown fringe is the classiest place in town for a drink – unlike its predecessor. Dress to be seen, order a Tropical Botanical (gin, coconut and mint) and act like you own the town. An excellent selection of Japanese share plates will ensure you stay vertical.

Hour Glass
BAR

(☑06-758 2299; www.facebook.com/thehour glass49; 49 Liardet St; tapas $4-10, mains $32-35; ⊗4pm-late Tue-Sat) On an unremarkable rise of Liardet St is this late-night tapas and craft-beer bar, with richly brocaded crimson drapes, straight-backed wooden chairs and interesting timber panelling. Plenty of craft beers, killer cocktails and even named lockers for expensive bottles if you're a regular. Check the Facebook page for tastings and informal jam sessions.

🛍 Shopping

Kina
ARTS, JEWELLERY

(☑06-759 1201; www.kina.co.nz; 101 Devon St W; ⊗9am-5.30pm Mon-Fri, 9.30am-4pm Sat, 11am-4pm Sun) Fabulous Kiwi crafts, jewellery, bath and beauty products plus art and design, as well as regular gallery exhibitions in a lovely shopfront on the main drag. It's the perfect spot to pick up a meaningful NZ souvenir.

ℹ️ Information

DOC (Department of Conservation; ☑06-759 0350; www.doc.govt.nz; 55a Rimu St; ⊗8am-4.30pm Mon-Fri) Info on regional national parks, tramping and camping.

New Plymouth i-SITE (☑06-759 6060; www. taranaki.co.nz; Puke Ariki, 1 Ariki St; ⊗9am-6pm Mon, Tue, Thu & Fri, to 9pm Wed, to 5pm Sat & Sun, closed public holidays) In the **Puke Ariki** (p234) building, with a fantastic interactive tourist-info database.

Phoenix Urgent Doctors (☑06-759 4295; www.phoenixdoctors.co.nz; 95 Vivian St; ⊗8.30am-8pm) Doctors by appointment and urgent medical help. Pharmacy on-site.

Taranaki Base Hospital (☑06-753 6139; www. tdhb.org.nz; 23 David St, Westown; ⊗24hr) Accident and emergency.

ℹ️ Getting There & Away

AIR

New Plymouth Airport (☑0800 144 129; www.newplymouthairport.com; Airport Dr) is 11km east of the centre off SH3. **Scott's Airport Shuttle** (☑0800 373 001, 06-769 5974; www.npairportshuttle.co.nz; per person $18-28, per 2 people $22-32) operates a door-to-door shuttle to/from the airport.

Airlines include the following:

Air New Zealand (☑06-357 3000, 0800 737 000; www.airnewzealand.co.nz) Daily direct flights to/from Auckland, Wellington and Christchurch, with onward connections.

Singapore Airlines (www.singaporeair.com) Flies between New Plymouth, Christchurch and Auckland.

Virgin Australia (www.virginaustralia.com) Flies the same routes as Air New Zealand.

BUS

Services run from the **Bus Centre** (cnr Egmont & Ariki Sts) in central New Plymouth. Standard fares (ie, no refund) are the cheapest option.

InterCity (www.intercity.co.nz) services include the following:

DESTINATION	COST	TIME (HR)	FREQUENCY (DAILY)
Auckland	from $43	6	2
Hamilton	from $33	3½-4	4
Palmerston North	from $28	4	1
Wellington	from $29	7	1
Whanganui	from $23	2½	1

TARANAKI & WHANGANUI NEW PLYMOUTH

Naked Bus (www.nakedbus.com) services ply similar routes and sometimes link up with other operators. Visit the website for routes and fares.

ⓘ Getting Around

BICYCLE

Cycle Inn (☑ 06-758 7418; www.cycleinn. co.nz; 133 Devon St E; per 2hr/day $10/20; ⊗ 8.30am-5pm Mon-Fri, 9am-4pm Sat, 10am-2pm Sun) rents out bicycles, as does Chaddy's Charters (p236) at Lee Breakwater.

BUS

Citylink (☑ 0800 872 287; www.taranakibus. info; tickets adult/child $3.70/2.30) services run Monday to Friday around New Plymouth, as well as north to Waitara and south to Oakura. Buses depart from the Bus Centre (p239).

CAR

Rent-a-Dent (☑ 06-757 5362, 1800 14 18 22; www.rentadent.co.nz; 592 Devon St E; ⊗ 8am-5pm Mon-Fri, to noon Sat) For cheap car hire, try Rent-a-Dent.

TAXI

Energy City Cabs (☑ 06-757 5580, 0800 14 15 25; www.energycabs.co.nz) Taxis in New Plymouth.

Around New Plymouth

There are some interesting places to visit heading north from New Plymouth along SH3, with various seaward turn-offs to high sand dunes and surf beaches.

⊙ Sights

About 5km past riverside summer hot spot **Urenui**, you'll find arguably the highlight of North Taranaki - a brewery called **Mike's** (☑ 06-752 3676; www.mikesbeer.co.nz; 487 Mokau Rd, Urenui; pizzas $18; ⊗ 10am-5pm). A little further on is the turn-off to **Pukearuhe** and **White Cliffs**, huge precipices resembling their Dover namesakes. From Pukearuhe boat ramp, you can tackle the **White Cliffs Walkway**, a three-hour loop walk with mesmerising views of the coast and mountains (Taranaki and Ruapehu). The tide can make things dicey along the beach: walk between two hours either side of low tide.

Continuing north towards Mokau, stop at the **Three Sisters** rock formation signposted just south of the Tongaporutu Bridge - you can traverse the shore at low tide. Two sisters stand somewhat forlornly off the coast: their other sister collapsed in a heap last decade, but a new sis is emerging from the eroding cliffs. Next to the sisters is **Elephant Rock** - you'll never guess what it looks like.

Pukeiti GARDENS
(☑ 0800 736 222; www.pukeiti.org.nz; 2290 Carrington Rd, New Plymouth; ⊗ 9am-5pm) FREE This sprawling garden, 23km south of New Plymouth, is home to masses of rhododendrons and azaleas. The flowers bloom between September and November, but it's worth a visit any time. Take a garden walk (45 minutes to two hours), or entertain the kids with the self-guided Treehouse Trail adventure. There's a cafe here, too.

Taranaki Aviation, Transport & Technology Museum MUSEUM
(TATATM; ☑ 06-752 2845; http://tatatm.tripod. com/museum; cnr SH3 & Kent Rd, New Plymouth; adult/child/family $7/2/16; ⊗ 10.30am-4pm Sat & Sun, school & public holidays) Around 9km south of New Plymouth is this roadside museum, with ramshackle displays of old planes, trains, automobiles and general household miscellany. Run by volunteer enthusiasts, the collection is always growing, thanks to donations. Many of the displays are interactive. Don't miss the chance to sit in the cockpit of the Harvard training plane!

Mt Taranaki & Around

ⓘ Getting There & Away

Drive yourself up and down Mt Taranaki, or opt for shuttle services running from New Plymouth up the national park's main access roads. InterCity (www.intercity.co.nz) and Naked Bus (www.nakedbus.com) run services through Stratford and Inglewood on their Whanganui–New Plymouth route.

Mt Taranaki (Egmont National Park)

A near-perfect 2518m volcanic cone dominating the landscape, Mt Taranaki is a magnet to all who catch his eye. According to Māori, Taranaki travelled from the North Island's volcanic plateau after he lost a battle with Mt Tongariro over the beautiful Mt Pihanga. Geologically, Taranaki is the youngest of three large volcanoes - including Kaitake and Pouakai - that stand along the same fault line. With the last eruption more than 350 years ago, experts say that the mountain is overdue for another go. But don't let that put you off - it's an absolute beauty and the highlight of any visit to the region, although trampers should check in with DOC information centres before attempting a climb as it's notoriously dangerous.

Access points for the mountain are North Egmont, Dawson Falls and East Egmont. There are DOC centres at North Egmont (p242) and Dawson Falls (p242); for accommodation and supplies head to Stratford or Inglewood.

🏃 Activities

Tramping

Due to its accessibility, Mt Taranaki ranks as the 'most climbed' mountain in NZ. Nevertheless, tramping on this mountain is dangerous and should not be undertaken lightly. It's crucial to get advice before departing and to leave your intentions with a Department of Conservation (DOC) visitor centre or i-SITE.

Most walks are accessible from North Egmont, Dawson Falls or East Egmont. Check out DOC's collection of detailed walk pamphlets ($1 to $1.50 each, or free if you print it off the web) or the free *Taranaki: A Walker's Guide* booklet for more info – although there are rumours the printed booklet might soon be discontinued.

From North Egmont, the main walk is the scenic **Pouakai Circuit**, a two- to three-day, 25km loop through alpine, swamp and tussock areas with awesome mountain views (a shorter and popular version is the day-long **Pouakai Crossing**, 19km one-way). Short, easy walks from here include the **Ngatoro Loop Track** (40 minutes), **Veronica Loop** (two hours) and **Nature Walk** (15-minute loop). The **Mt Taranaki Summit Climb** also starts from North Egmont. It's a 14km poled route taking five to six hours on the way up and three to four on the way down, and should not be attempted by inexperienced trampers, especially in icy conditions or snow.

East Egmont has the **Potaema Track** (wheelchair accessible; 30 minutes return) and **Stratford Plateau Lookout** (10 minutes return). A longer walk is the steep **Enchanted Track** (two to three hours return).

At Dawson Falls you can do several short walks, including **Wilkies Pools Loop** (1¼ hours return), whose new bridge provides an outlook back up towards the mountain and across the pools, or the excellent but challenging hike to **Fanthams Peak** (five hours return), which is snowed-in during winter. The **Kapuni Loop Track** (one-hour loop) runs to the impressive 18m **Dawson Falls** themselves. You can also see the falls

from the visitor centre via a 10-minute walk to a viewpoint.

The difficult 55km **Around-the-Mountain Circuit** takes three to five days and is for experienced trampers only. There are a number of huts en route, tickets for which should be purchased in advance.

The **York Road Loop Track** (up to three hours), accessible from York Rd north of Stratford, is a fascinating walk following part of a disused railway line.

You can tramp without a guide from January through to April when snowfalls are low, but at other times inexperienced climbers can check with DOC for details of local clubs and guides. It costs around $300 per day to hire a guide.

Skiing

Manganui Ski Area   SKIING
(www.skitaranaki.co.nz; off Pembroke Rd, East Egmont; daily lift passes adult/child $50/35) From Stratford take Pembroke Rd up to Stratford Plateau, from where it's a 1.5km (20-minute) walk to the small Manganui Ski Area. The Stratford i-SITE (p244) has daily weather and snow reports; otherwise check the webcam online. There's also shared-facilities ski-lodge accommodation here (adult/child/family $45/15/100), but to stay you need a group of 10, with at least five adults. For up-to-date information and speedy responses, check the Facebook page: www.facebook.com/Manganui.

👉 Tours

Top Guides Taranaki   TRAMPING
(☎0800 448 433; www.topguides.co.nz; half-/full-day tramps per person from $99/299) Guided Mt Taranaki tramps, from a half- to full-day – four trampers minimum. Shuttles between New Plymouth and the mountain are also available.

TARANAKI & WHANGANUI MT TARANAKI & AROUND

TARANAKI'S HEARTBREAK

According to Māori legend, Mt Taranaki belonged to a tribe of volcanoes in the middle of the North Island. But after a great battle with Mt Tongariro over Pihanga, the beautiful volcano near Lake Taupo, he was forced to leave. As he fled south (some say in disgrace; others say to keep the peace), Taranaki gouged out a wide scar in the earth, now the Whanganui River, and finally settled in the west in his current position. He remains here in majestic isolation, hiding his face behind a cloud of tears.

ℹ DECEPTIVE MOUNTAIN

Mt Taranaki might look small compared to mountains overseas, but this unassuming mountain has claimed more than 80 lives. The microclimate changes fast: from summery to white-out conditions almost in an instant. There are also precipitous bluffs and steep icy slopes.

There are plenty of short walks here, safe for much of the year, but for adventurous trampers January to March is the best time to go. Take a detailed topographic map (the Topo50 1:50,000 Mt Taranaki or Mt Egmont map is good) and consult a DOC officer for current conditions. You must register your tramping intentions with Dawson Falls or North Egmont DOC visitor centres on the mountain, New Plymouth i-SITE (p239) or online via www.adventure smart.org.nz.

Taranaki Tours
TOURS

(☑ 06-757 9888; www.taranakitours.com; per person from $145) Runs an around-the-mountain day tour, strong on Māori culture and natural history. Forgotten World Hwy tours, surf tours and mountain shuttle runs also available.

Beck Helicopters
SCENIC FLIGHTS

(☑ 0800 336 644, 06-764 7073; www.heli.co.nz; 4512 Mountain Rd, Eltham; flights per person from $295) Buzz around the big mountain on a scenic helicopter flight (and you thought it looked good from ground level!). Maximum four passengers.

🛏 Sleeping

Several DOC huts are scattered about the mountain wilderness, and are accessible via tramping tracks. Most cost $15 per night (Syme costs $5); purchase hut tickets in advance from DOC. BYO cooking, eating and sleeping gear. Bookings are not accepted – it's first come, first served.

On the road-accessible slopes of the mountain you'll find a hostel, two DOC-managed bunkhouses and some interesting lodges.

Camphouse
HOSTEL $

(☑ 06-756 0990; www.doc.govt.nz; Egmont Rd, North Egmont; per adult/child $25/10, exclusive use $600) Bunkhouse-style accommodation behind the North Egmont Visitor Centre in a historic 1860 corrugated-iron building, complete with gun slots in the walls (through

which settlers fired at local Māori during the Taranaki Land Wars). Enjoy endless horizon views from the porch. Sleeps 32 in four rooms, with communal facilities.

★ Ngāti Ruanui Stratford Mountain House
LODGE $$

(☑ 06-765 6100, 027 588 0228; www.stratford mountainhouse.co.nz; Pembroke Rd; d/f from $155/195; 🐾) This efficiently run lodge on the Stratford side of the big hill (15km from the SH3 turn-off and 3km to the Manganui Ski Area) has eight motel-style chalets, a twin room and a family room for four up a short, foresty path. Spa baths are a blessing on chilly nights, as is the fireplace in the mod, European-style restaurant (breakfast and lunch mains $12 to $39, dinner $31 to $42). Accommodation and meal packages also available (from $345).

ℹ Information

Dawson Falls Visitor Centre (☑ 06-443 0248; www.doc.govt.nz; Manaia Rd, Dawson Falls; ☺ 9am-4pm Thu-Sun, daily school holidays) On the southeastern side of the mountain, fronted by an awesome totem pole.

MetService (www.metservice.com) Mountain weather updates.

North Egmont Visitor Centre (☑ 06-756 0990; www.doc.govt.nz; Egmont Rd, North Egmont; ☺ 8am-4pm, reduced winter hr) Current and comprehensive national park info, and definitive details on tramping and huts.

ℹ Getting There & Away

There are three main entrance roads to Egmont National Park, all of which are well signposted. The closest to New Plymouth is North Egmont: turn off SH3 at Egmont Village, 12km south of New Plymouth, and follow Egmont Rd for 14km. From Stratford, turn off at Pembroke Rd and continue for 15km to East Egmont and the Manganui Ski Area. From the southeast, Manaia Rd leads up to Dawson Falls, 23km from Stratford.

There are no public buses to the national park, but there are a few shuttle/tour operators who will take you there for around $40/60 one way/return (usually cheaper for groups).

Eastern Taranaki Experience (p257) Mountain shuttle services as well as tours and accommodation. Based in Stratford.

Taranaki Tours New Plymouth to North Egmont return – good for day walks.

Top Guides Taranaki (p241) Mountain shuttle services, with pick-up points around New Plymouth. Picks up from accommodation between 7am and 7.20am. Mountain guides also available.

Inglewood

☑06 / POP 3250

Handy to Mt Taranaki on SH3, the little main-street town of Inglewood is a useful stop for supermarket supplies or a casual bite to eat.

◉ Sights

Fun Ho! National Toy Museum MUSEUM
(☑06-756 7030; www.funhotoys.co.nz; 25 Rata St; adult/child $7/3.50; ⊙10am-4pm; 🖟) Inglewood's cute Fun Ho! National Toy Museum exhibits (and sells) old-fashioned sand-cast toys. It doubles as the local visitor information centre. Good for big kids and hobbyists, too! Everybody shout, 'Fun Ho!'.

🛏 Sleeping & Eating

Inglebrook Villa & Gardens B&B $$
(☑027 271 8354, 06-756 6062; www.inglebrook. co.nz; s/d incl breakfast $140/170; 🖟) This early 1907 property is set on 300 sq metres of manicured trees and gardens with a lush outlook from the only room, the Garden Suite, which boasts double french doors and a patio. Love the timber-clad bathroom and brick fireplace in the lounge. Add $10 for a cooked breakfast. Sofa bed available in the lounge ($60 extra)

Caffe Windsor CAFE $$
(☑027 368 2738, 06-756 6665; www.caffewindsor. co.nz; 1 Kelly St; brunch mains $12-19, dinner $18-30; ⊙8.30am-5pm Mon-Thu, to late Fri & Sat, to 3pm Sun) Inside a fire-engine-red 1878 heritage building is one of Inglewood's first shops. Caffe Windsor sells eggs and waffles in the morning, old-school burgers and sandwiches during the day, and red Thai chicken curry at night (among other things).

Stratford

☑06 / POP 8991

A gateway town to Mt Taranaki and 40km southeast of New Plymouth on SH3, Stratford plays up its connection to namesake Stratford-upon-Avon, Shakespeare's birthplace, by naming its streets after bardic characters. The town is also home to NZ's first (and last) **glockenspiel clock**, which chimes four times a day (10am, 1pm, 3pm and 7pm). More impressive is the **Carrington Walkway**, accessible through the memorial gate at King Edward Park, which hugs the Pātea Stream and takes you across bridges and through farmland and a rhododendron dell.

◉ Sights

Percy Thomson Gallery GALLERY
(☑06-765 0917; www.percythomsongallery.org.nz; Prospero Pl, 56 Miranda St; ⊙10.30am-4pm Mon-Fri, to 3pm Sat & Sun) FREE Right next door to Stratford i-SITE, this progressive community gallery (named after the former mayor) displays eclectic local, regional and national art shows. New exhibitions every three to four weeks.

Taranaki Pioneer Village MUSEUM
(☑06-765 5399; www.pioneervillage.co.nz; SH3; adult/child $12/5; ⊙10am-4pm; 🖟) About 1km south of Stratford on SH3, the Taranaki Pioneer Village is a 4-hectare outdoor museum housing 40 historic buildings, with many dating back to the early 1850s. It's very bygone-era and even a little spooky! The Pioneer Express Train is a good way to see it if your feet need a rest ($5 or $3 with entry fee). There's a cafe here, too.

MAORI NZ: TARANAKI & WHANGANUI

Ever since Mt Taranaki fled here to escape romantic difficulties, the Taranaki region has had a turbulent history. Conflicts between local *iwi* (tribes) and invaders from the Waikato were followed by two wars with the government – first in 1860–61, and then again in 1865–69. Then there were massive land confiscations and an extraordinary passive-resistance campaign at Parihaka.

A drive up the Whanganui River Rd takes you into traditional Māori territory, passing the Māori villages of Atene, Koriniti, Ranana and Hiruharama along the way. In Whanganui itself, run your eyes over amazing indigenous exhibits at the Whanganui Regional Museum (p248), and check out the superb Māori carvings in Putiki Church (p248).

Over in Palmerston North, Te Manawa (p259) museum has a strong Māori focus, while the New Zealand Rugby Museum (p259) pays homage to Māori All Blacks, without whom the team would never have become back-to-back Rugby World Cup winners.

FORGOTTEN WORLD HIGHWAY

The remote 150km road between Stratford and Taumarunui (SH43) has become known as the Forgotten World Hwy. The drive winds through hilly bush country, passing Māori *pā* (fortified villages), abandoned coal mines and memorials to those long gone. Just a short section (around 12km) is unsealed road. Allow four hours and plenty of stops, and fill up with petrol at either end (there's no petrol along the route itself). Pick up the *Forgotten World Highway* pamphlet from i-SITEs or DOC visitor centres in the area.

Sights

The town of Whangamomona (population 40) is a highlight. This quirky village declared itself an independent republic in 1989 after disagreements with local councils. The town celebrates Republic Day in January every odd-numbered year with a themed extravaganza. Don't miss the grand old **Whangamomona Hotel** (☑ 06-762 5823; www.whanga-momonahotel.co.nz; 6018 Forgotten World Hwy, Whangamomona; s/d $120/150, lodge $175; ⊙ 9am-late), a pub offering simple accommodation and big country meals. Rental-house accommodation options include the **Whanga Bridge House** (☑ 06-762 5552; www.facebook.com/whangabridgehouse6025; 6025 Ohura Rd, Whangamomona; s/d incl breakfast $120/150), sleeping eight, and the **Whanga Butcher Shop** (☑ 06-762 5552; www.facebook.com/WhangaButcherShop; 6024 Ohura Road, Whangamomona; s/d $120/150), sleeping six, both run by the same folks.

Tours

If you're not driving, try a tour through the area with Eastern Taranaki Experience (p257) or Taranaki Tours (p242). See also Forgotten World Adventures (p209) in Taumarunui.

🛌 Sleeping

Regan House B&B $$
(☑ 06-765 4189, 022 412 3354; www.reganhouse.co.nz; 193 Regan St; s/d incl breakfast $100/150; 🅿️🛜) With only two suites available in this early 20th century house (one when family is staying), Regan House is a peaceful alternative to Stratford's limited, more commercial accommodation. Absurdly comfortable beds, manicured gardens and a generous cooked breakfast using eggs from the property's farm make this feel like home, sweet home. Located at the start of the Forgotten World Hwy.

Amity Court Motel MOTEL $$
(☑ 06-765 4496, 0800 496 313; www.amitycourtmotel.co.nz; 35 Broadway N; d/apt from $140/224; 🛜🚗) All stone-clad columns, jaunty roof angles, timber louvres and muted cave-colours, Amity Court Motel ups the town's accommodation standings. The two-bedroom apartments are a good set-up for families, while couples should ask for room 12 with the hot tub on the balcony. Electric car-charging station on-site.

ℹ️ Information

Stratford i-SITE (☑ 0800 765 6708, 06-765 6708; www.stratford.govt.nz; Prospero Pl,

Broadway S, Stratford; ⊙ 8.30am-5pm Mon-Fri, 10am-3pm Sat & Sun) All the local low-down, plus good advice on walks on Mt Taranaki. Down an arcade off the main street.

Surf Highway 45

Sweeping south from New Plymouth around the coastline to Hawera, the 105km-long SH45 is known as Surf Hwy 45. But don't take the name as gospel: while there is an abundance of black-sand beaches along the way, the road snakes inland through green paddocks and farmland, too. Pick up the *Surf Highway 45* brochure at visitor centres.

ℹ️ Getting There & Away

This part of NZ is delightfully untouristed and off the main bus routes. You'll need your own wheels to get around (cycling is a good option – the terrain is level most of the way).

Alternatively, local SouthLink (www.taranakibus.info) buses depart New Plymouth once on Fridays to Oakura, Okato and Opunake on SH45, before detouring inland to Hawera via Eltham. SouthLink also runs from New Plymouth to Hawera once daily Monday to Friday via Stratford on the inland route.

Oakura

06 / POP 1380

From New Plymouth, the first cab off the rank is laid-back Oakura, 15km southwest on SH45. For a town with not much more than a souvenir shop, petrol station and family medical centre, Oakura has a disproportionately high number of decent places to eat on your way through. Its broad sweep of beach is hailed by waxheads for its right-hander breaks, but it's also great for families (take sandals – that black sand gets scorching hot!).

🏃 Activities

Sharpen your wave skills with some lessons from **Vertigo Surf** (06-752 7363; www.vertigosurf.com; 2 Tasman Pde; lessons from $80; 9am-5.30pm Mon-Fri, to 4pm Sat & Sun) or **Tarawave Surf School** (021 119 6218; www.taranakisurfschool.com; 90min lessons per person from $50).

🛏 Sleeping & Eating

Oakura Beach Holiday Park   HOLIDAY PARK $
(06-752 7861; www.oakurabeach.com; 2 Jans Tce; campsites from $22, cabins $75-150; @ 🖥) Wedged between the cliffs and the sea, this better-than-average beachside park caters best to caravans, but self-contained units C11 and C12 have uninterrupted ocean views. Simple, elevated cabins and absolute beachfront spots for pitching a tent. Take the walk from the park through the native reserve to the *Gaerloch* shipwreck and try to imagine it in its former 345-tonne glory.

★ **Ahu Ahu Beach Villas**   BOUTIQUE HOTEL $$$
(06-752 7370; www.ahu.co.nz; 321 Ahu Ahu Rd; d & f $210-295, 2-bedroom lodge from $450; 🖥) Pricey on the pocket but with priceless views. Set on a knoll overlooking the ocean, these luxury, architecturally designed villas are superbly eccentric, with huge recycled timbers, bottles cast into walls, century-old lichen-covered French tile roofs and polished-concrete floors with inlaid paua shell. The lodge sleeps four and is the place for sunset drinks.

High Tide   CAFE $
(www.facebook.com/hightideoakura; 1136b SH45; lunch $9-15, pastries $3-5; 7am-2pm) Formerly a food caravan on Oakura Beach, High Tide grew so popular it moved to permanent digs. It's super-fresh cabinet-nosh-only here (try the smoked-salmon bagel or a French pastry), and the coffee is the best in town.

Staff are all smiles while local artwork, indoor festoon lights and patterned cushions add a charming boho surf vibe.

★ **Black Sand Pizzeria & Bistro**   PIZZA, BREAKFAST $$
(06-752 7806; www.facebook.com/blacksandOK; 1 Tasman Pde; pizza $15-20; 9am-late Tue-Sun summer, 5pm-late Thu & Fri and 9am-late Sat & Sun winter; 🖥) Reliable Black Sand is right on the beach and shares a building with the surf club. It's a surprising location to stumble upon authentic Napoli-style pizzas – all thin-based and blistered crusts – but these wood-fired beauties made in a custom Italian oven give the rest of Taranaki a run for its margherita. Bistro food, breakfast and beer on tap are also available.

Okato & Around

Between Oakura and Opunake, SH45 veers inland through Okato, with detours to sundry beaches along the way. There are legendary surf spots at **Stent Rd** (Stent Rd, Warea; 24hr), just south of Warea, and **Kumara Patch** (Komene Rd, Okato; 24hr), west of Okato. Near Pungarehu, Cape Egmont is home to a historic **lighthouse** (Cape Rd, Pungarehu; 24hr) FREE and associated **museum** (06-763 8507, 06-763 8489; www.southtaranaki.com; Bayly Rd, Warea; by donation; 11am-3pm Sat-Mon).

🛏 Sleeping & Eating

Stony River Hotel   PUB $$
(06-752 4454; www.stonyriverhotel.co.nz; 2502 SH45, Okato; tw/d/tr incl breakfast $110/120/170; 🖥) This lemon-yellow highway hotel dates back to 1875, when mailmen on horses would stop to rest on their way north. There are bright, super-tidy, country-style en suite rooms upstairs and a restaurant downstairs (mains $17 to $34), serving weekend lunches and dinner Wednesday to Sunday. The corner rooms have the best views. Don't miss Wednesday schnitzel nights with live oom-pah tunes.

★ **Cafe Lahar**   CAFE $
(06-752 4865; 64 Carthew St, Okato; mains $10-22; 8.30am-3pm Tue, to 4pm Wed & Thu, to 11pm Fri-Sun) Relaxed Lahar occupies an angular, black-trimmed timber box in Okato (hard to miss – there's not much else here). It's a lofty space with spinning fans, some tempting couches out the front and a menu ranging from pork sausages and beans, to tandoori chicken salad and pizzas on Friday, Saturday and Sunday nights. Good coffee and live music now and then.

Opunake

📱 06 / POP 1335

A sleepy summer town, Opunake is Taranaki's surfie epicentre, but it also has a sheltered family beach. There's not much happening on the main strip, but you can't go wrong grabbing some seriously good fish and chips and catching a film at the restored Everybody's Theatre.

🏃 Activities

Opunake Walkway WALKING

(Layard St; ☺ daylight hr) **FREE** Feel like stretching your pins? The Opunake Walkway is a signposted 7km, three-hour ramble around the Opunake waterfront, starting (or finishing) at Opunake Lake on Layard St.

Surfing With Murray SURFING

(📱 027 218 3377; murraybaylis@gmail.com; lessons from $60) Small-group, 1½-hour surfing lessons in the safe breaks of Opunake Beach. Boards and wetsuits provided; maximum four surf students (price drops to $60 for two people or more).

🛏 Sleeping & Eating

Opunake Beach Holiday Park HOLIDAY PARK $

(📱 0800 758 009, 06-761 7525; www.opunake beachnz.co.nz; 1 Beach Rd; d campsites/cabins/cottages $44/75/110; @🛜) Opunake Beach Holiday Park is a mellow spot behind the surf beach. Sites are grassy, the camp kitchen is big, the amenities block is cavernous and the waves are just a few metres away on the black-sand beach.

Headlands HOTEL $$

(📱 06-761 8358; www.headlands.co.nz; 4 Havelock St; r $130-250; 🛜) Just 100m back from the beach, Headlands is an upmarket, three-storey accommodation tower with a Euro-Indian bistro downstairs (mains $12 to $34; the food beats the decor). It's the flashest option in town, and the best rooms snare brilliant sunsets, but they also teeter on the bland side of modern.

⭐**Opunake Fish, Chips and More** FISH & CHIPS $

(📱 06-761 8478; www.facebook.com/Opunakefish chipsandmore; 61 Tasman St; fish & chips $3.50-10; ☺11am-8pm) This is as good as fish and chips gets. With a lengthy history (open since the 1960s), hand-cut chips, a range of fish (including fresh catches of the day to take home), smiling local owners and gluten-free options, one meal here and you'll instantly feel part of the Opunake community. Cheap, cheerful and nostalgic.

Sugar Juice Café CAFE $$

(📱06-761 7062; 42 Tasman St; brunch $5-21, dinner $25-39; ☺8am-4pm Sun-Wed, to 8pm Thu, to 9pm Fri & Sat, closed Mon Jun-Aug; 🖊) Happy, hippie and wholesome, Sugar Juice Cafe has some of the most reliable food on SH45. It's brimming with delicious, homemade, filling fare (try the southern-fried-chicken burger for dinner or a sausage roll from the display for lunch). Decent coffee and delicious cabinet food, as well as big brekkies and a courtyard – don't pass it by.

THE PARIHAKA MOVEMENT

From the mid-1860s Parihaka, a small Māori settlement east of SH45 near Pungarehu, became the centre of a peaceful resistance movement, one which involved not only other Taranaki tribes, but Māori from around the country. Its leaders, Te Whiti-o-Rongomai and Tohu Kākahi, were of both Taranaki and Te Āti Awa descent.

After the Land Wars, confiscation of tribal lands was the central problem faced by Taranaki Māori, and under Te Whiti's leadership a new approach to this issue was developed: resisting European settlement through nonviolent methods.

When the government started surveying confiscated land on the Waimate Plain in 1879, unarmed followers of Te Whiti, wearing the movement's iconic white feather in their hair, obstructed development by ploughing troughs across roads, erecting random fences and pulling survey pegs – all in good humour. Nevertheless, many were arrested and held without trial on the South Island. The protests continued and intensified. Finally, in November 1881, the government sent a force of more than 1600 troops to Parihaka. Its inhabitants were arrested or driven away, and the village was later demolished. Te Whiti and Tohu were arrested and imprisoned until 1883. In their absence Parihaka was rebuilt and the ploughing campaigns continued into the 1890s.

In 2006 the NZ government issued a formal apology and financial compensation to the tribes affected by the invasion and confiscation of Parihaka lands.

☆ Entertainment

Everybody's Theatre   CINEMA
(☑027 383 7926; www.everybodystheatre.co.nz;
72 Tasman St; adult/child $10/8; ☺screenings 1pm
& 7pm Wed & Sat, 7pm Fri & Sun) This restored
1920s theatre, run by volunteers, under-
went a major renovations in 2016. It cost
$250,000 to earthquake-proof the building
and at the time of writing $900,000 had
been spent to do it up. With couches downstairs and regular movie theatre seating upstairs, it shows the latest releases as well as
classic, foreign and fringe films on 'boutique
nights'.

ⓘ Information

Opunake Library (☑ 0800 111 323; www.
opunakenz.co.nz; 43 Tasman St; ☺9am-5pm
Mon-Fri, 9.30am-1pm Sat; ☏) Doubles as the
local visitor-information centre, with a couple
of internet terminals and free 24-hour wi-fi in
the forecourt.

Hawera

☑06 / POP 11,750

Don't expect much urban virtue from agricultural Hawera, the largest town in South
Taranaki. Still, it's a good pit stop to pick up
supplies, grab a coffee, visit the info centre,
stretch your legs or bed down for a night.
If you ain't nothin' but a hound dog, don't
miss Elvis.

◉ Sights

★KD's Elvis Presley Museum   MUSEUM
(☑06-278 7624, 027 498 2942; www.elvismuseum.
co.nz; 51 Argyle St; admission by donation; ☺by appointment) Elvis lives! At least he does at Kevin
D Wasley's astonishing museum, which houses more than 10,000 of the King's records and
a mind-blowing collection of Elvis memorabilia collected over nearly 60 years. 'Passion
is an understatement', says KD, who's grey
hair is slicked back and on theme. Admission
is by appointment – phone ahead.

Tawhiti Museum   MUSEUM
(☑06-278 6837; www.tawhitimuseum.co.nz; 401
Ohangai Rd; adult/child $15/5; ☺10am-4pm Fri-
Sun Feb-May & Sep-Dec, daily Jan, Sun only Jun-Aug)
The excellent Tawhiti Museum houses a collection of exhibits, dioramas and creepily lifelike human figures modelled on people from
the region. A large collection of tractors pays
homage to the area's rural heritage; there's
also a bush railway and a 'Traders & Whalers'
boat ride (extra charges for both). It's near
the corner of Tawhiti Rd, 4km north of town.

SNELLY!
....
Opunake isn't just about surf – it's also
the birthplace of iconic middle-distance
runner Sir Peter Snell (b 1938), who
showed his rivals a clean set of heels at
the 1960 Rome and 1964 Tokyo Olym-
pics. Old Snelly won the 800m gold in
Italy, then followed up with 800m and
1500m golds in Japan, as well as two
golds at the 1962 Commonwealth Games
in Perth, Australia. Legend! Check out his
bronze running statue outside the library.

Hawera Water Tower   TOWER, VIEWPOINT
(☑06-278 8599; www.southtaranaki.com; 55 High
St; adult/child/family $2.50/1/6; ☺8.30am-4pm
Mon-Fri, 10am-2pm Sat, Sun & public holidays) The
austere, 55m Hawera Water Tower is one of
few noteworthy attractions in quiet Hawera.
Grab the key from the neighbouring i-SITE
(p248), ascend the 215 steps, then scan the
horizon for signs of life (you can see the
coast and Mt Taranaki on a clear day).

🛏 Sleeping & Eating

Wheatly Downs Farmstay   FARMSTAY $
(☑06-278 6523; www.mttaranaki.co.nz; 484 Ararata Rd; campsites from $20, dm/s/tw $33/75/75,
d with/without bathroom $115/75) Set in a rural
idyll on a 350-acre sheep and cattle farm,
this heritage building is a classic with its
clunky wooden floors and no-nonsense fit-
tings. The affable owners might even ask if
you want to help feed the animals. To get
there, head past the turn-off to Tawhiti Museum and continue on Ararata Rd for 5.5km.
Pick-ups by arrangement.

Park Motel   MOTEL $$
(☑06-278 7275; www.theparkmotel.co.nz; 61 Waihi
Rd; d $140, 1-/2-bedroom apt $155/170; ℗) These
18 basic but clean rooms across the road
from King Edward Park and an aquatic cen-
tre make up our pick of the motels in Haw-
era. Consists of studio units and one- and
two-bedroom apartments; room number 8
may have a spa bath, but all rooms come
with homemade cookies.

Tairoa Lodge   B&B $$$
(☑06-278 8603; www.tairoa-lodge.co.nz; 3 Puawai
St; s/d $165/215, cottage d $245, extra adult/child
$50/30, all incl breakfast; ☏☒) Set on grassy
lawns, gorgeous old Tairoa is a photogenic
1875 Victorian manor house on the eastern
outskirts of Hawera, with three guest rooms
and two outlying cottages (two and three

bedrooms). Lashings of heritage style, bird-filled gardens (often full of wedding parties, too) and big cooked breakfasts await at the end of the bamboo-lined driveway.

Someday CAFE $$
(☑06-278 6097; www.facebook.com/somedaycafe hawera; 90 Princes St; dishes $9-19; ☺7am-5pm Mon-Fri, 9am-3pm Sat; 🛜) In a town short on decent places to eat, you can almost hear Someday cafe sigh at its surroundings. Around 20 can fit on the mid-century chairs and at the industrial communal table, where locals chat over cake and the best coffee around for miles and all-day brunch (try the generous ploughman's platter). Just passing through? Don't stop anywhere else.

ℹ Information

South Taranaki i-SITE (☑06-278 8599; www.southtaranaki.com; 55 High St; ☺8.30am-5pm Mon-Fri, 10am-3pm Sat & Sun; 🛜) Get the South Taranaki low-down. Extended summer weekend hours.

Whanganui

☑06 / POP 42,150

Before Whanganui was Whanganui, it was Petre, a town built at the mouth of the river in 1940. As one of New Zealand's oldest towns (and the fifth-largest until 1936), it's an amalgamation of Māori culture, heritage buildings – take a 60-minute self-guided tour with the free Whanganui Heritage Guide from the i-SITE (p252) – and a thriving local art community.

Despite the occasional flood, the wide Whanganui River is the lifeblood of the town, with regular markets, scenic walkways and old port buildings being turned into glass-art studios. There are few more appealing places to while away a sunny afternoon than the dog-free zone beneath Victoria Ave's leafy canopy.

⊙ Sights

★ **Waimarie Centre** MUSEUM
(☑0800 783 2637, 06-347 1863; www.waimarie.co.nz; 1a Taupo Quay; cruises adult/child/family $45/15/90; ☺10am-3pm Oct-Apr; 🚗) FREE The historical displays are interesting, but everyone's here for the PS *Waimarie,* the last of the Whanganui River paddle steamers. In 1900 it was shipped out from England and paddled the Whanganui until it sank ingloriously at its mooring in 1952. Submerged for 41 years, it was finally raised, restored,

then relaunched on the first day of the 21st century. It now offers two-hour tours up the river, boarding at 10.30am. Book in advance.

★ **Sarjeant on the Quay** GALLERY
(☑06-349 0506; www.sarjeant.org.nz; 38 Taupo Quay; ☺10.30am-4.30pm) FREE The elegant old neoclassical Sarjeant Gallery building in Queens Park is closed for earthquake-proofing. Until that work is finished, this estimable art collection is housed on Taupo Quay. There's not as much room here as up on the hill, so exhibits are limited (but revolving). There's more on show above the Whanganui i-SITE (p252) across the road. Fab gift shop, too, with lots of Whanganui glass.

★ **New Zealand Glassworks** GALLERY
(☑06-927 6803; www.nzglassworks.com; 2 Rutland St; ☺10am-4.30pm) FREE The pick of Whanganui's many glass studios. Watch glass-blowers working, check out the gallery, take a one-day glass-blowing course ($290, four people max) or a 30-minute 'Make a Paperweight' lesson ($80), or just hang out and warm up on a chilly afternoon.

Whanganui Regional Museum MUSEUM
(☑06-349 1110; www.wrm.org.nz; 62 Ridgway St; ☺10am-4.30pm) FREE When we visited, the original Queens Park museum was closed for earthquake strengthening but open for business on Ridgway St. Here you'll get a glimpse of one of NZ's better natural-history museums, including Māori exhibits, some vicious-looking *mere* (greenstone clubs) and colonial and wildlife installations.

Kai Iwi Beach BEACH
(Mowhanau Dr, off Rapanui Rd; ☺24hr; 🚗) Kai Iwi Beach is a wild ocean frontier, strewn with black sand, the ruin of a gun emplacement from WWII and masses of driftwood (you might see locals collecting it for their next 'piece'). There's also a big playground with a flying fox and plenty of paddle-friendly water for young kids.

Follow Great North Rd 4km north of town, then turn left onto Rapanui Rd and head seawards for 10km.

Putiki Church CHURCH
(St Paul's Memorial Church; ☑06-349 0508; www.visitwhanganui.nz; 20 Anaua St; per person $10; ☺service 9am Sun, tours 2pm Thu-Sun or by arrangement) Across the City Bridge from town and 1km towards the sea is the Putiki Church (aka St Paul's Memorial Church). It's unremarkable externally, but just like the faithful pew-fillers, it's what's inside that

Whanganui

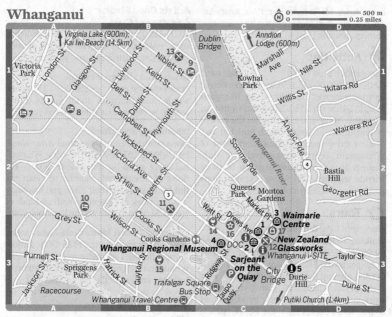

Whanganui

⊙ Top Sights
1 New Zealand Glassworks	C3
2 Sarjeant on the Quay	C3
3 Waimarie Centre	C3
4 Whanganui Regional Museum	C3

⊙ Sights
5 Durie Hill Elevator	D3

⊕ Activities, Courses & Tours
Wanganui City Guided Walking Tours	(see 12)
6 Whanganui River Road Tours	C1

⊜ Sleeping
7 151 on London	A1
8 Aotea Motor Lodge	A1
9 Braemar House YHA	B1
10 Browns Boutique B&B	A2
Tamara Backpackers Lodge	(see 6)

⊗ Eating
Big Orange	(see 4)
Ceramic Lounge	(see 4)
11 Mischief on Guyton	B2
12 Mud Ducks	C3
13 Yellow House Cafe	B1

⊙ Drinking & Nightlife
14 Frank Bar + Eatery	C3
15 Lucky Bar + Kitchen	B3

⊛ Entertainment
16 Savage Club	C3

⊚ Shopping
17 River Traders Market & Whanganui Farmers Market	C3

counts: the interior is magnificent, completely covered in Māori carvings and *tukutuku* (wall panels). Show up for Sunday service, or get some inside knowledge on a guided tour organised via the i-SITE (p252).

Durie Hill Elevator   TOWER, VIEWPOINT
(☎0800 92 64 26; www.visitwhanganui.nz; Anzac Pde; adult/child one way $2/1; ⊘8am-6pm Mon-

Fri, 10am-5pm Sat & Sun) Across City Bridge from downtown Whanganui, this elevator was built with grand visions for Durie Hill's residential future. Beyond an entrance lined with Māori carvings, a tunnel burrows 213m into the hillside, from where a 1919 elevator rattles 65.8m to the top.

At the summit you can climb the 176 steps of the War Memorial Tower and scan the horizon for Mt Taranaki and Mt Ruapehu. There's another lookout atop the lift machinery housing (just 41 steps).

🏃 Activities

Wanganui Horse Treks　　HORSE RIDING
(☑ 021 930 950, 06-345 3285; www.facebook.com/wanganuihorsetreks; 78 Wikitoria Rd, Whanganui Airport; 1/1½hr rides $80/120) Climb onto an agreeable horse and ride around the beaches and dunes at South Beach and Kai Iwi, a short drive southwest and northwest of Whanganui central respectively. A little cheaper if you can lasso a group of three friends together. Call for times, directions and bookings. Giddy-up!

☞ Tours

Wanganui City Guided Walking Tours　　WALKING
(☑ 06-349 3258; www.visitwhanganui.nz; 31 Taupo Quay; per person $10; ⊙10am & 2pm Sat & Sun Oct-Apr) Sign up for a 90-minute guided tour through old Whanganui, giving your legs a workout as you pass historic buildings and sights. Tours depart from the i-SITE (p252); book tickets inside.

🎊 Festivals & Events

Vintage Weekend　　CULTURAL
(☑ 021 261 3526; www.vintageweekend.co.nz; ⊙Jan) Time-travelling cars, clothes, music, markets, architecture and good times over three January days by the Whanganui River.

Artists Open Studios & Festival of Glass　　ART
(☑ 06-348 0157, 027 3042 126; www.openstudios.co.nz; ⊙Mar) Classy glass fest. Plenty of open studios, demonstrations and workshops.

Whanganui Literary Festival　　CULTURAL
(www.writersfest.co.nz; ⊙Sep-Oct) Thoughts, words, and thoughts about words. Every second September (odd-numbered years).

Whanganui River Week　　CULTURAL
(www.facebook.com/Whanganui-River-Week-156726904367057/; ⊙Nov) The wide Whanganui River got a bit too wide in 2015 – the flood aftermath took months to clean up. But locals still love their river, and celebrate it over a week in November with all kinds of events. Stay up to date via the Facebook page.

Cemetery Circuit Motorcycle Race　　SPORTS
(www.cemeterycircuit.co.nz; ⊙26 Dec) Pandemoniac Boxing Day motorcycle race around Whanganui's city streets. The southern hemisphere's version of the Isle of Man TT?

🛏 Sleeping

★**Anndion Lodge**　　HOSTEL $
(☑ 0800 343 056, 06-343 3593; www.anndionlodge.co.nz; 143 Anzac Pde; s/d/f/ste from $75/88/105/135; @🎇🍸🏊) Formerly run by Ann and Dion (Anndion, get it?), this hostel continues to attract travellers with its stereo systems, huge communal kitchen, pool tables, big TVs, spa, sauna, swimming pool, barbecue area and restaurant.

WHANGANUI OR WANGANUI?

Yeah, yeah, we know, it's confusing. Is there an 'h' or isn't there? Either way, the pronunciation is identical: 'wong-ga', not 'fong-ga' (as in the rest of the country when a 'w' and 'h' meet).

In the local dialect *whanga* (harbour) is pronounced 'wong-ga', which is how the original 'Wanganui' spelling came about. But in 1991 the New Zealand Geographic Board officially adopted the correct Māori spelling (with an 'h') for the Whanganui River and Whanganui National Park. This was a culturally deferential decision: the Pākehā-dominated town and region retained the old spelling, while the river area – Māori territory – adopted the new.

In 2009 the board assented that the town and region should also adopt the 'h'. This caused much community consternation; opinions on the decision split almost evenly (outspoken Mayor Michael Laws was particularly anti-'h'). Ultimately, NZ Minister for Land Information Maurice Williamson decreed that either spelling was acceptable, and that adopting the querulous 'h' is up to individual businesses or entities. A good old Kiwi compromise!

This middle ground held shakily until 2014, when the Wanganui District Council voted to ask the New Zealand Geographic Board to formalise the change to Whanganui. A public consultation process began, culminating in an announcement in late 2015 by Land Information Minister Louise Upston that the district's name would be officially changed to Whanganui. Whanderful!

Whanganui River

Top 10 Holiday Park HOLIDAY PARK $

(☑06-343 8402, 0800 272 664; www.wrivertop10. co.nz; 460 Somme Pde, Aramoho; unpowered/ powered sites $39/46, cabins/units from $76/130; ☎🅿️♿) This tidy Top 10 park sits on the Whanganui's west bank 6km north of Dublin Bridge. Facilities (pool, games room, jumping pillow) are prodigious. Kayak hire is also available: the owners shuttle you up river then you paddle back. Budget cabins by the river have big-dollar views, or opt for a glamping tent ($100) in summer. Local buses trundle past.

Tamara Backpackers Lodge HOSTEL $

(☑06-347 6300; www.tamaralodge.co.nz; 24 Somme Pde; dm/s/tr/q from $29/44/93/116, d & tw with/ without bathroom from $86/62; @☎) Tamara is a photogenic, mazelike, two-storey heritage house with a wide balcony, lofty ceilings, a kitchen, a TV lounge, free bikes, a leafy back garden and incredibly helpful staff who will tell you what to see and where to be seen. Ask for one of the doubles overlooking the river.

Braemar House YHA HOSTEL $

(☑06-348 2301; www.braemarhouse.co.nz; 2 Plymouth St; dm/s/tw/d $35/50/70/75, guesthouse incl breakfast s & d $140; @☎) Riverside Braemar brings together an 1895 Victorian B&B guesthouse and a reliable YHA backpackers (although there are separate lounge areas). Centrally located guesthouse rooms are floral and fancy; airy dorms conjure up a bit more fun out the back. Chooks patrol the lawns out in the yard.

★ **Browns Boutique B&B** B&B $$

(☑0273 082 495; www.brownsboutiquebnb.co.nz; 34 College St, College Estate; s/d incl breakfast $175/190) Owned by the same family for more than 50 years, this 1910 house was coincidentally built by an unrelated Brown. There are two rooms at the back with private entrances that look out onto the patio, and in addition to gorgeous decor and little touches (tiles made by a Moroccan-New Zealander, a typewriter for a guestbook), the free-range, gourmet breakfasts are divine.

The double drops to $175 per night for stays of three nights or more.

151 on London MOTEL $$

(☑0800 151 566, 06-345 8668; www.151onlondon. co.nz; 151 London St; d $130-180, 2-bedroom apt from $200; ☎♿) This snappy-looking spaceship of a motel wins plenty of fans with its architectural angles, quality carpets and linen, natty lime/silver/black colour scheme and big TVs.

At the top of the price tree are some excellent upstairs/downstairs apartment-style units sleeping six: about as ritzy as Whanganui accommodation gets. Cafe across the car park.

Aotea Motor Lodge MOTEL $$

(☑06-345 0303; www.aoteamotorlodge.co.nz; 390 Victoria Ave; d from $145, 1-bedroom ste from $215; ☎) On the upper reaches of Victoria Ave, this flashy, two-storey contemporary motel features roomy suites, lavish linen, leather chairs, dark timbers and plenty of marble and stone. Every room has a spa bath. Romance is never far away in Whanganui.

✖ Eating

★ **Mischief on Guyton** CAFE $

(☑06-347 1227; www.facebook.com/mischiefon guyton; 96 Guyton St; mains $10-23; ☺7.30am-3pm Mon-Fri) With cheeky signage and a flip calendar of quotes not suitable to print but good for a laugh with your coffee, Mischief on Guyton is true to its name. Step inside (or through to the courtyard) for a combined brunch and lunch menu featuring interesting dishes like the wonderfully named rockamorocca: oven-baked eggs with dukkah on pita bread.

★ **Yellow House Cafe** CAFE $

(The Yellow House; ☑06-3450083; www.yellowhouse cafe.co.nz; cnr Pitt & Dublin Sts; meals $11-19; ☺8am-4pm Mon-Fri, 8.30am-4pm Sat & Sun; ✈) Detour from the main drag for funky tunes, butterscotch pancakes, local art and courtyard tables beneath a chunky-trunk cherry blossom tree. Super-friendly staff bend over backwards to recommend what to do in town. Try a venison burger for lunch on the sunny terrace. If you want to give high tea a whirl, book in advance.

★ **Citadel** BURGERS $$

(☑06-344 7076; www.facebook.com/the-citadel. castlecliff; 14a Rangiora St, Castlecliff; burgers $12-19; ☺9am-8pm Thu & Sun-Mon, to 9pm Fri & Sat; ♿) Looking for the best burgers on the North Island? Community-minded Citadel, 10 minutes' drive from Whanganui centre, is a contender. Alongside classics, the Eh Monster is a feat of endurance. Order it (alongside loaded fries) and watch heads turn. Graffiti that looks like a children's book illustration covers the outdoor deck wall. Breakfast menu, kids' menu and wooden playground, too.

Big Orange CAFE $$

(☑06-348 4449; www.facebook.com/bigorange cafe; 51 Victoria Ave; meals $14-24; ☺7.30am-3pm Mon-Fri, 8am-3pm Sat & Sun; ☎♿) Inside a gorgeous old Whanganui red-brick building, Big Orange is a babbling espresso bar serving gourmet burgers, big breakfasts, muffins, cakes and sandwiches. The outdoor tables overlooking the roundabout are hot property, and from 5pm **Ceramic Lounge** (www.facebook.com/ceramicloungebar; mains $23-40; ⏱5pm-late Wed-Sat; 🛜) in the same building takes over with dinner and drinks. Ask about 'pay it forward' coffee.

🍷 Drinking & Nightlife

Frank Bar + Eatery   COCKTAIL BAR
(📞027 441 9577, 027 4222 555, 06-348 4808; www.facebook.com/pg/frankwhanganui; 98 Victoria Ave; burgers $18.50, platters $25-45; ⏱5-9pm Tue & Wed, to 10pm Thu, to midnight Fri & Sat) With DJs and events lined up every weekend and a solid cocktail list, we'll be Frank when we tell you that this is the place for a night out. The lofty space is split into an industrial-chic dining area with a mezzanine up above. Burgers and big share platters for eats. Happy hour is 6pm to 9pm Thursday to Saturday.

Lucky Bar + Kitchen   BAR
(📞021 126 3936; www.facebook.com/luckybarwhanganui; 53 Wilson St; mains $26-28; ⏱4pm-late Wed-Sat, kitchen closes 9pm) One of the few places for a night out in Whang, Lucky serves local fare worth eating, even if you're not into live music. With boxes stacked behind a small stage, round paper lanterns hanging from the ceiling and disco lighting, there's an endearing high-school vibe here, but all ages get up to dance when the tunes are right.

☆ Entertainment

Savage Club   LIVE MUSIC
(📞021 256 7647; www.whanganuimusiciansclub.co.nz; 65 Drews Ave; ⏱7pm 1st Fri of the month) The first Friday of every month is club night here; that means a scheduled performance from local and international stars, and even open mic earlier on. This is where the musos go for gigs. Search Whanganui Musicians Club on Facebook to see what's on. Better yet, it's BYO before 9pm.

🛍 Shopping

River Traders Market &
Whanganui Farmers Market   MARKET
(📞027 229 9616; www.therivertraders.co.nz; Moutoa Quay; ⏱9am-1pm Sat) Spend Saturday morning like a local at the River Traders Market, next to the Waimarie Centre, which is crammed with local arts and crafts. The Whanganui Farmers Market runs concur-

rently alongside, with loads of organic produce. Gather a picnic and enjoy under some trees by the river.

ℹ Information

DOC (Department of Conservation; 📞06-349 2100; www.doc.govt.nz; 34-36 Taupo Quay; ⏱8.30am-4.30pm Mon-Fri) For national park and regional camping info.

Whanganui Hospital (📞06-348 1234; www.wdhb.org.nz; 100 Heads Rd; ⏱24hr) Accident and emergency.

Whanganui i-SITE (📞06-349 0508, 0800 926 426; www.whanganuinz.com; 31 Taupo Quay; ⏱9am-5pm Nov-Apr, 9am-5pm Mon-Fri, to 4pm Sat & Sun May-Oct; 🛜) Tourist and DOC information (if DOC across the street is closed) in an impressive renovated riverside building (check out the old floorboards!). Sarjeant Gallery (p248) exhibition space upstairs; wi-fi lounge downstairs beside the lovely Mud Ducks (📞06-348 7626; www.facebook.com/MudDucks; 31 Taupo Quay; dishes $13-24; ⏱8.30am-4pm; 🛜) cafe.

ℹ Getting There & Away

AIR

Whanganui Airport (📞06-349 0001; www.whanganuiairport.co.nz; Airport Rd) is 4km south of town, across the river towards the sea. Air New Zealand (www.airnewzealand.co.nz) has daily direct flights to/from Auckland, with onward connections.

BUS

InterCity (www.intercity.co.nz) buses operate from the **Whanganui Travel Centre** (📞06-345 7100; 156 Ridgway St; ⏱8.15am-5.15pm Mon-Fri).

DESTINATION	COST	TIME (HR)	FREQUENCY (DAILY)
Auckland	from $33	8	1
Hamilton	from $31	5½	1
New Plymouth	from $17	2½	1-2
Palmerston North	from $18	1½	3-4
Wellington	from $24	4	2-3

ℹ Getting Around

BICYCLE

Bike Shed (📞06-345 5500; www.bikeshed.co.nz; cnr Ridgway & St Hill Sts; ⏱8am-5.30pm Mon-Fri, 9am-2pm Sat) Hires out city bikes from $35 per day, including helmet and lock. Also a good spot for info on the Mountains to Sea bike trail (www.mountainstosea.co.nz)

from Mt Ruapehu to Whanganui, which is part of the Nga Haerenga, New Zealand Cycle Trail (www.nzcycletrail.com).

BUS

Trafalgar Square Bus Stop (www.horizons. govt.nz; tickets adult/child $2.50/1.50) Horizons operates four looped council-run bus routes departing Trafalgar Sq shopping centre on Taupo Quay, including orange and purple routes past the Whanganui River Top 10 Holiday Park in Aramoho.

TAXI

Rivercity Cabs (☑ 06-345 3333, 0800 345 3333; www.whanganui.bluebubbletaxi.co.nz)

Whanganui National Park

The Whanganui River may not pay taxes or vote, but it has the same rights as a human being. That's because in early 2017 it became the first river to be legally recognised as a person, following a 140-year battle. The new legislation recognises the spiritual connection between Māori *iwi* and the river, considered an ancestor.

Curling 290km from Mt Tongariro to the Tasman Sea, it's the longest navigable river in New Zealand, and visitors traverse it by canoe, kayak, jetboat, and bike.

The native bush here is thick, podocarp, broad-leaved forest interspersed with ferns. Occasionally you'll see poplars and other introduced trees along the river, remnants of long-vanished settlements. There are also traces of Māori settlements, with old *pā* (fortified village) and *kainga* (village) sites, and Hauhau *niu* (war and peace) poles at the convergence of the Whanganui and Ohura Rivers at Maraekowhai.

History

In Māori legend the Whanganui River was formed when Mt Taranaki fled the central North Island for the sea after fighting with Mt Tongariro over the lovely Mt Pihanga, leaving a long gouge behind him. He turned west at the coast, finally stopping where he resides today. Mt Tongariro sent cool water to heal the gouge – and the Whanganui River was born.

Kupe, the great Polynesian explorer, is believed to have travelled 20km up the Whanganui around AD 800; Māori lived here by 1100. By the time Europeans put down roots in the late 1830s, Māori settlements lined the river valley. Missionaries sailed upstream and their settlements – at Hiruharama, Ranana, Koriniti and Atene – have survived to this day.

Steamers first tackled the river in the mid-1860s. In 1886 a Whanganui company established the first commercial steamer transport service. Others soon followed, utilising the river between Whanganui and Taumarunui.

New Zealand's contemporary tourism leviathan was seeded here. Internationally advertised trips on the 'Rhine of Māoriland' became so popular that by 1905, 12,000 tourists a year were making the trip upriver from Whanganui to Pipiriki or downriver from Taumarunui. The engineering feats and skippering ability required on the river became legendary.

From 1918 land upstream of Pipiriki was granted to returning WWI soldiers. Farming here was a major challenge, with many families struggling for years to make the rugged land productive. Only a few endured into the early 1940s.

The completion of the railway from Auckland to Wellington and improved roads ultimately signed river transport's death warrant; 1959 saw the last commercial riverboat voyage. Today, just one old-fleet vessel cruises the river – the PS Waimarie (p248).

◉ Sights

The scenery along the **Whanganui River Rd** en route to Pipiriki from Whanganui is camera conducive – stark, wet mountain slopes plunge into lazy jade stretches of the Whanganui River.

About 7km north of Parikino as the river and road bend into an obvious U-shape, cars slow to admire the **Oyster Cliffs**, where fossilised oysters jut from rock that used to be submerged in the ocean. If you cross a bridge and see the Moukuku Scenic Reserve sign, you've gone too far.

The Māori villages of **Atene, Koriniti, Ranana** and **Hiruharama** crop up as you travel further upstream – ask a local before you go sniffing around. Along the road you'll spot some relics of earlier settlements, such as the 1854 **Kawana Flour Mill** (☑ 04-472 4341; www.nzhistory.net.nz/media/photo/kawana -flourmill; 4075 Whanganui River Rd; ☺ dawn-dusk) **FREE** near Matahiwi and *pā* sites.

Pipiriki is beside the river at the north end of Whanganui River Rd. It's a rainy river town without much going on (no shops or petrol), but was once a humming holiday hot spot serviced by river steamers and paddleboats. Pipiriki is the end point for canoe trips coming down the river and the launching pad for jetboat rides.

Whanganui National Park Area

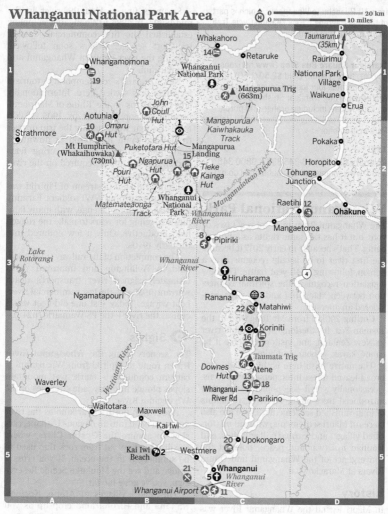

St Joseph's Church

CHURCH

(☏06-342 8190; www.compassion.org.nz; Whanganui River Rd; ⊙9am-5pm) FREE Around a corner in the Whanganui River Rd in Jerusalem, the picture-perfect, red-and-mustard spire of St Joseph's Church stands tall on a spur of land above a deep river bend. A French Catholic mission led by Suzanne Aubert established the Daughters of the Sisters of Compassion here in 1892. Slip off your shoes and explore the (slightly creepy) convent and Madeline-like dorms.

The sisters take in bedraggled travellers, offering 20 dorm-style beds (adults $20, children $5, linen $10 extra) and a simple kitchen – book ahead for the privilege. **Moutoa Island**, site of a historic 1864 battle, is just downriver.

Bridge to Nowhere

BRIDGE

(Whanganui River) FREE To say this bridge looks out of place is an understatement. With no roads on either side, you don't need to be a genius to figure out its name. Originally built so that horses could cross the river to Mangapurua Valley farmland that was provided to soldiers after WWI, thesoldiers deserted the poor soil in 1942, and the forest regained its natural posi-

Whanganui

tion. It's on the Mangapurua Track for trampers and mountain bikers, or it's a 40-minute walk from Mangapurua Landing, upstream from Pipiriki, accessible by jetboat or kayak.

Koriniti Marae   CULTURAL CENTRE
(☑ 021 115 1256; www.wrmtb.co.nz; Koriniti Pa Rd; ⊙ 9am-5pm) FREE Unless there's a *marae* (meeting house) function happening, you can wander around Koriniti Marae, between the Whanganui River Rd and the river (look for the signs). Gold coin *koha* (donation) welcome but not necessary.

🏃 Activities

Canoeing & Kayaking
The most popular stretch of river for canoeing and kayaking is the 145km downstream run from Taumarunui to Pipiriki. This has been added to the NZ Great Walks system as the **Whanganui Journey**. It's a Grade II river – easy enough for the inexperienced, with enough roiling rapids to keep things interesting. If you need a Great Walks Ticket, you must arrange one before you start paddling.

Taumarunui to Pipiriki is a five-day/four-night trip, **Ohinepane to Pipiriki** is a four-day/three-night trip, and **Whakahoro to Pipiriki** is a three-day/two-night trip. **Taumarunui to Whakahoro** is a popular overnight trip, especially for weekenders, or you can do a one-day trip from **Taumarunui to Ohinepane** or **Ohinepane to Whakahoro**. From Whakahoro to Pipiriki, 87km downstream, there's no road access so you're wed to the river for a few days. Most canoeists stop at Pipiriki.

The season for canoe trips is usually from October to Easter. Up to 5000 people make the river trip each year, mostly between Christmas and the end of January. During winter the river is almost deserted – cold currents run swift and deep as wet weather and short days deter potential paddlers.

To hire a two-person Canadian canoe for one/three/five days costs around $100/200/250 per person not including transport (around $50 per person). A single-person kayak costs about $70 per day. Operators provide you with everything you need, including life jackets and waterproof drums (essential if you go bottom-up).

You can also take guided canoe or kayak trips – prices start at around $350/850 per person for a two-/five-day guided trip.

Whanganui River Canoes   CANOEING, KAYAKING
(☑ 0800 408 888, 06-385 4176; www.whanganuirivercanoes.co.nz; Raetihi Holiday Park, 10 Parapara Rd, Raetihi; hire per person 3/4/5 days from $160/170/180, guided trips per person 3/4/5 days from $665/785/885) Kayak and canoe hire, plus all-inclusive guided trips. The one-day trip – jetboat to Bridge to Nowhere then canoe down to Pipiriki – is a good option if you're short on time.

Owhango Adventures   CANOEING, KAYAKING
(Map p280; ☑ 0800 222 663, 07-895 4854, 027 678 6461; www.canoewhanganuiriver.com; 2191 SH4, Owhango; trips 1/2/3/4/5 days per person

from $100/150/170/170/170, river guides per day $225) Myriad multiday options down the big river, with or without a river guide to point out the sights. Book your own DOC accommodation. Two- to five-night trips with four or more people are eligible for a free night's accommodation before departure.

Adrift Guided
Outdoor Adventures
CANOEING

(☑07-892 2751, 0800 462 374; www.adriftnz.co.nz; 53 Carroll St, National Park Village; trips 1/3 days adult $295/950, child $260/680) Paddle downstream with the experts on these guided multi-day canoe trips on the wide Whanganui River. Pick-up and drop-off from Adrift's base in National Park Village, unless arranged prior.

Unique Whanganui
River Experience
CANOEING, KAYAKING

(☑027 5544 426; www.uniquewhanganuiriver. co.nz; 3-/4-/5-day trips from $800/900/1100) All-inclusive guided five-day river trips with a knowledgable and experienced local. Based in Feilding.

Blazing Paddles
CANOEING, KAYAKING

(Map p280; ☑0800 252 946, 021 996 954; www. blazingpaddles.co.nz; 985 SH4, Piriaka; trips 1-7 days per person $75-250) DIY Whanganui River canoe experiences from the Taumarunui end of proceedings, from one hour to one week. Transport and equipment included; DOC accommodation/camping costs not included. Secure vehicle storage a bonus.

Taumarunui Canoe Hire
CANOEING, KAYAKING

(☑07-895 7483, 0800 226 634; www.taumarunui canoehire.co.nz; 292 Hikumutu Rd, Taumarunui; trips per person from $65) Based in Taumarunui, these guys offer unguided hire river trips with plenty of background support (maps, DOC tickets, jetboats etc). Paddles from two hours to eight days.

Canoe Safaris
CANOEING, KAYAKING

(☑0800 272 3353, 06-385 9237; www.canoesafaris. co.nz; 6 Tay St, Ohakune; canoe hire 3/4/5 days $185/200/210) Three- to five-day DIY river trips with all the requisite supports, based in Ohakune. River guides and Rangitikei and Mohaka river trips also available.

Yeti Tours
CANOEING, KAYAKING

(☑0800 322 388, 06-385 8197; www.yetitours. co.nz; 3 Burns St, Ohakune; hire 2-8 days $175-260, 2-6 day tours $420-895) Canoe and kayak hire, plus guided Whanganui River trips.

Jetboating

Hold onto your hats – jetboat trips give you the chance to see parts of the river that would otherwise take you days to paddle through. Jetboats depart from Pipiriki and Whanganui; four-hour tours start at around $125 to $150 per person. Most operators can also provide transport to the river ends of the Matemateāonga and Mangapurua Tracks.

Bridge to Nowhere Tours
OUTDOORS

(☑0800 480 308, 06-385 4622; www.bridgeto nowhere.co.nz; 11 Owairua Rd, Pipiriki; jetboating adult/child from $140/70, 2-day canoeing adult/ child from $235/165) Jetboat tours, canoeing, mountain biking, tramping – the folks at Bridge to Nowhere Lodge (p258) coordinate it all, with accommodation and accommodation plus meal packages in the middle of nowhere afterwards.

Whanganui Scenic
Experience Jet
BOATING, CANOEING

(☑0800 945 335, 06-342 5599; www.whanganui scenicjet.com; 1195 Whanganui River Rd; 2-8hr trips adult $80-200, child $60-160) Jetboat tours up river from Whanganui, plus longer expeditions into the national park with tramping detours. Canoe and canoe/jetboat combo trips also available.

Whanganui River
Adventures
BOATING, CANOEING

(☑0800 862 743, 06-385 3246; www.whanganui riveradventures.co.nz; 2522 Pipiriki-Raetihi Rd, Pipiriki; trips from $80) Jetboat rides up river from Pipiriki, with camping, cabins and a cottage at Pipiriki also available. The one-day jetboat-and-canoe combo ($160) gives you a good taste of the national park if you're in a hurry.

Tramping

Bridge to Nowhere Track
TRAMPING

(☑06-349 2100; www.doc.govt.nz; Whanganui National Park; ⊘daylight hrs) FREE The most popular track in Whanganui National Park is the 40-minute walk from Mangapurua Landing (30km upstream from Pipiriki by jetboat) to the long-lost Bridge to Nowhere (p254). Contact jetboat operators for transport (around $100 per person one way).

Atene Viewpoint Walk
& Atene Skyline Track
TRAMPING

(☑06-349 2100; www.doc.govt.nz; Whanganui River Rd; ⊘daylight hrs) FREE At Atene, on the Whanganui River Rd about 22km north of the SH4 junction, tackle the short Atene Viewpoint Walk – about a one-hour ascent.

The track travels through native bush and farmland along a 1959 roadway built by the former Ministry of Works and Development during investigations for a Whanganui River hydroelectric scheme (a dam was proposed at Atene that would have flooded the river valley almost as far as Taumarunui). The track ends on a black beech ridge – expect great views across the national park.

Matemateāonga Track   TRAMPING
(☑06-349 2100; www.doc.govt.nz; Whanganui National Park) FREE Three to four days from end to end, the 42km Matemateāonga Track gets kudos as one of NZ's best walks. Probably due to its remoteness, it doesn't attract the hordes of trampers that amass on NZ's more famous tracks. Penetrating deep into wild bush and hill country, it follows the crest of the Matemateāonga Range along the route of the Whakaihuwaka Rd. Work on the road began in 1911 to create a more direct link from Stratford to the railway at Raetihi. WWI interrupted progress and the road was never finished.

Mangapurua/ Kaiwhakauka Track   TRAMPING
(☑06-349 2100; www.doc.govt.nz; Whanganui National Park) FREE The Mangapurua/ Kaiwhakauka Track is a 40km trail between Whakahoro and the Mangapurua Landing, both on the Whanganui River. The track runs along the Mangapurua and Kaiwhakauka Streams (both Whanganui River tributaries). Between these valleys a side track leads to the 663m **Mangapurua Trig**, the area's highest point, from which cloudless views extend to the Tongariro and Egmont National Park volcanoes. The route also passes the amazing Bridge to Nowhere (p254). Walking the track takes 20 hours (three to four days).

Mountain Biking

The Whanganui River Rd and Mangapurua/Kaiwhakauka Track have been incorporated into the 317km **Mountains to Sea** Mt Ruapehu–Whanganui bike track (www.mountainstosea.co.nz), itself part of the Nga Haerenga, New Zealand Cycle Trail project (www.nzcycletrail.com). As part of the experience, from Mangapurua Landing on the Whanganui River near the Bridge to Nowhere, you catch a (prebooked) jetboat downstream to Pipiriki, then continue riding down the Whanganui River Rd. For repairs and info, try Bike Shed (p252) in Whanganui.

ℹ REMOTE TRACK ACCESS

The Matemateāonga and Mangapurua/Kaiwhakauka Tracks are brilliant longer tramps (downloadable from www.doc.govt.nz). Both are one-way tracks beginning (or ending) at remote spots on the river, so you have to organise jetboat transport to or from the river trailheads – ask any jetboat operator. Between Pipiriki and the Matemateāonga Track is around $50 per person; for the Mangapurua Track it's around $100.

☞ Tours

Whanganui River Road Tours   TOURS
(☑027 318 9803; www.whanganuiriverroad.com; per person from $80) Hosted by Rory of Tamara Backpackers Lodge (p251), this is a five-hour minibus ride up the River Rd with lots of stops and commentary. Or, you can take a truncated tour up to Pipiriki and back. Minimum four people on both tours, pick-up and drop-off available.

Eastern Taranaki Experience   TOURS
(☑06-765 7482, 027 4717136, 027 246 6383; www.eastern-taranaki.co.nz; 5 Verona Place, Stratford; per person incl lunch from $210) Departing Stratford in neighbouring Taranaki (with pick-ups in Whanganui), these day trips take you up the Whanganui River Rd to Pipiriki, from where you jetboat upstream to tramp to the Bridge to Nowhere, then make the return journey. Minimum six people. Multi-day tours also available.

Whanganui Tours   TOURS
(☑027 201 2472, 06-345 3475; www.whanganuitours.co.nz; per person $63) Join the mail carrier on the Whanganui River Rd to Pipiriki (pick-up between 7.30am and 8am), with lots of social and historical commentary. Only one person needed on weekdays, but minimum of three on weekends. Returns mid-afternoon. Ask about transport/cycling options from Jerusalem back down the road to Whanganui.

🛏 Sleeping

🛏 Whanganui National Park

Whanganui National Park has a sprinkling of huts, a lodge and numerous camping grounds (free to $15 per hut outside of the Great Walks season, which runs October to April). Along the Taumarunui–Pipiriki section are two huts classified as Great Walk Huts during summer

TARANAKI & WHANGANUI WHANGANUI NATIONAL PARK

ⓘ CAMPING & HUTS PASSES

Great Walk Tickets are required in Whanganui National Park from 1 October to 30 April for the use of huts (adult/child $22 or $22/free) and campsites (adult/child $6 to $20/free) between Taumarunui and Pipiriki. Outside the main season you'll only need a **Backcountry Hut Pass** (adult/child for one year $122/61, for six months $92/46), or you can pay on a night-by-night basis (adult/child $5/2.50). Passes and tickets can be purchased online (www.greatwalks.co.nz); via email (greatwalks@doc.govt.nz); by phone (0800 694 732); or at DOC offices in Whakapapa, Taumarunui, Ohakune or Whanganui (p252).

($32 per night) and Backcountry Huts in the off-season: **John Coull Hut** and **Tieke Kainga Hut**, which has been revived as a *marae* (you can stay here, but full *marae* protocol must be observed – eg no alcohol). The **Whakahoro Bunkroom** is also on this stretch of river. On the lower part of the river, **Downes Hut** is on the west bank, opposite Atene.

Bridge to Nowhere Lodge   LODGE $

(☑ 06-385 4622, 0800 480 308; www.bridgetonowhere.co.nz; Whanganui National Park; tent/cabins/dm $15/30/55) This remote lodge lies deep in the national park, 21km upriver from Pipiriki near the Matemateāonga Track. The only way to get here is by jetboat from Pipiriki or on foot. It has a licensed bar, and meals are quality home-cooked affairs. The lodge also runs jetboat, canoe and mountain-bike trips (p256). Transport/accommodation/meals packages available, including DB&B from $155.

🛏 Whanganui River Road

Along the River Rd there are a couple of lodges for travellers to bunk down in. There's also a free informal campsite with toilets and cold water at Pipiriki, and another one (even less formal) just north of Atene. Also at Pipiriki are a campsite, some cabins and a cottage run by Whanganui River Adventures (p256).

Kohu Cottage   RENTAL HOUSE $

(☑ 06-342 8178; www.whanganuiriver.co.nz/accommodation1/kohu-cottage; 3154 Whanganui River Rd, Koroniti; 1/2/3 nights per night $100/80/70) A snug little cream-coloured weatherboard cottage (over 100 years old!)

above the road in Koriniti, sleeping four people and a fifth for an extra $10. It has a basic kitchen and a wood fire for chilly riverside nights. Pay less per night the longer you stay.

Flying Fox   LODGE, B&B $$

(☑ 06-927 6809; www.theflyingfox.co.nz; Whanganui River Rd; campsites $15, summer glamping dm $60, d $90-240; 🛜) 🚗 Accessible only by boat or eponymous flying fox (park on the side of Whanganui River Rd and launch yourself across the river), this eco-attuned getaway is on the riverbank across from Koriniti. You can self-cater in the Brewers Cottage, James K or Glory Cart; opt for B&B ($120 per person); or pitch a tent in a bush clearing.

Rivertime Lodge   LODGE $$

(☑ 06-342 5595; www.rivertimelodge.co.nz; 1569 Whanganui River Rd; per person Nov-Apr $50-60) Rivertime is a simple riverside cottage with two bedrooms, a laundry, a wood heater, a lovely deck and no TV. Three additional en suite cabins sleeping three people each make this a lovely spot for a group of 10, but rooms are hired out exclusively to one group at a time, so you can have the outdoor dining area overlooking the riverbank all to yourself. DB&B packages from $105 per person.

🍴 Eating

There's not much in the way of food on the road, but the casual cafe **Matahiwi Gallery** (☑ 06-342 8112; www.facebook.com/Matahiwigallery; 3925 Whanganui River Rd, Matahiwi; snacks $4-8; ⓧ 9am-4pm Wed-Sun Oct-May) is a charming stop – call ahead to ensure it's open. Otherwise, pack a sandwich.

ⓘ Information

For national park information, try the affable Whanganui (p252) or Taumarunui (p210) i-SITEs, or check out www.doc.govt.nz and www.whanganuiriver.co.nz. Otherwise, a more tangible resource is the NZ Recreational Canoeing Association's *Guide to the Whanganui River* ($10; see http://rivers.org.nz/whanganui-guide).

DOC's **Pipiriki** (☑ 06-385 5022; www.doc.govt.nz; Owairua Rd, Pipiriki; ⓧ irregular) and **Taumarunui** (☑ 07-895 8201; www.doc.govt.nz; Cherry Grove Domain, Taumarunui; ⓧ irregular) centres are field bases rather than tourist offices, and aren't always staffed.

Mobile-phone coverage along the River Rd is patchy at best.

ⓘ Getting There & Away

From the north, there's road access to the Whanganui River at Taumarunui, Ohinepane and

Whakahoro, though the last of these is a long, remote drive on mostly unsealed roads. Roads to Whakahoro lead off from Owhango and Raurimu, both on SH4. There isn't any further road access to the river until Pipiriki.

From the south, the Whanganui River Rd veers off SH4 14km north of Whanganui, rejoining it at Raetihi, 91km north of Whanganui. It takes about two hours to drive the 79km between Whanganui and Pipiriki. The full circle from Whanganui through Pipiriki and Raetihi and back along SH4 takes four hours minimum (longer if you want to stop, explore and take photos). Alternatively, take a River Rd tour from Whanganui.

There are no petrol stations or shops along the River Rd.

Palmerston North

☑06 / POP 80,080

The rich farming region of Manawatu embraces the districts of Rangitikei to the north and Horowhenua to the south. The hub of it all, on the banks of the Manawatu River, is Palmerston North. Massey University, New Zealand's largest, informs the town's cultural and social structures and as a result 'Palmy' has an open-minded, rurally bookish vibe.

However, none of this impressed a visiting John Cleese who reportedly said, 'If you wish to kill yourself but lack the courage to, I think a visit to Palmerston North will do the trick'. The city exacted revenge with an exemplary sense of humour by naming a rubbish dump after him. We think Cleese needs to return (it has been over a decade now) to explore excellent mountain biking and lush walking tracks beyond the city and great coffee, beer and friendly locals within.

◎ Sights

★ New Zealand Rugby Museum   MUSEUM
(☑06-358 6947; www.rugbymuseum.co.nz; Te Manawa Complex, 326 Main St; adult/child/family $12.50/5/30; ⊙10am-5pm) Fans of the oval ball holler about the New Zealand Rugby Museum, an amazing space overflowing with rugby paraphernalia, from a 1905 All Blacks jumper to a scrum machine and the actual whistle used to start the first game of every Rugby World Cup. Of course, NZ won back-to-back Rugby World Cups in 2011 and 2015: quiz the staff about the All Blacks' 2019 prospects.

★ Te Manawa   MUSEUM
(☑06-355 5000; www.temanawa.co.nz; 326 Main St; ⊙10am-5pm, to 7.30pm Thu; ♠) FREE Te Manawa merges a museum and art gallery into one experience, with vast collections joining the dots between art, science and history. The museum has a strong Māori focus and includes plenty of social history, information on native animals and wetlands, and an interactive science display on Manawatu River. The gallery's exhibits change frequently. Kids under eight will get a kick out of the interactive play area. The New Zealand Rugby Museum is in the same complex.

The Square   PARK
(☑06-356 8199; www.pncc.govt.nz; The Square; ⊙24hr) FREE Taking the English village green concept to a whole new level, the Square is Palmy's heart and soul. The Square's Māori name, Te Marae o Hine, was chosen to symbolise all tribes and races living together peacefully, which they certainly do when the sun comes out and everyone gathers on the lawn to lunch. The 7 spacey hectares feature a clock tower, duck pond, giant chess set, Māori carvings, statues and trees of all seasonal dispositions and free wi-fi.

🏃 Activities

Swing into the i-SITE (p262) and pick up the *Discover City Walkways* booklet and printouts of suggested itineraries for shoppers, eaters, explorers and everything in between.

Lido Aquatic Centre   SWIMMING
(☑06-357 2684; www.lidoaquaticcentre.co.nz; 50 Park Rd; adult/child/family $5/4/13.50, hydroslide day passes $12; ⊙6am-8pm Mon-Thu, to 9pm Fri, 8am-8pm Sat & Sun) When the summer plains bake, dive into the Lido Aquatic Centre. It's a long way from the Lido Beach in Venice, but it has a 50m pool, water slides, a cafe and a gym.

➔ Tours

Tui Brewery Tours   TOURS
(☑06-376 0815; www.tuihq.co.nz; 5 Mara St, Mangatainoka; 40min tours per person from $20; ⊙11am-5pm Sun-Thu, to 6pm Fri & Sat Nov-Apr, closes 1hr later May-Oct) Even if you're more of a craft-beer fan than a drinker of the ubiquitous Tui, this boozy brewery tour (11.30am and 2.30pm) 40km east of Palmy is a doldrum-beating outing (book ahead). Check out the interesting old brewery and museum, and taste a Tui or three. Tours aside, order lunch inside (mains $18 to $22) and enjoy the grassy outdoor tables in the sunshine.

Feilding Saleyard Tours   TOURS
(☑06-323 3318; www.feildingsaleyards.co.nz/stockyardtours; 10 Manchester Sq, Feilding; tours $10; ⊙11am Fri) Local farmers instruct you in the

gentle art of selling livestock at this small town 19km north of the city centre. Watch the auction in action, which sees an average of 15,000 sheep and 1400 cattle sold every week. Tickets are purchased at the information centre in Manchester Sq, but the saleyard is in Manchester St at the Livestock Centre.

✦ Festivals & Events

Festival of Cultures   CULTURAL
(☑ 06-351 4100; www.festivalofcultures.co.nz; The Square; ☺ late Mar) A massive one-day arts, culture and lifestyle festival, with a food-and-craft market in The Square (p259).

Manawatu International
Jazz & Blues Festival   MUSIC
(www.mjc.org.nz; ☺ late May-early Jun) All things jazzy, bluesy and swingin' across various venues – including free jazz in various cafes and big events at the Globe Theatre and Regent on Broadway (p262) – as well as plenty of workshops.

⌷ Sleeping

@ the Hub   HOTEL $
(☑06-356 8880; www.atthehub.co.nz; 25 Rangitikei St; r $99-170; ☎) There are two @ the Hubs, one WEST (short-term accommodation) and one EAST (long-term). The latter is geared to students, but travellers can book anything from a serviced en suite with kitchenette and simple student shoebox to a three-bedroom family apartment. Great location but fairly sterile. Ask for a window room overlooking the Square, or risk no windows at all.

Peppertree Hostel   HOSTEL $
(☑ 06-355 4054; www.peppertreehostel.co.nz; 121 Grey St; dm/s/d/f $31/65/78/124; ☎) Inexplicably strewn with green-painted, succulent-filled boots, this endearing 100-year-old house is the best budget option in town. Mattresses are thick, the kitchen will never run out of spatulas and the piano and wood fire make things feel downright homey. Unisex bathrooms, but there is a gals-only dorm. Nine rooms and 35 beds.

Palmerston North
Holiday Park   HOLIDAY PARK $
(☑ 06-3580349;www.palmerstonnorthholidaypark. co.nz; 133 Dittmer Dr; campsites/cabins from $35/50, d/f units $95/105; ☎▣) About 2km from the Square, off Ruha St, this shady park with daisy-speckled lawns is quiet, affordable and right beside Victoria Esplanade gardens. Trees and gardens add calm, until the kids take over the playground!

Destiny Motel   MOTEL $$
(☑ 06-355 0050; www.destinymotel.co.nz; 127 Fitzherbert Ave; d/ste/2-bedroom from $145/165/259; ☑ ☎) Destiny's studios and suites pop with colours and patterns, making it stand out from the safe-but-boring colour schemes of most motels. Stylish, contemporary and with all the mod cons, it's more like a boutique hotel.

Primrose Manor   GUESTHOUSE $$
(☑ 06-355 4213; www.primrosemanor.co.nz; 123 Grey St; d $120-145; ☎) ✆ Managed by Peppertree Hostel next door, Primrose Manor is a more upmarket and endearing guesthouse. It has a fancy central communal kitchen and lounge with five guest rooms beyond, most with en suites and all with TVs. Help yourself to the fruit trees, but check before you book – when we visited renovations were underway and long-term tenants are common.

✕ Eating

★Saigon Corner   VIETNAMESE $
(☑ 06-355 4988; www.facebook.com/saigoncorner nz; 54 Princess St; mains $8.50-16; ☺ 11am-3pm & 5-8.30pm Tue-Sat, 11am-3pm Mon; ☑) The pick of Palmy cheap eats, this cheerful, casual Vietnamese restaurant nails all the classics: *pho, banh mi*, rice-paper rolls and noodle and rice dishes. Fresh and filled with locals, it's good to eat in or take away.

★Local   CAFE $
(☑06-280 4821; www.cafelocal.co.nz; 240 Broadway Ave; dishes $10-15; ☺7am-3.30pm Mon-Wed, to 7pm Thu & Fri, 8am-4pm Sat; ☎▣) Brilliant Local specialises in build-your-own meals. For breakfast, that means eggs with additions like potato herb hash and grilled salmon, and for lunch, wholesome bowls with your choice of protein on salad. Sharing the building with property brokers, Local scores top marks for the teal banquettes, tiled features and a roomy outdoor area. Don't leave without ordering curly fries.

Arranged Marriage   SOUTH INDIAN $$
(☑06-351 6300; www.arrangedmarriage.co.nz; 32b The Square; $16-23; ☺noon-2pm & 5-9.30pm Tue-Sun; ☑) A taste of Kerala right on The Square, this is the second restaurant from the Kathakali (p238) team in New Plymouth. The decor is fun and vibrant without being gaudy (love the coconut wall) and the food aromatic. You'll find butter chicken and vegetable korma here, but order the signature *dosa*. The $12 lunch deals are great, too.

Palmerston North

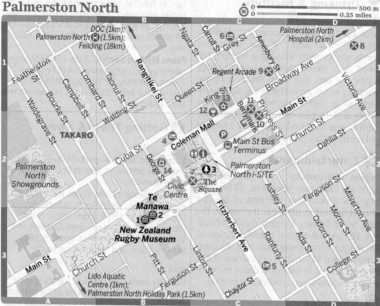

Palmerston North

◎ Top Sights
1 New Zealand Rugby Museum B3
2 Te Manawa B3

◎ Sights
3 The Square C2

⌂ Sleeping
4 @ the Hub B2
5 Destiny Motel C3
Peppertree Hostel .... (see 6)
6 Primrose Manor C1

✕ Eating
7 Arranged Marriage C2
8 Local D1

9 Nero Restaurant C1
10 Saigon Corner C2
11 Yeda C1

◉ Drinking & Nightlife
12 Brew Union C1

◉ Entertainment
13 Regent on Broadway C1

◉ Shopping
14 Bruce McKenzie Booksellers B2

Yeda   ASIAN **$$**
(☎06-358 3978; www.yeda.co.nz; 78 Broadway
Ave; mains $16-19; ⊘11am-9pm) Yeda feels a lit-
tle like a beer or uni hall, probably because
the long, minimalist room with concrete
floors is packed with students. It covers all
Asian bases, from Vietnamese *pho* to Thai
chicken and dumplings. Sip sake or an Asahi
while you wait (which won't be long). Ask
about Saturday afternoon cooking classes
($40 per person).

★Nero Restaurant   INTERNATIONAL **$$$**
(☎06-354 0312; www.nerorestaurant.co.nz; 36
Amesbury St; mains $39-44; ⊘11am-3pm & 5pm-
late Mon-Fri, 5pm-late Sat) Set in a refreshed
1918 Victorian with a manicured alfresco
dining area, Nero is the peak of fine dining
in Palmy. The chef and owner is an ambas-
sador for Beef & Lamb New Zealand, but
also serves dishes like sticky pork belly and
cauliflower steak with flair. Look out for the
dry-aged beef and say 'hi' to Truffles, the cat.

🍷 Drinking & Nightlife

⭐ Brew Union
MICROBREWERY

(📞06-280 3146; www.brewunion.co.nz; 41 Broadway Ave; ⏰11am-10pm) 🍴 An impressive warehouse formerly housing a butcher, followed by a record store and sports shop, is now the best spot for a drink in Palmy. Reaching across an entire block, the microbrewery-bar and restaurant has 21 beers on tap and 45 gins on the shelf. Come for a drink, stay for wood-fired pizza. Live DJs and music Friday through Sunday.

☆ Entertainment

Regent on Broadway
PERFORMING ARTS

(📞06-350 2100; www.regent.co.nz; 53 Broadway Ave) This theatre was the gem of the city when it opened in 1930, but it closed in the early '90s following a steady decline of visitors. The council stepped in and contributed $10 million to the restoration, and the community raised $1.7 million (an average of $25 for every person in the city!). Check the website for musicals, plays, ballet and beyond.

🛍 Shopping

⭐ Herb Farm
COSMETICS

(📞06 326 8633; www.homeoftheherbfarm.co.nz; Grove Rd, RD10; ⏰10am-4.30pm; ♿) Demand for Lynn Kirkland's homemade natural remedies led to the Herb Farm opening in 1993. Her daughter joined the business, and together they sell beautiful, natural skincare and health products on 1 hectare of fairytale-like gardens. Less than 20 minutes from central Palmy, grab a free-range, organic bite at the cafe ($13 to $22) and enjoy the serenity.

Bruce McKenzie Booksellers
BOOKS

(📞06-356 9922; www.bmbooks.co.nz; 37 George St; ⏰9am-5.30pm Mon-Fri, to 5pm Sat, 10am-4pm Sun) An excellent independent bookshop. Pick up that guide to NZ craft beer you've been looking for and browse through novels by NZ authors.

ℹ Information

DOC (Department of Conservation; 📞06-350 9700; www.doc.govt.nz; 28 North St; ⏰8am-4.30pm Mon-Fri) DOC information, 2km north of the Square.

Palmerston North Hospital (📞06-356 9169; www.midcentraldhb.govt.nz; 50 Ruahine St; ⏰24hr) Accident and emergency assistance.

Palmerston North i-SITE (📞0800 6262 9288, 06-350 1922; www.manawatunz.co.nz; The Square; ⏰9am-5.30pm Mon-Thu, to 7pm Fri & Sun, to 3pm Sat; 📶) A super-helpful source of tourist information, now hiring out electric bikes (hourly/half day/full day $30/45/65). Love the A4 printed guides to local walks, parks, shopping and more.

Palms Medical Centre (📞06-354 7737; www.careforyou.co.nz/the-palms; 445 Ferguson St; ⏰8am-8pm daily, GP 9am-5pm Mon-Fri) Urgent medical help, plus doctors by appointment and a pharmacy.

ℹ Getting There & Away

AIR

Palmerston North Airport (📞06-351 4415; www.pnairport.co.nz; Airport Dr) is 4km north of the town centre.

Air New Zealand (www.airnewzealand.co.nz) runs daily direct flights to Auckland, Christchurch and Wellington. Jetstar (www.jetstar.com) has flights to/from Auckland and Wellington. Originair (www.originair.nz) flies between Palmy and Nelson, down south.

BUS

InterCity (www.intercity.co.nz) buses operate from the **Main St bus terminus** on the east side of the Square; destinations include the following:

DESTINATION	COST	TIME (HR)	FREQUENCY (DAILY)
Auckland	from $42	9½	3
Napier	from $24	3½	3
Taupo	from $24	4	3
Wellington	from $22	2¼	9
Whanganui	from $18	1½	4

Naked Bus (www.nakedbus.com) services also depart the Main St bus terminus to most North Island hubs:

DESTINATION	COST	TIME (HR)	FREQUENCY (DAILY)
Auckland	from $28	10	2-4
Napier	from $22	2½	2-4
Taupo	from $15	4	2-3
Wellington	from $13	2½	2-4

TRAIN

KiwiRail Scenic Journeys (📞0800 872 467, 04-495 0775; www.kiwirailscenic.co.nz) runs long-distance trains between Wellington and Auckland, stopping at the retro-derelict **Palmerston North Train Station** (Mathews Ave), off Tremaine Ave about 2.5km north of the Square. From Palmy to Wellington, take the Northern Explorer ($69, 2½ hours) departing at 4.20pm Monday, Thursday and Saturday; or the Capital Connection ($35, two hours) departing Palmy at 6.15am Monday to Friday.

To Auckland, the Northern Explorer ($179, nine hours) departs at 10am on Tuesday, Friday and Sunday. Buy tickets from KiwiRail Scenic Journeys directly, or on the train and at the i-Site for the Capital Connection (no ticket sales at the station).

ⓘ Getting Around

TO/FROM THE AIRPORT

The Palmerston North–Feilding and Feilding–Palmerston North bus services travel via the airport. Taxis abound and **Super Shuttle** (☑ 0800 748 885, 09-522 5100; www.supershuttle.co.nz; tickets from $18) can whizz you into town in a minivan (prebooking required). A city-to-airport taxi costs around $20.

BICYCLE

Crank It Cycles (☑ 06-358 9810; www.crankit cycles.co.nz; 244 Cuba St; half/full day $35/50; ⊙ 8am-5.30pm Mon-Fri, 9.30am-3pm Sat, 10am-2pm Sun) hires out city bikes, including helmet and lock (deposit $50). You can also hire electric bikes from the i-SITE.

BUS

Horizons (☑ 06 9522 800, 0508 800 800; www.horizons.govt.nz; adult/child $2.50/1.50) Runs daytime buses departing from the Main St bus terminus on the east side of the Square. The Palmerston North–Feilding and Feilding–Palmerston North bus services now travel via the airport. Buy a GoCard on the bus or at the i-Site if you're in town for a while.

TAXI

Gold & Black Taxis (☑ 0800 351 2345, 06-351 2345; www.taxisgb.co.nz) Family-run local taxi outfit.

Around Palmerston North

Venture outside Palmerston North for landscapes and beaches in direct contrast with the faster, more corporate pace of the student city. About 12km east of town, SH2 dips into Manawatu Gorge. Māori named the gorge Te Apiti (the Narrow Passage), believing the big reddish rock near the centre of the gorge was its guardian spirit. It's an 11km, uphill slant to get to the viewpoints and takes around four hours one way. On the southwestern edge of the Gorge is the **Taratua Wind Farm**. North of the Gorge is **Te Āpiti Wind Farm**.

At the time of writing, the SH3 road through the Manawatu Gorge was closed due to landslips, but the walking tracks were open. Check before you go at the Palmerston North i-SITE or with the lo-cal Department of Conservation (call 06-350 9700).

South of Palmerston North is **Shannon** (population 1240) and **Foxton** (population 2650), quiet country towns en route to Wellington. **Foxton Beach** is one of a string of broad, shallow Tasman Sea beaches along this stretch of coast – other worthy beaches include **Himatangi**, **Hokio** and **Waikawa**. **Levin** (population 20,900) is more sizeable, but is too close to both Wellington and Palmerston North to warrant the through-traffic making an extended stop.

Park yourself in Palmy in the evening and treat the rest as day-trip terrain. Take your own car; otherwise InterCity (www.intercity.co.nz) and Naked Bus (www.nakedbus.com) services pass through Levin and Shannon (and sometimes Foxton) en route between Palmerston North and Wellington.

◉ Sights

Tararua Wind Farm   FARM
(☑ 027 244 1049; www.windenergy.org.nz/tararua -wind-farm; Hall Block Rd, Ballance; ⊙ 24hr) On the southwestern edge of Manawatu Gorge, about 40-minutes' drive from Palmerston North, is the Tararua Wind Farm, allegedly the largest wind farm in the southern hemisphere. It's on private land, but it's worth the drive up the winding, unsealed road for the views and to feel your car shake in the wind – even if you can't go past the 'private property' gate at the top.

Te Āpiti Wind Farm   LANDMARK
(☑ 0800 496 496; www.meridianenergy.co.nz/ about-us/te-apiti; Saddle Rd, Woodville; ⊙ 24hr) 🆓 Spinning north of Manawatu Gorge is Te Āpiti Wind Farm. The 55 turbines create enough power for around 39,000 New Zealand homes each year. It's on private land, but through the gate there is a public viewing platform with mesmerising views, just off Saddle Rd – ask the Palmerston North i-SITE for directions. It's more accessible than Tararua Wind Farm.

🏃 Activities

Timeless Horse Treks   HORSE RIDING
(☑ 027 446 8536, 06-376 6157; www.timelesshorse treks.co.nz; Gorge Rd, Ballance; 30/60/90min rides from $25/50/85; ➡) Flee Palmerston North and visit Timeless Horse Treks. Gentle trail rides take in the Manawatu River and surrounding hills. Palmy pick-up/drop-off available.

Taupo & the Ruapehu Region

Best Places to Eat

➜ Cadillac Cafe (p278)

➜ Storehouse (p274)

➜ Southern Meat Kitchen (p275)

➜ Spoon & Paddle (p275)

➜ Blind Finch (p289)

Best Places to Stay

➜ Station Lodge (p288)

➜ Braxmere (p277)

➜ River Lodge (p289)

➜ Lake Motel (p273)

➜ Ruapehu Country Lodge (p289)

Why Go?

Welcome to the New Zealand you've been waiting for, a picturesque landscape characterised as much by volcanic mountains as it is by bodies of water and native forest. Much of it is thanks to the Taupo Volcanic Zone – a line of geothermal activity that stretches via Rotorua to Whakaari (White Island) in the Bay of Plenty. It's beautiful, but it's what's on the inside that counts: thermal activity bubbling beneath the surface that's responsible for some of the North Island's star attractions, including the country's largest lake and the three snowcapped peaks of Tongariro National Park.

Thrill seekers are in for a treat – the area rivals Queenstown for outdoor escapades. And when the action finally exhausts you (or if you had a relaxing holiday in mind), try some therapeutic fly-fishing or soak the day away in a thermal bath. There's truly something for everyone in Taupo and the Ruapehu region.

When to Go

➜ Equally popular in winter and summer, there's not really a bad time to visit the centre of New Zealand.

➜ The ski season runs roughly from July to October, but storms and freezing temperatures can occur at any time on the mountains, and above 2500m there is a permanent snowcap.

➜ Due to its altitude, the Ruapehu region has a generally cool climate, with average high temperatures ranging from 0°C in winter up to around 24°C in summer.

➜ Lake Taupo is swamped with Kiwi holidaymakers from Christmas to late January, so it pays to book ahead for accommodation during this time.

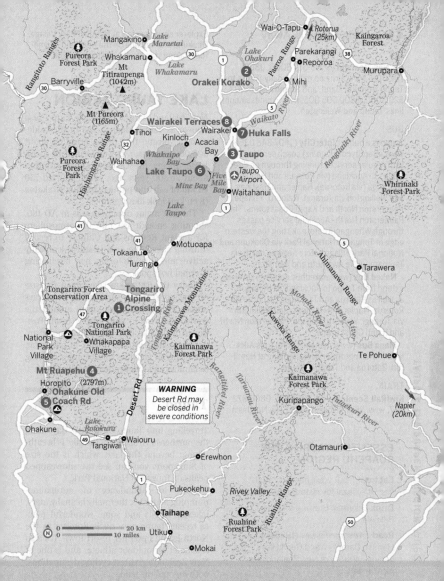

Taupo & the Ruapehu Region Highlights

❶ Tongariro Alpine Crossing (p282) Seeing why this is considered the best one-day tramp in New Zealand.

❷ Orakei Korako (p271) Rediscovering this volcanic 'lost valley'.

❸ Taupo (p266) Bungy jumping with a view towards Waikato River.

❹ Mt Ruapehu (p281) Skiing through fresh powder at Turoa or Whakapapa.

❺ Ohakune Old Coach Road (p287) Mountain biking over the 284m Hapuawhenua Viaduct.

❻ Lake Taupo (p269) Kayaking or cruising to the modern Māori rock carvings.

❼ Huka Falls (p269) Jetboating up the Waikato River to the base of the falls.

❽ Wairakei Terraces (p268) Soaking up the healing geothermal waters of these hot pools.

ⓘ Getting There & Away

AIR

Air New Zealand (☎ 09-357 3000, 0800 737 000; www.airnz.co.nz) has daily flights to Taupo from Auckland, and **Sounds Air** (☎ 03 520 3080, 0800 505 005; www.soundsair.com) links Taupo and Wellington.

BUS

Taupo is a hub for **InterCity** (☎ 07-348 0366; www.intercitycoach.co.nz) coach services, with regular services running through on direct routes to Auckland (via Rotorua and Hamilton), Tauranga (via Rotorua), Napier and Hastings, and Wellington via Turangi, Waiouru, Taihape, Palmerston North and Kapiti Coast towns. The Palmerston North–Auckland service passes through Whanganui before skirting the western edge of Tongariro National Park via Ohakune and National Park Village before heading north via Taumaranui, Te Awamutu and Hamilton.

Naked Bus (www.nakedbus.com/nz) services extend from Taupo to Auckland via Hamilton, as well as Rotorua and Tauranga, Gisborne via Rotorua, Napier and Hastings, and Wellington via Turangi, Waiouru, Taihape, Palmerston North and Kapiti Coast towns.

Mana Bus (www.manabus.com) runs Auckland to Wellington services stopping at Hamilton, Rotorua and Taupo en route.

TRAIN

KiwiRail Scenic (☎ 04-495 0775, 0800 872 467; www.kiwirailscenic.co.nz) The Northern

---

ESSENTIAL TAUPO & THE RUAPEHU REGION
....

Eat trout – but you'll have to catch it first! It's illegal for restaurants to serve it.

Drink Lakeman Brewing's Taupo Pale Ale.

Read *Awesome Forces* (1998) by Hamish Campbell and Geoff Hicks – the geological story of New Zealand in explosive detail.

Listen to the sonorous chirruping of tui along the Tongariro River Trail.

Watch *The Lord of the Rings* and *The Hobbit* movies, and spot Tongariro's movie-star mountains and rapids.

Go green and pedal Taupo's Craters MTB Park.

Go online www.greatlaketaupo.com, www.visitruapehu.com, www.national park.co.nz, www.visitohakune.co.nz

---

Explorer services stop at National Park Village, Ohakune and Taihape on the Auckland–Hamilton–Palmerston North–Wellington route.

LAKE TAUPO REGION

New Zealand's largest lake, Lake Taupo (also known as Taupo Moana), sits in the caldera of a volcano that began erupting about 300,000 years ago. It was formed by a collapse during the Oruanui super eruption about 26,500 years ago, which spurted 750 cu km of ash and pumice, making Krakatoa (8 cu km) look like a pimple.

The last major cataclysm was in AD 180, shooting enough ash into the atmosphere for ancient Romans and Chinese to record unusual skies. The area is still volcanically active and, like Rotorua, has fascinating thermal hot spots.

Today the 622-sq-km lake (about the size of Singapore) and its surrounding waterways attract fishing enthusiasts from around the world who visit to snag trophy trout. Positioned by the lake, both Taupo and Turangi are popular tourist centres. Taupo, in particular, has plenty of activities and facilities catering to families and independent travellers alike.

Taupo

☎ 07 / POP 32,900

Travelling into Taupo on a clear day along the northeastern shores of the lake is breathtaking: beyond the lake, which is the size of Singapore, you can see the snowcapped peaks of Tongariro National Park.

With an abundance of adrenaline-pumping activities, thermally heated waters, lakeside strolls and some wonderful places to eat, Taupo now rivals Rotorua as the North Island's premier resort town. It's also a magnet for outdoor athletes and is one of New Zealand's greatest cycling destinations, both on- and off-road.

The Waikato River, NZ's longest, starts at Lake Taupo in the township, before crashing its way through the Huka Falls and Aratiatia Rapids and then settling down for a sedate ramble to the west coast, just south of Auckland.

History

Let's start at the start, back in AD 180 when the Taupo eruption became the largest and most violent in recorded history. Debris was

Central Taupo

Central Taupo

⊙ Top Sights
1 Taupo Museum A2

✈ Activities, Courses & Tours
2 Big Sky Parasail.. A2
3 Canoe & Kayak..B1
  Ernest Kemp Cruises....................... (see 2)
  Fish Cruise Taupo .... (see 2)
4 Lake Fun Taupo.. A2
5 Pack & Pedal.. B2
6 Rafting NZ Adventure Centre................. B2
  Sail Barbary .... (see 2)
  Taupo Troutcatcher.......................... (see 4)
7 Taupo's Floatplane................................... A2

🛏 Sleeping
8 Finlay Jacks..C1
9 Haka Lodge C2

🍴 Eating
10 Bistro B2
11 Brantry D3
12 Malabar Beyond India B2
13 Merchant... C1
14 Pauly's Diner... B1
15 Replete Cafe & Store............................... B2
  Southern Meat Kitchen................ (see 12)
16 Spoon & Paddle C2
17 Storehouse.. B1

🍷 Drinking & Nightlife
18 Crafty Trout Brewing.............................. B1
19 Lakehouse B2
20 Vine Eatery & Bar.................................... B2

🛍 Shopping
  Kura Gallery .... (see 15)
21 Taupo Market... B1

deposited as far as 30,000 sq km and all of New Zealand was covered in ash, in some places up to 10m deep. Everything living was destroyed and there were reports from ancient Rome and China of unusual red sunsets. In the process, Lake Taupo formed in the volcanic caldera.

But Māori legend tells of Ngātoro-i-rangi, a priest who created the lake while searching for a place to settle. Climbing to the top of Mt Tauhara, he saw a vast dust bowl. He hurled a totara tree into it and fresh water swelled to form the lake. One of the early Māori, Tia, was first to explore the region. After Tia discovered the lake and slept beside it draped in his cloak, it became known as Taupō Nui a Tia (Great Cloak of Tia). Descendants of the original Ngāti Tūwharetoa inhabitants remain today.

Taupo & Wairakei

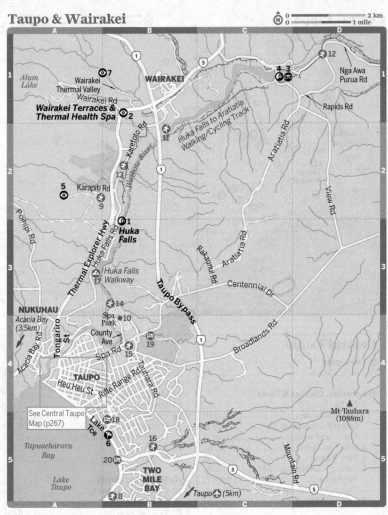

Europeans settled here in force during the East Coast Land War (1868–72), when Taupo was a strategic military base. A redoubt was built in 1869 and a garrison of mounted police remained until the defeat of Te Kooti later that year.

In the 20th century the mass ownership of the motorcar saw Taupo grow from a lakeside village of about 750 people to a large resort town, easily accessible from most points on the North Island. Today the population increases considerably at peak holiday times, when New Zealanders and international visitors alike flock to the 'Great Lake'.

◉ Sights

Many of Taupo's attractions are outside the town, with a high concentration around Wairakei to the north. The main attraction in the centre is the lake and everything you can do in, on and around it.

★ Wairakei Terraces & Thermal Health Spa
HOT SPRINGS
(☏ 07-378 0913; www.wairakeiterraces.co.nz; Wairakei Rd; thermal walk adult/child $15/7.50, pools $25, massage from $85; ⊗ 8.30am-9pm Oct-Mar, to 8.30pm Apr-Sep, closes 7pm Thu) ✿ Mineral-laden waters from the Wairakei

Taupo & Wairakei

geothermal steamfield cascade over silica terraces into pools (open to those 14 years and older) nestled in native gardens. For the price, we think there are better self-guided tours than the **Terraces Walkway** featuring a recreated Māori village, and artificially made geysers and silica terraces, but spending a few hours soaking in the therapeutic waters is well worthwhile.

Visit at dusk and watch the sunset over the pools. The evening **Māori Cultural Experience** (adult/child $104/52) includes a traditional challenge, welcome, concert, tour and *hāngi* meal and gives an insight into Māori life in the geothermal areas.

★**Huka Falls**   WATERFALL
(www.greatlaketaupo.com; Huka Falls Rd) Clearly signposted and with a car park and kiosk, these falls mark where NZ's longest river, the Waikato, is slammed into a narrow chasm, making a dramatic 11m drop into a surging crystal-blue pool at 220,000 litres per second. From the footbridge you can see the full force of this torrent that the Māori called Hukanui (Great Body of Spray).

★**Taupo Museum**   MUSEUM
(☏07-376 0414; www.taupodc.govt.nz; 4 Story Pl; adult/child $5/free; ⊙10am-4.30pm) With an excellent Māori gallery and quirky displays, which include a 1960s caravan set up as if the occupants have just popped down to the lake, this little museum makes an interesting rainy-day diversion. The centrepiece is an elaborately carved Māori meeting house, Te Aroha o Rongoheikume. Historical displays cover local industries, volcanic activity and a mock-up of a 19th-century shop.

Māori Rock Carvings   HISTORIC SITE
Accessible only by boat, these 10m-high carvings were etched into the cliffs near Mine Bay by master carver Matahi Whakataka-Brightwell in the late 1970s. They depict Ngātoro-i-rangi, the visionary Māori navigator who guided the Tūwharetoa and Te Arawa tribes to the Taupo area 1000 years ago. Go bright and early or take a sunset cruise.

**Wairakei Natural
Thermal Valley**   NATURAL FEATURE
(☏07-374 8004; www.wairakeitouristpark.co.nz; Wairakei Thermal Valley, off SH1; adult/child $10/5; ⊙9am-1hr before sunset) This thermal walk (around 1.8km) is on a secluded property and peaceful camping site, surrounded by peacocks and other animals (sites $18 to $21 per person, cabins $75 to 95, a cottage from $125, summer teepee from November to early April – depending on the weather – $65 to 85). Tickets are purchased from the **cafe** to explore mud pools, silica formations, the 'champagne cauldron' and rare and endangered plant life. Kids will get a kick out of pointing the loaned thermal laser gun.

Aratiatia Rapids   WATERFALL
(www.greatlaketaupo.com) Two kilometres off SH5, this was a spectacular part of the Waikato River until the government plonked a hydroelectric dam across the waterway, shutting off the flow. But the floodgates still open from October to March at 10am, noon, 2pm and 4pm and April to September at 10am, noon and 2pm. You can see the water surge through the dam from two good **vantage points** (off Aratiatia Rd).

Craters of the Moon
NATURAL FEATURE

(☑027 6564 684; www.cratersofthemoon.
co.nz; Karapiti Rd; adult/child/family $8/4/20;
⊘8.30am-5pm) This geothermal area sprang
to life when hydroelectric tinkering around
the power station caused water levels to fall.
The pressure shifted, creating new steam
vents and bubbling mud pools. The 2.7km
perimeter loop walk takes about 45 minutes
and affords great views down to the lake and
mountains beyond. There's a kiosk at the entrance, staffed by volunteers who keep an
eye on the car park.

🏃 Activities

Adrenaline addicts should look out for special deals that combine several activities for
a reduced price. Some operators offer backpacker discounts.

For megadiscounts on rafting, sailing to
the Māori Rock Carvings (p269), cultural
experiences and more, try booking through
www.bookme.co.nz or www.grabone.co.nz/
rotorua-taupo.

Adventure & Adrenaline

⭐**Taupo Bungy**
BUNGEE JUMPING

(☑0800 888 408; www.taupobungy.co.nz; 202 Spa
Rd; solo/tandem jump $169/338; ⊘9.30am-5pm)
On a cliff high above the Waikato River, this
picturesque bungy site is the North Island's
most popular. The courageous throw themselves off the edge of a platform, jutting 34m
out over the cliff, for a heart-stopping 47m
plunge. The 11m Cliffhanger swing is just as
terrifying (solo/tandem swing $145/290).

Skydive Taupo
SKYDIVING

(☑07-378 4662, 0800 586 766; www.skydivetaupo.
co.nz; Anzac Memorial Dr; 12,000ft/15,000ft jump
from $279/359) Packages available (from
$458), including a reduced-price second
jump for altitude junkies.

Rafting NZ Adventure
Centre
ADVENTURE SPORTS

(Adventure Centre; ☑0508 238 3688, 07-378
8482; www.theadventurecentre.co.nz; 47 Ruapehu St; ⊘9am-5pm Dec-May, 10am-5pm Jun-Nov)
With a handy location in central Taupo, this
well-run operation can hook you up with
everything from rafting on the Tongariro
River through to skydiving, jetboating and
bungy jumping, and more leisurely pursuits
such as lake cruises and fishing. Also home
of the **Adventure 6D Cinema**, where you
can virtually go rafting and plunge off waterfalls (adult/child $15/9).

Hukafalls Jet
ADVENTURE SPORTS

(☑07-374 8572, 0800 485 253; www.hukafallsjet.
com; 200 Karetoto Rd; adult/child $129/89) This
30-minute thrill ride takes you up the river to the spray-filled foot of the Huka Falls
and down to the Aratiatia Dam, all the
while dodging daringly and doing acrobatic
360-degree turns. Trips run all day, weather
dependent (prices include shuttle transport
from Taupo).

Rapids Jet
ADVENTURE SPORTS

(☑07-374 8066, 0800 727 437, 0274 308 730;
www.rapidsjet.com; Nga Awa Purua Rd; adult/
child $115/65; ⊘9am-5pm Oct-Mar, 10am-4pm
Apr-Sep) This sensational 35-minute ride
shoots along the lower part of the Aratiatia
Rapids – rivalling boat trips to Huka Falls
for thrills (and price!). The boat departs
from the end of the access road to the Aratiatia lookouts. Go down Rapids Rd and then
turn into Nga Awa Purua Rd.

Big Sky Parasail
ADVENTURE SPORTS

(☑0800 724 4759; www.bigskyparasail.co.nz;
Taupo Boat Harbour, Redoubt St; tandem/solo
$95/115; ⊘9am-6pm mid-Oct–May) Lofty para-
sailing flights from the lakefront. Choose
from 1000ft or 500ft, although according to
one instructor, the latter is 'like going halfway up a Ferris wheel'. Bookings essential.
Early bird special $85.

Rock'n Ropes
OUTDOORS

(☑0800 244 508, 07-374 8111; www.rocknropes.
co.nz; 65 Karetoto Rd; per person $20-70; ⊘weath-
er dependent) Beside **Huka Honey Hive** (☑07-
374 8553; www.hukahoneyhive.com; ⊘10am-5pm)
is this dare-devilish high-ropes course. With
high-flying bridges, trapeze, zipline and a
giant swing, you might be tempted to stay
on the ground – but know that everyone
from four to 86-years of age has given it a
go. Feeling brave? Check out the latest addition: the only five-storey free fall in the
country.

Walking & Cycling

Grab trail maps and hire bikes from **Pack
& Pedal** (☑07-377 4346; www.packandpedal
taupo.com; 5 Tamamutu St; 2hr/half-day/full-
day rental $30/40/60; ⊘8.30am-6pm Mon-Fri,
8.30am-5pm Sat, 9am-4pm Sun) or the i-SITE
(p276), including the *10 Great Rides* map.
You'll need to become a temporary member
of **Bike Taupo** (www.biketaupo.org.nz; $10 for
one week) to ride on local tracks. The bike
shops in town can sort out a temporary
membership.

ORAKEI KORAKO

A little off the beaten track, **Orakei Korako** (07-378 3131; www.orakeikorako.co.nz; 494 Orakei Korako Rd; adult/child $36/15; 8am-4.30pm) gets fewer visitors than other thermal areas. But since the destruction of the Pink and White Terraces, it's arguably the best thermal area left in New Zealand, with active geysers, stunning terraces, bubbling rainbow land and the country's only geothermal cave.

A walking track follows stairs and boardwalks around the colourful silica terraces for which the park is famous, and passes geysers and Ruatapu Cave (allow 1½ hours). This impressive natural cave has a jade-green pool, thought to have been used as a mirror by Māori women preparing for rituals (Orakei Korako means 'the Place of Adorning').

Entry includes the boat ride across the lake from the visitor centre. Take your phone if you're there during quieter periods – the ferry driver doesn't always do the best job of keeping a look out for those waiting for the return trip!

MudCake Cafe is located inside the visitor centre with basic food but a lovely terrace overlooking Lake Ohakuri.

Orakei Korako is about 30km from Taupo centre and just over 65km from Rotorua. There's no public transport, but you can also arrive with a splash via **New Zealand River Jet** (0800 748 375, 07-333 7111; www.riverjet.co.nz; Mihi Bridge, SH5; adult/child $179/99, incl entry to Orakei Korako).

There's nowhere to stay in the area, with most travellers visiting en route to/from Rotorua and Taupo. From Taupo, take SH1 towards Hamilton for 23km, and then travel for 14km from the signposted turn-off. From Rotorua the turn-off is on SH5, via Mihi.

Huka Falls Walkway   WALKING, CYCLING

(County Ave) Starting from the Spa Park car park at the end of County Ave (off Spa Rd), this scenic, easy walk is just over 3km one way to reach Huka Falls, following the east bank of the Waikato River. Continuing on from the falls is the 7km **Huka Falls to Aratiatia Rapids Walking Track** (another two-plus hours). The Taupo–Huka Falls–Aratiatia loop bike ride will take around four hours in total.

Craters MTB Park   MOUNTAIN BIKING

(www.biketaupo.org.nz; Karapiti Rd; 24hr) FREE For 50km of exciting off-road mountain-biking trails for all abilities, head to the Craters MTB Park, around 10 minutes' drive north of Taupo in the Wairakei Forest just before the Craters of the Moon entrance.

Don't forget to arrange a temporary membership with **Bike Taupo** before heading up there.

Great Lake Trail   WALKING, CYCLING

(www.greatlaketrail.com) A purpose-built 71km track from Whakaipo Bay to Waihaha in the remote northwestern reaches of the lake. The **W2K** section between Whakaipo and Kinloch has splendid views across the lake to Tongariro National Park.

Hot Springs

Soak in the hot pools at Wairakei Terraces (p268) or follow the locals to the Spa Thermal Park Hot Spring.

★ **Spa Thermal Park Hot Spring**   HOT SPRINGS

(Country Ave; 7am-8pm) FREE The hot thermal waters of the Otumuheke Stream meet the bracing Waikato River at this pleasant and well-worn spot under a bridge, creating a free spa bath with natural nooks. Take care: people have drowned trying to cool off in the fast-moving river. It's near the beginning of the Huka Falls Walkway, a couple of kilometres from the centre of town.

Taupo DeBretts Hot Springs   HOT SPRINGS

(07-378 8559; www.taupodebretts.co.nz; 76 Napier–Taupo Rd; adult/child $22/11; 8.30am-9.30pm;) A variety of therapeutic mineral-rich indoor and outdoor thermal pools and freshwater chlorinated pools. The kids will love the heated dragon slide, two curved racing hydroslides and the interactive 'Warm Water Playground', while adults can enjoy a great selection of treatments, such as relaxation massages.

Watersports

Lake Taupo is famously chilly, but in several places – such as **Hot Water Beach** (Lake Tce,

Hilltop) FREE, immediately south of the town centre – there are thermal springs just below the surface. You can swim right in front of the town, but Acacia Bay, 5km west, is a particularly pleasant spot. Even better and quieter is Whakaipo Bay, another 7km further on, an undeveloped waterfront reserve perfect for a lazy day.

Canoe & Kayak CANOEING, KAYAKING
(☑07-378 1003; www.canoeandkayak.co.nz/taupo; 54 Spa Rd; ⊘9am-5pm Mon-Fri, to 3pm Sat & Sun Nov-Mar, 9am-5pm Mon-Fri, to 3pm Sat Apr-Oct) Guided tours, including a two-hour trip on the Waikato River ($59) and a half-day to the Māori rock carvings for $99.

2 Mile Bay Sailing &
Watersports Centre SAILING, KAYAKING
(☑027 588 6588; www.sailingcentre.co.nz; Lake Tce; ⊘9am-10pm Nov-Apr, 9am-7pm Mon-Thu, to 8pm Fri-Sun May-Oct) A lakeside cafe-bar that pumps mellow Ben Harper tunes and hires out paddle boards, kayaks, windsurfers and canoes (from $30), sailboats ($75) and catamarans ($95); rates are per hour, or take an hour-long lesson for $50. Pizza available from 11am, or swing by from 4pm on a Sunday for local music jam sessions jutting over the lake.

Lake Fun Taupo BOATING
(☑0800 876 882; www.lakefuntaupo.co.nz; Taupo Marina, Ferry Rd; ⊘9am-9pm, weather dependent) Located at the marina about 500m from the i-SITE (p276), this outfit hires out single/double kayaks ($25/35 per hour), paddle boards ($30 per hour), self-drive motor boats (from $120 per hour) and jet skis ($150 per hour).

Fishing

Fish Cruise Taupo FISHING, CRUISE
(Launch Office; ☑07-378 3444; www.fishcruisetaupo.co.nz; Taupo Boat Harbour, 65 Redoubt St; ⊘9am-5pm Oct-Mar, 9.30am-3pm Apr-Sep) Representing a collective of 13 local boats, this booking office can hook you up with private charters whether you're looking for fishing on a small runabout, or a leisurely cruise on a yacht.

Taupo Troutcatcher FISHING
(☑0800 376 882; www.taupotroutcatcher.co.nz; Taupo Marina, Ferry Rd; per hour from $110; ⊘9am-9pm, weather dependent) Two decades of fishing experience on Lake Taupo adds up to a good choice of operator if you're looking to catch your dinner. Boats accommodating up to five or 10 people are both available.

☞ Tours

★**Sail Barbary** BOATING
(☑07-378 5879; www.sailbarbary.com; Taupo Boat Harbour, Redoubt St; adult/child $49-54/29-54; ⊘10.30am & 2pm year-round, plus 5pm Dec-Feb) 🖉 A classic 1926 yacht offering 2½-hour cruises to the Māori rock carvings daily. The evening cruises include buffet pizza and a drink. Being open to the elements, this is a more adventurous option, but custom-made waterproof, fleece-lined ponchos with hoods are handed out to anyone who's chilly.

Taupo Kayaking Adventures KAYAKING
(☑0274 801 231; www.tka.co.nz; 2/876 Acacia Bay Rd, Acacia Bay; tours from $60) Runs guided kayaking trips from its base in Acacia Bay to the Māori rock carvings, with the return trip taking around four hours ($100, including refreshments). Longer trips and walk/bike combos also available.

MĀORI NZ: TAUPO & THE RUAPEHU REGION

The North Island's central region is home to a group of mountains that feature in several Māori legends of lust and betrayal, which end with mountains fleeing to other parts of the island (just like in Mt Taranaki's sad tale (p241)).

Long after that was over, the *tohunga* (priest) Ngātoro-i-rangi, fresh off the boat from Hawaiki, explored this region and named the mountains that remained. The most sacred was Tongariro because it had at least 12 volcanic cones and was seen as the leader of all the other mountains.

The major *iwi* (tribe) of the region is Ngāti Tūwharetoa (www.tuwharetoa.co.nz), one of the few *iwi* in New Zealand that has retained an undisputed *ariki* (high chief). The current *ariki* is Sir Tumu Te Heuheu Tukino VIII, whose great-great-grandfather, Te Heuheu Tukino IV (a descendant of Ngātoro-i-rangi), gifted the mountains of Tongariro to New Zealand in 1887.

To discover the stories of local Māori and their ancestors, visit Taupō Museum (p269), the carved cliff faces at Mine Bay (p269) or Wairakei Terraces (p268).

Ernest Kemp Cruises BOATING
(☑07-378 3444, 021 669 139; www.ernestkemp.
co.nz; Taupo Boat Harbour, Redoubt St; adult/child
$35-44/10-22; ⊙10.30am & 2pm year-round,
5pm departure Oct-Apr) Board the *Ernest
Kemp* replica steamboat for a two-hour
cruise to view the Māori rock carvings, Hot
Water Beach, lakefront and Acacia Bay.
Lively commentary and complimentary
tea and coffee. Book at Fish Cruise Taupo
(p272). A special 90-minute cruise departs
at 12.30pm during school holidays (adult/
child $35/10). Check out the **cocktail
cruise**, too.

Taupo's Floatplane SCENIC FLIGHTS
(☑07-378 7500; www.tauposfloatplane.co.nz;
Taupo Boat Harbour, Ferry Rd; flights $109-955) Lo-
cated near the marina, the floatplane offers
a variety of trips, including quick flights over
the lake and longer forays over Mt Ruapehu
or Whakaari (White Island). The three-hour
'Taupo Trifecta' combines a scenic flight,
visit to Orakei Korako (p271) and jetboat
ride ($645).

✵ Festivals & Events

Wanderlust MUSIC, CULTURAL
(www.wanderlust.com/festivals/great-lake-taupo;
⊙Feb/Mar) A self-described 'all-out celebration of mindful living', four-day Wanderlust
combines relaxing and recharging music
with yoga, meditation and a focus on alternative therapies and natural health.

Graffiato Street Art Festival ART
(www.taupostreetart.co.nz; ⊙Oct) FREE Watch
local and international street artists create
large-scale works in the streets of Taupo
over three colourful days. Collect a Taupo
Street Art map from the i-SITE (p276) or
website and keep an eye out for art honour-
ing Māori *iwi* (tribes).

Lake Taupo Cycle Challenge SPORTS
(www.cyclechallenge.com; ⊙Nov) One of NZ's
biggest annual cycling events, the 160km
Lake Taupo Cycle Challenge sees some
10,000 people pedalling around the lake on
the last Saturday in November.

🛌 Sleeping

Taupo has plenty of accommodation, all
of which is in hot demand during late
December and January and during major
sporting events (book ahead). Campers
have the option of **Hipapatua** (Huka Falls
Rd) FREE, a scruffy spot beside the Waikato

River, after new camping laws came into
effect late 2017 to deal with tourism and
overcrowding.

Finlay Jacks HOSTEL $
(☑07-378 9292; www.finlayjacks.co.nz; 20 Taniwha
St; dm/s/d/f from $23/35/80/120; 🖭) Our pick
of Taupo's hostels, Finlay Jacks has turned an
ageing motel into a colourful hub for young
people. The largest rooms are 12-bed dorms,
but they feel smaller, with bunks separated
into lots of eight and four. Affordable private
rooms with en suites have super-comfy beds.
We love the pop-culture prints on the walls,
patterned bed covers and grassy lawn.

Haka Lodge HOSTEL $
(☑07-377 0068; www.hakalodge.com; 56 Kaimanawa St; dm $28-33, d $69, 1-bdrm apt $149; 🖭)
Haka Lodge has a fantastic, community feel
from the moment you walk in. We love the
custom, creak-proof wooden dorm bunks
with built-in storage and the 2nd-storey
barbecue deck beside the spotless, modern
kitchen. Check out their recipe for pikelets
(thin crumpets) on the wall of the kitchen.
Comfortable lounge with beanbags inside,
volleyball net, hammocks and spa pool
outside.

★**Waitahanui Lodge** MOTEL $$
(☑0800104321,07-3787183;www.waitahanuilodge.
co.nz; 116 SH1, Waitahanui; d $119-199; 🖭) Ten
kilometres south of Taupo, these five beach-
front, beach-hut-style units are ideally po-
sitioned for swimming, fishing and superb
sunsets. Pick of the bunch are the two abso-
lute-lakefront units, numbers three and four,
but all have lake access, sociable communal
areas plus free use of row boats and kayaks.
The units are all self-contained with kitchen-
ettes, or you can fire up the shared barbecue.
Fishing-rod hire half/full day $20/30.

★**Lake Motel** MOTEL $$
(☑07-378 4222, 021 951 808; www.thelakeonline.
co.nz; 63 Mere Rd; studio $125-175, 1-bdrm units
$145-185; @🖭) A reminder that 1960s and
'70s design wasn't all *Austin Powers*-style
groovaliciousness, this boutique motel is
crammed with furniture from the era's signature designers. The four one-bedroom
units sleep between two to four people and
have kitchenettes and living areas, and,
along with the two studios (maximum two
people), use of the garden. Look out for
paintings of well-known musos by the owners' son.
Bikes available to borrow free of charge.

Te Moenga Lodge
B&B **$$**

(☑ 07-378 0894, 021 680 863; www.temoenga.co.nz; 60 Te Moenga Park, Acacia Bay; r/6-bed apt incl breakfast $180/290-380; 🕸 🌊) As you drive to the very end of the street and park on top of the hill, two friendly border collie–golden retriever crosses will welcome you to Te Moenga. There are two studios, two separate chalets and an apartment for six. With Lake Taupo in front of you, it's possible you won't notice the stylish, homey decor. Best enjoy the view from the pool.

Reef Resort
RESORT **$$**

(☑ 0800 733 378, 07-378 5115; www.reefresort.co.nz; 219 Lake Tce; d/1-bdrm from $166-217/200-242; 🕸 🌊) Reef Resort stands out among Taupo's waterfront complexes for its classy, well-priced one- to three-bedroom apartments, centred on an appealing pool patio complete with thermal spa pool. It's worth paying a little extra for lake views. Cruiser bikes available to hire for $5 per hour.

Lake Taupo Holiday Resort
HOLIDAY PARK **$$**

(☑ 0800 332 121, 07-378 6860; www.laketauporesort.co.nz; 41 Centennial Dr; sites/cabins/units from $36/103/138; @ 🕸 🌊) This slick 8-ha park about 2.5km from the i-SITE has all mod cons, including a huge heated swimming pool – we're talking a thermally heated lagoon with a movie screen and bar – a jumping pillow, *pétanque,* basketball, volleyball and tennis courts, and an on-site shop. Manicured grounds, swish accommodation options and spotless facilities help make it a contender for camp of the year.

★ Acacia Cliffs Lodge
B&B **$$$**

(☑ 021 821 338, 07-378 1551; www.acaciacliffslodge.co.nz; 133 Mapara Rd, Acacia Bay; d $650-750; ⊘ closed May-Sep; @ 🕸) 🍃 This luxurious B&B, high above Acacia Bay, offers four contemporarily and artfully designed suites, three with grand lake views and one that compensates for the lack of them with a curvy bath and private garden. The chef-owner dishes up fine-dining fare at a heated table, with three-course dinners available (per person $95). Tariff includes breakfast, pre-dinner drinks, canapés and Taupo Airport transfer.

Serenity on Wakeman
B&B **$$$**

(☑ 027 454 6518; www.tauposerenity.co.nz; 57 Wakeman Rd, Acacia Bay; r $290-380; 🕸) Views of the lake don't get much better than this, but with only two rooms (technically, the third is reserved for groups), you'll have to book ahead. It's all in the details here, from bathrobes to breakfast on the deck. The upstairs suite has a private balcony, king bed and double spa bath. Luxurious, peaceful and romantic.

✖ Eating

Pauly's Diner
BURGERS **$**

(☑ 07-378 4315; www.paulysdiner.nz; 3 Paora Hape St; burgers $12-15; ⊘ 11.30am-8.30pm Wed-Sun & alternating Mon) Two brothers from Auckland set up this popular burger joint in an old fish and chipper, and it seems they've got the formula just right (selling out isn't uncommon). The shop only seats about a dozen, plus a few more outside, and specials are posted on Instagram (Dorito chip-fried chicken is a thing). Shakes and deep-fried goodies also available.

Merchant
DELI **$**

(☑ 07-378 4626; www.themerchant.co.nz; 114 Spa Rd; ⊘ 9am-6pm Mon & Sun, to 6.30pm Tue-Thu & Sat, to 7pm Fri) Championing NZ artisan producers and importing specialities from abroad, this grocery on the town fringe is a fruitful stop for those looking to stock up on supplies. Scenic Cellars is also located here, stocking craft beer and rare premium NZ wines, alongside single-malt whiskies and more. Ask for the incredibly knowledgable Lea if you don't know what to buy.

★ Storehouse
CAFE **$$**

(☑ 07-378 8820; www.facebook.com/storehousenz; 14 Runanga St; mains $13-18; ⊘ 7am-3.30pm Mon-Fri, 8am-3.30pm Sat, to 3pm Sun; 🕸 🍴) If you're looking for Taupo's coolest cafe, you've just found it. Setting the scene since 2013, Storehouse is located in an old plumbing store over two levels. Downstairs, indoor plants drape over warehouse beams, and upstairs a bike is inexplicably fastened to the wall. The breakfast salad bowl often sells out – guess that means we're having fried-chicken waffles.

★ Replete Cafe & Store
CAFE **$$**

(☑ 07-377 3011; www.replete.co.nz; 45 Heu Heu St; mains $13-18; ⊘ 8am-5pm Mon-Fri, to 4pm Sat & Sun; 🕸) "You don't come to Taupo without stopping for coffee here," a customer tells us, "It's an institution." He's not wrong. Established in 1993, Replete is split into a cafe and shop selling designer kitchenware, ceramics and souvenirs. The cafe cabinet is one of the best looking in town, while lunch has an Asian flair (Japanese bolognese or Sri Lankan curry, anyone?).

★ **Southern Meat Kitchen**   SOUTH AMERICAN $$
(SMK; ☑07-3783582; www.facebook.com/smktaupo; 40 Tuwharetoa St; mains $22-34; ⊙noon-midnight Wed-Sun, 4-11pm Mon & Tue) Calling all carnivores! SMK slow-cooks beef brisket, pulled pork and shredded chicken on an American wood-fire smoker – and you can order it by the half-pound (upgrade to a pound for $8). Arrives with mac 'n' cheese, slaw and rice. Save room for jalapeño-and-cheddar cornbread, served in a skillet with addictive honey butter. Beer tasting paddles for $15.

Spoon & Paddle   CAFE $$
(☑07-378 9664; www.facebook.com/spoonandpaddle; 101 Heu Heu St; mains $15-20; ⊙8am-4pm; 🛜🚼) Filling a 1950s house with colourful decor, this cafe feels like popping into a friend's place for brunch with a whole lot of strangers. Breakfast runs all day, and from 11.30am you can order tasty international numbers, including pork-belly *bao*, local beef-brisket soft-shell tacos or a lamb-shoulder salad bowl. Great coffee and a playground for the kids.

Bistro   MODERN NZ $$
(☑07-377 3111; www.thebistro.co.nz; 17 Tamamutu St; mains $26-39; ⊙5pm-midnight) Popular with locals – bookings are recommended – the Bistro focuses on doing the basics very, very well. That means harnessing local and seasonal produce for dishes such as bacon-wrapped Wharekauhau lamb, washed down with your pick from the small but thoughtful beer-and-wine list. Even the kids' menu is tempting.

Malabar Beyond India   INDIAN $$
(☑07-376 5456, 07-376 5454; www.malabartaupo.com; 2/40 Tuwharetoa St; mains $17-26; ⊙11.30am-1pm; 🍴🚼) Our pick of Indian restaurants in Taupo, Malabar has a broad menu but is especially good at vegetarian dishes, such as *dal makhani* made with black lentils and *akabari kofta* (cottage-cheese-and-almond dumplings). Friendly service in a warm space with handsome wooden chairs and a stone feature wall.

Brantry   MODERN NZ $$$
(☑07-378 0484; www.thebrantry.co.nz; 45 Rifle Range Rd; 3-course set menu $55-60; ⊙from 5.30pm Tue-Sat, daily from 5.30pm Dec-Jan) Operating out of an unobtrusive 1950s house, the Brantry continues its reign as one of the best in the region for well-executed, brilliant-value fine dining centred around a three-course menu. There's an impressive wine list

with friendly staff to help with difficult decisions. Sit in the covered al fresco dining area (blankets provided) or dine in the cellar.

🍷 **Drinking & Nightlife**

Crafty Trout Brewing   BREWERY
(☑07-989 8570; www.craftytrout.co.nz; 131-135 Tongariro St; mains $18-28, pizzas $14-49; ⊙Bier Kafe noon-late Wed-Mon, shop & brewery 10am-4pm Wed-Mon; 🛜) Somewhere between an alpine and a fishing lodge, only the five cuckoo clocks at Crafty Trout interrupt the German music. Comfy leather sofas and the sunny verandah are great places to dig into robust meals, including tasty fish and chips and wood-fired pizza, washed down with any of the 10 beers and ciders. Grab a porter-filled chocolate truffle for dessert.

Lakehouse   CRAFT BEER
(☑07-377 1545; www.lakehousetaupo.co.nz; 10 Roberts St; breakfast $9-20, mains $20-30; ⊙8am-late (kitchen closes 9pm)) Welcome to craft beer central, with a fridge full of interesting bottles, and nine taps serving a rotating selection of NZ brews. Order a tasting box of four beers ($15), partner them with a pizza or stone-grilled steak, and sit outside for lake views – and, if the clouds lift, glimpses of the mountains. Check the blackboard wall for daily specials.

Vine Eatery & Bar   WINE BAR
(☑07-378 5704; www.vineeatery.co.nz; 37 Tuwharetoa St; tapas $8-14, mains $17-39; ⊙11am-midnight) Wine glass chandeliers hang from the industrial ceiling at this restaurant-cum-wine bar, where you can sit in comfy booths, at raised stools or by the fire. Bottles are available to take home, with a zap-chilling service that cools them in five minutes. Share traditional tapas with a glass (there's whisky and craft beer, too) or linger longer with larger mains.

🛍 **Shopping**

Taupo Market   FOOD, CRAFTS
(☑027 306 6167, 07-3782 980; www.taupomarket.kiwi.nz; Redoubt St; ⊙9am-1pm Sat) Plenty of food stalls and trucks, local souvenirs, arts and crafts and a scattering of produce are all good reasons to make your first coffee of the day an al fresco espresso at this popular weekend market.

Kura Gallery   ART
(☑07-377 4068; www.kura.co.nz; 47a Heu Heu St; ⊙10am-5pm Mon-Fri, to 4pm Sat & Sun) This compact gallery represents more than 70

artists from around NZ. Works for sale include weaving, carving, painting and jewellery. Many items are imbued with a Māori or Pasifika influence.

❶ Information

Taupo i-SITE (☎ 0800 525 382, 07-376 0027; www.greatlaketaupo.com; 30 Tongariro St; ⏱ 9am-4.30pm May-Oct, 8.30am-5pm Nov-Apr) Handles bookings for accommodation, transport and activities; dispenses cheerful advice; and stocks Department of Conservation (DOC) and town maps.

❶ Getting There & Away

Taupo Airport (☎ 07-378 7771; www.taupo airport.co.nz; Anzac Memorial Dr) is 8km south of town. Expect to pay about $25 for a 12-minute cab from the airport to the centre of town.

Air New Zealand (p266) flies from Auckland to Taupo two to three times daily (50 minutes), and Sounds Air (p266) flies between Wellington and Taupo at least once per day except Tuesday and Wednesday (one hour).

InterCity (p266), **Mana Bus** (www.manabus. com) and **Naked Bus** (www.nakedbus.com/nz) services stop outside the **Taupo i-SITE**, where bookings can be made.

❶ Getting Around

Local Connector buses are run by **Busit!** (☎ 0800 4287 5463; www.busit.co.nz), including the Taupo North service running as far as Huka Falls and Wairakei, twice daily Monday to Friday.

Great Lake Shuttles (☎ 021 0236 3439; www.greatlakeshuttles.co.nz) offers charter services around the area, and can hook you up with **bike hire**.

Taxi companies include **Blue Bubble Taxis** (☎ 07-378 5100; www.taupo.bluebubbletaxi. co.nz) and **Top Cabs** (☎ 07-378 9250).

There are plenty of shuttle services operating year-round to Turangi and Tongariro National Park. Ask at the Taupo i-SITE which will best suit your needs as services vary according to season (ski or hike).

Turangi

☎ 07 / POP 3000

If you love trout, shout it out! Turangi is known as the 'Trout Fishing Capital of the World'. Perched on Lake Taupo's south and set on the Tongariro River, it's also a fantastic white-water rafting destination and is a short hop, ski and tramp from the ski fields and walking tracks of Tongariro National Park.

A small town, Turangi blossomed when the Tongariro Hydro Power Development was given the go-ahead in the 1960s. Over two years, the population quadrupled, peaking at 6500 people in 1968.

◉ Sights

Volcanic Activity Centre   MUSEUM
(www.volcanoes.co.nz; i-SITE, 1 Ngawaka Pl; adult/child $12/7; ⏱ 9am-4pm) This interactive science museum moved from Taupo to Turangi and it now adjoins the local i-SITE (p279). Learn about the area's geothermal activity with this excellent, if text-heavy, display. A favourite exhibit with kids is the Earthquake Simulator. You can also configure your own tornado then watch it wreak havoc, or see a simulated geyser above and below ground.

Tongariro National Trout Centre   AQUARIUM
(☎ 07-386 8085; www.troutcentre.com; SH1; adult/child $15/free; ⏱ 10am-4pm Dec-Apr, 10am-3pm May-Nov) Around 4km south of Turangi, this DOC-managed trout centre has a hatchery, an underwater viewing chamber, a museum with polished educational displays, a collection of rods and reels dating back to the 1880s, and freshwater aquariums displaying river life.

🏃 Activities

Aside from **trout fishing**, the Tongariro River Trail offers enjoyable walks from the centre of town, or cut down time by cycling. Further afield, good leg-stretchers include **Hinemihi's Track**, near the top of Te Ponanga Saddle, 8km west of Turangi on SH47 (15 minutes return); **Maunganamu Track**, 4km west of Turangi on SH41 (40 minutes return); and **Tauranga–Taupo River Walk** (30 minutes), which starts at Te Rangiita, 12km north of Turangi on SH1.

The Tongariro River has some superb Grade III rapids for **river rafting**, as well as Grade I stretches suitable for beginners in the lower reaches during summer.

★**Tongariro River Trail**   WALKING, CYCLING
(www.greatlaketaupo.com) The Tongariro River Trail is a 15km dual-use walking and cycling track starting from town and taking in the National Trout Centre en route upriver to the Red Hut suspension bridge. Walk the loop (four hours) or bike it (two hours) on easy terrain. Go in the morning to see the trout fishers knee-deep in the river.

Tongariro River Rafting RAFTING
(☑0800 101 024, 07-386 6409; www.trr.co.nz; 95 Atirau Rd; ☺9am-5pm) Test the white waters with a Grade II Gentle Family Float (adult/child $95/79) or splash straight into the Grade III white-water rapids ($139/125). Turangi's original rafting company also hires out mountain bikes (two hours free when you book a trip) and runs guided rides, including 42 Traverse, Tongariro River Trail, Tree Trunk Gorge and Fishers Track. Ask about multi-activity combos.

Rafting NZ RAFTING
(☑0800 865 226, 07-386 0352; www.raftingnew zealand.com; 41 Ngawaka Pl; ☺8am to 4-7pm, tour dependent) The main trips offered by this slick outfit are a four-hour, Grade III trip on the Tongariro River with an optional waterfall jump (adult/child $179/149), and a family float over more relaxed rapids (Grade II, $139/119, three hours base to base). Groups of four or more can tackle a two-day trip overnighting at a riverside camp (Grade III+, $410 per person).

🛏 Sleeping

Sportmans Lodge LODGE $
(☑07-386 8150, 0800 366 208; www.sportsmans lodge.co.nz; 15 Taupahi Rd; r $95-100, cottage $125; 🛜) Backing on to the river, this lodge is a hidden bargain for trout-fishing folk not bothered by punctuation. Tidy, compact rooms share a lounge with an open fire and a well-equipped kitchen, complete with a fishing wall of fame. The self-contained cottage sleeps four and just beside it is a path to a sunny picnic table.

Riverstone Backpackers HOSTEL $
(☑07-386 7004; www.riverstonebackpackers. com; 222 Te Rangitautahanga Rd; dm $35, t $76, d with/without bathroom $82/76; 🛜) This homey backpackers' hostel resides in a refitted house close to the town centre. Along with an enviable kitchen and comfortable lounge, it sports a stylish landscaped yard with a large wooden deck and pizza oven.

★ Braxmere MOTEL $$
(☑07-386 6449; www.braxmere.co.nz; 88 Waihi Rd, Tokaanu; unit $180; 🛜) Just 8km from Turangi on the southern fringes of Lake Taupo, Braxmere is a collection of 10 self-contained units with only a grassy lawn separating them from the lake. All are spacious one-bedroom numbers with decks and barbecues, the decor is maritime-chic and there's the added bonus of Lakeland House restaurant (p279)

Turangi

◉ Sights
1 Volcanic Activity Centre.....................B2

◐ Activities, Courses & Tours
2 Greig's Sporting World........................A1
3 Ian & Andrew Jenkins.........................B2
4 Rafting NZ..B1
5 Sporting Life...A2
6 Tongariro River Rafting......................A3
7 Tongariro River Trail...........................B3

◉ Sleeping
8 Creel Lodge...B2
9 Riverstone Backpackers....................B1
10 Sportmans Lodge...............................B1

◈ Eating
11 Cadillac Cafe..A1
Creel Tackle House & Cafe.........(see 8)

ⓘ Information
Turangi i-SITE.................................(see 1)

on-site. When we visited, there were plans for a private thermal pool.

Motuoapa Bay Holiday Park HOLIDAY PARK $$
(☑07-386 7162; www.motuoapabayholidaypark. co.nz; 2 Motuoapa Esplanade, Motuoapa; sites $20, cabins & units $70-140; 🛜) Around 8km

north of Turangi, this adorable holiday park not only boasts a lakeside location and assorted accommodation, but you can sleep in colourful VW Kombi vans and quirky wooden cabins shaped like boats (suitable for two to seven people). There are also self-contained motel units with one sleeping up to eight people.

Creel Lodge MOTEL $$
(☑07-386 8081, 0800 273 355; www.creel.co.nz; 183 Taupahi Rd; 1-/2-bdrm ste $140/145-155; 🛜) 🌱 Set in green and peaceful grounds, this heavenly hideaway backs onto a fine stretch of the Tongariro River. Nineteen spacious one- and two-bedroom suites sleeping two and four people respectively are named after fishing flies and local mountains. They have separate lounges, kitchens, soothing patios for sundowners and free use of barbecues. Creel Tackle House & Cafe is also on-site.

Tongariro Lodge LODGE $$$
(☑07-386 7946; www.tongarirolodge.co.nz; 83 Grace Rd; 1-bdrm chalet $175, 2-/5-bdrm villas from $269-750; 🛜) Three kilometres from Turangi on the Tongariro River, famed angler Tony Hayes established Tongariro Lodge in 1982. Across the 9-ha property are more affordable chalets with sunny decks and en suites, while larger, more luxurious options are ideal for groups and spoils.

✖ Eating

★**Cadillac Cafe** CAFE $$
(☑07-3860552; www.facebook.com/Thymeforfood cafe; 35 Turangi Town Centre; mains $9-20; ⊙8.30am-3pm) Step back in time at Cadillac with its array of vintage chairs, posters and impressive toy collection from the '50s and '60s. Retro games are available while you wait for your massive burger, sticky ribs or fish and chips. Just try to resist the Ameri-

---

ABOUT TROUT

Early European settlers who wanted to improve New Zealand's farming, hunting and fishing opportunities are responsible for the introduction of such ghastly wreckers as possums and rabbits. But one of their more benign introductions was that of trout – brown and rainbow – released into NZ rivers in the second half of the 19th century.

Today they are prized by sports anglers, who you'll find thigh-deep in limpid rivers and on the edge of deep green pools. Celebrities have also tried their luck in these North Island waters, including ex-American president Jimmy Carter, Michael Keaton, Harrison Ford and Liam Neeson – they all stay at the exclusive Tongariro Lodge.

Tall tales boast of Taupo trout weighing more than a sack of spuds and measuring the length of a surfboard. Truth be told, more than 28,000 legal trout are bagged annually, by both domestic and international fishing enthusiasts.

Trout fishing is highly regulated, with plenty of rules regarding where and how they're to be fished. Licences are required and can be bought online at www.doc.govt.nz or www.fishandgame.org.nz. Our advice is to seek out a guide. Most offer flexible trips, with $300 for a half-day a ballpark figure.

Creel Tackle House & Cafe (☑07-386 7929; www.creeltackle.com; 183 Taupahi Rd; lunch $10-15; ⊙cafe 8am-4pm, tackle shop 7.30am-5pm) Fishing equipment for hire, tips and coffee.

Bryce Curle Fly Fishing (☑07-386 6813, 027 204 9401; www.brycecurleflyfishing.com; 59 Kahotea Dr, Motuoapa; ⊙by appt) Turangi-based guide.

Flyfishtaupo (☑027 4450 223, 07-377 8054; www.flyfishtaupo.com) Guide Brent Pirie offers a range of fishing excursions, including seniors-focused 'Old Farts & Tarts' trips.

Greig's Sporting World (Barry Greig's Sporting World; ☑07-386 6911; www.greigsports.co.nz; 59 Town Centre; ⊙8.30am-5pm) Sells gear and handles bookings for guides and charters.

Sporting Life (☑07-386 8996; www.sportinglife-turangi.co.nz; The Mall, Town Centre; ⊙8.30am-5.30pm Mon-Sat, 9.30am-5pm Sun) Sports store laden with fishing paraphernalia, available to hire. Its website details the latest fishing conditions.

Ian & Andrew Jenkins (☑07-386 0840; www.tui-lodge.co.nz; Tui Lodge, 196 Taupahi Rd; ⊙by appt) Father and son fly-fishing guides.

Central Plateau Fishing (☑027 681 4134, 07-378 8192; www.cpf.net.nz) Turangi-based guide Brett Cameron.

can cakes in the rotating cabinet. Kids' and gluten-free menus available. Lots of outdoor seating.

Oreti Restaurant   MODERN NZ **$$**
(☑️07-386 7070, 0800 574 413; www.oretivillage.com; Mission House Dr, Pukawa; mains $29-36; ⊗6-8pm Wed-Sun or by appointment, closed Jun) With lake and mountain views, Oreti restaurant could get away with average food. But the kitchen doesn't compromise, serving fun filo pastry–wrapped prawns in shot glasses of sweet chilli and aioli and elegant mains like seared duck breast, sweet with parsnip and prunes. Where else on Lake Taupo do waitstaff wish you *bon appétit* to a jazzy French soundtrack?

Lakeland House   INTERNATIONAL **$$**
(☑️07-386 6442; www.braxmere.co.nz; 88 Waihi Rd, Tokaanu; mains lunch $20-40, dinner $27-40; ⊗10am-3pm & 6pm-late) Destination dining with a view across Lake Taupo with generous pastas, salads and chowder dominating the daytime menu. Craft beer from Tuatara Brewing is on tap, and come evening diners can salivate over pan-fried snapper with hollandaise and cajun tiger prawns followed by sticky date pudding with maple-and-walnut ice cream. Six kilometres from Turangi, just off SH41.

❶ Information

Turangi i-SITE (☑️07-386 8999, 0800 288 726; www.greatlaketaupo.com; 1 Ngawaka Pl; ⊗9am-4.30pm summer, 8.30am-4pm winter; 🛜) A good stop for information on Tongariro National Park, Kaimanawa Forest Park, trout fishing, and snow and road conditions. It issues DOC hut tickets, ski passes and fishing licences, and makes bookings for transport, accommodation and activities. Check out the Volcanic Activity Centre (p276) while you're here.

❶ Getting There & Away

InterCity (p266), **Mana Bus** (www.manabus. com) and **Naked Bus** (www.nakedbus.com/ nz) coaches stop outside the **Turangi i-SITE** on Ngawaka Pl. **Backyard Tours** (☑️022 314 2656, 07-386 5322; www.backyardtours.com) and **Turangi Alpine Shuttles** (☑️0272 322 135, 0508 427 677; www.alpineshuttles.co.nz) can both arrange transfers for the Tongariro Alpine Crossing.

❶ Getting Around

Rent bikes from basic to boss at **Central Plateau Cycles** (☑️07-386 0186; www.facebook. com/pg/Centralplateaucycles; 259/3 Te Rangitautahanga Rd; 2hr $20, half-/full-day hire $30/45; ⊗9am-5pm Mon-Fri, to 2pm Sat).

RUAPEHU REGION

One of New Zealand's premier destinations for adventure, one is never short of fresh air in the Ruapehu region. Tongariro National Park is a highlight and aside from tramping in summer and snow sports in winter, the Tongariro Alpine Crossing (p282) is considered one of the best day-long hikes in the world. If mountain-biking and kayaking sounds more up your alley, you can take these down the mountain at National Park Village and Ohakune.

❶ Getting There & Away

InterCity (p266) and **Naked Bus** (www.nakedbus. com/nz) call into Ohakune and National Park Village. National Park Village is also a stop on the *Northern Explorer* train service linking Auckland and Wellington.

Tongariro National Park

Even before you arrive in Tongariro National Park its three mighty volcanoes – Ruapehu (p281), Ngauruhoe (p281) and Tongariro (p281) – steal your breath from the horizon. It would be a wasted opportunity not to get closer, which is possible on the ski fields and during the other-worldly, day-long Tongariro Alpine Crossing (p282), as well as other walks to natural features. You don't have to cover all 796 sq km of the National Park to be awed by nature.

The National Park – New Zealand's first – was gifted by local Tuwharetoa Māori more than a century ago. Long before it was granted dual Unesco World Heritage status for its volcanic landscape and deep cultural importance, the Māori believed that the mountains were strong warriors who fought among each other. In the process, they created the landscape that attracts more than 200,000 visitors each year. Visit once and you'll understand why it was worth fighting for.

History

Established in 1887, Tongariro was New Zealand's first national park. The previous year, during the aftermath of the New Zealand Wars, the Native Land Court met to determine the ownership of the land around Tongariro. Ngāti Tūwharetoa chief Horonuku Te Heuheu Tukino IV pleaded passionately for the area to be left intact, mindful of Pākehā (white people) eyeing it up for grazing. "If our mountains of Tongariro are included in

Tongariro National Park & Around

Epic Cycle
Adventures
(2.5km)

Whakapapa River

Whanganui River

Lake Taupo

41 X 24

19 Tokaanu

23 Hautu

Owhango 12

Tongariro Forest Conservation Area

Tokaanu Power Station
Te Ponanga Saddle

Turangi
See Turangi Map (p277)

Lake Otamangakau

Tongariro 47

Otukou

Lake Rotopounamu

Mt Pihanga
(1325m)

Rangipo

Lake Rotoaira

Raurimu 6

Matariki Falls

Taurewa

42 Traverse

8

Tongariro Forest Conservation Area

47

Ketetahi Rd

46

Tongariro Alpine Crossing

Ketetahi Shelter

North Crater

4

Blue Lake

Central Crater

Emerald Lakes

Red Crater

Desert Rd

Tongariro River

Mangatepopo Rd

Mt Tongariro
(1967m)

10

14

Mangatepopo Hut

20

48

Tawhai Falls

South Crater

2

Mt Ngauruhoe
(2287m)

Oturere Hut

Tongariro Northern Circuit

National Park Village

4

Taranaki Falls

Tongariro National Park

Tama (1608m)

Kaimanawa Forest Park

Waikune

Whakapapa Village

Bruce Rd

Upper Tama Lake

Waihohonu Hut

Erua

Silica Rapids

Whakapapaiti Hut

Iwikau Village

18

Tongariro Northern Circuit

Ohinepango Springs

Mangaturuturu Hut

3

Crater Lake

15

Tukino Rd (4WD)

Round-the-Mountain Track

Warning
Desert Rd may be closed in severe conditions

Pokaka

16

Mt Ruapehu
(2797m)

Mangawhero Falls

17

Blyth Hut

Rangipo Hut

Horopito

Waitonga Falls

Mangaehuehu Hut

Tohunga Junction

Ohakune Old Coach Rd

Rangataua Conservation Area

Rangipo Desert

Desert Rd

Lake Moawhango

11

Ohakune Mountain Rd

Waihianoa River

1

Three Kings Range

Tohunga Rd

21

25

22

13

Ohakune

Rangataua 1

Lake Rotokura

Rotokura Ecological Reserve

49

Karioi

Tangiwai

Waiouru

5

0 ——— 10 km
0 ——— 5 miles

TAUPO & THE RUAPEHU REGION TONGARIRO NATIONAL PARK

the blocks passed through the court in the ordinary way," said the chief, "what will become of them? They will be cut up and sold, a piece going to one Pākehā and a piece to another."

In 1887 chief Horonuku ensured the land's everlasting preservation when he presented the area to the Crown for the purpose of a national park, the first in New Zealand and only the fourth in the world. With incredible vision for a man of his time, the chief realised that Tongariro's value lay in its priceless beauty and heritage, not as another sheep paddock.

Tongariro National Park & Around

Development of the national park was slow, and it was only after the main trunk railroad reached the region in 1909 that visitors arrived in significant numbers. Development mushroomed in the 1950s and 1960s as roads were sealed, tracks cut and more huts built.

◎ Sights

Mt Ruapehu
VOLCANO
(www.mtruapehu.com) Mt Ruapehu (2797m) is the North Island's highest mountain and one of the world's most active volcanoes. One year-long eruption began in March 1945, spreading lava over Crater Lake and sending clouds of ash as far as Wellington. During the heavy ashfalls, hundreds of cases of 'Ruapehu throat' were reported. On Christmas Eve 1953, the crater-lake lip collapsed and an enormous lahar (volcanic mudflow) swept away everything in its path, including a railway bridge. A crowded train plunged into the river, killing 151 people, making it one of NZ's worst tragedies.

Ruapehu also rumbled in 1969 and 1973, and significant eruptions occur with suspicious frequency. In 2007 a primary school teacher almost died when a rock was propelled through the roof of a trampers' shelter, crushing his leg.

Mt Tongariro
VOLCANO
(www.visitruapehu.com/explore/tongariro-national-park) Ongoing rumbles are reminders that all the volcanoes in the area are very much in the land of the living. The last major event was in 2012 when Mt Tongariro – the

northernmost and lowest peak in the park (1967m) – gave a couple of good blasts from its northern craters, causing a nine-month partial closure of the famous Alpine Crossing Track (p282). (To see video of recent eruptions, visit www.doc.govt.nz/eruption.)

Mt Ngauruhoe
VOLCANO
(☎ 07-892 3729; www.visitruapehu.com/explore/tongariro-national-park/volcanoes) Northeast of Ruapehu, Mt Ngauruhoe (2287m) is the national park's youngest volcano. Its first eruptions are thought to have occurred 2500 years ago. Until 1975 Ngauruhoe had erupted at least every nine years, including a 1954 eruption that lasted 11 months and disgorged 6 million cu m of lava. Its steam vents have temporarily cooled, suggesting that the main vent has become blocked.

🏃 Activities

Hiking
The DOC and i-SITE visitor centres at Whakapapa (p285), Ohakune (p290) and Turangi (p279) have maps and information on walks in the park, as well as current track and weather conditions. Each January, DOC offers an excellent guided-walks program in and around the park; ask at DOC centres for information or book online.

The safest and most popular time to tramp in the national park is December to March, when the tracks have usually been cleared of snow and the weather is more settled. In winter many of the tracks become full alpine adventures, requiring mountain-eering experience, an ice axe and crampons. Guided winter tramps are available with Adrift Outdoor Guided Adventures (p286).

The Tongariro Northern Circuit is a fa-vourite among more experienced trampers, but the park boasts over 14,000km of track to choose from. These range from short ambles to excellent day walks such as the **Whakapapa Valley** and **Tama Lakes Tracks**, both of which begin from the Tongariro National Park Visitor Centre (p285) at Whakapapa. There are also a number of challenging routes that should only be attempted by the fit, experi-enced and well equipped, such as the **Round the Mountain Track**, a remote 71km, four- to six-day tramp, circuiting Mt Ruapehu.

Scattered around the park's tramping tracks are 10 huts, most of which are $15 per person. However, as the Tongariro North-ern Circuit is a Great Walk, Mangatepopo, Oturere and Waihohonu huts are designated Great Walk huts ($36) during the Great Walk season (mid-October to April). Each hut has gas cookers, heating, cold running water and good old long-drop toilets, along with com-munal bunk rooms with mattresses. Camp-sites are located next to the huts; the $14 fee allows campers to use the hut facilities.

Great Walk hut tickets must be obtained in advance, either from the Tongariro Na-tional Park Visitor Centre (p285), **Great Walks Bookings** (☑0800 694 732; www. greatwalks.co.nz) or DOC visitor centres na-tionwide. It will pay to book early during the Great Walk season. In the low season, the huts become Standard huts ($5), the gas cookers are removed, and fees can be paid with Backcountry Hut Passes and tickets.

★**Tongariro Alpine Crossing**   TRAMPING (www.tongarirocrossing.org.nz) This popular crossing is lauded as NZ's finest one-day walk with more than 100,000 trampers finishing it yearly. It takes between six to eight hours to complete the 19.4km mixed terrain walk amid steaming vents and springs, stunning rock formations, peculiar moonscape basins, impossible scree slopes and vast views – the most iconic across the Emerald Lakes.

This is a fair-weather tramp. In poor conditions it is little more than an ardu-ous up-and-down, with only orange-tipped poles to mark the passing of the day. Strong winds see trampers crawl along the ridge of Red Crater, the high point of the trek, and can blow people off their feet. A sunny day could still be a gusty day, so check in with

your nearest information centre. The most crowded times on the track are the first nice days after Christmas and Easter, when there can easily be more than 1000 people strung out between the two road ends.

This is an alpine crossing, and it needs to be treated with respect. You need a reasonable level of fitness and you should be prepared for all types of weather. Shockingly ill-equipped trampers are legendary on this route – stupid shoes, no rain jackets, blue jeans soaked to the skin – we've seen it all. As well as prop-er gear, you'll need to stock up on water and snacks. If you're keen to undertake a guided tramp, contact Adrift Guided Outdoor Adven-tures (p286) or Adventure Outdoors (p286).

The Crossing starts at Mangatepopo Rd car park, off SH47, and finishes at Ketetahi Rd, off SH46. As of late 2017, a four-hour parking restriction at the Mangatepopo Rd car park has been implemented to resolve overcrowding. Those undertaking the cross-ing need to organise shuttle transport – of-ten your accommodation can provide a rec-ommendation. Shuttle services operate from Whakapapa Village, National Park Village, Turangi, Taupo, Ohakune and Raetihi.

ROUTE	ESTIMATED SUMMER WALK TIME (HR)
Mangatepopo Rd end to Mangatepopo Hut	¼
Mangatepopo Hut to South Crater	1½-2
South Crater to Emerald Lakes	1-1½
Emerald Lakes to Ketetahi Shelter	1½
Ketetahi Shelter to road end	1½

Tongariro Northern Circuit   TRAMPING (www.doc.govt.nz/tongarironortherncircuit) Cir-cumnavigating Ngauruhoe (p281), this 43km track takes four days from Whakapapa Vil-lage, Mangatepopo Rd or Ketetahi Rd, all reg-ularly serviced by shuttles. Although there's some moderate climbing, it's well marked and maintained, making it achievable for medium fitness levels. The weather can change sud-denly, so be prepared and check in with the visitor centre (p285) before you go.

As of late 2017, the Department of Conser-vation (DOC) has removed access signs to the Ngauruhoe and Tongariro summits to pre-serve the environment and respect the sanc-tity of the *maunga tapu* (sacred mountains).

The Northern Circuit passes plenty of the spectacular and colourful volcanic features that have earned the park its Unesco World Heritage Area status. Highlights include craters such as the **South Crater**, **Central Crater** and **Red Crater**; brilliantly colourful lakes, including the **Emerald Lakes**, **Blue Lake**, and the **Upper and Lower Tama Lakes**; the cold **Soda Springs**; and various other formations, including cones, lava flows and glacial valleys.

The traditional place to start and finish the tramp is Ngauruhoe Place in Whakapapa Village, just below the site of the park's visitor information centre. However, many trampers begin at Mangatepopo Rd to ensure they have good weather for the tramp's most dramatic day. This reduces it to a three-day tramp, with stays at Oturere and Waihohonu Huts, ending at Whakapapa Village.

ROUTE	ESTIMATED SUMMER WALK TIME (HR)
Whakapapa Village to Mangatepopo Hut	3-4
Mangatepopo Hut to Oturere Hut	5-6
Oturere Hut to Waihohonu Hut	3
Waihohonu Hut to Whakapapa Village	5-6

Round the Mountain Track   TRAMPING
(☎07-892 3729; www.doc.govt.nz) This off-the-beaten-track hike is a quieter alternative to the busy Tongariro Northern Circuit, but it's particularly tough, has some potentially tricky river crossings, and is not recommended for beginners or the unprepared. Looping around Mt Ruapehu (p281), the trail takes in diverse country from glacial rivers to tussocky moors to majestic mountain views. Allow at least four days to complete the 66.2km hike.

Six days is a realistic estimate for this hike if you're including side trips to the Blyth Hut or Tama Lakes.

You can get to the Round the Mountain trail from Whakapapa Village, the junction near Waihohonu Hut, Ohakune Mountain Rd or Whakapapaiti Hut. Most trampers start at Whakapapa Village and return there to finish the loop.

The track is safest from December to March when there is little or no snow, and less chance of avalanche. At other times of year, navigation is made difficult by snow covering the track, and full alpine gear (ice

> ### ⓘ MOUNTAIN SAFETY
> Many visitors to New Zealand come unstuck in the mountains. Compared to some overseas competitors, they might seem small at face value, but the weather can change dramatically in minutes, and rescues (and fatalities) are not uncommon. When heading out, you must be properly equipped and take safety precautions, including leaving your itinerary with a responsible person and checking in with the nearest visitor centre. Appropriate clothing is paramount. Think wool, and several layers of it, topped with a waterproof jacket and even waterproof pants. Gloves and a hat are good too, even in summer. And don't even think about wearing anything other than sturdy boots. Take plenty of water, snacks and sunscreen, especially on hot days.

axe, crampons and specialised clothing) is a requirement. To attempt the track you should prepare thoroughly. Take sufficiently detailed maps, check on the latest conditions, and carry clothing for all climes and more-than-adequate food supplies. Be sure to leave your plans and intended return date with a responsible person, and check in when you get back.

This track is served by Waihohonu, Rangipo, Mangaehuehu, Mangaturuturu and Whakapapaiti Huts, and a side trip can be made to Blyth Hut.

Walking Legends   TRAMPING
(☎ 021 545 068, 0800 925 569, 07-312 5297; www.walkinglegends.com) Guided tramps tackling the Tongariro Alpine Crossing (3½ days, $1590) and the Tongariro Northern Circuit (three days, $970).

Skiing
The linked Whakapapa and Turoa (p284) resorts straddle Mt Ruapehu and are New Zealand's two largest ski areas. Each offers similar skiing at an analogous altitude (around 2300m), with areas to suit every level of experience – from beginners' slopes to black-diamond runs for the pros. The same lift passes cover both ski areas.

Whakapapa Ski Area   SKIING
(☎07-892 4000; www.mtruapehu.com/winter/whakapapa; Bruce Rd; daily lift pass adult/child $119/69) Whakapapa Ski Area, on the northwestern slopes of Mt Ruapehu (p281), is NZ's

largest ski area, with more than 65 trails across 1050 hectares and a maximum altitude of 2300m. It's a good spot for beginners with some easy runs. The only accommodation is in private ski-club lodges so most visitors stay at Whakapapa or National Park Village.

Turoa Ski Area
SKIING

(☑ 06-385 8456; www.mtruapehu.com/winter/Turoa; Okahune Mountain Rd; daily lift pass adult/child $119/69) Turoa Ski Area on the south-western slopes of Mt Ruapehu (p281) has Australasia's longest vertical descent (722m!) and NZ's highest lift, the High Noon Express. Beginners are well catered for with gear hire, ski school, good learner areas and nice easy runs. The town of Ohakune is around 16km from Turoa, and is the most happening hub for après-ski good times.

Tukino Ski Area
SNOW SPORTS

(☑ 0800 885 466, 06-387 6294; www.tukino.org; Tukino Access Rd; day pass adult/child $65/35) Club-operated Tukino is on Mt Ruapehu's east side, 46km from Turangi and 35km from Waiouru. It's quite remote, 7km down a gravel road from the sealed Desert Rd (SH1), and you need a 4WD vehicle to get in (or call ahead to book a return shuttle from the 2WD car park, adult/child $20/10). It offers uncrowded, backcountry runs, mostly beginner and intermediate.

🕪 Tours

Mountain Air
SCENIC FLIGHTS

(☑ 0800 922 812; www.mountainair.co.nz; SH47; flights 15/25/35min $120/195/245; ⊙8am-7pm) Located just before the S48 turn-off, Mountain Air offers scenic flights from its base halfway between Whakapapa Village and National Park Village. Turangi and Taupo departures also available.

❶ Getting There & Away

Passing National Park Village and Ohakune are buses run by InterCity (p266) and **Naked Bus** (www.nakedbus.com/nz), and the *Northern Explorer* train run by KiwiRail Scenic (p266) stops at National Park Village.

The main gateway into Tongariro National Park is Whakapapa Village, but the park is also bounded by roads: SH1 (called the Desert Rd) to the east, SH4 to the west, SH46 and SH47 to the north and SH49 to the south.

Ohakune Mountain Rd leads up to the Turoa Ski Area from Ohakune. The Desert Rd is regularly closed when the weather is bad; detours will be in force. Likewise, Ohakune Mountain Rd and

Bruce Rd are subject to closures, and access beyond certain points may be restricted to 4WDs or cars with snow chains.

Ask your hotel or call the visitor centre if you're uncertain.

Whakapapa Village

☑ 07 / POP 100 (SUMMER), 300 (WINTER)

Located within the bounds of Tongariro National Park on the lower slopes of Mt Ruapehu, Whakapapa Village (pronounced 'fa-ka-pa-pa'; altitude 1140m) is the gateway to the park, home of the park's visitor centre, and the starting point for numerous walking tracks.

🕭 Activities

Tama Lakes Track
TRAMPING

(Ngauruhoe Pl) Part of the Tongariro Northern Circuit, starting at Whakapapa Village, this 17km-return track leads to the Tama Lakes, on the Tama Saddle between Ruapehu and Ngauruhoe (five to six hours return). The upper lake affords fine views of Ngauruhoe and Tongariro.

Taranaki Falls Track
TRAMPING

(Ngauruhoe Pl) A two-hour, 6km loop track heads from the village to Taranaki Falls, which plunge 20m over a 15,000-year-old lava flow into a boulder-ringed pool.

🛏 Sleeping

Whakapapa Village has limited accommodation, and during ski season prices skyrocket. Nearby options can be found in National Park Village and Ohakune, with the latter a much better base if you want to squeeze in some eating, drinking and shopping. The peak of summer over Christmas/New Year and around Easter also sees accommodation prices rise.

Whakapapa Holiday Park
HOLIDAY PARK $

(☑ 07-892 3897; www.whakapapa.net.nz; SH48; sites per person $23, dm $28, cabins $76-140, self-contained units $130-140; ☏) This popular park beside Whakapapanui Stream has a wide range of accommodation options, including campervan sites surrounded by beautiful beech forest (site 21 has a mountain view), a five-room, 32-bed backpackers' lodge and cabins sleeping up to six people (linen required) and self-contained two-bedroom units with en suites. The **store** stocks basic groceries. The huge communal kitchen was recently updated.

Chateau Tongariro Hotel HOTEL **$$$**
(☑07-892 3809, 0800 242 832; www.chateau.
co.nz; Bruce Rd; d $195-290, ste from $1000;
@🛜🐕) Despite its sublime setting, the
grandeur of this iconic 1929 hotel is a touch
faded, so it's worth checking out both the
Tongariro Wing and Heritage Wing before
deciding on a room. Still, the Chateau is
undeniably romantic, complete with **high
tea** (www.chateau.co.nz/chateau-high-tea;
high tea $32; ⊘11am-5pm) in the lounge over-
looking Mt Ngauruhoe, aperitifs in the foy-
er bar and dining in the grand **Ruapehu
Room** (www.chateau.co.nz/ruapehu-restaurant;
mains $30-43; ⊘6.30-10am, 6.30-9pm, noon-
2pm Sun).

🍴 Eating

Fergusson's Cafe CAFE **$**
(☑07-892 3809; www.chateau.co.nz/fergussons
-cafe; Bruce Rd; mains $8-15; ⊘6-11.30am; 🛜)
Fergusson's is a casual brunch spot with
outdoor tables, and proffers a daily buffet
breakfast (per person $12.50), sandwiches,
cakes and coffee. Just up and across the road
from Chateau Tongariro Hotel.

ℹ️ Information

Tongariro National Park Visitor Centre
(Whakapapa Visitor Centre; ☑07-892 3729;
www.doc.govt.nz/tongarirovisitorcentre; Bruce
Rd; ⊘8am-5pm daily last weekend Oct-Apr,
8.30am-4.30pm daily May-last Fri Oct) has
maps and info on all corners of the park, includ-
ing walks, huts and current skiing, track and
weather conditions. It's important to check in
with them before setting off to do the Tongariro
Alpine Crossing.

The *Walks in and around Tongariro National
Park* brochure provides a helpful overview of 30
walks and tramps in the park ($3). Exhibits on
the geological and human history of the area
should keep you busy for a couple of hours on a
rainy day.

Further national park information is available
from the i-SITEs in Ohakune (p290), Turangi
(p279) and Taupo (p276).

ℹ️ Getting There & Away

BUS
Tongariro National Park is well serviced by
shuttle operators, which travel between
Whakapapa Village, National Park Village,
Ohakune, Taupo and Turangi, as well as popular
trailheads. In summer tramping trips are their
focus, but in winter most offer ski-field shuttles.
Book your bus in advance to avoid unexpected
strandings.

Many shuttle operators are offshoots or
affiliates of accommodation providers, so ask
about transport when you book your stay. **Roam**
(☑021 588 734, 0800 762 612; www.roam.net.
nz; Whakapapa Holiday Park, Bruce Rd; adult/
child $35/25) is a local Whakapapa Village-
based company

Otherwise, try Taupo-based **Tongariro Expe-
ditions** (☑0800 828 763, 07-377 0435; www.
tongariroexpeditions.com) or Turangi-based
Turangi Alpine Shuttles (p279).

CAR
The main road up into Tongariro National Park
is SH48, which leads to Whakapapa Village and
continues further up the mountain as Bruce Rd
leading to the Whakapapa Ski Area.

National Park Village
☑07 / POP 200
The small sprawl of National Park Village is
the most convenient place to stay when tack-
ling New Zealand's best one-day tramp – the
Tongariro Alpine Crossing (p282) – with
more accommodation and eating options
than nearby Whakapapa.

National Park Village is busiest during the
ski season, but in summer it makes a quieter
base than Taupo for active travellers making
the most of nearby outdoor activities. A less-
er-known fact about the area is that it's a hot
spot for train enthusiasts. Who knew?

🏃 Activities
There's little to do in the village itself, its
major enticement being its proximity to
national park tramps, mountain-bike trails,
canoe trips on the Whanganui River and
winter skiing. Most accommodation in town
offers packages for shuttles to the Tongariro
Alpine Crossing (p282) as well as lift passes
and ski hire, sparing you the steeper prices
further up the mountain. The best ski gear
can be hired from **Eivins** (☑07-892 2843;
www.facebook.com/EivinsRentals; cnr SH4 & Wai-
marino Tokaanu Rd; ski hire from $26/33 half-/full
day, board hire from $32/40 half-/full day; ⊘7am-
6pm Thu-Mon Nov-Jun, daily Jul-Oct) and **Ski Biz**
(☑07-892 2717; www.skibiz.co.nz; 10 Carroll St;
⊘7.30-10.30am & 4-7pm summer, 7.30am-7pm, to
midnight Fri winter).

Daily shuttles leave from here to the Ton-
gariro Alpine Crossing and Whakapapa Vil-
lage in summer, and the ski area in winter.

When the conditions are favourable,
experienced outdoor climbers with their
own gear can find spots near Mangatepopo

Valley and Whakapapa Gorge. Otherwise head to the indoor climbing wall at National Park Backpackers.

My Kiwi Adventure MOUNTAIN BIKING
(☑021 784 202, 0800 784 202; www.mykiwi adventure.co.nz; 2 Findlay St; paddle boarding $50, mountain biking from $45; ⊘8am-5.30pm) Offers the only-in-National-Park activity of stand-up paddle boarding on Lake Otamangakau (November to April, 2½ hours). Trips include gear and shuttle transport. Plenty of mountain-biking adventures on standout local tracks, but we recommend the Tongariro Adventure Package ($75), which combines the Tongariro Alpine Crossing and biking the Old Coach Rd over two days. Stand-alone bike rental (half-/full day $35/55) also available.

Adventure Outdoors TRAMPING, KAYAKING
(☑0800 386 925, 027 242 7209; www.adventure outdoors.co.nz; 60 Carroll St; ⊘by appt) Offers guided trips on the Tongariro Alpine Crossing – in winter ($185) and in time for the summer sunrise ($345) – and negotiating the Whanganui or Whakapapa Rivers on inflatable two-person kayaks ($235). Wetsuits and lifejackets are all provided so you're good to go.

42 Traverse MOUNTAIN BIKING
(Map p280; Kapoors Rd (off SH47)) This four- to six-hour, 46km mountain-bike trail through the Tongariro Forest is one of the most popular one-dayers on the North Island. The Traverse follows old logging tracks, making for relatively dependable going, although there are plenty of ups and downs – more downs as long as you start from Kapoors Rd (off SH47) and head down to Owhango.

Adrift Guided Outdoor Adventures CANOEING, TRAMPING
(☑07-892 2751; www.adriftnz.co.nz; 53 Carroll St; ⊘by appt) Runs guided canoe trips on the Whanganui River (one/three days $295/950), and lots of different guided tramps in Tongariro National Park (two hours to three days, $115 to $950) including the Tongariro Alpine Crossing (from $195) and tramps to Crater Lake on Mt Ruapehu ($225). Half-day mountain-bike excursions ($205) are also available.

🛏 Sleeping

National Park Village is a town of budget and midrange accommodation. This makes sense, as you'll probably spend most of your time in the great outdoors.

Spring and summer prices (October to February) are generally more affordable than winter prices during the ski season and school holidays (March to September). To avoid missing out, book in advance.

Note that summer is becoming busier, especially with visitors undertaking the Tongariro Alpine Crossing (p282).

National Park Backpackers HOSTEL $
(☑07-892 2870; www.npbp.co.nz; 4 Findlay St; sites $15, dm $26-30, d $62-90; 🖭) This big, old board-and-batten YHA hostel has a large garden for lounging, a well-equipped kitchen and standard rooms. It's a good one-stop shop for booking activities in the area, and is home to the **Climbing Wall** (www.npbp.co.nz; 4 Findlay St; adult/child $15/10; ⊘9am-8pm) for when the weather turns to custard. Small **shop** on-site. Tip: ask about rooms with views of the snow-capped peaks.

Park Hotel HOTEL $$
(☑07-892 2748, 0800 800 491; www.the-park. co.nz; 2/6 Millar St; d/tw/f from $115/115/125; 🖭) Positioned on SH4, this is our pick when tackling Tongariro Crossing. Neat and super affordable, the twin, queen and family mezzanine rooms are quiet and comfortable. The B&B and two-night crossing packages are great value and once you've conquered the mountain, there are spa pools for soaking. **Spiral Restaurant & Bar** (mains $20 to $34) is a decent place to eat.

Discovery Lodge LODGE $$
(Map p280; ☑07-892 2744, 0800 122 122; www. discovery.net.nz; SH47; sites $18, cabins $60, d from $100, 1-bdrm from $160; 🖭) A fabulous base for the Tongariro Alpine Crossing, this complex has a range of rooms, from basic cabins and motel rooms through to upmarket chalets. An on-site **restaurant** has views of Ruapehu from the large deck, plus a **bar**, lounge and **shuttle transport**. Owner and world-class mountain runner Callum Harland holds the unofficial Crossing record at a mind-boggling 1 hour 25 minutes!

Tongariro Crossing Lodge LODGE $$
(☑07-892 2688; www.tongarirocrossinglodge. com; 27 Carroll St; d $189-209; 🖭) This pretty white weatherboard cottage is decorated with a baby-blue trim and rambling blooms in summer. The new owners have refreshed the six, spacious rooms – most of which have a living area. The two studios share a kitchen, another two are self-contained and

the remainder are great for families. Dotted with period furniture, there's a sunny deck and barbecue area, too.

Parkview Apartments APARTMENT $$$
(☑ 021 252 4930; www.parkviewnationalpark.com; 24 Waimarino–Tokaanu Rd; d $290; ☎) Stylish and thoroughly modern accommodation comes to National Park Village at these apartments. Both with two bedrooms and sleeping up to four people, or two adults and three children, the expansive windows make it easy to take in the beautiful alpine scenery, although indoor distractions such as big-screen TVs, gas fireplaces and contemporary kitchens make staying inside a temptation.

✖ Eating & Drinking

Station Cafe CAFE $$
(☑ 07-892 2881; www.stationcafe.co.nz; cnr Findlay St & Station Rd; lunch $15-28, dinner $29-35; ☺ 9am-9pm) This cosy little restored railway station is now one of the few places serving up half-decent sustenance in National Park Village. Eggy brunches, sandwiches, coffee and decadent cakes, plus a dinner menu that reads like a neighbourhood gastropub (pork tenderloin, sirloin steak, panko-crumbed chicken). Book ahead for the Sunday-night roast ($20).

Schnapps PUB
(☑ 07-892 2788; www.schnappsbarruapehu.com; cnr SH4 & Findlay St; ☺ noon-late) This popular pub has a meat-fest menu (meals $19 to $28), open fire, big-screen TV, pool table and a handy ATM. Things crank up on wintry weekends, and it's recently added a minigolf course out the front to entice kids of all ages (adult/child $11/6). Not in the mood to socialise? There's a bottle shop at the entrance.

ⓘ Information

There's no i-SITE in the village, so visit www.nationalpark.co.nz and www.visitruapehu.com for info. The nearest i-SITEs are in Taumarunui (p210) and Ohakune (p290).

ⓘ Getting There & Away

The Village lies at the junction of SH4 and SH47 at 825m above sea level, 15km from the hub of Whakapapa Village.

InterCity (☑ 09-583 5780; www.intercity.co.nz) buses stop at National Park Station at the Station Cafe, where the *Northern Explorer* train run by KiwiRail Scenic (p266) also pulls up.

Tongariro Crossing Shuttles (☑ 07-892 2993; www.tongarirocrossingshuttles.co.nz) offers a return shuttle from National Park Village to the Tongariro Alpine Crossing ($40) and Whakapapa for the Tongariro Northern Circuit ($35).

Ohakune

☑ 06 / POP 1000
Outdoor adventurists look no further: Ohakune pumps with snow enthusiasts in winter and trampers and mountain bikers in summer. The vibe is best when snow drifts down on **Turoa Ski Area** and people defrost together over a drink back in town. Despite the chill outside, the après-ski culture comes in hot every season.

When the snow clears the town quietens – and accommodation prices drop. It's the perfect time to ride along the fantastic Old Coach Road mountain-bike trail and provides easy access for exploring Whanganui National Park.

There are two distinct parts to Ohakune: the commercial hub is strung along the highway, but in winter the northern end around the train station, known as the Junction, is the epicentre of the action. The two are linked by the 2km **Mangawhero River Walkway**, a leafy amble along the riverbank.

✦ Activities

There are several scenic walks near the town, many starting from the Ohakune Mountain Rd, which stretches 17km from Ohakune to the Turoa Ski Area (p284) on Mt Ruapehu. The handy DOC brochure *Walks in and around Tongariro National Park* ($3), available from the Ruapehu i-SITE (p290), is a good starting point.

The Tongariro Alpine Crossing (p282) is readily accessible via regular shuttle services from Ohakune, while the Round the Mountain Track (p283) can be accessed by continuing on the Waitonga Falls Track (p288).

**★ Ohakune Old
Coach Road** MOUNTAIN BIKING
(www.ohakunecoachroad.co.nz; Marshalls Rd) One of NZ's best half-day (three to four hours) cycle rides, this gently graded route passes engineering features including the historic Hapuawhenua and Toanui viaducts – the only two remaining curved viaducts in the southern hemisphere. It also passes through ancient forests of giant rimu and totara that survived the Taupo blast of AD 180, being in the lee of Ruapehu. From the Ohakune

WORTH A TRIP

LAKE ROTOKURA

Lake Rotokura (☑07-892 3729; www.doc.govt.nz) is 12km southeast of Ohakune at Karioi, just off SH49 (karioi means 'places to linger'). It's one of two lakes in the Lake Rotokura Ecological Reserve: the first is Dry Lake, actually quite wet and perfect for picnicking; the furthest is Rotokura, tapu (sacred) to Māori, so eating, fishing and swimming are prohibited. It's a one-way, 1km walk from the start of the track to Rotokura, with an optional loop track around the lake. Allow an hour to admire ancient beech trees and waterfowl if you decide to do the whole stroll.

To get here, drive 11km southeast along SH49 from Ohakune, then 1km from the turn-off along Karioi Station Rd. Cross the railway line until you reach Rotokura car park.

railway station, ride down Old Coach Rd, turn right into Marshalls Rd and join the track.

Mountain Bike Station
MOUNTAIN BIKING
(☑0800 245 464, 06-385 9018; www.mountainbikestation.co.nz; Ohakune Shopping Centre, 27 Goldfinch St; ⊙7.30am-6pm Mon-Fri, 7am-6pm Sat & Sun Jul-Oct, 9am-6pm Nov-Jun) Rents mountain bikes (half/full day from $35/50) and provides cost-per-person transfers to biking routes, including to the Turoa Ski Field ($20), Horopito ($15) and Whanganui ($180). Longer bike and transport packages are also available. Often open longer during peak season, hours are subject to demand. Same building as SLR (☑06-385 9018; www.slr.co.nz; ⊙7.30am-6pm Mon-Fri, 7am-6pm Sat & Sun Jul-Oct, 9am-6pm Nov-Jun).

Waitonga Falls Track
TRAMPING
(www.doc.govt.nz; Ohakune Mountain Rd) The path to Waitonga Falls (1½ hours return, 4km), Tongariro's highest waterfall (39m), offers magnificent views of Mt Ruapehu. The track starts from Ohakune Mountain Rd.

Ruapehu Homestead
HORSE RIDING
(Map p254; ☑027 267 7057; www.ruapehuhomestead.kiwi.nz; cnr Piwara St & SH49, Rangataua; 30min-3hr adult $30-180, child $25-150; ⊙treks 10am, noon & 2pm) Four kilometres east of Ohakune (near Rangataua), Ruapehu Homestead offers guided treks around its

paddocks, as well as longer rides along the river and on backcountry trails with views of the mountain.

🛌 Sleeping

Station Lodge
HOSTEL $
(☑06-385 8797; www.stationlodge.co.nz; 60 Thames St; dm/r $28/70, apt $130-220, chalets $220-250; @🕏) 🌿 Housed in a lovely old villa with wooden floors and high ceilings, this excellent YHA hostel has a well-equipped kitchen, comfortable lounge, spa pool, and a garden with a pizza oven. If you're after privacy, apartments sleeping between two to six people and separate chalets (some with two bedrooms, gas fireplaces and private spa pools) are available.

LKNZ Lodge
HOSTEL $
(☑06-385 9169; www.lknz.co.nz; 1 Rata St; campsites $30, dm $23-28, d $65-99, f $159; 🕏) From budget to flashpacker, LKNZ rooms are spread over four lodges. During the ski season at least one is rented out by instructors. Tidy doubles with wooden bed-frames are a bargain and there's a drying room, 500 DVDs, bikes for hire, pay-per-use spa pools and a sauna and a cafe (open from 7.30am; try the nachos).

Ohakune Top 10 Holiday Park
HOLIDAY PARK $
(☑06-385 8561, 0800 825 825; www.ohakune.net.nz; 5 Moore St; sites $45, units $72-140; @🕏💧) 🌿 A bubbling stream borders this holiday park, which has a wide range of accommodation, including tidy motel units sleeping up to six people. Extras include a playground, barbecue area and private spa bath. Help yourself to the herbs growing out of plastic bottles on the wooden fence.

Powderhorn Chateau
HOTEL $$$
(☑06-385 8888; www.powderhorn.co.nz; cnr Thames St & Mangawhero Tce; r from $260; @🕏💧) At this Swiss-style chalet, guests stay in rooms where their favourite Lord of the Rings characters set up during filming. Peter Jackson booked out the eight-person apartment, but there are another 33 more affordable options. With woody interiors, possum-fur blankets and a spa-temperature indoor pool with an intercom to the bar, this is the place for mountain recovery and revelry.

Peaks Motor Inn
MOTEL $$
(☑0508 843 732, 06-385 9144; www.thepeaks.co.nz; cnr Mangawhero Tce & Shannon St; d/1-bdrm unit from $149/169; 🕏) This well-kept motel

offers spacious rooms with good bathrooms and full kitchens. Communal facilities include grassy lawns, a basic gym, large outdoor spa, and sauna. Check the website for good-value packages incorporating transport for the Tongariro Alpine Crossing.

⭐ **River Lodge**   B&B **$$$**
(Map p254; ☑021 292 2883, 06-385 4771; www.theriverlodge.co.nz; 206 Mangawhero River Rd; chalets incl breakfast $290, 1-/2-bdrm $260/290; 🛜) Just 8km from town, this charming property was designed with Mangawhero River in mind. Fish with direct access, laze in a hammock, borrow a picnic rug or walk along the barefoot-massage path. There are three double rooms in the house, one with a separate single bed, and two charismatic chalets for two with private spa pools and fireplaces.

⭐ **Ruapehu Country Lodge**   B&B **$$$**
(Map p254; ☑06-385 9594, 021 707 850; www.ruapehucountrylodge.co.nz; 630 Raetihi–Ohakune Rd; d $295; 🛜) Around 5km west of Ohakune on the road to Raetihi, Ruapehu Country Lodge is the perfect combination of country elegance and classy decor. You'll get a friendly welcome from Heather and Peter, as well as the alpacas beside the manicured driveway. Framed by expansive gardens on 2 hectares, the lodge is separated from the local golf course by a meandering river.

✕ Eating

⭐ **Eat Takeaway Diner**   CAFE **$**
(☑02041265520; www.facebook.com/eattakeawaydiner; 49 Clyde St; snacks & mains $9-14; ⏱8am-3pm, closed public holidays & Oct 23-31; 🛜✏) 🍃 Bagels, innovative salads, and tasty American and Tex Mex-influenced dishes combine with the best coffee in town at this modern spot on Ohakune's main drag. All white tiles and pops of blue, there's a strong focus on organic ingredients, sustainable practices and dietary requirement-friendly options, like the vegan 'cheeseburger', salad bowl and burrito.

⭐ **Blind Finch**   BURGERS, BREAKFAST **$$**
(☑06-385 8076; www.theblindfinch.co.nz; 29 Goldfinch St; burgers & breakfast $15.50; ⏱9am-10pm Jul-Oct; 4-10pm Mon-Fri, 9am-10pm Sat & Sun, Nov-Jun; 🛜) After tramping Mt Tongariro, skiing Mt Ruapehu or mountain biking, there's nothing better than these beast-sized burgers cooked on a custom-made manuka woodfire grill. Licensed until 2am, Blind Finch boasts a **bar** and regularly hosts impromptu jam sessions, burger bingo, trivia and events. More than half a dozen varieties of eggs Benedict for breakfast, available until 2pm.

Cyprus Tree   ITALIAN **$$**
(☑06-385 8857; www.cyprustree.co.nz; cnr Clyde & Miro Sts; mains $24-34; ⏱4.30pm-late Mon-Fri, 9am-late Sat & Sun) Open year-round, this restaurant and bar serves up Italian and Kiwi-influenced dishes: think wild venison on potato-and-herb rosti to slow-cooked lamb pappardelle. There's a special menu for little kids, and Ohakune's best range of NZ craft beers for big kids. Bar snacks from 3pm to 5pm. Couches next to the fire in winter, the outdoor deck in summer.

🍷 Drinking & Nightlife

Craft Haus   COFFEE
(☑06-385 8683, 022 3858 683; www.thecrafthaus.co.nz; 31 Thames St; drinks $3-5; ⏱10am-2pm Mon, Tue, Thu, Fri, 10am-5pm Sat & Sun) 'Local is the new black' says the sign on the brick wall at this coffee house-gallery-clothing store-brewery inside the heritage Ohakune train station, right on the platform. **Volcano Coffee** roasts out the back, **Ruapehu Brewing Co.** brews, **Opus Fresh** sells beautiful merino-wool pieces, and local arts and crafts are scattered about for sale.

Kitchen   CRAFT BEER
(☑06-385 8664; www.4thames.co.nz; 4 Thames St; mains $22-25; ⏱8am-6pm Mon-Fri, 7am-6pm Sat & Sun, to late during ski season) The friendly owner refers to the Kitchen as his 'bach (beach house)' with a bar attached'. Serving only NZ craft beer from more than 20 breweries, it's packed during winter and on the first weekend of September during a spring party. Local musicians and a simple, tasty menu that swings between Mexican and Asian fare.

SEEING ORANGE

If you're travelling northwest along the State Highway into Ohakune, the first thing you'll see is a **Big Carrot** (Rangataua Rd; ♿). This tribute to the carrot capital of the country goes back to the 1920s, when Chinese settlers cleared the land to grow them. Sit anywhere long enough with a view of the road and you're likely to see a truck overflowing with soil and specks of orange. There's even an annual **Carrot Carnival** (www.carrotcarnival.org.nz; ⏱early Jun).

RIVER VALLEY

River Valley (☑06-388 1444; www.
rivervalley.co.nz; Mangaohata Rd, Taihape;
☺7.30am-5pm) is an adventure centre
and lodge about 30km northeast of
Taihape (follow the signs from Taihape's
Gretna Hotel). Its popular half-day
white-water rafting trip tackles the thrilling Grade V rapids of Rangitikei River
($175). Horse treks are also offered,
taking in views of Mt Ruapehu, the Ruahine Range and the Rangitikei River (two
hours/half day $129/175).

Lodge **accommodation** is also available (sites per person $18, dorm $31,
doubles $169-175, B&B $199). Meals in
the **on-site restaurant** feature fresh
ingredients from the lodge's gardens.
Ask about multi-activity holidays.

❶ Information

Ruapehu i-SITE (☑0800 047 483, 06-385
8427; www.visitruapehu.com; 54 Clyde St;
☺8am-5.30pm) can make bookings for activities, transport and accommodation; DOC
officers are usually on hand from 10am to
4.30pm most days.

Visit Ohakune (www.visitohakune.co.nz) is
a useful website for 'The Mountain Town' and
around.

❶ Getting There & Away

InterCity (p266) has direct bus services from
Taupo and Auckland and passes through on
services between Palmerston North and Auckland and Wellington and Auckland, stopping on
Clyde St near the i-SITE. The *Northern Explorer*
train is run by KiwiRail Scenic (p266).

Dempsey Buses (☑06-385 4022; www.
dempseybuses.co.nz) is based locally, offering
services around the Ruapehu region, including
shuttles and buses servicing the Tongariro Alpine Crossing (leaving Ohakune at 7.15am in
summer at $50 per person), a daily shuttle to
the Ohakune Old Coach Rd, shuttles to the Turoa
ski field car park to hit the slopes or take a downhill Ohakune Mountain Rd ride, on-demand service to the 42nd Traverse bike ride and services
to and from the Mangapurua Track and Bridge
to Nowhere.

Waiouru

☑06 / POP 740

Waiouru (altitude 792m) is primarily an
army base and a refuelling stop for those
taking the 56km-long Desert Rd leading
to Turangi. In winter, the road occasionally closes due to snow. A barren landscape
of reddish sand with small clumps of tussock, the **Rangipo Desert** isn't actually a
desert. This unique landscape is in fact the
result of two million years of volcanic eruptions – especially the Taupo eruption about
2000 years ago that coated the land with
thick deposits of pumice and destroyed all
vegetation.

In town itself, there's not a lot other than
the National Army Museum.

◉ Sights

National Army Museum   MUSEUM
(☑06-387 6911; www.armymuseum.co.nz; cnr SH1
& Hassett Dr; adult/child $15/5; ☺9am-4.30pm)
🖉 At the south end of the town in a large,
concrete castle is the National Army Museum, which preserves the history of the NZ
military and its various campaigns, from
colonial times to the present. Its moving stories are well told through displays of arms,
uniforms, memorabilia and other collections. The on-site **cafe** is open 9am to 4pm.
For a truly memorable visit, attend the dawn
service on Anzac Day (25 April).

❶ Information

Waiouru i-SITE (☑06-387 5279; www.visit
ruapehu.com; National Army Museum, cnr SH1
& Hassett Dr; ☺9am-4.30pm) Local knowledge
and travel advice on Waiouru and the Ruapehu
region. Reservation services available, along
with souvenirs. Located in the iconic National
Army Museum.

❶ Getting There & Away

Waiouru is located at the junction of SH1 and
SH49, 27km east of Ohakune. InterCity (p266)
services Waiouru en route from Auckland to
Wellington. Multiple direct services leave in
the morning and evening from Auckland and
throughout the day from Wellington, taking 6¾
hours and 4¾ hours respectively.

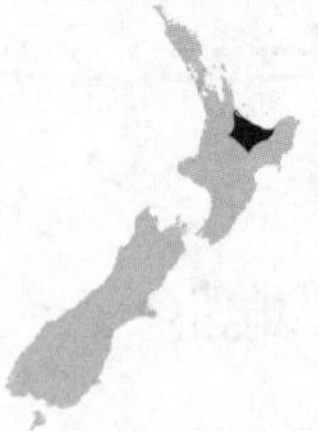

Rotorua & the Bay of Plenty

Best Places to Eat

➜ Macau (p315)

➜ Me & You (p315)

➜ Eightyeight (p320)

➜ Post Bank (p320)

➜ Grindz Café (p315)

Best Places to Stay

➜ Warm Earth Cottage (p323)

➜ Sport of Kings (p301)

➜ Asure Harbour View Motel (p314)

➜ Ohiwa Beach Holiday Park (p331)

➜ City Lights Boutique Lodge (p302)

Why Go?

Captain Cook named the Bay of Plenty when he cruised past in 1769, and plentiful it remains. Blessed with sunshine and sand, the bay stretches from Waihi Beach in the west to Opotiki in the east, with the holiday hubs of Tauranga, Mt Maunganui and Whakatane in between.

Offshore from Whakatane is New Zealand's most active volcano, Whakaari (White Island). Volcanic activity defines this region, and nowhere is this subterranean spectacle more obvious than in Rotorua. Here the daily business of life goes on among steaming hot springs, explosive geysers, bubbling mud pools and the billows of sulphurous gas responsible for the town's trademark eggy smell.

Rotorua and the Bay of Plenty are also strongholds of Māori tradition, presenting numerous opportunities to engage with NZ's rich indigenous culture: check out a power-packed concert performance, chow down at a *hāngi* (Māori feast) or skill up with some Māori arts-and-crafts techniques.

When to Go

➜ The Bay of Plenty is one of NZ's sunniest regions; Whakatane records a brilliant 2350 average hours of sunshine per year! In summer (December to February) maximums hover in the high 20s (Celsius). Everyone else is here, too, but the holiday vibe is heady and the beaches irresistible.

➜ Visit Rotorua any time: the geothermal activity never sleeps, and there are enough beds in any season.

➜ The mercury can slide below 5°C overnight here in winter, making the hot pools even more appealing. It's usually warmer on the coast, where you'll have the beaches all to yourself.

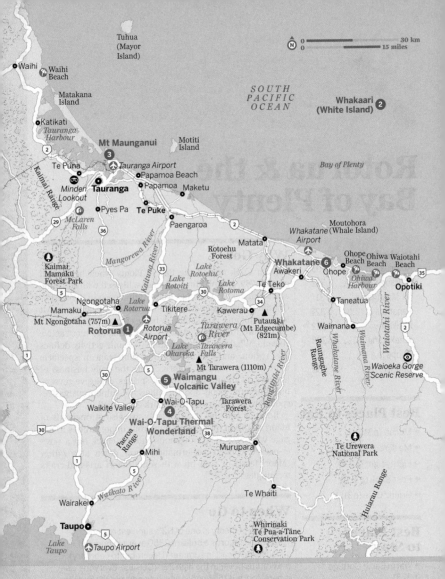

Rotorua & the Bay of Plenty Highlights

1 Rotorua (p293) Peering through the sulphurous steam at a unique town where geothermal activity, Māori culture and world-class mountain biking come together.

2 Whakaari (White Island) (p328) Stepping into the steaming crater of an active volcano 49km off the coast.

3 Mt Maunganui (p317) Lazing at the beach, carving up the surf and hiking up the signature mountain, then relaxing in the thermal pools before hitting the lively little strip of restaurants and bars.

4 Wai-O-Tapu Thermal Wonderland (p307) Marvelling at the unearthly hues of the region's most colourful geothermal attraction.

5 Waimangu Volcanic Valley (p307) Walking down through a spurting and sizzling valley to a blissfully peaceful lake.

6 Whakatane (p323) Soaking up the sunny small-town vibe where Māori culture and beach culture go hand in hand.

❶ Getting There & Away

Air New Zealand (p41) has direct flights from Tauranga and Rotorua to Auckland, Wellington and Christchurch. **Air Chathams** (☑ 0800 580 127; www.airchathams.co.nz) flies between Whakatane and Auckland.

InterCity (p41) and **Mana Bus** (☑ 09-367 9140; www.manabus.com) connect Rotorua and Tauranga to most major North Island cities, along with more limited services to other Bay of Plenty towns.

Aerolink Shuttles (☑ 0800 151 551; www.aerolink.nz) and **Luxury Airport Shuttles** (☑ 07-547 4444; www.luxuryairportshuttles.co.nz) both provide door-to-door shuttles between Auckland and Hamilton airports and the major Bay of Plenty towns.

ROTORUA

☑ 07 / POP 65,300

Catch a whiff of Rotorua's sulphur-rich air and you've already had an introduction to NZ's most dynamic geothermal area. The Māori revered this place, naming one of the most spectacular springs Wai-O-Tapu (Sacred Waters). Today 34% of the population is Māori, with cultural performances and traditional *hāngi* as big an attraction as the landscape itself.

The pervasive eggy odour hasn't prevented 'Sulphur City' becoming one of the most touristy spots on the North Island. Some say this steady trade has seduced the town into resting on its laurels while its famous attractions perpetually hike up their prices. It's certainly true that Rotorua's dining and bar scene lags well behind nearby Tauranga and Taupo. While the urban fabric of 'RotoVegas' isn't particularly appealing, where else can you see steam casually wafting out of drains and mud boiling in public parks?

History

The Rotorua area was first settled in the 14th century when the *Arawa* canoe, captained by Tamatekapua, arrived at Maketu in the central Bay of Plenty. Settlers took the tribal name Te Arawa to commemorate the vessel that had brought them here.

In the next few hundred years, subtribes spread and divided through the area (the main subtribe of Te Arawa who live in Rotorua today are known as Ngāti Whakaue). A flashpoint occurred in 1823 when the Arawa lands were attacked by Northland tribe Ngāpuhi, led by Hongi Hika, in the so-called

---

ESSENTIAL ROTORUA & THE BAY OF PLENTY

Eat a *hāngi* (earth-cooked) meal at one of the 'dinner and show' Māori cultural experiences in Rotorua.

Drink local craft beer from Rotorua's Croucher Brewing Co (p305).

Read *Tangata Whenua, An Illustrated History* (Atholl Anderson, Judith Binney & Aroha Harris, 2014) – a hefty but beautiful summation of all things Māori.

Listen to *Kora*, the eponymous rootsy album from Whakatane's soulful sons.

Watch *Utu* (Geoff Murphy, 1983), a classic NZ movie including a memorable eyeball-eating scene inspired by the death of Rev Carl Völkner in Opotiki in 1865.

Go green and negotiate the verdant bush-clad experience of Rotorua's Redwoods Treewalk (p298).

Go online www.rotoruanz.com, www.bayofplentynz.com

Musket Wars. After Te Arawa were defeated at Mokoia Island, the warring parties made their peace.

During the Waikato War (1863–64), Te Arawa threw in its lot with the government against its traditional Waikato enemies, preventing East Coast reinforcements getting through to support the Kingitanga (King Movement).

With peace in the early 1870s, word spread of scenic wonders, miraculous landscapes and watery cures for all manner of diseases. Rotorua boomed. Its main attraction was the fabulous Pink and White Terraces, formed by volcanic silica deposits. Touted at the time as the eighth natural wonder of the world, they were destroyed in the 1886 Mt Tarawera eruption.

⊙ Sights

⊙ City Centre

Rotorua Museum   NOTABLE BUILDING
(☑ 07-350 1814; www.rotoruamuseum.co.nz; Oruawhata Dr; adult/child $20/8) Constructed in a striking faux-Tudor style, Rotorua's most magnificent building opened in 1908 as an elegant spa retreat called the Bath House. In 1969 it was converted into a museum,

Rotorua

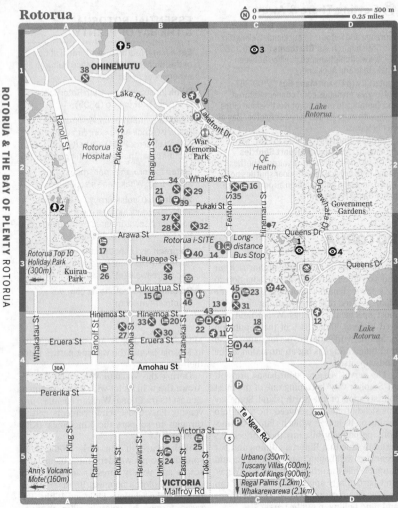

with an art gallery added later. Sadly it was closed in November 2016 after cracks were spotted following the major earthquake in Kaikoura, 650km away. Seismic strengthening was being planned at the time of research, but the work is expected to take years to complete.

Kuirau Park
PARK

(Ranolf St) Want some affordable geothermal thrills? Just west of central Rotorua is Kuirau Park, a volcanic area you can explore for free. It's a wonderful juxtaposition of genteel gardening and nature at its most unpredictable. Steam hisses and mud boils from fenced-off sections, while parents push strollers past duck-filled ponds and through the wisteria arbour. Occasional eruptions cover the park in mud, thwarting the best plans of the council's gardeners.

Take care around the active areas and keep your toddlers on a tight rein.

Lake Rotorua
LAKE

Lake Rotorua is the largest of the district's 18 lakes and is – underneath all that water – a spent volcano. Near the centre of the lake is **Mokoia Island**, which has for centuries

Rotorua

been occupied by various subtribes of the area. The lake can be explored by boat, with several operators situated at the lakefront.

Government Gardens   GARDENS
(Hinemaru St) The manicured Government Gardens surrounding the Rotorua Museum are a wonderful example of the blending of English (rose gardens, croquet lawns and bowling greens) and Māori traditions (carvings at the entrance and subtly blended into the buildings). Being Rotorua, there are steaming thermal pools scattered about, and it's well worth taking a walk along the active geothermal area at the lake's edge.

◉ Whakarewarewa

Rotorua's main drawcard is Whakarewarewa (pronounced 'fah-kah-*reh*-wah-*reh*-wah'), a geothermal reserve 3km south of the city centre. This area's full name is Te Whakarewarewatanga o te Ope Taua a Wāhiao, meaning 'The War Dance of the War Party of Wāhiao'. The area is as famous for its Māori cultural significance as for its steam and bubbling mud. There are more than 500 springs here, including some famed geysers.

The active area is split between the still-lived-in Māori village of Whakarewarewa (p296) and the Te Puia complex, which are separated from each other by a fence. Both offer cultural performances and geothermal activity galore; the village is cheaper to visit but Te Puia has a kiwi house and important Māori art institutions.

Te Puia   CULTURAL CENTRE
(☑07-348 9047; www.tepuia.com; Hemo Rd; adult/child $54/29, incl performance $69/35, Te Pō $125/63; ⊗8am-5pm) Te Puia dials up the heat on *Māoritanga* (things Māori) with explosive performances from both its cultural troupe and from **Pōhutu** (Big Splash), its famous geyser which erupts around 20 times a day, spurting hot water up to 30m skyward. You'll know when it's about to blow because the adjacent **Prince of Wales' Feathers** geyser will start up shortly before. Also here is the **National Carving School** and the

National Weaving School, where you can watch the students at work.

Daytime visits (*Te Rā*) include an informative guided tour of the entire complex (departing on the hour), which also features a *wharenui* (carved meeting house), a recreated precolonial village, a nocturnal kiwi enclosure and a large chunk of the Whakarewarewa thermal zone, including three major geysers and a huge pool of boiling mud. After the tour you're welcome to wander around at your leisure. It's well worth paying extra for the cultural performance (10.15am, 12.15pm and 3.15pm), incorporating a traditional welcome into the *wharenui* and a 45-minute *kapa haka* (traditional song and dance) concert.

The three-hour *Te Pō* (night) experience starts at 6pm and includes a cultural show and a *hāngi* meal, followed by a tour through the thermal zone on a people mover.

The exit is, inevitably, through the gift shop, which in this case gives you the opportunity to buy genuine Māori art and craft, along with beauty products made from Te Puia's mineral-rich mud.

Whakarewarewa   VILLAGE
(☑ 07-349 3463; www.whakarewarewa.com; 17 Tyron St; adult/child $40/18, incl hāngi $70/40; ☺ 8.30am-5pm) Unlike made-for-tourists experiences of Māori culture, Whakarewarewa is a living village where the local Tūhourangi/Ngāti Wāhiao people have resided for centuries. Villagers lead the tours (departing hourly from 9am to 4pm) and tell stories of their way of life amid the steamy bubbling pools, silica terraces and geysers. While most of the geothermal zone is across the fence in Te Puia, the view of the Pōhutu geyser is just as good from here, and considerably cheaper.

The admission also includes a cultural performance (daily at 11.15am and 2pm, with an additional show at 12.30pm from November to March) and a self-guided nature trail. The village shops sell authentic arts and crafts, and you can learn more about Māori traditions such as flax weaving, carving and *tā moko* (tattooing). Nearby you can eat tasty, buttery sweetcorn ($2) pulled straight out of the hot mineral pool – the only genuine geothermal *hāngi* meal in town.

Redwoods Whakarewarewa Forest   FOREST
(☑ 07-350 0110; www.redwoods.co.nz; Long Mile Rd) This magical forest park is 3km southeast of town on Tarawera Rd. From 1899,

170 tree species were planted here to see which could be grown successfully for timber. Mighty Californian redwoods (up to 72m high) give the park its grandeur today. Walking tracks range from a half-hour wander through the Redwood Grove to a whole-day route to the Blue and Green Lakes. Several walks start from the Redwoods i-SITE (p306), where you'll also find the spectacular Redwoods Treewalk (p298).

Aside from walking, the forest is great for picnics, and is acclaimed for its accessible mountain biking. There are close to 100km of tracks to keep bikers of all skill levels happy for days on end. Note that not all tracks in the forest are designated for bikers, so adhere to the signposts. Pick up a trail map at the i-SITE. Mountain Bike Rotorua (p299) and Planet Bike (p299) offer bike hire, across the park off Waipa State Mill Rd, where there are also toilets and a shower. At the time of research, a professional-standard BMX track was being constructed in this section of the park.

◎ Ohinemutu

Ohinemutu is a lakeside Māori village that is home to around 260 people. Highlights include the 1905 **Tama-te-Kapua Meeting House** (not open to visitors), many steaming volcanic vents, and the wonderful Māori-British mash-up that is St Faith's. Be respectful if you visit the village: the residents don't appreciate loud, nosy tourists wandering around taking photos of their private property.

St Faith's Anglican Church   CHURCH
(☑ 07-348 2393; Korokai St; admission by donation; ☺ 8am-6pm, services 9am Sun & 10am Wed) Consecrated in 1918, Ohinemutu's historic timber church is intricately decorated with Māori carvings, *tukutuku* (woven panels), painted scrollwork and stained-glass windows. One window features an etched image of Christ wearing a Māori cloak, appearing to walk on the waters of Lake Rotorua, visible through the glass. Behind the church is a military graveyard and memorial.

◎ Surrounds

Wingspan   BIRD SANCTUARY
(☑ 07-357 4469; www.wingspan.co.nz; 1164 Paradise Valley Rd, Ngongotaha Valley; adult/child $25/10; ☺ 9am-3pm) The Wingspan National Bird of Prey Centre is dedicated to conserv-

MĀORI NZ: ROTORUA & THE BAY OF PLENTY

The Bay of Plenty's Māori name, *Te Moana a Toi* (The Sea of Toi), recalls an early Polynesian voyager whose descendants first settled in Whakatane. Later (probably around the 13th or 14th century) the Mātaatua *waka* (canoe) made landfall in Whakatane, and it's from this migration that most of the Bay's tribes trace their ancestry. These include **Te Whakatōhea** (www.whakatohea.co.nz) of Opotiki, **Ngāti Awa** (www.ngatiawa.iwi.nz) of Whakatane, and **Ngāi Te Rangi** (www.ngaiterangi.org.nz), **Ngāti Pūkenga** (www.ngatipukenga.com) and **Ngāti Ranginui** (www.ranginui.co.nz) of the Tauranga area. **Te Arawa** (www.tearawa.iwi.nz) of Rotorua take their name from a different ancestral *waka*.

Tribes in this region were involved on both sides of the New Zealand Wars of the late 19th century, with those fighting against the government suffering considerable land confiscations that have caused legal problems right up to the present day.

There's a significant Māori population in the region, and many ways for travellers to engage with Māori culture. Whakatane has a visitor-friendly main-street marae (p323) (traditional meeting place) and Toi's Pā (p325), perhaps New Zealand's oldest *pā* (fortified village) site. Rotorua has Māori villages, *hāngi* (Māori feasts) and cultural performances aplenty.

ing threatened NZ raptors, particularly the kararea (NZ falcon). Learn about the birds in the museum display, then take a sneaky peek into the incubation area before walking through the all-weather aviary. Make sure you're here by 1.30pm for the 2pm flying display.

Paradise Valley Springs NATURE CENTRE
(☑07-348 9667; www.paradisevalleysprings.co.nz; 467 Paradise Valley Rd, Ngongotaha Valley; adult/child $30/15; ⊙8am-dusk, last entry 5pm) 🌿 At the foot of Mt Ngongotaha, 8km from Rotorua, this 6-hectare park has trout springs, big slippery eels, native birds and various land-dwelling animals such as deer, alpacas, possums and a pride of lions (fed at 2.30pm). There's also a coffee shop and an elevated treetop walkway.

Volcanic Hills Winery WINERY
(☑07-282 2018; www.volcanichills.co.nz; 176 Fairy Springs Rd, Fairy Springs; tastings 3/5 wines $9.50/15; ⊙11am-5.30pm) Perched at the top of the gondola, this winery-run bar gives you the opportunity to sample its vintages while soaking up stupendous lake views. The wine is made at the bottom of the hill from grapes sourced from NZ's main wine regions. You'll save a couple of dollars if you purchase your tasting as a combo with your gondola ticket.

Agrodome AGRICULTURAL CENTRE
(☑07-357 1050; www.agrodome.co.nz; 141 Western Rd, Ngongotaha; adult/child shows $36/19, tours $49/25, wagon ride $20/15, 4WD tour $99/89; ⊙8.30am-5pm) Learn everything you need to know about sheep at this model Kiwi farm.

Shows (9.30am, 11am and 2.30pm) include a parade of champion rams, lamb feeding, and shearing, milking and doggy displays. Yes, some of the jokes are corny, but it's still very entertaining. Farm tours on a tractor train depart at 10.40am, 12.10pm, 1.30pm and 3.40pm. You can also take a ride on a Clydesdale-drawn wagon or rev it up on a 4WD Back Country Adventure (10.45am, 12.15pm and 3.45pm).

Rainbow Springs NATURE CENTRE
(☑07-350 0440; www.rainbowsprings.co.nz; 192 Fairy Springs Rd, Fairy Springs; 24hr passes adult/child/family $40/20/99; ⊙8.30am-10pm) 🌿 The natural springs here are home to wild trout and eels, which you can peer at through an underwater viewer. There are interpretive walkways, a 'Big Splash' water ride and plenty of animals, including tuatara (a native reptile) and native birds. The **Kiwi Encounter** offers a rare peek into the lives of these endangered birds: excellent 30-minute tours (an extra $10 per person) have you tiptoeing through incubator and hatchery areas. There's also a free-flight exotic bird show at 11.30am.

Rainbow Springs is around 3km north of central Rotorua.

🏃 Activities

Adventure Sports

Rotorua Canopy Tours ADVENTURE SPORTS
(☑07-343 1001; www.canopytours.co.nz; 147 Fairy Springs Rd, Fairy Springs; 3hr tours adult/child $149/119; ⊙8am-8pm Oct-Apr, to 6pm May-Sep)

Explore a 1.2km web of bridges, flying foxes, zip-lines and platforms, 22m high in a lush native forest canopy 10 minutes out of town (they say that rimu tree is 1000 years old!), with plenty of native birds to keep you company. All trips depart from their office opposite the gondola.

Redwoods Treewalk
WALKING

(☑ 07-350 0110; www.treewalk.co.nz; Long Mile Rd, Whakarewarewa; adult/child $25/15; ⊗ 8.30am-9.30pm) 🍃 More than 500m is traversed on this walkway combining 23 bouncy wooden bridges suspended between century-old redwood trees. Most of the pathway is around 6m off the forest floor, but it ascends to 20m in some parts. It's at its most impressive at night when it's lit by striking wooden lanterns, hung from the trees.

Agroventures
ADVENTURE SPORTS

(☑ 07-357 4747; www.agroventures.co.nz; 1335 Paradise Valley Rd, Ngongotaha; 1/2/4 rides $49/85/129, bungy $129; ⊗ 9am-5pm) Agroventures is a hive of action, 9km north of Rotorua (free shuttles available). Start off with the 43m **bungy** and the **Swoop**, a 130km/h swing. The **Freefall Xtreme** simulates skydiving, and also here is the **Shweeb**, a monorail velodrome from which you hang in a clear capsule and pedal yourself along at speeds of up to 50km/h.

Alongside is the **Agrojet**, one of NZ's fastest jetboats, splashing and weaving around a very tight 1km course. Plus there's a **BMX** airbag and ramps for practising your jumps (two hours $30, BYO bike).

Skyline Rotorua
CABLE CAR

(☑ 07-347 0027; www.skyline.co.nz; 178 Fairy Springs Rd, Fairy Springs; adult/child gondola $30/15; ⊗ 9am-10pm) The cable car ride up the side of Mt Ngongotaha is only a teaser for the thrills on offer at the top. Most popular is the **luge**, which shoots along three different tracks (one/three/five/seven rides $14/28/38/45). For even speedier antics, try the **Sky Swing** (adult/child $89/74), the **Zoom Zipline** ($95/85) or the mountain-bike Gravity Park (p299). The summit also offers a restaurant, wine-tasting at the Volcanic Hills Winery (p297), a nature trail and stargazing sessions ($93/49).

Zorb
ADVENTURE SPORTS

(☑ 07-357 5100; www.zorb.com; 149 Western Rd, Ngongotaha; 1-/2-/3-person ride $45/70/90; ⊗ 9am-5pm, to 7pm Jan) The Zorb is 9km north of Rotorua on SH5 – look for the grassy hillside with large, clear, people-filled spheres rolling down it. There are three courses: 150m straight, 180m zigzag or 250m 'Drop'. Do your zorb strapped in and dry, or freestyle with water thrown in. And you can even rattle around with up to two friends inside.

Kawarau Jet
BOATING

(☑ 07-343 7600; www.kjetrotorua.co.nz; Lakefront Dr; 30min adult/child $85/54; ⊗ 9am-6pm) Speed things up on a jetboat ride with Kawarau Jet, which tears around the lake. Parasailing (30 minutes tandem/solo $85/115) is also available.

ROTORUA IN...

One Day

Start with a stroll through steamy **Kuirau Park** (p294) then head down to Ohinemutu to check out the carvings on the *wharenui* (meeting houses) and **St Faith's Anglican Church** (p296). Follow the lakefront to **Government Gardens** (p295) then cut through the park for a better look at the exterior of the **Rotorua Museum** (p293) and **Blue Baths** (p299). Grab a bite to eat in the town centre, then head to either **Whakarewarewa** (p296) or **Te Puia** (p295) for a cultural show and to gawk at the dependable Pōhutu geyser. In the evening, hit the **Eat Streat** section of Tutanekai St for a meal and a drink. Relax before bedtime with a lakeside mineral soak at the **Polynesian Spa** (p299).

Two Days

Too much geothermal excitement is barely enough! Spend the morning in **Waimangu Volcanic Valley** (p307) and/or **Wai-O-Tapu Thermal Wonderland** (p307). In the afternoon, drive down to **Lake Tarawera** (p307), stopping for a circuit of **Tikitapu** (the Blue Lake) on the way. In the evening, catch a concert and consume a *hāngi* (earth-cooked meal) at **Tamaki Māori Village** (p305) or **Mitai Māori Village** (p305).

Wall
CLIMBING

(☑07-350 1400; www.basementcinema.co.nz; 1140 Hinemoa St; adult/child $16/13, shoe hire $5; ⊘noon-10pm Mon-Fri, 10am-9pm Sat & Sun) Get limbered up at the Wall, a three-storey indoor climbing wall with overhangs aplenty.

Adventure Playground
OUTDOORS

(☑0800 782 396; www.adventureplayground.co.nz; 451 Ngongotaha Rd, Ngongotaha; ⊘from 10am) Horse trekking (one/two hours $65/120), clay-bird shooting (from $75) and self-drive 4WD tours (half-/full day $85/140) are all on offer at this versatile activities centre. Kids can take a 10-minute hand-held horse ride for $20.

OGO
ADVENTURE SPORTS

(☑07-343 7676; www.ogo.co.nz; 525 Ngongotaha Rd, Fairy Springs; 1/2/3 rides $45/80/99; ⊘9am-5pm) The OGO (about 5km north of town) involves careening down a grassy hillside in a big bubble, with water or without. Yes, it is very similar to the Zorb.

Mountain Biking

Between Redwoods Whakarewarewa Forest (p296) and the Skyline Rotorua MTB Gravity Park, Rotorua is well established as a mountain-biking and BMX destination. Additionally, the two-day, 48km Te Ara Ahi (Thermal by Bike) trail starts in Rotorua and heads south via various geothermal attractions to the Waikite Valley Thermal Pools (p310). This intermediate-level route is designated as one of the New Zealand Cycle Trail's 'Great Rides' (www.nzcycletrail.com). For more information, enquire at the Rotorua i-SITE or get online at www.riderotorua.com.

★ Skyline Rotorua MTB Gravity Park
MOUNTAIN BIKING

(☑07-347 0027; www.skyline.co.nz; 178 Fairy Springs Rd, Fairy Springs; 1/15/40 gondola uplifts with bike $30/59/110; ⊘9am-5.30pm) More evidence of Rotorua's status as a world-class mountain-biking destination is the network of 11 MTB tracks coursing down Mt Ngongotaha. There are options for riders of all experience levels, and access to the top of the park is provided by the Skyline gondola. Bike rental is available on-site from Mountain Bike Rotorua.

Mountain Bike Rotorua
MOUNTAIN BIKING

(☑07-348 4295; www.mtbrotorua.co.nz; Waipa State Mill Rd, Whakarewarewa; hire per 2hr/day from $35/60, guided rides from $130; ⊘9am-5pm) This outfit hires out bikes at the Waipa Mill car park entrance to the Redwoods Whakarewarewa Forest (p296), the starting point for the bike trails. You can also stop by their central Rotorua adventure hub (☑07-348 4290; www.mtbrotorua.co.nz; 1128 Hinemoa St; ⊘9am-5pm) for rentals, mountain-biking information and a cool little cafe, and they can fit you out with a bike at the Skyline MTB Gravity Park, too.

Planet Bike
CYCLING

(☑07-346 1717; www.planetbike.co.nz; 8 Waipa Bypass Rd, Whakarewarewa; hire per 2hr/day from $35/60) Bike hire (hardtail, full suspension, electric and kids' bikes) and guided mountain-bike rides (from $150) in the Redwoods Whakarewarewa Forest (p296).

Hiking

There are plenty of opportunities to stretch your legs around Rotorua, including the popular lakefront stroll (20 minutes). There are also a couple of good walks at Mt Ngongotaha: the easy 2.5km Ngongotaha Nature Loop through native forest, and the steep 5km return Jubilee Track to the (viewless) summit.

There are also dozens of more challenging tracks in the broader Rotorua Lakes area (p310).

Thermal Pools & Massage

Blue Baths
SWIMMING

(☑07-350 2119; www.bluebaths.co.nz; Queens Dr; adult/child $11/6; ⊘10am-6pm) The gorgeous Spanish Mission-style Blue Baths opened in 1933 (and, amazingly, were closed from 1982 to 1999) and they now regularly host special events (performances, weddings etc). If you feel like taking a dip, the pool is a fraction of the price of the nearby Polynesian Spa, but note that while it's geothermically heated, it's not mineral water.

Polynesian Spa
HOT SPRINGS

(☑07-348 1328; www.polynesianspa.co.nz; 1000 Hinemoa St; family pools adult/child $23/10, adult/deluxe pools $30/50, private pools per 30min from $20; ⊘8am-11pm) A bathhouse opened at these Government Gardens springs in 1882, and people have been taking to the waters ever since. Choose between the heated freshwater family pool, or the series of small adults-only mineral pools (36°C to 42°C) by the lake's edge. The deluxe option offers even more picturesque rock-lined lakeside pools and includes a free locker ($5 otherwise) and towel.

Spa treatments are also available, including massage, mud and beauty treatments.

Fishing

There's always good trout fishing to be had somewhere around Rotorua. Hire a guide or go solo: either way a licence (per day $20) is essential, and available from **O'Keefe's Anglers Depot** (☑07-346 0178; www.okeefesfishing.co.nz; 1113 Eruera St; ⊗8.30am-5pm Mon-Fri, 9am-2pm Sat). Note that not all of the Rotorua Lakes can be fished year-round; check with O'Keefe's or the i-SITE (p306).

Trout Man   FISHING
(☑ 021 951 174; www.waiteti.com; 14 Okona Cres, Ngongotaha; 2hr/day trips from $55/175) Learn to fish with experienced angler Harvey Clark.

Other Activities

aMAZEme   OUTDOORS
(☑07-357 5759; www.amazeme.co.nz; 1335 Paradise Valley Rd, Ngongotaha; adult/child/family $16/10/50; ⊗10am-4pm; ▣) This amazing 1.4km maze is constructed from immaculately pruned, head-high escallonia hedge. Lose yourself (or the kids) in the endless spirals. There's also a butterfly house and a small critter petting zoo.

☞ Tours

Happy Ewe Tours   CYCLING
(☑022 622 9252; www.happyewetours.com; departs 1148 Hinemaru St; adult/child $60/30; ⊗10am & 2pm) Saddle up for a three-hour, small-group bike tour of Rotorua, wheeling past 27 sights around the city. It's all flat and slow-paced, so you don't need to be at your physical peak (you're on holiday after all).

Foris Eco Tours   ECOTOUR
(☑07-542 5080; www.foris.co.nz; from $295) ✿ Check out ancient rainforest and native bird life in Whirinaki Te Pua-a-Tāne Conservation Park, or take a rafting and trout-fishing trip along the easy-going Rangitaiki River.

Elite Adventures   TOURS
(☑ 07-347 8282; www.eliteadventures.co.nz; half-/ full day from $155/290) Small-group tours covering a selection of Rotorua's major cultural and natural highlights.

Volcanic Air   TOURS
(☑07-348 9984; www.volcanicair.co.nz; Lakefront Dr; trips $95-1045) Offers a variety of float-plane and helicopter flights taking in Mt Tarawera and surrounding geothermal sites, including a 3½-hour flight over Whakaari.

Thermal Land Shuttle   TOURS
(☑0800 894 287; www.thermalshuttle.co.nz; departs 1167 Fenton St; adult/child from $65/33) Daily scheduled shuttles and tours around a selection of key sights, including Waimangu, Wai-O-Tapu, Waitomo Caves and stops on the Te Ara Ahi cycle trail. Transport-only or entry-inclusive options are available.

Rotorua Duck Tours   TOURS
(☑07-345 6522; www.rotoruaducktours.co.nz; 1241 Fenton St; adult/child $69/45; ⊗tours 11am, 1pm & 3.30pm Oct-Apr, 11am & 2.15pm May-Sep) Ninety-minute trips in an amphibious bi-ofuelled vehicle take in the major sites around town and head out onto three lakes (Rotorua, Okareka and Tikitapu/ Blue). Longer Lake Tarawera trips are also available.

Geyser Link Shuttle   TOURS
(☑03-477 9083; www.travelheadfirst.com; half-/ full day $82/135) Tours some of the major sights around Rotorua, including a half-day in Wai-O-Tapu or Waimangu, or a full day visiting both. Trips incorporating Hobbiton, Whakarewarewa and Mitai Māori Village are also available.

Mana Adventures   BOATING
(☑07-348 4186; www.manaadventures.co.nz; Lakefront Dr; ⊗9am-5pm) Down at the lake, Mana Adventures offers (weather permitting) rental pedal boats (adult/child $10/8 per 20 minutes), kayaks ($16/28 per half-hour/hour) and walking on water inside a giant inflatable ball ($11 per five minutes).

ᨑ Sleeping

Rotorua has plenty of motels (especially around Fenton St), holiday parks and an ever-changing backpacker scene. Ngongotaha, 7km northwest of the town centre, has some good B&Bs in its rural hinterland.

Crash Palace   HOSTEL **$**
(☑07-348 8842; www.crashpalace.co.nz; 1271 Hinemaru St; dm/s from $24/50, d with/without bathroom $78/70; @☏) Crash occupies a big, blue 1930s hotel near Government Gardens. The atmosphere strikes a balance between party and pristine, without too much of either. There's lots of art on the walls, a pool table and DJ console in the lobby, and a beaut terrace and thermally heated hot tub out the back. Limited off-street parking.

Waiteti Trout Stream Holiday Park   HOLIDAY PARK $

(☑07-357 5255; www.waiteti.com; 14 Okona Cres, Ngongotaha; sites/s/tw from $21/35/55, unit with/without bathroom $105/60; ☎) ⚡ This keenly maintained campground is a great option if you don't mind the 8km drive into town. Set in gardens abutting a trout-filled stream, it's a cute classic with character-filled motel units, compact cabins, a tidy backpackers' lodge (private rooms only) and beaut campsites by the water. Kayaks and dinghies are free, and you can book a fly-fishing lesson.

YHA Rotorua   HOSTEL $

(☑07-349 4088; www.yha.co.nz; 1278 Haupapa St; dm $26-31, with/without bathroom s $85/75, d from $94/84; @☎) ⚡ Bright and sparkling, this classy, purpose-built hostel is great for those wanting to get outdoors, with staff eager to assist with trip bookings, and bike storage and hire. Pricier rooms come with bathrooms, and there's a barbecue area and deck for hanging out on (though this ain't a party pad). Off-street parking is a bonus.

Funky Green Voyager   HOSTEL $

(☑07-346 1754; www.funkygreenvoyager.co.nz; 4 Union St, Victoria; dm $28-29, with/without bathroom s $70/47, d $78/66; ☎) ⚡ Green on the outside and the inside – due to several cans of paint and a dedicated environmental policy – the shoe-free Funky GV features laid-back tunes and plenty of sociable chat among a spunky bunch of guests and worldly-wise owners. The best rooms have bathrooms; dorms are roomy with quality mattresses and solid timber bunks.

Rotorua Central Backpackers   HOSTEL $

(☑07-349 3285; www.rotoruacentralbackpackers. co.nz; 1076 Pukuatua St; dm/s/d without bathroom $28/62/66; ☎) Built as flats in 1936, this heritage hostel retains original features including dark-wood skirting boards and door frames, deep bathtubs and geothermally powered radiators. Dorms have no more than six beds (and no bunks), plus there's a spa pool and barbecue. Perfect if you're not looking to party.

Rock Solid Backpackers   HOSTEL $

(☑07-282 2053; www.rocksolidrotorua.co.nz; 1140 Hinemoa St; dm from $27/60, d with/without bathroom $95/75; ☎) Cavernous Rock Solid occupies a former shopping mall: you might be bunking down in a florist or a delicatessen. Dorms over the street are sunny, and there's a big, bright kitchen. Downstairs is

the Wall (p299) rock-climbing facility, and the hostel's spacious lounge looks right out at the action. Free wi-fi, and table-tennis and pool tables seal the deal.

Base Rotorua   HOSTEL $

(☑07-348 8636; www.stayatbase.com; 1286 Arawa St; dm $30-33, r with/without bathroom $100/90; @☎⛱) A link in the Base chain, this huge hostel is ever-popular with partying backpackers who love the trashy Lava Bar (cheap meals, theme nights). It's a little shabby and dorms can be tight (up to 10 beds), but extras such as female-only dorms, en suites attached to most rooms and a thermally heated pool compensate.

Astray   MOTEL, HOSTEL $

(☑07-348 1200; www.astray.co.nz; 1202 Pukuatua St; dm/s $25/45, d with/without bathroom from $95/70; ☎) Even if you are 6ft 3in, Astray – a 'micro-motel' that would probably be more at home in Tokyo than Rotorua – is a decent budget bet. Clean, tidy, quiet, friendly and central: just don't expect acres of space.

★ Sport of Kings   MOTEL $$

(☑07-348 2135; www.sportofkingsmotel.co.nz; 6 Peace St, Fenton Park; units from $159; ☎⛱♿) Situated near the racecourse (if you hadn't already guessed), this friendly complex leads the motel pack with 16 spiffy, comfortable units. Some have their own thermal spas, while other guests can book one of the private tubs or splash about in the heated pool. Plus there's an electric-car charging station, a bike wash-down area and free daily newspapers.

All Seasons Holiday Park   HOLIDAY PARK $$

(☑07-345 6240; www.allseasonsrotorua.co.nz; 50-58 Lee Rd, Hannahs Bay; sites from $23, unit with/without bathroom $129/95; ⛄@☎⛱♿) ⚡ Jurassic Park meets holiday park at this dinosaur-themed campground, 8km northeast of the city centre. Kids will love the colourful concrete beasts, fanciful playground and covered heated pool. Their parents will appreciate the reasonable rates, the robes in the modern motel units, and the well-equipped campers' kitchen. It's near the airport but there aren't many flights, and none at night.

B&B @ the Redwoods   B&B $$

(☑07-345 4499; www.theredwoods.co.nz; 3 Awatea St, Lynmore; r $180-229; ☎) Like it says on the tin, this pleasant place offers three en-suite B&B rooms in a suburban house at the forest's edge. Two have views over the lake while the third faces the front garden. All have access to a large guest lounge where you can help yourself to a hot drink or share an evening glass of wine.

Aura   MOTEL $$

(☑ 07-348 8134; www.aurarotorua.co.nz; 1078 Whakaue St; unit from $145; ⏰☒) Plenty of Rotorua's motels have thermally heated freshwater spa pools but Aura differentiates itself with two natural mineral-water spas and a heated outdoor swimming pool. It's an older complex but it's been fully renovated, and the friendly owners can sort you out with a free Dutch-style bike for lakeside explorations.

Regal Palms   MOTEL $$

(☑ 07-350 3232; www.regalpalms.co.nz; 350 Fenton St, Glenholme; r from $185; ✳@⏰☒⛏) A large upmarket motel with resort ambitions, Regal Palms has tree-shaded gardens, a swimming pool, a gym, a sauna and kids' playground facilities including a mini-golf course. The rooms and apartments – all with spa baths – are spacious and modern, and there's an on-site lounge bar.

Rotorua Top 10 Holiday Park   HOLIDAY PARK $$

(☑ 07-348 1886; www.rotoruatop10.co.nz; 1495 Pukuatua St; sites from $55, unit with/without bathroom from $175/150; ✳@⏰☒⛏) Everything's kept spick and span at this small but perfectly formed holiday park. Facilities include a small outdoor pool, hot mineral spas and a super children's playground. Cabins are in good nick and have kettles, toasters and small fridges, or you can opt for a smart self-contained motel unit.

Victoria Lodge   MOTEL $$

(☑ 07-348 4039; www.victorialodge.co.nz; 10 Victoria St, Victoria; unit from $129; ⏰) The friendly Vic has seen a lot of competitors come and go, maintaining its foothold in the market with individual-feeling units with shallow thermally heated tubs. Fully equipped apartments can squeeze in seven, though four would be comfortable.

Sandi's Bed & Breakfast   B&B $$

(☑ 07-348 0884; www.sandisbedandbreakfast. co.nz; 103 Fairy Springs Rd, Fairy Springs; s/d incl breakfast $85/130; ⏰☒) Major renovations were underway when we last visited this friendly B&B, run by the well-humoured Sandi, who offers continental breakfasts and local advice with a ready smile. It's on a busy road a couple of kilometres north of town, so the best bets are the two bohemian chalets out the back.

Six on Union   MOTEL $$

(☑ 07-347 8062; www.sixonunion.co.nz; 6 Union St, Victoria; unit $129-180; @⏰☒) Hanging baskets and plastic flowers ahoy! This modest place has a pool and a hot tub, and small kitchenettes in all of the functional units. It's away from traffic noise, but still an easy walk into town.

Ann's Volcanic Motel   MOTEL $$

(☑ 07-347 1007; www.rotoruamotel.co.nz; 107 Malfroy Rd, Victoria; units from $129; ⏰) The larger rooms at this older motel feature courtyard spas and facilities for travellers with disabilities. Rooms close to the street can be a tad noisy. Free laundry facilities are a nice bonus.

★ City Lights Boutique Lodge   B&B $$$

(☑ 07-349 1413; www.citylights.nz; 56c Mountain Rd, Western Heights; r/cottage/apt/ste $275/275/285/355; ✳@⏰) Looking down on Rotorua from the slopes of Mt Ngongotaha, this upmarket lodge has three en-suite B&B rooms in the main house, a self-contained apartment attached to it and a separate garden cottage further down the drive. Plus there's a gym, a sauna and pet alpacas.

Quest Rotorua Central   APARTMENT $$$

(☑ 07-929 9808; www.questrotoruacentral.co.nz; 1192 Hinemoa St; apt from $210; ✳☒) Your quest for an upmarket, self-contained apartment ends at this modern four-storey block in the heart of the town centre. Double-glazing keeps the street noise at bay, although Rotorua isn't particularly noisy after dark anyway. Even the studio units are spacious and have full kitchen and laundry facilities.

Koura Lodge   B&B $$$

(☑ 07-348 5868; www.kouralodge.co.nz; 209 Kawaha Point Rd, Kawaha Point; r from $525; ⏰) Secluded on the lake's western shore, this upmarket lodge features spacious rooms and suites, and a two-bedroom apartment. Decks and balconies segue to lake views, and kayaking right from the property is possible. Gourmet breakfasts around the huge wooden table are perfect for meeting other travellers. A hot tub and sauna are added diversions.

Regent of Rotorua   BOUTIQUE HOTEL $$$

(☑ 07-348 4079; www.regentrotorua.co.nz; 1191 Pukaki St; s/d from $210/280; ✳⏰☒) A renovated 1960s motel, the Regent delivers glitzy glam in spades, with hip black-and-white decor, statement mirrors and feature wallpaper. Both the small outdoor and indoor pools are heated. If you tire of the well-regarded restaurant, Tutanekai St (known as Eat Streat) is a brief amble away.

Tuscany Villas MOTEL $$$
(⏹07-348 3500; www.tuscanyvillasrotorua.co.nz; 280 Fenton St, Glenholme; unit from $240; 🐾) With its Italian-inspired architecture and pointy conifers, this family-owned eye-catcher pitches itself at both corporate and leisure travellers, all of whom appreciate the plush furnishings, deep spa baths and free wi-fi.

🍴 Eating

The lake end of Tutanekai St – known as 'Eat Streat' – is a car-free strip of eateries beneath a canopy roof. There are plenty of other perfectly adequate options around town but few are memorable.

Le Café de Paris CAFE $
(⏹07-348 1210; www.facebook.com/cafedeparis rotorua; 1206 Hinemoa St; mains $10-18; ⏱7.30am-4pm Tue-Sat; 🐾) The greeting is *très français* but this little cafe walks a fine line between a traditional *crêperie* and the kind of cafe that Kiwi retirees gravitate to. *Galettes* (savoury crêpes) are cooked to order and served alongside toasted sandwiches and jam scones. The coffee's good too.

Coconut Cafe & Restaurant SOUTH INDIAN $
(⏹07-343 6556; www.coconutcafe.co.nz; 1240 Fenton St; mains $9-18; ⏱11am-3pm & 5-11pm; 🖊🍴) Owned by a friendly southern Indian family from Kerala, this riot of yellow and lime-green decor also serves up authentic dishes from Sri Lanka. Try the fish *moilee* (a hearty Keralan-style curry laced with coconut milk), and wash it down with a Kingfisher beer or a refreshing mango lassi.

Mistress of Cakes BAKERY $
(⏹07-345 6521; www.mistressofcakes.co.nz; Shop 2, 26 Lynmore Ave, Lynmore; snacks $5-8; ⏱8am-4pm Tue-Thu, 8am-6pm Fri, 9am-1pm Sat; 🐾) A coffee and a stonking sausage roll could be just the thing when you've been walking or mountain biking in the nearby Redwoods. It also sells muffins, slices, biscuits, scones and quiches.

Artisan Cafe CAFE $$
(⏹07-348 0057; www.artisancaferotorua.com; 1149 Tutanekai St; mains $11-24; ⏱7am-4pm; 🐾) A spinning wheel and a Mary Poppins-type

bicycle lend a folksy feel to Rotorua's best cafe. Yet there's nothing old-fashioned about the food, which includes cooked breakfasts, burgers, salads and a couple of vegan options. Even hardened blokes should consider ordering the Little Miss Bene, an eggs Benedict of agreeably modest proportions.

Atticus Finch INTERNATIONAL $$
(⏹07-460 0400; www.atticusfinch.co.nz; Eat Streat, 1106 Tutanekai St; lunch $16-20, shared plates $7.50-34; ⏱noon-2.30pm & 5pm-late; 🖊) Named after the righteous lawyer in *To Kill a Mockingbird*, the hippest spot on Eat Streat follows through with a Harper Lee cocktail and a Scout Sangria. Beyond the literary references, the menu of shared plates channels Asia and the Mediterranean rather than the American South, and a concise menu of NZ beer and wine imparts a local flavour.

Thai Restaurant THAI $$
(⏹07-348-6677; www.thethairestaurant.co.nz; 1141 Tutanekai St; mains $24-29; ⏱noon-2.30pm & 5pm-late; 🖊) Our pick of the global selection of ethnic eateries along Tutanekai St, the Thai overcomes an unimaginative name with excellent service and top-notch renditions of classics such as *pad thai* and green curry. The seafood dishes are particularly good.

Leonardo's Pure Italian ITALIAN $$
(⏹07-347 7084; www.leonardospure.co.nz; Eat Streat, 1099 Tutanekai St; mains $22-36; ⏱5pm-late; 🖊) Although it looks cavernous from the outside, Leonardo's is surprisingly pleasant inside, with dark wood, soft lighting and welcoming service. Sometimes the simple things are the best, and that's certainly the case with its traditional (ie creamless) *tagliatelle alla carbonara*. The desserts are more hit and miss.

Abracadabra Cafe Bar MEDITERRANEAN, MEXICAN $$
(⏹07-348 3883; www.abracadabracafe.com; 1263 Amohia St; mains $26-32, tapas $11-15; ⏱10.30am-11pm Tue-Sat, to 3pm Sun; 🐾🍴) Channelling Spain, Mexico and North Africa, Abracadabra is a magical cave of spicy delights, from beef-and-apricot tagine to chicken enchiladas. There's an attractive front deck and a great beer terrace out the back – perfect for sharing some tapas over a few local craft brews.

Third Place CAFE $$
(⏹07-349 4852; www.thirdplacecafe.co.nz; 35 Lake Rd, Ohinemutu; mains $15-20; ⏱7.30am-4pm; 🐾) This super-friendly cafe is away from the

hubbub and has awesome lake views. All-day breakfast/brunch sidesteps neatly between fish and chips, and a 'mumble jumble' of crushed kumara (sweet potato), green tomatoes and spicy chorizo topped with a poached egg and hollandaise sauce. Hangover? What hangover? Slide into a red-leather couch or score a window seat overlooking Ohinemutu.

Sabroso   LATIN AMERICAN $$

(☑ 07-349 0591; www.sabroso.co.nz; 1184 Haupapa St; mains $21-25; ⊙5-9pm Wed-Sun) This modest Latin American *cantina* – adorned with sombreros, guitars and salt-and-pepper shakers made from Corona bottles – serves zingy south-of-the-border fare. The black-bean chilli and the seafood tacos are excellent, as are the zesty margaritas. Booking ahead is highly recommended as Sabroso is *muy popular*. Buy a bottle of the owners' hot sauce to enliven your next Kiwi barbecue.

Fat Dog   CAFE $$

(☑ 07-347 7586; www.fatdogcafe.co.nz; 1161 Arawa St; mains breakfast $13-19, lunch & dinner $19-26; ⊙7am-9pm; 🔊🖟) With paw prints and silly poems painted on the walls, this is the town's most child-friendly cafe. During the day it dishes up burgers, nachos, salads and massive sandwiches; in the evening it's candlelit lamb shanks and venison. Fine craft brews are also served.

Lime Caffeteria   CAFE $$

(☑ 07-350 2033; www.limecafe.co.nz; 1096 Whakaue St; mains $13-25; ⊙7.30am-4.30pm) Occupying a quiet corner near the lake, this zesty cafe offers alfresco breakfasts and dishes with a welcome twist: try the mango chicken salad or prawn-and-salmon risotto in lime sauce. Classy counter snacks and good coffee.

Capers Epicurean   CAFE $$

(☑ 07-348 8818; www.capers.co.nz; 1181 Eruera St; mains brunch $13-23, dinner $23-26; ⊙7am-9pm; 🖟) This slick, barn-like cafe is perennially busy, with diners choosing from cabinets full of gourmet sandwiches, salads and cakes, and a blackboard menu of breakfasts and other tasty hot dishes. The deli section is stocked with relishes, jams and chocolates.

Urbano   BISTRO $$

(☑ 07-349 3770; www.urbanobistro.co.nz; 289 Fenton St, Glenholme; mains brunch $15-25, dinner $26-44; ⊙9am-11pm Mon-Sat, to 3pm Sun) This hip suburban diner, with a darkened

---

ROTORUA ON THE CHEAP

In NZ's ever-expanding quest for high-value tourism (ie targeted to the very rich), it can sometimes feel like the urge to fleece has gravitated from the sheep farms to the tourist attractions. Sadly, this is particularly true in Rotorua. However, there are still ways for the budget-conscious traveller to get a good whiff of this geothermal and cultural wonder.

Thermal activity can be seen free of charge in Kuirau Park (p294), Ohinemutu village (p296) and along the lakeshore by the Government Gardens (p295). If it's warm water you're after, eschew the pricey spas and take a dip at the Blue Baths (p299) or, for a mineral soak, go to Hell's Gate (p307). Many of the local motels and holiday parks also have their own thermally heated pools, some with actual mineral water.

There are lots of wonderful nature walks in the district; enquire at the Rotorua i-SITE (p306). If the Redwoods Treewalk (p298) is outside your budget, park by the road and wander into the forest at night for the magical sight of the lanterns illuminating the canopy.

If you can afford to visit just one of the ticketed geothermal areas, here's a guide for helping you choose:

Whakarewarewa (p296) An authentic experience of Māori life amid the steam.

Te Puia (p295) A slick combination of geothermal features and traditional Māori culture, but by far the most expensive.

Waimangu Volcanic Valley (p307) The best for feeling like you're among nature at its wildest, without the crowds.

Wai-o-Tapu Thermal Wonderland (p307) The most impressive and colourful geothermal features and also the cheapest, but usually the most crowded.

Hell's Gate (p307) More of the same but with the added bonus of a muddy foot bath at the end.

interior and streetside tables, offers casual cafe-style dining by day (cooked breakfasts, salads, burgers, curry of the day) and a more ritzy bistro vibe at night. Coffee comes in bucket-like proportions.

🍸 Drinking & Nightlife

Ponsonby Rd COCKTAIL BAR
(☑021 151 2036; www.ponsonbyrd.co.nz; Eat Streat, 1109 Tutanekai St; ⊙4pm-3am Tue-Sat; 🛜) Former TV weatherman turned Labour MP Tamati Coffey has introduced an approximation of flashy big-city style to Rotorua – the bar's name is a nod to an Auckland eating strip. Drenched in red light and trimmed with velvet, the decor is certainly vibrant, while the front terrace is perfect for cocktail-sipping and people-watching. Look forward to live music most weekends.

Brew CRAFT BEER
(☑07-346 0976; www.brewpub.co.nz; Eat Streat, 1103 Tutanekai St; ⊙11am-1am) Run by the lads from Croucher Brewing Co, Rotorua's best microbrewers, Brew sits in a sunny spot on 'Eat Streat'. Thirteen taps showcase the best of Croucher's brews as well as guest beers from NZ and overseas. Try the hoppy Sulfur City Pilsner with pizza or a burger. There's regular live music, too.

Pig & Whistle PUB
(☑07-347 3025; www.pigandwhistle.co.nz; 1182 Tutanekai St; ⊙11am-late; 🛜) Inside an art-deco former police station (look for the Māori motifs on the facade), this busy pub serves up frosty lager, big-screen TVs, a beer garden, live music and solid pub grub. The menu runs the gamut from harissa-spiced chicken salad to hearty burgers and fish and chips.

☆ Entertainment

Tamaki Māori Village TRADITIONAL MUSIC
(☑07-349 2999; www.tamakimaorivillage.co.nz; booking office 1220 Hinemaru St; adult/child $130/70) Tamaki offers a 3½-hour twilight Māori cultural experience with free transfers from Rotorua to its recreated pre-colonial village, 15km south of Rotorua. The encounter is very hands-on, taking you on an interactive journey through Māori history, arts, traditions and customs. The concert is followed by a *hāngi*.

Matariki TRADITIONAL MUSIC
(☑07-346 3888; www.novotelrotorua.co.nz; 11 Tutanekai St; concerts adult/child $35/18, incl hāngi $69/35) The Novotel's Māori cultural expe-

rience includes a performance of traditional song and dance followed by a *hāngi*. It's held in a separate building adjacent to the hotel, facing the lakeside park.

Mitai Māori Village TRADITIONAL MUSIC
(☑07-343 9132; www.mitai.co.nz; 196 Fairy Springs Rd, Fairy Springs; adult $116, child $23-58; ⊙6.30pm) This family-run outfit offers a popular three-hour evening event with a concert, *hāngi* and glowworm bush walk. The experience starts with the arrival of a *waka taua* (war canoe) and can be combined with a night-time tour of Rainbow Springs next door, including a walk through the kiwi enclosure. Pick-ups and a concert-only option are available.

Basement Cinema CINEMA
(☑07-350 1400; www.basementcinema.co.nz; 1140 Hinemoa St; adult/child $15/12; ⊙sessions vary) Oddly combined with a rock-climbing facility and a hostel, Basement offers offbeat, foreign-language and art-house flicks. Tickets are just $10 on Tuesdays.

🛍 Shopping

Rākai Jade ARTS & CRAFTS
(☑027 443 9295; www.rakaijade.co.nz; 1234 Fenton St; ⊙9am-5pm Mon-Sat) In addition to purchasing off-the-shelf *pounamu* (greenstone, jade) pieces, you can work with Rākai's on-site team of local Māori carvers to design and carve your own pendant or jewellery. A day's notice for 'Carve Your Own' experiences ($150) is preferred if possible; allow a full day.

Rotorua Night Market MARKET
(www.rotoruanightmarket.co.nz; Tutanekai St; ⊙5pm-late Thu) Tutanekai St is closed off on Thursday nights between Haupapa and Hinemoa Sts to allow this market to spread its wings. Expect local arts and crafts, souvenirs, cheesy buskers, coffee, wine and plenty of ethnically diverse food stalls for dinner.

Moko 101 ART
(☑021 165 7624; www.facebook.com/MOKO101; 1130a Hinemoa St; booking fee $50, tattooing per hour $150; ⊙10am-5pm Mon-Fri) Traditional *tā moko* (Māori tattooing) is offered here, albeit with modern tattooing equipment rather than stone chisels. Works from local Māori artists are also displayed for sale.

Mountain Jade ARTS & CRAFTS
(☑07-349 1828; www.mountainjade.co.nz; 1288 Fenton St; ⊙9am-6pm) Watch the carvers at work through the streetside window then

HAKA & HĀNGI

Māori culture is a big-ticket item in Rotorua and, although the experiences are commercialised, they're still a great introduction to authentic Māori traditions. The two big activities are *kapa haka* (traditional performing arts) concerts and *hāngi* (earth-cooked) feasts, often packaged together in an evening's entertainment featuring a *pōwhiri* (welcoming ceremony), the famous *haka* (war dance), *waiata* (songs) and *poi* dances, where women showcase their dexterity by twirling balls of flax.

Tamaki Māori Village (p305) and family-run Mitai Māori Village (p305) are established favourites, with the experience heightened due to their recreated precolonial village settings. Te Puia (p295) and Whakarewarewa (p296) offer the added thrill of being situated within an active geothermal zone. Both stage daytime shows; Te Puia also has an evening *hāngi*-and-show package while Whakarewarewa serves *hāngi*-cooked lunches.

Many of the big hotels also offer packages; these may lack the magical settings but they're usually considerably cheaper.

call in to peruse the high-end handcrafted greenstone jewellery and other objects. There's a second store at 1189 Fenton St.

ℹ️ Information

Lakes Primecare (☎ 07-348 1000; 1165 Tutanekai St; ⏰ 8am-10pm) Urgent medical care with a late-opening pharmacy next door.

Post Office (☎ 0800 081 190; www.nzpost. co.nz; 1218 Tutanekai St; ⏰ 9am-5pm Mon-Fri, to 1pm Sat) Centrally located.

Redwoods i-SITE (☎ 07-350 0110; www. redwoods.co.nz; Long Mile Rd, Whakarewarewa; ⏰ 8.30am-9.30pm) Sells tickets for the **Redwoods Treewalk** (p298), and provides information on **Redwoods Whakarewarewa Forest** (p296) and all of Rotorua.

Rotorua Hospital (☎ 07-348 1199; www. lakesdhb.govt.nz; Pukeroa Rd; ⏰ 24hr) Round-the-clock emergency department.

Rotorua i-SITE (☎ 07-348 5179; www.rotorua nz.com; 1167 Fenton St; ⏰ 7.30am-6pm; 📶) The hub for travel information and bookings, including Department of Conservation (DOC) walks. Also has a charging station, showers and lockers, and plenty of information on Rotorua's world-class mountain-biking scene.

ℹ️ Getting There & Away

AIR

Air New Zealand (p41) flies to/from Auckland, Wellington and Christchurch.

BUS

All of the **long-distance buses** (Fenton St) stop outside the Rotorua i-SITE, where you can arrange bookings.

InterCity (p41) destinations include Auckland (from $21, four hours, six daily), Hamilton (from $15, 1½ hours, five daily), Taupo (from $13, one

hour, four daily), Napier ($20, four hours, daily) and Wellington (from $26, 7½ hours, three daily).

Mana Bus (p293) has coaches to/from Auckland (from $21, four hours, five daily), Hamilton ($20, 1¾ hours, daily), Taupo ($23, one hour, two daily), Napier ($23, 3¼ hours, daily) and Wellington (from $25, 7¼ hours, two daily).

Baybus (☎ 0800 422 928; www.baybus. co.nz) operates the twice-daily Twin City Express service to/from Tauranga ($12.20, 1½ hours) and Mt Maunganui ($11.60, 1¾ hours) via Okere Falls ($3.90, 25 minutes).

ℹ️ Getting Around

TO/FROM THE AIRPORT

Rotorua Airport (ROT; ☎ 07-345 8800; www. rotorua-airport.co.nz; SH30) is located 9km northeast of town. **Super Shuttle** (☎ 09-522 5100; www.supershuttle.co.nz; 1st passenger/each additional passenger $21/5) offers a door-to-door airport service. Baybus route 10 stops at the airport hourly. A taxi to/from the town centre costs about $30.

Bus

Baybus has buses operating on 11 local routes from 6.30am to 6pm (cash fare $2.70, day pass $8.60). The most useful are route 1 to Ngongotaha (25 minutes, hourly) via Rainbow Springs/Skyline Gondola, 3 to the Redwoods (10 minutes, half-hourly), 10 to the airport (18 minutes, hourly) and 11 to Whakarewarewa (13 minutes, half-hourly).

Many local attractions offer free pick-up/drop-off shuttle services.

Car

The big-name car-hire companies vie for your attention at Rotorua Airport. Otherwise, try **Rent a Dent** (☎ 07-349 3993; www.rentadent.co.nz; 39 Fairy Springs Rd, Fairy Springs; ⏰ 8am-5pm Mon-Fri, to noon Sat).

Taxi
Rotorua Taxis (07-348 1111; www.rotorua taxis.co.nz) Well-established Rotorua taxi company.

ROTORUA LAKES

Lake Rotorua is the largest of 18 *roto* (lakes) scattered like splashes from an upturned wine glass to the north and east of the town of Rotorua. The district's explosive volcanic past and steamy present is on display at various interesting sites arrayed around the lakes and the three main rivers that connect them.

⊙ Sights

★ **Waimangu**
Volcanic Valley NATURAL FEATURE
(07-366 6137; www.waimangu.co.nz; 587 Waimangu Rd; adult/child walk $39/12, cruise $45/12; ⊙8.30am-5pm, last admission 3pm) Created during the eruption of Mt Tarawera in 1886, the Waimangu geothermal area spreads down a valley to **Lake Rotomahana** (Warm Lake). The experience is quite different from the other ticketed thermal areas as it involves a stroll down the lush, bush-lined valley, with a return by shuttle bus from either the 1.5km, 2.8km or 3.6km point. The last bus stop is by the lake, where it's possible to take a 45-minute boat cruise past steaming cliffs.

Highlights include the powdery blue **Inferno Crater Lake**, where overflowing water can reach 80°C, and **Frying Pan Lake**, the largest hot spring in the world. Waimangu (Black Water) refers to the dark water that once shot out of the mightiest geyser in the world, reaching heights of up to 400m during its eruptions from 1900 to 1904.

The site is 20 minutes south of Rotorua, 15km along SH5 (towards Taupo) and then 6km from the marked turn-off.

★ **Wai-O-Tapu Thermal**
Wonderland NATURAL FEATURE
(07-366 6333; www.waiotapu.co.nz; 201 Waiotapu Loop Rd; adult/child $33/11; ⊙8.30am-5pm) The most colourful of the region's geothermal attractions, Wai-O-Tapu (Sacred Waters) has a variety of features packed into a relatively compact area, with the highlights being the orange-rimmed, 65m-wide **Champagne Pool** and the unearthly lemon-lime-hued **Devil's Bath**. Just outside the gate (but requiring a ticket) is the **Lady Knox Geyser**,

which spouts off (with a little prompting from an organic soap) punctually at 10.15am and gushes up to 20m for about an hour (be here by 9.45am to see it).

You'll see a fair bit of the action on the shortest (1.5km) walking trail through the reserve but you're best to set aside at least a couple of hours for the full 3km loop track, which leads down to a waterfall spilling into **Lake Ngakoro**.

Wai-O-Tapu is 27km south of Rotorua along SH5 (towards Taupo), and a further 2km from the marked turn-off.

Lake Tarawera LAKE
(Tarawera Rd) Providing a mirror for Mt Tarawera (1110m), this pretty lake is a popular destination for swimming, fishing, boating and walks. It may look tranquil now, but it was a very different story on the night of 10 June 1886, when the volcano sprang into life, blanketing the surrounding countryside in ash and mud up to 20m thick. Water taxis and cruises leave from the Landing, 2km past the Buried Village.

Hell's Gate NATURAL FEATURE
(07-345 3151; www.hellsgate.co.nz; SH30, Tikitere; adult/child $35/18, pools $20/10, combo incl mud bath $90/45; ⊙8.30am-8.30pm) Known as Tikitere to the Ngāti Rangiteaorere people, this highly active geothermal reserve lies 16km northeast of Rotorua on the Whakatane road (SH30). It's not the most colourful of the Rotorua thermal areas but, among all the bubbling pools and steaming vents, there are some unique features such as a 2.4m-high mud volcano and the largest natural hot waterfall in the southern hemisphere. There's also a small but well-priced set of therapeutic outdoor mineral pools attached to the complex.

The diabolic name originated from a 1934 visit by Irish playwright George Bernard Shaw, who described it as the gateway to hell. However, Tikitere has long been known to local Māori as a place of healing. Warriors would ritually bathe in the hot waterfall to physically and spiritually cleanse themselves when returning from battle, and sulphur-infused water drawn from the pools was used as an insecticide and to heal septic wounds. After completing your loop of the complex, stop to soak your feet in the soothing warm mud in the designated place near the entrance.

There's also a cafe and a workshop where you can try your hand at woodcarving.

Rotorua Lakes

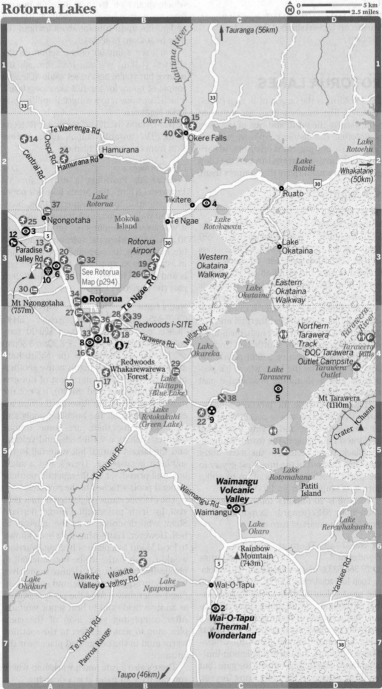

Rotorua Lakes

Te Wairoa, the Buried Village
ARCHAEOLOGICAL SITE

(☏07-362 8287; www.buriedvillage.co.nz; 1180 Tarawera Rd; adult/child $35/10; ⏱9am-5pm) The village of Te Wairoa was once the main staging post for Victorian-era tourists coming to visit the famous Pink and White Terraces on the shores of Lake Tarawera. When Mt Tarawera erupted in 1886, the entire village was covered in mud up to 2m thick. Today a museum houses objects dug from the ruins, and guides in period costume escort groups through the excavated sites. There's also a bush walk to the 30m Te Wairoa Falls.

🏃 Activities

Rafting, Kayaking & Sledging
There's plenty of white-water action around Rotorua, with the chance to take on the Grade V **Kaituna River**, complete with a startling 7m drop at Tutea Falls – the highest commercially rafted waterfall in the world.

Some companies head further out to the **Rangitaiki River** (Grade III–VI) and **Wairoa River** (Grade V), raftable only when the dam is opened every second Sunday. Sledging (in case you didn't know) is zooming downriver on a body board. Most operators can arrange transfers.

Rotorua Rafting
RAFTING

(☏0800 772 384; www.rotorua-rafting.co.nz; 761 SH33, Okere Falls; rafting $85-90) The minimum age for rafting the Grade V-rated Kaituna River is 13, but 10-year-olds are allowed on the Grade III-rated section of the river. Transfers from central Rotorua are included in the price.

River Rats
RAFTING, KAYAKING

(☏07-345 6543; www.riverrats.co.nz; Hangar 14s, Rotorua Airport, 837 Te Ngae Rd) 🚣 White-water rafting trips take on the Kaituna ($105), Wairoa ($129) and Rangitaiki ($139), including a scenic trip on the lower Rangitaiki (Grade II) that is good for youngsters ($139). Kayaking options include freedom hire (two hours from $30) and guided paddles to hot pools on Lake Rotoiti ($119). There's also exciting river sledging on the Kaituna ($129).

Waimarino Kayak Tours   KAYAKING
(☑ 07-576 4233; www.glowwormkayaking.com; departs Okere Falls Store, 757a SH33, Okere Falls; adult/child $130/85) Take a guided paddle on Lake Rotoiti to natural thermal pools and a glowworm cave.

Wet 'n' Wild   RAFTING
(☑ 07-348 3191; www.wetnwildrafting.co.nz; 58a Fryer Rd, Hamurana) Runs trips on the Kaituna ($99), Wairoa ($115) and Mokau ($160), as well as easy-going Rangitaiki trips (adult/child $140/120) and longer trips to remote parts of the Motu and Mohaka (two to five days, $650 to $1095).

Kaituna Cascades   RAFTING
(☑ 07-345 4199; www.kaitunacascades.co.nz; 18 Okere Falls Rd, Okere Falls) Rafting on the Kaituna ($95), Rangitaiki ($140) and Wairoa ($120) rivers, plus combos.

Kaituna Kayaks   KAYAKING
(☑ 021 277 2855; www.kaitunakayaks.co.nz; departs Rotorua Rafting, 761 SH33, Okere Falls; tandem trip $150, lessons per half-/full day from $100/220) Guided tandem white-water kayaking trips and lessons (cheaper for groups) on the Kaituna River.

Kaitiaki Adventures   RAFTING, HIKING
(☑ 07-357 2236; www.kaitiaki.co.nz) 🌿 Offers white-water rafting trips on the Kaituna ($109) and Wairoa ($138) rivers, plus sledging on a Grade III section of the Kaituna ($120). They also lead 4½-hour guided hikes up Mt Tarawera, including a walk around the crater's edge ($164). Prices include shuttles from central Rotorua; add-ons include a helicopter ride to the crater's edge.

Hiking
Numerous walks are outlined in DOC's *Walking and Hiking in Rotorua* booklet, which can be downloaded for free from its website (www.doc.govt.nz).

A good starting point is the blissfully beautiful 1½-hour (5.5km) **Blue Lake Track**, which circles around Lake Tikitapu.

The 10.5km **Eastern Okataina Walkway** (three hours one-way) goes along the eastern shoreline of Lake Okataina to Lake Tarawera and passes the Soundshell, a natural amphitheatre that has *pā* (fortified village) remains and several swimming spots. The 22.5km **Western Okataina Walkway**

(seven hours one-way) heads through the forest west of Lake Okataina to Lake Rotoiti.

The 6km **Northern Tarawera Track** (three hours one-way) connects to the Eastern Okataina Walkway, creating a two-day walk from either Ruato or Lake Okataina to Lake Tarawera with an overnight camp at either Humphries Bay (sites free) or **Tarawera Outlet** (☑ 07-323 6300; www.doc.govt.nz; adult/child $13/6.50). From Tarawera Outlet you can walk on to the 65m **Tarawera Falls** (two hours one-way, 5km). There's a forestry road into Tarawera Outlet from Kawerau, a timber town in the shadow of Putauaki (Mt Edgecumbe), off the road to Whakatane; access costs $5, with permits available from the Kawerau i-SITE (p311).

The **Okere Falls** are about 21km northeast of Rotorua on SH33, with an easy 1.2km track (30 minutes each way) past the 7m falls (popular for rafting), through native podocarp (conifer) forest and along the Kaituna River. Along the way is a lookout over the river at Hinemoa's Steps.

Just north of Wai-O-Tapu on SH5, the 2.5km **Rainbow Mountain Summit Track** (1½ hours one-way) is a strenuous walk up the peak known to Māori as Maunga Kakaramea (Mountain of Coloured Earth). There are spectacular views from the top towards Lake Taupo and Tongariro National Park.

Tarawera Trail   TRAMPING
(www.doc.govt.nz) Starting at the Te Wairoa car park on Tarawera Rd, this five- to six-hour track meanders 15km along Lake Tarawera and through forest to Hot Water Beach where there is **camping** (☑ 07-349 3463; www.whakarewarewa.com; adult/child $13/6.50) available. From here water taxis from Totally Tarawera can be prebooked to ferry you back to the Landing, where it's a 2km walk back to the car park.

Pick up a copy of DOC's *Tarawera Trail* brochure from the Rotorua i-SITE (p306) or download it from www.doc.govt.nz.

Other Activities
Waikite Valley Thermal Pools   HOT SPRINGS
(☑ 07-333 1861; www.hotpools.co.nz; 648 Waikite Valley Rd; adult/child $17/9, private pools 40min per person $20; ⊙ 10am-9pm) 🌿 Located in a verdant valley around 30km south of Rotorua, these pools provide a more low-key (not to mention cheaper) alternative to Rotorua's thermal baths. The outdoor pools range from a large family pool to small tubs, and private spas are also available. There's also

a cafe and neighbouring campsite (sites per adult/child from $22/11; pools free for campers).

To get here, turn off SH5 opposite the Wai-O-Tapu turn-off, and continue 6km; the gorgeous valley view as you come over the hill is enough to justify the drive in itself.

Farmhouse   HORSE RIDING
(☑ 07-332 3771; www.thefarmhouse.co.nz; 55 Sunnex Rd, Hamurana; 30min/1hr/2hr $35/55/95; 👶) New Zealand's biggest horse-riding complex offers short beginners' rides and longer treks through farmland and native bush, 16km northwest of central Rotorua. Small children can take a 15-minute pony ride ($25).

👉 Tours

Rotorua Paddle Tours   TOURS
(☑ 0800 787 768; www.rotoruapaddletours.co.nz; Rotorua Rafting, 761 SH33, Okere Falls; tours $80; ⊙ 9am, noon & 3pm) Keen to try stand-up paddle boarding without any waves to contend with? This outfit leads trips on the Blue Lake (Tikitapu) and on the channel between Lake Rotorua and Lake Rotoiti. Allow three hours for the round-trip, with one hour on the water. No experience required.

Totally Tarawera   CRUISE
(☑ 07-362 8080; www.totallytarawera.com; the Landing, 1375 Tarawera Rd; adult/child tour $65/30, water taxi $25/15) 🚤 Offers guided cruises on Lake Tarawera taking in cultural and geothermal sites (including Hot Water Beach and a natural bush hot pool), as well as a water taxi service between the Landing and Hot Water Beach, which is the terminus of the Tarawera Trail (p310); bookings are essential.

🛏 Sleeping

Blue Lake Top 10 Holiday Park   HOLIDAY PARK $$
(☑ 07-362 8120; www.bluelaketop10.co.nz; 723 Tarawera Rd; sites from $45, unit with/without bathroom from $130/80; @🛜👶) 🚤 Set alongside gorgeous Lake Tikitapu (aka the Blue Lake), 6km before you get to Lake Tarawera, this well-run holiday park has spotless facilities and a handy range of cabins and motel units.

🍴 Eating

Okere Falls Store   CAFE $
(☑ 07-362 4944; www.okerefallsstore.co.nz; 757a SH33, Okere Falls; snacks $7-15; ⊙ 7am-7pm, beer garden to 9pm Fri & Sat) 🚤 Around 20km from

---

WORTH A TRIP

WHIRINAKI TE PUA-A-TĀNE CONSERVATION PARK

This lush podocarp (conifer) forest park offers canyons, waterfalls, lookouts and streams, plus the **Oriuwaka Ecological Area** and **Arohaki Lagoon**. Walking tracks here vary in length and difficulty: the DOC booklet *Walks in Whirinaki Te Pua-a-Tāne Conservation Park* details walking and camping options. It's free online or you can pick one up at DOC's **Murupara office** (☑ 07-366 1080; www.doc.govt.nz; Main Rd, Murupara; ⊙ 9am-5pm Mon-Fri).

A good shortish walk is the 9.3km **Whirinaki Waterfall Loop Track** (three hours), which follows the Whirinaki River. Longer walks include the **Whirinaki Track** (two days), which can be combined with **Te Hoe Track** (four days). There's also a rampaging 16km **mountain-bike track**.

The conservation park is 90km southeast of Rotorua off SH38, en route to Te Urewera National Park (take the turn-off at Te Whaiti to Minginui). There are several camping areas and 10 backcountry huts (free to $15) in the park; pay at the DOC office.

Rotorua, this cafe-store is a handy refuelling stop near the top of the lake. Cool down on the raffish balcony with fruit smoothies and great views of Lake Rotoiti, or kick back in the beer garden with wine, local craft brews and home-baked savoury pies. It also hosts regular live music and a beer festival in October.

Landing Cafe   CAFE $$
(☑ 07-362 8502; The Landing, Tarawera Rd; mains $15-24; ⊙ 10am-8pm) Friendly waitstaff add extra sparkle to the lakeside setting at this cafe-cum-bar-cum-bistro, serving everything from bacon and eggs to pizza and curries.

ⓘ Information

Kawerau i-SITE (☑ 07-323 6300; www.kawerraunz.com; Plunkett St bus terminal; ⊙ 9am-4pm) The visitor centre at Kawerau, midway between Rotorua and Whakatane, has details on local accommodation and sells permits to access walks and camping at Tarawera Outlet and Tarawera Falls.

ⓘ Getting There & Away

The twice-daily Baybus (p306) *Twin City Express* service stops in Okere Falls en route between Rotorua ($3.90, 25 minutes) and Tauranga ($10, one hour).

Some of the major attractions and activity operators provide transfers from Rotorua, or you can try Geyser Link Shuttle (p300) or Thermal Land Shuttle (p300).

BAY OF PLENTY

The Bay of Plenty stretches along the pohutukawa tree-studded coast from Waihi Beach to Opotiki and inland as far as the Kaimai Range. This is where New Zealanders have come on holiday for generations, lapping up salt-tinged activities and lashings of sunshine.

ⓘ Getting There & Away

Towns and cities in the Bay of Plenty region are well connected by bus. Tauranga City Airport (p316) has flights to Auckland, Wellington and Christchurch, while Whakatane Airport (p329) has flights to Auckland. There are no passenger train services.

Tauranga

📞 07 / POP 138,000

Tauranga (pronounced 'toe-run-gah') has been booming since the 1990s and in 2017 it leapfrogged Dunedin to become NZ's fifth-biggest city. It's especially popular with retirees cashing up from Auckland's hyperkinetic real-estate market, along with young families who can no longer afford to buy there.

Its rapid rise has left it with traffic snarls on its arterial routes to rival even Auckland's. It also has NZ's busiest port, with petrol refineries and mountains of coal and lumber spoiling what was once a lovely view from the city centre to Mt Maunganui.

However, this growth has also brought with it fancy hotels and a terrific crop of restaurants and bars enlivening its vamped-up waterfront. Tauranga's city centre is never going to rival its beachside 'burbs, Mt Maunganui and Papamoa, for visitor appeal but if you're staying at the Mount, it's well worth popping over for a bite and a look around.

◉ Sights

Mills Reef Winery WINERY
(📞07-576 8800; www.millsreef.co.nz; 143 Moffat Rd, Bethlehem; ☺10am-5pm) Stately Mills Reef, 7km from the town centre at Bethlehem, has tastings of its award-winning wines. This isn't grape-growing country, so grapes are sourced from NZ's most acclaimed wine regions. There's also a refined restaurant that's open for brunch and lunch daily (mains $23 to $38).

The Elms HISTORIC BUILDING
(📞07-577 9772; www.theelms.org.nz; 15 Mission St; adult/child $15/7.50; ☺10am-4pm) Surrounded by mature trees and lovely gardens, Tauranga's original mission station incorporates the earliest buildings in the Bay of Plenty, along with one of the country's oldest oaks and first pianos. Fascinating guided tours tell the story of the mission, founded by Anglican priest Alfred Nesbit Brown in 1838, and its relations with local Māori. The property remained in the extended Brown family until 1997, retaining much of its original furniture, books and other chattels.

Tauranga Art Gallery GALLERY
(📞07-578 7933; www.artgallery.org.nz; cnr Wharf & Willow Sts; ☺10am-4.30pm) FREE The city's pre-eminent gallery isn't afraid to ruffle feathers with challenging exhibitions of contemporary work. The building itself is a former bank, although you'd hardly know it – it's an altogether excellent space with no obvious compromise. The gift shop is also worth a look.

Mission Cemetery CEMETERY
(Marsh St) Not far from The Elms mission house, this shady little cemetery has some interesting memorials relating to battles fought between local Māori and government forces in the 1860s. A prominent monument honours Rāwiri Puhirake, a Ngāi Te Rangi chief remembered for issuing a code of conduct for dealing mercifully with British civilians and wounded soldiers during the conflict.

Minden Lookout VIEWPOINT
(Minden Rd, Wairoa) On clear days this wooden viewing platform, located about 13km west of the city centre, provides a panorama of nearly the entire Bay of Plenty; see if you can spot Whaakari steaming away in the distance. To get here, take SH2 to Te Puna and turn south on Minden Rd; the lookout is about 3km up the road.

Monmouth Redoubt ARCHAEOLOGICAL SITE
(Monmouth St; ⊘24hr) FREE Shaded by huge pohutukawa trees, spooky Monmouth Redoubt was originally a Māori *pā* (fortified village), which was taken over and adapted by British soldiers during the New Zealand Wars. At the foot of the Redoubt, on the end of the Strand, is **Te Awanui**, a ceremonial *waka* (canoe) carved in 1972, on display in an open-sided building.

Robbins Park GARDENS
(Cliff Rd) At its best in late spring and summer, this verdant pocket of roses sits behind an ivy-covered colonnade on a cliff overlooking the harbour. The neighbouring greenhouse is packed with bromeliads and palms.

🏃 Activities

The free *Tauranga City Walkways* pamphlet (from the i-SITE) details walks around Tauranga and Mt Maunganui. History buffs should pick up the free *Historic Tauranga* brochure and stroll around the town's cache of historic sites.

★Waimarino
Adventure Park ADVENTURE SPORTS
(☑07-576 4233; www.waimarino.com; 36 Taniwha Pl, Bethlehem; park day pass adult/child $44/34; ⊘10am-5pm) On the banks of the Wairoa River, 8km west of town, Waimarino offers kayaking (including a customised kayak slide!), rock-climbing, pedal boats, water trampolines, a rope course and a human catapult called 'The Blob'. You can also hire kayaks here (per hour/day from $19/55) and take a paddle down the river to the harbour, or take a guided tour.

Adrenalin Forest ADVENTURE SPORTS
(☑07-929 8724; www.adrenalin-forest.co.nz; TECT All Terrain Park, Whataroa Rd, Ngawaro; adult/child $43/28; ⊘10am-2.30pm daily Oct-Mar, Wed-Sun Apr-Sep) About 30km from central Tauranga en route to Rotorua is this heart-starter: a series of high wires, flying foxes, platforms and rope bridges strung through a grove of tall conifers. There are six different routes of increasing difficulty to test your nerve.

Cycle Tauranga CYCLING
(☑07-571 1435; www.cycletauranga.co.nz; Harbour City Motor Inn, 50 Wharf St; 2hr/4hr/day $20/29/49) Has road-trail hybrid bikes for hire, including helmets, locks, saddlebags and maps. Tours are also available.

Dive Zone DIVING
(☑07-578 4050; www.divezonetauranga.co.nz; 213 Cameron Rd; trips from $150; ⊘8am-6pm Mon-Fri, 7.30am-4pm Sat, 7.30am-2pm Sun) PADI courses and trips to local wrecks and reefs, plus gear rental.

☞ Tours

Waimarino Kayak Tours KAYAKING
(☑07-576 4233; www.glowwormkayaking.com; 36 Taniwha Pl, Bethlehem) Kayak tours don't get more magical than an evening paddle across Lake McLaren to a canyon filled with glowworms ($130). Daytime tour options include Lake McLaren ($105), the Wairoa River ($75) and Tauranga Harbour ($120). Trips either start from or include transfers from Waimarino Adventure Park.

Bay Explorer CRUISE
(☑021 605 968; www.bayexplorer.co.nz; Strand Wharf; adult/child $150/65; ⊘departs 8am) This popular cruise incorporates wildlife-spotting – potentially including whales, dolphins and bird life – with the opportunity to go paddle boarding, kayaking and snorkelling around nearby Motiti Island.

Tauranga Tasting Tours TOURS
(☑07-544 1383; www.tastingtours.co.nz; tours $130) Whips around a local brewery, Mills Reef and Leveret Estate wineries, and back to town for cocktails.

🎊 Festivals & Events

National Jazz Festival MUSIC
(☑07-577 7460; www.jazz.org.nz; ⊘Easter) A five-day extravaganza of big blowers and scoobee-doobee-doo, with concerts galore.

Tauranga Arts Festival PERFORMING ARTS
(☑07-928 6213; www.taurangafestival.co.nz; ⊘Oct) Kicking off on Labour Day weekend in odd-numbered years, this 10-day festival showcases dance, comedy, theatre and other things arty.

🛏 Sleeping

Tauranga Tourist Park HOLIDAY PARK $
(☑07-578 3323; www.taurangatouristpark.co.nz; 9 Mayfair St; sites from $28, cabin with/without bathroom $88/58; 🛜) The layout at this harbourside holiday park feels a bit tight (don't expect rolling acres), but it's well maintained, clean and tidy. Aim for a site down by the bay under the pohutukawa trees.

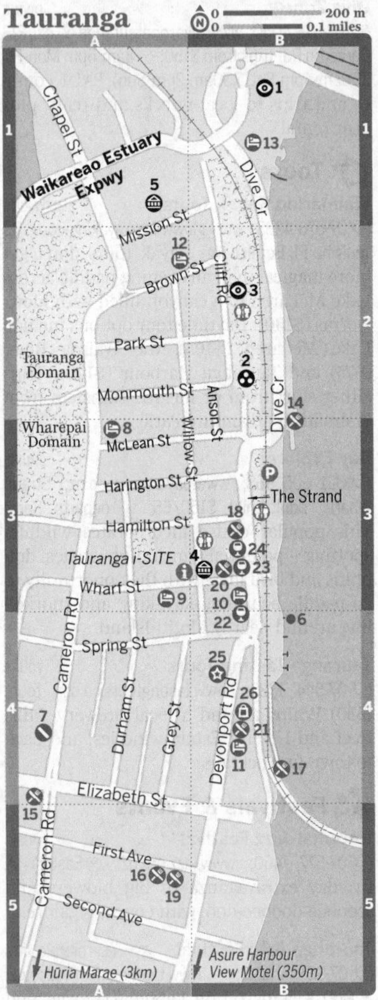

Tauranga

ROTORUA & THE BAY OF PLENTY TAURANGA

blues and greys along with the odd chandelier. Some of the upstairs rooms have gorgeous harbour views, and despite being on a quiet cul-de-sac it's only a short stroll to the centre. The friendly owners even deliver free newspapers to your door.

Hotel on Devonport HOTEL $$
(☑ 07-578 2668; www.hotelondevonport.net.nz; 72 Devonport Rd; r from $185; ✳ @ �🖥) City-centre Devonport is top of the town, with bay-view rooms, noise-reducing glass and slick interiors, all of which appeals to business travellers, air crew and upmarket weekenders. Guests have access to the gym at the venerable Tauranga Club, with whom they share the building.

Harbourside City Backpackers HOSTEL $
(☑ 07-579 4066; www.backpacktauranga.co.nz; 105 The Strand; dm $31, r with/without bathroom $90/86; @ �🖥) ✎ Soak up the sea air at this sociable hostel (a former hotel), directly above the Strand's bars and restaurants. Rooms are smallish but you'll spend more time on the awesome roof terrace anyway.

★ **Asure Harbour View Motel** MOTEL $$
(☑ 07-578 8621; www.harbourviewmotel.co.nz; 7 Fifth Ave East; unit from $155; �🖥) A fresh sea breeze has blown through this older-style motel and imbued it with a palette of pale

Harbour City Motor Inn
MOTEL $$
(☑ 07-571 1435; www.taurangaharbourcity.co.nz; 50 Wharf St; unit from $155; ❄ 🐾) With a winning location right in the middle of town (and with plenty of parking), this lemon-yellow motor inn has spa baths and kitchenettes in each room, and friendly staff who can offer sound advice on your itinerary.

City Suites
HOTEL $$
(☑ 07-577 1480; www.citysuites.co.nz; 32 Cameron Rd; units from $150; 🐾 🚻) The spacious rooms here (all with either a terrace or a balcony) have king-sized beds and full kitchens. A swimming pool, free wi-fi and secure underground parking complete the list of essentials for wandering business bods.

Roselands Motel
MOTEL $$
(☑ 07-578 2294; www.roselands.co.nz; 21 Brown St; unit from $149; 🐾) Spruced up with splashes of lime-green paint, slat-style beds and new TVs, this sweet, old-style motel is in a quiet but central location. Expect spacious units (all with kitchenettes) and friendly hosts.

850 Cameron
MOTEL $$
(☑ 07-577 1774; www.850motel.co.nz; 850 Cameron Rd, South Tauranga; units from $155; 🐾) This slick two-storey brick block offers a selection of modern, self-contained apartments ranging from studios to two-bedroom units with spa baths. All have kitchens, and the top-floor apartments have shiny metal-and-glass balconies, although the view is hardly inspiring: across the car park to the back of a medical centre.

Trinity Wharf
HOTEL $$$
(☑ 07-577 8700; www.trinitywharf.co.nz; 51 Dive Cres; r from $210; ❄ 🐾 🚻) This blocky three-storey number near the bridge has a slick, contemporary lobby – all white tiles and spiky pot plants – leading to the up-market in-house Halo Lounge & Dining. Amenities include an underutilised gym, infinity-edge swimming pool and free wi-fi. It's Tauranga's flashiest offering by far.

✕ Eating

★ Grindz Café
CAFE $
(☑ 07-579 0017; 50 First Ave; meals $10-19; ⊙8am-3.30pm; 🐾) The chatter of well-caffeinated patrons on Grindz' outside tables brings a welcome burst of street life to otherwise scrappy First Ave. Inside it's a roomy, split-level affair, with funky wallpaper, antiques and retro relics. Cooked breakfasts, muffins, cakes, smoothies and salads are the order of the day, including vegetarian and vegan options and excellent coffee.

Bobby's Fresh Fish Market
FISH & CHIPS $
(☑ 07-578 1789; 1 Dive Cres; fish & chips $6.20; ⊙8am-7pm) This local legend sells fresh fish as well as frying up arguably Tauranga's best fish and chips. Our pick, however, is the mussel fritters, fried up on a barbecue and served on white bread. Grab a seat among the expectant seagulls at the hexagonal outdoor tables on the water's edge.

The Med
CAFE $
(☑ 07-577 0487; www.medcafe.co.nz; 62 Devonport Rd; mains $9-19; ⊙7am-4pm; 🐾) Wonder Woman watches approvingly over the scrum of regulars enjoying terrific coffee and scrumptious all-day breakfasts. Order from the blackboard or from the cabinet crammed with sandwiches, salads, flans and cakes. Lunchtimes and weekends can be frantic but the on-to-it staff keep everything flowing.

★ Macau
ASIAN $$
(☑ 07-578 8717; www.dinemacau.co.nz; 59 The Strand; shared plates $10-33; ⊙11.30am-late) Zingy pan-Asian flavours take centre stage at Tauranga's top restaurant. Dishes – small and large – are all designed to be shared. Menu highlights include lamb-rib *sang choy bow* (lettuce wraps), crispy Sichuan-spiced aubergine, and moreish steamed buns with roasted pork belly. Stylish decor, Asian-inspired cocktails and a good craft-beer list complete the picture.

★ Me & You
CAFE $$
(☑ 07-577 0567; 48 First Ave; mains $15-19; ⊙7am-3.30pm; 🐾) Our favourite Tauranga cafe combines retro decor with an appealing front deck, and the hip baristas really know their way around the coffee machine. A huge array of counter food – including drool-inducing baked goods and a forever-changing range of fresh salads – combines with a menu including eggy breakfasts and delicious fruit smoothies.

Rye Bar & Grill
AMERICAN $$
(☑ 07-571 4138; www.ryekitchen.co.nz; 19 Wharf St; mains $23-40; ⊙4.30pm-late Tue-Thu, noon-late Fri-Sun) The cuisine of the USA's south is showcased at this rustic and relaxed spot on a pedestrian-friendly section of Wharf St. Grab an outdoor table and combine a burger, beef brisket or buttermilk fried chicken with a craft brew or whiskey.

Elizabeth Cafe & Larder   CAFE $$
(☎07-579 0950; www.elizabethcafe.co.nz; 247 Cameron Rd; mains $10-25; ⊗8am-3pm; 🖘) 'Eat, drink, enjoy' at Elizabeth, a hip cafe-bar on the ground floor of a four-storey city-centre office block. Many of the customers drift down from upstairs, but you don't need a suit to enjoy a knock-out eggs Benedict on potato rösti or the fish taco with a zingy Mexican slaw. Interesting industrial aesthetics and Peroni on tap complete the picture.

Harbourside   MODERN NZ $$
(☎07-571 0520; www.harboursidetauranga.co.nz; 150 The Strand; mains $24-39; ⊗11.30am-2.30pm & 5.30pm-late) In a wonderfully atmospheric 100-year-old boathouse at the end of the Strand, Harbourside is the place for a romantic dinner, with lapping waves and the overhead railway bridge arching out over the harbour. The Asian-style roast duck is hard to beat, or you can just swing by for a moody pre-dinner drink.

Somerset Cottage   MODERN NZ $$$
(☎07-576 6889; www.somersetcottage.co.nz; 30 Bethlehem Rd, Bethlehem; mains $33-43; ⊗11.30am-2.30pm Wed-Fri, 6-9pm Mon-Sat) Locals head to this elegant venue, incongruously situated across from a suburban mall, for a special treat. The food is highly seasonal, made from the best NZ ingredients and impressively executed without being too fussy. Standout dishes include baked cheese soufflé, duck with coconut kumara, and its famous liquorice ice cream.

🍸 Drinking & Nightlife

Brew   CRAFT BEER
(☎07-578 3543; www.brewpub.co.nz; 107 The Strand; 4-beer tasting rack $18; ⊗4pm-late Mon-Wed, 11am-late Thu-Sun) The long concrete bar here has room for plenty of elbows, and for plenty of glasses of Croucher's crafty seasonal ales and pilsners. The vibe is social, with communal tables, and good pizza and pub grub. Look forward to guest beers from around NZ, too.

Phoenix   BAR
(☎07-578 8741; www.thephoenixtauranga.co.nz; 67 The Strand; ⊗10.30am-late Mon-Fri, 8.30am-late Sat & Sun) At the northern end of the Strand, this sprawling gastropub pours Monteiths beers (once niche, now mainstream) and serves pizza and meaty pub meals. On weekends earnest youngsters with guitars strum covers to the dressed-up drinkers on the terrace.

Crown & Badger   PUB
(☎07-571 3038; www.crownandbadger.co.nz; 91 The Strand; ⊗9am-late) This particularly convincing black-painted Brit boozer does pukka pints and food along the lines of bangers and mash, and mini Yorkshire puds. Things get more lively on weekends with live bands.

☆ Entertainment

Rialto Cinemas   CINEMA
(☎07-577 0445; www.rialtotauranga.co.nz; Goddards Centre, 21 Devonport Rd; adult/child $17/11) Home to the Tauranga Film Society, the Rialto is the best spot in town to catch a flick – classic, off-beat, art-house or international. And you can sip a coffee or a glass of wine in the darkness. Tickets are discounted on Tuesdays.

🛍 Shopping

★Vinyl Destination   MUSIC
(☎027 412 7628; www.vinyldestination.co.nz; 52 Devonport Rd; ⊗9am-5pm) Not your ordinary record shop, this exceptionally hip establishment doubles as a cafe, a music venue and even a radio station (105.4FM). If there's anything interesting happening around town gig-wise, the clued-up staff here will certainly know about it.

ℹ Information

DOC Tauranga Office (☎07-578 7677; www. doc.govt.nz; 253 Chadwick Rd, Greerton; ⊗8am-4.30pm Mon-Fri) A field office rather than a visitor centre, but useful for information on walks and camping in the Kaimai Mamaku Forest Park.

Tauranga Hospital (☎07-579 8000; www. bopdhb.govt.nz; 829 Cameron Rd, Tauranga South; ⊗24hr) Emergency and other services.

Tauranga i-SITE (☎07-578 8103; www.bayof plentynz.com; 95 Willow St; ⊗8.30am-5pm; 🖘) Local tourist information, accommodation bookings, InterCity bus tickets and DOC maps.

ℹ Getting There & Away

AIR

Tauranga City Airport (TRG; ☎07-575 2456; www.taurangacityairport.co.nz; 73 Jean Batten Dr) is actually across the harbour in Mt Maunganui. Air New Zealand (p41) operates direct daily flights to Auckland, Wellington and Christchurch.

BUS

Coaches stop near the i-SITE on Wharf St.

InterCity (p41) destinations include Auckland ($22, 3¾ hours, three daily), Hamilton ($17, 1¾ hours, two daily), Taupo (from $22, three hours, two daily), Napier ($24, six hours, daily) and Wellington ($38, 9½ hours, daily).

Mana Bus (p293) has coaches to/from Auckland (from $15, 3½ hours, five daily), Hamilton ($13, two hours, daily), Katikati (from $15, 35 minutes, two daily) and Rotorua ($12, 1½ hours, daily).

Baybus (p306) has services to Mt Maunganui ($3.40, 28 minutes, every 15 minutes), Papamoa ($3.40, 30 minutes, hourly), Rotorua ($12.20, 1½ hours, two daily), Whakatane ($16, two hours, most days) and Katikati ($8.20, 50 minutes, two daily).

CAR

If you're heading to Cambridge on SH29, the Takitimu Dr toll road costs $1.80 per car. Heading east to Whakatane or south to Rotorua, there's also the option of the Tauranga Eastern Link ($2 per car), which begins near Papamoa. In both cases, free but slower alternative routes are possible. Tolls need to be paid online at www.nzta.govt.nz.

Getting Around

BICYCLE

Cycle Tauranga (p313) has road-trail hybrid bikes for hire, including helmets, locks, saddlebags and maps. Tours also available.

BUS

Tauranga's bright-yellow Baybus (p306) buses run on 14 different routes to most parts of the city.

CAR

Numerous car-rental agencies have offices in Tauranga, including cheapie **Rent a Dent** (07-578 1772; www.rentadent.co.nz; 19 Fifteenth Ave; 8am-5pm Mon-Fri, to noon Sat).

TAXI

Tauranga Mount Taxis (07-578 6086; www.taurangataxis.co.nz) A taxi from the centre of Tauranga to the airport or Mt Maunganui costs around $25.

Mt Maunganui

07 / POP 19,100

Occupying a narrow peninsula punctuated by a volcanic cone, the Mount is an uptempo beach town with thermal hot pools, lively cafes and hip bars. Despite being swallowed by Tauranga in 1989, it still retains a distinct identity, shaped largely by its sun-soaked surfy vibe.

Maunganui means 'big mountain', so Mt Maunganui is a rather strange name (Mt Big Mountain?), especially considering

that: a) it's not that big; and, b) its actual Māori name is Mauao, meaning 'caught by the dawn'.

Sunseekers flock to the Mount in summer, served by a cluster of high-rise apartment towers studding the spit. On the ocean side, long lovely Main Beach is popular with both surfers and swimmers, or you can cut across to the harbour side for a gentle dip at Pilot Bay Beach.

Sights

★ **Mauao** MOUNTAIN
Explore 232m-high Mt Maunganui itself on the walking trails winding around it and leading up to the summit of this extinct volcanic cone. The steep **summit walk** takes about 50 minutes (coming down is considerably quicker!). You can also clamber around the rocks on **Moturiki Island**, which adjoins the peninsula. The island and the base of Mauao comprise the **Mauao Base Track** (3.5km, 45 minutes), wandering through magical groves of pohutukawa trees that bloom between November and January.

Classic Flyers NZ MUSEUM
(07-572 4000; www.classicflyersnz.com; 9 Jean Batten Dr; adult/child/family $15/7.50/30; 9.30am-4pm;) Out near the airport, this interesting aviation museum showcases biplanes, retired US Air Force jets and the odd helicopter. Aside from the spitfires, kittyhawks, tiger moths and skyhawks, there's a buzzy on-site cafe and an excellent playground incorporating sections of fuselage. Plane freaks can take a nostalgic scenic flight on a DC3 (from $99) or a short blast in a biplane (from $355).

Activities

The Mount lays claim to being NZ's premier **surfing** town (they teach surfing at high school!). You can carve up the waves at **Main Beach**, which has beach breaks and a 100m artificial surf reef not far offshore.

Mount Hot Pools HOT SPRINGS
(07-577 8551; www.mounthotpools.co.nz; 9 Adams Ave; adult/child $14/9; 6am-10pm Mon-Sat, 8am-10pm Sun) If you've given your muscles a workout traipsing up and down Mauao, take a long relaxing soak at these thermally heated saltwater pools at the foot of the volcano. If the bustling family-friendly environment gets too much, private pools are available (from $32).

Mt Maunganui

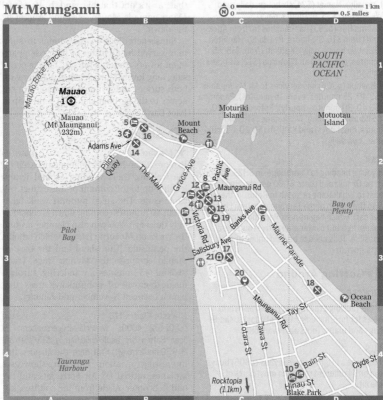

Hibiscus SURFING

(☎07-575 3792; www.surfschool.co.nz; Main Beach; 2hr/2-day lessons $75/165) Hires boards and offers a range of learn-to-surf lessons. Look for its van or red gazebo at Main Beach in summer.

Mount Surfshop SURFING

(☎07-575 9133; www.mountsurfshop.co.nz; 98 Maunganui Rd; 4hr board hire $30; ⊘9am-5pm Mon-Sat, 10am-5pm Sun) Hires surfboards and sells them alongside beachy threads and skateboards.

Rocktopia CLIMBING

(☎07-572 4920; www.rocktopia.co.nz; 9 Triton Ave; adult/child $17/13; ⊘9am-8pm; ⊕) This large climbing centre is split between Rock On, a large climbing wall painted like a bush-lined waterfall, and Clip n Climb, which is a little like a mini climbing theme park, featuring child-friendly challenges such as the 'Leap of Faith' and 'Vertical Drop Slide'.

Tauranga Tandem Skydiving SKYDIVING

(☎07-574 8533; www.tandemskydive.co.nz; 2 Kittyhawk Way; jumps 10,000/12,000ft $325/375) Offers exhilarating jumps with views as far as Whakaari (White Island) and Mt Ruapehu on the way down.

Baywave SWIMMING

(☎07-577 8550; www.bayvenues.co.nz; cnr Girven & Gloucester Rds; adult/child $7.50/5, hydroslide $4.90; ⊘6am-9pm Mon-Fri, 7am-7pm Sat & Sun) This large aquatic centre has a 25m swimming pool, a wave pool, a hydroslide and aqua aerobics, along with a fitness centre and a sauna.

☞ Tours

Aerius Helicopters SCENIC FLIGHTS

(☎0800 864 354; www.aerius.co.nz; Tauranga Airport; flights from $115) ✈ Aerial excursions to as far away as Lake Tarawera, Rotorua and Whakaari (White Island).

Mt Maunganui

🛏 Sleeping

Seagulls Guesthouse
HOSTEL $

(☑ 07-574 2099; www.seagullsguesthouse.co.nz; 12 Hinau St; dm/s from $34/70, d with/without bathroom $99/78; @ 🛜) Can't face another crowded, alcohol-soaked hostel? On a quiet street not far from town, Seagulls is a gem: an upmarket backpackers' spot where the emphasis is on peaceful enjoyment of one's surrounds rather than wallowing in excess. The best rooms have bathrooms and TVs.

Beachside Holiday Park
HOLIDAY PARK $

(☑ 07-575 4471; www.mountbeachside.co.nz; 1 Adams Ave; sites/on-site vans/cabins from $45/75/110) With three different camping areas nooked into the foot of Mt Maunganui itself, this community-run park has spectacularly positioned camping with all the requisite facilities. Plus it's right next to the Mount Hot Pools (discounts for campers) and a strip of eateries. Reception doubles as the local info centre.

Pacific Coast Lodge
HOSTEL $

(☑ 07-574 9601; www.pacificcoastlodge.co.nz; 432 Maunganui Rd; dm/r without bathroom from $30/88; @ 🛜) Set on the main road but a few blocks from the centre, this efficiently run, sharp-looking hostel is sociable but not party-focused, with drinkers gently encouraged to migrate into town after 10pm. Purpose-built bunk rooms are roomy and adorned with beachy murals. Free bikes and surfboards, too!

Mount Backpackers
HOSTEL $

(☑ 07-575 0860; www.mountbackpackers.co.nz; 87 Maunganui Rd; dm $30-40; @ 🛜) If you're after a no-frills dorm room that's handy for the beach and the bars, this main-drag hostel could be for you (pack the earplugs though). Extras include cheap surfboard and bike hire.

Westhaven Motel
MOTEL $$

(☑ 07-575 4753; www.westhavenmotel.co.nz; 27a The Mall; units from $130; 🛜) If you can look past the tatty blinds, thin towels and unremarkable decor, Westhaven is a spacious and surprisingly affordable option, especially for those travelling with families or groups of friends. It's handy for both the shops and the beach, and only a short stroll from the hot pools.

Mission Belle Motel
MOTEL $$

(☑ 07-575 2578; www.missionbellemotel.co.nz; 1 Victoria Rd; unit from $170; 🛜) With a distinctly Spanish Mission look – resembling something out of an old spaghetti-western movie – this family-run motel goes all modern inside, with especially good two-storey family suites with large bathtubs. Some of the studios are tiny but they all have kitchenettes. Note that the complex backs on to Astrolabe Brewbar (p321), so the rear units can be noisy.

Belle Mer
APARTMENT $$$

(☑ 07-575 0011; www.bellemer.co.nz; 53 Marine Pde; apt from $300; 🛜🏊) This flashy beachside complex offers one-, two- and three-bedroom apartments, some with seaview balconies and others opening on to private courtyards (though you'll more likely head for the pool terrace or the beach). Rooms are tastefully decorated and have everything you need for longer stays, including full kitchens and laundries.

✕ Eating

Mount Mainstreet
Farmers Market   MARKET $
(www.mountmaunganui.org.nz; Phoenix Car Park, Maunganui Rd; ⊙9am-1pm Sun) Roll up to the local farmers market for a Sunday-morning fix-me-up: fresh fruit and vegies, coffee, pastries, honey, cheese, juices... Arts and crafts are banned!

★ Eighteyeight   CAFE $$
(⌨07-574 0384; 88 Maunganui Rd; mains $14-20; ⊙7am-4.30pm) Don't come to this excellent little cafe if you're on a diet. Not that there aren't healthy options – it's just that the portions are so generous and the baked goods on the counter are completely irresistible. It's tiny inside so take a seat in the rear courtyard under the flower baskets.

★ Post Bank   BISTRO $$
(⌨07-575 4782; www.postbank.co.nz; 82 Maunganui Rd; mains $28-38; ⊙noon-2.30pm Tue-Fri, 5pm-late nightly) Bookcases crammed with an eclectic range of tomes give Post Bank the ambience of a gentlemen's club, but there's nothing stuffy about the food on offer. European influences pervade a menu playfully divided into Chapters 1, 2 and 3 and Epilogue. The smoothly professional team behind the bar concoct classy cocktails worthy of a 1920s speakeasy.

Fish Face   SEAFOOD $$
(⌨07-575 2782; www.fish-face.co.nz; 107 Maunganui Rd; mains $22-29; ⊙noon-9pm Wed-Mon, 4-9pm Tue; ▣) White walls emblazoned with funky fish cartoons set the scene for this fresh, fun and informal 'seafood and wine bar'. The menu splashes its way through multiple cuisines; hence blue cod comes either Moroccan-style or as part of a Balinese curry, or you can try a classic spaghetti marinara or kingfish ceviche. You really can't go wrong.

Smart India   INDIAN $$
(⌨07-574 9909; www.smartindia.co.nz; 245a Maunganui Rd; mains $17-23; ⊙11.30am-2.30pm & 5-10pm; ▨) It may not look promising from the outside but this colourful little Indian restaurant serves curries that rival even the lime and orange walls for zing. A tender, still-pink lamb *saagwala* (with spinach) is a highlight, as is a flavour-filled mushroom *mutter korma* (with peas). The service is excellent too. Call in at lunchtime for a $10 curry special.

Tay Street Beach Cafe   CAFE $$
(⌨07-572 0691; www.taystreetbeachcafe.co.nz; cnr Tay St & Marine Pde; breakfast $10-21, mains $19-29; ⊙7.30am-3pm Sun-Wed, to 9pm Thu-Sat) Around 2km south of Mauao, this beach-facing cafe is removed from the Mount's occasional bustle. Savvy locals crowd in for coffee in bright morning sunshine, linger

---

THE WRECK OF THE RENA

On 5 October 2011 the 47,000-tonne cargo ship MV *Rena*, loaded with 1368 containers and 1900 tonnes of fuel oil, ran aground on Astrolabe Reef, 22km off the coast of Mt Maunganui. The ship had been attempting to enter Tauranga Harbour, New Zealand's busiest port, but inexplicably hit one of the most consistently charted obstacles on the way. Pitched acutely on the reef with a rupturing hull, the *Rena* started spilling oil into the sea and shedding containers from its deck. Over subsequent days, disbelieving locals watched as oil slicks, containers, and dead fish and seabirds washed up on their glorious beaches.

The blame game began. The captain? The owners? The company that chartered the vessel? Thousands of volunteers pitched in to help with the clean-up. Salvors eventually managed to remove most of the oil from the ship, but on 8 January 2012 the *Rena* finally broke in two, spilling remnant oil and dozens more containers into the sea. The stern section subsequently slipped below the surface.

With the initial focus on preventing an oil spill, the elephant in the corner of the room – the *Rena* itself – seemed a problem too large. In 2017 the Environment Court of New Zealand ruled that the remainder of the boat should remain where it landed as removing it from the reef could cause further damage. The wreck is already teeming with fish and is a popular destination for divers.

The grounding was an environmental and economic disaster, but long-term impacts are hard to gauge: local businesses suffered at the time but are back in full swing, and the beautiful beaches are clean again. See www.astrolabereef.co.nz for information regarding boating, fishing and diving around the wreck.

over brunch classics, wolf down prawn tacos for lunch and return later in the week for an evening bistro meal. A good wine and craft-beer selection seals the deal.

Pronto
BURGERS $$

(☑ 07-572 1109; www.prontoburgers.co.nz; 7/1 Marine Pde; burgers $15-18; ☺ 9.30am-3pm Mon, to 8pm Tue-Sun; ⊕) Pronto's menu of gourmet burgers reads like it belongs in a bistro: chicken parmigiana, pulled lamb shoulder, chicken schnitzel, Moroccan chicken, pork belly... the peri peri chicken with chunky avocado is pretty hard to beat. Service can be patchy, though. Grab a streetside seat for ocean and mount views.

Mount Bistro
BISTRO $$$

(☑ 07-575 3872; www.mountbistro.nz; 6 Adams Ave; mains $36-38; ☺ 5.30-10pm Tue-Sun) The buttermilk-coloured Mount Bistro is on to a good thing: quality local meats (lamb, beef, venison, chicken) and fish creatively worked into classic dishes (lamb shanks, seafood chowder) and served with flair. It makes for a classy night out.

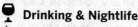 Drinking & Nightlife

★ Mount Social Club
BAR

(☑ 07-574 7773; www.mountsocialclub.co.nz; 305 Maunganui Rd; ☺ 8am-1am; 🖥⊕) ✦ A knowing blend of recycled materials, designer elements and lashings of utter kookiness, the Social is a visual feast. You can sit down to a proper meal inside but we prefer commandeering a bathtub couch in the courtyard, and we're certainly not ruling out dancing on the back of the day-glo truck when the band kicks in.

★ Hide
BAR

(☑ 07-572 0532; www.facebook.com/hide.thirstand hunger; 147b Maunganui Rd; ☺ 4-10pm Tue, noon-10pm Wed, Thu & Sun, noon-midnight Fri & Sat) Follow the sound of music and banter to this hip courtyard bar, tucked away behind the shops on the Mount's main street. It's the perfect place for a Moa beer and a burger on a balmy summer evening, and in the colder months they stoke up the open fire. We heartily endorse the chocolate rum Negroni.

★ Astrolabe Brewbar
PUB

(☑ 07-574 8155; www.astrolabe.co.nz; 82 Maunganui Rd; ☺ 9.30am-late; 🖥⊕) Astrolabe conjures up a funky retro bach (beach-hut) vibe, with floral carpets, bookshelves jammed with old novels, beach umbrellas and battered suitcases. If all that doesn't float your holiday boat, a Mac's Brewery beer might. Failing that, ask for a recommendation from the range of specialty gins and rums. There's even a playground for the kids, and stocks if they misbehave.

🛍 Shopping

Little Big Markets
MARKET

(www.littlebigevents.co.nz; Coronation Park; ☺ 9am-2pm 1st Sat of the month Oct-Mar) Arts, crafts and tasty food all feature at this monthly morning market.

ⓘ Information

The reception desk at Beachside Holiday Park (p319) doubles as an informal info centre; it's open from 8.30am to 8pm.

ⓘ Getting There & Away

AIR

Tauranga City Airport (p316) is actually in Mt Maunganui, 4km from central Tauranga.

BUS

The Mount's main bus stop is on Salisbury Ave, just off Maunganui Rd.

Baybus (p306) has daytime services to Tauranga ($3.40, 28 minutes, every 15 minutes), Papamoa ($3.40, 34 minutes, hourly) and Rotorua ($11.60, 1¾ hours, twice daily).

InterCity (p41) destinations include Auckland ($22, four hours, two daily), Hamilton ($17, 2¾ hours, daily), Rotorua ($10, 1½ hours, daily), Taupo ($16, three hours, daily) and Napier ($19, six hours, daily).

Mana Bus (p293) has daily coaches to/from Auckland ($24, 4¾ hours), Hamilton ($17, 2½ hours), Katikati ($26, 1¼ hours) and Rotorua ($6, 1¼ hours).

CAR

Mt Maunganui is connected to Tauranga by bridge, or accessible from the south via SH2. For car hire, try Rite Price Rentals (☑ 07-575 2726; www.ritepricerentals.co.nz; 63 Totara St; ☺ 8am-5pm Mon-Sat, to noon Sun).

Papamoa
☑ 07 / POP 20,100

Papamoa is a burgeoning 'burb next to Mt Maunganui, separated by just an empty paddock or two, destined for subdivision. With big new houses on pristine streets, parts of Papamoa have the air of a gated community, but the beach beyond the sheltering dunes is awesome – you can't blame folks for moving in.

🏃 Activities

Blokart Recreation Park   ADVENTURE SPORTS
(📞07-572 4256; www.blokartrecreationpark.co.nz; 176 Parton Rd; blokarts 30min/1hr $30/50, drift karts 15min $25; ⊗10am-4.30pm Sat & Sun) Forget all that pesky water, this custom-built speedway is the place to attempt land-sailing (blokarts are like seated windsurfers on wheels). There are also electric-powered drift karts, so action is possible even when there's no wind. Both activities are loads of fun, easily mastered and highly recommended.

🛏 Sleeping & Eating

Beach House Motel   MOTEL $$
(📞07-572 1424, 0800 429 999; www.beachhouse motel.co.nz; 224 Papamoa Beach Rd; unit from $155; 🐕🛏) With its angular corrugated-iron exterior and tasteful cane furnishings, this upmarket motel offers an immaculate version of the Kiwi bach (beach house) holiday, relaxed and close to the water. Outside there's a small pool for when the beach is too windy, and flowers poking up from an old dinghy.

Papamoa Beach Resort   HOLIDAY PARK $$
(📞07-572 0816; www.papamoabeach.co.nz; 535 Papamoa Beach Rd; sites from $24, unit with/without bathroom $153/93; @🛏🐕) 🍴 This sprawling resort is a spotless, modern complex, primed and priced beyond its caravan-park origins, with luxurious self-contained villas tucked directly behind the dunes. Small children will love the playground, the jumping pillow and the summertime kids' club.

Bluebiyou   CAFE $$
(📞07-572 2099; www.bluebiyou.co.nz; 559 Papamoa Beach Rd; mains breakfast $16-20, lunch $19-26, dinner $22-37; ⊗10am-late) Bluebiyou is a casual, breezy bistro riding high on the dunes, serving big brunches, a whole heap of Italian-influenced dishes (bruschetta, pizza, pasta), seafood specialities and tapas. The delicately battered oysters are excellent. Drop by on Sunday afternoons for live music, happy-hour drinks and food specials.

ℹ Getting There & Away

Baybus (p306) has services to Mt Maunganui ($3.40, 50 minutes) and Tauranga ($3.40, 30 minutes) at least hourly, along with a bus to Whakatane ($14, 1½ hours) most days.

Katikati

📞07 / POP 4060

'Katikat' to the locals, this busy little stop on the highway was the only planned Ulster (Irish Scots) settlement in the world, and it celebrates this history with a series of colourful murals. There are now more than 60 murals brightening up the town centre, along with some wonderful street sculpture (look for *Barry, a Kiwi Bloke* sitting reading his newspaper on a park bench near the information centre).

👁 Sights

Haiku Pathway   PARK
(www.katikati.co.nz) Built as a millennium project, this unusual attraction consists of boulders inscribed with haiku verses wending through a pretty park flanking the Uretara River, just behind the main drag.

Katikati Bird Gardens   BIRD SANCTUARY
(📞07-549 0912; www.birdgardens.co.nz; 263 Walker Rd East, Aongatete; adult/child $10/8.50; ⊗10am-4.30pm daily Oct-May, Sat & Sun Jun-Sep; ♿) About 7km south of town, this gorgeous 4-hectare private garden is all aflap with native and exotic bird life (ever seen a kawaupaka?). Admission includes a packet of grain, which will ensure your immediate popularity upon arrival; have your camera handy for pigeon-on-head snaps. There's a cafe and gift shop here, too, plus boutiquey cottage accommodation (double B&B $175).

Western Bay Museum   MUSEUM
(📞07-549 0651; www.nzmuseum.com; 32 Main Rd; adult/child $5/2; ⊗10am-4pm) Housed in a former fire station, this little regional museum displays a selection of Māori artefacts from the local tribe, Ngāi Te Rangi, along with temporary exhibitions devoted to aspects of the town's heritage. Don't miss the old Katikati Jail in the grounds, a compact hut with room for only two prisoners at a time.

Leveret Estate   WINERY
(📞07-552 0795; www.wineportfolio.co.nz; 2389 SH2, Aongatete; ⊗9.30am-5pm) Transplanting Cape Dutch architecture from South Africa's wine country to SH2, 8km south of Katikati, this excellent winery is open for tastings and stock-ups. They make some particularly lovely (and well-priced) sauvignon blanc, chardonnay, pinot noir and late-harvest viognier.

👉 Tours

Katikati Mural Tours   CULTURAL
(☑ 07-549 5250; www.muraltown.co.nz; depart 36
Main Rd; per person $10; ☺ 11am Sat & Sun Oct-
Mar) Guided tours depart from the information centre, taking in some of the 60-plus
murals dotting the town. Bookings aren't
necessary.

🛏 Sleeping

Kaimai View Motel   MOTEL $$
(☑ 07-549 0398; www.kaimaiview.co.nz; 84 Main
Rd; unit from $135; 🐕🖥) This motel offers neat
rooms (all named after NZ native trees) with
CD players, kitchenettes and, in the larger
rooms, spa baths. The namesake views ex-
tend over the back fence.

★ Warm Earth Cottage   COTTAGE $$$
(☑ 07-549 0962; www.warmearthcottage.co.nz;
202 Thompsons Track, Aongatete; r $290) Re-
ignite your romance or simmer in simple
pleasures at this rural idyll, 5km south of
town then 2km west of SH2. Two pretty,
electricity-less cottages sit by the swimmable Waitekohe River. Fire up the barbecue,
melt into a wood-fired outdoor bath, or
chew through a book in the lovely guest
lounge-library. Big DIY breakfasts are included in the price.

🍴 Eating & Drinking

Ambria   BISTRO $$
(☑ 07-549 2272; www.ambria.co.nz; 5/62 Main
Rd; mains lunch $17-20, dinner $26-37; ☺ 5pm-late
Tue & Wed, 11am-2pm & 5pm-late Thu-Sun) Sur-
prisingly atmospheric, Ambria is a hip bar-
eatery in a nondescript shopping strip on
the eastern side of town. Grab a seat over-
looking the river and order a glass of Kiwi
wine to wash down your roasted confit duck
with kumara mash. Gourmet pizzas straddle
the lunch and dinner menus.

Talisman Hotel   PUB
(☑ 07-549 3218; www.talismanhotel.co.nz; 7 Main
Rd; ☺ 11am-late) The Talisman is better than
your average small-town boozer, with an at-
tractive garden bar and a bistro.

ℹ Information

Katikati Information Centre (☑ 07-549
1658; www.katikati.org.nz; 36 Main Rd;
☺ 8am-5pm Mon-Fri, 10am-2pm Sat & Sun;
🛜) Sells guides to the town's numerous
murals (from $5); guided mural tours depart
from here.

ℹ Getting There & Away

Three InterCity (p41) coaches a day stop here en
route to Auckland (from $17, 3¼ hours), Thames
(from $15, 1¼ hours), Waihi ($15, 29 minutes),
Tauranga (from $15, 35 minutes) and Mt Maun-
ganui ($15, 45 minutes).

Mana Bus (p293) has a daily coach to/from
Auckland ($18, 2¾ hours), Waihi ($26, 20
minutes), Tauranga ($26, 35 minutes), Mt Maun-
ganui ($26, 1¼ hours) and Rotorua (from $10,
2¾ hours).

Baybus (p306) has two buses a day to Tauran-
ga ($8.20, 50 minutes) and Thursday-only ser-
vices to Waihi ($5, 30 minutes) and Waihi Beach
($5, 58 minutes).

Whakatane

☑ 07 / POP 18,800

A true pohutukawa paradise, Whakatane
(pronounced 'fah-kah-*tah*-neh') sits on a
natural harbour at the mouth of the river
of the same name. It's the hub of a produc-
tive agricultural district, but there's much
more to Whakatane than farming – blissful
beaches, a sunny main-street vibe and vol-
canic Whakaari offshore for starters. And
it's consistently one of the sunniest spots
in the country – although in 2016 it narrowly
forfeited its long-held title of 'NZ's sunniest
town' to Blenheim.

◎ Sights

Mataatua   HISTORIC BUILDING
(☑ 07-308 4271; www.mataatua.com; 105 Muriwai
Dr; adult/child 1hr tour $49/15, incl walk $98/30;
☺ 10am-4pm Dec-Feb, to 2pm Mar-Nov) FREE
Mataatua is a large, fantastically carved
1875 *wharenui* (meeting house) that is the
centrepiece of Te Mānuka Tūtahi *marae*
(traditional meeting place). The remarkable
story of 'the house that came home' is told in
the neighbouring visitor centre through dis-
plays and a fascinating eight-minute movie.
To visit the *wharenui* you'll need to take an
hour-long guided tour (usually at noon and
2pm; call ahead), which starts with a *powhi-
ri* (traditional welcoming ceremony).

In 1879 Mataatua was dismantled and
sent to Sydney, much to the consternation of
the local Ngāti Awa people whose ancestors
it embodied. Adding insult to injury, it was
re-erected inside out, exposing its precious
interior carvings to the harsh Australian ele-
ments. After a stint in Melbourne it was sent
to London and ended up spending 40 years
in the Victoria & Albert Museum cellars.

Whakatane

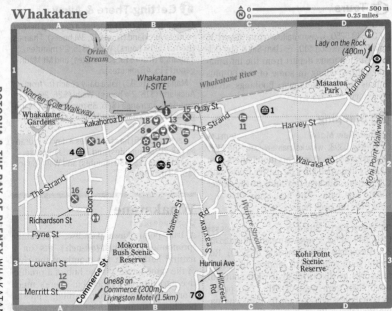

Whakatane

⊙ Sights

1 Mataatua	C1
2 Muriwai's Cave	D1
3 Pōhaturoa	B2
4 Te Kōputu a te whanga a Toi	A2
5 Te Pāpaka & Puketapu	B2
6 Wairere Falls	C2
7 Whakatane Observatory	B3

✪ Activities, Courses & Tours

8 Diveworks	B2
White Island Tours	(see 11)

⚏ Sleeping

9 Tuscany Villas	B2
10 Whakatane Hotel	B2
11 White Island Rendezvous	C2
12 Windsor Lodge Backpackers	A3

⊗ Eating

13 L'Epicerie	B2
14 Niko Niko	A2
Peejay's Cafe	(see 11)
15 Roquette	B1
16 Soulsa	A2

⊙ Drinking & Nightlife

17 Craic	B2
18 Office Bar & Grill	B2

✪ Entertainment

Boiler Room	(see 17)
19 WhakaMax Movies	B2

After 71 years in the Otago Museum, where it was cut down to fit the space, it finally came home in 2011.

Visits can be combined with the 90-minute 'Footsteps of Our Ancestors' walking tour, taking in nearby sites of cultural significance.

Wairere Falls　　　　　　　　WATERFALL
(Toroa St) Tumbling down the cliffs behind town, picture-perfect Te Wairere occupies a deliciously damp nook, and once powered flax and flour mills and supplied Whaka-

tane's drinking water. It's a gorgeous spot, and goes almost completely unheralded: in any other country there'd be a ticket booth, interpretive audiovisual displays and a hot-dog van!

Te Kōputu a te whanga a Toi　　MUSEUM
(Whakatane Library & Exhibition Centre; ☎07-306 0509; www.whakatanemuseum.org.nz; 49 Kakahoroa Dr; ⊙9am-5pm Mon-Fri, 10am-2pm Sat & Sun) FREE Attached to the library, this impressive museum and gallery has artfully presented

displays on early Māori and European settlement in the area. Some of the Māori *taonga* (treasures) travelled from a distant Pacific island on the *Mātaatua* canoe more than 700 years ago. Other displays focus on Whakaari (White Island) and Moutohora (Whale Island). The gallery presents a varied series of NZ and international exhibitions.

Te Pāpaka & Puketapu
VIEWPOINT

(Hillcrest & Seaview Rds) On the cliff tops behind the town are a pair of ancient Ngāti Awa *pā* (fortified village) sites – Te Pāpaka (The Crab) and Puketapu (Sacred Hill) – both of which offer sensational (and very defensible) outlooks over Whakatane. Look for the track leading up from the car park at the top of Seaview Rd to the first, then cross Hillcrest Rd for the track to the second.

Muriwai's Cave
CAVE

(Te Ana o Muriwai; 35 Muriwai Dr) This partially collapsed cave once extended 122m into the hillside and was the home of Muriwai, a famous seer and sister of Toroa, captain of the Mātaatua *waka* (canoe). Along with Wairere Falls and a rock in the harbour-mouth, the cave was one of three landmarks Toroa was told to look for by his father Irakewa before setting out from their Polynesian homeland. Carvings of the siblings flank the entry.

Pōhaturoa
LANDMARK

(cnr The Strand & Commerce St) Beside a roundabout on The Strand is Pōhaturoa, a large *tapu* (sacred) rock outcrop, where birth, death, war and *moko* (tattoo) rites were performed. The Treaty of Waitangi was signed here by Ngāti Awa chiefs in 1840. There's also a monument to respected Ngāti Awa chief Te Hurinui Apanui (1855–1924).

Whakatane Observatory
OBSERVATORY

(☎07-308 6495; www.whakatane.info/business/whakatane-astronomical-society; 17 Hurinui Ave; adult/child $15/5; ⊙7.30pm Tue & Fri) Up on a hill top behind the town, this observatory offers abundant Bay of Plenty star-spotting when the sky is clear.

🏃 Activities

The *Whakatāne Walkways Guide*, available from the i-SITE, details some highly scenic walks easily accessible from the town centre. The mother of them all is the **Ngā Tapuwae o Toi (Footsteps of Toi) Walkway**, a 16km loop that takes between five and seven hours to complete. Starting in town it quickly joins

the spectacular **Kōhī Point Walkway**: a bushy track with panoramic cliff-top views and a genuine 'gasp' moment when you first set eyes on **Otarawairere Bay**. A short detour rewards you with amazing views from **Toi's Pā** (Kapua-te-rangi), reputedly the oldest *pā* (fortified village) site in NZ. After 7km (about three hours) you'll reach Ohope, where you can catch the bus back to Whakatane if there aren't any more kilometres left in your legs.

A flatter option is the **Warren Cole Walkway** (one hour return), starting from the Landing Rd bridge and following the Whakatane River past Whakatane Gardens and Muriwai's Cave.

Onepū Mountain Bike Park
MOUNTAIN BIKING

(SH30, Te Teko) FREE Bump and grind your way around 15km of trails in this patch of forest, 30km southwest of Whakatane on the way to Rotorua. There are even some BMX-type jumps to try. For information on this and other cycling tracks, pick up a copy of the *Whakatāne Cycling Guide* from the i-SITE.

👉 Tours

⭐White Island Tours
TOURS

(☎0800 733 529; www.whiteisland.co.nz; 15 The Strand; 5½hr trips adult/child $219/130) 🍃 The only official boat trip to Whakaari, with wildlife-spotting en route, an excellent 1½-hour tour of the island and a picnic lunch. Moutohora (Whale Island) tours are also available (adult/child $99/59).

White Island Flights
SCENIC FLIGHTS

(☎07-308 7760; www.whiteislandflights.co.nz; Whakatane Airport; flights $249) Fixed-wing scenic flights over Whakaari, with lots of photo opportunities. A Whakaari/Mt Tarawera combo flight costs $339.

Diveworks
DIVING

(☎0800 354 7737, 07-308 2001; www.whaleislandtours.com; 96 The Strand; diving incl gear from $215) As well as guided eco tours to Moutohora (p327), Diveworks delves into the waters around it, including the wreck of the 44m *Seafire*. Other trips head to the Rurima Islands for crayfish and as far out as Whakaari.

Frontier Helicopters
SCENIC FLIGHTS

(☎0800 804 354; www.whiteislandvolcano.co.nz; Whakatane Airport; tour $695) Catch a helicopter out to Whakaari and land in the active volcano's crater for a one-hour guided walk.

🛏 Sleeping

Windsor Lodge Backpackers HOSTEL $
(☏ 07-308 8040; www.windsorlodge-backpackers.
co.nz; 10 Merritt St; dm $25, with/without bath-
room s $84/49, d $88/68; @ 🛜) This hostel
occupies a converted funeral parlour, so a
restful sleep is on the cards. Rooms range
from serviceable dorms to a couple of private en-suite rooms out the front. The large
internal courtyard is great for summertime
socialising.

Whakatane Hotel PUB $
(☏ 07-307 1670; www.whakatanehotel.co.nz; 79 The
Strand; s $75, d with/without bathroom $85/75; 🛜)
This lovely old art-deco pub has basic but
decent rooms upstairs. It's what you'd expect
from pub accommodation of its era: rooms
have high ceilings, many share bathrooms
and there's a communal kitchen. Expect
noise from the bar downstairs.

One88 on Commerce MOTEL $$
(☏ 07-307 0915; www.one88oncommerce.co.nz;
188 Commerce St; unit from $149; 🛜) Located a
10-minute walk from the town centre, this
modern motel has sparkling, spacious units
and extra-large super-king suites. Most options feature spa baths and private courtyards along with kitchenettes and huge flat-
screen TVs.

White Island Rendezvous MOTEL $$
(☏ 07-308 9500; www.whiteislandrendezvous.
co.nz; 15 The Strand E; s/d from $99/140; 🛜)
🖉 Run by the on-the-ball White Island

Tour people (cheaper rates for guests), this
immaculate complex includes a vaguely
Tuscan-looking main block, a 'micro-village'
of stylish corrugated-iron cabins, and B&B
rooms in a charming villa next door. There
are lots of balconies and decks for inhaling
the sea air, and some units have spa baths.

Tuscany Villas MOTEL $$
(☏ 07-308 2244; www.tuscanyvillas.co.nz; 57 The
Strand E; unit from $159; ❄ 🛜) This motel may
be a long way from Florence, but it still
offers a few rays of Italian sunshine with
wrought-iron balconies, an outdoor pizza
oven and a summertime wine bar. Rooms
are luxurious and comfy, with super-king
beds and spa pools.

Livingston Motel MOTEL $$
(☏ 07-308 6400; www.livingston.co.nz; 42 Landing
Rd; unit from $130; 🛜) It's a bit of a hike into
town, but this spotless, ranch-style motel
is the pick of the half-dozen dotted along
Landing Rd. Expect spacious, well-kept
units, comfy beds and large spas in executive suites.

Captain's Cabin APARTMENT $$
(☏ 07-308 5719; www.captainscabin.co.nz; 23 Muriwai Dr; d/tr $135/160) On the serene side of
town, with sparkling water views, this home-
ly self-contained unit is perfect if you're
hanging around for a few days (cheaper for
two nights or more). A cosy living area clev-
erly combines bedroom, lounge, kitchen and
dining room, with a second smaller room
and bijou bathroom – all sweetly decorated
along nautical lines.

🍴 Eating

Peejay's Cafe CAFE $
(☏ 07-308 9588; www.whiteisland.co.nz; 15 The
Strand E; mains $10-19; ⏱ 6.30am-4pm) Part
of the White Island Rendezvous complex,
our favourite Whakatane cafe serves a
mean kedgeree and tasty baked goods,
including a delicious ginger slice. Ginger
features prominently in many of the dishes, no doubt aiming to settle the stomachs
of those about to catch the boat to Whakaari. It gets frantic around tour-check-in
time but it's a pleasantly laid-back spot
otherwise.

Julian's Berry Farm CAFE $
(☏ 07-308 4253; www.juliansberryfarm.co.nz; 12
Huna Rd, Coastlands; mains $5-20; ⏱ 8.30am-
5.30pm Nov-Feb; ♿) Pick-your-own berry
farms are a Kiwi summer tradition. Kids

THE NAMING OF WHAKATANE

Whakatane's name originated some six
centuries ago, 200 years after the original
Māori settlers arrived here. The warrior
Toroa and his family sailed into the estuary in a huge ocean-going *waka* (canoe),
the *Mātaatua*. As the men went ashore
to greet local leaders, the tide turned,
and the *waka* – with all the women on
board – drifted out to sea. Toroa's daughter, Wairaka, cried out '*E! Kia whakatāne
au i ahau!*' (Let me act as a man!) and,
breaking the traditional *tapu* (taboo)
on women steering a *waka*, she took up
the paddle and brought the boat safely
ashore. A whimsical statue of Wairaka,
the Lady on the Rock, stands proudly
at the mouth of Whakatane's harbour in
commemoration of her brave deed.

MOUTOHORA (WHALE ISLAND)

It's quite unusual for the English version of a Māori place name to be an exact translation but this volcanic island, 9km off the coast near Whakatane, really does look like a cartoon whale from certain angles. It's one of the less active members of the Taupo Volcanic Zone, although there are hot springs along its shore. The summit is 353m high and the island has several historic sites, including an ancient *pā* (fortified village) site, a quarry and a camp.

Moutohora was once the site of a Ngāti Awa village but in 1867 it passed into European ownership. Since 1965 it has been a DOC-protected wildlife refuge for seabirds and shorebirds, and it's now completely predator free. In 1999, 40 tieke (the once-endangered North Island saddleback) were released; they now number around 1500. Fur seals are also frequently spotted.

The island's protected status means landing is restricted to a handful of licensed operators, departing from Whakatane.

White Island Tours (p325) runs half-day tours to the island (adult/child $99/59), incorporating a visit to a NZ fur seal colony and bird-watching.

Diveworks (p325) offers a two-hour circumnavigation of the island (adult/child $90/70) or a four-hour trip including a guided tour of the island ($120/75).

KG Kayaks (p329) heads to the island by catamaran and then unloads the kayaks for a wildlife-spotting paddle around the shoreline, entering sea caves when the conditions are right (per person $195).

love it, but if you'd prefer to leave the back-breaking work to someone else, order from the cafe and grab a seat on the large sunny terrace. Berries make their way into most things, including muffins, hot cakes, smoothies and ice cream. There's also mini-golf and a petting farm.

Niko Niko SUSHI $
(07-307 7351; 43 Kakahoroa Dr; sushi $2-3; 9am-6pm) This quick-fire sushi joint sits on a sunny corner tucked between The Strand and the waterfront. Order a couple of gorgeously presented chilli-chicken rolls and hit the sunny outdoor tables. Priced from $11 to $15, the extra-long sushi rolls are good value.

Soulsa MODERN NZ $$
(07-307 8689; www.soulsa.co.nz; 14 Richardson St; mains $33; 5.30-9pm Mon-Sat) Seasonal produce is creatively transformed into tasty dishes at this modern restaurant, serving everything from Asian-style broths to gamey Kiwi classics such as venison with kumara. There's also a good wine list.

L'Epicerie CAFE $$
(07-308 5981; www.lepicerie.co.nz; 73 The Strand; mains $10-20; 7.30am-4pm;) *Sacré bleu!* This classic French cafe in central Whakatane is a real surprise, serving terrific omelettes, croissants and crepes at communal tables. Fabulous coffee and deli shelves crammed with preserves, breads, mustards and deliciously stinky French cheeses complete a very Gallic scene. Try an excellent *galette* (savoury pancake) for a leisurely breakfast.

Roquette MEDITERRANEAN $$
(07-307 0722; www.roquette-restaurant.co.nz; 23 Quay St; mains lunch $22-37, dinner $30-37; 10am-late Mon-Sat) Ritzy Roquette serves up refreshing Mediterranean-influenced fare with lots of summery salads, risotto and fish dishes. It's a modern waterside restaurant with lots of glass, good coffee and efficient staff to boot. Try the chargrilled lamb salad or the prawn-and-chorizo *arancini*. Call in before 6pm for a good-value early-bird menu (main plus wine $23).

Drinking & Nightlife

Craic IRISH PUB
(07-282 3058; www.whakatanehotel.co.nz; Whakatane Hotel, 79 The Strand; 11am-late) The Craic is a busy locals' boozer of the Irish ilk; good for a pint or two, or a mug of hot chocolate if you're feeling subpar. Inside there are lots of cosy nooks, but when the sun's shining, the street tables are the place to be.

DON'T MISS

WHAKAARI (WHITE ISLAND)

New Zealand's most active volcano lies 49km off the Whakatane coast, easily identified on clear days by its constant white plume of steam. This small island is estimated to be between 150,000 to 200,000 years old and was originally formed from three separate volcanic cones. The two oldest have been eroded, while the younger cone has risen up between them. Mt Gisborne is the highest point on the island, at 321m, but beneath the waterline the mountain descends a further 440m to the seabed.

Sights

Visiting Whakaari is an absolutely unforgettable once-in-a-lifetime experience. Licensed tours land directly in the crater and steer gingerly between chimneys of bright-yellow sulphur and steaming vents (temperatures of 600°C to 800°C have been recorded). You won't see any lava (it's not that kind of volcano) but you will get to touch and taste pure sulphur, and clean your 10c coins in an acidic thermal stream.

Tours also visit the ruins of a sulphur factory that operated on the island from 1923 to 1933. The volcanic atmosphere has corroded the metal but preserved the wood, leaving a photogenic tumble of remains. A previous attempt at mining on the island ended in tragedy; in 1914 all 10 men stationed here disappeared without a trace, the only survivor being Pete the camp cat (subsequently dubbed 'Peter the Great').

Visits to the island aren't without risk, but nobody has died here since then. Significant events happen every two to 10 years, usually taking the form of an ash eruption. Hard hats must be worn at all times and gas masks are provided; the fumes aren't dangerous but can irritate the throat.

Despite the harsh conditions, the island is home to a thriving gannet colony and the waters around it abound with marine life.

Tours

All tours depart from Whakatane and are subject to the weather and volcanic activity. Bookings are essential but trips can't be confirmed until the night before.

White Island Tours (p325) has the only boats permitted to land on the island and an enthusiastic crew of highly informative guides. The entire trip takes five to six hours, including upwards of an hour on the island and a picnic lunch while docked offshore. The tour keeps a watchful eye for marine wildlife on the 90-minute (each-way) boat journey.

Frontier Helicopters (p325) offers a two-hour tour from Whakatane, circling the volcano for a bird's-eye view before landing in the crater for a tour.

Aerius Helicopters (p318) offers a similar experience, departing from Mt Maunganui ($870 per person).

Office Bar & Grill BAR
(☑ 07-307 0123; www.whakatane.info/business/office-bar-grill; 82 The Strand; ☺ 10am-late) The Office is a no-frills sports bar that does what it does well: racing, beer, big meals with chips and salad, and live bands and/or DJs later in the week.

☆ Entertainment

Boiler Room LIVE MUSIC
(☑ 07-282 3058; www.facebook.com/BoilerRoom Whakatane; George St) Open for events only, the large gritty band room at the Whakatane Hotel hosts DJs, live bands and the occasional Kiwi stand-up comic.

WhakaMax Movies CINEMA
(☑ 07-308 7623; www.whakamax.co.nz; 99 The Strand; adult/child $14/9) Right in the middle of The Strand, WhakaMax screens new-release movies. Cheaper tickets before 5pm and on Tuesdays.

ⓘ Information

Whakatane i-SITE (☑ 07-306 2030; www.whakatane.com; cnr Quay St & Kakahoroa Dr; ☺ 8.30am-5.30pm Mon-Fri, 9am-4pm Sat & Sun; ☎) Free wi-fi (including on the terrace outside the building after hours), tour bookings, accommodation and general DOC enquiries. Also bike hire (two hours, $10) for exploring nearby coastal pathways.

ⓘ Getting There & Away

AIR

Whakatane Airport (WHK; 216 Aerodrome Rd, Thornton) is in Thornton, 9km west of town. Air Chathams (p293) has two to three flights a day between Whakatane and Auckland.

BUS

Baybus (p306) has services to Ohope ($3.40, 30 minutes, seven daily except Sunday), Opotiki ($9.50, 45 minutes, two per week), Papamoa ($14, 1½ hours, most days) and Tauranga ($16, two hours, most days).

On most days InterCity (p41) has a coach to Auckland ($38, six hours), Hamilton ($34, 3½ hours), Rotorua ($23, 1½ hours), Opotiki ($15, 35 minutes) and Gisborne ($16, three hours), stopping outside the i-SITE.

Ohope

♪ 07 / POP 2760

Just 6km over the hill from Whakatane, Ohope has an extraordinarily gorgeous, just-short-of-endless beach, perfect for lazing or surfing. It's backed by sleepy Ohiwa Harbour, a top spot for kayaking and fishing.

🏃 Activities

Salt Spray Surf School SURFING
(♪ 021 149 1972; www.saltspraysurfschool.co.nz; West End Rd; 2hr lessons from $70) Rents boards and wet suits, and offers lessons for beginners, including targeted classes for kids and women.

☞ Tours

KG Kayaks KAYAKING
(♪ 027 272 4073; www.kgkayaks.co.nz; 1 Kutarere Wharf Rd, Kutarere; tour from $85, 1/2/3hr hire from $25/45/65) Although it's based on the southern shores of the Ohiwa Harbour between Ohope and Opotiki, KG rents kayaks from a shed at Port Ohope in summer. Its 2½-hour guided Coastal Adventure departs Ohope Beach for a paddle around secluded bays. It also offers daytime and moonlight excursions on Ohiwa Harbour, and longer trips to Moutohora (p327).

🛌 Sleeping

Moanarua Beach Cottage B&B $$
(♪ 07-312 5924; www.moanarua.co.nz; 2 Hoterini St; d $180) Well-travelled owners Miria and Taroi are adept at combining a warm welcome with information on local Māori heritage, art and culture. Accommodation is in a self-contained garden cottage trimmed with Māori design. Taroi can hook visitors up with bike and kayak rental, and arrange fishing and boating trips.

Ohope Beach Top 10 Holiday Park HOLIDAY PARK $$
(♪ 07-312 4460; www.ohopebeach.co.nz; 367 Harbour Rd; sites from $21, unit with/without bathroom from $163/78; 🐕🌊♿🚣) 🐾 This vast complex is the very model of a modern holiday park, with a raft of family-friendly facilities: sports courts, mini-golf, jumping pillow, pool with hydroslides... Plus shady sites and some great apartments peeking over the dunes. It's busy as a woodpecker in summer (with prices to match).

Aquarius Motel MOTEL $$
(♪ 07-312 4550; www.aquariusmotel.co.nz; 103 Harbour Rd; unit from $135; 🐕) Aquarius consists of a series of small blocks of units spreading back from the main road towards the beach (no need for a swimming pool). Rooms are simple but they all have kitchens.

🍴 Eating

Ohiwa Oyster Farm FISH & CHIPS $
(♪ 07 312 4565; www.whakatane.info/business/ohiwa-oyster-farm; 111 Wainui Rd; meals $7.30-12; ⏱10am-6.30pm) Perched over a swampy back-reach of Ohiwa Harbour (serious oyster territory), this classic roadside fish shack is perfect for a fish-and-chip picnic or to stock up on pots of oysters. Keep an eye out for stingrays hanging around the water's edge hoping for a feed.

Moxi CAFE $$
(♪ 021 283 1330; www.moxicafe.co.nz; 23 Pohutukawa Ave; mains breakfast $12-18, lunch $18-24; ⏱7am-3.30pm) Cobbled together out of shipping containers but with a very flash louvred roof, this mainly open-air cafe is Ohope's best. Portions aren't large and the service is so-so but the food is delicious and the coffee is first-rate. There's also craft beer and wine on offer, making it a great spot for a post-beach tipple.

Cadera MEXICAN $$
(♪ 07-312 6122; www.facebook.com/Cadera.ohope; 19 Pohutukawa Ave; mains $18-25; ⏱4-10pm Tue & Wed, 4pm-midnight Thu, 11am-midnight Fri-Sun) Perfectly suited to its beachy setting, this relaxed restaurant-bar has the obligatory Frida Kahlo print on the wall and a menu of Mexican favourites (nachos, burritos, quesadillas). The tacos are particularly yummy.

Fisherman's Wharf
BISTRO $$

(☑07-312 4017; www.facebook.com/fishermans wharfcafe; 340 Harbour Rd; mains $28-33; ⊗5.30-8.30pm Wed-Sat) Look forward to stellar harbour views from the spacious deck of this relaxed, beachy restaurant. Meals include excellent steaks and seafood – try the fish tacos – and there's a decent beer and wine selection to ease you into another Ohope evening. Takeaway fish and chips are available from a handy window outside.

✪ Getting There & Away

Baybus (p306) route 122 makes the short hop across the hill from Whakatane to Ohope ($3.40, 30 minutes, seven per day, no Sunday services), while 147 continues on to Opotiki ($9.50, 45 minutes) on Mondays and Wednesdays.

InterCity (p41) has a coach most days to Auckland ($39, 6½ hours), Hamilton ($34, four hours), Rotorua ($23, two hours), Opotiki ($15, 25 minutes) and Gisborne ($16, three hours).

Opotiki

☑07 / POP 4180

Set out in a tidy grid pattern within the embrace of two rivers, Opotiki is a worn-around-the-edges kind of town with a scattering of historic buildings and a couple of exceptional beaches nearby (Ohiwa and Waiotahi). Aside from the beaches, its main appeal is as a gateway to both the East Coast and a series of mountain-biking trails in the hinterland. Māori traditions are alive and well here, with more than half of the population claiming Māori descent.

◉ Sights

Pick up the *Historic Opotiki* brochure from the i-SITE (or download it from www. opotikinz.com) for the lowdown on the town's heritage buildings.

Hukutaia Domain
FOREST

(501 Woodlands Rd; ⊗daylight hours) FREE Around 8km south of town, this small but verdant patch of forest is home to around 1500 varieties of native plants, which can be seen on a 20-minute circuit. The most important specimen is Taketakerau, a sacred 23m puriri tree estimated to be more than 2000 years old. It was once used as a burial place for the distinguished dead of the Upokorehe *hapū* (subtribe) of Whakatōhea; the remains have since been reinterred elsewhere.

Hiona St Stephen's Church
CHURCH

(☑07-315 8319; www.hiona.org.nz; 124 Church St) White wooden St Stephen's (1862) is an Anglican church with a timber-lined interior and *tukutuku* (woven flax) panels in the sanctuary. Reverend Carl Völkner, known by the local Whakatōhea tribe to have acted as a government spy during the New Zealand Wars, was executed by Māori here in 1865. In 1992 the governor-general granted Mokomoko, the man the government in turn hanged for his 'murder', a full pardon, which is displayed in the lobby.

Hours vary but the church is usually open in the morning and until around 2pm.

Opotiki Museum
MUSEUM

(☑07-315 5193; www.opotikimuseum.org.nz; 123 Church St; adult/child $10/5; ⊗10am-4pm Mon-Fri, to 2pm Sat) Run by volunteers, Opotiki's museum has heritage displays including Māori artefacts, militaria, recreated shopfronts (barber, carpenter, printer...), and agricultural items including tractors and a horse-drawn wagon. The admission charge includes entry to the Shalfoon & Francis general store a few doors down (you may have to ask for it to be opened for you).

Founded in the 1860s, the store closed its doors in 2000 and the shelves are still piled high with old grocery and hardware products. Handbags, sticky-tape dispensers, sets of scales, books – you name it, they had it. An amazing collection.

🏃 Activities

Motu Trails
MOUNTAIN BIKING

(www.motutrails.co.nz) One of the New Zealand Cycle Trail's 'Great Rides', Motu Trails comprises three trails around Opotiki – the easy **Dunes Trail** (10km), the intermediate **Motu Road Trail** (67km) and the advanced **Pakihi Track** (44km). All of these distances are one way, necessitating shuttles, but parts of the trails can be combined to form the **Motu Trails Loop** (91km).

For bike hire, camping and lodge accommodation, and shuttle services see www. motucycletrails.com or www.hireandshuttle. co.nz.

Travel Shop
OUTDOORS

(☑07-315 8881; www.travelshop.co.nz; 104 Church St; hire 4/8hr $30/40; ⊗9am-5pm Mon-Fri) This main-street travel agency rents bikes, kayaks and surfboards.

🛏 Sleeping

⭐ **Ohiwa Beach Holiday Park** HOLIDAY PARK **$**
(☎07-315 4741; www.ohiwaholidays.co.nz; Ohiwa
Harbour Rd; sites from $21, unit with/without bath-
room from $95/65; 🐕 ⚄ 🖶) Blissfully squeezed
into a remote corner between Ohiwa Harbour and a gorgeous ocean beach, 14km west
of Opotiki, this large holiday park distils the
essence of the Kiwi summer: pohutukawa
trees, phoenix palms, manicured lawns, rolling waves and endless sands. There are only
a handful of units but there's ample space
to pitch a tent. Bring coins for the showers.

Opotiki Beach House HOSTEL **$**
(☎07-315 5117; www.opotikibeachhouse.co.nz;
7 Appleton Rd, Waiotahi Beach; dm/s/d from
$30/49/68; 🐕) This cruisy, shoe-free beach-
side pad has a sunny, hammock-hung deck,
sea views and a *very* wide sandy backyard.
Beyond the dorms and breezy lounge are
decent doubles and a quirky caravan (sleeps
two) for those who want a real taste of the
Kiwi summer holiday. It's right by Waiotahi
Beach, about 5km west of town.

Central Oasis Backpackers HOSTEL **$**
(☎07-315 5165; centraloasis@hotmail.com; 30
King St; dm/s/d $25/35/56; 🐕) Occupying a
19th-century wooden house, this central
hostel is a snug spot with spacious rooms,
a crackling fire and a lush garden to hang
out in. There's also a handy coffee caravan –
open to the public – serving organic coffee,
tea and fresh juices.

Island View Holiday Park HOLIDAY PARK **$$**
(☎07-315 7519; www.islandviewholiday.co.nz; 6
Appleton Rd, Waiotahi Beach; dm & sites $25, unit
with/without bathroom from $140/80; 🐕⚄) A
rustic driftwood fence sets a Robinson Cru-
soe vibe at this chilled-out holiday park.
Cabins open onto shared decks with barbe-
cues and their own toilet blocks, meaning
that what you sacrifice in privacy you stand
to gain in sociability. Plus there are free kay-
aks, hammocks slung between trees, a vol-
leyball court and a swimming pool.

Eastland Pacific Motor Lodge MOTEL **$$**
(☎07-315 5524; www.eastlandpacific.co.nz; 44 St
John St; unit from $125; 🐕) Bright, clean East-
land is a well-kept motel with units that are
simple but pleasantly kitted out. Some have
spa baths and, at $160, the two-bedroom
units are top value.

🍴 Eating

Two Fish CAFE **$**
(☎07-315 5448; 102 Church St; mains $7-21;
⏱8am-2.50pm Mon-Fri, to 1.50pm Sat) Decent
eating options are thin on the ground in
Opotiki, but this happy wee cafe serves up
robust homemade burgers, chowder, toasties, steak sandwiches, salads and a jumbo
selection in the cabinet. The coffee's excellent too. Grab a seat in the retro-groovy interior or in the courtyard.

☆ Entertainment

DeLuxe Theatre CINEMA
(☎07-315 6110; www.deluxetheatre.co.nz; 127
Church St; adult/child $14/7) Dating from
1926, this beguiling community-run cinema shows recent movies and hosts the odd
concert.

ℹ Information

The **Opotiki i-SITE** (☎ 07-315 3031; www.
opotikinz.com; 70 Bridge St; ⏱9am-4.30pm
Mon-Fri, to 1pm Sat & Sun; 🐕) and **DOC** (☎07-
315 1001; www.doc.govt.nz; 70 Bridge St;
⏱9am-4.30pm Fri) are in the same building.
The i-SITE takes bookings for activities and
transport, and stocks the indispensable free
East Coast booklet *Pacific Coast Highway*. Showers are available, too ($3).

ℹ Getting There & Away

BUS

Baybus (p306) route 147 ($9.50) heads to
Whakatane (55 minutes) and Ohope (45 min-
utes) twice daily on Mondays and Wednesdays.
Route 150 heads east along the coast as far as
Potaka on Tuesdays and Thursdays.

InterCity (p41) has a coach most days to
Auckland ($42, 6¾ hours), Hamilton ($34, 4¼
hours), Rotorua ($23, 2¼ hours), Whakatane
($15, 44 minutes) and Gisborne ($16,
two hours).

CAR

Travelling east from Opotiki there are two
routes: SH2, crossing the spectacular Waioeka
Gorge, or SH35 around East Cape. The SH2
route offers some day walks in the Waioeka
Gorge Scenic Reserve, with the gorge getting
steeper and narrower as you travel inland,
before the route crosses typically green, rolling hills, dotted with sheep, on the descent to
Gisborne.

The East Coast

Why Go?

New Zealand is known for its mix of wildly divergent landscapes, but on the East Coast it's the sociological contours that are most pronounced. There's a full spectrum of NZ life here, from the earthy settlements on the East Cape to Havelock North's moneyed, wine-soaked streets.

Māori culture is never more visible than it is on the East Coast. Exquisitely carved *marae* (meeting house) complexes dot the landscape, and *te reo* and *tikanga* (the language and customs) are alive and well.

Intrepid types will have no trouble losing the tourist crowds – along the Pacific Coast Hwy, through rural back roads, on remote beaches or in the mystical wilds of Te Urewera. And when the call of the wild gives way to caffeine withdrawal, you can get a quick fix in Gisborne or Napier. You'll also find plenty of wine here: the Hawke's Bay region is striped with vine rows.

Best Places to Eat

➜ Mister D (p356)

➜ Bistronomy (p356)

➜ Crawford Road Kitchen (p343)

➜ Maina (p360)

➜ Elephant Hill (p361)

Best Places to Stay

➜ Stranded in Paradise (p337)

➜ St Andrews Escape (p360)

➜ Millar Road (p360)

➜ Ahi Kaa Motel (p342)

➜ Kiwiesque (p355)

When to Go

➜ The East Coast basks in a warm, mainly dry climate. Temperatures in summer (from roughly December to March) around balmy Napier and sunny Gisborne nudge 25°C; in winter (around June to August) they rarely dip below 8°C.

➜ The Hawke's Bay region enjoys mild, dry, grape-growing conditions year-round, with an average annual rainfall of just 800mm. Harvest time is autumn (March to May).

➜ In winter, heavy downpours sometimes wash out sections of the Pacific Coast Hwy (SH35) around the East Cape: check road conditions at either end (Opotiki or Gisborne) before you hit the highway.

ⓘ Getting There & Around

The region's only airports are in Gisborne and Napier. Air New Zealand (www.airnewzealand.co.nz) flies to both towns from Auckland and Wellington, and also to Napier from Christchurch. Regular InterCity (www.intercity.co.nz) and Naked Bus (https://nakedbus.com) services ply State Hwy 2 (SH2) and State Hwy 5 (SH5), connecting Gisborne, Opotiki, Wairoa, Napier and Hastings with all the main centres.

Transport is limited around the East Cape and Te Urewera. Bay Hopper (www.baybus.co.nz) runs between Opotiki and Potaka/Cape Runaway on Tuesday and Thursday afternoon ($17, two hours). **Cooks Couriers** (p338) runs between Te Araroa and Opotiki on Tuesdays and Thursdays, and between Gisborne and Hicks Bay daily Monday to Saturday. Call for prices and departure/arrival times. Otherwise, arrange to have your own wheels.

EAST CAPE

📓 06 & 07

The slow-paced East Cape is a unique and special corner of New Zealand. It's a quiet place, where everyone knows everyone, and community ties are built on rural enterprise and a shared passion for the ocean. Horse riding, tractors on the beach, fresh fish for dinner – it's all part of daily life here.

Inland, the wild Raukumara Range forms the Cape's jagged spine. Tracing the fringe of the land, the 327km Pacific Coast Hwy (SH35) runs from Opotiki to Gisborne. Lonely shores lie strewn with driftwood, while picture-postcard sandy bays lure just a handful of visitors.

Pacific Coast Hwy

The winding 327km Pacific Coast Hwy around the North Island's easternmost point has long been a road-trip rite of passage for New Zealanders. If you like scenic drives and don't mind that attractions are few and far between, you'll find the journey intrepid and captivating. You can drive it in a day if you must, but an overnighter (or longer) is more rewarding.

If you're short on time, head for Gisborne via SH2 from Opotiki – a 147km, 2½-hour alternative via the **Waioeka Gorge**, where you'll find the two- to three-hour loop walk leading off from the historic **Tauranga Bridge**.

Both routes are covered in the excellent *Pacific Coast Highway Guide,* available at Gisborne (p344) and Opotiki (p330) i-SITEs. Set off with a full petrol tank, and stock up on snacks and groceries – shops and petrol stations are in short supply. Sleeping and eating options are also pretty spread out: plan accordingly.

⊙ Sights

Along the coast east of Opotiki, there are hazy views across to **Whakaari** (White Island), a chain-smoking active volcano. The desolate beaches at **Torere, Hawai** and **Omaio** are steeply shelved and littered with flotsam. Check out the magnificent *whakairo* (carving) on the Torere school gateway. Hawai marks the western boundary of the Whānau-ā-Apanui tribe, whose *rohe* (traditional land) extends to Cape Runaway.

Around 42km east of Opotiki the road crosses the broad pebbly expanse of the **Motu River**, the first river in New Zealand to be designated as a protected wilderness area.

Some 67km east of Opotiki, the fishing town of **Te Kaha** once sounded the death knell for passing whales. Here you'll find a shop, holiday park, hostel, B&B and resort.

Around 24km east of Te Kaha, stop at **Papatea Bay** to see the gateway of **Hinemahuru Marae**, intricately carved with images of WWI Māori soldiers. At blink-and-you'll-miss-it **Raukokore**, the 1894 Anglican

The East Coast Highlights

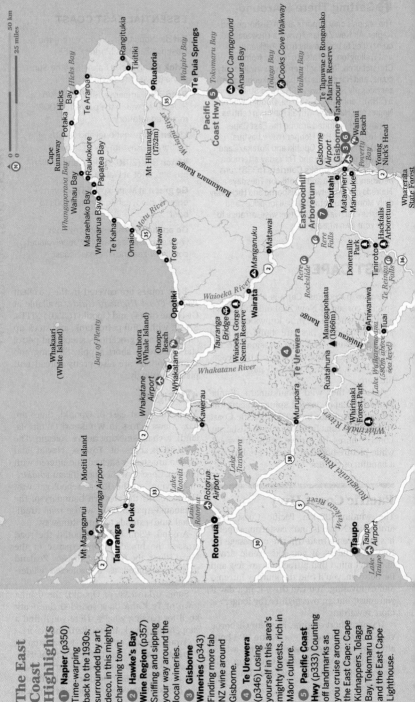

1 Napier (p350)
Time-warping back to the 1930s, surrounded by art deco, in this mighty charming town.

2 Hawke's Bay Wine Region (p357)
Sniffing and sipping your way around the local wineries.

3 Gisborne Wineries (p343)
Finding more fab NZ wine around Gisborne.

4 Te Urewera (p346)
Losing yourself in this area's mighty forests, rich in Māori culture.

5 Pacific Coast Hwy (p333)
Counting off landmarks as you cruise around the East Cape: Cape Kidnappers, Tolaga Bay, Tokomaru Bay and the East Cape Lighthouse.

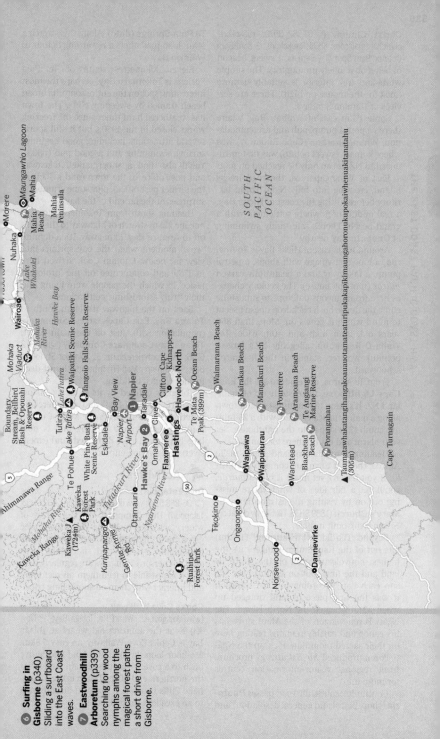

SOUTH PACIFIC OCEAN

6 Surfing in Gisborne (p340)
Sliding a surfboard into the East Coast waves.

7 Eastwoodhill Arboretum (p339)
Searching for wood nymphs among the magical forest paths a short drive from Gisborne.

Christ Church ([☎]07-352 3979; ruakokore.
church@gmail.com; SH35, Raukokore; ⊙8am-8pm
Oct-Apr, 9am-5pm May-Sep) is a sweet beacon
of belief on a lonely promontory. The simple
white-and-grey interior is suitably demure
(look for the mouse on high). There are services at 11am on Sundays.

Some 17km east of **Waihau Bay**, where
there's a petrol pump, pub and accommodation, **Whangaparaoa** (Cape Runaway) was
where kumara (sweet potato) was first introduced to NZ. It can only be reached on foot.

East of Whangaparaoa, the road tracks
inland, crossing into hilly Ngāti Porou territory before hitting the coast at **Hicks Bay**,
a real middle-of-nowhere settlement with a
grand beach. There's safe sandy swimming
at **Onepoto Bay** nearby.

Around 10km east of Hicks Bay is **Te Araroa**, a lone-dog village with shops, a petrol
pump, a takeaway and a beautifully carved
marae (meeting house). The geology changes here from igneous outcrops to sandstone
cliffs: the dense bush backdrop doesn't seem
to mind which it grows on. More than 350
years old, 20m high and 40m wide, **Te-
Waha-O-Rerekohu**, allegedly NZ's largest
pohutukawa tree, stands in the Te Araroa
schoolyard.

From Te Araroa, drive out to see the **East
Cape Lighthouse**, the easterly tip of mainland NZ. It's 21km (30 minutes) east of town
along a mainly unsealed road, with a 25-min-
ute climb (750 steps!) to the lighthouse. Set
your alarm and get up there for sunrise.

Heading through farmland south of Te
Araroa, the first town you come to is **Tikitiki**. If you haven't yet made it into a *marae*,
you'll get a fair idea of what you're missing out on by visiting the extraordinary **St
Mary's Church** (1889 SH35, Tikitiki; by donation;
⊙9am-5pm), built in 1924.

Beyond Tikitiki, **Mt Hikurangi** (1752m)
juts out of the Raukumara Range – it's the
highest nonvolcanic peak on the North Island and the first spot on Earth to see the
sun each day. According to local tradition
it was the first piece of land dragged up
when Maui snagged the North Island. The
Ngāti Porou version of the Māui story has
his canoe and earthly remains resting here
on their sacred mountain. Pick up the Ngāti Porou-produced *Mt Hikurangi* brochure
from regional visitor-information centres
for more info.

Continuing south, the road passes **Ruato-
ria** (shop, petrol and general desolation) and

Te Puia Springs (ditto). Along this stretch a
14km loop road offers a rewarding detour to
Waipiro Bay.

Eleven kilometres south of Te Puia
Springs is **Tokomaru Bay**, perhaps the most
interesting spot on the entire route, its broad
beach framed by sweeping cliffs. The town
has weathered hard times since the freezing
works closed in the 1950s, but it still sports
several attractions including good beginner
surfing, swimming and a good pub (p338).
You'll also find a supermarket, takeaway
and post office in the town (and a B&B in
the former post office), plus some crumbling
surprises at the far end of the bay.

Heading south from Tokomaru Bay is a
bucolic 22km stretch of highway to the turn-
off to **Anaura Bay**, 6km away. It's a definite
'wow' moment when the bay springs into
view far below. Captain Cook arrived here
in 1769 and commented on the 'profound
peace' in which the people were living and
their 'truly astonishing' cultivations.

Back on the highway it's 14km south to
Tolaga Bay, East Cape's largest community
(population 830). Just off the main street,
Tolaga Bay Cashmere Company ([☎]06-862
6746; www.cashmere.co.nz; 31 Solander St, Tolaga
Bay; ⊙10am-4pm Mon-Fri) inhabits the art-deco
former council building.

Tolaga is defined by its amazing historic wharf. Built in 1929 and commercially
functional until 1968, it's the longest in the
southern hemisphere (660m), and is now
largely restored after dedicated (and expensive!) preservation efforts.

🏃 Activities

Dive Tatapouri
DIVING

([☎]06-868 5153; www.divetatapouri.com; 532 SH35,
Tatapouri) Dive Tatapouri offers an array of
watery activities including dive trips (price
given upon application), reef-ecology tours
(adult/child $45/20) and snorkelling trips
($70 per person). Stingrays are regularly seen
and it is possible to feed them on reef tours
and interact with them on snorkelling trips.

Cooks Cove Walkway
TRAMPING

(www.doc.govt.nz; Wharf Rd, Tolaga Bay; ⊙Nov-
Jul) Near the amazing old wharf at Tolaga
Bay is Cooks Cove Walkway, an easy 5.8km,
2½-hour loop through farmland and native
bush to a cove where the captain landed. At
the northern end of the beach is the Tatara-
hake Cliffs Lookout, a sharp 10-minute walk
to an excellent vantage point.

Wet 'n' Wild Rafting   RAFTING
(☎0800 462 7238, 07-348 3191; www.wetnwild rafting.co.nz; 2- to 5-day tours $995-1095) Based on the outskirts of Rotorua, Wet 'n' Wild Rafting also offers multiday excursions on the Motu River, with the longest taking you 100km down the river. The two-day tour requires you to be helicoptered in, and therefore costs nearly as much as the five-day trip.

🛏 Sleeping

★**Stranded in Paradise**   HOSTEL $
(☎06-864 5870; www.stranded-in-paradise.net; 21 Potae St, Tokomaru Bay; campsites per person $18, dm/s/d/f $32/48/75/96; ⑨) Up on the hill behind town, the 12-bed Stranded in Paradise scores points for views, eco-loos and free wifi. There are two tricky loft dorm rooms, a double downstairs and three wave-shaped cabins. Tenters have a panoramic knoll (astonishing bay views!) on which to pitch.

Anaura Bay Motor Camp   CAMPGROUND $
(☎06-862 6380; www.tairawhitigisborne.co.nz; Anaura Bay Rd, Anaura Bay; sites per adult/child from $20/11; ⑨🐾) Friendly Anaura Bay Motor Camp is all about the location – right on the beachfront by the little stream where Captain Cook once stocked up with water. There's a decent kitchen, showers and toilets.

There's also a standard Department of Conservation (DOC) campsite here for fully self-contained campers only (adult/child $8/4). Open October to April.

Morepork's Nest   HOSTEL $
(☎06-391 8954; myradawn5@gmail.com; 57 Waione Rd, Te Araroa; dm $25, campervan or tent sites per person $15; ⑨) Surrounded by bird-filled gardens, there's basic but character-laden accommodation in this amazing 135-year-old former convent. Kitchen and bathroom facilities are shared, and there's room in the lovely grounds for campervans and tents. Does the old saxophone on the wall still work?

Tolaga Bay Holiday Park   HOLIDAY PARK $
(☎06-862 6716; www.tolagabayholidaypark.co.nz; 167 Wharf Rd, Tolaga Bay; sites per adult/child from $16/10, cabins $60-100; ⑨) Tolaga Bay Holiday Park is right next to the wharf. The stiff ocean breeze tousles Norfolk Island pines as open lawns bask in the sunshine. It's a special spot. Cabins are rustic and facilities include shared kitchens and blocks with washing facilities and toilets.

Hicks Bay Motel Lodge   MOTEL $
(☎06-864 4880; www.hicksbaymotel.co.nz; 5198 SH35, Hicks Bay; dm $40, d $89-171, 2-bedroom units $165; ⑨🍴) Knockout views distract

---

MĀORI NZ: THE EAST COAST

The main *iwi* (tribes) in the region are Te Whānau-ā-Apanui (www.apanui.co.nz; west side of East Cape), Ngāti Porou (www.ngatiporou.com; east side of East Cape), Ngāti Kahungunu (www.kahungunu.iwi.nz; the coast from Hawke's Bay down) and Ngāi Tūhoe (www.ngaituhoe.iwi.nz; inland in Te Urewera).

Ngāti Porou and Ngāti Kahungunu are the country's second- and third-biggest *iwi*, respectively. In the late 19th century they produced the great leaders James Carroll (the first Māori cabinet minister) and Apirana Ngata (who was briefly acting prime minister). Ngata, whose face adorns New Zealand's $50 note, worked tirelessly in parliament to orchestrate a cultural revival within Māoridom. The region's magnificent carved *marae* (meeting houses) are part of his legacy.

Māori life is at the forefront around the East Cape, in sleepy villages centred upon the many *marae* that dot the landscape. Living in close communities, drawing much of their livelihoods from the sea and the land, the *tangata whenua* (local people) of the Cape offer a fascinating insight into what life might have been, had they not been so vigorously divested of their land in the 19th century.

You will meet Māori wherever you go. For accommodation with Māori flavour, consider Hikihiki's Inn (p347). For an intimate introduction to *Māoritanga* (things Māori), take a guided tour with Long Island Guides (p359) or **Waimarama Tours** (☎021 057 0935; www.waimaramamaori.co.nz; 2-4hr tours per person from $95, transport from $40).

For a more passive brush with the culture, visit Gisborne's Tairawhiti Museum (p339) and C Company Memorial House (p339), **Otatara Pā** (☎06-834 3111; www.doc.govt.nz; off Springfield Rd; ⏰24hr) FREE in Napier and Tikitiki's St Mary's Church (p336).

from the mildly barracks-like ambience at this 50-year-old motel squatting high above the bay. The clean, old-fashioned rooms are nothing flash, although the restaurant (mains $21 to $35, open for breakfast and dinner), shop, pool and glowworm grotto compensate.

Nga Puriri
COTTAGE $$

(06-864 4035; www.thepuriris.co.nz; 5138 Te Araroa Rd, Hicks Bay; d incl breakfast $160;) Overlooking Hicks Bay, this wee self-contained weatherboard cottage is a delight, with room for two and breakfast eggs from the chooks (chickens) next door. There's safe sandy swimming at Onepoto Bay nearby.

Waikawa B&B
B&B $$

(07-325 2070; www.waikawa.net; 7541 SH35, Te Kaha; d/units from $110/130, extra person $35;) About 7km north of Te Kaha, magical Waikawa B&B sits on a private rocky cove with views of the sunset and Whakaari (White Island). The artful buildings blend weathered timber, corrugated iron and paua (shell) inlay to great effect. There are two B&B options here – a double room, and a two-bedroom self-contained bach (simple cottage) sleeping up to six wanderers.

Tui Lodge
B&B $$

(07-325 2922; tuilodge@yahoo.co.nz; 200 Copenhagen Rd, Te Kaha; s/d incl breakfast $155/175) Tui Lodge is a capacious, modern guesthouse that sits in groomed 3-acre gardens, irresistible to tui and many other birds. Delicious meals are available by arrangement, as are horse trekking, fishing and diving trips.

Eating

Cottle's Cafe & Bakery
BAKERY $

(06-862 6484; cnr Cook & Monkhouse Sts, Tologa Bay; pies $4-5; 7am-4pm) Decent coffee and excellent savoury pies make Cottle's an essential stop on Tologa Bay's main drag. The bacon-and-egg pie is deservedly popular all around East Cape, but we reckon the fish one is just as good. Grab a pie to go and devour it while taking in views of the Tologa Bay Wharf.

Pacific Coast Macadamias
ICE CREAM $

(07-325 2960; www.macanuts.co.nz; 8462 SH35, Whanarua Bay; snacks $5-12; 10am-3pm 26 Dec-Mar, Sat & Sun 1-24 Dec;) Heaven is a tub of homemade macadamia-and-honey ice cream at Pacific Coast Macadamias, accompanied by views along one of the most spectacular parts of the coast. Toasted sand-

wiches and nutty sweet treats make this a great lunch stop. Call ahead to check it's open – hours can be very sketchy outside of summer (from roughly December to March).

Waihau Bay Lodge
PUB FOOD $$

(07-325 3805; www.thewaihaubaylodge.co.nz; Orete Point Rd, Waihau Bay; mains $25-35; 4pm-late Sun-Wed, from 2pm Thu-Sat) A two-storey timber pub by the pier, serving hefty meals and offering accommodation ranging from campsites ($15) to four-bed dorms (from $35 per person), en suite doubles ($140) and roomy en suite units sleeping eight (double $195, extra person $30).

Te Puka Tavern
PUB FOOD $$

(06-864 5465; www.tepukatavern.co.nz; 135 Beach Rd, Tokomaru Bay; mains $15-28; 11am-late;) The well-run pub with cracker ocean views is a cornerstone of the community, keeping everyone fed and watered, and offering visitors a place to stay.

Four natty split-level, self-contained units sleep up to six (doubles $160, extra person $30) and there's room for four campervans (powered sites $15, unpowered sites free).

Shopping

East Cape Manuka Company
FOOD

(06-864 4824; www.eastcapemanuka.co.nz; 4464 Te Araroa Rd, Te Araroa; 9am-3pm Oct-Apr, Mon-Fri May-Sep) The progressive East Cape Manuka Company sells soaps, oils, creams and honey made from potent East Cape manuka. It's a good stop for a coffee, a slice of cheesecake or a delicious manuka honey smoothie (meals and snacks $6 to $15). Check out the busy bees at work in the wall display.

Getting There & Away

By far the most fun way to experience the Pacific Coast Hwy is with your own wheels (motorised or pedal-powered). Otherwise, Bay Hopper (www. baybus.co.nz) runs between Opotiki and Potaka/ Cape Runaway on Tuesday and Thursday afternoons. **Cooks Couriers** (021 371 364, 06-864 4711) runs between Te Araroa and Opotiki on Tuesdays and Thursdays, and between Gisborne and Hicks Bay daily Monday to Saturday.

Gisborne
06 / POP 47,734

'Gizzy' to her friends, Gisborne (pronounced *Gis*-born, not Gis-bun) is a pretty place, squeezed between surf beaches and a sea of chardonnay, and it proudly claims to be the first city on Earth to see the sun each day. It's a good place to put your feet up for a few days, hit the beach and sip some wine.

If you're into festivals, make a dance-music-and-DJ date for late December, or experience the best of the local food, wine and beer scene in October. Across other times of the year, walking in an arboreal wonderland or exploring New Zealand's best regional museum are fine reasons to visit the country's most remote city.

History

The Gisborne region has been settled for more than 700 years. A pact between two migratory *waka* (canoe) skippers, Paoa of the *Horouta* and Kiwa of the *Takitimu*, led to the founding of Turanganui a Kiwa (now Gisborne). Kumara (sweet potatoes) flourished in the fertile soil and the settlement blossomed.

In 1769 this was the first part of NZ sighted by Captain Cook's expedition on the *Endeavour*. Eager to replenish supplies and explore, they set ashore, much to the amazement of the locals. Setting an unfortunate benchmark for intercultural relations, the crew opened fire when the Māori men performed their traditional blood-curdling challenge, killing six of them.

The *Endeavour* set sail without provisions. Cook, perhaps in a fit of petulance, named the area Poverty Bay as 'it did not afford a single item we wanted'.

European settlement began in 1831 with whaling and farming; missionaries followed. In the 1860s battles between settlers and Māori erupted. Beginning in Taranaki, the Hauhau insurrection spread to the East Coast, culminating in the battle of Waerenga a Hika in 1865.

To discover Gisborne's historical spots, pick up the *Historic Walk* pamphlet from Gisborne i-SITE (p344).

⊙ Sights

★ **Tairawhiti Museum**   MUSEUM
(☏06-867 3832; www.tairawhitimuseum.org.nz; Kelvin Rise, Stout St; adult/child $5/free; ⊙10am-4pm Mon-Sat, from 1.30pm Sun) The Tairawhiti Museum, with its fab gallery extension, focuses on East Coast Māori and colonial history. It is Gisborne's arts hub, with rotating exhibits and excellent historic photographic displays. There's also a maritime wing, with displays on *waka* (canoes), whaling and Cook's Poverty Bay, although these pale in comparison to the vintage surfboard collection. There's also a shop, and a cafe overlooking Kelvin Park. Outside is the reconstructed **Wyllie Cottage** (1872), Gisborne's oldest house.

Footrot Flats Statue   STATUE
(Peel St, outside HB Williams Memorial Library) Gisborne is already well endowed with statues, but this one commemorating the hugely popular Footrot Flats cartoons (p344) by Gisborne local, the late Murray Ball, is our new favourite. Wal, the series' archetypal Kiwi farmer, stands with his devoted canine companion, 'The Dog', looking on. For more on *Footrot Flats*, see www.footrotflats.com, or check out the 1986 movie *Footrot Flats: The Dog's Tale* (Murray Ball).

C Company
Memorial House   CULTURAL CENTRE
(www.ngatamatoa.co.nz; 10 Stout St; ⊙noon-3pm Tue-Fri & Sun, from 10am Sat) This cultural centre commemorates the dedication and commitment of the famed 28th (Māori) Battalion of the New Zealand Army that fought bravely in the European and North African theatres in WWII. In particular the role of Māori men from the East Coast who made up the battalion's C Company is brought to life with poignant photos and stories.

Gisborne Farmers Market   MARKET
(☏027 251 8608; www.gisbornefarmersmarket. co.nz; cnr Stout & Fitzherbert Sts; ⊙9.30am-12.30pm Sat) Stock up on fresh fruit, macadamia nuts (and macadamia nut paste!), smallgoods (cooked meats and meat products), honey, herbs, coffee, wine, bread, pastries, fish, cheese and Gisborne oranges...all of it locally grown or procured.

Titirangi Reserve   PARK
(www.gdc.govt.nz; Titirangi Dr, off Queens Dr; ⚐) High on a hill overlooking Gisborne, Titirangi was once a *pā* (fortified village). Reach it via Queens Dr, or on the track from the **Cook Monument** (Kaiti Beach Rd). Near the **lookout** (Titirangi Dr) at the top is yet another Cook edifice, at **Cook's Plaza** (Titirangi Dr). Adjacent is a modest pohutukawa tree planted by Princess Diana in 1983.

Eastwoodhill Arboretum   GARDENS
(☏06-863 9003; www.eastwoodhill.org.nz; 2392 Wharekopae Rd, Ngatapa; adult/child/family $15/2/28; ⊙9am-5pm; ⚐) An arboreal nirvana, Eastwoodhill Arboretum is the largest

Gisborne

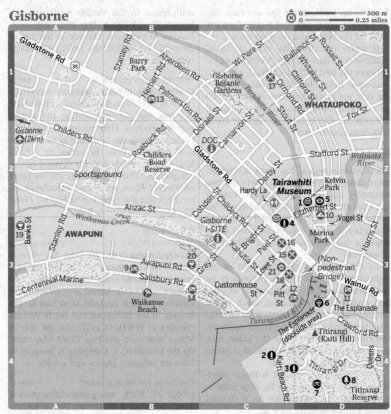

collection of northern-hemisphere trees and shrubs in the southern hemisphere. It's staggeringly beautiful, and you could easily lose a day wandering around the 25km of themed tracks in this pine-scented paradise. It's well signposted, 35km northwest of Gisborne.

There's basic accommodation in bunks and private rooms (dorm bed $35, double room $120 and twin room $70, all including garden admission). Meals are available by arrangement, or you can use the fully equipped kitchen (BYO food as there aren't any shops nearby).

East Coast Museum
of Technology   MUSEUM
(ECMOT; ☎ 027 221 5703; www.ecmot.org.nz; SH2, Makaraka; adult/child $5/1; ☺10am-4pm Sun-Fri, from 1pm Sat) Think analogue rather than digital; old-age rather than space-age. About 5km west of the town centre, this improbable medley of farm equipment, fire engines

and sundry appliances has found an appropriate home in a motley old milking barn and surrounding outhouses. Dig the millennium welcome sign!

🏃 Activities

Water Sports
Surfing is de rigueur in Gisborne, with the teenage population looking appropriately shaggy. **Waikanae Beach** and **Roberts Road** are good for learners; experienced surfers get tubed south of town at the **Pipe**, or east at **Sponge Bay** and **Tuamotu Island**. Further east along SH35, **Wainui** and **Makorori** also have quality breaks.

There's safe swimming between the flags at Waikanae and **Midway Beach**.

Rere Rockslide   SWIMMING
(Wharekopae Rd; ☺daylight hours) This natural phenomenon occurs in a section of the Rere River 50km northwest of Gisborne along

Gisborne

◉ Top Sights
1 Tairawhiti Museum D2

◉ Sights
   C Company Memorial House ....(see 1)
2 Cook Monument..................................C4
3 Cook's Plaza.......................................C4
4 Footrot Flats Statue............................C3
5 Gisborne Farmers Market....................D2
6 Gisborne Wine Centre D3
7 Titirangi Lookout................................D4
8 Titirangi Reserve D4

🛏 Sleeping
9 Ahi Kaa Motel....................................B3
10 Gisborne District Council....................D2
11 Gisborne YHA D3
12 Portside Hotel....................................C3

13 Teal Motor Lodge...............................B1
14 Waikanae Beach Top 10 Holiday
    Park B3

✖ Eating
   Crawford Road Kitchen.................(see 6)
15 Frank & Albie's C3
16 Muirs Bookshop & Cafe C3
17 Neighbourhood Pizzeria C1
   PBC Cafe ....(see 21)
18 USSCO Bar & Bistro C3

◉ Drinking & Nightlife
19 Smash Palace..................................... A3
20 Sunshine Brewery B3

◉ Entertainment
21 Dome Cinema..................................... C3

Wharekopae Rd. Grab a tyre tube or boogie board to cushion the bumps and slide down the 60m-long rocky run into the pool at the bottom. Three kilometres downriver, the **Rere Falls** send a 20m-wide curtain of water over a 5m drop; you can walk behind it if you don't mind getting wet.

Walking On Water Surf School   SURFING
(WOW; ☑ 06-863 2969, 022 313 0213; www.wow surfschool.com; 2hr/3-day/4-day lessons per person from $60/140/185; 🚸) Surfing is just like walking on water, right? Wrong. It's even harder than that – but these guys know how to turn the most naive novice into an upstanding surfer in no time. Kids' lessons and gear hire, too.

Walking
There are many miles of walks to tackle around Gisborne, starting with a gentle stroll along the river. The Gisborne i-SITE (p344) can provide you with brochures for the *Historic Walk* and the *Walking Trails of Gisborne City.*

Winding its way through farmland and forest with commanding views, the **Te Kuri Walkway** (two hours, 5.6km, November to July) starts 4km north of town at the end of Shelley Rd.

👉 Tours

Haurata High Country Walks   TRAMPING
(☑ 06-867 8452; www.haurata.co.nz; walks unguided/guided per person from $15/25) Take a tramp in the hills with Haurata, which offers guided or unguided short and long day walks through the gorgeous high country behind Gisborne. Meals, farmhouse accommodation and hot-tub soaks also available. Haurata's 'Aerial Station' property is around 65km northwest of Gisborne. Allow 70 minutes for the drive.

Tairāwhiti Tours   CULTURAL
(☑ 021 276 5484; www.tairawhititours.co.nz; tours per person from $225) Excellent 5½-hour guided tours around Gisborne, digging into history, wine, food and culture (all the interesting stuff). Discounts are available for groups.

Cycle Gisborne   CYCLING
(☑ 06-927 7021; www.cyclegisborne.com; tours from $125, bicycle hire per day from $50) Half-day to multiday guided cycle tours around local sights and further afield, including wineries and Eastwoodhill Arboretum (p339). Bike hire also available (with maps and advice on tap).

✩ Festivals & Events

First Light Wine & Food Festival   WINE, FOOD
(www.firstlightwineandfood.co.nz; ⊘ Oct) Cellar-door spectacular, with local winemakers and foodies pooling talents. Buses leave from the Gisborne i-SITE (p344), and transport revellers between the venues.

Rhythm & Vines   MUSIC, WINE
(R&V; www.rhythmandvines.co.nz; ⊘ Dec) A huge event on Gizzy's music calendar, R&V is a three-day festival leading up to New Year's Eve, featuring big-time local and international bands and DJs. Local accommodation feels the squeeze.

🛏 Sleeping

Gisborne YHA HOSTEL **$**
(☏06-867 3269; www.yha.co.nz; 32 Harris St; dm/s/d/f $29/52/68/130; @ 🛜 🔁 🏠) A short wander across the river from town, this rambling, mustard-coloured 1925 charmer houses a well-kept hostel. The rooms are large and comfy (even the 10-bed dorm in the attic), while a shared outdoor deck and lawns kindle conversation. There's a family en suite unit, and surfboard and bike hire are also available.

**Waikanae Beach
Top 10 Holiday Park** HOLIDAY PARK **$**
(☏0800 867 563, 06-867 5634; www.gisborneholidaypark.co.nz; 280 Grey St; sites per person from $27, cabins & units d $95-150; 🛜 🔁 🏠) Right by the beach and an easy 10-minute walk to town, this grassy holiday park offers basic cabins, better units and grassy lanes for pitching tents and parking vans. Surfboards and bikes are for hire, and a swimming pool was added in late 2017.

Portside Hotel HOTEL, APARTMENT **$$**
(☏0800 767 874, 06-869 1000; www.portsidegisborne.co.nz; 2 Reads Quay; d/apt from $165/235; @ 🛜 🔁) The wandering business traveller's hotel of choice in Gisborne, Portside offers three levels of sassy two-bedroom apartments, right by the river mouth where the big ships come and go. Charcoal-and-cream colour scheme, with little glass-fronted balconies.

Ahi Kaa Motel MOTEL **$$**
(☏06-867 7107; www.ahikaa.co.nz; 61 Salisbury Rd; d $140-170; @ 🛜) 🅿 An uptown motel offering on a quiet backstreet, a short sandy-footed stroll across the road from Waikanae Beach. Fancy linen, tasteful bathrooms, double glazing, outdoor showers, recycled timbers, solar power and recycling savvy – nice one!

Teal Motor Lodge MOTEL **$$**
(☏0800 838 325, 06-868 4019; www.teal.co.nz; 479 Gladstone Rd; d/f from $150/205; 🛜 🔁) With super street appeal on the main drag (500m into town), the vaguely alpine (and just a bit *Mad Men*) Teal boasts a solid offering of tidy, family-friendly units plus a saltwater swimming pool and immaculate lawns to run around on.

Knapdale Eco Lodge LODGE **$$$**
(☏06-862 5444; www.knapdale.co.nz; 114 Snowsill Rd, Waihirere; d incl breakfast from $420; 🛜) 🅿 Indulge yourself at this rural idyll, complete with lake, farm animals and home-grown produce. The modern lodge is filled with international artwork, its glassy frontage flowing out to an expansive patio with brazier, barbecue and pizza oven. Five-course dinners by arrangement ($95). To get here head 10km northwest of Gisborne, via Back Ormond Rd.

🍴 Eating

Neighbourhood Pizzeria PIZZA **$**
(☏06-868 7174; www.neighbourhoodpizzeria.co.nz; 9 Ballance St; pizzas $10-18; ⏰4.30-8.30pm) Serving pies out of a hip caravan, Neighbourhood Pizzeria draws loyal locals most nights for what we reckon are among the country's best pizzas. Traditional flavours like margherita segue to pork and jalapeño or chicken and chorizo. Mozzarella comes from nearby Waimata, and the adjacent area includes an excellent weekday cafe and a cool store selling vintage and retro collectables.

Frank & Albie's CAFE **$**
(☏06-867 7847; www.frankandalbie.co.nz; 24 Gladstone Rd; mains $6-10; ⏰7am-2.30pm Mon-Fri) 'We cut lunch, not corners' is the motto at Frank & Albie's, a neat little hipster nook on Gisborne's main drag (check out the old art-deco leadlighting above the door). Nifty plywood benches, recycled timber tables and dinky white stools set the scene for super sandwiches, coffee, teas and smoothies.

Muirs Bookshop & Cafe CAFE **$**
(☏06-867 9741; www.muirsbookshop.co.nz; 62 Gladstone Rd; meals $5-14; ⏰8.30am-3.30pm Mon-Fri, 9am to 3pm Sat) Situated above a beloved, age-old independent bookseller in

GISBORNE WINERIES

With hot summers and fertile loam soils, the Waipaoa River valley to the northwest of Gisborne is one of New Zealand's foremost grape-growing areas. The region is traditionally famous for its chardonnay, and is increasingly noted for Gewürztraminer and pinot gris. See www.gisbornewine.co.nz for a cellar-door map. Opening hours scale back out of peak season. Four of the best:

Millton (☑06-862 8680; www.millton.co.nz; 119 Papatu Rd, Manutuke; ⊙10am-5pm, reduced winter hours) ✔

Matawhero (☑06-867 6140; www.matawhero.co.nz; Riverpoint Rd, Matawhero; ⊙noon-4pm Sat & Sun)

Kirkpatrick Estate (☑06-862 7722; www.kew.co.nz; 569 Wharekopae Rd, Patutahi; ⊙open by appointment) ✔

Bushmere Estate (☑06-868 9317; www.bushmere.com; 166 Main Rd, Matawhero; ⊙11am-3pm Wed-Sun Sep-May)

a lovely heritage building, this simple cafe offers a small but sweet selection of counter food and cakes. Fans of fine espresso and literature may need to be forcibly removed. Over-street balcony for balmy days. Show up around 9.30am for the best chance of a freshly baked chocolate brioche.

★**Crawford Road Kitchen** BISTRO $$
(☑06-867 4085; www.crawfordroadkitchen.co.nz; Shed 3, 50 The Esplanade; shared plates $11-25; ⊙11am-9pm Tue-Thu, to 10pm Fri & Sat, to 5pm Sun) Attached to the **Gisborne Wine Centre** (☑06-867 4085; www.gisbornewinecentre.co.nz; Shed 3, 50 The Esplanade; ⊙11am-9pm Tue-Sat, to 5pm Sun), this bistro combines culinary smarts and international flavours with an interesting location beside Gisborne's inner harbour. Good-value shared plates could include feta-crusted lamb with beetroot puree or baked snapper with harissa and quinoa, and the excellent wine list features around 15 local wines by the glass. Craft beers are also proudly Gisborne-brewed.

PBC Cafe CAFE $$
(☑06-863 3165; 38 Childers Rd; mains breakfast $15-25, lunch $20-32; ⊙7am-3pm Mon-Fri, from 8am Sat & Sun; ☑) The creaky old grandeur of the Poverty Bay Club for gentlemen (1874) is reason enough to visit, and this cafe inside certainly adds impetus with appealing counter food, all-day brunch, pizza, blackboard specials and reasonable prices. Love the big pew along the outside wall. There's the Dome Cinema (p344) and a sweet little gift shop here, too.

USSCO Bar & Bistro MODERN NZ $$$
(☑06-868 3246; www.ussco.co.nz; 16 Childers Rd; mains $36-45; ⊙4.30pm-late Mon-Sat) Housed in the restored Union Steam Ship Company building (hence USSCO), this place is all class. Kitchen skills shine on a highly seasonal menu featuring the likes of roast duck with kumara (sweet potato) fondant, and the devilishly good desserts are always a highlight. Look forward to local wines, NZ craft beers, generous portions and multi-course deals.

🍷 Drinking & Nightlife

★**Smash Palace** BAR
(☑06-867 7769; www.smashpalacebar.com; 24 Banks St; ⊙3-8pm Tue, Thu & Sun, to 11pm Wed & Fri, noon-11pm Sat) Get juiced at the junkyard: an iconic drinking den in Gisborne's industrial wastelands (make as much noise as you like!), full to the gunwales with ephemera and its very own DC3 crash-landed in the beer garden. Occasional live music; vinyl sessions Sunday afternoons.

★**Sunshine Brewery** MICROBREWERY
(☑06-867 7777; www.sunshinebrewery.co.nz; 49 Awapuni Rd; ⊙noon-8pm Mon-Sat) Bottling up a clutch of quality beers including the excellent Electron IPA, Gisborne's own craft brewery has a fab tasting room near Waikanae Beach. Pizza from Neighbourhood Pizzeria (p342) is also served. Try one with the hoppy Offshore Indian Pale Lager. Sunshine's more interesting brews fall under its Sunrise Project banner. Tasting paddles (five beers) are $15.

☆ Entertainment

★ Dome Cinema   CINEMA, BAR
(☑08-324 3005; www.domecinema.co.nz; 38
Childers Rd; tickets $14; ⊙from 5pm Wed-Sun)
The excellent Dome is located inside the
charming old Poverty Bay Club building
(1874): beanbags and art-house flicks now
occupy the glass-domed ballroom. There's
a cool bar next door serving beer, wine and
pizza amid black-painted floorboards. The
PBC Cafe (p343) is also here.

❶ Information

DOC (Department of Conservation; ☑06-869
0460; www.doc.govt.nz; 63 Carnarvon St;
⊙8am-4.30pm Mon-Fri)
Gisborne Hospital (☑06-869 0500; www.tdh.
org.nz; 421 Ormond Rd, Riverdale; ⊙24hr)
Gisborne i-SITE (☑06-868 6139; www.
gisbornenz.com; 209 Grey St; ⊙8.30am-
5.30pm Mon-Fri, 9am-5pm Sat, 10am-4pm
Sun; ☎) Beside a doozy of a Canadian totem
pole, this information centre has all and sundry,
including a travel desk, internet access, bike
hire and toilets.
Post Office (www.nzpost.co.nz; 127 Gladstone
Rd; ⊙9am-5pm Mon-Fri, to noon Sat)
Three Rivers Medical (☑06-867 7411; www.
3rivers.co.nz; 75 Customhouse St; ⊙8am-8pm
Mon-Fri, 9am-6pm Sat & Sun) Doctors and
dentists available by appointment.

❶ Getting There & Around

AIR
Gisborne Airport (www.eastland.co.nz/
gisborne-airport; Aerodrome Rd, Awapuni) is
3km west of the city. Air New Zealand (www.
airnewzealand.co.nz) flies to/from Auckland
and Wellington.

BUS
InterCity and Naked Bus services depart from
Gisborne i-SITE, with daily buses to the following
destinations.

DESTINATION	COMPANY	PRICE	DURATION
Auckland	InterCity	$85	9hr
Napier	InterCity	$45	4hr
Opotiki	InterCity	$31	2hr
Opotiki	Naked Bus	$22	2hr
Rotorua	InterCity	$60	5hr
Rotorua	Naked Bus	$28	4½hr
Taupo	Naked Bus	$25	6hr
Wairoa	InterCity	$29	1½hr

Gisborne Airport Car Rental is an agent for nine
car-hire companies including big brands and
local outfits.

THE STORY OF FOOTROT FLATS

From 1976 to 1994, the *Footrot Flats* cartoon strip by long-time Gisborne resident Murray
Ball (1939–2017) ran in newspapers across New Zealand, and compilation books of the
series sold millions throughout NZ and Australia. Oddly, it was also a big hit in Denmark.

At its heart, *Footrot Flats* is the story of the relationship between Wallace 'Wal' Footrot
and his loyal border collie, nicknamed 'The Dog' in a fine example of Kiwi understatement. A revolving cast of characters includes Darlene 'Cheeky' Hobson, Wal's hairdresser
girlfriend; Horse, an irascible and fierce tomcat based on an actual feline that lived at
Ball's farm; and Prince Charles, a very spoilt Welsh corgi owned by Wal's Aunt Dolly. Not
the most farm-savvy of canines, Prince Charles often needs to be taught the finer points
of rural life by The Dog.

Life in the country is the ongoing background of the cartoon strip – along with quintessential NZ locations like the local rugby club in the fictional town of Raupo – and
this proudly rural sensibility is a big reason why *Footrot Flats* was such a big hit with
city dwellers and countryfolk alike. New Zealand is still a young country, and many
late-20th-century Kiwis could easily identify with a country lifestyle in their family history
from just a couple of generations earlier.

Beyond the gentle humour, cartoonist Ball was a fierce opponent of inequality, and
over its lifespan, *Footrot Flats* also incorporated subtle commentary on environmental-
ism. The series was at its peak in the mid-1980s, spawning a feature-length animated
film in 1986, and an Auckland theme park which was open from 1986 to 1991. Charles M
Schulz, creator of the *Peanuts* comic strip, and Ball were mutual admirers, and Schulz
penned an introduction to the only *Footrot Flats* compilation to be published in the United States.

WORTH A TRIP

MAHIA PENINSULA

Between Gisborne and Napier, the Mahia Peninsula's eroded hills, sandy beaches and vivid blue sea resemble the Coromandel, but without the tourist crowds and with the bonus of dramatic cliffs.

It's an enduring holiday spot for East Coasters, who come for boaty, beachy stuff, and you can get in on the action if you have your own transport. A day or two could be spent exploring the scenic reserve and the bird-filled Maungawhio Lagoon, hanging out at the beach (Mahia Beach at sunset can be spectacular), or even playing a round of golf. Mahia has several small settlements offering between them a few guesthouses, a holiday park, a bar-bistro and a couple of stores.

In recent years, the peninsula's eastern edge has become the launch location for New Zealand's very own rocket company. Check Rocket Lab's website (www.rocketlabusa. com) for information on this innovative and surprising Kiwi startup.

See www.voyagemahia.co.nz for accommodation listings.

The peninsula is a short detour east of the road between Gisborne and Wairoa (SH2). Turn off at Nuhaka – the main settlements are about 20km away. No buses run here – you'll need your own vehicle.

CAR

Gisborne Airport Car Rental (☑ 0800 144 129; www.gisborneairportcarhire.co.nz) Agent for nine car-hire companies including big brands and local outfits.

TAXI

Gisborne Taxis (☑ 0800 505 555, 06-867 2222; www.gisbornetaxis.co.nz)

South of Gisborne

From Gisborne heading south towards Napier, you can take the coast road or the inland road. The coastal route is a marginally better choice, being quicker and offering occasional views out to sea. However, SH36 (Tiniroto Rd) is also an interesting drive (or bike route) with several good stopping points along the way.

⊙ Sights

Doneraille Park, 49km from Gisborne, is a peaceful bush riverside reserve with freedom camping for self-contained vehicles. **Hackfalls Arboretum** (☑ 06-863 7083; www. hackfalls.org.nz; 187 Berry Rd, Tiniroto; adult/child $10/free; ⊙ 9am-5pm) is a 3km detour from the turn-off at the Tiniroto Tavern. The snow-white cascades of **Te Reinga Falls**, 12km further south, are well worth a stop.

The busier SH2 route heads inland and soon enters the **Wharerata State Forest** (beware of logging trucks). Just out of the woods, 55km from Gisborne, **Morere Hot Springs** (☑ 06-837 8856; www.morere

hotsprings.co.nz; SH2, Morere; adult/child $12/6, private pools $15/10, nonswimmers $3; ⊙ 10am-5pm, extended hours Dec-Feb) burble up from a fault line in the **Morere Springs Scenic Reserve**.

From Gisborne on SH2, keep an eye out for the brightly painted **Taane-nui-a-Rangi Marae** on the left. You can get a decent view from the road; don't enter unless invited.

Continuing south, SH2 leads to Nuhaka at the northern end of Hawke's Bay. From here it's west to Wairoa or east to the seasalty Mahia Peninsula. Not far from the Nuhaka roundabout is **Kahungunu Marae** (www.kahungunu.iwi.nz/our-marae; cnr Ihaka & Mataira Sts, Nuhaka).

🛌 Sleeping & Eating

Morere Hot Springs Lodge & Cabins   BUNGALOW **$**
(☑ 06-837 8824; www.morerelodge.co.nz; SH2, Morere; d $100-120, extra person $30; 🐕🅿) A farmy enclave where the lambs gambol and the dog wags her tail at you nonstop. Sleeping options include a classic 1917 farmhouse (sleeps 12) with kitchen and sweet sleep-out, another two-bedroom farmhouse (sleeps four) and two photogenic cabins. Great value. Pizzas and other evening meals are available by arrangement.

ⓘ Getting There & Away

Drive the SH2 south of Gisborne, running close to the coast, or take SH36 inland via Tiniroto. Either way you'll end up in Wairoa.

InterCity (www.intercity.co.nz) buses take the SH2, departing daily from **Gisborne i-SITE** (p344) for Napier (from $14, four hours) via Wairoa (from $10, 1½ hours).

Te Urewera

Shrouded in mist and mysticism, Te Urewera encompasses 2127 sq km of virgin forest cut with lakes and rivers. The highlight is Lake Waikaremoana (Sea of Rippling Waters), a deep crucible of water encircled by the Lake Waikaremoana Track, one of New Zealand's Great Walks. Rugged bluffs drop away to reedy inlets, the lake's mirror surface disturbed only by mountain zephyrs and the occasional waterbird taking to the skies.

History

The name Te Urewera still has the capacity to make Pākehā (white) New Zealanders feel slightly uneasy – and not just because it translates as 'The Burnt Penis'. There's something primal and untamed about this wild woodland, with its rich history of Māori resistance.

The local Ngāi Tūhoe people – prosaically known as the 'Children of the Mist' – never signed the Treaty of Waitangi and fought with Rewi Maniapoto at Orakau during the Waikato Wars. The army of Te Kooti took refuge here during running battles with government troops. The claimant of Te Kooti's spiritual mantle, Rua Kenana, led a thriving community beneath the sacred mountain Maungapohatu (1366m) from 1905 until his politically motivated 1916 arrest. This effectively erased the last bastion of Māori independence in the country. Maungapohatu never recovered, and only a small settlement remains today. Nearby, Ruatahuna's extraordinary Mataatua Marae celebrates Te Kooti's exploits.

Tūhoe remain proud of their identity and traditions, with around 40% still speaking *te reo* (the language) on a regular basis.

In 2014, following a settlement under the Treaty of Waitangi, administration of Te Urewera was passed to the Te Urewera Board comprising both Tūhoe and the NZ government. Tūhoe and this board lead the formulation of annual plans for Te Urewera, and work with the Department of Conservation (DOC) to maintain tracks and visitor facilities in the area.

TE KOOTI

Māori history is littered with mystics, prophets and warriors, one of whom is the celebrated Te Kooti (rhymes with naughty, not booty).

In 1865 he fought with the government against the Hauhau (adherents of the Pai Marire faith, founded by another warrior-prophet) but was accused of being a spy and imprisoned on the Chatham Islands without trial.

While there, Te Kooti studied the Bible and claimed to receive visions from the archangel Michael. His charismatic preaching and 'miracles' – including producing flames from his hands (his captors claimed he used phosphorus from the head of matches) – helped win over the Pai Marire to his distinctly Māori take on Christianity.

In 1867 Te Kooti led an astounding escape from the Chathams, hijacking a supply ship and sailing to Poverty Bay with 200 followers. En route he threw a doubter overboard as a sacrifice. Upon their safe arrival, Te Kooti's disciples raised their right hands in homage to God rather than bowing submissively; *ringa tu* (upraised hand) became the name of his church.

Te Kooti requested a dialogue with the colonial government but was once again rebuffed, with magistrate Reginald Biggs demanding his immediate surrender. Unimpressed by Pākehā (white person) justice, Te Kooti commenced a particularly effective guerrilla campaign – starting with killing Biggs and around 50 others (including women and children, both Māori and Pākehā) at Matawhero near Gisborne.

A four-year chase ensued. Eventually Te Kooti took refuge in the King Country, the Māori king's vast dominion where government troops feared to tread.

Proving the pointlessness of the government's approach to the whole affair, Te Kooti was officially pardoned in 1883. By this time his reputation as a prophet and healer had spread and his Ringatu Church was firmly established. Today it claims more than 16,000 adherents.

🏃 Activities

There are dozens of walks within Te Urewera's vast boundaries, most of which are outlined in DOC's *Lake Waikaremoana Walks* pamphlet ($2). Plenty of short walks kick off from near the eastern end of the lake or the Waikaremoana Holiday Park, or tackle the longer Lake Waikaremoana Track.

Lake Waikaremoana Track

This 46km, three- to four-day Great Walk scales the spectacular Panekire Bluff (1180m), with open panoramas interspersed with fern groves and forest. The walk is rated as moderate, with the only difficult section being the Panekire ascent, and during summer it can get busy.

Although it's a year-round track, winter rain deters many people and makes conditions much more challenging. At this altitude (580m above sea level), temperatures can drop quickly, even in summer. Walkers should take portable stoves and fuel as there are no cooking facilities en route.

There are five **huts** (adult/child $32/free) and **campsites** (adult/child $14/free) spaced along the track, all of which must be pre-booked through DOC, regardless of the season. Book at regional DOC offices, i-SITEs or online at www.greatwalks.co.nz.

If you have a car, it is safest to leave it at the Waikaremoana Holiday Park or Big Bush Holiday Park, and then take a water taxi to either trailhead. Alternatively, you can take the fully catered, three-night guided tour offered by the enthusiastic and experienced **Walking Legends** (📞 0800 925 569, 07-312 5297; www.walkinglegends.com; per person $1490-1590) or **Te Urewera Treks** (📞 07-929 9669; www.teureweratreks.co.nz/home; per person $1500) 🌿.

Propel yourself onto the track either clockwise from just outside **Onepoto** in the south, or anticlockwise from **Hopuruahine Suspension Bridge** in the north. Estimated walking times:

ROUTE	TIME (HR)
Onepoto to Panekire Hut	5
Panekire Hut to Waiopaoa Hut	3-4
Waiopaoa Hut to Marauiti Hut	4-5
Marauiti Hut to Waiharuru Hut	1½
Waiharuru Hut to Whanganui Hut	2
Whanganui Hut to Hopuruahine Suspension Bridge	2

Walks Near Lake Waikareiti

With its untouched islands, **Lake Waikareiti** is an enchanting place. Starting near the far eastern end of Lake Waikaremoana, it's an hour's walk to its shore.

Accessed from the track to Lake Waikareiti, the more challenging **Ruapani Circuit Track** (a six-hour loop) passes through wetlands and dense, virgin forest. Also from Lake Waikareiti it's a three-hour walk to the **Sandy Bay Hut** at the northern end of the lake.

🛏 Sleeping

There are more than 30 huts and campsites within Te Urewera, most of which are very basic, plus the Waikaremoana Holiday Park. There is also a B&B in the area in the pretty village of Tuai.

Waikaremoana Holiday Park   HOLIDAY PARK $
(📞 06-837 3826; www.doc.govt.nz/waikaremoana-holiday-park; 6249 Lake Rd/SH38; unpowered/powered campsites from $36/42, cabins/chalets d from $65/130; 🌐) Right on the shore, this place has Swiss-looking chalets, fisher's cabins and campsites, most with watery views, plus an on-site shop. New chalets opened in late 2017 are tucked into the native forest.

Hikihiki's Inn   B&B $$$
(📞 06-8373 701; www.hikihiki.co.nz; 9 Rotten Row, Tuai; s/d $140/255) In the sweet lakeside settlement of Tuai, 6km from Onepoto, this little weatherboard gem serves as a B&B run by a charming and friendly '100% Kiwi' host.

ℹ Information

Te Urewera Visitor Centre (Te Kura Whenua Paradise; 📞 06-837 3803; www.ngaituhoe.iwi.nz; 6249 Lake Rd; ⊙ 8.30am-4pm) Opened by the Ngāi Tūhoe people in 2017, this spectacular new lakeside visitor centre includes a cafe, and displays and galleries on the natural and cultural history of Te Urewera. Visitor information and Department of Conservation information on the Lake Waikaremoana Track are available, and Great Walk bookings can be made. Enquire about rowboat hire to explore nearby Lake Waikareiti.

ℹ Getting There & Away

Lake Waikaremoana is about an hour (64km) from Wairoa on SH38, which continues through to Rotorua – the entire SH38 route is named the **Te Urewera Rainforest Route**. Around 95km of the entire 195km Wairoa–Rotorua route is unsealed: it's a four-hour, bone-rattling drive (but a great adventure!).

Lake Waikaremoana Track

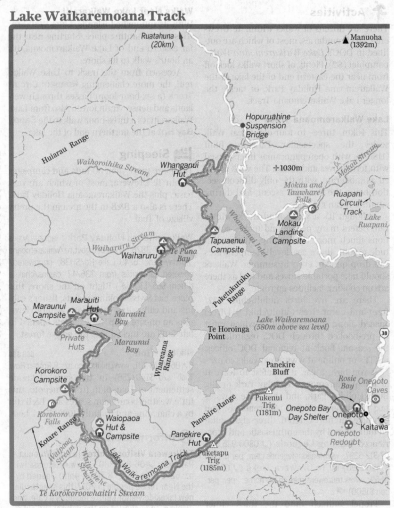

Big Bush Water Taxi (🕿 0800 525 392, 06-837 3777; www.lakewaikaremoana.co.nz/water-taxi; per person one way $50-60) will boat you to either Onepoto or Hopuruahine trailhead, with hut-to-hut backpack transfers for the less gung-ho. It also runs minibus shuttles to and from Wairoa (from $50 per person one-way).

HAWKE'S BAY

Hawke Bay, the name given to the body of water that stretches from the Mahia Peninsula to Cape Kidnappers, looks like it's been bitten out of the North Island's eastern flank. Add an

apostrophe and an 's' and you've got a region that stretches south and inland to include fertile farmland, surf beaches, mountainous ranges and forests. With food, wine and architecture the prevailing obsessions, it's smugly comfortable but thoroughly appealing, and is best viewed through a rosé-tinted wine glass.

Wairoa & Around

The small river town of Wairoa (population 4260) is trying hard to shake its rough-edged rep. Not scintillating enough to warrant an extended stay, the town does have a

(☑06-838 3108; www.facebook.com/pg/Wairoa Museum; 142 Marine Pde, Wairoa; ☺10am-4pm Mon-Fri, to noon Sat) FREE inside an old bank.

⊙ Sights

The stretch of highway between Wairoa and Napier traipses through unphotogenic farmland and forestry blocks for much of its 117km. Most of it follows a railway line, currently only used for freight – you'll realise what a travesty this is when you pass under the Mohaka Viaduct (1937), the highest rail viaduct (97m) in Australasia.

Occupied by early Māori, Lake Tutira has walkways and a bird sanctuary. At Tutira village, just north of the lake, Pohokura Rd leads to the wonderful Boundary Stream Scenic Reserve, a major conservation area. Three loop tracks start from the road, ranging in length from 40 minutes to three hours. Also along this road you'll find the Opouahi and Bellbird Bush Scenic Reserves, which both offer rewarding walks. See www.doc.govt.nz for info on all of these reserves.

Off Waipatiki Rd, 34km outside Napier, Waipatiki Beach is a beaut spot boasting a low-key campsite and the 64-hectare Waipatiki Scenic Reserve. Further down the line, White Pine Bush Scenic Reserve, 29km from Napier on SH2, bristles with kahikatea and nikau palms. Tangoio Falls Scenic Reserve, 27km north of Napier, has Te Ana Falls, stands of wheki-ponga (tree ferns) and native orchids. Again, www.doc.govt.nz has the lowdown on these reserves. Between White Pine and Tangoio Reserves the Tangoio Walkway (three hours return) follows Kareaara Stream.

The highway surfs the coast for the last 20km, with impressive views towards Napier. Hawke's Bay wine country starts in earnest at the mouth of the Esk River.

❶ Information

Wairoa i-SITE (☑06-838 7440; www.visit wairoa.co.nz; cnr SH2 & Queen St; ☺8.30am-5pm Mon-Fri, 10am-4pm Sat & Sun) The spot for local info, including advice on Lake Waikaremoana and accommodation around town.

❶ Getting There & Away

The closest sizeable town to Te Urewera (p346), Wairoa is 98km southwest of Gisborne and 117km northeast of Napier. InterCity (www.intercity. co.nz) buses trundle in from Gisborne (1½ hours, from $10) and Napier (2¼ hours, from $14).

couple of points of interest, including an exceptional (and exceptionally early-opening) pie shop called Oslers (☑06-838 8299; 116 Marine Pde, Wairoa; pies $4-5, meals $7-15; ☺8am-4pm Mon-Fri, to 2.30pm Sat & Sun). The arty Eastend Cafe (☑06-838 6070; eastendcafe@xtra.co.nz; 250 Marine Pde, Wairoa; meals $7-20; ☺7am-3pm Mon-Fri, 8am-4pm Sat & Sun) is part of the revamped Gaiety Cinema & Theatre (☑06-838 3104; www.gaietytheatre.co.nz; 252 Marine Pde, Wairoa; tickets from $10; ☺10am-10pm Thu-Sun) complex – the town's cultural hub. Other diversions include the plaque-studded River Walkway, and the Wairoa Museum

Hawke's Bay

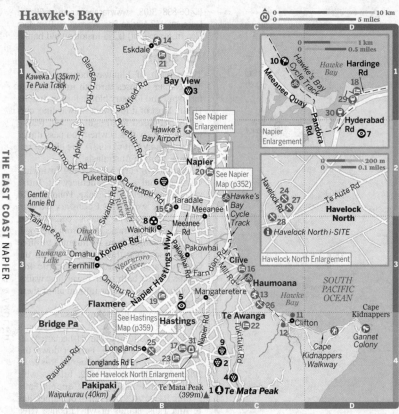

Napier

♪ 06 / POP 63,100

The Napier of today – a charismatic, sunny, composed city with the air of an affluent English seaside resort – is the silver lining of the dark cloud that was the deadly 1931 earthquake. Rebuilt in the popular architectural styles of the time, the city retains a unique concentration of art-deco buildings. Don't expect the Chrysler Building – Napier is resolutely low-rise – but you will find amazingly intact 1930s facades and streetscapes, which can provoke a *Great Gatsby*-esque swagger in the least romantic soul. Linger a while to discover some of regional New Zealand's best restaurants and also a few excellent wineries less visited than the bigger names around nearby Hastings and Havelock North.

History

The Napier area has been settled since around the 12th century and was known to Māori as Ahuriri (now the name of a suburb of Napier). By the time James Cook eyeballed the scene in October 1769, Ngāti Kahungunu was the dominant tribe, controlling the whole coast down to Wellington.

In the 1830s whalers hung around Ahuriri, establishing a trading base in 1839. By the 1850s the Crown had purchased – often by dubious means – 1.4 million acres of Hawke's Bay land, leaving Ngāti Kahungunu with less than 4000 acres. The town of Napier was planned in 1854 and obsequiously named after the British general and colonial administrator Charles Napier.

At 10.46am on 3 February 1931, the city was levelled by a catastrophic earthquake (7.9 on the Richter scale). Fatalities in Napier and nearby Hastings numbered 258. Napier

Hawke's Bay

suddenly found itself 40 sq km larger, as the earthquake heaved sections of what was once a lagoon 2m above sea level (Napier airport was once more 'port', less 'air'). A fevered rebuilding program ensued, resulting in one of the world's most uniformly art-deco cities.

◉ Sights

Napier's claim to fame is undoubtedly its architecture, and a close study of these treasures could take several days (especially if you're stopping to eat). Beyond the edge of town, the Hawke's Bay wineries are a treat.

★ **MTG Hawke's Bay** MUSEUM, THEATRE
(Museum Theatre Gallery; ☎06-835 7781; www.mtghawkesbay.com; 1 Tennyson St; ⊙10am-5pm) FREE The beating cultural heart of Napier is the smart-looking MTG. It's a gleaming-white museum-theatre-gallery space by the water, and it brings live performances, film screenings and regularly changing gallery and museum displays together with touring and local exhibitions. Napier's public library – which has free wi-fi access – was set to be relocated to the building in early 2018.

★ **Daily Telegraph Building** ARCHITECTURE
(☎06-834 1911; www.heritage.org.nz/the-list/details/1129; 49 Tennyson St; ⊙9am-5pm Mon-Fri) The Daily Telegraph is one of the stars of Napier's art-deco show, with superb zigzags, fountain shapes and a symmetrically patterned facade. If the front doors are open, nip inside and ogle the painstakingly restored foyer (it's a real-estate office these days).

Sea Walls PUBLIC ART
(Artists for Oceans) Painted as part of street-art festivals held in 2016 and 2017, almost 50 colourful and thought-provoking murals are scattered across Napier. Pick up the *Sea Walls: Artists for Oceans* map from the Napier i-SITE (p357) or the National Aquarium of New Zealand (p353) to begin your own discovery of various works reinforcing and celebrating the well-being of our oceans' ecosystems.

Bluff Hill Lookout VIEWPOINT
(Lighthouse Rd) The convoluted route to the top of Bluff Hill (102m) goes up and down like an elevator on speed (best to drive), but rewards with expansive views across the port. Bring a picnic or some fish and chips.

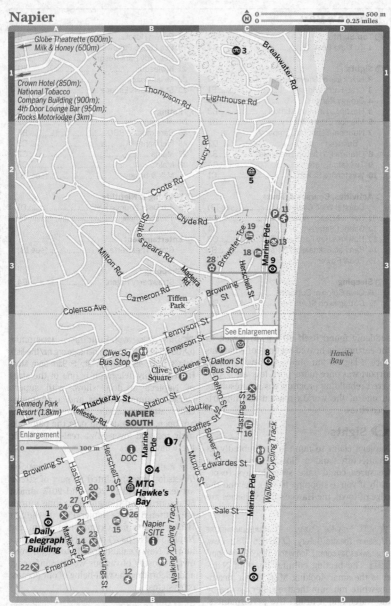

Globe Theatrette (600m);
Milk & Honey (600m)

Crown Hotel (850m);
National Tobacco
Company Building (900m);
4th Door Lounge Bar (950m);
Rocks Motorlodge (3km)

Thompson Rd

Lighthouse Rd

Breakwater Rd

Coote Rd

Clyde Rd

Shakespeare Rd

Madeira Rd

Milton Rd

Cameron Rd

Tiffen Park

Colenso Ave

Brewster Tce

Marine Pde

Herschell St

Browning St

Tennyson St

Emerson St

Clive Sq
Bus Stop

Clive
Square

Dickens St

Dalton St
Bus Stop

Hawke
Bay

Kennedy Park
Resort (1.8km)

Thackeray St

Wellesley Rd

Station St

NAPIER
SOUTH

Vautier St

Raffles St

Dalton St

Hastings St

Bower St

Munro St

Edwardes St

Sale St

Walking/Cycling Track

Marine Pde

Enlargement

Browning St

Hastings St

Herschell St

Marine Pde

DOC

MTG
Hawke's
Bay

Napier
i-SITE

Market St

Hastings St

Emerson St

**Daily
Telegraph
Building**

National Tobacco Company Building

ARCHITECTURE

(☏06-834 1911; www.heritage.org.nz/the-list/details/1170; cnr Bridge & Ossian Sts, Ahuriri; ⊙lobby 9am-5pm Mon-Fri) Around the shore at Ahuriri, the National Tobacco Compa-

ny Building (1932) is arguably the region's deco masterpiece, combining art-deco forms with the natural motifs of art nouveau. Roses, raupo (bulrushes) and grapevines frame the elegantly curved entrance. During business hours, pull on the leaf-

Napier

shaped brass door handles and enter the first two rooms.

National Aquarium of New Zealand
AQUARIUM

(☏06-834 1404; www.nationalaquarium.co.nz; 546 Marine Pde; adult/child/family $20/10.50/57; ☺9am-5pm, feedings 10am & 2pm, last entry 4.30pm) Inside this modern complex with its stingray-inspired roof are piranhas, terrapins, eels, kiwi, tuatara and a whole lotta fish. Snorkellers can swim with sharks ($100), or sign up for a 'Little Penguin Close Encounter' ($70).

Marine Parade
STREET

Napier's elegant seaside avenue is lined with huge Norfolk Island pines, and dotted with

motels and charming timber villas. Along its length are parks, quirky **sunken gardens** (Marine Pde; ☺24hr) **FREE**, a mini-golf course, a skate park, a sound shell, a swim centre and an aquarium. Near the north end of the parade is the **Tom Parker Fountain** (Marine Pde) **FREE**, best viewed at night when it's lavishly lit. Next to it is the **Pania of the Reef** (Marine Pde) **FREE** sculpture.

Napier Prison
HISTORIC BUILDING

(☏06-835 9933; www.napierprison.com; 55 Coote Rd; adult/child/family $20/10/50; ☺9am-5pm) On the run from the law? Assuage your guilt with a tour of the grim 1906 Napier Prison on the hill behind the town. There's a self-guided audio set-up, available in 16 languages.

🏃 Activities

Napier's pebbly ocean beach isn't safe for swimming. Instead, to cool off, locals head north of the city to **Westshore Beach** (off Ferguson Ave, Westshore), or to the surf beaches south of Cape Kidnappers.

Mountain Valley
ADVENTURE SPORTS

(☏06-834 9756; www.mountainvalley.co.nz; 408 McVicar Rd, Te Pohue; horse treks/rafting/fishing per person from $70/109/250) About 60km north of Napier on SH5, Mountain Valley is a hub of outdoorsy action: horse trekking, white-water rafting, kayaking and fly-fishing. There's also simple accommodation on-site (campsites/dorms/doubles from $16/22/100).

Ocean Spa
SWIMMING

(☏06-835 8553; www.oceanspanapier.co.nz; 42 Marine Pde; adult/child $11/8, private pools 30min $13/10; ☺6am-10pm Mon-Sat, from 8am Sun) A spiffy waterfront complex that features a lane pool, hot pools, a beauty spa and a gym. Exhausting...

👉 Tours

If you haven't got time for a guided or self-guided art-deco walking tour, just take to the streets – particularly Tennyson and Emerson. Remember to look up!

Deco Centre
CULTURAL

(☏06-835 0022; www.artdeconapier.com; 7 Tennyson St; ☺9am-5pm; 🚲) Start your explorations at the Deco Centre, which runs daily one-hour guided deco walks ($19) departing the Napier i-SITE (p357) at 10am; and daily two-hour tours ($21) leaving the Deco Centre at 2pm. There's also a little shop here, plus brochures for the self-guided *Art Deco*

Walk ($10), *Art Deco Scenic Drive* ($3) and *Marewa Meander* ($3).

Other options include a minibus tour ($5, 1¼ hours), vintage car tour ($110, 1¼ hours) and the kids' Art Deco Explorer treasure hunt ($5).

Hawke's Bay Scenic Tours TOURS
(☑06-844 5693, 027 497 9231; www.hbscenic tours.co.nz; tours from $55) A grape-coloured bunch of tour options including the 2½-hour 'Napier Whirlwind' ($55), full-day Hawke's Bay scenic tour ($140), and a 4½-hour wine and brewery jaunt ($100).

Absolute de Tours BUS
(☑06-844 8699; www.absolutedetours.co.nz; tours 90min/half-day from $50/70) Runs quick-fire bus tours of the city, Marewa and Bluff Hill in conjunction with the Deco Centre (p353), as well as half-day tours of Napier and Hastings.

Grape Escape WINE
(☑021 227 7211, 0800 100 489; www.grapeescape. net.nz; tours from $90) Respected half-day winery tours, visiting four or five cellar doors; or

take a six-hour tour with a lunch stop ($95). The outfit also runs extremely fancy six-hour luxury wine tours for couples, if you're feeling honeymoony ($895 per couple).

✵ Festivals & Events

Art Deco Weekend CULTURAL
(www.artdeconapier.com; ⊙Feb) In the third week of February, Napier and Hastings co-host the sensational Art Deco Weekend. Around 125 events fill the week (dinners, picnics, dances, balls, bands, Gatsby-esque fancy dress), many of which are free. Expect around 40,000 art-deco fans!

🛏 Sleeping

Napier YHA HOSTEL $
(☑06-835 7039; www.yha.co.nz; 277 Marine Pde; dm/s/d from $30/45/69; ⟩) Napier's friendly YHA is housed in a lovely old timber beach-front villa with a seemingly endless ramble of rooms. There's a fabulous reading nook and a sunny rear courtyard. Staff can help with bookings and local info. It's the best of several hostels along Marine Pde. Bike hire $20 per day.

CYCLE THE BAY

The 200km network of Hawke's Bay Trails (www.nzcycletrail.com/hawkes-bay-trails) – part of the national Nga Haerenga, New Zealand Cycle Trails project – offers cycling opportunities from short, city scoots to hilly, single-track shenanigans. Dedicated cycle tracks encircle Napier, Hastings and the coastline, with landscape, water and wine themes. Pick up the *Hawke's Bay Trails* brochure from the **Napier i-SITE** (p357) or online.

Napier itself is very cycle-friendly, particularly along Marine Pde, where you'll find **Fishbike** (☑0800 131 600, 06-833 6979; www.fishbike.nz; 22 Marine Pde, Pacific Surf Club; bike hire per half/full day $30/40, tandems per hr $35; ⊙9am-5pm) renting comfortable bikes – including tandems for those willing to risk divorce. **Napier City Bike Hire** (☑021 959 595, 0800 245 344; www.bikehirenapier.co.nz; 117 Marine Pde; half-day kids/city/mountain-bike hire from $20/25/30, full day from $25/35/40; ⊙9am-5pm) is another option.

Mountain bikers head to **Pan Pac Eskdale MTB Park** (☑06-873 8793; www.hawkes baymtb.co.nz; off SH5; 3-week permits $10) for a whole lot of fun in the forest: see the website or call for directions. You can hire mountain bikes from **Pedal Power** (☑06-844 9771; www.avantiplus.co.nz/pedalpower; 340 Gloucester St, Taradale; half-/full day from $30/50; ⊙8am-5.30pm Mon-Fri, 9am-3pm Sat, 10am-3pm Sun), just out of the city centre, or from Napier City Bike Hire.

Given the conducive climate, terrain and multitudinous tracks, it's no surprise that numerous cycle companies pedal fully geared-up tours around the bay, with winery visits near-mandatory. Operators include the following:

Bike About Tours (☑06-845 4836, 027 232 4355; www.bikeabouttours.co.nz; tours half/full day from $25/30)

Coastal Wine Cycles (☑06-875 0302; www.winecycles.co.nz; 41 East Rd, Te Awanga; tours per day $40; ⊞)

On Yer Bike Winery Tours (☑06-650 4627; www.onyerbikehb.co.nz; full-day tours $55)

Tākaro Trails (☑06-835 9030; www.takarotrails.co.nz; day rides from $40)

Criterion Art Deco Backpackers HOSTEL $
(06-835 2059; www.criterionartdeco.co.nz; 48 Emerson St; dm/s/d/f without bathroom from $29/53/66/112, d with bathroom from $85;) The owners have spent a lot of money sprucing up this 1st-floor, ruby-red city-centre hostel – Napier's best Spanish Mission specimen – which has a beaut little balcony over Emerson St and an amazing old fireplace in the lounge area. A super-charming hostel in a top spot.

Kennedy Park Resort HOLIDAY PARK $
(0800 457 275, 06-843 9126; www.kennedypark.co.nz; 1 Storkey St; sites from $53, cabins & units $65-173;) Less a campground and more an entire suburb of holidaymakers, this complex is top dog on the Napier camping scene. It's the closest campsite to town (2.5km out, southwest of the centre) and has every facility imaginable, plus a swathe of cabin and unit configurations. And a karaoke machine!

Seaview Lodge B&B B&B $$
(027 235 0202, 06-835 0202; www.aseaviewlodge.co.nz; 5 Seaview Tce; r $150-190;) This grand Victorian villa (1890) is queen of all she surveys – which is most of the town and a fair bit of ocean. The elegant rooms have tasteful period elements and feature either a separate or en suite bathroom. It's hard to resist a sunset tipple on the verandah, which opens off the relaxing guest lounge.

★**Kiwiesque** B&B $$$
(06-836 7216; www.kiwiesque.com; 347 SH 5, Eskdale; d $295-345;) Located in rural Eskdale, around 18km north of Napier, Kiwiesque offers accommodation right beside expansive vineyards. For independent travellers, the best options are the four suites in the property's modern woolshed-influenced building. Breakfast packed with seasonal produce is included, bathrooms are elegant, and outdoor decks offer vineyard views. Eco-aware design includes double glazing and sheep-wool insulation in the walls.

Pebble Beach Motor Inn MOTEL $$$
(0800 723 224, 06-835 7496; www.pebblebeach.co.nz; 445 Marine Pde; r $219-315;) Unlike the majority of NZ motels, this one is truly owner-operated – the motel operators actually own the building – so maintenance and service top the list of staff priorities. There are 25 immaculate rooms over three levels, all with kitchens, spas, balconies and ocean views. Full to capacity most nights. Ask the friendly owners about the 'hole in one' golf story.

Scenic Hotel Te Pania HOTEL $$$
(06-833 7733; www.scenichotels.co.nz; 45 Marine Pde; d from $190, 1-/2-bedroom ste from $260/342;) Looking like a mini UN HQ by the sea, the refurbished, curvalicious, six-storey Te Pania has instant retro appeal. Rooms are far from retro, however, with designer linen, leather lounges and floor-to-ceiling windows that slide open for lungfuls of sea air.

Crown Hotel HOTEL $$$
(06-833 8300; www.thecrownnapier.co.nz; 1-/2-bedroom apt from $239/369;) The conversion of this 1932 Ahuriri pub into a ritzy apartment-style hotel must have broken a few fishers' hearts. The new wing features muted tones, nice wallpaper and linen, and super sea views. There's a cafe downstairs for your morning coffee shot and lots of other restaurants within walking distance.

Masonic Hotel HOTEL $$$
(06-835 8689; www.masonic.co.nz; cnr Tennyson St & Marine Pde; r $239-649;) The art-deco Masonic is the heart of the old town, with its accommodation, restaurants and bars taking up most of a city block. A much-needed refurb has revived the old stager, with stripy carpets and quirky wallpaper adorning the original bones. All 42 rooms and suites have bathrooms; the best have sea views and access to the roof terrace.

✕ Eating

Hapī VEGAN $
(06-561 0142; www.hapi.nz; 89 Hastings St; mains $12-14; 7am-4pm;) Welcome to Hapī, where virtuous and vital vegan flavours are also damn tasty. Breakfast bowls packed with *acai, chia* and quinoa team up with superior snacks like polenta fries or chipotle tofu tacos, and the drinks list of cold-pressed organic elixirs and plant-based smoothies is equally beneficial and bargain-priced.

Cafe Ujazi CAFE $
(06-835 1490; www.facebook.com/ujazicafe; 28 Tennyson St; mains $10-22; 8am-5pm;) The most bohemian of Napier's cafes, Ujazi folds back its windows and lets the alternative vibes spill out onto the pavement. It's a long-established, consistent performer offering blackboard meals and hearty counter food (vegetarian and vegan a speciality). Try the classic *rewana* special – a big breakfast on traditional Māori bread. Oooh – homemade limeade!

★ Mister D
MODERN NZ $$

(☑06-835 5022; www.misterd.co.nz; 47 Tennyson St; mains $25-36; ⊙7.30am-4pm Sun-Wed, to late Thu-Sat) This long, floorboarded room with its green-tiled bar is the pride of the Napier foodie scene. Hip and slick but not un-affordable, with quick-fire service delivering the likes of pulled pork with white polenta or roast-duck risotto. Addictive doughnuts are served with syringes full of chocolate, jam or custard (DIY injecting). Bookings essential.

Milk & Honey
CAFE $$

(☑06-833 6099; www.themilkandhoney.co.nz; 19 Hardinge Rd, Ahuriri; mains & shared plates $15-34; ⊙7am-9pm) One of the best options in the good eating and drinking hub around sea-side Ahuriri village, Milk & Honey combines ocean and boardwalk views with a versatile all-day menu. Hawke's Bay beers and wines feature along with delicate seafood ceviche or a Japanese-influenced chicken salad. After dark the emphasis turns to shared plates like crispy prawns and fish sliders.

Throughout afternoons and evenings from November to March, pizza and Asian dumplings are available next door from Milk & Honey's Pizza/Pazzi and The Hatch.

Greek National Cafe
GREEK $$

(☑06-833 6069; www.greeknationalcafe.nz; 112 Emerson St; mains $20-29; ⊙5-9pm Tue-Thu, 4-10pm Fri, 5-10pm Sat; ☑) Operated as a Kiwi diner serving steak and seafood for many decades, the National Cafe was reopened in 2017 by descendants of the original Greek owners. A few dishes from its heritage hey-day linger, but now the emphasis is firmly on authentic flavours. Settle into the retro 1960s decor and partner meze and char-grilled octopus with ouzo, wine and retsina.

Be sure to order the *kessaria* pies with gooey cheese and pine nuts.

★ Bistronomy
MODERN NZ $$$

(☑06-834 4309; www.bistronomy.co.nz; 40 Hastings St; mains lunch $22-28, dinner six/nine courses $75/100; ⊙noon-late Fri-Sun, from 5pm Wed & Thu; ☑) ✦ Bistronomy is proof that some of NZ's best food can be enjoyed outside the country's biggest cities. The finely judged seasonal tasting menus, which could include sumac-cured kingfish or chicken poached in kawakawa (a NZ forest herb), are highly recommended; they're great-value experiences you'll definitely talk about when you get back home. Lunch is slightly less formal, but equally excellent.

Pacifica
MODERN NZ $$$

(☑06-833-6335; www.pacificarestaurant.co.nz; 209 Marine Pde; five courses without/with wine pairings $65/115; ⊙6-10pm Tue-Sat) ✦ Judged NZ'S top restaurant in 2017 by *Cuisine* mag-azine, Pacifica is a showcase for chef Jeremy Rameka's affinity with *kai moana* (seafood). The decor is surprisingly relaxed, and the good-value $65 five-course menu could in-clude a mousse of mussels and scallops, or lemonfish marinated in coconut cream. A second menu including other proteins is available, as are recommended wine pairings.

🍸 Drinking & Nightlife

Monica Loves
BAR

(☑06-650 0240; www.monicaloves.co.nz; 39 Tennyson St; ⊙3-11pm Wed-Thu, to midnight Fri & Sat) Big-city laneway style comes to Napier at this bar tucked away off Tennyson St. Look for the big neon sign proclaiming 'Who shot the barman?' and you're in the right place for top cocktails, a beer list with regular sur-prises on the taps, and a knowingly Hawke's Bay-centric wine list.

4th Door Lounge Bar
COCKTAIL BAR

(☑06-834 0835; www.threedoorsup.co.nz/the-4th -door; 3 Waghorne St, Ahuriri; ⊙5pm-late Wed-Sat) The 4th Door offers an alternative to Ahuri-ri's waterfront bars. It's a classy, moody lit-tle nook, perfect for a pre-dinner drink, or a nightcap. Occasional live jazz and piano tunes on weekends.

Emporium
BAR

(☑06-835 0013; www.emporiumbar.co.nz; Mason-ic Hotel, cnr Tennyson St & Marine Pde; ⊙7am-late; ☎) Napier's most civilised bar, Emporium is super atmospheric, with its marble-topped bar, fab art-deco details and old-fashioned relics strewn about. Brisk staff, creative cocktails, good coffee, NZ wines, bistro fare (plates $17 to $36) and a prime location seal the deal.

Thirsty Whale
BAR

(☑06-835 8815; www.thethirstywhale.co.nz; 62 West Quay, Ahuriri; ⊙11am-late Mon-Fri, from 9am Sat & Sun; ☎) Does a whale drink? Or just fil-ter krill? Either way, this big dockside bar is a sporty spot to join some fellow mammals for a brew or a bite (mains $12 to $39). Be-neath 'Hawke's Bay's biggest screen' is the place to watch the All Blacks.

DON'T MISS

HAWKE'S BAY WINERIES

Once upon a time, this district was most famous for its orchards. Today it's vines that have top billing, with Hawke's Bay now New Zealand's second-largest wine-producing region (behind Marlborough). Expect excellent Bordeaux-style reds, shiraz and chardonnay. Pick up the *Hawke's Bay Winery Guide* map or the *Hawke's Bay Trails* cycling map from Hastings (p361) or **Napier** i-SITEs, or download them from www.winehawkes bay.co.nz. A few of our faves:

Black Barn Vineyards (☑06-877 7985; www.blackbarn.com; Black Barn Rd, Havelock North; ☺cellar door 10am-4pm, restaurant 10am-5pm Sun-Wed & to 9pm Thu-Sat (reduced hours Apr-Oct))

Mission Estate Winery (☑06-845 9354; www.missionestate.co.nz; 198 Church Rd, Taradale; ☺9am-5pm Mon-Sat, 10am-4.30pm Sun)

Crab Farm Winery (☑06-836 6678; www.crabfarmwinery.co.nz; 511 Main North Rd, Bay View; ☺10am-5pm daily, plus 6pm-late Fri)

Te Mata Estate (☑06-877 4399; www.temata.co.nz; 349 Te Mata Rd, Havelock North; ☺9am-5pm Mon-Fri, from 10am Sat) ✎

Craggy Range (☑06-873 0141; www.craggyrange.com; 253 Waimarama Rd, Havelock North; ☺10am-6pm, closed Mon & Tue Apr-Oct)

☆ Entertainment

Globe Theatrette CINEMA
(☑06-833 6011; www.globenapier.co.nz; 15 Hardinge Rd, Ahuriri; tickets adult/child $16/14; ☺1pm-late Tue-Sun) A vision in purple, this boutique 45-seat cinema screens art-house flicks in a sumptuous lounge with ready access to up-market snacks and drinks.

Cabana Bar LIVE MUSIC
(☑06-835 1102; www.cabana.net.nz; 11 Shakespeare Rd; ☺6pm-late Wed-Sat) This legendary music venue of the '70s, '80s and '90s died in 1997, but thanks to some forward-thinking rock fans, it's risen from the grave to save the day for Napier's gig lovers. Expect Led Zep tribute acts, NZ original bands and karaoke nights.

ℹ Information

City Medical Napier (☑06-878 8109; www.hawkesbay.health.nz; 76 Wellesley Rd; ☺24hr) Round-the-clock medical assistance.

DOC (Department of Conservation; ☑06-834 3111; www.doc.govt.nz; 59 Marine Pde; ☺9am-4.15pm Mon-Fri) Maps, advice and passes.

Napier i-SITE (☑06-834 1911; www.napiernz.com; 100 Marine Pde; ☺9am-5pm, extended hours Dec-Feb; 🖥) Central, helpful and right by the bay.

Napier Post Office (www.nzpost.co.nz; 1 Dickens St; ☺9am-5pm Mon-Fri, 9.30am-12.30pm Sat)

ℹ Getting There & Away

AIR

Hawke's Bay Airport (www.hawkesbay-airport.co.nz; SH2) is 8km north of the city.

Air New Zealand (☑0800 737 000; www.airnewzealand.co.nz) flies direct to/from Auckland, Wellington and Christchurch. Jetstar links Napier with Auckland, and Sounds Air has direct flights to Blenheim three times a week.

BUS

InterCity (www.intercity.co.nz) buses can be booked online or at the **i-SITE**. Naked Bus (https://nakedbus.com) tickets are best booked online. Some Naked Bus services are operated by ManaBus.

Both companies depart from **Clive Sq bus stop**, with daily services (several daily for Hastings) to the following:

DESTINATION	COMPANY	PRICE	DURATION
Auckland	InterCity	$50	7½hr
Auckland	Naked Bus	$26	9hr
Gisborne	InterCity	$43	4hr
Hastings	InterCity	$15	30min
Palmerston North	InterCity	$18	3hr
Taupo	InterCity	$18	2hr
Taupo	Naked Bus	$15	2hr
Wairoa	InterCity	$14	2¼hr
Wellington	InterCity	$33	5½hr
Wellington	Naked Bus	$23	5hr

ⓘ Getting Around

BICYCLE

Bikes (including tandems and children's) can be hired from Fishbike (p354) or Napier City Bike Hire (p354).

BUS

GoBay (www.hbrc.govt.nz) local buses (fitted with bike racks) run many times daily between Napier, Hastings and Havelock North. Napier to Hastings (adult/child $4.20/2) takes 30 minutes (express) or 55 minutes (all stops). Buses depart **Dalton St bus stop**.

CAR

See www.rentalcars.com for car-hire deals with companies at Hawke's Bay Airport, including the big brands and local outfits. **RAD Car Hire** (☑ 06-834 0688, 0800 736 823; www.radcar hire.co.nz; Hawke's Bay Airport, SH2; ☺7am-5pm Mon-Fri, to 1pm Sat, 9am-noon Sun) is also at the airport.

TAXI

A city–airport taxi or pre-booked airport shuttle costs around $20 to $25. Try **Blue Bubble Taxis** (☑06-835 7777, 0800 228 294; www. hawkes-bay.bluebubbletaxi.co.nz) or the door-to-door **Super Shuttle** (☑0800 748 885; www.supershuttle.co.nz; one-way $20, extra person $5).

Hastings & Around

☑06 / POP 77,900

Positioned at the centre of the Hawke's Bay fruit bowl, busy Hastings is the commercial hub of the region, 20km south of Napier. A few kilometres of orchards still separate it from Havelock North, with its prosperous village atmosphere and the towering backdrop of Te Mata Peak.

Imbibing and dining around the area's restaurants, breweries and vineyards, and trawling good farmers markets and seasonal fruit stands are fine foodie-focused reasons to explore, and balance can be provided by biking or tramping around Te Mata's spectacular natural profile.

◉ Sights

Like Napier, Hastings was devastated by the 1931 earthquake and also boasts some fine art-deco and Spanish Mission buildings, built in the aftermath. Main-street highlights include the Westerman's Building (cnr Russell St & Heretaunga St E), arguably the bay's best example of the Spanish Mission style, although there are myriad architectur-

al gems here. The i-SITE (p361) stocks the *Art Deco Hastings* brochure ($1), detailing two self-guided walks.

★ **Te Mata Peak**   PARK
(☑06-873 0080; www.tematapark.co.nz; off Te Mata Rd, Havelock North; ☺5am-10pm) Rising dramatically from the Heretaunga Plains 16km south of Havelock North, Te Mata Peak (399m) is part of the 1-sq-km **Te Mata Trust Park**. The summit road passes sheep tracks, rickety fences and vertigo-inducing stone escarpments, cowled in a bleak, lunar-meets-Scottish-Highlands atmosphere. On a clear day, views from the lookout fall away to Hawke Bay, the Mahia Peninsula and distant Mt Ruapehu.

The park's 30km of tracks offer walks ranging from 30 minutes to two hours: pick up the *Te Mata Park's Top 5 Walking Tracks* brochure from local i-SITEs. Mountain biking is also popular.

Hastings Farmers Market   MARKET
(☑027 697 3737; www.hawkesbayfarmersmarket. co.nz; Showgrounds, Kenilworth Rd; ☺8.30am-12.30pm Sun) If you're around on Sunday, the Hastings market is mandatory. Bring an empty stomach, some cash and a roomy shopping bag.

Hastings City Art Gallery   GALLERY
(HCAG; ☑06-871 5095; www.hastingscityartgallery. co.nz; 201 Eastbourne St E; ☺10am-4.30pm) FREE The city's neat little gallery presents contemporary NZ (including Māori) and international art in a bright, purpose-built space. Expect some wacky stuff (much wackier than Hastings itself...).

🏃 Activities

Hawke's Bay Farmyard Zoo   HORSE RIDING
(☑06-875 0244; www.farmyardzoo.co.nz; 32 East Rd, Haumoana; farm admission adult/child/family $10/7/35, horse rides 1/2hr $70/100; ☺10am-5pm; ●) Little kids might enjoy patting the farm animals and having a pony ride ($5) at this farmy place 13km west of central Hastings, while older folks can saddle up for a slow-paced horseback jaunt through the coastal countryside.

Airplay Paragliding   PARAGLIDING
(☑06-845 1977; www.airplay.co.nz; 1-day courses $220) Te Mata Peak is a paragliding hot spot, with updraughts aplenty. Airplay offers full-day beginners' courses if you're keen to take the drop.

Hastings

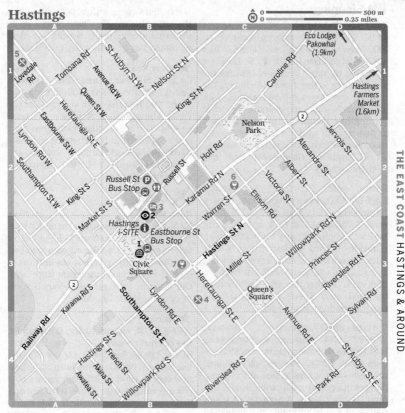

👉 Tours

Long Island Guides   GUIDED TOUR, CULTURAL
(📞06-874 7877; www.longislandtoursnz.com; half-day tours per person from $248) Customised Hawke's Bay tours across a wide range of interests including Māori culture, tramping, kayaking, horse riding, fishing and, inevitably, food and wine.

Prinsy's Tours   WINE
(📞06-845 3703, 0800 004 237; www.prinsystours.co.nz; half-/full-day tours from $90/110) Affable half- or full-day wine jaunts, with laypeople's explanations, at four or five wineries. Door-to-door delivery a bonus.

🎊 Festivals & Events

Hastings Blossom Parade   CULTURAL
(www.facebook.com/HastingsBlossomParade; ⊙Sep) The Hastings Blossom Parade is a petalled spring fling, infamous for its 12-person 'riot' in 1960 when a few local teen-

agers got a bit hot under the collar and were arrested for a few hours. The annual flowery celebration happens in the second half of September, featuring parades, arts, crafts and visiting artists.

🛏 Sleeping

Eco Lodge Pakowhai
HOSTEL $

(☑027 298 8910; www.ecolodge-pakowhai.co.nz; 1000 Pakowhai Rd, Hastings; dm/s from $27/70, d with/without bathroom $80/70; 🛜) 🍴 The same family has tilled this land since 1885, but the attitude here is very forward-thinking. The talkative owner cuts carbon emissions with solar panels, rainwater-collection systems, worm farms, double-glazing...and is expert at finding farm work for travellers. Accommodation comprises neat cabins or dorms in an old farmhouse. Good weekly rates; free wi-fi and laundry.

Rotten Apple
HOSTEL $

(☑06-878 4363; www.rottenapple.co.nz; Upstairs, 114 Heretaunga St E, Hastings; dm/tw/d $26/70/70, weekly $125/140/140; @🛜) This central-city, 1st-floor option is a fairly fruity affair, with settled-in orchard workers paying weekly rates. There's a bit of deck, a decent kitchen and sociable vibes, and staff can help you find work (sorting the rotten apples from the good ones). There's a dedicated 'quiet room' if you don't want to par-tay.

Cottages on St Andrews
COTTAGES $$

(☑06-877 1644; www.cottagesonstandrews.nz; 14 St Andrews Rd, Havelock North; units $160, cottages $320; 🛜❄🐾) Modern self-contained two-bedroom cottages feature at this versatile spot in a quiet rural location around 1km from Havelock North. A heated pool, tennis court and a kids' adventure playground all maximise the appeal to travelling families, and there are also lambs, llamas and other farmyard critters to say g'day. A cheaper studio unit is also available.

Clive Colonial Cottages
COTTAGE $$

(☑06-870 1018; www.clivecolonialcottages.co.nz; 198 School Rd, Clive; d from $175; 🛜) A two-minute walk to the beach and almost equidistant from Hastings, Napier and Havelock, these three tasteful kitchen cottages encircle a courtyard garden on a 2-acre spread. Communal areas include a barbecue, a giant chess set and a snooker room. Bikes on-site; track at your doorstep.

★ St Andrews Escape
B&B $$$

(☑06-877 1525; www.standrewsescape.co.nz; 172 St Andrews Rd, Havelock North; d $210-250, cottages $250; 🛜) Four lodge rooms with unique decor combine with a stand-alone cottage at this property near orchards and a compact lake around 3km from Havelock North. Our favourite accommodation in the main house is the 'Retro' room with a 1960s vibe, while the self-contained Te Whare (sleeps up to three) has Kiwiana design accents. Two-night minimum stay from Thursday to Saturday.

★ Millar Road
VILLA $$$

(☑06-875 1977; www.millarroad.co.nz; 83 Millar Rd, Hastings; villas/houses from $500/800; 🛜❄) Set in the Tuki Tuki Hills with vineyard and bay views, Millar Road is architecturally heaven-sent. Two plush villas (each sleep four) and a super-stylish house (sleeps eight) are filled with NZ-made furniture and local artworks. Explore the 20-hectare grounds or look cool by the pool.

🍴 Eating

Rush Munro's
ICE CREAM $

(☑06-878 9634; www.rushmunro.co.nz; 704 Heretaunga St W, Hastings; ice cream $4-7; ⊙noon-5pm Mon-Fri, from 11am Sat & Sun, extended hours Dec-Feb) Rush Munro's is a Hastings institution, serving locally made ice cream since 1926. Our favourite is the manuka honey, best enjoyed in the shaded garden.

★ Maina
CAFE $$

(☑06-877 1714; www.maina.co.nz; 11 Havelock Rd, Havelock North; mains $12-24; ⊙7am-11pm Mon-Fri, from 8am Sat, 9am-3pm Sun; 🍴) 🍴 Blur the line between breakfast and lunch at the best new cafe in Hawke's Bay. This former post office is infused with stylish retro Kiwiana decor, and highlights include Te Mata mushrooms on organic sourdough or creamy pulled pork croquettes. Pizza and an ever-evolving selection of salads are also good, and superior homestyle baking includes perfect mid-morning coffee and doughnuts.

★ Opera Kitchen
CAFE $$

(☑06-870 6020; www.eatdrinksharehb.co.nz; 306 Eastbourne St E, Hastings; mains $13-30; ⊙7.30am-4pm Mon-Fri, 9am-3pm Sat & Sun; 🍴) Located in a high-ceilinged heritage building – formerly the HB Electric Power Board – our favourite Hastings cafe serves up sophisticated breakfast and lunch dishes with international accents. Spend a few hours browsing the design magazines and feasting on smoked fishcakes with a toasted nori sauce or Korean fried chicken with miso caramel. Heavenly pastries, great coffee and efficient staff.

Bareknuckle BBQ
BARBECUE $$

(☑021 773 303; www.bareknucklebbq.co.nz; 1091 Riverslea Rd South, Longlands; snacks & mains $13-28; ⊙11am-10pm Fri, to 5pm Sat) This authentic American barbecue place around 4km southwest of Hastings is hugely popular with locals. Pitmaster Jimmy Macken knows his stuff – Bareknuckle's barbecue was hand-built near the Texas-Mexico border – and he turns out fine brisket, ribs and pulled pork. Other dishes enjoyed in the raffish and ram-shackle garden include tacos, and local craft beers are always on tap.

Alessandro's PIZZA $$

(☑ 06-877 8844; www.alessandrospizzeria.co.nz; 24 Havelock Rd, Havelock North; mains $20-27; ⊙4.30-9pm Tue-Sun) Excellent Alessandro's does handmade wood-fired pizzas, thin and flavoursome, just like back in Napoli. Order the *noci e pere* (pear, Gorgonzola, mozzarel-la, walnuts and truffle honey) with a mean *affogato* for dessert. Snappy interior design; Peroni beer on tap.

★ Elephant Hill MODERN NZ $$$

(☑ 06-872 6060; www.elephanthill.co.nz; 86 Clift-on Rd, Te Awanga; mains $36-42; ⊙cellar door 11am-5pm Nov-Mar, to 4pm Apr-Oct, restaurant noon-3pm & 6-9pm daily Nov-Mar, Thu-Sat Apr-Oct) 🍴 There's plenty of great vineyard dining around Hawke's Bay, but Elephant Hill in the beachy surroundings of Te Awanga is something special. Huge picture windows provide unencumbered views of Cape Kid-nappers and vineyards, and Elephant Hill's award-winning wines partner supremely with seasonal dishes like Thai-style grilled gamefish with squid, or beef tartare with mustard ice-cream and truffle mayonnaise. Exquisite.

Malo MODERN NZ $$$

(☑ 06-877 2009; www.malo.co.nz; 4 Te Aute Rd, Havelock North; mains $36-38; ⊙7-11am & 4pm-late) 🍴 Hotel restaurants can be hit-and-miss, but Malo at the Porters Boutique Hotel in Havelock North hits the right notes. Har-nessing truckloads of regional and season-al Hawke's Bay produce, the open kitchen turns out dishes with local lamb and ven-ison, fresh oysters, tuna and kingfish from the raw bar, and beer snacks like Vietnam-ese rolls, sashimi and dumplings nightly from 4pm.

🍸 Drinking & Nightlife

★ GodsOwn Brewery CRAFT BEER

(☑ 027 931 1042; www.godsownbrewery.co.nz; 3672 SH 50, Maraekakaho; ⊙3-10pm Thu & Fri, from noon Sat & Sun) 🍴 This super micro-brewery 22km east of Hastings is run from a safari tent, a caravan and a few outdoor tables. On a compact brewing set-up, tra-ditional European beer styles like *biere de gardes* and *saisons* are crafted; the shel-tered valley includes its own hop vines. Spent grain from the brewing process is used for tasty wood-fired flatbreads ($10 to $20).

Common Room BAR

(☑ 027 656 8959; www.commonroombar.com; 227 Heretaunga St E, Hastings; ⊙3pm-late Wed-Sat) There's pretty much nothing wrong with this hip little bar in central Hastings: cheery staff, bar snacks, craft beer, local wines, a creative retro interior, a garden bar, Persian rugs, live music and a tune-scape ranging from jazz to alt-country to indie. All the right stuff! Open Sundays as well from De-cember to March.

Brave Brewing Co CRAFT BEER

(☑ 027 460 8414; www.facebook.com/bravebeer; 408 Warren St; ⊙4-9pm Thu, from noon Fri-Sun) Brave's cool and compact tasting room on the edge of central Hastings showcases its own brews – ask if the Tigermilk IPA is avail-able – and regular guest beers from brewing mates around the country. Curious beer fans should order a four-beer tasting paddle, and partner the different brews with delicious gourmet burgers ($15) from the on-site Carr's Kitchen.

🛍 Shopping

Strawberry Patch FOOD

(☑ 06-877 1350; www.strawberrypatch.co.nz; 76 Havelock Rd, Havelock North; ⊙9am-5.30pm) Pick your own berries in season (late No-vember to April), or visit year-round for fresh produce, picnic supplies, coffee and real fruit ice cream ($4).

ℹ Information

Hastings i-SITE (☑ 06-873 0080; www.hawkesbaynz.com; Westermans Bldg, cnr Rus-sell St & Heretaunga St E; ⊙9am-5pm Mon-Fri, to 3pm Sat, 10am-2pm Sun) The usual array of maps, brochures and bookings.

Hastings Memorial Hospital (☑ 06-878 8109; www.hawkesbay.health.nz; Omahu Rd, Camber-ley; ⊙24hr)

Havelock North i-SITE (☑ 06-877 9600; www.havelocknorthnz.com; 1 Te Aute Rd; ⊙10am-5pm Mon-Fri, to 3pm Sat, to 2pm Sun; 🐾) Local info in a cute little booth.

KARIN WASSMER/SHUTTERSTOCK ©

1 & 3. Pacific Coast Highway (p333)

This 327km route has long been a rite of passage for New Zealanders. Sights en route include Christ Church (p336) in Raukokore, a sweet beacon of relief on a lonely promontory, and the historic Tauranga Bridge (p333).

2. Lake Waikaremoana Track (p347)

This 46km, three- to four-day Great Walk is a year-round track that scales the spectacular Panekire Bluff.

4. Napier (p350)

Destroyed by a devastating earthquake in 1931, Napier was rebuilt in the popular architectural styles of the time and retains a unique concentration of art deco buildings.

SLYELLOW/SHUTTERSTOCK ©

ⓘ Getting There & Away

Napier's Hawke's Bay Airport (p357) is a 20-minute drive from Hastings. **Air New Zealand** (☑ 06-873 2200; www.airnewzealand.co.nz; 117 Heretaunga St W, Hastings; ☺ 9am-5pm Mon-Fri) flies from Napier to Auckland, Wellington and Christchurch.

InterCity buses stop at the **Russell St bus stop**. Book InterCity (www.intercity.co.nz) and Naked Bus (https://nakedbus.com) buses online or at the i-SITE.

ⓘ Getting Around

GoBay (www.hbrc.govt.nz) local buses (with bike racks) run between Hastings, Havelock North and Napier. Daily Hastings to Napier buses (adult/child $4.20/2) take 30 minutes (express) or 55 minutes (all stops). Hastings to Havelock North buses run Monday to Saturday (adult/child $2.90/1.50, 35 minutes). Buses depart from the **Eastbourne St bus stop**.

Hastings Taxis (☑ 0800 875 055, 06-878 5055; www.hastingstaxis.co.nz) is the local cab outfit.

Cape Kidnappers

From mid-September to late April, Cape Kidnappers (named when local Māori tried to kidnap Captain Cook's Tahitian servant boy) erupts with squawking gannets. These big ocean birds usually nest on remote islands but here they settle for the mainland, completely unfazed by human spectators.

The birds nest as soon as they arrive, and eggs take about six weeks to hatch, with chicks arriving in early November. In March the gannets start their migration; by May they're gone.

Early November to late February is the best time to visit. Take a tour or the walkway to the **colony** (☑ 06-834 3111; www.doc. govt.nz; off Clifton Rd, Clifton; ☺ Nov-Jun) FREE: it's about five hours return from Clifton. En route are interesting cliff formations, rock pools, a sheltered picnic spot and the gaggling gannets themselves. The walk is tide-dependent: leave no earlier than three hours after high tide; start back no later than 1½ hours after low tide.

ⓕ Tours

Gannet Beach Adventures   ECOTOUR
(☑ 06-875 0898, 0800 426 638; www.gannets. com; 475 Clifton Rd, Clifton; adult/child/family $44/24/106; ⓐ) Ride along the beach on a tractor-pulled trailer before wandering out on the cape for 90 minutes. This four-hour, guided return trip departs from the Clifton waterfront, and is both good fun and great value.

Gannet Safaris   ECOTOUR
(☑ 06-875 0888; www.gannetsafaris.co.nz; 396 Clifton Rd, Te Awanga; adult/child $80/40; ⓐ) Overland 4WD trips across farmland into the gannet colony. Three-hour tours depart at 9.30am and 1.30pm. Pick-ups from Napier and Hastings cost extra (adult/child additional $32/16).

ⓘ Getting There & Away

No regular buses go to Clifton, but it's just a short drive from Hastings (20km). Alternatively tour operators will transport you for an additional fee, or you could bike it.

Central Hawke's Bay

Grassy farmland stretches south from Hastings, dotted with the grand homesteads of Victorian pastoralists. It's a untouristy area (aka 'Lamb Country'), rich in history and deserted beaches. The main regional town is **Waipukurau** (aka 'Wai-puk'; population 3750) – not exactly thrilling but a functional hub for petrol, motels, a supermarket and the Central Hawke's Bay Information Centre (p365) with adjunct coffee booth.

Look for the handy *Limestone Route* driving map at the Napier and Hastings i-SITEs before you set off.

⊙ Sights

There are no fewer than six windswept beaches along the coast here: **Kairakau**, **Mangakuri**, **Pourerere**, **Aramoana**, **Blackhead** and **Porangahau**. The first five are good for swimming, and between the lot they offer a range of sandy, salty activities including surfing, fishing and driftwoody, rock-pooly adventures. Between Aramoana and Blackhead Beach lies the DOC-managed **Te Angiangi Marine Reserve** – bring your snorkel.

It's a nondescript hill in the middle of nowhere, but the place with the world's longest name is good for a photo op. Believe it or not, **Taumatawhakatangihangakoauauotamateaturipukakapikimaungahoronukupokaiwhenuakitanatahu** is the abbreviated form of 'The Brow of a Hill where Tamatea, the Man with the Big Knees, Who Slid, Climbed and Swallowed Mountains, Known as Land Eater, Played his Flute to his Brother'. To get there, fuel up in Waipukurau and drive 40km to the Mangaorapa junction on Rte 52. Turn left and go 4km towards Porangahau. At the intersection with the signposts, turn right and continue 4.3km to the sign.

Onga Onga, a historic village 16km west of Waipawa, has interesting Victorian and Edwardian buildings. Pick up a pamphlet for a self-guided walking tour from the info centre in Waipukurau.

Central Hawke's Bay Settlers Museum   MUSEUM

(☑ 06-857 7288; www.chbsettlersmuseum.co.nz; 23 High St, Waipawa; adult/child $5/1; ☉ 10am-4pm) The Central Hawke's Bay Settlers Museum in Waipawa has pioneer artefacts, informative 'homestead' displays and a good specimen of a river *waka* (canoe). Look for the anchor of the ill-fated schooner *Maroro* out the front.

✕ Eating

★ Paper Mulberry Café   CAFE $

(☑ 06-856 8688; www.papermulberrycafe.co.nz; 89 SH2, Pukehou; snacks $4-10, lunch mains $10-17; ☉ 7am-4pm) Halfway between Waipawa and Hastings, this retro cafe-gallery in a 100-year-old, aquamarine-coloured church serves excellent coffee, smoothies and homespun food (unbeatable fudge). Well worth a stop for a chomp, a browse through the local crafts on the side tables and to warm your buns by the wood heater in winter.

De La Mama   BURGERS $

(☑ 021 261 0180; www.facebook.com/DeLaMama Waipawa; 85 High St, Waipawa; burgers $10-15; ☉ noon-8pm Wed-Sun, from 5pm Tue) Look for the wall-covering Latin-themed mural and you've found this surprising place serving up some of the best burgers in the land. The New York and Cuban ones are our favourites, and it's pretty well mandatory to combine a few *churros* (Spanish fried-dough sweets) and a coffee before you continue north or south.

❶ Information

Central Hawke's Bay Information Centre

(☑ 06-858 6488; www.lambcountry.co.nz; Railway Esplanade, Waipukurau; ☉ 9am-4pm Mon-Fri, to 1pm Sat) Helpful visitor centre in the old railway station (with coffee booth on one side).

❶ Getting There & Away

InterCity (www.intercity.co.nz) and Naked Bus (https://nakedbus.com) pass through Waipawa and Waipukurau on their Wellington–Napier routes.

Kaweka & Ruahine Ranges

The remote Kaweka and Ruahine Ranges separate Hawke's Bay from the Central Plateau. These forested wildernesses offer some of the North Island's best tramping. See www.doc.govt.nz for track, hut and campsite info on Ruahine Forest Park and the downloadable pamphlet *Kaweka Forest Park & Puketitiri Reserves*.

⚑ Activities

An ancient 136km Māori track, now known as the **Gentle Annie Road**, runs inland from Omahu near Hastings to Taihape, via Otamauri and Kuripapango (where there's a basic but charming DOC campsite, adult/child $6/3). This isolated route takes around three hours (or a couple of days by bike).

Kaweka J, the highest point of the Kaweka Range (1724m), can be reached by a three- to five-hour tramp from the end of Kaweka Rd; from Napier take Puketitiri Rd then Whittle Rd. The drive is worthwhile in itself; it's partly unsealed and takes three hours return.

Enjoy a soak in **natural hot pools** (☑ 06-834 3111; www.doc.govt.nz; off Makahu Rd; ☉ daylight hours) `FREE` before or after the three-hour walk on **Te Puia Track**, which follows the picturesque **Mohaka River.** From Napier, take Puketitiri Rd, then Pakaututu Rd, then Makahu Rd. Parts of the road can be dicey – bring a 4WD if you've got one.

The Mohaka River can be rafted with **Mohaka Rafting** (☑ 027 825 8539, 06-839 1808; www.mohakarafting.com; day trips $115-210, 3 days per 2 people $3850).

Wellington Region

Best Places to Eat

➡ Noble Rot (p384)

➡ Shepherd (p384)

➡ Logan Brown (p386)

➡ Loretta (p384)

➡ Whitebait (p386)

Best Places to Stay

➡ QT Museum Wellington (p381)

➡ Ohtel (p381)

➡ City Cottages (p380)

➡ Dwellington (p378)

➡ YHA Wellington City (p378)

Why Go?

If your New Zealand travels thus far have been all about the great outdoors and sleepy rural towns, Wellington will make for a lively change of pace. Art-house cinemas, hip bars, live bands and endless cafes all await you in NZ's cultural capital.

Wellington is the crossing point between the North and South Islands, so travellers have long been passing through these parts. The likes of Te Papa and Zealandia now stop visitors in their tracks, while myriad other urban attractions reveal themselves over the course of a longer sojourn.

Less than an hour away to the north, the Kapiti Coast has a slower, beachy vibe, with Kapiti Island nature reserve a highlight. An hour away to the northeast over the Rimutaka Range, the Wairarapa plains are dotted with quaint towns and wineries, hemmed in by a rugged, wild coastline.

When to Go

➡ Wellington has a bad rep for blustery, cold, grey weather, but this isn't the whole story: 'Windy Welly' breaks out into blue skies and T-shirt temperatures at least several days a year, when you'll hear locals exclaim, 'You can't beat Wellington on a good day'.

➡ November to April are the warmer months here, with average maximums hovering around 20°C. From May to August it's colder and wetter – daily temperatures lurk around 12°C.

➡ The Kapiti Coast and Wairarapa are a different story – both warmer and less windy, with more blue-sky days to bask in.

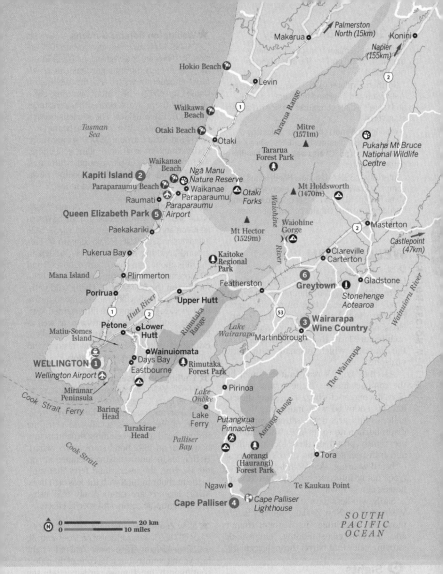

Wellington Region Highlights

1 Wellington (p368) Drowning in a sea of craft beer and top-notch coffee in New Zealand's most artsy, bohemian and political city.

2 Kapiti Island (p393) Hiking through native bush filled with some of the country's rarest bird species and perhaps even chancing upon a real live kiwi on a nocturnal walk.

3 Wairarapa Wine Country (p397) Struggling to maintain a straight line on your bicycle as you tour the wineries around Martinborough.

4 Cape Palliser (p399) Scaling the lighthouse steps on this wild and remote headland.

5 Queen Elizabeth Park (p393) Rambling through the dunes near beachy Paekakariki.

6 Greytown (p398) Soaking up the genteel, heritage ambience of the Wairarapa's prettiest town.

ⓘ Getting There & Away

Wellington is a major transport hub, being the North Island port for the interisland ferries (p391).

Northern Explorer (p391) trains run between Wellington and Auckland three times a week, and there's a daily commuter service to Palmerston North.

Wellington Airport (p390) is serviced by international and domestic airlines, while Kapiti Coast Airport (p392) also welcomes a handful of domestic routes.

InterCity (p391) is the main North Island bus company, travelling just about everywhere. Mana Bus (p391) also has services to Auckland, including an overnight sleeper with bunk beds.

WELLINGTON

📞 04 / POP 208,000

On a sunny, windless day, Wellington is up there with the best of them. For starters it's lovely to look at, sitting on a hook-shaped harbour ringed with ranges that wear a cloak of snow in winter. Victorian timber architecture laces the bushy hillsides above the harbour, which resonate with native birdsong.

As cities go, it's really rather small but the compact nature of the downtown area gives it a bigger-city buzz and, being the capital, it's endowed with museums, theatres, galleries and arts organisations completely disproportionate to its size. Wellingtonians are rightly proud of their kickin' caffeine and craft-beer scene, and there's no shortage of beard-wearing, skateboard-lugging, artsy types doing interesting things in old warehouses across town.

Sadly, windless days are not the norm for Wellington. In New Zealand the city is infamous for two things: its frequent tremors and its umbrella-shredding, hairstyle-destroying gales that barrel through regularly.

⊙ Sights

★ **Mt Victoria Lookout**   VIEWPOINT
(Lookout Rd) The city's most impressive viewpoint is atop 196m-high Mt Victoria (Matairangi), east of the city centre. You can take the No 20 bus most of the way up, but the rite of passage is to sweat it out on the walk (ask a local for directions or just follow your nose). If you've got wheels, take Oriental Pde along the waterfront and then scoot up Carlton Gore Rd. Aside from the views there are some rather interesting info panels.

★ **Wellington Botanic Gardens**   GARDENS
(📞04-499 4444; www.wellington.govt.nz; 101 Glenmore St, Thorndon; ⊙ daylight hours) FREE These hilly, 25-hectare botanic gardens can be *almost* effortlessly visited via the Wellington Cable Car (p372) – nice bit of planning, eh? – although there are several other entrances hidden in the hillsides. The gardens boast a tract of original native forest, the beaut Lady Norwood Rose Garden, 25,000 spring tulips and various international plant collections. Add in fountains, a playground, sculptures, a duck pond, a cafe and city skyline views, and you've got a grand day out indeed.

★ **Zealandia**   WILDLIFE RESERVE
(📞04-920 9213; www.visitzealandia.com; 53 Waiapu Rd, Karori; adult/child/family exhibition only $9/5/21, full admission $20/10/46; ⊙9am-5pm; 🚼) 🐾 This ground-breaking ecosanctuary is hidden in the hills about 2km west of town: buses 3 and 20 stop nearby, or see the Zealandia website for info on the free shuttle. Living wild within the fenced valley are more than 30 native bird species, including rare little spotted kiwi, takahe, saddleback, hihi and kaka, as well as NZ's little dinosaur, the tuatara. An excellent exhibition relays NZ's natural history and world-renowned conservation story.

★ **Wellington Museum**   MUSEUM
(📞04-472 8904; www.museumswellington.org.nz; 3 Jervois Quay, Queens Wharf; ⊙10am-5pm; 🚼) FREE For an imaginative, interactive experience of Wellington's social and maritime history, head to this beguiling little museum, housed in an 1892 bond store on the wharf. Highlights include a moving documentary on the *Wahine,* the inter-island ferry that sank in the harbour in 1968 with the loss of 51 lives. Māori legends are dramatically told using tiny holographic actors and special effects.

★ **New Zealand Parliament**   HISTORIC BUILDING
(📞04-817 9503; www.parliament.nz; Molesworth St; ⊙9.30am-4.30pm) FREE New Zealand might be a young country but it has one of the oldest continuously functioning parliaments in the world and has chalked up more than its share of firsts, including being the first to give women the vote (in 1893) and the first to include an openly transsexual Member of Parliament (in 1999). You can learn all about NZ's unique version of democracy on a free guided tour.

Te Papa   MUSEUM
(📞04-381 7000; www.tepapa.govt.nz; 55 Cable St; tours adult/child $20/10; ⊙10am-6pm; 🚼) 🐾 FREE New Zealand's national museum is hard to miss, taking up a sizeable chunk of

the Wellington waterfront. 'Te Papa Tongare-wa' loosely translates as 'treasure box' and the riches inside include an amazing collection of Māori artefacts and the museum's own colourful *marae* (meeting place); natural history and environment exhibitions; Pacific and NZ history galleries; themed hands-on 'discovery centres' for children; and Toi Art, a revitalised home for the National Art Collection, which opened in 2018. Big-name temporary exhibitions incur an admission fee, although general admission is free.

Introductory and Māori Highlights tours depart from the information desk on level two; it pays to book ahead.

Weta Cave   WORKSHOP
(☑04-909 4100; www.wetanz.com; 1 Weka St, Miramar; single tour adult/child $25/12, both tours $45/20; ⊙9am-5.30pm) Academy Award-winning special-effects and props company Weta Workshop has been responsible for bringing the likes of *The Lord of the Rings*, *The Hobbit*, *King Kong*, *District 9* and *Thor: Ragnarok* to life. Learn how they do it on entertaining 45-minute guided tours, starting every half-hour; bookings recommended. Weta Cave is 8km east of the city centre: drive, catch bus 31 or book transport ($40 return) with your admission.

City Gallery Wellington   GALLERY
(☑04-913 9032; www.citygallery.org.nz; Civic Sq; ⊙10am-5pm) FREE Housed in the monumental old library in Civic Sq, Wellington's much-loved City Gallery does a cracking job of securing acclaimed contemporary international exhibitions, as well as unearthing up-and-comers and supporting those at the forefront of the NZ scene. Charges may apply for major exhibits.

Pukeahu National
War Memorial Park   MEMORIAL
(☑04-385 2496; www.mch.govt.nz; Buckle St, Mt Cook; ⊙hall 10am-5pm) It seems strangely fitting that NZ's National War Memorial should be a musical instrument and contain as its centrepiece not a statue of a soldier, but of a grieving mother and her children. The statue is contained within the **Hall of Memories** at the base of the 51m-high, 49-bell, art-deco **Carillon** (1932). It's flanked by a sobering and oddly tranquil park with a prominent **Australian Memorial** consisting of 15 red sandstone columns.

Space Place   OBSERVATORY
(☑04-910 3140; www.museumswellington.org.nz; 40 Salamanca Rd, Kelburn; adult/child/family $13/8/39; ⊙4-11pm Tue & Fri, 10am-11pm Sat,

10am-5.30pm Sun) Located in the Carter Observatory at the top of the Botanic Gardens (p368), this full-dome planetarium offers regular space-themed multimedia shows (eg *We Are Aliens, Dynamic Earth, Matariki Dawn*) and stargazing sessions. Check the website for show times.

Otari-Wilton's Bush   GARDENS
(☑04-499 4444; www.wellington.govt.nz; 160 Wilton Rd, Wilton; ⊙daylight hours) FREE The only botanic gardens in NZ specialising in native flora, Otari features more than 1200 plant species including an extant section of native bush containing the city's oldest trees (such as an 800-year-old rimu). There's also an information centre, an 18m-high canopy walkway, 11km of walking trails and some beaut picnic areas. It's located about 5km northwest of the centre and is well signposted; bus 14 passes the gates.

St Mary of the Angels   CHURCH
(☑04-473 8074; www.smoa.org.nz; 17 Boulcott St; ⊙7am-6pm) Closed for seismic strengthening and restoration from 2013 to 2017, this pretty Catholic parish church is looking downright heavenly. Built in 1922, it was the first Gothic-style church in the world to have been constructed using reinforced concrete. The motto of the Marist order, *Sub Mariæ Nomine* ('under the name of Mary'), adorns

Wellington

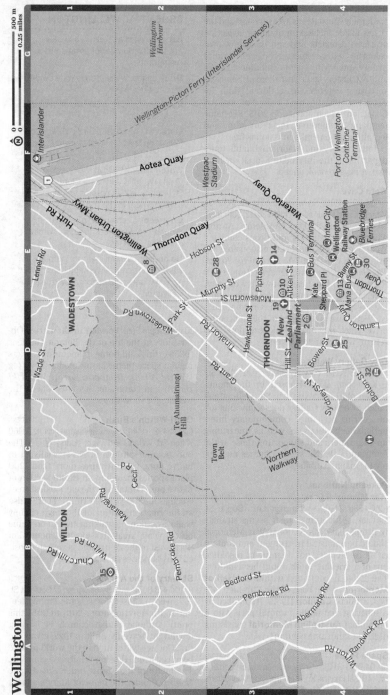

500 m
0.25 miles

Wellington Harbour

Wellington-Picton Ferry (Interislander Services)

Interislander

Aotea Quay

Westpac Stadium

Waterloo Quay

Port of Wellington Container Terminal

Hutt Rd

Wellington Urban Mwy

Thorndon Quay

Lennel Rd

WADESTOWN

Hobson St

Murphy St

28

Wade St

Wadestown Rd

Park St

Molesworth St

Tinakori Rd

Hawkestone St

Hill St

Pipitea St

Aitken St

14

Bus Terminal

InterCity

Wellington Railway Station

Bunny St

Bluebridge Ferries

30

Kate Sheppard Pl

Mana Bus

13

Thorndon Quay

Lambton Quay

10

THORNDON

New Zealand Parliament

19

2

Bowen St

25

Bolton St

32

Grant Rd

Cecil Rd

Mairangi Rd

WILTON

Churchill Rd

W'lton Rd

15

Pembroke Rd

Bedford St

Pembroke Rd

Abermarle Rd

Te Ahumairangi Hill

Town Belt

Northern Walkway

Wilton Rd

Randwick Rd

Sydney St W

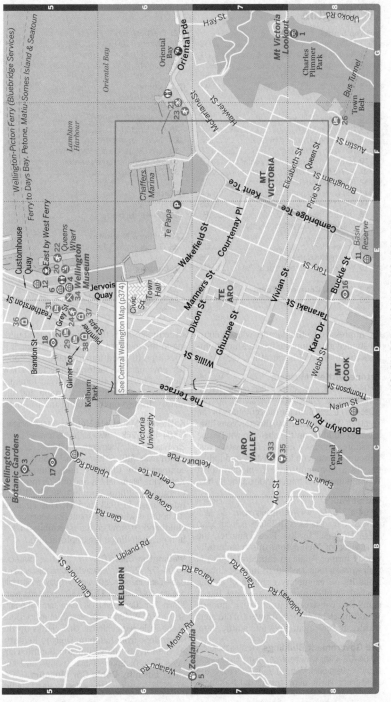

Wellington

the impressive Gothic facade, while colourful stained glass imported from Munich imbues the interior with warmth.

Petone Settlers Museum   MUSEUM
(☑04-568 8373; www.petonesettlers.org.nz; The Esplanade, Petone; ⊙10am-4pm Wed-Sun Apr-Nov, daily Dec-Mar) FREE Built for the centenary of the Treaty of Waitangi in 1940, this gorgeous little art-deco building on the shell-strewn Petone foreshore contains a fun and fascinating wee museum focusing on local history and industry. It's a 15-minute drive from downtown Wellington, or a 23-minute ride on the 83 bus.

Old St Paul's   CHURCH
(☑04-473 6722; www.oldstpauls.co.nz; 34 Mulgrave St, Thorndon; tours $5-7.50; ⊙9.30am-5pm) FREE Designed by Rev Fred Thatcher, the first vicar of Wellington, this wonderfully woody former Anglican cathedral (1866) is well worth a look. Despite its modest dimensions it's an exemplary example of Gothic Revival architecture, with a ceiling like a ship's hull constructed from native timbers. Inside are claret carpets, drawers of old altar textiles, brassy organ pipes and a little shop.

Old Government Buildings   HISTORIC BUILDING
(☑04-472 4341; www.heritage.org.nz; 55 Lambton Quay; ⊙9am-5pm Mon-Fri) FREE Across the road from Parliament, this grand Italianate

structure (1876) is the largest wooden building in the southern hemisphere, although it does a pretty good impersonation of stone. It's now part of Victoria University's law faculty. Check out the magnificent hanging staircase, the former cabinet room and the history displays on the ground and 1st floors.

Katherine Mansfield House HISTORIC BUILDING
(☑04-473 7268; www.katherinemansfield.com; 25 Tinakori Rd, Thorndon; adult/child $8/free, guided tours $10; ⊙10am-4pm Tue-Sun) Often compared to Chekhov and Maupassant, Katherine Mansfield is one of NZ's most distinguished authors. Born in 1888, she died of tuberculosis in 1923 aged 34. This Tinakori Rd house is where she spent five years of her childhood. It now contains exhibits in her honour, including a biographical film.

Wellington Cable Car   CABLE CAR
(☑04-472 2199; www.wellingtoncablecar.co.nz; Cable Car Lane, rear 280 Lambton Quay; adult/child one way $4/2, return $7.50/3.50; ⊙departs every 10min, 7am-10pm Mon-Fri, 8.30am-9pm Sat & Sun; ⛟) One of Wellington's big-ticket attractions is the little red cable car that clanks up the steep slope from Lambton Quay to Kelburn. At the top are the Wellington Botanic Gardens (p368), Space Place (p369) and the small but nifty **Cable Car Museum** (☑04-475 3578; www.museumswellington.org.nz; 1A Up-

land Rd, Kelburn; ⊙9.30am-5pm) **FREE**. The last of these evocatively depicts the cable car's story since it was built in 1902 to open up hilly Kelburn for settlement. Ride the cable car back down the hill, or wander down through the gardens.

Wellington Zoo   ZOO
(☑04-381 6755; www.wellingtonzoo.com; 200 Daniell St, Newtown; adult/child $24/12; ⊙9.30am-5pm; ⊕) ✿ Committed to conservation, research and captive breeding, Wellington Zoo is home to a menagerie of native and exotic wildlife, including lions and tamarins. The nocturnal house has kiwi and tuatara. 'Close encounters' allow you to meet the big cats, red pandas, giraffes and mischievous meerkats (for a fee). The zoo is 4km south of the centre; catch bus 10 or 23.

New Zealand Cricket Museum   MUSEUM
(☑04-385 6602; www.nzcricketmuseum.co.nz; Museum Stand, Basin Reserve, Mt Cook; admission by donation; ⊙during cricket matches) Tucked under a stand at the Basin Reserve, the NZ Cricket Museum is a must-see for fans of the old game. It's only open during cricket matches or by special appointment; check the website for details.

National Library of New Zealand   MUSEUM
(☑0800 474 300; www.natlib.govt.nz; 70 Molesworth St, Thorndon; ⊙8.30am-5pm Mon-Sat) **FREE** As well as being a wonderful resource for researchers, the National Library has various exhibition spaces including the **Turnbull Gallery**, displaying rare books and ephemera. The highlight is **He Tohu** (The Signs), opened in 2017 to house three of NZ's most treasured documents: the 1835 Declaration of Independence of the United Tribes of NZ, the 1840 Treaty of Waitangi and the 1893 Women's Suffrage Petition. Interesting multimedia displays outline the significance of these documents to the nation.

Bucket Fountain   FOUNTAIN
(Cuba Mall; ⊙24hr; ⊕) Cuba Mall's landmark (and sneakily splashy) fountain mocks the surrounding commerce with its Zen-like tilt-and-pour processes. The kids will be mesmerised!

New Zealand Portrait Gallery   GALLERY
(☑04-472 2298; www.nzportraitgallery.org.nz; Shed 11, Customhouse Quay; ⊙10.30am-4.30pm) **FREE** Housed in a heritage red-brick warehouse on the waterfront, this excellent gallery presents a diverse range of NZ portraiture and caricature from its own collection and frequently changing guest exhibitions.

Dowse Art Museum   GALLERY
(☑04-570 6500; www.dowse.org.nz; 45 Laings Rd, Lower Hutt; ⊙10am-5pm; ⊕) **FREE** A beacon of culture and delight, the excellent Dowse is worth visiting for its jaunty architecture alone. It's a family-friendly, accessible art museum showcasing NZ art, craft and design, with a nice cafe to boot. The only permanent showcase is a carved *pataka* (traditional raised storehouse). It's a 20-minute drive, 30-minute ride on bus 83 or short train trip from central Wellington.

Wellington Cathedral of St Paul   CATHEDRAL
(☑04-472 0286; www.wellingtoncathedral.org.nz; cnr Hill & Molesworth Sts; ⊙8am-5pm Sun-Fri, 10am-4pm Sat) **FREE** At 88m long and 18m high, this modern Anglican cathedral exudes quasi-Moorish architectural vibes inside its lofty interiors. It first opened its doors in 1964 but wasn't completed until 1998 – which makes it even more surprising that the exterior is looking so shabby. Look out for the lovely wooden Lady Chapel, a 1905 church which was moved here from Paraparaumu and tacked to the cathedral's side in 1991.

Ngā Taonga Sound & Vision   ARCHIVES
(☑04-384 7647; www.ngataonga.org.nz; 84 Taranaki St; screenings adult/child $10/8; ⊙library noon-4pm Mon-Fri) **FREE** Ngā Taonga is a vortex of NZ moving images into which you could get sucked for days. Its library holds tens of thousands of titles: feature films, documentaries, short films, home movies, newsreels, TV programs, advertisements... There are regular screenings in the cinema (check the website for the schedule), and a viewing library (free) where you can watch films until you're square-eyed. If the library is closed, there's a media player in the on-site cafe.

Academy Galleries   GALLERY
(☑04-499 8807; www.nzafa.com; 1 Queens Wharf; ⊙10am-5pm) **FREE** The showcase of the esteemed New Zealand Academy of Fine Arts (founded 1882), the Academy Galleries presents frequently changing exhibitions by NZ artists, from canvases to ceramics to photography.

Nairn Street Cottage   MUSEUM
(☑04-384 9122; www.museumswellington.org.nz; 68 Nairn St, Mt Cook; adult/child $8/4; ⊙noon-4pm Sat & Sun) Just a five-minute amble from the top of Cuba St, Wellington's oldest cottage (1857) has been carefully restored, complete with an organic garden and chooks (chickens). Admission is by tour only (on the hour noon to 3pm), retelling stories of early settlers and life in the mid-19th century.

Central Wellington

🏃 Activities

Wellington's harbour offers plenty of opportunities to get active: kayaking, paddle boarding, sailing, windsurfing... (Wellington is windy: might as well make the most of it!). Back on dry land there's rock climbing, cycling and high-wire walking to keep you entertained. Pick up the *Wellington City Cycle Map* for bike-trail info.

Switched On Bikes   CYCLING
(📱022 075 8754; www.switchedonbikes.co.nz; Queens Wharf; city & mountain bike hire 1hr/4hr/day $15/40/60, electric $20/45/75, guided tours from $95; ⊘9am-5pm) If you're short on puff on those notorious Wellington hills, these guys rent out electric bikes for cruising the city or taking on guided tours around the harbour. Look for their shipping-container base near the end of the wharf.

Wellington Ocean Sports   WATER SPORTS
(📱04-939 6702; www.oceansports.org.nz; 115 Oriental Pde; harbour sails per person $40; ⊘booking office 9am-5pm) Harness Wellington's infamous wind on a one-hour harbour sailing trip, departing most weekends (weather dependent) – no experience required! Ask

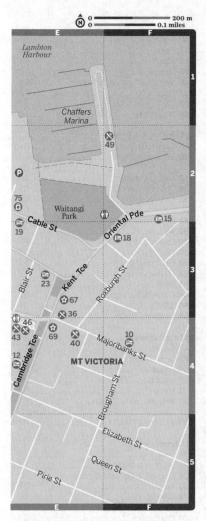

Makara Peak
Mountain Bike Park
MOUNTAIN BIKING

(www.makarapeak.org; 116 South Karori Rd, Karori; ⊙daylight hours) In hilly Karori, 7km west of the city centre, this excellent 230-hectare park is laced with 45km of single-track, ranging from beginner to extreme. The nearby **Mud Cycles** (☑04-476 4961; www.mudcycles.co.nz; 424 Karori Rd, Karori; half-day/full-day/weekend bike hire from $35/60/100; ⊙9.30am-6.30pm Mon-Fri, 10am-5pm Sat & Sun) has mountain bikes for hire. To get here by public transport, catch bus 3.

Freyberg Pool & Fitness Centre
SWIMMING

(☑04-801 4530; www.wellington.govt.nz; 139 Oriental Pde; pool adult/child $6/3.70; ⊙6am-9pm; ⛲) Built in 1963, modernist Freyberg Pool is the most striking piece of architecture on Oriental Bay. As well as a big indoor pool there's a gym, spa, and aerobics, yoga and pilates classes.

Adrenalin Forest
ADVENTURE SPORTS

(☑04-237 8553; www.adrenalin-forest.co.nz; Okowai Rd, Porirua; adult/child 3hr $43/28; ⊙10am-2.30pm daily Oct-Apr, Wed-Sun May-Sep) Walk out on the high wire on this web of cables, suspension bridges and platforms strung between a copse of high pines. It's located 21km north of central Wellington; catch the train to Porirua then the 230 bus.

Wild Winds
WATER SPORTS

(☑04-473 3458; www.wildwinds.co.nz; 2 Hunter St; 2hr lesson $110; ⊙10am-5.30pm Mon-Fri, to 3pm Sat) With all this wind and water, Wellington was made for windsurfing and kiteboarding. Tackle one or both with an introductory lesson.

On Yer Bike
CYCLING

(☑04-384 8480; www.avantiplus.co.nz/wellington; 181 Vivian St; city/mountain/electric bike per day $30/40/60; ⊙8.30am-5.30pm Mon-Sat) Quality bike hire in the city centre.

Tours

Kiwi Coastal Tours
DRIVING

(☑021 464 957; www.kiwicoastaltours.co.nz; 3/5hr tours $150/250) Excellent 4WD exploration of the rugged south coast in the company of a local Māori guide with plenty of stories to tell.

Walk Wellington
WALKING

(☑04-473 3145; www.walkwellington.org.nz; departs Wellington i-SITE, 111 Wakefield St; tour $20; ⊙10am daily year-round, plus 5pm Mon, Wed & Fri Dec-Mar) Informative and great-value two-hour walking tours focusing on the city and waterfront, departing from the i-SITE (p390). Book online, by phone or just turn up.

about stand-up paddle boarding, windsurfing, *waka ama* (outrigger canoeing) and kayaking sessions.

Ferg's Kayaks
KAYAKING, CLIMBING

(☑04-499 8898; www.fergskayaks.co.nz; Shed 6, Queens Wharf; ⊙10am-8pm Mon-Fri, 9am-6pm Sat & Sun) Stretch your tendons with indoor rock-climbing (adult/child $21/17), cruise the waterfront wearing in-line skates (one/two hours $20/25) or go for a paddle in a kayak (one/two hours $25/35) or on a stand-up paddle board (one/two hours $30/40). There's also bike hire (hour/day from $20/80) and guided kayaking trips.

Central Wellington

Zest Food Tours FOOD & DRINK
(☏04-801 9198; www.zestfoodtours.co.nz; departs Wellington i-SITE, 111 Wakefield St; tours from $185) Runs 3½- to five-hour small-group foodie tours around the city, plus day tours over the hills into the Wairarapa wine region.

Flat Earth DRIVING
(☏04-472 9635; www.flatearth.co.nz; half-/full-day tours from $95/385) An array of themed small-group guided tours: city highlights, Māori treasures, arts, wilderness and Middle Earth filming locations. Martinborough wine tours also available.

DAYS BAY & MATIU/SOMES ISLAND

Wellingtonians have been taking day trips across the harbour to Days Bay since the 1880s. At the bay there's a beach, a park and a cafe, and a boatshed with kayaks and bikes for hire. A 10-minute walk from Days Bay leads to Eastbourne, a beachy township with cafes, a cute pub, a summer swimming pool and a playground.

The sweet little **East by West Ferry** (☑04-499 1282; www.eastbywest.co.nz; Queens Wharf; return adult/child $23/12) plies the 20- to 30-minute route 16 times a day on weekdays and eight times on weekends; some sailings stop in Petone and Seatoun as well.

Three or four of the daily ferries also stop at Matiu/Somes Island in the middle of the harbour, a DOC-managed reserve that is home to weta, tuatara, kakariki and little blue penguins, among other critters. The island is rich in history, having once been a prisoner-of-war camp and quarantine station. Take a picnic lunch, or even stay overnight in the basic campsite (adult/child $13/6.50) or at one of the two DOC cottages (sole-occupancy $200): book online at www.doc.govt.nz or at the **DOC Wellington Visitor Centre** (p390).

Te Wharewaka o Pōneke CULTURAL
(☑04-901 3333; www.wharewakaoponeke.co.nz; Taranaki Wharf, 2 Taranaki St; tours walking $30-40, 2hr waka $100, 3hr waka & walk $125) Get set for (and maybe a little bit wet on) a two-hour paddle tour in a Māori *waka* (canoe) around Wellington's waterfront, with lots of cultural insights along the way. Call for the latest tour times and bookings – minimum numbers apply.

Hop On Hop Off BUS
(☑0800 246 877; www.hoponhopoff.co.nz; departs 101 Wakefield St; adult/child $45/30; ☺departs 9.30am, 11am, 12.30pm & 2.30pm) Flexible 1½-hour scenic loop of the city with 11 stops en route. Tickets are valid for 24 hours.

South Coast Shuttles DRIVING
(☑04-389 2161; www.southcoastshuttles.co.nz; departs Wellington i-SITE, 111 Wakefield St; 2½hr tours $55; ☺tours 10am & 1pm) Offers scheduled daily city highlights tours including the south coast, Mt Victoria, Weta Cave and Otari-Wilton's Bush.

Rover Rings DRIVING
(☑04-471 0044; www.wellingtonrover.co.nz; adult/child tours from $95/50) Half- to full-day tours of *Lord of the Rings* locations in and around the city.

Wellington Movie Tours TOURS
(☑027 419 3077; www.adventuresafari.co.nz; adult/child tours from $45/30) Half- and full-day tours with more props, clips, and Middle Earth film locations than you can shake a staff at.

✵ Festivals & Events

Check at the Wellington i-SITE (p390) for comprehensive events listings.

Summer City CULTURAL
(www.wellington.govt.nz; ☺Jan-Mar; 🅰) A summertime city-wide events bonanza – many free and outdoor happenings, including the lovely 'Gardens Magic' concerts. The Wellington Pasifika Festival and Waitangi Day celebrations also fall under the Summer City umbrella.

Fringe CULTURAL
(https://fringe.co.nz/; ☺Feb-Mar) Three weeks of way-out-there experimental visual arts, music, dance and theatre. Although it's held around the same time as the biennial New Zealand Festival, Fringe is held every year.

New Zealand Festival CULTURAL
(www.festival.co.nz; ☺Feb-Mar) A month-long biennial (even years; around mid-February to mid-March) spectacular of theatre, dance, music, visual arts and literature. International acts aplenty. A real 'kick up the arts'!

NZ International Comedy Festival COMEDY
(www.comedyfestival.co.nz; ☺Apr-May) Three weeks of hysterics. World-famous-in-NZ comedians, and some truly world-famous ones, too.

Wellington Jazz Festival MUSIC
(www.jazzfestival.co.nz; ☺mid-Jun) Five days of finger-snappin' bee-boppin' good times around the capital – an antidote for winter chills.

Matariki CULTURAL
(www.tepapa.govt.nz; ☺mid-Jun–mid-Jul) Celebrates the Māori New Year, with a free festival of dance, music and other events at Te Papa (p368).

New Zealand International Film Festival FILM
(www.nzff.co.nz; ☺Jul-Aug) Roving two-week indie film fest screening the best of NZ and international cinema.

Beervana
BEER
(www.beervana.co.nz; Westpac Stadium; ⊘Aug)
A barrel-load of craft-beer aficionados roll
into town for a weekend of supping and
beard-stroking.

Wellington on a Plate
FOOD & DRINK
(www.wellingtononaplate.com; ⊘Aug) Lip-
smacking roster of gastronomic events, and
bargains aplenty held over 17 days at restaurants around the city.

Spring Festival
FAIR
(www.wellington.govt.nz; ⊘Sep; ﹢) Tiptoe
through the tulips in the Wellington Botanic
Gardens and Otari-Wilton's Bush, with plenty
of free and kid-friendly walks and activities.

★ World of WearableArt
FASHION
(WOW; www.worldofwearableart.com; TSB Bank Arena; ⊘Sep-Oct) A two-week run of spectacular
garments (dresses or sculptures – it's a fine
line) displayed in a spectacular show. Tickets
are hot property; hotel beds anywhere near
the city sell out weeks in advance.

🛌 Sleeping

Accommodation in Wellington is more expensive than in regional areas, but there are
plenty of options close to the city centre. Free
parking spots are a rarity – ask in advance
about options. Wellington's budget accommodation largely takes the form of multistorey
hostel megaliths. Motels dot the city fringes.
Self-contained apartments are popular, and often offer bargain weekend rates. Book well in
advance in summer and during major events.

★ Dwellington
HOSTEL $
(☑04-550 9373; www.thedwellington.co.nz; 8
Halswell St, Thorndon; dm/r from $29/85; P🐕) Two
conjoined heritage houses have been reinvent-
ed to create this terrific modern hostel, sandwiched between the US and Chinese embassies.
There are no en suites, but the rooms are
clean, bright and comfortable, and there's free
wi-fi and breakfast. The location is handy for
the ferries, trains and intercity buses, but a fair
hike from the after-dark fun around Cuba St.

★YHA Wellington City
HOSTEL $
(☑04-801 7280; www.yha.co.nz; 292 Wakefield
St; dm/s from $36/87, d with/without bathroom
$134/99; @🐕) ✔ The trusty YHA wins points
for fantastic communal areas including two
big kitchens and dining areas, and separate
rooms for games, reading and watching
movies. Sustainable initiatives (recycling,
composting and energy-efficient hot water)
abound, and there's a comprehensive booking
service and espresso machine at reception.

★Moana Lodge
HOSTEL $
(☑04-233 2010; www.moanalodge.co.nz; 49 Moana Rd, Plimmerton; dm/s/d from $38/70/96;
P🐕) In Plimmerton, 25km north of central Wellington (30 minutes by train), this
exceptional hostel justifies the schlep with
sea views and a little sandy beach just across
the road. The lovely old house is immaculate
and inviting, with an affable host who will
happily steer you towards the local sights.

Cambridge Hotel
HOSTEL, HOTEL $
(☑04-385 8829; www.cambridgehotel.co.nz; 28
Cambridge Tce; dm $26-40, s with/without bath-
room from $99/69, d $119/89; 🐕) Built in 1883,
the Cambridge is the consummate corner
pub, with old-fashioned budget rooms
above; it's hard to believe that the Queen
stayed here in the 1960s. All of the hotel
rooms have fridges and kettles, and some
have tiny bathrooms. The backpacker wing
has a snug kitchen-lounge and dorms with
little natural light but sky-high ceilings.

Trek Global
HOSTEL $
(☑04-471 3480; www.trekglobal.net; 9 O'Reilly
Ave; dm/s from $23/59, d with/without bathroom
$89/79; P@🐕) ✔ A highlight of this back-
lane hostel is the funky and welcoming foyer
hang-out and snug TV lounge. The sleeping
quarters and kitchens are squeezed between
rabbit-warren corridors. It's relatively quiet
with clean rooms and laudable extras such
as bike hire, parking ($20 per day) and a
women-only dorm with a suntrap terrace.

Wellington Top 10
Holiday Park
HOLIDAY PARK $
(☑04-568 5913; www.wellingtontop10.co.nz; 95
Hutt Park Rd, Seaview; sites from $35, units with/
without bathroom $120/70; P🐕﹢) Located
16km northeast of central Wellington, the
Top 10 offers the closest camping to the city.
Family-friendly facilities include communal
kitchens, a games room and a playground,
but the industrial back-block location de-
tracts. Follow the signs off SH2 for Petone
and Seaview, or catch bus 83.

Nomads Capital
HOSTEL $
(☑04-978 7800; www.nomadsworld.com; 118
Wakefield St; dm/r from $32/120; 🐕) ✔ Smack
bang in the middle of town, Nomads has
good security, spick-and-span rooms with
en suites and an on-site cafe-bar. Kitchen
and lounge spaces are short on elbow room,
but slick service, heritage features and the
hot location stop you from dwelling on the
negatives. Plus they offer free breakfasts and
light dinners.

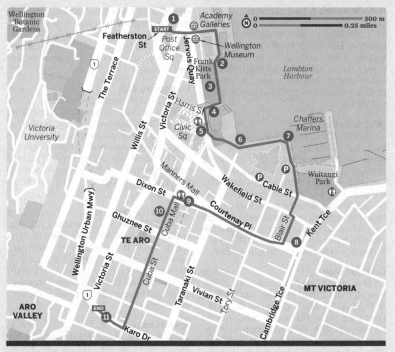

🚶 City Walk
City Sculpture

START POST OFFICE SQ
END KARO DR
LENGTH 2.8KM; ONE HOUR

Get started in windswept Post Office Sq, where Bill Culbert's **1 SkyBlues** twirls into the air. Cross Jervois Quay and pass between the Academy Galleries and Wellington Museum. At the Queens Wharf waterfront, turn right, past the big shed to the **2 Water Whirler**, the largely lifeless needle of kooky kineticist Len Lye that whirrs crazily into life on the hour several times a day.

Continue along the promenade below the **3 mast of the Wahine**, which tragically sank in Wellington Harbour in 1968. Around the corner are the white, rather whale-like forms of the **4 Albatross Fountain**. Detour up onto the flotsamy **5 City to Sea Bridge** and check out the collection of weathered wooden sculptures here.

Back on the waterfront, continue past the *whare waka* (canoe house), to the mooring of the **6 Hikitia**, the world's oldest working crane ship – something of a sculpture in itself. Strip to your undies and jump off the diving platform, or perhaps just keep on trucking along the wharf, past the naked bronze form of **7 Solace in the Wind** leaning over the harbour fringe.

Turn right and wander through the landscaped wetlands of Waitangi Park before crossing Cable St and cutting along Chaffers St, and then Blair St with its century-old warehouses.

At Courtenay Pl look to your left, to check out the leggy form of the industrial-cinematic **8 Tripod**, before turning right. Continue along to wedge-shaped **9 Te Aro Park** with its canoe prow and trip hazards.

Turn left when you hit Cuba St, heading up the pedestrian mall. Watch out for the sly, sloshy **10 Bucket Fountain** (p373) – it exists solely to splash your legs.

Change down a gear and window-shop all the way to the top of Cuba St, where a remnant heritage precinct is bisected by the controversial inner-city bypass. Bookend your sculpture walk with Regan Gentry's brilliant but ghostly outline of a demolished house, **11 Subject to Change**. Alongside is the curious 7.5m-deep Tonks' Well, dating from the 1860s.

Hotel Waterloo & Backpackers   HOSTEL $
(☎04-473 8482; www.hotelwaterloo.co.nz; 1 Bunny St; dm $25-35, s with/without bathroom from $99/72, d $119/89; @🖢) 🅿 Housed in an art-deco hotel (1937) at the railway end of town, this budget hotel and hostel has tidy rooms and plenty of capacious, character-filled communal areas (be sure to check out the bar).

★City Cottages   RENTAL HOUSE $$
(☎0210739232;www.wellingtoncityaccommodation. co.nz; 5 & 7 Tonks Gr; cottage $170-200; P🖢) These two tiny 1880 cottages squat amid a precious precinct of historic buildings. Clever conversion has transformed them into self-contained one-bedroom pads, comfortable for two but sleeping up to four (thanks to a sofa bed). It's not the quietest location but it's hip and exceedingly convenient. They also rent a modern two-bedroom studio and a historic townhouse (sleeping 10) nearby.

Gourmet Stay   HOTEL $$
(☎04-801 6800; www.gourmetstay.co.nz; 25 Frederick St; r with/without bathroom from $189/159; P🖢) A bit like a dorm-less hostel for grown-ups, this backstreet hotel has 13 rooms, all with different configurations, spread between two neighbouring buildings. Most have en suites and all of them are tastefully designed, with nice linen and natty art. A free continental breakfast is provided and a blackboard lists foodie tips around town.

Gilmer Apartment Hotel   HOTEL $$
(☎04-978 1400; www.10gilmer.co.nz; 10 Gilmer Tce; apt from $118; P🖢) There's a hip, artsy vibe to this 62-unit inner-city apartment hotel. Sizes range from studios to two-bedroom apartments, and they all have their own kitchens and laundries. The nonrefundable advance-purchase rates are a steal for this part of town.

Booklovers B&B   B&B $$
(☎04-384 2714; www.booklovers.co.nz; 123 Pirie St, Mt Victoria; s/d from $180/220; ❄🖢) Author Jane Tolerton's elegant, book-filled B&B has three queen guest rooms (one with an extra single bed). A bus service runs past the front gate to Courtenay Pl and the train station, and the city's 'green belt' begins right next door. Free wi-fi and street parking.

Capital View Motor Inn   MOTEL $$
(☎04-385 0515; www.capitalview.co.nz; 12 Thompson St, Mt Cook; unit from $140; P🖢) Many of the 21 rooms in this neat, well-maintained mini-tower building near the top of Cuba St do indeed enjoy capital views – especially the large, good-value penthouse (sleeps five). All are self-contained and spruce, and there's free parking.

Apollo Lodge   MOTEL $$
(☎04-385 1849; www.apollolodge.co.nz; 49 Majoribanks St, Mt Victoria; unit from $150; P🖢) Within staggering distance of Courtenay Pl, Apollo Lodge is a loose collation of a couple of dozen varied units, ranging from studios to family-friendly two-bedroom units with full kitchens to long-stay apartments. It's good value for a location this close to the city.

WELLINGTON IN...

Two Days
To get a feel for the lie of the land, walk (or drive) up to the **Mt Victoria Lookout** (p368), or ride the cable car up into the **Wellington Botanic Gardens** (p368). After lunch on boho-hipster Cuba St, catch some Kiwi culture at **Te Papa** (p368) or the **Wellington Museum** (p368). Top off the day by doing the rounds of the city's numerous craft-beer bars.

   The next day, reconstitute with coffee and an eggy infusion at **Fidel's** (p385), a real Wellington institution, then head to **Zealandia** (p368) to be with the birds and learn about New Zealand conservation. Alternatively, walk the halls with a different species of birdbrain on a tour of **Parliament** (p368). Grab a meal at one of the central city's excellent restaurants, before catching some live music, or a movie at the gloriously restored **Embassy Theatre** (p388).

Four Days
Shake and bake the two-day itinerary, then decorate with the following: hightail it out of Wellington for a seal-spotting safari to wild **Cape Palliser** (p399), followed by a wine-tasting or two around **Martinborough** (p396) in the middle of Wairarapa Wine Country. The next day, head to **Paekakariki** (p393) on the Kapiti Coast for an ocean swim before wandering through the dunes of **Queen Elizabeth Park** (p393) next door.

CityLife Wellington
HOTEL $$

(☑04-922 2800; www.heritagehotels.co.nz; 300 Lambton Quay; apt from $162; 🛜) 🚗 It's big and more than a little corporate but this apartment-style hotel, right in the commercial heart of the city, has a range of plush studio, one- and two-bedroom apartments. Some have full kitchen and in-room laundry facilities, and some offer harbour glimpses.

Victoria Court Motor Lodge
MOTEL $$

(☑04-385 7102; www.victoriacourt.co.nz; 201 Victoria St; unit from $165; P🛜) Three-tier, lemon-yellow Victoria Court continues to deliver satisfaction in the city, with spacious studios and apartments with kitchenettes. There are two disabled-access units, and larger units sleep up to five. It's just a short stumble to Cuba St. Free on-site parking.

Quality Hotel
HOTEL $$

(☑04-385 2156; www.cqwellington.com; 223 Cuba St; ste from $183; P🛜🍽) A lopsided proposition, the high-rise Quality is joined to its lesser-quality sibling, the heritage Comfort Hotel, by way of a shared reception and facilities including an in-house bar, restaurant, pool and parking ($30 per night). Expect snazzy, spacious suites but be prepared for hit-and-miss service.

★ Ohtel
BOUTIQUE HOTEL $$$

(☑04-803 0600; www.ohtel.nz; 66 Oriental Pde, Oriental Bay; r from $229; ❋🛜) 🚗 Ever feel like you've walked into a design magazine? This bijou hotel has 10 individually decorated rooms with immersive NZ scenes plastered above the bath-tubs and original, mid-century, Scandi-style furniture and ceramics, avidly collected by the architect-owner. The best rooms have decks and harbour views.

★ QT Museum Wellington
HOTEL $$$

(☑04-802 8900; www.qtwellington.com; 90 Cable St; r/apt from $215/296; ❋🛜🍽) That there's a hippopotamus theme to the decor says a lot about the quirkiness of this art-filled hotel. In the hotel wing, black lifts open on to darkened corridors leading to flamboyantly decorated rooms. The apartment wing is marginally more restrained but equally luxurious, and the units have kitchenettes and laundry facilities.

Edgewater Lodge
B&B $$$

(☑04-388 4446; www.edgewaterwellington.co.nz; 423 Karaka Bay Rd, Karaka Bay; r from $290; P🛜) True to its name, the Edgewater is a big modern house set just across the road from a little beach. It's a 15-minute drive from the city but handy for the movie-making enclave of Miramar – which might explain the Hobbity paraphernalia scattered about. One of the three rooms has a large sea-gazing deck, while another has its own external entrance.

Joyce's B&B
B&B $$$

(☑04-499 7338; www.joycesbnb.nz; 46 Aurora Tce, Kelburn; r $215; P🛜) Perched above the motorway on *steeep* Aurora Tce, Joyce's is but a short stumble from the city. The two rooms have private bathrooms and one of them is like a little flat, with its own separate kitchen, laundry and an adjoining second bedroom. The free parking is a rare treat this close to the centre.

Bolton Hotel
HOTEL $$$

(☑04-472 9966; www.boltonhotel.co.nz; 12 Bolton St; r from $297; 🛜🍽) Visiting diplomats and corporate types flock to the Bolton, filling 139 rooms spread over 19 floors. Rooms come in all shapes and sizes, but share a common theme of muted tones, fine linens and colourful artwork. Most have full kitchens; some come with park or city views. It's independent and just a bit arty.

At Home
APARTMENT $$$

(☑04-802 0858; www.athomewellington.com; L4, 181 Wakefield St; apt from $229; ❋🛜) You'd be forgiven for thinking the worst, entering this commercial building, ascending in the lift and walking along the featureless corridor to the cluttered reception. After the unpromising lead-up, the bright and spacious apartments come as a welcome surprise. All have kitchens, laundries and a writing desk, and the location couldn't be more central.

InterContinental Wellington
HOTEL $$$

(☑04-472 2722; www.intercontinental.com; 2 Grey St; r from $293; 🛜🍽) Occupying a big 1980s-style marble-clad tower in the city centre, the InterContinental offers all the usual five-star trimmings you'd expect from the international brand – including a gym, pool and an excellent restaurant.

Copthorne Hotel
HOTEL $$$

(☑04-385 0279; www.millenniumhotels.com; 100 Oriental Pde, Oriental Bay; d from $219; 🛜🍽) This multistorey gleamer has a terrific location facing off with the harbour. Business bods surf through the lobby on a pervasive wave of slickness, while active types head for the heated indoor pool or free workouts at the Freyberg fitness centre across the road.

🍴 Eating

Wellington offers a bewildering array of eating options: contemporary cafes, upmarket restaurants and oodles of noodle houses. Stiff competition keeps standards high.

RUDMER ZWERVER/SHUTTERSTOCK ©

1. Kapiti Island (p393)
The dominant feature of the Kapiti Coast, the island is home to a remarkable range of birds.

2. Castlepoint (p401)
This is a truly end-of-the-world place, affording unique swimming, walking and caving opportunities.

3. Urban Wellington (p368)
Victorian timber architecture laces the bushy hillsides above a hook-shaped harbour.

4. Wellington Botanic Gardens (p368)
Twenty-five hectares of gardens and original native forest await at the end of a cable-car ride.

WELLINGTON FOR CHILDREN

Let's cut to the chase: Welly's biggest hit for kids is Te Papa (p368), with the whole caboodle looking like it's curated by a team of five-year-old geniuses. It has interactive activities galore, more creepy, weird and wonderful things than you can shake a squid at, and heaps of special events for all ages. See the dedicated Kids & Families page on the website for proof of Te Papa's prowess in this department.

Conveniently located either side of Te Papa are Frank Kitts Park and Waitangi Park, both with playgrounds and in close proximity to roller skates, ice creams, and life-saving espresso for the grown-ups.

A ride up the cable car (p372) and a lap around the Wellington Botanic Gardens (p368) will get the wee ones pumped up. When darkness descends head to Space Place (p369) to gaze at galaxies far, far away. On a more terrestrial plane, kids can check out some crazy New Zealand critters at the Wellington Zoo (p373) or Zealandia (p368).

Little Penang   MALAYSIAN $

(☑04-382 9818; www.facebook.com/littlepenang; 40 Dixon St; mains $12-17; ⊙11am-3pm & 5-9pm Mon-Fri, 11am-9pm Sat; ☑) Among a bunch of great Malaysian diners, Little Penang steals the show with its fresh-flavoured, fiery street food. Order a *nasi lemak* with the good eggy, nutty, saucy stuff; or go for the bargain $9 roti bread with curry. And don't bypass the curry puffs. The lunchtime rush can border on the absurd.

Havana Coffee Works   CAFE $

(☑04-384 7041; www.havana.co.nz; 163 Tory St; snacks $4-8; ⊙7am-5pm Mon-Fri) Continuing Wellington's unwavering obsession with all things Cuba, this fantastic roastery and 'First Class' coffee lounge offers heart-jolting coffee and smiles all round. Nibbles are limited to the likes of scones, bagels, cakes and pies from the warmer. There's also a takeaway counter in the roastery.

Midnight Espresso   CAFE $

(☑04-384 7014; www.facebook.com/midnight espresso; 178 Cuba St; mains $8-17; ⊙7.30am-3am; ☑) Let it all hang out after midnight at this devilishly good late opener. Munch on some cheesy lasagne, sticky date pudding or spinach-and-basil muffins if you must, but caffeine is really where it's at. Dig the little brass repair plates in the old floorboards and the pinball machine.

KK Malaysian Restaurant   MALAYSIAN $

(☑04-385 6698; www.kkmalaysian.co.nz; 54 Ghuznee St; mains $13-16; ⊙11.30am-9.30pm Mon-Sat, 5-9.30pm Sun; ☑) The still-life vegetables and distressed Tuscan wall finishes here are a bit odd, but ignore the decor and focus on the food – some of the best Malaysian in the capital. Couples meet after work for a *roti chanai* (curry and bread) and students slurp laksa lunches, all just a few metres from Cuba St. Good vegetarian options, too.

Gelissimo Gelato   ICE CREAM $

(☑04-385 9313; www.gelissimo.co.nz; Taranaki Wharf, 11 Cable St; single scoop $5; ⊙8am-5.30pm Mon-Fri, 10.30am-5.30pm Sat & Sun) The hottest thing in coldness is the gelato and sorbet made by Graham, who grew up in a fruiterer's shop and sure knows his apples (and raspberries, and chocolate...). It's a bit hard to find, nooked in behind the huge Mac's brew bar.

★Noble Rot   FRENCH $$

(☑04-385 6671; www.noblerot.co.nz; 6 Swan Lane; mains $29-34; ⊙4pm-late) Noble Rot thinks of itself as a wine bar, but this cosy nook serves some of Wellington's best food, too. A French influence pervades the menu (charcuterie, duck parfait, smoked-cheese souffle, slow-cooked lamb), alongside a few distinctly Kiwi touches such as spaghetti with *puha* (a native green vegetable). Needless to say, the wine list is exceptional.

★Shepherd   CONTEMPORARY $$

(☑04-385 7274; www.shepherdrestaurant.co.nz; 1/5 Eva St; mains $26-30; ⊙5.30pm-late Wed-Sun) This good Shepherd leads the way with on-trend contemporary cuisine, guiding its eager flock through fusion flavours, unusual produce and pickled accompaniments. A long bar on one side and an open kitchen on the other, with an assortment of brightly painted stools and high tables in between. The vibe is young and edgy, and the food is thrilling.

★Loretta   CAFE $$

(☑04-384 2213; www.loretta.net.nz; 181 Cuba St; mains $13-28; ⊙9am-10pm Tue-Sun; ☑) From breakfast (waffles, crumpets, cereal) through lunch (sandwiches, fritters, soup) and into dinner (pizzas, roast chicken, schnitzel), Loretta has won leagues of fans with her classy, well-proportioned offerings served in bright, airy surrounds. We recommend splitting a pizza and grain-filled salad between two. Bookings for lunch only.

Field & Green BRITISH $$

(☏04-384 4992; www.fieldandgreen.co.nz; 262 Wakefield St; mains $14-33; ⊗8am-10pm Wed-Sat, to 3pm Sun) 'European soul food' is their slogan, but it's the best of British that dominates here, including Red Leicester scones, Welsh rarebit, kedgeree, fish-finger sarnies, bacon butties with HP sauce and pan-fried pork chops. It's actually way more sophisticated than it sounds, with a Scandi-chic sensibility to the decor and accomplished London-born chef Laura Greenfield at the helm.

WBC FUSION $$

(☏04-499 9379; www.wbcrestaurant.co.nz; Level 1, 107 Victoria St; small plates $14-18, large $25-28; ⊗10.30am-late Tue-Sat) At the Wholesale Boot Company (wonder why they use the acronym?), flavours from Thailand, China and Japan punctuate a menu filled with the best of NZ produce, including freshly shucked oysters and clams (served raw, steamed or tempura-battered) and game meats (tahr tacos, *kung pow* venison). Everything is packed with flavour and designed to be shared.

Prefab CAFE $$

(☏04-385 2263; www.pre-fab.co.nz; 14 Jessie St; mains $11-26; ⊗7am-4pm Mon-Sat; 🐾) A big industrial-minimalist space houses the city's slickest espresso bar and roastery, owned by long-time Wellington caffeine fiends. Beautiful house-baked bread features on a menu of flavourful, well-executed offerings. Dogs doze on the sunny terrace while the staff efficiently handle the bustle inside.

Nikau Cafe CAFE $$

(☏04-801 4168; www.nikaucafe.co.nz; City Gallery, Civic Sq; mains $15-27; ⊗7am-4pm Mon-Sat) 🌿 An airy affair at the sophisticated end of Wellington's cafe spectrum, Nikau consistently dishes up simple but sublime stuff (pan-fried halloumi, legendary kedgeree). Refreshing aperitifs, divine sweets, charming staff and a sunny courtyard complete the package. The organic, seasonal menu changes daily.

Capitol ITALIAN $$

(☏04-384 2855; www.capitolrestaurant.co.nz; 10 Kent Tce, Mt Victoria; mains brunch $10-27, lunch $18-27, dinner $28-38; ⊗noon-3pm & 5.30-9.30pm Mon-Fri, 9.30am-3pm & 5.30-9.30pm Sat & Sun) This consistent culinary star serves simple, seasonal fare using premium local ingredients, with a nod to classic Italian cuisine (try the homemade *tagliolini* or the

parmesan-crusted lamb's liver). The dining room is a bit cramped and noisy, but elegant nonetheless.

Fidel's CAFE $$

(☏04-801 6868; www.fidelscafe.com; 234 Cuba St; mains brunch $9-22, dinner $13-26; ⊗8am-10pm; 🌿) A Cuba St institution for caffeine-craving alternative types, Fidel's cranks out eggs any which way, pizza and super salads from its itsy kitchen, along with Welly's best milkshakes. Revolutionary memorabilia adorns the walls of the low-lit interior, and there's a small outdoor area and a street-facing booth for takeaway coffees. The ever-busy crew copes with the chaos admirably.

Aro Cafe CAFE $$

(☏04-384 4970; www.arocoffee.co.nz; 90 Aro St, Aro Valley; mains brunch $9-23, dinner $23-28; ⊗7.30am-4pm Mon & Tue, 7.30am-4pm & 5.30-10pm Wed-Fri, 9am-4pm & 5.30-10pm Sat, 9am-5pm Sun) If this stretch of Aro St – and this long-running licensed cafe in particular – were any more photogenic it'd be a crime. Order from the cabinet or take a seat and someone will bring you a menu. The coffee's great too. In the evening it transitions into a neighbourhood bistro.

Mt Vic Chippery FISH & CHIPS $$

(☏04-382 8713; www.thechippery.co.nz; 5 Majoribanks St, Mt Victoria; meals $12-20; ⊗noon-8.30pm; 🌿) At this backwater fish shack it's fish and chips by numbers: 1. Choose your fish (from at least three varieties). 2. Choose your coating (beer batter, panko crumb, tempura...). 3. Choose your chips (five varieties!). 4. Add aioli, coleslaw, salad or sauce, and a quality soft drink. 5. Chow down inside or take away. There are burgers and battered sausages too.

Caffe L'affare CAFE $$

(☏04-385 9748; www.laffare.co.nz; 27 College St; mains $15-20; ⊗8am-4pm; 🌿) One of Wellington's pioneering coffee-roasting cafes (since 1990), L'affare is still doing things well. Its mod-industrial lines and backstreet vibes feel as fresh as ever. Aside from predictably good bean-brews, expect cooked breakfasts, soups, burgers, short ribs, steaks and salads. Look for the patriotic row of NZ flags and the sunny scatter of tables out the front.

Tatsushi JAPANESE $$

(☏04-472 3928; www.facebook.com/tatsushi392; 99 Victoria St; mains $9-19, set menus $29-34; ⊗11.30am-2.30pm Mon-Sat & 6-10pm Tue-Sat) This compact space is reassuringly dominated by an open kitchen from which authentic Japanese dishes such as super-fresh sashimi, homemade *kumiage* tofu, *chazuke* soup, squid *sunomono* (dressed salad) and moreish *karaage* chicken emerge. They also sell sushi and bento boxes to go.

Sweet Mother's Kitchen   AMERICAN $$
(☑04-385 4444; www.sweetmotherskitchen.co.nz; 5 Courtenay Pl; mains $11-27; ☺8am-10pm; ☑) Perpetually brimming with cool cats, Sweet Mother's serves dubious but darn tasty takes on the Deep South, such as burritos, nachos, pulled-pork po'boys, jambalaya, fried chicken and Key lime pie. It's cheap and cute, with craft beer and good sun.

Great India   INDIAN $$
(☑04-384 5755; www.greatindia.co.nz; 141 Manners St; mains $17-29; ☺noon-2pm & 5-9pm; ☑) This is not your average curry joint. While a tad more expensive than its competitors, Great India consistently earns its moniker with its distinctly flavoured offerings. The super-spicy chicken vindaloo will straighten your curls.

Ombra   VENETIAN $$
(☑04-385 3229; www.ombra.co.nz; 199 Cuba St; dishes $6-19; ☺10am-11pm; ☑) This stylish *bacaro* (taverna) dishes up mouth-watering *cicheti* (Venetian tapas) in warm, uptempo surrounds. Assess the on-trend distressed interior while sipping an aperitif, then share tasty morsels like *fritto miso* (fried fish), meatballs, *pizzette* (mini-pizza) and gnocchi. Round things off with a sumptuous tiramisu or honey-and-spiced-fig *panna cotta*.

Regal   CHINESE $$
(☑04-3846656;www.facebook.com/regal.restaurant; Level 1, 7 Courtenay Pl; mains $16-31; ☺11am-2.30pm & 5.30-10.30pm; ☑) Regal is the pick of the Chinese restaurants clustered around Courtenay Pl, packing in the punters for late-night plates and weekend yum cha. Speed, volume, quality and brassy interior design – just what you want from a Chinese restaurant – plus excellence in the departments of steamed prawn dumplings, barbecue pork buns and spicy Szechuan tofu. Booking advised.

Scopa   ITALIAN $$
(☑04-384 6020; www.scopa.co.nz; cnr Cuba & Ghuznee Sts; pizza $15-25, mains $20-31; ☺8am-late; ☑) Authentic pizza, pasta and gnocchi make dining at this modern *cucina* a pleasure. The *bianche* (white) pizzas change things up a bit, as does the *pizzaiolo* – pizza of the week. Monday night meatballs; weekday lunchtime pasta specials ($12); Peroni on tap.

Aunty Mena's   VEGETARIAN $$
(☑04-382 8288; 167 Cuba St; meals $12-19; ☺noon-9pm Mon-Sat; ☑) This cheery noodle house

cranks out tasty vegie and vegan Malaysian and Chinese dishes (including kick-ass dumplings) in easy-clean, overlit surrounds.

★**Whitebait**   SEAFOOD $$$
(☑04-385 8555; www.white-bait.nz; 1 Clyde Quay Wharf; mains $38; ☺5.30pm-late year-round, plus noon-3pm Wed-Fri Nov-Mar) Neutral colours and gauzy screens set an upmarket tone for this top-rated seafood restaurant. All the fish is sustainably sourced and deftly prepared, with a scattering of quality non-fishy options rounding out the contemporary menu. Early diners (seatings before 6.30pm) can take advantage of a good-value set 'bistro' menu ($55 for an oyster, entree, main and petit four).

★**Logan Brown**   CONTEMPORARY $$$
(☑04-801 5114; www.loganbrown.co.nz; 192 Cuba St; mains $39-45; ☺noon-2pm Wed-Sat & 5pm-late Tue-Sun; ☎) ✒ Deservedly ranked among Wellington's best restaurants, Logan Brown oozes class without being overly formal. Its 1920s banking-chamber dining room is a neoclassical stunner – a fitting complement to the produce-driven modern NZ cuisine. The three-course bistro menu ($45) won't hurt your wallet too badly (but the epic wine list might force a blow-out). There's also a great-value $25 main-plus-wine lunch deal.

Charley Noble   MEDITERRANEAN $$$
(☑04-282 0205; www.charleynoble.co.nz; 1 Post Office Sq; mains $26-52; ☺7am-late Mon-Fri, 5pm-late Sat & Sun) Bustling to the point of mild chaos once the after-work crowd descends, this cavernous establishment occupies the gloriously renovated Huddart Parker building. Solo diners should opt for a seat by the large open kitchen for a first-row view of the culinary action. Highlights include shucked-to-order oysters and wood-fired meats.

Ortega Fish Shack   SEAFOOD $$$
(☑04-382 9559; www.ortega.co.nz; 16 Majoribanks St, Mt Victoria; mains $34-39; ☺5.30pm-late Tue-Sat) Mounted trout, salty portraits, marine-blue walls and Egyptian floor tiles cast a Mediterranean spell over Ortega – a magical spot for a seafood dinner. Fish comes many ways (including as zingy sashimi), while desserts continue the Mediterranean vibes with Catalan orange crêpes and one of Welly's best cheeseboards.

☙ Drinking & Nightlife

Wellingtonians love a late night. The inner city is riddled with bars, with high concentrations around raucous Courtenay Pl, bohemian Cuba St and along the waterfront.

A creative live-music scene keeps things thrumming, along with great NZ wines and even better craft beer. See www.craft beercapital.com for beery propaganda. For gig listings see www.undertheradar.co.nz and www.eventfinder.co.nz.

★**Dirty Little Secret**   ROOFTOP BAR
(📞021 0824 0298; www.dirtylittlesecret.co.nz; Level 8, 7-8 Dixon St; ⊗4pm-late Mon-Thu, noon-late Fri-Sun; 📶) While it's not strictly a secret (it's packed to the gills on balmy evenings) this hip bar atop the historic Hope Gibbons Ltd building plays hard to get, with a nondescript entrance on Taranaki St next to Jack Hackett's Irish Pub. Expect craft beer, slugged-together cocktails, loud indie music and plastic awnings straining to keep the elements at bay.

★**Golding's Free Dive**   CRAFT BEER
(📞04-381 3616; www.goldingsfreedive.co.nz; 14 Leeds St; ⊗noon-11pm; 📶) Hidden down a busy little back alley near Cuba St, gloriously garish Golding's is a bijoux craft-beer bar with far too many merits to mention. We'll single out ex-casino swivel chairs, a nice wine list, a ravishing Reuben sandwich, and pizza from Pomodoro (📞04-3812929; www.pizzapomodoro.co.nz; 13 Leeds St; pizza $16-26; ⊗noon-2pm Wed-Fri & 5-9pm daily; 🍴) next door. Blues, Zappa and Bowie conspire across the airways.

★**Hawthorn Lounge**   COCKTAIL BAR
(📞04-890 3724; www.hawthornlounge.co.nz; Level 1, 82 Tory St; ⊗5pm-3am) This classy cocktail bar has a 1920s speakeasy feel, suited-up in waistcoats and wide-brimmed fedoras. Sip a whisky sour and play poker, or watch the behind-the-bar theatrics from the Hawthorn's mixologists, twisting and turning classics into modern-day masterpieces. Open 'til the wee small hours.

★**Library**   BAR
(📞04-382 8593; www.thelibrary.co.nz; Level 1, 53 Courtenay Pl; ⊗5pm-late) You'll find yourself in the right kind of bind at moody, bookish Library, with its velveteen booths, board games and swish cocktails. An excellent all-round drink selection is complemented by a highly shareable menu of sweet and savoury treats. There's live music on occasion.

Garage Project Taproom   CRAFT BEER
(📞04-802 5324; www.garageproject.co.nz; 91 Aro St, Aro Valley; ⊗3-10pm Tue-Thu, noon-10pm Fri-Sun) The actual microbrewery occupies a former petrol station just down the road (68 Aro St) where they serve craft beer by the litre, petrol-pump style. If you'd rather consume your brew on premises in less industrial quantities, head to this narrow graffiti-lined

bar. Order a tasting flight or chance your arm on the Pernicious Weed or Venusian Pale Ale.

Motel   COCKTAIL BAR
(📞04-384 9084; www.motelbar.co.nz; Forresters Lane; ⊗5pm-late Mon-Sat) The back-lane location, retro neon sign and unpromising staircase generate a suitably seedy NYC-in-the-'70s first impression but inside is a louche, low-lit tiki bar, where the barstaff shake up fruity cocktails before a backdrop of giant clams, Polynesian-style statues and pineapple lights. Campy, fun and a great place for a sneaky rendezvous.

Fortune Favours   CRAFT BEER
(📞04-595 4092; www.fortunefavours.beer; 7 Leeds St; ⊗11am-11pm) The bold and the beautiful head to the rooftop of this old warehouse to sup on beer brewed in the shiny vats downstairs. Along with seven of their own concoctions, they serve guest brews, wine and cocktails.

S&M's   GAY
(📞04-802 5335; www.scottyandmals.co.nz; 176 Cuba St) Don't get excited, there's nothing fetishistic about Scotty and Mal's upmarket bar, unless your fetish happens to be dark wood, chandeliers and fabulous cocktails. It's a great place for a quiet drink; don't come expecting a crowd.

Counterculture   BAR
(📞04-891 2345; www.counterculture.co.nz; 211 Victoria St; unlimited games $5; ⊗noon-10pm Mon-Fri, 10am-10pm Sat & Sun; 📶🍴) Who doesn't secretly love a board game? Assume an ironic stance if you must, but here's the chance to embrace your inner games nerd in public. There are almost 400 games to choose from, staff to advise on rules, and craft beers and cocktails to take the edge off your ugly competitive streak.

Fork & Brewer   CRAFT BEER
(📞04-472 0033; www.forkandbrewer.co.nz; 20a Bond St; ⊗11.30am-late Mon-Sat) Aiming to improve on the 'kebab at 2am' experience, F&B offers excellent burgers, pizzas, pies, share plates and meaty mains to go along with its crafty brews (of which there are dozens – the Low Blow IPA comes highly recommended). Oh, and dark-beer doughnuts for dessert!

Laundry   BAR
(📞04-384 4280; www.laundry.net.nz; 240 Cuba St; ⊗4pm-2am) Tumble into this lurid-green, junk-shop juke joint any time of the day or night for a tipple and a plate of jerk chicken. Regular live music and DJs offset Southern-style bar food and carnival-esque decor

pasted up with a very rough brush. There's also a backyard complete with a caravan.

Little Beer Quarter
CRAFT BEER

(☑ 04-803 3304; www.littlebeerquarter.co.nz; 6 Edward St; ⊘ 3.30pm-late Sun & Mon, noon-late Tue-Sat) Buried in a back lane, lovely LBQ is warm, inviting and moodily lit in all the right places. Well-curated taps and a broad selection of bottled beer pack a hoppy punch. There are good cocktails, wines, and whiskies, too, plus zesty bar food. Call in for a $20 pizza and pint on Monday nights.

Rogue & Vagabond
CRAFT BEER

(☑ 04-381 2321; www.rogueandvagabond.co.nz; 18 Garrett St; ⊘ 11am-late) Fronting onto a precious pocket park, the Rogue is a lovably scruffy, colourful, kaleidoscopic craft-beer bar with heaps going on – via 18 taps including two hand-pulls. Voluminous, chewy-crust pizza, burgers, po' boys, alcoholic milkshakes and regular, rockin' gigs add further appeal. Swill around on the patio or slouch on the lawn.

Havana
BAR

(☑ 04-384 7039; www.havanabar.co.nz; 32a-34 Wigan St; mains $25-28; ⊘ 11.30am-late) Go out of your way to find Havana, a mighty fine needle in Welly's hospitality haystack, hidden down a side street in two weathered old cottages sharing a groovy backyard. Fortify yourself with tapas and top-shelf booze, then have a chinwag, smoke a cigar, carouse or all of the above. Dinner is a treat.

Hashigo Zake
CRAFT BEER

(☑ 04-384 7300; www.hashigozake.co.nz; 25 Taranaki St; ⊘ noon-late; 🛜) This bricky bunker is the HQ for a zealous beer-import business, splicing big-flavoured international brews into a smartly selected NZ range. Hop-heads stand elbow to elbow around the bar, ogling the oft-changing taps and brimming fridges, and squeeze into the sweet little side-lounge on live-music nights.

Southern Cross
PUB

(☑ 04-384 9085; www.thecross.co.nz; 39 Abel Smith St; ⊘ 8am-late; 🖶) Welcoming to all – from frenetic five-year-olds to knitting nanas – the democratic Cross rambles through a series of colourful rooms, combining a lively bar, a dance floor, a pool table and the best garden bar in town. There's good beer on tap, food for all budgets and regular events (gigs, quiz nights, karaoke, coffee groups).

Matterhorn
BAR

(☑ 04-384 3359; www.matterhorn.co.nz; 106b Cuba St; ⊘ 3pm-late Mon-Fri, 10am-late Sat & Sun)

Founded in 1963 as a Swiss cafe, the 'Horn peaks with its reputable food (tapas and dinner), snappy service and regular live music. The sultry, designerly interior still holds up, the wine list is as long as your leg, and it's still the best place for a drink on Cuba Mall.

Ivy
GAY & LESBIAN

(☑ 04-282 1580; www.ivybar.co.nz; 63 Cuba St; ⊘ 7pm-late Tue-Sat) Descend the stairs to the clubbiest of Wellington's queer venues. It attracts a fun young crowd including plenty of mic-hogging young lesbians on karaoke nights.

☆ Entertainment

Wellington has a lively theatre scene and is the home of large national companies such as the Royal NZ Ballet and the NZ Symphony Orchestra. Most shows can be booked via **Ticketek** (www.ticketek.co.nz), **Ticketmaster** (www.ticketmaster.co.nz) and **TicketDirect** (www.ticketdirect.co.nz). Discounted same-day tickets for productions are sometimes available at the i-SITE (p390).

Movie times are listed in the daily *Dominion Post* and at www.flicks.co.nz. There are some excellent indie cinemas here, plus the usual mainstream megaplexes.

★ Embassy Theatre
CINEMA

(☑ 04-384 7657; www.embassytheatre.co.nz; 10 Kent Tce; ⊘ 10am-late) Wellywood's cinema mother ship is an art-deco darling, built in the 1920s. Today she screens mainly mainstream films with state-of-the-art sound and vision. Be sure to check out the glamorous Black Sparrow cocktail bar at the rear.

Light House Cinema
CINEMA

(☑ 04-385 3337; www.lighthousecinema.co.nz; 29 Wigan St; adult/child $18/13; ⊘ 10am-late; 🛜) Tucked away near the top end of Cuba St, this small, stylish cinema throws a range of mainstream, art-house and foreign films up onto the screens in three small theatres. High-quality snacks. Tuesday tickets $11.50.

San Fran
LIVE MUSIC

(☑ 04-801 6797; www.sanfran.co.nz; 171 Cuba St; ⊘ 3pm-late Tue-Sat) This much-loved, mid-size music venue is moving to a new beat; it has boarded the craft-beer bandwagon and rocks out smoky, meaty food along the way. Gigs still rule, dancing is de rigueur, and the balcony gets good afternoon sun.

Michael Fowler Centre
CONCERT VENUE

(☑ 04-801 4231; www.venueswellington.com; 111 Wakefield St) The city's major concert hall stages regular performances by the **NZ Sympho-**

ny Orchestra (www.nzso.co.nz), **Orchestra Wellington** (www.orchestrawellington.co.nz) and assorted pop stars and contemporary musicians. The i-SITE (p390), near the entrance, acts as an outlet for Ticketek and Ticketmaster.

St James Theatre THEATRE
(☑ 04-801 4231; www.venueswellington.com; 77 Courtenay Pl) This grand old heritage theatre hosts big-ticket productions such as the **Royal NZ Ballet** (www.rnzb.org.nz) and **NZ Opera** (www.nzopera.com), plus the odd rocker and comedian.

Circa Theatre THEATRE
(☑ 04-801 7992; www.circa.co.nz; 1 Taranaki St) This attractive waterfront theatre has two auditoriums in which it shows everything from edgy new works to Christmas panto.

Meow LIVE MUSIC
(☑ 04-385 8883; www.welovemeow.co.nz; 9 Edward St; ⊙4pm-late Tue-Fri, 6pm-late Sat) Truly the cat's pyjamas, Meow goes out on a limb to host a diverse range of gigs and performances: country, ragtime, DJs, acoustic rock, jazz, poetry... At the same time the kitchen plates up good-quality, inexpensive food at any tick of the clock. Mishmashed retro decor; cool craft beers.

BATS THEATRE
(☑ 04-802 4175; www.bats.co.nz; 1 Kent Tce) Wildly alternative but accessible BATS presents cutting-edge and experimental NZ theatre – varied, cheap and intimate – in its revamped theatre.

🛍 Shopping

Wellington supports a host of independent shops including scores of design stores and clothing boutiques. Despite cheap imports and online shopping, there's still plenty that's Kiwi-made here. Retailers fly their home-grown flags with pride.

★**Unity Books** BOOKS
(☑ 04-499 4245; www.unitybooks.co.nz; 57 Willis St; ⊙9am-6pm Mon-Sat, 11am-5pm Sun) Sets the standard for every bookshop in the land, with dedicated NZ tables piled high.

Underground Market MARKET
(www.undergroundmarket.co.nz; under Frank Kitts Park, Jervois Quay; ⊙10am-4pm Sat) On Saturday mornings (and the occasional Sunday) the car park under Frank Kitts Park is filled with stalls selling interesting craft, artsy gifts, clothes by up-and-coming designers, and nibbles – plus the inevitable dreamcatchers and tie-dye that's de rigueur in such settings.

Bello GIFTS & SOUVENIRS
(☑ 04-385 0058; www.bello.co.nz; 140 Willis St; ⊙10am-6pm Mon-Fri, to 4pm Sat & Sun) A sweet little boutique full of gorgeous things – not the least of which are the charming staff, who will point you in the direction of designer glassware, refined fragrances, floaty scarves and luxurious homewares.

Slow Boat Records MUSIC
(☑ 04-385 1330; www.slowboatrecords.co.nz; 183 Cuba St; ⊙9.30am-5.30pm Sat-Thu, to 7.30pm Fri) Country, folk, pop, indie, metal, blues, soul, rock, Hawaiian nose-flute music – it's all here at Slow Boat, Wellington's long-running music shop and Cuba St mainstay.

Moore Wilson's FOOD & DRINKS
(☑ 04-384 9906; www.moorewilsons.co.nz; 93 Tory St; ⊙7.30am-7pm) A call-out to self-caterers: this positively swoon-inducing grocer is one of NZ's most committed supporters of independently produced and artisanal produce. If you want to chew on the best of Wellington and NZ, here's your chance. Head upstairs for dry goods, wine, beer and kitchenware.

Mandatory CLOTHING
(☑ 04-384 6107; www.mandatory.co.nz; 108 Cuba St; ⊙10am-6pm Mon-Fri, to 4.30pm Sat, noon-4pm

WELCOME TO WELLYWOOD

In recent years Wellington has stamped its name firmly on the world map as the home of New Zealand's dynamic film industry, earning itself the nickname 'Wellywood'. Acclaimed director Sir Peter Jackson still calls Wellington home; the success of his *The Lord of the Rings* films and subsequent productions such as *King Kong, The Adventures of Tintin* and *The Hobbit* have made him a powerful Hollywood player, and have bolstered Wellington's reputation.

Canadian director James Cameron is also in on the action; shooting has commenced for his four *Avatar* sequels, the first of which is due for a 2020 release. Cameron and his family are NZ residents, with landholding in rural Wairarapa. They have that in common with Jackson, who also has a property there.

Movie buffs can experience some local movie magic by visiting the Weta Cave (p369) or one of many film locations around the region – a speciality of local guided-tour companies.

WELLINGTON REGION WELLINGTON

Sun) Fancy duds for dudes: great service and sharp tailoring for the capital's cool cats.

Harbourside Market
MARKET
(☑ 04-495 7895; www.harboursidemarket.co.nz; cnr Cable & Barnett Sts; ☺ 7.30am-1pm Sun) Around 25,000 locals visit this market every Sunday. Why? Well, it's in a scenic spot next to Te Papa, and you can find everything here from a jar of raspberry jam to an heirloom carrot to a cinnamon roll. There's lots of cooked meals for lunch, too.

Old Bank
SHOPPING CENTRE
(☑ 04-922 0600; www.oldbank.co.nz; 233-237 Lambton Quay; ☺ 9am-6pm Mon-Fri, 11am-3pm Sat & Sun) This dear old building on a wedge-shaped city site is home to an arcade of indulgent, high-end shops, predominantly jewellers and boutiques. Check out the fab tiled floors and Corinthian columns.

Kura
ART
(☑ 04-802 4934; www.kuragallery.co.nz; 19 Allen St; ☺ 10am-6pm Mon-Fri, 11am-4pm Sat & Sun) Contemporary Māori and NZ art: painting, ceramics, jewellery and sculpture. A gorgeous gallery – come for a look even if you're not buying.

Wellington Night Market
MARKET
(☑ 022 074 2550; www.wellingtonnightmarket. co.nz; Left Bank, Cuba Mall; ☺ 5-11pm Fri & Sat) Nocturnal fun and games on Cuba St, with international foods aplenty and more buskers and performers than you have eyes and ears. On Saturdays it moves a block down the road to the corner of Manners St.

Hunters & Collectors
CLOTHING
(☑ 04-384 8948; www.facebook.com/huntersand collectorswellington; 134 Cuba St; ☺ 10.30am-6pm) Beyond the best-dressed window in NZ you'll find off-the-rack and vintage clothing (punk, skate, Western and mod), plus shoes and accessories.

Vault
GIFTS & SOUVENIRS
(☑ 04-471 1404; www.thevaultnz.com; 2 Plimmer Steps; ☺ 9.30am-5.30pm Mon-Thu, 9.30am-7pm Fri, 11am-4.30pm Sat & Sun) Exquisite jewellery, clothing, bags, ceramics, cosmetics – a lovely shop with lots of beautiful NZ-made things.

David Jones
DEPARTMENT STORE
(☑ 04-912 0700; www.davidjones.com.au; 165-177 Lambton Quay; ☺ 9am-6pm Sat-Thu, to 8pm Fri) Established in 1863 this was Kirkcaldie & Stains, New Zealand's answer to Harrods, until 2016. Now it's an outpost of the popular Australian brand. Bring your travel documents with you for tax-free shopping.

ℹ️ Information

EMERGENCY & IMPORTANT NUMBERS

Ambulance, fire service & police	☑ 111
Lifeline Aotearoa	☑ 0800 543 354
Sexual Abuse Help Foundation	☑ 04-801 6655
Wellington Central Police Station	☑ 04-381 2000

INTERNET ACCESS
Free wi-fi is available throughout most of Wellington's Central Business District (CBD; www. cbdfree.co.nz).

MEDICAL SERVICES
Wellington Accident & Urgent Medical Centre (☑ 04-384 4944; www.wamc.co.nz; 17 Adelaide Rd, Mt Cook; ☺ 8am-11pm) No appointment necessary; also home to an after-hours pharmacy.

Wellington Regional Hospital (☑ 04-385 5999; www.ccdhb.org.nz; Riddiford St, Newtown; ☺ 24hr) Has a 24-hour emergency department; 1km south of the city centre.

UFS Pharmacy (☑ 04-384 9499; www.ufs. co.nz; 45 Courtenay Pl; ☺ 8am-6pm Mon-Fri, 10am-2pm Sat) Handy city-centre pharmacy.

POST
Post Office (☑ 0800 081 190; www.nzpost. co.nz; 2 Manners St; ☺ 9am-5.30pm Mon-Fri, to 3pm Sat; 🖥️)

TOURIST INFORMATION
DOC Wellington Visitor Centre (☑ 04-384 7770; www.doc.govt.nz; 18 Manners St; ☺ 9.30am-5pm Mon-Fri, 10am-3.30pm Sat) Maps, bookings, passes and information for local and national walks (including Great Walks), parks, huts and camping.

Wellington i-SITE (☑ 04-802 4860; www. wellingtonnz.com; 111 Wakefield St; ☺ 8.30am-5pm; 🖥️) After an earthquake chased it out of its regular digs, the i-SITE has taken over the Michael Fowler Centre's old booking office. It looks like it will be here for the foreseeable future, but check its website for the latest. Staff book almost everything here, and cheerfully distribute Wellington's *Official Visitor Guide*, along with other maps and helpful pamphlets.

ℹ️ Getting There & Away

AIR
Wellington is an international gateway to NZ.
Wellington Airport (WLG; ☑ 04-385 5100; www.wellingtonairport.co.nz; Stewart Duff Dr, Rongotai) has the usual slew of airport accoutrements: info kiosks, currency exchange, ATMs, car-rental desks, shops, espresso... If you're in transit or have an early flight, note that you can't linger overnight inside the terminal.

Domestic services include:

Air New Zealand (⌨ 0800 737 000; www. airnewzealand.co.nz) Flies to/from Auckland, Hamilton, Tauranga, Rotorua, Gisborne, Napier, New Plymouth, Palmerston North, Kapiti Coast, Nelson, Blenheim, Christchurch, Timaru, Queenstown, Dunedin and Invercargill.

Golden Bay Air (www.goldenbayair.co.nz) Takaka

Jetstar (www.jetstar.com) Auckland, Nelson, Christchurch and Dunedin.

Sounds Air (⌨ 0800 505 005; www.sounds air.com) Taupo, Blenheim, Picton, Nelson and Westport.

BOAT

On a clear day, sailing into Wellington Harbour or into Picton in the Marlborough Sounds is magical. Cook Strait can cut up rough, but the big ferries handle it well, and offer the distractions of sport lounges, cafes, bars, information desks and cinemas.

Car-hire companies allow you to pick up and drop off vehicles at ferry terminals. If you arrive outside business hours, arrangements can be made to collect your vehicle from the terminal car park.

There are two ferry options:

Bluebridge Ferries (⌨ 04-471 6188; www. bluebridge.co.nz; 50 Waterloo Quay; adult/ child/car/campervan/motorbike from $53/27/120/155/51; ☎) Up to four sailings between Wellington and Picton daily (3½ hours).

Interislander (⌨ 04-498 3302; www.inter islander.co.nz; Aotea Quay; adult/child/car/ campervan/motorbike from $56/28/149/ 181/84) Up to five sailings between Wellington and Picton daily; crossings take 3¼ to 3½ hours. A free shuttle bus heads from platform 9 at Wellington Railway Station to Aotea Quay, 50 minutes before every daytime sailing and returns 20 minutes after every arrival.

BUS

Wellington is a major terminus for North Island bus serves.

InterCity (⌨ 04-385 0520; www.intercity. co.nz) coaches depart from platform 9 at Wellington Railway Station. Destinations include Auckland (from $28, 11¼ hours, three daily), Rotorua (from $26, 7½ hours, three daily), Taupo (from $26, six, hours, four daily), Napier (from $19, 5¼ hours, two daily) and Palmerston North (from $15, 2¼ hours, six daily).

Mana Bus (⌨ 09-367 9140; www.manabus.com) departs from Bunny St, opposite the railway station. It has two daily services to Auckland (from $25, 11½ hours), Hamilton (from $30, nine hours), Rotorua (from $25, 7¼ hours), Taupo (from $23, 6¼ hours) and Palmerston North (from $15, two hours), one of which is an overnight sleeper service where you can pay extra for a bed.

TRAIN

Metlink (⌨ 0800 801 700; www.metlink.org. nz) commuter trains head as far as Paekakariki ($10.50, 46 minutes, every 30 minutes), Paraparaumu ($12, 55 minutes, every 30 minutes), Waikanae ($13, one hour, every 30 minutes) and Masterton ($18, 1¾ hours, six on weekdays, two on weekends).

Three days a week the **Northern Explorer** (www.greatjourneysofnz.co.nz) heads to/ from Palmerston North (from $59, two hours), Ohakune (from $79, five hours), National Park Village (from $79, 5¼ hours), Hamilton (from $139, 8½ hours) and Auckland (from $139, 11 hours).

The daily **Capital Connection** heads from Palmerston North ($35, two hours), Waikanae ($15, 55 minutes) and Paraparaumu ($10, 48 minutes) to Wellington on weekday mornings, returning in the evening.

ⓘ Getting Around

Metlink is the one-stop shop for Wellington's regional bus, train and harbour ferry networks; there's a handy journey planner on its website. You can pay by cash or use **Snapper** (www. snapper.co.nz), an integrated prepaid smartcard. The Snapper fares are cheaper ($1.66 for a one-zone trip as opposed to $2) but the card costs $10, so it's probably not worth purchasing for a short stay.

TO/FROM THE AIRPORT

Wellington Airport is 6km southeast of the city. **Wellington Combined Shuttles** (⌨ 04-387 8787; www.co-opshuttles.co.nz; 1/2/3 passengers $20/26/32) provides a door-to-door minibus service (15 minutes) between the city and airport. It's cheaper if two or more passengers are travelling to the same destination. Shuttles meet all arriving flights.

The **Airport Flyer** (⌨ 0800 801 700; www. airportflyer.co.nz; cash fare to city $9; ☎) bus runs between the airport, Wellington Railway Station and Lower Hutt every 20 minutes (every 10 minutes in peak hours) from around 7am to 9pm.

A taxi between the city centre and the airport takes around 15 minutes and costs about $30.

BICYCLE

If you're fit or keep to the flat, cycling is a viable option. If you'd like some extra help on the hills, consider an electric bike. They're available from Switched On Bikes (p374) and On Yer Bike (p375), while Ferg's Kayaks (p375) only hires the pedal-powered version.

BUS

Frequent and efficient **Metlink** buses cover the whole Wellington region, running between approximately 6am and 11.30pm. Major **bus terminals** (Lambton Quay) are near the Wellington

Railway Station, and on Courtenay Pl near the Cambridge Tce intersection. Pick up route maps and timetables from the **i-SITE** (p390) and convenience stores, or online.

Metlink also runs **After Midnight** buses, departing from two city stops (Courtenay Pl and Manners St) between midnight and 4.30am Saturday and Sunday, following a number of routes to the outer suburbs. There's a set $6.50 fare for most trips.

CAR & MOTORCYCLE

There are a lot of one-way streets in Wellington, and parking gets tight (and pricey) during the day. If you've got a car or a caravan, park on the outskirts and walk or take public transport into the city centre. Freedom camping is permitted for self-contained vehicles at Evans Bay marina, 3km southeast of the city centre.

Along with the major international rental companies, Wellington has various lower-cost operators including **Apex Car Rental** (☑04-385 2163; www. apexrentals.co.nz; 186 Victoria St; ☺8am-5pm), **Jucy Rentals** (☑0800 399 736; www.jucy.co.nz; 13 Jean Batten St, Rongotai; ☺8am-6pm) and **Omega Rental Cars** (☑04-472 8465; www. omegarentalcars.com; 77 Hutt Rd; ☺8am-5pm). Most agencies have offices both at the airport and in the city centre. If you plan on exploring both the North and South Islands, most companies suggest you leave your car in Wellington and pick up another one in Picton after crossing Cook Strait. This is a common (and more affordable) practice, and car-hire companies make it a painless exercise.

There are often cheap deals on car relocation from Wellington to Auckland, as most renters travel in the opposite direction. The catch is that you may have only 24 or 48 hours to make the journey.

TAXI

Packed taxi ranks can be found on Courtenay Pl, at the corner of Dixon and Victoria Sts, on Featherston St, and outside the railway station. Major operators include **Green Cabs** (☑0800 464 7336; www.greencabs.co.nz) and **Wellington Combined Taxis** (☑04-384 4444; www.taxis. co.nz). There are also plenty of Uber drivers in the city.

TRAIN

Metlink (p391) operates five train routes running through Wellington's suburbs to regional destinations. Trains run frequently from around 6am to 11pm, departing Wellington Railway Station. The lines are as follows:

Johnsonville via Ngaio and Khandallah

Kapiti via Porirua, Plimmerton, Paekakariki and Paraparaumu

Melling via Petone

Hutt Valley via Waterloo to Upper Hutt

Wairarapa via Featherston, Carterton and Masterton

Timetables are available from convenience stores, the train station, Wellington i-SITE (p390) and online. Fares are stage-based; there's a handy calculator on the Metlink site. A Day Rover ticket ($14) allows unlimited off-peak and weekend travel on all lines except Wairarapa.

KAPITI COAST

With long, driftwood- and pumice-strewn, crowd-free beaches, the Kapiti Coast acts as a summer playground and suburban extension for Wellingtonians. The region takes its name from Kapiti Island, a wildlife sanctuary 5km offshore from Paraparaumu.

The mountainous Tararua Forest Park forms a dramatic backdrop along the length of the coastline and has some accessible day walks and longer tramps.

The Kapiti Coast makes an easy day trip from Wellington, though if you're after a few restful days there's enough of interest to keep you entertained.

❶ Information

The Kapiti Coast's official visitor centre is the Paraparaumu i-SITE (p395), at the unappealing, sprawling Coastlands shopping area (www. coastlands.co.nz; banks, ATMs, post office, supermarkets...).

❶ Getting There & Away

Access to the the the Kapiti Coast is a snap: it's just a short drive away from Wellington, there are good bus and train connections to Auckland and Wellington, and there's an airport in Paraparaumu.

AIR

Kapiti Coast Airport (☑04-298 1013; www. kapiticoastairport.co.nz; 60 Toru Rd) is in central Paraparaumu. Sounds Air (p391) and **Air2There** (☑0800 777 000; www.air2there. com) fly to Blenheim and Nelson.

BUS

InterCity (p391) coaches stop at the major Kapiti Coast towns. Destinations include Wellington, Napier, New Plymouth, Taupo and Auckland.

Metlink (p391) runs local bus services around Paraparaumu and Waikanae – they're particularly handy for getting from the railway station to the beach.

CAR & MOTORCYCLE

Getting here from Wellington is a breeze by car: just follow SH1. After Paekakariki the Kapiti Expressway takes over; note, older satellite navigation devices might not include this route, which opened in 2017.

WORTH A TRIP

KAPITI ISLAND

Kapiti Island is the coastline's dominant feature, a 10km by 2km slice that has been a protected reserve since 1897. Predator-free since 1998 (22,500 possums were eradicated here in the 1980s), it's now home to a remarkable range of birds, including many species that are extinct on the mainland.

To visit the island, you must make your arrangements in advance with one of two licensed operators. Remember to reconfirm your arrangements on the morning of departure, as sailings are weather-dependent. All boats depart from Paraparaumu Beach, which can be reached by train.

Tours

The island is open to day walkers (there are some fab trails here), limited each day to 100 people at **Rangatira**, where you can hike up to the 521m high point, Tuteremoana; and 60 visitors at the **northern end**, which has short, gentle walks to viewpoints and around a lagoon.

Family-run **Kapiti Island Nature Tours** (☏ 021 126 7525; www.kapitiislandnaturetours.co.nz; departs Kapiti Boating Club, Marine Pde; transport only $80) ✔ run day tours ($180 including boat and lunch) to look at the island's birds (incredible in range and number), seal colony, history and Māori traditions. Overnight stays (from $384, including boat, meals and accommodation) include an after-dark walk in the bush to spot the rare little spotted kiwi. **Kapiti Explorer** (☏ 027 655 4739; www.kapitiexplorer.nz; departs Kapiti Boating Club, Marine Pde; adult/child return from $75/40; ☺ Sep-May) runs to and from Kapiti Island. Guided walks are $12 extra; fares include DOC landing permit.

Information

More information about Kapiti Island can be found in DOC's *Kapiti Island Nature Reserve* brochure (downloadable from www.doc.govt.nz), or in person at the DOC Wellington Visitor Centre (p390).

TRAIN

Metlink (p391) commuter trains between Wellington and the coast are more convenient and more frequent than buses. Services run from Wellington to Waikanae (generally half-hourly 5am to midnight), stopping in Paekakariki and Paraparaumu en route.

Three days a week the scenic Northern Explorer (p391) train stops in Paraparaumu, heading to Palmerston North (from $59, one hour), Ohakune (from $79, 3¾ hours), National Park (from $79, 4½ hours), Hamilton (from $119, 7¼ hours) and Auckland (from $119, 9¾ hours).

The Capital Connection (p391) heads from Palmerston North to Wellington on weekday mornings, returning in the evening; stops include Paraparaumu and Waikanae.

Paekakariki

☏ 04 / POP 1670

The first stop-worthy Kapiti Coast town you come to heading north from Wellington is cute little Paekakariki, 41km north of the capital. It's an arty seaside village stretched along a black-sand beach, serviced by a train station.

◉ Sights

★ **Queen Elizabeth Park**   PARK
(☏ 04-292 8625; www.gw.govt.nz/qep; MacKay's Crossing, SH1; ☺ 8am-dusk; 🚻) ✔ One of the last relatively unchanged areas of dune and wetland along the Kapiti Coast, this undulating 650-hectare beachside park offers swimming, walking, cycling and picnicking opportunities, as well as a **tram museum** (☏ 04-292 8361; www.wellingtontrams.org.nz; MacKay's Crossing; admission by donation; ☺ 11am-4pm Sat & Sun, daily Jan) and horse riding outfit. There are three entrances: off Wellington Rd in Paekakariki, at MacKay's Crossing on SH1, and off the Esplanade in Raumati to the north.

🏃 Activities

Stables on the Park   HORSE RIDING
(☏ 06-364 3336; www.stablesonthepark.co.nz; MacKay's Crossing, SH1; pony/horse rides from $25/60) Mandy and friends run guided rides on well-mannered horses. The 90-minute trek will have you trotting along the beach with views of Kapiti Island before heading inland on park tracks. Beginners are welcome. Call for bookings.

🛏 Sleeping & Eating

Paekakariki Holiday Park HOLIDAY PARK $
(📞04-292 8292; www.paekakarikiholidaypark.
co.nz; 180 Wellington Rd; sites from $18, unit
with/without bathroom from $95/70; @🛜) You
couldn't say that this large, leafy park is fully engaged with NZ's contemporary holiday
park zeitgeist, but it is well located, 1.5km
north of the township at the southern entrance to Queen Elizabeth Park (good for
tramping and biking). Tidy hedges demar-
cate tent and campervan sites, and there's
a range of cabins and tourist flats available.

Finn's HOTEL $$
(📞04-292 8081; www.finnshotel.co.nz; 2 Beach Rd; r
$145-165; 🛜) Finn's is a flashy beige suit in this
low-key railway village, but redeems itself with
spacious rooms, big bistro meals, a cafe area,
craft beer on tap and an in-house 26-seat cin-
ema. Double glazing keeps the highway at bay.

Beach Road Deli CAFE $
(📞04-902 9029; www.beach-road-deli.com; 5
Beach Rd; mains $11-17; ⏱7.30am-4pm Tue-Thu,
Sat & Sun, to 8.30pm Fri; 🍴) This bijou deli and
wood-fired pizzeria, stocked with cheese
and home-baked bread and pastries, is heav-
en-sent for the highway traveller or prospec-
tive picnicker. The coffee's good too.

Paraparaumu

📞04 / POP 25,600
Busy Paraparaumu is the Kapiti Coast's ma-
jor commercial and residential hot spot. It's
a tale of two towns: the main town on the
highway, with its deeply unappealing shop-
ping-mall sprawl; and Paraparaumu Beach,
with its waterside park and walkway, decent
swimming and winning view out to Kapiti

Island (island boat trips set sail from here).
If you're into craft beer or cars, you're in the
right town!

The correct pronunciation is 'Pah-ra-pah-
ra-*oo*-moo', meaning 'scraps from an oven',
which is said to have originated when a
Māori war party attacked the settlement and
found only scraps of food remaining. It's a
bit of a mouthful to pronounce; locals usual-
ly just corrupt it into 'Para-pa-ram'.

👁 Sights

Tuatara Brewery BREWERY
(📞04-296 1953; www.tuatarabrewing.co.nz; 7 Shef-
field St; ⏱3-7pm Wed & Thu, 11am-7pm Fri-Sun)
Visit the oldest and most famous of Welling-
ton's craft breweries at its industrial-estate
premises where you can slurp a pint or two
and chew some bar snacks (biersticks, na-
chos, pizza). Book in advance for an enlight-
ening Saturday afternoon tasting experience,
matching four beers with canapes ($35).

Our Lady of Lourdes statue STATUE
(access from 16 Taranaki St) Paraparaumu's odd-
est claim to fame is surely this 14m-high stat-
ue of the Madonna, looming over the town
from a 75m-high hill. It was commissioned by
the local Catholic priest in 1958 for the 100th
anniversary of the Lourdes apparitions. While
the statue itself is in good nick, it's reached
by a scrappy path through a dishevelled part
of town and the 14 *Stations of the Cross* that
line the route are in a sorry state of repair.

Southward Car Museum MUSEUM
(📞04-297 1221; www.southwardcarmuseum.co.nz;
Otaihanga Rd; adult/child $18/5; ⏱9am-4.30pm)
This huge hangar-like museum has one of
Australasia's largest collections of antique
and unusual cars. Check out the DeLorean,

MĀORI NZ: WELLINGTON REGION

Referred to in legends as the 'mouth of Maui's fish' and traditionally called Te Whanganui-
a-Tara, the Wellington area became known to Māori in the mid-19th century as 'Pōneke'
(a transliteration of Port Nick, short for Port Nicholas, its English name at the time).

The major *iwi* (tribes) of the region were Te Āti Awa and Ngāti Toa. Ngāti Toa was the *iwi*
of Te Rauparaha, who composed the now famous *Ka Mate haka*. Like most urban areas the
city is now home to Māori from many *iwi*, sometimes collectively known as Ngāti Pōneke.

New Zealand's national museum, Te Papa (p368), presents excellent displays on
Māori culture, traditional and modern, as well as a colourful *marae* (traditional meeting
place). In its gift shop you can see excellent carving and other crafts, as you can in both
Kura (p390) and **Ora** (📞04-384 4157; www.oragallery.co.nz; 23 Allen St; ⏱9am-6pm Mon-
Sat, 10am-4pm Sun) galleries nearby.

Te Wharewaka o Pōneke (p377), Kapiti Island Nature Tours (p393) and Kiwi Coastal
Tours (p375) offer intimate insights into the Māori culture of the rugged coast around
Wellington.

WELLINGTON REGION PARAPARAUMU

the German-built 1897 Lux and the 1950 gangster Cadillac complete with bullet holes. The museum is signposted from the expressway.

✕ Eating

Marine Parade Eatery CAFE $$
(☑ 04-892 0098; www.marineparadeeatery.com; 50 Marine Pde; mains breakfast $15-20, lunch $23-25, dinner $27-32; ⊙ 7.30am-4pm Sat-Thu, to 9pm Fri; 🖐) Affecting something of a Robinson Crusoe look, this fresh-as-a-daisy cafe offers a sophisticated international menu and terrific views of Kapiti Island out the front window. The seafood laksa (coconut noodle soup) is delicious and they also serve *chia*-seed porridge, bagels, pulled-lamb burgers, coconut-poached chicken and meze platters.

The Social PUB FOOD $$
(☑ 04-298 3955; www.mysocial.co.nz; 8 Kapiti Lights; mains $17-30; ⊙ 11am-late) Despite its insalubrious location in a car park near the mall, this breezy modern pub is a good place to drink, watch the rugby or catch a band. The food's surprisingly ambitious too, featuring the likes of jerk chicken burgers, chickpea-battered fish and chips, and harissa, pea and squid pasta.

ⓘ Information

Paraparaumu i-SITE (☑ 04-298 8195; www.kapiticoast.govt.nz; Coastlands Mall, Main Rd; ⊙ 9am-5pm) Kapiti Coast information, maps and brochures, including the *Kāpiti Walking & Cycling* pamphlet with the low-down on coastal trails and tracks.

Waikanae

☑ 04 / POP 10,600

Beachy Waikanae has long been a retiree stamping ground but in recent times it has transformed into a growing, go-ahead town, bolstered by first-home-buyer flight from unaffordable Wellington. It's a cheery seaside enclave, good for some salt-tinged R&R and natural-realm experiences.

⦿ Sights

Ngā Manu NATURE RESERVE
(☑ 04-293 4131; www.ngamanu.co.nz; 74 Ngā Manu Reserve Rd; adult/child/family $18/8/38; ⊙ 10am-5pm; 🖐) 🖊 Waikanae's main visitor lure, Ngā Manu Nature Reserve is a 15-hectare bird sanctuary dotted with picnic areas, bushwalks, aviaries and a nocturnal house with kiwi, owls and tuatara. The reserve's endangered long-fin eels are fed at 2pm daily; guided bird-feeding tours run at 11am daily (adult/child $25/10 including admission).

Hemi Matenga Memorial Park Scenic Reserve FOREST
(www.doc.govt.nz; off Tui Cres) FREE This 330-hectare reserve overlooking Waikanae contains a large remnant of native kohekohe forest. The reserve rises steeply from 150m to its highest point, Te Au (514m), a hike of three to four hours. The **Kohekohe Walk** is also here, an easy 30-minute amble on a well-formed path.

⌲ Tours

Waikanae Estuary Bird Tours BIRDWATCHING
(☑ 04-905 1001; www.kapitibirdtours.co.nz; 2hr tours $25) 🖊 The Waikanae Estuary is a hot spot for birds, with around 66 species visiting during the year. You can expect to see around 20 of them on these personalised outings with a passionate guide.

🛏 Sleeping & Eating

Kapiti Gateway Motel MOTEL $$
(☑ 04-902 5876; www.kapitigateway.co.nz; 114 Main Rd; unit from $125; 🖐≋🖐) This tidy and welcoming motel may look old-fashioned from the outside but the rooms have been updated and there's a solar-heated pool, free wi-fi and Sky TV. All rooms have at least a microwave and a kettle, and some have full kitchens.

Long Beach CAFE $$
(☑ 04-293 6760; www.longbeach.net.nz; 40 Tutere St; mains breakfast $13-24, lunch $17-25, dinner $16-33; ⊙ 9am-11pm; 🖐🖐🖐) Grab a seat in the large conservatory or the herb garden attached to this attractive, family-friendly cafe-bar. It's a sunny spot for an afternoon wine or craft beer, accompanied by live music on Sundays. The extensive menu includes cooked breakfasts, pizza, pub grub and bistro-style dishes.

THE WAIRARAPA

☑ 06

The Wairarapa is the large tract of land east and northeast of Wellington, beyond the Tararua and Rimutaka Ranges. It is named after Wairarapa Moana – otherwise known as Lake Wairarapa, translating as 'sea of glistening waters'. This shallow 80-sq-km lake and the surrounding wetland is the focus of much-needed ecological restoration, redressing generations of livestock grazing. Fields of fluffy sheep still abound, as do vineyards and the associated hospitality that have turned the region into a decadent weekend retreat.

In recent years this picturesque slice of New Zealand's rural heartland has gained an unlikely Hollywood connection, with block-buster movie directors Sir Peter Jackson and James Cameron both putting down roots here.

Activities

Rimutaka Cycle Trail   CYCLING
(www.nzcycletrail.com/trails/rimutaka-cycle-trail) The 115km, three-day Rimutaka Cycle Trail is one of the Nga Haerenga New Zealand Cycle Trail 'Great Rides'. The trail kicks off at the head of Wellington Harbour before scaling the Rimutaka Ranges, then spilling out around the western end of Palliser Bay.

Getting There & Away

From Wellington, Metlink (p391) commuter trains run to Masterton (six times daily on weekdays, twice daily on weekends), calling at seven Wairarapa stations including Featherston and Carterton (though notably not Greytown or Martinborough).

Tranzit Coachlines runs the InterCity (p391) service between Masterton and Palmerston North ($21, two hours) five days a week (no Monday or Saturday buses, but two on Fridays).

Getting Around

Metlink (p391) bus 200, operated by Tranzit Coachlines, heads from Masterton to Cartertown, Greytown and Featherston seven times on weekdays and three times on Saturdays. All of the Saturday buses continue on to Martinborough, but only one of the weekday services does. On weekdays a further five buses connect Martinborough to the train station at Featherston.

Beyond the main towns, you'll need your own vehicle; many of this area's notable sights are out on the coast and along rural roads. As is often the case, getting there is half the fun: the drive up over the ranges from Wellington is particularly scenic.

Martinborough

📞 06 / POP 1470
Laid out in the shape of a Union Jack with a leafy square at its centre, Martinborough (Wharekaka) is a photogenic town with some charming old buildings, surrounded by a patchwork of pasture and pinstripe grapevines. It is famed for its wineries, which draw in visitors to nose the pinot noir, pair it up with fine food and snooze it off at boutique accommodation.

With most of its cellar doors arranged around the perimeter of the town grid, Martinborough provides a uniquely accessible experience for oenophiles. It's quite possible to walk around the major wineries, but the classic Martinborough sight is of gaggles of merry pedal-powered punters getting ever more wobbly as the afternoon progresses.

Sights

Martinborough Brewery   BREWERY
(📞 06-306 6249; www.martinboroughbeer.com; 10 Ohio St; tasting paddle from $10, tour $5; ⏰ 11am-7pm Thu-Mon Mar-Nov, Thu-Tue Dec-Feb) It's hard to go anywhere in NZ these days and not find a craft brewery bubbling away in the corner. Martinborough is no exception. The brewery counters the town's prevailing wine vibe with its range of meaty brews (dark beers a speciality). Sip a tasting paddle or a pint on the sunny terrace out the front. Brewery tours by arrangement.

Activities

The most ecofriendly way to explore the Wairarapa's wineries is by bicycle, as the flat landscape makes for puff-free cruising. Rental bikes are comfortable cruisers with saddlebags for your booty. Suffice to say, you ought to pay greater attention to your technique, and to the road, as the day wears on.

Rental outfitters include **Green Jersey Explorer Tours** (📞 06-306 6027; www.greenjersey.co.nz; 16 Kitchener St; 6hr guided tours incl lunch $120, bike hire per day $40; 🚲), **Indi Bikes** (📞 027 306 6090; www.indibikesmartinborough.co.nz; 1-6 seater $35-190 per day; ⏰ 10am-5.30pm Fri-Sun), Martinborough Top 10 Holiday Park (p397) and Martinborough Wine Merchants (p398).

Tours

Zest Food & Wine Tours   FOOD & DRINK
(📞 04-801 9198; www.zestfoodtours.co.nz; per person incl lunch $595) Exclusive small-group tours (two to four guests) around Martinborough and Greytown, with the focus squarely on quality wine and food. Pricey, but worth it if you want a really personalised experience. The tour starts from the Featherston railway station and includes the train from Wellington.

Martinborough Wine Tours   WINE
(📞 06-306 8032; www.martinboroughwinetours.co.nz; per couple incl lunch $575) An upmarket 'Martinborough in a Day' tour for couples, with tastings at five wineries, a bit of history, an olive farm visit and a fine wine-matched lunch. Less fancy half-/full-day tours also available (per person $85).

Festivals & Events

Toast Martinborough   FOOD & DRINK
(📞 06-306 9183; www.toastmartinborough.co.nz; Memorial Sq; from $89; ⏰ Nov) A hugely popular wine, food and music event held on the third Sunday in November; book in advance.

WAIRARAPA WINE COUNTRY

Wairarapa's world-renowned wine industry was nearly crushed in infancy. The region's first vines were planted in 1883, but in 1908 the prohibition movement put a cap on that corker of an idea. It wasn't until the late 1970s that winemaking was revived, after Martinborough's terroir was discovered to be similar to that of Burgundy, France. A few vineyards sprang up, the number since ballooning to around 30 across the region. Martinborough is the undisputed hub of the action, but vineyards around Gladstone and Masterton are also on the up. Pinot noir is the region's most acclaimed variety, but sauvignon blanc also does well, as do aromatics and shiraz.

Wairarapa's wineries thrive on visitors: well-oiled cellar doors swing wide open for tastings. Most wineries charge a tasting fee (although many will waive it if you purchase a bottle); others are free. Some have a cafe or restaurant, while others will rustle up a picnic platter to be enjoyed in their gardens. Winter hours wind back to the minimum.

The *Wairarapa Visitor Guide* (available from local i-SITEs and many other locations) has maps to aid your navigations. Read all about it at www.winesfrommartinborough. com. A few of our favourites:

Ata Rangi (☑06-306 9570; www.atarangi.co.nz; 14 Puruatanga Rd; tastings $5, waived with purchase; ⊙1-3pm) One of the region's pioneering winemakers. Great drops across the board and a cute cellar door, also selling honey and olive oil.

Coney Wines (☑06-306 8345; www.coneywines.co.nz; 107 Dry River Rd; ⊙11am-4pm Fri-Sun Dec-Mar, Sat & Sun Oct, Nov & Apr-Jul) Fingers crossed that your tasting host will be the inimitable Tim Coney, an affable character who makes a mighty shiraz and may sing at random. It's also home to the excellent Trio Cafe; bookings recommended.

Haythornthwaite Wines (☑06-306 9889; www.ht3wines.co.nz; 45 Omarere Rd; tastings $5; ⊙11am-5pm) Sustainable, hands-on winery producing complex drops including cherry-like pinot noir and gorgeous gewürztraminer. If the weather's fine, the tasting will be served at the outdoor tables.

Martinborough Vineyard (☑06-306 9955; www.martinborough-vineyard.co.nz; 57 Princess St; tasting $5, waived with purchase; ⊙11am-4pm daily Oct-May, Fri-Tue Jun-Sep) The first vineyard to plant pinot noir in the region, this vineyard is a local legend with a sterling international reputation.

Poppies Martinborough (☑06-306 8473; www.poppiesmartinborough.co.nz; 91 Puruatanga Rd; ⊙11am-4pm Fri-Tue) Delectable handcrafted wines served by the label's passionate winemaking and viticulturalist duo. Savour their wines alongside a well-matched platter in the stylishly simple cellar.

🛌 Sleeping

Claremont MOTEL $$
(☑06-306 9162; www.theclaremont.co.nz; 38 Regent St; unit from $145; 🖥) A classy accommodation enclave 15 minutes' walk from town, the Claremont has two-storey, self-contained units in great nick, modern studios with spa baths, and sparkling two-bedroom apartments, all at reasonable rates (even cheaper in winter and/or midweek). It's surrounded by tidy gardens with barbecue areas, and they also offer bike hire.

Martinborough
Top 10 Holiday Park HOLIDAY PARK $$
(☑0800 780 909; www.martinboroughholidaypark. com; 10 Dublin St; sites from $42, unit with/without bathroom from $139/80; 🖥🛝) Just five minutes' walk from town, this appealing campsite has grapevine views, shady trees and the town pool over the back fence. Cabins are simple but great value, freeing up your dollars for the cellar door. Good-quality bikes, including tandems and child seats, are available for hire.

Old Manse B&B $$$
(☑06-306 8599; www.oldmanse.co.nz; 19 Grey St; r $230-255; 🖥) Oozing historic charm, this venerable villa has five en-suite rooms painted in bold colours. Two are larger than the others but they're all a decent size. Plus there's a cedar hot tub in the garden with views over the vines.

Peppers Parehua RESORT $$$
(☑06-306 8405; www.peppers.co.nz; New York St West; cottage from $272; 🖥🏊) Martinborough's ritziest accommodation comprises 28 free-standing cottages scattered around

398

WELLINGTON REGION GREYTOWN

an ornamental lake surrounded by vines. All have fully equipped kitchens and open fireplaces, and some have private cedar hot tubs. The complex also includes a tennis court and restaurant.

Aylstone Retreat BOUTIQUE HOTEL $$$
(06-306 9505; www.aylstone.co.nz; 19 Huangarua Rd; r $290;) Set among the vines on the edge of the village, this elegant retreat is a winning spot for the romantically inclined. Seven en-suite rooms exude flowery French-provincial charm and share a posh reading room. The whole shebang is surrounded by micro-mansion gardens sporting lawns, box hedges and chichi furniture.

Eating

Café Medici CAFE $$
(06-306 9965; www.cafemedici.co.nz; 9 Kitchener St; lunch mains $9-23, dinner $30-36; 8.30am-4pm daily & 6.30pm-late Fri & Sat) A perennial favourite among townsfolk and regular visitors, this airy cafe has a sunny courtyard and great coffee. Tasty, home-cooked food includes muffins, big brunch dishes such as Spanish eggs, delicious prawn linguine, and Med-flavoured dinner options such as Moroccan lamb tagine.

Village Cafe CAFE $$
(06-306 8814; www.facebook.com/thevillagecafemartinborough; 6 Kitchener St; mains $10-24; 8am-4pm) 'The heart of Martinborough' might be overstating things just a little but this busy, central cafe is undoubtedly popular, serving eggy breakfasts, big salads, a mean Reuben sandwich, and pizza. Lofty mess-hall vibes, mellow tunes and occasional live music.

Pinocchio BISTRO $$$
(06-306 6094; www.pinocchiomartinborough.co.nz; 3 Kitchener St; mains $36-38; 6pm-late Wed-Fri) Odd name aside, there's much to love about this upmarket but relaxed little restaurant. Expect modern, produce-led country dishes such as pulled lamb with peas, and their signature confit duck with duck-liver parfait and pumpkin.

Drinking & Nightlife

Micro Wine Bar WINE BAR
(06-306 9716; www.facebook.com/microwinebar; 14c Ohio St; 4pm-late Thu-Mon) Moreish little Micro packs a punch with its excellent wine list (mostly local with some far-flung stars), notable craft-beer selection and yummy nibbles. The tasting flights are a good way to sample the vineyards that got away ($20 for five whites, $25 for reds). Catch the sun

streetside or head to the courtyard. Vinyl spins on the vintage 1970s stereo.

Martinborough Hotel PUB
(06-306 9350; www.martinboroughhotel.co.nz; Memorial Sq; 2pm-late Mon-Fri, noon-late Sat & Sun) This handsome 1882 hotel is an elegant place to sip a quiet beer at the end of a hard day's wine tasting. Most of the space is given over to diners, though; grab a seat on the terrace on a sunny day. Upstairs there are attractive bedrooms.

Entertainment

Circus CINEMA
(06-306 9442; www.circus.net.nz; 34 Jellicoe St; adult/child $16/11; 3pm-late Wed-Mon) Lucky old Martinborough has its own stylish arthouse cinema. This modern, micro-sized complex has two comfy studio theatres and a cafe opening out on to a sunny, somewhat Zen garden. Reasonably priced food (mains $22 to $34) includes bar snacks, pizzas and mains with seasonal vegies. Take your wine into the cinema with you.

Shopping

Martinborough Wine Merchants WINE
(06-306 9040; www.martinboroughwinemerchants.com; 6 Kitchener St; 9.30am-6pm) Adjoining the Village Cafe, this large store is an excellent place to buy local wine and maybe taste some, too. They also sell olive oil and chocolate, and rent out bikes ($25/35 per half/full day) for cellar-door adventures.

Information

Martinborough i-SITE (06-306 5010; www.wairarapanz.com; 18 Kitchener St; 9am-5pm) Small, helpful and cheery, the local info centre stocks wine-region maps and plenty of local brochures.

Greytown

06 / POP 2200

The prettiest of several small towns along SH2, Greytown (Te Hupenui) is home to a permanent population of urbane locals and waves of Wellington weekenders. It was the country's first planned inland town: intact Victorian buildings line the main street with interesting historic plaques on many of them (pick up the *Historic Greytown* brochure for a handy map). Within the old buildings you'll find accommodation, cafes, restaurants and some swanky shopping.

In 1890 Greytown became the first town in NZ to celebrate Arbor Day, bequeathing

CAPE PALLISER

The Wairarapa coast is rugged, remote and sparsely populated. A trip to climb the 250 steps to the candy-striped 1897 **Cape Palliser Lighthouse** (Cape Palliser Rd) is a must-do if you can spare the time and have your own wheels. The drive to the Cape takes around 80 minutes from Martinborough, but depending on stops you could take half to a full day. There's no public transport.

From Martinborough, the road wends through picturesque farmland before hitting the coast. This section of the drive is impossibly scenic, hugging the coast between wild ocean on one side and sheer cliffs on the other. Look for shadows of the South Island, visible on a clear day. You'll pass the **Putangirua Pinnacles** (www.doc.govt.nz) FREE en route. Standing like giant organ pipes, these 'hoodoos' were formed by rain washing silt and sand away, exposing the underlying bedrock. It's an eerie landscape, perfectly suited for its starring role as the approach to the Paths of the Dead in *The Lord of the Rings: The Return of the King*. The car park is signposted off Cape Palliser Rd. From here it's an easy 1½-hour walk to the lookout, or take the 3½-hour loop track past hills and coastal viewpoints.

As you approach Cape Palliser (Matakitakiakupe) you'll reach the wind-worn fishing village of **Ngawi**. The first things you'll notice here are the rusty bulldozers on the beach, used to drag fishing boats ashore.

On the way there or back, take a short detour to the crusty waterside settlement of **Lake Ferry**, overlooking **Lake Onoke**. The lake empties directly to the sea through grey, shingled dunes, with big black-backed gulls circling overhead. The **Lake Ferry Hotel** (06-307 7831; www.lakeferryhotel.co.nz; 2 Lake Ferry Rd, Lake Ferry; noon-3pm & 5-9pm Mon-Fri, 11am-9pm Sat & Sun;) is an old-school pub with a beaut outdoor terrace upon which to sit, sip, and snack on some fish and chips. Basic accommodation is also available.

it a legacy of magnificent mature trees. The mountain ash in the grounds of St Luke's Anglican Church is the last survivor of three saplings that mysteriously sprouted after being stolen in 1856 from a delivery carted by hand, over the Rimutakas. Greytown's other historic claim to fame was as the site of a Māori Parliament that held two sessions at nearby Pāpāwai Marae in the 1890s.

⊙ Sights

Cobblestones Museum   MUSEUM
(06-304 9687; www.cobblestonesmuseum.org.nz; 169 Main St; adult/child $7/3; 10am-4pm daily Oct-May, Thu-Mon Jun-Sep;) Occupying the site of an old coach stop, complete with its original stables and well-worn cobbled courtyard, this endearing museum comprises an enclave of transplanted period buildings and donated old-time objects, dotted around pretty grounds just begging for a lie-down on a picnic blanket. There's a blacksmiths, a school, a fire station, a church, a wool shed... Wairarapa colonial history in tangible form.

Stonehenge Aotearoa   MONUMENT
(06-377 1600; www.stonehenge-aotearoa.co.nz; 51 Ahiaruhe Rd, Ahiaruhe; adult/child $10/5, tour $20/5; 10am-4pm daily Jan, Wed-Sun Feb-Apr & Sep-Dec, Sat & Sun May-Aug) About 10km east of Greytown in a farmer's backyard, this full-scale ad-aptation of England's Stonehenge is orientated for its southern hemisphere location on a grassy knoll overlooking the Wairarapa Plain. Its mission: to bring the night sky to life, even in daylight. The pre-tour talk and audiovisual presentation are excellent, and the henge itself a surreal (and delightfully eccentric) sight.

🛏 Sleeping

Greytown Campground   CAMPGROUND $
(06-304 9387; www.greytowncampground.co.nz; Kuratawhiti St; sites/cabins from $15/65;) This simple camping option is scenically spread through Soldiers Memorial Park, 650m from the main street. As well as shady sites, accommodation options include a gypsy caravan, a glamping tent and two handkerchief-sized cabins with bunk beds. Plus there are bush walks, tennis courts and a massive kids' playground nearby.

Oak Estate Motor Lodge   MOTEL $$
(06-304 8188; www.oakestate.co.nz; 2 Hospital Rd; unit from $140;) A stand of gracious roadside oaks and pretty gardens shield this smart complex of red-roofed units at the southern end of town. Choose from studio, one- and two-bedroom options. Expect tasteful interiors and white doves strutting about on the lawns. There's free wi-fi, although the signal is not strong.

Eating

Food Forest Organics VEGAN $
(☑06-304 9790; www.foodforestorganics.co.nz;
101 Main St; mains $12-14; ⊙9.30am-4.30pm Wed-
Sun; 🖋) The ecofriendly sentiments in *Avatar* weren't an aberration for director James
Cameron. The Wairarapa local is a committed vegan, and this health-food-store-cum-
cafe features many organic products from
the Cameron Family Farms (fresh produce,
nuts, honey, beeswax candles, moisturisers,
bath salts). Call in at lunchtime for a delicious plant-based quesadilla, lasagne or
borscht; seating is limited.

French Baker BAKERY $
(☑06-304 8873; www.frenchbaker.co.nz; 81 Main
St; mains $7-16; ⊙7.30am-3.30pm) Buttery
croissants, tempting tarts and authentic
breads – this artisan bakery is le real McCoy.
Grab and go from the cabinet, or tuck into
a ham-and-cheese croissant, soup or spaghetti bolognese, capped off with a silky flat
white coffee.

Saluté TAPAS, PIZZA $$
(☑06-304 9825; www.salute.net.nz; 83 Main St;
tapas $9-19, pizza $21, mains lunch $18-24, dinner
$36-38; ⊙noon-late Wed-Fri, 11.30am-late Sat
& Sun) A neat red iron-clad house on the
main street, Saluté will suit you down to the
ground if you like things saucy, succulent,
crisp, charred and fried, along with lashings of olive oil and wedges of lemon. For
non-sharing types there a few stand-alone
mains, and moderately priced pizza is available throughout the day.

Drinking & Nightlife

Greytown Hotel PUB
(☑06-304 9138; www.greytownhotel.co.nz; 33
Main St; ⊙10am-late; 🖥) One of New Zealand's oldest hotels (1863), the 'Top Pub' is
looking tidy for its age. There are still simple rooms with shared bathrooms upstairs,
while downstairs there's a cosy bar and a
restaurant serving pub meals. It's one of the
few places in Greytown with any signs of life
after 9pm, with occasional live music on Saturday nights.

Shopping

Imperial Productions TOYS
(☑06-304 9625; www.imperialproductions.co.nz;
5 McMaster St) A cute old-fashioned shop for
a cute old-fashioned town, Imperial sells
beautiful rendered traditional toy soldiers
and other figurines. Keep an eye out for the
tiny Māori warriors.

Information

Greytown Information Centre (89 Main St;
⊙2-4pm Fri, 11am-3pm Sat & Sun) This volunteer-staffed centre is housed in Greytown's
historic town hall (1869).

Masterton & Around

☑06 / POP 23,400

The Wairarapa's main hub, Masterton
(Whakaoriori) is an unremarkable, unselfconscious little city getting on with the
business of life. Nobody was more surprised
than the Mastertonians themselves when
it was rated New Zealand's most beautiful
city in the 2017 *Keep NZ Beautiful Awards*.
It does, however, have rivers on two flanks,
a lovely central park and some striking
20th-century buildings. Plus there are some
interesting natural attractions in the surrounding area.

To the southwest is **Carterton**, one of
a clutch of small rural towns punctuating
SH2. It boasts by far the best hanging flower
baskets of the lot, along with some good second-hand shops, cafes and craft breweries.

Sights

**Pukaha Mt Bruce
National Wildlife Centre** WILDLIFE RESERVE
(☑06-375 8004; www.pukaha.org.nz; 85379 SH2;
adult/child $20/6, incl guided walk $45/25; ⊙9am-
4.30pm) 🖋 About 30km north of Masterton,
this 10-sq-km centre is one of NZ's most
successful wildlife and captive breeding
centres. The scenic 1½-hour loop walk gives
a good overview. There's also a kiwi house
here and a series of aviaries for viewing other native birds. Tuatara are also on show,
and the eels are fed daily at 1.30pm. Guided
walks depart at 11am and 2pm daily; book
in advance.

Queen Elizabeth Park PARK
(www.cityofmasterton.co.nz; Dixon St, Masterton)
Planted in 1877, Queen Elizabeth Park is perfect for stretching your legs. Walk around
the lake, dump someone on the see-saw, see
if the little train is running or practise your
slip catches on the cricket oval.

**Aratoi Wairarapa Museum
of Art & History** MUSEUM
(☑06-370 0001; www.aratoi.co.nz; 6 Dixon St, Masterton; admission by donation; ⊙10am-4.30pm)
Hushed and refined, this small but splendid
gallery hosts an impressive program of exhibitions and events (and has a busy cafe and
a shop).

Tararua Forest Park   NATURE RESERVE
(www.doc.govt.nz) FREE The turn-off to the main eastern entrance of the Tararua Forest Park is just south of Masterton on SH2; follow Norfolk Rd about 15km to the gates. Mountain streams dart through virgin forest in this area, known as **Holdsworth**. A recreation area has swimming holes, picnic spots and campsites. Another popular section is the **Waiohine Gorge**, although it's reached by a narrow, unsealed road; look for the turn-off south of Carterton.

Wool Shed   MUSEUM
(📞06-378 8008; www.thewoolshednz.com; 12 Dixon St, Masterton; adult/child $10/2; ⏰10am-4pm) Occupying two historic woolsheds, this baaaa-loody marvellous little museum is dedicated to NZ's sheep-shearing and wool-production industries. Smell the lanolin! It's also a good spot to pick up a home-knitted hat.

🎊 Festivals & Events

Golden Shears   CULTURAL
(www.goldenshears.co.nz; Masterton War Memorial Stadium, 2 Dixon St; day pass $15; ⏰Mar) Masterton's main claim to immortality is the nearly 60-year-old sheep-shearing competition, the international Golden Shears, held over three days in the first week of March.

**Wairarapa Wines
Harvest Festival**   FOOD & DRINK
(📞027 477 4717; www.wairarapaharvestfestival.co.nz; The Cliffs, Dakins Rd, East Taratahi; adult/child $50/free; ⏰Mar) Celebrates the beginning of the harvest with an extravaganza of wine, food and family fun. It's held at a remote riverbank setting 10 minutes from Carterton on a Saturday in mid-March (shuttles depart from all the major towns, from $15). Tickets go on sale at the end of the preceding November – be quick!

🛏 Sleeping

Mawley Holiday Park   HOLIDAY PARK $
(📞06-378 6454; www.mawleypark.co.nz; 5 Oxford St, Masterton; sites from $36, unit with/without bathroom from $100/70) 🐾 This amenable, clean camping ground is spread across the verdant banks of the Waipoua River, just north of the town centre. Units range from basic cabins (bring your own linen) to self-contained two-bedroom units.

Cornwall Park Motel   MOTEL $$
(📞06-378 2939; www.cornwallparkmotel.co.nz; 119 Cornwall St, Masterton; unit from $120; 📶🐾) Hide yourself away on the backstreets in this tidy motel. The neat brick units are warm

CASTLEPOINT

On the coast 68km east of Masterton, Castlepoint is a truly awesome, end-of-the-world place, with a reef, the lofty 162m-high **Castle Rock**, some safe swimming and walking tracks. There's an easy (but sometimes ludicrously windy) 30-minute return walk goes across the reef to the lighthouse, where 70-plus shell species are fossilised in the cliffs. A one-hour return walk runs to a huge limestone cave (take a torch), or take the 1½-hour return track from **Deliverance Cove** to Castle Rock. Keep well away from the lower reef when there are heavy seas.

and comfortable, set among manicured lawns centred on a large old elm tree.

🍴 Eating

⭐**Clareville Bakery**   CAFE $
(📞06-379 5333; www.theclarevillebakery.co.nz; 3340 SH2, Clareville; mains $6-22; ⏰7.30am-4pm Mon-Sat; 👶) Located on SH2 immediately northeast of Carterton, this brilliant bakery-cafe is famous for its sourdough bread, lamb-cutlet pie, open steak sandwich and lavash-style crackers – but everything displayed on the counter is borderline irresistible. There's garden seating, a play area for the kids and regular live-music evenings.

Gladstone Inn   PUB FOOD $$
(📞06-372 7866; www.gladstoneinn.co.nz; 571 Gladstone Rd, Gladstone; pizza $17-20, mains $27-32; ⏰11am-late Tue-Sun; 👶) Gladstone, 18km south of Masterton, is less a town, more a state of mind. There's very little here except a handful of vineyards and this classic old timber inn, haven to thirsty locals, bikers, Sunday drivers and lazy afternoon sippers who hog the tables in the glorious garden bar by the river. There's the odd crafty beer on tap, too.

ℹ Information

DOC Masterton Office (📞06-377 0700; www.doc.govt.nz; 220 South Rd, Masterton; ⏰9am-4.30pm Mon-Fri) A regional office rather than a visitor centre, but you can still call in for Wairarapa-wide DOC information, including advice on tracks.

Masterton i-SITE (📞06-370 0900; www.wairarapanz.com; 6 Dixon St, Masterton; ⏰9.30am-4.30pm) Can sort you out with local information, including a copy of the *Wairarapa Visitor Guide*, and advice on accommodation.

Marlborough & Nelson

Best Places to Eat

➡ Arbour (p417)

➡ Hopgood's (p428)

➡ Rock Ferry (p417)

➡ Cod & Lobster (p428)

➡ Boat Shed Cafe (p431)

Best Places to Stay

➡ Hopewell (p413)

➡ Bay of Many Coves
Resort (p411)

➡ Lemon Tree Lodge (p422)

➡ Zatori Retreat (p442)

➡ St Leonards (p416)

Why Go?

For many travellers, Marlborough and Nelson will be their introduction to what South Islanders refer to as the 'Mainland'. Having left windy Wellington, and made a white-knuckled crossing of Cook Strait, folk are often surprised to find the sun shining and the temperature 10°C warmer.

These top-of-the-South neighbours have much in common beyond an amenable climate: both boast renowned coastal holiday spots, particularly the Marlborough Sounds, Abel Tasman National Park and Kaikoura. There are two other national parks (Kahurangi and Nelson Lakes) amid more mountain ranges than you can poke a Leki stick at.

The two regions also have an abundance of produce, from game and seafood to summer fruits, and most famously the grapes that work their way into the wine glasses of the world's finest restaurants. Keep your penknife and picnic set at the ready.

When to Go

➡ The forecast is good: Marlborough and Nelson soak up some of New Zealand's sunniest weather, with January and February the warmest months when daytime temperatures average 22°C.

➡ July is the coldest, averaging 12°C. However, the top of the South sees some wonderful winter weather, with frosty mornings often giving way to sparklingly clear skies and T-shirt temperatures.

➡ The rumours are true: it is wetter and more windswept the closer you get to the West Coast.

➡ From around Christmas to mid-February, the top of the South teems with Kiwi holidaymakers, so plan ahead during this time and be prepared to jostle for position with a load of jandal (flip-flop)–wearing families.

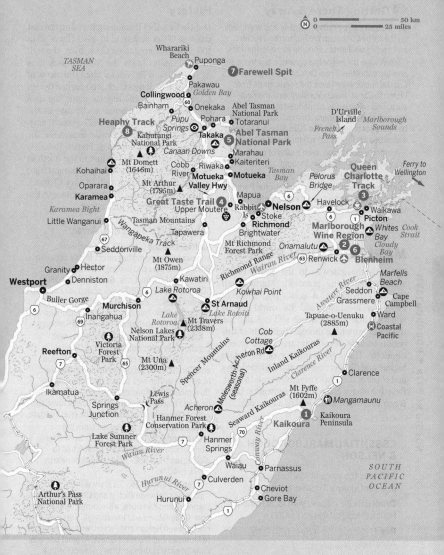

TASMAN
SEA

Wharariki
Beach   Puponga

7 Farewell Spit

Pakawau

Collingwood   *Golden Bay*

Bainham   Onekaka   Abel Tasman
National Park
Pupu   Pohara   Totaranui
Heaphy Track   Springs
Kahurangi   **Takaka**   **Abel Tasman**
National Park   **5 National Park**

Canaan Downs   Marahau
Mt Domett   Cobb   Riwaka   Kaiteriteri
(1646m)   River   **Motueka**   *Tasman
Bay*

Kohaihai   Mt Arthur   **Motueka**
(1795m)   **Valley Hwy**

Oparara   Mapua   *Pelorus
Bridge*
Karamea   **Great Taste Trail 4**   Rabbit   **Nelson**   Havelock
Upper Moutere   Is   **Stoke**
Karamea Bight   **Richmond**
Little Wanganui   Tapawera   Brightwater   **Marlborough**
Wine Region
Tasman Mountains   Mt Richmond   Onamalutu
Forest Park   Renwick
Seddonville   Mt Owen   Richmond Range
(1875m)   Wairau River   63

Granity   Hector   Kawatiri   *Kowhai Point*
Westport   Denniston   Lake Rotoroa
Buller Gorge   6
Murchison   *Lake
Rotoroa*   **St Arnaud**
Inangahua   69   *Lake Rotoiti*   Cob
Nelson Lakes   Mt Travers   Cottage
Reefton   Victoria   National Park   (2338m)
Forest   Mt Una
Park   (2300m)   Spencer Mountains
65   Moloneworth-Acheron Rd
(seasonal)
Ikamatua   Lewis
Pass
Springs   Acheron   Inland Kaikouras
Junction   Hanmer Forest
7   Conservation Park   70
Lake Sumner   Hanmer
Forest Park   Springs
Waiau River   Waiau   Parnassus

Arthur's Pass   *Hurunui River*   7   Culverden
National Park   Cheviot
Hurunui   1   Gore Bay

*D'Urville
Island*   *Marlborough
Sounds*
*French
Pass*
**Queen
Charlotte
Track**   Ferry to
Wellington
3
Waikawa
Picton
1   *Whites
Bay*   *Cook
Strait*
Marlborough   2 6   *Cloudy
Bay*
2   **Blenheim**

Marfells
Beach
Seddon   Cape
Grassmere   Campbell
Tapuae-o-Uenuku   Ward
(2885m)
**Coastal
Pacific**

Clarence River   Clarence
Mt Fyffe   1
(1602m)   Mangamaunu
Seaward Kaikouras   Kaikoura
1   Peninsula
Kaikoura   Kaikoura

Conway River

SOUTH
PACIFIC
OCEAN

Awatere River

Avon River

Marlborough & Nelson Highlights

1 Kaikoura (p418) Getting
up close to wildlife, including
whales, seals, dolphins and
albatrosses.

**2 Marlborough Wine
Region** (p416) Nosing your
way through the wineries.

3 Queen Charlotte Track
(p409) Tramping or biking in
the Marlborough Sounds.

4 Great Taste Trail (p431)
Eating and drinking your way
along this popular cycle trail.

**5 Abel Tasman National
Park** (p435) Kayaking or
tramping in this postcard-
perfect park.

**6 Omaka Aviation
Heritage Centre** (p413)

Getting blown away at one of
New Zealand's best museums.

7 Farewell Spit (p442)
Driving through a dunescape
with gannets and godwits for
company.

8 Heaphy Track (p443)
Reaching the wild West Coast
on foot, crossing through
Kahurangi National Park.

ⓘ Getting There & Away

Cook Strait can be crossed slowly and scenically on the ferries between Wellington and Picton, and swiftly on flights servicing key destinations.

InterCity is the major bus operator, but there are also local shuttles. From October to May, KiwiRail's *Coastal Pacific* train takes the scenic route from Picton to Christchurch, via Blenheim and Kaikoura. This service was suspended following the November 2016 Kaikoura earthquake, but should be operational again in late 2018. Check KiwiRail's website (www.kiwirail.co.nz) for the latest update.

Renting a car is easy, with a slew of car-hire offices in Picton and depots throughout the region.

Popular coastal areas such as the Marlborough Sounds and Abel Tasman National Park are best navigated on foot or by kayak, with water-taxi services readily available to join the dots.

MARLBOROUGH REGION

Picton is the gateway to the South Island and the launching point for Marlborough Sounds exploration. A cork's pop south of Picton is Blenheim and its world-famous wineries, and further south still is Kaikoura, the whale-watching mecca. Highlights of this region include negotiating the famed Queen Charlotte Track by tramping or mountain biking, and discovering the many hidden bays and coves of the Marlborough Sounds by boat. Relaxing over a glass of local sauvignon blanc is recommended at the end of a busy day.

ESSENTIAL MARLBOROUGH & NELSON

Eat amid the vines at Marlborough's excellent vineyard restaurants.

Drink pale ale infused with local Riwaka hops at Hop Federation (p432).

Read *How to Have a Beer* (2017) by Alice Galletly.

Listen to the dawn chorus in Nelson Lakes National Park (p444).

Watch the horizon to spot whales around Kaikoura.

Celebrate at the Marlborough Wine & Food Festival (p414).

Go green at Lochmara (p411) learning about its eco-protection programs.

Go online www.marlboroughnz.com, www.nelsonnz.com, www.kaikoura.co.nz

---

History

Long before Abel Tasman sheltered on the east coast of D'Urville Island in 1642 (more than 100 years before James Cook blew through in 1770), Māori knew the Marlborough area as Te Tau Ihu o Te Waka a Māui (the prow of Māui's canoe). It was Cook who named Queen Charlotte Sound; his reports made the area the best-known sheltered anchorage in the southern hemisphere. In 1827 French navigator Jules Dumont d'Urville discovered the narrow strait now known as French Pass. His officers named the island just to the north in his honour. In the same year a whaling station was established at Te Awaiti in Tory Channel, which brought about the first permanent European settlement in the district.

ⓘ Getting There & Away

Air New Zealand (☑ 0800 747 000; www.airnewzealand.co.nz) has direct flights between Blenheim airport and Wellington and Auckland with onward connections. **Soundsair** (☑ 0800 505 005, 03-520 3080; www.soundsair.co.nz; 10 London Quay; ⊙ 7.30am-5.30pm Mon-Thu & Sat, to 7pm Fri, 9am-7pm Sun) connects Blenheim with Wellington, Paraparaumu, Napier and Kaikoura.

KiwiRail Scenic (☑ 0800 872 467; www.greatjourneysofnz.co.nz) runs the *Coastal Pacific* service daily each way between Picton and Christchurch via Blenheim and Kaikoura. Note this service was suspended following the November 2016 Kaikoura earthquake, but should be operating again by late 2018. Check KiwiRail's website (www.kiwirail.co.nz) for the latest update.

Buses serving Picton depart from the **Interislander** (☑ 0800 802 802; www.interislander.co.nz; Auckland St; adult/child to Wellington from $52/32) terminal or nearby i-SITE (p407).

InterCity (☑ 03-365 1113; www.intercity.co.nz) runs buses between Picton and Christchurch via Blenheim and Kaikoura, with connections to Dunedin, Queenstown and Invercargill. Services also run between Nelson and Picton, with connections to Motueka and the West Coast. At least one bus daily on each of these routes connects with a Wellington ferry service. **Naked Bus** (☑ 0900 625 33; https://nakedbus.com) runs south to Christchurch, Dunedin and Queenstown.

Picton

☑ 03 / POP 4360

Half asleep in winter, but hyperactive in summer (with up to eight fully laden ferry arrivals per day), boaty Picton clusters around a deep gulch at the head of Queen

Charlotte Sound. It's the main traveller port for the South Island, and the best base for tackling the Marlborough Sounds and Queen Charlotte Track. Over the last few years this little town has really bloomed, and offers visitors plenty of reasons to linger even after the obvious attractions are knocked off the list.

⊙ Sights

Lookout
VIEWPOINT

The lookout on the **Tirohanga Track** has beautiful, wide-ranging views of Picton and Queen Charlotte.

Edwin Fox Maritime Museum
MUSEUM

(☑03-573 6868; www.edwinfoxsociety.co.nz; Dunbar Wharf; adult/child $15/5; ⊙9am-5pm) Purportedly the world's ninth-oldest surviving wooden ship, the *Edwin Fox* was built near Calcutta and launched in 1853. During its chequered career it carried troops to the Crimean War, convicts to Australia and immigrants to NZ. This museum has maritime exhibits, including this venerable old dear.

Eco World Aquarium
AQUARIUM

(☑03-573 6030; www.ecoworldnz.co.nz; Dunbar Wharf; adult/child/family $24/12/67; ⊙9.30am-7.30pm) 🐾 The primary purpose of this centre is animal rehabilitation: all sorts of critters come here for fix-ups and rest-ups, and the odd bit of hanky-panky! Special specimens include NZ's 'living dinosaur' – the tuatara – as well as blue penguins, geckos and giant weta. Fish-feeding time (11am and 2pm) is a splashy spectacle. Sharing the ageing building is the **Picton Cinema** (☑03-573 6030; www.pictoncinemas.co.nz; Dunbar Wharf; tickets adult/child $16/11), screening mainstream and edgy flicks.

🏃 Activities

The majority of activity happens around the Marlborough Sounds, but landlubbers will still find enough to occupy themselves, including some lovely walks. A free i-SITE map details many of these, including an easy 1km track to **Bob's Bay**. The **Snout Track** (three hours return) continues along the ridge offering superb water views. Climbing a hill behind the town, the **Tirohanga Track** is a two-hour leg-stretching loop offering the best view in the house.

For town explorations, hire bikes for the whole family from Wilderness Guides (p409).

Go Dive Marlborough
DIVING

(☑03-573 7831; https://godive.co.nz; 66 Wellington St; diving from $220) Offers dive trips around the Sounds taking in marine reserves and also the wreck of the MS *Mikhail Lermontov*, which sank in 1986. Diver training and snorkelling trips ($95) to hand-feed fish are also available.

☞ Tours

Escape to Marlborough
TOURS

(☑0800 6937 2273; www.escapetomarlborough.co.nz; adult/child $69.50/15.50; ⊙8am-6pm) Hop-on, hop-off bus services running at hourly intervals and linking Picton and Blenheim, stopping at 18 key attractions, vineyards and breweries. There are two routes, both taking eight hours in full, and it's possible to change onto the other service en route. Direct transport to Blenheim or Blenheim airport and bespoke wine tours are also offered.

Marlborough Tour Company
TOURS

(☑0800 990 800, 03-577 9997; www.marlboroughtourcompany.co.nz; Town Wharf; adult/child $155/59; ⊙departs 1.30pm) Runs the 3½-hour 'Seafood Odyssea' cruise to a salmon farm, complete with an ocean bounty and sauvignon blanc tasting. Other tour options include a full day discovering Marlborough wine.

🛌 Sleeping

★ Jugglers Rest
HOSTEL $

(☑03-573 5570; www.jugglersrest.com; 8 Canterbury St; dm $33, d $75-85; ⊙closed Jun-Sep; @🖘) 🐾 Jocular hosts keep all their balls in the air at this well-run, ecofriendly, bunk-free backpackers. Peacefully located a 10-minute walk from town, or even less on a free bike. Cheery gardens are a good place to socialise with fellow travellers, especially during the occasional circus-skills shows.

Buccaneer Lodge
LODGE $

(☑03-573 5002; www.buccaneerlodge.co.nz; 314 Waikawa Rd, Waikawa; d $110; 🖘) This Waikawa Bay lodge offers four redecorated en-suite rooms, some with expansive views of the Sounds from the 1st-floor balcony. Town transfers, bike hire and home-baked bread come courtesy of kindly owners Mel and Phil. A smaller downstairs room ($80) is also available.

Tombstone Backpackers
HOSTEL $

(☑03-573 7116; www.tombstonebp.co.nz; 16 Gravesend Pl; dm $31-36, d with/without bathroom $91/84, apt $120; @🖘) Rest in peace

Picton

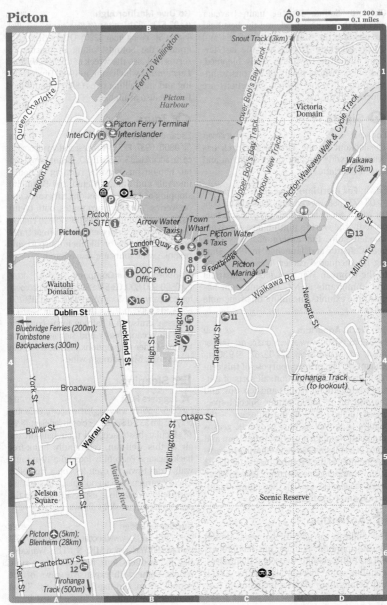

in a smart dorm, double room or self-contained apartment. Also on offer are a spa overlooking the harbour, free breakfast, a sunny reading room, table tennis, free internet, ferry pick-up and drop-off...the list goes on.

Sequoia Lodge Backpackers HOSTEL $
(☏0800 222 257, 03-573 8399; www.sequoialodge.co.nz; 3a Nelson Sq; dm $29-31, d with/without bathroom $84/74; ☏) This well-managed backpackers in a colourful Victorian house is a little out of the centre, but has bonuses

Picton

including free wi-fi, hammocks, barbecues, a hot tub and nightly chocolate pudding. Complimentary breakfast May to October. In the special Netflix room, you can fire up your video-on-demand content of choice. Family rooms are good for groups (from $100 for three people).

Picton Top 10 Holiday Park   HOLIDAY PARK $
(☑ 03-573 7212, 0800 277 444; www.pictontop10.co.nz; 70 Waikawa Rd; sites from $48, units $78-165; @ 🌐 🐕 🔥) About 500m from town, this compact, well-kept park has plenty of lawn and picnic benches, plus crowd-pleasing facilities including a playground, barbecue area and swimming pool.

Gables B&B   B&B $$
(☑ 03-573 6772; www.thegables.co.nz; 20 Waikawa Rd; d $175-195, units $230; @ 🌐) This historic B&B (once home to Picton's mayor) has three individually styled rooms in the main house and two homey self-contained units out the back. Lovely hosts show good humour (ask about the Muffin Club) and provide excellent local advice.

Harbour View Motel   MOTEL $$
(☑ 03-573 6259, 0800 101 133; www.harbourviewpicton.co.nz; 30 Waikawa Rd; d $140-240; 🌐) Its

elevated position means this motel commands good views of Picton's mast-filled harbour from its smart, self-contained studios with timber decks.

Whatamonga Homestay   HOMESTAY $$$
(☑ 03-573 7192; www.whsl.co.nz; 425 Port Underwood Rd; d incl breakfast $360-390; @ 🌐) Follow Waikawa Rd, which becomes Port Underwood Rd, for 8km and you'll bump into this classy waterside option – two self-contained units with king-sized beds and balconies with magic views. Two other rooms under the main house share a bathroom. Free kayaks, dinghies and fishing gear are available. Minimum two-night stay.

✕ Eating

Picton Village Bakkerij   BAKERY $
(☑ 03-573 7082; www.facebook.com/PictonVillageBakery; cnr Auckland & Dublin Sts; bakery items $2-8; ⊘ 6am-4pm Mon-Fri, to 3.30pm Sat; 🖊) Dutch owners bake trays of European goodies here, including interesting breads, filled rolls, cakes and custardy, tarty treats. The savoury pies are very good – ask if the chicken, chilli and cream cheese one is available (trust us, it's a winning combination). An excellent stop before or after the ferry, or to stock a packed lunch.

Café Cortado   CAFE $$
(☑ 03-573 5630; www.cafecortado.co.nz; cnr High St & London Quay; mains $17-35; ⊘ 8am-late Nov-Apr, 8am-late Wed-Sun May-Oct) Pleasant corner cafe and bar with views of the harbour through the foreshore's pohutukawa and palms. This consistent performer turns out fish dishes, homemade cheeseburgers and decent pizza. There's a surprisingly eclectic selection of local Marlborough wines and a few craft beers on tap. Kick off with the breakfast burrito and come back for a dinner of beer-battered blue cod.

ⓘ Information

DOC Picton Office (☑ 03-520 3002; www.doc.govt.nz; 14 Auckland St; ⊘ 9am-4.30pm Mon-Fri) This Department of Conservation office is largely a field office and offers only hut and camp tickets and local tramping information.

Picton i-SITE (☑ 03-520 3113; www.marlboroughnz.com; foreshore; ⊘ 8am-5pm) All vital tourist guff including maps, Queen Charlotte Track information, lockers and transport bookings. Dedicated DOC counter.

ℹ️ Getting There & Away

AIR

Soundsair (p404) flies between Picton and Wellington (adult/child from $99/89); a shuttle bus to/from the airstrip at Koromiko is available.

BOAT

There are two operators crossing Cook Strait between Picton and Wellington, and although all ferries leave from more or less the same place, each has its own terminal. The main transport hub (with car-rental depots) is at the **Interislander Terminal** (Auckland St), which also has a cafe and internet facilities.

Bluebridge Ferries (☎ 0800 844 844, 04-471 6188; www.bluebridge.co.nz; adult/child to Wellington from $53/27; 🐕) crossings take just over three hours, and the company has up to four sailings in each direction daily. Cars cost from $120 and campervans from $155. The sleeper service arrives in Picton at 6am.

Interislander (p404) crossings take just over three hours; there are up to six sailings in each direction daily. Cars are priced from $121, campervans (up to 5.5m) from $153, motorbikes $56, bicycles $15.

Local transport for the Queen Charlotte Track is provided by a wide range of water-based transport options based in Picton.

BUS

Buses serving Picton depart from the Interislander (p404) ferry terminal or the nearby i-SITE (p407).

InterCity (☎ 03-365 1113; www.intercity.co.nz; outside Interislander Ferry Terminal, Auckland St) runs south to Christchurch twice daily ($56, 5½ hours) via Blenheim ($12, 30 minutes) and Kaikoura ($21, 2½ hours), with connections to Dunedin, Queenstown and Invercargill. Services also run to/from Nelson ($23, 2¼ hours), with connections to Motueka and the West Coast. At least one bus daily on each of these routes connects with a Wellington ferry service.

Escape to Marlborough (p405) runs hourly services linking Picton to Blenheim ($12.50) and Blenheim airport ($17.50). A good local shuttle company is **Marlborough Sounds Shuttles** (☎ 03-573 7122; www.marlborough soundsshuttles.co.nz).

TRAIN

KiwiRail Scenic (p404) runs the *Coastal Pacific* service daily each way between Picton and Christchurch via Blenheim and Kaikoura connecting with the Interislander (p404) ferry. Note this service was suspended following the November 2016 Kaikoura earthquake, but was planned to be back up and running in late 2018. Check KiwiRail's website (www.kiwirail.co.nz) for the latest update.

ℹ️ Getting Around

Shuttle services around town and beyond are offered by **A1 Picton Shuttles** (☎ 022 018 8472; www.a1pictonshuttles.co.nz).

Renting a car in Picton is easy and competitively priced (as low as $50 per day), with numerous rental companies based at the Interislander (p404) ferry terminal and many others within a short walk. **Ace** (☎ 03-573 8939; www.acerentalcars.co.nz; Interislander Ferry Terminal) and **Omega** (☎ 03-573 5580; www.omegarentalcars.com; 1 Lagoon Rd) are reliable local operators. Most agencies allow drop-offs in Christchurch; if you're planning to drive to the North Island, most companies suggest you leave your car at Picton and pick up another one in Wellington after crossing Cook Strait.

Marlborough Sounds

The Marlborough Sounds are a maze of peaks, bays, beaches and watery reaches, formed when the sea flooded deep river valleys after the last ice age. They are very convoluted: Pelorus Sound, for example, is 42km long but has 379km of shoreline.

Many spectacular locations can be reached by car. The wiggly 35km route along **Queen Charlotte Drive** from Picton to Havelock is a great Sounds snapshot, but if you have a spare day, head out to **French Pass** (or even **D'Urville Island**) for some big-picture framing of the Outer Sounds. Roads are predominantly narrow and occasionally unsealed; allow plenty of driving time and keep your wits about you.

There are loads of tramping, kayaking, boating and biking opportunities, and there's diving as well – notably the wreck of the *Mikhail Lermontov,* a Russian cruise ship that sank in Port Gore in 1986.

🎯 Sights & Activities

Motuara Island   WILDLIFE RESERVE
(www.doc.govt.nz; Queen Charlotte Sound) 🍃
This DOC-managed, predator-free island reserve is chock-full of rare NZ birds including Okarito kiwi (rowi), native pigeons (kereru), saddleback (tieke) and king shags. You can get here by water taxi and with tour operators working out of Picton.

Sea Kayak Adventures   KAYAKING, BIKING
(☎ 03-574 2765, 0800 262 5492; www.nzsea kayaking.com; cnr Queen Charlotte Dr & Anakiwa Rd; half-/1-day guided paddles $90/125) Guided and 'guided then go' kayaking with bike/

hike options around Queen Charlotte, Kenepuru and Pelorus Sounds. Also offers kayak and mountain-bike rental (half/full day $40/60).

👉 Tours

★**Wilderness Guides**   TOURS
(📞0800 266 266, 03-573 5432; www.wilderness guidesnz.com; Town Wharf, Picton; 1-day guided trips from $130, kayak/bike hire per day $60) Host of the popular and flexible one- to three-day 'multisport' trips (kayak/tramp/cycle) plus many other guided and independent biking, tramping and kayaking tours, including a remote Ship Cove paddle. Mountain bikes and kayaks for hire, too.

Cougar Line   TOURS
(📞03-573 7925, 0800 504 090; www.cougarline. co.nz; Town Wharf, Picton; track round trips $105, cruises from $85) Queen Charlotte Track transport, plus various half- and full-day cruise/walk trips, including the rather special (and flexible) eco-cruise to Motuara Island and a day walk from Resolution Bay to Furneaux Lodge.

Marlborough Sounds
Adventure Company   TOURS
(📞03-573 6078, 0800 283 283; www.marlborough sounds.co.nz; Town Wharf, Picton; half-/5-day guided packages $95/2420, kayak hire per half day from $40) Bike-tramp-kayak trips, with options to suit every inclination and interest. Bikes, kayaks and camping equipment are also available for rent. Trip durations range from half days to five days, and the popular Kayak & Hike option combines one day of kayaking, one day of tramping and an overnight stay in the Sounds.

Beachcomber Cruises   TOURS
(📞03-573 6175, 0800 624 526; www.beachcomber cruises.co.nz; Town Wharf, Picton; mail runs $101, cruises from $85, track round trips $103) Two- to eight-hour cruise adventures, including the classic 'Magic Mail Run', plus walking, biking and resort lunch options and round-trip track transport.

E-Ko Tours   TOURS
(📞03-573 8040, 0800 945 354; www.e-ko.nz; Town Wharf, Picton; dolphin swimming/viewing $165/135) Half-day 'swim with dolphins' trips, and various other wildlife tours including trips to Motuara Island (p408). Tours are cheaper if you don't want to get in the water with the wildlife.

🛏 Sleeping

Some Sounds sleeping options are accessible only by boat and are deliciously isolated, but the most popular are those on (or just off) the Queen Charlotte Track. Some places close over winter; call ahead to check.

There are over 30 DOC camping grounds throughout the Sounds (many accessible only by boat), providing water and toilet facilities but not much else.

Ask at Picton i-SITE (p407) about local bachs (simple holiday homes) for rent, of which there are many.

ℹ Getting There & Away

The Marlborough Sounds are most commonly explored from Picton, where boat operators congregate at the centrally located Town Wharf. They offer everything from lodge transfers to cruises taking in sites such as Ship Cove and Motuara Island bird sanctuary, to round-trip Queen Charlotte Track transport and pack transfers that allow trampers to walk without a heavy burden. Bikes and kayaks can also be transported.

ℹ Getting Around

Sounds travel is invariably quicker by boat (for example, Punga Cove from Picton by car takes two to three hours, but just 45 minutes by boat). Fortunately, an armada of vessels offer scheduled and on-demand boat services, with the bulk operating out of Picton for the Queen Charlotte Sound, and some from Havelock for Kenepuru and Pelorus Sounds.

Options to get around include **Arrow Water Taxis** (📞03-573 8229, 027 444 4689; www. arrowwatertaxis.co.nz; Town Wharf, Picton), a **float plane** (📞021 704 248, 03-573 9012; www.nz-scenic-flights.co.nz; Ferry Terminal, Picton; flights from $110) service, Kenepuru Water Taxi (p413), Pelorus Sound Water Taxi (p413) and **Picton Water Taxis** (📞03-573 7853, 027 227 0284; www.pictonwatertaxis. co.nz; Waterfront, cnr London Quay & Wellington St, Picton).

Queen Charlotte Track

One of New Zealand's classic walks – and now one of its Great Rides, too – the meandering, 70km Queen Charlotte Track offers gorgeous coastal scenery on its way from historic Ship Cove to Anakiwa, passing through a mixture of privately owned land and DOC reserves. Access depends on the cooperation of local landowners; respect their property by utilising designated campsites and

Marlborough Sounds

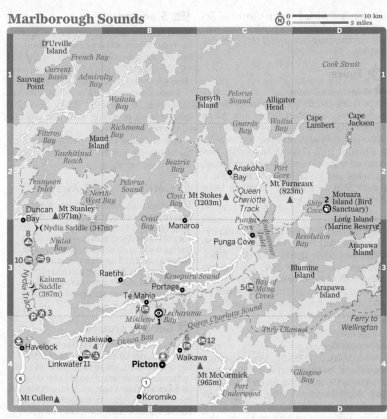

toilets, and carrying out your rubbish. Your purchase of the **Track Pass** ($10 to $18), available from the Picton i-SITE (p407) and track-related businesses, provides the co-op with the means to maintain and enhance the experience for all.

Activities

Queen Charlotte is a well-defined track, suitable for people of average fitness. Numerous boat and tour operators service the track, allowing you to tramp the whole three- to five-day journey, or to start and finish where you like, on foot or by kayak or bike. We're talking mountain biking here, and a whole lot of fun for fit, competent off-roaders. Part of the track is off limits to cyclists from 1 December to the end of February, but there is still good riding to be had during this time.

Ship Cove is the usual (and recommended) starting point – mainly because it's easier

to arrange a boat from Picton to Ship Cove than vice versa – but the track can be started from Anakiwa. There's a public phone at Anakiwa but not at Ship Cove.

Estimated walk times:

TRACK SECTION	DISTANCE (KM)	DURATION (HR)
Ship Cove to Resolution Bay	4.5	1½-2
Resolution Bay to head of Endeavour Inlet	10.5	2½-3
Endeavour Inlet to Camp Bay/Punga Cove	12	3-4
Camp Bay/Punga Cove to Torea Saddle/ Portage	24	6-8
Torea Saddle/Portage to Te Mahia Saddle	7.5	3-4
Te Mahia Saddle to Anakiwa	12.5	3-4

Marlborough Sounds

🛏 Sleeping

There are lots of great day-trip options, allowing you to base yourself in Picton. There's also plenty of accommodation spaced along the way; boat operators will transport your luggage along the track.

There are six DOC campsites, all with toilets and a water supply but no cooking facilities, and a variety of resorts, lodges, backpackers and guesthouses. Unless you're camping, book your accommodation waaay in advance, especially in summer.

Anakiwa 401 HOSTEL $
(☑️03-574 1388; www.anakiwa401.co.nz; 401 Anakiwa Rd; s/q $75/200, d $100-120; 📶) At the southern end of the track, this former schoolhouse is a soothing spot to rest and reflect. There are two doubles (one with en suite), one twin and a beachy self-contained unit. Jocular owners will have you jumping off the jetty for joy and enjoying espresso and ice cream from their green caravan (open afternoons). Free bikes and kayaks.

Smiths Farm Holiday Park HOLIDAY PARK $
(☑️03-574 2806; www.smithsfarm.co.nz; 1419 Queen Charlotte Dr, Linkwater; campsites per person from $18, cabins $65, units $115-150; @📶) 🌿 Located on the aptly named Linkwater flat between Queen Charlotte and Pelorus, friendly Smiths makes a handy base camp for the track and beyond. Well-kept cabins and motel units face out onto the bushy hillside, while livestock nibble around the lush camping lawns. Short walks extend to a waterfall and magical glow-worm dell.

Mistletoe Bay HOLIDAY PARK $
(☑️03-573 4048; www.mistletoebay.co.nz; Onahau Bay; campsites adult/child $16/10, dm/d $40/80, linen $7.50; 📶) 🌿 Surrounded by bushy hills, Mistletoe Bay offers attractive camping with no-frills facilities. There are also eight modern cabins ($140) sleeping up to six, plus a bunkhouse and modern shared kitchen. Environmental sustainability abounds, as does the opportunity to jump off the jetty, kayak in the bay, or tramp the Queen Charlotte Track.

⭐ **Te Mahia Bay Resort** RESORT $$
(☑️03-573 4089; www.temahia.co.nz; 63 Te Mahia Rd; d $160-258; 📶) This lovely low-key resort is within cooee (shouting distance) of the Queen Charlotte Track in a picturesque bay on Kenepuru Sound. It has a range of delightful rooms-with-a-view, our pick of which are the great-value heritage units. The on-site shop has precooked meals, pizza, cakes, coffee and camping supplies (wine!), plus there is kayak hire and massage.

Lochmara Lodge RESORT $$
(☑️03-573 4554, 0800 562 462; www.lochmara lodge.co.nz; Lochmara Bay; units $99-300; 📶) 🌿 Set in lush surroundings, this arty eco-retreat can either be reached via the Queen Charlotte Track or from Picton aboard the lodge's water taxi ($30 one way). There are en-suite doubles, units and chalets, an excellent cafe and restaurant, plus a bathhouse for spa and massage services. Recent additions are **Lochmara's** (☑️03-573 4554; www. lochmara.co.nz; Lochmara Bay; day trips from $40) 🌿 wildlife conservation activities and an interesting underwater observatory.

⭐ **Bay of Many Coves Resort** RESORT $$$
(☑️0800 579 9771, 03-579 9771; www.bayofmany coves.co.nz; Bay of Many Coves; 1-/2-/3-bedroom apt $860/1090/1435; 📶🏊) These stylish and secluded apartments feature all mod cons and private balconies overlooking the water. As well as upmarket cuisine, there are various indulgences such as massage, a spa and a hot tub. Kayaking and bush walks are also on the cards, as are adventures in the Sounds organised by the charming, hands-on owners and staff.

Mahana Lodge LODGE $$$
(☑️03-579 8373; www.mahanalodge.co.nz; Camp Bay, Endeavour Inlet; d $250; ⊘closed Jun-Aug) 🌿 This beautiful property features a pretty waterside lawn and purpose-built lodge with four en-suite doubles. Ecofriendly initiatives include bush regeneration, pest trapping

and an organic veggie garden. In fact, feel-good factors abound: free kayaks, home baking and a blooming conservatory where prearranged evening meals are served (three courses $75).

ⓘ Information

The best place to get track information and advice is Picton i-SITE (p407), which also handles bookings for transport and accommodation. Also see the Queen Charlotte Track website (www.qctrack.co.nz) and the Queen Charlotte Track Land Cooperative website (www.qctlc.com).

ⓘ Getting There & Away

Picton water taxis can drop you off and pick you up at numerous locations along the track.

Kenepuru & Pelorus Sounds

Kenepuru and Pelorus Sounds, to the west of Queen Charlotte Sound, are less populous and therefore offer fewer traveller services, including transport. There's some cracking scenery, however, and those with time to spare will be well rewarded by their explorations.

Havelock is the hub of this area, the western bookend of the 35km Queen Charlotte Drive (Picton being the eastern one) and the self-proclaimed 'Greenshell Mussel Capital of the World'. While hardly the most rock-and-roll of New Zealand towns, Havelock offers most necessities, including accommodation, fuel and food.

⊙ Sights

If a stroll through the streets of Havelock leaves you thinking that there *must* be more to this area, you're right – and to get a taste of it you need go no further than the **Cullen Point Lookout**, a 10-minute drive from Havelock along the Queen Charlotte Drive. A short walk leads up and around a headland overlooking Havelock, the surrounding valleys and Pelorus Sound. And of course, there's plenty to see and do exploring the Marlborough Sounds themselves.

🏃 Activities

Pelorus Eco Adventures   KAYAKING
(☑03-574 2212, 0800 252 663; www.kayak-newzealand.com; Blue Moon Lodge, 48 Main Rd, Havelock; per person $180) Float in an inflatable kayak on scenic Pelorus River, star of the barrel scene in *The Hobbit*. Wend your

way down exhilarating rapids, through crystal-clear pools and past native forest and waterfalls. No experience required; minimum two people. Tours last around four to five hours.

Nydia Track   TRAMPING
(www.doc.govt.nz) The Nydia Track (27km, 10 hours) starts at Kaiuma Bay and ends at Duncan Bay (or vice versa). You'll need water and road transport to complete the journey; Havelock's Blue Moon Lodge runs a shuttle to Duncan Bay.

Around halfway along is beautiful Nydia Bay, where there's a **DOC campsite** (www.doc.govt.nz; adult/child $6/3) and **Nydia Lodge** (☑03-520 3002; www.doc.govt.nz; Nydia Bay; dm $15, minimum charge $60), an unhosted 50-bed lodge. Also in Nydia Bay, **On the Track Lodge** (☑03-579 8411; www.onthetracklodge.nz; Nydia Bay; dm $60, s $90-120, d $140-180) 🌿 is a tranquil, eco-focused affair offering everything from packed lunches to evening meals and a hot tub.

👉 Tours

Pelorus Mail Boat   CRUISE
(☑03-574 1088; www.themailboat.co.nz; Jetty 1, Havelock Marina; adult/child $128/free; ⊗departs 9.30am Nov-Apr, Tue, Thu & Fri May-Oct) Popular full-day boat cruise through the far reaches of Pelorus Sound on a genuine NZ Post delivery run. Bookings essential; BYO lunch. Picton and Blenheim pick-up and drop-off available.

🛏 Sleeping

There's plenty of accommodation around Kenepuru and Pelorus, much of which is accessible off the Queen Charlotte Track. There are also some picturesque DOC campgrounds (most full to bursting in January), a few remote lodges and the very handy Smiths Farm Holiday Park (p411) at Linkwater, the crossroads for Queen Charlotte and Kenepuru, where you'll find a petrol station with snacks. Havelock also has a couple of decent offerings.

Blue Moon Lodge   HOSTEL $
(☑0800 252 663, 03-574 2212; www.bluemoonhavelock.co.nz; 48 Main Rd, Havelock; dm $33, r with/without bathroom from $96/82; @🅰) 🌿 This pleasant and relaxed lodge has homey rooms in the main house, a spa family unit (from $130), and cabins and a bunkhouse in the yard. Notable features include a sunny barbecue deck, inflatable kayak trips on the Pelorus River, and Nydia Track transport.

★**Hopewell**   LODGE **$$**
(📞03-573 4341; www.hopewell.co.nz; 7204 Ke-
nepuru Rd, Double Bay; dm/cottages $40/240, d
with/without bathroom $150/110; @ 🛜) Beloved
of travellers, remote Hopewell sits waterside
surrounded by native bush. Savour the long,
winding drive to get there, or take a water
taxi from Te Mahia ($25). Stay a couple of
days, so you can chill out or enjoy the roll-
call of activities: mountain biking, kayaking,
sailing, fishing, eating gourmet pizza, soak-
ing in the outdoor hot tub and more.

Havelock Garden Motels   MOTEL **$$**
(📞03-574 2387; www.gardenmotels.com; 71 Main
Rd, Havelock; d $125-160; 🛜) Set in a large,
graceful garden complete with dear old trees
and blooms galore, these 1960s units have
been tastefully revamped to offer homey
comforts. Local activities are happily booked
for you.

ℹ️ Information

Havelock i-SITE (📞03-577 8080; www.marl-
boroughnz.com; 61 Main Rd, Havelock; ⊙9am-
4.30pm Sep-May) This helpful wee visitor
centre shares its home with the **Eyes On Nature**
museum, chock-full of frighteningly lifelike, full-
size replicas of birds, fish and other critters.

For a complete list of visitor services, visit
www.pelorusnz.co.nz, which covers Havelock,
Kenepuru and Pelorus Sounds, and the extremi-
ties of French Pass and D'Urville Island.

ℹ️ Getting There & Away

InterCity (p404) runs daily buses from Picton
to Havelock via Blenheim ($17, one hour), and
from Havelock to Nelson ($17, 1¼ hours). Buses
depart from near the **Havelock i-SITE**.

ℹ️ Getting Around

Both **Kenepuru Water Taxi** (📞 03-573 4344,
021 132 3261; www.kenepuru.co.nz; 7170 Kenepuru Rd, Raetihi) and **Pelorus Sound Water
Taxi** (📞 0508 4283 5625, 027 444 2852; www.
pelorussoundwatertaxis.co.nz; Pier C, Havelock
Marina) offer transport and sightseeing trips
around the area.

Blenheim

📞03 / POP 31,300

Blenheim is an agricultural town 29km
south of Picton on the pretty Wairau Plains
between the Wither Hills and the Richmond
Ranges. The last decade or so has seen town
beautification projects, the maturation of
the wine industry and the addition of a

PELORUS BRIDGE

A peaky pocket of deep, green forest
tucked between paddocks of bog-stand-
ard pasture, 18km west of Havelock, this
scenic reserve contains one of the last
stands of river-flat forest in Marlborough. It survived only because a town
planned in 1865 didn't get off the ground
by 1912, by which time obliterative
logging made this little remnant look
precious. Visitors can explore its many
tracks, admire the historic bridge, take a
dip in the limpid Pelorus River (alluring
enough to star in Peter Jackson's *The
Hobbit*), and partake in some home baking at the cafe. The fortunate few can
stay overnight in DOC's small but perfectly formed **Pelorus Bridge Campground** (📞03-571 6019; www.doc.govt.nz;
Pelorus Bridge, SH6; unpowered/powered
sites per person $9/18), with its snazzy fa-
cilities building. Come sundown keep an
eye out for long-tailed bats – the reserve
is home to one of the last remaining
populations in Marlborough.

landmark museum significantly increase the
town's appeal to visitors.

Check out the new riverside development,
including compact parks, walkways and a
pedestrian footbridge, on the northeastern
edge of the town centre.

⊙ Sights

★**Omaka Aviation
Heritage Centre**   MUSEUM
(📞 03-579 1305; www.omaka.org.nz; 79 Aerodrome
Rd, Omaka; adult/child/family both exhibitions
$30/16/99; ⊙9am-5pm Dec-Mar, 10am-5pm Apr-
Nov) This exceptionally brilliant museum
houses film-director Peter Jackson's collection of original and replica Great War aircraft, brought to life in a series of dioramas
that depict dramatic wartime scenes, such
as the death of the Red Baron. A new wing
houses Dangerous Skies, a WWII collection.
Vintage biplane flights are available (10/20
minutes, $250/380 for one or two people).

A cafe and shop are on site, and next door
is **Omaka Classic Cars** (📞03-577 9419; www.
omakaclassiccars.co.nz; Aerodrome Rd, Omaka;
adult/child $15/free; ⊙10am-4pm), which hous-
es more than 100 vehicles dating from the
'50s to the '80s.

Pollard Park PARK
(Parker St) Ten minutes' walk from town, this 25-hectare park boasts beautiful blooming and scented gardens, a playground, tennis courts, croquet and a nine-hole golf course. It's pretty as a picture when lit up on summer evenings. Five minutes away, on the way to or from town, is the extensive **Taylor River Reserve**, a lovely place for a stroll.

Activities

Wither Hills Farm Park WALKING
In a town as flat as a pancake, this hilly 11-sq-km park provides welcome relief, offering over 60km of walking and mountain-biking trails with grand views across the Wairau Valley and out to Cloudy Bay. Pick up a map from the i-SITE (p418) or check the information panels at the many entrances including Redwood St and Taylor Pass Rd.

Avantiplus CYCLING
(☑ 03-578 0433; www.bikemarlborough.co.nz; 61 Queen St; hire per half/full day from $25/40; ⊙ 8am-5.30pm Mon-Fri, 10am-2pm Sat) Rents bikes; extended hire and delivery by arrangement. E-bikes and tandems also available if you want to ease the load.

Tours

Wine tours are generally conducted in a minibus, last between four and seven hours, take in four to seven wineries and range in price from $65 to $95 (with a few grand tours up to around $200 for the day, including a winery lunch).

★ Driftwood Eco-Tours KAYAKING, ECOTOUR
(☑ 03-577 7651; www.driftwoodecotours.co.nz; 749 Dillons Point Rd; kayak & 4WD tours $200) Go on a kayak or 4WD tour for fascinating natural history on and around the ecologically and historically significant Wairau Lagoon, 10 minutes' drive from Blenheim. Rare birds and the muppetty royal spoonbill may well be spotted. The semi self-contained 'Retreat' provides accommodation for up to four (double/quad $250/450), while the 'treehouse' offers accommodation for up to three (double/triple $200/250).

Breakfast is an extra $20 per person, and both accommodation options are next to the Opawa River.

Bike2Wine TOURS
(☑ 0800 653 262, 03-572 8458; www.bike2wine. co.nz; 9 Wilson St, Renwick; standard/tandem per day $30/60, pick-ups from $10; ⊙ 10am-5.30pm) An alternative to the usual minibus tours – get around the grapes on two wheels. This operator offers self-guided, fully geared and supported tours. New owners are keeping up the same levels of stellar service and it's just a short ride to a good range of vineyards around Renwick.

Sounds Connection TOURS
(☑ 03-573 8843, 0800 742 866; www.sounds connection.co.nz; tours from $75) Wine-based excursions exploring the best of the area's wineries and vineyard restaurants. Also incorporating boat excursions on the Marlborough Sounds.

Bubbly Grape Wine Tours TOURS
(☑ 027 672 2195, 0800 228 2253; www.bubblygrape. co.nz; tours $100-195) Three different tours including a gourmet lunch option.

Highlight Wine Tours TOURS
(☑ 027 434 6451, 03-577 9046; www.highlightwine tours.co.nz; tours $115-130) Visit a chocolate factory, too. Custom tours available.

Festivals & Events

Marlborough Wine & Food Festival FOOD & DRINK
(☑ 03-577 9299; www.wine-marlborough-festival. co.nz; tickets $62; ⊙ mid-Feb) Held at Brancott (p416) vineyard, this is an extravaganza of local wine, fine food and entertainment. Book accommodation well in advance.

Sleeping

Blenheim's budget beds fill with long-stay seasonal workers; hostels will help find work and offer weekly rates. Numerous mid-range motels can be found on Middle Renwick Rd west of the town centre, and SH1 towards Christchurch.

Central Blenheim

Blenheim Top 10 Holiday Park HOLIDAY PARK $
(☑ 03-578 3667, 0800 268 666; www.blenheim top10.co.nz; 78 Grove Rd; sites $42, cabins $79-89, units $135; @⊛⊛) Ten minutes' walk to town, this holiday park spreads out under and alongside the main road bridge over the Opawa River. Ask for the quietest spot available. Cabins and units are tidy but plain-Jane, set in a sea of asphalt. Fun-time diversions include a spa, a pool, a playground and bike hire.

Grapevine Backpackers HOSTEL $
(☑ 03-578 6062; www.thegrapevine.co.nz; 29 Park Tce; dm $26-27, s/d/tr $62/70/84; ⊛) Located

Marlborough Wine Region

Marlborough Wine Region

MARLBOROUGH & NELSON BLENHEIM

inside an old maternity home a 10-minute walk from the town centre, Grapevine has respectable rooms set aside for travellers. The kitchen is tight, but offset by free canoes and a peaceful barbecue deck by the Opawa River. Bike hire is $25 per day.

171 on High   MOTEL **$$**
(☎0800 587 856, 03-579 5098; www.171onhigh motel.co.nz; 171 High St; d $170-210; ☎) A welcoming option close to town, these tasteful, splash-o-colour studios and apartments are bright and breezy in the daytime, warm and shimmery in the evening. Expect a wide complement of facilities and 'extra mile' service.

🛏 Wine Region

Watson's Way Lodge   LODGE **$**
(☎03-572 8228; www.watsonswaylodge.com; 56 High St, Renwick; tents/campervans $15/18, dm $30, d & tw $88-99; ☺closed Aug & Sep; @☎) This traveller-focused lodge has spick-and-span en-suite rooms in a sweetly converted bungalow with a full kitchen and comfy lounge. There are also spacious leafy gardens dotted with fruit trees and hammocks, an outdoor claw-foot bath, bikes for hire (guest/public rate $18/28 per day) and local information aplenty.

MARLBOROUGH WINERIES

Marlborough is NZ's vinous colossus, producing around three-quarters of the country's wine. At last count, there were 244 sq km of vines planted – that's more than 28,000 rugby pitches! Sunny days and cool nights create the perfect conditions for cool-climate grapes: world-famous sauvignon blanc, top-notch pinot noir, and notable chardonnay, riesling, gewürztraminer, pinot gris and bubbly. Drifting between tasting rooms and dining among the vines is a quintessential South Island experience.

A Taste of the Tastings

Around 35 wineries are open to the public. Our picks of the bunch provide a range of high-quality cellar-door experiences, with most being open from around 10.30am till 4.30pm (some scale back operations in winter). Wineries may charge a small fee for tasting, normally refunded if you purchase a bottle. Pick up a copy of the *Marlborough Wine Trail* map from Blenheim i-SITE (p418), also available online at www.wine-marlborough. co.nz. If your time is limited, pop into Wino's (p418) in Blenheim, a sterling one-stop shop for some of Marlborough's finer and less common drops.

Auntsfield Estate (☑03-578 0622; www.auntsfield.co.nz; 270 Paynters Rd; ⊙by appointment 11am-4.30pm Mon-Fri late Oct-Easter)

Bladen (☑03-572 9417; www.bladen.co.nz; 83 Conders Bend Rd; ⊙11am-4.30pm late Oct-Apr)

Brancott Estate Heritage Centre (☑03-520 6975; www.brancottestate.com; 180 Brancott Rd; ⊙10am-4.30pm)

Clos Henri Vineyard (☑03-572 7293; www.clos-henri.com; 639 State Hwy 63, RD1; ⊙10am-4pm Mon-Fri Oct-Apr)

Cloudy Bay (☑03-520 9147; www.cloudybay.co.nz; 230 Jacksons Rd; ⊙10am-4pm) ✿

Forrest (☑03-572 9084; www.forrest.co.nz; 19 Blicks Rd; ⊙10am-4.30pm)

Framingham (☑03-572 8884; www.framingham.co.nz; 19 Conders Bend Rd, Renwick; ⊙10.30am-4.30pm) ✿

Huia (☑03-572 8326; www.huiavineyards.com; 22 Boyces Rd; ⊙10am-5pm Nov-Mar) ✿

Saint Clair Estate (☑03-570 5280; www.saintclair.co.nz; 13 Selmes Rd, Rapaura; ⊙9am-5pm Nov-Apr, 11am-4pm May-Oct)

★**St Leonards**　　　　　　COTTAGE **$$**
(☑03-577 8328; www.stleonards.co.nz; 18 St Leonards Rd; d incl breakfast $150-340; 🖥🐕) Tucked into the 4.5-acre grounds of an 1886 homestead, these five stylish and rustic cottages offer privacy and a reason to stay put. Each is unique in its layout and perspective on the gardens and vines. Our pick is the capacious and cosy Woolshed, exuding agricultural chic. Resident sheep, chickens and deer await your attention.

Olde Mill House　　　　　　B&B **$$**
(☑03-572 8458; www.oldemillhouse.co.nz; 9 Wilson St, Renwick; d $175-195; 🖥) On an elevated section in otherwise flat Renwick, this charming old house is a treat. New owners are keeping standards high at this welcoming B&B infused with stately decor, and home-grown fruit and homemade jams and pickles are offered for breakfast. Free bikes, an outdoor spa and gardens make this a tiptop choice in the heart of the wine country.

Marlborough Vintners Hotel　　HOTEL **$$$**
(☑0800 684 190, 03-572 5094; www.mvh.co.nz; 190 Rapaura Rd; d from $315; 🖥) ✿ Sixteen architecturally designed suites make the most of valley views and boast wet-room bathrooms and abstract art. The stylish reception building has a bar and restaurant opening out on to a cherry orchard and organic veggie garden.

🍴 Eating & Drinking

★**Burleigh**　　　　　　　　DELI **$**
(☑03-579 2531; www.facebook.com/theburleighnz; 72 New Renwick Rd; pies $6; ⊙7.30am-3pm Mon-Fri, 9am-1pm Sat) The humble pie rises to stratospheric heights at this fabulous deli; try the sweet pork-belly or savoury steak and blue cheese, or perhaps both. Fresh-filled

Spy Valley Wines (☑03-572 6207; www.spyvalleywine.co.nz; 37 Lake Timara Rd, Waihopai Valley; ☺10.30am-4.30pm mid-Oct to mid-May, 10.30am-4.30pm Mon-Fri mid-May to mid-Oct) 🍷

Te Whare Ra (☑03-572 8581; www.twrwines.co.nz; 56 Anglesea St, Renwick; ☺11am-4pm Mon-Fri Nov–mid-Mar) 🍷

Vines Village (☑03-579 5424; www.thevinesvillage.co.nz; 193 Rapaura Rd; ☺10am-5pm)

Wairau River (☑03-572 9800; www.wairauriverwines.com; 11 Rapaura Rd; ☺10am-5pm) 🍷

Yealands Estate (☑03-575 7618; www.yealandsestate.co.nz; cnr Seaview & Reserve Rds, Seddon; ☺10am-4.30pm) 🍷

Wining & Dining

Wairau River Restaurant (☑03-572 9800; www.wairauriverwines.com; cnr Rapaura Rd & SH6, Renwick; mains $21-27; ☺noon-3pm) Modishly modified mud-brick bistro with wide veranda and beautiful gardens with plenty of shade. Order the chilli salt prawns or the double-baked blue-cheese soufflé. Relaxing and thoroughly enjoyable.

Rock Ferry (☑03-579 6431; www.rockferry.co.nz; 130 Hammerichs Rd; mains $25-29; ☺11.30am-3pm) Pleasant environment inside and out, with a slightly groovy edge. The compact summery menu – think miso-marinated salmon with an Asian slaw or the organic open steak sandwich topped with a creamy spinach and anchovy spread – is accompanied by wines from Marlborough and Otago. Leave room for dessert and coffee in the garden.

Wither Hills (☑03-520 8284; www.witherhills.co.nz; 211 New Renwick Rd; mains $27-30, platters $22-24; ☺11am-4pm) Simple, well-executed food in a stylish space. Pull up a beanbag on the Hockneyesque lawns and enjoy confit duck, local king salmon, or a cheese and charcuterie platter, before climbing the ziggurat for impressive views across the Wairau.

Arbour (☑03-572 7989; www.arbour.co.nz; 36 Godfrey Rd, Renwick; mains $37-39; ☺5-11pm Tue-Sat Aug-Jun; ☑) Located in the thick of Renwick wine country, this elegant restaurant offers 'a taste of Marlborough' by focusing on local produce fashioned into contemporary, crowd-pleasing dishes. Settle in for a three-, four- or multiple-course à la carte offering ($75/85/99), or an end-of-the-day nibble and glass or two from the mesmerising wine list.

baguettes, local sausage, French cheeses and great coffee also make tempting appearances. Avoid the lunchtime rush.

Gramado's BRAZILIAN $$
(☑03-579 1192; www.gramadosrestaurant.com; 74 Main St; mains $28-40; ☺4pm-late Tue-Sat) Injecting a little Latin American flair into the Blenheim dining scene, Gramado's is a fun place to tuck into unashamedly hearty meals such as lamb *assado*, feijoada (smoky pork and bean stew) and Brazilian-spiced fish. Kick things off with a caipirinha, of course.

Scotch Wine Bar WINE BAR
(☑03-579 1176; www.scotchbar.co.nz; 24-26 Maxwell Rd; ☺4pm-late) A versatile and sociable spot in central Blenheim, Scotch offers local wines, craft beer on tap and shared plates ($18 to $30), including spiced lamb and hummus, and steamed buns crammed

with Japanese-style fried chicken. Pop next door and buy wine from a stellar selection, including many local Marlborough tipples, either to be enjoyed in the bar or at home.

Moa Brewing Company CRAFT BEER
(☑03-572 5146; www.moabeer.com; 258 Jacksons Rd, Rapaura; tastings $8; ☺11am-5pm) Take a break from wine-tasting at Moa's laid-back beer-tasting room amid Rapaura's rural vineyards. You won't find any giant flightless moa roaming around, but there's still plenty of other bird life in the gardens. Food trucks often rock up Friday to Sunday, and there's usually a few seasonal brews on tap. Travelling beer geeks should try Moa's excellent sour beers.

Dodson Street CRAFT BEER
(☑03-577 8348; www.dodsonstreet.co.nz; 1 Dodson St; ☺11am-11pm) Pub and garden with a beer-hall ambience and suitably Teutonic

menu (mains $17 to $27) featuring pork knuckle, bratwurst and schnitzel (its pizza and burgers are also good). The stars of the show are the 24 taps pouring quality, ever-changing craft beer from around Marlborough and the rest of NZ. A tasting of five brews is $10.

🛍 Shopping

Wino's   WINE

(☑ 03-578 4196; www.winos.co.nz; 49 Grove Rd; ⊙ 10am-7pm Sun-Thu, to 8pm Fri & Sat) If your time is limited, pop into Wino's, a sterling one-stop shop for some of Marlborough's finer and less common drops.

ⓘ Information

Blenheim i-SITE (☑ 03-577 8080; www. marlboroughnz.com; Railway Station, 8 Sinclair St; ⊙ 9am-5pm Mon-Fri, to 3pm Sat, 10am-3pm Sun) Information on Marlborough and beyond. Wine-trail maps and bookings for everything under the sun.

Wairau Hospital (☑ 03-520 9999; www. nmdhb.govt.nz; Hospital Rd)

ⓘ Getting There & Away

AIR

Marlborough Airport (www.marlborough airport.co.nz; Tancred Cres, Woodbourne) is 6km west of town on Middle Renwick Rd.

Air New Zealand (p404) has direct flights to/from Wellington and Auckland with onward connections. Soundsair (p404) connects Blenheim with Wellington, Paraparaumu, Napier and Kaikoura.

BUS

InterCity (p404) buses run daily from the Blenheim i-SITE to Picton (from $10, 30 minutes) and Nelson (from $22, 1¾ hours). Buses also head down south to Christchurch (from $41, six hours, four daily) via Kaikoura.

Naked Bus (p404) sells bargain seats on some of the same services, and on its own buses on major routes.

TRAIN

KiwiRail Scenic (p404) runs the daily *Coastal Pacific* service (October to May), stopping at Blenheim en route to Picton heading north, and Christchurch via Kaikoura heading south. At the time of research, this service was suspended due to track damage from the November 2016 Kaikoura earthquake, but was scheduled to relaunch in late 2018. Check the website for the latest update.

ⓘ Getting Around

BICYCLE

Avantiplus (p414) rents bikes; extended hire and delivery by arrangement. **Bike2Wine** (p414) also rents bikes to explore nearby vineyards.

BUS

Blenheim Shuttles (☑ 03-577 5277, 0800 577 527; www.blenheimshuttles.co.nz) Offers shuttles around Blenheim and the wider Marlborough region.

TAXI

Marlborough Taxis (☑ 03-577 5511) Four-wheeled rescue is offered by Marlborough Taxis.

Kaikoura

☑ 03 / POP 2080

Take SH1 129km southeast from Blenheim (or 180km north from Christchurch) and you'll encounter Kaikoura, a pretty peninsula town backed by the snow-capped Seaward Kaikoura Range. Few places in the world are home to such a variety of easily spottable wildlife: whales, dolphins, NZ fur seals, penguins, shearwaters, petrels and several species of albatross live in or pass by the area.

Marine animals are abundant here due to ocean-current and continental-shelf conditions: the seabed gradually slopes away from the land before plunging to more than 800m where the southerly current hits the continental shelf. This creates an upwelling of nutrients from the ocean floor into the feeding zone.

History

In Māori legend, Kaikoura Peninsula (Taumanu o Te Waka a Māui) was the seat where the demigod Māui placed his feet when he fished the North Island up from the depths. The area was heavily settled by Māori, with excavations showing that the area was a moa-hunter settlement about 800 to 1000 years ago. The name Kaikoura comes from 'kai' (food/eat) and 'koura' (crayfish).

James Cook sailed past the peninsula in 1770, but didn't land. His journal states that 57 Māori in four double-hulled canoes came towards the *Endeavour*, but 'would not be prevail'd upon to put along side'.

In 1828 Kaikoura's beachfront was the scene of a tremendous battle. A northern Ngāti Toa war party, led by chief Te Rauparaha, bore down on Kaikoura, killing or capturing several hundred of the local Ngāi Tahu tribe.

Europeans established a whaling station here in 1842, and the town remained a whaling centre until 1922, after which time farming and fishing sustained the community. It was in the 1980s that wildlife tours began to transform Kaikoura into a lively tourist town with excellent marine mammal viewing.

In November 2016, a powerful 7.8 magnitude earthquake struck the region, but following the reestablishment of vital transport links (in some cases ongoing into 2018), Kaikoura is again looking forward to a positive future.

◉ Sights

Point Kean Seal Colony   WILDLIFE RESERVE
At the end of the peninsula, seals laze around on the rocks lapping up all the attention. Give them a wide berth (10m), and never get between them and the sea – they will attack if they feel cornered and can move surprisingly fast. Since the uplift of the coastline during the 2016 earthquake, the seals have moved further from the road and car park, so keep a close eye on tides.

Kaikoura Museum   MUSEUM
(☏03-319 7440; https://kaikoura-museum.co.nz; 96 West End; adult/child $12/6; ⊙10am-4pm) Housed in a modern building designed to resemble a crayfishing pot, the Kaikoura Museum is one of NZ's best provincial museums. The region's geology and natural and coastal histories are illuminated with well-curated exhibitions – highlights include the fossilised remains of a plesiosaur – and there are poignant displays on the November 2016 earthquake that struck the region. The 'New Normal' section consists of more than 30 individual 'mini exhibitions' about the earthquake's impact, contributed by local residents.

Fyffe House   HISTORIC BUILDING
(www.heritage.org.nz; 62 Avoca St; adult/child $10/free; ⊙10am-5pm Oct-Apr, to 4pm Thu-Mon May-Sep) Kaikoura's oldest surviving building, Fyffe House's whale-bone foundations were laid in 1844. Proudly positioned and fronted with a colourful garden, the little two-storey cottage offers a fascinating insight into the lives of colonial settlers. Interpretive displays are complemented by historic objects, while peeling wallpaper and the odd cobweb lend authenticity. Cute maritime-themed shop.

✚ Activities & Tours

Wildlife Watching
Wildlife tours are Kaikoura's speciality, particularly those involving whales (including sperm, pilot, killer, humpback and southern right), dolphins (Hector's, bottlenose and dusky – a particularly social species sometimes seen in the hundreds) and NZ fur seals. There's also plenty of bird life, including albatrosses and blue penguins. During summer, book your tour a few weeks ahead, and allow some leeway for lousy weather.

★ Albatross Encounter   BIRDWATCHING
(☏03-319 6777, 0800 733 365; www.encounter kaikoura.co.nz; 96 Esplanade; adult/child $125/60; ⊙tours 9am & 1pm year-round, plus 6am Nov-Apr) 🐾 Even if you don't consider yourself a bird-nerd, you'll love this close encounter with pelagic species such as shearwaters, shags, mollymawks and petrels. It's the various albatross species, however, that steal the show. Just awesome.

Whale Watch Kaikoura   WILDLIFE WATCHING
(☏0800 655 121, 03-319 6767; www.whalewatch. co.nz; Railway Station; 3½hr tours adult/child $150/60) 🐾 With knowledgable guides and fascinating on-board animation, Kaikoura's biggest operator heads out on boat trips (with admirable frequency) in search of some of the big fellas. It'll refund 80% of your fare if no whales are sighted (success rate: 95%). If this trip is a must for you, allow a few days' flexibility in case the weather turns to custard.

Seal Kayak Kaikoura   KAYAKING
(Levi's Pedal Kayaks; ☏027 261 0124, 0800 387 7325; www.sealkayakkaikoura.com; 2 Beach Rd; tours from $59) Sightseeing, seal encounters and fishing trips using pedal kayaks, which provide the option of propelling the craft either with your arms or legs.

South Pacific Whale Watch   WHALE WATCHING
(☏0800 360 886; www.southpacificwhales.co.nz; 72 West End; per person $350-650) Offers a wide range of whale-watching and flightseeing trips by helicopter.

Seal Swim Kaikoura   ECOTOUR
(☏03-319 6182, 0800 732 579; www.sealswim kaikoura.co.nz; 58 West End; adult/child $110/70, viewing $55/35; ⊙Oct-May) 🐾 Take a (warmly wet-suited) swim with Kaikoura's healthy population of playful seals – including very cute pups – on two-hour guided snorkelling tours (by boat) run by the Chambers family.

Kaikoura

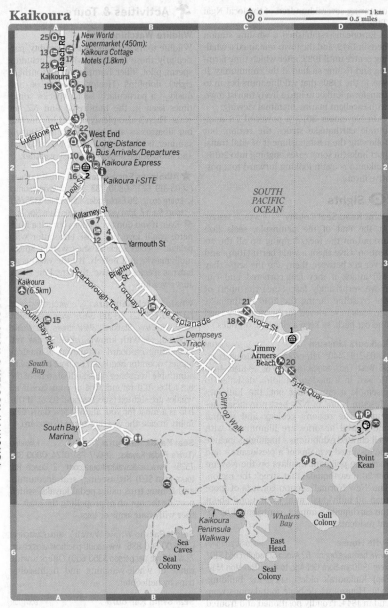

Dolphin Encounter ECOTOUR

(📞0800 733 365, 03-319 6777; www.encounter
kaikoura.co.nz; 96 Esplanade; swim adult/child
$175/160, observation $95/50; ⏰tours 8.30am
& 12.30pm year-round, plus 5.30am Nov-Apr) 🐬

Claiming NZ's highest success rate (90%) for
both locating and swimming with dolphins,
this operator runs feel-good three-hour
tours, which often encounter sizeable pods of
sociable duskies – the classic Kaikoura treat.

Kaikoura

⊙ Sights
1 Fyffe House...C4
2 Kaikoura Museum..................................A2
3 Point Kean Seal Colony........................D5

⊙ Activities, Courses & Tours
Albatross Encounter.....................(see 4)
4 Dolphin Encounter................................B3
5 Kaikoura Fishing Tours..........................A5
6 Kaikoura Helicopters............................A1
7 Kaikoura Kayaks...................................A3
8 Kaikoura Peninsula Walkway................D5
9 Seal Kayak Kaikoura.............................A1
10 Seal Swim Kaikoura..............................A2
South Pacific Whale Watch..........(see 10)
11 Whale Watch Kaikoura...........................A1

⊙ Sleeping
12 Albatross Backpacker Inn......................A3
13 Alpine Pacific Holiday Park....................A1

14 Anchor Inn Motel..................................B3
15 Bay Cottages..A4
Lemon Tree Lodge.....................(see 10)
16 SkyHi Hostel Lodge...............................A2
17 Sunrise Lodge......................................A1

⊗ Eating
18 Green Dolphin.......................................C4
19 Hislops Wholefoods Cafe......................A1
20 Kaikoura Seafood BBQ..........................C4
21 Pier Hotel..C3
22 Zephyr...A2

⊙ Drinking & Nightlife
23 Emporium Brewing................................A1

⊙ Shopping
24 Coastal Sports......................................A2
25 Cods & Crayfish....................................A1

Wings over Whales   SCENIC FLIGHTS
(☑ 03-319 6580, 0800 226 629; www.whales.co.nz;
30min flights adult/child $180/75) Light-plane
flights departing from Kaikoura Airport,
8km south of town on SH1. Spotting success
rate: 95%.

Kaikoura Helicopters   SCENIC FLIGHTS
(☑ 03-319 6609; www.worldofwhales.co.nz; Whale-
way Station Rd; 15/60min flights $100/490) Relia-
ble whale-spotting flights (standard tour 30
minutes, $220 each for three or more peo-
ple), plus jaunts around the peninsula, Mt
Fyffe and peaks beyond. Ask about flights
taking in the area's spectacular post-earthquake landscapes from above.

Tramping

★**Kaikoura Peninsula Walkway**   WALKING
Starting from town, this must-do three- to
four-hour loop heads out to Point Kean,
along the cliffs to South Bay, then back to
town over the isthmus (or in reverse, of
course). En route you'll see fur seals and
red-billed seagull and shearwater colonies.
Lookouts and interesting interpretive panels abound. Collect a map at the i-SITE
(p424) or follow your nose.

Kaikoura Coast Track   TRAMPING
(☑ 03-319 2715; www.kaikouratrack.co.nz; 356
Conway Flat Rd, Ngaroma; $200) This easy two-
day, 26km, self-guided tramp across private farmland combines coastal and alpine
views. The price includes two nights' cottage
accommodation, including one night before

actually beginning the tramp, and pack
transport; BYO sleeping bag and food. Starts
45km south of Kaikoura.

Kaikoura Wilderness Walks   TRAMPING
(☑ 0800 945 337, 03-319 6966; www.kaikoura
wilderness.co.nz; day walks $250-795) 🍃 A
choice of three guided day walks through
the privately owned Puhi Peaks Nature Reserve high in the Seaward Kaikoura range.
Most accessible is the Valley of the Feathers
walk (four hours), climbing to Totara Saddle
and taking in views of the changes wrought
on the landscape by the 2016 earthquake.

Other Activities

There's a safe swimming **beach** on the Esplanade, and a small surf break has been
formed nearby following the 2016 earthquake. Decent **surfing** can be found around
the area, particularly at **Mangamaunu
Beach** (15km north of town), where there's
a 500m point break. Water-sports gear hire
and advice are available from **Board Silly
Surf & SUP Adventures** (☑ 027 418 8900,
0800 787 352; www.boardsilly.co.nz; 9 Hawthorne
Rd, Mangamaunu; 3hr lessons $80, board & suit
from $40) and **Coastal Sports** (☑ 03-319
5028; www.coastalsports.co.nz; 24 West End;
⊙ 9am-5.30pm Mon-Sat, 10am-5pm Sun, extended
hours late Oct-Easter).

For town riding, hire bicycles from the
i-SITE (p424) or Coastal Sports. While you're
there, ask about the Kowhai Trail to the foot
of Mt Fyffe.

MARLBOROUGH & NELSON KAIKOURA

Clarence River Rafting
RAFTING

(☑03-319 6993; www.clarenceriverrafting.co.nz; 1/3802 SH1, at Clarence Bridge; half-day trips adult/child $120/80) Raft the rapids of the Clarence River and experience the spectacular uplift and changes to the landscape following the 2016 Kaikoura earthquake. Half-day trips incorporate 2½ hours on the water, while longer journeys include a three- to five-day adventure with wilderness camping (adult/child $1400/900). Based on SH1, 35km north of Kaikoura near the Clarence Bridge. Grade II; all gear provided.

Kaikoura Kayaks
KAYAKING

(☑0800 452 456, 03-319 7118; www.kaikoura kayaks.nz; 19 Killarney St; 3hr tours adult/child $99/70; ⊙tours 8.30am, 12.30pm & 4.30pm Nov-Apr, 9am & 1pm May-Oct; ⏺) Excellent, family friendly, guided sea-kayak tours to view fur seals and explore the peninsula's coastline. Kayak fishing and other on-demand trips available, plus freedom kayak and paddle-board hire. Ask about visiting Hope Springs, a sulphurous, bubbling section of the ocean that was discovered following the 2016 earthquake.

Kaikoura Fishing Tours
FISHING

(☑0800 246 6587, 027 524 5687; www.kaikoura -fishing-tours.co.nz; 2hr per person $120) Serious about scenery and seafood. Your catch is filleted ready for dinner.

✵ Festivals & Events

Kaikoura Seafest
FOOD & DRINK

(☑0800 473 2337; www.seafest.co.nz; adult/child $45/15; ⊙Oct) This annual one-day celebration in early October combining seafood, wine, beer and music is always a whale of a good time. Fancy dress is encouraged so don't be surprised to see a few folk dressed as penguins, dolphins or other denizens of the deep. Book ahead for accommodation.

🛏 Sleeping

SkyHi Hostel Lodge
GUESTHOUSE $

(☑03-319 5538; www.skyhi.nz; 11 Churchill St; s/d/tr $55/72/105; ⏺) More guesthouse than hostel, SkyHi combines simple but spotless rooms and shared bathrooms with a modern kitchen, spacious guest lounge, and a conservatory with excellent mountain and ocean views. Usually patrolled by the affable owner's friendly cat, the sunny garden and barbecue area is a great place to relax. Pick-ups from the i-SITE (p424) are available on request.

Sunrise Lodge
HOSTEL $

(☑03-319 7444; sunrisehostel@xtra.co.nz; 74 Beach Rd; dm $34-36, d $90; ⏺) In a modern house a short walk from good cafes and restaurants, Sunrise has spotless four- and six-bed dorms, doubles and sunny outdoor chairs and tables.

Alpine Pacific Holiday Park
HOLIDAY PARK $

(☑0800 692 322, 03-319 6275; www.alpine-pacific. co.nz; 69 Beach Rd; sites from $50, cabins $85, units & motels $152-215; @🛜🏊) This compact and proudly trimmed park copes well with its many visitors and offers excellent facilities, including a pool, hot tubs and a barbecue pavilion. Rows of cabins and units are a tad more stylish than the average, and mountain views can be enjoyed from many angles.

Albatross Backpacker Inn
HOSTEL $

(☑0800 222 247, 03-319 6090; www.albatross -kaikoura.co.nz; 1 Torquay St; dm $34-36, tw/d/tr $79/84/105; ⏺) 🐾 This arty backpackers resides in three sweet buildings, one a former post office. It's colourful and close to the beach but sheltered from the breeze. As well as a laid-back lounge with musical instruments for jamming, there are decks and verandas to chill out on.

★ Kaikoura Cottage Motels
MOTEL $$

(☑0800 526 882, 03-319 5599; www.kaikoura cottagemotels.co.nz; cnr Old Beach & Mill Rds; d $140-200; ⏺) This enclave of eight modern tourist flats looks mighty fine, surrounded by attractive native plantings. Oriented for mountain views, the spick-and-span self-contained units sleep four between an open-plan studio-style living room and one private bedroom. Proud and lovely hosts seal the deal.

Bay Cottages
MOTEL $$

(☑0800 556 623, 03-319 7165; www.baycottages. co.nz; 29a South Bay Pde; cottages $120-200; ⏺) Here's a great-value option in South Bay, a few kilometres south of town. Five cottages sleeping up to four all feature a kitchen, lounge area and free Netflix. The surrounding area is private and quiet. Various walkways start in South Bay, and fishing charters leave nearby from Kaikoura's new harbour. A barbecue to cook your fish on is also available.

★ Lemon Tree Lodge
B&B $$$

(☑03-319 7464; www.lemontree.co.nz; 31 Adelphi Tce; s $280, d $280-320; ⏺) Enjoying superb ocean and mountain views, Lemon Tree Lodge combines four charming and stylish rooms in the main house with two quiet and secluded garden units. Our favourites are the Ocean View Suites with expansive windows and private balconies showcasing brilliant Pacific vistas. The well-travelled and friendly owners have plenty of great advice on how best to enjoy the region.

Anchor Inn Motel
MOTEL $$$

(☑ 03-319 5426; www.anchorinn.co.nz; 208 Esplanade; d $185-255; 🕏) The Aussie owners liked this Kaikoura motel so much they bought it and moved here. The sharp and spacious units are a pleasant 15-minute walk from town and about 10 seconds from the ocean. The motel reopened in December 2017 after a post-earthquake makeover.

✕ Eating

Pier Hotel
PUB FOOD $$

(☑ 03-319 5037; www.thepierhotel.co.nz; 1 Avoca St; lunch $16-25, dinner $29-40; ⊙ 11am-late) Situated in the town's primo seaside spot, with panoramic views, the historic Pier Hotel is a friendly and inviting place for a drink and respectable pub grub, including crayfish (half/whole $50/100). Great outside area for sundowners with vistas of the Inland Kaikoura mountain range. You'll find beers here from Kaikoura's two craft breweries: Emporium Brewing and the Kaikoura Brewing Company.

Hislops Wholefoods Cafe
CAFE $$

(☑ 03-319 6971; www.hislops-wholefoods.co.nz; 33 Beach Rd; breakfast & lunch mains $12-19, dinner mains $26-36; ⊙ 8.30am-8pm Wed-Sat, to 4pm Sun; 🖉) 🍃 Organic ingredients shine at this long-established Kaikoura eatery. Come for breakfast on the shaded deck and enjoy hotcakes with blueberries or spicy harissa eggs, or book for dinner and partner organic and biodynamic NZ wines with the lamb salad or local seafood. Throughout the day, home-style baking blurs the line between healthy and tasty, and the coffee is always good.

★ Green Dolphin
MODERN NZ $$$

(☑ 03-319 6666; www.greendolphinkaikoura. com; 12 Avoca St; mains $28-39; ⊙ 5pm-late) Kaikoura's consistent top-ender dishes up high-quality local produce including seafood, beef, lamb and venison. There are also lovely homemade pasta dishes. The hefty drinks list demands attention, featuring exciting aperitifs, craft beer from Three Boys Brewery in Christchurch, interesting wines and more. Booking ahead is definitely rec-

---

---

ommended. Ask for a window table to experience a sunlit Kaikoura dusk.

Zephyr
BISTRO $$$

(☑ 03-319 6999; www.zephyrrestaurant.co.nz; 40 West End; mains $29-37; ⊙ 5.30pm-late Tue-Sat, reduced hours Easter-late Oct) 🍃 Focusing on a concise and seasonal menu, Zephyr's modern dining room is a good place to enjoy seafood chowder, mushroom-crusted venison or local fish and crayfish with a gourmet spin. The wine and beer list is equally focused and well curated.

🍷 Drinking & Nightlife

Emporium Brewing
MICROBREWERY

(☑ 03-319 5897; www.emporiumbrewing.co.nz; 57a Beach Rd; ⊙ 10am-8pm) Fill up a takeaway rigger or buy bottles of Emporium's tasty brews at this simple taproom. Our favourite is the award-winning Angry Sky Red IPA. There's also an on-site minigolf course. Check out the hole featuring the 'earthquake cows', three bovine locals that were stranded precariously on a tiny 'island' of farmland for three days following the 2016 earthquake.

ⓘ Information

Kaikoura i-SITE (☑03-319 5641; www.
kaikoura.co.nz; West End; ⊙9am-5pm Mon-Fri,
to 4pm Sat & Sun, extended hours Dec-Mar)
Helpful staff make tour, accommodation and
transport bookings, and help with DOC-related
matters.

ⓘ Getting There & Away

BUS

InterCity (p404) buses have traditionally run
between Kaikoura and Nelson once daily (3¾
hours), and Picton (2¼ hours) and Christchurch
(from $26, 2¼ hours) twice daily. The bus stop is
next to the i-SITE – tickets and info inside.

Note the service north to Picton was suspended following the 2016 earthquake, but normal
schedules were expected to return following the
full reopening of SH1 north to Picton in 2018.
Check the InterCity website for the latest.

Kaikoura Express (☑0800 500 929; www.
kaikouraexpress.co.nz; adult one way/return
$35/60, child $30/50) – aka the 'Red Bus' –
runs a convenient service (2¾ hours) linking
Christchurch and Kaikoura. Buses leave from
the i-SITE.

TRAIN

KiwiRail Scenic (p404) runs the daily *Coastal
Pacific* service stopping at Kaikoura en route to
Picton (2¼ hours), and Christchurch (2¾ hours)
and vice versa.

Note this service was suspended following the
2016 Kaikoura earthquake, but should be operating again by late 2018. Check KiwiRail's website (www.kiwirail.co.nz) for the latest update.

ⓘ Getting Around

Kaikoura Shuttles (☑03-319 6166; www.
kaikourashuttles.co.nz) will run you around the
local sights as well as to and from the airport.
It can also get you to the starting point of the
Kaikoura Coast Track. For local car hire, contact
Kaikoura Rentals (☑03-319 3311; www.
kaikourarentals.co.nz; 94 Churchill St).

NELSON REGION

The Nelson region is centred upon Tasman
Bay. It stretches north to Golden Bay and
Farewell Spit, and south to Nelson Lakes. It's
not hard to see why it's such a popular travel
destination for international and domestic
travellers alike: not only does it boast three
national parks (Kahurangi, Nelson Lakes
and Abel Tasman), it can also satisfy nearly
every other whim, from food, wine and beer,
art, craft and festivals, to that most precious
of pastimes for which the region is well
known: lazing about in the sunshine.

ⓘ Getting There & Away

Nelson is the region's primary gateway, with
competitive domestic airline connections, and
comprehensive bus services linking it with all
major South Island towns.

Abel Tasman Coachlines (☑03-548 0285;
www.abeltasmantravel.co.nz)

Golden Bay Coachlines (☑03-525 8352;
www.gbcoachlines.co.nz)

Trek Express (☑027 222 1872, 0800 128 735;
www.trekexpress.co.nz)

Nelson

☑03 / POP 46,440

Dishing up a winning combination of beautiful surroundings, sophisticated art and culinary scenes, and lashings of sunshine, Nelson is hailed as one of New Zealand's most
'liveable' cities. In summer it fills up with
local and international visitors, who lap up
its diverse offerings.

⊙ Sights

Nelson has an inordinate number of galleries, most of which are listed in the *Art
& Crafts Nelson City* brochure (with walk-
ing-trail map) available from the i-SITE
(p429). A fruitful wander can be had by
starting at the woolly **Fibre Spectrum**
(☑03-548 1939; www.fibrespectrum.co.nz; 280
Trafalgar St; ⊙9am-5pm Mon-Fri, 9.30am-2.30pm
Sat), before moving on to *The Lord of the
Rings* jeweller **Jens Hansen** (☑03-548 0640;
www.jenshansen.com; 320 Trafalgar Sq; ⊙9am-
5pm Mon-Fri, to 2pm Sat year-round, 10am-1pm Sun
late Oct-Easter) and glass-blower **Flamedaisy**
(☑03-548 4475; www.flamedaisy.co.nz; 324 Trafalgar Sq; ⊙10am-4pm Mon-Sat) nearby. Other interesting local creations can be found at the
Nelson Market (p429) on Saturday.

★ **World of WearableArt
& Classic Cars Museum**   MUSEUM
(WOW; ☑03-547 4573; www.wowcars.co.nz; 1 Cadillac Way; adult/child $24/10; ⊙10am-5pm) Nel-
son is the birthplace of NZ's most inspiring
fashion show, the annual World of WearableArt Awards. You can see 70 or so current
and past entries in this museum's several
sensory-overloading galleries, including a
glow-in-the-dark room. Look out for the
'Bizarre Bras'.

More car than bra? Under the same roof are more than 100 mint-condition classic cars and motorbikes. Exhibits change, but may include a 1959 pink Cadillac, a yellow 1950 Bullet Nose Studebaker convertible and a BMW bubble car.

The World of WearableArt Awards show began humbly in 1987 when Suzie Moncrieff held an offbeat event featuring art that could be worn and modelled. Folks quickly cottoned on to the show's creative (and competitive) possibilities. You name it, they've shown that a garment can be made from it: wood, metal, shells, cable ties, dried leaves, ping-pong balls... The festival (p378) now has a new home in Wellington.

Between the galleries, cafe and art shop, allow a couple of hours if you can.

⭐**Tahuna Beach**   BEACH
(🚻) Nelson's primo playground takes the form of an epic sandy beach (with lifeguards in summer) backed by dunes, and a large grassy parkland with a playground, an espresso cart, a hydroslide, bumper boats, a roller-skating rink, a model railway, and an adjacent restaurant strip. Weekends can get very busy!

McCashin's Brewery   BREWERY
(📞03-547 5357; www.mccashins.co.nz; 660 Main Rd, Stoke; ⊗7am-6pm Mon-Wed, 7am-10pm Thu & Fri, 9am-10pm Sat, 9am-8pm Sun) A groundbreaker in the new era of craft brewing in NZ, which started way back in the 1980s. Visit the historic cider factory for a tasting, cafe meal or tour.

Founders Heritage Park   MUSEUM
(📞03-548 2649; www.founderspark.co.nz; 87 Atawhai Dr; adult/child/family $7/5/15; ⊗10am-4.30pm) Two kilometres from the city centre, this park comprises a replica historic village with a museum, gallery displays, and artisan products such as chocolate and clothing. It makes for a fascinating wander, which you can augment with a visit to the on-site **Park Life Brewery** (📞03-548 4638; www.facebook.com/parklifebrewing; 87 Atawhai Dr; ⊗9am-4.30pm Mon-Fri, to 5.30pm Sat & Sun). Check its Facebook page for occasional Food Truck Fridays from 5pm (late October to Easter).

Suter Art Gallery   GALLERY
(www.thesuter.org.nz; 208 Bridge St; ⊗9.30am-4.30pm) FREE Adjacent to **Queen's Gardens** (Bridge St), Nelson's public art gallery presents changing exhibitions, floor talks, mu-sical and theatrical performances, and films. The Suter reopened after a fabulous redevelopment in late 2016 and now features an arthouse cinema and a great riverside cafe. Check the website to find out what's on.

Christ Church Cathedral   CHURCH
(www.nelsoncathedral.org; Trafalgar Sq; ⊗9am-6pm) FREE The enduring symbol of Nelson, the art-deco Christ Church Cathedral lords it over the city from the top of Trafalgar St. The best time to visit is during the 10am and 7pm Sunday services when you can hear the organist and the choir in song.

Nelson Provincial Museum   MUSEUM
(📞03-548 9588; www.nelsonmuseum.co.nz; cnr Trafalgar & Hardy Sts; adult/child $5/3; ⊗10am-5pm Mon-Fri, to 4.30pm Sat & Sun) This modern museum space is filled with cultural heritage and natural history exhibits that have a regional bias, as well as regular touring exhibitions (for which admission fees vary). It also features a great rooftop garden.

🏃 **Activities**

Walking & Cycling
There's plenty of walking and cycling to be enjoyed in and around the town, for which the i-SITE (p429) has maps. The classic walk from town is to the **Centre of NZ** atop the **Botanical Reserve** (Milton St); if you enjoy that then ask about the **Grampians**.

Nelson has two of the New Zealand Cycle Trail's 23 Great Rides: **Dun Mountain Trail** (www.heartofbiking.org.nz), an awesome but challenging one-day ride ranging over the hills to the south of the city; and the Great Taste Trail (p431) offering a blissfully flat meander through beautiful countryside dotted with wine, food and art stops.

Gentle Cycling Company   CYCLING
(📞03-929 5652, 0800 932 453; www.gentle cycling.co.nz; 411 Nayland Rd, Stoke; day tours from $95) Self-guided cycle tours along the Great Taste Trail, with drop-ins (and tastings) at wineries, breweries, cafes and occasional galleries. Bike hire (from $30) and shuttles also available.

Trail Journeys   CYCLING
(📞03-540 3095, 0800 292 538; www.trailjourneys nelson.co.nz; 37-39 Halifax St; full-day tours from $89) Trail Journeys offers a range of self-guided cycle tours around Nelson city, and beyond along the Great Taste Trail. It's located next to the i-SITE (p429) in central

Central Nelson

Nelson and there are two other conveniently located depots at Mapua Wharf and Kaiteriteri.

Paragliding, Hang Gliding & Kiteboarding

Nelson is a great place for adrenaline activities, with plenty of action in summer, particularly around the rather divine Tahuna Beach (p425). Tandem paragliding costs around $180, introductory kitesurfing starts at $150, and paddle-board hire is around $20 per hour.

Kite Surf Nelson   KITESURFING
(☑0800 548 363; www.kitesurfnelson.co.nz; lessons from $175) Learn to kite surf at Tahunanui, or hire a stand-up paddle board.

Nelson Paragliding   PARAGLIDING
(☑03-544 1182; www.nelsonparagliding.co.nz; Ngawhatu Recreation Ground, Stoke; tandem paragliding $220) Get high in the sky over Tahunanui with Nelson Paragliding.

Other Activities

Cable Bay Kayaks   KAYAKING
(☑03-391 0010; www.cablebaykayaks.co.nz; Cable Bay Rd, Hira; half-/full-day guided trips $90/150) Fifteen minutes' drive from Nelson city, Greig and the team offer richly rewarding guided sea-kayaking trips exploring the local coastline, where you'll likely meet local marine life (snorkelling gear on board helps). You might even enter a cave.

Moana SUP   WATER SPORTS
(☑027 656 0268; www.moananzsup.co.nz; lessons from $70) Learn SUP with the guys at Moana, or hire a board if you're already enlightened.

⛵ Tours

Nelson Tours & Travel   TOURS
(☑027 237 5007, 0800 222 373; www.nelsontoursandtravel.co.nz) CJ and crew run various small-group, flexible tours honing in on

Central Nelson

Nelson's wine, craft beer, art and scenic highlights. The five-hour 'Best of Both Worlds' ($140) tour includes beer, wine and lunch at the heritage Moutere Inn. Day tours of Marlborough wineries also available ($250).

✷ Festivals & Events

Nelson Jazz Festival MUSIC
(www.nelsonjazzfest.co.nz; ⊘ Jan) More scoo-be-doo-bop events over a week in January than you can shake a leg at. Features local and national acts.

Nelson Arts Festival PERFORMING ARTS
(www.nelsonartsfestival.co.nz; ⊘ Oct) Over two weeks in October; events include a street carnival, exhibitions, cabaret, writers, theatre and music.

⊨ Sleeping

Prince Albert HOSTEL $
(☏0800 867 3529, 03-548 8477; www.theprincealbert.co.nz; 113 Nile St; dm $27-29, s/d/tw $50/85/85; ☎) A five-minute walk from the city centre, this lively, well-run backpackers has roomy en-suite dorms surrounding a sunny courtyard. Private rooms are upstairs in the main building, which also houses an English-style pub where guests can meet the locals and refuel with a good-value meal.

Bug Backpackers HOSTEL $
(☏03-539 4227; www.thebug.co.nz; 226 Vanguard St; dm $26-29, d $69-95; @☎) A buzzy hostel about 15-minutes' walk from town, occupying a converted villa, a modern

building next door and a self-contained unit sleeping up to four. The VW-themed Bug boasts an unashamedly bold colour scheme, a homey backyard and jovial owners. Free bikes, wi-fi and pick-ups/drop-offs.

Tasman Bay Backpackers HOSTEL $
(☏0800 222 572, 03-548 7950; www.tasmanbaybackpackers.co.nz; 10 Weka St; sites from $20, dm $28-30, d $76-88; @☎) This well-designed, friendly hostel has airy communal spaces with a 100% Kiwi music soundtrack, hypercoloured rooms, a sunny outdoor deck and a well-used hammock. Good freebies: wi-fi, decent bikes, breakfast during winter, and chocolate pudding and ice cream year-round.

Brook Valley Holiday Park HOLIDAY PARK $
(☏03-548 0399; 600 Brook St; unpowered/powered sites per person $10/17) Holiday park in a rural setting around 4km from central Nelson, sitting near trails up to Dun Mountain and across to the Pelorus River. The park's future existence seems to be in perpetual limbo, so check ahead.

Sussex House B&B $$
(☏03-548 9972; www.sussex.co.nz; 238 Bridge St; d $170-190, tr $180; ☎) In a relatively quiet riverside spot, only a five-minute walk to town, this creaky old lady dates back to around 1880. The five tastefully decorated rooms feature upmarket bedding, period-piece furniture and en-suite bathrooms, except one room that has a private bathroom down the hall. Enjoy local fruit at breakfast in the grand dining room.

MARLBOROUGH & NELSON NELSON

Te Maunga House
B&B $$

(📞 021 201 2461; www.nelsoncityaccommodation. co.nz; 15 Dorothy Annie Way; s $80-100, d $125-140; ⊗ closed May-Oct; 🐾) Aptly named (The Mountain), this grand old family home has exceptional views and a well-travelled host. Two doubles and a twin have a homey feel with comfy beds and their own bathrooms. Your hearty breakfast can be walked off up and down *that* hill, a very steep 10-minute climb with an extra five minutes to town.

Beaches Motor Inn
MOTEL $$

(📞 0800 332232, 03-546 8008; www.beachesmotor inn.co.nz; 69-71 Tahunanui Dr, Tahunanui; d from $169; 🐾) Sixteen smart, well-equipped units closer to the road than the beach but still handy to all of Tahunanui's watery attractions. All units have patios or balconies, and free wi-fi.

Cedar Grove Motor Lodge
MOTEL $$

(📞 03-545 1133; www.cedargrove.co.nz; cnr Trafalgar & Grove Sts; d $160-210; 🐾) A big old cedar landmark, this smart, modern block of spacious apartments is just a three-minute walk to town. Its range of studios and doubles are plush and elegant, with full cooking facilities.

Palazzo Motor Lodge
MOTEL $$$

(📞 03-545 8171, 0800 472 5293; www.palazzomotor lodge.co.nz; 159 Rutherford St; d $210-335; 🐾) This modern, Italian-tinged motor lodge offers stylish studios and one- and two-room apartments featuring enviable kitchens with decent cooking equipment, classy glassware and a dishwasher. Its comfort and convenient location easily atone for the odd bit of dubious art.

✕ Eating

Falafel Gourmet
MIDDLE EASTERN $

(📞 03-545 6220; 195 Hardy St; meals $11-19; ⊗ 10am-4pm Mon-Sat; 🍴) A cranking joint dishing out the best kebabs for miles around. They're healthy, too!

★ Cod & Lobster
SEAFOOD, BISTRO $$

(📞 03-546 4300; www.codandlobster.com; 300 Trafalgar St; mains $22-36; ⊗ 11am-11pm) Stellar cocktails and NZ's biggest selection of gin make Cod & Lobster's corner bar an essential destination, but this heritage space also serves up excellent food. Unsurprisingly, seafood is the main focus, so enliven your palate with Bloody Mary oyster shooters before moving on to Louisiana-style prawns with spicy sausage or the good-value seafood platter ($40 for two people).

Urban Oyster
MODERN NZ $$

(📞 03-546 7861; www.urbaneatery.co.nz; 278 Hardy St; dishes $11-27; ⊗ 4pm-late Mon, 11am-late Tue-Sat) Slurp oysters from the shell, or revitalise with sashimi and ceviche, then sate your cravings with street-food dishes such as kung pao Sichuan fried chicken or smoked-pork empanadas with charcoal shrimp mayo. Black butchers' tiles, edgy artwork and a fine wine list all bolster this metropolitan experience, and craft beers come courtesy of Golden Bear Brewing in nearby Mapua.

DeVille
CAFE $$

(📞 03-545 6911; www.devillecafe.co.nz; 22 New St; meals $12-21; ⊗ 8am-4pm Mon-Sat, 9am-3pm Sun; 🍴) Most of DeVille's tables lie in its sweet walled courtyard, a hidden boho oasis in the inner city and the perfect place for a meal or morning tea. The food's good and local – from fresh baking to a chorizo-burrito brunch, Caesar salad and proper burgers, washed down with regional wines and beers. Open late for live music Fridays in summer.

Morri Street Cafe
CAFE $$

(📞 03-548 8110; www.morrisonstreetcafe.co.nz; 244 Hardy St; mains $11-21; ⊗ 7.30am-3.30pm Mon-Fri, 8.30am-4pm Sat & Sun; 🍴) Shared tables, colourful local art and a quieter atrium at the back all combine to make Morri Street a top place for a leisurely breakfast or lunch. You may have to share the buzzy space with a few locals having impromptu business meetings, but it's a price worth paying for dishes including Moroccan eggs and a good pulled-pork burger.

Indian Café
INDIAN $$

(📞 03-548 4089; www.theindiancafe.com; 94 Collingwood St; mains $13-20; ⊗ noon-2pm Mon-Fri, 5pm-late daily; 🍴) This saffron-coloured Edwardian villa houses an Indian restaurant that keeps the bhajis raised with impressive interpretations of Anglo-Indian standards such as chicken tandoori, rogan josh and beef Madras. Share the mixed platter to start, then mop up your mains with one of 10 different breads.

★ Hopgood's
MODERN NZ $$$

(📞 03-545 7191; www.hopgoods.co.nz; 284 Trafalgar St; mains $36-39; ⊗ 5.30pm-late Mon-Sat) Tongue-and-groove-lined Hopgood's is perfect for a romantic dinner or holiday treat. The food is decadent and skilfully prepared but unfussy, allowing quality local ingredients to shine. Try the duck breast with chestnut polenta or the lamb rump with a mint and caper dressing. The five-course tasting menu ($95) affords the full Hopgood's experience. Desirable, predominantly Kiwi wine list. Bookings advisable.

🍷 Drinking & Nightlife

Craft Beer Depot CRAFT BEER
(☑03-548 2126; www.craftbeerdepot.nz; 70 Achilles Ave; ⊗noon-9pm Tue-Thu, to 10pm Fri & Sat, to 8pm Sun) Concealed behind the bus station, Craft Beer Depot is a rustic and loads-of-fun showcase of the best of NZ craft beer. Ten taps dispense brews from around the country, and a back room has plenty more bottled beers. Foosball, old sofas and occasional Friday and Saturday food trucks combine with some of the most beer-savvy bartenders in NZ.

Free House CRAFT BEER
(☑03-548 9391; www.freehouse.co.nz; 95 Collingwood St; ⊗3-11pm Mon-Fri, noon-11pm Sat & Sun) Tastefully converted from its original more reverent purpose, this former church is now home to an excellent, oft-changing selection of NZ craft beers. Munch on Brazilian-influenced bar snacks on the outside deck, and visit on a Friday or Saturday afternoon from noon to 6pm to browse the racks of vinyl at the Free House's excellent Family Jewels Records pop-up store.

Rhythm & Brown BAR
(☑03-546 6319; www.facebook.com/rhythmandbrown.nz; 19 New St; ⊗4pm-late Tue-Sat) Nelson's slinkiest late-night drinking den, where classy cocktails, fine wines and craft beer flow from behind the bar and sweet vinyl tunes drift from the speakers. Regular Saturday-night microgigs in a compact, groovy space.

☆ Entertainment

Theatre Royal THEATRE
(☑03-548 3840; www.theatreroyalnelson.co.nz; 78 Rutherford St; ⊗box office 10am-4pm Mon-Fri) State-of-the-art theatre in a charmingly restored heritage building. This 'grand old lady of Nelson' boasts a full program of local and touring drama, dance and musical productions. Visit the website for the current program and bookings (or book online at www.ticketdirect.co.nz), or visit the box office.

🛍 Shopping

Nelson Farmers Market MARKET
(☑022 010 2776; www.nelsonfarmersmarket.org.nz; Maitai Blvd, Paru Paru Rd; ⊗8am-2pm Wed) Relocated in late 2017 to a leafy riverside location, this market is full to bursting with local produce to fill your picnic hamper.

IN PURSUIT OF HOPPINESS

The Nelson region lays claim to the title of craft-brewing capital of New Zealand. World-class hops have been grown here since the 1840s, and around a dozen breweries are spread between Nelson and Golden Bay.

Pick up a copy of the *Nelson Craft Beer Trail* map (available from the i-SITE and other outlets, and online at www.craftbrewingcapital.co.nz) and wind your way between brewers and pubs. Top picks for a tipple include Free House and the Craft Beer Depot in Nelson, Hop Federation (p432) in Riwaka, and the Townshend Brewery at Motueka's Toad Hall (p433).

Nelson Market MARKET
(☑03-546 6454; www.nelsonmarket.co.nz; Montgomery Sq; ⊗8am-1pm Sat) Don't miss Nelson Market, a big, busy weekly market featuring fresh produce, food stalls, fashion, local arts, crafts and buskers.

ℹ Information

After Hours & Duty Doctors (☑03-546 8881; 98 Waimea Rd; ⊗8am-10pm)
Nelson Hospital (☑03-546 1800; www.nmdhb.govt.nz; Waimea Rd)
Nelson i-SITE (☑03-548 2304; www.nelsonnz.com; cnr Trafalgar & Halifax Sts; ⊗9am-5pm Mon-Fri, to 4pm Sat & Sun) A slick centre complete with DOC information desk for the low-down on national parks and tracks (including Abel Tasman and Heaphy). Pick up a copy of the *Nelson Tasman Visitor Guide*.

ℹ Getting There & Away

Book Abel Tasman Coachlines, InterCity, KiwiRail Scenic and Interisland ferry services at the **Nelson SBL Travel Centre** (☑03-548 1539; www.nelsoncoachlines.co.nz; 27 Bridge St; ⊗7am-5.15pm Mon-Fri) or the i-SITE.

AIR

Nelson Airport is 5km southwest of town, near Tahunanui Beach. A taxi from there to town will cost around $30 or **Super Shuttle** (☑0800 748 885, 03-547 5782; www.supershuttle.co.nz) offers door-to-door service for around $20.
Air New Zealand (☑0800 737 000; www.airnewzealand.co.nz) Direct flights to/from Wellington, Auckland and Christchurch.
Air2There (☑0800 777 000, 04-904 5133; www.air2there.com) Flies to/from Paraparaumu.

Jetstar (☑ 09-975 9426, 0800 800 995; www.jetstar.com) Flies to/from Auckland and Wellington.

Originair (☑ 0800 380 380; www.originair. co.nz) To/from Palmerston North.

Soundsair (☑ 0800 505 005, 03-520 3080; www.soundsair.com) To/from Wellington and Paraparaumu.

BUS

Abel Tasman Coachlines (p424) operates bus services to Motueka ($14, one hour), and Kaiteriteri and Marahau (both $21, two hours). These services also connect with Golden Bay Coachlines (p424) services for Takaka and around. Transport to/from the three national parks is provided by Trek Express (p424).

InterCity (☑ 03-548 1538; www.intercity. co.nz; Bridge St) runs from Nelson to most key South Island destinations including Picton ($23, two hours), Kaikoura ($52, 3½ hours) and Greymouth ($40, six hours).

ⓘ Getting Around

BICYCLE

Bikes are available for hire from **Nelson Cycle Hire & Tours** (☑ 03-539 4193; www.nelsoncyclehire.co.nz; Nelson Airport; bike hire per day $45), among many other cycle tour companies.

BUS

Nelson Suburban Bus Lines (SBL; ☑ 03-548 3290; www.nbus.co.nz; 27 Bridge St) operates NBUS local services from the **Central Bus Stop** (Wakatu Lane) between Nelson and Richmond via Tahunanui and Bishopdale until about 7pm weekdays and 4.30pm on weekends. It also runs the **Late Late Bus** (www.nbus. co.nz; Trafalgar St; ⊙ hourly 10pm-3am Fri & Sat) from Nelson to Richmond via Tahunanui on Friday and Saturday nights, departing from the Westpac Bank on Trafalgar St. Maximum fare for these services is $4.

TAXI

Nelson City Taxis (☑ 03-548 8225; www. nelsontaxis.co.nz)

Sun City Taxis (☑ 03-548 2666; www.suncity taxis.co.nz)

Ruby Coast & Moutere Hills

From Richmond, south of Nelson, there are two routes to Motueka: the quicker, busier route along the Ruby Coast, and the inland route through the Moutere Hills. If you're making a round trip from Nelson, drive one route out, and the other on the way back.

The two highways aren't particularly far apart, and the whole area can be explored by bicycle on the Great Taste Trail, so named for the many wineries and other culinary (and art) stops along the way. The *Nelson Wine Guide* pamphlet (www.wine nelson.co.nz) will help you find them. Other useful resources for this area are the *Nelson Art Guide* and *Nelson's Creative Pathways* pamphlets.

◉ Sights

The Ruby Coast route begins on SH60 and skirts around Waimea Inlet before diverting along the well signposted **Ruby Coast Scenic Route**. Although this is the quickest way to get from Nelson to Motueka (around a 45-minute drive), there are various distractions waiting to slow you down. Major attractions include Rabbit Island recreation reserve, and **Mapua**, near the mouth of the Waimea River, home to arty shops and eateries.

The inland **Moutere Highway** (signposted at Appleby on SH60) is a pleasant alternative traversing gently rolling countryside dotted with farms, orchards and lifestyle blocks. Visitor attractions are fewer and further between, but it's a scenic and fruitful drive, particularly in high summer when roadside stalls are laden with fresh produce. The main settlement along the way is **Upper Moutere**. First settled by German immigrants and originally named Sarau, today it's a sleepy hamlet with a couple of notable stops. Look for the *Moutere Artisans* trail guide (www.moutereartisans.co.nz).

Rabbit Island/Moturoa   BEACH, FOREST
(⊙ dawn-dusk) Around 9km from Richmond on SH60 is the signposted turn-off to Rabbit Island/Moturoa, a recreation reserve offering estuary views from many angles, sandy beaches and quiet pine forest trails forming part of the Great Taste Trail. The bridge to the island closes at sunset; overnight stays are not allowed.

Höglund Art Glass   GALLERY
(☑ 03-544 6500; www.hoglundartglass.com; 52 Lansdowne Rd, Appleby; ⊙ 10am-5pm) Ola, Marie and their associates work the furnace to produce internationally acclaimed glass art. The process is amazing to watch, and the results beautiful to view in the gallery. Their jewellery and penguins make memorable souvenirs if their signature vases are too heavy to take home.

GREAT TASTE TRAIL

In a stroke of genius inspired by great weather and easy topography, the Tasman region has developed one of New Zealand's most popular cycle trails. Why is it so popular? Because no other is so frequently punctuated by stops for food, wine, craft beer and art, as it passes through a range of landscapes from bucolic countryside to estuary boardwalk.

The 174km **Great Taste Trail** (www.heartofbiking.org.nz) stretches from Nelson to Kaiteriteri, with plans afoot to propel it further inland. While it can certainly be ridden in full in a few days, stopping at accommodation en route, it is even more easily ridden as day trips of various lengths. Mapua is a great place to set off from, with bike hire from **Wheelie Fantastic** (☑03-543 2245; www.wheeliefantastic.co.nz; 151 Aranui Rd, Mapua; self-guided tours from $65, bike hire per day from $50) or **Trail Journeys** (p425) and a ferry ride over to the trails of **Rabbit Island**. The trail also passes through thrilling **Kaiteriteri Mountain Bike Park** (p433).

Nelson's many other cycle-tour and bike-hire companies can get you out on the trail, with bike drops and pick-ups.

✖ Eating & Drinking

Smokehouse FISH & CHIPS $
(☑0800 540 2280; www.smokehouse.co.nz; Mapua Wharf, Mapua; fish & chips $8-12; ☺11am-8pm) Visit this Mapua institution to order fish and chips and eat them on the wharf while the gulls eye off your crispy bits. Get some delicious wood-smoked fish and pâté to go.

★ **Boat Shed Cafe** MODERN NZ $$
(☑03-540 2656; www.boatshedcafe.co.nz/mapua; 33 Toru St, Mapua; shared plates $15-20, mains $31; ☺10.30am-late; ☑) 🍴 Look past the slightly odd location – the cafe's waterfront pavilion is reached by travelling through the Mapua Leisure Park – and focus on views of nearby Rabbit Island (p430) and a menu combining diverse international influences. Flavours include Vietnamese beef tartare, fish carpaccio and one of the South Island's best gourmet cheeseburgers, and the surprising drinks list is exceedingly local.

Jester House CAFE $$
(☑03-526 6742; www.jesterhouse.co.nz; 320 Aporo Rd, Tasman; meals $16-21; ☺9am-4.30pm) Long-standing Jester House is reason alone to take this coastal detour, as much for its tame eels as for the peaceful sculpture gardens that encourage you to linger over lunch. A short, simple menu puts a few twists into staples (venison burger, lavender shortbread), and there are local beers and wines. It's 8km to Mapua or Motueka.

Moutere Inn PUB
(☑03-543 2759; www.mouterinn.co.nz; 1406 Moutere Hwy, Upper Moutere; ☺noon-8pm Mon & Tue, to 9pm Wed & Sun, to 11pm Thu-Sat) Reputedly NZ's oldest pub, complete with retro decor, the Moutere Inn is a welcoming establishment serving thoughtful meals ($13 to $32; homemade burgers, potato gnocchi) and predominantly local and NZ craft beer. Sit in the sunshine with a beer-tasting platter, or settle in on music nights with a folksy bent. Rooms are available if you need to rest your head.

ⓘ Getting There & Away

InterCity (p430) buses service Nelson and Motueka, but to access the Ruby Coast and Moutere Hills you'll need your own transport. Biking the Great Taste Trail is a good way of exploring.

Motueka

☑ 03 / POP 7600

Motueka (pronounced mott-oo-ecka, meaning 'Island of Weka') is a bustling agricultural hub, and a great base from which to explore the Nelson region. It has vital amenities, ample accommodation, cafes and roadside fruit stalls, all in a beautiful river and estuary setting. Stock up here if you're en route to Golden Bay or the Abel Tasman and Kahurangi National Parks. Tasty distractions before you leave town include local craft beers and ciders served in a leafy garden cafe, and an excellent Sunday morning farmers market. Airborne thrill seekers are spoilt for choice.

Motueka

Motueka

Activities, Courses & Tours
1 Bike Shed A2

Sleeping
2 Equestrian Lodge Motel B3
3 Laughing Kiwi A3
4 Motueka Top 10 Holiday Park B1

Eating
5 Motueka Sunday Market B2
6 Precinct Dining Co A2

Drinking & Nightlife
7 Sprig & Fern B2

Sights & Activities

While most of Mot's drawcards are out of town, there are a few attractions worth checking out, the buzziest of which is the active aerodrome, home to some of the country's best skydiving. It's a good place to soak up some sun and views, and watch a few folks drop in.

While you might not realise it from the high street, Motueka is just a stone's throw from the sea. Eyeball the waters (with birds and saltwater baths) along the **estuary walkway** (which can also be cycled; hire bikes from the **Bike Shed** (☑03-929 8607; www.motuekabikeshed.co.nz; 132 High St; half-/

full-day hire from $30/40)). Follow your nose or obtain a town map from the i-SITE (p433), where you can also get the *Motueka Art Walk* pamphlet detailing sculptures, murals and occasional peculiarities around town.

Hop Federation BREWERY
(☑03-528 0486; www.hopfederation.co.nz; 483 Main Rd, Riwaka; ⊙11am-6pm) Pop in for tastings and fill a flagon to go at this teeny-weeny but terrific craft brewery 5km from Mot. A mixed sampler pack of four different brews ($15) is good value. Our pick of the ales is the Red IPA. And note the cherry stall across the road.

★ **Skydive Abel Tasman** ADVENTURE SPORTS
(☑03-528 4091, 0800 422 899; www.skydive.co.nz; Motueka Aerodrome, 60 College St; jumps 13,000/16,500ft $319/409) Move over, Taupo: we've jumped both and think Mot takes the cake. Presumably so do the many sports jumpers who favour this drop zone, some of whom you may see rocketing in. Photo and video packages are extra. Excellent spectating from the front lawn.

Sleeping

Eden's Edge Lodge HOSTEL $
(☑03-528 4242; www.edensedge.co.nz; 137 Lodder Lane, Riwaka; d/tw/tr with bathroom $120/120/150; 🐕) 🅿 Surrounded by farmland 4km from Motueka, this lodge's facilities include smart rooms and relaxed communal areas. Breakfast is included – with organic eggs from the owners' hens – and there are fresh herbs aplenty in the garden for cooking up in the spotless kitchen. Hire a bike for nearby beer, ice-cream and coffee stops along the Great Taste Trail.

Motueka Top 10 Holiday Park HOLIDAY PARK $
(☑03-528 7189; www.motuekatop10.co.nz; 10 Fearon St; sites from $40, cabins $65-150, units & motels $165-457; @🐕🏊) 🅿 Close to town and the Great Taste Trail, this place is packed with grassy, green charm – check out those lofty kahikatea trees! Shipshape communal amenities include a swimming pool, spa and jumping pillow, and there are ample accommodation options from smart new cabins to an apartment sleeping up to 11. On-site bike hire, plus local advice and bookings freely offered.

Laughing Kiwi HOSTEL $
(☑03-528 9229; www.laughingkiwi.co.nz; 310 High St; dm $29, d with/without bathroom $76/68; 🐕) Compact, low-key YHA hostel with rooms spread between an old villa and a pur-

pose-built backpacker lodge with a smart kitchen/lounge. The self-contained bach is a good option for groups of up to four ($180).

Equestrian Lodge Motel MOTEL $$
(☑0800 668 782, 03-528 9369; www.equestrian lodge.co.nz; Avalon Ct; d $148-178, q $199-255; 🛜🐕) No horses, no lodge, but no matter. This excellent motel complex is close to town (off Tudor St) and features expansive lawns, rose gardens, and a heated pool and spa alongside a series of continually refreshed units. Cheerful owners will hook you up with local activities.

Resurgence LODGE $$$
(☑03-528 4664; www.resurgence.co.nz; 574 Riwaka Valley Rd; d lodge from $695, chalets from $595; @🛜🐕) 🍃 Choose a luxurious en-suite lodge room or a self-contained chalet at this magical green retreat. It's a 15-minute drive from Abel Tasman National Park, and a 30-minute walk from the picturesque source of the Riwaka River. Lodge rates include aperitifs and a four-course dinner as well as breakfast; chalet rates are for B&B, with dinner an extra $120.

The lodge is 18km northwest of Motueka.

✕ Eating & Drinking

★ **Toad Hall** CAFE $$
(☑03-528 6456; www.toadhallmotueka.co.nz; 502 High St; mains $16-23; ⊙8am-5pm Easter-Oct, 8am-6pm Mon & Tue, to 10pm Wed-Sun Oct-Easter) This fantastic cafe serves excellent breakfast and lunch dishes (think potato hashcakes and pork-belly burgers). Also on offer are smoothies, juices, baked goods, pies and selected groceries. Look forward to live music and pizza on Friday and Saturday nights in summer. Have a drink at its new tap room, with beers and ciders brewed on site by **Townshend Brewery**.

Precinct Dining Co CAFE $$
(☑03-528 5332; www.precinctdining.com; 108 High St; breakfast & lunch mains $10-18, dinner mains $24-30; ⊙9am-3pm Mon, 9am-late Tue-Sat) At the northern end of town, Precinct Dining Co is a relaxed and versatile slice of well-priced cosmopolitan cool. Kick off with eggs Benedict and pea-and-chorizo smash for brunch, before returning at dinner for fish with local Golden Bay clams or a rustic pumpkin risotto with toasted walnuts. Good coffee and a savvy drinks list seal the deal.

Sprig & Fern CRAFT BEER
(☑03-528 4684; www.sprigandfern.co.nz; Wallace St; ⊙2pm-late) A member of the local Sprig & Fern brewery family, this backstreet tav-

ern is the pick of Motueka's drinking holes. Small and pleasant, with two courtyards, it offers 20 hand-pulled brews, simple food (pizza, platters and an awesome burger; meals $15 to $25) and occasional live music.

ⓘ Information

Motueka i-SITE (☑03-528 6543; www. motuekaisite.co.nz; 20 Wallace St; ⊙9am-4.30pm Mon-Fri, to 4pm Sat & Sun) An endlessly busy info centre with helpful staff handling bookings from Kaitaia to Bluff and providing local national-park expertise and necessaries. DOC information and bookings are also available.

ⓘ Getting There & Away

Bus services depart from **Motueka i-SITE**. Abel Tasman Coachlines (p424) runs daily from Nelson (where you can connect to other South Island destinations via InterCity (p404)) to Motueka (one hour), Kaiteriteri (25 minutes) and Marahau (30 minutes). These services connect with Golden Bay Coachlines (p424) services to Takaka (1¼ hours) and other Golden Bay destinations including Totaranui in Abel Tasman National Park, Collingwood, and on to the Heaphy Track trailhead. Note that from May to September all buses run less frequently.

Kaiteriteri

☑03 / POP 790
Known simply as 'Kaiteri', this seaside hamlet 13km from Motueka is the most popular resort town in the area. During the summer holidays its golden swimming beach feels more like Noumea than New Zealand, with more towels than sand. Consider yourself warned. Kaiteri is also a major departure point for Abel Tasman National Park transport, although Marahau is the main base.

✦ Activities

Kaiteriteri Mountain Bike Park MOUNTAIN BIKING
(www.kaiteritembpark.org.nz) Extensive MTB park with tracks to suit all levels of rider. See Trail Journeys (p434) opposite the beach for bike rental and advice.

⌂ Sleeping & Eating

Kaiteri Lodge LODGE $
(☑03-527 8281; www.kaiterilodge.co.nz; Inlet Rd; dm $35, d $80-160; @🛜) Modern, purpose-built lodge with small, simple dorms and en-suite doubles. The nautical decor adds some cheer to the somewhat lazily

maintained communal areas. The sociable **Beached Whale** (☑ 03-527 8281; www.kaiteri lodge.co.nz; Inlet Rd; dinner $18-28; ⊙ 4pm-late, reduced hours May-Oct) bar is on site – it's a popular location for backpacker bus trips.

Torlesse Coastal Motels MOTEL $$
(☑ 03-527 8063; www.torlessemotels.co.nz; 8 Ko-tare Pl, Little Kaiteriteri Beach; d $190-210, q $300-350; ☎) Just 200m from Little Kaiteriteri Beach (around the corner from the main beach) is this congregation of roomy hill-side units with pitched ceilings, full kitchens and laundries. Most have water views, and there's a ferny barbecue area and spa.

Kai BISTRO $$
(☑ 03-527 8507; www.experiencekaiteriteri.co.nz; cnr Inlet & Sandy Bay Rds; mains $15-33, shared platters $18-32; ⊙ 7.30am-9pm, reduced hours Apr-Nov) For-merly called Shoreline, this cafe-restaurant near the beach has re-emerged as Kai, a mod-ern and stylish bistro. Breakfast and lunch op-tions include buttermilk pancakes and bagels with salmon, while dinner is (slightly) more formal with fish, beef and lamb dishes. Errat-ic winter hours, but the adjacent **Goneburg-er** booth is usually open to dispense burgers, wraps and coffee to holidaying families.

⊙ Getting There & Away

Kaiteriteri is serviced by Abel Tasman Coach-lines (p424). Services include Motueka ($11, 20 minutes) and Nelson ($21, 90 minutes).

Trail Journeys (☑ 03-548 0093; www.trail journeysnelson.co.nz; 3 Kaiteriteri-Sandy Bay Rd) offers bike rental and advice on negotiating the Great Taste Trail (p431). It also has mountain bikes to rent for the nearby Kaiteriteri Mountain Bike Park (p433).

Marahau

☑ 03 / POP 120

Just up the coast from Kaiteriteri and 18km north of Motueka, Marahau is the main gateway to Abel Tasman National Park. It's less of a town, more of a procession of holi-day homes and tourist businesses.

🏃 Activities

Abel Tasman Horse Trekking HORSE RIDING
(☑ 03-527 8232; https://abeltasmanhorsetrekking. co.nz; Ocean View Chalets, 305 Sandy Bay-Marahau Rd; 2hr ride per person $95) If you're in an equine state of mind, head here for the chance to belt along the beach on four legs. Offers two-hour beach rides (for those 12 years and old-

er), with training for newbie riders. Younger ones can be led around a paddock on a pony for 30 minutes ($35) after helping to brush and saddle up their mount.

🛏 Sleeping

Barn HOSTEL $
(☑ 03-527 8043; www.barn.co.nz; 14 Harvey Rd; un-powered/powered sites per person $20/22, dm $32, d & tw $89; @☎) This backpackers has hit its straps with comfortable dorms, a toilet block and a grassy camping field added to a mix of microcabins, alfresco kitchens and barbecue areas. The barn itself is the hub – the communal kitchen and lounge area are good for socialising, as is the central deck, which has a fireplace. Activity bookings and secure parking available.

Abel Tasman Lodge MOTEL $$
(☑ 03-527 8250; www.abeltasmanlodge.co.nz; 295 Sandy Bay-Marahau Rd; d $145-195, q $200-260; @☎) 🍃 Enjoy halcyon days in this renovat-ed arc of 15 studios and self-contained units with groovy styling and cathedral ceilings, opening onto landscaped gardens. There's also a communal kitchen for self-caterers, plus spa and sauna. Cuckoos, tui and bell-birds squawk and warble in the bushy sur-rounds, and some of the cool interior decor is styled after local bird life.

Ocean View Chalets CHALET $$
(☑ 03-527 8232; www.accommodationabeltasman. co.nz; 305 Sandy Bay-Marahau Rd; d $145-245, q $299; ☎) On a leafy hillside affording plen-ty of privacy, these cheerful, cypress-lined chalets are 300m from the Coast Track with views out to Fisherman Island. All except the cheapest studios are self-contained; breakfast and packed lunches available.

🍴 Eating

Fat Tui BURGERS $
(☑ 03-527 8420; cnr Marahau-Sandy Bay & Marahau Valley Rds; burgers $14-17; ⊙ noon-8pm late Oct-Easter, Wed-Sun May-late Oct) Everyone's heard about this bird, based in a caravan that ain't rollin' anywhere fast. Thank goodness. Super-lative burgers, such as the Cowpat (beef), the Ewe Beaut (lamb) and Roots, Shoots & Leaves (vegie). Fish and chips, and coffee, too.

Hooked CAFE $$
(☑ 03-527 8576; www.hookedonmarahau.co.nz; 229 Marahau-Sandy Bay Rd; lunch $15-20, dinner $26-32; ⊙ 8am-10pm Dec-Mar, 8-11am & 3-10pm Oct, Nov & Apr) This popular place reels them

in, so dinner reservations are recommended. The art-bedecked interior opens on to an outdoor terrace with distracting views. Lunch centres on salads and seafood, while the dinner menu boasts fresh fish of the day – ask if bluenose is available – green-lipped mussels and NZ lamb shanks. Pop in for happy hour drinks from 4pm to 6pm.

Park Cafe CAFE **$$**
(☑ 03-527 8270; www.parkcafe.co.nz; Harvey Rd; lunch $12-22, dinner $17-36; ☺ 8am-late mid-Sep–May; ✍) At the Coast Track trailhead, this breezy cafe is perfect for fuelling up or restoring the waistline. High-calorie options include the big breakfast, burgers and cakes, but there are also seafood and salad options plus wood-fired pizza Wednesday through Saturday evenings. Enjoy in the room with a view or the sunny courtyard garden. Check Facebook for occasional live music listings.

❶ Getting There & Away

Marahau is serviced by Abel Tasman Coachlines (p424). Services include Motueka ($11, 30 minutes) and Nelson ($21, two hours).

Abel Tasman National Park

Coastal Abel Tasman National Park blankets the northern end of a range of marble and limestone hills that extend from Kahurangi National Park. Various tracks in the park include an inland route, although the Coast Track is what everyone is here for – it's New Zealand's most popular Great Walk.

Even if you're not keen on tackling the walk, kayaking or cruising amid Abel Tasman's hidden coves and beaches is accessible to all visitors.

🏃 Activities

Abel Tasman Coast Track

This is arguably NZ's most beautiful Great Walk – 60km of sparkling seas, golden sand, quintessential coastal forest, and hidden surprises such as Cleopatra's Pool. Such pulling power attracts around 30,000 overnight trampers and kayakers per year, each of whom stay at least one night in the park. A major attraction is the terrain: well cut, well graded and well marked. It's almost impossible to get lost here and the track can be tramped in sneakers.

You will, however, probably get your feet wet, as this track features long stretches of beach and crazy tides. In fact the tidal differences in the park are among the greatest in the country, up to a staggering 6m. At Torrent and Bark Bays, it's much easier and more fun to doff the shoes and cross the soggy sands, rather than take the high-tide track. At Awaroa Bay you have no choice but to plan on crossing close to low tide. Tide tables are posted along the track and on the DOC website; regional i-SITEs also have them.

It's a commonly held belief that the Coast Track ends at Totaranui, but it actually extends to a car park near Wainui Bay. The entire tramp takes only three to five days, although with water taxi transport you can convert it into an almost endless array of

MARLBOROUGH & NELSON ABEL TASMAN NATIONAL PARK

THE BEACH BOUGHT BY 30,000 NEW ZEALANDERS

When the 800m arc of Awaroa Bay in the northern reaches of Abel Tasman National Park was offered for sale by a private owner in late 2015, there was concern overseas buyers could secure the sheltered slice of paradise. But following a few chats over a few beers on Christmas Day 2015, up stepped two proud South Islanders to rally the public of NZ and instigate the biggest crowd-funding campaign the country has ever seen.

Against the threat of offshore purchasers winning the tender for the 7 hectares of coastal perfection, Duane Major and Adam Gard'ner – both regular summertime visitors to the bays and coves of Abel Tasman National Park – launched a campaign on the NZ crowdfunding website, Givealittle, to secure the beach for all New Zealanders.

By the time the tender deadline was reached on 15 February 2016, 29,239 private donors had raised $2,259,923, and, along with significant corporate donations and $350,000 from the NZ government, the winning tender of more than $2.8 million was reached.

Less than five months later, on 10 July 2016, Awaroa Bay was officially incorporated into Abel Tasman National Park. With its now-protected status, there are ongoing efforts to restore the beach's sand dune ecosystem, and native plant species are being repopulated to improve the natural habitat for coastal birds, including oystercatchers, dotterel and godwits.

Abel Tasman National Park

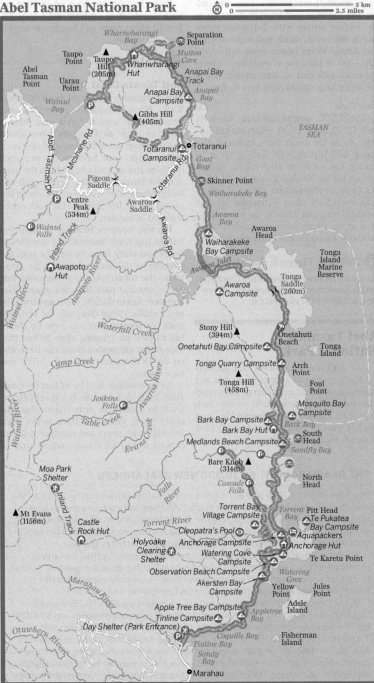

options, particularly if you combine it with a kayak leg. If you can only spare a couple of days, a rewarding option is to loop around the northern end of the park, tramping the Coast Track from Totaranui, passing Anapai Bay and Mutton Cove, overnighting at Whariwharangi Hut, then returning to Totaranui via the Gibbs Hill Track. This will give you a slice of the park's best features (beaches, seals, coastal scenery) while being far less crowded than other segments.

The track operates on DOC's Great Walks Pass. Children are free but bookings are still required. Book online (www.doc.govt.nz), contact the **Nelson Marlborough Bookings Helpdesk** (📞03-546 8210), or book in person at the Nelson, Motueka or Takaka i-SITES or DOC offices, where staff can offer suggestions to tailor the track to your needs and organise transport at each end. Book your trip well ahead of time, especially huts between December and March.

This track is so well trodden that a topographical map isn't essential for navigation. The map within DOC's *Abel Tasman Coast Track* brochure provides sufficient detail, and you can readily buy more illuminating maps at local visitor centres.

Other Activities

⭐ **Abel Tasman Canyons**   ADVENTURE
(📞03-528 9800, 0800 863 472; www.abeltasman canyons.co.nz; Motueka; full-day trips $269) Few Abel Tasman visitors see the Torrent River, but here's your chance to journey down its staggeringly beautiful granite-lined canyon, via a fun-filled combination of swimming, sliding, abseiling, zip-lining and big leaps into jewel-like pools. Other trips explore Kahurangi National Park and Richmond Forest Park, and combo adventures including kayaking or sky diving are also available.

🚗 Tours

Tour companies usually offer free Motueka pick-up/drop-off, with Nelson pick-up available at extra cost.

Wilsons Abel Tasman   OUTDOORS
(📞03-528 2027, 0800 223 582; www.abeltasman. co.nz; 409 High St, Motueka; walk/kayak from $62/90) This long-standing, family owned operator offers an impressive array of cruises, walking, kayaking and combo tours. Overnight stays are available at Wilsons' lodges in pretty Awaroa and Torrent Bay for guided-tour guests.

Offers an Explorer Pass for unlimited boat travel on three days over a seven-day period (adult/child $150/75).

Abel Tasman Eco Tours   TOURS
(📞03-528 0946, 0800 223 538; www.abeltasman ecotours.co.nz; Marahau; day tours adult/child $189/120) Take an ecology focused day trip with marine scientist Stew Robertson, either cruising around the coast in a boat, or on a five-hour tramping trip in the Wainui Valley. Stew's a passionate natural history buff and really knows his stuff.

Abel Tasman Charters   BOATING
(📞0800 223 522, 027 441 8588; www.abeltasman charters.co.nz; 6hr tours $285) Offers a six-hour trip combining walking, kayaking, swimming and cruising in Abel Tasman National Park from Stephen's Bay (near Kaiteriteri).

Abel Tasman Tours & Guided Walks   WALKING
(📞03-528 9602; www.abeltasmantours.co.nz; Riwaka; tours from $295) Small-group, day-long walking tours (minimum two people) that include a packed lunch and water taxis.

🛏 Sleeping

Along the Abel Tasman Coast Track are four Great Walk huts ($38) with bunks, heating, flush toilets and limited lighting, but no cooking facilities. There are also 19 designated Great Walk campsites ($14). An interesting alternative is Aquapackers (p438), a catamaran moored permanently in Anchorage Bay.

As the Coast Track is a Great Walk, all huts and campsites must be booked in advance year-round, either online through **Great Walks Bookings** (📞0800 694 732; www.doc.govt.nz) or at DOC visitor centres nationwide. Hut tickets and annual passes cannot be used on the track, and there is a two-night limit on stays in each hut or campsite, except for Totaranui campsite, which has a one-night limit. Penalty fees apply to those who do not have a valid booking, and you may be required to leave the park if caught.

Totaranui Campsite   CAMPGROUND $
(📞03-528 8083; www.doc.govt.nz; Oct-Apr $15, May-Sep $10) An extremely popular facility with a whopping capacity (850 campers) and a splendid setting next to the beach backed by some of the best bush in the park. A staffed DOC office has interpretive displays, flush toilets, cold showers and a public phone. Note there's a one-night limit here.

Aquapackers   HOSTEL **$$**
(☑ 0800 430 744; www.aquapackers.co.nz; Anchorage; dm/d $85/245; ☺ closed May-Sep) The specially converted 13m *Catarac* (catamaran), moored permanently in Anchorage Bay, provides unusual but buoyant backpacker accommodation for 22. Facilities are basic but decent; prices include bedding, dinner and breakfast. Bookings essential.

ⓘ Getting There & Away

The closest big town to Abel Tasman is Motueka, with nearby Marahau the southern gateway. Although Wainui is the official northern trailhead, it is more common to finish in Totaranui, either skipping the northernmost section or looping back to Totaranui over Gibbs Hill Track. All gateways are serviced by either Abel Tasman Coachlines (p424) and Golden Bay Coachlines (p424).

ⓘ Getting Around

Once you hit the park, it is easy to get to/ from any point on the track via numerous tour companies and water-taxi operators offering scheduled and on-demand services, either from Kaiteriteri or Marahau. Typical one-way prices

PADDLING THE ABEL TASMAN

The Abel Tasman Coast Track has long been tramping territory, but its coastal beauty makes it an equally seductive spot for sea kayaking, which can easily be combined with walking and camping.

A variety of professional outfits are able to float you out on the water, and the possibilities and permutations for guided or freedom trips are vast. You can kayak from half a day up to three days, camping, or staying in DOC huts, bachs, even a floating backpackers, either fully catered or self-catering. You can kayak one day, camp overnight then walk back, or walk further into the park and catch a water taxi back.

Most operators offer similar trips at similar prices. Marahau is the main base, but trips also depart from Kaiteriteri. There are numerous day-trip options, including guided trips often departing Marahau and taking in bird-filled Adele Island (around $200). There are also various multiday guided trips, with three days a common option, costing anything from $260 to $750 depending on accommodation and other inclusions.

Freedom rentals (double-kayak and equipment hire) are around $75/115 per person for one/two days; all depart from Marahau with the exception of Golden Bay Kayaks (p441), which is based at Tata Beach in Golden Bay.

Instruction is given to everyone, and most tour companies have a minimum age of either eight or 14 depending on the trip. None allow solo hires. Camping gear is usually provided on overnight trips; if you're disappearing into the park for a few days, most operators provide free car parking.

November to Easter is the busiest time, with December to February the absolute peak. You can, however, paddle all year round, with winter offering its own rewards; the weather is surprisingly amenable, the seals are more playful, and there's more bird life and less haze.

Following are the main players in this competitive market (shop around):

Abel Tasman Kayaks (☑ 0800 732 529, 03-527 8022; www.abeltasmankayaks.co.nz; Main Rd, Marahau; guided tours from $150)

Kahu Kayaks (☑ 0800 300 101, 03-527 8300; www.kahukayaks.co.nz; 11 Marahau Valley Rd; self-guided/guided tours from $75/215)

Kaiteriteri Kayaks (☑ 0800 252 925, 03-527 8383; www.seakayak.co.nz; Kaiteriteri Beach; ☺ adult/child from $80/60)

Marahau Sea Kayaks (☑ 0800 529 257, 03-527 8176; www.msk.co.nz; Abel Tasman Centre, Franklin St, Marahau; tours from $150)

R&R Kayaks (☑ 0508 223 224; www.rrkayaks.co.nz; 279 Sandy Bay-Marahau Rd; tours from $135)

Sea Kayak Company (☑ 0508 252 925, 03-528 7251; www.seakayaknz.co.nz; 506 High St, Motueka; tours from $85)

Tasman Bay Sea Kayaking (☑ 0800 827 525; www.tasmanbayseakayaking.co.nz; Harvey Rd, Marahau; tours from $110)

Wilsons Abel Tasman (p437)

from either Marahau or Kaiteriteri: Anchorage and Torrent Bay ($37), Bark Bay ($42), Awaroa ($47) and Totaranui ($49). Getting around on the water is best accomplished with **Abel Tasman Aqua Taxi** (☑03-527 8083, 0800 278 282; www.aquataxi.co.nz; Marahau-Sandy Bay Rd, Marahau) or **Marahau Water Taxis** (☑03-527 8176, 0800 808 018; www.marahauwater-taxis.co.nz; Abel Tasman Centre, Franklin St, Marahau).

Golden Bay

From Motueka, SH60 takes a stomach-churning meander over Takaka Hill to Golden Bay, a small region mixing rural charm, artistic endeavour, alternative lifestyles and a fair share of transient folk spending time off the grid.

For the visitor its main attractions are access to both the Abel Tasman and Kahurangi National Parks, along with other natural wonders including Farewell Spit and a swathe of beautiful beaches. Look out for (or download) DOC's *Walks in Golden Bay* brochure to kick-start your adventures.

ⓘ Getting There & Away

Golden Bay is well serviced by Golden Bay Coachlines (p424), with daily runs between Nelson and the Heaphy Track via Motueka and Takaka, but to get to quiet corners you'll need to be wily or have your own wheels.

Takaka Hill

☑03

Takaka Hill (791m) butts in between Tasman Bay and Golden Bay. It looks pretty bushy but closer inspection reveals a remarkable marble landscape formed by millions of years of erosion. Its smooth beauty is revealed on the one-hour drive over the hill road (SH60), a steep, winding route punctuated by spectacular lookout points and a smattering of other interesting stops.

Just before the summit is the turn-off to **Canaan Downs Scenic Reserve**, reached at the end of an 11km gravel road. This area stars in both *The Lord of the Rings* and *The Hobbit* movies, but **Harwoods Hole** is the most famous feature here. It's one of the largest *tomo* (caves) in the country at 357m deep and 70m wide, with a 176m vertical drop. It's a 30-minute walk from the car park. Allow us to state the obvious: the cave is off limits to all but the most experienced cavers.

◉ Sights & Activities

Mountain bikers with intermediate-level skills can venture along a couple of loop tracks, or head all the way down to Takaka via the titillating **Rameka Track**. Also close to the top, the **Takaka Hill Walkway** is a three-hour loop through marble karst rock formations, native forest and farmland. For more walks, see DOC's brochure *Walks in Golden Bay*.

Ngarua Caves   CAVE

(☑03-528 8093; www.ngaruacaves.co.nz; SH60; adult/child $20/8; ⏱45min tours hourly 10am-4pm Oct-Apr, phone ahead other months) Just below the summit of Takaka Hill (literally) are the Ngarua Caves, a rock-solid attraction, where you can see myriad subterranean delights including moa bones. Access is restricted to tours – you can't go solo spelunking.

Takaka

☑03 / POP 1240

Boasting New Zealand's highest concentration of yoga pants, dreadlocks and bare feet in the high street, Takaka is a lovable little town and the last 'big' centre before the road west ends at Farewell Spit (p442). You'll find most things you need here, and a few things you don't, but we all have an unworn tie-dyed tank top in our wardrobe, don't we?

Beyond the town's past and present as a bit of a hippie enclave, an interesting new arts cooperative and Takaka's very own distillery (p441) are adding a more contemporary and diverse sheen.

◉ Sights

Many of Takaka's sights can readily be reached via bicycle, with hire and maps available from the time-warped Quiet Revolution Cycle Shop (p440) on the main street.

Anatoki Salmon   HATCHERY

(☑0800 262 865, 03-525 7251; www.anatoki salmon.co.nz; 230 McCallum Rd; ⌖) Here's your chance to catch a salmon and have it smoked for lunch or prepared as super-fresh sashimi. Rods and instructions are provided, but the fish pretty well catch themselves anyway. Other attractions beyond fishing include hand-feeding tame eels, a petting zoo for the kids and minigolf. There's no entrance fee, but expect to pay around $35 to $55 for your salmon.

Rawhiti Cave

CAVE

(www.doc.govt.nz) The ultimate in geological eye-candy around these parts are the phytokarst features of Rawhiti Cave, a 15-minute drive from Takaka (reached via Motupipi, turning right into Glenview Rd, then left into Packard Rd and following the signs). The rugged two-hour-return walk (steep in places; dangerous in the wet) may well leave you speechless (although we managed 'monster', 'fangs' and even 'Sarlacc').

Te Waikoropupū Springs

SPRING

(www.doc.govt.nz) The largest freshwater springs in the southern hemisphere and some of the clearest in the world, 'Pupū Springs' is a colourful little lake refreshed with around 14,000L of water per second surging from underground vents. From Takaka, head 4km northwest on SH60 and follow the signs inland for 3km from Waitapu Bridge. There are illuminating information panels at the car park and a 30-minute forest loop taking in the waters, which are sacred and therefore off limits.

Grove Scenic Reserve

VIEWPOINT

(www.doc.govt.nz) Around a 10-minute drive from Takaka (signposted down Clifton Rd), you will find this crazy limestone maze punctuated by gnarled old rata trees. The walkway takes around 10 minutes and passes an impressive lookout.

Activities

Golden Bay Air

SCENIC FLIGHTS

(03-525 8725, 0800 588 885; www.goldenbayair.co.nz; Takaka Airfield, SH60) Offering scenic and charter flights around Golden Bay and surrounds.

Pupu Hydro Walkway

TRAMPING

(www.doc.govt.nz; Pupu Valley Rd) This enjoyable two-hour circuit follows an old water race through beech forest, past engineering and gold-mining relics to the restored (and operational) Pupu Hydro Powerhouse, built in 1929. It's 9km from Takaka at the end of Pupu Valley Rd; just follow the signs at the Te Waikoropupū Springs junction.

Adventure Flights
Golden Bay

SCENIC FLIGHTS

(0800 150 338, 03-525 6167; www.adventureflightsgoldenbay.co.nz; Takaka Airfield, SH60; from $40) Look forward to scenic and charter flights in the area around Golden Bay.

Quiet Revolution Cycle Shop

CYCLING

(03-525 9555; www.quietrevolution.co.nz; 11 Commercial St; bike hire per day $30-65; ⊙9am-5pm Mon-Fri, to 12.30pm Sat) You'll get personal service at this most proper of bike shops. Town- and mountain-bike hire, plus top-notch servicing and sales. Local ride maps and a car relocation service for the Heaphy Track in winter, too.

Sleeping

Golden Bay Kiwi Holiday Park

HOLIDAY PARK $

(03-525 9742; www.goldenbayholidaypark.co.nz; 99 Tukurua Rd, Tukurua; unpowered/powered sites $43/47, d cabins from $98; @🛜) Eighteen kilometres north of Takaka with a quiet beach right out front, this gem of a park has acres of grass, graceful shade trees and hedgerows, easily atoning for tight communal facilities. There are tidy, family friendly cabins for budget travellers, and luxury beach houses sleeping up to four ($195 to $315).

Kiwiana

HOSTEL $

(0800 805 494, 03-525 7676; www.kiwianabackpackers.co.nz; 73 Motupipi St; tent sites per person $24, dm $30, s/d $55/70; @🛜) Beyond the welcoming garden is a cute cottage where rooms are named after classic Kiwiana (the jandal, Buzzy Bee...). The garage has been converted into a convivial lounge, with wood-fired stove, table tennis, pool table, music, books and games; free bikes for guest use.

★ Adrift

COTTAGE $$$

(03-525 8353; www.adrift.co.nz; 53 Tukurua Rd, Tukurua; d $378-585; 🛜) 🌿 Adrift on a bed of beachside bliss is what you'll be in one of these five cottages dotted within landscaped grounds, right on the beach. Tuck into your breakfast hamper, then self-cater in the fully equipped kitchen, dine on the sunny deck, or soak in the spa bath. A minimum two-night stay usually applies. Also available is a stylish studio.

Eating & Drinking

Dangerous Kitchen

CAFE $$

(03-525 8686; www.thedangerouskitchen.co.nz; 46a Commercial St; mains $13-30; ⊙9am-8.30pm Mon-Sat; 🌿) 🌿 DK serves largely healthy, good-value fare such as felafel, pizza, bean burritos, pasta, great baking and juices as well as local wines and craft beer. It's mellow and musical, with a sunny courtyard out back and people-watching out front. Check out the quirky, Instagram-worthy mural near the entrance, and ask about occasional live music.

★ **Mussel Inn** PUB
(☑03-525 9241; www.musselinn.co.nz; 1259 SH60, Onekaka; all-day snacks $5-19, dinner $24-30; ⊙11am-late, closed mid-Jul–mid-Sep) You will find one of NZ's most beloved brewery-taverns halfway between Takaka and Collingwood. The Mussel Inn is rustic NZ at its most genuine, complete with creaking timbers, a rambling beer garden with a brazier, regular music and other events, and hearty, homemade food. Try the signature 'Captain Cooker', a brown beer brewed naturally with manuka.

Dancing Sands Distillery DISTILLERY
(☑03-525 9899; www.dancingsands.com; 46a Commercial St; ⊙10am-4pm Mon-Sat) 🍸 Here's a surprise – an award-winning distillery tucked down a laneway off Takaka's main street. Its Sacred Spring gin is crafted from water from the same aquifer that feeds the pristine waters of the nearby Pupū Springs, and variations include NZ's first barrel-aged gin, and gin flavoured with chocolate or saffron. Other standout Dancing Sands tipples include rum and vodka.

ⓘ Information

Golden Bay Area DOC Office (☑03-525 8026; www.doc.govt.nz; 62 Commercial St; ⊙1-3pm Mon-Fri) Information on Abel Tasman and Kahurangi National Parks, the Heaphy Track, Farewell Spit and Cobb Valley. Sells hut passes.
Golden Bay Visitor Centre (☑03-525 9136; www.goldenbaynz.co.nz; Willow St; ⊙10am-3pm Mon-Fri, to 2pm Sat) A friendly little centre with all the necessary information, including the exemplary free visitor map. Bookings and DOC passes.

ⓘ Getting There & Away

Golden Bay Air (p440) flies at least once and up to four times daily between Wellington and Takaka (one way adult/child from $169/129).

Golden Bay Coachlines (p424) departs from Takaka and runs through to Collingwood ($21, 25 minutes), the Heaphy Track ($35, one hour), Totaranui ($24, one hour) and over the hill to Motueka ($28, 1¼ hours) and Nelson ($38, 2¼ hours).

Pohara

☑03 / POP 550
About 10km northeast of Takaka is pintsized Pohara, a beachy village with a population that quadruples over summer. It has more flash holiday homes than other parts of Golden Bay, but an agreeable air persists

nonetheless, aided by decent food and lodging, and a beach that at low tide is as big as Heathrow's runway.

Pohara lies close to the northern gateway of Abel Tasman National Park. The largely unsealed road into the park passes **Tarakohe Harbour** (Pohara's working port), followed by **Ligar Bay**. It's worth climbing to the Abel Tasman lookout as you pass by.

🏃 Activities

The next settlement along from Pohara is **Tata Beach**, where **Golden Bay Kayaks** (☑03-525 9095; www.goldenbaykayaks.co.nz; 29 Cornwall Pl, Tata Beach; half-day guided tours adult/child from $85/50, freedom hire from $55; 🖐) offers freedom rental of kayaks and stand-up paddle boards, as well as guided trips into Abel Tasman National Park.

Signposted from the Totaranui Rd at Wainui Bay is a leafy one-hour return walk to the best cascade in the bay: **Wainui Falls**.

🛏 Sleeping & Eating

Pohara Beach Top 10
Holiday Park HOLIDAY PARK $
(☑0800 764 272, 03-525 9500; www.poharabeach.com; 809 Abel Tasman Dr; sites $49, cabins & units $81-169; @🖐) Lining grassy parkland between the dunes and the main road, this place is in prime position for some beach time. Sites are nice and there are some beaut cabins, but be warned – this is a favourite spot for NZ holidaymakers so it goes a bit mental in high summer. General store and takeaway on site.

★ **Sans Souci Inn** LODGE $$
(☑03-525 8663; www.sanssouciinn.co.nz; 11 Richmond Rd; s/d $95/120, units from $160; ⊙closed Jul–mid-Sep; 🖐) 🍽 Sans Souci means 'no worries' in French, and this will be your mantra too after staying in one of the seven Mediterranean-flavoured, mud-brick rooms. Guests share a plant-filled, mosaic bathroom with composting toilets, and an airy lounge and kitchen that open onto a semitropical courtyard. Dinner in the restaurant is highly recommended (bookings essential; mains $35 to $37); breakfast by request.

Ratanui LODGE $$$
(☑03-525 7998; www.ratanuilodge.com; 818 Abel Tasman Dr; d from $235; @🖐🏊) A romantic haven close to the beach, this boutique lodge is styled with Victorian panache. It features myriad sensual stimulants such as perfumed rose gardens, a swimming pool,

FAREWELL SPIT

Bleak, exposed and positively sci-fi, Farewell Spit is a wetland of international importance and renowned bird sanctuary – the summer home of thousands of migratory waders, notably the godwit, Caspian tern and Australasian gannet. Walkers can explore the first 4km of the spit via a network of tracks (see DOC's *Farewell Spit & Puponga Farm Park* brochure; $2 or downloadable from www.doc.govt.nz). Beyond that point access is limited to trips with the brilliant **Farewell Spit Eco Tours** (📞0800 808 257, 03-524 8257; www.farewellspit.com; 6 Tasman St; tours $130-165), scheduled according to tides.

The spit's 35km beach features colossal, crescent-shaped dunes, from where panoramic views extend across Golden Bay and a vast low-tide salt marsh.

At the foot of the spit is a hilltop visitor-centre-cum-cafe – a convenient spot to write a postcard over a coffee, especially on an inclement day.

a spa, a massage service, cocktails and a candelabra-lit restaurant showcasing local produce (open to the public; bookings required). Free bikes, too.

ℹ Getting There & Away

Golden Bay Coachlines (p424) runs daily from Takaka to Pohara ($17, 15 minutes) on the way to Totaranui.

Collingwood & Around

📞03 / POP 240

Far-flung Collingwood is the last town in Golden Bay, and has a real end-of-the-line vibe. It's busy in summer, though for most people it's simply a launch pad for the Heaphy Track or Farewell Spit.

◉ Sights & Activities

Whariki Beach   BEACH

Remote, desolate Whariki Beach is along an unsealed road, then a 20-minute walk from the car park over farmland (part of the DOC-administered Puponga Farm Park). It's a wild introduction to the West Coast, with mighty dune formations, looming rock islets and a seal colony at its eastern end (look out for seals in the stream on the walk here). As inviting as a swim may seem, there are strong undertows – what the sea wants, the sea shall have...

Cape Farewell Horse Treks   HORSE RIDING

(📞03-524 8031; www.horsetreksnz.com; McGowan St, Puponga; treks from $80) Befitting a frontier, this is the place to saddle up: Cape Farewell Horse Treks is en route to Whariki Beach. Treks in this wind-blown country range from 1½ hours (to Pillar Point) to three hours (to Whariki Beach), with longer (including overnight) trips by arrangement.

🛏 Sleeping & Eating

★Innlet Backpackers
& Cottages   HOSTEL $

(📞03-524 8040, 027 970 8397; www.theinnlet. co.nz; 839 Collingwood-Puponga Rd, Pakawau; dm/ s/d $35/69/80, cabins from $95; ⊗closed Jun-Aug; 🐾) 🚲 This leafy charmer is 10km from Collingwood on the way to Farewell Spit. The main house has elegant backpacker rooms, and there are self-contained options including a cottage sleeping six. Enjoy the garden, explore the local area on a bike or in a kayak, or venture out for a tramp on the property. Check the website for occasional three-night specials.

Somerset House   HOSTEL $

(📞03-524 8624; www.backpackerscollingwood. co.nz; 10 Gibbs Rd; dm/s/d incl breakfast $32/50/78; ⊗closed May-Oct; @🐾) A small, low-key hostel in a bright, historic building on a hill with views from the deck. Get tramping advice from the charming owners, who offer track transport, free bikes and kayaks, freshly baked bread for breakfast, and your fourth night's stay free.

★Zatori Retreat   LODGE, HOSTEL $$

(📞03-524 8692; www.zatori.co.nz; 2321 Takaka-Collingwood Rd; s/d/f with shared bathroom $60/120/210, ste with breakfast $229-399; 🐾) 🚲 This former maternity hospital has been transformed into a stylish and relaxing retreat. Chic suites are arrayed around a spacious lounge area enlivened with colourful artworks from Asia, and looking out onto brilliant views of Farewell Spit. A separate wing houses rooms with shared bathrooms for budget travellers. Massage services, kayaks and paddle boards are available, and there's a restaurant-bar.

M.A.D Skool Café CAFE $

(☑ 021 107 6312; www.facebook.com/MADSkool
Cafe; 7 Tasman St; snacks & mains $5-18; ⊙ 8am-
8pm; ☑) ✦ One part quirky art gallery, one
part vegetarian and vegan cafe, M.A.D Skool
has the best coffee in town and a tasty selection of food including burgers, fish and
chips and a healthy array of vegan and vegetarian bites. Opening hours can be somewhat flexible, especially outside of summer.

ⓘ Getting There & Away

Golden Bay Coachlines (p424) runs twice daily
from Takaka to Collingwood ($21, 25 minutes).

Kahurangi National Park

Kahurangi – 'blue skies' in one of several
translations – is the second largest of New
Zealand's national parks, and also one
of its most diverse. Its most eye-catching
features are geological, ranging from windswept beaches and sea cliffs to earthquake-
shattered slopes and moraine-dammed
lakes, and the smooth, strange karst forms
of the interior tableland.

Around 85% of the 4520 sq km park is
forested, and more than 50% of NZ's plant
species can be found here, including more
than 80% of its alpine plant species. Among
the park's 60 bird species are great spotted
kiwi, kea, kaka and whio (blue duck). There
are creepy cave weta, weird beetles and a
huge, leggy spider, but there's also a majestic and ancient snail known as Powelliphan-
ta – something of a flag bearer for the park's
animal kingdom. If you like a field trip filled
with the new and strange, Kahurangi National Park will certainly satisfy.

🕭 Activities

The best-known tramp in Kahurangi is the
Heaphy Track. The more challenging **Wangapeka** is not as well known as the Heaphy, but many consider it a more enjoyable
tramp. Taking about five days, the track
starts 25km south of Karamea at Little Wanganui and runs 52km east to Rolling River
near Tapawera. There's a chain of huts along
the track.

The Heaphy and Wangapeka, however,
are just one part of a 650km network of
tracks that includes excellent full-day and
overnight tramps such as those in the **Cobb
Valley** and **Mt Arthur/Tablelands**. See
www.doc.govt.nz for detailed information
on all Kahurangi tracks.

Heaphy Track

The Heaphy Track is one of the most popular tracks in the country. A Great Walk in
every sense, it traverses diverse terrain –
dense native forest, the mystical Gouland
Downs, secluded river valleys, and beaches dusted in salt spray and fringed by
nikau palms.

Although quite long, the Heaphy is well
cut and benched, making it easier than any
other extended tramp found in Kahurangi National Park. That said, it may still be
found arduous, particularly in unfavourable
weather.

Tramping from east to west most of the
climbing is done on the first day, and the
scenic beach walk is saved for the end, a fitting and invigorating grand finale.

The track is open to mountain bikers
between May and October. Factoring in distance, remoteness and the possibility of bad
weather, this epic journey is only suited to
well-equipped cyclists with advanced riding
skills. A good port of call for more information is the Quiet Revolution Cycle Shop
(p440) in Takaka.

A strong tramper could walk the Heaphy
in three days, but most people take four or
five days. For a detailed track description,
see DOC's *Heaphy Track* brochure. Estimated walking times:

ROUTE	TIME (HR)
Brown Hut to Perry Saddle Hut	5
Perry Saddle Hut to Gouland Downs Hut	2
Gouland Downs Hut to Saxon Hut	1½
Saxon Hut to James Mackay Hut	3
James Mackay Hut to Lewis Hut	3½
Lewis Hut to Heaphy Hut	2½
Heaphy Hut to Kohaihai River	5

⭐ Tours

Bush & Beyond TRAMPING
(☑ 021 027 08209, 03-543 3742; www.heaphytrack
guidedwalks.co.nz) ✦ Specialising in Kahurangi, the area's original guiding company
(beginning in 1993) offers eco-aware and
natural-history-orientated hikes around
the national park ranging from Mt Arthur
or Cobb Valley walks (two days from $700)
through to a guided six-day Heaphy Track
package ($1900). Accommodation and
meals included. It operates year-round but
the best walking is from October to March.

Kahurangi Guided Walks TRAMPING
(☑ 03-391 4120; www.kahurangiwalks.co.nz) Offers all-inclusive, week-long Heaphy hikes ($1950), plus one- to five-day trips in Abel Tasman National Park ($250 to $1750).

🛏 Sleeping

Seven designated Great Walk huts ($34) lie along the Heaphy Track, which have bunks and a kitchen area, heating, flush toilets and washbasins with cold water. Most but not all have gas rings; a couple have lighting. There are also nine Great Walk campsites ($14), plus the beachside **Kohaihai Campsite** (www.doc.govt.nz; per person $8) at the West Coast trailhead. The two day shelters are just that; overnight stays are not permitted.

As the Heaphy is a Great Walk, all huts and campsites must be booked in advance year-round. Bookings can be made online through **Great Walks Bookings** (☑ 0800 694 732; www.doc.govt.nz) or at DOC visitor centres nationwide.

ℹ Information

In person, the best spot for detailed Heaphy Track information and bookings is the DOC counter at Nelson i-SITE (p429). Closer to the Golden Bay end of the track, hut tickets, bookings and other track information can be obtained in Takaka at the Golden Bay Area DOC Office (p441) or Golden Bay Visitor Centre (p441). See also www.heaphytrack.com and DOC's *Heaphy Track* brochure.

ℹ Getting There & Away

The two road ends of the Heaphy Track are an almost unfathomable distance apart: 463km to be precise. From Takaka, you can get to the Heaphy Track (via Collingwood) with Golden Bay Coachlines (p424) ($35, 9.15am, one hour) from December to March.

The Kohaihai trailhead is 15km from the small town of Karamea. **Karamea Express** (☑ 03-782 6757; info@karamea-express.co.nz; Heaphy Track trailhead transport per person $20) departs from the shelter at 1pm and 2pm for Karamea from October to the end of April ($20). Booking ahead is essential. **Karamea Connections** (☑ 03-782 6767; www.karameaconnections.co.nz) offers on-demand pick-ups.

Heaphy Bus (☑ 0800 128 735, 0272 221 872; www.theheaphybus.co.nz) offers a round-trip shuttle service – drop-off at Brown Hut and pickup from Kohaihai ($160) – and other on-demand local track transport.

Heaphy Track Help (☑ 03-525 9576; www.heaphytrackhelp.co.nz) offers car relocations

(around $300, depending on the direction and time), food drops, shuttles and advice.

Adventure Flights Golden Bay (p440) will fly you back to Takaka from Karamea (or vice versa) for $240 to $265 per person (up to five people). **Golden Bay Air** (☑ 0800 588 885; www.goldenbayair.co.nz) flies the same route ($149 to $179 per person), as does Helicopter Charter Karamea (p453), which will take up to six passengers for $1400. With five passengers and mountain bikes the cost is $1600.

Nelson Lakes National Park

Nelson Lakes National Park surrounds two lakes – Rotoiti and Rotoroa – fringed by sweet-smelling beech forest with a backdrop of greywacke mountains. Located at the northern end of the Southern Alps, and with a dramatic glacier-carved landscape, it's an awe-inspiring place to get up on high.

Part of the park, east of Lake Rotoiti, is classed as a 'mainland island' where a conservation scheme aims to eradicate introduced pests (rats, possums and stoats), and regenerate native flora and fauna. It offers excellent tramping, including short walks, lake scenery and one or two sandflies... The park is flush with bird life, and famous for brown-trout fishing.

The human hub of the Nelson Lakes region is the small, low-key village of **St Arnaud**.

🏃 Activities

Many spectacular walks allow you to appreciate this rugged landscape, but before you tackle them, stop by the DOC Nelson Lakes Visitor Centre for maps, track/weather updates and to pay your hut or camping fees.

There are two fantastic day hikes to be had. The five-hour **Mt Robert Circuit Track** starts at Mt Robert car park – a short drive away from St Arnaud, serviced by Nelson Lakes Shuttles (p445) – and circumnavigates the mountain. The optional side trip along Robert Ridge offers staggering views into the heart of the national park. Alternatively, the **St Arnaud Range Track** (five hours return), on the east side of the lake, climbs steadily to the ridge line adjacent to Parachute Rocks. Both tracks are strenuous, but reward with jaw-dropping vistas of glaciated valleys, arête peaks and Lake Rotoiti. Only attempt these tramps in fine weather.

At other times they are both pointless (no views) and dangerous.

There are also plenty of shorter (and flatter) walks from Lake Rotoiti's Kerr Bay and the road end at Lake Rotoroa. These and the longer day tramps are described in DOC's *Walks in Nelson Lakes National Park* pamphlet ($2).

The fit and well equipped can embark upon longer hikes such as the **Lake Angelus Track**. This magnificent two-to-three-day tramp follows Robert Ridge to Lake Angelus, where you can stay at the fine Angelus Hut (adult/child $20/10, bookings essential late November to April; backcountry pass/tickets valid the rest of the year) for a night or two before returning to St Arnaud via one of three routes. Pick up or download DOC's *Angelus Hut Tracks & Routes* pamphlet ($2) for more details. And if you've heard about **Blue Lake**, seek advice from the visitor centre before you even so much as contemplate it.

Rainbow SNOW SPORTS
(☑ 03-521 1861, snow phone 0832 226 05; www.skirainbow.co.nz; daily lift pass adult/child $80/39) The sunny Nelson region has a ski area, just 100km away (a similar distance from Blenheim). Rainbow borders the Nelson Lakes National Park, with varied terrain, minimal crowds and good cross-country skiing. Chains are often required. St Arnaud is the closest town (32km) and the season usually lasts from mid-July to mid-October. Ski and snowboard rental is available.

🛌 Sleeping

Kerr Bay DOC Campsite CAMPGROUND $
(www.doc.govt.nz; unpowered/powered sites per person $18/21) Near the Lake Rotoiti shore, the hugely popular Kerr Bay campsite has powered sites, toilets, hot showers, a laundry and a kitchen shelter. It's an inspiring base for your adventures, but do book in advance. Overflow camping is available around at DOC's **West Bay Campsite** (☑ 03-521 1806; www.doc.govt.nz; adult/child $13/6.50; ⊙ mid-Dec–Apr), which is more basic.

Travers-Sabine Lodge HOSTEL $
(☑ 03-521 1887; www.nelsonlakes.co.nz; Main Rd, St Arnaud; dm/d $32/75; 🛜) This hostel is a great base for outdoor adventure – being a short walk to Lake Rotoiti – inexpensive, clean and comfortable. It also has particularly cheerful Technicolor linen in the dorms, doubles and family room. The owners are experienced adventurers themselves, so tips come as standard; tramping equipment available for hire.

★ Alpine Lodge LODGE $$
(☑ 03-521 1869; www.alpinelodge.co.nz; Main Rd, St Arnaud; d $180-229; @ 🛜) Family owned and a consistent performer, this large lodge complex offers a range of accommodation, the pick of which is the split-level doubles with mezzanine bedroom and spa. If nothing else, go for the inviting in-house restaurant – a snug affair sporting an open fire, mountain views, good food (meals $15 to $32, takeaway pizza $20) and local beer.

ℹ Information

DOC Nelson Lakes Visitor Centre (☑ 03-521 1806; www.doc.govt.nz; View Rd; ⊙ 8am-4.30pm, to 5pm Dec-Apr) The Nelson Lakes Visitor Centre proffers park-wide information (weather, activities) and hut passes, plus displays on park ecology and history.

ℹ Getting There & Away

Nelson Lakes Shuttles (☑ 027 222 1872, 03-540 2042; www.nelsonlakesshuttles.co.nz) runs a weekly scheduled service between Nelson and the national park from December to February (Tuesday at 10am; $45), and on-demand the rest of the year. The service returns to Nelson at 11am on Fridays from December to February. It will also collect/drop off at Kawatiri Junction on SH63 to meet other bus services heading between Nelson and the West Coast, and offers services from St Arnaud through to Picton, Kaikoura, Hanmer Springs and other top-of-the-South destinations on demand. Try also Trek Express (p424), which regularly plies such routes.

ℹ Getting Around

Rotoiti Water Taxis (☑ 021 702 278; www.rotoitiwatertaxis.co.nz; Kerr Bay) Runs to/from Kerr Bay and West Bay to the southern end of Lake Rotoiti (three/four passengers $100/120). Kayaks, canoes and rowing boats can be hired from $50 per half-day; fishing trips and scenic lake cruises are available by arrangement.

The West Coast

Why Go?

Nowhere is solitude sweeter than on the West Coast. A few marvels pull big crowds – like Franz Josef and Fox Glaciers, and the magnificent Pancake Rocks – but you'll need jet-boats, helicopter rides and tramping trails to explore its inner realms. Hemmed in by the Southern Alps and the savage Tasman Sea, the West Coast forms almost 9% of New Zealand's land area but contains less than 1% of its population.

Nineteenth-century European settlers in this region faced great hardships as fortunes built on gold, coal and timber wavered. A chain of ghost towns and forlorn pioneer cemeteries were left in their wake, and only the hardiest remained. Present-day Coasters exhibit the same grit, softened with ironic humour and unquestioning hospitality. Time spent in these indomitable communities will have you spinning yarns of the wild West Coast long into the future.

Best Places to Eat

➡ Snake Bite Brewery (p472)
➡ Aurora (p465)
➡ Lake Matheson Cafe (p476)
➡ Ramble + Ritual (p465)
➡ Cow Shed (p449)

Best Places to Stay

➡ Theatre Royal Hotel (p462)
➡ Rough & Tumble Lodge (p452)
➡ Drifting Sands (p464)
➡ Te Waonui Forest Retreat (p472)
➡ Bazil's Hostel (p452)
➡ Old Slaughterhouse (p452)

When to Go

➡ December through February is peak season, so book accommodation at least a couple of months ahead during this period.

➡ The shoulder months of October/November and March/April are increasingly busy, particularly around Punakaiki, Hokitika and the Glaciers.

➡ The West Coast has plenty of sunshine but serious rainfall (in places, up to 5m annually).

➡ May to September has fewer crowds and cheaper accommodation; though mild (for NZ), it's reliably rainy.

➡ All year round, backcountry trampers should check conditions with local DOC (Department of Conservation) office staff. Rivers are treacherous and snow hangs around longer than you think.

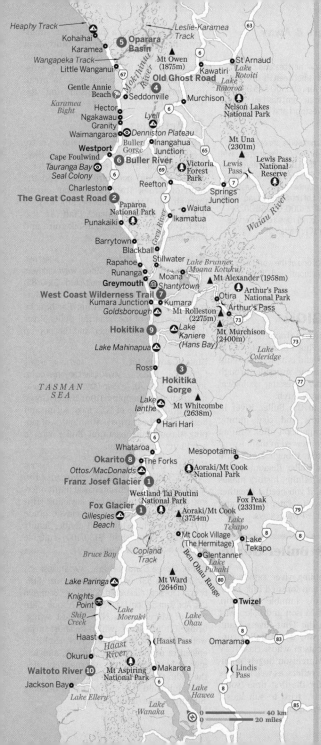

The West Coast Highlights

1 Glacier Country (p468) Soaring above Franz Josef and Fox Glaciers before a guided walk on glistening ice.

2 The Great Coast Road (p455) Admiring salt-licked beaches and the dramatic Pancake Rocks along an unforgettable 100km drive.

3 Hokitika Gorge (p463) Gawping at vibrant turquoise waters from a lofty swing bridge.

4 Gold-Rush History (p451) Delving into the past on the tough Old Ghost Road, or in mining towns like Reefton.

5 Oparara Basin (p454) Craning your neck at limestone formations girded by dense forest.

6 Buller River (p448) Getting wet 'n' wild taking on the rapids of this mighty river.

7 West Coast Wilderness Trail (p459) Enjoying equal measures of views and history by bike or on foot.

8 Okarito (p467) Kayaking through rainforest channels before joining a kiwi-spotting walk.

9 Hokitika (p465) Hunting out authentic local *pounamu* in working studios.

10 Waiatoto River (p477) Jetboating deep into Haast's World Heritage wilderness.

ⓘ Getting There & Away

AIR

Air New Zealand (www.airnewzealand.com) has two flights most days between Hokitika and Christchurch. **Sounds Air** (☑0800 505 005, 03-520 3080; www.soundsair.com) has two to three flights daily between Westport and Wellington.

BUS

Major and extensive bus networks are operated by **Atomic Travel** (☑03-349 0697; www.atomictravel.co.nz), **InterCity** (☑03-365 1113; www.intercity.co.nz) and **Naked Bus** (☑09-979 1616; www.nakedbus.com), connecting a number of West Coast destinations with the rest of the South Island. **West Coast Shuttle** (☑027 492 7000, 03-768 0028; www.westcoastshuttle.co.nz) runs a daily service between Greymouth and Christchurch.

TRAIN

The TranzAlpine (p458), one of the world's great train journeys, links Greymouth and Christchurch.

BULLER REGION

Forest and coast unite in dramatic form in the Buller Region. This northwesterly expanse of the South Island is a promised land for trampers. Trails wend riverside through primeval forest, some accessing geological marvels like the Oparara Arch.

Gold was found in the Buller River in the mid-19th century, and coal mining scorched the landscape soon after. Mining history is carefully conserved in main towns Westport and Reefton, though agriculture and tourism are the Buller Region's prime moneymakers today. Mining history makes a pleasant diversion, if you need a breather from muddy trails, white-water rafting, and kayaking tannin-stained waterways.

Murchison & Buller Gorge

☑03 / POP 492

In Murchison, tumbling river rapids add freshness to the air and forested hills beckon bushwalkers. This humble township, 125km southwest of Nelson and 95km east of Westport, lies on the 'Four Rivers Plain'. The mightiest waterway is the Buller, running alongside Murchison, whose class II-IV rapids have made Murchison hugely popular with experienced rafters, as well as those testing the waters for the first time (some jetboat operators have trips to suit kids... and risk-averse grown-ups).

Unless you have a passion for small-town history and antiques, Murchison itself won't excite you. But a day or two spent rafting or tramping here is a satisfying, adrenaline-drenched way to break up journeys between Nelson and the West Coast.

🏃 Activities

Ask at the Murchison Information Centre (p449) about local walks, such as the **Skyline Walk**, a 90-minute tramp through fern-filled beech and podocarp forest, and the **Johnson Creek Track**, a two-hour circuit through pine forest to the 'big slip', formed during the 1929 earthquake. Staff can also hook you up with mountain-bike hire and trout-fishing guides.

★**Wild Rivers Rafting**   RAFTING
(☑0508 467 238, 03-789 8953; www.wildriversrafting.co.nz; 2hr rafting adult/child $160/85) White-water rafting with Bruce and Marty on the particularly exciting Earthquake Rapids section of the beautiful Buller River (good luck with 'gunslinger' and the 'pop-up toaster'!).

Buller Canyon Jet   ADVENTURE SPORTS
(☑03-523 9883; www.bullercanyonjet.co.nz; adult/child $110/70; ☉Sep-May; 🚼) Launching from the whopping 110m Buller Gorge Swingbridge is one of NZ's most scenic and best-value jetboat trips – 40 minutes of ripping through the beautiful Buller with a good-humoured captain.

Ultimate Descents   RAFTING
(☑03-523 9899, 0800 748 377; www.rivers.co.nz; 38 Waller St; 🚼) Murchison-based outfit offering white-water rafting and kayaking trips on the Buller, including the classic grade III-IV gorge trip ($160), and gentler family excursions (adult/child $130/100) suitable for kids aged five or more.

Buller Gorge Swingbridge ADVENTURE SPORTS
(☑0800 285 537; www.bullergorge.co.nz; SH6; bridge crossing adult/child $10/5; ☉8am-7pm Dec-Apr, 9am-5.30pm May-Nov; 🚼) About 15km west of Murchison is NZ's longest swingbridge (110m), across which lie short bushwalks taking in the White Creek Faultline, epicentre of the 1929 earthquake, and former gold-mining sites. Alternatively, ride the 160m Cometline Flying Fox, either seated (adult/child $30/15) or forward-facing 'Supaman' style (adult $60).

👉 Tours

Natural Flames Experience   TOURS
(📞0800 687 244, 027 698 7244; www.natural
flames.co.nz; 34 Waller St; adult/child $95/65) Who
would have thought oil-drilling history would
be a high point of your trip? This informative
half-day 4WD and bushwalking tour through
verdant valleys, beech forest and capped oil
wells arrives at a hot spot where natural gas
seeping out of the ground has been burning
since 1922. Boil a billy on the flames and cook
pancakes before returning to civilisation.

🛌 Sleeping

**Kiwi Park Motels
& Holiday Park**   MOTEL, HOLIDAY PARK $
(📞03-523 9248, 0800 228 080; www.kiwipark.co.nz;
170 Fairfax St; unpowered/powered sites from $20/27,
cabins $70-85, motels $145-225; @🛜📶) A veritable Noah's Ark of emus, lambs and aston-
ishingly sociable ducks lift this leafy holiday
park from ordinary to family holiday heaven.
Endlessly helpful hosts preside over a campervan and tent area graced with mature trees,
basic cabins, roomy motel units and a kitchen
hewn from native timber. All these acres of
green space are just 1km south of town.

Lazy Cow   HOSTEL $
(📞03-523 9451; www.lazycow.co.nz; 9 Waller St;
dm $32-35, d & tw $90-110; 🛜) It's easy to be a
lazy cow here, with all the comforts of home
in a stress-free, small-scale package. Four-
bed dorms and private rooms all have electric blankets and guests are welcomed with
free muffins or cake, which you can enjoy in
the backyard or cosy lounge.

Order a pizza straight to your room from
the excellent adjoining **Cow Shed** (📞03-523
9523; http://lazycow.co.nz/eating; 37 Waller St;
mains $18-24; ⊙5-9pm Mon-Fri; 🅿) restaurant.

Riversong Cottages   COTTAGE $$
(📞03-523 9011; www.riversong.co.nz; 30 Fairfax St;
studio $110, unit from $180; 🛜) Boutique studio
and two-bedroom units open out to a big,
grassy yard and vegetable garden at this re-
laxed and refined set-up, and hosts Arran and
Alexia offer service with a personal touch.

🍴 Eating

Zen's Kitchen   CAFE, VEGAN $
(📞022 645 3756; www.zenskitchen.co.nz; 38
Waller St; snacks $5-10; ⊙10am-4pm Wed-Sun late
Oct-Easter; 🅿) Check out this retro yellow-and-
white caravan for tasty burgers made with
sourdough ciabatta buns and crammed with

vegan ingredients including spiced soy and
mushroom patties and cashew garlic aioli. In
cooler months, daily soup specials are on of-
fer, and fresh homestyle baking could include
savoury brioches or still-warm chocolate and
blueberry brownies. All organic and all good.

ℹ Information

Murchison Information Centre (📞03-523
9350; www.visitmurchison.nz; 47 Waller St;
⊙10am-5pm daily Dec-Mar, 10am-4pm Mon-Fri
Apr & Oct-Nov, closed May-Sep) Helpful tourist
centre that can assist with activity and hotel
bookings and offer bags of local info.

ℹ Getting There & Away

Daily Intercity (p448) and Naked Bus (p448)
services travelling from Picton ($47, three
hours) and Nelson (from $29, two hours) pass
through Murchison, with one continuing to West-
port (from $24, 1½ hours) on the West Coast.
During the peak tramping season **Trek Express**
(📞027 222 1872, 0800 128 735; www.trek
express.co.nz) passes through, between Nelson
and the Wangapeka/Heaphy Tracks.

Buses stop at Beechwoods Cafe on Waller St.

Reefton

📞03 / POP 1026

In Reefton town, nostalgia permeates every
period building and forlorn mining hut.
Reefton's gold-mining hey-day is never far
from mind, with museums dedicated to the
gold rush and a ghost town, 23km south, dat-
ing to this lost era. Early adoption of the elec-
tricity grid and street lighting gave Reefton
its tag line 'the town of light', but these days
it's the great outdoors that shines brightest.
Reefton is a good base for mountain biking,
tramping and rafting, if the good ol' days
aren't enough of an enticer to swing by.

◉ Sights

With loads of crusty, century-old buildings
situated within a 200m radius, Reefton is well
worth a stroll. To find out who lived where
and why, undertake the short **Heritage Walk**
outlined in the *Historic Reefton* leaflet, avail-
able from the Reefton i-SITE (p450).

Waiuta   GHOST TOWN
(www.waiuta.org.nz; off SH7) Remote Waiuta is
one of the West Coast's most famous ghost
towns. Spread over a square kilometre or so
of plateau, this once-burgeoning gold town
was abandoned in 1951 after the mineshaft
collapsed. Waiuta grew quickly after a gold

THE WEST COAST REEFTON

MĀORI NZ: THE WEST COAST

Early Māori forged paths through to the alps' mountains and river valleys to the West Coast in search of highly prized *pounamu* (greenstone), which they carved into tools, weapons and adornments. Admire and buy classy carvings created by town artists or polish your own stone at Bonz 'N' Stonz (p463).

discovery in 1905 but these days the forest-shrouded settlement is reduced to a big old rusty boiler, an overgrown swimming pool, stranded brick chimneys and the odd intact cottage, which face off against Mother Nature who has sent in the strangleweed.

🏃 Activities

Pick up the *Walks and Tracks of Reefton* leaflet detailing the **Golden Fleece Walk** (15 minutes), **Powerhouse Walk** (25 minutes) and other easy strolls.

Surrounding Reefton is the 206,000-hectare **Victoria Forest Park** (NZ's largest forest park), which sports hidden historic sites, such as the old goldfields around Blacks Point. Starting at Blacks Point, the enjoyable **Murray Creek Track** is a five-hour return trip. A number of walks, from 90 minutes to three hours, begin in or around the ghost town of Waiuta (p449), 23km south of Reefton.

Longer tramps in the Forest Park include the three-day **Kirwans** or two-day **Big River Track**, both of which can be traversed on a mountain bike. Pick up the free *Reefton Mountain Biking ('the best riding in history')* leaflet for more information; bikes can be hired from **Reefton Sports Centre** (☑ 03-732 8593; 56 Broadway; bike rental per day $30; ⊙ 9am-5pm Mon-Fri, 10am-1pm Sat, 11am-2pm Sun), where you can also enquire about legendary trout fishing in the environs.

🛏 Sleeping & Eating

⭐ **Reef Cottage B&B**   B&B $$
(☑ 03-732 8440; www.reefcottage.co.nz; 51-55 Broadway; d incl breakfast $150-170; 🐾) Enjoy total immersion into olde worlde Reefton at this converted 1887 solicitor's office. Compact rooms are furnished in period style, with modern touches like swish bathrooms and a well-equipped guest kitchen. In our favourite room, a burglar-proof money vault has been converted into the bathroom – privacy guaranteed! There's extra elbow room in the communal lounge and garden, too.

Full cooked breakfasts at the cafe next door are included in the price.

Future Dough Co.   BAKERY $$
(☑ 03-732 8497; www.thefuturedoughco.co.nz; 31 Broadway; snacks $3-8, meals $13-20; ⊙ 8am-5pm) This wooden-floored tea room gets by far the most daytime traffic in Reefton, whether for a fresh loaf and homemade shortbread, or a bigger feed of sausage breakfasts, toasties and whitebait lunches. But we're here for the seriously good coffee and jammy, cinnamon-dusted Linzer slice.

ℹ Information

Reefton i-SITE (☑ 03-732 8391; www.reefton.co.nz; 67-69 Broadway; ⊙ 9.30am-5pm Mon-Fri, 9.30am-2pm Sat, 9.30am-1pm Sun) This i-SITE has helpful staff, and you can visit a compact recreation of a mine inside (gold coin entry).

ℹ Getting There & Away

East West Coaches (☑ 03-789 6251; www.eastwestcoaches.co.nz) East West Coaches stops near the i-SITE in Reefton every day except Saturday on the run between Westport ($20, 1¼ hours) and Christchurch ($60, four hours).

Westport & Around

☑ 03 / POP 4035

The 'capital' of the northern West Coast is Westport. The town's fortunes have waxed and waned on coal mining, but in the current climate it sits quietly stoked up on various industries, including dairy and, increasingly, tourism. It boasts respectable hospitality and visitor services, and makes a good base for exploring the fascinating coast north to Denniston, Charming Creek, Karamea and the Heaphy Track.

👁 Sights

The most riveting sights are beyond Westport's city walls, particularly heading north on SH67, which passes **Granity**, **Ngakawau** (home to the well named Charming Creek) and **Hector**, where stands a monument to Hector's dolphins, NZ's smallest, although you'll be lucky to see them unless your timing is impeccable. It's also worth poking around **Seddonville**, a small bush town on the Mokihinui River. This small dot on the map is about to get slightly bigger, being the northern trailhead for the thrilling Old Ghost Road.

Coaltown Museum MUSEUM
(www.coaltown.co.nz; 123 Palmerston St; adult/child $10/2; ⊙9am-5pm Mon-Fri, 10am-4pm Sat & Sun) Westport's 'black gold' is paid homage at this remarkably interesting museum, adjoining the i-SITE. A replica mine, well-scripted display panels and an excellent selection of photographs and pioneer ephemera allow for an informative trip into the coal-blackened past. Best of all are the Denniston displays, including a whopping brake drum and panels explaining the daily tribulations of miners.

Denniston Plateau HISTORIC SITE
(www.doc.govt.nz; Denniston Rd) Six hundred metres above sea level, Denniston was once NZ's largest coal town, with 1500 residents in 1911. By 1981 there were eight. Its claim to fame was the fantastically steep Denniston Incline, which hurtled laden wagons down a 45-degree hillside. Display panels bring the plateau's history to life and trails provide a direct route into the past: the **Town Walk** (40 minutes) loops around the old township while the **Bridle Path** (5½ hours return) follows old coal transportation routes.

🏃 Activities

Westport is good for a stroll – the i-SITE (p453) can direct you to the **Millennium Walkway** and **North Beach Reserve**. The most exciting excursion hereabouts is cave rafting with Underworld Adventures (p456) in Charleston, although mountain biking is gaining momentum as a popular pastime among local and visiting backcountry adventurers. The folk at Habitat Sports offer bike rental, maps and advice.

⭐**Old Ghost Road** TRAMPING, CYCLING
(www.oldghostroad.org.nz) One of the gnarliest of NZ's cycling and tramping trails, the 85km Old Ghost Road follows a historic miners' track that was started in the 1870s but never finished as the gold rush petered out. Following a painstaking, volunteer-led build, the gruelling track now traverses native forests, tussock tops, river flats and valleys.

The southern trailhead is at Lyell, 50 minutes' drive (62km) east of Westport along the scenic Buller Gorge (SH6). The DOC campsite and day walks here have long been popular, with visitors drawn in by readily accessible historic sites, including a graveyard secreted in the bush. The northern trailhead is at Seddonville, 45 minutes' drive (50km)

north of Westport off SH67, from where the track sidles along the steep-sided and utterly stunning Mokihinui River. Joining the two ends is an alpine section, with entrancing views from sunrise to sunset.

The track is dual use, but favours trampers (allow five days). For advanced mountain bikers who can handle narrow trails and plenty of jolts, it is pretty much the Holy Grail, completed in two to four days, preferably from Lyell to Seddonville. The four huts along the way need to be booked in advance on the Old Ghost Road website, which also details a range of other ways to experience the track other than an end-to-end ride or tramp. Day trips from either end are a rewarding, flexible way in, particularly from the West Coast end via the inimitable Rough & Tumble Lodge (p452).

Being a long and remote track through wild terrain, conditions can change quickly, so check the trail website for status. Westport's **Buller Adventures** (📞0508 486 877; www.bulleradventures.com; 193 Palmerston St), **Habitat Sports** (📞03-788 8002; www.habitatsports.co.nz; 234 Palmerston St, Westport; bike rental from $35; ⊙9am-5pm Mon-Fri, 9am-1pm Sat) and **Hike n Bike Shuttle** (📞027 446 7876; www.hikenbikeshuttle.co.nz; shuttle from $40) provide bike and equipment hire, shuttles and other related services.

⭐**Cape Foulwind Walkway** WALKING
(www.doc.govt.nz) Screaming gulls and rasping waves are the soundtrack to tramps around Cape Foulwind (45 minutes to one hour each way), as wind-battered a walk as its name promises. The trail traverses buttercup-speckled farmland, which carpets the coastal hills between Omau and Tauranga Bay. Towards the southern end is the **seal colony** where – depending on the season – up to 200 fur seals loll on the rocks. Further north the walkway passes a replica astrolabe (a navigational aid) and lighthouse.

Charming Creek Walkway TRAMPING, CYCLING
(www.doc.govt.nz) Starting from either Ngakawau (30km north of Westport), or near Seddonville, a few kilometres further on, this is one of the best day walks on the coast, taking around six hours return. Following an old coal line through the Ngakawau River Gorge, it features rusty relics galore, tunnels, a suspension bridge and waterfall, and lots of interesting plants and geological formations.

🛏 Sleeping

⭐ Bazil's Hostel — HOSTEL $

(☎03-789 6410; www.bazils.com; 54 Russell St, Westport; dm $32, d with/without bathroom $110/72; 🛜) Mural-painted Bazil's has homey, well-maintained dorm and private rooms in a sociable setting. It's managed by worldly types who offer surfing lessons (three hours $80; board and suit hire per day $45), rainforest SUP trips, and social activities aplenty. So do you want the yoga class ($8), something from the pizza oven ($10), or a little of both?

⭐ Old Slaughterhouse — HOSTEL $

(☎027 529 7640, 03-782 8333; www.oldslaughterhouse.co.nz; SH67, Hector; tent sites $22, dm/s/d $40/70/88; ⊙Oct-Jun) 🌿 Perched on a hillside 32km north of Westport, this lodge and chalets gaze across epic views of the Tasman Sea. Powered largely by a waterwheel, the central lodge has a roomy lounge, shared kitchen, reading nooks and a deck where you can luxuriate in the lack of wi-fi. A steep, 10-minute walk from the car park bolsters its off-the-grid charm.

Carters Beach Top 10 Holiday Park — HOLIDAY PARK, MOTEL $

(☎03-789 8002, 050 893 7876; www.top10westport.co.nz; 57 Marine Pde, Carters Beach; unpowered/powered site from $20/47, units $72-215; @🛜🐾) Right on Carters Beach and located 4km from Westport and 12km to Tauranga Bay, this tidy complex has pleasant sites as well as comfortable cabins and motel units. It's a good option for tourers seeking a peaceful stop-off with a swim (or on foul-weather days, a games room and playground to distract the kids).

Gentle Annie Seaside Accommodation — HOLIDAY PARK $

(☎0274 188 587, 03-782 1826; www.gentleannie.co.nz; De Malmanche Rd, Mokihinui; sites from $12, s/d from $30/60, cottages $110-180; 🛜) Family-run since the 1970s, Gentle Annie's campsite and self-contained cottages cluster at the Mokihinui River mouth. The beach isn't so gentle, but the atmosphere is restful: guests can tramp to Gentle Annie Point for stirring coast views, gather driftwood for a beach bonfire, and retreat to a rustic-chic cottage (we especially liked Remu House, with its huge open-plan lounge and fireplace).

Archer House — B&B $$

(☎0800 789 877, 03-789 8778; www.archerhouse.co.nz; 75 Queen St, Westport; d incl breakfast $195-245; 🛜) This beautiful 1880s heritage building, formerly the home of a goldfields trader, has original features galore. There are three individually decorated rooms (each one a work of art) with private bathrooms and three tastefully attired lounges in which to swirl a glass of complimentary wine while admiring English stained glass, Moroccan lights, tiled fireplaces and the flourishing garden.

Miners on Sea — CABIN, APARTMENT $$

(☎03-782 8664; www.minersonsea.co.nz; 117 Torea St (SH6), Granity; pods d/tr $85/100, chalets $195-245) This place knows what bikers passing through Granity need: serviceable and clean 'pod' rooms (with shared kitchen and bathroom facilities), and adjoining Tommyknockers (☎03-782 8664; www.minersonsea.co.nz; 117 Torea St (SH6), Granity; snacks from $4, mains $18-39; ⊙11am-8pm) for easy-to-reach booze and food. More upmarket are the modern, self-contained studio chalets: fireplaces, gleaming bathrooms and marine-themed trimmings that befit their sea-facing location. Breakfast platters cost $17.

Omau Settlers Lodge — MOTEL $$

(☎03-789 5200; www.omausettlerslodge.co.nz; cnr Cape Foulwind & Omau Rds, Cape Foulwind; d incl breakfast $145-175; 🛜) Relaxation is the mantra at this faultless motel near Cape Foulwind. Beds are plump, bathrooms are glossy and fragrant, plus there's a hot tub surrounded by bush. Chatty hosts Karen and Lee offer superb service, and lay out a satisfying continental breakfast. Ask nicely and you might get a lift to the end of Cape Foulwind Walkway.

⭐ Rough & Tumble Lodge — LODGE $$$

(☎03-782 1337; www.roughandtumble.co.nz; Mokihinui Rd, Seddonville; d incl continental breakfast $210, extra person $50; 🛜) 🌿 With invigorating views of river and bush, this luxe tramping lodge sits at the West Coast end of the Old Ghost Road, at a bend in the Mokihinui River. Its five split-level quad rooms have silver birch banisters, posh bathrooms and verdant views. Bonus: profits are poured back into the maintenance of the walking track.

🍴 Eating

PR's Cafe — CAFE $

(☎03-789 7779; 124 Palmerston St, Westport; mains $10-20; ⊙7am-4.30pm Mon-Fri, to 3pm Sat & Sun; 🛜) Westport's sharpest cafe has a cabinet full of sandwiches and pastries, and a counter groaning under the weight of cakes (Dutch apple, banoffee pie) and cookies. An all-day menu delivers carefully composed meals such as salmon omelette oozing with dill aioli, spanakopita, and fish and chips.

Star Tavern PUB FOOD $$
(☑ 03-789 6923; 6 Lighthouse Rd, Cape Foulwind;
meals $9-30; ⊙ 4pm-late Mon-Fri, noon-late Sat &
Sun) The floor space cleared to make room
for pool and table tennis ensures a convivial
huddle at the bar inside the Star Tavern. A
small dining hall adjoins it, where you can
tuck into plates of ham, fish and chips, or
sizeable steaks lashed with garlic butter. Hey,
you can walk it off around Cape Foulwind.

ⓘ Information

Buller Hospital (☑ 03-788 9030; Cobden St,
Westport; ⊙24hr)
DOC Westport Office (☑03-788 8008; www.
doc.govt.nz; 72 Russell St, Westport; ⊙8-
11am & 2-4.30pm Mon-Fri) DOC bookings and
information can be obtained from the i-SITE.
For curly questions, visit this field office.
Westport i-SITE (☑03-789 6658; www.buller.
co.nz; 123 Palmerston St, Westport; ⊙9am-5pm
Mon-Fri, 10am-4pm Sat & Sun; ☎) Information
on local tracks, walkways, tours, accommoda-
tion and transport. Self-help terminal for DOC
information and hut and track bookings.

ⓘ Getting There & Away

AIR
Sounds Air (p448) has two to three flights daily
to/from Wellington.

BUS
InterCity (p448) buses reach Nelson (from
$36, 3½ hours) and Greymouth (from $21, 2¼
hours). Change in Greymouth for Franz Josef or
Fox Glacier (from $39, six hours). Similar prices
on the same routes are available through Naked
Bus (p448). Buses leave from the i-SITE.

East West Coaches (p450) Operates a service
through to Christchurch, via Reefton and the
Lewis Pass, every day except Saturday, depart-
ing from the Caltex petrol station.

Karamea Express (p455) Links Westport and
Karamea ($35, two hours, Monday to Friday May
to September, plus Saturday from October to
April). It also services Kohaihai twice daily dur-
ing peak summer, and other times on demand.
Wangapeka transport is also available.

Trek Express (p449) Passes through Westport
on its frequent high-season tramper transport
link between Nelson and the Wangapeka/
Heaphy Tracks.

ⓘ Getting Around

BICYCLE
Hire bikes and obtain advice from Habitat
Sports (p451).

TAXI
Buller Taxis (☑ 03-789 6900)

Karamea & Around
☑ 03 / POP 575
Friendly tramping hub Karamea is colour-
ful, pint-sized, and perched by the enticing
wilderness of Kahurangi National Park. As
the beginning (or end) point of the Heaphy
and Wangapeka Tracks, it's common to see
trampers gearing up for adventure (or shuf-
fling wearily to the pub). You can delve into
the national park on much shorter walks,
in particular around the 35 million-year-old
Oparara Basin, whose rainforest hides lime-
stone caverns and natural rock arches.

Driving north from Westport, Karamea is
98 scenic (and petrol station–free) kilometres
along SH67 (fill your tank before you set out).

⊙ Sights

★**Scotts Beach** BEACH
It's almost an hour's walk each way from Ko-
haihai over the hill to Scotts Beach – a wild,
empty shoreline shrouded in mist, awash
in foamy waves, strewn with driftwood and
backed by nikau palm forest. Wander in
wonder, but don't even think about dipping
a toe in – there are dangerous currents at
work here.

🏃 Activities

The outdoor wonderland of nikau palms,
moss-clad forests and stunning shores is the
prime reason to visit Karamea. Trampers can
launch into the Heaphy Track or embark on
trails around the imposing Oparara Basin.
Flexible and friendly **Karamea Outdoor
Adventures** (☑03-782 6181; www.karamea
adventures.co.nz; Bridge St, Karamea; guided kay-
ak/riverbug trips from $70, 2hr biking trips from
$35) offers guided and freedom kayaking
and riverbug trips, plus mountain-bike hire,
horse treks and caving.

Never swim at Karamea's beaches, where
currents are wild and waves smash the
shore. If you must dip a toe in some water,
ask at the information centre about freshwa-
ter swimming spots like river holes.

Helicopter Charter Karamea SCENIC FLIGHTS
(☑03-782 6111; www.helicharterkaramea.com; 78
Aerodrome Rd, Karamea) Helicopter Charter
Karamea offers flights through to the
northern trailhead in Golden Bay: up to
six passengers $1450; up to five passengers
with mountain bikes $1600. Ask about
other drop-off/pick-ups, including the Old
Ghost Road.

OPARARA BASIN

Lying within Kahurangi National Park, the Oparara Basin is a hidden valley concealing limestone arches and caves within a thick forest of massive, moss-laden trees. The valley's signature sight is the 200m-long, 37m-high **Oparara Arch**, spanning the picturesque Oparara River, tannin-stained a fetching shade of caramel, which wends alongside the easy walkway (45 minutes return). The main car park, a 25km drive northeast of Karamea (very rough and narrow in places) is the trailhead for walks of various lengths, and there are excellent information panels here, too.

At the cave mouth of the Oparara Arch walk, some trampers continue uphill for lofty views but it's steep and treacherous (especially after rain), so we advise against it.

The smaller but no less stunning **Moria Gate Arch** (43m long, 19m high) is reached via a simply divine forest loop walk (1½ hours), which also passes the **Mirror Tarn** (itself 15 minutes from the car park).

Just a 10-minute walk from the second car park are the **Crazy Paving and Box Canyon Caves**. Take your torch to enter a world of weird subterranean shapes and rare, leggy spiders. Spiders, caves, darkness...sound like fun?

Beyond this point are the superb **Honeycomb Hill Caves and Arch**, accessible only by guided tours (3-/5-/8-hour tours $95/150/240) run by the **Karamea Information & Resource Centre** (p455). Ask about other guided tours of the area, and also about transport for the **Oparara Valley Track**, a rewarding five-hour independent tramp through ancient forest, along the river, popping out at the **Fenian Walk** car park.

To drive to the valley from Karamea, travel 10km along the main road north and turn off at McCallum's Mill Rd, where signposts will direct you a further 14km up and over into the valley along a road that is winding, gravel, rough in places and sometimes steep. Don't attempt it with a campervan.

Tramping

Hats off to the Karamea community who established the very pleasant **Karamea Estuary Walkway**, a long-as-you-like stroll bordering the estuary and Karamea River. The adjacent beach can be reached via Flagstaff Rd, north of town. Both feature plenty of bird life and are best walked at sunset. The Karamea Information & Resource Centre (p455) has various maps, including the free *Karamea* brochure, which details other walks such as **Big Rimu** (one hour return to a whopping tree) and the **Zig Zag** (one hour return), which accesses lookouts over peaceful farmland.

Longer walks around Karamea include the **Fenian Walk** (four hours return, bring a torch) leading to **Cavern Creek Cave**, **Tunnel Cave** and **Adams Flat**, where there's a replica gold-miner's hut; and the first leg of the **Wangapeka Track** to Belltown Hut. The Wangapeka Track is a four-to-six-day backcountry trip suitable for highly experienced trampers only.

The West Coast road ends 14km from Karamea at **Kohaihai**, the western trailhead (and most commonly, the finish point) of the Heaphy Track (p443), where there's also a **DOC campsite** (www.doc.govt.nz; Kahurangi National Park; sites per adult/child $8/4). A day walk or overnight stay can readily be had from here. Walk to Scotts Beach (p453) (two hours return), or go as far as the fabulous new Heaphy Hut (five hours) and stay a night or two before returning.

This section can also be mountain-biked, as can the whole track (two to three days) from May to September; ask at Westport's Habitat Sports (p451) for bike hire and details.

Helicopter Charter Karamea (p453) offers flights through to the northern trailhead in Golden Bay: up to six passengers $1450; up to five passengers with mountain bikes $1600. (Ask about other drop-off/pick-ups, including the Old Ghost Road.)

Sleeping & Eating

Karamea Farm Baches CABIN $
(☑ 03-782 6838; www.karameafarmbaches.com; 17 Wharf Rd, Karamea; d/tr/q $99/129/157; 🛜)
🍃 These seven 1960s self-contained baches push reuse and recycle to the limit, from period wallpaper and grandma's carpet to organic vegetables grown on site. Light on luxury but brimming with old-school charm.

Wi-fi signal reaches all but one of the baches.

Rongo Dinner, Bed & Breakfast   B&B $$

(☑ 03-782 6667; http://rongo.nz; 130 Waverley St, Karamea; half-board s/d $90/180; 🛜) 🍴 Rongo's rainbow-coloured exterior draws you in, while its free-spirited vibe lengthens your stay. Formerly a backpacker hostel, Rongo retains a slouchy, neo-hippie ethos but these days wows guests with zero-kilometre cuisine whipped up by a French chef (breakfasts and dinners included in the price).

Last Resort   LODGE $$

(☑ 03-782 6617, 0800 505 042; www.lastresort karamea.co.nz; 71 Waverley St, Karamea; dm $37, d/tw with shared bathroom $74, r for 2/3/4 guests with private bathroom $107/127/147, studio from $130; 🛜) Enclosed by greenery some 600m west of Market Cross, this rambling resort suits most budgets, with a choice of rooms with and without private bathrooms. At the posher end of the price range are self-contained two-bedroom cottages (from $155) complete with spa tub. Bonus points for laundry facilities and a comfy communal lounge with TV and tea-making.

The attached cafe (☑ 03-782 6617; www.lastresortkaramea.co.nz; 71 Waverley St, Karamea; snacks from $4, mains $15-30; ⊙ 7.30am-11pm) is the best place in town for a feed.

Karamea Village Hotel   PUB FOOD $$

(☑ 03-782 6800; www.karameahotel.co.nz; cnr Waverley St & Wharf Rd, Karamea; meals $15-34; ⊙ 11am-11pm) Here lie simple pleasures and warm hospitality: a game of pool, a pint of ale, and a choice of roast dinners, nachos and beer-battered whitebait, to a soundtrack of local gossip and dinging pokie machines.

ℹ Information

Karamea Information & Resource Centre
(☑ 03-782 6652; www.karameainfo.co.nz; Market Cross; ⊙ 9am-5pm Mon-Fri, 10am-1pm Sat & Sun, shorter hours May-Dec) This excellent, community-owned centre has the local low-down, internet access, maps and DOC hut tickets. It also doubles as the petrol station.

ℹ Getting There & Away

Karamea Express (☑ 03-782 6757; info@karamea-express.co.nz) links Karamea and Westport ($35, two hours, Monday to Friday May to September, plus Saturday from October to April). On Mondays and Saturdays, this service connects to a shuttle to Kohaihai ($20). Wangapeka transport is also available. Bookings essential – services are by demand outside peak season.

Heaphy Bus (☑ 0800 128 735, 03-540 2042; www.theheaphybus.co.nz), based in Nelson,

services both ends of the Heaphy Track, as well as the Wangapeka.

Fly from Karamea to Takaka with Helicopter Charter Karamea (p453), **Golden Bay Air** (☑ 0800 588 885; www.goldenbayair.co.nz) or **Adventure Flights Golden Bay** (☑ 0800 150 338, 03-525 6167; www.adventureflightsgolden bay.co.nz; from $185) starting from $150 per person, then tramp back on the Heaphy Track; contact the Karamea Information & Resource Centre for details.

Based at **Rongo, Karamea Connections** (☑ 03-782 6667; www.karameaconnections. co.nz) runs track and town transport, including services to Heaphy, Wangapeka, Oparara Basin and Westport on demand. Fares vary by group number and destination; for a group of four going from Karamea to the Oparara Basin (with a later pick-up at the Fenian Track), you can expect to pay $25 per head ($10 extra for bikes).

THE GREAT COAST ROAD

One hundred kilometres of salty vistas line the road between Westport and Greymouth. One of New Zealand's most beautiful drives, the Great Coast Road meanders past foaming surf and shingle beaches on one side, and forbidding, overhanging cliffs on the other. The best-known stop along this inspiring stretch of SH6 is Punakaiki's geologically fascinating Pancake Rocks. But there are numerous wind-whipped lookouts where you can pull over to gaze at waves smashing against haggard turrets of stone.

Fill up in Westport or Greymouth if you're low on petrol and cash.

Charleston & Around

The northernmost section of the Great Coast Road plies gold-mining history, dreamy coast and quiet farmland on its way between Westport and Punakaiki's Pancake Rocks. Roughly midway is Charleston, an 1860s gold-rush boom town that once boasted 80 hotels, three breweries and hundreds of thirsty gold-diggers staking claims along the Nile River. There's not much left now except a motel, camping ground, a clutch of local houses, and the brilliant Underworld Adventures (p456), with whom you can explore some utterly amazing hidden treasures.

South of Charleston is where the Great Coast Road becomes truly enthralling, with a series of dramatic bays. Drive as slowly as the traffic behind you will allow.

◉ Sights & Activities

Mitchells Gully Gold Mine   HISTORIC SITE
(☑03-789 6257; http://mitchellsgullygoldmine.
co.nz; SH6, Charleston; adult/child $10/free;
☺9am-4pm) For a true taste of the region's
gold-mining past, swing into Mitchells Gully
Gold Mine, 3km north of Charleston. You'll
get a friendly primer on the 1860s mining
days and then explore mining tunnels and
railway tracks on a pleasant, 40-minute
bush walk, goggling at Charleston's last remaining waterwheel and stamping battery
along the way.

If you're staying in the area, reserve a spot
on a night-time glowworm tour (adult/child
$25/5).

Underworld Adventures   CAVING
(☑03-7888168,0800116686;www.caverafting.com;
SH6, Charleston) Glow with the flow on black-
water rafting trips deep into glowworm-filled
Nile River Caves (adult/child $185/150, four
hours). This friendly Charleston-based operator also runs cave excursions without rafting (adult/child $120/87.50). Short on time?
Take the rainforest train ride (adult/child
$25/20), a 1½-hour return journey depart-
ing two or three times daily. The centre and
its cafe are 26km south of Westport.

Kids aged 10 and over can raft, while the
cave tours suit anyone who can walk on slippery surfaces for a couple of hours.

The Adventure Caving trip ($350, five
hours) includes a 40m abseil into Te Tahi
cave system, with rock squeezes, waterfalls,
prehistoric fossils and trippy cave formations.

🛏 Sleeping

Beaconstone Eco Lodge   HOSTEL $
(☑027 3341136; www.beaconstoneecolodge.
co.nz; Birds Ferry Rd, SH6; dm $40, d & tw $96-104;
☺Oct-Apr; 🐾) 🍃 Set on 42 serene hectares,
17km south of Westport, this solar-powered, energy-efficient lodge is both eco- and
guest-friendly. Fashioned from sustainably
sourced native timber and featuring comfy
beds and a laid-back communal area, the
lodge's style is Americana cool meets West
Coast charm. Bush walks lead right from the
doorstep. Book ahead.

ⓘ Getting There & Away

InterCity (p448) and Naked Bus (p448) services
ply this leg of the Great Coast Road once a day,
stopping at Charleston on their way between
Westport (from $10, 25 minutes) and Greymouth
(from $16, two hours), via Punakaiki (around
$13, 40 minutes).

Punakaiki & Paparoa National Park

Located midway between Westport and
Greymouth is Punakaiki, a small settlement
beside the rugged 38,000-hectare Paparoa
National Park. Most visitors come for a
quick squiz at the Pancake Rocks, layers of
limestone that resemble stacked crepes. But
these are just one feature of the impressive,
boulder-sprinkled shoreline. Pebble beaches
(keep an eye out for greenstone) are kissed
by spectacular sunsets and there are some
riveting walking trails into the national park.

◉ Sights

Paparoa National Park is blessed with high
cliffs and empty beaches, a dramatic mountain range, crazy limestone river valleys,
diverse flora, and a profusion of bird life,
including weka and the Westland petrel, a
rare sea bird that nests only here.

★Pancake Rocks   NATURAL FEATURE
(www.doc.govt.nz; SH6) Punakaiki's claim
to fame is Dolomite Point, where a layer-
ing-weathering process called stylobedding
has carved the limestone into what looks
like piles of thick pancakes. Aim for high
tide (tide timetables are posted at the visitor
centre; hope that it coincides with sunset)
when the sea surges into caverns and booms
menacingly through blowholes. See it on a
wild day and be reminded that Mother Nature really is the boss.

Allow 20 minutes for the straightforward
walk, which loops from the highway out to
the rocks and blowholes (or 40 minutes if
you want to take photos). Parts of the trail
are suitable for wheelchair access.

🏃 Activities

Tramps around Punakaiki include the **Tru-
man Track** (30 minutes return) and the
Punakaiki–Porari Loop (3½ hours), which
goes up the spectacular limestone Pororari
River gorge before popping over a hill and
coming down the bouldery Punakaiki River
to rejoin the highway.

Surefooted types can embark on the **Fox
River Cave Walk** (three hours return), 12km
north of Punakaiki and open to amateur explorers. BYO torch and sturdy shoes.

The Paparoa National Park Visitor Centre
(p457) has free maps detailing other tramps
in the area. Note that many of Paparoa's inland walks are susceptible to river flooding

so it is vital that you obtain updates from the centre before you depart, and always heed warning signs and roped-off trails.

Punakaiki Canoes KAYAKING
(☑ 0800 271 383, 03-731 1870; www.riverkayaking.co.nz; SH6; 2hr canoe hire adult/child $50/10, then $5 per hr) This outfit rents canoes near the Pororari River bridge, for gentle, super-scenic paddling for all abilities. The rental shop is signposted near the river at the north end of Punakaiki.

Punakaiki Horse Treks HORSE RIDING
(☑ 03-731 1839, 021 264 2600; www.pancake-rocks.co.nz; SH6, Punakaiki; 2½hr ride $180; ◷ mid-Oct–early May) Trek through the beautiful Punakaiki Valley right onto the beach on these guided horseback tours, suitable for all experience levels. Private rides start at $220 (minimum two people).

🛏 Sleeping & Eating

★**Punakaiki Beach Hostel** HOSTEL $
(☑ 03-731 1852; www.punakaikibeachhostel.co.nz; 4 Webb St; sites per person $22, dm/d $32/89; 🛜) The ambience is laid-back but Punakaiki Beach is efficiently run. This spick-and-span 24-bed hostel has all the amenities a traveller could need, from laundry to a shared kitchen to staff who smile because they mean it. Comfy dorm rooms aside, the en-suite bus ($140) is the most novel stay, but cutesy Sunset Cottage ($150) is also worth a splurge.

Te Nikau Retreat HOSTEL $
(☑ 03-731 1111; www.tenikauretreat.co.nz; 19 Hartmount Pl; dm $32, d $85-110, cabins $120-210; 🛜) 🍃 Checking in to Te Nikau feels instantly restorative. Kindly staff establish a relaxing tone, and charming wooden lodges (dorms and private cabins) are tucked into rainforest, a short walk from the beach. Our favourite is tiny Stargazer: it's little more than a double bed in a low hut but glass roof panels allow you to count constellations on clear nights.

Hydrangea Cottages COTTAGE $$$
(☑ 03-731 1839; www.pancake-rocks.co.nz; SH6; cottages $245-485; 🛜) On a hillside overlooking the Tasman, these six standalone and mostly self-contained cottages are built from salvaged timber and stone. Each is distinct, like 'Miro' with splashes of colour and bright tiles, and two-storey 'Nikau' with a private, sea-facing deck. Occasional quirks like outdoor bathtubs add to the charm. It's 800m south of Pancake Rocks and the visitor centre.

Pancake Rocks Cafe CAFE $$
(☑ 03-731 1122; www.pancakerockscafe.com; 4300 Coast Rd (SH6), Punakaiki; mains $10-26; ◷ 8am-5pm, to 10pm Dec-Feb; ✎) Almost inevitably, pancakes are the pride of the cafe opposite the Pancake Rocks trail, heaped with bacon, berries, cream and other tasty toppings. Even better are the pizzas, from whitebait to four cheese (with a few good veggie options, too). Time a visit for summer open-mic nights from 6pm on Fridays.

ⓘ Information

Paparoa National Park Visitor Centre (☑ 03-731 1895; www.doc.govt.nz; SH6, Punakaiki; ◷ 9am-5pm Oct-Nov, to 6pm Dec-Mar, to 4.30pm Apr-Sep) Across the road from the Pancake Rocks walkway, the visitor centre has information on the national park and track conditions, and handles bookings for some local attractions and accommodation, including hut tickets.

Punakaiki Promotions (www.punakaiki.co.nz) Online directory of accommodation, activities and tide times.

ⓘ Getting There & Away

InterCity (p448) and Naked Bus (p448) services travel daily north to Westport (from $16, one hour), and south to Greymouth (from $11, 45 minutes) and Fox Glacier (from $37, 5½ hours). Buses stop long enough for passengers to admire the Pancake Rocks.

Barrytown & Around

The southernmost stretch of the Great Coast Road, between Punakaiki and Greymouth, carves a path between rocky bays and the steep, bushy Paparoa Ranges. Sleepy, sparsely populated Barrytown is the main settlement along this section of the SH6, but expansive views provide an excuse to stop and take it all in. Set out on a clear day and you can see as far as the Southern Alps.

🗡 Courses

★**Barrytown Knifemaking** KNIFEMAKING
(☑ 03-731 1053, 0800 256 433; www.barrytownknifemaking.com; 2662 SH6, Barrytown; classes $160; ◷ Tue-Sun by arrangement) Fashion your very own knife on a day-long course in Barrytown, 17km south of Punakaiki. Under the expert tutelage of Steve and Robyn, who host the courses in their home, you'll hand-forge the steel blade and craft its handle from native rimu timber. Bonuses include

axe-throwing, a big swing, and a stream of entertainingly bad jokes from Steve. Bookings essential.

🛏 Sleeping

⭐ Breakers
B&B $$$

(🕿03-762 7743; www.breakers.co.nz; 1367 SH6, Nine Mile Creek, Rapahoe; d incl breakfast $275-385; 🕝) Crafted to tug at the heart strings of surfers and beach bunnies, every room at Breakers has a sea view and easy access down to the shore. Tucked into a hillside nook 14km north of Greymouth, all four self-contained units are tasteful and modern, with decks for sighing over the sunset.

Ti Kouka House
B&B $$$

(🕿03-731 1460; www.tikoukahouse.co.nz; 2522 SH6, Barrytown; d incl breakfast $350; 🕝) Across the highway from the beach, quirky Ti Kouka House has a one-of-a-kind design against a rainforest backdrop. Recycled building materials are accented with driftwood, stained glass and sculptures, creating an ambience somewhere between artist's studio and nature retreat. You'll want to move in permanently, but you'll have to settle for a stay in one of three individually decorated rooms.

ⓘ Getting There & Away

InterCity (p448) and Naked Bus (p448) services ply this leg of the Great Coast Road once a day, stopping at Barrytown on their way between Westport (from $17, 1¾ hours) and Greymouth (from $10, 20 minutes), via Punakaiki (from $10, 15 minutes).

GREYMOUTH REGION

Bookending the magnificent alpine highway Arthur's Pass and sitting roughly halfway along the West Coast road, Greymouth and its surrounds are more of a transit point than a destination.

Largest town Greymouth (to the Māori 'Māwhera', wide river mouth) is big on services but light on attractions, though the classy brewery and historic village Shantytown merit a visit. Inland, Kumara is a common stop-off for cyclists on the West Coast Wilderness Trail, Lake Brunner is a soothing getaway for fishing or bird-watching, and remote Blackball is firmly in trampers' eyelines as a starting point for the Pike29 Memorial Track, a 45km 'Great Walk' destined to open in 2019. Even by NZ's standards, the Greymouth region is a standout for friendliness; its down-to-earth folks might be reason enough to dawdle here before you travel on.

Greymouth

🕿03 / POP 13,371 (DISTRICT)

Greymouth is the largest town on the West Coast and the region's 'Big Smoke'. For locals it's a refuelling and shopping pit stop, for travellers it's a noteworthy portal to tramping trails. Arriving on a dreary day, it's no mystery why Greymouth, crouched at the mouth of the imaginatively named Grey River, is sometimes the butt of jokes. But with gold-mining history, a scattering of jade shops, and worthy walks in its surrounds, it pays to look beyond the grey.

◉ Sights

Shantytown
MUSEUM

(🕿03-762 6634; www.shantytown.co.nz; Rutherglen Rd, Paroa; adult/child/family $33/16/78; ⊙8.30am-5pm; 🚼) Good fun for kids and young-of-heart travellers, Shantytown is a recreated 1860s gold-mining town, 10km south of Greymouth. Peer inside a church, workshops and gory hospital (shield the kids' eyes), all painstakingly crafted to evoke the spirit of the era. Take cheesy souvenir pics in period costume and try gold-panning, but the highlight is a steam-train ride into the bush (five to seven daily).

Monteith's Brewing Co
BREWERY

(🕿03-768 4149; www.monteiths.co.nz; cnr Turumaha & Herbert Sts; guided tour $25; ⊙tours 4 daily, tasting room & bar 11am-8pm May-Oct, to 9pm Nov-Mar) The original Monteith's brewhouse is brand HQ: glossy and a wee bit corporate, but it delivers a high-quality experience. Plan ahead for one of four daily guided tours (25 minutes, including generous samples) or DIY in the industrial-chic tasting room and bar, complete with roaring fire.

🏃 Activities

⭐ TranzAlpine
RAIL

(🕿04-495 0775, 0800 872 467; www.greatjourneys ofnz.co.nz; one way adult/child from $119/83) The TranzAlpine is one of the world's great train journeys. It traverses the Southern Alps between Christchurch and Greymouth, through Arthur's Pass National Park, from the Pacific Ocean to the Tasman Sea. Dramatic landscapes span its 223km length,

WEST COAST WILDERNESS TRAIL

One of 22 NZ Cycle Trails (www.nzcycletrail.com), the 136km **West Coast Wilderness Trail** (www.westcoastwildernesstrail.co.nz) stretches from Greymouth to Ross, following gold-rush trails, reservoirs, old tramways and railway lines, forging new routes cross-country. Suitable for intermediate riders, the trail reveals dense rainforest, glacial rivers, lakes and wetlands, and views from the snow-capped mountains of the Southern Alps to the wild Tasman Sea.

The trail is gently graded most of the way, and although the full shebang takes a good four days by bike, it can easily be sliced up into sections of various lengths, catering to every ability and area of interest. Novice riders can tackle the fairly easy 'Big Day Out' from Kawhaka to Kaniere, which takes in major highlights over seven hours, or a four-hour ride following Kumara's gold trails.

Bike hire, transport and advice are available from the major setting-off points. In Hokitika, contact **Wilderness Trail Shuttle** (☑ 03-755 5042, 021 263 3299; www.wildernesstrailshuttle.co.nz) and in Greymouth **Trail Transport** (☑ 03-768 6618; www.trailtransport.co.nz; bike hire per day from $50, shuttle transport $28-65).

from the flat, alluvial Canterbury Plains, through alpine gorges, an 8.5km tunnel, beech-forested river valleys and a lake fringed with cabbage trees.

The train leaves Greymouth daily at 2.05pm on an unforgettable five-hour journey, whatever the weather (and if it's raining on one coast, it's probably fine on the other).

Point Elizabeth Walkway WALKING
(www.doc.govt.nz) Accessible from Dommett Esplanade in Cobden, 6km north of Greymouth, this enjoyable walkway (three hours return) skirts around a richly forested headland in the shadow of the Rapahoe Range to an impressive ocean lookout, before continuing on to the northern trailhead at Rapahoe (11km from Greymouth) – small town, big beach, friendly local pub.

🛌 Sleeping

★ **Global Village** HOSTEL $
(☑ 03-768 7272; www.globalvillagebackpackers.co.nz; 42 Cowper St; dm/d $32/80; @🖥) Collages of African and Asian art on its walls, and a passionate traveller vibe at its core. Global Village also has free kayaks – the Lake Karoro wetlands reserve is a short walk away – and mountain bikes for guests, and relaxation comes easy with a spa, sauna, barbecue and fire pit.

Greymouth Seaside
Top 10 Holiday Park HOLIDAY PARK, MOTEL $
(☑ 03-768 6618, 0800 867 104; www.top10greymouth.co.nz; 2 Chesterfield St; sites $40-46, cabins $60-125, motel r $110-374; 🖥🐾) Well positioned for walks on the adjacent beach and

2.5km south of the town centre, this large park has various tent and campervan sites, simple cabins and deluxe sea-view motels. A playground and TV room keep kids entertained on rainy days, there's a full quota of amenities like laundry, plus unexpected comforts like underfloor heating in the communal showers.

Ardwyn House B&B $
(☑ 03-768 6107; ardwynhouse@hotmail.com; 48 Chapel St; s/d incl breakfast from $65/110; 🖥) As much a homestay as a B&B, Ardwyn House has old-fashioned rooms with quaint trimmings (including ship's wheel-style headboards) that share a bathroom. The property perches amid steep gardens on a dead-end street just south of the train station.

Mary, the well-travelled host, cooks a splendid breakfast.

Paroa Hotel HOTEL $$
(☑ 03-762 6860, 0800 762 6860; www.paroa.co.nz; 508 Main South Rd, Paroa; units $149-300; 🖥) A family affair since 1954, from kitchen to reception, the venerable Paroa has benefitted from a makeover. Sizeable units with great beds are decorated in fetching monochrome and share a garden. The hotel's warm service continues inside the noteworthy bar and restaurant. It's opposite the Shantytown turn-off.

🍴 Eating

Recreation Hotel BISTRO $$
(☑ 03-768 5154; www.rechotel.co.nz; 68 High St; mains $17 to $26; ⏱ 11am-late) A strong local following fronts up to 'the Rec' for its smart

Greymouth

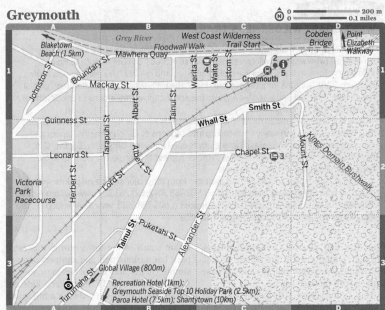

Greymouth

◎ Sights
1 Monteith's Brewing Co A3

✦ Activities, Courses & Tours
2 TranzAlpine...C1

🛌 Sleeping
3 Ardwyn House C2

🍸 Drinking & Nightlife
4 DP1 Cafe C1

ⓘ Information
5 Greymouth i-SITE C1
West Coast Travel Centre............(see 2)

public bar serving good pub grub, such as a daily roast, burgers and local fish and chips amid pool tables and the TAB.

DP1 Cafe   CAFE
(104 Mawhera Quay; ⊙8am-5pm Mon-Fri, 9am-5pm Sat & Sun; 🛜) A stalwart of the Greymouth cafe scene, this quayside java joint is awash in local artwork. Hip clientele and friendly staff make it an excellent place to mingle (while sipping the best espresso in town). Swing in for the $6 morning muffin and coffee special, or a caramel slice at any other hour.

ⓘ Information

Grey Base Hospital (☏03-769 7400; High St)
Greymouth i-SITE (☏03-768 7080, 0800 767 080; www.westcoasttravel.co.nz; 164 Mackay St, Greymouth Train Station; ⊙9am-5pm Mon-Fri, 10am-4pm Sat & Sun; 🛜) The helpful crew at the train station can assist with all manner of advice and bookings, including those for DOC huts and walks. See also www.westcoast nz.com.

ⓘ Getting There & Away

BUS
All buses stop outside the train station. InterCity (p448) has daily buses north to Westport (from $21, 2¼ hours) and Nelson (from $40, six hours), and south to Franz Josef and Fox Glaciers (around $30, 3½ hours). Naked Bus (p448) runs the same route. Both companies offer connections to destinations further afield.

Atomic Travel (p448) runs daily between Greymouth and Christchurch, as does West Coast Shuttle (p448) – around $50 fare.

Combined with the i-SITE in the train station, the **West Coast Travel Centre** (☏03-768 7080; www.westcoasttravel.co.nz; 164 Mackay St, Greymouth Train Station; ⊙9am-5pm Mon-Fri, 10am-4pm Sat & Sun; 🛜) books local and national transport, and offers luggage storage.

TRAIN

The view-laden TranzAlpine (p458) train connection to Christchurch leaves Greymouth daily at 2.05pm.

ⓘ Getting Around

Greymouth Taxis (☎03-768 7078) A taxi to Shantytown will cost you around $35 (one way).
Trail Transport (p459) Bike rental and shuttle transport focusing on the West Coast Wilderness Trail.

Blackball

📞03 / POP 330

Ramshackle Blackball is a shadow of its mining glory days, but this spirited town offers more than meets the eye. Around 25km upriver of Greymouth, Blackball was established in 1866 to service gold diggers; coal mining kicked in between 1890 and 1964. The National Federation of Labour (a trade union) was conceived here, born from influential strikes in 1908 and 1913.

Blackball remains fiercely proud of its trade union history – just check out the old posters in **Formerly the Blackball Hilton** (☎03-732 4705, 0800 425 225; www.blackballhilton. co.nz; 26 Hart St; s/d incl breakfast $55/110; ☎). This century-old hotel is a major talking point: it changed its name to avoid a legal battle with a certain hotel chain. Another claim to fame is **Blackball Salami Co** (☎03-732 4111; www.blackballsalami.co.nz; 11 Hilton St; salami packs from $9; ⊗8am-4pm Mon-Fri, 9am-2pm Sat), whose smoky meats are renowned up and down the West Coast.

Sleepy Blackball is likely to be stirred up by the opening of the Pike29 Memorial Track (probably in 2019), which will bring a new influx of trampers.

🏃 Activities

The **Croesus Track** (www.doc.govt.nz), linking inland Blackball with coastal Barrytown, has put Blackball on the map for trampers. Suitable for experienced trampers, the Croesus follows an old mining track that dates to the late 19th century, an 18km, one- to two-day trek crossing the Paparoa Ranges (climbing as high as 1km above sea level). From 2019, the Croesus Track will link to a new Great Walk, the **Pike29 Memorial Track**, a two- to three-day tramping trail between Blackball and Punakaiki spanning 45km (one to two days for advanced cyclists).

ⓘ Getting There & Away

It's half an hour's drive east (25km) to Blackball from Greymouth on the West Coast Hwy (SH7); you'll need your own wheels.

Lake Brunner

Expect your pulse to slow almost as soon as you arrive at Lake Brunner. Named for England-born explorer Thomas Brunner, this 40 sq km expanse of sapphire water lies 35km southeast of Greymouth. The lake is large but main settlement Moana (on its northern shore) is minuscule; nonetheless it brims with accommodation options to suit families and trout-fishing enthusiasts drawn to this sedate spot.

Brunner is a scenic place to idle away a day or two strolling lakeside tracks, fishing or bird-watching. Book ahead in summer (and note that it's whisper-quiet in winter).

🏃 Activities

One of many lakes in the area, Brunner is a tranquil spot for bush walks, bird-spotting and various water sports, including boating and fishing. Indeed, the local boast is that the lake and Arnold River are 'where the trout die of old age', which suggests this is a largely untouched spot for you to dangle a rod. Greymouth i-SITE (p460) can hook you up with a guide.

🛏 Sleeping

**Lake Brunner
Country Motel**   MOTEL, CAMPGROUND $
(☎03-738 0144; www.lakebrunnermotel.co.nz; 2014 Arnold Valley Rd; sites $35-40, cabins $65-75, cottages d $130-155; ☎) Birdsong, flower beds and six acres of greenery...feeling relaxed yet? At this motel and campground, 2km from Lake Brunner, choose from powered and unpowered sites, and plain, unvarnished cabins, all of which share bathrooms and kitchen facilities. More plush are the self-contained cottages, complete with floral trimmings and nice bathrooms.

ⓘ Getting There & Away

Reach Lake Brunner via the SH7 turn-off at Stillwater, a journey of 36km from Greymouth. It can also be reached from the south via Kumara Junction. The TranzAlpine (p458) train pulls into Moana train station daily on its way between Christchurch and Greymouth. Atomic Travel (p448) shuttles also pass through daily on the same journey.

Kumara

📞 03 / POP 309

Once upon a time, folks piled into Kumara's two theatres, waltzing until dawn and roaring with delight at travelling circus acts that passed through this gold-rush town. But with the glittering 1880s long faded into memory, only a threadbare settlement remains, near the western end of Arthur's Pass (30km south of Greymouth). Thanks to local enthusiasm for Kumara's boom time, display panels around town tell stories of feisty figures from history while the Theatre Royal Hotel and other converted period properties offer a glimpse of life in the gold-flecked past.

In recent times Kumara's main claim to fame is as a supporter of the multisport **Coast to Coast race** (www.coasttocoast. co.nz). Held each February, the strong, the brave and the totally knackered run, cycle and kayak a total of 243km all the way across the mountains to Christchurch, with top competitors dusting it off in just under 11 hours.

🛌 Sleeping & Eating

Jacksons Retreat HOLIDAY PARK $
(📞 03-738 0474; www.jacksonsretreat.co.nz; Jacksons, SH73, Kumara; powered/unpowered sites $48/44, cabins from $90, apt $180; 🛜) 🅿️ Nestled beside the Taramakau River, 63km southeast of Greymouth, is the tiny settlement of Jacksons. The exceptional holiday park here is a worthy stop along Arthur's Pass. Rugged views provide a backdrop for well-groomed campervan sites, tidy cabins (with shared bathrooms) and spacious self-contained apartments. There are undercover tents ($55) for a night under canvas without exposure to the elements.

⭐ **Theatre Royal Hotel** HOTEL $$$
(📞 03-736 9277; www.theatreroyalhotel.co.nz; 81 Seddon St, SH73, Kumara; d from $180; 🛜) Themed around colourful figures from Kumara's past, rooms at the beautifully restored Theatre Royal Hotel are reason enough to stay in town. We especially loved the feminine flourishes of Barbara Weldon's room, honouring a former lady of the night (good soundproofing). Motel-style miners cottages ($200 to $280), sleeping up to four, are brand new but have vintage finishes such as clawfoot tubs.

The opulence continues in the hotel's apartments (from $239): have a full-on Marie Antoinette fantasy in the boutique apartments (complete with four-poster beds) or bed down in the old Bank of New Zealand building (gold was once weighed in what's now the bathroom).

Stop for game specials or afternoon tea in the Theatre Royal's **restaurant** (📞 03-736 9277; www.theatreroyalhotel.co.nz; 81 Seddon St, SH73, Kumara; lunch mains $16-25, dinner mains $22-33; ⏰ 11am-8pm Sun-Thu, to late Fri & Sat), whose adjoining bar is a great spot for a yarn with the locals.

ℹ️ Getting There & Away

West Coast Shuttle (p448) passes through Kumara (not to be confused with Kumara Junction, close to the coast) on its daily service from Christchurch to Greymouth ($55, 3½ hours) – but most travellers arrive by car or bike.

WESTLAND

Bookended by Mount Aspiring National Park to its south and the rugged Great Coast Road to its north, Westland is one of New Zealand's most thinly populated regions.

Amid this tapestry of farmland and rainforest, the most remarkable (and famous) features are Franz Josef and Fox Glaciers. Though currently in retreat, these frosty monoliths framed by granite cliffs hook thousands of adventure-seekers, many of whom stick around for pulse-thudding pursuits like mountain biking the West Coast Wilderness Trail, tramping the Copland Track, soaring above national parks by helicopter, or tiptoeing through the bush on kiwi-spotting walks.

There's culture, too, if you like it quaint and low-key: gold-rush sights in Ross, jade-carving classes in Hokitika and art galleries in lonely locales all provide brain fodder for days when you want to hang up your tramping boots.

Hokitika

📞 03 / POP 3078

This sweet seaside town has a glint in its eye: indigenous *pounamu* (greenstone), carved and buffed to a shine by a thriving community of local artists. Shopping for greenstone, glassware, textiles and other home-grown crafts inspires droves of visitors to dawdle along Hokitika's streets, which are dotted with grand buildings from its 1860s gold-rush days.

Radiant sunsets and a glowworm dell add extra sparkle to this coastal idyll, though many visitors prefer to work up a sweat:

Hokitika accesses the West Coast Wilderness Trail as well as view-laden tramps at Lakes Kaniere and Mahinapua.

◉ Sights

★ Hokitika Gorge   GORGE

(www.doc.govt.nz) Water this turquoise doesn't come easy. Half a million years of glacial movement sculpted Hokitika's porcelain-white ravine; the rock 'flour' ground over millennia intensifies the water's dazzling hue. A lookout at the swingbridge is only 10 minutes' walk from the car park, but you'll want to spend a full hour admiring and photographing the scene (until the sandflies chase you away). It's a scenic 35km drive south of Hokitika, well signposted from Stafford St (past the dairy factory).

Lake Mahinapua   LAKE

(www.doc.govt.nz; SH6, Ruatapu) Serene Lake Mahinapua and its diverse forests lie 10km south of Hokitika. The scenic reserve, gazetted in 1907, has a picnic area and DOC campsite that bask in mountain views, and the shallow, lagoon-fed water is warm enough for a paddle. There are several short walks (an hour return or less) signposted along the shore.

Lake Kaniere   LAKE

(www.doc.govt.nz) Lying at the heart of a 7000-hectare scenic reserve, beautiful Lake Kaniere is 8km long, 2km wide, 195m deep, and freezing cold (as you'll discover if you swim). You may prefer to camp or picnic at Hans Bay (www.doc.govt.nz; Hans Bay Rd, Lake Kaniere; sites per adult/child $8/4), peer at Dorothy Creek Falls (4km south of the campground), or undertake one of numerous canoe walks, ranging from the 15-minute Canoe Cove Walk to the seven-hour return gut-buster up Mt Tuhua. It's 20km southeast of central Hokitika.

Sunset Point   VIEWPOINT

(Gibson Quay) A visit to stunning Sunset Point is a quintessential Hokitika experience: watch the day's light fade away, observe whitebaiters casting nets, munch fish and chips, or stroll around the quayside shipwreck memorial.

Glowworm Dell   NATURAL FEATURE

(SH6) At nightfall, bring a torch (or grope your way) into this grotto on the northern edge of town, signposted off the SH6. The dell is an easy opportunity to glimpse legions of glowworms (aka fungus gnat larvae), which emit an other-worldly blue light. An information panel at the entrance will further illuminate your way.

National Kiwi Centre   BIRD SANCTUARY

(☑ 03-755 5251; www.thenationalkiwicentre.co.nz; 64 Tancred St; adult/child $24/12; ⊙ 9am-5pm Dec-Feb, to 4.30pm Mar-Nov; 🐾) Tiptoe through the darkened kiwi house to watch these iconic birds rummage for tasty insects, or stare a tuatara – a reptile unchanged for 225 million years – in its beady eyes. Time your visit for eel feeding time (three times a day, usually 10am, noon and 3pm) when you can hold out scraps of meat for these slithery critters to grab from a pair of tongs (or, shudder, your bare hands).

🏃 Activities

Hokitika is a great base for walking and cycling. Download DOC's brochure *Walks in the Hokitika Area,* and visit Hokitika Cycles & Sports World (☑ 03-755 8662; www.hokitikasportsworld.co.nz; 33 Tancred St; bike rental per day $55; ⊙ 9am-5pm) for bike rental and advice on tracks, including the West Coast Wilderness Trail (p459).

Bonz 'N' Stonz   ART

(www.bonz-n-stonz.co.nz; 16 Hamilton St; carving per hour $30, full-day bone/jade workshop $80/180) Design, carve and polish your own *pounamu* (greenstone), bone or paua (shellfish) masterpiece, with tutelage from Steve. Prices vary with materials and design complexity. Bookings recommended, and 'laughter therapy' included in the price.

West Coast Treetops Walkway   OUTDOORS

(☑ 0508 8733 8677, 03-755 5052; www.treetopsnz.com; 1128 Woodstock-Rimu Rd; adult/child $38/15; ⊙ 9am-5pm Oct-Mar, 9am-4pm Apr-Sep) Visitors strolling along this wobbly steel walkway, 450m long and 20m off the ground, can enjoy an unusual perspective on the canopy of native trees, featuring many old rimu and kamahi. The highlight is the 40m-high tower, from which extend views across Lake Mahinapua, the Southern Alps and Tasman Sea. Wheelchair-friendly.

🎊 Festivals & Events

★ Wildfoods Festival   FOOD & DRINK

(www.wildfoods.co.nz; ⊙ Mar) Finding the West Coast's seafood scene a little samey? Give your tastebuds the equivalent of a defibrillator shock at this one-day festival of daredevil eating in early March. Fish eyes, pigs' ears and huhu beetle grubs usually grace the menu. Don't worry, there are local and international food stands to expunge the lingering taste of blood casserole...

Hokitika

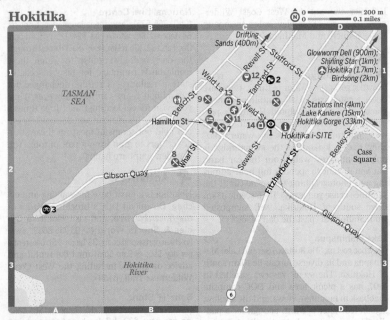

Driftwood & Sand
ART

(Hokitika Beach; ⊙Jan) Free spirits and budding artists transform flotsam and jetsam into sculptures on Hokitika Beach during this three-day, volunteer-led festival. Participants range from beginners to pros, and accordingly their creations span the full spectrum from enigmatic to delightfully daft.

🛏 Sleeping

★ Drifting Sands
B&B $

(☑021 0266 5154; www.driftingsands.nz; 197 Revell St; d & tr $99-125, f $200; ⑨) Natural tones and textures, upcycled furniture and hip vibes make this boutique beachside guesthouse a winner on style and location. Heightening the feel-good factor, there's a lounge warmed by a log burner and fresh bread every morning, plus free bike hire. One night isn't enough.

Birdsong
HOSTEL $

(☑03-755 7179; www.birdsong.co.nz; 124 Kumara Junction Hwy; dm $34, s/d with shared bathroom $69/85, d with private bathroom $119, all incl breakfast; ⑨) Sigh at sea views from the shared lounge and kitchen of this adorable hostel, 2.5km north of town. Rooms are themed around native bird life, hosts welcome guests with wit, and our only gripe is that

bathrooms could be bigger (with better privacy than saloon-style doors).

Shining Star
HOLIDAY PARK, MOTEL $$

(☑03-755 8921; 16 Richards Dr; sites per adult/child $20/10, d $119-149, f $185; ⑨🐾) Attractive and versatile beachside spot with everything from camping to log-lined cabins facing the sea. Kids will love the menagerie, including pigs and alpacas straight from Dr Doolittle's appointment book. Parents might prefer the spa or sauna ($15).

Stations Inn
MOTEL $$

(☑03-755 5499; www.stationsinnhokitika.co.nz; 11 Blue Spur Rd; d $170-300; ⑨) A hotel has stood on these rolling hills, 4km southeast of Hokitika, since the 1860s. Today it's a smart, modern motel complex with plush units featuring king-sized beds (the larger units have a spa bath). With an on-site **restaurant** (☑03-755 5499; www.stationsinnhokitika.co.nz; 11 Blue Spur Rd; mains $32 to $42; ⊙6-10pm Tue-Sun), patio, pond and waterwheel out the front, the Stations Inn conjures the right measure of nostalgia along with bang-up-to-date amenities.

Teichelmann's B&B
B&B $$$

(☑03-755 8232; www.teichelmanns.nz; 20 Hamilton St; s/d incl breakfast $235-280; ⑨) Once home to surgeon, mountaineer and profes-

Hokitika

sional beard-cultivator Ebenezer Teichel-mann, this B&B holds on to its venerable history but adds first-rate hospitality and splashes of complimentary port. Its six rooms each have an airy, restorative ambience, replete with great beds, quality cotton sheets and private bathrooms; the best enjoy fern-filled garden views. For added privacy, request self-contained Teichy's Cottage.

✕ Eating & Drinking

★ Ramble + Ritual   CAFE $
(☑03-755 6347; 51 Sewell St; snacks $3-8, meals $8-15; ⊘7.30am-4pm Mon-Fri; ✍) Tucked away near the **Clock Tower** (cnr Weld & Sewell Sts), this gallery-cum-cafe is a stylish spot to linger while hobnobbing with friendly staff and punters. Let's see, will it be a Gruyère and mushroom slice, superfood salad, or a ginger oaty munched in between gulps of super-strength coffee?

Dulcie's Takeaways   FISH & CHIPS $
(cnr Gibson Quay & Wharf St; fish & chips $6-12; ⊘11am-9pm Tue-Sun) Net yourself some excellent fish and chips (try the turbot, blue cod or fried oysters), then scoff them down the road at Sunset Point for an extra sprinkle of sea salt.

★ Aurora   MODERN NZ $$
(☑03-755 8319; http://aurorahoki.co.nz; 19 Tancred St; breakfast $10, mains $18-40; ⊘8am-11pm) Breakfast egg-and-bacon ciabattas, Thai-style mussels, mid-afternoon tapas, desserts crowned with rich ice cream...from morning until closing time, everything at Aurora is beautifully plated and served with cheer.

Fat Pipi   PIZZA $$
(www.fatpipi.co.nz; 89 Revell St; pizzas $20-30; ⊘noon-2.30pm Wed-Sun, 5-9pm daily; ✍) Purists might balk at flavour combos like smoked chicken and apricot, but Fat Pipi bakes Hokitika's best pizza. There are versions for veggies and gluten-free diners, and garlicky whitebait pizza adds a local twist. Sweet tooth? Try dessert pizza heaped with blueberry, caramel and crumble. Enjoy it in the garden bar, or grab a takeaway and nibble at Sunset Point (p463).

West Coast Wine Bar   WINE BAR
(www.westcoastwine.co.nz; 108 Revell St; ⊘4pm-late Wed-Sat) Upping Hoki's sophistication factor, this weeny joint packs a fridge full of fine wine and craft beer. Sip it in the hidden-away back garden, laden with murals and dangling antlers.

🔒 Shopping

Hokitika has a buzzing arts and crafts scene centred on carving and polishing *pounamu* into ornaments and jewellery. Be aware that some galleries sell jade imported from Europe and Asia, so ask before you buy.

Along for the ride are woodworkers, textile weavers and glass-blowers, all represented at classy boutiques in the centre of town.

Hokitika Craft Gallery   ARTS & CRAFTS
(☑03-755 8802; www.hokitikacraftgallery.co.nz; 25 Tancred St; ⊘9.30am-5pm) The town's best one-stop shop, this co-op showcases a wide range of local work, including *pounamu* (greenstone), jewellery, flax handbags, hand-coloured silk scarves, ceramics and woodwork.

Waewae Pounamu   ARTS & CRAFTS
(☑03-755 8304; www.waewaepounamu.co.nz; 39 Weld St; 8am-5pm) This stronghold of NZ *pounamu* (greenstone) displays traditional and contemporary designs in its main-road gallery-boutique.

Hokitika Glass Studio   ARTS & CRAFTS
(☑03-755 7775; www.hokitikaglass.co.nz; 9 Weld St; ⊘8.30am-5pm) Art and souvenirs from garish to glorious: glass eggs, multicoloured bowls and animal ornaments. And yes, they

secure these fragile objects in oodles of protective wrapping. Watch the blowers at the furnace on weekdays.

❶ Information

Hokitika i-SITE (☑03-755 6166; www.hokitika. org; 36 Weld St; ⊗8.30am-5pm Mon-Fri, 10am-4pm Sat & Sun) One of NZ's best i-SITEs offers extensive bookings, including all bus services. Also holds DOC info, although you'll need to book online or at DOC visitor centres further afield.

See also www.westcoastnz.com.

Westland Medical Centre (☑03-755 8180; www.westlandmedical.co.nz; 54a Sewell St; ⊗8am-4.45pm Mon & Wed-Fri, 9am-4.45pm Tue) Call ahead for appointments, or use the after-hours phone service (24 hours). In urgent cases, use the weekend walk-in service at 10am and 5pm.

❶ Getting There & Away

AIR

Hokitika Airport (www.hokitikaairport.co.nz; Airport Dr, off Tudor St) is 1.5km east of the town centre. **Air New Zealand** (www.airnewzealand. com) has two flights most days to/from Christchurch.

BUS

One InterCity (p448)/Naked Bus (p448) service leaves from the Kiwi Centre on Tancred St, then outside the i-SITE, daily for Greymouth (around $15, 45 minutes) and Fox and Franz Josef Glaciers (from $29, 2–2½ hours). For Nelson (from $42, seven hours), change buses in Greymouth. For Christchurch, bus to Greymouth and take the TranzAlpine (p458).

❶ Getting Around

Hokitika Taxis (☑03-755 5075)

Ross

☑ 03 / POP 297

When folks sensed gold in these hills in the mid-1860s, the township of Ross was hurriedly established. It soon ballooned to 2500 people and reached giddy heights of fame with the discovery of the 'Honourable Roddy' gold nugget, weighing in at nearly 3kg.

It's the start or finish point of the West Coast Wilderness Trail (p459), but gold-rush history makes Ross an entertaining stopoff along drives between Hokitika and the West Coast glacier towns.

The **Water Race Walk** (one hour return) starts near the **heritage centre** (☑03-755 4077; 4 Aylmer St; $2; ⊗9am-4pm Dec-Mar, to 2pm Apr-Nov), passing old gold diggings, caves, tunnels and a cemetery. Hire a gold pan ($10) from the centre and head to Jones Creek to look for Roddy's great, great grandnuggets.

There are plain rooms upstairs at the **Empire Hotel** (☑03-755 4005; 19 Aylmer St; ⊗10am-late) but seaside **Top 10 Holiday Park Ross Beach** (☑03-429 8277, 021 428 566; https://rossbeachtop10.co.nz; 145 Ross Beach Rd; site unpowered/powered $40/50, dm $35, pod with/without bathroom from $125/99; ☎), 3km north of town, is our pick.

Hari Hari

☑ 03 / POP 330

The most famous visitor to blunder into Hari Hari was Australian aviator Guy Menzies, who crash-landed his biplane after being blown off course during his solo flight across the Tasman Sea in 1931. Menzies finished his record-breaking flight by landing

---

WHITEBAIT FEVER

If you visit the West Coast between September and mid-November, you're sure to catch a whiff of whitebait fever. The West Coast is gripped by an annual craze for tiny, transparent fish, and netting buckets of whitebait is an all-consuming, highly competitive passion. Firstly there's money in it (from $60 to $70 per kilo along the coast, and much more elsewhere), then there's the satisfaction of netting more than your neighbours. Riverbanks bustle with baiters from Karamea to Haast, but ask a whitebaiter if they're catching much and they'll likely say no...to throw you off the scent of their best whitebaiting spots.

In season you'll see whitebait sold from backdoors and served in cafes and restaurants. They mostly surface in a pattie, made best with just an egg, and accompanied by a wedge of lemon or perhaps mint sauce. We've seen them topping pizzas and salads, too.

Whitebait are the young of native fish, including inanga, kokopu, smelt and eels. Conservationists say they shouldn't be eaten at all, with some species threatened or in decline. The DOC applies stiff penalties for anyone breaching their rules on whitebaiting season and the size of nets, and they urge locals to keep their catch small.

upside down in a swamp, miraculously unharmed. You're more likely to cruise through this dozy little town in between the West Coast glaciers and Hokitika, stretching your legs on the **Hari Hari Coastal Walk** (www.doc.govt.nz; Wanganui River) or getting cake and a cuppa from the **Pukeko Store** (☑03-753 3192; 37 Main Rd (SH6); snacks from $4; ☺7.30am-5pm; ☏☑).

Two motel options are signposted right on the highway; our pick is cheerful, well-run **Flaxbush Motels** (☑03-753 3116; www.flaxbushmotels.co.nz; 29 Main St (SH6); d $65-120; ☏).

Whataroa

☑ 03 / POP 288

Though it looks humdrum, Whataroa is a gateway to rare natural wonders. Strung out along the SH6, 30km north of Franz Josef Glacier, this nondescript town is the departure point for tours of NZ's only nesting site for the kōtuku (white heron). Their wings as delicately pretty as a bridal veil, these rare birds hold a special significance for Māori, who treasure their feathers and use 'kōtuku' as a compliment describing seldom-seen guests. When the birds roost between late September and February, **White Heron Sanctuary Tours** (☑03-753 4120, 0800 523 456; www.whiteherontours.co.nz; Main Rd; adult/child $150/75; ☺tours late Sep-Feb) ✈ offers exclusive access to a viewing hide.

Other worthwhile activities include **Alpine Fault Tours** (☑03 753 4236, 0800 556 244; http://alpinefaulttours.co.nz; 70 Main Rd (SH6); adult/child $50/20; ☺by arrangement), which buses small groups to where the Australian and Pacific plates meet. Here you can stand astride two tectonic plates, marvelling at Mother Nature's might, and listen to engaging commentary on the forces that created the Southern Alps. A bird's-eye view is possible through **Glacier Country Scenic Flights** (☑0800 423 463, 03-753 4096; www.glacieradventures.co.nz; cnr SH6 & Scally Rd; flights $225-525); lifting off from Whataroa Valley, these guys give you more mountain-gawping for your buck than many of the operators flying from the glacier townships.

The folks at White Heron Sanctuary Tours run a good-value **motel** (☑03-753 4120, 0800 523 456; www.whiteherontours.co.nz; Main Rd; d with/without bathroom $130/80). Alternatively there's a cheery motel in Hari Hari, 30km east, and abundant (though pricier) options in Franz Josef, 30km southwest.

GREENSTONE SYMBOLS

The West Coast has a thriving community of artists sourcing *pounamu* (greenstone) and carving it into sculptures and jewellery, particularly in Hokitika and Greymouth. It's considered luckier to buy greenstone for others, rather than yourself, and a few recurring shapes carry distinctive meanings.

Koru Whirl reminiscent of a fern shoot, signifying the life journey: creation, growth and travel.

Toki A rectangular shape harking to traditional Māori tools; a symbol of courage and strength.

Pikorua Contemporary 'twist' design symbolising the continuity of bonds between family or friends.

Hei matau Curved fish hook design with a variety of meanings: health, safe travel and prosperity.

Okarito

☑ 03 / POP 30

Huddled against a lagoon, the seaside hamlet of Okarito has a restorative air. Barely 10km from SH6, Okarito Lagoon is the largest unmodified wetland in NZ. More than 76 bird species preen and glide among its waterways, including gossamer-winged kōtuku (white heron). Hiding out in the forest are rowi kiwi, the rarest species of NZ's iconic land-bird – for a great chance of seeing one in the wild, hook up with the South Island's only licensed kiwi-tour operator, based in the village.

Okarito has no shops, limited visitor facilities and patchy phone reception, so stock up and book before you arrive.

◉ Sights & Activities

From a car park on the Strand you can begin the easy **Wetland Walk** (20 minutes), a longer mission along the **Three Mile Pack Track** (three hours, with the coastal return route tide dependent, so check in with the locals for tide times), and a jolly good puff up to **Okarito Trig** (1½ hours return), which rewards the effort with spectacular Southern Alps and Okarito Lagoon views (weather contingent).

★ **Okarito Kiwi Tours** WILDLIFE

(☏03-753 4330; www.okaritokiwitours.co.nz; 53 The Strand; 3-5hr tours $75) ✍ Spotting the rare kiwi in Okarito's tangle of native forest isn't easy, but bird-whisperer Ian has a 98% success rate for his small-group evening tours. Patience, tiptoeing and fine weather are essential. If you have your heart set on a kiwi encounter, book ahead and be within reach of Okarito for a couple of nights, in case of poor weather.

★ **Okarito Kayaks** KAYAKING

(☏03-753 4014, 0800 652 748; www.okarito.co.nz; 1 The Strand; kayak rental half-/full day $65/75; ⊙hours vary) This hands-on operator hires out kayaks for paddles across Okarito's shallow lagoon, in the company of strutting waterfowl and beneath a breathtaking mountainscape. Personalised guided kayaking trips (from $100) are ideal for getting to know the landscape; otherwise honest advice on weather, tides and paddling routes are gamely offered.

Okarito Boat Eco Tours WILDLIFE

(☏03-753 4223; www.okaritoboattours.co.nz; 31 Wharf St; ⊙late Oct-May) Runs bird-spotting lagoon tours, the most fruitful of which is the 'early bird' ($80, 1½ hrs, 7.30am). The popular two-hour 'ecotour' offers deeper insights into this remarkable natural area ($90, 9am and 11.30am), or there's an afternoon 'wetlands tour' ($70, 2.30pm) if you aren't a morning person. Book at least 24 hours in advance.

🛏 Sleeping

Code Time Lodge APARTMENT $$

(☏021 037 2031; www.codetimelodge.co.nz; 8 Albert St; apt $150-250; 🕾) Driftwood decorations and soft colour schemes impart a dreamy air to the Code Time Lodge, whose two roomy, self-contained apartments (kitchen included) are kept toasty by log-burning stoves.

Okarito Beach House LODGE $$

(☏03-753 4080; www.okaritobeachhouse.com; 29 The Strand; d & tw $115-165; 🕾) Though it's on the main street rather than the beach, there's a reviving feel to Okarito Beach House: airy, bamboo-trimmed doubles and twins (priced by size), a pleasant shared kitchen, and a dining room table carved from the biggest log you've ever seen. The charming self-contained 'Hutel' ($195, sleeping two people) offers added privacy.

ℹ Getting There & Away

Okarito is 10km north off SH6 between Franz Josef and Whataroa. You'll need your own wheels to get there.

WESTLAND TAI POUTINI NATIONAL PARK

With colossal mountains, forests and glaciers, Westland Tai Poutini National Park clobbers visitors with its mind-bending proportions. Reaching from the West Coast to the razor peaks of the Southern Alps, the park's supreme attractions are twin glaciers Franz Josef and Fox, served by townships 23km apart. Out of more than 60 glaciers in the park, only these two are easily accessible.

The glaciers are the most majestic handiwork of the West Coast's ample precipitation. Snowfall in the glaciers' broad accumulation zones fuses into clear ice at 20m depth, and then creeps down the steep valleys. Nowhere else at this latitude do glaciers descend so close to the ocean.

But the glaciers are as fragile as they are amazing to behold. Rising temperatures have beaten the glaciers into retreat, reducing opportunities to view them on foot and clanging a death knell for their long-term future if climate change continues unchecked.

Franz Josef Glacier

☏03 / POP 441

Franz Josef's cloak of ice once flowed from the mountains right to the sea. Following millennia of gradual retreat, the glacier is now 19km inland and accessible only by helicopter. Swarms of small aircraft from Franz Josef Glacier village, 5km north, lift visitors to views of sparkling ice and toothy mountains. Many land on the glacier to lead groups to blue-tinged caves and crevasses. A glacier experience is the crowning moment for thousands of annual visitors, but walking trails, hot pools, and adventure sports from quad biking to clay target shooting keep adrenaline pulsing.

Geologist Julius von Haast led the first European expedition here in 1865, and named the glacier after the Austrian emperor. The dismal forecast of a rainier, warmer future spells more shrinkage for Franz Josef, whose trimlines (strips of vegetation on the valley walls) mark out decades of dramatic glacial retreat.

◉ Sights

West Coast Wildlife Centre WILDLIFE RESERVE

(☏03-752 0600; www.wildkiwi.co.nz; cnr Cron & Cowan Sts; day pass adult/child/family $38/20/85, incl backstage pass $58/35/145;

⏱8am-5pm) 🕊 The purpose of this feel-good attraction is breeding two of the world's rarest kiwi – the rowi and the Haast tokoeka. The entry fee is well worthwhile by the time you've viewed the conservation, glacier and heritage displays, hung out with kiwi in their ferny enclosure, and met the five resident tuatara (native reptiles). The backstage pass into the incubating and rearing area is a rare opportunity to learn how a species can be brought back from the brink of extinction.

🏃 Activities

Independent Walks

A series of walks start from the glacier car park, 5km from the village. **Sentinel Rock** (20 minutes return) reveals either impressive views of the glacier valley or a mysterious panorama swallowed by mist and cloud. **Kā Roimata o Hine Hukatere Track** (1½ hours return), the main glacier valley walk, leads you to the best permissible view of the terminal face.

Other walks include the **Douglas Walk** (one hour return), off the Glacier Access Rd, which passes moraine piled up by the glacier's advance in 1750, and **Peters Pool**, a small kettle lake. The **Terrace Track** (30 minutes return) is an easy amble over bushy terraces behind the village, with Waiho River views. Two good rainforest walks, **Callery Gorge Walk** and **Tatare Tunnels** (both around 1½ hours return), start from Cowan St – bring a torch for the latter.

Much more challenging walks, such as the five-hour **Roberts Point Track** and eight-hour **Alex Knob Track**, are detailed, along with all the others, in DOC's excellent *Glacier Region Walks* booklet ($2, or download at www.doc.govt.nz/Documents/parks-and-recreation/tracks-and-walks/west-coast/glacier-region-walks.pdf).

A rewarding alternative to driving to the glacier car park is the richly rainforested **Te Ara a Waiau Walkway/Cycleway**, starting from near the fire station at the south end of town. It's a one-hour walk (each way) or half that by bicycle. Leave your bikes at the car park – you can't cycle on the glacier walkways. When we passed through, bike hire wasn't easy to come by and folks were recommending rental from Fox Glacier Lodge (p476) (per hour/half-day $5/15), 24km south. Ask in the i-SITE (p473) for the latest.

FRANZ OR FOX?

If skies are blue and choppers are flying, seize the chance to helihike either glacier. Weather changes quickly, sometimes grounding aircraft for days and inflicting tourist heartbreak. Franz Josef is the more popular of the two glaciers, its steepness intensifying the drama of crevasses and ice formations, while Fox is longer and faster-moving (not that you'll notice). The two major operators offering helihikes on the glaciers have primo standards on safety and technical expertise. More popular Franz Josef Glacier Guides is a well-oiled machine, while family-run Fox Glacier Guiding (p473) prides itself on a friendly, personalised experience. They're comparable on price (around $450 for a helihike with three hours on the ice) and both offer photo-ops in the famous blue ice caves (though Franz' caves are bigger).

Guided Walks & Helihikes

Franz Josef Glacier Guides (📞03-752 0763, 0800 484 337; www.franzjosefglacier.com; 63 Cron St) runs small group walks with experienced guides (boots, jackets and equipment supplied). With dazzling blue ice, photo ops in ice caves, and helicopter rides to and from the ice, this might be one of your most memorable experiences in NZ. The standard trip involves three hours of guided rambling on the ice ($459); the daring can seize an ice pick for a five-hour ice-climbing tour (adults only, $575). If you don't need to get on the ice, choose a three-hour guided valley walk (adult/child $75/65). **Glacier Valley Eco Tours** (📞0800 925 586; www.glaciervalley.co.nz; 22 Main Rd; adult/child $75/37.50) 🕊 offers a similar experience, a 3½-hour ramble by the river and into native forest. Conservation-focused commentary on local flora and geological forces enlivens the journey, which is rewarded by a steaming cuppa sipped in view of the glacier face.

Aerial Sightseeing & Skydiving

Forget sandflies and mozzies, the buzzing you're hearing is a swarm of small aircraft. The most affordable scenic flights involve 10 or 12 minutes in the air above Franz Josef Glacier (around $120 to $165) but it's worth paying for 20 minutes or more to get a snow landing or to view both Franz Josef and Fox Glaciers (from $245). Pricier, 40-minute

Franz Josef Glacier & Village

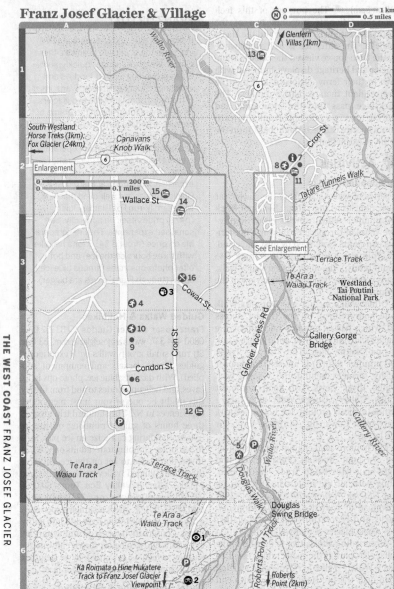

flights enjoy the most eye-popping views (around \$370 to \$460), swooping around Aoraki/Mt Cook. Fares for children under 12 years usually cost around 70% of the adult price. Shop around: most operators are situated on the main road.

Skydive Franz   SKYDIVING
(☎ 03-752 0714, 0800 458 677; www.skydivefranz. co.nz; Main Rd) Claiming NZ's highest jump (19,000ft, 80 to 90 seconds freefall; \$559), this company also offers 16,500ft for \$419, 13,000ft for \$319 and 9000ft for \$249. With

Franz Josef Glacier & Village

◉ Sights
1 Peters Pool	B6
2 Sentinel Rock	B6
3 West Coast Wildlife Centre	B3

◉ Activities, Courses & Tours
4 Air Safaris	B3
5 Alex Knob Track	C5
Franz Josef Glacier Guides	(see 8)
6 Glacier Country Helicopters	B4
7 Glacier Country Kayaks	C2
Glacier Helicopters	(see 4)
8 Glacier Hot Pools	C2
9 Glacier Valley Eco Tours	B4
10 Skydive Franz	B4

◉ Sleeping
11 58 on Cron	C2
12 Franz Josef Glacier YHA	B5
13 Franz Josef Top 10 Holiday Park	C1
14 Rainforest Retreat	B2
15 Te Waonui Forest Retreat	B2

◉ Eating
16 Alice May	B3
Snake Bite Brewery	(see 4)

◉ Drinking & Nightlife
Monsoon	(see 14)

Aoraki/Mt Cook in your sights, this could be the most scenic jump you ever do.

Air Safaris SCENIC FLIGHTS
(☑0800 723 274, 03-752 0716; www.airsafaris.co.nz; Main Rd) Franz' only fixed-wing flyer offers 50-minute 'grand traverse' ($370) flights that expose breathtaking views of Franz Josef and Fox Glaciers, Aoraki/Mt Cook, and far-flung valleys, lakes and waterways en route. Charge your camera.

Glacier Helicopters SCENIC FLIGHTS
(☑03-752 0755, 0800 800 732; www.glacierhelicopters.co.nz; Main Rd; 20-40min flights $245-460) This reliable operator has been running scenic flights since 1970. Shorter flights take you to one of the glaciers, while the 40-minute option reaches both, as well as soaring to spectacular views of Aoraki/Mt Cook. There's a brief snow landing on each trip.

Glacier Country Helicopters SCENIC FLIGHTS
(☑03-752 0203, 0800 359 37269; www.glaciercountryhelicopters.co.nz; 10 Main Rd; 12-45min flights $165-465) Based in Franz Josef, this family-owned and operated company offers four different scenic options, including an affordable 12-minute flight ($165) over Franz Josef.

Other Activities

★ Glacier Country Kayaks KAYAKING
(☑03-752 0230, 0800 423 262; www.glacierkayaks.com; 64 Cron St; 3hr kayak adult/child $115/70) Enjoy a change of pace from chopper rides and sheer-faced glaciers on a guided kayak trip on Lake Mapourika (10km north of Franz). The 'kayak classic' is three hours of bird-spotting and mountain views, plus a short bush walk. The summer-only 'sunset classic' ($125) is at the golden hour (no cameras, but guides snap pictures and share them for free).

One-hour 'discovery' tours are a good option for novices (adult/child $85/65). Guided stand-up paddle boarding on offer, too (from $85).

Glacier Hot Pools HOT SPRINGS
(☑03-752 0099; www.glacierhotpools.co.nz; 63 Cron St; adult/child $28/24; ⊙11am-9pm, last entry 8pm) Cleverly set into a pretty rainforest on the edge of town, this stylish and well-maintained outdoor hot-pool complex is perfect après-hike or on a rainy day. Private pools also available, and hour-long massages cost from $140.

South Westland Horse Treks HORSE RIDING
(☑0800 187 357, 03-752 0223; www.horsetreknz.com; Waiho Flats Rd; 1/1½/2hr trek $90/145/170) This trekking company runs equine excursions across farmland and through rainforest, some with fantastic glacier views along the way, beginning at a location 5km west of town. Beginners welcome.

🛌 Sleeping

Franz Josef Top 10 Holiday Park HOLIDAY PARK $
(☑0800 467 8975, 03-752 0735; www.franzjoseftop10.co.nz; 2902 Franz Josef Hwy; sites $45-47, cabins $78-83, units $128-160; 🕸🐾) With such voluminous sleeping options, this spacious holiday park has no room for frills. Tents and motorhomes enjoy free-draining grassy sites away from the road, while travellers who prefer four walls can choose good-value cabins (sharing the well-maintained bathroom and kitchen areas) or trim self-contained units. It's 1.5km north of the township.

THE WEST COAST FRANZ JOSEF GLACIER

Franz Josef Glacier YHA
HOSTEL $

(☑03-752 0754; www.yha.co.nz; 2-4 Cron St; dm from $32, d with/without bathroom from $150/125; ☎) Functional and friendly, the YHA has warm, spacious communal areas, family rooms, a large free sauna, and a booking desk for transport and activities. It has 103 beds, but you'll still need to book ahead.

58 on Cron
MOTEL $$

(☑0800 662 766, 03-752 0627; www.58oncron. co.nz; 58 Cron St; d $175-245; ☎) Guests staying in these 16 comfortable motel units, from petite doubles to family suites that sleep six, enjoy sweet service and a barbecue area. Bonus: you won't forget the motel's address.

★ Te Waonui Forest Retreat
HOTEL $$$

(☑0800 696 963, 03-752 0555; www.tewaonui. co.nz; 3 Wallace St; d incl breakfast & dinner from $749; ☺Sep-Apr; @☎) 🖉 Luxurious Te Waonui is filled with design flourishes that evoke the land: twinkly lights suggest glowworms, coal-black walls nod to the mining past, and local stone provides an earthy backdrop. Beyond the gorgeous, greenery-facing rooms, the prime draws are the five-course degustation dinner (included in the price) and the nightly Māori cultural show.

★ Glenfern Villas
APARTMENT $$$

(☑0800 453 633, 03-752 0054; www.glenfern. co.nz; SH6; d $265-299; ☎) Forming something of a tiny, elite village 3km north of town, Glenfern's one- and two-bedroom villas are equipped with every comfort from quality beds to plump couches, gleaming kitchenettes and private decks where you can listen to birdsong. Book well ahead.

✕ Eating & Drinking

★ Snake Bite Brewery
ASIAN, FUSION $$

(☑03-752 0234; www.snakebite.co.nz; 28 Main Rd; mains $18-25; ☺7.30am-10.30pm) Snake Bite's motley Asian meals awaken tastebuds after their long slumber through the West Coast's lamb-and-whitebait menus. Choices include nasi goreng (fried rice), Thai- and Malaysian-style curries and salads of calamari and carrot that zing with fresh lime. Try the mussel fritters with wasabi mayo. Between courses, glug craft beers on tap or 'snakebite' (a mix of cider and beer).

Alice May
MODERN NZ $$

(☑03-752 0740; www.facebook.com/alicemayfranz josef; cnr Cowan & Cron Sts; mains $22-33; ☺4pm-late) Piling on the charm with its faux-Tudor decor, Alice May is the classiest restaurant in town. Sure, the menu includes meaty NZ

GLACIERS FOR DUMMIES

Hashtag a few of these suckers into your social media posts and make yourself look like a #geologist #geek.

Ablation zone Where the glacier melts.

Accumulation zone Where the ice and snow collects.

Bergschrund A large crevasse in the ice near the glacier's starting point.

Blue ice As the accumulation zone (névé) snow is compressed by subsequent snowfalls, it becomes firn and then blue ice.

Calving The process of ice breaking away from the glacier terminal face.

Crevasse A crack in the glacial ice formed by the stress of competing forces.

Firn Partly compressed snow en route to becoming blue ice.

Glacial flour Finely ground rock particles in the milky rivers flowing off glaciers.

Icefall When a glacier descends so steeply that the upper ice breaks into a jumble of ice blocks.

Kettle lake A lake formed by the melt of an area of isolated dead ice.

Moraine Walls of debris formed at the glacier's sides (lateral moraine) or end (terminal moraine).

Névé Snowfield area where firn is formed.

Seracs Ice pinnacles formed, like crevasses, by the glacier rolling over obstacles.

Terminus The final ice face at the bottom of the glacier.

favourites, but usually with a gourmet twist, like pork roasted in wine and star anise, brie-topped chicken or rosemary and pumpkin risotto. Try to snag an outdoor or window table for sigh-worthy mountain views.

Monsoon BAR
(☑03-752 0220; www.monsoonbar.co.nz; 46 Cron St; mains $15-33; ☺11am-11pm) Sip drinks in the sunshine or within the cosy, chalet-style bar of the **Rainforest Retreat** (☑03-752 0220, 0800 873 346; www.rainforestretreat.co.nz; 46 Cron St; sites $39-48, dm $30-39, d $69-220; ☞), usually packed to the rafters with a sociable crowd of travellers. Bar snacks, burgers and posh pizzas (like chorizo and prawn) ensure you needn't move from your comfy spot by the fire.

ⓘ Information

Franz Josef Health Centre (☑ appointment booking 0800 7943 2584, direct 03-752 0700; 97 Cron St; ☺8.30am-6pm Mon-Fri) South Westland's main medical centre. After hours, calls connect to a local nurse.

Franz Josef i-SITE (☑ 0800 354 748; www.glaciercountry.co.nz; 63 Cron St; ☺8.30am-6pm) Helpful local centre offering advice and booking service for activities, accommodation and transport in the local area and beyond.

Westland Tai Poutini National Park Visitor Centre (☑03-752 0360; www.doc.govt.nz; 69 Cron St; ☺8.30am-6pm Dec-Feb, to 5pm Mar-Nov) Insightful exhibits, weather information, maps, and all-important track updates and weather forecasts.

ⓘ Getting There & Away

Direct InterCity (p448) and Naked Bus (p448) services along SH6 pass through once daily, northwards to Hokitika ($29, 2½ hours) and Greymouth (around $29, four hours) and south to Haast (from $23, 3¼ hours), stopping at Fox Glacier ($10, 40 minutes) on the way. Book ahead for fares as low as $1. A direct daily bus also reaches Queenstown (from $62, 8½ hours). For Nelson or Christchurch, change services in Greymouth.

Book at the i-SITE or YHA (p472). The bus stop is opposite the Fern Grove Four Square supermarket.

Glacier Motors (☑ 03-752 0725; Main Rd; ☺8am-7.30pm) After hours, there's a a 24-hour diesel and petrol pump.

ⓘ Getting Around

Glacier Shuttles & Charters (☑0800 999 739) runs scheduled shuttle services to the glacier car park (return trip $12.50). You can also charter return transport to Lake Matheson, Okarito or Fox Glacier ($55 per person, minimum two people).

ⓘ GLACIER SAFETY

The only way to get close to or on to the ice safely is with a guided tour. Both glacier terminal faces are roped off to prevent people being caught in icefalls and river surges, which can flood the valleys in a matter of minutes. Obey warning signs and stay out of roped-off areas (even if you see guides leading walkers that way...they know where to tread safely, you don't).

Fox Glacier
☑ 03 / POP 400

Descending from the brooding Southern Alps, impassable Fox Glacier seems to flow steadily, ominously towards the township below. But in this fragile landscape it's the glacier that's at risk: despite hints of advance in recent years, this 12km glacier (named for former New Zealand PM Sir William Fox) has been steadily retreating over the past century.

Compared with the glacier, the eponymous township isn't nearly so dramatic. Surrounded by farmland, its cafes and tour operators are strung along the main road, along with dozens of motels catering to visiting crowds that descend between November and March. Most are here to helihike or embark on scenic flights, but flying weather is never guaranteed on the turbulent West Coast. Fortunately Fox Glacier has tramping trails, skydiving and remnants of pioneers past to keep you busy while waiting for skies to clear.

ⓞ Sights

Fox Glacier Lookout VIEWPOINT
(Glacier Access Rd) On a clear day, this is one of the best land-based positions from which to see Fox Glacier (though its retreat may mean you see just a snippet).

⚡ Activities

Glacier Walks & Helihikes
The only way on to the ice is by taking a helihiking trip, run by the superb **Fox Glacier Guiding** (☑03-751 0825, 0800 111 600; www.foxguides.co.nz; 44 Main Rd). Independent walks offer a chance to explore the valley – raw and staggeringly beautiful even in its ice-less lower reaches – and get as close to

Fox Glacier & Village

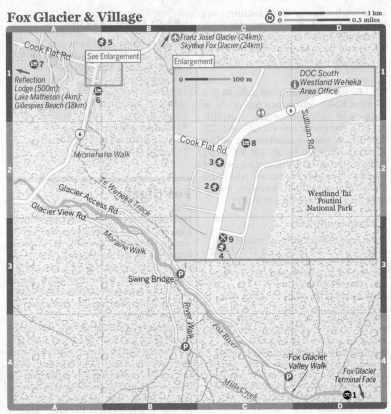

the glacier's terminal face as safety allows. They're also a good option if unstable weather is keeping helicopters grounded.

It's 1.5km from Fox Village to the glacier turn-off, and a further 2km to the car park, which you can reach under your own steam via **Te Weheka Walkway/Cycleway**, a pleasant rainforest trail starting just south of the Bella Vista motel. It's 2½ hours return on foot, or an hour by bike (leave your bikes at the car park – you can't cycle on the glacier walkways). Hire bikes from Fox Glacier Lodge (p476) (per hour/half-day $5/15).

From the car park, the terminal-face viewpoint is around 40 minutes' walk, depending on current conditions. Obey all signs: this place is dangerously dynamic.

Short return walks near the glacier include the half-hour **Moraine Walk** (over a major 18th-century advance) and 20-minute **Minnehaha Walk**. The fully accessible **Riv-**er Walk Lookout Track (20 minutes return) starts from the Glacier View Rd car park and allows people of all abilities the chance to view the glacier.

Pick up a copy of DOC's excellent *Glacier Region Walks* booklet ($2, or download at www.doc.govt.nz/Documents/parks-and-recreation/tracks-and-walks/west-coast/glacier-region-walks.pdf), which provides maps and illuminating background reading.

Other Walks

★**Lake Matheson**   TRAMPING
(www.doc.govt.nz) The famous 'mirror lake' can be found about 6km down Cook Flat Rd. Wandering slowly (as you should), it will take 1½ hours to complete the circuit. The best time to visit is early morning, or when the sun is low in the late afternoon, although the presence of the Lake Matheson Cafe (p476) means that any time is a good time.

Fox Glacier & Village

Copland Track   TRAMPING

(www.doc.govt.nz) About 26km south of Fox Glacier, along SH6, is the trailhead for the Copland Track, a seven-hour tramp (moderate fitness required) to legendary Welcome Flat, where thermal springs bubble up next to DOC's serviced Welcome Flat Hut. The hut and adjacent camping ground are extremely popular so book in advance either online or in person at DOC visitor centres.

Gillespies Beach   TRAMPING

(www.doc.govt.nz) Follow Cook Flat Rd for its full 21km (final 12km unsealed) to remote Gillespies Beach, a wind-blasted length of slate-grey sand and shingle near an old mining settlement. Interesting walks from here include a 30-minute, partly sheltered circuit to a rusting **gold dredge** from 1932, and a 3½-hour return walk to **Galway Beach**, a seal hang-out. Don't disturb them.

Aerial Sightseeing & Skydiving

Short heliflights (10 to 20 minutes) offer a spectacular vantage point over Fox Glacier with a snow landing up top. On a longer flight (30 to 50 minutes) you can also enjoy sky-high sightseeing over Franz Josef Glacier and Aoraki/Mt Cook. Ten-minute joy flights cost from around $120, but we recommend 20 minutes or more in the air (from $245). Children are admitted, though age restrictions vary; expect to pay around 70% of the adult price. Shop around: most operators are situated on the main road in Fox Glacier village.

Helicopter Line   SCENIC FLIGHTS

(📞0800 807 767, 03-751 0767; www.helicopter.co.nz; cnr SH6 & Cook Flat Rd; 20-50min flights $245-640) Whisking travellers to giddy heights since 1986, this well-established operator has a big menu of scenic flight options. The 50-minute flight taking in Aoraki/Mt Cook and Tasman Glacier (NZ's longest glacier) is noteworthy for the comparatively long amount of time spent in the air.

Skydive Fox Glacier   SKYDIVING

(📞0800 0080, 0800 751 0080; www.skydivefox.co.nz; Fox Glacier Airfield, SH6) Eye-popping scenery abounds on leaps from 16,500ft ($399), 13,000ft ($299) or 9000ft ($249)... between 30 and 65 seconds of freefall, depending on height. The airfield is three minutes' walk from the village centre.

Fox & Franz Josef
Heliservices   SCENIC FLIGHTS

(📞03-751 0866, 0800 800 793; www.scenic-flights.co.nz; 44 Main Rd; 20-40min flights $245-455) Locally run operator zipping sightseers up and down the glaciers, always with a snow landing. A two-glacier flight ($325) is over all too quickly, but longer flights also soar around Aoraki/Mt Cook.

Mountain Helicopters   SCENIC FLIGHTS

(📞03-751 0045, 0800 369 423; www.mountainhelicopters.co.nz; 43 Main Rd; 10-40min flights $119-440) Private company owned by locals for more than three decades, offering flights over Fox and Franz Josef Glaciers. Options range from a 10-minute taster to a 40-minute all-rounder with views of Fox Glacier and Aoraki/Mt Cook.

🛏 Sleeping

★ Fox Glacier Top 10
Holiday Park   HOLIDAY PARK $

(📞03-751 0821, 0800 154 366; www.fghp.co.nz; Kerr Rd; sites $45-52, cabins from $75, units $144-280; 🌐👶) Inspiring mountain views and ample amenities lift this reliable chain holiday park above its local competition. Grassy tent and hard campervan sites access a quality communal kitchen and dining room, and trim cabins (no private bathroom) and upscale self-contained units offer extra comfort. A spa pool, playground with trampoline and double-seater fun bikes pile on the family fun factor.

Westhaven   MOTEL $$

(📞0800 369 452, 03-751 0084; www.thewesthaven.co.nz; 29 Main Rd (SH6); d $178-311; @🌐) A classy combo of corrugated steel and local stone, Westhaven's 23 smart units are filled with home comforts (underfloor heating, neat kitchenettes) and priced by size. 'Superior' suites have spa baths.

Reflection Lodge
B&B $$$

(☑03-751 0707; www.reflectionlodge.co.nz; 141 Cook Flat Rd; d incl breakfast $230; ☎) The gregarious hosts of this ski-lodge-style B&B go the extra mile to make your stay a memorable one. Blooming gardens complete with alpine views and a Monet-like pond seal the deal.

Fox Glacier Lodge
B&B, MOTEL $$$

(☑0800 369 800, 03-751 0888; www.foxglacier lodge.com; 41 Sullivan Rd; unpowered/powered sites $30/40, d $175-235; ☎) Beautiful timber adorns this lodge both inside and out, imparting a mountain-chalet vibe. Similarly woody self-contained mezzanine units have spa baths and gas fires, and all guests can enjoy the communal barbecue and laundry facilities. A hearty continental breakfast is included for guests staying in the lodge, or costs $15 otherwise.

✕ Eating

★ Lake Matheson Cafe
MODERN NZ $$

(☑03-751 0878; www.lakematheson.com; Lake Matheson Rd; breakfast & lunch $10-21, dinner $29-35; ⊙8am-late Nov-Mar, to 3pm Apr-Oct) Next to Lake Matheson, this cafe does everything right: sharp architecture that maximises inspiring mountain views, strong coffee, craft beers and upmarket fare. Bratwurst breakfasts are a good prelude to rambling the lake, the pizzas are heaped with seasonal ingredients, and seafood risotto is topped with salmon sourced down the road in Paringa.

Last Kitchen
CAFE $$

(☑03-751 0058; cnr Sullivan Rd & SH6; mains $25-35; ⊙4-9.30pm) Making the most of its sunny corner location with outside tables, the Last Kitchen serves locally sourced produce sprinkled with European flavour: creamy chicken Alfredo, heavily topped burgers and ginger lamb bulk out the mainly carnivorous menu.

❶ Information

DOC South Westland Weheka Area Office
(☑03-751 0807; SH6; ⊙10am-2pm Mon-Fri) This is no longer a general visitor-information centre, but has the usual DOC information and hut tickets, with weather and track updates posted on the board outside.

Activity operators and accommodation providers are slick at providing information (and usually a booking service for transport and activities elsewhere), but you can also find info online at www.glaciercountry.co.nz. Ask your accommodation provider about transport bookings, or try Fox Glacier Guiding (p473), which also offers postal and currency-exchange services.

Fox Glacier Health Centre (☑03-751 0836, 24hr 0800 794 325; SH6) Clinic opening hours are displayed at the centre, or ring the 0800 number for 24-hour assistance.

❶ Getting There & Away

Direct InterCity (p448) and Naked Bus (p448) services along SH6 trundle through Fox Glacier once a day, heading south to Haast (from $20, 2½ hours) and north to Hokitika ($53, 3¼ hours) and Greymouth ($61, 4½ hours), stopping at Franz Josef ($10, 40 minutes) on the way. Book ahead for fares as low as $1. A direct daily bus also reaches Queenstown (from $59, 7¾ hours). For Nelson or Christchurch, transfer in Greymouth.

Most buses stop outside the Fox Glacier Guiding (p473)Skydiving building.

Fox Glacier Motors (☑03-751 0823; 52 Main Rd (SH6)) If you're heading south along the coast, it's your last chance for fuel before Haast, 120km away.

HAAST REGION

The isolated Haast region bookends the West Coast road. Upon approaching its forests, wetlands and sweeping beaches, your phone signal gets thinner as the wildlife gets correspondingly richer: kahikatea swamp forests, twisted rata trees aflutter with birdlife, and squabbling colonies of seals and penguins.

As a fitting prelude to the natural beauty surrounding Haast, part of Te Wāhipounamu–Southwest New Zealand World Heritage Area, jaw-dropping views line both routes to the region. Linking Haast to Fox Glacier and the rest of the West Coast, a scenic 120km stretch of highway is chopped through lowland forest, with views inland to sheer-sided valleys and intermittent but grand views seaward. Winding south is the fearsome Haast Pass Hwy (p478), 145 jagged kilometres that inspire gasps of wonder (as well as a tight grip on the steering wheel).

Haast

☑03 / POP 240

A small township at the yawning mouth of the Haast River, Haast acts as a springboard to forests, sand dunes, craggy coast and tree-knotted lakes. Only in 1965 was Haast linked to the rest of the West Coast Hwy and the untouched feel endures. It's a handy stop for filling the tank and tummy if you're travelling between Otago and the West Coast glaciers, but we'd recommend sticking around at least long enough for a river cruise and one blazing sunset.

If you're heading north, check your fuel gauge as Haast petrol station is the last one before Fox Glacier.

Activities

Waiatoto River Safaris
CRUISE
(📞 0800 538 723, 03-750 0780; www.riversafaris. co.nz; 1975 Haast-Jackson Bay Rd, Hannahs Clearing; adult/child $199/139; ⏰ trips 10am, 1pm & 4pm Nov-Mar, 11am Apr-Oct) 🅿 These two-hour river cruises offer an exhilarating taste of Haast's wilderness. Knowledgable operators Wayne and Ruth point out bird life and features of the dramatic landscape as the jetboat buzzes past World Heritage forest, in areas otherwise only accessible by helicopter. Birds chatter, ducks race alongside the boat, and there's the occasional white-knuckle rapid on this generally gentle-paced journey.

The base is 19km southwest of Haast Junction.

Ship Creek
WALKING
(www.doc.govt.nz) Two contrasting walks begin at Ship Creek, 15km north of Haast, each with interesting interpretive panels. Stroll sand dunes, stunted forest and driftwood-strewn beaches on the **Dune Lake Walk** (30 minutes return), before embarking on the enchanting **Kahikatea Swamp Forest Walk** (20 minutes return), along boardwalks that hover above glistening marshland (the bird-watching's superb).

Haast Heli
SCENIC FLIGHTS
(📞 03-750 0111; www.haastheli.co.nz; cnr Marks Rd & Hwy 6; per person from $160-475) This small helicopter outfit whooshes thrill seekers high and above primeval Hanging Lakes valley (30 minutes), or to Mt Aspiring (one hour). Prices depend on group size (max four).

Sleeping & Eating

Haast Lodge
LODGE $
(📞 03-750 0703, 0800 500 703; www.haastlodge. com; Marks Rd; sites from $16, dm $28, d & tw $65, tr $70, units from $140; 🖥) Covering all accommodation bases, Haast Lodge offers clean, well-maintained facilities that include a pleasant communal area for lodge users and campervanners, and compact, modern motel units at the Aspiring Court next door.

Haast River Motels & Holiday Park
HOLIDAY PARK, MOTEL $$
(📞 0800 624 847, 03-750 0020; www.haastriver motels.co.nz; 52 Haast Pass Hwy (SH6), Haast township; sites $44-48, d $128, units $155-232; 🖥) Easy-going staff, a reasonable free wi-fi allowance (500MB), and roomy motel units with dive-in beds. This holiday park ticks a lot of boxes. Campervan guests are kept happy with on-site facilities like a laundry, a games room, and a book and DVD-filled lounge surveyed by mounted deer heads.

Wilderness Lodge Lake Moeraki
LODGE $$$
(📞 03-750 0881; www.wildernesslodge.co.nz; SH6, Lake Moeraki; s $520-770, d $840-1240, incl breakfast & dinner; 🖥) 🅿 At the southern end of Lake Moeraki, 31km north of Haast, you'll find one of NZ's best nature lodges. In a verdant setting on the edge of the Moeraki River, it offers comfortable rooms and four-course dinners, but the real delights are the outdoor activities, such as kayak trips and coastal walks, guided by people with conservation in their blood.

Hard Antler
PUB FOOD $$
(📞 03-750 0034; Marks Rd, Haast township; mains $14-30; ⏰ 11am-late) Antlers and a wall of fame of local fishing folk establishes the hunting-lodge vibe of Haast's best boozer. Service is gruff but meaty main courses (venison stew, burgers and tasty grilled blue cod) are served all day. Vegetarians, we hope you like nachos.

ℹ Information

DOC Haast Visitor Centre (📞 03-750 0809; www.doc.govt.nz; cnr SH6 & Jackson Bay Rd; ⏰ 9am-6pm Nov-Mar, to 4.30pm Apr-Oct) Wall-to-wall regional information and free screenings of Haast landscape film *Edge of Wilderness*. With outdoor water features and a brimming museum, it's more attractive than the average info centre. Sells insect repellent.

General regional information and visitor services listings can be found on www.haastnz.com.

ℹ Getting There & Away

Naked Bus (p448) and Intercity (p448) buses stop on Marks Rd (opposite Wilderness Accommodation) on their daily runs from Queenstown ($36, 4¾ hours) to Franz Josef and Fox Glaciers (from $23, 3½ hours).

HAAST PASS HWY

The 145km road careening between the West Coast and Central Otago is a spectacular drive. It takes roughly 2½ hours from Haast to Wanaka, but allow more time to drive this Southern Alpine saddle if you want to stop at lookouts and waterfall trails.

Heading inland from Haast, the highway (SH6) snakes alongside the Haast River, crossing the boundary into Mt Aspiring National Park. The further you go, the narrower the river valley becomes, until the road clambers around sheer-sided valley walls streaked with waterfalls and scarred by rock slips. Princely sums are involved in keeping this highway clear, and even so it sets plenty of traps for unwary drivers. Stop at signposted lookouts and short walkways to admire the scenery, such as small, graceful **Fantail Falls** (10 minutes return) and aptly named **Thunder Creek Falls** (one hour return). These are detailed in DOC's booklet *Walks along the Haast Highway* ($2), but sufficient detail is provided at the trailheads. The highway tops out at the 563m mark, shortly after which you will reach food and fuel at Makarora. Hello Otago!

Early Māori travelled this route in their quest for *pounamu*, naming it Tioripātea, meaning 'Clear Path'. Northern chief Te Puoho led troops across the pass in 1836 to raid southern tribes. German geologist Julius von Haast led a party of Europeans across in 1863 – hence the name of the pass, river and township – but evidence suggests that Scottish prospector Charles Cameron may have pipped Haast at the post. It was clearly no mean feat: the terrain is such that the Haast Pass Hwy wasn't opened until as late as 1965.

Jackson Bay & Around

Most travellers drive northeast from Haast Junction towards epic Fox and Franz Josef Glaciers, but the road less travelled makes an interesting detour. Steering southwest, 45km from Haast, find the pocket-sized outpost of Jackson Bay, towered over by the Southern Alps. There's no through road: this fishing hamlet is truly the end of the line.

Farms here stand testament to some of the hardiest souls who ever attempted settlement in New Zealand. Migrants arrived in 1875 under a doomed settlement scheme, their farming and timber-milling aspirations shattered by never-ending rain and the lack of a wharf, not built until 1938. Until the 1950s, the only way to reach Haast overland was via bush tracks from Hokitika and Wanaka. Supplies came by an infrequent coastal shipping service.

Unless you're in the market for whitebait, present-day Jackson Bay has few attractions other than a couple of lovely and lonely walking trails.

🏃 Activities

Near Okuru, 10km west of Haast, is the **Hapuka Estuary Walk** (20 minutes return), a winding boardwalk that loops through a sleepy wildlife sanctuary with good interpretation panels en route.

The road continues west to Arawhata Bridge, where a turn-off leads to the **Lake Ellery Track** (www.doc.govt.nz), 3.5km south along an unsealed road. A one-hour round trip takes you through mossy beech forest to a lookout over peaceful Lake Ellery. There's not much besides a picnic bench when you arrive, but you'll likely have it to yourself.

From the end of Jackson Bay Rd begins the **Wharekai Te Kou Walk** (www.doc.govt.nz), 40 minutes return, to Ocean Beach, a tiny bay with some interesting rock formations. The muddy three- to four-hour **Smoothwater Bay Track**, following an old pioneers' track, also begins nearby.

🍴 Eating

Cray Pot SEAFOOD $$
(📞 03-750 0035; Haast-Jackson Bay Rd; mains $12-38; ⊙ noon-4pm Oct-Dec, to 7pm Jan-Apr, hours may vary) Spotty opening hours are the only blight on this brightly painted caravan diner overlooking Jackson Bay. Cray Pot serves honest seafood, from big portions of fish and chips ($19) to crayfish tails with potato salad (from $65), as well as whitebait, green-lipped mussels and local blue cod, served with homegrown vegies and herbs.

ℹ️ Getting There & Away

Jackson Bay is 45km southwest of Haast along a sealed road. There are no transport services, so you'll need your own vehicle.

Christchurch & Canterbury

Best Places to Eat

➡ Pegasus Bay (p513)

➡ Supreme Supreme (p495)

➡ Little High Eatery (p495)

➡ Oxford (p521)

➡ Twenty Seven Steps (p496)

Best Places to Stay

➡ Halfmoon Cottage (p504)

➡ Eco Villa (p493)

➡ Peel Forest DOC Campsite (p524)

➡ Woodbank Park Cottages (p511)

➡ Lake Tekapo Lodge (p528)

Why Go?

Nowhere in New Zealand is changing and developing as fast as post-quake Christchurch. The scaffolding is coming down, the hospitality scene is flourishing and the central city is once again drawing visitors to its pedestrian-friendly streets.

A short drive from the city, Banks Peninsula conceals idyllic hidden bays and beaches that provide the perfect backdrop for wildlife cruises, with a sunset return to the attractions of pretty Akaroa. To the north are the vineyards of the Waipara Valley and the relaxed ambience of Hanmer Springs, while westwards, the Canterbury Plains morph quickly into the dramatic wilderness of the Southern Alps.

Canterbury's attractions include tramping along alpine valleys and over passes around Arthur's Pass, and mountain biking around the turquoise lakes of Mackenzie Country. During winter (June to September), attention switches to the ski fields. Throughout the seasons, Aoraki/Mt Cook, the country's tallest peak, stands sentinel over this diverse region.

When to Go

➡ Canterbury is one of NZ's driest regions, as moisture-laden westerlies from the Tasman Sea dump their rainfall on the West Coast before hitting the eastern side of the South Island. Visit from January to March for hot and settled weather, with plenty of opportunities to get active amid the region's spectacular landscapes.

➡ The shoulder seasons of October to November and March to May can be cool and dry, and blissfully uncrowded. Come prepared for all weather; snow is still possible on the mountains.

➡ Hit the winter slopes from July to October at Mt Hutt or on one of Canterbury's smaller club ski fields.

Christchurch & Canterbury Highlights

1 **Christchurch** (p479) Experiencing the dynamic rebuilding and re-emergence of the city post-earthquake.

2 **Botanic Gardens** (p486) Meandering through Christchurch's beautiful green heart.

3 **Mt John** (p527) Marvelling at the otherworldly views of Mackenzie Country and the surreal azure blue of Lake Tekapo from the top.

4 **Hanmer Springs** (p509) Soaking in the soothing waters at this famous hot spring.

5 **Banks Peninsula** (p502) Admiring the surf-bitten edges from Summit Rd before descending to the quaint Gallic ambience of Akaroa.

50 km
25 miles

SOUTH
PACIFIC
OCEAN

481

TASMAN SEA

Mahinapua
Ross
Hokitika Gorge

Mt Bryce
(2188m)

Mt Whitcombe
(2635m)

Mt Tyndall
(2524m)

Mt Arrowsmith
(2795m)

Mt D'Archiac
(2865m)

Elie de
Beaumont
(3116m)

Mt Tasman
(3498m)

Westland Tai Poutini
National Park

MalteBrun
(3154m)

Aoraki/Mt Cook
(3724m)

Aoraki/Mt Cook
National Park

Mt Cook
Village

Mt Sefton
(3151m)

Haritari

Lake Ianthe

Whataroa

Okarito

Franz Josef

Fox Glacier

Bruce Bay

Paringa

Haast

Mesopotamia

The Thumbs
(2545m)

Two Thumb Range

Craigieburn
Forest Park

Lake
Coleridge

Lake
Heron

Rakaia River

Mt Somers

Rangitata River

Ben McLeod
(1952m)

Fox Peak
(2331m)

Peel Forest

Geraldine

Fairlie

Burkes
Pass

Lake
Tekapo

Lake
Tekapo

Mt John 3

Lake
Pukaki

Lake
Ohau

Glentanner

Ben Ohau Range

Ruataniwha
Conservation
Park

Twizel 7

Southern Alps

Porters
Pass
(945m)

Windwhistle

Mt Hutt

Methven

Mayfield

Rakaia Gorge

Darfield

Glentunnel

Dunsandel

Rakaia

Ashburton

Tinwald

Rangitata

Temuka

Pleasant
Point

Timaru

Albury

Hunter Hills

Waimate

Lake
Benmore

Glenavy

Pukeuri

Lake
Ellesmere

Waitaki River

6 Aoraki/Mt Cook
(p531) Gazing at
the cloud-piercing
silhouette of NZ's
highest peak.

7 Alps 2 Ocean
Cycle Trail (p532)
Cycling the best
bits of the trail from
unspoiled Twizel.

ℹ️ Getting There & Away

AIR

Christchurch's international airport is the South Island's main hub. Air New Zealand flies here from 15 domestic destinations, while Jetstar has flights from Auckland and Wellington. Air New Zealand also flies between Timaru and Wellington.

BUS

Christchurch is the hub for coaches and shuttles heading up the coast as far as Picton, down the coast to Dunedin (and on to Te Anau), over the Alps to Greymouth and inland down to Queenstown.

TRAIN

The *TranzAlpine* service connects Christchurch and Greymouth, and the *Coastal Pacific* chugs north to Picton, with ferry connections across Cook Strait to the North Island.

CHRISTCHURCH

🖉 03 / POP 375,000

Welcome to a vibrant city in transition, coping creatively with the aftermath of NZ's second-worst natural disaster. Traditionally the most English of NZ cities, Christchurch's heritage heart was all but hollowed out following the 2010 and 2011 earthquakes that left 186 people dead.

Today Christchurch is in the midst of an epic rebuild that has completely reconstructed the city centre, where over 80% of buildings needed to be demolished after the quake. Scaffolding and road cones will be part of Christchurch's landscape for a while yet, but don't be deterred; exciting new buildings are opening at an astonishing pace, and most sights are open for business.

Curious travellers will revel in this chaotic, crazy and colourful mix, full of surprises and inspiring in ways you can't even imagine. And despite all the hard work and heartache, the locals will be only too pleased to see you.

History

The first people to live in what is now Christchurch were moa (bird) hunters, who arrived around 1250. Immediately prior to colonisation, the Ngāi Tahu tribe had a small seasonal village on the banks of the Avon called Ōtautahi.

When British settlers arrived in 1850 it was an orderly Church of England project; the passengers on the 'First Four Ships' were dubbed 'the Canterbury Pilgrims' by the British press. Christchurch was meant to be a model of class-structured England in the South Pacific, not just another scruffy colonial outpost. Churches were built rather than pubs, the fertile farming land was deliberately placed in the hands of the gentry, and wool made the elite of Christchurch wealthy.

In 1856 Christchurch officially became NZ's first city, and a very English one at that. Town planning and architecture assumed a close affinity with the 'Mother Country' and English-style gardens were planted, earning it the nickname, the 'Garden City'. To this day, Christchurch in spring is a glorious place to be.

◉ Sights

The majority of Christchurch's key sights rebounded soon after the 2011 earthquakes. Today there is more to see than ever. The centre is graced by numerous notable arts institutions and museums, as well as the stunning Botanic Gardens and Hagley Park. Inner-city streets conceal art projects and pocket gardens, dotted among a thinned-out cityscape featuring remnant stone buildings and the sharp, shiny architecture of the new.

◎ City Centre

★ **Christchurch Art Gallery** GALLERY
(Te Puna o Waiwhetu; 🖉03-941 7300; www.christchurchartgallery.org.nz; cnr Montreal St & Worcester Blvd; ⊙10am-5pm Thu-Tue, to 9pm Wed) FREE Damaged in the earthquakes, Christchurch's fantastic art gallery has reopened brighter and bolder, presenting a stimulating mix of local and international exhibitions. Collection items range from the traditional to the startlingly contemporary – think light installations and interactive sculptures.

Free guided tours (one hour) take place at 11am and 2pm daily.

★ **Quake City** MUSEUM
(🖉03-366 5000; www.quakecity.co.nz; 299 Durham St N; adult $20, child accompanied/unaccompanied free/$8; ⊙10am-5pm) A must-visit for anyone interested in understanding the impact of the Canterbury earthquakes, this compact museum tells stories through photography, video footage and various artefacts, including the remnants of ChristChurch Cathedral's celebrated rose window and other similarly moving debris. There are exhibits aimed at engaging both adults and children. Most affecting of all is the film featuring survivors recounting their own experiences.

Christchurch

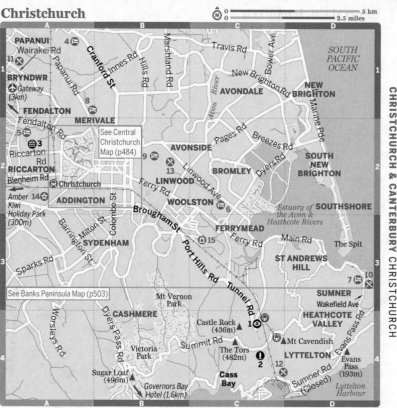

Christchurch

⊙ Sights
1	Christchurch Gondola	C4
2	Pioneer Women's Memorial	C4
3	Riccarton House & Bush	A2

🛏 Sleeping
4	Christchurch Top 10	A1
5	Fendalton House	A2
6	Haka Lodge	C2
7	Le Petit Hotel	D3
8	Merivale Manor	A1
9	Old Countryhouse	B2

⊗ Eating
10	Bohemian Bakery	D3
	Christchurch Farmers Market	(see 3)
	Freemans	(see 12)
11	Kinji	A1
	Lyttelton Coffee Company	(see 12)
12	Lyttelton Farmers Market	C4
	Roots	(see 12)
13	Under the Red Verandah	B2

🍸 Drinking & Nightlife
	Civil and Naval	(see 12)
	The Brewery	(see 15)
	Village Inn	(see 10)
	Wunderbar	(see 12)

🎭 Entertainment
14	AMI Stadium	A2
	Hollywood Cinema	(see 7)

🛍 Shopping
	Henry Trading	(see 12)
	London St Bookshop	(see 12)
15	Tannery	C3

ℹ Information
	Lyttelton Visitor Information Centre	(see 12)

ℹ Transport
	Black Cat	(see 12)

Central Christchurch

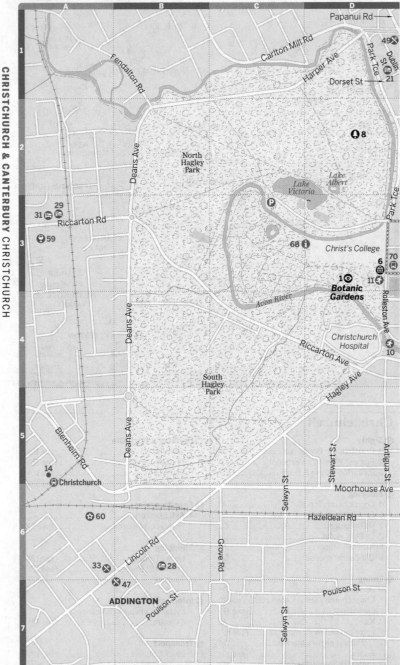

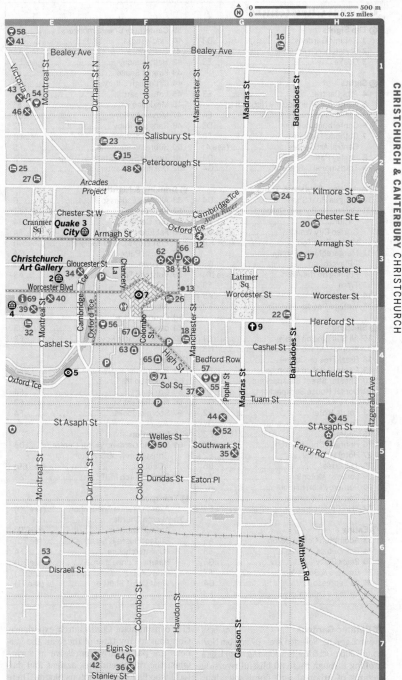

Central Christchurch

★ **Botanic Gardens**   GARDENS
(www.ccc.govt.nz; Rolleston Ave; ☺7am-9pm Nov-Feb, to 8.30pm Oct & Mar, to 6.30pm Apr-Sep) FREE Strolling through these 30 blissful riverside hectares of arboreal and floral splendour is a consummate Christchurch experience. Gorgeous at any time of the year, the gardens are particularly impressive in spring when the rhododendrons, azaleas and daffodil woodland are in riotous bloom. There are thematic gardens to explore, lawns to

sprawl on, and a playground adjacent to the **Botanic Gardens Visitor Centre** ([✆]03-941 7590; ⊘9am-4pm), which also contains a lovely **cafe** and gift shop.

Guided walks ($10, 1½ hours) depart at 1.30pm (October to May) from the gate near Canterbury Museum, or hop aboard the 'Caterpillar' electric shuttle.

Canterbury Earthquake National Memorial
MEMORIAL

(Oi Manawa; www.canterburyearthquakememorial.co.nz; Oxford Tce) Unveiled in 2017, this moving monument comprises a 100m-long memorial wall, curved along the south bank of the Avon and engraved with the names of the 185 people who died as a result of the 22 February 2011 earthquake. On the opposite bank, a shady park provides a space for reflection and remembrance. The memorial's Māori name, Oi Manawa, means 'tremor or quivering of the heart'.

Hagley Park
PARK

(Riccarton Ave) Wrapped around the Botanic Gardens, Hagley Park is Christchurch's biggest green space, stretching for 165 hectares. Riccarton Ave splits it in two, while the Avon River snakes through the northern half. It's a great place to stroll, whether on a foggy autumn morning, or a warm spring day when the cherry trees lining Harper Ave are in flower. Joggers make the most of the tree-lined avenues year-round.

Transitional Cathedral
CHURCH

(www.cardboardcathedral.org.nz; 234 Hereford St; entry by donation; ⊘9am-5pm Apr-Oct, to 7pm Nov-Mar) Universally known as the Cardboard Cathedral due to the 98 cardboard tubes used in its construction, this interesting structure serves as both the city's temporary Anglican cathedral and as a concert venue. Designed by Japanese 'disaster architect' Shigeru Ban, the entire building was constructed in 11 months.

Arts Centre
HISTORIC BUILDING

(www.artscentre.org.nz; 2 Worcester Blvd; ⊘10am-5pm) [FREE] Dating from 1877, this enclave of Gothic Revival buildings was originally Canterbury College, the forerunner of Canterbury University. The buildings are slowly reopening to the public after extensive restoration work due to quake damage, with the entire site due to reopen by 2019. Inside you'll find an array of shops, cafes and museums and galleries, as well as the i-SITE (p499). Exhibition spaces play host to regular concerts, markets and events.

Canterbury Museum
MUSEUM

([✆]03-366 5000; www.canterburymuseum.com; Rolleston Ave; ⊘9am-5.30pm Oct-Mar, to 5pm Apr-Sep; [♿]) [FREE] Yes, there's a mummy and dinosaur bones, but the highlights of this museum are more local and more recent. The Māori galleries contain some beautiful *pounamu* (greenstone) pieces, while Christchurch Street is an atmospheric walk through the colonial past. The reproduction of Fred & Myrtle's gloriously kitsch Paua Shell House embraces Kiwiana at its best, and kids will enjoy the interactive displays in the Discovery Centre (admission $2). Free guided tours (one hour) depart from the foyer at 3.30pm on Tuesdays and Thursdays.

Christchurch Gondola
CABLE CAR

(www.welcomeaboard.co.nz/gondola; 10 Bridle Path Rd; return adult/child $28/12; ⊘10am-5pm) Take a ride to the top of Mt Cavendish (500m) on this 862m cable car for wonderful views over the city, Lyttelton, the Banks Peninsula and the Canterbury Plains. At the top there's a cafe and the child-focused *Time Tunnel* ride, which recounts the history of the area. You can also walk to Cavendish Bluff Lookout (30 minutes return) or the **Pioneer Women's Memorial** (one hour return).

ESSENTIAL CHRISTCHURCH & CANTERBURY

Eat salmon spawned in the shadow of NZ's tallest mountains.

Drink some of NZ's finest pinot noir and riesling from the Waipara Valley.

Read *Decline and Fall on Savage Street* (2017), a poetic fictionalisation of the 2011 quake by local South Island author Fiona Farrell.

Listen to the soulful tones and uplifting beats of Christchurch's Ladi6.

Watch *The Changeover* (Miranda Harcourt & Stuart McKenzie, 2017), a silver screen adaptation of Margaret Mahy's 1984 novel, set and shot in Christchurch.

Go green at the ecofriendly Okuti Garden (p504) on Banks Peninsula.

Go online www.christchurchnz.com, www.mtcooknz.com, www.midcanterbury nz.com, www.visithurunui.co.nz

Cathedral Square SQUARE

Christchurch's city square stands at the heart of the rebuilding efforts, with the remains of Christchurch Cathedral emblematic of what has been lost. The February 2011 earthquake brought down the 63m-high spire, while subsequent earthquakes in June 2011 and December 2011 destroyed the prized stained-glass rose window. Other heritage buildings around the square were also badly damaged, but one modern landmark left unscathed is the 18m-high metal sculpture *Chalice,* designed by Neil Dawson. It was erected in 2001 to commemorate the new millennium.

The much-loved Gothic cathedral has been at the centre of a battle between those who seek to preserve what remains of Christchurch's heritage, the fiscal pragmatists, and those ideologically inclined to things new. In 2012 the Anglican Diocese announced that the cathedral was to be demolished, but work was stayed when heritage advocates launched court proceedings. Eventually, in September 2017, the church leadership voted to preserve the building after the government and Christchurch City Council banded together to offer significant financial support. It's thought that the rebuild could take up to 10 years, with an estimated cost of $104 million.

Central Art Gallery GALLERY

(☑ 03-366 3318; www.thecentral.co.nz; Arts Centre, 2 Worcester Blvd; ⊙ 10am-5pm Tue-Sun) FREE Housed in the Arts Centre's beautifully restored 1916 Library building, the Central Art Gallery exhibits contemporary works by established and emerging NZ artists.

⊙ Other Suburbs

Riccarton House & Bush HISTORIC BUILDING

(www.riccartonhouse.co.nz; 16 Kahu Rd, Riccarton; ⊙ 9am-4pm Sun-Fri, to 1pm Sat) FREE Historic Riccarton House (1856) sits proudly amid 12 hectares of pretty parkland and forest beside the Avon River. The grounds host the popular Christchurch Farmers Market (p496) on Saturdays; the rest of the week you can visit the lovely restaurant on the ground floor.

The biggest draw, however, is the small patch of bush behind the house. Enclosed by a vermin-proof fence, this is the last stand of kahikatea floodplain forest in Canterbury.

Kahikatea is NZ's tallest native tree, growing to heights of 60m; the tallest trees here are a mere 30m and around 300 to 600

years old. A short loop track heads through the heart of the forest.

The majority of the house is only accessible on a guided tour, departing at 2pm Sunday to Friday (adult/child $18/5, one hour); shorter tours (adult/child $8/free) run every half hour between 10am and 12.30pm on Saturdays.

Orana Wildlife Park ZOO

(☑ 03-359 7109; www.oranawildlifepark.co.nz; 793 McLeans Island Rd, McLeans Island; adult/child $34.50/9.50; ⊙ 10am-5pm) Orana is an 'open range' zoo, and you'll know exactly what that means if you opt to jump in the cage for the lion encounter (per person $45). There's an excellent, walk-through native bird aviary, a nocturnal kiwi house, and a reptile exhibit featuring tuatara. Most of the 80-hectare grounds are devoted to Africana, including rhinos, giraffes, zebras, cheetahs and gorillas.

Willowbank Wildlife Reserve ZOO

(☑ 03-359 6226; www.willowbank.co.nz; 60 Hussey Rd, Northwood; adult/child $29.50/12; ⊙ 9.30am-7pm Oct-Apr, to 5pm May-Sep) ♠ Willowbank focuses on native NZ critters (including kiwi), heritage farmyard animals and hands-on enclosures with wallabies, deer and lemurs. There's also a recreated Māori village, the setting for the evening Ko Tane (p491). It's 10km north of town, near the airport.

International Antarctic Centre MUSEUM

(☑ 0508 736 4846, 03-357 0519; www.iceberg.co.nz; Christchurch Airport, 38 Orchard Rd; adult/child $39/19; ⊙ 9am-5.30pm) As one of only five 'gateway cities' to Antarctica, Christchurch has played a special role in Antarctic exploration since expeditional ships to the icy continent began departing from Lyttelton in the early 1900s. This huge complex, built for the administration of the NZ, US and Italian Antarctic programs, gives visitors the opportunity to learn about Antarctica in a fun, interactive environment.

Attractions include the Antarctic Storm chamber (where you can get a taste of -18°C wind chill), face-to-face encounters with resident little blue penguins, and a meet-and-greet with rescue huskies (Friday to Sunday only). The 'Xtreme Pass' (adult/child $59/29) includes the '4D theatre' (a 3D film with moving seats and a water spray) and a joyride on a Hägglund all-terrain amphibious Antarctic vehicle. An optional extra is the Penguin Backstage Tour (adult/child

$25/15), which allows visitors behind the scenes of the Penguin Encounter.

A free shuttle to the centre departs from outside Canterbury Museum (p487) at 9am, 11am, 1pm and 3pm, returning at 10am, noon, 2pm and 4pm.

🏃 Activities

Boating

Antigua Boat Sheds   BOATING, KAYAKING
(📞03-366 5885; www.boatsheds.co.nz; 2 Cambridge Tce; ☺9am-5pm) Dating from 1882, the photogenic green-and-white Antigua Boat Sheds hires out rowing boats ($35), kayaks ($12),

canoes ($35) and bikes (adult/child $10/5); all prices are per hour. There's also a good cafe.

Punting on the Avon   BOATING
(www.punting.co.nz; 2 Cambridge Tce; adult/child $28/12; ☺9am-6pm Oct-Mar, 10am-4pm Apr-Sep)
🚣 If rowing your own boat down the Avon sounds a bit too much like hard work, why not relax in a flat-bottomed punt while a strapping lad in Edwardian clobber glides you peaceably through the Botanic Gardens. Tours depart year-round from the Antigua Boat Sheds; during the warmer months alternative trips run from sites at Mona Vale and Worcester Bridge.

THE CHRISTCHURCH EARTHQUAKES

Christchurch's seismic nightmare began at 4.35am on 4 September 2010. Centred 40km west of the city, a 40-second, 7.1-magnitude earthquake jolted Cantabrians from their sleep, and caused widespread damage to older buildings in the central city. Close to the quake's epicentre in rural Darfield, huge gashes erupted amid grassy pastures, and the South Island's main railway line was bent and buckled. Because the tremor struck in the early hours of the morning when most people were home in bed, there were no fatalities, and many Christchurch residents felt that the city had dodged a bullet.

Fast forward to 12.51pm on 22 February 2011, when central Christchurch was busy with shoppers and workers enjoying their lunch break. This time the 6.3-magnitude quake was much closer, centred just 10km southeast of the city and only 5km deep. The tremor was significantly greater, and many locals report being flung violently and almost vertically into the air. The peak ground acceleration exceeded 1.8, almost twice the acceleration of gravity.

When the dust settled after 24 traumatic seconds, NZ's second-largest city had changed forever. The towering spire of the iconic ChristChurch Cathedral lay in ruins; walls and verandas had cascaded down on shopping strips; and two multistorey buildings had pancaked. Of the 185 deaths (across 20 nationalities), 115 occurred in the six-storey Canterbury TV building, where many international students at a language school were killed. Elsewhere, the historic port town of Lyttelton was badly damaged; roads and bridges were crumpled; and residential suburbs in the east were inundated as a process of rapid liquefaction saw tons of oozy silt rise from the ground.

In the months that followed literally hundreds of aftershocks rattled the city's traumatised residents (and claimed one more life), but the resilience and bravery of Cantabrians quickly became evident. From the region's rural heartland, the 'Farmy Army' descended on the city, armed with shovels and food hampers. Social media mobilised 10,000 students, and the Student Volunteer Army became a vital force for residential clean-ups in the city's beleaguered eastern suburbs. Heartfelt aid and support arrived from across NZ, and seven other nations sent specialised urban-search-and-rescue teams.

The impact of the events of a warm summer's day in early 2011 will take longer than a generation to resolve. Entire streets and neighbourhoods in the eastern suburbs have had to be abandoned, and Christchurch's heritage architecture is irrevocably damaged. Families in some parts of the city have been forced to live in substandard accommodation, waiting for insurance claims to be settled. Around 80% of the buildings within the city centre's famed four avenues have been or are still due to be demolished. Amid the doomed, the saved, and the shiny new builds are countless construction sites and empty plots still strewn with rubble.

Plans for the next 20 years of the city's rebuild include a compact, low-rise city centre, large green spaces, and parks and cycleways along the Avon River. It's estimated that the total rebuild and repair bill could reach $40 or even $50 billion.

To find out more about the effects of the quakes, and to hear survivors tell their experiences of that time in their own voices, visit the highly recommended Quake City (p482).

Walking

The i-SITE (p499) provides information on walking tours as well as self-guided options, including the rewarding Avon River Walk, which takes in major city sights, and several excellent trails around the Port Hills.

For long-range city views, take the walkway from the Sign of the Takahe on Dyers Pass Rd. The various 'Sign of the...' places in this area were originally roadhouses built during the Depression as rest stops. This walk leads up to the Sign of the Kiwi, through Victoria Park and then along the view-filled Summit Rd to Scotts Reserve.

You can walk to Lyttelton on the Bridle Path (1½ hours), which starts at Heathcote Valley (take bus 28). The Godley Head Walkway (two hours return) begins at Taylors Mistake, crossing and recrossing Summit Rd, and offers beautiful views on a clear day.

Walks in Christchurch and throughout Canterbury are well detailed at www.christchurchnz.com.

Cycling

Being mostly flat and boasting more than 300km of cycle trails, Christchurch is a brilliant place to explore on two wheels. For evidence, look no further than the free *Christchurch City Cycle Map*, available around town or downloadable from www.ccc.govt.nz/cycling.

The i-SITE (p499) can advise on bicycle hire and guided tours.

There's some great off-road riding around the Port Hills, while towards Banks Peninsula you'll find the best section of the Little River Trail (p504), one of NZ's Great Rides.

Vintage Peddler Bike Co   CYCLING
(☑ 03-365 6530; www.vintagepeddler.co.nz; 7/75 Peterborough St; half-/full-day hire from $25/30) Take to two retro wheels on these funky vintage bicycles. Helmets, locks and local knowledge are all supplied. It also offers small-group cycling tours.

City Cycle Hire   CYCLING
(☑ 03-377 5952; www.cyclehire-tours.co.nz; city bike half/full day from $25/35, touring bike per week from $140) Offers door-to-door delivery of on- and off-road city bikes and touring bikes. Will also meet you with a bike at the top of the gondola if you fancy a 16km descent ($70 including gondola ride; 1½ hours).

Swimming & Surfing

Despite having separate names for different sections, it's one solid stretch of sandy beach that spreads north from the estuary of the Avon and Heathcote Rivers. Closest to the city centre is New Brighton, with a distinctive pier reaching 300m out to sea. On either side, South New Brighton and North Beach are quieter options. Waimairi, a little further north, is our personal pick.

The superstar is Sumner, 12km from the city centre on the south side of the estuary. Its beachy vibe, eateries and art-house cinema make it a satisfying spot for a day trip.

Further east around the headland, isolated Taylors Mistake has the cleanest water of any Christchurch beach and some good surf breaks. Beginners should stick to Sumner or New Brighton.

Other Activities

Margaret Mahy Family Playground   PLAYGROUND
(cnr Manchester & Armagh Sts; 🚻) Named after beloved Kiwi children's author Margaret Mahy, this magical playground has four separate themed zones – peninsula, forest, wetlands and plains. From a splash park to a giant spiral slide, you'll find plenty to keep the kids (and kids at heart) entertained.

☞ Tours

★ Tram   TRAM
(☑ 03-366 7830; www.welcomeaboard.co.nz; adult/child $25/free; ⊗ 9am-6pm Sep-Mar, 10am-5pm Apr-Aug) Excellent driver commentary makes this so much more than just a tram ride. The beautifully restored old dears trundle around a 17-stop loop, departing every 15 minutes, taking in a host of city highlights,

including Cathedral Sq and New Regent St. The full circuit takes just under an hour, and you can hop on and hop off all day.

TranzAlpine RAIL

(☑ 03-341 2588, 0800 872 467; www.kiwirailscenic.co.nz; one way from $119) The *TranzAlpine* is one of the world's great train journeys, traversing the Southern Alps between Christchurch and Greymouth, from the Pacific Ocean to the Tasman Sea, passing through Arthur's Pass National Park. En route is a sequence of dramatic landscapes, from the flat, alluvial Canterbury Plains to narrow alpine gorges, an 8.5km tunnel, beech-forested river valleys, and a lake fringed with cabbage trees.

The 4½-hour journey is unforgettable, even in bad weather (if it's raining on one coast, it's probably fine on the other). The train departs Christchurch at 8.15am and Greymouth at 2.05pm.

Guided City Walks WALKING

(☑ 0800 423 783; www.walkchristchurch.nz; Rolleston Ave; adult/child $20/free; ⊙10.30am & 1pm) Departing from the red kiosk outside Canterbury Museum, these 2½-hour tours offer a leisurely stroll around the city's main sights in the company of knowledgable guides.

Hassle Free Tours BUS

(☑ 03-385 5775; www.hasslefree.co.nz) Explore Christchurch in an open-top double-decker bus on a one-hour highlights tour ($35) or three-hour discovery tour ($69). Tours depart outside Canterbury Museum. Regional options include a 4WD alpine safari, Kaikoura whale-watching, and visiting the location of Edoras from the *Lord of the Rings* trilogy.

Caterpillar Botanic Gardens Tour OUTDOORS

(☑ 0800 88 22 23; www.welcomeaboard.co.nz; adult/child $20/9; ⊙10am-3.30pm Oct-Mar, 11am-3pm Apr-Sep) Hop aboard the 'Caterpillar' electric shuttle for a tour of Christchurch's stunning Botanic Gardens (p486).

Garden City Helicopters SCENIC FLIGHTS

(☑ 03-358 4360; www.helicopters.net.nz; 73-93 Grays Rd; 20min per pserson $199) Scenic flights above the city and Lyttelton let you observe the impact of the earthquake and the rebuilding efforts.

Ko Tane CULTURAL

(☑ 03-359 6226; www.kotane.co.nz; 60 Hussey Rd, Northwood; adult/child $135/67.50; ⊙5.15pm) Rousing Māori cultural performance by members of the Ngāi Tahu tribe comprising a *pōwhiri* (welcome), the famous *haka,* a buffet *hāngi* (earth-oven) meal, and plenty of *waiata ā ringa* (singing and dancing). At Willowbank Wildlife Reserve (p488).

✷✷ Festivals & Events

Check www.ccc.govt.nz/events and www.christchurchnz.com/events for comprehensive festivals and events listings.

CHRISTCHURCH IN...

Two Days

After breakfast at **C1 Espresso** (p495), take some time to walk around the regenerating city centre, visit **Quake City** (p482) and wander through **Cathedral Sq** (p488). Make your way to **Christchurch Art Gallery** (p482), then gather picnic supplies at **Canterbury Cheesemongers** (p495). After lunch, visit the excellent **Canterbury Museum** (p487) and take a walk through the lovely **Botanic Gardens** (p486). That evening, explore the Victoria St restaurant strip or head to **Smash Palace** (p497) for beer and a burger amid the hipsters.

Start day two at **Addington Coffee Co-op** (p496) and then head up Mt Cavendish on the **gondola** (p487) for views and a walk at the top. Continue to Lyttelton for lunch at **Lyttelton Coffee Company** (p501) before returning through the tunnel and around to Sumner for a late-afternoon swim or stroll, then stop for dinner and catch a flick at the **Hollywood Cinema** (p498).

Four Days

Follow the two-day itinerary, then on day three head to Akaroa (p505) to explore its wildlife-rich harbour and walk its pretty streets, enjoying stupendous views on the way there and back again. On day four, visit **Orana Wildlife Park** (p488) and **Riccarton House & Bush** (p488) before finishing the day with shopping, beer and pizza at the **Tannery** (p499) in Woolston.

World Buskers Festival PERFORMING ARTS
(www.worldbuskersfestival.com; ⊙Jan) National and international talent entertain passers-by for 10 days in mid-January. Shows span stand-up comedy, burlesque, music and circus arts. Check the website for locations – and don't forget to throw money in the hat.

KidsFest FAIR
(www.kidsfest.org.nz; ⊙Jul) If family fun is a priority, consider planning your travels around NZ's biggest children's festival. KidsFest offers a smorgasbord of munchkin-friendly shows, workshops and parties, held during the winter school holidays.

Christchurch Arts Festival PERFORMING ARTS
(www.artsfestival.co.nz; ⊙mid-Aug–mid-Sep) Month-long biennial arts extravaganza celebrating music, theatre and dance. The next festival will be held in 2019.

NZ Cup & Show Week SPORTS
(www.nzcupandshow.co.nz; ⊙Nov) Various horse races, fashion shows, fireworks and the centrepiece A&P Show, where the country comes to town. Held over a week in mid-November.

Garden City SummerTimes MUSIC
(www.summertimes.co.nz; ⊙Dec-Mar) Soak up the summer buzz at a huge array of outdoor concerts, festivals and markets.

🛏 Sleeping

🛏 City Centre

All Stars Inn on Bealey HOSTEL $
(📞03-366 6007; www.allstarsinn.com; 263 Bealey Ave; dm $34-39, d $85, with bathroom $110; 🅿@🛜) Large, well-designed rooms are the hallmark of this purpose-built complex on the city fringe. Dorms have fridges, USB points and individual lights; some have en suites, too. Private rooms are similarly well equipped. It's a 25-minute walk to the centre of town.

YHA Christchurch HOSTEL $
(📞03-379 9536; www.yha.co.nz; 36 Hereford St; dm/s/d from $30/75/90; @🛜) Smart, well-run 100-plus-bed hostel conveniently located near Canterbury Museum and the Botanic Gardens. Dorms and doubles include many with en suite bathrooms. If it's full, Christchurch's other YHA is one street away (5 Worcester Blvd).

Around the World Backpackers HOSTEL $
(📞03-365 4363; www.aroundtheworld.co.nz; 314 Barbadoes St; dm $25-41, d $74-85; 🅿@🛜) Friendly, well-run hostel with good facilities, Kiwiana decor and sunny back garden (complete with hammock and barbecue). Rooms are small but clean; doubles have TVs and homey decorative touches.

Dorset House Backpackers HOSTEL $
(📞03-366 8268; www.dorset.co.nz; 1 Dorset St; dm $34, d $84-89; 🅿@🛜) 🐾 Built in 1871, this tranquil wooden villa has a sunny deck, a large regal lounge with a pool table, and great kitchen facilities. Dorms feature beds instead of bunks, and private rooms are small but spotless. It's a short stroll to Hagley Park and the Victoria St restaurant strip.

Chester Street Backpackers HOSTEL $
(📞03-377 1897; www.chesterst.co.nz; 148 Chester St E; dm/d $36/72; @🛜) This relaxed wooden villa is painted in bright colours and has a sunny front room for reading. Vinnie the house cat is a regular guest at hostel barbecues in the peaceful wee garden.

CHRISTCHURCH FOR CHILDREN

There's no shortage of kid-friendly sights and activities in Christchurch. If family fun is a priority, consider planning your travels around NZ's biggest children's festival, KidsFest. It's held every July and is chock-full of shows, workshops and parties. The annual World Buskers Festival is also bound to be a hit with young 'uns.

The impressive Margaret Mahy Family Playground (p490) is a must for anyone with small people in tow. For picnics and open-air frolicking, visit the Botanic Gardens (p486); there's a playground beside the cafe, and little kids will love riding on the Caterpillar train. Extend your nature-based experience with a wildlife encounter at Orana Wildlife Park (p488) or the Willowbank Wildlife Reserve (p488), or get them burning off excess energy in a rowing boat or kayak from the Antigua Boat Sheds (p489). Fun can be stealthily combined with education at the International Antarctic Centre (p488), the Discovery Centre at Canterbury Museum (p487) and Quake City (p482).

If the weather's good, hit the beaches at Sumner or New Brighton.

Foley Towers
HOSTEL $

(☎ 03-366 9720; www.backpack.co.nz/foley.html; 208 Kilmore St; dm $31-34, d $72, with bathroom $78; P @ 🛜) Sheltered by well-established trees, Foley Towers provides a range of well-maintained rooms and dorms encircling a quiet, flower-filled garden. Friendly, helpful staff will provide the latest local info.

★ Eco Villa
GUESTHOUSE $$

(☎ 03-595 1364; www.ecovilla.co.nz; 251 Hereford St; d $116-270, without bathroom $95-150; P 🛜) 🖋 There are only eight rooms in this beautifully renovated villa, each individually decorated with luxe fittings and muted colours. The lovely shared lounge, kitchen and dining room all emphasise the focus on sustainable, ecofriendly design, as does the lush edible garden (with twin outdoor bathtubs!). Be sure to try the delicious vegan breakfasts (per person $20).

BreakFree on Cashel
HOTEL $$

(☎ 03-360 1064; www.breakfreeoncashel.co.nz; 165 Cashel St; d $115-248; P 🛜) 🖋 This large, modern hotel in the heart of the CBD has options to suit all budgets. Rooms are compact and sharply designed, with high-tech features like smart TVs and sci-fi pod bathrooms.

Pomeroy's on Kilmore
B&B $$

(☎ 03-374 3532; www.pomeroysonkilmore.co.nz; 282 Kilmore St; r $145-195; P 🛜) Even if this cute wooden house wasn't the sister and neighbour of the city's best craft-beer pub, it would still be one of our favourites. Three of the five elegant, en suite rooms open onto a sunny garden. Rates include breakfast at Little Pom's (p497) cafe next door.

Focus Motel
MOTEL $$

(☎ 03-943 0800; www.focusmotel.com; 344 Durham St N; r $160-250; P 🛜) Sleek and centrally located, this friendly motel offers studio, one- and two-bedroom units with big-screen TVs, iPod docks, kitchenettes and super-modern decor. There's a guest barbecue and laundry, and pillow-top chocolates sweeten the deal.

CentrePoint on Colombo
MOTEL $$

(☎ 03-377 0859; www.centrepointoncolombo.co.nz; 859 Colombo St; r/apt from $155/189; P 🛜) The friendly Kiwi-Japanese management has imbued this centrally located motel with style and comfort. Little extras such as stereos, blackout curtains and spa baths (in the deluxe rooms) take it to the next level.

GAP FILLER

Starting from the ground up after the earthquakes, the Gap Filler folks fill the city's empty spaces with creativity and colour. Projects range from temporary art installations, performance spaces and gardens, to a minigolf course scattered through empty building sites, to the world's first giant outdoor arcade game. Gaps open up and get filled, so check out the Gap Map on the website (www.gapfiller.org.nz), or simply wander the streets and see what you can find.

★ George
HOTEL $$$

(☎ 03-379 4560; www.thegeorge.com; 50 Park Tce; r $490-525, ste $795-1050; P @ 🛜) 🖋 The George has 53 luxe rooms in a defiantly 1970s-looking building on the fringe of Hagley Park. Discreet staff attend to every whim, and ritzy extras include huge TVs, luxury toiletries and two highly rated in-house restaurants – Pescatore and 50 Bistro.

Hotel Montreal
HOTEL $$$

(☎ 03-943 8547; www.hotelmontreal.co.nz; 363 Montreal St; d from $550; P 🛜) Handy to all the city sights and Victoria St's restaurants, this upmarket hotel occupies a revamped apartment building. Swanky suites are boldly styled in black, grey and gold, with plush lounge areas, kitchenettes and balconies in all rooms. There's also a light-filled in-house restaurant and a gym. Good deals are available in the low season.

Heritage Christchurch
HOTEL $$$

(☎ 03-983 4800; www.heritagehotels.co.nz; 28-30 Cathedral Sq; ste $300-450; 🛜) 🖋 Still standing grandly on Cathedral Sq, the 1909 Old Government Building owes its survival to a thorough strengthening when it was converted to a hotel in the 1990s. After a three-year post-earthquake restoration its spacious suites are more elegant than ever. All have separate bedrooms and full kitchens.

🛏 Merivale

Merivale Manor
MOTEL $$

(☎ 03-355 7731; www.merivalemanor.co.nz; 122 Papanui Rd; d $169-249; P 🛜) A gracious 19th-century Victorian mansion is the hub of this elegant motel, with units both in the main house and in the more typical motel-style blocks lining the drive. Accommodation ranges from studios to two-bedroom apartments.

Fendalton

Fendalton House
B&B $$

(☑03-343 1661; www.fendaltonhouse.co.nz; 28a Kotare St; r $195; P🅿️🛜) There's only one guest room at this friendly, homestay-style B&B nestled among the leafy streets of Fendalton. Rates include a generous cooked breakfast.

Riccarton

Amber Kiwi Holiday Park
HOLIDAY PARK $

(☑03-348 3327, 0800 348 308; www.amberpark. co.nz; 308 Blenheim Rd, Riccarton; sites $43-47, units $84-220; P🅿️🛜🐾) Lovely gardens and close proximity to the city centre make this urban holiday park a great option for campervaners and campers. Tidy cabins and more spacious motel units are also available.

Lorenzo Motor Inn
MOTEL $$

(☑03-348 8074; www.lorenzomotorlodge.co.nz; 36 Riccarton Rd; d $160-175, apt $250; P✳️🛜) There's a Mediterranean vibe to this trim two-storey motel – the best of many on the busy Riccarton Rd strip. Rooms range from studios to two-bedroom apartments; some have spa baths and little balconies, or sweet sitting areas.

Roma on Riccarton
MOTEL $$

(☑03-341 2100; www.romaonriccarton.co.nz; 38 Riccarton Rd; d $143-183, apt $260; P✳️🛜) One of the many motels along the Riccarton Rd strip, this modern two-storey block offers clean, well-proportioned units ranging from studios to two-bedroom apartments.

Addington

★ Jailhouse
HOSTEL $

(☑03-982 7777, 0800 524 546; www.jail. co.nz; 338 Lincoln Rd, Addington; dm $30-39, s/d $85/89; @🛜) From 1874 to 1999 this was Addington Prison; it's now one of Christchurch's most appealing and friendly hostels. Private rooms are a bit on the small side – they don't call them cells for nothing – but there are plenty of communal spaces to relax outside of your room. Perks include a TV room, unlimited free wi-fi and bikes for rent.

Sumner

Le Petit Hotel
B&B $$

(☑03-326 6675; www.lepetithotel.co.nz; 16 Marriner St, Sumner; d $139-179; P@🛜) Relaxed coffee-and-croissant breakfasts, friendly owners, elegant furnishings and close proximity to Sumner Beach make this charming B&B a definite *oui*. Request an upstairs room with a view.

Other Suburbs

Jucy Snooze Christchurch
HOSTEL $

(☑03-903 0070; www.jucysnooze.co.nz; 5 Peter Leeming Rd; dm/d $39/129; P✳️🛜) Only a 10-minute walk from the airport, this new flashpackers offers Japanese-style capsule beds in place of traditional dorms. The 'pods' are cosy and private, with nice touches like USB-charge points and individual lights. There are also tiny but spotless double rooms, with surprisingly spacious en suites and flat-screen TVs. It's a 25-minute bus ride to the city centre.

Haka Lodge
HOSTEL $

(☑03-980 4252; www.hakalodge.com; 518 Linwood Ave, Woolston; dm/d/apt $29/79/170; P🛜) 🖋 Sprawled across three floors of a charming suburban house, Haka Lodge offers colourful bunk-free dorms and cheery doubles. Bonuses include a comfy lounge with wood-burning fireplace, large communal kitchen, and a bird-filled garden with barbecue. It's the kind of place you could happily stay awhile.

Old Countryhouse
HOSTEL $

(☑03-381 5504; www.oldcountryhousenz.com; 437 Gloucester St, Linwood; dm $36-38, d $99, with bathroom $122; P@🛜🧖) Spread between three separate villas, 2km east of Cathedral Sq, this chilled-out hostel has bright dorms, a reading lounge, and a lovely garden with native ferns and lavender. A spa pool and sauna heat things up.

Christchurch Top 10
HOLIDAY PARK $

(☑03-352 9176; www.christchurchtop10.co.nz; 39 Meadow St, Papanui; sites $30-55, units from $75, with bathroom from $85; P@🛜🧖) 🖋 Family owned and operated for nearly 50 years, this large holiday park has a wide range of accommodation along with various campervan nooks and grassy tent sites. It has a raft of facilities, including a pool, games room and bike hire. Enthusiastic staff can help with travel advice and bookings.

Airport Gateway MOTEL $$

(📞03-358 7093; www.airportgateway.co.nz; 45 Roydvale Ave, Burnside; d $160-300; P🐕🖥🛜) Handy for early flights, this large motel offers a variety of rooms with good facilities. The newer superior rooms are very comfortable; budget rooms are showing their age, but are clean and well proportioned. Airport transfer is available 24 hours a day at no extra charge.

✕ Eating

✕ City Centre

★**Supreme Supreme** CAFE $

(📞03-365 0445; www.supremesupreme.co.nz; 10 Welles St; mains breakfast $7-20, lunch $12-22; ⏱7am-3pm Mon-Fri, 8am-3pm Sat & Sun; 🍴) With so much to love, where to start? Perhaps with a cherry and pomegranate smoothie, a chocolate-fish milkshake or maybe just an exceptional espresso, alongside a fresh bagel, a goji bowl or even pulled corn-beef hash. One of NZ's original and best coffee roasters comes to the party with a right-now cafe of splendid style, form and function.

C1 Espresso CAFE $

(www.c1espresso.co.nz; 185 High St; mains $10-22; ⏱7am-10pm; 🛜) 🍴 C1 sits pretty in a grand former post office that somehow escaped the cataclysm. Recycled materials fill the interior (Victorian oak panelling, bulbous 1970s light fixtures) and tables spill onto a little square. Eggy brekkies and bagels are available all day, while sliders and curly fries slip onto the menu at lunch.

Caffeine Laboratory CAFE $

(www.caffeinelab.co.nz; 1 New Regent St; mains $10-22; ⏱7am-3pm Mon-Fri, from 8am Sat & Sun; 🍴) The small-scale, corner C-lab is hooked on coffee, but also cooks up delicious brunches like brioche French toast, house-smoked salmon or chipotle pulled pork. Around lunch, the menu switches to tasty hipster classics like fried chicken and mac 'n' cheese.

Mexicano's MEXICAN $

(📞03-365 5330; www.mexicanos.co.nz; 131 Victoria St; dishes $7-29; ⏱11.30am-late; 🍴) Spicing up Victoria St's burgeoning dining scene, this cheap and cheeky Mexican joint dishes up inauthentic but tasty tacos, fried chicken and hand-hacked guacamole alongside respectable margaritas and a volley of tequila shots. Day of the Dead decor and a retractable roof add more devil-may-care attitude.

Canterbury Cheesemongers DELI $

(📞03-379 0075; www.cheesemongers.co.nz; rear, 301 Montreal St; ⏱9am-5pm Tue-Fri, to 4pm Sat) Pop in to gather up artisanal cheese, bread and accompaniments, such as pickles and smoked salmon, then get your espresso to go and head down the road to the Botanic Gardens for the perfect picnic lunch.

★**Little High Eatery** FOOD HALL $$

(www.littlehigh.co.nz; 255 St Asaph St; dishes $5-20; ⏱7am-10pm Mon-Wed, 8am-midnight Thu-Sat, 8am-10pm Sun; 🛜) Can't decide whether you want sushi, pizza or Thai for dinner? At Little High, you won't have to choose – this stylish new food hall is home to eight different gourmet businesses, offering everything from dumplings to burgers. Stop in for your morning coffee or swing by for a late-night mojito in the beautifully outfitted space.

Unknown Chapter CAFE $$

(www.unknownchaptercoffee.co.nz; 254 St Asaph St; mains $14-22; ⏱6.30am-4pm; 🍴) Polished concrete, reclaimed timber tables, hanging plants and floor-to-ceiling windows give this newcomer an urban hipster vibe. Drop in for your morning caffeine hit, or visit at lunchtime for gourmet sandwiches, tasty salads and an irresistible cake cabinet.

Fiddlesticks MODERN NZ $$

(📞03-365 0533; www.fiddlesticksbar.co.nz; 48 Worcester Blvd; mains breakfast $12-20, lunch $20-40, dinner $25-45; ⏱8am-late Mon-Fri, from 9am Sat & Sun; 🛜) Sidle into Fiddlesticks for sophisticated, hearty meals from breakfast to supper. The cosy formal dining room is perfect for intimate dinners, but we like the glassed-in patio attached to the curvy cocktail bar – especially during weekend brunches, when you might be tempted to order a cheeky mimosa alongside your eggs.

Black Betty CAFE $$

(📞03-365 8522; www.blackbetty.co.nz; 165 Madras St; mains $14-20; ⏱7.30am-4pm Mon-Fri, from 8am Sat & Sun; 🛜) Black Betty's industrial-chic warehouse is a popular destination for students from the nearby college. Friendly service, great food and a laid-back atmosphere are all pluses, but the biggest attraction is the coffee from specialty roaster Switch Espresso – try pour-over, syphon, aeropress or traditional espresso brews.

Rangoon Ruby
BURMESE $$

(☑022 028 0920; www.facebook.com/Rangoon RubyChch; 819 Colombo St; dishes $13-21; ⏱5.30-9.30pm Mon-Sat; ☑) Rangoon Ruby is the latest iteration of longtime Christchurch fave Bodhi Tree, which has been wowing locals with the nuanced flavours of Burmese cuisine for more than a decade. Feel-good food comes in sharing-sized dishes and sings with zing. Standouts include *le pet thoke* (pickled tea-leaf salad) and *ameyda nut* (slow-cooked beef curry).

Bamboozle
ASIAN $$

(☑03-366 9991; www.bamboozlerestaurant. co.nz; 151 Cambridge Tce; mains $18-46; ⏱noon-2pm Mon-Fri & 5.30pm-late Mon-Sun) Asian fusion is the name of the game at Bamboozle, where talented chefs conjure up innovative spins on traditional dishes. Their stylish new premises is all cool green and classy glass.

Lotus Heart
VEGETARIAN $$

(☑03-377 2727; www.thelotusheart.co.nz; 363 St Asaph St; mains $14-25; ⏱7.30am-3pm Tue-Sun & 5-9pm Fri & Sat; ☑) 🌱 Run by students of Indian spiritual leader Sri Chinmoy, this colourful vegetarian eatery serves a range of cuisines, from tasty curries and dosas, to pizzas, nachos and burgers. Organic, vegan and gluten-free options abound, and you can quench your thirst with freshly squeezed juices, smoothies and a wide tea selection.

★ Twenty Seven Steps
MODERN NZ $$$

(☑03-366 2727; www.twentysevensteps.co.nz; 16 New Regent St; mains $34-40; ⏱5pm-late) 🌱 Overlooking the pastel-coloured New Regent St strip, this elegant restaurant showcases locally sourced seasonal ingredients. Mainstays include modern renditions of lamb, beef, venison and seafood, as well as outstanding risotto. Delectable desserts and friendly waitstaff seal the deal; reservations are advised.

King of Snake
ASIAN $$$

(☑03-365 7363; www.kingofsnake.co.nz; 145 Victoria St; mains $27-43; ⏱11am-late Mon-Fri, 4pm-late Sat & Sun) Dark wood, gold tiles and purple skull-patterned wallpaper fill this hip restaurant and cocktail bar with just the right amount of sinister opulence. The interesting fusion menu gainfully plunders the cuisines of Asia – from India to Korea – to delicious, if pricey, effect.

Saggio di Vino
EUROPEAN $$$

(☑03-379 4006; www.saggiodivino.co.nz; 179 Victoria St; mains $40-46; ⏱5pm-late) An elegant Italo-French restaurant that's up there with Christchurch's best. Expect delicious, modern takes on classics like duck *a l'orange* or fillet of beef, plus seasonal degustation menus (five courses from $105, with paired wines $155). The well-laden cheese trolley offers the perfect finale.

⚔ Merivale

Gatherings
MODERN NZ $$$

(☑021 02 93 5641; www.gatherings.co.nz; 2 Papanui Rd; lunch mains $10-14, dinner 5-course tasting menu $65, with matched wines $110; ⏱noon-2pm & 4-11pm Wed-Sat; ☑) 🌱 Thoughtful, seasonal vegetarian dishes are the focus at this petite restaurant on the edge of the Papanui Rd dining strip. The set five-course tasting menu changes regularly, with a focus on sustainable, local produce and unique flavour combinations. At lunch, offerings include simple but well-executed staples like grilled cheese or soup.

⚔ Riccarton

Christchurch Farmers Market
MARKET $

(www.christchurchfarmersmarket.co.nz; 16 Kahu Rd, Riccarton; ⏱9am-1pm Sat) 🌱 Held in the pretty grounds of Riccarton House (p488), this excellent farmers market offers a tasty array of organic fruit and veg, South Island cheeses and salmon, local craft beer and ethnic treats.

⚔ Addington

Addington Coffee Co-op
CAFE $

(☑03-943 1662; www.addingtoncoffee.org.nz; 297 Lincoln Rd, Addington; meals $7-22; ⏱7.30am-4pm Mon-Fri, from 9am Sat & Sun; 📶☑) You will find one of Christchurch's biggest and best cafes packed to the rafters most days. A compact shop selling fair-trade gifts jostles for attention with delicious cakes, gourmet pies, legendary breakfasts (until 2pm) and, of course, excellent coffee. An on-site launderette completes the deal for busy travellers.

Mosaic by Simo
MOROCCAN $

(☑03-338 2882; www.mosaicbysimo.co.nz; 300 Lincoln Rd, Addington; tapas & mains $8-19; ⏱9am-9pm Mon-Sat; ☑) This deli-cafe is popular for its takeaway *bocadillos* (toasted wraps filled with a huge selection of Middle

Eastern– and African-inspired fillings, sauces and toppings). Other tasty offerings include super-generous platters, *merguez* sausages and tagines.

✕ Sumner

Bohemian Bakery
BAKERY $
(☑ 021 070 6271; www.bohemianbakery.co.nz; 43 Nayland St, Sumner; pastries $4-6; ⊙ 7.30am-4pm Wed-Sun) The kitchen at this petite bakery is entirely open, so you can see the bakers at work crafting delicious yeasty treats all day long. Grab one of their famed cinnamon rolls and head to the beach.

✕ Other Suburbs

Kinji
JAPANESE $$
(☑ 03-359 4697; www.kinjirestaurant.com; 279b Greers Rd, Bishopdale; mains $16-24; ⊙ 5.30-10pm Mon-Sat) Despite being hidden away in suburbia, this acclaimed Japanese restaurant has a loyal following, so it's wise to book. Tuck into the likes of sashimi, grilled ginger squid and venison *tataki*, but save room for the green tea tiramisu, a surprising highlight.

Under the Red Verandah
CAFE $$
(www.utrv.co.nz; 29 Tancred St, Linwood; mains $15-25; ⊙ 7.30am-3pm Mon-Fri, 8.30am-3pm Sat & Sun; ☑) This lucky suburban backstreet boasts a lovely sunny cafe, beloved by locals and travellers alike. Take a seat under the namesake veranda and tuck into baked goodies, oaty pancakes, homemade pies and eggs multiple ways.

Burgers & Beers Inc
BURGERS $$
(www.burgersandbeersinc.co.nz; 355 Colombo St, Sydenham; burgers $14-18; ⊙ 11am-late) Quirky gourmet burgers – try the Woolly Sahara Sand Hopper (Moroccan-spiced lamb with lemon yoghurt) or the Shagged Stag (venison with plum chutney) – and an ever-changing selection of Kiwi craft beers give you reason to head south.

Hello Sunday
CAFE $$
(☑ 03-260 1566; www.hellosundaycafe.co.nz; 6 Elgin St, Sydenham; mains $13-23; ⊙ 7.30am-4.30pm Mon-Fri, from 8.30am Sat & Sun; ☎☑) Spread across two rooms of a restored old post office building, this popular cafe is a great spot for all-day brunches, spectacular salads and excellent coffee. If you're feeling decadent, try the white chocolate and peanut butter waffles, topped with vanilla candy floss – wow!

☕ Drinking & Nightlife

☕ City Centre

★ Smash Palace
BAR
(☑ 03-366 5369; www.thesmashpalace.co.nz; 172 High St; ⊙ 3pm-late Mon-Thu, from noon Fri-Sun) Epitomising the spirit of transience, tenacity and resourcefulness that Christchurch is now known for, this deliberately downcycled and ramshackle beer garden is an intoxicating mix of grease-monkey garage, trailer-trash park and proto-hipster hangout, complete with a psychedelic school bus, edible garden and blooming roses. There's craft beer, chips, Cheerios, and burgers made from scratch ($11 to $15).

★ Pomeroy's Old Brewery Inn
PUB
(☑ 03-365 1523; www.pomspub.co.nz; 292 Kilmore St; ⊙ 3pm-late Tue-Thu, from noon Fri-Sun) For fans of great beer, Pomeroy's is perfect for supping a drop or two alongside a plate of proper pork crackling. Among this British-style pub's many endearing features are regular live music, a snug, sunny courtyard and Victoria's Kitchen, serving comforting pub food (mains $25 to $40). The newest addition, pretty Little Pom's cafe, serves excellent brunch fare ($9 to $25) until mid-afternoon.

Fat Eddie's
BAR
(☑ 03-595 5332; www.fateddiesbar.co.nz; cnr Hereford St & Oxford Tce; ⊙ 2pm-late) Seven years after the quakes, jazz bar Fat Eddie's has re-opened in a brand-new building on the riverfront. With comfy couches, retro styling, a big dance floor, live music most nights and a wraparound balcony perfect for sunset drinks, there's no doubt this new iteration will be more popular than ever.

Dux Central
BAR
(☑ 03-943 7830; www.duxcentral.co.nz; 6 Poplar St; ⊙ 11am-late) Pumping a whole lot of heart back into the flattened High St precinct, the epic new Dux complex comprises a brew bar serving its own and other crafty drops, the Emerald Room wine bar, Upper Dux restaurant and the Poplar Social Club cocktail bar, all housed within the confines of a lovingly restored old building.

Boo Radley's
BAR
(☑ 03-366 9906; www.booradleys.co.nz; 98 Victoria St; ⊙ 4pm-late) An intimate, speakeasy vibe makes Boo's an alluring late-night hang-out. Southern-style decor meshes with

bourbons galore and American comfort food like sliders, fried chicken and curly fries (snacks $7 to $24). There's regular live music, too.

Merivale

Vesuvio
WINE BAR

(☑ 03-355 8530; www.vesuvio.co.nz; 4 Papanui Rd, Merivale; ⊘ 3pm-late) Half-hidden at the back of a busy cluster of eateries, this European-style wine bar is the perfect spot for a pre-dinner *aperitivo* – though the thoughtful selection of local and imported wines, excellent antipasti boards (from $19) and regular live jazz might mean you end up settling in for the night.

Riccarton

Volstead Trading Company
BAR

(www.volstead.co.nz; 55 Riccarton Rd, Riccarton; ⊘ 4-11pm Mon-Wed, from noon Thu-Sun) Tucked away inside a suburban shopping strip, this cosy bar combines comfy old sofas from your last student flat with quirky murals and a wide range of craft beers on tap. The complementary beer-food menu features tasty sliders, burritos and fried chicken.

Sumner

Village Inn
PUB

(☑ 03-326 6973; www.thevillageinnsumner.co.nz; 41b Nayland St, Sumner; ⊘ noon-late Tue-Fri, from 11am Sat & Sun) This new addition on Sumner's main shopping strip has a sunny courtyard, good pub grub (mains $16 to $22) and live music on Sunday afternoons.

Other Suburbs

The Brewery
CRAFT BEER

(www.casselsbrewery.co.nz; 3 Garlands Rd, Woolston; ⊘ 8am-late) An essential destination for beer-loving travellers, the Cassels & Sons' brewery crafts beers using a wood-fired brew kettle, resulting in big, bold ales. Tasting trays are available for the curious and the indecisive, live bands perform regularly, and the food – including wood-fired pizzas ($20 to $26) – is top-notch, too.

Allpress Espresso
COFFEE

(110 Montreal St, Sydenham; ⊘ 7.30am-3.30pm Mon-Fri) Hidden behind a nondescript facade down the industrial end of Montreal St, the Christchurch branch of this famous Kiwi coffee roastery does a mean espresso – just

as you'd expect. If you're feeling peckish, there are also fresh light lunch options and smoothies on offer.

⭐ Entertainment

For live music and club listings, see www.undertheradar.co.nz and www.christchurchmusic.org.nz.

Isaac Theatre Royal
THEATRE

(☑ 03-366 6326; www.isaactheatreroyal.co.nz; 145 Gloucester St; ⊘ box office 10am-5pm Mon-Fri) This century-old dear survived the quakes and emerged restored to full glory in 2014. Its heritage features are enjoyed by patrons venturing inside for everything from opera and ballet to contemporary theatre and rock concerts.

Alice Cinema
CINEMA

(☑ 03-365 0615; www.alice.co.nz; 209 Tuam St; adult/child $15/11) This delightful two-screen art-house cinema can be found within the long-standing and excellent Alice In Videoland video-store.

Court Theatre
THEATRE

(☑ 03-963 0870; www.courttheatre.org.nz; Bernard St, Addington; ⊘ box office 9am-8.15pm Mon-Thu, to 10.15pm Fri, 10am-10.15pm Sat) Christchurch's original Court Theatre was an integral part of the city's Arts Centre, but it was forced to relocate to this warehouse after the earthquakes. The new premises are much more spacious; it's a great venue to see popular international plays and works by NZ playwrights.

darkroom
LIVE MUSIC

(www.darkroom.bar; 336 St Asaph St; ⊘ 7pm-late Thu-Sat) A hip combination of live-music venue and bar, darkroom has lots of Kiwi beers and great cocktails. Live gigs are frequent – and frequently free.

Hollywood Cinema
CINEMA

(www.hollywoodcinema.co.nz; 28 Marriner St, Sumner; adult/child $17/12) Screens art-house and blockbuster flicks in the seaside suburb of Sumner.

AMI Stadium
STADIUM

(Rugby League Park; www.crfu.co.nz; 95 Jack Hinton Dr, Addington) After the stadium at Lancaster Park was irreparably damaged during the 2011 earthquake, Canterbury Rugby Union shifted its home games to Rugby League Park, taking the name AMI Stadium with it. The Crusaders play here from late February to July in the Super Rugby tournament, while from July to September, Canterbury plays in NZ's domestic rugby championship.

🔒 Shopping

★ **Tannery** SHOPPING CENTRE
(www.thetannery.co.nz; 3 Garlands Rd, Woolston; ⊙10am-5pm) In a city mourning the loss of its heritage, this postearthquake conversion of a 19th-century tannery couldn't be more welcome. The Victorian buildings have been beautifully restored, and are crammed with all manner of delightful boutiques selling everything from surfboards to vintage clothing to exquisite homewares.

When you're tired of shopping, stop by The Brewery (p498) for an afternoon pick-me-up. There are also several cafes and an art-house cinema on site.

Scorpio Books BOOKS
(⌚03-379 2882; www.scorpiobooks.co.nz; BNZ Centre, 120 Hereford St; ⊙9am-6pm Mon-Fri, 10am-5pm Sat & Sun) Excellent independent bookstore Scorpio Books is now back in the inner city after six years in Riccarton.

New Regent St MALL
(www.newregentstreet.co.nz) This pretty little stretch of pastel Spanish Mission–style shops was described as NZ's most beautiful street when it was completed in 1932. Fully restored post-earthquake, it's once again a delightful place to stroll, and has become something of a hub for quality cafes, bars and restaurants.

Ballantynes DEPARTMENT STORE
(www.ballantynes.com; cnr Colombo & Cashel Sts; ⊙9am-5.30pm Mon-Fri, to 5pm Sat, 10am-5pm Sun) A venerable Christchurch department store selling men's and women's fashions, cosmetics, travel goods, stationery and speciality NZ gifts.

Crossing SHOPPING CENTRE
(⌚027 506 8149; www.thecrossing.co.nz; 166 Cashel St; ⊙9am-6pm Mon-Wed, to 8pm Thu, 10am-5pm Sat & Sun) Opened in 2017, this shiny new complex fronting the Cashel St pedestrian mall is home to all manner of local and international retailers.

Colombo Mall MALL
(www.thecolombo.co.nz; 363 Colombo St, Sydenham; ⊙9am-5.30pm Mon-Sat, 10am-5pm Sun) Within walking distance of the CBD, this hip little mall is home to a few interesting, independent shops, an art-house cinema and a range of culinary delights – you'll find macarons, crêpes, dumplings, sushi, salads, craft beer and good coffee.

ℹ️ Information

EMERGENCY & IMPORTANT NUMBERS

Emergency (police, fire, ambulance)	☑111
Country code	☑64
International access code	☑00

MEDICAL SERVICES

24-Hour Surgery (☑03-365 7777; www.24hoursurgery.co.nz; 401 Madras St) No appointment necessary.

Christchurch Hospital (☑03-364 0640, emergency dept 03-364 0270; www.cdhb.govt.nz; 2 Riccarton Ave) Has a 24-hour emergency department.

Urgent Pharmacy (☑03-366 4439; cnr Bealey Ave & Colombo St; ⊙6-11pm Mon-Fri, from 9am Sat & Sun)

TOURIST INFORMATION

Airport i-SITE (☑03-741 3980; www.christchurchnz.com; International Arrivals Hall; ⊙8am-6pm)

Christchurch i-SITE (☑03-379 9629; www.christchurchnz.com; Arts Centre, 28 Worcester Blvd; ⊙8.30am-5pm)

ChristchurchNZ (www.christchurchnz.com) Official tourism website for the city and region.

DOC Visitor Centre (☑03-379 4082; www.doc.govt.nz; Arts Centre, 28 Worcester Blvd; ⊙9am-4.45pm) Information on South Island national parks, including walk and hut bookings; located within the i-SITE.

ℹ️ Getting There & Away

AIR

Christchurch Airport (CHC; ☑03-358 5029; www.christchurchairport.co.nz; 30 Durey Rd) The South Island's main international gateway, with regular flights to Australia, China, Fiji and Singapore. Facilities include baggage storage, car-rental counters, ATMs, foreign-exchange offices and an **i-SITE**.

Air New Zealand (☑0800 737 000; www.airnewzealand.co.nz) Direct flights to/from Auckland, Wellington, Dunedin and Queenstown. Code-share flights with smaller regional airlines head to/from Blenheim, Hamilton, Hokitika, Invercargill, Napier, Nelson, New Plymouth, Palmerston North, Paraparaumu, Rotorua and Tauranga.

Jetstar (☑0800 800 995; www.jetstar.com) Flies to/from Auckland and Wellington.

BUS

Tourist-oriented services generally stop outside the Canterbury Museum on Rolleston Ave; local and some long-distance services depart from the inner-city **Bus Interchange** (cnr Lichfield & Colombo Sts).

Akaroa French Connection (☑0800 800 575; www.akaroabus.co.nz; Rolleston Ave; return adult/child $50/35) Daily service to Akaroa.

Akaroa Shuttle (☑ 0800 500 929; www. akaroashuttle.co.nz; Rolleston Ave; adult/child one way $35/30, return $50/40; ⊘Oct-Apr) Daily service to Akaroa.

Atomic Shuttles (☑03-349 0697; www.atomic travel.co.nz; Lichfield St) Destinations include Picton ($40, 5¼ hours), Greymouth ($50, 3¾ hours), Timaru ($25, 2½ hours), Dunedin ($35, 5¾ hours) and Queenstown ($55, seven hours).

Budget Buses & Shuttles (☑03-615 5119; www.budgetshuttles.co.nz; Rolleston Ave; ⊘Mon-Sat) Offers a door-to-door shuttle to Geraldine ($57) and Timaru ($50), along with cheaper scheduled runs (from $27).

Hanmer Connection (☑03-382 2952, 0800 242 663; www.hanmerconnection.co.nz; Rolleston Ave; adult/child one way $30/20, return $50/30) Daily coach to/from Hanmer Springs via Amberley and Waipara.

InterCity (☑ 03-365 1113; www.intercity. co.nz; Lichfield St) New Zealand's widest and most reliable coach network. Coaches head to Timaru (from $14, 2½ hours), Dunedin (from $21, six hours), Queenstown (from $47, eight to 11 hours), Te Anau (from $63, 10¾ hours) and Picton (from $26, 5¼ hours) at least daily.

West Coast Shuttle (☑03-768 0028; www. westcoastshuttle.co.nz; Lichfield St) Daily bus to/from the West Coast stopping at Springfield ($32, 1¼ hours), Arthur's Pass ($42, 2¾ hours) and Greymouth ($55, four hours).

TRAIN

Christchurch Railway Station (www.great journeysofnz.co.nz; Troup Dr, Addington; ⊘ticket office 6.30am-3pm) is the terminus for two highly scenic train journeys, the hero of which is the TranzAlpine (p491). The other, the *Coastal Pacific*, runs along the east coast from Christchurch to Picton, stopping at Waipara, Kaikoura and Blenheim. The service was not operating at the time of research due to damage sustained in the 2016 quake, but was expected to recommence in mid-2018. Contact **Great Journeys of New Zealand** (☑0800 872 467; www.greatjourneysofnz.co.nz) for updates.

❶ Getting Around

TO/FROM THE AIRPORT

Christchurch Airport Located 10km from the city centre. A taxi into town costs $45 to $65. Alternatively, the airport is well served by public buses (www.metroinfo.co.nz). The purple line bus heads through Riccarton (20 minutes) to the central Bus Interchange (30 minutes) and on to Sumner (1¼ hours). Bus 29 heads through Fendalton (10 minutes) to the Bus Interchange (30 minutes). Both services cost $8.50 (pay the driver) and run every 30 minutes from approximately 7am to 11pm. Shuttle services are available for around $25 per person.

CAR & MOTORCYCLE

Most major car- and campervan-rental companies have offices in Christchurch, as do numerous smaller local companies. Operators with national networks often want cars from Christchurch to be returned to Auckland because most renters travel in the opposite direction, so you may find a cheaper price on a northbound route.

Local options include the following:

Ace Rental Cars (☑03-360 3270; www.ace rentalcars.co.nz; 20 Abros Pl, Burnside)

Hitch Car Rental (☑03-357 3074; www.hitch carrentals.co.nz; 545 Wairakei Rd)

New Zealand Motorcycle Rentals & Tours (☑09-486 2472; www.nzbike.com)

New Zealand Rent a Car (☑03-961 5880; www.nzrentacar.co.nz; 26b Sheffield Cres, Burnside)

Omega Rental Cars (☑03-377 4558; www. omegarentalcars.com; 158 Orchard Rd, Harewood)

Pegasus Rental Cars (☑03-358 5890; www. rentalcars.co.nz; 154 Orchard Rd, Harewood)

PUBLIC TRANSPORT

Christchurch's **Metro bus network** (☑03-366 8855; www.metroinfo.co.nz) is inexpensive, efficient and comprehensive. Most buses run from the inner-city Bus Interchange.

Pick up timetables from the i-SITE (p499) or the Interchange. Tickets (adult/child $4/2) can be purchased on board and include one free transfer within two hours. Alternatively, Metrocards allow unlimited travel for two hours/one day/one week for $2.55/5.10/25.50. Cards are available from the Interchange; they cost $10 and must be loaded with a minimum of $10 additional credit.

TAXI

Blue Star (☑03-379 9799; www.bluestartaxis. org.nz)

First Direct (☑03-377 5555; www.firstdirect. net.nz)

Gold Band (☑03-379 5795; www.goldband taxis.co.nz)

AROUND CHRISTCHURCH

Lyttelton

📞 03 / POP 3100

Southeast of Christchurch, the prominent Port Hills slope down to the city's port on Lyttelton Harbour. Christchurch's first European settlers landed here in 1850 to embark on their historic trek over the hills. Nowadays a 2km road tunnel makes the journey considerably quicker.

Lyttelton was badly damaged during the 2010 and 2011 earthquakes, and many of the town's heritage buildings along London St were subsequently demolished. Today, however, Lyttelton has re-emerged as one of Christchurch's most interesting communities. The town's arty, independent and bohemian vibe is stronger than ever, and it is once again a hub for great bars, cafes and shops. It's well worth catching the bus from Christchurch and getting immersed in the local scene, especially on a sunny Saturday morning when the farmers market's buzzing.

✕ Eating

Lyttelton Farmers Market MARKET $
(www.lyttelton.net.nz; London St; ⊙10am-1pm Sat) Every Saturday morning food stalls take the place of cars on Lyttelton's main street. Stock up alongside locals on fresh bread, baked goods, flowers, cheeses, local produce and good coffee.

Lyttelton Coffee Company CAFE $$
(📞03-328 8096; www.lytteltoncoffee.co.nz; 29 London St; mains $12-20; ⊙7am-4pm Mon-Fri, 8am-4pm Sat & Sun; 📶📷) Local institution Lyttelton Coffee Company has risen from the rubble and continues its role as a stalwart of the London St foodie scene, serving consistently great coffee and wholesome food in its cavernous, exposed-brick warehouse space.

Freemans ITALIAN $$
(📞03-328 7517; www.freemansdiningroom.co.nz; 47 London St; mains breakfast $16-18, lunch $20-27, dinner $24-39; ⊙3pm-late Wed-Fri, from 9am Sat, from noon Sun; 📷) Freemans consistently pleases with fresh pasta, top-notch pizzas, local wines and craft beers from Christchurch's Three Boys Brewery. Grab a spot on the deck for great harbour views and Sunday afternoon jazz from 3pm.

★**Roots** MODERN NZ $$$
(📞03-328 7658; www.rootsrestaurant.co.nz; 8 London St; 5-/8-/12-course degustation $90/125/185, incl wine $140/205/305; ⊙6-11pm Tue-Sat, plus noon-2pm Fri & Sat) 🍃 Let chef-owner Giulio Sturla take you on a magical tasting tour with his renowned degustation menus, which champion all things local and seasonal. Dishes can also be accompanied by carefully paired wines, should you choose to splurge. Reserve ahead.

🍷 Drinking & Nightlife

Civil and Naval BAR
(📞03-328 7206; www.civilandnaval.co.nz; 16 London St; ⊙10am-11pm Sun-Thu, to 1am Fri & Sat) Steadfast staff at this compact, bijou bar serve a quality selection of cocktails, fine wines and craft beers, while the kitchen keeps patrons civil with an eclectic range of tapas ($6 to $18).

MĀORI NZ: CHRISTCHURCH & CANTERBURY

Only 14% of NZ's Māori live on the South Island, and of those, half live in Canterbury. The first major tribe to become established here were Waitaha, who were subsequently conquered and assimilated into the Ngāti Māmoe tribe in the 16th century. In the following century, they in turn were conquered and subsumed by Ngāi Tahu (www.ngaitahu.iwi. nz), a tribe that has its origins in the East Coast of the North Island. Today, Ngāi Tahu is considered to be one of Māoridom's great success stories, with a reputation for good financial management, sound cultural advice and a portfolio including property, forestry, fisheries and many high-profile tourism operations.

There are many ways to engage in Māori culture in Canterbury. Artefacts can be seen at Canterbury Museum (p487), Akaroa Museum (p505), Okains Bay Māori & Colonial Museum (p503) and South Canterbury Museum (p519). Willowbank Wildlife Reserve (p488) in Christchurch has a replica Māori village and an evening cultural show. Further south in Timaru, the Te Ana Māori Rock Art Centre (p519) has interactive displays and arranges tours to see centuries-old work in situ.

Governors Bay Hotel · PUB

(☑ 03-329 9433; www.governorsbayhotel.co.nz; 52 Main Rd, Governors Bay; ⊙ 11am-late; ⛾) A scenic 9km drive from Lyttelton is one of NZ's oldest operational pubs (1870). You couldn't ask for a more inviting deck and garden in which to quaff an afternoon tipple. The food is good, too, covering all the classic pub-grub bases (mains $25 to $39).

Upstairs are chicly renovated rooms with shared bathrooms (double rooms $119 to $169).

Wunderbar · BAR

(☑ 03-328 8818; www.wunderbar.co.nz; 19 London St; ⊙ 5pm-late Mon-Fri, 1pm-3am Sat & Sun) Wunderbar is a top spot to get down, with regular live music covering all spectra, and clientele to match. The kooky decor and decapitated dolls' heads alone are worth the trip. Enter via the stairs in the rear car park.

🛍 Shopping

London St Bookshop · BOOKS

(48 London St; ⊙ 10am-4pm Tue-Sun) Dimly lit and crammed full of intriguing volumes, this charming second-hand bookshop is a bibliophile's dream.

Henry Trading · ARTS & CRAFTS

(☑ 03-328 8088; www.henrytrading.co.nz; 33 London St; ⊙ 10am-4pm Tue-Sun) This tiny but perfectly curated store stocks a range of lovely homewares and gifts, many made by local producers, as well as a sweet line in artisanal Lyttelton souvenirs.

ℹ Information

Lyttelton Visitor Information Centre (☑ 03-328 9093; www.lytteltonharbour.info; 20 Oxford St; ⊙ 10am-4pm) Friendly staff can provide information on accommodation, local walks and ferry departures.

ℹ Getting There & Away

Lyttelton is 15km from Christchurch CBD via the Lyttelton Tunnel. At the time of writing, Summit Rd between Sumner and Lyttelton was still closed.

Bus Buses 28 and 535 run from Christchurch to Lyttelton (adult/child $4/2, 30 minutes).

Ferry From Lyttelton, **Black Cat** (☑ 03-328 9078; www.blackcat.co.nz; 5 Norwich Quay) provides ferries to sheltered Quail Island (adult/child return $30/15, 10 minutes, once daily October to April only), as well as to sleepy Diamond Harbour (adult/child one way $6.50/3.20, 10 minutes, hourly).

Banks Peninsula

☑ 03 / POP 4750

Gorgeous Banks Peninsula (Horomaka) was formed by two giant volcanic eruptions about eight million years ago. Harbours and bays radiate out from the peninsula's centre, giving it an unusual cogwheel shape. The historic town of Akaroa, 80km from Christchurch, is a highlight, as is the absurdly beautiful drive along Summit Rd around the edge of one of the original craters. It's also worth exploring the little bays that dot the peninsula's perimeter.

The waters around Banks Peninsula are home to the smallest and one of the rarest dolphin species, the Hector's dolphin, found only in NZ waters. A range of tours depart from Akaroa to spot these and other sealife, including white-flippered penguins, orcas and seals.

History

James Cook sighted the peninsula in 1770, believing it to be an island. He named it after the naturalist Sir Joseph Banks.

In 1831, Onawe *pa* (fortified village) was attacked by the Ngāti Toa chief Te Rauparaha and in the massacres that followed, the local Ngāi Tahu population was dramatically reduced. Seven years later, whaling captain Jean Langlois negotiated the purchase of Banks Peninsula from the survivors and returned to France to form a trading company. With French-government backing, 63 settlers headed for the peninsula in 1840, but only days before they arrived, panicked British officials sent their own ship to raise the flag at Akaroa, claiming British sovereignty under the Treaty of Waitangi. Had the settlers arrived two years earlier, the entire South Island could have become a French colony, and NZ's future might have been quite different.

The French did settle at Akaroa, but in 1849 their land claim was sold to the New Zealand Company, and in 1850 a large group of British settlers arrived. The heavily forested land was cleared and soon farming became the peninsula's main industry.

◉ Sights

Hinewai Reserve · FOREST

(www.hinewai.org.nz; 632 Long Bay Rd) 🍃 Get a glimpse of what the peninsula once looked like with a stroll through this privately owned 1250-hectare nature reserve, which has been replanted with native forest. Pick

Banks Peninsula

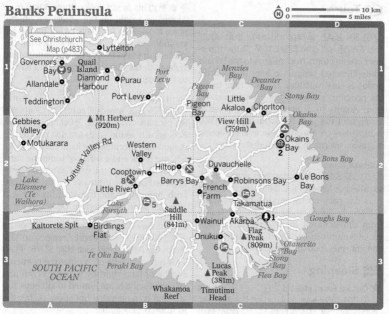

up a map outlining the walking tracks at the visitor centre, a short walk from the main entrance.

Okains Bay Māori & Colonial Museum MUSEUM
(www.okainsbaymuseum.co.nz; 1146 Okains Bay Rd, Okains Bay; adult/child $10/2; ⊙10am-5pm) Northeast of Akaroa, this museum has a respectable array of European pioneer artefacts, but it is the nationally significant Māori collection, featuring a replica *wharenui* (meeting house), *waka* (canoes), stone tools and personal adornments, that make this a worthwhile detour. Note the cute shop down the road.

🏃 Activities

Akaroa i-SITE (p508) stocks pamphlets on walks around Akaroa township, taking in the old cottages, churches and gardens that lend Akaroa its character. The six-hour Skyline Circuit also starts from town, and there are many more rewarding walks throughout the peninsula.

Banks Peninsula Track TRAMPING
(☑03-304 7612; www.bankstrack.co.nz; 2-/3-days from $195/260; ⊙Oct-Apr) This privately owned and maintained 29km three-day tramp traverses farmland and forest along the dramatic coast east of Akaroa. Fees include transport

Banks Peninsula

◎ Sights
1 Hinewai Reserve.................................C3
2 Okains Bay Māori & Colonial Museum...C2

🛏 Sleeping
3 Coombe Farm...................................C2
4 Okains Bay Camping Ground............C2
5 Okuti Garden....................................B2
6 Onuku Farm Hostel..........................C3

🍴 Eating
7 Hilltop Tavern.................................B2
8 Little River Cafe & Gallery................B2

🍷 Drinking & Nightlife
9 Governors Bay Hotel.........................A1

from Akaroa and hut accommodation. The two-day option covers the same ground only faster, for experienced hikers.

Bone Dude ART
(☑03-329 0947; www.thebonedude.co.nz; 111 Poranui Beach Rd, Birdlings Flat; from $60; ⊙1-4pm Fri, 10am-1pm Sat) Creative types should consider booking a session with the Bone Dude, who'll show you how to carve your own bone pendant (allow three hours). Sessions are limited to seven participants, so book ahead.

⛅ Tours

Pohatu Plunge   WILDLIFE
(📞 03-304 8542; www.pohatu.co.nz; tours adult/
child $75/55, self-drive $25/12) 🚗 Runs three-
hour evening tours from Akaroa to the Pohatu
white-flippered penguin colony (a self-drive
option is also available). The best time to see
the penguins is during the breeding season
from August to January, but it is possible
throughout the year. Sea kayaking and 4WD
nature tours are also available, as is the option
of staying overnight in a secluded cottage.

Tuatara Tours   WALKING
(📞 03-962 3280; www.tuataratours.co.nz; per person $1695; ⊙ Nov-Apr) You'll only need to carry
your day pack on the guided Akaroa Walk,
a leisurely 39km, three-day guided tramp
from Christchurch to Akaroa via the gorgeous Summit Ridge. Good accommodation
and gourmet food are included.

🛏 Sleeping

⭐ **Onuku Farm Hostel**   HOSTEL $
(📞 03-304 7066; www.onuku.co.nz; Hamiltons Rd,
Onuku; sites per person from $12.50, dm/d from
$20/70; ⊙ Oct-Apr; 🅿 @ 📶) Set on a working
farm 6km south of Akaroa, this blissfully
isolated backpackers has a grassy camping
area, simple, tidy rooms in a farmhouse and
'stargazer' cabins with translucent roofing
($40 for two, BYO bedding). Tonga Hut af-
fords more privacy and breathtaking sea
views ($80). Ask about the swimming-with-
dolphins tours (from $110), kayaking trips
(from $40) and the Skytrack walk.

⭐ **Halfmoon Cottage**   HOSTEL $
(📞 03-304 5050; www.halfmoon.co.nz; SH75, Barrys Bay; dm/s/d $33/64/80; ⊙ closed Jun-Aug;

LITTLE RIVER TRAIL

One of the Great Rides of the NZ Cycle
Trail, this easy-graded, 49-km cycle
trail (www.littleriverrailtrail.co.nz)
runs from Hornby, on the outskirts of
Christchurch, to Little River at the base
of the Banks Peninsula. It rolls across
rural plains, past weathered peaks and
along the shores of Lake Ellesmere –
home to NZ's most diverse bird population – and its smaller twin, Lake Forsyth.
The best section of track can be enjoyed
as a return ride from Little River, where
there is a cafe and bike hire.

🅿 @ 📶) This pretty 1896 cottage, 12km from
Akaroa and right on the water, is a blissful
place to spend a few days lazing on the big
verandas or in the hammocks dotting the
gardens. It offers proper home comforts and
style, with the bonus of bicycles and kayaks
to take exploring.

Okuti Garden   HOSTEL $
(📞 03-325 1913; www.okuti.co.nz; 216 Okuti Valley
Rd; per adult/child $50/25; ⊙ Oct-Apr; 🅿 📶) 🚗
Ecologically sound creds are just part of this
delightfully eccentric package that includes
a house truck and a series of romantic yurts
dotted throughout colourful gardens. Freshly picked herbs, a pizza oven, a fire-warmed
bath, hammocks and free-roaming chickens
give this place some serious *Good Life* vibes.

Okains Bay Camping Ground   CAMPGROUND $
(📞 03-304 8789; www.okainsbaycamp.co.nz; 1357
Okains Bay Rd; sites per adult/child $12/6; 🅿 🚿)
This tidy camp sits on a pine-tree-peppered
swathe of land right by a lovely beach and
estuary. Facilities are limited to kitchens, toilets and coin-operated hot showers, but the
location is unbeatable.

Coombe Farm   B&B $$
(📞 03-304 7239; www.coombefarm.co.nz; 18 Old
Le Bons Track, Takamatua Valley; d $180-220; 🅿 📶)
Choose between the private and romantic
Shepherd's Hut – complete with outdoor
bath – or the historic farmhouse lovingly re-
stored in shades of Laura Ashley. After a luxe
breakfast you can take a walk to the nearby
waterfall, or drive the five minutes into Akaroa.

🍴 Eating

Little River Cafe & Gallery   CAFE $
(📞 03-325 1944; www.littlerivergallery.com; SH75,
Little River; mains $13-22; ⊙ 7.30am-4pm Mon-
Fri, to 4.30pm Sat & Sun) On SH75 between
Christchurch and Akaroa, the flourishing set-
tlement of Little River is home to this fantastic
combo of contemporary art gallery, shop and
cafe. It's top-notch in all departments, with
some particularly delectable home baking on
offer as well as yummy deli goods to go.

Barrys Bay Cheese   CHEESE $
(📞 03-304 5809; www.barrysbaycheese.co.nz;
5807 Christchurch-Akaroa Rd; cheese $7-11;
⊙ 9am-5pm) This award-winning cheese fac-
tory has a small store attached where you
can taste its cheesy goodness and pick up
supplies for seaside picnics. Large windows
give you a sneak peek into where the magic
happens. It's 12km from Akaroa.

★ **Hilltop Tavern** PUB FOOD $$
(☑ 03-325 1005; www.thehilltop.co.nz; 5207 Christchurch-Akaroa Rd; pizzas $24-26, mains $22-30; ☺ 10am-late, reduced hours May-Sep) Craft beer, wood-fired pizzas, a pool table and occasional live bands seal the deal for locals and visitors alike at this historic pub. Enjoy stunning views of Akaroa harbour and the peninsula – especially at sunset.

❶ Getting There & Away

From October to April the Akaroa Shuttle (p500) runs daily services from Christchurch to Akaroa (departing at 8.30am), returning to Christchurch at 3.45pm. Check the website for Christchurch pick-up options. Scenic tours from Christchurch exploring Banks Peninsula are also available.

Akaroa French Connection (p500) has a year-round daily departure from Christchurch at 9am, returning from Akaroa at 4pm.

Akaroa

☑ 03 / POP 624

Akaroa (Long Harbour) was the site of the country's first French settlement and descendants of the original French pioneers still reside here. It's a charming town that strives to recreate the feel of a French provincial village, down to the names of its streets and houses. Generally it's a sleepy place, but the peace is periodically shattered by hordes descending from gargantuan cruise ships. The ships used to dock in Lyttelton but since the earthquakes Akaroa has been a popular substitute. Even when Lyttelton's back on its feet, the ships will be reluctant to leave.

◎ Sights

★ **Giant's House** GARDENS
(www.thegiantshouse.co.nz; 68 Rue Balguerie; adult/child $20/10; ☺ 12-5pm Jan-Apr, 2-4pm May-Dec) An ongoing labour of love by local artist Josie Martin, this whimsical garden is really one giant artwork, a combination of sculpture and mosaics that cascades down a hillside above Akaroa. Echoes of Gaudí and Miró can be found in the intricate collages of mirrors, tiles and broken china, and there are many surprising nooks and crannies to discover. Martin also exhibits her paintings and sculptures in the lovely 1880 house, the former residence of Akaroa's first bank manager.

★ **Akaroa Museum** MUSEUM
(www.akaroamuseum.org.nz; cnr Rues Lavaud & Balguerie; ☺ 10.30am-4.30pm) FREE An arduous post-quake revamp has rewarded Akaroa with a smart, contemporary regional museum. Learn about the various phases of the peninsula's settlement, from the Māori to the French, and view interesting temporary exhibitions. The 20-minute historical film screening in the adjacent restored courthouse is worth a look, too. Note the donation box.

Old French Cemetery CEMETERY
The first consecrated burial ground in Canterbury, this hillside monument makes for a poignant wander. Follow the trail (up the hill) off Rue Brittan.

St Patrick's Catholic Church CHURCH
(www.akaroacatholicparish.co.nz; 29 Rue Lavaud; ☺ 8am-7pm) Akaroa's Catholic church (1863) is a cute, frilly edged old dear, featuring richly coloured stained glass imported from Stuttgart.

St Peter's Anglican Church CHURCH
(46 Rue Balguerie) Graciously restored in 2015, this 1864 Anglican gem features extensive exposed timbers, stained glass and an historic organ. Well worth a peek whether you're godly or not.

⭐ Activities

Akaroa Adventure Centre OUTDOORS
(☑ 03-304 7784; www.akaroa.com; 74a Rue Lavaud; ☺ 9am-5pm) Rents sea kayaks and stand-up paddle boards (per hour/day $20/60), paddle boats (per hour $30), bikes (per hour/day $15/65) and fishing rods (per day $10). Based at the i-SITE (p508); open later in summer (December through March).

☞ Tours

Akaroa Guided Sea Kayaking Safari KAYAKING
(☑ 021 156 4591; www.akaroakayaks.com; per person from $115) Paddle serenely around the harbour on these guided kayaking tours, which cater for beginners and experienced paddlers alike. Slip into the water at 7.30am for a three-hour sunrise safari, or if early starts aren't your thing, try the 11.30am highlights tour.

Eastern Bays Scenic Mail Run DRIVING
(☑ 03-304 8526; tours $80; ☺ departs 9am Mon-Fri) Travel along with the ex-conservation-ranger postie to visit isolated communities and bays on this 120km, five-hour mail delivery service. Departs from the i-SITE (p508); bookings are essential as there are only eight seats available.

Akaroa

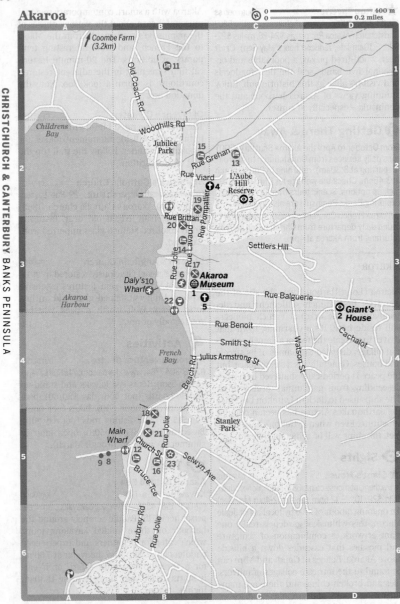

Black Cat Cruises BOATING
(☎03-304 7641; www.blackcat.co.nz; Main Wharf; nature cruises adult/child $75/30, dolphin swims adult/child $160/130) As well as a two-hour nature cruise, Black Cat offers a three-hour 'swimming with dolphins' experience. Wetsuits and snorkelling gear are provided, plus hot showers back on dry land. Observers can tag along (adult/child $85/45) but only 12 people can swim per trip, so book ahead.

Akaroa

Akaroa Dolphins
BOATING

(☑ 03-304 7866; www.akaroadolphins.co.nz; 65 Beach Rd; adult/child $80/40; ⊙12.45pm year-round, plus 10.15am & 3.15pm Oct-Apr) Two-hour wildlife cruises on a comfortable 50ft catamaran, complete with a complimentary drink, home baking and, most importantly, the company of an extraordinary wildlife-spotting dog.

Fox II Sailing
BOATING

(☑ 0800 369 7245; www.akaroafoxsail.co.nz; Daly's Wharf; adult/child $80/40; ⊙ departs 10.30am & 1.30pm Jan-May) Enjoy the scenery, observe the marine wildlife, learn some history and try your hand at sailing on *Fox II*, a gaff-rigged ketch built in 1922.

Akaroa Sailing Cruises
BOATING

(☑ 0800 724 528; www.aclasssailing.co.nz; Main Wharf; adult/child $75/37.50; ⊙ departs 10.15am & 1.15pm Oct–mid-May) Set sail for a 2½-hour hands-on cruise around the harbour on a gorgeous 1946 A-Class yacht.

✨ Festivals & Events

French Fest
FOOD & DRINK

(www.akaroa.com/akaroa-french-fest; ⊙Oct) This Gallic-inspired, two-day celebration features historical re-enactments, markets, activities and – *bien sûr* – plenty of food and wine. It's held biennially in odd-numbered years.

⊟ Sleeping

Chez la Mer
HOSTEL $

(☑ 03-304 7024; www.chezlamer.co.nz; 50 Rue Lavaud; dm $34, d $76, with bathroom $86; ☎) Pretty in pink, this historic building houses a friendly backpackers with well-kept rooms and a shaded garden, complete with fish pond, hammocks and barbecue. There's also a cosy lounge and kitchen, and free bikes for loan.

Akaroa Top 10 Holiday Park
HOLIDAY PARK $

(☑ 0800 727 525, 03-304 7471; www.akaroa-holiday park.co.nz; 96 Morgans Rd; sites $40-47, units $82-125; @☎☎⚑) Grandstand views of the harbour and peninsula hills are the main drawcard at this basic holiday park. Cabins and motel units are dated but tidy, while the facilities blocks are due for an overhaul.

Akaroa Village Inn
APARTMENTS $$

(☑ 03-304 1111; www.akaroavillageinn.co.nz; 81 Beach Rd; units $135-245; P☎) Right on the harbour front, this sprawling complex offers one- and two-bedroom units of varying levels of luxury. The water-view apartments are obviously the pick of the bunch, but ask to see a few, as they are individually owned, and furnishings vary widely.

La Rochelle
MOTEL $$

(☑ 03-3048762, 0800452762; www.larochellemotel. co.nz; 1 Rue Grehan; d/q $170/260; P☎) Tidy, modern and reasonably priced, La Rochelle has a range of compact motel units within walking distance of the main village. Each room has a kitchenette and opens onto a small private patio or balcony.

Tresori Motor Lodge
MOTEL $$

(☑ 03-304 7500; www.tresori.co.nz; cnr Rue Jolie & Church St; d $135-205; ☎) There are 12 tidy, modern units at this friendly motel set one block back from the esplanade. All have kitchenettes, but given the proximity to Akaroa's cafe and restaurant strip, you needn't worry about using them.

★ Beaufort House
B&B $$$

(☑ 03-304 7517; www.beauforthouse.co.nz; 42 Rue Grehan; r $395; ☺ closed Jun-Aug; P ☎) Tucked away on a quiet street behind gorgeous gardens, this lovely 1878 house is adorned with covetable artwork and antiques. Of the five individually decorated rooms only one is without an en suite, compensated by a large private bathroom with a claw-foot tub just across the hall. A lovely breakfast is included.

✖ Eating

Peninsula General Store
CAFE, DELI $

(☑ 03-304 8800; www.peninsulageneralstore.co.nz; 40 Rue Lavaud; ☺ 9am-4pm Thu-Mon) Not only does this darling little corner store sell fresh bread, organic local produce and groceries, it also does the best espresso in the village.

Akaroa Boucherie & Deli
DELI $

(67 Rue Lavaud; ☺ 10am-5.30pm Mon-Fri, 9am-4pm Sat) A dream scenario for picnickers and self-caterers, this sharp butcher's shop and deli peddles all manner of local produce from bread, salmon, cheese and pickles, to delicious pies, smallgoods and, of course, meat.

Akaroa Fish & Chips
FISH & CHIPS $

(59 Beach Rd; meals $10-20; ☺ 11am-7.30pm) This is a suitably salty seaside location for tucking into blue cod, scallops, oysters and other deep-fried goodies. You can eat in or take your prize across the road to the harbour's edge. Either way, expect to be circled by seagulls.

Trading Rooms
FRENCH $$$

(☑ 03-304 7656; www.thetradingrooms.co.nz; 71 Beach Rd; mains lunch $19-29, dinner $28-39; ☺ 10am-3pm Thu-Mon, 5-10pm Fri-Mon) Decked out in francophile dark timbers and burgundy, this is an atmospheric spot to linger over a refined meal. French cuisine such as snails

and cassoulet dominate, although at lunch the Gallic guard drops a little to reveal burgers and gourmet club sandwiches.

Little Bistro
FRENCH $$$

(☑ 03-304 7314; www.thelittlebistro.co.nz; 33 Rue Lavaud; mains $22-40; ☺ 5.30-11pm Tue-Sat) A decent bet for refined food, this place serves a classic bistro-style menu featuring local seafood, South Island wines and Canterbury craft beers. The menu changes seasonally, but usually includes favourites such as crusted lamb or local salmon.

🍷 Drinking & Nightlife

Harbar
BAR

(83 Rue Jolie; ☺ 5-9.30pm) Sporadic opening hours, dictated by weather and demand, should not deter you from attempting a sundowner at Akaroa's favourite waterside bar. There's no better location for a summer evening (December to March).

☆ Entertainment

Akaroa Cinema & Café
CINEMA

(☑ 03-304 8898; www.cinecafe.co.nz; cnr Rue Jolie & Selwyn Ave; adult/child $15/10) Grab a beer and settle in to watch an art-house, classic or foreign flick with high-quality sound and projection.

ⓘ Information

Akaroa i-SITE & Adventure Centre (☑ 03-304 7784; www.akaroa.com; 74a Rue Lavaud; ☺ 9am-5pm) A helpful hub offering free maps, info and bookings for activities, transport etc. Doubles as the post office.

ⓘ Getting There & Away

From October to April the Akaroa Shuttle (p500) runs daily services from Christchurch to Akaroa (departs 8.30am), returning to Christchurch at 3.45pm. Check the website for Christchurch pick-up options. Scenic tours from Christchurch exploring Banks Peninsula are also available.

Akaroa French Connection (p500) has a year-round daily departure from Christchurch at 9am, returning from Akaroa at 4pm.

NORTH CANTERBURY

South of Kaikoura, SH1 crosses the Hundalee Hills and heads into Hurunui District, an area known for its wine and for the thermal resort of Hanmer Springs. It's also the start of the Canterbury Plains, a vast, flat, richly agricultural area partitioned by distinctive braided rivers. The region is bounded to the west by the Southern Alps. If you're crossing into Canterbury from either Westport or Nelson, the most direct route cuts through the Alps on the beautiful Lewis Pass Hwy (SH7).

Lewis Pass

The northernmost of the three main mountain passes connecting the West Coast to the east, 864m-high Lewis Pass is not as steep as the others (Arthur's and Haast), but the drive is arguably just as scenic. Vegetation comprises mainly beech (red and silver) and kowhai trees growing along river terraces.

After the closure of SH1 north of Kaikoura due to the November 2016 earthquake, Lewis Pass became the main route between Picton and Christchurch. (The SH1 was still closed at the time of research, though it was due to reopen in late 2017.) From Lewis Pass the highway wiggles east for 62km before reaching the turn-off to Hanmer Springs.

⊙ Sights

Marble Hill   FOREST
(www.doc.govt.nz; SH7) Located within Lewis Pass Scenic Reserve, Marble Hill is home to one of NZ's most beautiful DOC camping grounds – a row of sites tucked into beech forest, overlooking a grassy meadow and encircled by snow-capped mountains.

This special place represents a landmark victory for NZ's conservation movement. Back in the 1970s, this significant forest was saved from the chop by a 341,159-signature petition known as the 'Maruia Declaration', which played a part in the Department of Conservation's establishment in 1987.

⚡ Activities

The area has some interesting **tramps**, passing through beech forest backed by snow-capped mountains, lakes and alpine tarns. Popular tracks include the **St James Walkway** (66km; four to five days) and those through **Lake Sumner Forest Park**; see the DOC pamphlet *Lake Sumner & Lewis Pass* ($2). Subalpine conditions apply; make sure you sign the intentions books at the huts.

Maruia Springs   HOT SPRINGS
(☑ 03-523 8840; www.maruiasprings.co.nz; SH7; adult/child $40/18; ⊙ 8am-9pm) Maruia Springs is a small hot spring resort on the banks of the Maruia River. The water temperature varies between 36°C and 42°C across a variety of pools, including outdoor rock pools, indoor baths, a sauna and a cold plunge pool. It's a magical setting during winter (June to September) but mind the sandflies in summer (December to March).

❶ Getting There & Away

East West Coaches (☑ 03-789 6251; www.eastwestcoaches.co.nz) runs between Christchurch and Westport via the Lewis Pass daily except Saturday (adult/child $60/45, five hours), stopping at Maruia Springs and the St James Walkway.

Hanmer Springs

☑ 03 / POP 840

Ringed by mountains, pretty Hanmer Springs has a slightly European feel, enhanced by the fact that many of the streets are named after English spa towns (Bath, Harrogate, Leamington). The town is the main thermal resort on the South Island, and it's a pleasantly low-key spot to indulge yourself, whether by soaking in hot pools, dining out, or being pampered in the spa complex. If that all sounds too soporific, fear not; there are plenty of family-friendly outdoor activities on offer, including a few to get the adrenaline pumping.

⚡ Activities

★ **Hanmer Springs Thermal Pools**   HOT SPRINGS
(☑ 03-315 0000; www.hanmersprings.co.nz; 42 Amuri Ave; adult/child $24/12, locker per 2hr $2; ⊙ 10am-9pm; ⛹) ✎ Māori legend has it that these hot springs are the result of embers from Mt Ngauruhoe in the North Island falling from the sky. Whatever their origin, visitors flock to Hanmer Springs year-round to soak in the warming waters. The main complex consists of a series of large pools of various temperatures.

Hanmer Forest Park   TRAMPING, MOUNTAIN BIKING
(www.visithurunui.co.nz) Trampers and mountain bikers will find plenty of room to move within the 130 sq km expanse of forest abutting Hanmer Springs. The easy Woodland Walk starts 1km up Jollies Pass Rd and goes through Douglas fir, poplar and redwood stands before joining Majuba Walk, which leads to Conical Hill Lookout and then back towards town (1½ hours).

The Waterfall Track is an excellent half-day tramp starting at the end of McIntyre

Hanmer Springs

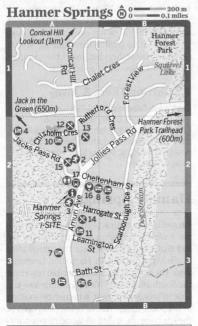

Hanmer Springs

Rd. The i-SITE (p512) stocks a *Forest Park Walks* booklet and a mountain-biking map (both $3).

Hanmer Springs Spa
SPA

(☏ 03-3150029, 0800873529; www.hanmersprings.co.nz; 42 Amuri Ave; ☺10am-7pm) If you're looking to be pampered, you've come to the right place. Hanmer Springs Spa offers every kind of treatment you would expect from an international-standard spa, from facials (from $90) to hot-stone massages ($180) to full-body treatments ($320).

Mt Lyford Alpine Resort
SKIING

(☏ 0274 710 717, 03-366 1220; www.mtlyford.co.nz; day passes adult/child $75/35; ☺lifts 9am-4pm) Around 60km from both Hanmer Springs and Kaikoura, this is more of a 'resort' than most NZ ski fields, with accommodation and eating options. There's a good mix of runs and a terrain park.

A shuttle service runs from Mt Lyford village (a 45-minute drive from Hanmer Springs) during the season – enquire at **Hanmer Springs Adventure** (☏0800 368 7386, 03-315 7233; www.hanmeradventure.co.nz; 20 Conical Hill Rd; ☺9am-5pm).

Hanmer Springs Ski Area
SKIING

(☏ 027 434 1806; www.skihanmer.co.nz; day passes adult/child/family $60/30/130) Only 17km from town via an unsealed road, this small complex has runs to suit all levels of ability. The Adventure Centre provides shuttles during the ski season (adult/child return $40/32) and also has gear for rent.

Hanmer Springs Attractions
ADVENTURE SPORTS

(☏03-3157046, 0800661538; www.welcomeaboard.co.nz; 839 Hanmer Springs Rd; ☺9am-5pm) Bungy off a 35m-high bridge ($169), jet-boat the Waiau Gorge (one hour, adult/child $125/70), explore the Waiau River in a raft (two hours, adult/child $169/99) or inflatable canoe (five hours, adult/child $249/169), or get dirty on a quad bike (two hours, adult/child $169/99). The activities base is next to the bridge near the turn-off from SH7, but there's also a **booking office** (☏03-315 7346, 0800 661 538; www.welcomeaboard.co.nz; 12 Conical Hill Rd; ☺9am-5pm) in town.

Sleeping

Hanmer Springs has a wide range of accommodation options, from basic camping through to luxury B&Bs and swanky apartments. If you're planning on staying awhile, check out websites like www.alpineholiday homes.co.nz and www.hanmerholidayhomes. co.nz for local rentals.

Kakapo Lodge
HOSTEL **$**

(☑03-315 7472; www.kakapolodge.co.nz; 14 Amuri Ave; dm $33, d $76, with bathroom $95; P⓪) The YHA-affiliated Kakapo has a cheery owner, a roomy kitchen and lounge, chill-busting underfloor heating and a 1st-floor sundeck. Bunk-free dorms (some with bathrooms) and spotless double rooms are available.

Jack in the Green
HOSTEL **$**

(☑03-315 5111; www.jackinthegreen.co.nz; 3 Devon St; sites per person $20, dm $32, d $76, with bathroom $92; P⓪) This charming converted old home is a 10-minute walk from the town centre. Large rooms (no bunks), relaxing gardens and a cosy lounge area are the main drawcards. For extra privacy, book an en suite garden 'chalet'.

Hanmer Springs Top 10
HOLIDAY PARK **$**

(☑03-315 7113, 0800 904 545; www.hanmersprings top10.co.nz; 5 Hanmer Springs Rd; sites $40-48, units from $89, with bathroom from $145; P@⓪⛺) This family-friendly park is just a few minutes' walk from the town's eponymous pools. Kids will love the playground and jumping pillow. Take your pick from basic cabins (BYO everything) to attractive motel units with everything supplied.

★Woodbank Park Cottages
COTTAGE **$$**

(☑03-315 5075; www.woodbankcottages.co.nz; 381 Woodbank Rd; d $190-225; P✱) Nestled among the trees, these two plush cottages are a six-minute drive from Hanmer but feel a million miles away. Decor is crisp and modern, with wraparound wooden decks that come equipped with gas barbecues and rural views. Log-burning fireplaces and well-stocked kitchens seal the deal.

Chalets Motel
MOTEL **$$**

(☑03-315 7097; www.chaletsmotel.co.nz; 56 Jacks Pass Rd; d $160-195; P⓪) Soak up the mountain views from these tidy, reasonably priced, freestanding wooden chalets, set on the slopes behind the town centre. All chalets have full kitchens; the larger spa unit is the pick of the bunch.

Scenic Views
MOTEL **$$**

(☑03-315 7419, 0800 843 974; www.hanmer scenicviews.co.nz; 2 Amuri Ave; d $160-235, apt from $245; P✱⓪⛺) An attractive timber-and-stone complex offering modern stu-

dios and apartments, most with sunny balconies or patios. Try for one of the two spa rooms, which have heavenly mountain views.

Rosie's
B&B **$$**

(☑03-315 7095; www.rosiesbandbhanmer.co.nz; 9 Cheltenham St; s/d $90/140; P⓪) Rosie has left the building but the hospitality continues at this homey, good-value B&B. Guests have use of a cosy shared lounge and kitchen; rates include a continental breakfast.

Tussock Peak Motor Lodge
MOTEL **$$**

(☑03-315 5191, 0800 887 762; www.tussockpeak. co.nz; 2 Leamington St; d $160-180; ⓪) Modern, spotless and central, Tussock Peak has colourful decor and friendly service. Units come in studio or one- and two-bedroom incarnations; some have spa baths and balconies.

Cheltenham House
B&B **$$$**

(☑03-315 7545; www.cheltenham.co.nz; 13 Cheltenham St; r $235-280; P⓪) This large 1930s house has room for both a billiard table and a grand piano. There are four art-filled suites in the main house and two in cosy garden cottages. Cooked gourmet breakfasts are delivered to the rooms and wine is served in the evening.

St James
APARTMENT **$$$**

(☑0508 785 2637, 03-315 5225; www.thestjames. co.nz; 20 Chisholm Cres; d $225-270, apt from $320; P✱⓪) Luxuriate in a stylish modern apartment with all the mod cons, including an iPod dock and fully equipped kitchen. Sizes range from studios to two-bedroom apartments; most have mountain views.

✗ Eating

Hanmer Springs Bakery
BAKERY **$**

(☑03-315 7714; www.hanmerbakery.co.nz; 16 Conical Hill Rd; pies $4.80-5.80, rolls from $4.50; ⊙6am-4pm) In peak season queues stretch out the door for this humble bakery's meat pies and filled rolls.

Coriander's
INDIAN **$$**

(☑03-315 7616; www.corianders.co.nz; Chisholm Cres; mains $16-22; ⊙noon-2pm & 5-10pm Tue-Sun, 5-10pm Mon; ☑) Spice up your life at this brightly painted North Indian restaurant complete with *bhangra*-beats soundtrack. There are plenty of tasty lamb, chicken and seafood dishes to choose from, plus a fine vegetarian selection. The lunch special ($14) is good value.

MOLESWORTH STATION

Filling up 1807 mountainous sq km between Hanmer Springs and Blenheim, Molesworth Station is NZ's largest farm, with the country's largest cattle herd (up to 10,000). It's also an area of national ecological significance and the entire farm is now administered by DOC (Map p415; ☑03-572 9100; www.doc.govt.nz; Gee St, Renwick).

Visits are usually only possible when the Acheron Rd through the station is open from November to early April (weather permitting; check with DOC or at the Hanmer Springs i-SITE). Note that the gates are only open from 7am to 7pm. Pick up DOC's *Molesworth Station* brochure from the i-SITE or download it from the website.

Overnight camping (adult/child $6/3) is permitted in certain areas (no open fires allowed). There are also a couple of basic DOC huts (adult/child $5/2.50).

Molesworth Heritage Tours (☑027 201 4536, 03-315 7401; www.molesworth.co.nz; tours $198-770; ☺Oct-May) leads 4WD coach trips to the station from Hanmer Springs. Day tours include a picnic lunch, but there's also a five-hour 'no frills' option. From the Blenheim side, **Molesworth Tours** (☑03-572 8025; www.molesworthtours.co.nz) offers one- to four-day all-inclusive heritage and 4WD trips ($220 to $1487), as well as four-day fully supported (and catered) mountain-bike adventures ($1460).

Powerhouse Cafe
CAFE $$

(☑03-315 5252; www.powerhousecafe.co.nz; 8 Jacks Pass Rd; brunch mains $15-24; ☺7.30am-3pm) Delicious cakes and good-quality coffee are on the menu at this local favourite, tucked away off the main street. Power up with a huge High Country breakfast or try the Highland Fling – caramelised, whisky-sodden porridge topped with banana. Lunch offerings are equally palatable.

Malabar
ASIAN $$

(☑03-315 7745; www.malabar.co.nz; 5 Conical Hill Rd; mains $28-35; ☺5-10pm Tue-Sun plus noon-2.30pm Sat) This cheery restaurant on the main drag presents Asian cuisine from Beijing to Bangalore, although the emphasis is more on the Indian. All dishes are designed to be shared; a limited takeaway menu is also available.

No. 31
MODERN NZ $$$

(☑03-315 7031; www.restaurant-no31.nz; 31 Amuri Ave; mains $37-40; ☺5-11pm) Substantial servings of good-quality, albeit conservative, cuisine are on offer in this pretty wooden cottage. The upmarket ambience befits the prices, though you're also paying for the location, directly opposite the hot springs. Book ahead on weekends.

Drinking & Nightlife

Monteith's Brewery Bar
PUB

(☑03-315 5133; www.mbbh.co.nz; 47 Amuri Ave; ☺9am-11pm) This large, slightly worn pub is the town's busiest watering hole. The kitchen serves decent pub-style meals all day (mains $22 to $35). Live musicians kick off from 4pm Sundays.

Information

Hanmer Springs i-SITE (☑03-315 0020, 0800 442 663; www.visithanmersprings.co.nz; 40 Amuri Ave; ☺10am-5pm) Books transport, accommodation and activities.

Getting There & Away

The **main bus stop** is near the corner of Amuri Ave and Jacks Pass Rd.

Hanmer Connection (p500) Runs a daily bus to/from Christchurch via Waipara and Amberley, departing Christchurch at 9am and Hanmer Springs at 4.30pm.

Hanmer Tours & Shuttle (☑03-315 7418; www.hanmertours.co.nz) runs daily buses to/from Culverden ($15, 30 minutes), Waikari ($15, 45 minutes), Waipara ($20, one hour), Amberley ($20, one hour), Christchurch city centre ($35, two hours) and Christchurch Airport ($45, two hours).

Waipara Valley

☑03 / POP 5200

Conveniently stretched along SH1 60km north of Christchurch, this resolutely rural area makes for a tasty pit stop. The valley's warm dry summers followed by cool autumn nights have proved a winning formula for growing grapes, olives, hazelnuts and lavender. While Waipara accounts for less than 3% of NZ's vines, it nonetheless produces some of the country's finest cool-climate wines, including riesling, pinot noir and gewürztraminer.

Of the region's 30 or so wineries, around a dozen have cellar doors to visit, four with restaurants. To explore the valley's bounty fully, pick up a copy of the *North Canterbury Wine Region* map (or download it from www.waiparavalleynz.com). Otherwise, you'll spot several of the big players from the highway. The area's main towns are tiny Waipara and slightly larger Amberley, but you're likely to spend most of your time in the countryside between the two.

⊙ Sights

★ Pegasus Bay   WINERY
(☑ 03-314 6869; www.pegasusbay.com; Stockgrove Rd; ⊘ restaurant noon-4pm Thu-Mon, tastings 10am-5pm daily) It's fitting that Waipara Valley's premier winery should have the loveliest setting and one of Canterbury's best restaurants (mains $34 to $43). Verdant manicured gardens set the scene, but it's the contemporary NZ menu and luscious paired wines that steal the show.

Black Estate   WINERY
(☑ 03-314 6085; www.blackestate.co.nz; 614 Omihi Rd, SH1; ⊘ 10am-5pm, shorter hours Jun-Oct) ⌘ Perched on a hillside overlooking the valley, this striking black barn is home to some excellent drops – try the pinot noirs from the winery's three nearby vineyards, each of which have a distinctive terroir of their own. The attached light-filled restaurant offers stunning views and food that champions local producers (mains $38 to $44).

Brew Moon   BREWERY
(☑ 03-314 8036; www.brewmoon.co.nz; 12 Markham St, Amberley; ⊘ 3pm-late Wed-Fri, from noon Sat & Sun) The variety of craft beers available to taste at this wee brewery never wanes. Stop in to fill a rigger (flagon) to take away, or sup an ale alongside a tasty wood-fired pizza in the cosy bar area (pizzas $10 to $20).

⌂ Sleeping & Eating

Old Glenmark Vicarage   B&B $$$
(☑ 03-314 6775; www.glenmarkvicarage.co.nz; 161 Church Rd, Waipara; d $230, barn d $210; ℗ 🕏 ☲) There are two divine options in this beautifully restored vicarage: cosy up with bed

and breakfast in the main house, or lounge around in the character-filled, converted barn that sleeps up to six (perfect for families or groups). The lovely gardens and swimming pool are a blessed bonus.

★ Little Vintage Espresso   CAFE $
(20 Markham St, Amberley; breakfast $10-19; ⊘ 7am-4pm Mon-Sat; 🕏) This petite white-washed cottage just off SH1 has the best coffee in town, with food to match. All-day breakfasts, gourmet sandwiches and delectable homemade cakes are all on offer.

Pukeko Junction   CAFE, DELI $$
(☑ 03-314 8834; www.pukekojunction.co.nz; 458 Ashworths Rd, SH1, Leithfield; mains $7.50-20; ⊘ 9am-4.30pm Tue-Sun; ⌘) A deservedly popular roadside stop, this bright, friendly cafe in Leithfield (south of Amberley) serves delicious bakery fare, like gourmet sausage rolls and tarts filled with goat's cheese, leek and walnut. The attached shop stocks an excellent selection of local wines.

❶ Getting There & Away

Hanmer Connection (p500) One daily bus stops in Waipara on request on the road between Hanmer Springs ($20, 50 minutes) and Christchurch ($20, 1¼ hours).

Hanmer Tours & Shuttle Runs a daily shuttle to/from Hanmer Springs ($20), Christchurch city centre ($15) and Christchurch Airport ($25).

InterCity (p500) Coaches head to/from Picton (from $34, seven hours), Kaikoura (from $28, 1¾ hours) and Christchurch (from $11, one hour) at least daily. Travel times to Picton will shorten once the SH1 reopens north of Kaikoura.

The *Coastal Pacific* train from Christchurch to Picton stops at Waipara; however, at the time of research the train was not running due to track damage as a result of the 2016 Kaikoura earthquake. The train is expected to resume operations in mid-2018; see www.railnewzealand.com for updates.

CENTRAL CANTERBURY

While the dead-flat agricultural heartland of the Canterbury Plains blankets the majority of the region, there's plenty of interest for travellers in the west, where the Southern Alps soar to snowy peaks. Here you'll find numerous ski fields and some brilliant wilderness walks.

Unusually for NZ, the most scenic routes avoid the coast, with most places of interest accessed from one of two spectacular roads: the Great Alpine Highway (SH73), which wends from the Canterbury Plains deep into the mountains and over to the West Coast, and the Inland Scenic Route (SH72), which skirts the mountain foothills on its way south towards Tekapo.

Selwyn District

📍 03 / POP 56,400

Named after NZ's first Anglican bishop, this largely rural district has swallowed an English map book and regurgitated place names such as Lincoln, Darfield and Sheffield. Yet any illusions of Britain are quickly dispelled by the looming presence of the snow-capped Southern Alps, providing a rugged retort to 'England's mountains green'.

The highly scenic Great Alpine Hwy pierces the heart of the district on its journey between Christchurch and the West Coast. On the Canterbury Plains, it passes through the small settlement of Springfield, notable for a monument to local Rewi Alley (1897–1987), who became a great hero of the Chinese Communist Party.

Selwyn's numerous ski fields may not be the country's most glamorous, but they provide plenty of thrills for ski bunnies. **Porters** (📞 03-318 4731; www.skiporters.co.nz; daily lift passes adult/child weekend $99/69, midweek $79/49; ⏰ lifts 9am-4pm) is the main commercial field; club fields include **Mt Olympus** (📞 03-318 5840; www.mtolympus.co.nz; daily lift passes adult/child $75/35), **Cheeseman** (📞 03-344 3247, snow phone 03-318 8794; www.mtcheeseman.co.nz; daily lift passes adult/child $79/39; ⏰ lifts 9am-4.30pm, shorter hours midweek), **Broken River** (📞 03-318 8713; www.brokenriver.co.nz; daily lift passes adult/child $75/35; ⏰ lifts 9am-4pm), **Craigieburn Valley** (📞 03-318 8711; www.craigieburn.co.nz; daily lift passes adult/child $75/35) and **Temple Basin** (📞 03-377 7788; www.templebasin.co.nz; daily lift passes adult/child $69/35).

🏃 Activities

Rubicon Valley Horse Treks HORSE RIDING
(📞 03-318 8886; www.rubiconvalley.co.nz; 534 Rubicon Rd, Springfield) Operating from a sheep farm 6km from Springfield, Rubicon offers a variety of horse treks to suit both beginner and advanced riders, including hour-long farm rides ($55), two-hour river or valley rides ($98), two-hour sunset rides ($120) and six-hour mountain trail rides ($285).

🛏 Sleeping & Eating

Smylies Accommodation HOSTEL $
(📞 03-318 4740; www.smylies.co.nz; 5653 West Coast Rd, Springfield; dm/s/d $38/60/90; 🅿 🛜) 🍃 This well-seasoned, welcoming, YHA-associated hostel has a piano, manga comics galore, a DVD library and a wood-burning fire in the large communal kitchen. As well as traditional dorms, there are also self-contained motel units ($105) and a three-bedroom cottage ($280). Winter packages (June to September), including ski-equipment rental and ski-field transport, are available.

Famous Sheffield Pie Shop BAKERY $
(📞 03-318 3876; www.sheffieldpieshop.co.nz; 51 Main West Rd, Sheffield; pies $5-6; ⏰ 6.30am-4pm Mon-Fri, from 7.30am Sat & Sun) Blink and you'll miss this stellar roadside bakery, a purveyor of more than 20 varieties of pies, from traditional beef to more experimental flavour combinations – think whisky and venison, or chicken, camembert and apricot. While you're here, snaffle a bag of the exemplary afghan biscuits – such cornflakey, chocolatey goodness!

ⓘ Getting There & Away

Public transport is limited in Selwyn District, so it's best have your own transport.

Arthur's Pass

📍 03 / POP 30

Having left the Canterbury Plains at Springfield, the Great Alpine Hwy heads over Porter's Pass through the mountainous folds of the Torlesse and Craigieburn Ranges and into Arthur's Pass.

Māori used this pass to cross the Southern Alps long before its 'discovery' by Arthur Dobson in 1864. The Westland gold rush created the need for a dependable crossing over the Alps from Christchurch, and the coach road was completed within a year. Later, the coal and timber trade demanded a railway, duly completed in 1923.

Today it's an amazing journey. Successive valleys display their own character, not least the spectacular braided Waimakariri River Valley, encountered as you enter the national park proper.

Arthur's Pass village is 4km from the actual pass. At 900m, it's NZ's highest-altitude settlement and a handy base for tramps, climbs and skiing. The weather, however, is a bit of a shocker. Come prepared for rain.

⊙ Sights

★ Arthur's Pass
National Park NATIONAL PARK

(www.doc.govt.nz) Straddling the Southern Alps, known to Māori as Ka Tiriti o Te Moana (Steep Peak of Glistening White), this vast alpine wilderness became the South Island's first national park in 1929. Of its 1144 sq km, two-thirds lies on the Canterbury side of the main divide; the rest is in Westland. It is a rugged, mountainous area, cut by deep valleys, and ranging in altitude from 245m at the Taramakau River to 2408m at Mt Murchison.

There are plenty of well-marked day tramps throughout the park, especially around Arthur's Pass village. Pick up a copy of DOC's *Discover Arthur's Pass* booklet to read about popular tramps, including: the **Arthur's Pass Walkway**, a reasonably easy track from the village to the Dobson Memorial at the summit of the pass (2½ hours return); the one-hour return walk to **Devils Punchbowl** falls; and the steep walk to beautiful views at **Temple Basin** (three hours return). More challenging, full-day options include the **Bealey Spur** track and the classic summit hike to **Avalanche Peak**.

The park's many multiday trails are mostly valley routes with saddle climbs in between, such as **Goat Pass** and **Cass-Lagoon Saddles Tracks**, both two-day options. These and the park's longer tracks require previous tramping experience as flooding can make the rivers dangerous and the weather is extremely changeable. Always seek advice from DOC before setting out.

Cave Stream Scenic Reserve CAVE

(www.doc.govt.nz) Near Broken River Bridge, 2km northeast of Castle Hill, you'll find this 594m-long cave. As indicated by the information panels in the car park, the walk through the cave is an achievable adventure, but only with a foolproof torch and warm clothing, and definitely only if the water level is less than waist deep where indicated. Heed all notices, take necessary precautions and revel in the spookiness.

Castle Hill/Kura Tawhiti LANDMARK

Scattered across lush paddocks around 33km from Springfield, these limestone formations reach up to 30m high, and look so otherworldly they were named 'treasure from a distant land' by early Māori. A car park (with toilets) provides easy access to a short walk into the strange rock garden (10 minutes), favoured by rock climbers and photographers.

🛌 Sleeping

Camping is possible near the basic **Avalanche Creek Shelter** (www.doc.govt.nz; SH73; adult/child $8/4; P), opposite the DOC, where there's running water, tables, a sink and toilets. You can also camp for free at **Klondyke Corner** (www.doc.govt.nz; SH73) or **Hawdon Shelter** (www.doc.govt.nz; Mount White Rd, off SH37), 8km and 24km south of Arthur's Pass respectively, where facilities are limited to toilets and stream water for boiling. If you're not camping, there are plenty of accommodation options in Arthur's Pass village and surrounds.

Mountain House YHA HOSTEL $

(☑ 03-318 9258; www.trampers.co.nz; 83 Main Rd; dm/d $33/92, motel units $165; P🖥) Spread around the village, this excellent suite of accommodation includes a well-kept hostel, two upmarket motel units and two three-bedroom cottages with log fires ($340, for up to eight people). The enthusiastic manager runs a tight ship and can provide extensive local tramping information.

Arthur's Pass Village B&B B&B $$

(☑ 021 394 776; www.arthurspass.org.nz; 72 School Tce; d $140-160; P🖥) This lovingly restored former railway cottage is now a cosy B&B, with two well-appointed guest rooms. Breakfast on free-range bacon and eggs, pancakes and freshly baked bread, while enjoying the company of the friendly owners. Delicious home-cooked dinners are also available ($35).

Arthur's Pass Alpine Motel MOTEL $$

(☑ 03-318 9233; www.apam.co.nz; 52 Main Rd; d $130; P🖥) On the southern approach to the village, this cabin-style motel complex combines the homey charms of yesteryear with the beauty of double-glazing and the advice of active, enthusiastic hosts.

Flock Hill Lodge MOTEL, HOSTEL $$

(☑ 03-318 8196; www.flockhill.co.nz; Great Alpine Hwy, Craigieburn Valley; dm/s/d $35/55/90, cottages $170-200; P@🖥) Near Craigieburn Forest Park and Lake Pearson, this historic high-country sheep station offers a genuine taste of rural life in its Shearers' Quarters bunkhouse, set in a picturesque farmyard. Tidy cottage units enjoy a more manicured garden setting.

Wilderness Lodge LODGE $$$

(☑ 03-318 9246; www.wildernesslodge.co.nz; Cora Lynn Rd, Bealey; half board s $569-770, d $938-1240; P🖥) 🌿 For tranquillity and natural grandeur, this midsize alpine lodge tucked into beech forest just off the highway takes some beating. It's a class act, with a focus on immersive, nature-based experiences. Two daily guided activities (such as tramping and kayaking) are included in the tariff, along with gourmet breakfast and dinner.

✗ Eating

Arthur's Pass Store & Cafe   CAFE $

(85 Main Rd; breakfast & lunch $7-24; ⊘8am-5pm; 🛜) You want it, this is your best chance, with odds-on for egg sandwiches, hot chips, decent coffee, basic groceries and petrol.

Wobbly Kea   CAFE $$

(www.wobblykea.co.nz; 108 Main Rd; breakfast $10-17, mains $24-26; ⊘9am-8pm) Don your big-eatin' pants for brunch, lunch or dinner at the Wobbly Kea, which offers a short menu of simple but tasty home-cooked meals, such as meaty stew and curry. Pricey pizza ($33) is available to take away, as are fish and chips.

❶ Information

DOC Arthur's Pass Visitor Centre (☑ 03-318 9211; www.doc.govt.nz; 80 Main Rd; ⊘8.30am-4.30pm) Helpful staff can provide advice on suitable tramps and the all-important weather forecast. Detailed route guides and topographical maps are also available, as are locator beacons for hire. Before you leave, log your trip details on AdventureSmart (www.adventuresmart.org.nz) via the on-site computer.

❶ Getting There & Away

Fill your fuel tank before you leave Springfield (or Hokitika or Greymouth, if you're coming from the west). There's a pump at Arthur's Pass Store but it's expensive and only operates from 8am until 5pm.

Buses depart from various stops all a stone's throw from the store – check with the bus company for the latest information.

From Arthur's Pass, Atomic Shuttles (p500) has buses heading to/from Christchurch ($40, 2¼ hours), Springfield ($40, one hour), Lake Brunner ($40, 50 minutes) and Greymouth ($40, 1¼ hours).

West Coast Shuttle (p500) has buses stopping at Arthur's Pass head to/from Christchurch ($42, 2¾ hours) and Greymouth ($32, 1¾ hours).

TranzAlpine (☑ 04-495 0775, 0800 872 467; www.greatjourneysofnz.co.nz/tranzalpine; fares from $119) has one train daily in each direction that stops in Arthur's Pass, heading to/from Springfield (1½ hours) and Christchurch (2½ hours), or Lake Brunner (one hour) and Greymouth (two hours).

Methven

☑03 / POP 1700

Methven is busiest in winter (June to September), when it fills up with snow bunnies heading to nearby Mt Hutt. At other times tumbleweeds don't quite blow down the main street – much to the disappointment of the wannabe gunslingers arriving for the raucous October rodeo. Over summer (December to March) it's a low-key and affordable base for trampers and mountain bikers heading into the spectacular mountain foothills.

🏃 Activities

Most people come to Methven for the nearby ski slopes, but there are plenty of other activities nearby. Ask at the i-SITE (p518) about local walks (including the town heritage trail and Methven Walk/Cycleway) and longer tramps, horse riding, mountain biking, fishing, clay-shooting, archery, golfing, scenic helicopter flights, and jetboating through the nearby Rakaia Gorge.

Rakaia Gorge Walkway   WALKING

(www.doc.govt.nz; Rakaia Gorge Bridge, SH72) Following river terraces into the upper gorge, this well-graded tramp passes through forest and past the historic ferryman's cottage and coal mines, with plenty of pretty picnic spots. The highlight is the lookout at the end with epic alpine views. The walk is four hours return, but a shorter tramp to the lower lookout (one hour return) is also worthwhile.

Black Diamond Safaris   SKIING

(☑ 027 450 8283; www.blackdiamondsafaris.co.nz) Provides access to uncrowded club ski fields by 4WD. Prices start at $150 for transport, safety equipment and familiarisation, while $275 includes a lift pass, lunch and a guide.

Methven Heliski   SKIING

(☑03-302 8108; www.methvenheli.co.nz; Main St; 5-run day trips $1075) Epic guided, all-inclusive backcountry heliski trips, featuring five runs averaging drops of 750 to 1000 vertical metres.

Discovery Jet   BOATING

(☑ 021 538 386, 0800 538 2628; www.discoveryjet.co.nz; Rakaia Gorge Bridge, SH72; adult/child $99/75) A speedy, exhilarating way to explore the Rakaia Gorge is via jetboat. Discovery Jet, based downstream of the bridge, offer a 45-minute blood-pumping ride with twists, turns and 360-degree spins, all with a backdrop of majestic mountain scenery. Shorter joyrides are also available.

Skydiving Kiwis SKYDIVING
(📞 0800 359 549; www.skydivingkiwis.com; Ashburton Airport, Seafield Rd) Offers tandem jumps from 6000ft ($235), 9000ft ($285), 12,000ft ($335) and 13,000ft ($360) departing Ashburton Airport.

🛏 Sleeping

Book ahead during the ski season, especially for budget accommodation. Prices can rise significantly in winter (June to September); some places close in the summer months from December through February.

Alpenhorn Chalet HOSTEL $
(📞 03-302 8779; www.alpenhorn.co.nz; 44 Allen St; dm $30, d $65-85; 🅿 @ 🛜) This small, inviting home has a leafy conservatory housing an indoor spa pool, a log fire and complimentary espresso coffee. Bedrooms are spacious and brightly coloured, with lots of warm, natural wood; one double room has an en suite bathroom.

Rakaia Gorge Camping Ground CAMPGROUND $
(📞 03-302 9353; 6686 Arundel-Rakaia Gorge Rd; sites per adult/child under 12yr $8.50/free) There are no powered sites here, only toilets, showers and a small kitchen shelter, but don't let that put you off. This is the best camping ground for miles, perched picturesquely above the ultra-blue Rakaia River, and a good base for exploring the area. Amenities closed May to September.

Mt Hutt Bunkhouse HOSTEL $
(📞 03-302 8894; www.mthuttbunkhouse.co.nz; 8 Lampard St; dm $31, d $68-80, cottage $280-350; 🅿 🛜) Enthusiastic on-site owners run this basic, well-equipped, bright and breezy hostel. There's a comfy lounge, and a large garden sporting a barbecue and a volleyball court. The cottage (sleeps up to 18) is economical for large groups.

Big Tree Lodge HOSTEL $
(📞 03-302 9575; www.bigtreelodge.co.nz; 25 South Belt; dm $35-40, d $75-90, apt $110-180; 🅿 🛜) Once a vicarage, this relaxed hostel has bunk-free dorms and wood-trimmed bathrooms. Tucked just behind is Little Tree Studio, a self-contained unit sleeping up to four people.

Redwood Lodge HOSTEL, LODGE $$
(📞 03-302 8964; www.redwoodlodge.co.nz; 3 Wayne Pl; s $55-65, d $86-149; 🅿 @ 🛜 🐾) Expect a warm welcome and no dorms at this charming and peaceful family-friendly lodge. Most rooms are en suite, and bigger

DON'T MISS

MT HUTT

One of the highest ski areas in the southern hemisphere, **Mt Hutt** (📞 03-302 8811; www.nzski.com/mt-hutt; day lift passes adult/child $99/50; ⏰ 9am-4pm) has the largest skiable area of any of NZ's commercial fields (365 hectares). The ski field is only 26km from Methven but in wintry conditions the drive takes about 40 minutes; allow two hours from Christchurch. Road access is steep: be extremely cautious in lousy weather.

Methven Travel (p518) runs shuttle buses from Methven during the ski season ($20). Half of the terrain is suitable for intermediate skiers, with a quarter each for beginning and advanced skiers. The longest run stretches for 2km. Other attractions include chairlifts, heliskiing and wide-open faces that are good for learning to snowboard. The season usually runs from mid-June to mid-October.

rooms can be reconfigured to accommodate families. The large shared lounge is ideal for resting ski-weary limbs.

Whitestone Cottages RENTAL HOUSE $$$
(📞 03-928 8050; www.whitestonecottages.co.nz; 3016 Methven Hwy; cottages $175-255; 🅿 🛜) When you just want to spread out, cook a meal, do your laundry and have your own space, these four large freestanding cottages in leafy grounds are just the ticket. Each sleeps six in two en suite bedrooms. Rates are for two people; each extra person is $35

🍴 Eating & Drinking

Cafe 131 CAFE $
(131 Main St; mains $10-19; ⏰ 7.30am-5pm; 🛜) Polished timber and leadlight windows lend atmosphere to this conservative but reliable local favourite. Highlights include good coffee, hearty all-day breakfasts and tasty home baking, with a tipple on offer should you fancy it. Free wi-fi is a nice bonus.

★ Dubliner BISTRO $$
(📞 03-302 8259; www.dubliner.co.nz; 116 Main St; meals $19-34; ⏰ 4.30pm-late) This atmospheric Irish bar and restaurant is housed in Methven's lovingly restored old post office. Great food includes pizza, Irish stew and other hearty fare suitable for washing down with a pint of craft beer.

Aqua
JAPANESE $$

(📞03-302 8335; 112 Main St; mains $9-23; ⏰11.30am-2pm & 5.30-9pm Thu-Sun) A ski-season stalwart with unpredictable hours at other times (ring ahead), this tiny restaurant sports kimono-clad waitresses and traditional Japanese cuisine, including *yakisoba* (fried noodles), ramen (noodle soup) and *izakaya* (Japanese pub-eatery)-style small plates to share, with ice-cold beer or warming sake.

Blue Pub
PUB

(📞03-302 8046; www.thebluepub.co.nz; 2 Barkers Rd; ⏰11am-late; 📶) Have a drink at the bar, crafted from a huge slab of native timber, or tuck into robust meals in the quieter cafe (mains $24 to $36). Afterwards, challenge the locals to a game of pool or listen to regular live music.

☆ Entertainment

Cinema Paradiso
CINEMA

(📞03-302 1975; www.cinemaparadiso.co.nz; 112 Main St; adult/child $17/12; ⏰Wed-Sun) Quirky 35-seat cinema with an art-house slant.

ℹ Information

Medical Centre (📞03-302 8105; The Square, Main St; ⏰8.30am-5.30pm)

Methven i-SITE (📞03-302 8955; www.methvenmthutt.co.nz; 160 Main St; ⏰9.30am-5pm daily Jul-Sep, 9am-5pm Mon-Fri, 10am-3pm Sat & Sun Oct-Jun; 📶) Ask staff here about local walks and other activities.

ℹ Getting There & Away

Methven Travel (📞0800 684 888, 03-302 8106; www.methventravel.co.nz; 160 Main St) Runs shuttles between Methven and Christchurch Airport (adult/child $45/27.50) four times a week from October to June, increasing to three times daily during the ski season. Also runs shuttles up to Mt Hutt ski field from June to September (adult return $20, kids free with paying adult).

Mt Somers

📞03 / POP 2650

The small settlement of Mt Somers sits on the edge of the Southern Alps, beneath the mountain of the same name. The biggest drawcard to the area is the **Mt Somers track** (26km), a two-day tramp circling the mountain, linking the popular picnic spots of Sharplin Falls and Woolshed Creek. Trail highlights include volcanic formations, Māori rock drawings, deep river canyons and botanical diversity. The route is subject to sudden weather changes, so precautions should be taken.

There are two DOC huts on the track: Pinnacles Hut and Woolshed Creek Hut (adult/child $15/7.50). Hut tickets and information are available at Mt Somers General Store and Staveley Store.

🛏 Sleeping & Eating

Mt Somers Holiday Park
HOLIDAY PARK $

(📞03-303 9719; www.mountsomers.co.nz; 87 Hoods Rd; sites from $20, cabin $55, with bathroom $80; 🅿) This small, friendly park offers pleasant sites in leafy grounds along with standard (bring your own linen) and en suite cabins. All guests have access to basic shared kitchen and lounge areas.

Staveley Store & Cafe
CAFE $$

(📞03-303 0859; 2 Burgess Rd, Staveley; mains $6-11; ⏰9am-4pm Apr-Nov) Call into this cute little country store for the best coffee for miles around, as well as tasty lunch rolls, delectable cakes, gourmet ice cream and locally sourced groceries. Also sells hut tickets for the Mt Somers track.

Stronechrubie
BISTRO $$

(📞03-303 9814; www.stronechrubie.co.nz; cnr Hoods Rd & SH72; mains bistro $18-28, restaurant $39-41; ⏰bistro 5.30pm-late Thu-Sat, restaurant 6.30pm-late Wed-Sat, Sun lunch by appointment; 📶) This motel complex offers comfortable chalets overlooking bird-filled gardens (doubles $120 to $160), but it's the up-and-coming culinary hub that's the main draw here. Enjoy a more formal meal in the lauded, long-standing restaurant, or head to the flash new bar and bistro for modern, tapas-style fare alongside lovely wines and craft beer. Reservations recommended.

ℹ Information

Mt Somers General Store (📞03-303 9831; 61 Pattons Rd; ⏰7am-5.30pm Mon-Fri, 8am-5.30pm Sat, 9am-5pm Sun) Hut tickets for the Mt Somers track, plus information, petrol and basic groceries.

ℹ Getting There & Away

There are no public buses to/from Mt Somers village, so you will need your own transport.

SOUTH CANTERBURY

After crossing the Rangitata River into South Canterbury, SH1 and the Inland Scenic Route (SH72) narrow to within 8km of each other at the quaint town of Geraldine.

Here you can choose to take the busy coastal highway through the port city of Timaru, or continue inland on SH79 into Mackenzie Country, where NZ's tallest peaks rise above powder-blue lakes.

The Mackenzie Basin is a wild, tussock-strewn bowl at the foot of the Southern Alps, carved out by ancient glaciers. It takes its name from the legendary James 'Jock' McKenzie, who ran his stolen flocks in this then-uninhabited region in the 1840s.

Director Sir Peter Jackson made the most of this rugged and untamed landscape while filming the *Lord of the Rings,* choosing Mt Cook Village as the setting for Minas Tirith and a sheep station near Twizel as Gondor's Pelennor Fields.

Timaru

📞 03 / POP 26,000

Trucking on along the SH1 through Timaru, travellers could be forgiven for thinking that this small port city is merely a handy place for food and fuel halfway between Christchurch and Dunedin. Drop the anchors, people! Straying into the CBD reveals a remarkably intact Edwardian precinct boasting some good dining and interesting shopping, not to mention a clutch of cultural attractions and lovely parks, all of which sustain at least a day's stopover.

The town's name comes from the Māori name Te Maru, meaning 'place of shelter'. No permanent settlement existed here until 1839, when the Weller brothers set up a whaling station. The *Caroline,* a sailing ship that transported whale oil, gave the picturesque bay its name.

⊙ Sights

★ Aigantighe Art Gallery   GALLERY
(www.timaru.govt.nz/community/facilities/art -gallery; 49 Wai-iti Rd; ⊘10am-4pm Tue-Fri, from noon Sat & Sun) FREE One of the South Island's largest public galleries, this 1908 mansion houses a notable collection of NZ and European art across various eras, alongside temporary exhibitions staged by the gallery's ardent supporters. The Gaelic name means 'at home' and is pronounced 'egg-and-tie'.

Sacred Heart Basilica   CHURCH
(7 Craigie Ave, Parkside) Roman Catholic with a definite emphasis on the Roman, this beautiful neoclassical church (1911) impresses with multiple domes, Ionian columns and richly coloured stained glass. Its architect, Francis Petre, also designed the large basilicas in Christchurch (now in ruins) and Oamaru. Inside, there's an art-nouveau feel to the plasterwork, which includes intertwined floral and sacred-heart motifs. There are no set opening hours; try the side door.

Caroline Bay Park   PARK, BEACH
(Marine Pde) Fronting the town, this expansive park ranges over an Edwardian-style garden under the Bay Hill cliff, then across broad lawns to low sand dunes and the beach itself. It has something for everyone between the playground, skate park, soundshell, ice-cream kiosk, minigolf, splash park and myriad other attractions.

Te Ana Māori Rock Art Centre   MUSEUM
(📞03-684 9141; www.teana.co.nz; 2 George St; adult/child $22/11, tours $130/52; ⊘10am-3pm) Passionate Ngāi Tahu guides bring this innovative multimedia exhibition about Māori rock paintings to life. You can also take a three-hour excursion (departing at 2pm, November to April) to see isolated rock art in situ; prior booking is essential.

Timaru Botanic Gardens   GARDENS
(cnr King & Queen Sts; ⊘8am-dusk) Established in 1864, these gardens are a restful place to while away an hour or two, with a pond, lush lawns, shady trees, a playground and vibrant floral displays. With luck you'll arrive during rhododendron or rose bloom time. Enter from Queen St, south of the city centre.

South Canterbury Museum   MUSEUM
(http://museum.timaru.govt.nz; Perth St; admission by donation; ⊘10am-4.30pm Tue-Fri, 1-4.30pm Sat & Sun) Historic and natural artefacts of the region are displayed here. Highlights include the Māori section, a full-scale model of a ship's cabin from 1859, and a replica of the aeroplane designed and flown by local pioneer aviator and inventor Richard Pearse. It's speculated that his mildly successful attempts at flight came before the Wright brothers' famous achievement in 1903.

✷ Festivals & Events

Timaru Festival of Roses   CULTURAL
(www.festivalofroses.co.nz; ⊘Nov/Dec) Featuring a market day, concerts and family fun, this week-long celebration capitalises on Timaru's obsession with all things rosy. The festival is held annually for one week at the end of November or early December.

Timaru

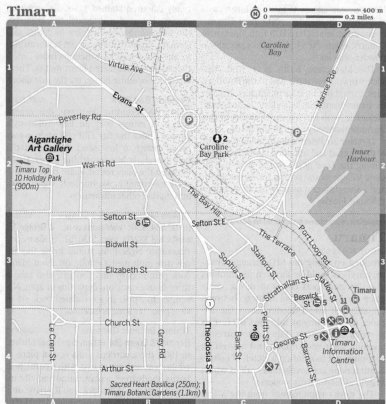

🛏 Sleeping

Timaru Top 10 Holiday Park   HOLIDAY PARK **$**
(☑03-684 7690; www.timaruholidaypark.co.nz; 154a Selwyn St, Marwiel; sites $40-44, units from $65, with bathroom from $99; P✿) 🅿 Tucked away in the suburbs, this excellent holiday park has clean, colourful amenities and a host of accommodation options throughout mature, leafy grounds. Helpful staff go out of their way to assist with local advice and bookings.

Grosvenor   HOTEL **$**
(☑03-687 9190; www.thegrosvenor.co.nz; 26 Cains Tce; s/d from $90/115; P✿) In a heritage building right in the centre of town, this good-value budget hotel offers clean, no-frills rooms with comfy beds, fridge and TV. The quirky Mondrian-styled corridors give the place a hip vibe.

Sefton Homestay   B&B **$$**
(☑03-688 0017; www.seftonhomestay.co.nz; 32 Sefton St, Seaview; r $130-140; ✿) Set back behind a pretty garden, this imposing heritage house has two guest rooms: one with an en suite, and a larger bedroom with an adjoining sun lounge and a bathroom across the hall. Swap travel stories over a glass of port in the guest sitting room.

Glendeer Lodge   B&B **$$$**
(☑03-686 9274; www.glendeer.co.nz; 51 Scarborough Rd, Scarborough; d $210-260; P✿) 🅿 Set on five acres 4km south of Timaru, this purpose-built lodge is a peaceful option away from busy SH1. Walk to the lighthouse, relax in the garden watching fallow deer nibbling the paddock, then retire to the plush, self-contained lodge offering three en suite rooms. The owners' fly-fishing guiding business lends a wilderness vibe.

🍴 Eating & Drinking

Arthur Street Kitchen   CAFE **$**
(www.arthurstkitchen.co.nz; 8 Arthur St; mains $9-19; ⏰7am-5pm Mon-Fri, 9am-3pm Sat; ☑) Timaru's hippest coffee house follows the recipe

Timaru

for success: namely great coffee, contemporary cafe fare, good tunes and a mix of arty inside and sunny outside seating. Made with flair and care, the food offering includes grainy salads, refined sandwiches and pastry treats, plus an à la carte breakfast and lunch menu.

★**Oxford** MODERN NZ **$$**
(☏03-688 3297; www.theoxford.co.nz; 152 Stafford St; mains $26-32; ◷10am-late Mon & Wed-Fri, 9.30am-late Sat & Sun) This sophisticated corner restaurant honours its 1925 building with stylish monochrome decor and a feature wall commemorating the day Timaru went bust. The menu offers high-class comfort food, starring local produce like venison, beef and salmon, while an alluring drinks list encourages you to pop in for pinot and cheese, or a glass of sticky wine alongside golden syrup pudding.

Koji JAPANESE **$$**
(☏03-686 9166; 7 George St; mains $21-31; ◷11.30am-2pm & 5-9pm) Despite its unassuming exterior, this split-level restaurant does a jolly good job of creating a Japanese vibe. Sit in the downstairs dining room or at the cute bar, or better still head up to the upper level and watch flames rise from the teppanyaki grill. Delicious dishes include sashimi, tempura, *gyoza* and *takoyaki* complete with dancing bonito flakes.

Speight's Ale House PUB
(☏03-686 6030; www.timarualehouse.co.nz; 2 George St; ◷11.30am-late; 🖥) The pub most likely to be registering a pulse of an evening, this enterprise – housed in an interesting 1870s stone warehouse – redeems its overly ostentatious branding with friendly staff and a sunny courtyard, including bean bags for slumping in.

ℹ Information

Timaru Information Centre (☏03-687 9997; www.southcanterbury.org.nz; 2 George St; ◷10am-4pm Mon-Fri, to 3pm Sat & Sun; 🖥) Across from the train station (trains in this area only carry freight, not passengers), the visitor centre shares its building with the Te Ana Māori Rock Art Centre (p519). There's free wi-fi throughout Timaru's CBD and Caroline Bay Park.

ℹ Getting There & Away

AIR

Air New Zealand (p499) flies from Timaru's Richard Pearse Airport to/from Wellington and Auckland at least once daily.

BUS

Atomic Shuttles (p500) Stops by the Timaru Information Centre twice daily, en route to Christchurch ($25, 2½ hours), Oamaru ($20,1¼ hours) and Dunedin ($25, 2¾ hours).

Budget Buses & Shuttles (p500) offers shuttles to Christchurch, either door-to-door ($47) or scheduled runs from Timaru Information Centre to Christchurch's Canterbury Museum ($27).

InterCity (p500) stops outside the train station. Services run to the following destinations:

DESTINATION	FARES FROM	DURATION (HR)	FREQUENCY
Christchurch	$29	2½	2 daily
Dunedin	$34	3	2 daily
Gore	$49	6	daily
Oamaru	$23	1	2 daily
Te Anau	$52	8	daily

Inland & Mackenzie Country

Heading to Queenstown and the southern lakes from Christchurch means a turn off SH1 onto SH79, a scenic route towards the high country and the Aoraki/Mt Cook National Park's eastern foothills. The road

522

GREG BRAVE/SHUTTERSTOCK ©

TRAVELLIGHT/SHUTTERSTOCK ©

CHANACHAI PANICHPATTANAKIJ/GETTY IMAGES ©

1. Aoraki/Mt Cook National Park (p531)

This spectacular national park is home to the mighty Aoraki/Mt Cook – at 3724m, the tallest peak in Australasia.

2 & 3. Christchurch (p482)

Christchurch is a vibrant city of transition, boasting old sites such as the Botanic Gardens (p486) as well as new, post-earthquake attractions like the Transitional Cathedral (p487).

4. Lake Tekapo (p527)

The Church of the Good Shepherd (p527) stands watch over this turquoise lake, born of a hydropower scheme completed in 1953.

passes through Geraldine and Fairlie before joining SH8, which heads over Burkes Pass to the sparkling blue Lake Tekapo.

The expansive high ground from which the scenic peaks of Aoraki/Mt Cook National Park escalate is known as Mackenzie Country, after the legendary James 'Jock' McKenzie, who ran his stolen flocks in this then-uninhabited region in the 1840s. When he was finally caught, other settlers realised the potential of the land and followed in his footsteps. The first people to traverse the Mackenzie were the Māori, trekking from Banks Peninsula to Otago hundreds of years ago.

Peel Forest

♩ 03 / POP 180

Tucked away between the foothills of the Southern Alps and the Rangitata River, Peel Forest is a small but important remnant of indigenous podocarp (conifer) forest. Many of the totara, kahikatea and matai trees here are hundreds of years old and are home to an abundance of bird life, including riflemen, kereru (wood pigeons), bellbirds, fantails and grey warblers. There's a small settlement, mostly to serve the visitors who come to tramp, ride and raft the beautiful surrounds.

A road from nearby Mt Peel sheep station leads to Mesopotamia, the run of English writer Samuel Butler in the 1860s. His experiences here partly inspired his famous satire *Erewhon* ('nowhere' backwards, almost).

◉ Sights

St Stephen's Church   CHURCH
(1200 Peel Forest Rd) Sitting in a pretty glade right next to the general store, this gorgeous little Anglican church (1885) has a warm wooden interior and some interesting stained glass. Look for St Francis of Assisi surrounded by NZ flora and fauna (get the kids to play spot the tuatara).

🏃 Activities

Big Tree Walk (30 minutes return) is a gentle stroll through the forest to a particularly fine example of a totara, which is 31m tall, has a circumference of 9m and is over 1000 years old. There are also trails to **Emily Falls** (1½ hours return), **Rata Falls** (two hours return) and **Acland Falls** (one hour return). Pick up the *Peel Forest Area*

brochure from Peel Forest Store or download it from the DOC website (www.doc.govt.nz).

★ **Rangitata Rafts**   RAFTING
(☏0800 251 251; www.rafts.co.nz; Rangitata Gorge Rd; ⊙Oct-May) Begin your adventure in the stupendously beautiful braided Rangitata River valley before heading on an exhilarating two-hour ride through the gorge's Grade V rapids ($215, minimum age 15). A gentler alternative route encounters only Grade II rapids ($175, minimum age six).

Peel Forest Horse Trekking   HORSE RIDING
(☏03-696 3703; www.peelforesthorsetrekking.co.nz; 1hr/2hr/half day/full day $65/120/220/320, multiday $800-1450) Ride through lush forest on short rides or multiday treks with experienced guides. Accommodation packages are available in conjunction with Peel Forest Lodge.

Hidden Valleys   RAFTING
(☏03-696 3560; www.hiddenvalleys.co.nz; ⊙Sep-May) They may be based in Peel Forest but this crew doesn't limit itself to rafting the Rangitata. Multiday expeditions head to the Waimakariri, Waiau, Landsborough, and Grey and Waiatoto Rivers, peaking with a five-day trip ($1650) down the Clarence near Kaikoura. Shorter, child-friendly trips on the Rangitata River are also available (adult $105 to $200, child $75 to $180).

🛏 Sleeping & Eating

★ **Peel Forest DOC Campsite** CAMPGROUND $
(☏03-696 3567; www.peelforest.co.nz; sites per adult/child powered $21/10.50 unpowered $18/9, cabins $50-80) Near the Rangitata River, around 3km beyond Peel Forest Store, this lovely camping ground is equipped with basic two- to four-berth cabins (bring your own sleeping bag), hot showers and a kitchen. Check in at the store.

Peel Forest Lodge   LODGE $$$
(☏03-696 3703; www.peelforestlodge.co.nz; 96 Brake Rd; d $380, additional adult/child $40/20; ▣🕏) This delightful log cabin hidden in the forest has four rooms and sleeps eight people. It only takes one booking at a time, so you and your posse will have the place to yourself. The cabin is fully self-contained, but meals can be arranged, as can horse treks, rafting trips and other explorations of the beautiful surrounds.

Peel Forest Store
CAFE **$$**

(📞 03-696 3567; www.peelforest.co.nz; 1202 Peel Forest Rd; mains lunch $6-19, dinner $20-29; ⊘ cafe 9.30am-4.30pm daily, bar 6pm-late Wed-Sat; 🛜) Your one-stop shop for basic groceries, hut tickets, internet access and DOC campsite (p524) bookings. The attached cafe has good espresso coffee and does a roaring trade in toasties and burgers come lunchtime. There's occasionally live music in the evenings; check the website for dates.

🅘 Getting There & Away

Atomic Shuttles (p500) and InterCity (p500) buses will get you as close as Geraldine, but you'll need your own transport or a lift to get to Peel Forest itself.

Geraldine
📞 03 / POP 2300

Consummately Canterbury in its dedication to English-style gardening, pretty Geraldine has a village vibe and an active arts scene. In spring (September to November), duck behind the war memorial on Talbot St to the River Garden Walk, where green-fingered locals have gone completely bonkers planting azaleas and rhododendrons. If you've still got energy to burn, try the well-marked trails in Talbot Forest on the town fringe.

🅞 Sights & Activities

Geraldine Historical Museum
MUSEUM

(📞 03-693 7028; 5 Cox St; ⊘10am-3pm Mon-Sat, from 12.30pm Sun) **FREE** Occupying the photogenic Town Board Office building (1885), this cute little museum tells the town's story with an eclectic mix of exhibits, including an extensive collection of photographs.

Geraldine Vintage Car & Machinery Museum
MUSEUM

(📞 03-693 8756; 178 Talbot St; adult/child $15/free; ⊘ 9.30am-4pm Oct-May, 10am-4pm Sat & Sun Jun-Sep) Rev-heads will enjoy this lovingly maintained vintage car collection, featuring a 1907 De Dion-Bouton and a gleaming 1926 Bentley. There's also a purpose-built Daimler used for the 1954 royal tour, plus some very nice Jags, 1970s muscle cars and all sorts of farm machinery.

Big Rock Canyons
ADVENTURE SPORTS

(📞0800 244 762; www.bigrockcanyons.co.nz; tours from $360; ⊘Oct-Apr) Offers slippy, slidey day-long adventures in the Kaumira Canyon near Geraldine, as well as in five other canyons with varying degrees of difficulty. Pick up is available in Geraldine or Christchurch.

🛏 Sleeping

Geraldine Kiwi Holiday Park
HOLIDAY PARK **$**

(📞03-693 8147; www.geraldineholidaypark.co.nz; 39 Hislop St; sites $36-40, d $52-135; 🅿@🛜) 🌿 This top-notch holiday park is set amid well-established parkland right in the centre of town. Tidy accommodation ranges from budget cabins to plusher motel units, plus there's a TV room and playground.

Rawhiti Backpackers
HOSTEL **$**

(📞03-693 8252; www.rawhitibackpackers.co.nz; 27 Hewlings St; dm/s $34/50, d $78-84; 🅿🛜) On a hillside on the edge of town, this former maternity hospital is now a sunny and spacious hostel with well-maintained communal areas, bright rooms, a lemon tree and two cute cats.

Scenic Route Motor Lodge
MOTEL **$$**

(📞03-693 9700; www.motelscenicroute.co.nz; 28 Waihi Tce; d $135-150; 🅿🛜) Only five minutes' walk from the town centre, these modern motel rooms have double-glazing, flat-screen TVs and even stylish wallpaper. Larger studios have spa baths.

🍴 Eating

Long overdue to be lauded 'Cheese & Pickle Capital of NZ', Geraldine is paradise for self-caterers. Numerous artisan producers line the Four Peaks Plaza; seek out a bag of Heartland potato chips, made just down the road. There's an excellent **farmers market** (St Mary's Church car park; ⊘9am-12.30pm Sat Oct-Apr) 🌿, and, if you're not in the mood to DIY, there are also a few good cafes in town.

★Talbot Forest Cheese
DELI **$**

(www.talbotforestcheese.co.nz; Four Peaks Plaza, Talbot St; cheeses $5-10; ⊘9am-5pm; 🌿) This little shop not only showcases the plethora of cheeses made on-site (including delicious parmesan and gruyère), it doubles as a deli with all you need for a tasty picnic.

Verde
CAFE **$**

(📞03-693 9616; 45 Talbot St; mains $9-18; ⊘9am-4pm; 🌿) Down the lane beside the old post office and set in beautiful gardens, this excellent cafe is one of Geraldine's best eateries.

Drop in for coffee and cake, or linger over a lazy lunch of salads, soup, sandwiches and the like.

Barker's of Geraldine
DELI $

(☑03-693 9727; www.barkers.co.nz; Four Peaks Plaza, Talbot St; preserves $4-10; ⊙9am-5.30pm Oct-Apr, to 5pm May-Sep; ☑) Putting the pickle into the Cheese & Pickle Capital is Barker's, long-standing producer of favourite fruity preserves, including raspberry jam, tamarillo chutney and cherry juice. Buy some bread and cheese and find a picnic bench.

Running Duck
BURGERS $$

(☑ 03-693 8320; www.therunningduck.co.nz; 1 Peel St; burgers $8-19; ⊙8am-4pm Mon, Wed & Thu, 8am-8pm Fri, 9am-4pm Sat & Sun) A welcome addition to the Geraldine culinary scene, this hipster burger joint is the perfect setting to feast on tasty gourmet burgers and crispy fries, topped with chef Al's special spicy sauce.

☆ Entertainment

Geraldine Cinema
CINEMA

(☑03-693 8118; www.geraldinecinema.co.nz; 78 Talbot St; adult/child $12/8) Snuggle into an old sofa to watch a Hollywood favourite or an art-house surprise at this ageing dame, built in 1924. There's also occasional live music, usually with a folk, blues or country spin.

ℹ Information

Geraldine Visitor Information Centre (☑ 03-693 1101; www.southcanterbury.org.nz; 38 Waihi Tce; ⊙8am-5.30pm) Located inside the Kiwi Country visitor complex. See also www.gogeraldine.co.nz.

ℹ Getting There & Away

Atomic Shuttles (p500) runs daily services to the following:

DESTINATION	FARE	DURATION (HR)
Christchurch	$30	2
Cromwell	$35	4½
Lake Tekapo	$25	1¼
Queenstown	$35	5
Twizel	$30	2

Budget Buses & Shuttles (p500) offers a door-to-door shuttle to Christchurch ($57), along with a cheaper scheduled run ($47).

InterCity (p500) runs daily services to the following:

DESTINATION	FARES FROM	DURATION (HR)
Christchurch	$32	2¼
Cromwell	$40	4¾
Lake Tekapo	$21	1¼
Mt Cook Village	$38	3
Queenstown	$42	5¾

Fairlie
☑03 / POP 720

Leafy Fairlie describes itself as 'the gateway to the Mackenzie', but in reality this wee, rural town feels a world away from tussocky Mackenzie Country over Burkes Pass, to the west. The bakery and picnic area make it a good lunchtime stop.

◉ Sights & Activities

The information centre can provide details on nearby tramping and mountain-biking tracks. The main ski resort, Mt Dobson (☑03-281 5509; www.mtdobson.co.nz; daily lift passes adult/child $82/28), lies in a 3km-wide treeless basin 26km northwest of Fairlie. There's also a club ski field 29km northwest at Fox Peak (☑03-685 8539, snow phone 03-688 0044; www.foxpeak.co.nz; daily lift passes adult/child $60/10) in the Two Thumb Range.

Fairlie Heritage Museum
MUSEUM

(www.fairlieheritagemuseum.co.nz; 49 Mt Cook Rd; adult/child $6/free; ⊙9.30am-5pm) A somewhat dusty window on to rural NZ of old, this museum endears with its farm machinery, model aeroplanes, dodgy dioramas and eclectic ephemera. Highlights include the homespun gyrocopter, historic cottage and new automotive wing featuring mint-condition tractors. The attached cafe bakes a good biscuit.

🛏 Sleeping & Eating

Musterer's
MOTEL $$

(☑03-685 8284; www.musterers.co.nz; 9 Gordon St; units $110-260; P🐾) On the western edge of Fairlie, these stylish self-contained cottages afford all mod cons with the bonus of a shared barbecue area and woolshed 'lounge' – complete with donkeys, goats and a pony to pet. Units are plush and spacious; the larger ones come complete with their own wood-fired hot tub ($45 extra) for a stargazing soak.

★Fairlie Bakehouse
BAKERY $

(☑03-685 6063; www.liebers.co.nz; 74 Main St; pies $5-7; ⊙7.30am-4.30pm Mon-Sat, to 4pm Sun; ☑) Famous for miles around and probably the top-ranking reason to stop in Fairlie, this terrific little bakery turns out exceptional pies, including the legendary salmon and bacon. On the sweet side, American doughnuts and raspberry cheesecake elbow their way in among Kiwi classics, such as custard squares and cream buns. Yum.

ℹ Information

Fairlie Heartland Resource & Information Centre (☑03-685 8496; www.fairlienz.com; 67 Main St; ☺10am-4pm Mon-Fri) Has maps and brochures, and can advise on nearby activities.

ℹ Getting There & Away

Atomic Shuttles (p500) runs daily services to the following:

DESTINATION	FARE	DURATION
Christchurch	$30	2½hr
Cromwell	$35	3½hr
Geraldine	$20	40min
Lake Tekapo	$20	40min
Queenstown	$50	4½hr

InterCity (p500) runs daily services to the following:

DESTINATION	FARES FROM	DURATION
Christchurch	$33	3¼hr
Cromwell	$39	4hr
Lake Tekapo	$13	40min
Mt Cook	$87	2½hr
Queenstown	$40	5hr

Lake Tekapo

☑03 / POP 369

Born of a hydropower scheme completed in 1953, today Tekapo is booming off the back of a tourism explosion, although it has long been a popular tour-bus stop on the route between Christchurch and Queenstown. Its popularity is well deserved: the town faces out across the turquoise lake to a backdrop of snow-capped mountains.

Such splendid Mackenzie Country and Southern Alps views are reason enough to linger, but there's infinitely more to see if you wait till dark. In 2012 the Aoraki Mackenzie area was declared an International Dark Sky Reserve, one of only 12 in the world, and Tekapo's Mt John – under light-pollution-free skies – is the ultimate place to experience the region's glorious night sky.

◉ Sights

Church of the Good Shepherd CHURCH (Pioneer Dr; ☺9am-5pm) The picture window behind the altar of this pretty stone church (built in 1935) gives worshippers a distractingly divine view of the lake and mountains; needless to say, it's a firm favourite for weddings. Come early in the morning or late afternoon to avoid the peace-shattering crowds – this is the prime debarkation point for tour buses.

Nearby is a statue of a collie, a tribute to the sheepdogs that helped develop Mackenzie Country.

🏃 Activities

Lake Tekapo is a great base for outdoor activities enthusiasts. In winter (June to September), snow bunnies can go downhill skiing at Mt Dobson (p526) and **Roundhill** (☑021 680 694, snow phone 03-680 6977; www.roundhill.co.nz; daily lift passes adult/child $84/36), and cross-country skiing on the Two Thumb Range.

When the Mackenzie Basin was scoured out by glaciers, **Mt John** (1029m) remained as an island of tough bedrock in the centre of a vast river of ice. Nowadays, a road leads to the summit, or you can tramp via a circuit track (2½ hours return) for rewarding views. To extend it to an all-day tramp, continue on to Alexandrina and McGregor Lakes.

AORAKI MACKENZIE INTERNATIONAL DARK SKY RESERVE

The stars really do seem brighter in Mackenzie Country. A unique combination of clear skies and next to no light pollution makes this region one of the best stargazing sites in the world – a fact that led to 4367 sq km of Aoraki/Mt Cook National Park and the Mackenzie Basin being declared the southern hemisphere's only International Dark Sky Reserve in 2012.

If you're up for some amateur stargazing, all you'll need are a cloud-free night and some warm clothes. For best results, time your visit to coincide with a new moon, when the skies will be at their darkest. For those who'd like a bit more guidance, your best bet is to join one of the nightly tours of the Mt John Observatory run by **Earth & Sky** (☑03-680 6960; www.earthandsky.co.nz; SH8) ✎.

OFF THE BEATEN TRACK

RUATANIWHA CONSERVATION PARK

Stretched between Lake Pukaki and Lake Ohau, this 368-sq-km **protected area** (www.doc.govt.nz) includes the rugged Ben Ohau Range along with the Dobson, Hopkins, Huxley, Temple and Maitland Valleys. It offers plenty of tramping and mountain-biking opportunities, as detailed in DOC's *Ruataniwha Conservation Park* pamphlet (available online), with several day trails close to Twizel.

DOC huts and camping areas are scattered throughout the park, and a more comfortable stay is available at Lake Ohau Lodge (p530). Passing through these parts is the Alps 2 Ocean Cycle Trail (p532), a great way to survey the majestic surroundings.

The free town map details this and other walks in the area, along with cycling tracks, including **Cowan's Hill** and those in **Lake Tekapo Regional Park**.

Mackenzie Alpine Horse Trekking — HORSE RIDING
(☑ 0800 628 269; www.maht.co.nz; Godley Peaks Rd; 30min/1hr/2hr/day $45/70/110/310; ⊘ Oct-May) Located on the road to Mt John, these folks run various treks taking in the area's amazing scenery, catering for everyone from novice to experienced riders.

Tekapo Springs — SPA
(☑ 03-680 6550; www.tekaposprings.co.nz; 6 Lakeside Dr; pools adult/child $25/14, ice skating $18/13; ⊘10am-9pm) There's nothing nicer on a chilly day than soaking in the thermal waters of these landscaped outdoor pools, with views over the lake to the snow-capped mountains beyond. Pools range in temperature from 28°C to 40°C, and include an artificial beach and aqua play area. There's also a steam room and sauna ($6 extra), along with a day spa.

Tekapo Helicopters — SCENIC FLIGHTS
(☑ 03-680 6229; www.tekapohelicopters.co.nz; SH8) For a bird's-eye view of the surrounds, check out the five different options here, from a 20-minute flight ($215) to an hour-long trip taking in Aoraki/Mt Cook, and Fox and Franz Josef Glaciers ($525). All flights include an alpine landing.

Air Safaris — SCENIC FLIGHTS
(☑03-680 6880; www.airsafaris.co.nz; SH8) Awe-inspiring views of Aoraki/Mt Cook National Park's peaks and glaciers are offered on the 'Grand Traverse' fixed-wing flight (adult/child $370/250); there are also various other flights available, including similar trips in a helicopter.

🛏 Sleeping

Lake Tekapo Motels & Holiday Park — HOLIDAY PARK, MOTEL $
(☑03-680 6825; www.laketekapo-accommodation.co.nz; 2 Lakeside Dr; sites $44-56, dm $36-40, d $100-170; P🐾🛜) With a prime position right on the lakefront, this sprawling complex has something for everyone. Backpackers get the cosy, log-cabin lodge, while others can enjoy cute Kiwi 'bachs', basic cabins, and smart en suite units with particularly good views. Campervaners and campers are spoilt for choice, and share the sparkling amenities block.

Tailor Made Tekapo Backpackers — HOSTEL $
(☑03-680 6700; www.tekapohostelnz.com; 11 Aorangi Cres; dm $28-40, d $87-100, d without bathroom $77-99; 🛜) Spread over three well-tended houses on a peaceful street five minutes' walk from town, this sociable hostel offers bright dorms (with no bunks) and cosy doubles. There's also a large garden complete with barbecue, hammock, chickens and bunnies, plus tennis and basketball courts next door for the energetic.

★Lake Tekapo Lodge — B&B $$$
(☑03-680 6566; www.laketekapolodge.co.nz; 24 Aorangi Cres; r $300-495; 🛜) This fabulously designed, luxurious B&B is filled to the brim with covetable contemporary Kiwi art, and boasts painterly views of the lake and mountains from the sumptuous rooms and lounge. Fine-dining evening meals are available by prior arrangement.

Chalet Boutique Motel — APARTMENT $$$
(☑03-680 6774; www.thechalet.co.nz; 14 Pioneer Dr; units $205-330; P🛜) The 'boutique motel' tag doesn't do justice to this collection of attractive accommodation options in three adjacent properties beside the lake. The wonderfully private 'Henkel hut' is a stylish option for lovebirds. Charming hosts will happily provide all the local information you need.

🍴 Eating & Drinking

★Astro Café — CAFE $
(Mt John University Observatory; mains $6-14; ⊘9am-6pm Oct-Apr, 10am-5pm May-Sep, weather dependent) This glass-walled pavilion atop

Mt John has spectacular 360-degree views across the entire Mackenzie Basin – it's quite possibly one of the planet's best locations for a cafe. Tuck into bagels with local salmon or fresh ham-off-the-bone sandwiches; the coffee and cake are good, too.

Kohan   JAPANESE $$
(☑ 03-680 6688; www.kohannz.com; SH8; dishes $6-20, bento $28-39; ⏱ 11am-2pm daily, plus 6-9pm Mon-Sat; ☎) Despite its basic decor, this is one of Tekapo's best dining options, both for its distracting lake views and its authentic Japanese food, including fresh-off-the-boat sashimi. Leave room for the handmade green-tea ice cream.

Run 76   CAFE $$
(☑ 03-680 6910; www.run76laketekapo.co.nz; SH8; mains $13-22; ⏱ 7.30am-4pm; ☎☑) Classic breakfast dishes (until 2.30pm), a cabinet full of cakes, pies and sandwiches, good espresso and free wi-fi are all reasons to visit this petite cafe. Gourmet deli items – including freshly baked ciabatta – will tempt the self-catering crew.

Mackenzie's Bar & Grill   BAR
(☑ 03-680 6886; SH8; ⏱ 10am-late) While full immersion on the menu front is not necessarily advisable, this tidy gastro-pub-style establishment is a safe bet for a few cold ones and some bar snacks. The views are grand, particularly from the deck overlooking the lake.

ⓘ Information

Kiwi Treasures & Information Centre (☑ 03-680 6686; SH8; ⏱ 8am-5.30pm Mon-Fri, to 6pm Sat & Sun) This little gift shop doubles as the post office and info centre with local maps and advice, plus bookings for nearby activities and national bus services.

Tekapo Springs Sales & Information Centre (☑ 03-680 6579; SH8; ⏱ 10am-6pm) The folks from Tekapo Springs dispense brochures and advice, as well as taking bookings for their own complex down the road.

See also www.tekapotourism.co.nz.

ⓘ Getting There & Away

Atomic Shuttles (p500) runs daily services to the following:

DESTINATION	FARE	DURATION
Christchurch	$35	3¼hr
Cromwell	$30	3hr
Geraldine	$25	1¼hr
Queenstown	$45	4hr
Twizel	$20	40min

Cook Connection (☑ 0800 266 526; www.cookconnect.co.nz) has a shuttle service to Mt Cook village ($40, 2¼ hours).

InterCity (p500) runs daily services to the following:

DESTINATION	FARES FROM	DURATION
Christchurch	$35	3¾hr
Cromwell	$35	2¾hr
Geraldine	$20	1hr
Mt Cook village	$84	1½hr
Queenstown	$35	4hr

Twizel
☑ 03 / POP 1200

Pronounced 'twy-zel' but teased with 'Twizzel' and even 'Twizzelsticks' by outsiders, Twizel gets the last laugh. The town was built in 1968 to service construction of the nearby hydroelectric power station, and was due for obliteration in 1984 when the project was completed. But there was no way the locals were upping their twizzlesticks and relinquishing their relaxed, mountain country lifestyle.

Today the town is thriving with a modest boom in holiday-home subdivisions and recognition from travellers that – as plain Jane as it may be – Twizel is actually in the middle of everything and has almost everything one might need (within reason).

🏃 Activities

Twizel sits amid some spectacular country offering all sorts of adventure opportunities. **Lake Ruataniwha** is popular for rowing, boating and windsurfing. Nearby tramping and cycling trails are illustrated on the excellent town map (available from the information centre (p531), including a nice river ramble. Twizel is also the best hub for rides on the Alps 2 Ocean Cycle Trail (p532).

Fishing in local rivers, canals and lakes is big business; enquire at the information centre about local guides, and ask them about swimming in **Loch Cameron** while you're at it (but don't tell them we tipped you off!).

☞ Tours

OneRing Tours   TOURS
(☑ 0800 213 868, 03-435 0073; www.lordoftheringstour.com; cnr Ostler & Wairepo Sts) How often do you get the opportunity to charge around like a mad thing wielding replica *LOTR* gear? Not often enough! A range of tours is

LAKE PUKAKI LOOKOUT

The largest of the Mackenzie's three alpine lakes, Pukaki is a vast jewel of totally surreal colour. On its shore, just off SH8 between Twizel and Lake Tekapo, is a well-signed and perennially popular lookout affording picture-perfect views across the water all the way up to snow-capped Aoraki/Mt Cook and its surrounding peaks.

Beside the lookout, the **Lake Pukaki Visitor Centre** (www.mtcookalpine salmon.com; SH8; ⏱8.30am-5.30pm Oct-Jun, 9am-5pm Jul-Sep) is actually an outpost of Mt Cook Alpine Salmon, the highest salmon farm on the planet, which operates in a hydroelectric canal system some distance away. The visitor centre offers the opportunity to pick up some sashimi ($10) or a smoked morsel for supper.

available – head to the sheep station used for the location of the Battle of the Pelennor Fields (adult/child $89/59), or take a lunchtime visit to Laketown (adult/child $119/89), as seen in the *Hobbit* films.

There's also a breakfast tour (adult/child $109/89) or an adults-only twilight tour ($139); enjoy beer, wine and nibbles as the sun sets over Gondor.

Helicopter Line   SCENIC FLIGHTS
(☏03-435 0370; www.helicopter.co.nz; Pukaki Airport, Harry Wigley Dr) Flights range from the hour-long Aoraki/Mt Cook Discovery ($765) to the 25-minute Alpine Express ($300), with several options in between. All but the shortest guarantee snow landings.

🛏 Sleeping

Twizel Holiday Park   HOLIDAY PARK $
(☏03-435 0507; www.twizelholidaypark.co.nz; 122 Mackenzie Dr; sites from $40, units $60-180; P🐾) Offers green, flower-filled grounds, with grassed sites and tidy communal facilities. Basic rooms are available in an old converted maternity hospital. The modern, self-contained cottages are particularly good value. Bike hire is also available.

⭐ **Lake Ohau Lodge**   LODGE $$
(☏03-438 9885; www.ohau.co.nz; Lake Ohau Rd; s $110-216, d $118-237; P🐾) Idyllically sited on the western shore of remote Lake Ohau, 42km west of Twizel, accommodation includes everything from budget rooms with shared facilities to upmarket rooms with decks and mountain views.

The lodge is the buzzy wintertime hub of the Ohau Ski Field (running from June to September); in summer (December to February) it's a quieter retreat. Half-board packages are available (the nearest dining options are in Twizel).

Omahau Downs   LODGE, COTTAGE $$
(☏03-435 0199; www.omahau.co.nz; SH8; d $150-165, cottages from $155; ⏱closed Jun-Aug; P🐾) This farmstead, 2km north of Twizel, has three cosy, self-contained cottages (one sleeping up to 15), and a lodge with sparkling, modern rooms and a deck looking out at the Ben Ohau Range.

Mountain Chalets   CHALET $$
(☏03-435 0785; www.mountainchalets.co.nz; Wairepo Rd; d $130-170; P🐾) Wood-panelled ceilings add a rustic quality to these cosy, well-equipped, self-contained A-frame chalets, available as studios or one- and two-bedroom units.

Heartland Lodge   B&B, APARTMENT $$$
(☏03-435 0008; www.heartland-lodge.co.nz; 19 North West Arch; d $300-360, apt $190; P🐾) On the leafy outskirts of town, this elegant modern house offers spacious, en suite rooms and a comfortable, convivial communal space. Friendly hosts prepare a cooked breakfast using organic, local produce where possible. The adjacent 'retreat' apartment sleeps up to six and has its own kitchenette (breakfast is not provided).

🍴 Eating

⭐ **Shawty's**   CAFE $$
(☏03-435 3155; www.shawtys.co.nz; 4 Market Pl; mains brunch $12-20, dinner $28-36; ⏱8.30am-late; 🐾) The town centre's social hub and hottest meal ticket serves up big breakfasts, gourmet pizzas and fancy lamb racks as the sun goes down. A considerate kids' menu, cocktails, al fresco dining and occasional live music make it all the more appealing.

High Country Salmon   SEAFOOD $$
(☏0800 400 385; www.highcountrysalmonfarm. co.nz; SH8; salmon per kg from $60; ⏱8am-6pm) The glacial waters of this floating fish farm, 3km from Twizel, produce mighty delicious fish, available to buy as fresh whole fillets and smoked portions. Our pick is the hot-smoked salmon, flaked into hot pasta, per-

haps with a dash of cream. There's also a small cafe selling sashimi and other salmon-inspired dishes.

Poppies Cafe CAFE $$
(📞03-435 0848; www.poppiescafe.com; 1 Benmore Pl; mains brunch $10-21, dinner $27-38; ⏰9am-9pm; 🐾) A favourite with locals, this well-run cafe serves up classic brunch faves and good coffee in the mornings, while come evening you'll find tasty curries, fresh fish and pasta dishes on the menu. Craft beer encourages a wee sup and snack, if you're not going the whole hog. It's south of town just off SH8.

🛍 Shopping

Twizel Bookshop BOOKS
(📞027 464 5062; www.twizelbookshop.co.nz; 12b Market Pl; ⏰9am-5pm Mon-Fri, shorter hours Sat & Sun) A sweet, well-curated bookshop offering both new and second-hand titles.

ℹ Information

Twizel Information Centre (📞03-435 3124; www.twizel.info; Market Pl; ⏰8.30am-5pm Mon-Fri, 10am-3pm Sat) Can advise on tramping and cycling paths in the area, as well as book accommodation. Also offers bike hire (one hour/three hours/full day $25/35/45).

ℹ Getting There & Away

Atomic Shuttles (p500) runs daily services to the following:

DESTINATION	FARE	DURATION
Christchurch	$35	4hr
Cromwell	$30	2hr
Geraldine	$25	2hr
Lake Tekapo	$20	45min
Queenstown	$30	3hr

Cook Connection (p529) runs daily shuttle services to Mt Cook village (one way/return $28/51, one hour).

InterCity (p500) runs daily services to the following:

DESTINATION	FARES FROM	DURATION
Christchurch	$38	5¼hr
Cromwell	$28	2hr
Lake Tekapo	$13	50min
Mt Cook village	$78	1hr
Queenstown	$40	3hr

Naked Bus (www.nakedbus.com) services Christchurch and Queenstown/Wanaka.

Aoraki/Mt Cook National Park

📷 03 / POPULATION 200

The spectacular 700-sq-km Aoraki/Mt Cook National Park is part of the Southwest New Zealand (Te Wāhipounamu) World Heritage Area, which extends from Westland's Cook River down to Fiordland. More than one-third of the park has a blanket of permanent snow and glacial ice; of the 23 NZ mountains over 3000m, 19 are in this park. The highest is mighty Aoraki/Mt Cook – at 3724m, the tallest peak in Australasia. Among the region's other great peaks are Sefton, Tasman, Silberhorn, Malte Brun, La Perouse, Hicks, De la Beche, Douglas and the Minarets.

Aoraki/Mt Cook is a wonderful sight, assuming there's no cloud in the way. Most visitors arrive on tour buses, stop at the Hermitage hotel for photos, and then zoom off back down SH80. Hang around to soak up this awesome peak and the surrounding landscape, and to try the excellent short walks in the area, including to the Tasman Glacier.

History

Known to Māori as Aoraki (Cloud Piercer), after an ancestral deity in Māori mythology, the mountain was given its English name in 1851, in honour of explorer Captain James Cook.

This region has always been the focus of climbing in NZ. On 2 March 1882 William Spotswood Green and two Swiss alpinists failed to reach the summit of Cook after an epic 62-hour ascent. Two years later a trio of local climbers – Tom Fyfe, George Graham and Jack Clarke – were spurred into action by the news that two well-known European alpinists were coming to attempt Cook, and set off to climb it before the visitors. On Christmas Day 1894 they ascended the Hooker Glacier and north ridge to stand on the summit.

In 1913 Australian climber Freda du Faur became the first woman to reach the summit. New Zealander Edmund Hillary first climbed the south ridge in 1948; Hillary went on to become the first person to reach the summit of Mt Everest. Since then, most of the daunting face routes have been climbed.

👁 Sights

⭐ **Aoraki/Mt Cook National Park Visitor Centre** MUSEUM
(📞03-435 1186; www.doc.govt.nz; 1 Larch Grove; ⏰8.30am-5pm Oct-Apr, to 4.30pm May-Sep) **FREE** Arguably the best DOC visitor centre

DON'T MISS

ALPS 2 OCEAN CYCLE TRAIL

One of the best Great Rides within the New Zealand Cycle Trail (www.nzcycletrail.com), the 'A2O' serves up epic vistas on its way from the foot of the Southern Alps all the way to the Pacific Ocean at Oamaru.

New Zealand's highest mountain – Aoraki/Mt Cook – is just one of many stunning sights. Others include braided rivers, glacier-carved valleys, turquoise hydro-lakes, tussock-covered highlands and lush farmland. Off-the-bike activities include wine tasting, penguin spotting, glider flights and soaking in al fresco hot tubs. Country hospitality, including food and accommodation, along with shuttles and other services, make the whole trip easy to organise and enjoy.

The trail is divided into nine easy-to-intermediate sections across terrain varying from canal paths, quiet country roads, old railway lines and expertly cut cross-country track, to some rougher, hilly stuff for the eager. The whole journey takes around four to six days, but it can easily be sliced into short sections.

Twizel is an excellent base for day rides. Options include taking a shuttle to Lake Tekapo (p527) for a five- to six-hour, big-sky ride back to Twizel, or riding from Twizel out to Lake Ohau Lodge (p530) for lunch or dinner. Both rides serve up the sublime lake and mountain scenery for which the Mackenzie is famous.

The trail is well supported by tour companies offering bike hire, shuttles, luggage transfers and accommodation. These include Twizel-based **Cycle Journeys** (☏03-435 0578, 0800 224 475; www.cyclejourneys.co.nz; 3 Benmore Pl; all-inclusive packages from $1250) and **Jollie Biker** (☏027 223 1761, 03-435 0517; www.thejolliebiker.co.nz; 193 Glen Lyon Rd; bike hire per day from $50). The Alps 2 Ocean website (www.alps2ocean.com) has comprehensive details.

in NZ. It not only dispatches all necessary information and advice on tramping routes and weather conditions, it also houses excellent displays on the park's natural and human history. It's a fabulous place to commune with the wilderness, even on a rainy day. Most activities can be booked here.

Tasman Glacier   GLACIER
(www.doc.govt.nz) At 27km long and up to 4km wide, the Tasman is the largest of NZ's glaciers, but it's melting fast, losing hundreds of metres of length each year. It is also melting from the surface, shrinking around 150m in depth since it was first surveyed in 1891. Despite this considerable shrinkage, at its thickest point the ice is still estimated to be over 600m deep.

In its lower section the melts have exposed rocks, stones and boulders, which form a solid unsightly mass on top of the ice.

Tasman Lake, at the foot of the glacier, started to form only in the early 1970s and now stretches to 7km. The ongoing effects of climate change are expected to extend it much further in the next decade. The lake is covered by a maze of huge icebergs, which are continuously being sheared off the glacier's terminal face. On 22 February 2011 the Christchurch earthquake caused a 1.3km-long, 300m-high, 30-million-tonne chunk of

ice to break off, causing 3.5m waves to roll into the tourist boats on the lake at the time (no one was injured). You can kayak on Tasman Lake with Glacier Kayaking (p533).

In the glacier's last major advance (17,000 years ago), the glacier crept south far enough to carve out Lake Pukaki. A later advance did not reach out to the valley sides, so there's a gap between the outer valley walls and the lateral moraines of this later advance. The unsealed Tasman Valley Rd, which branches off Mt Cook Rd 800m south of Mt Cook village, travels through this gap. From the Blue Lakes shelter, 8km along the road, the Tasman Glacier View Track (30 minutes return) climbs interminable steps to an aptly rewarding viewpoint on the moraine wall, with a side trip to Blue Lakes on the way.

Sir Edmund Hillary Alpine Centre   MUSEUM
(www.hermitage.co.nz; Hermitage, Terrace Rd; adult/child $20/10; ☺7am-8.30pm Oct-Mar, 8am-7pm Apr-Sep) This multimedia museum opened just three weeks before the 2008 death of the man regarded by many as the greatest New Zealander of all time. The main attraction is a cinema and domed digital planetarium that screens films all day, including the *Mt Cook Magic* 3D movie and a fascinating 75-minute documentary about Sir Ed's conquest of Everest. The foyer houses memora-

bilia both from St Ed's various expeditions and from the Hermitage (p536) hotel itself, which was originally built in 1884.

🏃 Activities

Hiking & Climbing

Various easy tramps from the village are outlined in the (multilingual) *Walking & Cycling Tracks* pamphlet available from the Aoraki/Mt Cook National Park Visitor Centre (p531) and online. On the trails, look for the thar, a Himalayan goat; the chamois, smaller and of lighter build than the thar, and originally hailing from Europe; and red deer, also European. Summertime (December through March) brings into bloom the Mt Cook lily, a large mountain buttercup, and mountain daisies, gentians and edelweiss.

Longer tramps are only recommended for those with mountaineering experience, as tracks and conditions at higher altitudes can become dangerous. Highly changeable weather is typical: Aoraki/Mt Cook is only 44km from the coast and weather conditions rolling in from the Tasman Sea can mean sudden storms.

As for climbing, there's unlimited scope for the experienced, but those without experience must go with a guide. Regardless of your skills, take every precaution – more than 200 people have died in climbing accidents in the park. The bleak *In Memoriam* book in the Visitor Centre begins with the first death on Aoraki/Mt Cook in 1907; since then more than 80 climbers have died on the peak.

Check with the park rangers before attempting any climb and always heed their advice. If you're climbing, or even going on a longer tramp, fill out an intentions card before starting out so rangers can check on you if you're overdue coming back. Sign out again when you return. The Visitor Centre also hires locator beacons (per three/seven days $30/40).

If you intend to stay at any of the park's huts, it's essential to register your intentions at the Visitor Centre and pay the hut fees. Walkers can use the public shelter in Mt Cook village, which has running water, toilets and coin-operated showers. Note that this shelter cannot be used for overnight stays.

⭐ Sealy Tarns Track — TRAMPING
The walk to Sealy Tarns (three to four hours return) branches off the Kea Point Track and continues up the ridge to Mueller Hut (dorm $36), a comfortable 28-bunk hut with gas, cooking facilities and long-drop toilets.

Hooker Valley Track — TRAMPING
Perhaps the best of the area's day walks, this track – three hours return from the DOC White Horse Hill Campground (p536) – heads up the Hooker Valley and crosses three swing bridges to the Stocking Stream and the terminus of the Hooker Glacier. After the second swing bridge, Aoraki/Mt Cook totally dominates the valley, and you may see icebergs floating in Hooker Lake.

Kea Point Track — TRAMPING
The trail to Kea Point (two hours return from the visitor centre) is lined with native plants and ends with excellent views of Aoraki/Mt Cook, the Hooker Valley, and the ice faces of Mt Sefton and the Footstool. Despite the name, you're no more likely to see a kea (bird) here than anywhere else. If you do, don't feed it.

Alpine Guides — CLIMBING
(📞03-435 1834; www.alpineguides.co.nz; 98 Bowen Dr; beginners climbing course from $2350) Offers guided climbs and mountaineering courses for all skill levels, along with ski-touring, including heli options. It also stocks outdoor clothing and mountaineering gear, and rents ice axes, crampons, day packs and sleeping bags.

Southern Alps Guiding — ROCK CLIMBING, SNOW SPORTS
(📞03-435 1890; www.mtcook.com; Old Mountaineers' Cafe, Bowen Dr) Offers mountaineering instruction and guiding, plus three- to four-hour helihiking trips on Tasman Glacier year-round ($550). From June to October heliskiers can head up the Tasman, Murchison and Mannering Glaciers for a series of 5km to 15km runs (four runs, from $1150; extra runs per person from $125).

Alpine Recreation — TRAMPING
(📞0800 006 096, 03-680 6736; www.alpinerecreation.com; guided tramps 2/4/6 days from $790/1690/2490) Based in Lake Tekapo, these folks organise high-altitude guided tramps, as well as mountaineering courses and ski touring. Also on offer are guided ascents of Aoraki/Mt Cook, Mt Tasman and other peaks.

Other Activities

Glacier Kayaking — KAYAKING
(📞03-435 1890; www.mtcook.com; Old Mountaineers' Cafe, Bowen Dr; per person $250; ⊙Oct-Apr) Suitable for paddlers with just an ounce of experience, these guided kayaking trips head out on the terminal lake of the Tasman or Mueller Glaciers. With luck there will be

Aoraki/Mt Cook National Park

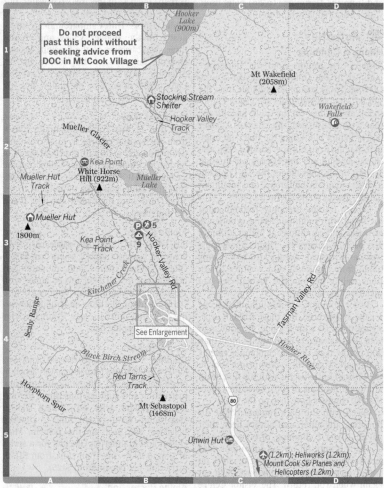

icebergs to negotiate, but regardless there will be spectacular scenery, with a fascinating geology lesson thrown in. Trips last four to six hours, depending on conditions; book at the Old Mountaineers' Cafe (p536).

Big Sky Stargazing STARGAZING
(☑ 03-435 1809, 0800 686 800; www.hermitage. co.nz; Hermitage, Terrace Rd; adult/child $90/45) NZ's southern sky is introduced with a 45-minute presentation in the Alpine Centre's digital planetarium. Afterwards participants venture outside to study the real deal with telescopes, binoculars and an astronomy guide.

👉 Tours

Mount Cook Ski Planes and Helicopters SCENIC FLIGHTS
(☑ 03-430 8026; www.mtcookskiplanes.com; Mt Cook Airport) Get an aerial view of Mt Cook and surrounding glaciers via ski plane or helicopter with this outfit, based at Mt Cook Airport. Most flights include a snow or glacier landing; options include the 45-minute Grand Circle (adult/child $560/425) and the 35-minute Tasman Experience (adult/child $310/245). Flight-seeing without a landing is a cheaper option – for a taster, try the 10-minute Lower Tasman Loop ($99).

Aoraki/Mt Cook National Park

Glacier Explorers   BOATING
(📞03-435 1641; www.glacierexplorers.com; Hermitage, Terrace Rd; adult/child $170/87; ☺Sep-May) Head out on the terminal lake of the Tasman Glacier for this small-boat tour, which gets up close and personal with old icebergs and crazy moraines. Includes a 30-minute walk. Book at the activities desk at the Hermitage (p536).

Helicopter Line   SCENIC FLIGHTS
(📞03-435 1801; www.helicopter.co.nz; Glentanner Park, Mt Cook Rd) Departing from Glentanner Park, the Helicopter Line offers 20-minute Alpine Vista flights ($240), an exhilarating 35-minute flight over the Ben Ohau Range ($360), and a 40-minute Mountains High flight over the Tasman Glacier and alongside Aoraki/Mt Cook ($450). All feature snow landings.

Heliworks   SCENIC FLIGHTS
(📞03-435 1460, 0800 666 668; www.heliworks.nz; Mt Cook Airport; flights per person $280-590) Offers a range of scenic helicopter flights over some of NZ's most majestic scenery, all with a glacier landing. The 55-minute Aoraki/Mt Cook Ultimate flight ($580) circumnavigates the country's highest peak.

Tasman Valley 4WD & Argo Tours   TOURS
(📞0800 686 800; www.mountcooktours.co.nz; adult/child $49/29) Offers year-round, 90-minute Argo (8WD all-terrain vehicle) tours to the Tasman Glacier and its terminal lake, with alpine flora and an interesting commentary along the way. Book online or at the Hermitage (p536) activities desk.

🛏 Sleeping

Mt Cook YHA HOSTEL $

(📞03-435 1820; www.yha.co.nz; 1 Bowen Dr; dm/d $40/140; 🅿🛜) 🏊 Handsomely decked out in pine, this excellent hostel has a free sauna, a drying room, log fires, a large kitchen and friendly, helpful staff. Rooms are clean and warm, although some are a tight squeeze (particularly the twin bunk rooms).

**DOC White Horse
Hill Campground** CAMPGROUND $

(📞03-435 1186; www.doc.govt.nz; Hooker Valley Rd; sites per adult/child $13/6.50; 🅿) Located 2km up the Hooker Valley from Mt Cook village, this self-registration camping ground has a basic shelter with (cold water) sinks, tables and toilets, along with blissful views and close proximity to various walking tracks.

Glentanner Park Centre HOLIDAY PARK $

(📞03-435 1855; www.glentanner.co.nz; State Hwy 80; sites $22-25, dm $40, units $110, without bathroom $210; 🅿@🍴🛜) 🏊 On the northern shore of Lake Pukaki, 22km south of Mt Cook village, this is the nearest fully equipped camping ground to the national park. Features include cabins and motel units, a bunk room, a cafe and free-roaming rabbits.

★ Aoraki/Mt Cook Alpine Lodge LODGE $$

(📞03-435 1860; www.aorakialpinelodge.co.nz; Bowen Dr; d $169-240; 🅿🛜) This lovely family-run lodge has en suite rooms, including some suitable for families and two with kitchenettes; most have views. The huge lounge and kitchen area also has a superb mountain outlook, as does the barbecue area – a rather inspiring spot to sizzle your dinner.

Aoraki Court Motel MOTEL $$$

(📞03-435 1111; www.aorakicourt.co.nz; 26 Bowen Dr; d $375-455; 🅿🛜) While they wouldn't command these prices elsewhere, this clump of modern motel units offers classy decor, all the requisite mod cons and good views. Some units have spa baths, and there are bikes for hire.

Hermitage HOTEL $$$

(📞03-435 1809; www.hermitage.co.nz; Terrace Rd; r $235-525; 🅿@🛜) Completely dominating Mt Cook village, this famous hotel offers awesome views. While the corridors in some of the older wings can seem a little hospital-like, all of the rooms have been renovated to a reasonable standard (the cheapest do not have mountain views). In addition to the on-site shop and Alpine Centre, there are three dining options of reasonable standard.

🍴 Eating & Drinking

Old Mountaineers' Cafe CAFE $$

(www.mtcook.com; Bowen Dr; mains breakfast $9-15, lunch $14-26, dinner $24-35; ⏱10am-9pm; 🛜) 🏊 Encouraging lingering with books, memorabilia and mountain views through picture windows, the village's best eatery also supports local and organic suppliers via an all-day menu offering salmon and bacon pies, cooked breakfasts, burgers and pizza.

Chamois Bar & Grill PUB

(www.mountcookbackpackers.co.nz; Bowen Dr; ⏱4pm-late; 🛜) Upstairs in Mt Cook Backpacker Lodge, this large bar offers basic pub meals (mains $15 to $30), a pool table, a big-screen TV and the occasional live gig, but the views are its best feature. Come at sunset and watch the mountains change colour.

ℹ Information

The Aoraki/Mt Cook National Park Visitor Centre (p531) is the best source of local information. The nearest ATM and supermarket are in Twizel.

ℹ Getting There & Away

Mt Cook village's small airport only serves aerial sightseeing companies. Some of these may be willing to combine transport to the West Coast (ie Franz Josef) with a scenic flight, but flights are heavily dependent on weather.

If you're driving, fill up at Lake Tekapo or Twizel. There is a self-service pump at Mt Cook, but it's expensive.

Cook Connection (p529) runs shuttle services to Lake Tekapo ($40, 1½ hours) and Twizel ($28, 45 minutes).

InterCity (p500) coaches stop at the Hermitage; however, they are operated as part of a 'tour' and can be pricey – you might be better off catching a shuttle back to Twizel and picking up an InterCity connection from there.

DESTINATION	FARES FROM	DURATION (HR)
Christchurch	$213	5¼
Lake Tekapo	$87	1¼
Queenstown	$184	4¾

Dunedin & Otago

Best Places to Eat

➜ Riverstone Kitchen (p547)

➜ Fleur's Place (p549)

➜ No 7 Balmac (p558)

➜ Bracken (p558)

➜ Courthouse Cafe & Larder (p568)

Best Places to Stay

➜ Pen-y-bryn Lodge (p547)

➜ Oliver's (p569)

➜ Pitches Store (p567)

➜ Old Bones Backpackers (p546)

➜ Hogwartz (p555)

Why Go?

Otago has attractions both urban and rural, from quirky towns to world-class wineries and some of the country's most accessible wildlife. Its historic heart is Dunedin, home to a vibrant student culture and arts scene. From the town's stately Edwardian train station it's possible to catch the famous Taieri Gorge Railway inland, and continue on two wheels along the craggily scenic Otago Central Rail Trail.

Those seeking colonial New Zealand can soak up the frontier atmosphere of gold-rush towns such as Clyde, St Bathans, Naseby and cute-as-a-button Ophir. For wildlife, head to the Otago Peninsula, where penguins, albatross, sea lions and seals are easily sighted. Seaside Oamaru has a wonderful historic precinct, resident penguin colonies and a quirky devotion to steampunk culture.

Unhurried and overflowing with picturesque scenery, Otago is generous to explorers who are after a more leisurely style of holiday.

When to Go

➜ February and March have sunny, settled weather (usually...), and the juicy appeal of fresh apricots, peaches and cherries.

➜ At Easter, hook yourself a 'Southern Man' at the biennial Middlemarch Singles Ball, or drown your sorrows at the Clyde Wine & Food Festival.

➜ Take to two wheels on the Otago Central Rail Trail during the quieter month of September.

➜ In November, watch the pros battle it out on the Highlands Motorsport Park, then ride graciously into the past on a penny farthing bicycle at Oamaru's Victorian Heritage Celebrations.

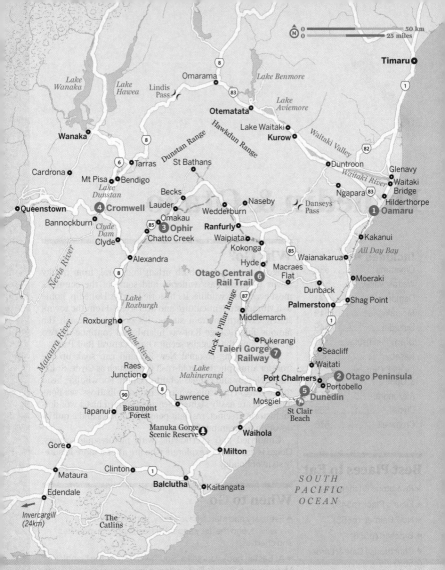

Dunedin & Otago Highlights

1 **Oamaru** (p541) Delving into its heritage past and a possible steampunk future.

2 **Otago Peninsula** (p561) Peering at penguins, admiring albatross and staring at seals.

3 **Ophir** (p566) Exploring New Zealand's gold-mining heritage in a quaint backcountry village.

4 **Cromwell** (p570) Taste-testing some of the planet's best pinot noir in the wineries scattered around the fruit bowl of the south.

5 **Dunedin** (p549) Sampling local beers and bopping to local bands in the city's bars and cafes.

6 **Otago Central Rail Trail** (p565) Cycling through breathtaking vistas of brown and gold on the route of a defunct train line.

7 **Taieri Gorge Railway** (p555) Winding through gorges, alongside canyons and across tall viaducts on this snaking heritage railway.

ⓘ Getting There & Away

Air New Zealand (☑ 0800 737 000; www.airnewzealand.co.nz) flies from Dunedin to Christchurch, Wellington and Auckland, and **Jetstar** (☑ 0800 800 995; www.jetstar.com) flies to Wellington and Auckland.

The only train services are heritage trips (p555) from Dunedin to Middlemarch or Palmerston.

The main bus routes follow SH1 or SH8.

WAITAKI DISTRICT

The broad, braided Waitaki River provides a clear dividing line between Otago and Canterbury to the region's north. The Waitaki Valley is a direct but less-travelled route from the Southern Alps to the sea, featuring freaky limestone formations, Māori rock paintings and ancient fossils. The area is also one of NZ's newest winemaking regions, and a major component of the new Alps 2 Ocean Cycle Trail (p532), which links Aoraki/Mt Cook National Park to the coast. The district's main town, Oamaru, is a place of penguins, steampunk and glorious heritage architecture.

Omarama

☑ 03 / POP 270

At the head of the Waitaki Valley, sleepy Omarama is surrounded by mountain ranges and fabulous landscapes. Busy times include the rodeo (28 December) and the sheepdog trials (March).

◉ Sights

Clay Cliffs Paritea LANDMARK
(Henburn Rd; vehicles $5) This bizarre moonscape is the result of two million years of erosion on layers of silt and gravel that were exposed along the active Ostler fault line. The cliffs are on private land; pay your entrance fee via the honour box at the gate. To get to the cliffs, head north from town for 3km on SH8, turn left onto Quailburn Rd, and then turn left after 3km onto unsealed Henburn Rd (the route is well signposted).

🏃 Activities

Omarama Hot Tubs SPA
(☑ 03-438 9703; www.hottubsomarama.co.nz; 29 Omarama Ave, SH8; per 1-/2-/3-/4-person tub $52/90/114/136, pod $75/140/180/200; ☺ 11am-late) If your legs are weary after mountain biking or tramping, or you just want to cosy up with your significant other, these private, wood-fired hot tubs could be just the ticket. Choose between a 90-minute soak in a tub (each has its own dressing room) or a two-hour session in a 'wellness pod', which includes a sauna.

The chemical-free glacier and snow-melt water is changed after each booking, and the used water is recycled for irrigation. The concept is Japanese, but with the surrounding mountain ranges, the lakeside setting and a pristine night sky, you could only be on the South Island of NZ. Therapeutic massages (30/60/90 minutes $60/100/150) and other treatments are also available.

Glide Omarama GLIDING
(☑ 03-438 9555; www.glideomarama.com; Airport Rd, Omarama Airfield) The area's westerlies and warm summer thermals allow for world-class gliding over the hills and spectacular Southern Alps, and a national gliding meet is held here in December or January. This outfit offers lessons and scenic flights ranging from 30 minutes ($358) to five hours ($1475).

🛏 Sleeping & Eating

Buscot Station FARMSTAY $
(☑ 027 222 1754; www.bbh.co.nz; 912 SH8; campsite/dm/s/d $10/26/44/63; ℗) For a completely different and uniquely Kiwi experience, grab a room in the home-style farmhouse attached to a huge sheep and cattle station, or a bed in the large dormitory out the back. The sunset views are terrific and there's plenty of acreage for quiet explorations. Look for it on SH8, 10km north of Omarama.

Omarama Top 10
Holiday Park HOLIDAY PARK $
(☑ 03-438 9875; www.omaramatop10.co.nz; 1 Omarama Ave, SH8; campsites $40-45, units with/without bathroom $145/80; ℗ 🐕 🖶) ♿ Facilities are good at this holiday park, squeezed between the highway and a stream. Standard cabins are on the cosy side, but larger en suite cabins and self-contained motel units are also available.

Wrinkly Rams CAFE $$
(☑ 03-438 9751; www.thewrinklyrams.co.nz; 24-30 Omarama Ave, SH8; mains $12-30; ☺ 7am-4.30pm; 🐕) Restaurants attached to tourist attractions can be dodgy, but the meals here are perfectly fine (the coffee is hit and miss, though). Big glass windows and outside

tables give a nice view of the mountains while you eat. Wines from the nearby Waitaki Valley also feature.

ⓘ Information

Omarama Hot Tubs (p539) doubles as the tourist office, and can assist with accommodation and transport info. See www.discover omarama.co.nz for more details.

ⓘ Getting There & Away

The road from Omarama to Cromwell heads over the striking Lindis Pass.

Atomic Shuttles (p560) services stop in Omarama for a break before continuing on to Christchurch ($40, five hours), Lake Tekapo ($20, 1¾ hours), Twizel ($20, 20 minutes), Cromwell ($25, 1½ hours) and Queenstown ($35, 2½ hours).

InterCity (p560) runs two coaches a day to/ from Christchurch (from $30, 4¾ hours), Twizel (from $10, 25 minutes), Cromwell (from $23, 1½ hours) and Queenstown (from $32, 2½ hours), and one to/from Mt Cook Village ($78, 1¼ hours).

Naked Bus (p560) runs daily services to/ from Christchurch (4¾ hours), Lake Tekapo (1¼ hours), Cromwell (2½ hours) and Queenstown (3¼ hours). Prices vary.

Waitaki Valley

Wine, waterskiing and salmon-fishing are just some of the treats on offer along this little-travelled route. Coming from Omarama, the winding SH83 passes a series of glassy blue lakes. For a scenic detour along the north bank, leave the highway at Otematata and cross over Benmore Dam, then cross back over Aviemore Dam to rejoin the route.

A succession of sleepy little towns line the highway, peppered with rustic old bank buildings and pubs. One of the most appealing is tiny **Kurow**, the hometown of World Cup–winning retired All Blacks captain Richie McCaw. From almost-as-cute

Duntroon, adventurous (and appropriately insured) drivers can take the unsealed road over Danseys Pass to Naseby.

Although they've got a way to go to attain the global reputation enjoyed by their colleagues in Central Otago, a few winemaking pioneers in Waitaki Valley are producing wine of which international experts are taking notice.

◉ Sights

◉ Kurow

Kurow Heritage & Information Centre MUSEUM
(☑ 03-436 0950; www.kurow.org.nz; 57 Bledisloe St, Kurow; ☺ 9.30am-4pm Mon-Fri year-round, plus 11am-3pm Sat & Sun Nov-Mar) FREE Local hero Richie McCaw rates a mention at this very sweet community-run museum, which mostly features artefacts and curios from Kurow's more distant past. Staff are knowledgable and friendly, and can give excellent advice on local activities and routes.

Pasquale Kurow Winery WINERY
(☑ 03-436 0443; www.pasquale.co.nz; 5292 Kurow-Duntroon Rd, SH83; ☺ 10am-5pm Nov-Mar) The valley's most impressive winery, Pasquale produces killer pinot noir, pinot gris and riesling, as well as less common varietals such as Gewürztraminer and *arneis*. Drop in for a wine-tasting session ($10, refundable upon purchase) and an antipasto and cheese platter.

◉ Duntroon & Around

Takiroa Māori Rock Painting Site ARCHAEOLOGICAL SITE
(SH83) FREE Hidden within the honeycomb cliffs lining the highway, this well-signposted site, 3km west of Duntroon, features centuries-old drawings of mystical creatures, animals and even a sailing ship.

MĀORI NZ: DUNEDIN & OTAGO

The early Māori history of Otago echoes that of Canterbury (p501), with Ngāi Tahu the dominant tribe at the time the British arrived. One of the first parcels of land that Ngāi Tahu sold was called the Otago block, a 1618-sq-km parcel of land that changed hands in 1844 for £2400. The name Otago reflects the Ngāi Tahu pronunciation of Ōtākou, a small village on the far reaches of the Otago Peninsula, where there's still a *marae* (meeting place).

Dunedin's Otago Museum (p554) has the finest Māori exhibition on the South Island, including an ornately carved *waka taua* (war canoe) and finely crafted *pounamu* (greenstone). Māori rock art can still be seen in situ in the Waitaki Valley (p541).

Maerewhenua Māori
Rock Painting Site ARCHAEOLOGICAL SITE
(Livingstone-Duntroon Rd) FREE Sheltered by an impressive limestone overhang, this site contains charcoal-and-ochre paintings dating to before the arrival of Europeans in NZ. Head east from Duntroon and take the first right after crossing the Maerewhenua River; the site is on the left after about 400m.

Vanished World Centre MUSEUM
(www.vanishedworld.co.nz; 7 Campbell St, Duntroon; adult/child $10/free; ⊙10am-4pm) Perhaps there wouldn't be quite so many bad dolphin tattoos and dancing penguin films if more people stopped in Duntroon to check out this small but interesting volunteer-run centre. Once you see the 25-million-year-old fossils of shark-toothed dolphins and giant penguins, they suddenly don't seem so cute.

Pick up a copy of the *Vanished World Trail* map ($6.50) outlining 20 different interesting geological locations around the Waitaki Valley and North Otago coast.

🏃 Activities

Awakino Skifield SKIING
(☑021 890 584; www.skiawakino.com; Awakino Skifield Rd; daily lift pass adult/child $55/27) Situated high above Kurow, Awakino is a small player on the NZ ski scene, but worth a visit for intermediate skiers who fancy some peace and quiet. Weekend lodge-and-ski packages are available.

🛈 Getting There & Away

There's no public transport along this route. You'll need your own car or bike.

Oamaru

☑03 / POP 13,000

Nothing moves very fast in Oamaru. Tourists saunter, locals linger and penguins waddle. Even the town's recently resurrected heritage modes of transport – penny farthings and steam trains – reflect an unhurried pace. Most travellers come here for the penguins, but hang around and you'll sense the wellspring of eccentricity bubbling under the surface. Put simply, Oamaru is *cool*.

Down by the water, a neighbourhood of once-neglected Victorian buildings now swarms with oddballs, antiquarians and bohemians of all stripes, who run offbeat galleries, quirky shops, hip music venues and even an 'urban winery'. Most visible are the steampunks, their aesthetic boldly celebrating the past and the future with an ethos of 'tomorrow as it used to be'.

Away from the docks, Oamaru's whitestone buildings harbour an increasing array of cafes and bars, while up on the clifftops a few excellent accommodation options have taken hold. You may find yourself lingering longer than expected in this laid-back coastal town.

History

Oamaru used to be rich and ambitious. In its 1880s heyday, Oamaru was about the same size as Los Angeles was at the time. Refrigerated meat-shipping had its origins nearby and the town became wealthy enough to erect the imposing buildings that grace Thames St today. However, the town overreached itself and spent the end of the 19th century teetering on the verge of bankruptcy.

Economic decline in the 20th century meant that there wasn't the impetus to swing the wrecking ball with the same reckless abandon that wiped out much of the built heritage of NZ's main centres. It's

ESSENTIAL DUNEDIN & OTAGO

Eat nectarines, apricots, peaches, plums and cherries from Central Otago.

Drink pinot noir from Central Otago and the Waitaki Valley.

Read *To the Is-land* (1982), the first volume of Otago author Janet Frame's lyrical autobiography.

Listen to *Tally Ho! Flying Nun's Greatest Bits*, a 2011 compilation marking the 30th anniversary of Dunedin's iconic record label.

Watch *In My Father's Den* (2004), set in Central Otago.

Celebrate at Oamaru's Victorian Heritage Celebrations (p546) in late November.

Go green and tiptoe down to Otago Peninsula beaches in search of rare yellow-eyed penguins.

Go online www.dunedinnz.com, www.centralotagonz.com

GUNTSOOPHACK YUKTAHNON/SHUTTERSTOCK ©

MARKUS GANN/SHUTTERSTOCK ©

1. Otago Peninsula (p561)

Only half an hour's drive from downtown Dunedin, this small sliver of land is home to diverse wildlife.

2-4. Dunedin (p549)

Hilly Dunedin – home to the steepest street in the world, Baldwin St (p554; pictured bottom right) – features urban wonders like Dunedin Railway Station (p550; pictured bottom left) that are a mere stone's throw away from natural beauties such as the Tunnel Beach Walkway (p555; pictured top right).

3

MARTIAN977/SHUTTERSTOCK ©

Oamaru

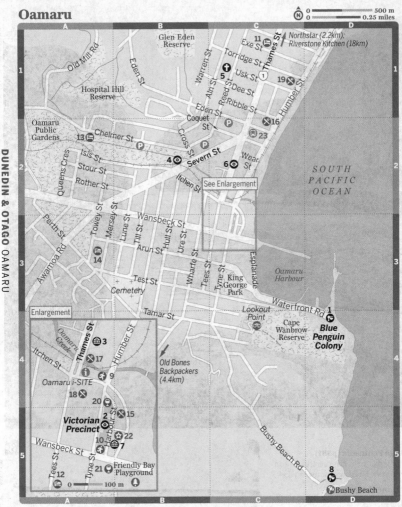

only in recent decades that canny creative types have cottoned on to the uniqueness of Oamaru's surviving Victorian streetscapes and have started to unlock this otherwise unremarkable town's potential for extreme kookiness.

⊙ Sights

★**Victorian Precinct**   AREA

Consisting of only a couple of blocks centred on Harbour and Tyne Sts, this atmospheric enclave has some of NZ's best-preserved Victorian commercial buildings. Descend on

a dark and foggy night and it's downright Dickensian. It's also ground zero for all that is hip, cool and freaky in Oamaru, and one of the best places to window-shop in the entire South Island.

Wander around during the day and you'll discover antiquarian bookshops, antique stores, galleries, vintage-clothing shops, kooky gift stores, artist studios, old-fashioned lolly shops and artisan bookbinders. At night there are some cute little bars, and you might even see a penguin swaggering along the street – we did!

Oamaru

The precinct is at its liveliest on Sundays when the excellent **Oamaru farmers market** is in full swing. Note that some shops and attractions are closed on Mondays.

★**Blue Penguin Colony**   BIRD SANCTUARY
(☑ 03-433 1195; www.penguins.co.nz; 2 Waterfront Rd; adult/child $30/15; ⊙ 10am-2hr after sunset)
📖 Every evening the tykes from the Oamaru little penguin colony surf in and wade ashore, heading to their nests in an old stone quarry near the waterfront. Stands are set up on either side of the waddle route. General admission will give you a good view of the action but the premium stand (adult/child $45/22.50), accessed by a boardwalk through the nesting area, will get you closer.

You'll see the most penguins (up to 250) in November and December. From March to August there may be only 10 to 50 birds. They arrive in clumps called rafts just before dark (around 5.30pm in midwinter and 9.30pm midsummer), and it takes about an hour for them all to come ashore; nightly viewing times are posted at the i-SITE (p548). Use of cameras is prohibited and you're advised to dress warmly.

To understand the centre's conservation work and its success in increasing the penguin population, take the daytime, behind-the-scenes tour (adult/child self-guided $10/5 or guided $16/8); packages that combine night viewing and the daytime tour are also available.

Do not under any circumstances wander around the rocks beside the sea here at night looking for penguins. It's damaging to their environment and spoils studies into the human effects on the birds.

St Patrick's Basilica   CHURCH
(☑ 03-434 8543; www.cdd.org.nz/st-patrick -oamaru; 68 Reed St) If you've ever fantasised about being transported back to Ancient Rome, stroll through the Corinthian columns and into this gorgeous Catholic church (built in 1873). Renowned architect Francis Petre went for the full time warp with this one, right down to a coffered ceiling and cupola above the altar.

Thames St   AREA
Oamaru's main drag owes its expansive girth to the need to accommodate the minimum turning circle of a bullock cart. The town's grand pretensions reached their peak in the late 19th century in a series of gorgeous buildings constructed from the milky local limestone (known as Oamaru stone or whitestone), with their forms reflecting the fashion of the times; there's a particular emphasis on the neoclassical.

Impressive examples include the Forrester Gallery (at No 9, built 1883), the ANZ Bank (No 11, 1871), the Waitaki District

Council building (No 20, 1883), the North Otago Museum (No 60, 1882), the Courthouse (No 88, 1883) and the Opera House (No 92, 1907).

Steampunk HQ
GALLERY

(☑ 027 778 6547; www.steampunkoamaru.co.nz; 1 Itchen St; adult/child $10/2; ☺ 10am-5pm) Discover an alternative past – or maybe a quirky version of the future – at this fascinating art project celebrating steampunk culture. Ancient machines wheeze and splutter, and the industrial detritus of the last century or so is repurposed and reimagined to creepy effect. Bring a $2 coin to fire up the sparking, space-age locomotive out the front.

Yellow-Eyed Penguin Colony
BIRD SANCTUARY

(Bushy Beach Rd) FREE Larger and much rarer than their little blue cousins, yellow-eyed penguins waddle ashore at Bushy Beach in the late afternoon to feed their young. In order to protect these endangered birds, the beach is closed to people from 3pm onwards, but there are hides set up on the cliffs (you'll need binoculars for a decent view). The best time to see them is two hours before sunset.

Oamaru Public Gardens
GARDENS

(Severn St; ☺ dawn-dusk) Opened in 1876, these beautiful gardens are a lovely place to stroll and relax, with expansive lawns, waterways, bridges and a children's playground.

Forrester Gallery
GALLERY

(☑ 03-433 0853; www.culturewaitaki.org.nz; 9 Thames St; ☺ 10.30am-4.30pm Mon-Fri, from 1pm Sat & Sun; ☝) FREE Housed in a temple-like former bank building, the Forrester Gallery stages excellent temporary exhibitions of local and NZ art. The 'wonderlab', upstairs, hosts interactive exhibitions especially designed for children.

Whitestone City
MUSEUM

(☑ 0508 978 663; www.whitestonecity.com; 12 Harbour St, Seaward Side; adult/child $20/10; ☺ 10am-6pm) Opened in 2017, this brandnew attraction brings Oamaru's heyday to life. Stroll through the replica Victorian streetscape, visit the schoolroom complete with slates and schoolmistress, play old-fashioned games in the dimly lit saloon, and take a ride on the pièce de résistance – a penny-farthing carousel.

North Otago Museum
MUSEUM

(☑ 03-433 0852; www.culturewaitaki.org.nz; 58-60 Thames St; ☺ 1-4.30pm Mon-Fri) FREE The museum is currently preparing for a move to a larger exhibition space (scheduled for 2019); in the interim, a limited selection of exhibits are open to view in this one-room space, including Māori and Pākehā (white person) artefacts and a collection of antique printing presses.

🏃 Activities

Vertical Ventures
CYCLING, ROCK CLIMBING

(☑ 03-434 5010; www.verticalventures.co.nz; 4 Wansbeck St) Rent a mountain bike (from $45 per day), or join guided mountain-biking trips, including the Alps 2 Ocean Cycle Trail (seven days including transport, food and accommodation from $2995). The 'vertical' part comes in the form of rock-climbing day trips (from $150 per person).

Oamaru Steam & Rail
RAIL

(www.oamaru-steam.org.nz; adult/child/family return $8/3/20; ☺ 11am-3pm Sun; ☝) On Sundays, take a half-hour ride on a vintage steam train from the Victorian Precinct to the waterfront.

🎊 Festivals & Events

Victorian Heritage Celebrations
CULTURAL

(www.vhc.co.nz; ☺ mid-Nov) Five days of costumed capers and historical hijinks, culminating in a grand fete.

🛏 Sleeping

⭐ Old Bones Backpackers
HOSTEL $

(☑ 03-434 8115; www.oldbones.co.nz; Beach Rd; r $100, campervans per person $25; @ 🛜) Five kilometres south of Oamaru on the coast road, this top-notch dorm-free hostel has tidy rooms off a huge, sunny, central space. Listen to the surf crashing over the road while relaxing in front of the wood-burning fire, or book one of the hot tubs (from $90) and drift into ecstasy while gazing at the stars.

Oamaru Backpackers
HOSTEL $

(☑ 021 190 0069; www.oamarubackpackers. co.nz; 47 Tees St; dm/s $30/50, d $75-90; ℙ 🛜) A stone's throw from the Victorian quarter, this recently renovated hostel has lovely, individually decorated rooms and a great dorm with privacy curtains and individual outlets. Best of all is the view of the harbour from the giant windows in the airy, light-filled lounge.

Oamaru Top 10 Holiday Park
HOLIDAY PARK $

(☑ 03-434 7666; www.oamarutop10.co.nz; 30 Chelmer St; sites $40-45, units with/without bath-

RIVERSTONE

It's well worth taking the 14km trip from Oamaru to this idiosyncratic complex, hidden along the unassuming short stretch of SH1 between the braided mouth of the Waitaki River and SH83 turn-off.

First and foremost it's the home of **Riverstone Kitchen** (☑03-431 3505; www.riverstonekitchen.co.nz; 1431 Glenavy-Hilderthorpe Rd, SH1, Waitaki Bridge; breakfast $16-22, lunch $22-32, dinner $28-34; ⊙9am-late Thu-Sat, to 5pm Sun-Mon), a sophisticated restaurant that outshines any in Oamaru itself. A riverstone fireplace and polished concrete floors set the scene for a menu that's modern without being overworked. Much of the produce comes from the extensive on-site kitchen gardens (go for a stroll, they're impressive), plus locally sourced venison, pork, salmon and beef. It's a smashing brunch option, with excellent coffee and legendary truffled scrambled eggs. Save room for dessert, too.

Next door, behind a set of fake heritage shopfronts, **Riverstone Country** (☑03-431 3872; 1431 Glenavy-Hilderthorpe Rd, SH1, Waitaki Bridge; ⊙9am-5.30pm) is literally packed to the rafters with gifts, crafts, homewares, fake flowers, garden ornaments and Christmas decorations. Outside, there's an aviary stocked with canaries, lorikeets and guinea pigs.

If this all points to an eccentric mind at the helm, take a look at the moated **castle** at the rear of the complex. The castle is the brainchild of Dot Smith, one of the owners of Riverstone, and is destined to be a private home – construction was completed in mid-2017. At the time of research there was no public access to the castle itself, but that is due to change; check with the restaurant for an update during your visit.

If you're looking for a good place to stay nearby, **Waitaki Waters** (☑03-431 3880; www.campingoamaru.co.nz; 305 Kaik Rd, Waitaki Bridge; sites/cabins from $15/45; P☎) is a holiday park with sparkling facilities, manicured hedges and a peaceful location 3km off SH1. Cabins are simple but well maintained; bring your own bedding.

room from $110/75; P@☎) Grassy and well maintained, this Top 10 has trees out the back and is right next door to the lush public gardens. Standard cabins are basic, but the other units (with varying levels of self-contained comfort) are much nicer.

Highfield Mews MOTEL $$
(☑03-434 3437; www.highfieldmews.co.nz; 244 Thames St; units from $190; P☎@☎) ✎ The units at this flash new motel are basically smart apartments, with kitchens, desks, stereos, tiled bathrooms and outdoor furniture. The larger, one-bedroom units come with spa baths.

★**Pen-y-bryn Lodge** B&B $$$
(☑03-434 7939; www.penybryn.co.nz; 41 Towey St; r $600-725; P☎) Well-travelled foodie owners have thoroughly revitalised this beautiful 1889 residence. There are two rooms in the main house but we prefer the three recently and luxuriously refurbished ones in the rear annexe. Predinner drinks and canapés are served in the antique-studded drawing room, and you can arrange a four-course dinner in the fabulous dining room (from $125 per person).

✖ Eating

Harbour St Bakery BAKERY $
(☑03-434 0444; www.harbourstreetbakery.com; 4 Harbour St; pies $5.50; ⊙10am-4pm Tue-Sun) Selling both European-style bread and pastries and Kiwi meat pies, this petite Dutch bakery covers its bases well. Grab a seat outside and watch Oamaru's heritage streetlife scroll past like an old-time movie.

Whitestone Cheese Factory DELI, CAFE $
(☑03-434 8098; www.whitestonecheese.com; 3 Torridge St; platters $14.50; ⊙9am-5pm Mon-Fri, 10am-4pm Sat & Sun) The home of award-winning artisanal cheeses, Whitestone is a local culinary institution and the factory-door cafe is a fine place to challenge one's arteries. As well as fulfilling self-caterers' cheese dreams, the petite cafe offers a couple of cheesy options to eat-in, including cheese scones, cheesecake, and tasting platters of six different cheeses, as well as tea and coffee.

Steam CAFE $
(www.facebook.com/steamoamaru; 7 Thames St; mains $10-13; ⊙7.30am-4.30pm Mon-Fri, 8am-2.30pm Sat & Sun; ☎) This popular little cafe near the Victorian quarter specialises in

coffees and fruit juices, and it's a good spot to stock up on freshly ground beans for your own travels. Check the counter cabinet for the day's culinary choices, including freshly baked muffins, croissants and the like.

Tees St CAFE $$

(☑ 03-434 7004; www.teesst.com; 3 Tees St; mains $13-18; ☉ 7am-3pm Mon-Fri, from 8.30am Sat & Sun; ☎) An ornate Victorian draper's shop provides a suitably gracious ambience for this hip little cafe. A concise brunch menu offers the usual suspects, from eggs to pancakes to a delectable chia pudding. Great coffee and homemade pastries complete the picture.

Midori JAPANESE $$

(☑ 03-434 9045; www.facebook.com/Midori JapaneseSushiBarAndRestaurant; 1 Ribble St; sushi $12-17, mains $18-29; ☉ 10.30am-8.30pm Mon-Wed, 10.30am-9pm Thu-Fri, 11am-9pm Sat, noon-8.30pm Sun) Midori, housed in a heritage stone building, serves sashimi and sushi that makes the most of fresh local seafood. Other carefully prepared dishes include teriyaki salmon and blue cod, udon soup and a variety of bento boxes. If you just want to grab and go, there's also a takeaway menu available.

🍷 Drinking & Nightlife

Scott's Brewing Co. BREWERY

(☑ 03-434 2244; www.scottsbrewing.co.nz; 1 Wansbeck St; ☉ 11am-8.30pm Mon-Tue, to 9.30pm Wed & Sun, to 11pm Thu-Sat) Drop into this old waterfront warehouse to sample the output of Oamaru's premier craft brewers. Slouch against the counter for a tasting or head out onto the sunny deck for a pint and a pizza.

Criterion Hotel PUB

(☑ 03-434 6247; www.criterionhotel.co.nz; 3 Tyne St; ☉ 11am-late Mon-Fri, from 10am Sat & Sun) The most Victorian of the Victorian Precinct's watering holes, this corner beauty has a good beer selection and plenty of local wines. There's usually live music on Fridays.

☆ Entertainment

★ Penguin Club LIVE MUSIC

(www.thepenguinclub.co.nz; Emulsion Lane, off Harbour St; cover charge varies) Tucked down an atmospheric alley off a 19th-century street, the Penguin's unusual location

matches its acts: everything from touring Kiwi bands to punky/grungy/rocky/country locals.

Oamaru Opera House THEATRE

(☑ 03-433 0779; www.oamaruoperahouse.co.nz; 90 Thames St; ☉ ticket office 10am-4pm Mon-Fri, to 1pm Sat) First opened in 1907 and now beautifully restored to its original glory, Oamaru's opera house hosts a variety of shows, including music, dance, theatre and comedy. The main auditorium seats 500-plus patrons under the stunning 1900s cupola and chandelier, while the smaller Inkbox theatre is home to more intimate performances.

ℹ Information

Oamaru i-SITE (☑ 03-434 1656; www.visit oamaru.co.nz; 1 Thames St; ☉ 9am-5pm; ☎) Friendly staff here can offer mountains of information including details on local walking trips and wildlife, plus daily penguin-viewing times. There's also bike hire ($28/40 per half/full day) and an interesting 10-minute film on the history of the town.

ℹ Getting There & Away

Oamaru sits on the main SH1 coastal route between Christchurch (3¼ hours) and Dunedin (1½ hours).

Most buses and shuttles depart from the **Lagonda Tearooms** (☑ 03-434 8716; www. facebook.com/LagondaTeaRooms; 191 Thames St; ☉ 9am-4.30pm; ☎). Both the tearooms and the i-SITE take bookings.

Atomic Shuttles (p560) runs buses to/from Christchurch ($35, four hours), Timaru ($20, 1¼ hours) and Dunedin ($20, 1½ hours), twice daily.

Coast Line Tours (p560) runs shuttles to/from Dunedin (adult/child $30/12); pick up at your accommodation. Detours to Moeraki and Dunedin Airport can be arranged.

InterCity (p560) runs two daily coaches to/from Christchurch (from $22, four hours), Timaru (from $15, one hour), the Moeraki turn-off (from $11, 28 minutes) and Dunedin (from $15, 1½ hours), and one to Te Anau (from $30, 6½ hours).

Naked Bus (p560) runs daily buses to/from Christchurch (four hours), Timaru (1¼ hours), Moeraki (35 minutes) and Dunedin (1¾ hours). Fares fluctuate widely; check the website for deals.

The *Seasider* tourist train, operated by Dunedin Railways (p555), is a scenic way to travel to Dunedin.

Moeraki

☑ 03 / POP 60

The name Moeraki means 'a place to sleep by day', which should give you some clue as to the pace of life in this little fishing village. You might be surprised to learn that this was one of the first European settlements in NZ, with a whaling station established here in 1836. Since then, Moeraki has nurtured the creation of several national treasures, from Frances Hodgkins' paintings to author Keri Hulme's *The Bone People*, and Fleur Sullivan's cooking.

Apart from Fleur's eponymous restaurant, the main reason travellers stop in town is the **Moeraki Boulders** (Te Kaihinaki), beloved of photographers and children alike. It's a pleasant 45-minute walk along the beach from the village to the boulders. Head in the other direction on the **Kaiks Wildlife Trail** and you'll reach a cute old wooden **lighthouse**. You might even spot yellow-eyed penguins and fur seals (be sure to keep your distance).

🛏 Sleeping & Eating

Riverside Haven Lodge & Holiday Park CAMPGROUND $

(☑03-439 5830; www.riversidehaven.nz; 2328 Herbert Hampden Rd/SH1, Waianakarua; sites from $8, dm $28-33, d with/without bathroom from $98/88; 🕏) 🌢 Nestled in a loop of the Waianakarua River, 12km north of the Moeraki turn-off, this pretty riverside property offers both bucolic camping sites and colourful lodge rooms, some with en suites. Kids will love the playground and farm animals; parents will love the spa and peaceful vibe.

Moeraki Beach Motel MOTEL $

(☑03-439 4862; www.moerakibeachmotels.co.nz; cnr Cleddy & Haven Sts; units from $115; 🅿🕏) The four split-level units at this wood-lined motel are spacious and comfortable. Each has two bedrooms, a full kitchen and a balcony with views over the water.

★Fleur's Place SEAFOOD $$$

(☑03-439 4480; www.fleursplace.com; Old Jetty, 169 Haven St; mains $18-44; ⊙10.30am-late Wed-Sun) There's a rumble-tumble look about it, but this quirky tin-and-timber fishing hut houses one of the South Island's best – and most popular – seafood restaurants. Head for the upstairs deck and tuck into fresh shellfish, tender blue cod and other recently landed ocean bounty. Bookings are strongly recommended.

❶ Getting There & Away

Moeraki is on SH1, a 30-minute drive from Oamaru and one hour from Dunedin. All of the buses travelling between the two stop on SH1 by the Moeraki turn-off. From here it's about a 2km walk to both the centre of the village and to the boulders.

DUNEDIN

☑ 03 / POP 127,000

Two words immediately spring to mind when Kiwis think of their seventh-largest city: 'Scotland' and 'students'. The 'Edinburgh of the South' is immensely proud of its Scottish heritage, never missing an opportunity to break out the haggis and bagpipes on civic occasions. In fact the very name Dunedin is derived from the Scottish Gaelic name for Edinburgh – Dùn Èideann – and the city even has its own tartan.

Just like the Scots, Dunedin locals love a drink, and none more so than the students that dominate Dunedin in term time. The country's oldest university provides plenty of student energy to sustain the local bars.

Dunedin is an easy place in which to while away a few days. Weatherboard houses ranging from stately to ramshackle pepper its hilly suburbs, and bluestone Victorian buildings punctuate the compact city centre. It's a great base for exploring the wildlife-rich Otago Peninsula, which officially lies within the city limits.

History

The first permanent European settlers, two shiploads of pious, hard-working Scots, arrived at Port Chalmers in 1848, including the nephew of Scotland's favourite son, Robbie Burns. A statue of the poet dominates The Octagon, the city's civic heart.

In the 1980s Dunedin spawned its own internationally influential indie music scene, with Flying Nun Records and the 'Dunedin sound'. Music is not Dunedin's only creative outlet. In 2014, the city became the first in New Zealand to be designated a UNESCO City of Literature, reflecting the city's literary heritage and culture.

Dunedin & the Otago Peninsula

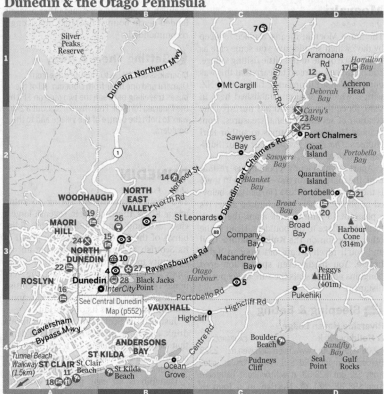

⊙ Sights

⊙ City Centre

★**Toitū Otago Settlers Museum**   MUSEUM
(☑03-477 5052; www.toituosm.com; 31 Queens
Gardens; ◔10am-5pm) **FREE** Storytelling is the
focus of this excellent interactive museum,
which traces the history of human settlement
in the South Island. The engrossing Māori
section is followed by a large gallery where
floor-to-ceiling portraits of Victorian-era settlers stare out from behind their whiskers
and lace. Other displays include a recreated
passenger-ship cabin, an impressive vintage
car collection and a fascinating array of obso-
lete technology, like the first computer used
to draw the lottery in Dunedin.

Dunedin Railway Station   HISTORIC BUILDING
(22 Anzac Ave) Featuring mosaic-tile floors
and glorious stained-glass windows, Dunedin's striking bluestone railway station
(built between 1903 and 1906) claims to
be NZ's most photographed building. Head
upstairs for the New Zealand Sports Hall
of Fame (p553), a small museum devoted to the nation's obsession, and the **Art
Station** (☑03-477 9465; www.otagoartsociety.
co.nz; Dunedin Railway Station, 22 Anzac Ave;
◔10am-4pm) **FREE**, the local Art Society's
gallery and shop. The station is the departure point for several popular scenic rail
journeys (p555).

Dunedin Public Art Gallery   GALLERY
(☑03-474 3240; www.dunedin.art.museum; 30
The Octagon; ◔10am-5pm) **FREE** Gaze upon
local and international art – including a
small collection of Impressionists – at this
expansive and airy gallery. Only a fraction
of the collection is displayed at any given
time, with most of the space given over to
often-edgy temporary exhibitions.

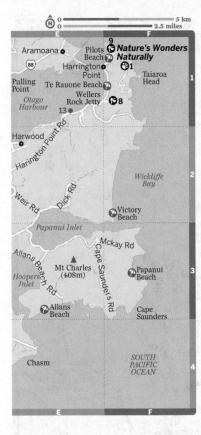

St Paul's Cathedral CHURCH
(www.stpauls.net.nz; Moray Pl; ⊙10am-4pm Oct-Apr, to 3pm May-Sep) Even in Presbyterian Dunedin, the 'established church' (aka the Church of England) gets the prime spot on The Octagon. A Romanesque portal leads into the Gothic interior of this beautiful Anglican cathedral, where soaring white Oamaru-stone pillars spread into a vaulted ceiling. The main part of the church dates from 1919 although the sanctuary was left unfinished until 1971, hence the slightly jarring modern extension. The massive organ (3500 pipes) is said to be one of the finest in the southern hemisphere.

Dunedin Chinese Garden GARDENS
(☏03-477 3248; www.dunedinchinesegarden. com; cnr Rattray & Cumberland Sts; adult/child $9/free; ⊙10am-5pm) Built to recognise the contribution of Dunedin's Chinese community, this walled garden was constructed in Shanghai before being dismantled and re-assembled in its current location. The tranquil confines contain all of the elements of a classical Chinese garden, including ponds, pavilions, rockeries, stone bridges and a tea house. There's also a small display on the

Central Dunedin

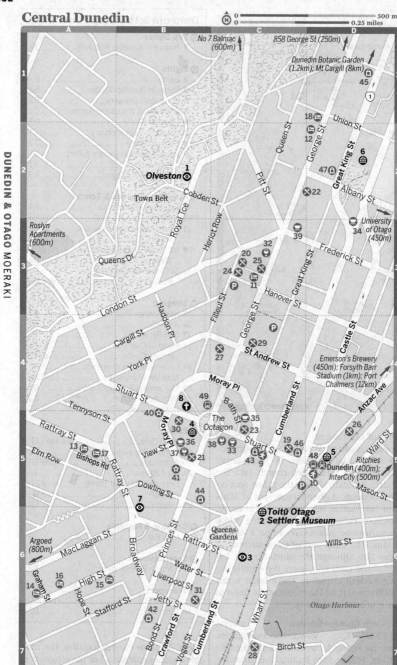

0 500 m
0 0.25 miles

No 7 Balmac (600m)

858 George St (250m)

Dunedin Botanic Garden (1.2km); Mt Cargill (8km)
45

18
12

6

47

22

39

University of Otago (450m)
34

Olveston 1

Town Belt

Roslyn Apartments (600m)

Queens Dr

32
20
25
24
11

29
27
St Andrew St

Moray Pl

8
49
40
4
30
35
23
36
38
33
37
21
43 9
41
19 46
48 5
Dunedin InterCity (500m)
Ritchies (400m)
26
10
44

Emerson's Brewery (450m); Forsyth Barr Stadium (1km); Port Chalmers (12km)

London St
Cargill St
York Pl
Stuart St
Tennyson St
Rattray St
Elm Row
13
17
Bishops Rd

7

Toitū Otago
2 Settlers Museum

Queens Gardens

3

Argoed (800m)

MacLaggan St
14
16
15
31

42

28

St Kilda (3km); St Clair (4km); Dunedin (27km)

Manor Pl

Otago Harbour

Birch St

Central Dunedin

history of the local Chinese community. An informative audioguide is included in the entry price.

Speight's Brewery BREWERY
(☏ 03-477 7697; www.speights.co.nz; 200 Rattray St; adult/child $29/13; ⊘ tours noon, 2pm, 4pm Apr-Sep, plus 5pm, 6pm & 7pm Oct-Mar) Speight's has been churning out beer on this site since the late 19th century. The 90-minute tour gives an insight into the history of the building, the company and the brewing process, and finishes up in the tasting room for a guided sampling session.

New Zealand Sports Hall of Fame MUSEUM
(☏ 03-477 7775; www.nzhalloffame.co.nz; Dunedin Railway Station, 22 Anzac Ave; adult/child $6/2; ⊘ 10am-4pm) At the New Zealand Sports Hall of Fame you can try to match

bike-champ Karen Holliday's average speed of 45.629km/h, or check out the high-stepping style of iconic All Black fullback George Nepia.

◉ North Dunedin

★**Olveston** HOUSE
(☏ 03-477 3320; www.olveston.co.nz; 42 Royal Tce, Roslyn; adult/child $20/11; ⊘ tours 9.30am, 10.45am, noon, 1.30pm, 2.45pm & 4pm) Although it's a youngster by European standards, this spectacular 1906 mansion provides a wonderful window into Dunedin's past. Entry is via fascinating guided tours; it pays to book ahead. There's also a pretty little garden to explore (entry free).

Until 1966 Olveston was the family home of the wealthy Theomin family, notable patrons of the arts who were heavily involved with endowing the Public Art Gallery. This artistic bent is evident in Olveston's grand interiors, which include works by Charles Goldie and Frances Hodgkins (a family friend). A particular passion was Japanese art, and the home is liberally peppered with exquisite examples. The family was Jewish, and the grand dining table is set up as if for Shabbat dinner.

Otago Museum
MUSEUM

(☑ 03-474 7474; www.otagomuseum.nz; 419 Great King St, North Dunedin; ⊙ 10am-5pm) 🖋 **FREE** The centrepiece of this august institution is Southern Land, Southern People, showcasing Otago's cultural and physical past and present, from geology and dinosaurs to the modern day. The Tāngata Whenua Māori gallery houses an impressive *waka taua* (war canoe), wonderfully worn old carvings, and some lovely *pounamu* (greenstone) weapons, tools and jewellery. Other major galleries include Pacific Cultures, People of the World (including the requisite mummy), Nature, Maritime and the Animal Attic.

The newly renovated Tūhura Otago Community Trust Science Centre reopened in December 2017 to much fanfare, boasting 45 new hands-on interactive science displays, a refreshed Tropical Forest butterfly enclosure and a 7.5m-high double helix slide.

Guided tours depart from the information desk at 11am, 1pm, 2pm and 3pm daily (per person $15).

Emerson's Brewery
BREWERY

(☑ 03-477 1812; www.emersons.co.nz; 70 Anzac Ave; tour per person $28; ⊙ tours 10.30am, 12.30pm, 3.30pm & 5.30pm, restaurant 10am-late, cellar door 10am-6pm Sun-Wed, to 8pm Thu-Sat) Opened in 2016, this impressive brick-and-glass structure is the flash new home of Emerson's, the microbrewery founded by local-boy-made-good Richard Emerson in 1992. Forty-five-minute tours take you behind the scenes of the brewing process, ending with the all-important tasting. There's also a cellar door where you can fill a rigger with your favourite drop – or, if you'd like to linger longer, drop into the cavernous restaurant for hearty meals (mains $28 to $32).

University of Otago
HISTORIC BUILDING

(www.otago.ac.nz; 362 Leith St) Founded in 1869, the University of Otago is New Zealand's oldest. Today the university is home to some 18,000 students, and is well worth a wander, with many magnificent bluestone buildings

to admire. The historic heart – bounded by Leith, St David and Castle Sts – is the most photogenic part of the campus. Check the university website for a self-guided tour map.

Dunedin Botanic Garden
GARDENS

(☑ 03-471 9275; www.dunedinbotanicgarden. co.nz; cnr Great King St & Opoho Rd, North Dunedin; ⊙ dawn-dusk) **FREE** Dating from 1863, these 30 hectares of peaceful, grassy and shady green space include rose gardens, rare natives, a rhododendron dell, an exotic bird aviary, a playground and a cafe. Kids love tootling about on the Community Express 'train' (adult/child $3/1) and feeding the ducks (pick up free duck food at the park information centre).

Baldwin St
LANDMARK

(North East Valley) The world's steepest residential street (according to the *Guinness Book of World Records*), at its peak Baldwin St has a gradient of 1 in 2.86 (19°). The slope is the setting for several local events, the most amusing being the annual Jaffa Race, where some 25,000 jaffas are rolled down the street each July for charity.

To reach the street from the city centre, head 2km north up Great King St to where the road branches sharp left to Timaru. Get in the right-hand lane and continue straight ahead. This becomes North Rd, and Baldwin St is on the right after 1km.

🏃 Activities

Swimming, Surfing & Diving

St Clair and St Kilda are both popular swimming beaches (though you need to watch for rips at St Clair). Both have consistently good left-hand breaks, and you'll also find good surfing further south at Blackhead, and at Aramoana on Otago Harbour's North Shore.

Esplanade Surf School
SURFING

(☑ 0800 484 141; www.espsurfschool.co.nz; 1 Esplanade, St Clair; 90min group lesson $60, private instruction $120) Operating from a van parked at St Clair Beach in summer whenever the surf is up (call at other times), this experienced crew provides board hire and lessons to suit all levels.

St Clair Hot Salt Water Pool
SWIMMING

(www.dunedin.govt.nz; Esplanade, St Clair; adult/ child $6.50/3; ⊙ 6am-7pm Mon-Fri, from 7am Sat & Sun Oct-Mar) This heated, outdoor pool sits on the western headland of St Clair Beach.

Walking

The **Otago Tramping & Mountaineering Club** (www.otmc.co.nz) organises regular day and overnight tramps in the surrounding area, including to the Silver Peaks Reserve north of Dunedin. Nonmembers are welcome, but must contact trip leaders beforehand.

Tunnel Beach Walkway WALKING

(Tunnel Beach Rd, Blackhead) This short but extremely steep pathway (15 minutes down, 30 back up) brings you to a dramatic stretch of coast where the wild Pacific has carved sea stacks, arches and unusual formations out of the limestone. Strong currents make swimming here dangerous, but the views are spectacular.

The walkway takes its name from a hand-hewn stone tunnel at the bottom of the track, which civic father John Cargill had built to give his family access to secluded beachside picnics.

The track is 7km southwest of central Dunedin. Head south on Princes St and continue as it crosses under the motorway and then a railway bridge. Turn right at the next traffic lights onto Hillside Rd and follow it until the end, then make a quick left then right onto Easther Cres. Stay on this road for 3.5km (it changes name several times) then look for Tunnel Beach Rd on the left.

Mt Cargill-Bethunes
Gully Walkway WALKING

(www.doc.govt.nz; Norwood St, Normanby) Yes, it's possible to drive up 676m Mt Cargill, but that's not the point. The track (four hours, 8.5km return) starts from Norwood St, which is accessed from North Rd. From Mt Cargill, a trail continues to the 10-million-year-old, lava-formed Organ Pipes and, after another half-hour, to Mt Cargill Rd on the other side of the mountain.

Other Activities

Dunedin Railways RAIL

(☑03-477 4449; www.dunedinrailways.co.nz; Dunedin Railway Station, 22 Anzac Ave; ⊙office 8am-5pm Mon-Fri, 8.30am-3pm Sat & Sun) Two scenic heritage train journeys set off from Dunedin's railway station. The best is the **Taieri Gorge Railway**, with narrow tunnels, deep gorges, winding tracks, rugged canyons and viaduct crossings. The four-hour return trip aboard 1920s heritage coaches travels to Pukerangi (one Mt Cargill-Bethunes Gully Walkwayway/return $61/91), 58km away. Some trains carry on to Middlemarch

($77/115, six hours return) – handy for the Otago Central Rail Trail.

The **Seasider** heads north, partly along the coast, as far as Oamaru ($72/109, seven hours return), although it's possible to get off the train at Moeraki ($66/99) for a two-hour stop before hopping on the return train. Shorter trips head as far as Palmerston ($59/89, four hours return). Aim for a seat on the right-hand side of the train for better sea views.

Cycle World CYCLING

(☑03-477 7473; www.cycleworld.co.nz; 67 Stuart St; per day from $50; ⊙8.30am-6pm Mon-Fri, 9.30am-3.30pm Sat, 10am-3pm Sun) Bike rental, repair and information.

🛏 Sleeping

🛏 City Centre

★**Hogwartz** HOSTEL $

(☑03-474 1487; www.hogwartz.co.nz; 277 Rattray St; dm/s/d from $32/50/74, d with bathroom $86, studio $120; P@🖤) The Catholic bishop's residence from 1872 to 1999, this beautiful building is now a fascinating warren of comfortable and sunny rooms, many with harbour views. Shared bathrooms include welcome touches like waterfall showers and underfloor heating. The old coach house and stables house swankier en suite rooms and apartments.

Chalet Backpackers HOSTEL $

(☑03-479 2075; www.chaletbackpackers.co.nz; 296 High St; dm/s/d from $21/44/66; P@🖤) At the top of the High St hill, this rambling old building offers sweeping views of the city from its sunny lounge and dining room; there's also a compact garden, pool table, piano and rumours of a ghost. Rooms are ageing but tidy.

315 Euro MOTEL $$

(☑03-477 9929; www.eurodunedin.co.nz; 315 George St; apt from $160; P@🖤) This sleek complex is accessed by an unlikely looking alley off Dunedin's main retail strip. Choose from modern studios or larger one-bedroom apartments with full kitchens and laundries. Double glazing keeps George St's incessant buzz at bay.

Dunedin Palms Motel MOTEL $$

(☑03-477 8293; www.dunedinpalmsmotel.co.nz; 185-195 High St; units from $169; P🖤) Located a mercifully short stroll up from the city centre, the Palms has smartly renovated studios and one- and two-bedroom units arrayed around a central car park.

Brothers Boutique Hotel   HOTEL $$$
(☑03-477 0043; www.brothershotel.co.nz; 295 Rattray St; r $190-395; P🐾) Rooms in this 1920s Christian Brothers residence have been refurbished beyond any monk's dreams, while still retaining many unique features. The chapel room even has its original arched stained-glass windows. There are great views from the rooftop units. Rates include a continental breakfast and an evening drink.

Fletcher Lodge   B&B $$$
(☑03-474 5551; www.fletcherlodge.co.nz; 276 High St; s/d/apt from $310/350/650; P🐾) 🐾 Originally home to one of NZ's wealthiest industrialists, this gorgeous red-brick mansion is just minutes from the city, but the secluded gardens feel wonderfully remote. Rooms are elegantly trimmed with antique furniture and ornate plaster ceilings.

🛏 North Dunedin

Kiwi's Nest   HOSTEL $
(☑03-471 9540; www.kiwisnest.co.nz; 597 George St, North Dunedin; dm $28, s w/without bathroom $68/48, d $88/68, apt $105; P@🐾) This wonderfully homey two-storey house has a range of tidy centrally heated rooms, some with en suites, fridges and kettles. Plus it's a flat walk to The Octagon – something few Dunedin hostels can boast.

★ 858 George St   MOTEL $$
(☑03-474 0047; www.858georgestreetmotel.co.nz; 858 George St, North Dunedin; units from $150; P🐾) 🐾 Designed to blend in harmoniously with the neighbourhood two-storey Victorian houses, this top-quality motel complex has modern units ranging in size from studios to two bedrooms. Studios are fitted with microwaves, fridges, toasters and kettles, while the larger units also have stove tops or full ovens.

★ Bluestone on George   APARTMENT $$$
(☑03-477 9201; www.bluestonedunedin.co.nz; 571 George St, North Dunedin; apt from $230; P@🐾) 🐾 If you're expecting an imposing old bluestone building, think again: this four-storey block couldn't be more contemporary. The elegant studio units are decked out in muted tones, with kitchenettes, laundry facilities and decks or tiny balconies – some with harbour views. There's also a small gym and a guest lounge.

🛏 St Clair

Majestic Mansions   APARTMENT $$
(☑03-456 5000; www.st-clair.co.nz; 15 Bedford St, St Clair; 1-/2-bedroom apt from $139/199; P🐾) One street back from St Clair Beach, this venerable 1920s apartment block has been thoroughly renovated, keeping the layout of the original little flats but sprucing them up with feature wallpaper and smart furnishings. Each has kitchen and laundry facilities.

Hotel St Clair   HOTEL $$$
(☑03-456 0555; www.hotelstclair.com; 24 Esplanade, St Clair; r $214-409; P🐾) Soak up St Clair's surfy vibe from the balcony of your chic room in this contemporary medium-rise hotel. All but the cheapest rooms have ocean views, and the beach is only metres from the front door.

🛏 Other Suburbs

Leith Valley Touring Park   HOLIDAY PARK $
(☑03-467 9936; www.leithvalleytouringpark.co.nz; 103 Malvern St, Woodhaugh; sites per person $19, units with/without bathroom from $99/49; P🐾) 🐾 This holiday park is surrounded by native bush studded with walks, glowworm caves and a creek. Self-contained motel units are spacious, while tourist flats are smaller but have a more rustic feel (BYO linen).

Argoed   B&B $$
(☑03-474 1639; www.argoed.co.nz; 504 Queens Dr, Belleknowes; s/d from $150/210; P🐾) Roses and rhododendrons encircle this gracious two-storey wooden villa, built in the 1880s. Each of the three charmingly old-fashioned bedrooms has its own bathroom, though only one is en suite. Guests can relax in the conservatory or tinkle the ivories of the grand piano in the lounge.

Roslyn Apartments   APARTMENT $$$
(☑03-477 6777; www.roslynapartments.co.nz; 23 City Rd, Roslyn; apt from $225; P🐾) Unbeatable city and harbour views are the trump card at these modern apartments, just a short walk from Roslyn's eating strip. Each has full kitchen and laundry facilities.

🍴 Eating

Cafes and restaurants are clustered around The Octagon and all along George St. Uphill from the centre, Roslyn has some good eating choices, while the beachy ambience of St Clair is great for a lazy brunch or sunset drinks.

City Centre

★ Otago Farmers Market
MARKET **$**

(www.otagofarmersmarket.org.nz; Dunedin Railway Station; ⊗8am-12.30pm Sat) This thriving market is all local, all edible (or drinkable) and mostly organic. Grab a freshly baked pastry and a flat white to sustain you while you browse, and stock up on fresh meat, seafood, vegies and cheese for your journey. Sorted.

Modaks Espresso
CAFE **$**

(☑03-477 6563; 337-339 George St; mains $9-21; ⊗7.30am-2.30pm Mon-Fri, from 8am Sat & Sun; ☑) This funky little place with mismatched formica tables, plastic animal heads and lounge chairs for slouching in is popular with students and those who appreciate sweet indie pop while they nurse a pot of tea. Plump, toasted bagels warm the insides in winter.

Best Cafe
FISH & CHIPS **$**

(www.facebook.com/bestcafedunedin; 30 Stuart St; takeaways $6-10, mains $11-26; ⊗11am-2.30pm & 5-8pm Mon-Sat) Serving up fish and chips since 1932, this local stalwart has its winning formula down pat, complete with vinyl tablecloths, hand-cut chips and curls of butter on white bread.

Miga
KOREAN **$$**

(☑03-477 4770; www.facebook.com/migadunedin; 4 Hanover St; mains lunch $10-15, dinner $16-42; ⊗11.30am-2pm & 5pm-late Mon-Sat) Settle into a booth at this attractive brick-lined eatery, and order claypot rice or noodle dishes from the extensive menu. Japanese dishes include tempura, *katsu* and incredible ramen soups, made with fresh noodles. Otherwise go for broke and cook a Korean barbecue right at your table.

Vogel St Kitchen
CAFE **$$**

(☑03-477 3623; www.vogelstkitchen.co.nz; 76 Vogel St; brunch $13-25, pizzas $24; ⊗7.30am-3pm Mon-Thu, to 4pm Fri, 8.30am-4pm Sat & Sun; ☜) In the heart of Dunedin's warehouse precinct, Vogel St Kitchen offers smashing breakfasts and wood-fired pizzas in a cavernous two-storey redbrick building. It gets especially busy on weekends, when local residents make the most of large shared tables for long lazy brunches.

Paasha
TURKISH **$$**

(☑03-477 7181; www.paasha.co.nz; 31 St Andrew St; mains lunch $12-24, dinner $21-36; ⊗11.30am-3pm & 5-9pm Mon-Wed, 11.30am-late Thu-Sun; ☖) Authentic kebabs, dips and salads are on the menu at this long-running Dunedin favourite. It's a top place for takeaways, and most nights the spacious and warm interior is filled with groups drinking Efes beer and sharing heaving platters of tasty Turkish goodness.

Etrusco at the Savoy
ITALIAN **$$**

(☑03-477 3737; www.etrusco.co.nz; 8a Moray Pl; mains $15-27; ⊗5.30pm-late) New Zealand has very few dining rooms to match the Edwardian elegance of the Savoy, with its moulded ceilings, stained-glass crests, brass chandeliers, green Ionian columns and fabulously over-the-top lamps. Pizza and pasta might seem like an odd fit, but Etrusco's deliciously rustic Italian dishes absolutely hold their own.

Saigon Van
VIETNAMESE **$$**

(☑03-474 1445; www.saigonvannz.com; 66a St Andrew St; mains $9-23; ⊗11.30am-2pm & 5-9pm Tue-Sun; ☑) The decor looks high-end Asian, but the prices are more moderate than you'd expect. Try the combination spring rolls and a bottle of Vietnamese beer to recreate lazy nights in Saigon. The bean-sprout-laden *pho* (noodle soup) and salads are also good.

Izakaya Yuki
JAPANESE **$$**

(☑03-477 9539; 29 Bath St; dishes $4-12; ⊗5pm-late Mon-Sun plus noon-2pm Thu & Fri) Cute and cosy, with a huge array of small dishes on which to graze, Yuki is a lovely spot for supper or a relaxed, drawn-out Japanese meal. Make a night of it with sake or Asahi beer, sashimi, teppanyaki and multiple plates of *kushiyaki* (grilled skewers).

DUNEDIN & OTAGO MOERAKI

JUST GIVE ME THE COFFEE & NO ONE WILL GET HURT

Dunedin has some excellent coffee bars in which you can refuel and recharge:

The Fix (www.thefixcoffee.co.nz; 15 Frederick St; ⊗7am-4pm Mon-Fri, 8am-noon Sat)

Mazagran Espresso Bar (36 Moray Pl; ⊗8am-6pm Mon-Fri, to 2pm Sat)

Insomnia by Strictly Coffee (☑03-479 0017; www.strictlycoffee.co.nz; 23 Bath St; ⊗7am-4pm Mon-Fri)

Allpress (☑03-477 7162; www.nz. allpressespresso.com; 12 Emily Siedeberg Pl; ⊗8am-4pm Mon-Fri)

★ **Bracken** MODERN NZ $$$
(☑03-477 9779; www.brackenrestaurant.co.nz; 95 Filleul St; 5/7/9-course menu $79/99/120, with matched wines $134/164/200; ⊘6-9pm Tue-Sat) 🍴 Bracken's seasonal tasting menus offer a succession of pretty little plates bursting with flavour. While the dishes are intricate, nothing's overly gimmicky, and the setting, in an old wooden house, is classy without being too formal.

Plato MODERN NZ $$$
(☑03-477 4235; www.platocafe.co.nz; 2 Birch St; mains lunch $20-28, dinner $29-38; ⊘noon-2pm Wed-Sat, from 11am Sun, plus 6pm-late daily) The kooky decor (including collections of toys and beer tankards) gives little indication of the seriously good food on offer at this relaxed eatery by the harbour. Fresh fish and shellfish feature prominently in a lengthy menu full of international flavours and subtle smoky elements. Servings are enormous.

Scotia SCOTTISH $$$
(☑03-477 7704; www.scotiadunedin.co.nz; 199 Stuart St; mains $31-38; ⊘5pm-late Tue-Sat) Occupying a cosy heritage townhouse, Scotia toasts all things Scottish with a wall full of single-malt whisky and hearty gourmet fare like sous vide duck breast and smoked beef fillet. The two Scottish Robbies – Burns and Coltrane – look down approvingly on a menu that also includes haggis and whisky-laced pâté.

✕ North Dunedin

Everyday Gourmet CAFE, DELI $
(www.everydaygourmet.net.nz; 466 George St, North Dunedin; mains $10-19; ⊘7.40am-4.30pm Mon-Fri, 8am-3.30pm Sat; 🛜) Apart from cooked breakfasts and pasta, most of the good stuff beckons from the counter of this excellent bakery-style cafe and deli. It's light, bright and extremely popular, with good coffee and friendly staff.

✕ St Clair

Starfish CAFE $$
(☑03-455 5940; www.starfishcafe.co.nz; 7/240 Forbury Rd, St Clair; mains $11-30; ⊘7am-5pm Sun-Tue, to late Wed-Sat) Part of the growing restaurant scene at St Clair Beach, Starfish is a popular all-day eatery offering decadent brunch dishes, good coffee and a great buzz. Pop in for a quick lunch on the balcony overlooking the beach, or drop by in the evening for a hearty dinner accompanied by a glass of wine or wide selection of craft beer.

Esplanade ITALIAN $$
(☑03-456 2544; www.esplanade.co; 2 Esplanade, St Clair; mains $21-26; ⊘9am-late Mon-Fri, from 8.30am Sat & Sun) A prime position overlooking St Clair Beach is only the beginning at this relaxed Italian cafe-restaurant. Drop in during the morning for an espresso and a *panino*, or come by in the evening for authentic thin-crust pizzas washed down with an aperol spritz. At sunset the windows offer the perfect frame as lavender twilight descends over the beach.

✕ Other Suburbs

★ **No 7 Balmac** CAFE $$
(☑03-464 0064; www.no7balmac.co.nz; 7 Balmacewen Rd, Maori Hill; mains brunch $14-26, dinner $29-45; ⊘7am-late Mon-Fri, 8.30am-late Sat, 8.30am-5pm Sun; 🛜) We wouldn't recommend walking to this sophisticated cafe at the top of Maori Hill, but luckily it's well worth the price of a cab. The fancy cafe fare stretches from smashing brunches to the likes of confit duck and slow-braised lamb. If you're on a diet, avoid eye contact with the cake cabinet.

🍷 Drinking & Nightlife

★ **Aika + Co** BAR
(www.facebook.com/aikaandcompany; 357 George St; ⊘10am-late Mon-Sat) With a new name but the same tiny space, 'Dunedin's littlest bar' might only be 1.8m wide, but it's still big enough to host regular live bands. There are just six bar stools, so patrons spill out into an adjacent laneway. By day, it's a handy caffeine-refuelling spot, as well as offering juices, milkshakes, baked goods and simple bar snacks.

Inch Bar BAR
(☑03-473 6496; 8 Bank St, North East Valley; ⊘3pm-late) Make the short trek from town to this cavelike little bar for its selection of Kiwi craft beers and tasty tapas, and the cute little indoor/outdoor beer garden. Despite its diminutive dimensions, it often hosts live music on Thursday, Friday and Saturday nights.

Albar BAR
(☑03-479 2468; 135 Stuart St; ⊘11am-late) This former butcher is now a bohemian bar, with

a dark, atmospheric interior and cosy booths, illuminated by a single chandelier. Punters are drawn in by the many single-malt whiskies and interesting tap beers, as well as the cheap tapas-style snacks (from $7).

Carousel COCKTAIL BAR
(☑03-477 4141; www.carouselbar.co.nz; 141 Stuart St; ☺5pm-late Wed-Sat) Monochrome tartan wallpaper, a roof deck and great cocktails leave the classy clientele looking pleased to be seen somewhere so deadly cool. DJs spin deep house until late from Thursday through to Saturday, and there's often live jazz on Friday evenings from 8.30pm. It's upstairs.

Pequeno COCKTAIL BAR
(☑03-477 7830; www.pequeno.co.nz; behind 12 Moray Pl; ☺7pm-late Tue, Wed & Sat, from 6pm Thu, from 5pm Fri) Down the alley opposite the Rialto Cinema, Pequeno attracts a sophisticated crowd with leather couches, a cosy fireplace and an excellent wine and cocktail list. Music is generally laid-back, with regular live acts.

Speight's Ale House PUB
(☑03-471 9050; www.thealehouse.co.nz; 200 Rattray St; ☺11.30am-late) Busy even in the non-university months, the Ale House is a favourite of strapping young lads in their cleanest dirty shirts. It's a good spot to watch the rugby on TV and to try the full range of Speight's beers; there are also decent pub meals on offer.

Pop CLUB
(14 The Octagon; ☺10pm-late Wed-Sat) A late-night Dunedin staple, Pop serves great martinis and prides itself on seriously good DJs playing funk and house. It's downstairs.

☆ Entertainment

Forsyth Barr Stadium STADIUM
(www.forsythbarrstadium.co.nz; 130 Anzac Ave) Constructed for the 2011 Rugby World Cup, this is the only major stadium in NZ with a fully covered roof. It's the home ground of the Highlanders Super 15 rugby team (www.thehighlanders.co.nz) and the Otago rugby team (www.orfu.co.nz), and also plays host to international sporting matches, concerts and shows.

Fortune Theatre THEATRE
(☑03-477 8323; www.fortunetheatre.co.nz; 231 Stuart St; adult/child $45/17.50; ☺box office

UNESCO CITY OF LITERATURE

Dunedin was designated a UNESCO City of Literature in 2014, in recognition of the profound creative energy of this small southern city. If you'd like to explore Dunedin's literary side during your stay, check out the City of Literature office's website (www.cityofliterature.co.nz) for information about readings, launches and other literary events.

Nowhere is Dunedin's bookishness more evident than in the city's bookstores, whose number seems at odds with Dunedin's relatively small population. As well as the usual chain stores and the excellent **University Book Shop** (☑03-477 6976; www.unibooks.co.nz; 378 Great King St, North Dunedin; ☺8.30am-5.30pm Mon-Fri, 10am-4pm Sat, 11am-3pm Sun), be sure to seek out some of the city's abundance of secondhand bookshops, which are all packed to the ceiling with intriguing volumes. Our favourites include **Dead Souls** (☑021 0270 8540; www.deadsouls.co.nz; 393 Princes St; ☺10am-6pm), **Scribes** (☑03-477 6874; 546 Great King St; ☺10am-5pm Mon-Fri, to 4.30pm Sat & Sun) and **Hard to Find Books** (☑03-471 8518; www.hardtofind.co.nz; 20 Dowling St; ☺10am-6pm).

10.30am-5pm Mon-Fri, 4.30-7.30pm Sat, 1.30-4pm Sun) The world's southernmost professional theatre company has been staging dramas, comedies, pantomimes, classics and contemporary NZ productions for over 40 years. Shows are performed – watched over by the obligatory theatre ghost – in an old Gothic-style Wesleyan church.

Rialto Cinemas CINEMA
(☑03-474 2200; www.rialto.co.nz; 11 Moray Pl; adult/child $16/10) Screens blockbusters and art-house flicks. Tickets are cheaper on Tuesdays.

🛍 Shopping

Gallery De Novo ART
(☑03-474 9200; www.gallerydenovo.co.nz; 101 Stuart St; ☺9.30am-5.30pm Mon-Fri, 10am-3pm Sat & Sun) This interesting, contemporary, fine-art gallery is worth a peek whether you're likely to invest in a substantial piece of Kiwi art or not.

Stuart Street Potters
Co-operative
ARTS & CRAFTS

(☑03-471 8484; 14 Stuart St; ☺10am-5pm Mon-Fri, 9am-3pm Sat) If you're after a unique souvenir, this sweet store stocks locally crafted pottery and ceramic art.

❶ Information

The **Dunedin i-SITE** (☑03-474 3300; www.isite dunedin.co.nz; 50 The Octagon; ☺8.30am-5pm Apr-Oct, to 6pm Nov-Mar) incorporates the **DOC Visitor Centre** (Department of Conservation; ☑03-474 3300; www.doc.govt.nz; 50 The Octagon; ☺8.30am-5.30pm), providing a one-stop shop for all of your information needs, including Great Walks and hut bookings.

Dunedin Hospital (☑03-474 0999; www.southerndhb.govt.nz; 201 Great King St)

Urgent Doctors (☑03-479 2900; www.dunedinurgentdoctors.co.nz; 95 Hanover St; ☺8am-10pm) There's also a late-night pharmacy next door.

❶ Getting There & Away

AIR

Air New Zealand (p539) flies to/from Auckland, Wellington and Christchurch.

Jetstar (p539) flies to/from Auckland and Wellington.

Virgin Australia (☑0800 670 000; www.virginaustralia.com) flies to/from Brisbane, Australia.

BUS

Buses and shuttles leave from the Dunedin Railway Station, except where we've noted otherwise.

Atomic Shuttles (☑03-349 0697; www.atomic travel.co.nz) Buses to/from Christchurch ($35, six hours), Queenstown ($45, 4½ hours), Timaru ($25, three hours) and Oamaru ($20, two hours), twice daily.

Catch-a-Bus (☑03-449 2024; www.trail journeys.co.nz) Bike-friendly shuttles to/from key Rail Trail towns, including Middlemarch ($45, one hour), Ranfurly ($49, two hours), Alexandra ($56, 3¼ hours), Clyde ($56, 3½ hours) and Cromwell ($60, 3¾ hours).

Coast Line Tours (☑03-434 7744; www.coastline-tours.co.nz) Shuttles to Oamaru depart from The Octagon (one way/return $30/55, two hours); detours to Dunedin Airport and Moeraki can be arranged.

InterCity (☑03-471 7143; www.intercity.co.nz) Coaches to/from Christchurch (from $42, six hours), Oamaru (from $23, 1½ hours), Cromwell (from $23, 3¼ hours), Queenstown (from $26, 4¼ hours) and Te Anau (from $38, 4½ hours) at least daily. Departs 7 Halsey St.

Naked Bus (www.nakedbus.com; prices vary) Daily buses head to/from Christchurch (six hours), Timaru (three hours), Gore (2½ hours) and Invercargill (3¾ hours).

Ritchies (☑03-443 9120; www.alpine connexions.co.nz) Shuttles head to/from Clyde ($50, three hours), Cromwell ($50, 3¼ hours), Wanaka ($50, four hours) and Queenstown ($50, 4½ hours), as well as key stops on the Otago Central Rail Trail.

TRAIN

The heritage tourist trains operated by Dunedin Railways (p555) can be used as a transport connection. The *Taieri Gorge Railway* heads to Middlemarch twice a week, while the *Seasider* is an option for Moeraki and Oamaru.

❶ Getting Around

TO/FROM THE AIRPORT

Dunedin Airport (DUD; ☑03-486 2879; www.dnairport.co.nz; 25 Miller Rd, Momona; 🛜) is 27km southwest of the city. There is no public transport to the airport. A standard taxi ride to/from the city costs around $90. For door-to-door shuttles, try **Kiwi Shuttles** (☑03-487 9790; www.kiwishuttles.co.nz; per 1/2/3/4 passengers $20/36/48/60) or **Super Shuttle** (☑0800 748 885; www.supershuttle.co.nz; per 1/2/3/4 passengers $25/40/50/60) – book in advance.

BUS

Dunedin's **GoBus** (☑03-474 0287; www.orc.govt.nz; adult $2.60-15.30) network extends across the city. It's particularly handy for getting to St Clair, St Kilda and Port Chalmers, and as far afield as Palmerston or the Otago Peninsula. Buses run regularly Monday to Friday, with reduced services on weekends.

Individual tickets are available from the bus driver; for longer stays, invest in a GoCard – purchase from bus drivers, from the council offices in The Octagon, or from University Book Shop (p559) – which offers reduced fares.

CAR

The big international rental companies all have offices in Dunedin; local outfits include **Hanson Rental Vehicles** (☑03-453 6576; www.hanson.net.nz; 313 Kaikorai Valley Rd) and **Ezi Car Rental** (☑03-486 1245; www.ezicarrental.co.nz; Dunedin Airport).

TAXI

There are several taxi companies in Dunedin; options include **Dunedin Taxis** (☑0800 50 50 10, 03-477 7777; www.dunedintaxis.co.nz), **Southern Taxis** (☑03-476 6300; www.southern taxis.co.nz) and **Green Cabs** (☑0800 46 47 336; www.greencabs.co.nz).

AROUND DUNEDIN

Port Chalmers

☑ 03 / POP 1370

Little Port Chalmers is only 13km from central Dunedin but it feels a world away. Somewhere between working class and bohemian, Port Chalmers has a history as a port town but has long attracted Dunedin's arty types. The main drag, George St, is home to a handful of cafes, design stores and galleries, perfect for a half-day's worth of wandering, browsing and sipping away from the city crush.

⊙ Sights

Orokonui Ecosanctuary   WILDLIFE RESERVE
(☑ 03-482 1755; www.orokonui.org.nz; 600 Blueskin Rd; adult/child $19/9.50; ⊙ 9.30am-4.30pm) 🐾 From the impressive visitors centre there are great views over this 307-hectare predator-free nature reserve, which encloses cloud forest on the mountainous ridge above Port Chalmers and stretches to the estuary on the opposite side. Its mission is to provide a mainland refuge for species usually exiled to offshore islands for their own protection. Visiting options include self-guided explorations, hour-long 'highlights' tours (adult/child $35/17.50; 11am and 1.30pm daily) and two-hour 'forest explorer' tours (adult/child $50/35; 11am daily).

Rare bird species finding sanctuary here include kiwi, takahe and kaka, while reptiles include tuatara and Otago skinks.

Orokonui is a well-signposted 6km drive from the main road into Port Chalmers.

🏃 Activities

Traditional rock climbing (nonbolted) is popular at Long Beach and the cliffs at Mihiwaka, both accessed via Blueskin Rd north of Port Chalmers.

Hare Hill   HORSE RIDING
(☑ 03-472 8496; www.horseriding-dunedin.co.nz; 207 Aramoana Rd, Deborah Bay; treks $95-195) Horse treks include thrilling beach rides and harbour views.

🛏 Sleeping & Eating

Billy Brown's   HOSTEL $$
(☑ 03-472 8323; www.billybrowns.co.nz; 423 Aramoana Rd, Hamilton Bay; d $150, additional person $50; ⊙ Sep-May) On a farm 5km along the road from Port Chalmers, this backpacker fave no longer offers dorm accommodation, but the whole rustic lodge is available to rent for groups from one to eight people. There's a lovely lounge with a cosy wood-burner and plenty of retro vinyl to spin.

Union Co.   CAFE $
(2 George St; mains $8-15; ⊙ 8am-3pm) Great coffee, delicious baked goods and a sunny corner position make this the pick for your morning caffeine fix.

Carey's Bay Hotel   PUB FOOD $$
(☑ 03-472 8022; www.careysbayhotel.co.nz; 17 Macandrew Rd, Carey's Bay; mains $19-30; ⊙ 10am-late) Just around the corner from Port Chalmers you'll find this historic pub, popular with locals for its hearty meals and unbeatable location – on sunny days grab a table out the front for first-class views over the sparkling water.

❶ Getting There & Away

On weekdays buses (adult/child $6/3.60, 30 minutes, half-hourly) travel between Dunedin and Port Chalmers between 6.30am and 9.30pm (11.30pm on Friday). On weekends buses run hourly between 8.30am and 11.30pm on Saturday, and 9.30am and 5.30pm on Sunday.

Otago Peninsula

POP 4210

It's hard to believe that the Otago Peninsula – a picturesque haven of rolling hills, secluded bays, sandy beaches and clifftop vistas – is only half an hour's drive from downtown Dunedin. As well as interesting historical sites and wild walking trails, this small sliver of land is home to the South Island's most accessible diversity of wildlife, including albatross, penguins, fur seals and sea lions. The peninsula's only town is the petite Portobello, and despite a host of tours exploring the region, it maintains its quiet rural air.

⊙ Sights

The Otago Peninsula is one of the best places on the South Island for wildlife spotting, from penguins to albatross to sea lions.

★ Nature's Wonders Naturally   WILDLIFE RESERVE
(☑ 03-478 1150; www.natureswonders.co.nz; Taiaroa Head; adult/child Argo $99/45, coach $45/22.50; ⊙ tours from 10.15am) What makes the improbably beautiful beaches of this coastal sheep farm different from other important wildlife

habitats is that (apart from pest eradication and the like) they're left completely alone. Many of the multiple private beaches haven't suffered a human footprint in years. The result is that yellow-eyed penguins can often be spotted (through binoculars) at any time of the day, and NZ fur seals laze around rocky swimming holes, blissfully unfazed by tour groups passing by.

Depending on the time of year, you might also see whales and little penguin chicks.

The tour is conducted in 'go-anywhere' Argo vehicles by enthusiastic guides, at least some of whom double as true-blue Kiwi farmers. A less bumpy coach option is also available, though you won't see as much.

Royal Albatross Centre & Fort Taiaroa
BIRD SANCTUARY

(☑ 03-478 0499; www.albatross.org.nz; Taiaroa Head; adult/child albatross $50/15, fort $25/10, combined $55/20; ⏱ 10.15am-dusk) Taiaroa Head, at the peninsula's northern tip, has the world's only mainland royal albatross colony, along with a late 19th-century military fort. The only public access to the area is by guided tour. There's an hour-long albatross tour and a 30-minute fort tour available, or the two can also be combined. Otherwise you can just call into the centre to look at the displays and have a bite in the cafe.

Albatross are present on Taiaroa Head throughout the year, but the best time to see them is from December to March, when one parent is constantly guarding the young while the other delivers food throughout the day. Sightings are most common in the afternoon when the winds pick up; calm days don't see as many birds in flight.

Little penguins swim ashore at Pilots Beach (just below the car park) around dusk to head to their nests in the dunes. For their protection, the beach is closed to the public every evening, but viewing is possible from a specially constructed wooden platform (adult/child $35/10). Depending on the time of year, 50 to 300 penguins might waddle past.

Fort Taiaroa was built in 1885 in response to a perceived threat of Russian invasion. Its **Armstrong Disappearing Gun** was designed to be loaded and aimed underground, then popped up like the world's slowest jack-in-the-box to be fired.

Larnach Castle
CASTLE

(☑ 03-476 1616; www.larnachcastle.co.nz; 145 Camp Rd; adult/child castle & grounds $31/10, grounds only $15.50/5; ⏱ 9am-7pm Oct-Mar, to 5pm Apr-Sep) 🅿 Standing proudly on top of a hill overlooking the peninsula, this gorgeous Gothic Revival mansion was built in 1871 by Dunedin banker, merchant and Member of Parliament William Larnach. The castle fell into disrepair after Lanarch's death, until it was purchased by the Barker family in 1967, and a long period of restoration began. The four floors are now filled with intricate woodwork and exquisite antique furnishings, and the crenellated tower offers expansive views.

A self-guided tour brochure is provided, or you can buy an iPhone app ($6) that digitally peoples the rooms with costumed actors. After lording it about in the mansion, take a stroll through the pretty gardens or settle in for high tea in the ballroom cafe.

Glenfalloch Woodland Garden
GARDENS

(☑ 03-476 1006; www.glenfalloch.co.nz; 430 Portobello Rd, Macandrew Bay; ⏱ 8am-dusk) FREE Make time to pause at these lush, well-tended gardens, filled with flowers and swaying, mature trees, including a 1000-year-old matai. Walking tracks meander through dense forest, with peeks of the harbour visible from all angles. There's also a good restaurant on-site. The Portobello bus stops out the front.

Penguin Place
BIRD SANCTUARY

(☑ 03-478 0286; www.penguinplace.co.nz; 45 Pakihau Rd, Harington Point; adult/child $54/16; ⏱ tours from 10.15am Oct-Mar, 3.45pm Apr-Sep) On private farmland, this reserve protects nesting sites of the rare yellow-eyed penguin/hoiho. The 90-minute tours focus on penguin conservation and close-up viewing from a system of hides. Bookings are recommended.

🏃 Activities

A popular walking destination is beautiful **Sandfly Bay**, reached from Seal Point Rd (one hour return). You can also follow a trail from the end of Sandymount Rd to the **Sandymount summit** and on to the impressive **Chasm and Lovers Leap** (one hour return). Note that this track is closed from September to mid-October for lambing. Pick up or download the helpful DOC *Dunedin Walks* brochure to plan your tramp.

☞ Tours

Back to Nature Tours
BUS

(☑ 0800 286 000; www.backtonaturetours.co.nz) 🅿 The full-day Royal Peninsula tour (adult/child $193/125) heads to points of interest around Dunedin before hitting the Otago

Peninsula. Stops include Larnach Castle's gardens (castle entry is extra), Penguin Place and the Royal Albatross Centre. There's also a half-day option that visits various beaches ($83/55) and another tackling the Lovers Leap walking track ($89/55). Will pick up from your accommodation.

Wild Earth Adventures KAYAKING
(☑ 03-489 1951; www.wildearth.co.nz; per person $115) Offers guided tours in double sea kayaks, with wildlife often sighted en route. Tours take between three hours and a full day, with pick-ups from The Octagon in Dunedin.

Elm Wildlife Tours WILDLIFE
(☑ 03-454 4121; www.elmwildlifetours.co.nz; tours from $103) 🖋 Well-regarded, small-group, wildlife-focused tours, with options to add the Royal Albatross Centre or a Monarch Cruise. Pick-up and drop-off from Dunedin is included.

Monarch Wildlife Cruises & Tours BOATING
(☑ 03-477 4276; www.wildlife.co.nz) 🖋 One-hour boat trips departing from Wellers Rock Wharf (adult/child $53/22), as well as half-day ($92/35) and full-day ($250/124) tours cruising right along the harbour from Dunedin. You may spot sea lions, penguins, albatross and seals. The full-day option includes admission to the Royal Albatross Centre and Penguin Place.

🛏 Sleeping & Eating

McFarmers Backpackers HOSTEL $
(☑ 03-478 0389; mcfarmers@xtra.co.nz; 774 Portobello Rd, Broad Bay; s/d $55/70) On a working sheep farm with harbour views, the rustic timber lodge and self-contained cottage here are steeped in character and feel instantly like home. The Portobello bus goes past the gate.

★ Portobello Motel MOTEL $$
(☑ 03-478 0155; www.portobellomotels.com; 10 Harington Point Rd, Portobello; units from $160; P 🐾 🛜) These sunny, modern units are thoughtfully decorated and outfitted with all mod cons. The studio units are the pick of the bunch, each with small private decks overlooking the bay. Spacious one- and two-bedroom versions are also available, but lack the views.

Larnach Castle B&B $$$
(☑ 03-476 1616; www.larnachcastle.co.nz; 145 Camp Rd; d stable/lodge/estate $160/320/510; P @ 🛜) 🖋 Larnach Castle's pricey backgarden lodge has 12 unique, whimsically decorated rooms with views. Less frivolous are the atmospheric rooms in the 140-year-old stables (bathrooms are shared). A few hundred metres from the castle, Camp Estate has luxury suites worthy of a romantic splurge. Each option includes breakfast and castle entry; dinner in the castle is extra ($70).

Portobello Hotel & Bistro PUB FOOD $$
(☑ 03-478 0759; www.portobellohotelandbistro.co.nz; 2 Harington Point Rd, Portobello; mains lunch $13-23, dinner $23-36; ⏱ 11.30am-11.30pm) Refreshing thirsty travellers since 1874, the Portobello pub is still a popular pit stop. Grab a table in the sun and tuck into seafood chowder, a burger or a fillet of freshly caught blue cod.

1908 Cafe CAFE, BISTRO $$
(☑ 03-478 0801; www.1908cafe.co.nz; 7 Harington Point Rd, Portobello; mains lunch $14-24, dinner $31-34; ⏱ noon-2pm & 6-10pm, closed Mon & Tue Apr-Oct) Salmon, venison and steak are joined by fresh fish and blackboard specials at this casual eatery. Cafe fare, such as soup and toasted sandwiches, are served at lunch. As the name suggests, the building originally opened as a tearoom in 1908, and many of the original features are still in place.

❶ Getting There & Away

Portobello is a scenic 20km drive from Dunedin along the harbour.

On weekdays, buses make the journey from Dunedin's Cumberland St to Portobello Village from 7.30am to 10.30pm (adult/child $6/3.60, one hour, half-hourly), with four services continuing to Harrington Point at the tip of the peninsula. On Saturdays the service reduces to hourly from 8.30am.

Once on the peninsula, it's tough to get around without your own transport. Most tours will pick you up from your Dunedin accommodation.

There's no petrol available on the peninsula.

CENTRAL OTAGO

Rolling hills that turn from green to gold in the relentless summer sun provide a backdrop to a succession of tiny, charming gold-rush towns where farmers mingle with Lycra-clad cyclists in lost-in-time pubs. As well as being one of the country's top wine regions, the area provides fantastic opportunities for those on two wheels, whether mountain biking along old gold-mining trails or traversing the district on the Otago Central Rail Trail.

Middlemarch

📞 03 / POP 153

With the Rock and Pillar Range as an impressive backdrop, the small town of Middlemarch is the terminus of both the Taieri Gorge Railway and the Otago Central Rail Trail. It's famous in NZ for the Middlemarch Singles Ball (held across Easter in odd-numbered years), where southern men gather to entice city gals to the country life.

🏃 Activities

Both **Cycle Surgery** (📞 03-464 3630; www. cyclesurgery.co.nz; Swansea St; rental per day from $35; ⏰ depot Oct-Apr) and **Trail Journeys** (📞 03-464 3213; www.trailjourneys.co.nz; 20 Swansea St; rental per day from $45; ⏰ depot Oct-Apr) have depots on Middlemarch's main street, providing bike rental and logistical support to riders on the Otago Central Rail Trail (p565). This includes shuttles, bag transfers and an accommodation booking service. They also have depots in Clyde, at the other end of the trail, to drop off your bikes.

🛏 Sleeping & Eating

Otago Central Hotel   B&B $$
(📞 027 544 4800; www.otagocentralhotelhyde. com; SH87, Hyde; d with/without bathroom from $170/130; ⏰ Oct-Apr) Most of the tidy rooms in this cool old hotel, 27km along the trail from Middlemarch, have private bathrooms, but only some are en suite. It's no longer a working pub, so the $50 set dinner is the only meal for many miles around.

There's a very sweet pop-up 'honesty cafe' on the veranda for passing rail-trailers.

Kissing Gate Cafe   CAFE $
(📞 03-464 3224; 2 Swansea St; mains $8-18; ⏰ 8.30am-4pm; 🖥) Sit out under the fruit trees in the pretty garden of this cute little wooden cottage and tuck into a cooked breakfast, meat pie, zingy salad or some home baking. Nana-chic at its best.

ⓘ Getting There & Away

Middlemarch is an hour's scenic drive from Dunedin.

Both of the main cycle companies offer shuttles to Dunedin, Pukerangi and the Rail Trail towns. In the warmer months, Trail Journey's

Catch-a-Bus (📞 03-449 2150; www.trail journeys.co.nz; ⏰ Oct-Apr) has scheduled daily services to/from Dunedin ($45, one hour), Ranfurly ($27, one hour), Alexandra ($55, 2¼ hours), Clyde ($55, 2½ hours) and Cromwell ($59, three hours).

The scenic **Taieri Gorge Railway** (📞 03-477 4449; www.dunedinrailways.co.nz; ⏰ Sun May-Sep, Fri & Sun Oct-Apr) has only limited runs between Dunedin and Middlemarch (one way/return $77/115, three hours); most services end at Pukerangi Station, 20km away.

Ranfurly

📞 03 / POP 663

After a series of fires in the 1930s, Ranfurly was rebuilt in the architectural style of the day, and a few attractive art-deco buildings still line its sleepy main drag. The teensy town is trying hard to cash in on this meagre legacy, calling itself the 'South Island's art-deco capital'. There's even an **Art Deco Museum** in the admittedly fabulous Centennial Milk Bar building on the main street.

Most travellers come through Ranfurly as part of a journey on the Otago Central Rail Trail (p565), which passes right through town.

🛏 Sleeping

Hawkdun Lodge   MOTEL $$
(📞 03-444 9750; www.hawkdunlodge.co.nz; 1 Bute St; s/d from $113/150; 🖥) 🖥 This smart boutique motel is the best option in the town centre by far. Even studio units are spacious, with kitchenettes, sitting areas and en suites. Travelling chefs can flex their skills in the smart guest kitchen and dining area.

Peter's Farm Lodge   LODGE $$
(📞 03-444 9811; www.petersfarm.co.nz; 113 Tregonning Rd, Waipiata; per adult/child $60/45) On a sheep farm 13km south of Ranfurly, this rustic 1882 farmhouse offers comfy beds, hearty barbecue dinners ($25) and free pick-ups from the Rail Trail. Kayaks, fishing rods and gold pans are all available, so it's worth staying a couple of nights. Further beds are available in neighbouring Tregonning Cottage (1882).

Kokonga Lodge   B&B $$$
(📞 03-444 9774; www.kokongalodge.co.nz; 33 Kokonga-Waipiata Rd; s/d $240/295; 🖥🖥) Just off SH87 between Ranfurly and Hyde, this upmarket rural property offers six contemporary en suite rooms, one of which was

DON'T MISS

OTAGO CENTRAL RAIL TRAIL

Stretching from Dunedin to Clyde, the Central Otago rail line linked small, inland gold-field towns with the big city from the early 20th century through to the 1990s. After the 150km stretch from Middlemarch to Clyde was permanently closed, the rails were ripped up and the trail resurfaced. The result is a year-round, mainly gravel trail that takes bikers, walkers and horse riders along a historic route containing old rail bridges, viaducts and tunnels.

With excellent trailside facilities (toilets, shelters and information), few hills, gob-smacking scenery and profound remoteness, the trail attracts well over 25,000 visitors annually. March is the busiest time, when there are so many city slickers on the track that you might have to wait 30 minutes at cafes en route for a panini. Consider September for a quieter ride.

The trail can be followed in either direction. The entire trail takes approximately four to five days to complete by bike (or a week on foot), but you can obviously choose to do as short or as long a stretch as suits your plans. There are also easy detours to towns such as Naseby and St Bathans.

Mountain bikes can be rented in Dunedin, Middlemarch, Alexandra and Clyde. Any of the area's i-SITEs can provide detailed information. See www.otagocentralrailtrail.co.nz and www.otagorailtrail.co.nz for track information, recommended timings, accommodation options and tour companies.

Due to the popularity of the trail, a whole raft of sleeping and eating options has sprung up in remote locales en route, although some stops are less well served than others.

occupied by Sir Peter Jackson when he was filming *The Hobbit* in the area. The Rail Trail passes nearby.

✕ Eating & Drinking

Maniototo Cafe   CAFE $
(☑ 03-444 9023; www.maniototocafe.co.nz; 1 Pery St; mains $7-14; ☺ 7am-4.30pm Mon-Fri, 8am-5pm Sat & Sun) Attached to the Four Square supermarket, this sunny cafe is a good lunch option, with a tempting array of salads, sandwiches, sausage rolls and cakes.

Waipiata Country Hotel   PUB
(☑ 03-444 9470; www.waipiatahotel.co.nz; 29 Main St, Waipiata; ☺ 10am-late; ☎) Around 10km from Ranfurly, this friendly country pub right on the rail trail is a great spot to quench your post-ride thirst. It also offers good pub meals – like deer and beer pies and tasty burgers – and has rooms available if you're too tired to pedal any further (per person from $70).

ⓘ Information

Ranfurly i-SITE (☑ 03-444 1005; www.centralotagonz.com; 3 Charlemont St; ☺ 9am-5pm; ☎) Call into the Ranfurly i-SITE in the old train station to pick up a copy of the free *Rural Art Deco – Ranfurly Walk* brochure. While you're there, check out the short film about the rail trail and interesting local history displays.

ⓘ Getting There & Away

Ranfurly sits on route 85, 1¾ hours drive from Dunedin. In the warmer months, Trail Journey's Catch-a-Bus (p564) passes through Ranfurly on its way between Cromwell ($52, two hours) and Dunedin ($49, two hours).

Naseby

☑ 03 / POP 120

Cute as a button, surrounded by forest and dotted with 19th-century stone buildings, Naseby is the kind of small settlement where life moves slowly. That the town is pleasantly obsessed with the fairly insignificant world of NZ curling (a Winter Olympic sport resembling shuffleboard on ice) indicates there's not much else going on. It's that lazy small-town vibe, along with good mountain-biking and walking trails through the surrounding forest, that makes Naseby an interesting stopover for rail trailers.

🏃 Activities

Naseby Ice Luge   SNOW SPORTS
(☑ 03-444 9270; www.lugenz.com; 1057 Channel Rd; adult/child $35/25; ☺ 10am-4pm Jun-Aug) Hurtle 360m down a hillside on a wooden sled during winter. Weather dependent; call ahead, bookings recommended.

WORTH A TRIP

ST BATHANS

A 17km detour north from SH85 heads into the foothills of the imposing Dunstan Mountains and on to diminutive St Bathans. This once-thriving gold-mining town of 2000 people is now home to only half a dozen permanent residents living amid a cluster of cutesy 19th-century buildings, almost all of which have 'For Sale' signs in front of them. There's not much in town but the historic **Vulcan Hotel** (☑03-447 3629; stbathans.vulcanhotel@xtra.co.nz; Main St; r per person $60) – an atmospheric (and famously haunted) spot to drink, eat or stay. Considering St Bathans' tiny population, you'll find the bar here reasonably busy on a Friday night as thirsty farmers from around the valley descend en masse.

The **Blue Lake** is an accidental attraction: a large hollow filled with blue water that has run off abandoned gold workings. Walk along the sculpted cliffs to the lookout for a better view of the alien landscape (one hour return).

Maniototo Curling International
SNOW SPORTS
(☑03-444 9878; www.curling.co.nz; 1057 Channel Rd; adult/child per 90min $35/15; ⊘10am-5pm May-Oct, 9am-7.30pm Nov-Apr) All year round you can shimmy after curling stones at this indoor ice rink; tuition is available. In winter there's also an outdoor ice rink to skate around.

🛏 Sleeping

Royal Hotel
PUB $
(☑03-444 9990; www.naseby.co.nz; 1 Earne St; dm $40, d with/without bathroom $110/80; 🐾) One of two historic pubs in town, the 1863 Royal Hotel sports the royal coat of arms and what just might be NZ's most rustic garden bar. Rooms are simple but clean.

Naseby Lodge
APARTMENT $$
(☑03-444 8222; www.nasebylodge.co.nz; cnr Derwent & Oughter Sts; 1-/2-bedroom apt $170/260) Constructed of environmentally friendly straw-bale walls sheathed in rustic corrugated iron, these free-standing modern apartments are smart and spacious, with fully equipped kitchens and underfloor heating in the bathrooms. There's also a good restaurant on-site.

Old Doctor's Residence
B&B $$$
(☑03-444 9775; www.olddoctorsresidence.co.nz; 58 Derwent St; r/ste $295/350; 🐾) 🍽 Old doctors take note: this is how to reside! Sitting behind a pretty garden, this gorgeous 1870s house offers two luxurious guest rooms and a lounge where wine and nibbles are served of an evening. The suite has a sitting room and an en suite bathroom, while the smaller room's bathroom is accessed from the corridor.

ℹ Information

Naseby Information Centre (☑03-444 9961; www.nasebyinfo.org.nz; Old Post Office, Derwent St; ⊘11am-2pm Fri, Sun & Mon, to 4pm Sat, extended hours summer)

ℹ Getting There & Away

The Ranfurly–Naseby Rd leaves SH85, 4km north of Ranfurly. There's no public transport and cyclists should factor in a 12km detour from the Rail Trail (many accommodation providers will collect you if you ask). From Naseby, you can wind your way on unsealed roads northeast through spectacular scenery to Danseys Pass and through to Duntroon in the Waitaki Valley.

Lauder, Omakau & Ophir

Separated by 8km of SH85, tiny **Lauder** (population 12) and larger **Omakau** (population 260) are good stops if you're a hungry cyclist in need of a feed and a bed. However, the area's real gem is **Ophir** (population 50), 2km from Omakau across the Manuherikia River.

Gold was discovered here in 1863 and the town swiftly formed, named after the biblical place where King Solomon sourced his gold. By 1875, the population hit over 1000 but when the gold disappeared, so did the people. Ophir's fate was sealed when the railway bypassed it in 1904, leaving its main street trapped in time.

The most photogenic of Ophir's heritage buildings is the 1886 **post office** (www.historic.org.nz; 53 Swindon St, Ophir; ⊘9am-noon Mon-Fri). At the far end of town, the road heads over the heritage-listed 1870s **Dan O'Connell Bridge**, a bumpy but scenic crossing that loops back to SH85.

Ophir lays claim to the country's widest range of recorded temperatures: from -21.6°C to 35°C.

🛏 Sleeping & Eating

Blacks Hotel
PUB $$

(📞03-447 3826; www.blackshotel.co.nz; 170 Swindon St, Ophir; r $155; 🅿🛜) The sunny terrace of this popular local watering hole is a great spot to enjoy a pint or a pub-style meal (mains $23 to $30). Out the back is a row of simple, clean en suite rooms.

Chatto Creek Tavern
HERITAGE HOTEL $$

(📞03-447 3710; www.chattocreektavern.co.nz; 1544 SH85, Chatto Creek; dm/s/d without bathroom $60/100/130; 🅿🛜) Dating from 1886, this attractive stone hotel sits right beside the Rail Trail and highway, 10km southwest of Omakau. Pop in for 'wabbit' pie and other hearty pub meals (mains $19 to $34), or rest your weary calf muscles in a dorm bed or double room. Rates include breakfast. Informal camping is also possible.

⭐ Pitches Store
B&B $$$

(📞03-447 3240; www.pitches-store.co.nz; 45 Swindon St, Ophir; r $295; ⊙restaurant 10am-late daily Dec-Apr, 10am-3pm Mon, Sun & Thu, 10am-late Fri & Sat May & Aug-Nov) Formerly a general store and butcher, this heritage building has been sensitively transformed into six elegant guest rooms and a humdinger of a **cafe-restaurant** (mains lunch $15 to $18 and dinner $33 to $37). Exposed stone walls may speak of the past but the menu offers contemporary gourmet fare – it was named Silver Fern Farms Best Regional Restaurant in 2016 and 2017.

Stationside Cafe
CAFE $

(📞03-447 3580; Lauder-Matakanui Rd, Lauder; mains $8-18; ⊙8am-5pm Oct-Apr) Country hospitality is on show at this great little trailside place with wonderfully charming hosts. Options include tasty breakfasts, healthy salads and soups, as well as a mouth-watering selection of just-baked scones, cakes and muffins.

❶ Getting There & Away

There's no public transport to these parts but many of the bike crews servicing the Otago Central Rail Trail provide shuttles, and many accommodation providers can pick you up from the trail if you enquire in advance.

Alexandra

📞03 / POP 4800

Unless you've come especially for the Easter Bunny Hunt or the springtime Blossom Festival and NZ Merino Shearing Championships, the main reason to visit unassuming Alexandra is mountain biking. It's the biggest Otago Central Rail Trail (p565) settlement by far, offering more eating and sleeping options than the rest of the one-horse (or fewer) towns on the route. It's also the start of the new Roxburgh Gorge Trail.

Alex, as it's known to the locals, marks the southeastern corner of the acclaimed Central Otago wine region. Of the dozen wineries in the immediate vicinity, only a handful are open for tastings. These are detailed on the *Central Otago Wine Map*, available from the i-SITE (p568).

⊙ Sights

Central Stories
MUSEUM

(📞03-448 6230; www.centralstories.com; 21 Centennial Ave; by donation; ⊙10am-4pm) Central Otago's history of gold mining, winemaking, fruit growing and sheep farming is covered in this excellent regional museum and gallery, which shares a building with the i-SITE (p568).

🏃 Activities

As well as the obvious – the Otago Central Rail Trail – walkers and mountain bikers will love the old gold trails weaving through the hills; collect maps from the i-SITE. The **Alexandra–Clyde 150th Anniversary Walk** (12.8km, three hours one way) is a riverside trail that's fairly flat, with ample resting spots and shade.

Roxburgh Gorge Trail
MOUNTAIN BIKING

(www.cluthagold.co.nz; suggested track maintenance donation per person $10) Opened to considerable fanfare in 2013, this well-constructed cycling and walking track was intended to connect Alexandra to Roxburgh Dam. As access through some of the farmland in the middle section wasn't successfully negotiated, however, riding the 'full trail' requires prearranging a scenic 13km jetboat ride (adult/child $95/55) through the local information centres or directly with Clutha River Cruises (p568).

Altitude Bikes
CYCLING

(📞03-448 8917; www.altitudeadventures.co.nz; 88 Centennial Ave; per day from $30; ⊙8.30am-5.30pm Mon-Fri, 9am-1pm Sat) Rents bikes in conjunction with Henderson Cycles and organises logistics for riders on the Otago Central, Clutha Gold and Roxburgh Gorge Trails.

ALEXANDRA TO MILTON ON THE SH8

Heading south from Alexandra, SH8 winds along rugged, rock-strewn hills above the Clutha River as it passes Central Otago's famous orchards. In season (roughly December to March) roadside fruit stalls sell just-picked stone fruit, cherries and berries. En route are a scattering of small towns, many dating from gold-rush days.

Thirteen kilometres south of Alexandra, the historic **Speargrass Inn** (☑03-449 2192; www.speargrassinn.co.nz; 1300 Fruitlands Roxburgh Rd, SH8, Fruitlands; r $180; ☺cafe 8.30am-4pm Sat-Thu, 8.30am-late Fri, closed May-Sep; ☎) has three handsome rooms in a block out the back, set in attractive gardens. The original 1869 building houses a charming cafe (mains $18 to $26). It's an excellent place to stop for coffee and cake or a more substantial meal.

Further south, the Clutha broadens into **Lake Roxburgh**, with a large hydroelectric power station at its terminus, before rushing past Roxburgh itself. Call into the friendly **i-SITE** (☑03-446 8920; www.centralotagonz.com; 120 Scotland St; ☺9am-5pm daily Nov-Apr, Mon-Fri May-Oct) for information on mountain biking, water sports and seasonal fruit-picking work in the surrounding apple and stone-fruit orchards.

Before you leave Roxburgh, drop into **Jimmy's Pies** (☑03-446 9012; www.jimmyspies.co.nz; 143 Scotland St; pies $4-6.50; ☺7.30am-5pm Mon-Fri), renowned across the South Island since 1959. If you're at a loss to which of the 20 different varieties of pies to choose try the apricot chicken – you're in orchard country after all.

Continuing south from Roxburgh, the road passes through **Lawrence** and the **Manuka Gorge Scenic Reserve**, a picturesque route through wooded hills and gullies. SH8 joins SH1 near **Milton**.

Clutha River Cruises BOATING
(☑0800 258 842; www.clutharivercruises.co.nz; boat ramp, Dunorling St; adult/child $95/55; ☺2.30pm Oct-May) Explore the scenery and history of the region on a 2½-hour heritage cruise. They also run the jetboat transfer for cyclists on the Roxburgh Gorge Trail (p567).

🛌 Sleeping & Eating

Marj's Place HOSTEL $
(☑03-448 7098; www.marjsplace.co.nz; 5 Theyers St; dm/s/d without bathroom $30/45/90; ☎) The standard varies widely between the three neighbouring houses that comprise this sprawling hostel. The 'homestay' has private rooms, a Finnish sauna and a spa bath. It's much nicer than the 'backpackers' across the road, which is let mainly to seasonal workers.

Asure Avenue Motel MOTEL $$
(☑03-448 6919; www.avenue-motel.co.nz; 117 Centennial Ave; units from $142; ⓟ☎) The pick of the motels on the main drag, these clean, modern units have all the mod cons – and some have full kitchens, too. Studio, one- and two-bedroom apartments are available.

★**Courthouse Cafe & Larder** CAFE $
(☑03-448 7818; www.packingshedcompany.com; 8 Centennial Ave; mains $11-23; ☺6.30am-4.30pm Mon-Fri, 8am-4pm Sat) Fairy lights and bounteous botanical displays dispel any lingering austerity in this stone courthouse building, dating from 1878. The counter groans under the weight of an extraordinary array of baked goods (cakes, doughnuts, croissants and more), which compete with gourmet brunch and lunch options – and if Jack's rolled ice cream happens to be on the menu when you visit, you'd best save room!

ℹ️ Information

Alexandra i-SITE (☑03-262 7999; www.centralotagonz.com; 21 Centennial Ave; ☺9am-5pm; ☎) Pick up a free map; friendly staff can also help with activity bookings and accommodation.

ℹ️ Getting There & Away

Alexandra lies on SH8, around 2½ hours' drive from Dunedin and 1¼ hours from Queenstown.

InterCity (p560) coaches head to/from Dunedin (from $22, three hours), Roxburgh (from $14, 34 minutes), Clyde (from $10, nine minutes), Cromwell (from $11, 24 minutes) and Queenstown (from $14, 1½ hours).

A daily Atomic Shuttles (p560) bus heads to/from Dunedin ($40, three hours), Roxburgh ($20, 30 minutes), Cromwell ($20, 30 minutes) and Queenstown ($30, 1¾ hours).

Catch-a-Bus (p560) runs door-to-door shuttles to Cromwell ($25, 30 minutes), Clyde ($15, 10 minutes), Ranfurly ($43, one hour), Middlemarch ($55, two hours) and Dunedin ($56, 3¼ hours).

Clyde

📞 03 / POP 1010

More charming than his buddy Alex, 8km down the road, Clyde looks more like a 19th-century gold-rush film set than a real town. Set on the banks of the emerald-green Clutha River, Clyde retains a friendly, small-town feel, even when holidaymakers arrive in numbers over summer. It's also the trailhead of the Otago Central Rail Trail (p565).

◉ Sights

Clyde Historical Museums   MUSEUM
(5 Blyth St; by donation; ⊙2-5pm Tue-Sun) This volunteer-run local museum showcases Māori and Victorian exhibits, and traces the construction of the Clyde Dam. You can also peep into the old council chambers. A second building, housed in the Herb Factory complex at 12 Fraser St, was closed for renovations when we visited.

🏃 Activities

Pick up a copy of *Walk Around Historic Clyde* from the Alexandra i-SITE (p568). The **Alexandra–Clyde 150th Anniversary Walk** (12.8km, three hours one way) is a riverside trail that's fairly flat, with ample resting spots and shade.

Trail Journeys   CYCLING
(📞03-449 2150; www.trailjourneys.co.nz; 16 Springvale Rd; rental per day from $45; ⊙9am-5pm Mon-Fri May-Oct, 8am-5pm daily Nov-Apr) 🚲 Right by the Otago Central Rail trailhead, Trail Journeys rents bikes and arranges cycling tours, baggage transfers and shuttles. It also has a depot in Middlemarch (p564).

🎉 Festivals & Events

Clyde Wine & Food Festival   WINE, FOOD
(www.promotedunstan.org.nz; adult/child $15/10; ⊙10.30am-4.30pm Easter Sun) Held in the main street on Easter Sunday each year, this local festival showcases the region's produce and wines.

🛌 Sleeping & Eating

Postmaster's House   B&B $$
(📞03-449 2488; www.postofficecafeclyde.co.nz; 4 Blyth St; d with/without bathroom $125/95; ▣ 🛜)

Antique furnishings are dotted around the large and lovely rooms in this pretty stone cottage. Two of the three rooms share a bathroom; the third has its own.

Dunstan House   B&B $$
(📞03-449 2295; www.dunstanhouse.co.nz; 29 Sunderland St; s/d without bathroom from $110/130, d/ste with bathroom from $190/260; ⊙Oct-Apr; 🛜) This restored late-Victorian balconied inn has lovely bar and lounge areas, and stylish rooms decorated in period style. The less expensive rooms share bathrooms but are just as comfortable and atmospheric.

⭐ Oliver's   B&B $$$
(📞03-449 2600; www.oliverscentralotago.co.nz; Holloway Rd; r/ste from $235/535; ▣ 🛜) 🌿 Oliver's fills an 1860s merchant's house and stone stables with luxurious rooms decked out with old maps, heritage furniture and claw-foot baths. Most of the rooms open onto a secluded garden courtyard.

Bank Cafe   CAFE $
(www.bankcafe.co.nz; 31 Sunderland St; mains $10-19; ⊙9am-4pm) Grab a table inside or out and tuck into cakes, slices, waffles and delicious burgers. The robust takeaway sandwiches are perfect for lunch on two wheels.

⭐ Oliver's   MODERN NZ $$
(📞03-449 2805; www.oliverscentralotago.co.nz; 34 Sunderland St; mains lunch $21-26, dinner $26-41; ⊙restaurant noon-2pm & 6pm-late, bar noon-late) Housed in a gold-rush era general store, this classy complex incorporates a craft brewery, bar and bakery-cafe within its venerable stone walls. The restaurant shifts gears from on-trend cafe fare at lunchtime to a bistro showcasing the best local, seasonal produce in the evenings, with dishes like smoked rabbit and barley risotto or roast lamb rump.

ℹ️ Getting There & Away

InterCity (p560) coaches head to/from Dunedin (from $22, three hours), Roxburgh (from $14, 45 minutes), Alexandra (from $10, nine minutes), Cromwell (from $10, 14 minutes) and Queenstown (from $14, 1½ hours).

Catch-a-Bus (p564) runs door-to-door shuttles to/from Cromwell ($25, 20 minutes), Alexandra ($15, 10 minutes), Ranfurly ($43, 1½ hours), Middlemarch ($55, 2½ hours) and Dunedin ($56, 3½ hours) during the main cycling season.

Cromwell

☑ 03 / POP 4150

Cromwell has a charming lakeside historic precinct, a great weekly farmers market and perhaps the South Island's most over-the-top 'big thing' – a selection of giant fruit by the highway, representing the area's extensive fruit-growing industry.

It's also at the very heart of the prestigious Central Otago wine region (www.cowa.org.nz), known for its extraordinarily good pinot noir and, to a lesser extent, riesling, pinot gris and chardonnay. The Cromwell Basin – which stretches from Bannockburn, 5km southwest of Cromwell, to north of Lake Dunstan – accounts for over 70% of Central Otago's total wine production. Pick up the *Central Otago Wine Map* for details of upwards of 50 local wineries.

⊙ Sights

Cromwell Heritage Precinct

HISTORIC BUILDING

(www.cromwellheritageprecinct.co.nz; Melmore Tce) When the Clyde Dam was completed in 1992 it flooded Cromwell's historic town centre, 280 homes, six farms and 17 orchards. Many historic buildings were disassembled before the flooding and have since been rebuilt in a pedestrianised precinct beside Lake Dunstan. While some have been set up as period museum pieces (stables and the like), others house a few good cafes, galleries and some interesting shops. In summer the area plays host to an excellent weekly farmers market.

Carrick

WINERY

(☑ 03-445 3480; www.carrick.co.nz; Cairnmuir Rd, Bannockburn; ⊙ 11am-5pm) Around a dozen or so Bannockburn wineries are open to the public; several offer notable dining. Carrick is up there with the best, with an art-filled restaurant opening out on to a terrace and lush lawns, and a willow-framed view of the Carrick mountains. The seasonal menu (including excellent share platters) is a pleasurable complement to the wine range, which includes an intense, spicy pinot noir – the flagship drop – as well as a rich, toasty chardonnay and citrusy aromatic varietals.

Bendigo Historic Reserve

HISTORIC SITE

(www.doc.govt.nz; Bendigo) Gold was first discovered in Bendigo in 1862; relics from this era can be seen at this historic reserve, accessible via a gravel road off SH8, just north of Lake Dunstan. Sights include mine shafts and tunnels, machinery, dams and water races, as well as the crumbled stone remnants of Crippletown, Logantown and Welshtown, where the miners lived.

🏃 Activities

Highlands Motorsport Park

ADVENTURE SPORTS

(☑ 03-445 4052; www.highlands.co.nz; cnr SH6 & Sandflat Rd; ⊙ 10am-5pm) Transformed from a paddock into a top-notch 4km racing circuit in just 18 months, this revheads' paradise hosted its first major event in 2013. The action isn't reserved just for the professionals, with various high-octane experiences on offer, along with an excellent museum.

Budding speed freaks can start out on the **go-karts** ($45 per 10 minutes) before taking a 200km/h ride in the **Highlands Taxi** ($129 for up to four people), completing three laps of the circuit as a passenger in a **Porsche GT3** ($295), or having a go at the wheel of a **V8 muscle car** ($395).

If you'd prefer a less racy experience, the **National Motorsport Museum** (adult/child $25/10) showcases racing cars and displays about Kiwi legends such as Bruce McLaren, Possum Bourne, Emma Gilmour and Scott Dixon. Family groups can opt for the **Jurassic Safari Adventure**, a trip in a safari van through a forest inhabited by dinosaurs ($99 per family including museum entry). There's also free **minigolf** and a good cafe.

🛱 Tours

Goldfields Jet

ADVENTURE

(☑ 03-445 1038; www.goldfieldsjet.co.nz; SH6; adult/child $115/59; ⊙ 9am-5pm) Zip through the Kawarau Gorge on a 40-minute jet-boat ride.

Central Otago Motorcycle Hire

TOURS

(☑ 03-445 4487; www.comotorcyclehire.co.nz; 271 Bannockburn Rd; per day from $185) The sinuous and hilly roads of Central Otago are perfect for negotiating on two wheels. This crew hires out motorbikes and advises on improbably scenic routes. Is also offers guided trail-bike tours (from $195) and extended road tours (from $575).

Bannockburn Historic Goldfields Tours

WALKING

(☑ 03-445 1559; www.bannockburngold.co.nz; per person $15-29) Informative guided tours exploring Bannockburn's gold-mining heritage.

✨ Festivals & Events

Highlands 101 SPORTS
(www.highlands.co.nz/highlands-501; ⊘Nov) A weekend-long motorsports festival at Highlands Park, culminating in a 101-lap endurance race.

Highlands Festival of Speed SPORTS
(www.highlands.co.nz; ⊘Apr) Two days of classic motor racing, held in early April.

🛌 Sleeping

Cromwell Top 10 Holiday Park HOLIDAY PARK $
(☑03-445 0164; www.cromwellholidaypark.co.nz; 1 Alpha St; sites $42-46, units with/without bathroom from $115/75; P@🖀) The size of a small European nation and packed with cabins and self-contained units of various descriptions, all set in tree-lined grounds.

Carrick Lodge MOTEL $$
(☑03-445 4519; www.carricklodge.co.nz; 10 Barry Ave; units $140-220; P🖀) One of Cromwell's more stylish motels, Carrick has spacious, modern units and is just a short stroll from the main shopping complex. Executive units have spa baths and views over the golf course.

★ Burn Cottage Retreat B&B, COTTAGE $$$
(☑03-445 3050; www.burncottageretreat.co.nz; 168 Burn Cottage Rd; cottage $235-265; P🖀) Set among walnut trees and gardens 3km northwest of Cromwell, this peaceful retreat has three luxurious, self-contained cottages with classy decor, spacious kitchens and modern bathrooms.

🍴 Eating

Grain & Seed Café CAFE $
(Melmore Tce; meals $10-14; ⊘9am-4pm) Set in a beautiful stone building that was once Jolly's Grain Store, this cafe serves up tasty muffins and big, inexpensive meals. Grab an outside table beside the lake for great views.

Black Rabbit Kitchen & Bar CAFE $$
(☑03-445 1553; 430a Bannockburn Rd, Bannockburn; mains $23-28; ⊘8am-6pm Sun-Thu, till late Fri & Sat) A welcome addition to the tiny hamlet of Bannockburn, this rustic chic cafe-bar offers great brunches, good coffee, an extensive wine list and a sunny deck on which you can happily while away the afternoon.

Bannockburn Hotel PUB FOOD $$
(☑03-445 0615; www.bannockburnhotel.com; 420 Bannockburn Rd, Bannockburn; mains $22-29; ⊘4-10pm Tue-Wed, from noon Thu-Sun) A recent refurbishment has turned this historic Bannockburn watering hole into a stylish modern pub with a tapas-inspired sharing menu and a wine list longer than your arm. It's 5km out of town, but it operates a free courtesy bus.

Mt Difficulty BISTRO $$
(☑03-445 3445; www.mtdifficulty.co.nz; 73 Felton Rd, Bannockburn; mains $34-39; ⊘tastings 10.30am-4.30pm, restaurant noon-4pm) As well as making our favourite NZ pinot noir, Mt Difficulty is a lovely spot for a leisurely lunch looking down over the valley. There are large wine-friendly platters to share, but save room for the decadent desserts.

🛍 Shopping

Cromwell Farmers Market MARKET
(www.cromwellheritageprecinct.co.nz; ⊘9am-1pm Sun) In summer the Cromwell Heritage Precinct plays host to an excellent farmers market, running every Sunday from Labour weekend (late October) to Easter.

ℹ️ Information

Cromwell i-SITE (☑03-445 0212; www.centralotagonz.com; 2d The Mall; ⊘9am-7pm Jan-Mar, to 5pm Apr-Dec) Stocks the *Walk Cromwell* brochure, covering local cycling and walking trails, including the nearby gold-rush ghost town of Bendigo.

ℹ️ Getting There & Away

Daily Atomic Shuttles (p560) buses head to/from Queenstown ($15, 1¼ hours), Alexandra ($20, 30 minutes), Roxburgh ($30, 1½ hours), Dunedin ($35, 3½ hours) and Christchurch ($40, 6¼ hours).

Catch-a-Bus (p564) runs door-to-door shuttles to Clyde ($25, 20 minutes), Alexandra ($25, 30 minutes), Ranfurly ($52, 1¾ hours), Middlemarch ($59, 2¾ hours) and Dunedin ($60, 3¾ hours) during the main cycling season.

InterCity (p560) runs coaches to Queenstown (from $11, one hour, four daily), Fox Glacier (from $44, 6¼ hours, one daily), Christchurch (from $51, 7¼ hours, two daily), Alexandra (from $12, 24 minutes, two daily) and Dunedin (from $22, 3½ hours).

Naked Bus (p560) runs buses from Queenstown (one hour) and Wanaka (45 minutes) stop in Cromwell before continuing to Omarama (1¼ hours), Lake Tekapo (three hours) and Christchurch (7½ hours). Prices vary.

Ritchies (p560) runs scheduled shuttles to/from Wanaka ($22, 45 minutes), Queenstown Airport ($22, one hour) and Queenstown CBD ($22, 1¼ hours).

Queenstown & Wanaka

Best Places to Eat

➜ Bespoke Kitchen (p586)

➜ Chop Shop (p597)

➜ Kai Whakapai (p604)

➜ Kika (p604)

➜ Public Kitchen & Bar (p586)

Best Places to Stay

➜ EcoScapes (p594)

➜ Hidden Lodge (p585)

➜ Wanaka Bakpaka (p603)

➜ Lime Tree Lodge (p604)

➜ YHA Queenstown Lakefront (p583)

Why Go?

Few people come to Queenstown to wind down. The self-styled 'adventure capital of the world' is a place where visitors come to throw their inhibitions out the window...and throw themselves out of planes and off mountain tops and bridges.

The region has a cinematic backdrop of mountains and lakes and a smattering of valley towns just as enticing as Queenstown itself. Wanaka may resemble Queenstown – lakeside setting, a fringe of mountains, a lengthy menu of adventures – but it runs at a less frenetic pace. Glenorchy is even more sedate, and yet it's the final stop for many on their way into arguably the finest alpine tramping terrain in NZ. History makes its home in gold-rush Arrowtown, where the main-street facades still hint at past glory. Settle in for dinner and a drink after the crowds disperse – the following day there'll be plenty more opportunities to dive back into Queenstown's action-packed whirlwind.

When to Go

➜ The fine and settled summer weather from January to March is the perfect backdrop to Queenstown's active menu of adventure sports and outdoor exploration. March also brings the Gibbston Wine & Food Festival to Queenstown Gardens.

➜ Gold returns to Arrowtown in autumn (March to May) with a vivid display of colour in the turning of the leaves.

➜ In late June the Queenstown Winter Festival celebrates the coming of the ski season. From June to August, the slopes of the four ski fields surrounding Queenstown and Wanaka are flush with skiers and snowboarders.

➜ The winter play season ends in a flourish from late August with Queenstown's Gay Ski Week and the Remarkables Ice & Mixed Festival.

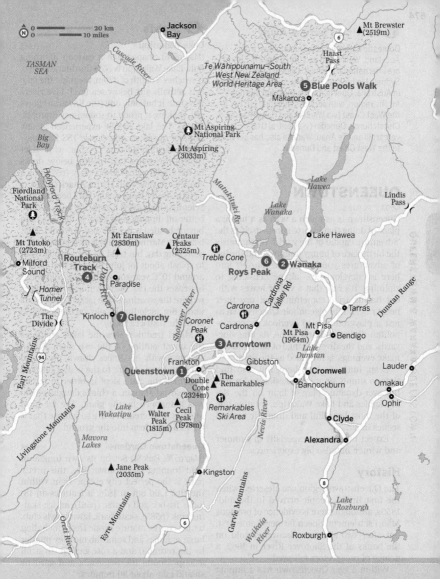

Queenstown & Wanaka Highlights

1 **Queenstown** (p574)
Taking the literal leap into any number of once-in-a-lifetime activities in the 'adventure capital of the world'.

2 **Wanaka** (p599) Scaling a waterfall *via ferrata* before dining among the lakeside town's bevy of interesting eateries.

3 **Arrowtown** (p595) Spending a day in a lower gear

strolling this historic gold-rush town before discovering a couple of very chic bars.

4 **Routeburn Track** (p592) Tramping high into the mountains on arguably the greatest of NZ's Great Walks.

5 **Blue Pools Walk** (p607) Taking a short stroll to a luminous bloom of river colour just outside of Makarora.

6 **Roys Peak** (p601) Snapping *that* photo, but continuing to the summit of this mountain with drone-like views over Lake Wanaka.

7 **Glenorchy** (p590) Discovering that Paradise really is just around the corner at one of NZ's most enticing tramping bases.

ℹ️ Getting There & Away

Domestic flights head to Queenstown from Auckland, Wellington and Christchurch. There are international flights to Queenstown from Sydney, Melbourne, Brisbane and the Gold Coast in Australia. Queenstown is the main bus hub for the region, with services radiating out to the West Coast (via Wanaka and Haast Pass), Christchurch, Dunedin (via Central Otago), Invercargill and Te Anau. Wanaka also has services to the West Coast and Dunedin.

QUEENSTOWN

📱 03 / POP 12,500

Queenstown is as much a verb as a noun, a place of doing that likes to spruik itself as the 'adventure capital of the world'. It's famously the birthplace of bungy jumping, and the list of adventures you can throw yourself into here is encyclopedic – alpine heliskiing to ziplining. It's rare that a visitor leaves without having tried something that ups their heart rate, but to pigeonhole Queenstown as just a playground is to overlook its cosmopolitan dining and arts scene, its fine vineyards, and the diverse range of bars that can make evenings as fun-filled as the days.

Leap, lunge or luge here, but also find time to simply sit at the lakeside and watch the ever-dynamic play of light on the Remarkables and Lake Wakatipu, creating one of the most beautiful and dramatic natural scenes in NZ.

Expect big crowds, especially in summer and winter, but also big experiences.

History

The Queenstown region was deserted when the first British people arrived in the mid-1850s, although there is evidence of previous Māori settlement. Sheep farmers came first, but after two shearers discovered gold on the banks of the Shotover River in 1862, a deluge of prospectors followed.

Within a year Queenstown was a mining town with streets, permanent buildings and a population of several thousand. It was declared 'fit for a queen' by the NZ government; hence Queenstown was born. Lake Wakatipu was the principal means of transport, and at the height of the boom there were four paddle steamers and 30 other craft plying the waters.

By 1900 the gold had petered out and the population was a mere 190. It wasn't until the 1950s that Queenstown became a popular holiday destination.

👁️ Sights

Lake Wakatipu LAKE
(Map p576) Shaped like a cartoon lightning bolt, Lake Wakatipu is NZ's third-largest lake. It reaches a depth of 379m, meaning the lake bed actually sits below sea level. Five rivers flow into it but only one (the Kawarau) flows out, making it prone to sometimes dramatic floods. The lake can be experienced at any number of speeds: the classic TSS Earnslaw (p581) steamboat trip, a spin with KJet (p578), the water taxi (p590), below decks in the Underwater Observatory (p575), or a shark's-eye view with Hydro Attack (p578).

If the water looks clean, that's because it is. Scientists have rated it as 99.9% pure – you're better off dipping your glass in the lake than buying bottled water. It's also very cold. That beach by Marine Pde may look tempting on a scorching day, but trust us – you won't want to splash about for long in water that hovers around 10°C year-round. Because cold water increases the risk of drowning, local bylaws require the wearing of life jackets in all boats under 6m, including kayaks, on the lake (and all of the district's lakes).

Māori tradition sees the lake's shape as the burnt outline of the evil giant Matau sleeping with his knees drawn up. Local lad Matakauri set fire to the bed of bracken on which the giant slept in order to rescue his beloved Manata, a chief's daughter who was kidnapped by the giant. The fat from Matau's body created a fire so intense that it burnt a hole deep into the ground.

Queenstown Gardens PARK
(Map p576; Park St) Set on its own tongue of land framing Queenstown Bay, this pretty park is the perfect city escape right within the city. Laid out in 1876, it features an 18-'hole' frisbee golf course (p581), an ice-skating rink (p585), skate park, lawn-bowls club, tennis courts, mature exotic trees (including large sequoias and some fab monkey puzzles by the rotunda) and a rose garden. To stroll a loop around the peninsula and gardens should take about 30 minutes.

Skyline Gondola CABLE CAR
(Map p576; 📱03-441 0101; www.skyline.co.nz; Brecon St; adult/child return $35/22; ⊙9am-9pm) Hop aboard for fantastic views as the gondola squeezes through pine forest to its grandstand location 400m above Queenstown. At the top there's the inevitable cafe, restaurant, souvenir shop and observation deck, as well as the Queenstown Bike Park (p580), Skyline Luge (p581), Ledge Bungy (p577), Ledge Swing (p577) and Ziptrek

Ecotours (p581). At night there are Māori culture shows from Kiwi Haka (p589) and stargazing tours (including gondola, adult/child $93/49).

Walking trails include the **Skyline Loop track** through the Douglas firs (30 minutes return). The energetic (or frugal) can forgo the gondola and hike to the top on the Tiki Trail, while the popular Ben Lomond Track climbs on another 940m.

Kiwi Birdlife Park   ZOO
(Map p576; ☑03-442 8059; www.kiwibird.co.nz; Brecon St; adult/child $49/24; ☺9am-5pm, shows 11am, 1.30pm & 4pm) These two hectares are home to 10,000 native plants, tuatara and scores of birds, including kiwi, kea, NZ falcons, parakeets and extremely rare black stilts. Stroll around the aviaries, watch the conservation show and tiptoe quietly into the darkened kiwi houses. Kiwi feedings take place five times a day.

Underwater Observatory   VIEWPOINT
(Map p578; ☑03-442 6142; www.kjet.co.nz; Marine Pde; adult/child $10/5; ☺8.30am-dusk) Six windows showcase life under the lake in this reverse aquarium (the people are behind glass) beneath the KJet office. Large brown trout abound, and look out for freshwater eels and scaup ducks, which dive past the windows – especially when the coin-operated food-release box is triggered. A KJet trip (p578) gets you free entry.

🏃 Activities

Head to Shotover St to get a handle on the baffling array of activities on offer in Queenstown. This street, particularly the two blocks between Stanley and Brecon Sts, is wall-to-wall with adventure-tour operators selling their products, interspersed with travel agencies and 'information centres' hawking the very same products. Adding to the confusion is the fact that some stores change their name from summer to winter, while some tour operators list street addresses that are primarily their pick-up points rather than distinct shopfronts for the business.

If you're planning on tackling several activities, various combination tickets are available, including those offered by **Queenstown Combos** (Map p578; ☑03-442 7318; www.combos.co.nz; The Station, cnr Shotover & Camp Sts).

Hiking & Climbing

The Department of Conservation (DOC) publishes a dedicated *Wakatipu Walks* brochure, as well as the *Head of Lake Wakatipu* brochure, which covers trails closer to

Glenorchy. Between them, they outline more than 60 day walks in the area, including **Ben Lomond** (Map p576; www.doc.govt.nz), **Queenstown Hill** (Map p576) and the **Tiki Trail** (Map p576) FREE. They can be downloaded from the DOC website (www.doc.govt.nz), or picked up from DOC's Queenstown visitor centre (p589).

Ultimate Hikes   TRAMPING
(Map p578; ☑03-450 1940; www.ultimatehikes.co.nz; The Station, Duke St entrance; ☺Nov-Apr) 🏄 If you like your adventure with a little comfort, Ultimate Hikes offers three-day guided tramps on the Routeburn (from $1375) and Milford (from $2130) Tracks, staying in its own well-appointed private lodges. It also runs day walks on both tracks (from $179) and a couple of combinations of tracks. Prices include transfers from Queenstown, meals and accommodation.

Guided Walks New Zealand   TRAMPING
(☑03-442 3000; www.nzwalks.com; unit 29, 159 Gorge Rd) Guided walks ranging from half-day nature walks near Queenstown (adult/child $109/69) to a day on the Routeburn Track ($199/140) and the full three-day Hollyford Track (from $1895/1495). Also offers snowshoeing in winter.

Climbing Queenstown   CLIMBING
(Map p578; ☑027 477 9393; www.climbingqueenstown.com; 9 Shotover St; from $179) Rock-climbing, mountaineering and guided

Queenstown

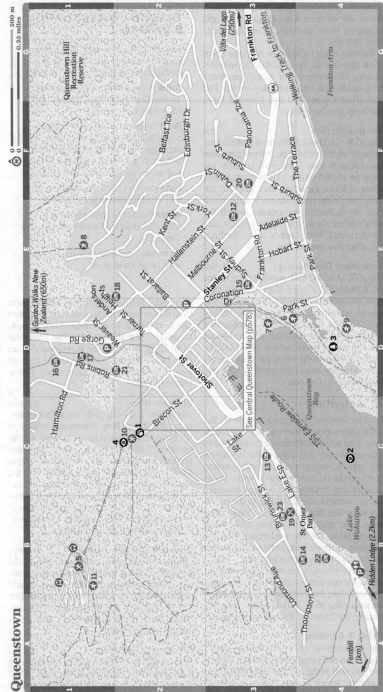

Queenstown Hill Recreation Reserve

Frankton Rd

Villa del Lago (250m)

Panorama Tce

The Terrace

Suburb St

Suburb St

Dublin St

Frankton Arm

Walking Track to Frankton

Belfast Tce

Edinburgh Dr

York St

Kent St

Adelaide St

Hobart St

Park St

Hallenstein St

Melbourne St

Sydney St

Frankton Rd

Park St

Ballarat St

Stanley St

Coronation Dr

Anderson Heights

Turner St

Weaver St

Gorge Rd

Robins Rd

Guided Walks New Zealand (650m)

Hamilton Rd

Shotover St

Brecon St

Lake St

See Central Queenstown Map (p578)

TSS Earnslaw Route

Queenstown Bay

Lake Esp

Brunswick St

St Omer Park

Lomond Ave

Lake Wakatipu

Thompson St

Hidden Lodge (2.2km)

Fernhill (1km)

500 m
0.25 miles

N

0
0

Queenstown

trekking and snowshoeing trips in the Remarkables. Trips depart from (and can be booked at) Outside Sports (p579).

Bungy & Swings

Shotover Canyon Swing & Fox   ADVENTURE SPORTS
(Map p578; ☑ 03-442 6990; www.canyonswing.co.nz; 34 Shotover St; swing $229, fox $169, swing & fox combo $299) ⌀ Pick from any number of jump styles – backwards, in a chair, upside down – and then leap from a 109m cliff above the Shotover River, with 60m of free fall and a wild swing across the canyon at 150km/h. The Canyon Fox, new in 2016, can have you whizzing across the Shotover Canyon, more than 180m above the river.

The price includes transfer from the Queenstown booking office, and if you liked the swing the first time, you can go again for $45.

AJ Hackett Bungy   BUNGY JUMPING
(Map p578; ☑ 0800 286 4958, 03-450 1300; www.bungy.co.nz; The Station, cnr Camp & Shotover Sts) The bungy originator now offers jumps from three sites in the Queenstown area, with giant swings available at two of them. It all started at the historic 1880 **Kawarau Bridge** (adult/child $195/145), 23km from Queenstown, which became the world's first commercial bungy site in 1988. The 43m leap has you plunging towards the river, and is the only bungy site in the region to offer tandem jumps.

The Kawarau Bridge site also features the **Kawarau Zipride** (adult/child $50/40, 3-/5-ride

pack $105/150), a zipline along the riverbank that reaches speeds of 60km/h. Multi-ride packs can be split between groups, making it a far cheaper alternative to the bungy.

The closest options to Queenstown are the **Ledge Bungy** (Map p576; adult/child $195/145) and **Ledge Swing** (Map p576; adult/child $160/110), set just beneath the top station of the Skyline Gondola. The drop is 47m, but it's 400m above town. In winter you can even leap into the dark.

Last but most airy is the **Nevis Bungy** (Map p578; ☑ 0800 286 4958; www.bungy.co.nz; The Station, cnr Camp & Shotover Sts; $275), the highest leap in New Zealand. From Queenstown, 4WD buses will transport you onto private farmland where you can jump from a specially constructed pod, 134m above the Nevis River. The **Nevis Swing** (Map p578; ☑ 0800 286 4958; www.bungy.co.nz; solo $195, tandem per person $175) starts 160m above the river and cuts a 300m arc across the canyon on a rope longer than a rugby field – yes, it's the world's biggest swing.

If you're keen to try more than one AJ Hackett experience, enquire about the range of combo tickets.

White-Water Rafting

Queenstown Rafting   RAFTING
(Map p578; ☑ 03-442 9792; www.queenstownrafting.co.nz; 35 Shotover St; rafting/helirafting $229/339) ⌀ Rafts year-round on the churning Shotover River (Grades III to V) and calmer Kawarau River (Grades II to III). Half-day trips give you two to three hours on the water. Helirafting trips are an exciting

Central Queenstown

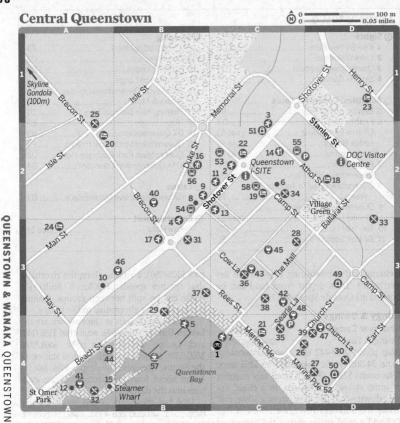

alternative, and there are multiday trips on the Landsborough River. Rafters must be at least 13 years old and weigh more than 40kg.

Family Adventures
RAFTING

(☑03-442 8836; www.familyadventures.co.nz; adult/child $189/120; ☺Oct-Apr; ⛟) Gentle (Grades I to II) rafting trips on the Shotover River, suitable for children three years and older. Trips depart from Browns Ski Shop (39 Shotover St).

Jetboating

Shotover Jet
BOATING

(☑03-442 8570; www.shotoverjet.com; Gorge Rd, Arthurs Point; adult/child $145/75; ✍) Half-hour jetboat trips through the narrow Shotover Canyon, with lots of thrilling 360-degree spins and reaching speeds of 85km/h.

Skippers Canyon Jet
BOATING

(☑03-442 9434; www.skipperscanyonjet.co.nz; Skippers Rd; adult/child $145/85; ✍) A 30-minute jetboat blast through the remote and hard-

to-access Skippers Canyon, among the narrowest gorges on the Shotover River. Trips pick up from Queenstown, taking around three hours in total.

KJet
BOATING

(☑03-442 6142; www.kjet.co.nz; adult/child $129/69) Skim, skid and spin around Lake Wakatipu and the Kawarau and Lower Shotover Rivers on these one-hour trips, leaving from the main town pier.

Hydro Attack
BOATING

(☑0508 493 762; www.hydroattack.co.nz; Lapsley Butson Wharf; $149; ☺9am-6pm Nov-Mar, 10am-4.30pm Apr-Oct) That shark you see buzzing about Lake Wakatipu is the Hydro Attack – jump inside, strap yourself in and take a ride. This 'Seabreacher X' watercraft can travel at 80km/h on the water, dive 2m underneath and then launch itself nearly 6m into the air. It's mesmerising to watch, let alone travel inside.

Central Queenstown

Mountain Biking

Since the opening of the Queenstown Bike Park in 2011, Queenstown has been entrenched as an international destination for mountain bikers. Your best bets for hiring serious wheels in the bike park are **Vertigo Bikes** (Map p578; ☑03-442 8378; www.vertigo bikes.co.nz; 4 Brecon St; rental half/full day from $39/59; ☺8am-7pm) and **Outside Sports** (Map p578; ☑03-441 0074; www.outsidesports. co.nz; 9 Shotover St; ☺8.30am-8pm).

The **Queenstown Trail** links five scenic cycling routes that radiate out like spokes to Arrowtown, Gibbston, Jack's Point, Lake Hayes and along the shores of Lake Wakatipu – 120km of trails in total. The trail

is suitable for cyclists of all levels. Bike-hire places such as **ChargeAbout** (☑03-442 6376; http://chargeabout.co.nz; Hilton Hotel, 79 Peninsula Rd, Kelvin Heights; ebike half/full day $79/119; ☺10am-5pm) and Arrowtown Bike Hire (p596) typically offer packages that include shuttle-bus pick-ups from Gibbston – ride one way, sip a few wines and get a designated driver for the return trip.

Queenstown Bike Park   MOUNTAIN BIKING
(Map p576; ☑03-441 0101; www.skyline.co.nz; Skyline Gondola; half/full day incl gondola $70/95; ☺Sep-May) More than 30 different trails – from easy (green) to extreme (double black) – radiate out from the top of the

Skyline Gondola. Once you've descended the 400m of vertical, simply jump on the gondola and do it all over again. The best trail for novice riders is the 6km-long **Hammy's Track**, which is studded with lake views and picnic spots.

Skiing & Snowboarding

Queenstown has two excellent ski fields: **The Remarkables** (☎03-442 4615; www.nzski.com; daily lift pass adult/child $119/55) and **Coronet Peak** (☎03-442 4620; www.nzski.com; Coronet Peak Rd; daily lift pass adult/child $119/55). If you fancy a change of scenery, there's also Cardrona Alpine Resort (p606) and Treble Cone (p599) near Wanaka. Coronet Peak is the only field to offer night skiing, which is an experience not to be missed if you strike a starry night. Roads around Queenstown become almost commuter busy on ski mornings and evenings, so taking the **NZSki Snowline Express** (Map p578; www.nzski.com) can mean one less vehicle holding up the show.

The ski season generally lasts from around June to September. In winter, shops throughout Queenstown are full of ski gear for purchase and hire; Outside Sports (p579) and **Small Planet Outdoors** (Map p578; ☎03-442 5397; www.smallplanetsports.com; 15-17 Shotover St; ⊗9am-7pm Oct-May, 8am-9pm Jun-Sep) are reliable options.

Even outside of the main ski season, heliskiing is an option for serious, cashed-up skiers; try **Harris Mountains Heli-Ski** (Map p578; ☎03-442 6722; www.heliski.co.nz; The Station, cnr Shotover & Camp Sts; from $990), **Alpine Heliski** (Map p578; ☎03-441 2300; www.alpine-heliski.com; 37 Shotover St; 3-8 runs $940-1340; ⊗Jul-Sep) or **Southern Lakes Heliski** (Map p578; ☎03-442 6222; www.heliskinz.com; Torpedo 7, 20 Athol St; from $1050).

Skydiving, Gliding & Parasailing

NZone   ADVENTURE SPORTS
(Map p578; ☎03-442 5867; www.nzoneskydive.co.nz; 35 Shotover St; from $299) Jump out of a perfectly good airplane from 9000,12,000 or 15,000ft...in tandem with someone who actually knows what they're doing.

Queenstown Paraflights   ADVENTURE SPORTS
(Map p578; ☎03-441 2242; www.paraflights.co.nz; solo $159, tandem/triple per person $129/99) Take a solo, tandem or triple paraflight, zipping along 200m above the lake, pulled behind a boat. Departs from the town pier.

GForce Paragliding   PARAGLIDING
(Map p576; ☎03-441 8581; www.nzgforce.com; incl gondola $219) Tandem paragliding from the top of the gondola (9am departures are $20 cheaper).

Other Activities

If you've heard it can be done, it's likely that it can be done in Queenstown. Short of us writing an adventure encyclopedia, check in at the i-SITE (p589) if you're interested in the likes of golf, minigolf, sailing or diving.

QUEENSTOWN IN...

Two Days

Fuel up at **Bespoke Kitchen** (p586) before riding the **Skyline Gondola** (p574) to get the lay of the land; have a go on the **luge** here, or let gravity take you back to town on the **Queenstown Bike Park** (p580). Take an afternoon leap from the **Kawarau Bridge Bungy** (p577) or squeeze through canyons in the **Shotover Jet** (p578), two of Queenstown's signature activities. Have a sunset drink at **Atlas Beer Cafe** (p588) before taking the three steps to **Public Kitchen & Bar** (p586) for dinner, followed by a bar hop – **Zephyr** (p588), **World Bar** (p588), **Smiths Craft Beer House** (p588) – to round out the day.

The next day begin at **Yonder** (p586) before devoting the morning to skiing, skydiving, white-water rafting or riverboarding. In the afternoon, take to two wheels on the Queenstown Trail (p579), or try your hand at the **Frisbee golf** course in the Queenstown Gardens. Have dinner at **Blue Kanu** (p586) before winding down with a quiet fireside wine at **Bardeaux** (p588).

Four Days

Follow the two-day itinerary, then head to Arrowtown (p595). Brunch at **Chop Shop** (p597), stroll Buckingham St and then continue on to the Gibbston wineries (p582). Return to Arrowtown for an evening at **Blue Door** (p598) or **La Rumbla** (p598). The following day, drive along the lakeshore to tiny Glenorchy (p590). Have lunch at the **Glenorchy Cafe** (p595) and then drive to the **Routeburn Track** (p592) trailhead for a short tramp on one of NZ's finest trails.

Frisbee Golf
OUTDOORS

(Map p576; www.queenstowndiscgolf.co.nz; Queenstown Gardens) FREE A series of 18 chain baskets set among the trees of Queenstown Gardens. Local sports stores – and the Queenstown Ice Arena (p585) – sell or rent frisbees and scorecards.

Ziptrek Ecotours
ADVENTURE SPORTS

(Map p576; ✆03-441 2102; www.ziptrek.co.nz; Skyline Gondola) 🌿 Incorporating a series of ziplines (flying foxes), this thrill-ride takes you whirring through the forest canopy, from treetop platform to treetop platform, high above Queenstown. Choose from the two-hour four-line Moa tour (adult/child $139/89) or the gnarlier and faster three-hour six-line Kea option ($189/139) that end back at the base of the gondola.

Skyline Luge
ADVENTURE SPORTS

(Map p576; ✆03-441 0101; www.skyline.co.nz; Skyline Gondola; 2/3/5 rides incl gondola adult $49/52/56, child $37/42/46; ⏰from 10am, closing times vary btwn 6pm & 9pm) 🌿 Ride the gondola to the top, then hop on a three-wheeled cart to ride 800m of track. Your first run must be on the easy Blue Track then you're allowed to advance to the Red Track, with its banked corners and tunnel. Children must be over 135cm in height to ride the Red Track.

🖝 Tours

Lake Cruises
TSS Earnslaw
BOATING

(Map p578; ✆0800 656 501; www.realjourneys. co.nz; Steamer Wharf, Beach St) The stately, steam-powered TSS *Earnslaw* was built in the same year as the *Titanic* (but with infinitely better results). Climb aboard for the standard 1½-hour Lake Wakatipu tour (adult/child $65/22), or take a 3½-hour excursion to the high-country Walter Peak Farm for $80/22 where there are sheepdog and shearing demonstrations.

Scenic Flights
Air Milford
SCENIC FLIGHTS

(✆03-442 2351; www.airmilford.co.nz; 3 Tex Smith Lane, Queenstown Airport) Options include a Milford Sound flyover (adult/child $440/265), a fly-cruise-fly combo (from $510/305), and longer flights to Doubtful Sound (summer only) and Aoraki/Mt Cook.

Over The Top
SCENIC FLIGHTS

(✆03-442 2233; www.flynz.co.nz; 10 Tex Smith Lane, Frankton) Offers a range of helicopter flights, from a picnic on a peak near town (per person $770) to a flight to a high-country sheep

station (from $4400) to an Ultimate Milford flight with four landings (from $7400). From July to October it offers heliskiing.

Glenorchy Air
SCENIC FLIGHTS

(✆03-442 2207; www.glenorchyair.co.nz; Queenstown Airport, Frankton) Scenic trips from Queenstown or Glenorchy include a Milford Sound fly-cruise-fly option (adult/child from $460/295), an Aoraki/Mt Cook flyover ($655/375) and a couple of *Lord of the Rings*–themed flights (from $395/195).

Sunrise Balloons
BALLOONING

(✆03-442 0781; www.ballooningnz.com; adult/child $545/345) One-hour sunrise flights, including a champagne breakfast on landing. Allow four hours for the entire experience.

Winery Tours
New Zealand Wine Tours
WINE

(✆0800 666 778; www.nzwinetours.co.nz; from $235) Small-group (maximum seven people) or private winery tours, including lunch – platter, degustation or à la carte, depending on the tour – and an 'aroma room' experience.

Appellation Central Wine Tours
WINE

(✆03-442 0246; www.appellationcentral.co.nz; tours $199-265) Take a tipple at four or five wineries in Gibbston, Bannockburn and Cromwell, including platter lunches at a winery restaurant.

Cycle de Vine
CYCLING

(✆0800 328 897; http://m.queenstown-trails. co.nz; tour $155; ⏰Oct–mid-May) Cruise around Gibbston on a retro bicycle. Tours take in three different wineries and a picnic snack beside the Kawarau River. Pick-ups from your Queenstown accommodation.

Milford Sound Tours
Day trips from Queenstown to Milford Sound via Te Anau take 12 to 13 hours, including a two-hour cruise on the sound. Bus-cruise-flight options are also available, as is pick-up from the Routeburn Track trailhead at the Divide. It's a long day in the saddle, so you might consider visiting Milford from Te Anau. Another way to speed things up are plane or helicopter sightseeing flights to Milford. A number of these offer landings at Milford Sound with cruise options.

BBQ Bus
TOURS

(✆03-442 1045; http://bbqbus.co.nz; adult/child $220/110) Small-group bus tours to Milford Sound (maximum 15 people), including a BBQ lunch followed by a cruise. Te Anau drop-offs and pick-ups are $40 cheaper.

DON'T MISS

EXPLORING THE GIBBSTON VALLEY

Queenstown's adrenaline junkies might be happiest dangling off a giant rubber band, but as they're plunging towards the Kawarau River, they might not realise they're in the heart of Gibbston, one of Central Otago's main wine subregions, accounting for around 20% of plantings.

Strung along Gibbston Hwy (SH6) is an interesting and beautiful selection of vineyards. Almost opposite the Kawarau Bridge, a precipitous 2km gravel road leads to **Chard Farm** (☑03-442 6110; www.chardfarm.co.nz; Chard Rd, Gibbston; ☉10am-5pm Mon-Fri, 11am-5pm Sat & Sun), the most picturesque of the wineries. A further 1km along SH6 is **Gibbston Valley** (☑03-442 6910; www.gibbstonvalley.com; 1820 Gibbston Hwy/SH6, Gibbston; ☉10am-5pm), the area's oldest commercial winery. As well as tastings, it has a restaurant, cheesery, tours of NZ's largest wine cave and bike hire. It also operates its own bus from Queenstown – you could always take the bus and then hire a bike to get between cellar doors.

Another 3km along SH6, **Peregrine** (☑03-442 4000; www.peregrinewines.co.nz; 2127 Gibbston Hwy/SH6, Gibbston; ☉11am-5pm) has an impressive, award-winning cellar door – a bunker-like building with a roof reminiscent of a falcon's wing in flight. As well as tastings, you can take a stroll through the adjoining barrel room.

The **Gibbston River Trail**, part of the Queenstown Trail, is a walking and cycling track that follows the Kawarau River for 11km from the Kawarau Bridge, passing all of the wineries. From Peregrine, walkers (but not cyclists) can swing onto the **Peregrine Loop** (one hour, 2.7km), which crosses over old mining works on 11 timber and two steel bridges, one of which passes through the branches of a willow tree. A 30-minute loop trail from Waitiri Creek Wines heads to **Big Beach** on the Kawarau River, with views of Nevis Bluff.

While you're in the area, be sure to call into the rustic **Gibbston Tavern** (☑03-409 0508; www.gibbstontavern.co.nz; 8 Coalpit Rd, Gibbston; ☉11am-8pm), just off the highway past Peregrine. It stocks Gibbston wines, fires up good pizzas and has a small art gallery.

If you're keen to explore the valley's wineries without needing to contemplate a drive afterwards, consider staying among the vines in **Kinross Cottages** (☑0800 131 101; www.kinrosscottages.co.nz; 2300 Gibbston Hwy/SH6, Gibbston; r $275-325; ☜), where the heritage-looking cottages are a front for modern, luxurious studio rooms. It has its own cellar door, representing five Central Otago vineyards, plus a general store with good meals.

Ask at the **Queenstown i-SITE** (p589) for maps and information about touring the area.

Real Journeys TOURS
(Map p578; ☑0800 656 501; www.realjourneys. co.nz; Steamer Wharf, Beach St) 🐋 Runs a host of trips, including the TSS Earnslaw (p581) cruises and activities at Walter Peak Farm, as well as day and overnight tours to Milford and Doubtful Sounds.

Other Tours

Nomad Safaris DRIVING
(Map p578; ☑03-442 6699; www.nomadsafaris.co.nz; 37 Shotover St; adult/child from $185/90) Runs 4WD tours into hard-to-get-to backcountry destinations such as Skippers Canyon and Macetown, as well as a trip through Middle Earth locations around Glenorchy and the Wakatipu Basin. You can also quad-bike through a sheep station on Queenstown Hill ($245).

Off Road Adventures DRIVING
(Map p578; ☑03-442 7858; www.offroad.co.nz; 61a Shotover St) Exciting off-road trips by quad bike (from $199) or dirt bike (from $289), with exclusive access to a 4500-hectare property along the Kawarau River and Nevis Range.

🎉 Festivals & Events

Gibbston Wine & Food Festival WINE, FOOD
(www.gibbstonwineandfood.co.nz; ☉Mar) Gibbston comes to Queenstown Gardens for a day in mid-March.

Queenstown Winter Festival SPORTS
(www.winterfestival.co.nz; ☉Jun) Four days of wacky ski and snowboard activities, live music, comedy, fireworks, a community carnival, parade, ball and plenty of frigid frivolity in late June.

LUMA Southern Light Project LIGHT SHOW
(http://luma.nz; Queenstown Gardens; ☉Jun) Four nights of illumination throughout the Queenstown Gardens over the Queen's Birthday public-holiday weekend. It began in 2015 with four light installations, and had grown to 38 by 2017.

Remarkables Ice & Mixed Festival SPORTS
(www.iceandmixedfestival.co.nz; ☉Aug) How often do you get to take your ice axe to a festival? This winter event gives you the

opportunity to climb alongside top-notch and rookie climbers on the iced walls of the Remarkables.

Gay Ski Week   LGBT
(www.gayskiweekqt.com; ☺ Aug/Sep) The South Island's biggest and best gay-and-lesbian event, held in late August/early September.

Queenstown Jazzfest   MUSIC
(http://queenstownjazzfest.co.nz; ☺Oct) Labour Day–weekend celebration of all things sax-y, with performances around the city and beyond.

🛏 Sleeping

Lakefront accommodation isn't difficult to come by in Queenstown, but midpriced rooms are few and far between. Queenstown's hostels are competitive, however, often with an intriguing selection of extras – free GoPro hire, in-house saunas etc. Hostels such as the YHA Queenstown Lakefront, **Hippo Lodge** (Map p576; ☎03-442 5785; www.hippolodge.co.nz; 4 Anderson Heights; dm $30-34, d without bathroom $88-96, with bathroom $96-104; P@☎) and Butterfli Lodge have views the equal of any of the town's hotels.

Prices fluctuate widely at most places, so check hotel websites to see about discounts.

Goodstays   ACCOMMODATION SERVICES $$$
(Map p578; ☎ 03-409 0537; www.goodstays.co.nz; 1st fl, 19 Camp St; ☺8.30am-5pm Mon-Fri) Has a huge variety of holiday homes and apartments, all listed on its website, with prices ranging from around $210 to $1350 per night. Minimum stays apply to all listings, ranging from three to five days.

🛏 Central Queenstown

★YHA Queenstown Lakefront   HOSTEL $
(Map p576; ☎03-442 8413; www.yha.co.nz; 88-90 Lake Esplanade; dm/s/d without bathroom from $30/80/102; P☎) 🌿 This large lakefront hostel, fresh from a refit in 2017, has basic but neat-as-a-pin bunkrooms and an industrial-size kitchen with window benches to absorb the view. The TV room is filled with beanbags and there are even a couple of massage chairs in the lounge. Lakeview suites get a shared balcony (and some traffic noise).

Adventure Q2 Hostel   HOSTEL $
(Map p578; ☎03-409 0862; http://adventureq2.co.nz; 5 Athol St; dm with/without bathroom from $35/33, d from $115; ☎) Opened in 2016, this sister hostel to Adventure Queenstown Hostel is pretty much its twin (complete with

the ski rentals, free GoPro hire etc), but with sturdier bunks, disabled-access bathrooms and an elevator in case you're tired of lugging around that rock-heavy backpack.

Haka Lodge   HOSTEL $
(Map p578; ☎03-442 4970; www.hakalodge.com; 6 Henry St; dm/r without bathroom from $33/99, apt $229; P☎) Part of a small Kiwi chain of higher-brow hostels, the warren-like Haka has cosy dorms with solid bunks that include large lockable storage chests, privacy curtains, personal lights and electrical sockets. There's a one-bedroom apartment attached, with its own kitchen, spacious lounge, laundry facilities and private deck where you can watch paragliders swirl down from the gondola.

Adventure Queenstown Hostel   HOSTEL $
(Map p578; ☎03-409 0862; www.aqhostel.co.nz; 36 Camp St; dm with/without bathroom $34/32, d from $110; @☎) Run by experienced travellers (as the photos displayed throughout testify), this central hostel has spotless dorms, a modern kitchen (complete with bread-maker) and balconies that are like a window onto the city. Free stuff includes use of bikes, frisbees and even GoPros. Private rooms have en suite bathrooms, as do some of the dorms.

Butterfli Lodge   HOSTEL $
(Map p576; ☎ 03-442 6367; www.butterfli.co.nz; 62 Thompson St; dm/s/d $34/73/77; P☎) This little hostel sits on a quiet hillside west of the town centre, ruled over by Jimmy the cat. There are no bunks but no en suites either. The views from the deck are like a sightseeing tour in themselves.

Flaming Kiwi Backpackers   HOSTEL $
(Map p576; ☎03-442 5494; www.flamingkiwi.co.nz; 39 Robins Rd; dm/s/d without bathroom $36/76/84; P☎) Close to the town centre but still quietly removed, this friendly hostel offers tidy dorms with a locker for every bed, three kitchens, unlimited wi-fi and a bottle of sunblock at reception. The lounge is like being back at home, and there are free bikes, frisbees and international phone calls to around 30 countries.

Bumbles   HOSTEL $
(Map p576; ☎03-442 6298; www.bumblesbackpackers.co.nz; cnr Lake Esplanade & Brunswick St; campsite/dm/r $25/35/76; P@☎) Enjoying a prime lakeside location, this popular wee hive has a supremely laid-back vibe. All of the rooms share bathrooms, and even the dorms get lake views.The beanbag-filled lounge has a colourful mural on one side and a more colourful vista of the Remarkables out the other. There's limited space for tents out the back.

★ **Creeksyde Queenstown Holiday Park & Motels** HOLIDAY PARK $$
(Map p576; ☎03-442 9447; www.camp.co.nz; 54 Robins Rd; sites from $55, d without bathroom from $83, units from $139; P 🛜) 🅿 In a garden setting, this pretty and extremely well-kept holiday park has accommodation ranging from small tent sites along the creek to fully self-contained motel units. It claims to be the 'world's first environmentally certified holiday park' and a number of the powered sites were switched to solar power in 2017.

Lomond Lodge MOTEL $$
(Map p578; ☎03-442 8235; www.lomondlodge. com; 33 Man St; from $145; P🛜) This mid-range motel on the fringe of the town centre has small but smartly designed rooms with a newly landscaped, sunny terrace and BBQ area out back. It's worth plumping for one of the upstairs Lakeview rooms ($220), which come with lookout-worthy balconies.

Queenstown Motel Apartments MOTEL $$
(Map p576; ☎03-442 6095; www.qma.co.nz; 62 Frankton Rd; units $145-225; P🛜) This well-run, sunlit spot is like two distinct properties in one – smallish but comfortable newer units out front and cheaper 1970s-style units (with newly renovated bathrooms) lined along the back. It has good views across the lake to Cecil Peak and Walter Peak. No children under 18.

Eichardt's Private Hotel BOUTIQUE HOTEL $$$
(Map p578; ☎03-441 0450; www.eichardts.com; Marine Pde; apt/ste from $1200/1500; 🛜) Dating from 1867, this restored hotel enjoys an absolute lakefront location. Each of the five giant suites – lake view or mountain view – has a fireplace, king-sized bed, heated floor, lake-sized bathtub and views. Four nearby apartments are equally luxurious.

Dairy BOUTIQUE HOTEL $$$
(Map p578; ☎03-442 5164; www.thedairy.co.nz; cnr Brecon & Isle Sts; r from $439; P🛜) Its dining room was once a corner store, but the Dairy is now a luxury B&B with 13 rooms packed with classy touches such as designer bed linen, silk cushions and luxurious mohair rugs. Rates include cooked breakfasts and complimentary NZ bubbly on arrival. There are discounts in winter.

Queenstown Park Boutique Hotel BOUTIQUE HOTEL $$$
(Map p576; ☎03-441 8441; www.queenstownpark. co.nz; 21 Robins Rd; r from $380; P🛜) 🅿 White curtains billow over beds decked out in luxurious linen at this very chic 19-room hotel. The 'Remarkables' rooms overlook a park to

the namesake mountain range (there aren't any lake views), while the 'Gondola' rooms are smaller but have courtyards or balconies. All have kitchenettes, and there's free wine and nibbles during 'canapé hour' (6pm to 7pm).

QT Queenstown BOUTIQUE HOTEL $$$
(Map p576; ☎03-450 3450; www.qthotelsand resorts.com/queenstown; 30 Brunswick St; r from $323) Queenstown's newest luxury hotel opened in December 2017 and sits just a touch above the lakefront hotels along Lake Esplanade, creating even more expansive views. There are 69 rooms with standalone bathtubs and gel beds. The top-floor Remarkable King rooms get the best of the views.

Amity Lodge Motel MOTEL $$$
(Map p576; ☎03-442 7288; www.amitylodge.co.nz; 7 Melbourne St; units from $195; P🛜) In a quiet street around a five-minute walk up from the town centre, this angular white block has renovated one- and two-bedroom apartments and friendly owners. The triple-glazing is more about keeping out the cold than noise.

Coronation Lodge LODGE $$$
(Map p576; ☎03-441 0860; www.coronationlodge.co. nz; 10 Coronation Dr; d $199-259, with kitchenette $219-289; P🛜) Right beside Queenstown Gardens, this tidy block with 11 rooms has basement parking, double-glazed windows, wooden floors and Turkish rugs. Larger rooms have kitchenettes. The attractive little wood-lined breakfast room at the front serves both cooked ($17) and continental ($13) options. There are ski lockers and drying rooms in winter.

🛏 Surrounds

Queenstown Top 10 Holiday Park HOLIDAY PARK $
(☎03-442 9306; www.qtowntop10.co.nz; 70 Arthurs Point Rd, Arthurs Point; sites from $48, units with/without bathroom from $95/85; P🛜🚗) 🅿 High above the Shotover River, this relatively small and extremely neat park with better-than-the-norm motel units is 10 minutes' drive from the hustle and bustle of Queenstown. There's bike storage, a ski drying room and a complimentary shuttle bus into town. Fall out of your campervan straight onto the famous Shotover Jet.

★ **Little Paradise Lodge** LODGE $$
(☎03-442 6196; www.littleparadise.co.nz; Glenorchy–Queenstown Rd, Mt Creighton; s/d $90/140, units $180; P) This isolated and peaceful lodge, almost midway between Queenstown and Glenorchy, is a whimsical gem. From the toilet-cistern aquariums

QUEENSTOWN WITH CHILDREN

While Queenstown is brimming with activities, some of them have age restrictions that may exclude the youngest in your group. Nevertheless, you shouldn't have any trouble keeping the littlies busy.

All-age attractions include the Kiwi Birdlife Park (p575) and lake cruises on the TSS Earnslaw (p581). The small ones in your group will love watching the duck dives from the Underwater Observatory (p575). There's a good beachside **playground** (Map p576; ⌖) near the entrance to the Queenstown Gardens (p574) on Marine Pde. Also in the gardens, **Queenstown Ice Arena** (Map p576; ☑03-441 8000; www.queenstownicearena.co.nz; 29 Park St; entry incl skate hire $19; ⊘10am-5pm mid-Apr–mid-Oct) is great for a rainy day, and a round of Frisbee golf (p581) will easily fill in a couple of hours. The Skyline Gondola (p574) offers a slow-moving activity with a dizzying view. Small children can also ride the luge (p581) with an adult, but need to be at least 110cm in height to go it alone.

Family Adventures (p578) runs gentle rafting trips suitable for three-year-olds. Under-fives can ride on the Shotover Jet (p578) for free, provided they're over 1m in height, and six-year-olds can tackle the ziplines with Ziptrek Ecotours (p581). Children as young as eight can tackle the Kawarau Zipride (p577), though eight- and nine-year-olds must ride tandem with an adult.

For more ideas and information, including details of local babysitters, visit the i-SITE (p589) or www.kidzgo.co.nz.

(complete with fish) to the huge garden with 3000 roses, monkey puzzle trees and the Swiss owner's own sculptural work, you won't have seen a place like it. There are two rooms in the main house and a unit out back.

If you're not staying, you can still wander the gardens ($15), which straddle the 45th parallel.

★ **Hidden Lodge**　　　　　　B&B $$$
(☑03-442 6636; www.hiddenlodgequeenstown. co.nz; 28 Evergreen Pl, Sunshine Bay; r from $395; P@☎) The well-named Hidden Lodge is literally the last place west in Queenstown. Tucked away in Sunshine Bay, it has enormous rooms, unfettered lake and mountain views, complimentary beer and wine and a new outdoor hot tub. A quiet escape that is indeed a hidden gem.

Villa del Lago　　　　　　APARTMENT $$$
(☑03-442 5727; www.villadellago.co.nz; 249 Frankton Rd, Queenstown East; apt from $360; P☎) Clinging to the slopes between the highway and the lake, these spacious one- to three-bedroom apartments have lake-facing terraces, incredible views and all the mod cons, including full kitchens, laundries and gas fires. The water taxi (p590) can stop at the private jetty, or you can walk along the lake to Queenstown in 25 minutes.

✖ Eating

Dining runs the full gamut in Queenstown's city centre, from refined to rough and ready, silver service to takeaways from the side of a

public toilet. There's a multitude of international cuisine on offer, and a good selection of restaurants riffing on modern interpretations of NZ food. For most of the year, it's wise to make a reservation.

✖ Central Queenstown

Fergbaker　　　　　　BAKERY $
(Map p578; 40 Shotover St; items $5-10; ⊘6.30am-4.30am) The sweeter sister of Fergburger (p587) bakes all manner of tempting treats – and though most things look tasty with 3am beer goggles on, it withstands the daylight test admirably. Goodies include inventive pies (venison and portobello mushroom) and breads (pinot, fig and cranberry), filled rolls and a sugary wealth of sweet treats. If you're after gelato, call into **Mrs Ferg** next door.

Caribe Latin Kitchen　　　　　　MEXICAN $
(Map p578; ☑03-442 6658; www.caribelatinkitchen. com; 36 Ballarat St; mains $8-15) One of the mall's more characterful and colourful restaurants, Caribe is a small nook dishing out quality tacos, quesadillas and burritos stuffed fuller than a piñata. The tiled decor plays to a Day of the Dead theme, and the few tables are brighter than a Mexican sun. Excellent value.

Erik's Fish & Chips　　　　　　FISH & CHIPS $
(Map p578; ☑03-441 3474; www.eriksfishandchips. co.nz; 12 Earl St; fish $5-10; ⊘noon-9pm) A pair of food trucks squeezed into a laneway

QUEENSTOWN ON A BUDGET

➡ Play frisbee golf (p581) for free in Queenstown Gardens.

➡ Shun the gondola and hike to a view on Queenstown Hill (p575) or the Tiki Trail (p575); for a free and full day out to Queenstowns' finest view, continue along the Ben Lomond Track (p575).

➡ Fuel up at Fergbaker (p585), Taco Medic, **Empanada Kitchen** (Map p578; ☑ 021 0279 2109; www. theempanadakitchen.com; 60 Beach St; empanadas $5.50; ⊘10am-5pm) or Caribe Latin Kitchen (p586).

➡ Skip an organised lake tour and ride the water taxi (p590) across to Kelvin Heights.

between buildings – order your hoki, dory or blue cod from one, and eat inside the other. Ever fancied a deep-fried kiwi fruit to finish your meal? You've come to the right place...

Rehab
HEALTH FOOD $
(Map p578; ☑03-442 5294; www.therehabstory. com; 33 Camp St; bowls $12-14; ⊘8.30am-8pm Mon-Fri, 9am-7pm Sat & Sun; ☜☑) If the hard living of Queenstown is wearing you out, pop into Rehab for a Buddha bowl, miso and edamame broth bowl, kale and cashew wrap, or something from its raw bakery – instant recovery in a bowl of locally sourced ingredients.

Taco Medic
FAST FOOD $
(Map p578; ☑ 03-442 8174; www.tacomedic.co.nz; 3 Searle Lane; tacos $7; ⊘11am-10pm) Taco Medic began life as a food truck, but has put on the handbrake to become a stylishly simple bolthole eatery. Cosy up to the bar and choose from seven tacos made with local free-farmed meats and a changing fish-of-the-day taco. The food truck, parked now at the airport, also still rolls them out.

★ Bespoke Kitchen
CAFE $$
(Map p578; ☑03-409 0552; www.bespokekitchen. co.nz; 9 Isle St; mains $11-19; ⊘8am-5pm; ☜) Occupying a light-filled corner site near the gondola, Bespoke delivers everything you'd expect of a smart Kiwi cafe. There's a good selection of counter food, beautifully presented cooked options, a range of outside seating in sight of the mountains and, of course, great coffee. In 2015, within six months of opening, it was named NZ's cafe of the year.

★ Public Kitchen & Bar
MODERN NZ $$
(Map p578; ☑03-442 5969; www.publickitchen. co.nz; Steamer Wharf, Beach St; dishes $12-46; ⊘11am-late; ☜) You can't eat closer to the water than at this excellent lakefront eatery where local is law: Cardrona lamb, Fiordland wild venison, Geraldine pork, South Island fish. Grab a group and order a selection of plates of varying sizes from the menu. The meaty dishes, in particular, are excellent.

Yonder
CAFE $$
(Map p578; ☑03-409 0994; www.yonderqt.co.nz; 14 Church St; brunch $9-23; ⊘7.30am-late; ☜) With a menu inspired by 'the things we've loved around our travels', this new cafe brings to the table a cosmopolitan assortment of dishes: bacon butties, kimchi bowls, tuna poke bowls. There are power points and USB ports by many of the indoor tables, but when the sun's out you'll want to be on the outdoor patio.

Blue Kanu
MODERN NZ $$
(Map p578; ☑03-442 6060; www.bluekanu.co.nz; 16 Church St; mains $28-38; ⊘4pm-late) Disproving the rule that all tiki houses are inherently tacky, Blue Kanu serves up a food style it calls 'Polynasian' – *bibimbap* in one hand, fried chicken pineapple buns in the other. It's relaxed and personable, capable of making you feel like a regular in minutes. The marriage of the Polynesian decor and the chopsticks sounds impossible to pull off, but it works.

Vudu Cafe & Larder
CAFE $$
(Map p578; ☑03-441 8370; www.vudu.co.nz; 16 Rees St; breakfast $15-23, lunch $19-23; ⊘7.30am-6pm) Excellent home-style baking combines with great coffee and the sort of breakfasts that make bacon and eggs seem very passé (try the French-toast pudding) at this ever-popular cafe. Admire the huge photo of a far less populated Queenstown from an inside table, or head outside to graze by the lake. Service can be slow, but that's the weight of numbers.

The Cow
ITALIAN $$
(Map p578; ☑03-442 8588; www.facebook.com/ thecowrestaurant; Cow Lane; mains $25-29, pizza $23-27; ⊘noon-midnight) Forget seasonal menus and daily specials; this tried-and-trusted Queenstown stalwart has been dishing up an unchanged menu of pizza and spaghetti for four decades. The reason it's thrived for so long is that everything on the short menu is just like *nonna* used to make.

Winnie's
PIZZA $$
(Map p578; ☑ 03-442 8635; www.winnies.co.nz; 1st fl, 7 Ballarat St; mains $20-37; ⊘noon-late; ☜) It's a Tardis-like journey leaving the mall and

finding Winnie's – part pizza joint and part bar, looking a little like a '50s diner with a drinking habit. Pizzas come in various accents – Moroccan, Mexican, Chinese – along with burgers, nachos, chicken wings and salads. Whatever the blurring of genres, it's undeniably fun and alive.

Fergburger BURGERS **$$**
(Map p578; ☑03-441 1232; www.fergburger. com; 42 Shotover St; burgers $12-19; ⊘8am-5am) Who knew a burger joint could ever be a destination restaurant? Such are the queues at Fergburger that it often looks like an All Blacks scrum out the front. The burgers are as tasty and satisfying as ever, but the wait can be horrendous and the menu has more choices than the place has seats.

Rata MODERN NZ **$$$**
(Map p578; ☑ 03-442 9393; www.ratadining.co.nz; 43 Ballarat St; mains $35-44, 2-/3-course lunch $28/38; ⊘noon-late) After gaining Michelin stars for restaurants in London, New York and LA, chef-owner Josh Emett now wields his exceptional but surprisingly unflashy cooking back home in this upmarket but informal back-lane eatery. Native bush, edging the windows and in a large-scale photographic mural, sets the scene for a short menu showcasing the best seasonal NZ produce.

Bazaar Interactive Marketplace MODERN NZ **$$$**
(Map p576; ☑ 03-450 1336; https://bazaar restaurant.co.nz; 6th fl, Rydges Lakeland Resort, 38-54 Lake Esplanade; breakfast $34, dinner $79; ⊘6-10am & 6-10pm) From one of the loftiest perches along the lakeshore, this new restaurant features a series of 'stations' where chefs turn out the likes of Asian noodles, seafood, wood-fired pizzas and grills, as well as stations of charcuterie and cheese. It's the perfect spot to watch life on the lake begin or end for the day.

Botswana Butchery MODERN NZ **$$$**
(Map p578; ☑03-442 6994; www.botswana butchery.co.nz; 17 Marine Pde; lunch mains $17-34, dinner $35-55; ⊘noon-late) Named as one of NZ's top 100 restaurants in 2017, this swish lakefront place is one of the flag-bearers of Queenstown high-end dining. Despite that, it doesn't come across as too sniffy, especially at lunch when prices drop and a casual air pervades. Evenings are predominantly but not exclusively meaty – a 1.4kg cut of Cardrona lamb, anyone?

✕ Surrounds

Boat Shed CAFE **$$**
(☑03-441 4146; www.boatshedqueenstown.com; Sugar Lane, Frankton; mains $15-26; ⊘8am-5pm; 🐾) Occupying a historic NZ Railways shipping office right by the lake, this great little cafe serves excellent, artfully arranged breakfasts and the likes of prawn and chorizo pasta for lunch. It's the perfect pit stop if you're cycling or walking the lakeside trail.

Wakatipu Grill EUROPEAN **$$$**
(☑03-450 9400; www.queenstownhilton.com; Hilton Queenstown, Peninsula Rd, Kelvin Heights; mains $28-47; ⊘6-10.30am Mon-Fri, 6-11am Sat & Sun, 6-9.30pm daily) The Hilton sprawls along the lakeside by the Kawarau River outlet, and part of the fun of visiting its signature restaurant is the water-taxi (p590) ride. As the name implies, there's always a decent selection of steak on the menu, but much more besides, including locally sourced fish and lamb.

Gantley's MODERN NZ **$$$**
(☑03-442 8999; www.gantleys.co.nz; 172 Arthurs Point Rd, Arthurs Point; 2-/3-course dinner $65/75, 6-/8-course degustation $95/130, with paired wines $160/215; ⊘6-10pm) Gantley's French-influenced menu and highly regarded wine list justify the 7km journey from Queenstown. The atmospheric dining experience is showcased in a stone-and-timber building, built in 1863 as a wayside inn and surrounded by beautiful gardens. The degustation options are the menu's centrepiece. Reservations are essential, and free pick-up from Queenstown is available by arrangement.

🍷 Drinking & Nightlife

Unsurprisingly for a city that plays hard by day, there are plenty of nightlife options in Queenstown, and they are as varied as the adventures. There are character-filled pubs, smooth-as-velvet wine bars, a new jazz lounge, a pair of frigid ice bars and a couple of high-quality craft-beer bars. Most places advertise themselves as opening until late, which generally means around 4am.

★ Smiths Craft Beer House CRAFT BEER
(Map p578; ☑03-409 2337; www.smithscraftbeer. co.nz; 53 Shotover St; ⊘noon-late) It's back to basics in everything but the taps, with bare concrete floors and industrial tables and chairs, but up to 20 creative craft beers on tap. The folks behind the bar will chat brews as long as you'll listen, and there's a menu (mains $17 to $20) of burgers and po'boys to mop up the suds.

★**Zephyr** BAR

(Map p578; [☎]03-409 0852; www.facebook.com/zephyrqt; Searle Lane; ⊗7pm-4am) Queenstown's coolest indie rock bar is located – as all such places should be – in a dark, grungy, concrete-floored space off a back lane. There's a popular pool table and live bands on Wednesday nights. Beer comes only in bottles, and there's a permanently rockin' soundtrack.

★**Atlas Beer Cafe** BAR

(Map p578; [☎]03-442 5995; www.atlasbeercafe.com; Steamer Wharf, Beach St; ⊗10am-late) There are usually around 20 beers on tap at this pint-sized lakefront bar, headlined by brews from Dunedin's Emerson's Brewery and Queenstown's Altitude. There are tasting paddles (with tasting notes) with four beers of your choice available. It serves excellent cooked breakfasts ($10 to $20) and simple substantial fare such as steaks, burgers and chicken parmigiana ($20).

1789 LOUNGE

(Map p578; [☎]03-450 0045; www.sofitel-queenstown.com; 8 Duke St; ⊗4pm-midnight Sun-Thu, to 1am Fri & Sat) Tucked into a corner of the Sofitel, this velvet-smooth new jazz lounge is named for the French Revolution, with a bloody colour scheme to suit. There are around 350 wines by the bottle and 50 by the glass, live jazz sessions on Friday and Saturday evenings and jazz piano on Wednesday and Sunday.

Bunker COCKTAIL BAR

(Map p578; [☎]03-441 8030; www.thebunker.co.nz; 14 Cow Lane; ⊗5pm-4am) Bunkered upstairs rather than down, this chichi little bar clearly fancies itself the kind of place that Sean Connery's James Bond might frequent, if the decor is anything to go by. Best of all is the outside terrace, with couches, a fire in winter and a projector screening classic movies onto the wall of a neighbouring building.

Vinyl Underground CLUB

(Map p578; www.facebook.com/Vinylunderground qt; 12 Church St; ⊗8pm-late) Enter the underworld, or at least the space under the World Bar, to find the heartbeat of Queenstown's nightlife. Inside the concrete bunker – the bar alone must weigh several tonnes – projectors screen dance clips onto a faux brick wall, and DJs spin from 10pm. There's a pool table in the back room.

Rhino's Ski Shack BAR

(Map p578; [☎]03-441 3329; www.rhinosskishack.com; Cow Lane; ⊗3pm-late) This vibey basement bar serves Rhino's house lager on tap ($5), hot rum in the ski months and empanadas. Animal pelts, snowshoes and skis line the recycled wood–lined walls, giving it an appropriately rustic ski-lodge-bar feel.

World Bar BAR

(Map p578; [☎]03-450 0008; www.theworldbar.co.nz; 12 Church St; ⊗11.30am-2.30am) Queenstown's legendary party hub before it was destroyed by fire in 2013, the World Bar is well and truly getting its groove back. Decor swings between degrees of eclectic, from the mounted moose head with halo, to the cocktails that come in teapots. The food's good, there are regular DJs and the outdoor area is prime real estate on balmy afternoons and evenings.

Bardeaux WINE BAR

(Map p578; [☎]03-442 8284; www.goodgroup.co.nz; Eureka Arcade, Searle Lane; ⊗4pm-4am) This small, cavelike wine bar is all class. Under a low ceiling are plush leather armchairs and a fireplace made from Central Otago schist. Whisky is king here, but the wine list is extraordinary, especially if you're keen to drop $4500 on a bottle once in your life. It's surprisingly relaxed for a place with such lofty tastes.

Pub on Wharf PUB

(Map p578; [☎]03-441 2155; www.pubonwharf.co.nz; 88 Beach St; ⊗10am-late) Ubercool interior design combines with handsome woodwork and lighting fit for a hipster hideaway, with fake sheep heads to remind you that you're still in NZ. Mac's beers on tap, scrummy nibbles and a decent wine list make this a great place to settle in for the evening. There's live music nightly and comedy occasionally.

☆ Entertainment

Pick up a copy of *The Source* (www.sourcemag.nz), a free monthly publication with articles and details of goings-on around Queenstown.

Sherwood LIVE MUSIC

(☎03-450 1090; www.sherwoodqueenstown.nz; 554 Frankton Rd) The faux-Tudor architecture might have you expecting lutes and folk ballads, but the Sherwood is Queenstown's go-to spot for visiting musos. Many of NZ's bigger names have performed here; check the website for coming gigs.

Kiwi Haka TRADITIONAL MUSIC

(Map p576; [☎]03-441 0101; www.skyline.co.nz; Skyline Gondola; adult/child incl gondola $77/52) For a traditional Māori cultural experience, head to the top of the gondola for one of the 30-minute shows that include the famed *haka*. There are usually four shows per night; bookings are essential.

Shopping

Romer Gallery PHOTOGRAPHY
(Map p578; ☑021 171 1771; www.romer-gallery.com;
15 Earl St; ☺8.30am-5pm) Stunning gallery
of large-format, perspex-finished NZ landscapes from renowned Queenstown-based
photographer Stephan Romer. Images are
up to $15,000 a pop, but they display a rare
beauty.

Vesta ARTS & CRAFTS
(Map p578; ☑03-442 5687; www.vestadesign.
co.nz; 19 Marine Pde; ☺10am-5.30pm) Arguably
Queenstown's most interesting store, inside inarguably the town's oldest building.
Vesta sells a collection of prints, glassware,
jewellery and homewares as fascinating as
the original wallpaper and the floorboards
warped by time in the 1864 wooden cottage.

Bound Books & Records BOOKS
(Map p578; ☑03-442 5601; www.facebook.com/
boundqueenstown; 3 Church St; ☺10am-6pm Mon-
Sat) Interesting and varied collection of NZ
books, fiction and quality vinyl.

Information

DOC Visitor Centre (Map p578; ☑03-442
7935; www.doc.govt.nz; 50 Stanley St;
☺8.30am-4.30pm) Head here to pick up
Routeburn Track bookings and backcountry hut
passes. Posts weather and tramper alerts, has
good day-walk advice and sells maps.

Queenstown i-SITE (Map p578; ☑03-442
4100; www.queenstownisite.co.nz; cnr Shotover & Camp Sts; ☺8.30am-8pm) Friendly
and informative despite being perpetually
frantic, the saintly staff here can help with
bookings and information on Queenstown,
Gibbston, Arrowtown and Glenorchy.

Getting There & Away

AIR

Air New Zealand (☑0800 737 000; www.air
newzealand.co.nz) flies direct to Queenstown
from Auckland, Wellington and Christchurch.
Jetstar (☑0800 800 995; www.jetstar.com)
also flies the Auckland route.

Various airlines offer direct flights to Queenstown from Sydney, Melbourne, Brisbane and the
Gold Coast in Australia.

BUS

Most buses and shuttles stop on Athol St or
opposite the i-SITE; check when you book.
Atomic Travel (Map p578; ☑03-349 0697;
www.atomictravel.co.nz) Daily (except Tuesday) bus to and from Cromwell ($15, one
hour), Omarama ($35, 2¼ hours), Twizel ($30,

3¼ hours), Tekapo ($45, four hours) and
Christchurch ($55, 7¼ hours).
Catch-a-Bus South (☑03-479 9960; www.
catchabussouth.co.nz) Door-to-door daily bus
from Invercargill ($60, 3¼ hours) and Bluff
($75, 3¾ hours), heading via Gore ($61, 2½
hours) three times a week.
InterCity (Map p578; ☑03-442 4922; www.
intercity.co.nz) Daily coaches to/from Wanaka
(from $17, 1¾ hours), Franz Josef (from
$62, eight hours), Dunedin (from $26, 4¼
hours), Invercargill (from $49, 2½ hours) and
Christchurch (from $55, 8½ to 11½ hours).
Naked Bus (Map p578; www.nakedbus.com)
Buses daily to Wanaka (from $17, 1¾ hours),
Cromwell (from $11, one hour), Te Anau (from
$10, 2½ hours), Franz Josef (from $62, eight
hours) and Christchurch (from $55, 8½ hours).
Ritchies (Map p578; ☑03-443 9120; www.
alpineconnexions.co.nz) Buses head to/from
Dunedin ($50, 4½ hours, daily), with stops at
towns along the route on request.
Ritchies Connectabus Wanaka (Map p578;
☑0800 405 066; www.connectabus.com; ☎)
Heads to/from Wanaka five times daily ($35,
two hours). Does hotel pick-ups and has free
wi-fi on board.

HIKERS' & SKIERS' TRANSPORT

Buckley Track Transport (☑03-442 8215;
www.buckleytracktransport.nz) Shuttles
between Queenstown and the Routeburn and
Greenstone & Caples Tracks, as well as Te Anau
Downs (for the Milford Track).
EasyHike (☑027 370 7019; www.easyhike.
co.nz) Offers a car-relocation service for the
Milford, Routeburn and Kepler Tracks, dropping
you at the start and shifting your car to the
end. It can also kit you out entirely for the hike,
offering a range of packages up to a 'Premium'
service that includes booking your hut tickets,
track transport, backpack, food, rain gear,
cooking pots and first-aid kit.
Glenorchy Journeys (p595) Shuttles from
Queenstown and Glenorchy to the Routeburn,
Greenstone & Caples and Rees-Dart Tracks.
Info & Track (Map p578; ☑03-442 9708; www.
infotrack.co.nz; 37 Shotover St; ☺7.30am-9pm)
During the Great Walks season, this agency
provides transfers to the trailheads of the
Routeburn, Greenstone & Caples and Rees-Dart
Tracks. In winter it morphs into Info & Snow and
heads to the Cardrona, Coronet Peak, Remarkables and Treble Cone ski fields instead.
Kiwi Discovery (Map p578; ☑03-442 7340;
www.kiwidiscovery.com; 37 Camp St) Offers
trailhead transport for the Milford, Routeburn
and Kepler Tracks. In winter it runs buses to the
four ski fields around the area.
NZSki Snowline Express (p580) During the ski
season shuttles depart from outside the Snow

Centre on Duke St every 20 minutes from 8am until 11.30am (noon for Coronet Peak), heading to both Coronet Peak and the Remarkables (return $20). Buses return as they fill up, from 1.30pm onwards. They also leave on the hour from 4pm to 7pm for night skiing at Coronet Peak, returning on the half-hour from 5.30pm to 9.30pm.

Trackhopper ([☑] 021-187 7732; www.track hopper.co.nz) Offers a handy car-relocation service for the Routeburn, Milford, Greenstone and Rees-Dart Tracks, driving you to one end of the track and leaving your car for you at the other. Prices start from $160, plus fuel.

Tracknet (Map p578; [☑] 03-249 7777; www. tracknet.net) This Te Anau–based outfit offers Queenstown connections to the Routeburn, Greenstone Caples, Kepler, Hollyford and Milford Tracks throughout the Great Walks season. Its Invercargill bus service can connect with transport to the Rakiura Track on Stewart Island. Charter transport to trailheads during winter can also be arranged.

ⓘ Getting Around

TO/FROM THE AIRPORT

Queenstown Airport (ZQN; [☑] 03-450 9031; www.queenstownairport.co.nz; Sir Henry Wrigley Dr, Frankton) is 7km east of the town centre.

Blue Bubble Taxis ([☑] 0800 228 294; www. queenstown.bluebubbletaxi.co.nz) and **Green Cabs** ([☑] 0800 464 7336; www.greencabs. co.nz) charge around $45 to $50 for trips between the airport and town.

Ritchies Connectabus (Map p578; [☑] 03-441 4471; www.connectabus.com) has an airport service that runs every 15 minutes to Queenstown ($12), while also running four times daily to Cromwell ($22, one hour) and Wanaka ($35, 1½ hours).

Super Shuttle ([☑] 0800 748 885; www.super shuttle.co.nz) runs a door-to-door shuttle service from Queenstown Airport to the city ($20).

BOAT

Queenstown Water Taxis (Map p578; [☑] 03-441 1124; www.queenstownwatertaxis.co.nz; Steamer Wharf, Beach St; ⊙10am-9.30pm Sun-Thu, to 10.30pm Fri & Sat) Crosses the lake from the city centre to the Hilton Hotel (and requested stops in between) on the Kelvin Peninsula (adult/child $10/5). Pay the driver on the boat in cash.

PUBLIC TRANSPORT

Ritchies Connectabus has various colour-coded routes, reaching Sunshine Bay, Fernhill, Arthurs Point, Frankton and Arrowtown. A day pass (adult/child $33/17) allows travel on the entire network. Pick up a route map and timetable from the i-SITE (p589). Buses leave from beside the clock tower on Camp St.

AROUND QUEENSTOWN

Glenorchy

[☑] 03 / POP 360

Perhaps best known as the gateway to the Routeburn Track, Glenorchy sits on a rare shelf of flat land at the head of Lake Wakatipu. The small town is a great option if you want to be beside the lake and the mountains but prefer to stay once removed from the bustle and bluster of Queenstown. The tramping around Glenorchy is sensational, and the town is also a base for horse treks, jetboat rides, helicopter flights and skydives. It's Queenstown on sedatives.

There's often a sense of déjà vu when you arrive in Glenorchy, with areas around the town featuring heavily in the *Lord of the Rings* trilogy, as well as being the setting for Jane Campion's *Top of the Lake* BBC series.

The town centre sits slightly back from the lake, so be sure to wander down to the wharf, where the Humboldt Mountains rise from the opposite shore.

🏃 Activities

Shuttles from Queenstown to the Routeburn, Rees-Dart and Greenstone & Caples Tracks pass through Glenorchy; you can be picked up here along the way. Other activities on offer include farm tours, fly-fishing and guided photography tours; enquire at the Queenstown i-SITE (p589) or the Glenorchy Information Centre & Store (p595).

Hiking

DOC's *Head of Lake Wakatipu* and *Wakatipu Walks* brochures detail more than 60 day walks in the area. Both brochures can be downloaded from the DOC website (www.doc.govt.nz). Two of the best short tracks are the **Routeburn Flats** (three hours), which follows the first section of the Routeburn Track, and **Lake Sylvan** (one hour 40 minutes).

Another good wander, especially if you like your birds, is the **Glenorchy Walkway**, which starts in the town centre and loops around Glenorchy lagoon, switching to boardwalks for the swampy bits. It's split into the Southern Circuit (30 minutes) and the Northern Circuit (one hour) and there are plenty of seats along the way, well positioned for views over the water to the mountains.

Before setting out on any longer tramps, call into DOC's Queenstown visitor centre (p589) for the latest track conditions and

Queenstown Region

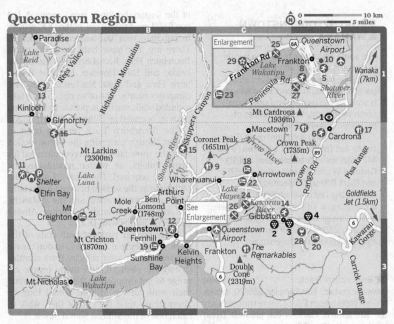

Queenstown Region

◎ Sights
1 Cardrona Distillery & Museum	D1
2 Chard Farm	C3
3 Gibbston Valley	C3
4 Peregrine	D2

◈ Activities, Courses & Tours
5 Air Milford	D1
6 Backcountry Saddle Expeditions	D2
7 Cardrona Alpine Resort	D2
8 ChargeAbout	D1
9 Coronet Peak	C2
10 Glenorchy Air	D1
11 Greenstone & Caples Tracks	A2
12 Guided Walks New Zealand	B3
13 High Country Horses	A1
14 Kawarau Bridge Bungy	C2
Kawarau Zipride	(see 14)
Over The Top	(see 5)
15 Skippers Canyon Jet	B2
16 Skydive Paradise	A2
17 Snow Farm	D2
Spa at Millbrook	(see 22)
The Cardrona	(see 1)

⌂ Sleeping
18 Arrow Private Hotel	C2
Arrowfield Apartments	(see 18)
19 Hidden Lodge	B3
20 Kinross Cottages	D3
21 Little Paradise Lodge	A2
22 Millbrook Resort	C2
23 Villa del Lago	C1
Waiorau Homestead	(see 1)

⊗ Eating
24 Amisfield Bistro & Cellar Door	C2
25 Boat Shed	C1
26 Graze	C2
27 Wakatipu Grill	D1

⌾ Drinking & Nightlife
28 Gibbston Tavern	D3

⌾ Entertainment
29 Sherwood	C1

ⓘ Transport
Super Shuttle	(see 10)

to purchase detailed maps. Another good resource is Lonely Planet's *Hiking & Tramping in New Zealand*.

For track snacks or meals, stock up on groceries in Queenstown, though you'll also find a small selection of trail-perfect fodder at **Mrs Woolly's General Store** (64 Oban St; ☺10am-5.30pm). Track transport is at a premium during the Great Walks season (late October through April), so try to book in advance.

MĀORI NZ: QUEENSTOWN & WANAKA

The same transition, from moa hunter to Waitaha, to Ngāti Māmoe to Ngāi Tahu rule, took place here as in other parts of the South Island. Lake Wakatipu is shrouded in legend, and sites to its north were highly valued sources of *pounamu* (greenstone).

The Ngāi Tahu *iwi* (tribe) owns **Shotover Jet** (p578), **Dart Stables** (☑03-442 5688; www.dartstables.com; Coll St), **Guided Walks New Zealand** (p575) and **Dart River Wilderness Jet** (p594), the last of which offers a cultural component with its excursions. Other cultural insights are offered by **Kiwi Haka** (p589), which performs nightly atop the gondola in Queenstown.

★**Routeburn Track**   TRAMPING
(www.doc.govt.nz; huts/camping $65/20, outside of Great Walks season $15/5) Some trampers say the Routeburn Track is the greatest Great Walk of all. The 32km, two- to four-day tramp is a high-level mountain route with fantastic views all the way – expansive panoramas of other ranges, and near-at-hand views of mirror-like tarns, waterfalls, fairy glades lined with plush moss, and gnarled trees with long, straggly, lichen beards.

The track can be started from either end. From the Routeburn Flats end, you'll walk along the top of **Routeburn Gorge** and then ascend past the impressive **Routeburn Falls**. Arriving at alpine **Lake Harris** is a stunning mountain moment, as is the moment you rise onto **Harris Saddle** with its vast view. From here, if you have any energy left, you can make a steep 1½- to two-hour detour up **Conical Hill**. On a clear day you can see waves breaking at Martins Bay, far away on the west coast, but it's not worth the climb on a cloudy or windy day. Shortly before you reach the Divide, a highly recommended one-hour detour heads up to the **Key Summit**, where there are views of the Hollyford Valley and the Eglinton and Greenstone Valleys.

During the Great Walks season (late October through April) you'll need to book ahead, which can be done online through **Great Walks Bookings** (☑0800 694 732; www.greatwalks.co.nz). You'll then need to call into the DOC visitor centre in either Queenstown or Te Anau to collect actual tickets, either the day before or on the day of departure. Outside of the season, bookings aren't required, but you'll still need to visit one of the DOC centres to purchase your hut and campsite tickets. There are four basic huts along the track: Routeburn Flats, Routeburn Falls, Lake Mackenzie and Lake Howden. Both the Routeburn Flats and Lake Mackenzie huts have campsites nearby. The other option is to take a guided walk, staying at private lodges along the way, operated by Ultimate Hikes (p575).

The Routeburn Track remains open in winter, though traversing the alpine section after the snow falls is not recommended for casual hikers, as winter mountaineering skills are required. There are 32 avalanche paths across the section between Routeburn Falls and Lake Howden, and the avalanche risk continues through to spring. Always check conditions with DOC.

There are car parks at both ends of the track, but they're unattended, so don't leave any valuables in your vehicle. Track shuttles (p589) are plentiful, and many people arrange to get dropped at the Divide to start their walk after a Milford Sound tour, or alternatively time the end of their walk to catch one of the Milford Sound buses.

ROUTE	ESTIMATED WALKING TIME (HR)
Routeburn Shelter to Routeburn Flats Hut	1½-2½
Routeburn Flats Hut to Routeburn Falls Hut	1-1½
Routeburn Falls Hut to Lake Mackenzie Hut	4½-6
Lake Mackenzie Hut to Howden Hut	3-4
Howden Hut to the Divide	1-1½

Greenstone & Caples Tracks   TRAMPING
(www.doc.govt.nz; huts/camping $15/5) Looping through a pair of lush valleys, with a crossing over a subalpine pass, these two tracks combine for a moderate four- or five-day tramp. There are basic DOC-run huts along the way; backcountry hut passes must be purchased in advance.

The tracks link with the Routeburn Track via a short connecting track at Lake McKellar – you can either follow the Routeburn's tail end down to the Divide, or (if you've prebooked) take the track back towards the Glenorchy side of the mountains. From McKellar Hut, it's about an hour's tramp to Lake Howden Hut on the Routeburn Track, which is another hour from the Divide.

Access to the Greenstone and Caples Tracks is from a car park at the end of Greenstone Station Rd.

ROUTE	ESTIMATED WALK-ING TIME (HR)
Greenstone car park to Mid Caples Hut	2½
Mid Caples Hut to McKellar Hut	6-7
McKellar Hut to Greenstone Hut	4½-6½
Greenstone Hut to Greenstone car park	3-5

Rees-Dart Track TRAMPING
(www.doc.govt.nz; hut/campsite $15/5) This demanding four- to five-day horseshoe route from near the head of Lake Wakatipu takes you through valleys and over an alpine pass, with the possibility of a side trip to the Dart Glacier if you're suitably equipped and expe-

rienced. Most people go up the Rees Track first and come back down the Dart.

Access by vehicle is possible as far as Muddy Creek on the Rees side, from where it's six to eight hours' walk to Shelter Rock Hut. Hut passes must be purchased in advance for the three basic DOC huts (Shelter Rock, Dart and Daleys Flat).

ROUTE	ESTIMATED WALK-ING TIME (HR)
Muddy Creek to Shelter Rock Hut	6-8
Shelter Rock Hut to Dart Hut	4-6
Dart Hut to Daleys Flat Hut	5-7
Daleys Flat Hut to Paradise	5½-7½

Other Activities

Skydive Paradise ADVENTURE SPORTS
(☑03-442 8333; www.skydiveparadise.co.nz; Glenorchy Airfield, Glenorchy-Queenstown Rd) Tandem skydiving above some of the planet's

Routeburn, Greenstone & Caples Tracks

THE ROAD TO PARADISE

Road signs in Glenorchy promote the town as the 'Gateway to Paradise' and it is...literally. Paradise lies around 15km north of Glenorchy, near the start of the Dart Track.

The road from Glenorchy to Paradise, which is unsealed from the Kinloch turn-off, heads up the broad Rees Valley, edging along the foot of the Richardson Range. Approaching Paradise it cuts through a beautiful section of beech forest on the shores of Diamond Lake before fording the River Jordan – how's that for a biblical entrance to paradise! – and arriving at Paradise. There's not much here (ok, there's pretty much nothing here); it's just paddocks. But it sure is pretty!

most spectacular mountain scenery, taking the leap from either 12,000ft ($335) or 15,000ft ($409).

Heli Glenorchy SCENIC FLIGHTS
(☎0800 435 449; www.heliglenorchy.co.nz; 35 Mull St) It takes the best part of a day to drive from Glenorchy to Milford Sound, but it's only 15 minutes by helicopter. Heli Glenorchy has a three-hour Milford Sound heli-cruise-heli package ($825) and a wilderness drop-off so that you can walk the last few kilometres of the Milford Track to Giant's Gate Falls before being whisked back over the mountains ($865).

High Country Horses HORSE RIDING
(☎03-442 9915; www.high-country-horses.co.nz; 243 Priory Rd) Has more equine options than the Auckland Cup, from tootling around Glenorchy on a 30-minute carriage ride (adult/child $50/25) to an overnight 'Around the Mountain' trek ($675).

Tours

Private Discovery Tours DRIVING
(☎03-442 2299; www.privatediscoverytours. co.nz; half/full day from $190/350) A range of 4WD tours, including exclusive access to Mt Earnslaw Station, a high-country sheep property in a remote valley between Mts Earnslaw and Alfred, complete with Middle Earth movie locations. Prices include pick-up from Queenstown. Also runs a couple of day-walk tours.

Dart River Wilderness Jet BOATING
(☎03-442 9992; www.dartriver.co.nz; 45 Mull St; adult/child from $249/139) The only jetboat operator on the Dart River, with trips in-

cluding a 30-minute walk through the rainforest. Also offers jetboat rides combined with a river descent in an inflatable three-seater 'funyak' (departs 8.45am, adult/child from $339/239). Prices include Queenstown pick-ups, which depart an hour before each trip.

Sleeping

Kinloch Lodge LODGE $$
(☎03-442 4900; www.kinlochlodge.co.nz; Kinloch Rd, Kinloch; dm $39, d with/without bathroom from $175/115; ☎) 🅿 Just 3km from Glenorchy, but 26km by road, Kinloch Lodge is the perfect escape if getting away from it all to Glenorchy isn't getting away from it all enough. The wonderfully remote 1868 lodge has small rooms with shared bathrooms, while rooms in the YHA-associated hostel are comfy and colourful. The open-air hot tub has cracking mountain and lake views.

Glenorchy Motel MOTEL $$
(☎0274 368 531; www.glenorchymotels.co.nz; 87 Oban St; r from $150; ☎) Given the full nip and tuck by new owners in 2017, the eight rooms here have some design savvy, an outdoor hot tub has been added, and there's a wood sauna out the back if you need to thaw some limbs after a day on the trails.

★**EcoScapes** CABIN $$$
(☎03-442 4900; http://ecoscapes.nz; Kinloch Rd, Kinloch; r $395; ☎) 🅿 Opened in 2017, these twin contemporary cabins are in utter contrast to the historic Kinloch Lodge next door. Built using passive design, they feature blonde woods, ultra-modern furnishings and feel almost like a city apartment plonked into the wilderness.

Eating

Queenie's Dumplings DUMPLINGS $
(☎03-442 6070; http://queeniesdumplings.wixsite. com/queeniesdumplings; 27 Mull St; 9 dumplings $13.50, noodle soup $15; ⏱11am-4pm) Where else would you expect to find an authentic little dumpling joint than far-flung, rural Glenorchy? Choose from seven types of dumplings, or a handful of noodle soups.

Glenorchy Cafe CAFE $$
(GYC; ☎03-442 9978; 25 Mull St; mains $12-20; ⏱10am-4.30pm Sun-Fri, to 1.30am Sat) Grab a sunny table out the back of this cute little cottage and tuck into cooked breakfasts, sandwiches and soup. Head inside on Saturday night to partake in pizza and beer underneath the oddball light fixtures.

ℹ Information

Glenorchy Information Centre & Store (☏03-409 2049; www.glenorchy-nz.co.nz; 42-50 Mull St; ⊙8.30am-9pm) Attached to the Glenorchy Hotel, this little shop is a good source of weather and track information. Fishing rods and mountain bikes can be hired, and it sells tramping supplies, including gas canisters and a good selection of maps. It also has a bottle shop, bless it.

ℹ Getting There & Away

Glenorchy lies at the head of Lake Wakatipu, a scenic 40-minute (46km) drive northwest from Queenstown, winding around bluffs and coves with sweeping views over the lake and its frame of mountains. There are no bus services, but there are trampers' shuttles (p589) during the Great Walks season (late October to April). Shuttles pick up from the Glenorchy Hotel, which offers free parking to trampers.

Glenorchy Journeys (☏03-409 0800; www.glenorchyjourneys.co.nz) Runs shuttles from Queenstown and Glenorchy to the Routeburn, Greenstone & Caples and Rees-Dart Tracks.

Arrowtown

☏03 / POP 2450

Beloved by day-trippers from Queenstown, exceedingly quaint Arrowtown sprang up in the 1860s following the discovery of gold in the Arrow River. Today its pretty, tree-lined avenues retain more than 60 of their original gold-rush buildings, and history is so ingrained here that even the golf course wraps around the ruined cottages and relics of the town's gold-mining heyday. But don't be fooled by the rustic facades; Arrowtown has a thriving contemporary scene, with chic modern dining, a cool cinema and a couple of drinking dens to rival the finest in Queenstown.

The pace in Arrowtown is very different to that of Queenstown, just 20km away. Strolling Buckingham St, with its gold-era facades, is the major activity here, and when you need something more, there are gentle bike rides along the valleys, or an expanding network of walks along the Arrow River and Bush Creek.

◉ Sights

Arrowtown Gaol HISTORIC BUILDING
(Cardigan St) FREE With gold rushes came lawlessness. Arrowtown's prisoners were originally manacled to logs, but in 1876 this schist jail, now surrounded by homes, was constructed. The building was used as a jail as recently as 1987 when two men were held here for drunkenness. The jail is locked, but

you can grab the key ($5 deposit) from the visitor information centre (p598).

Chinese Settlement HISTORIC SITE
(Buckingham St; ⊙24hr) FREE Strung along the creek, near the site of Arrowtown's first gold find, is NZ's best example of an early Chinese settlement. Interpretive signs explain the lives of Chinese miners during and after the gold rush (the last resident died in 1932), while restored huts and the only remaining Chinese store in the southern goldfields make the story more tangible. Subjected to significant racism, the Chinese often had little choice but to rework old tailings rather than seek new claims.

Lakes District Museum & Gallery MUSEUM
(☏03-442 1824; www.museumqueenstown.com; 49 Buckingham St; adult/child $10/3; ⊙8.30am-5pm) Exhibits cover the gold-rush era and the early days of Chinese settlement around Arrowtown. Kids are kept engaged by the likes of a 'Crack the Code' game they can play as you wander the exhibits. You can also rent pans here to try your luck panning for gold on the Arrow River ($3); you're more likely to find some traces if you head away from the town centre.

🏃 Activities

The information centre stocks a *Cycling & Walking Trail* brochure ($1) outlining some excellent tracks in the area. One particularly good cycling route is the **Arrow River Bridges Ride** (12km) from Arrowtown to the Kawarau Bridge, which traverses various purpose-built suspension bridges and a tunnel cut under the highway. If you have more time and energy, you can connect onto the Gibbston River Trail at the Kawarau Bridge to cycle past a string of cellar doors.

Local walks range from hour-long strolls along Bush Creek and the Arrow River to a climb along the **Big Hill Trail** (12km, five to six hours) that meets the Arrow River closer to Macetown.

Arrowtown Bike Hire CYCLING
(☏0800 224 473; www.arrowtownbikehire.co.nz; 59 Buckingham St; half-/full-day rental $42/55, e-bikes $80/120; ⊙8.30am-5.30pm daily Sep-Apr, Tue-Sat May-Aug) Hires bikes (including e-bikes) and provides great advice about local trails. If you fancy tackling the 16km Arrow River Bridges ride through to the Gibbston wineries, the company will collect you, your companions and your bikes for $79. Multiday rentals are also available, and bikes can be delivered to your Arrowtown accommodation. Find the entrance on Romans Lane.

Arrowtown

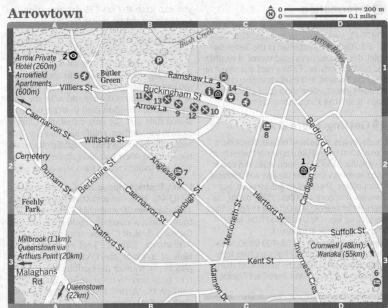

Arrowtown

Sights

1 Arrowtown Gaol.................................D2
2 Chinese Settlement.........................A1
3 Lakes District Museum &
   Gallery...C1

Activities, Courses & Tours

4 Arrowtown Bike Hire.......................C1
   Arrowtown Time
   Walks....................................... (see 3)
5 Dudley's Cottage...............................A1
   Queenstown Bike
   Tours...(see 5)

Sleeping

6 Arrowtown Holiday Park D3

7 Arrowtown Lodge B2
8 Shades of Arrowtown.........................C2

Eating

9 Chop Shop...B1
10 La Rumbla..C1
11 Saffron..B1
12 Slow Cuts..B1
13 Terra Mia..B1

Drinking & Nightlife

   Blue Door ....(see 11)
14 Fork & Tap C1

Entertainment

   Dorothy Browns.............................(see 11)

Dudley's Cottage   OUTDOORS
(☑ 03-409 8162; www.dudleyscottagenz.com; 4
Buckingham St; ⊙ 9am-5pm) Call into this historic cottage for a gold-panning lesson ($10, plus an extra $5 if you're keen to rent a pan and give it a go). If you've already got golden skills, rent a pan and shovel ($6) or sluice box ($35) and head out on your own.

Queenstown Bike Tours   CYCLING
(☑ 03-442 0339; www.queenstownbiketours.co.nz; Dudley's Cottage, 4 Buckingham St; half/full day $45/55) From straightforward bike rentals to

a Gibbston Wine Tour package ($195, September to April only) that includes bike hire, lunch in Gibbston, tastings at four vineyards and return transport to Arrowtown to save you wobbling back. E-bikes available.

Tours

Arrowtown Time Walks   WALKING
(☑ 021 782 278; www.arrowtowntimewalks.com; adult/child $20/12) Guided walks (1½ hours) depart from the museum on demand, tracing a path through Arrowtown's golden past, point-

ing out places of interest along the way and delving into gold-rush history. Book through the website, or in person at the museum.

🛏 Sleeping

Arrowtown Holiday Park   HOLIDAY PARK $
(☑ 03-442 1876; www.arrowtownholidaypark.co.nz; 12 Centennial Ave; sites/units from $42/135, r without bathroom $69) Close to the town centre, this small holiday park offers a cul de sac of en suite cabins and a gleaming amenities block with coin-operated showers. When it's not booked up by school groups, budget travellers can get a room in Oregon Lodge – each room has two sets of bunks and shares the communal kitchen and bathrooms.

Arrowtown Lodge   B&B $$
(☑ 03-442 1101; www.arrowtownlodge.co.nz; 7 Anglesea St; r/cottage $195/395; 🖥) From the outside, the guest rooms look like heritage cottages, but inside they're cosy and modern, with en suite bathrooms. There are three rooms, including a large cottage that has its own separate outdoor living space and spa. A continental breakfast is provided, and Buckingham St is a two-minute walk from the lodge's back entrance.

Shades of Arrowtown   MOTEL $$
(☑ 03-442 1613; www.shadesofarrowtown.co.nz; cnr Buckingham & Merioneth Sts; units from $150; 🖥) Tall shady trees and a garden setting give these stylish bungalow-type cottages a relaxed air. Some have full kitchens and spa baths. The two-bedroom, self-contained cottage is good value if you're travelling with the whole clan.

Arrowfield Apartments   RENTAL HOUSE $$$
(☑ 03-442 0012; www.arrowfield.co.nz; 115 Essex Ave, Butel Park; houses from $250; 🖥🖳) Lining a quiet crescent in a new development at Arrowtown's edge, these 10 spacious townhouses, identical in all but colour, have internal garages, full kitchens, underfloor heating, gas fires and three bedrooms. Bedroom doors can be locked off for a smaller, cheaper rental.

Arrow Private Hotel   BOUTIQUE HOTEL $$$
(☑ 021 414 141; www.thearrow.co.nz; 63 Manse Rd; ste from $395; 🖥) Five understated but luxurious suites feature at this modern property on Arrowtown's outskirts. Accommodation is chic and contemporary with huge picture windows showcasing the surrounding countryside. The suites are framed around an old stone cottage that has an open fire, armchairs and a selection of spirits and local wines. The Queenstown Trail goes right by the door.

Millbrook Resort   RESORT $$$
(☑ 03-441 7000; www.millbrook.co.nz; Malaghans Rd; r from $265; 🖥🖳) 🏊 Further from Arrowtown in aesthetics than kilometres, this massive manicured resort is a town unto itself. Rooms range from studios to luxury homes overlooking the fairways of the resort's golf course, which has been rated among the top 10 courses in NZ. At the end of the day, take your pick from four restaurants, or relax at the spa (☑ 03-441 7017; www.millbrook.co.nz; Malaghans Rd; treatments from $79).

🍴 Eating

Slow Cuts   RIBS, BURGERS $
(☑ 03-442 0066; 46-50 Buckingham St; mains $11-14; ⊙ noon-9pm) From the *amigas* at La Rumbla comes Slow Cuts, dishing up fast food in slow motion. There are rotisserie chickens, burgers, ribs, smashed fries and a good small list of local wines.

★ Chop Shop   CAFE $$
(☑ 03-442 1116; www.facebook.com/thechopshop foodmerchants; 7 Arrow Lane; mains $20-30; ⊙ 8am-3pm) Perhaps the tables are a little tightly packed, and the open kitchen does take up half the space, but we're splitting hairs. This place is uniformly fabulous (and uniformly popular) – from the internationally inspired menu (pork dumplings, Turkish eggs, smoked pork-hock hash) to the interesting decor (pressed-tin bar, cool wallpaper, chandeliers made from bicycle wheels and chains). Great coffee, too.

La Rumbla   TAPAS $$
(☑ 03-442 0509; www.facebook.com/larumbla. arrowtown; 54 Buckingham St; tapas $11-24; ⊙ 4pm-late Tue-Sun) Tucked behind the post office, this little gem does a brilliant job of bringing the bold flavours and late-dining habits of Spain to sleepy little Arrowtown. Local produce is showcased in tasty bites on an ever-changing menu, and the cocktail list goes long and strong in the evening.

Terra Mia   ITALIAN $$
(☑ 03-409 8378; www.facebook.com/arrowtown. co.nz; 28-30 Buckingham St; pizza $23-29, mains $23-25; ⊙ 8am-5pm daily, 6-9pm Thu-Sat) Opened in 2016, Terra Mia pairs traditional Italian cooking (and good espresso) with wines from Gibbston Valley (p582) in a large open space that feels like a traditional trattoria. There's a small Italian pantry up the back with antipasto goods, Italian beers and Gibbston Valley wines.

WORTH A TRIP

LAKE HAYES

Around 14,000 years ago, little Lake Hayes was joined to the Frankton Arm of Lake Wakatipu. Now it sits in quiet isolation, its often-mirror-perfect reflections of the surrounding hills and mountains leading some to claim it as the most photographed lake in New Zealand. It's a great place for an easy stroll, with the 8km, bike-friendly **Lake Hayes Walkway** looping right around it. Allow two to three hours to walk it.

On the lake's eastern flank is **Amisfield Bistro & Cellar Door** (☑03-442 0556; www.amisfield.co.nz; 10 Lake Hayes Rd; 3-/5-course menu $75/95; ⊗ cellar door 10am-6pm, restaurant noon-8pm), a match for any of the wineries in nearby Gibbston, though it's the bistro that's the real showstopper. In 2017 it was named as one of NZ's top 100 restaurants, so you can feel reassured leaving yourself in the hands of the chefs when you order – there's no menu; you simply pick three or five courses and await whatever the chefs decide. Wine tastings are free if you purchase a bottle, or $10 otherwise.

Hidden in a natural depression across the highway, south of the lake, is **Lake Hayes Estate**, established in the 1990s as a more affordable, less touristy residential option to Queenstown. It's worth dropping by for a bite at **Graze** (☑03-441 4074; www.grazenz.co.nz; 1 Onslow Rd, Lake Hayes Estate; brunch $13-25, dinner $20-34; ⊗ 7.30am-5pm Mon, to late Tue-Sun; ⓐ), an unexpectedly stylish cafe-bar at the heart of the estate. Its offerings run the gamut from morning coffee to dinner to a beer from its own attached microbrewery.

Lake Hayes is 4km south of Arrowtown, on the road to Frankton.

Saffron　　　　　　　　MODERN NZ $$$
(☑03-442 0131; www.saffronrestaurant.co.nz; 18 Buckingham St; lunch $18-29, dinner $25-49; ⊗noon-3pm & 6pm-late) Walking into Saffron is like stepping out of town, with its formal, clean-lined setting providing a contrast to Buckingham St's gunslinger appearance. Expect lamb, wild boar and fish, with both the portions and the soundtrack having a bit more spunk than you might expect from the setting.

🍸 Drinking & Nightlife

★ **Blue Door**　　　　　　　　BAR
(☑03-442 0415; www.facebook.com/TheBlueDoor Bar; 18 Buckingham St; ⊗4pm-late; ⓐ) The only indications that you're here are the unmarked blue doors – push them open and it's like stepping into a prohibition-era speakeasy. The cool little bar has a formidable wine list and enough rustic ambience to keep you mellow for the evening. Low ceilings, an open fire and abundant candles create an intimate setting.

Fork & Tap　　　　　　　　PUB
(☑03-442 1860; www.theforkandtap.co.nz; 51 Buckingham St; ⊗11am-11pm) Built as a bank in the 1870s, Fork and Tap's currency is now craft beer, with up to 19 suds on tap. Add in good food, including shared meat and cheese platters, and a large sunny, kid-friendly back garden, and you have the pick of Arrowtown's pubs. Grab a tasting paddle of four 150mL beers of your choice for $14.

There's Irish music every Wednesday night, and live music in the garden on summer Sunday evenings.

☆ Entertainment

Dorothy Browns　　　　　　　　CINEMA
(☑03-442 1964; www.dorothybrowns.com; 18 Buckingham St; adult/child $18.50/15) This is what a cinema should be like: wide, ultra-comfortable seating with fine local wine, cheese boards and olives available to accompany the mostly art-house films on offer. Most screenings in the main theatre have an intermission – the perfect opportunity to tuck into a tub of gourmet ice cream.

The cinema doubles as a neat little bookstore with quality reads.

ⓘ Information

Arrowtown Visitor Information Centre (☑03-442 1824; www.arrowtown.com; 49 Buckingham St; ⊗8.30am-5pm) Shares premises with the Lakes District Museum & Gallery (p595). Sells maps and a selection of NZ books.

ⓘ Getting There & Away

Ritchies Connectabus (p590) runs regular services from around 7am to 10pm on its No 10 route from Frankton to Arrowtown ($15). From Queenstown, you'll need to catch a No 11 bus to Frankton and change there.

WANAKA

☑ 03 / POP 6480

So long described as Queenstown's smaller and more demure sibling, Wanaka now feels grown up enough to have moved out of home and asserted its own identity.

What it does share with Queenstown is the fact that they're both lake and mountain towns bristling with outdoors and adventure opportunities. Wanaka's list of adventure options is impressive by almost any measure, except against the Queenstown ruler. The breadth and selection of adventures here might not be as comprehensive, but the lakefront is more natural and less developed – complete with a day-at-the-beach feel on sunny days – and the town centre has a more soulful atmosphere.

Despite constant growth – in both size and costs – Wanaka retains a fairly laid-back, small-town atmosphere. Days are invarably active here, but evenings are an invite into a wave of new eateries and some truly quirky bars.

◉ Sights

★ National Transport & Toy Museum
MUSEUM

(☑03-443 8765; www.nttmuseumwanaka.co.nz; 891 Wanaka–Luggate Hwy/SH6; adult/child $18/5; ◷8.30am-5pm; ⛟) Mixing Smurfs with Studebakers and Skidoos (and an authentic MiG jet fighter flown by the Polish Air Force) is this completely eclectic and absorbing collection of more than 60,000 items. Suitably, it's as jumbled as a toy box, making it all a bit of a treasure hunt, but it's a nostalgic journey even if you're only young enough to remember as far back as the Sylvanian Families.

Wanaka Station Park
PARK

Wanaka Station Park is a piece of Wanaka that existed before Wanaka did. This remnant of the sheep station that once covered the town area and beyond is a beautiful, well-hidden park space with trees far more impressive (just less photogenic) than That Wanaka Tree nearby – giant sequoias, Himalayan cedars, a large walnut tree, an enormous rhododendron hedge and the station's surviving orchard, with pears and apples that are free for picking.

Warbirds & Wheels
MUSEUM

(www.warbirdsandwheels.com; 11 Lloyd Dunn Ave, Wanaka Airport; adult/child $20/5; ◷9am-5pm) Dedicated to NZ combat pilots, the aircraft they flew and the sacrifices they made, this museum features a replica of a Hawker Hurricane, a de Havilland FB5 Vampire and twin rows of gleaming classic cars – pride of place goes to the 1934 Duesenberg Model J, described as the finest car ever made in the USA. There's a retro **diner** attached.

Puzzling World
AMUSEMENT PARK

(☑03-443 7489; www.puzzlingworld.com; 188 Wanaka–Luggate Hwy/SH84; adult/child $20/14, Great Maze only $16/12; ◷8.30am-5.30pm; ⛟) A 3D Great Maze and lots of fascinating brain-bending visual illusions to keep people of all ages bemused, bothered and bewildered. Even the cafe tables come equipped with puzzles. It's en route to Cromwell, 2km from town.

Wanaka Beerworks
BREWERY

(☑03-443 1865; www.wanakabeerworks.co.nz; 891 Wanaka–Luggate Hwy/SH6; ◷tasting room 11am-4.30pm) Push past the Barbies to get to the beer – the tasting room for the Wanaka Beerworks is rather incongruously at the rear of the toy museum gift shop. Get a tasting paddle of six beers from the craft brewer's two labels – Wanaka Beerworks and Jabberwocky – or try them from the tap or bottle. Tours of the brewing process ($15), which is out of sight otherwise, run at 2pm Monday to Saturday and include tastings.

★ Activities

Wanaka might not have bridges to leap off, but you could still bottle the adrenaline here. For powder monkeys it's the gateway to the **Treble Cone** (☑03-443 1406; www.treble cone.com; daily lift pass adult/child $110/55), Cardrona (p606), Snow Farm (p606) and Harris Mountains (p580) ski areas, and it's the last stop before Tititea/Mt Aspiring National Park for those in hiking boots.

Hiking

For walks close to town, including various lakeside wanders, download DOC's *Wanaka Outdoor Pursuits* brochure from its website (www.doc.govt.nz). Roys Peak (p600) is usually Wanaka's tramp *du jour,* though you can get lofty views with far less effort atop **Mt Iron** (527m, 1½ hours return) – it's a rather grandiose name for what's really just a hill.

For something low-level, the **Glendhu Bay Track** bobbles along the western shore of Lake Wanaka, passing That Wanaka Tree and **Rippon** (☑03-443 8084; www.rippon.co.nz; 246 Mt Aspiring Rd; ◷11am-5pm) before rolling into Glendhu Bay after three to four hours on foot. It's also a good track for a gentle mountain-bike ride.

Wanaka

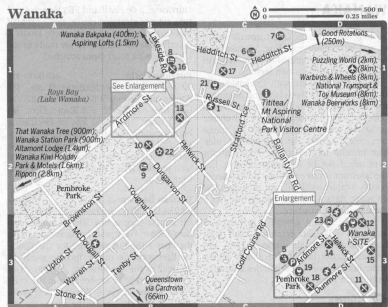

⊕ 0   500 m
0   0.25 miles

Wanaka

⊕ Activities, Courses & Tours
1 Adventure Consultants	C1
2 Aspiring Guides	A3
3 Deep Canyon	D2
4 Outside Sports	D3
5 Paddle Wanaka	C3
Wild Walks	(see 2)

⊜ Sleeping
6 Archway Motels	C1
7 Criffel Peak View	C1
8 Lakeside	B1
9 YHA Wanaka	B2

⊗ Eating
10 Charlie Brown	B2
11 Federal Diner	D3
12 Francesca's Italian Kitchen	D3
13 Francesca's Wood-Fired Pizza	B2
14 Kai Whakapai	D3

15 Kika	D3
16 Landing	B1
17 Red Star	C1
18 White House Restaurant & Bar	D3

⊕ Drinking & Nightlife
19 Gin & Raspberry	D3
20 Lalaland	D3
21 Woody's	C1

⊕ Entertainment
22 Cinema Paradiso	B2

ⓘ Transport
23 InterCity	D3
Naked Bus	(see 23)
Ritchies	(see 23)
Ritchies Connectabus Wanaka	(see 23)

★ Roys Peak
TRAMPING

Roys Peak is Wanaka's big-ticket walk, though many people come just to climb to the saddle that forms the podium for one of the most popular travel photos in NZ. The views are incredible, but the 1578m peak (five hours return) shouldn't be taken lightly as it requires a 1200m climb. The saddle is about three-quarters of the way up.

At busy times the car park overflows with vehicles, so come early.

Wild Walks
TRAMPING

(☎03-443 9422; www.wildwalks.co.nz; 58 McDougall St) Runs a range of interesting and remote guided tramps, from a lap of the Gillespie Pass Circuit (p607), from $1715, to an 'assisted trek' to Cascade Saddle, from $355, in which a guide leads you to the tricky and precipitous pass and you then walk out on your own through the Dart Valley. Winter turns to glacier and snow walks.

Aspiring Guides   ADVENTURE SPORTS
(☑03-443 9422; www.aspiringguides.com; 58 Mc-Dougall St) This crew offers a multitude of options, including guided tramping on around a dozen wilderness routes, mountaineering and ice-climbing courses, guided ascents of Tititea/Mt Aspiring and Aoraki/Mt Cook, and off-piste ski trips (one- to five-day back-country expeditions).

Climbing & Mountaineering
Excellent rock climbing can be found at Hospital Flat, around 20km from Wanaka towards Tititea/Mt Aspiring National Park, and the adjoining Diamond Lake Conservation Area.

Wanaka Rock Climbing   CLIMBING
(☑022-015 4458; www.wanakarock.co.nz) Introductory rock-climbing course (half/full day $203/293), a half-day abseiling intro on 40m-high rock walls ($203) and guided climbs around the region.

Basecamp Wanaka   CLIMBING
(☑03-443 1110; www.basecampwanaka.co.nz; 50 Cardrona Valley Rd; day pass adult/child $21/18; ⊙noon-7pm Mon-Fri, 10am-5pm Sat & Sun) Indoor climbing wall at the town edge where even fearless tots can have a go on the Clip 'n Climb automatic belay system (from $10, booking recommended).

Adventure Consultants   ADVENTURE SPORTS
(☑03-443 8711; www.adventureconsultants.com; 20 Brownston St) Highly respected mountain guiding outfit (it's been leading climbs on Everest for decades, if you have money and mountain skills to burn...) offering treks to Brewster Glacier (two days, from $890) and Gillespie Pass (three days, $1250).

Mountain Biking
Hundreds of kilometres of tracks and trails in the region are open to mountain bikers. Download DOC's *Wanaka Outdoor Pursuits* brochure, which describes a range of mountain-bike rides, including the popular **Deans Bank Track** (12km).

One particularly scenic route is the **Newcastle Track** (12km), which follows the raging blue waters of the Clutha River from Albert Town to the Red Bridge on Kane Rd. You can make it a 30km loop by joining the **Upper Clutha River Track** at Luggate.

The **Glendhu Bay Track** provides easy riding along the shore of Lake Wanaka, while a local favourite is **Sticky Forest**, with around 30km of purpose-built trails through pine forest.

Bike rental is easy to find in town – try **Outside Sports** (☑03-443 7966; www.outside sports.co.nz; 17/23 Dunmore St; half/full day from $30/50; ⊙bike rentals 9am-6pm) for a quality dual-suspension or downhill mountain bike, or if you prefer the boost of an e-bike, head to **Good Rotations** (☑03-443 4349; www.goodrotations.co; 34 Anderson Rd; half/full day from $45/89; ⊙11am-5pm Tue-Fri).

Other Activities
★**Wildwire Wanaka**   ADVENTURE SPORTS
(☑027 430 1332; www.wildwire.co.nz) The Italian world of *via ferrata* – climbing using the likes of iron rungs, plank bridges and cables – arrives in Wanaka, scaling the cliffs beside (and sometimes across) Twin Falls. Make the half-day climb partway up the falls ($249), or go the whole hog on Lord of the Rungs ($595), the world's highest waterfall *via ferrata,* with a helicopter flight back down.

Pioneer Rafting   RAFTING
(☑03-443 1246; www.ecoraft.co.nz; payment by donation) 🕊 Raft on the high-volume Clutha, with Grade II to III rapids, incorporating a spot of gold panning and bird-watching. The operation is based on non-commercial principles – you don't pay for the trip per se, you donate a sum of money of your choosing towards Pioneer Rafting's river conservation projects.

Deep Canyon   ADVENTURE SPORTS
(☑03-443 7922; www.deepcanyon.co.nz; 100 Ardmore St; from $240; ⊙Oct-Apr) Climb, walk, leap, zip-line and abseil your way through narrow, wild gorges – 10 options on offer, from novice to 'oh God'.

Paddle Wanaka   KAYAKING
(☑0800 926 925; www.paddlewanaka.co.nz; Ardmore St; ⊙9am-6pm Oct-Easter) Rents kayaks ($20 per hour) and stand-up paddle boards (SUP, $20 per hour) and offers guided paddle-powered tours of the lake (half/full day $135/275) and the rapids of the Clutha River (half day $189). For something unique, how about a heli-SUP trip to a remote mountain lake?

Skydive Wanaka   SKYDIVING
(☑03-443 7207; www.skydivewanaka.com; 14 Mustang Lane, Wanaka Airport; from $229) Grab some airtime, jumping from 9000ft, 12,000ft, or going the whole banana with a 15,000ft leap and 60 seconds of free fall.

MT ASPIRING NATIONAL PARK

Verdant valleys, alpine meadows, braided glacial rivers, craggy mountains and more than 100 glaciers make Tititea/Mt Aspiring National Park an outdoor enthusiast's paradise. Protected as a national park in 1964, and later included in the Te Wāhipounamu (Southwest New Zealand) World Heritage Area, the park now blankets 3555 sq km along the Southern Alps, from the Haast River in the north to its border with Fiordland National Park in the south. Lording it over all is colossal Tititea/Mt Aspiring (3033m), the highest peak outside the Aoraki/Mt Cook area.

While the southern end of the national park near Glenorchy includes famed tramps such as the **Routeburn** (p592) and **Greenstone & Caples** (p593) Tracks, there are plenty of blissful short walks and more demanding multiday tramps in the **Matukituki Valley**, close to Wanaka; see DOC's *Matukituki Valley Tracks* brochure, which can be downloaded from its website (www.doc.govt.nz).

The dramatic **Rob Roy Track** (10km, three to four hours return) takes in glaciers, waterfalls and lush rainforest, and is among the most scenic and spectacular of all New Zealand's day tramps. It's a moderate walk, but some parts are quite steep. The **West Matukituki Valley Track** goes on to the Aspiring Hut (four to five hours return; peak/off-peak $30/25 per night), a scenic walk over mostly grassy flats. For overnight or multiday tramps offering great views of Mt Aspiring, continue up the valley to the Liverpool Hut (three to four hours from Aspiring Hut; $15 per night) and French Ridge Hut (four to five hours from Aspiring Hut; $25 per night).

Many of these tramps are prone to snow and avalanche risk and can be treacherous. It is extremely important to consult with the DOC staff at the **Tititea/Mt Aspiring National Park Visitors Centre** (p605) in Wanaka and to purchase hut tickets before heading off. You should also register your intentions on www.adventuresmart.org.nz.

The Matukituki Valley tracks begin from Raspberry Creek at the end of Mt Aspiring Rd, 50km from Wanaka. The road is unsealed for 30km and involves nine creek fords. It's usually fine in a 2WD, except in very wet conditions (check at the visitor centre).

Hatch   FISHING
(☑ 03-443 8446; www.hatchfishing.co.nz; half/full day $450/790, 2 anglers $490/850) Guided fly-fishing on Lakes Wanaka and Hawea and the surrounding rivers, which are excellent for trout. There's also the option of accessing remote spots by helicopter or jetboat, or overnight backcountry trips, staying in huts.

🕝 Tours

Scenic Flights

Aspiring Helicopters   SCENIC FLIGHTS
(☑ 03-443 7152; www.aspiringhelicopters.co.nz; Cattle Flat Station, 2211 Mt Aspiring Rd) A range of flight options, from a 20-minute buzz over Lake Wanaka ($185) to a three-hour flight to Milford Sound ($1250), choppering along the sound's length and making four landings.

Southern Alps Air   SCENIC FLIGHTS
(☑ 03-443 4385, 0800 345 666; www.southernalps air.co.nz; 12 Lloyd Dunn Ave, Wanaka Airport) Flights over Aoraki/Mt Cook, taking in Tasman, Fox and Franz Josef Glaciers (adult/child $485/320), along with Milford Sound flyovers ($455/300), Milford

fly-cruise combos ($540/355) and whirls over Tititea/Mt Aspiring and Lake Wanaka ($290/200).

Other Tours

Wanaka Bike Tours   CYCLING
(☑ 03-443 6363; www.wanakabiketours.co.nz; from $199) Guided trips along the shores of Lake Hawea, the Clutha River bike trail, or into the mountains above Lake Wanaka. Also has helibiking options.

Eco Wanaka Adventures   OUTDOORS
(☑ 03-443 2869; www.ecowanaka.co.nz) 🎋 Trips include a full-day walk to the Rob Roy Glacier ($275), a four-hour cruise and walk on Mou Waho Island ($225) to find a lake within a lake, and a full-day cruise-4WD combo ($454). Also offers helihikes.

Ridgeline Adventures   DRIVING
(☑ 0800 234 000; www.ridgelinenz.com) 🎋 Choose from a range of 4WD explorations, be it a 'safari' through farming country ($229), a 4WD/jetboat/helicopter combo ($846), or a drive to a romantic dinner for two on a remote hilltop overlooking Lake Wanaka ($375).

⚜ Festivals & Events

TUKI MUSIC
(www.tukifestival.nz; ⊙ Feb) New incarnation of the former Rippon Festival, moving up the road to Glendhu Bay in 2018, but featuring the same ilk of big-name Kiwi bands and musicians. It's held every second year, in even-numbered years.

Warbirds over Wanaka AIR SHOW
(☑ 03-443 8619, 0800 496 920; www.warbirdsover wanaka.com; Wanaka Airport; 3 days from adult/child $190/35, daily entry from $70/15) Held every second Easter (in even-numbered years), this incredibly popular international airshow attracts upwards of 50,000 people.

🛌 Sleeping

★ Wanaka Bakpaka HOSTEL $
(☑ 03-443 7837; www.wanakabakpaka.co.nz; 117 Lakeside Rd; dm $31, d with/without bathroom $92/74; ℗@✆) The only lakeside hostel in town delivers million-dollar views at backpacker prices. Amenities are top-shelf and it's worth paying a bit extra for the en suite double with the gorgeous views, though you can also just lap it all up from the wide lounge windows. There are bikes for hire and the hot-water bottles come free.

YHA Wanaka HOSTEL $
(☑ 03-443 1880; www.yha.co.nz; 94 Brownston St; dm $30-38, d with/without bathroom from $108/93; @✆) 🍃 This Wanaka stalwart is older than many of its guests, and it's mellowed comfortably with age. It has a mix of dorms and private rooms, but best of all are the large lounge, with commanding lake and mountain views, and the quiet reading room. The giant topo map in the lounge is great for planning tramps.

Wanaka Kiwi Holiday Park & Motels HOLIDAY PARK $
(☑ 03-443 7766; www.wanakakiwiholidaypark.nz; 263 Studholme Rd North; campsites $25-27, units with/without bathroom from $124/80; ℗✆) This charming and relaxing campground is tucked under Roys Peak, with grassy terraced sites for tents and campervans, lots of trees and pretty views. Facilities include a barbecue area with heaters, and free unlimited wi-fi, plus spa pool and sauna ($5). Older-style motel units have all been renovated, and the newest budget cabins are warm and cosy with wooden floors.

Altamont Lodge LODGE $
(☑ 03-443 8864; www.altamontlodge.co.nz; 121 Mt Aspiring Rd; s/d $79/99; ✆) At the quiet end of town, Altamont is like a hostel for grown-ups.

There are no dorms but the tidy little rooms share spotless bathrooms and a spacious, well-equipped kitchen. Pine-lined walls give it a ski-lodge ambience, while the spa pool and roaring fire in the lounge with its views of Roys Peak will warm you up post-slopes.

Criffel Peak View B&B $$
(☑ 03-443 5511; www.criffelpeakview.co.nz; 98 Hedditch St; s/d/apt from $140/170/280; ℗✆) Situated in a quiet cul-de-sac, this excellent B&B has three rooms sharing a large lounge with a log fire and a sunny wisteria-draped deck. The charming hostesses live in a separate house behind, which also has a self-contained two-bedroom apartment attached.

Archway Motels MOTEL $$
(☑ 03-443 7698; www.archwaymotels.co.nz; 64 Hedditch St; units/chalets from $135/155; ✆) Classically old-school motel with clean and spacious units and chalets, a short uphill walk from the town centre. Cedar hot tubs with mountain views give this place an extra edge. Also has two large self-contained caravans ($125) on site.

★ Lime Tree Lodge LODGE $$$
(☑ 03-443 7305; www.limetreelodge.co.nz; 672 Ballantyne Rd; d $395-595; ℗✆🖼) Quietly removed from town, this intimate lodge has four luxury rooms and two suites. Outside there's a pool, spa, tennis court and pitch-and-putt golf, while the lodge is centred on an inviting living area with open kitchen where the in-house chef prepares meals. There are pre-dinner drinks with the owners – former local sheep-station owners – each night.

★ Aspiring Lofts B&B $$$
(☑ 03-443 7856; www.aspiringlofts.co.nz; 42 Manuka Cres; s/d $220/240; ✆) Perched on a rise overlooking the lake, this modern house has two upmarket rooms in the loft above the garage. Each has its own private balcony to make the most of the views – sit out at night in winter and you can watch the lights as Treble Cone is groomed. You can also stargaze through the roof of the bathroom.

★ Lakeside APARTMENT $$$
(☑ 03-443 0188; www.lakesidewanaka.co.nz; 9 Lakeside Rd; apt from $295; ✆🖼) Luxuriate in a modern apartment in a prime position overlooking the lake, right by the town centre. All 23 apartments have three bedrooms, but can be rented with only one or two bedrooms open. The swimming pool is a rarity in these parts, and if you hire ski gear through the website it can be delivered to your door.

Alpine View Lodge
B&B $$$

(☑ 03-443 7111; www.alpineviewlodge.co.nz; 23 Studholme Rd South; d from $195, cottage $290; 🛜) In a peaceful, rural setting on the edge of town, this excellent lodge has three B&B rooms, one of which has its own private deck with mountain views. Little extras include homemade shortbread in the rooms and a hot tub. Alternatively, you can opt for the fully self-contained two-bedroom cottage, which opens onto the garden.

✖ Eating

Charlie Brown
CRÊPES $

(www.charliebrowncrepes.co.nz; 28 Dungarvon St; crêpes $6-11; ☺ 9am-9pm, shorter hours off-season) Started by a Frenchman in 2016 and taken over by, well, another Frenchman a year later, this retro caravan purveys French crêpes and savoury galettes, with a permanent menu and a seasonal specials board. Grab a crêpe before you head into Cinema Paradiso (p605) – it's right across the road.

Red Star
BURGERS $

(☑ 03-443 9322; https://redstarburgerbar. mobi2go.com; 26 Ardmore St; burgers $12-17; ☺ 11.30am-9pm) The burger menu is exhaustive and inventive – beef, chicken, venison, fish and veggie burgers on crunchy toasted buns. Grab a seat on the terrace and sup on a craft beer with your craft burger.

★ Francesca's Italian Kitchen
ITALIAN $$

(☑ 03-443 5599; www.fransitalian.co.nz; 93 Ardmore St; mains $20-32; ☺ noon-3pm & 5pm-late) Pretty much the matriarch of Wanaka eateries, the perennially busy and cavernous Francesca's has the big flavours and easy conviviality of an authentic Italian family trattoria. Even simple things such as pizza, pasta and polenta chips are exceptional. It also runs a **pizza food truck** (☑ 0800 4647 4992; www.francescaspizzas. com; pizza $10-20; ☺ 4-9pm) on Brownston St.

★ Kai Whakapai
CAFE $$

(☑ 03-443 7795; cnr Helwick & Ardmore Sts; mains $19-26; ☺ 7am-11pm; 🖥) As Wanaka as *that* tree, this local institution is where the town seems to congregate on a sunny evening for a liquid sundowner over excellent pizza or salad. Locally brewed craft beers are on tap and there are Central Otago wines as well.

Federal Diner
CAFE $$

(☑ 03-443 5152; www.federaldiner.co.nz; 47 Helwick St; breakfast $10-19, mains $22-40; ☺ 7am-4pm Mon & Tue, to 9pm Wed-Sun; 🛜) When it's this hidden away and still this popular, you know to expect good things. This cosmopoli-

tan cafe delivers robust breakfasts, excellent coffee, legendary scones, gourmet sandwiches and salads. In the evenings the menu shifts to substantial dishes such as baked gnocchi and slow-roasted lamb shoulder.

★ Kika
TAPAS $$$

(☑ 03-443 6535; http://kika.nz; 2 Dunmore St; plates $12-55; ☺ 5.30pm-late) The baby sister to Francesca's has grown up fast, vaulting within just a year of opening to become the only Wanaka eatery named among New Zealand's top 100 restaurants in 2017. It's a Mediterranean mix of modern Italian food, served tapas style in a casual dining space. Stuck what to choose? Let the chefs decide with the Just Feed Me menu ($62).

White House Restaurant & Bar
MEDITERRANEAN $$$

(☑ 03-443 9595; 33 Dunmore St; mains $25-45; ☺ 4-10.30pm Tue-Sat) This curious restaurant is, well, yeah, in a house – a white one – looking as though someone dropped a casual eatery into the lounge room of an art-deco home. The ever-changing menu ranges through a selection of bruschetta and the likes of lamb with puy lentils, or linguine with surf clams.

Landing
MODERN NZ $$$

(☑ 03-443 5099; www.thelandinglakewanaka. co.nz; 1st fl, 80 Ardmore St; mains $26-35; ☺ 5pm-late Tue-Sun) Looking over the lake from an upstairs perch, the Landing is a stylish place where both menus and views change with the seasons. Expect local meats and fish served in innovative ways. The wine list is strong on Central Otago drops, and there's typically a Wanaka craft beer on tap.

🍷 Drinking & Nightlife

Lalaland
COCKTAIL BAR

(☑ 03-443 4911; www.facebook.com/Lalaland wanaka; 1st fl, 99 Ardmore St; ☺ 4pm-2.30am) Before Ryan Gosling and Emma Stone popularised the term, there was already this Lalaland in Wanaka. Sink into a comfy chair at the little, low-lit palace/bordello, where bar staff concoct elixirs to suit every mood. The lake view might be better at other upstairs Ardmore St bars, but can they top this playlist or cocktail list? Entry via the rear stairs.

Gin & Raspberry
COCKTAIL BAR

(☑ 03-443 4216; www.ginandraspberry.co.nz; 1st fl, 155 Ardmore St; ☺ 3pm-late) If you're in the swing for bling, this lush bar is like stepping into a Baz Luhrmann film set. Among the gilded mirrors, grand piano (yes, you can ask to play it) and purple mood lighting, classic movies provide a backdrop to classic cocktails (including various martinis). The gin collection is impressive and the deck is the perfect sunset perch.

Woody's BAR
(☑03-443 5551; www.facebook.com/woodys wanaka; Post Office Lane, 33 Ardmore St; ☺4pm-2.30am) The mainstays of Post Office Lane are this sports bar and neighbouring **Barluga**, sharing a courtyard and operating more or less in tandem, especially when there's a DJ event on. Woody's is the sporting partner, with pool tables and outside fireplace, while Barluga has the leather armchairs and sophistication...until the wicked cocktails and killer back-to-back beats smash that illusion.

☆ Entertainment

Ruby's CINEMA
(☑03-443 6901; www.rubyscinema.co.nz; 50 Cardrona Valley Rd; adult/child $19/13) How very Wanaka that an art-house cinema should adjoin an indoor climbing wall. Channelling a lush New York or Shanghai vibe, Ruby's has a whiff of cinema's glory days. Watch a movie from a reclining leather chair with a warming blanket over your knees, or just chill in the red-velvet lounge with local craft beers and wine or classic cocktails.

Ruby's is in the Basecamp Wanaka (p601) building on the outskirts of town.

Cinema Paradiso CINEMA
(☑03-443 1505; www.paradiso.net.nz; 72 Brownston St; adult/child $15/9.50) Sprawl on a comfy couch, or recline in a dentist's chair or an old Morris Minor at this Wanaka institution, screening the best of Hollywood and art-house flicks. At intermission head to the lobby for freshly baked cookies (simply follow your nose), though the homemade ice cream is just as enticing.

❶ Information

Wanaka i-SITE (☑03-443 1233; www.lake wanaka.co.nz; 103 Ardmore St; ☺8am-7pm summer, to 5pm winter) Lakefront office that's ever helpful, but always busy.

Tititea/Mt Aspiring National Park Visitor Centre (☑03-443 7660; www.doc.govt.nz; cnr Ardmore St & Ballantyne Rd; ☺8.30am-5pm daily Nov-Apr, Mon-Sat May-Oct) In an A-framed building on the edge of the town centre, this DOC office takes hut bookings and offers advice on tracks and conditions. Be sure to call in before undertaking any wilderness tramps.

Wanaka Medical Centre (☑03-443 0710; www.wanakamedical.co.nz; 23 Cardrona Valley Rd; ☺9am-6pm Mon-Fri) is the place to go if you need to patch up any adventure mishaps.

❶ Getting There & Away

Queenstown is Wanaka's main transport link to the outside world, but bus services do range out from here to Dunedin and up the West Coast.

InterCity (p589) coaches depart from outside the log cabin on the lakefront, with daily services to Cromwell (from $10, 35 minutes), Queenstown (from $17, two hours), Lake Hawea (from $10, 20 minutes), Makarora (from $12, 1½ hours) and Franz Josef (from $43, six hours).

Naked Bus (p589) runs services to Queenstown (from $17, two hours), Cromwell (from $10, 35 minutes) and Franz Josef (from $43, six hours).

Ritchies (p589) links Wanaka with Dunedin ($50, four hours), transferring to an InterCity coach at Cromwell.

Ritchies Connectabus Wanaka (p589) heads to/from Queenstown five times daily ($35, two hours) via Cromwell ($22, 45 minutes) and Queenstown Airport. Free wi-fi on board. Call ahead for a hotel pick-up.

❶ Getting Around

Adventure Rentals (☑03-443 6050; www. adventurerentals.co.nz; 51 Brownston St) hires cars and 4WDs (the latter is the best option if you're heading to Tititea/Mt Aspiring National Park), while **Yello** (☑03-443 5555; www.yello. co.nz) operates taxis and scheduled winter shuttles to Cardrona and Treble Cone ski fields ($35 return). Bikes can be hired from Outside Sports (p601) or Good Rotations (p601).

AROUND WANAKA

Cardrona

Gouged between the Crown and Criffel Ranges, the cute settlement of Cardrona reached its zenith in the 1870s at the height of the gold rush, when its population numbered more than 1000. Today it's effectively a ski field balanced atop a pub, albeit perhaps the most recognisable and evocative pub in New Zealand.

Cardrona wakes with a jolt for the ski season, but even if you're not here for powder, it's well worth a visit. Drink in the views and the beer, take a horse ride through the open tussock country, be slightly bemused at the bra fence and understand that a distillery rightly belongs here since the landscape is so reminiscent of the Scottish Highlands.

◉ Sights

Cardrona Distillery & Museum   DISTILLERY

(☑ 03-443 1393; www.cardronadistillery.com; 2125 Cardrona Valley Rd; tours $25; ⊙ 9.30am-5pm) Matching the ever-so-Scottish setting is this single-malt distillery. Enter past the fence of bras (Bra-drona!) and you'll find the beautiful cellar door inside a building of local schist rock. Have a sip of the orange liqueur and award-winning gin, or take the 75-minute distillery tour, which leaves on the hour from 10am to 3pm. You probably won't want to hang around waiting for the whisky to be ready – the first release is due in 2025.

✦ Activities

Cardrona Alpine Resort   SKIING

(☑ 03-443 8880, snow report 03-443 7007; www.cardrona.com; Cardrona Skifield Access Rd; day lift pass adult/child Jul & Aug $110/60, Jun, Sep & Oct $99/50; ⊙ 8.30am-4pm Jun-Oct) Well organised and professional, this 345-hectare ski field offers runs to suit all abilities (25% beginners, 25% intermediate, 30% advanced, 20% expert) at elevations ranging from 1670m to 1860m. Cardrona has several high-capacity chairlifts (including a new Chondola in 2017), beginners' tows and extreme snowboard terrain.

Buses run from Wanaka and Queenstown during ski season.

In summer, the mountain bikers take over. The **Cardrona Peak to Pub**, from the ski fields to the Cardrona Hotel, is a classic NZ ride with 1270m of descent – the resort runs shuttles back up the mountain.

The Cardrona   HORSE RIDING

(☑ 03-443 1228; www.thecardrona.co.nz; 2125 Cardrona Valley Rd) Guided horse rides through the Cardrona Valley, including a High Country Pub ride ($149) that'll have you tying up at the Cardrona Hotel hitching rail for a beer. Also runs quad-bike tours and winter snowmobiling trips onto the Pisa Range.

Snow Farm   SKIING

(☑ 03-443 7542; www.snowfarmnz.com; Snow Farm Access Rd; day trail pass adult/child $40/20, snowshoe day trail pass $20/10; 🐾) In winter this is home to fantastic cross-country skiing and snowshoeing, with 55km of groomed ski trails and 24km of snowshoe trails. Lessons and ski hire are available.

Backcountry Saddle Expeditions   HORSE RIDING

(☑ 03-443 8151; www.backcountrysaddles.co.nz; 2416 Cardrona Valley Rd; adult/child $90/70) Two-hour horse treks across Mt Cardrona Station on Appaloosa horses. Also now runs quad-bike tours ($149).

🛏 Sleeping

Waiorau Homestead   B&B $$$

(☑ 03-443 2225; www.waiorauhomestead.co.nz; 2127 Cardrona Valley Rd; r from $250; 🐾🖥) Tucked away in a private, bucolic nook near the Snow Farm, this lovely stone house, fringed by an old stand of conifers, has deep verandas and three luxurious guest bedrooms, each with their own bathroom. Rates include a full cooked breakfast. Enquire about the cheaper self-contained cabin ($170 to $190); the owners usually rent it on Airbnb.

🍷 Drinking & Nightlife

Cardrona Hotel   PUB

(☑ 03-443 8153; www.cardronahotel.co.nz; 2310 Cardrona Valley Rd; 🐾) The wood-panelled facade looks like a film set, but it's the real deal – NZ's most photographed pub is a gold-rush relic from 1863. The sense of history is palpable (note the exposed mine shaft over which the pub was built) and things get busy in the après-ski thawing hours.

The meals are good (mains $23 to $36) and there are 16 lovingly restored rooms ($195) if you want to stay the night.

ⓘ Getting There & Away

There are no scheduled bus services to Cardrona, but winter ski shuttles are offered by Yello (p605) and Ridgeline Adventures (p602) in Wanaka, and Kiwi Discovery (p589) in Queenstown.

The 45km drive from Queenstown to Cardrona along the Crown Range Rd is one of the South Island's most scenic drives. Topping out at 1076m, it's the highest sealed road in NZ. There are some great places to stop and ogle the view, particularly at the Queenstown end of the road. However, the road is narrow and winding, and needs to be tackled with care in poor weather. In winter it's sometimes closed after heavy snows, and you'll often need snow chains for your tyres.

Lake Hawea

☑ 03 / POP 2175

People looking to escape the bright lights of Queenstown typically gravitate to Wanaka; those looking to escape the slightly less bright lights of Wanaka come to Lake Hawea.

This small town, 15km north of Wanaka, is strung along the southern shore of its 141-sq-km namesake. Separated from Lake Wanaka by a narrow strip of land called the Neck, the blue-grey Lake Hawea (with an average water temperature of just 9°C) is 35km long and 410m deep. It's particularly popular with fisherfolk looking to do battle with its trout and landlocked salmon. The lake was raised 20m in 1958 when it was dammed to facilitate the power stations downriver.

There's little here, but that's the town's appeal.

Sleeping

Lake Hawea Holiday Park HOLIDAY PARK $
(☑ 03-443 1767; www.haweaholidaypark.co.nz; SH6; campsites from $18, units with/without bathroom $140/80; P⊕) On the lakeshore, this spacious and peaceful old-fashioned holiday park is a favourite of fishing and boating enthusiasts. Units range from a block of basic cabins with vividly coloured doors to motel units and cottages. There's bike hire (half/full day $30/40), fishing-rod hire and even a fish smoker if you do land something.

Lake Hawea Hotel HOTEL $$$
(☑ 03-443 1224; www.lakehawea.co.nz; 1 Capell Ave; r from $220; P⊕) Every player wins a prize, with all 12 rooms having unbeatable views across the lake, but they're rather pricey for what's basically an upmarket motel. There's a large bar and **restaurant** (mains $19 to $36), arrayed around an enormous double fireplace, that has equally stellar vistas.

There's also a hostel (dorm from $25) and camping (from $12 per person) out the back.

Getting There & Away

InterCity (☑ 03-442 4922; www.intercity.co.nz) coaches stop at the Lake Hawea dam (SH6) daily, heading to/from Queenstown (from $20, two hours), Cromwell (from $14, one hour), Wanaka (from $10, 20 minutes), Makarora (from $10, 1¼ hours) and Franz Josef (from $40, six hours).

Makarora
☑ 03 / POP 40

Just 20km from Haast Pass, where the West Coast begins its wild ways, remote Makarora is very much a last frontier – and it certainly feels like it. Traffic to and from the West Coast rolls through, but then Makarora settles back to silence.

Activities

★**Blue Pools Walk** TRAMPING
Far and away the most popular walk in the Makarora area is the 750m (30-minute return) track to the luminously blue pools at the point where the Makarora and Blue Rivers converge. The water is so clear you can see the trout seemingly suspended in it. The trailhead is around 8km north of the Makarora Tourist Centre.

Wilkin Valley Track TRAMPING
The Wilkin Valley Track starts from SH6 and heads along the Wilkin River to Kerin Forks Hut (four to five hours, 15km). Another day's walk up the valley will bring you to Top Forks Hut (six to eight hours, 15km), from where the picturesque Lakes Diana, Lucidus and Castalia (one hour, 1½ hours and three hours respectively) can be reached.

Gillespie Pass TRAMPING
The three-day Gillespie Pass tramp loops through the Young, Siberia and Wilkin Valleys. This is a high pass (1501m) with avalanche danger in winter and spring. With the option of a jetboat ride down the Wilkin to complete it, it rates as one of NZ's most memorable tramps.

Siberia Experience ADVENTURE
(☑ 03-443 4385; www.siberiaexperience.co.nz; Makarora Tourist Centre, 5944 Haast Pass–Makarora Rd/SH6; adult/child $395/299) This thrill-seeking extravaganza combines a 25-minute scenic flight, a three-hour tramp through a remote valley and a half-hour jetboat trip down the Wilkin and Makarora Rivers in Titītea/Mt Aspiring National Park.

Information

Makarora Tourist Centre (☑ 03-443 8372; www.makarora.co.nz; 5944 Haast Pass–Makarora Rd/SH6; ⊙ summer 8am-late, winter 9am-5.30pm; ⊕) A large all-in-one complex incorporating a cafe, bar, shop, information centre, camping ground (unpowered/powered sites $15/17), dorms ($30), cabins with kitchenettes ($85) and self-contained chalets (from $128).

Getting There & Away

InterCity (p589) has daily coaches to/from Queenstown (from $24, 3½ hours), Cromwell (from $19, 2¼ hours), Wanaka (from $12, 1½ hours), Lake Hawea (from $10, 1¼ hours) and Franz Josef (from $36, 4¾ hours).

Fiordland & Southland

Best Places to Eat

➡ Kepler's (p616)

➡ Batch (p626)

➡ Louie's (p626)

➡ Elegance at 148 on Elles (p626)

➡ Whistling Frog Cafe & Bar (p631)

➡ Orepuki Beach Cafe (p623)

Best Places to Stay

➡ Te Anau Lodge (p616)

➡ Newhaven Holiday Park (p632)

➡ Southern Comfort Backpackers (p625)

➡ Bushy Point Fernbirds (p626)

➡ Slope Point Accommodation (p629)

Why Go?

Brace yourself for sublime scenery on a breathtaking scale.

Fiordland National Park's mountains, forests and mirror-smooth waters hold visitors in thrall. Framed by kilometre-high cliffs, Milford Sound was clawed away by glaciers over millennia. Leading here is the Milford Hwy, which reveals a magnificent alpine view at every bend. Shying away from attention is Doubtful Sound, the pristine 'place of silence' (which leaves many admiring visitors speechless, too).

From here, a chain of towns characterised by friendliness and fresh seafood is strung along the Southern Scenic Route. The road snakes through Southland to the Catlins, where meadows roll to golden bays and saw-tooth cliffs are speckled with dozing seals.

Then there's the end of the line – Stewart Island/Rakiura, an isolated isle home to seafarers and a flock of rare birds, including New Zealand's beloved icon, the kiwi.

When to Go

➡ Visit from December to April for the best chance of settled weather in Fiordland's notoriously fickle climate (although chances are, you'll still see rain!).

➡ Late October to late April is the Great Walks season for the Milford, Kepler, Routeburn and Rakiura Tracks – book in advance if you want to hike these popular routes.

➡ Stewart Island/Rakiura's changeable weather can bring four seasons in a day, at any time of year. But the temperature is mild: winter (June to August) averages around 10°C and summer (December to February) 16.5–18°C, with highs in the mid-20s.

Fiordland & Southland Highlights

1 **Milford Sound** (p619)
Being overwhelmed by your first glimpse of Mitre Peak rising from the inky waters of the fiord.

2 **Milford Track** (p612)
Tramping through a World Heritage wilderness.

3 **Catlins Waterfalls** (p631)
Feeling the mist from forest waterfalls on road trips through peaceful Owaka and Papatowai.

4 **Doubtful Sound** (p621)
Embracing silence when the boat engine snaps off on this remote cruise.

5 **Stewart Island/Rakiura** (p633) Savouring solitude on NZ's 'third island', a bird haven.

6 **Kaka Point** (p632)
Squinting at penguins or watching sea lions sunbathe on the rock-studded coast.

7 **Invercargill** (p624)
Embracing your inner petrol-head at themed museums before sampling the dining scene.

8 **Slope Point** (p629)
Tramping to sea-ravaged cliffs at the South Island's southernmost point.

9 **Te Waewae Bay** (p623)
Marvelling at nature on this surf-battered stretch of coast.

❶ Getting There & Away

Invercargill is the main transport hub, with flights to/from Wellington, Christchurch and Stewart Island/Rakiura, and buses from as far afield as Queenstown and Dunedin. Te Anau has direct bus connections with Queenstown, Dunedin and Christchurch.

FIORDLAND

If you picture New Zealand, it might just be Fiordland National Park that flashes into your mind's eye. Part of the Te Wāhipounamu (Southwest New Zealand) World Heritage Area, this formidable tract of mountains and forest spanning 26,000 sq km has deeply recessed sounds (technically fiords) that spider inland from the Tasman Sea.

Some of the South Island's most iconic destinations are here. Along the world-famous Milford Hwy, views of mountains and mirror lakes are only surpassed in beauty by the road's end point, Milford Sound. Here, granite giants cast their reflection in waters where dolphins and penguins frolic. Even more secluded is Doubtful Sound: the Māori-named 'place of silence' is teeming with wildlife, larger than Milford Sound, but much less visited.

ESSENTIAL FIORDLAND & SOUTHLAND

Eat Bluff oysters, a New Zealand gourmet obsession, followed by Stewart Island salmon, whitebait and blue cod.

Drink Hokonui Moonshine Whisky (p628) in Gore or a sheep's milk flat white at Invercargill's **Blue River Dairy** (☑ 03-211 5150; www.blueriverdairy.co.nz; 111 Nith St; ⊙10am-2pm Tue-Sat).

Read poems by Hone Tuwhare (1922–2008), who drew inspiration from the landscapes of the Catlins.

Listen to roaring surf in Te Waewae, the crackle of static on road trips (radio signal is patchy), and dead silence in Doubtful Sound.

Watch *The World's Fastest Indian* (Roger Donaldson, 2005), to understand Invercargill's devotion to the legacy of Burt Munro.

Go online www.fiordland.org.nz, https://southlandnz.com

Cruises enter the watery wilderness but walkers can delve deepest into Fiordland either on the multiday Milford, Kepler and Hollyford Tracks or shorter walks, easily reached from the highway.

Te Anau

🎵 03 / POP 1911

Picturesque Te Anau is the main gateway to Milford Sound and three Great Walks: the Milford, Kepler and Routeburn Tracks. Far from being a humdrum stopover, Te Anau is stunning in its own right. The township borders Lake Te Anau, New Zealand's second-largest lake, whose glacier-gouged fiords spider into secluded forest on its western shore. To the east are the pastoral areas of central Southland, while west across Lake Te Anau lie the rugged mountains of Fiordland.

Te Anau is popular with fly-by sightseers and long-haul trampers alike. This has encouraged a sizeable accommodation scene and a decent array of places to eat. While Te Anau doesn't party nearly as hard as effervescent Queenstown, there are plenty of places to sink a few beers – which taste all the better after a long day of tramping, kayaking or driving the unforgettable Milford Hwy.

⊙ Sights

Te Anau Glowworm Caves CAVE
(☑ 0800 656 501; www.realjourneys.co.nz; adult/child $83/22) Stare up at constellations of glowworms on an underground boat ride. Once present only in Māori legends, this 200m-long cave system was rediscovered in 1948. Its sculpted rocks, waterfalls and whirlpools are impressive by themselves, but the bluish sparkle of glowworms, peculiar territorial larvae who lure prey with their come-hither lights, is the main draw.

Reach the caves on a 2¼-hour guided tour with Real Journeys (p615), via a lake cruise, walkway and a short boat ride. Tours depart from its office on Lakefront Dr.

🏃 Activities

Te Anau is the gateway to three Great Walks – the Kepler, Milford and Routeburn (p592) – and the less visited but equally worthy Hollyford. Detailed information can be found in Lonely Planet's *Hiking & Tramping New Zealand* guide, and from the helpful folk at the Fiordland National Park Visitor Centre (p617), where you can also register your intentions via the AdventureSmart

Te Anau

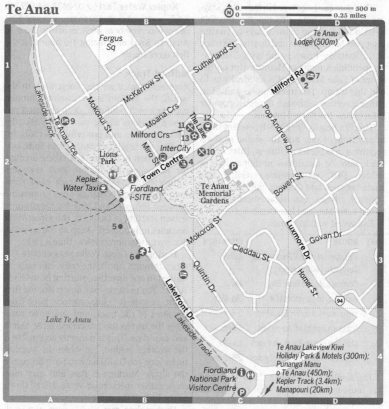

Te Anau

🟢 Activities, Courses & Tours
1 Fiordland Jet	B3
2 Fiordland Tours	D1
3 Real Journeys	B2
4 Rosco's Milford Kayaks	B2
5 Southern Lakes Helicopters	B3
6 Wings & Water	B3

🛏 Sleeping
7 Keiko's Cottages	D1
8 Te Anau Lakefront Backpackers	B3
9 Te Anau Top 10	A2

✕ Eating
10 Kepler's	C2
11 Sandfly Cafe	B2

🍸 Drinking & Nightlife
Black Dog Bar	(see 13)
12 Ranch Bar & Grill	C2

☆ Entertainment
13 Fiordland Cinema	C2

FIORDLAND & SOUTHLAND TE ANAU

website (www.adventuresmart.org.nz), so there's a record of your planned route in case of emergency.

Kepler Track

Opened in 1988, the Kepler is one of NZ's best-planned tracks and now one of its most popular. The route takes the form of a mod-erately strenuous 60km loop beginning and ending at the Waiau River control gates at the southern end of Lake Te Anau. It features an all-day tramp across the mountaintops taking in incredible panoramas of the lake, the Jackson Peaks and the Kepler Mountains. Along the way it traverses rocky ridges, tussock lands and peaceful beech forest.

The route can be covered in four days, staying in the three huts, although it is possible to reduce the tramp to three days by continuing past Moturau Hut and leaving the track at the Rainbow Reach swing bridge. However, spending a night at Moturau Hut on the shore of Lake Manapouri is an ideal way to end this tramp. The track can be walked in either direction, although the most popular is Luxmore–Iris Burn–Moturau.

This is a heavily weather-dependent track at any time of year and the alpine sections require a good level of fitness. Parts of the track may be hazardous or impassible in winter. DOC recommends tackling this route between late October and April – and strongly advises against attempting it between early May and late October.

Estimated walking times:

DAY	ROUTE	DURATION
1	Fiordland National Park Visitor Centre to control gates	45min
1	Control gates to Brod Bay	1½hr
1	Brod Bay to Luxmore Hut	3½-4½hr
2	Luxmore Hut to Iris Burn Hut	5-6hr
3	Iris Burn Hut to Moturau Hut	5-6hr
3	Moturau Hut to Rainbow Reach	1½-2hr
4	Rainbow Reach to control gates	2½-3½hr

The Kepler is officially a Great Walk and you must obtain a Great Walk pass for the Luxmore Hut, Iris Burn Hut and Moturau Hut in advance. It pays to book well in advance, either online via DOC's **Great Walks Bookings** (☎0800 694 732; www.greatwalks. co.nz) or in person at a DOC visitor centre. In the low season (inadvisable for all but the most experienced NZ trampers) the huts revert to the 'serviced' category. There are campsites at **Brod Bay** (☑national park centre 03-249 7924; www.doc.govt.nz; tent sites late Oct–mid Apr $20, rest of year $5) and **Iris Burn** (www.doc.govt.nz; tent sites late Oct–mid Apr $20, rest of year $5).

The recommended map for this tramp is 1:60,000 *Parkmap 335-09 (Kepler Track)*.

Conveniently, the track begins under an hour's walk from the Fiordland National Park Visitor Centre, via the lakeside track alongside the Manapouri-Te Anau Rd (SH95). There's a car park and shelter near the control gates. **Tracknet** (☑0800 483 262; www.tracknet.net) and **Topline Tours** (☑03-249 8059; www.toplinetours.co.nz; 32 Caswell Rd) both run shuttles to and from both the control gates and the Rainbow Reach trailheads.

Kepler Water Taxi (☑03-249 8364, 027 249 8365; www.keplerwatertaxi.co.nz; each way $25) offers morning boat services across Lake Te Anau to Brod Bay, slicing 1½ hours off the first day's tramp.

Milford Track

Routinely touted as 'the finest walk in the world', the Milford is an absolute stunner, complete with rainforest, deep glaciated valleys, a glorious alpine pass surrounded by towering peaks and powerful waterfalls, including the legendary Sutherland Falls, one of the loftiest in the world. All these account for its popularity: almost 7500 trampers complete the 54km-long track each summer. Soon after bookings open (sometime between February and May, for the summer season starting in October), this Great Walk becomes fully booked - keep an eye on www. doc.govt.nz/milfordtrack to time it right.

During the Great Walks season (late October through April), the track can only be walked in one direction, starting from Glade Wharf. You must stay at Clinton Hut the first night, despite it being only one hour from the start of the track, and you must complete the trip in the prescribed three nights and four days. This is perfectly acceptable if the weather is kind, but when the weather turns sour you'll still have to push on across the alpine Mackinnon Pass and may miss some rather spectacular views. It's all down to the luck of the draw.

During the Great Walk season, the track is also frequented by guided tramping parties, which stay at cosy, carpeted lodges with hot showers and proper food. If that sounds appealing, contact Ultimate Hikes (p616), the only operator permitted to run guided tramps on the Milford.

The track is covered by 1:70,000 *Parkmap 335-01 (Milford Track)*.

Estimated walking times:

DAY	ROUTE	DURATION
1	Glade Wharf to Glade House	20min
1	Glade House to Clinton Hut	1hr
2	Clinton Hut to Mintaro Hut	6hr
3	Mintaro Hut to Dumpling Hut	6-7hr
3	Side trip to Sutherland Falls	1½hr return
4	Dumpling Hut to Sandfly Point	5½-6hr

The Milford Track is officially a Great Walk. Between late October and mid-April, you need to book each of your three nights in the huts ($70): Clinton Hut, Mintaro Hut

Kepler Track

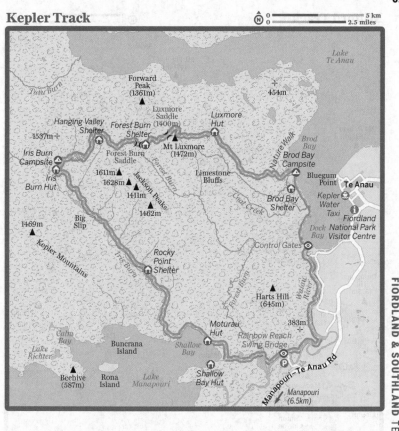

and Dumpling Hut. Hut passes must be obtained in advance, either online via DOC's Great Walks Bookings (p612) or in person at a DOC visitor centre. Book early to avoid disappointment as the entire season books up very quickly.

DOC advises against tackling the Milford Track between early May and late October because of the significant risk of avalanches and floods, and the fact that bridges at risk of avalanche are removed. It's wet, very cold, and snow conceals trail markers. If you're a well-equipped tramping pro considering the Milford Track out of season, get DOC advice on weather conditions. During this low season, huts revert to the 'serviced' category ($15), and restrictions on walking the track in four days are removed.

The track starts at Glade Wharf, at the head of Lake Te Anau, accessible by a 1½-hour boat trip from Te Anau Downs, itself 29km from Te Anau on the road to Milford

Sound. The track finishes at Sandfly Point, a 15-minute boat trip from Milford Sound village, from where you can return by road to Te Anau, around two hours away. You will be given options to book this connecting transport online, at the same time as you book your hut tickets.

Tracknet offers transport from Queenstown and Te Anau to meet the boats at Te Anau Downs and Milford Sound. There are other options for transport to and from the track, including a float-plane hop from Te Anau to Glade Wharf with **Wings & Water** (☎03-249 7405; www.wingsandwater.co.nz; Lakefront Dr). Fiordland i-SITE (p617) and the Fiordland National Park Visitor Centre (p617) can advise on options to best suit you. **Safer Parking** (☎03-249 7198; www.saferparking.co.nz; 48 Caswell Rd; per day per motorbike/car/motorhome $4/9/10) is a good option for stashing your vehicle while you hike.

Milford Track

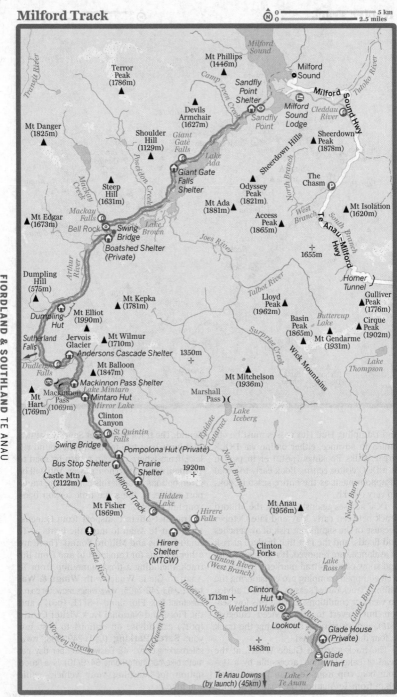

Hollyford Track

The four- to five-day (each way), 56km Hollyford Track is an easy to moderate tramp through the lower Hollyford – the longest valley in Fiordland National Park – to remote Martins Bay. Track upgrades and improved transport services, combined with the fact that it's a low-level hike achievable year-round (weather permitting), have resulted in more trampers discovering the splendid mountain and lake vistas, forest, extensive bird life and magical coast that make the Hollyford so special. Even so, the track averages only 4000 trampers a year, making it a good option for those in search of solitude.

The track is basically one way (unless combined with the super-challenging, 88km Pyke–Big Bay Route). The majority of trampers turn tail and retrace their steps, or fly out from the airstrip at Martins Bay. Allow some time in the bay to view a seal colony and get a sneaky peak at a penguin, if you're lucky. This will more than make up for some of the most demonic sandflies in NZ.

The best maps for this tramp are *CA09 (Alabaster)* and *CA08 (Milford Sound/Piopiotahi)*. DOC produces a *Hollyford Track* brochure.

Trampers have the use of six DOC huts on the track, ranging from serviced ($15) to standard ($5). Camping ($5) is permitted next to the huts, although sandflies will prevent this from being remotely enjoyable. Tickets should be obtained in advance online from DOC Visitor Centres.

Tracknet (p612) and **Trips & Tramps** (☑03-249 7081, 0800 305 807; www.tripsandtramps.com) both run shuttles to the Hollyford trailhead. Nine kilometres (two hours' walk) shy of the trailhead is Gunn's Camp (p618), a good bolthole before or after the feat with car storage available.

Fly Fiordland (☑0800 359 346; www.flyfiordland.com; 52 Town Centre; up to 4 passengers $620) flies between Te Anau and the Martins Bay airstrip.

Short Walks

Te Anau's **Lakeside Track** makes for a very pleasant stroll or cycle in either direction – north to the marina and around to the Upukerora River (about an hour return), or south past the Fiordland National Park Visitor Centre and on to the control gates and start of the Kepler Track (50 minutes).

Day tramps in the national park are readily accessible from Te Anau. Kepler Water Taxi (p612) and **Fiordland Outdoors** (☑0800 347 4538; www.fiordlandoutdoors.co.nz) can scoot you over to Brod Bay, from where you can walk back along the Lakeside Track to Te Anau (two to three hours). During summer, Trips & Tramps offers small-group, guided day hikes on the Kepler and Routeburn, among other tracks (as well as shuttles to and from trailheads). Real Journeys (p622) runs guided day hikes (adult/child $195/127, November to mid-April) along an 11km stretch of the Milford Track. Various day walks can also be completed by linking with regular bus services run by Tracknet (p612).

For self-guided adventures, pick up DOC's *Fiordland National Park Day Walks* brochure ($2) from the Fiordland i-SITE (p617) or Fiordland National Park Visitor Centre (p617), or download it at www.doc.govt.nz.

⌖ Tours

★ **Real Journeys**   TOURS
(☑0800 656 501; www.realjourneys.co.nz; 85 Lakefront Dr; ☉7.30am-8.30pm Sep-May, 8am-7pm Jun-Aug) ✎ You can count on sharp service and well-organised tours from this major player, which offers cruises on Doubtful and Milford Sounds on its big menu of tours, walks and outdoor activities – always with sensitivity to local wildlife. Other highlights are guided day-walks on the Milford Track and tours of the Te Anau Glowworm Caves (p610).

Fiordland Jet   ADVENTURE SPORTS
(☑0800 253 826; www.fjet.nz; 84 Lakefront Dr; adult/child $139/70) Thrilling 90-minute jet-boating trips on the Upper Waiau River (in *Lord of the Rings*, the River Anduin), zipping between mountain-backed beech forest, with commentary on the area's natural (and fictional) highlights.

Fiordland Tours   TOURS
(☑0800 247 249; www.fiordlandtours.co.nz; 208 Milford Rd; adult/child from $149/69) Runs small-group bus and Milford Sound cruise tours (15 passengers or less), departing from Te Anau and stopping at scenic view points along the way. It also provides track transport and guided day walks on the Kepler Track.

Hollyford Track   TRAMPING
(☑03-442 3000; www.hollyfordtrack.com; adult/child from $1895/1495; ☉late Oct-late Apr) ✎ Brimming with insight into Māori history and Fiordland wildlife, this Ngāi Tahu–owned operator leads small-group (less than 16 people) three-day guided trips on the Hollyford staying at private huts/lodges. The journey is

shortened with a jetboat trip down the river and Lake McKerrow on day two, and ends with a scenic flight to Milford Sound.

Ultimate Hikes   TRAMPING
(☑03-450 1940, 0800 659 255; www.ultimate hikes.co.nz; 5-day tramps incl food dm/s/d $2295/3330/5390; ☺Nov–mid-Apr) ✎ Booking yourself onto a guided tramp of the Milford Track with Queenstown-based Ultimate Hikes puts route planning and logistics in the capable hands of an experienced operator. The guides' expert knowledge of fauna and flora enhances the journey, and walkers will overnight in lodges with hot showers and proper food.

Southern Lakes Helicopters SCENIC FLIGHTS
(☑03-249 7167; www.southernlakeshelicopters. co.nz; Lakefront Dr) Offering flights over Te Anau for 30 minutes ($240) and longer trips with landings over Doubtful, Dusky and Milford Sounds (from $685), this operator's quarter-century of experience in Fiordland will reassure nervous flyers.

🛏 Sleeping

⭐**Te Anau Lakefront Backpackers**   HOSTEL $
(☑03-249 7713, 0800 200 074; www.teanauback packers.co.nz; 48-50 Lakefront Dr; tent sites $20, dm $35, d with/without bathroom from $98/88; 🖧) Tidy dorm and private rooms with a lakefront location hoist this backpackers to the top spot among Te Anau's budget beds. Gaze at the lake through huge windows, let the staff fill your brain with local tips, or snooze in a game- and book-filled lounge with Dexter, the adopted house cat.

Te Anau Lakeview Kiwi Holiday Park & Motels   HOLIDAY PARK $
(☑0800 483 262, 03-249 7457; www.teanauholiday park.co.nz; 77 Te Anau–Manapouri Rd; unpowered/ powered sites $23/24, dm/s/d without bathroom $35/40/80, units $125-306; @🖧) This 9-hectare grassy lakeside holiday park has plenty of space to pitch your tent or park your van. It also has a wide range of accommodation from basic dorms through to tidy cabins and the rather swanky Marakura two-bedroom motels with enviable lake and mountain views. Friendly staff will hook you up with local activities and transport.

Te Anau Top 10   HOLIDAY PARK $$
(☑03-249 7462, 0800 249 746; www.teanautop10. co.nz; 128 Te Anau Tce; powered sites from $50, cabins without bathroom $62-99, units with bathroom $150-236; @🖧✈) Accommodation at this lakefront holiday park covers all budgets: motel units have slate-grey decor and compact kitchens, while private tent sites and well-priced cabins share modern kitchen facilities and bathrooms. Lake-facing hot tubs, a playground, bike hire and barbecue area are perfect when the sun's out, while a games room and sauna provide wet-weather distractions for parents and kids alike.

Keiko's Cottages   B&B $$
(☑03-249 9248; www.keikos.co.nz; 228 Milford Rd; d from $175; ☺closed Jun-Aug; 🖧) Surrounded by Japanese-style flower gardens, complete with babbling water features and fish pond, Keiko's self-contained cottages are private, comfortable and decorated with feminine flair. The welcome is ebullient and breakfast ($30 per person) poses a difficult choice: Kiwi-style or a full Japanese banquet? The spa and sauna are worthy extras. Wi-fi vouchers cost extra.

⭐**Te Anau Lodge**   B&B $$$
(☑03-249 7477; www.teanaulodge.com; 52 Howden St; with breakfast s $225-350, d $250-375, tr $300-400; 🖧) In a sea of functional but fusty motels, Te Anau's former Sisters of Mercy Convent distinguishes itself with unique history. Each chamber carries a whisper of its previous function, from the elegant 'Music Room' to the lavish 'Mother Superior'. Sip complimentary wine in a fireside chesterfield, collapse on a king-size bed, then awaken to an ample continental breakfast.

🍴 Eating

⭐**Sandfly Cafe**   CAFE $
(☑03-249 9529; 9 The Lane; mains $7-20; ☺7am-4.30pm; 🖧) As popular with locals as travellers, Sandfly serves the town's best espresso alongside breakfasts, light meals of pasta or club sandwiches, and an impressive rack of sweet treats from caramel slices to berry friands (almond-flour cakes). Sun yourself on the lawn, or try to get maximum mileage out of the free 15 minutes of wi-fi.

⭐**Kepler's**   SOUTH AMERICAN $$$
(☑03-249 7909; 90 Town Centre; mains $29-40; ☺5-9pm) Mountains of crayfish, mouthwatering ceviche and perfectly seared steaks are whisked to tables at this efficient but friendly family-run place. South American flair permeates the menu (quinoa-crusted orange roughy, Chilean malbec); we suggest the whopping roast lamb with a generous pour of merlot.

🍷 Drinking & Entertainment

Ranch Bar & Grill PUB
(📞 03-249 8801; www.theranchbar.co.nz; 111 Town Centre; ⏱ 8am-late) An open fire and chalet-style eaves heighten the appeal of this popular local pub, most loved for its hefty Sunday roast dinners ($15), Thursday jam nights and sports matches on big screens. Show up for big pancake breakfasts (until 11.30am) or generous schnitzels and mostly meaty mains ($20 to $42) at other times.

Fiordland Cinema CINEMA
(📞 03 249 8844; www.fiordlandcinema.co.nz; 7 The Lane; 🎬) In between regular showings of the excellent *Ata Whenua/Fiordland on Film* (adult/child $10/5), essentially a 32-minute advertisement for Fiordland scenery, Fiordland Cinema serves as the local movie house.

The **Black Dog Bar** (📞 03-249 9089; www.blackdogbar.co.nz; 7 The Lane; ⏱ 10am-late; 🎬), next to the cinema, is the town's most sophisticated watering hole.

ℹ️ Information

Fiordland i-SITE (📞 03-249 8900; www.fiordland.org.nz; 19 Town Centre; ⏱ 8.30am-8pm Dec-Mar, to 5.30pm Apr-Nov) The official information centre, offering activity, accommodation and transport bookings.

Fiordland National Park Visitor Centre (DOC; 📞 03-249 7924; www.doc.govt.nz; cnr Lakefront Dr & Te Anau–Manapouri Rd; ⏱ 8.30am-4.30pm) Can assist with Great Walks bookings, general hut tickets and information, with the bonus of a natural-history display and a shop stocking tramping supplies and essential topographical maps for backcountry trips.

Fiordland Medical Centre (📞 03-249 7007; 25 Luxmore Dr; ⏱ 8am-5.30pm Mon-Fri, 9am-noon Sat, 10-10.30am & 5-5.30pm Sun) If you need medical help after hours, the centre's number will give the info of an on-call GP.

ℹ️ Getting There & Away

InterCity (📞 03-442 4922; www.intercity.co.nz; Miro St) runs services to Milford Sound ($22 to $44, three hours, two to three daily) and Queenstown ($21 to $49, 3¼ hours, four daily), and daily morning buses to Gore ($20 to $40, 1¾ hours), Dunedin ($25 to $49, 4½ hours) and Christchurch ($31 to $81, 11 hours). Buses depart from a stop on Miro St, at the Town Centre end.

Naked Bus (https://nakedbus.com) has daily bus services to Queenstown (from $30, 2¾ hours) and one daily morning bus to Milford Sound (from $32, 2¼ hours). Services depart from Te Anau Lakeview Kiwi Holiday Park.

Topline Tours (p612) offers year-round shuttles between Te Anau and Manapouri ($20), and, from November to March, transfers from Te Anau to the Kepler Track trailheads at the control gates ($5) and the Rainbow Reach swing bridge ($8).

From November to April Te Anau–based **Tracknet** (p612) has at least three daily scheduled buses to/from Te Anau Downs ($28, 30 minutes), the Divide ($41, 1¼ hours) and Milford Sound ($53, 2¼ hours), one bus to/from Manapouri ($25, 30 minutes) and four daily to Queenstown ($47, 2¾ hours). In winter, services are by demand. Buses depart from near the Te Anau Lakeview Kiwi Holiday Park.

Milford Hwy

Sometimes the journey is the destination, and that's certainly true of the 119km stretch of road between Te Anau and Milford Sound (SH94). The Milford Hwy offers the most easily accessible experience of Fiordland in all its diversity, taking in expanses of beautiful beech forest, gentle river valleys, mirror-like lakes, exquisite alpine scenery and ending at arguably New Zealand's most breathtaking vista, Milford Sound.

The journey should take 2½ hours each way, but expect to spend time dawdling along walking trails and maxing out your camera's memory card. Most travellers embark on the Milford Hwy as a day trip from Te Anau, with a cruise on Milford Sound to break up the return journey. But the prospect of longer tramps or camping beneath jagged mountains might entice you to stay.

👁 Sights & Activities

Leaving Te Anau north along the Milford Hwy (SH94), the road meanders through rolling farmland atop the lateral moraine of the glacier that once gouged out Lake Te Anau. At the 29km mark it passes **Te Anau Downs**, where boats for the Milford Track depart. From here, an easy 45-minute return walk leads through forest to **Lake Mistletoe** (Te Anau Downs), a small glacier-formed lake.

The road then heads into the **Eglinton Valley**, at first pocketed with sheepy pasture, then reaching deeper wilderness immersion as it crosses the boundary into Fiordland National Park: knobby peaks, thick beech forest, lupin-lined river banks and grassy meadows.

Just past the **Mackay Creek Campsite** (at 51km) are the **Eglinton Flats**, a wide-open space exposing truly epic views of Pyramid Peak (2295m) and Ngatimamoe Peak

HUMBOLDT FALLS & GUNN'S CAMP

Three kilometres north of the Divide, look out for a northeasterly detour off SH94. Follow the unsealed road (leading to the Hollyford Track) for 8km to reach **Gunn's Camp**. Blow dust off antique agricultural implements in the **museum** (Hollyford Rd; adult/child $2/free; ⊙hours vary), or consider an overnight stay in an unvarnished cabin, heated by a wood-fired stove. A further 9km northeast of here begins the Hollyford Track, where you will find the track to **Humboldt Falls** (off Hollyford Rd) (30 minutes return). It's an easy 1.2km tramp through rainforest to a viewing platform where you can spy this distant 275m-high cascade.

(2164m). The most popular roadside stop is **Mirror Lakes** (SH94) (at 58km). A short boardwalk (five minutes' walk) overlooks glassy waters, their surface interrupted by occasional mallards. If you're lucky enough to stop by on a calm, clear day, the lakes perfectly reflect the mountains across the valley.

At the 77km mark, after an enchanting stretch of forest-framed road, is **Cascade Creek** and **Lake Gunn**. This area was known to Māori as O Tapara, and a stopover for parties heading to Anita Bay in search of *pounamu* (greenstone). The bewitching **Lake Gunn Nature Walk** (SH94) (45 minutes return) loops through tall red beech forest. Moss-clung logs and a chorus of birdsong create a fairy-tale atmosphere, and side trails lead to quiet lakeside beaches.

At 84km you pass across the **Divide**, the lowest east–west pass in the Southern Alps; from here the highway narrows and weaves. The roadside shelter is used by trampers either finishing or starting the Routeburn or Greenstone and Caples Tracks. From here you can embark on a marvellous three-hour return walk along the start of the Routeburn, climbing up through beech forest to the alpine tussockland of **Key Summit**. On a good day the views of the Humboldt and Darran Mountains are sure to knock your socks off, and the nature walk around the boggy tops and stunted beech is a great excuse to linger.

From the Divide, the road falls into the beech forest of the Hollyford Valley (stop at **Pop's View** (SH94) for a great outlook...if you can get a parking space). The road climbs through a cascade-tastic valley to the **Homer Tunnel**, 101km from Te Anau and framed by a high-walled, ice-carved amphitheatre. Begun as a relief project in the 1930s and completed in 1953, the tunnel is one way (traffic lights direct vehicle flow – patience required). Dark, rough-hewn and dripping with water, the 1270m-long tunnel emerges at the head of the spectacular **Cleddau Valley**. Any spare 'wows' might pop out about now. Kea (alpine parrots) hang around the tunnel entrance looking for food from tourists, but don't feed them as it's bad for their health.

About 10km before Milford Sound, the wheelchair- and pram-friendly **Chasm Walk** (SH94) (20 minutes return) affords staggering views over the churning Cleddau River. Pebbles caught in its frenetic currents have hollowed boulders into shapes reminiscent of a Salvador Dalí scene. Along the final 9km to Milford Sound, watch for glimpses of Mt Tutoko (2723m), Fiordland's highest peak, above the beech forest.

🛏 Sleeping

There are eight basic DOC campsites (per adult/child $8/4) along the highway. All are scenic but also popular with sandflies. If you prefer four walls to canvas or campervans, find more robust accommodation at **Knob's Flat** (📞03-249 9122; www.knobsflat.co.nz; 6178 SH94; unpowered tent or campervan sites per adult/child $20/10, d $130-150), or reserve a frontier-feel cabin at **Gunn's Camp** (www.gunnscamp.org.nz; Hollyford Rd; unpowered tent/campervan sites per person from $15, cabins $70, bed linen extra $7.50). Otherwise, you're better off returning to the abundant accommodation choices in Te Anau, 119km south.

❶ Getting There & Away

Check when you book bus tickets whether the operator is purely A-to-B or incorporates scenic lookouts.

InterCity (p617) runs twice-daily bus services to Milford Sound from Te Anau ($22 to $44, three hours) and Queenstown (from $44, six hours).

Naked Bus (p617) runs daily morning buses from Te Anau to Milford Sound (from $32, 2¼ hours).

From November to April Te Anau–based **Tracknet** (p612) has at least three daily scheduled buses to/from Te Anau Downs ($28, 30 minutes), the Divide ($41, 1¼ hours) and Milford Sound ($53, 2¼ hours). Two continue to Queenstown ($92, five hours). In winter (June to August), services are by demand.

Milford Sound

📞 03 / POP 120

The pot of gold at the end of Milford Hwy (SH94) is sublime Milford Sound (Piopiotahi). Rising above the fiord's indigo water is Mitre Peak (Rahotu), the deserved focal point of millions of photographs. Tapering to a cloud-piercing summit, the 1692m-high mountain appears sculpted by a divine hand.

In truth, it's the action of glaciers that carved these razor-edge cliffs. Scoured into the bare rock are pathways from tree avalanches, where entangled roots dragged whole forests down into darkly glittering water. When rain comes (and that's often), dozens of temporary waterfalls curtain the cliffs. Stirling and Lady Bowen Falls gush on in fine weather, with rainbows bouncing from their mists when sunlight strikes just right.

By 2019, Milford Sound will receive an estimated one million annual visitors – an almighty challenge to keep its beauty pristine. But out on the water, all human activity – cruise ships, divers, kayakers – seems dwarfed into insignificance.

🏃 Activities

Rosco's Milford Kayaks
KAYAKING

(📞 03-249 8500, 0800 476 726; www.roscosmilford kayaks.com; 72 Town Centre, Te Anau; trips $99-199; ⏰ Nov-Apr) Rosco, a colourful character seasoned by decades of kayaking experience, leads guided, tandem-kayak trips such as the 'Morning Glory' ($199), a challenging paddle the full length of the fiord to Anita Bay, and the 'Stirling Sunriser' ($195), which ventures beneath the 151m-high Stirling Falls. Beginners can take it easy on a two-hour paddle on the sound ($109).

Descend Scubadiving
DIVING

(📞 027 337 2363; www.descend.co.nz; dives incl gear $345) Black coral, more than 150 species of fish, the possibility of dolphins... Milford Sound is as beautiful underwater as is it above. Descend's six-hour trips offer a sampler of both realms: cruising on Milford Sound in a 7m catamaran and two dives along the way. There are excursions for experienced divers and novices. Transport, equipment, hot drinks and snacks included.

👉 Tours

Fiordland's most accessible experience is a cruise on Milford Sound, usually lasting 90 minutes or more. A slew of companies have booking desks in the flash cruise terminal, a 10-minute walk from the main car park, but it's always wiser to book ahead.

Each cruise company claims to be quieter, smaller, bigger, cheaper or in some way preferable to the rest. What really makes a difference is timing. Most bus tours aim for 1pm sailings, so if you avoid that time of day there will be fewer people on the boat, fewer boats on the water and fewer buses on the road.

If you're particularly keen on wildlife, opt for a cruise with a nature guide on board. These are usually a few minutes longer than the standard 'scenic' cruises, and often on smaller boats. Most companies offer coach transfers from Te Anau for an additional cost. Day trips from Queenstown make for a very long 13-hour day.

Arrive 20 minutes before departure. All cruises visit the mouth of the sound, just 15km from the wharf, poking their prows into the choppy waves of the Tasman Sea. Shorter cruises visit fewer en route 'highlights', which include Bowen Falls, Mitre Peak, Anita Bay and Stirling Falls.

Only visitable on trips run by Southern Discoveries and Mitre Peak Cruises, **Milford Discovery Centre** (www.southerndiscoveries. co.nz; Harrison Cove; adult/child $36/18; ⏰ 9am-4pm), New Zealand's only floating underwater observatory, showcases interactive displays on the natural environment of the fiord. The centre offers a chance to view corals, tube anemones and bottom-dwelling sea perch from 10m below the waterline.

⭐ Real Journeys
BOATING

(📞 0800 656 501, 03-249 7416; www.realjourneys. co.nz) 🚣 Milford's biggest and most venerable operator runs a popular 1¾-hour scenic cruise (adult/child from $76/22). More specialised is the 2½-hour nature cruise (adult/child from $88/22), which hones in on wildlife with commentary from a nature guide. Overnight cruises are also available, from which you can kayak and take nature tours in small boats en route.

Overnight trips depart from the cruise terminal in the mid-afternoon and return around 9.30am the following day. The *Milford Wanderer,* modelled on an old trading scow, accommodates 36 passengers in two- and four-bunk cabins with shared bathrooms (dorm/single/double $339/681/778). The *Milford Mariner* sleeps 60 in more-up-market single ($803) or double ($918) en suite cabins. Cheaper prices apply from

April through to September; food included but coach transport from Te Anau is extra.

Gilded with a long list of awards since it was founded in 1954, Real Journeys continues to be involved in local conservation efforts, from its minimal-impact cruises to fundraisers and charitable donations.

Cruise Milford
BOATING

(☏0800 645 367; www.cruisemilfordnz.com; adult/child from $95/18; ⏱10.45am, 12.45pm & 2.45pm) Offering a more personal touch than some of the big-boat tours, Cruise Milford's smaller vessels head out three times a day on 1¾-hour cruises, divulging great info from tectonics to wildlife.

Go Orange
BOATING

(☏03-442 7340, 0800 505 504; www.goorange.co.nz; adult/child from $45/15; ⏱9am, 12.30pm & 3pm) These low-cost two-hour cruises along the full length of Milford Sound include a complimentary breakfast, lunch or snack.

To see the sound from water level, book a trip with this operator's kayaking arm (☏03-442 7340; www.goorangekayaks.co.nz; ⏱Sep-Apr), such as the 'Milford Must Do' ($149, four hours on the water).

Mitre Peak Cruises
BOATING

(☏0800 744 633, 03-249 8110; www.mitrepeak.com; adult/child from $70/17) Two-hour cruises in smallish boats (maximum capacity 75), allowing closer waterfall and wildlife viewing than larger vessels. The 4.30pm cruise is a good choice because many larger boats are heading back at this time.

🛏 Sleeping

★Milford Sound Lodge
LODGE $$$

(☏03-249 8071; www.milfordlodge.com; SH94; powered campervan sites $60, dm $40, chalets $415-465; 🛜) Alongside the Cleddau River, 1.5km from the Milford hub, this lodge feels simultaneously rustic and chic. Luxurious chalets have the wow factor, with either jaw-on-the-floor mountain views or a river-side setting, while the forest-clad campervan area and clean, no-frills dorm rooms (sleeping five to 11 people) suit smaller budgets. Book far in advance for November to April.

ℹ Information

It's better to book a cruise in advance (and essential if you want an overnight cruise or a cruise-and-kayak combo). Otherwise, head straight to the cruise terminal to find booking desks for all the tour operators.

Although it's run by Southern Discoveries, the **Discover Milford Sound Information Centre** (☏03-249 7931; www.southerndiscoveries.co.nz; SH94; ⏱8am-4pm) near Milford's main car park sells tickets for most of the tour and cruise companies, as well as for scenic flights and InterCity buses. There's also a mediocre cafe attached.

ℹ Getting There & Away

BUS

InterCity (p617) runs twice-daily bus services to Milford Sound from Te Anau ($22-44, three hours) and Queenstown (from $44, six hours), onto which you can add a cruise or scenic flight when you book.

Naked Bus (p617) runs daily morning buses from Te Anau to Milford Sound (from $32, 2¼ hours) and coach-and-cruise packages from Queenstown (from $111).

From November to April Te Anau–based Tracknet (p612) has at least three daily scheduled buses to/from Te Anau Downs ($28, 30 minutes), the Divide ($41, 1¼ hours) and Milford Sound ($53, 2¼ hours). In winter (June to August), services are by demand.

CAR

Fill up with petrol in Te Anau before setting off. There are no petrol stations on the road to Milford Sound, and you'll want to avoid the high prices at Milford's self-serve petrol pump (the next closest, near Gunn's Camp (p618), is also costly and only accepts cash).

Snow chains must be carried on ice- and avalanche-risk days from May to November (there will be signs on the road), and can be hired from service stations in Te Anau.

Manapouri

☏03 / POP 400

Manapouri, 20km south of Te Anau, is the jumping-off point for cruises to Doubtful Sound. Most visitors head straight to the boat harbour for the ferry to the West Arm of Lake Manapouri, known to early Māori as Roto Ua or 'rainy lake', and later as Moturau, the 'many island lake'.

But little Manapouri has a few tricks up its sleeve. The town can't compete with Te Anau's abundance of restaurants and motels but it has mountain-backed lake views easily as lovely as those enjoyed by its bigger, more popular sibling. At 440m, Lake Manapouri is the second-deepest lake in New Zealand. And with far fewer overnight visitors than Te Anau, you can enjoy the spectacular sunsets all to yourself.

🏃 Activities

The **Kepler Track** is accessible from the northern end of Lake Manapouri at Rainbow Reach, 10km north of town. Manapouri is also a staging point for the remote **Dusky Track**, a highly challenging 84km tramp taking eight to 10 days. For more information contact DOC.

By crossing the Waiau River at Pearl Harbour (p622) you can embark on day walks as detailed in DOC's *Fiordland Day Walks* brochure. A classic circuit with glimmering lake views (and occasional steep parts) is the **Circle Track** (3½ hours), which can be extended to **Hope Arm** (five to six hours return). You can cross the river aboard a hired row boat or water taxi from **Adventure Manapouri** (☑ 03-249 8070, 021 925 577; www.adventuremanapouri.co.nz; row boat hire per day $40, water taxi per person return $20), which also offers guided walks and fishing tours.

Running between the northern entrance to Manapouri township and Pearl Harbour, the one-hour **Frasers Beach** walk offers picnic and swimming spots as well as fantastic views across the lake.

Adventure Kayak & Cruise   KAYAKING
(☑ 0800 324 966, 03-249 6626; http://kayaksandcruises.co.nz; 33 Waiau St; ☺ Oct-Apr) Rents kayaks from $50 per day for paddles on Lake Manapouri. In the interests of safety, it will only rent to groups of two or more (who have prior paddling experience), and it provides VHF radios free of charge. It also offers cruises on Lake Manapouri (prices depend on program and group size).

🛏 Sleeping & Eating

Possum Lodge   HOLIDAY PARK $
(☑ 03-249 6623; www.possumlodge.co.nz; 13 Murrell Ave; campervan sites $34-39, dm $25, units with/without bathroom $110/59; 🛜) Nestled into forest by the lake, Possum Lodge is old-fashioned in the best kind of way. Hospitable hosts preside over basic cabins, timeworn motels, enviably green campervan sites, laundry facilities and a fully equipped kitchen. Peace, quiet and a short walk to the riverbank: what more could you need? Oh that's right, unlimited wi-fi...done.

Freestone Backpackers   HOSTEL $
(☑ 03-249 6893; www.freestone.co.nz; 270 Hillside Rd; dm $25, d with/without bathroom $86/75; 🛜) Sprinkled across a hillside about 3km east of town, these cabins are styled like little hunting lodges (antlers, potbelly stoves);

OFF THE BEATEN TRACK

SOUTHERN SCENIC ROUTE

The Southern Scenic Route skirts lonesome beaches, forest-clad lakes and jaw-dropping lookout points, cutting a lazy arc from Queenstown to Te Anau, Manapouri, Tuatapere, Riverton and Invercargill. From Invercargill it continues east and then north through the Catlins to Dunedin. Yes, there are more direct routes than this 610km meander, but we can't think of a better excuse to dawdle through the South Island. See www.southernscenicroute.co.nz or pick up the free *Southern Scenic Route* map to join all the dots.

the loftiest have terraces with ringside seats to the best mountain sunsets for miles. Bathrooms are basic and communal. A converted family home offers another eight beds for singles, doubles and twins, with communal facilities including a full kitchen.

The Church   PUB FOOD $$
(☑ 03-249 6001; www.facebook.com/pg/manapouri.co.nz; 23 Waiau St; mains $17-25; ☺ 11am-10pm Sun-Thu, to midnight Fri & Sat) No need to head up to Te Anau for a satisfying feed and a few beers, hurrah! Plates heavy with steaks, burgers and butter chicken are hauled to tables in this converted church building, now a merry pub with exceptionally welcoming staff.

ⓘ Getting There & Away

Topline Tours (p612) offers year-round shuttles between Te Anau and Manapouri ($20).

Tracknet (p612) runs one daily bus to/from Te Anau ($25, 30 minutes) from November to April, and on demand at other times of the year.

Doubtful Sound

Remote Doubtful Sound is humbling in size and beauty. Carved by glaciers, it's one of New Zealand's largest fiords – almost three times the length of more popular Milford. Boats gliding through this maze of forested valleys have good chances of encountering fur seals and Fiordland penguins. Aside from haunting birdsong, Doubtful Sound deserves its Māori name, Patea, the 'place of silence'.

Until relatively recently, Doubtful Sound was isolated from all but intrepid explorers. Even Captain Cook only observed it from off the coast in 1770, because he was 'doubtful' whether winds would be sufficient to blow the ship back to sea. Access improved when the road over Wilmot Pass opened in 1959 to facilitate construction of West Arm power station.

Boat and coach transfers from Manapouri to Deep Cove are easily organised through tour operators, but time-consuming enough to deter some travellers...ideal for those who want to enjoy the silence.

☞ Tours

Day cruises allow about three hours on the water (once you've factored in transport time to the sound). Overnight cruises are pricey but preferable; they include meals plus the option of fishing and kayaking, depending on the weather.

★ Real Journeys CRUISE
(☎0800 656 501; www.realjourneys.co.nz) 🚢 A family-run tourism trailblazer, Real Journeys is ecofriendly, and just plain friendly. One-day 'wilderness cruises' (adult/child from $250/65) include a three-hour journey aboard a modern catamaran with a specialist nature guide. The overnight cruise, which runs from September to May, is aboard the *Fiordland Navigator*, which sleeps 70 in en suite cabins (quad-share per adult/child from $419/210, single/double from $1171/1338).

Fiordland Expeditions CRUISE
(☎0508 888 656, 03-249 9005; www.fiordland expeditions.co.nz; dm/s/d/tr from $645/1340/1420/2130; 🐕) A classy operator offering overnight cruises on the *Tutoko II* (maximum 14 passengers). It's a standard Doubtful Sound program plus fishing for your dinner and a welcome drink of bubbly. Fiordland Expeditions also operates cruises in winter (June to August), if more time on the water (a full two days) and absolute tranquillity appeal.

Deep Cove Charters CRUISE
(☎03-249 6828; https://doubtfulsoundcruise. nz; s $550, cabins tw/d $1300/1400) Overnight cruises on board the *Seafinn* (maximum 12 passengers) run by home-grown crew who nimbly tailor the cruise to the day's weather and wildlife-spotting conditions. There are options to kayak and fish but they had us at 'crayfish lunch and venison supper included'.

Doubtful Sound Kayak KAYAKING
(☎03-249 7777, 0800 452 9257; www.fiordland adventure.co.nz; day tours $299; ⊙Oct-Apr) Runs day trips to Doubtful Sound, including four hours paddling time, suitable for beginners or seasoned kayakers.

❶ Getting There & Away

Getting to Doubtful Sound involves boarding a boat at **Pearl Harbour** (Waiau St, Manapouri) in Manapouri for a one-hour trip to West Arm power station, followed by a 22km (40-minute) drive over Wilmot Pass to Deep Cove (permanent population: two), where you hop aboard a boat for your cruise on the sound. Manapouri is the easiest place to base yourself, although Te Anau (20km) and Queenstown (170km) pick-ups are readily organised through the cruise-boat operators.

CENTRAL SOUTHLAND

Sandwiched between world-famous Fiordland National Park and the scene-stealing Catlins, Central Southland is often forgotten about by travellers. But its peaceful farmland and savage coast form a memorable contrast, while its seam of small-town quirk is heaps of fun.

There's Gore, with a proud history of moonshine distilling; oyster-mad Bluff; and Tuatapere, as famous for challenging tramping trails as it is for sausages. Invercargill, the closest thing to a city slicker in Central Southland, has a long-standing revhead culture and a slew of impressive museums dedicated to classic cars, fast bikes and big diggers. Confused? This is a region where departing the beaten track is inevitable and going local reaps big rewards.

Tuatapere

🌐 03 / POP 558
Formerly a timber-milling town, sleepy Tuatapere is gently shaken awake by trampers who pass through before embarking on the Hump Ridge or Dusky Tracks. The town's early woodcutters were very efficient, so only a remnant of a once-large tract of native podocarp (conifer) forest remains.

Still capitalising on a 1988 victory in a sausage-making competition, Tuatapere styles itself as New Zealand's sausage capital – scoff some snags, ride the rapids of the Waiau River by jetboat, and you'll do this low-slung town justice.

🏃 Activities

Hump Ridge Track

This three-day, 61km track is rich in natural and cultural history, from coastal and alpine scenery to the relics of a historic timber town. The tramping days are long (up to nine hours on the first two days, ascending 890m on the first) and the terrain suits intermediate-level trampers. There's bird life aplenty, and the chance to see Hector's dolphins on the lonely windswept coast. En route the path crosses a number of towering historic wooden viaducts, including NZ's highest.

To hike the track you need to book through the Tuatapere Hump Ridge Track Information Centre. Packages include transport to the trailhead (at Rarakau, 19km from Tuatapere) and comfortable lodge accommodation. The tramp is possible year-round and operates in three seasonal bands, priced accordingly (from $175), with guided tramps also available. Advance bookings are essential.

Dusky Track

A swathe of wilderness surrounds Lake Hauroko, west of Tuatapere, reached by a mostly unsealed 32km road. Lined with dark, brooding, steeply forested slopes, it's the deepest lake in NZ (462m). The challenging, 84km Dusky Track between here and Lake Manapouri begins (or ends) on its northern shores. An epic one-way journey of eight to 10 days, the Dusky Track only suits trampers at the top of their game: you'll wobble across three-wire bridges and wade through mud.

Book a boat with Tuatapere-based **Lake Hauroko Tours** (☑0800 376 174, 03-225 5677; www.duskytrack.co.nz; track transport $99; ☺Nov-Apr) to access the trailhead (Mondays and Thursdays scheduled, other days by arrangement). Trips & Tramps (p615) offers transport ($50 per head) from Te Anau to **Clifden Suspension Bridge**, 12km north of Tuatapere, timed to meet boats near their launching point to the Dusky Track trailhead.

🚌 Tours

Wairaurahiri Wilderness Jet   BOATING
(☑0800 270 556; www.river-jet.co.nz; 17 Main Street, Otautau; day tours from $230) Offers jet-boat rides on the Wairaurahiri River, packaged together with a guided forest walk (total six hours). Other options include a jetboat-helicopter combo or overnighting at the remote Waitutu Lodge.

ℹ️ Information

Tuatapere Hump Ridge Track Information Centre (☑0800 486 774, 03-226 6739; www.humpridgetrack.co.nz; 31 Orawia Rd; ☺7.30am-6pm Nov-Mar, limited hours Apr-Oct) Assists with local information, Hump Ridge hut passes and transport. Call ahead if you're passing through between April and October.

ℹ️ Getting There & Away

Tuatapere is on the meandering Southern Scenic Route between Queenstown and Dunedin. It's 200km south of Queenstown and 80km west of Invercargill.

Buses must be booked through the Tuatapere Hump Ridge Track Information Centre; with demand, services go to/from Queenstown ($95, three hours), Te Anau ($50, 1½ hours) and Invercargill ($60, one hour).

Te Waewae & Colac Bays

Between Tuatapere and Riverton on SH99, a section of the Southern Scenic Route, these long, moody bays set a steely glare towards Antarctica. Colac Bay has a small but dedicated following among hardy surfers, but most travellers simply stop for a brisk dip or beach stroll before continuing the drive.

Driving west to east along SH99, pause at **McCracken's Rest** (SH99), the most impressive lookout point along the Southern Scenic Route. Admire views of wind-lashed Te Waewae Bay (and, if you're lucky Hector's dolphins and southern right whales). Seven kilometres further, stroll along the sparkly sands at Orepuki, aka **Gemstone Beach**, before continuing a further 4km towards **Monkey Island** (off SH99, Orepuki), a former Māori whaling lookout.

If you're travelling from the east, driving this stretch of SH99 provides a first glimpse of the snowcapped Southern Alps descending into the sea, framing the western end of the bay.

🍴 Eating

⭐ **Orepuki Beach Cafe**   CAFE $$
(☑03-234 5211; www.facebook.com/pg/orepuki beachcafe; cnr Dudley St & Stafford St (SH99), Orepuki; mains $19-29; ☺9am-5pm Sun-Thu, to 11pm Fri & Sat; ☑) What's this? A beacon of gastronomic hope, beaming out good vibes and delicious aromas along a desolate stretch of highway? This chipper cafe has soups, samosas, risottos and a rack of

homemade cakes. Bigger feeds, like salmon fettuccine and lamb with plum sauce, have a sprinkling of sophistication, but the atmosphere is pure seaside charm.

ⓘ Getting There & Away

Te Waewae and Colac Bays extend between Tuatapere and Invercargill, along SH99. There is no public transport along this remote stretch of coast.

Riverton

📱 03 / POP 1430

Quiet little Riverton (in Māori, Aparima) is worth a detour for its dreamy bay views and gripping museum of local history. If near-Antarctic swimming takes your fancy, the long, broad sands of **Taramea Bay** are good for a dip; otherwise we suggest a stroll along **Palmerston St**, studded with cafes and 19th-century buildings. Riverton makes a good lunch stop if you're driving the Southern Scenic Route, or a pleasantly laid-back day trip from Invercargill, 38km east.

ⓞ Sights

★ **Te Hikoi Southern Journey**   MUSEUM
(📱 03-234 8260; www.tehikoi.co.nz; 172 Palmerston St; adult/child $8/free; ⓞ 10am-4pm Apr-Sep, to 5pm Oct-Mar) Oh, that all small-town museums could be this good! This riveting museum starts with a 16-minute film dramatising key events in the region's history, including the arrival of the first European seal hunters (fiercely met by the local Māori). Legends behind the landscape are entertainingly told, as are anecdotes about characters from cabbage-tree rum distillers to the first recorded Pākehā (white European) Māori, James Caddell.

✕ Eating

★ **Beach House**   MODERN NZ $$
(📱 03-234 8274; http://beachhouseriverton.co.nz; 126 Rocks Hwy; mains lunch $17-32, dinner $27-39; ⓞ 10am-10pm Wed-Sun, to 4pm Mon & Tue; 🛜🅿️) Looking over Taramea Bay, Beach House is a stylish, comfortable cafe famous for seafood, especially its creamy chowder studded with juicy mussels and hunks of salmon. On a sunny day with a warm breeze wafting off Foveaux Strait, the outside tables are a must. The other 90% of the time, retire inside to admire the view through the windows.

ⓘ Getting There & Away

Riverton is on SH99, the section of the Southern Scenic Route between Tuatapere (47km) and Invercargill (36km). There are no public transport connections.

Invercargill

📱 03 / POP 51,700

Don't underestimate Invercargill... Sure, it usually serves as a pit stop between Fiordland and the Catlins (or en route to Stewart Island/Rakiura), but its combination of motor-sport mania, historic buildings and friendly folk might win you over.

Invercargill has long been a revhead's heaven, thanks in part to local legend Burt Munro, who claimed an overland speed world record by motorcycle, but now there's a trio of motoring museums and attractions. A craft brewery and a scattering of good restaurants might also lengthen your stay in this slow-burner of a city.

ⓞ Sights

The streets of Invercargill boast a slew of 19th-century buildings. Eighteen landmarks are described in the *Invercargill Heritage Trail* brochure while the *Short Walks* brochure details various walks in and around the town; get both from the i-SITE (p626).

★ **Bill Richardson Transport World**   MUSEUM
(📱 03-217 0199; www.transportworld.co.nz; 491 Tay St; adult/child $25/15; ⓞ 10am-5pm; ♿) A kingdom of shiny chrome lies beyond the doors of Transport World, touted as the largest private automotive museum on the planet. Across 15,000 sq m of warehouse space you'll find classic cars, hulking tractors and vintage petrol pumps (even the bathrooms are on theme). Kids' play areas, a miniature movie theatre, displays of fashions of yesteryear and a great cafe round out Transport World as a crowd-pleaser, rather than just one for the petrol-heads.

Revved up for more? Smaller museum **Classic Motorcycle Mecca** (📱 03-217 0199; www.transportworld.co.nz; 25 Tay St; adult/child $20/10; ⓞ 10am-5pm) holds a collection of bikes, while **Dig This** (📱 03-217 0199; www.transportworld.co.nz; 84 Otepuni Ave; ⓞ 9am-6pm Wed-Sun; ♿) puts you behind the controls of a bulldozer to dig ditches and stack tyres.

A 'Turbo Pass' (adult/child $40/20) grants access to both Transport World and Classic Motorcycle Mecca.

Invercargill

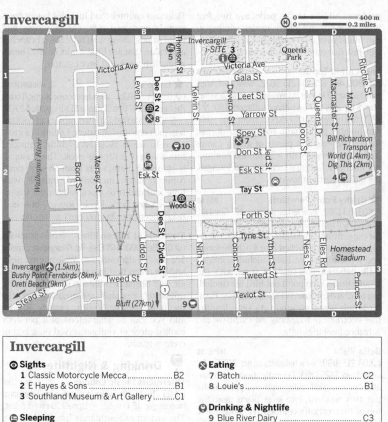

Invercargill

⊙ Sights
1 Classic Motorcycle Mecca	B2
2 E Hayes & Sons	B1
3 Southland Museum & Art Gallery	C1

🛏 Sleeping
4 Bella Vista	D2
5 Southern Comfort Backpackers	B1
6 Victoria Railway Hotel	B2

🍴 Eating
7 Batch	C2
8 Louie's	B1

🍸 Drinking & Nightlife
9 Blue River Dairy	C3
10 Tillermans Music Lounge	B2

Southland Museum & Art Gallery MUSEUM
(☏03-219 9069; www.southlandmuseum.com; Queens Park, 108 Gala St; ⊙9am-5pm Mon-Fri, from 10am Sat & Sun) **FREE** Adjoining the local visitor centre in a big white pyramid (à la the Louvre?), Invercargill's cultural hub has permanent displays on Southland's natural and human history, recounting plenty of maritime exploits. The museum's rock stars are undoubtedly the tuatara, NZ's unique lizard-like reptiles, unchanged for 220 million years. Slow-moving patriarch Henry, more than 110 years old, holds a world record for living in captivity more than 46 years.

E Hayes & Sons MUSEUM
(☏03-218 2059; www.ehayes.co.nz; 168 Dee St; ⊙7.30am-5.30pm Mon-Fri, 10am-4pm Sat & Sun) **FREE** Hardware shops aren't usually a must-

see, but this one holds a piece of motoring history. In among the aisles of bolts, barbecues and brooms in this classic art-deco building are more than 100 items of motoring memorabilia, including the actual motorbike on which the late Burt Munro broke the world speed record (as immortalised in the 2005 film *The World's Fastest Indian*, starring Sir Anthony Hopkins).

🛏 Sleeping

⭐ Southern Comfort
Backpackers HOSTEL $
(☏03-2183838;www.southerncomfortbackpackers. com; 30 Thomson St, Avenal; dm/d from $32/72; @) With a mix of snug and swish, this large Victorian house has a lounge with fireplace, fully equipped kitchen and peaceful

gardens. Adding to the perks are two free bikes, laundry and a herb garden where you can pluck your own garnish. A restful package, just five minutes' walk from town.

Invercargill Top 10 HOLIDAY PARK $

(☑0800 486 873, 03-215 9032; www.invercargill top10.co.nz; 77 McIvor Rd, Waikiwi; campervan sites from $42, units $105, d without bathroom $80; ☎) 🖉 You know what to expect from this well-run holiday park chain: backpacker dorms, modern motels and plenty of grassy camping space, always with well-tended communal kitchens, laundry facilities and lounges. It's 6.5km north of town.

★ Bushy Point Fernbirds B&B $$

(☑03-213 1302; www.fernbirds.co.nz; 197 Grant Rd, Otatara; s/d incl breakfast $160/170) 🖉 A haven for the ornithologically inclined, this 25-year-old guesthouse is tucked into a private forest and wetland reserve. Rates include a guided walk between 600-year-old trees with the affable hosts, who point out bird life (including fernbirds, of course) along the way. Fernbirds only hosts one group at a time, lending this ecofriendly hideaway an exclusive air. Advance bookings only.

Bella Vista MOTEL $$

(☑03-217 9799; www.bellavista.co.nz; 240 Tay St; units from $125; ☎) Friendly hosts, reasonable prices and tidy, well-equipped units put this modern, two-level place near the top of Invercargill's competitive motel pack. Units range from cosy studios with tea- and toast-making facilities, to two-bedroom apartments with full kitchens (from $165).

Victoria Railway Hotel HOTEL $$

(☑0800 777 557, 03-218 1281; www.hotel invercargill.com; cnr Leven & Esk Sts; r $145-195; ☎) This beautifully restored 1896 building is awash in nostalgia. With old portraits and an old-fashioned bar, the dining area feels like a snapshot of more genteel times, amplified by kind, personalised service. The 11 rooms aren't as stately as the common areas, though comfy beds, crimson drapes and sloped ceilings are refined enough to encourage dreams of a grander past.

✖ Eating

★ Batch CAFE $$

(☑03-214 6357; 173 Spey St; mains $13-20; ☺7am-4pm Mon-Fri, from 8am Sat & Sun; ☎🖉) Large, shared tables, a relaxed beachy ambience, and top-notch coffee and smoothies give this cafe its reputation as Southland's best.

Delicious counter food includes bagels, generously crammed rolls, cheese scones and great salads, along with full-blown brunches and cakes that are little works of art. There's a smallish wine and beer list, too.

★ Louie's MODERN NZ $$

(☑03-214 2913; www.facebook.com/pg/Louies Restaurant; 142 Dee St; tapas $13-16, mains $29-32; ☺5.30pm-late Wed-Sat) Part tapas and cocktail bar, part chic fusion eatery, Louie's is a great place to while away an evening, snuggled into a sofa or a fireside nook. The seasonally changing menu veers from creative tapas (venison tacos, muttonbird, mussels with lime and chilli) to more substantial mains. Slow-cooked pork, locally sourced blue cod, magnificent steaks...you can't go wrong.

Elegance at 148 on Elles FRENCH, BRITISH $$$

(☑03-216 1000; 148 Elles Rd, Georgetown; mains $28-38; ☺6-11pm Mon-Sat) Welcome to 1984, and we mean that in a completely affectionate way. Elegance is the sort of old-fashioned, upmarket, regional restaurant where the menu is vaguely French, vaguely British, and you can be guaranteed of a perfectly cooked piece of venison served on a bed of creamy mash.

🍷 Drinking & Nightlife

Tillermans Music Lounge BAR, CLUB

(☑03-218 9240; www.facebook.com/tillermans. invercargill; 16 Don St; ☺11pm-3.30am Fri & Sat) The saviour of Southland's live-music scene, Mr Tillerman's venue hosts everything from thrash to flash, with a battered old dance floor to show for it. Visit the fun downstairs Vinyl Bar, which is open from 8pm, to find out what's coming up.

ℹ Information

Invercargill i-SITE (☑03-211 0895; www.invercargillnz.com; Queens Park, 108 Gala St; ☺8.30am-5pm Mon-Fri, to 4pm Sat & Sun) Sharing the Southland Museum (p625) pyramid, the i-SITE can help with general enquiries and is a godsend if you're stuck for Stewart Island/Rakiura or Catlins accommodation options. Staff are brimming with insights into local tramping trails, and can advise on transport.

ℹ Getting There & Away

AIR

Air New Zealand (www.airnewzealand.com) flights link Invercargill to Christchurch (from $159) and Wellington (from $208) multiple times per day.

Stewart Island Flights (p638) connects Invercargill to Stewart Island/Rakiura three times a day year-round.

BUS
Buses leave from the Invercargill i-SITE, where you can also book your tickets.

Catch-a-Bus South (☑ 03-214 4014, 24hr 027 449 7994; www.catchabussouth.co.nz) offers scheduled shuttle services at least daily to Bluff ($22, 35 minutes), Queenstown and Queenstown Airport ($60, 3–3¼ hours), Gore ($28, 1½ hours) and Dunedin ($57 to $60, 3½ hours). Bookings essential; reserve by 4pm on the day before you travel.

InterCity (☑ Dunedin 03-471 7143; www.intercity.co.nz) runs direct coaches to and from Gore ($1 to $13, one hour, two daily), Queenstown Airport ($49, 3½ hours, daily) and Queenstown (from $38, 3¾ hours, daily).

Naked Bus (p617) runs twice daily buses to and from Gore ($1 to $13, 50 minutes, two daily), Dunedin (from $24, 3½ hours) and Queenstown (from $35, 3¾ hours).

ⓘ Getting Around

Invercargill Airport (☑ 03-218 6920; www.invercargillairport.co.nz; 106 Airport Ave) is 3km west of central Invercargill. The door-to-door **Executive Car Service** (☑ 03-214 3434; https://executivecarservice.co.nz) costs around $15 from the city centre; more for residential pick-up. By taxi it's around $20; try **Blue Star Taxis** (☑ 03-217 7777; www.bluestartaxis.co.nz; 158 Tay St).

Bluff

☑ 03 / POP 1794

Mention Bluff to any New Zealander and we bet they'll think of oysters. Bluff is Invercargill's port, windswept and more than a little bleak, located at the end of a protruding strip of land, 27km south of the city. Bluff's bulging bivalves are among the South Island's most prized produce, guzzled with gusto between March and August, and feted with a festival in May.

Outside oyster season, the main reason folk come here is to catch the ferry to Stewart Island/Rakiura, catch some maritime nostalgia at the museum, or pose for photos beside the Stirling Point signpost.

⊙ Sights

Bluff Maritime Museum   MUSEUM
(☑ 03-212 7534; 241 Foreshore Rd; adult/child $3/1; ⊙ 10am-3.30pm Mon-Fri year-round, plus 12.30-4.30pm Sat & Sun Oct-Apr; 🖐) Salty tales

---

BLUFF OYSTERS

Bluff oysters are in huge demand from the minute they come into season (late March to late August). Top restaurants as far away as Auckland compete to be the first to add them to their menus. As oysters go, they're whoppers. Don't expect to be able to slurp one down in a dainty gulp – these beasts take some chewing. If you want to know what all the fuss is about, you can buy fresh or battered Bluff oysters when they're in season from Fowlers Oysters. Up by the signpost for **Stirling Point** (off SH1) is **Oyster Cove** (☑ 03-212 8855; www.oystercove.co.nz; 8 Ward Pde; half-dozen oysters $39, mains $18-40; ⊙ 11am-7.30pm; 🖐), where you can guzzle oysters while admiring sea views through floor-to-ceiling windows. Or time your visit for the annual Bluff Oyster & Food Festival in May.

---

whisper from the portholes, driftwood and barnacle-clung planks displayed at Bluff's small museum. The best part is clambering aboard the *Monica* and posing at the control of this 1909 oystering ship, though steam and pump engines (which clank to action at the touch of a button) come a close second.

The museum also houses interesting displays on Bluff history and on the annual tītī (muttonbird) harvest, an important tradition for local Māori.

⚡ Festivals & Events

Bluff Oyster & Food Festival   FOOD & DRINK
(www.bluffoysterfest.co.nz; ⊙ May) Celebrate Bluff's most famous export at this one-day winter festival, with oyster-eating contests, live music and other mollusc-themed merriment.

✕ Eating

Fowlers Oysters   SEAFOOD **$$**
(☑ 03-212 8792; www.facebook.com/fowlersoysters; Ocean Beach Rd; half-dozen cooked $14.50, dozen raw from $24; ⊙ 9am-7pm Mar-Aug) Whether you like your oysters battered or freshly shucked, stop at Fowlers during oyster season for the best bivalves on the South Island. It's on the left-hand side as you head into Bluff. Battered blue cod and hot dogs are available for those squeamish about slurping on molluscs.

WORTH A TRIP

GORE

Around 66km northeast of Invercargill, Gore (population 12,033) struts to its own beat. The town declares itself New Zealand's 'home of country music', and when it isn't strumming its way through the **Gold Guitar Awards** (www.goldguitars.co.nz; ⊙ early Jun) – for which you'll need to book your beds well in advance – it celebrates moonshine-distilling history, vintage aircraft and local art with a trio of distinctive museums.

The **Hokonui Heritage Centre** (☑ 03-208 7032; 16 Hokonui Dr; ⊙ 8.30am-5pm Mon-Fri, 9.30am-4pm Sat, 1-4pm Sun) **FREE** incorporates the Gore Visitor Centre, the Gore Historical Museum and the **Hokonui Moonshine Museum** (☑ 03-208 9907; www.hokonuiwhiskey.com; 16 Hokonui Dr; adult/child $5/free; ⊙ 8.30am-5pm Mon-Fri, 9.30am-4pm Sat, 1-4pm Sun). Together they celebrate the town's proud history of fishing, farming and illegal distilleries. The Historical Museum exhibits a more-intriguing-than-average collection, ranging from a taxidermied mollymawk bird to grandfather clocks and sparkling antiques, alongside tender homages to local passions such as angling and country music. Admission to the Moonshine Museum includes a wee dram of local whisky.

Nicknamed the 'Goreggenheim', the **Eastern Southland Gallery** (☑ 03-208 9907; www. facebook.com/easternsouthlandgallery; 14 Hokonui Dr; ⊙ 10am-4.30pm Mon-Fri, 1-4pm Sat & Sun) **FREE** has an impressive treasury of contemporary New Zealand art, including a large Ralph Hotere collection, as well as fascinating indigenous folk art from West Africa and Australia.

Aircraft from the 1920s and '30s are lovingly restored and showcased at the **Croydon Aviation Heritage Centre** (☑ 03-208 6046; www.experiencemandeville.com/museum; 1558 Waimea Hwy, SH94; adult/child $10/free; ⊙ 9.30am-4.30pm Mon-Fri, 11am-3pm Sat & Sun) warehouse, 16km northwest of Gore on SH94 (towards Queenstown). You can also book a flight in a two-seater 1930s Tiger Moth biplane or other diminutive aircraft (from $150 for a 15-minute flight).

❶ Getting There & Away

Catch-a-Bus South (☑ 03-479 9960; www. catchabussouth.co.nz) offers scheduled shuttle services to Invercargill ($22, 30 minutes, four daily), Gore ($44, two hours, one or two daily) and Dunedin ($75, four hours, one or two daily). With prior notice, daily buses from Invercargill to Queenstown Airport ($75, 3½ hours) and Queenstown ($70, 3¾ hours) can include pick-up in Bluff.

Stewart Island Experience (p636) runs a shuttle between Bluff and Invercargill connecting with its Stewart Island/Rakiura ferry. Transfers from Te Anau and Queenstown to Bluff are available from late October to late April. It also offers secure vehicle storage by the ferry terminal ($10 for 24 hours).

THE CATLINS

The Catlins' meandering roads thread together a medley of pretty-as-a-picture landscapes. Bypassed entirely by SH1, this southeasterly swathe of the South Island is a road-tripper's dream. Narrow, winding roads weave past golden-sand bays, zip through bucolic meadows and trace boulder-studded coast, while gravelly detours expose you to startled sheep and even more startled farmers. Eventful

drives are part of the fun of reaching beauty spots like Roaring Bay (p632), moodily monochromatic Purakaunui Falls (p631) and forlorn Waipapā Lighthouse. But numerous natural stunners – like Lake Wilkie (p631) and Nugget Point (p632) – are only a short, flat walk from the car park. Too easy.

Over centuries, semi-nomadic Māori came to the Catlins to make canoes from local timber. In the 19th century, European whalers and sealers arrived (the region is named after a whaling captain). Though increasingly popular with visitors, the sparse Catlins retain a faraway feel – especially when an Antarctic southerly blasts in...

Flora & Fauna

The Catlins is a wonderful place for independent wildlife watching. Fur seals and sea lions laze along the coast, while in spring migratory southern right whales are occasionally spotted. Dolphins are also frequent visitors.

Unlike much of Southland, tall kahikatea, totara and rimu forests still exist in the Catlins. Prolific bird life includes tui, bellbird, kereru (wood pigeon), the endangered yellow-eyed penguin and the rare mohua (yellowhead).

ℹ Information

Get maps and local tips at the small Owaka Museum & Catlins Information Centre (p631) and the even smaller **Waikawa Museum & Information Centre** (☑ 03-246 8464; waikawa museum@hyper.net.nz; 604 Niagara–Waikawa Rd; museum admission by donation; ⊙10am-5pm). En route to the Catlins, you can also grab lots of info from the i-SITEs in Invercargill and **Balclutha** (☑ 03-418 0388; www.cluthanz.com; 4 Clyde St, Balclutha; ⊙ 8.30am-5pm Mon-Fri, 9.30am-3pm Sat & Sun).

For further information, see www.catlins.org. nz and www.catlins-nz.com.

There are no banks in the Catlins but there's an ATM at the **Four Square** (☑ 03-415 8201; 3 Ovenden St; ⊙7.30am-7pm) supermarket in Owaka. Most businesses accept credit cards but we recommend bringing some cash.

ℹ Getting There & Away

There is no public transport in the Catlins area so you'll need your own vehicle to get around. From Invercargill you can reach the westerly end of the Catlins, Fortrose, on a 45km drive. From Dunedin, it's an 80km drive southwest to Balclutha, the Catlins' easterly gateway town.

Curio Bay & Around

Chasing sun and surf, droves of holiday-makers descend on Curio Bay in summer. For beach-lovers the focal point is Porpoise Bay, a reliably wave-lashed arc of sand and arguably the best swimming beach in the Catlins. Blue penguins nest in the dunes and in summer (December to February) Hector's dolphins come here to rear their young.

Nearby, other natural curiosities merit a visit: a Jurassic-age forest lies just south in Curio Bay while 15km west is the trailhead for a short walk to Slope Point, South Island's most southerly point.

Curio Bay is whisper-quiet in winter (June to August). Regardless of the season, it's handy to bring food provisions and a full tank of fuel along this sparse stretch of coast.

◉ Sights & Activities

⭐**Slope Point**   LANDMARK
(Slope Point Rd, Haldane) South Island's true southerly point lies not in Bluff, as many mistakenly believe, but at the end of a 20-minute hike through cliffside meadows. From the trailhead, walk towards the sea and veer left along the fencing; a humble signpost marks this spectacular spot where blackened rocks tumble into turquoise sea while waves smash and swirl below.

Signs south from Haldane point the way. The car park at the start of the track is 4km south of Slope Point Accommodation, along a gravel road.

Petrified Forest   NATURAL FEATURE
(Curio Bay) Marvel at the rare phenomenon of fossilised forest, extending south of Curio Bay. Preserved by silica in the ashy floodwaters that submerged these Jurassic-era trees, craggy stumps create a dramatic contrast with the frothing waves. The petrified forest is visible for around four hours either side of low tide.

Yellow-eyed penguins waddle ashore here an hour or so before sunset. Do the right thing and keep your distance.

Waipapā Lighthouse   LIGHTHOUSE
(Waipapā Lighthouse Rd, Otara) FREE Standing on a desolate but beautiful point surrounded by farmland, this 13.4m lighthouse was built after the SS *Tararua* disaster, an 1881 shipwreck that claimed 131 lives. The lighthouse was built three years later, to avert future tragedy on these rocky shores. The beach below is home to fur seals and sea lions (keep a safe distance). The turn-off to Waipapā Point is at Otara, 12km southeast of Fortrose.

Catlins Surf   SURFING
(☑ 03-246 8552; www.catlins-surf.co.nz; 601 Curio Bay Rd; 2hr lesson $60, full gear hire per 3½hr/day $45/65) Based at the Curio Bay Holiday Park, this surf school offers lessons on Porpoise Bay, much to the amusement of any passing dolphins. If you're already confident on the waves, you can hire a board, wet suit (very necessary) and flippers. Owner Nick also offers stand-up paddle boarding tuition ($75, 2½ hours).

🛏 Sleeping

Slope Point Accommodation GUESTHOUSE $
(☑ 03-246 8420; www.slopepoint.co.nz; 164 Slope Point Rd, Slope Point; tent sites from $15, powered sites $30, d with/without bathroom $90/50; 🐾) In the midst of a working farm 4km north of Slope Point, this family-run accommodation plunges you into the rhythms of rural life: calf feeding time, scampering pets, and kids eager to introduce you to their favourite lamb. Double rooms and self-contained units are cosy and modern, while grassy tent pitches and gravel campervan sites will satisfy campers.

The Catlins

Lazy Dolphin Lodge   HOSTEL $

(☑ 03-246 8579; www.lazydolphinlodge.co.nz; 529 Curio Bay Rd; dm/r without bathroom $40/90; @ 🖀) This perfect hybrid of seaside holiday home and hostel has light-filled bedrooms sporting cheerful linen. There are two kitchens and lounges, but you'll want to hang out upstairs on the deck overlooking Porpoise Bay. A path at the rear of the property leads directly to the beach.

Curio Bay Accommodation   APARTMENT $$

(☑ 03-246 8797; www.curiobay.co.nz; 521a Curio Bay Rd; apt from $190) Three plush units are on offer here – one apartment attached to the hosts' house, and two similar units down the road. All are self-contained, decorated in rustic, beachy style, with big windows and sun-drenched decks right next to the beach. There's also an old-fashioned Kiwi bach, sleeping up to six people.

ⓘ Getting There & Away

There is no public transport to Curio Bay. The area's western entry point is Fortrose, a 45km drive east from Invercargill; the eastern end of the region is its focal point, Curio and Porpoise Bays, 4km south of Waikawa. A 9km section of the road between Haldane and Curio Bay is unsealed.

Papatowai & Around

Nature shows off some of her best angles at Papatowai, which is perched at a meeting of forest, sea and the Tahakopa River. The leafy village has barely 40 inhabitants but swells with holidaymakers in summer, drawn by a languid vibe and glittering views of water-

falls and golden bays. Adding to the low-key delight, trails to beauty spots are easy peasy: Matai or McLean Falls are reached by an easy tramp, and walkers of all levels can idle around lustrous Lake Wilkie.

A couple of days in Papatowai satisfies most visitors. You'll soon find yourself drawn east to gorgeous Purakaunui Falls (along the road to Owaka) and the jagged coast of Kaka Point, or west to the wild surf of Curio Bay.

⊙ Sights

Cathedral Caves   CAVE

(www.cathedralcaves.co.nz; 1069 Chaslands Hwy; adult/child $5/1; ⊙ Nov–May) Cutting back into cliffs right on the beach, the huge, arched Cathedral Caves were carved out of the limestone by 160 million years of waves. Named for their acoustic properties, they are only accessible for two hours at either side of low tide (tide timetables are posted on the website, at the highway turn-off and at visitor information centres) – and even then they can be closed at short notice if the conditions are deemed dangerous.

Lost Gypsy Gallery   GALLERY

(☑ 021 122 8102; www.thelostgypsy.com; 2532 Papatowai Hwy; $5; ⊙ 10am–5pm Thu–Tue mid-Oct–Apr) Fashioned from remaindered bits and bobs, artist Blair Somerville's intricately crafted automata are wonderfully irreverent. The bamboozling collection inside a converted bus (free entry) is a teaser for the carnival of creations through the gate (young children not allowed, sorry...). The buzz, bong and bright lights of the organ are bound to tickle your ribs. Espresso caravan and wi-fi on-site.

🏃 Activities

Four kilometres west of Papatowai, an easy walk along moss-scented pathways and boardwalks takes you out onto the waters of dazzling **Lake Wilkie** (Chaslands Hwy) (30 minutes return). If you're pressed for time but want a photo of this Ice Age mirror lake, it's a 10-minute return walk to a lookout point. A further 7km west is the turn-off to **McLean Falls** (off Rewcastle Rd, Chaslands), reached by a thrilling walk along fern-fringed trails. Allow 40 minutes to walk to the falls and back; the car park is 4km from the main highway along a rough road.

Catlins Wildlife Trackers   WILDLIFE
(☑ 0800 228 5467, 03-415 8613; www.catlins-ecotours.co.nz; 744 Catlins Valley Rd, Tawanui) 🖉 Running since 1990, Catlins Wildlife Trackers offers customised guided walks and tours with a focus on ecology. Want to see the beloved mohua, penguins, sea lions or other wildlife? Mary and Fergus will track them down for you. Half-day tours cost $150 per adult (or $75 for kids). A three-night/two-day package costs $1200 (including all food, accommodation and transport).

🛏 Sleeping & Eating

Hilltop   LODGE $
(☑ 03-415 8028; 77 Tahakopa Valley Rd, Papatowai; d with/without bathroom $110/100) High on a hill 1.5km out of town, with native forest at the back door and surrounded by a sheep farm, these two shipshape cottages command spectacular views of the Tahakopa Valley and coast. Rent by the room or the whole house; the en suite double is the pick of a very nice bunch.

★ **Mohua Park**   COTTAGE $$$
(☑ 03-415 8613; www.catlinsmohuapark.co.nz; 744 Catlins Valley Rd, Tawanui; cottages $225; 🖥) 🖉 Situated on the edge of a peaceful 14-hectare nature reserve (7km off the highway), these four spacious self-contained cottages offer peace, quiet and privacy. Instead of TV, you'll watch birds flitting through the forest on your doorstep and sigh at views of rolling hills.

★ **Whistling Frog Cafe & Bar**   CAFE $$
(☑ 03-415 8338; www.whistlingfrogcafe.com; 9 Rewcastle Rd, Chaslands; mains $18-23; ⊙8.30am-9.30pm Nov-Mar, 10am-6pm Apr-Oct; 🖥) Colourful and fun, the Frog is the best dining option in the Catlins, offering craft beer on tap and crowd-pleasing meals, often garnished with flowers from the garden. We're talking

seafood chowder, wood-fired pizza, gourmet burgers, craft-beer-battered blue cod, and vegie feeds like risotto and big salads. Excellent coffee and breakfast spreads, too. Ribbit!

It's located at the **Catlins Kiwi Holiday Park** (Whistling Frog Holiday Resort; ☑ 03-415 8338; www.catlinskiwiholidaypark.com; 9 Rewcastle Rd, Chaslands; sites from $46, units from $165, without bathroom from $110; 🖥), near McLean Falls.

ℹ Getting There & Away

There is no public transport in the Catlins. Papatowai is a pleasant 36km drive east from Waikawa, or 25km west of Owaka.

Owaka & Around

The Catlins' main town is an ideal base for exploring the region. Ruggedly rocky Kaka Point is 24km east by road, while in the other direction lustrous waterfalls like Purakaunui are a short drive away. Languid Owaka township may be tiny but it has a top-quality museum and a supermarket and petrol station (no vain boast in these parts).

Four kilometres southeast of Owaka town is **Pounawea**, a beautiful hamlet on the edge of the Catlins River Estuary. Just across the inlet is **Surat Bay**, notable for the sea lions that lie around the beach between here and **Cannibal Bay**, an hour's beach-walk away.

◉ Sights

★ **Purakaunui Falls**   WATERFALL
(Purakaunui Falls Rd) If you only see one waterfall in the Catlins, make it this magnificent cascade down three tiers of jet-black rock. It's an easy 15-minute clamber to reach the falls from the small parking area.

Purakaunui Falls are almost equidistant between Owaka and Papatowai (respectively 15km and 12km by road).

Owaka Museum & Catlins Information Centre   MUSEUM
(☑ info centre 03-415 8371, museum 03-415 8323; www.owakamuseum.org.nz; 10 Campbell St, Owaka; museum adult/child $5/free; ⊙9.30am-4.30pm Mon-Fri, 10am-4pm Sat & Sun) Vaguely canoe-shaped in honour of the town name (Owaka means 'place of the canoe'), this state-of-the-art museum is a pleasant surprise. Salty tales of shipwrecks are well explained in short video presentations, Māori and settler stories grippingly displayed, and an interesting array of artefacts exhibited. It doubles as the main information centre for the Catlins.

🏃 Activities

Catlins River–Wisp Loop Track TRAMPING
(www.doc.govt.nz) This 24km loop comprises two 12km sections: the low-level, well-formed Catlins River Walk (five to six hours), and the Wisp Loop Walk (four to five hours), a higher-altitude tramp with a side trip to Rocky Knoll boasting great views and sub-alpine vegetation.

Catlins Horse Riding HORSE RIDING
(📱027 629 2904; www.catlinshorseriding.co.nz; 41 Newhaven Rd, Owaka; 1-/2-/3-hr rides $70/110/150) Explore the idiosyncratic coastline and landscapes on four legs. Learners' treks and the full gallop available, and trips are tailored to your level of experience. Full safety briefing (and glorious coastal views) included. Book ahead. Full-day treks also available (per person $230 to $260).

🛏 Sleeping

★**Newhaven Holiday Park** HOLIDAY PARK $
(📱03-415 8834; www.newhavenholiday.com; 324 Newhaven Rd, Surat Bay; unpowered/powered sites from $35/40, units from $70, with bathroom from $110; 🛜) This exemplary holiday park has a choice of cabins and self-contained units and bags of camping space set among low hills at the entrance to Surat Bay. Communal bathrooms are improbably fragrant, the kitchen's well equipped and there's a merry village atmosphere throughout. A little footpath leads down to the beach for easy seal-spotting, too.

Split Level HOSTEL $
(📱03-415 8868; www.thesplitlevel.co.nz; 9 Waikawa Rd, Owaka; dm $33, d with/without bathroom $82/74, tr with bathroom $99; 🛜) Very much like staying at a mate's house, this tidy two-level home has a comfortable lounge with a large TV and leather couches, and a well-equipped kitchen. Dorm rooms are spotless and there are en suites for those who want privacy but the perks of a sociable hostel setting.

Pounawea Grove Motel MOTEL $$
(📱03-415 8339; www.pounaweagrove.co.nz; 5 Ocean Grove, Pounawea; d or tw $140; 🛜) More sophisticated than the average motel, Pounawea Grove has a boutique feel thanks to its roomy units with sharp, modern bathrooms and plush textiles. Throw in a warm welcome and the bucolic estuary setting, and a relaxing stay is almost guaranteed.

ℹ️ Getting There & Away

You'll need your own wheels to reach Owaka, at the heart of the public-transport-free Catlins. The town is 30km south of Balclutha, a gateway town to the Catlins on Hwy 1.

Kaka Point & Around

The township might be sedate but the views at Kaka Point, 23km east of Owaka, are among the most mesmerising in the Catlins. The primary draws of this small coastal community are Nugget Point, a remarkable rock-studded peninsular shoreline, and Roaring Bay, where (with good timing) you can spot yellow-eyed penguins (hōiho). A much more common sight are sea lions and fur seals, which you'll see basking on beaches and camouflaging themselves among the rocks.

◎ Sights

★**Nugget Point** NATURAL FEATURE
(off Nugget Point Rd) Reach one of the South Island's most jaw-dropping coastal lookouts via the 900m Nugget Point (Tokatā) walkway. Wave-thrashed cliffs give way abruptly to sapphire waters dotted with toothy islets known as the Nuggets. The track to the lighthouse is dotted with poetic placards, and you can spot seals and sea lions lolling below. Look out for bird life, such as soaring tītī (muttonbird) and spoonbills huddling in the lee of the breeze.

It's 9km south of Kaka Point township, just past the Roaring Bay car park.

Roaring Bay VIEWPOINT
(Nugget Point Rd) Your best chance of spotting rare yellow-eyed penguins (hōiho) is from a hide at Roaring Bay, 8km south of Kaka Point's main drag. The hide is accessible throughout daylight hours but suggested viewing times are posted on a noticeboard at the car park. Penguin behaviour changes seasonally but times are usually before 7am or after 3pm or 4pm; ask locally or at your guesthouse.

🛏 Sleeping

Nugget View & Kaka Point Motels MOTEL $$
(📱03-412 8602, 0800 525 278; www.catlins.co.nz; 11 Rata St, Kaka Point; units $110-180; 🛜) Unpolished but amply comfortable, the nine units at this motel park range from economy studios to more modern apartments with spa baths. The largest sleeps up to four and all except one have a sea-view veranda.

♀ Drinking & Nightlife

Point Cafe & Bar PUB

(📞03-412 8800; 58 Esplanade, Kaka Point; ⊙10am-8pm Jun-Aug, longer hours Sep-May) A one-stop shop for souvenirs, takeaway fried everything or decent full-blown meals of blue cod or lamb shank (mains $18 to $29), the Point is best for a beer at a window seat facing the sea.

⊕ Getting There & Away

Kaka Point is a 23km drive east of Owaka. Approaching from the north, it's 20km south of Balclutha on Hwy 1. You'll need your own vehicle – there is no public transport in the Catlins area.

STEWART ISLAND (RAKIURA)

📞03 / POPULATION 378

If you make the short but extremely rewarding trip to Stewart Island/Rakiura you'll have one up on most New Zealanders, many of whom maintain an active curiosity about the country's 'third island' without ever going there.

Travellers who make the effort are rewarded with a warm welcome from both the local Kiwis and the local kiwi. This is arguably the best place to spy the country's shy, feathered icon in the wild. Don't be surprised if the close-knit community of islanders quickly know who you are – especially if you mingle over a beer at NZ's southernmost pub in Oban, the island's only settlement.

Stewart Island/Rakiura offers plenty of outdoor adventures including kayaking and tramping. A major impetus for such excursions is bird life. The island is a bird sanctuary of international repute, and even amateur spotters will be distracted by the glorious squawking, singing and flitting of feathery flocks.

History

Stewart Island's Māori name is Rakiura (Glowing Skies), and you only need to catch a glimpse of a spectacular blood-red sunset or the aurora australis to see why. According to myth, New Zealand was hauled up from the ocean by Māui, who said, 'Let us go out of sight of land, far out in the open sea, and when we have quite lost sight of land, then let the anchor be dropped'. The North Island was the fish that Māui caught, the South

Island his canoe and Rakiura was the anchor – Te Punga o te Waka o Māui.

There is evidence that parts of Rakiura were occupied by moa (bird) hunters as early as the 13th century. The tītī (muttonbird) on adjacent islands were an important seasonal food source for the southern Māori.

The first European visitor was Captain Cook. Sailing around the eastern, southern and western coasts in 1770 he mistook it for the bottom end of the South Island and promptly named it South Cape. In 1809 the sealing vessel *Pegasus* circumnavigated Rakiura and named it after its first officer, William Stewart.

In June 1864 Stewart and the adjacent islets were bought from local Māori for £6000. Early industries were sealing, timber-milling, fish-curing and shipbuilding, with a short-lived gold rush towards the end of the 19th century. Today the island's economy is dependent on tourism and fishing.

Flora & Fauna

With an absence of mustelids (ferrets, stoats and weasels) and large areas of intact forest, Stewart Island/Rakiura has one of the largest and most diverse bird populations of anywhere in NZ. Even in the streets of Oban the air resonates with birds such as tui, bellbirds and kaka, which share their island home with weka, kakariki, fernbirds, robins and Rakiura tokoeka/kiwi. There are also plenty of shore- and seabirds, including dotterels, shags, mollymawks, prions, petrels and albatross, as well as the tītī (muttonbird), which is seen in large numbers during breeding season. Ask locals about the evening parade of penguins on cliffs near the wharf; and *please* – don't feed the birds. It's bad for them.

Exotic animals include two species of deer, the red and the Virginia (whitetail), introduced in the early 20th century, as were brush-tailed possums, which are now numerous throughout the island and destructive to the native bush. Stewart Island/Rakiura also has NZ fur seals, NZ sea lions and elephant seals dawdling on its beaches and rocky shores.

Beech, the tree that dominates much of NZ, is absent from Stewart Island/Rakiura. The predominant lowland bush is podocarp forest, with exceptionally tall rimu, miro and totara forming the canopy. Because of mild winters, frequent rainfall and porous soil, most of the island is a lush forest, thick with vines and carpeted in deep green ferns and mosses.

Stewart Island/Rakiura (North)

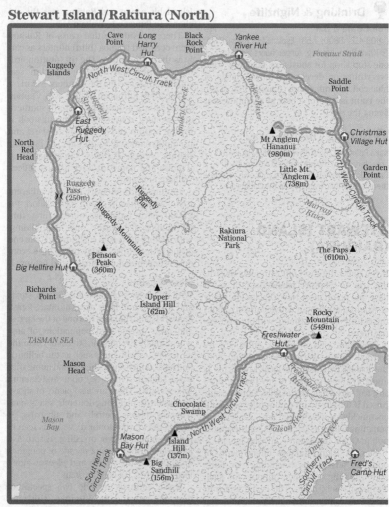

◉ Sights

★ Ulva Island   WILDLIFE RESERVE

A tiny paradise covering only 269 hectares, Ulva Island/Te Wharawhara is a great place to see lots of native NZ birds. Established as a bird sanctuary in 1922, it remains one of Stewart Island/Rakiura's wildest corners. The island was declared rat-free in 1997 and three years later was chosen as the site to release endangered South Island saddlebacks.

Today the air is bristling with birdsong, which can be appreciated on walking tracks in the island's northwest as detailed in *Ulva: Self-Guided Tour* ($2), available from the

Rakiura National Park Visitor Centre (p638). Many paths intersect amid beautiful stands of rimu, miro, totara and rata. Any water-taxi company will run you to the island from Golden Bay wharf, with scheduled services offered by Ulva Island Ferry (p638). To get the most out of Ulva Island, go on a tour with Ulva's Guided Walks (p636).

Rakiura Museum   MUSEUM

(☏ 03-219 1221; www.rakiuramuseum.co.nz; 9 Ayr St, Halfmoon Bay; adult/child $2/50c; ⊙ 10am-1.30pm Mon-Sat, noon-2pm Sun Oct-Apr, 10am-noon Mon-Fri, 10am-1.30pm Sat, noon-2pm Sun

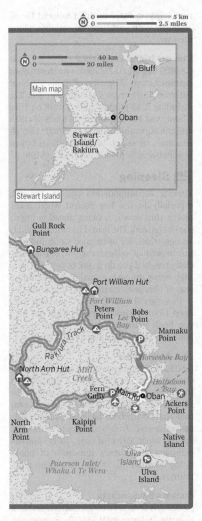

around beautiful beaches before climbing over a 250m-high forested ridge and traversing the sheltered shores of Paterson Inlet/Whaka ā Te Wera. It passes sites of historical interest, including Māori sites and sawmilling relics, and introduces many common sea and forest birds.

Rakiura Track is 32km long, but adding in the road sections at either end bumps it up to 39km, conveniently forming a circuit from Oban. It's a well-defined loop requiring a moderate level of fitness, suitable for tramping year-round. Being a Great Walk, it has been gravelled to eliminate most of the mud for which the island is infamous.

There are two Great Walk huts ($22 to $24) en route, which need to be booked in advance, either via the DOC website or in person at the Rakiura National Park Visitor Centre (p638). There is a limit of two consecutive nights in any one hut. Camping ($6) is permitted at the 'standard' campsites near the huts, and also at Māori Beach.

Ackers Point   WALKING

This three-hour return walk features an amble around the bay to a bushy track passing the historic 1835 **Stone House** at **Harrold Bay** before reaching **Ackers Point Lighthouse**, where there are wide views of Foveaux Strait and the chance to see blue penguins and a tītī (muttonbird) colony.

Observation Rock   WALKING

This short but quite sharp 15-minute climb through Oban's backstreets reaches the Observation Rock lookout where there are panoramic views of Paterson Inlet, Mt Anglem and Rakeahua. The track is clearly marked from the end of Leonard Rd, off Ayr St.

North West Circuit Track   TRAMPING

(www.doc.govt.nz) The North West Circuit Track is Stewart Island/Rakiura's legendary tramp, a demanding coastal epic around a remote and natural coastline featuring isolated beaches, sand dunes, birds galore and miles of mud. It's 125km, and takes nine to 11 days, although there are several options for shortening it involving boats and planes.

The track begins and ends in Oban. There are well-spaced huts along the way, all of which are 'standard' ($5) except for two Great Walk Huts ($22 to $24), which must be booked in advance. A North West Circuit Pass ($35), available at the national park visitor centre, provides for a night in each of the 'standard' huts.

May–Sep) Historic photographs are the stars of this small museum focused on local natural and human history, and featuring Māori artefacts, whaling gear and household items.

Big plans are in the works for a revamped, state-of-the-art Rakiura Museum in a new location. The new museum was slated to open at the end of 2018 or early 2019.

🏃 Activities

★ Rakiura Track   TRAMPING

(www.doc.govt.nz) One of NZ's nine Great Walks, the three-day Rakiura Track is a peaceful and leisurely loop that sidles

FIORDLAND & SOUTHLAND KAKA POINT & AROUND

Locator beacons are advised and be sure to call into DOC for up-to-date information and to purchase the essential topographical maps. You should also register your intentions at AdventureSmart (www.adventuresmart.org.nz) as this is no easy walk in the park.

Tours

Ulva's Guided Walks WALKING
(027 688 1332, 03-219 1216; www.ulva.co.nz) Focused firmly on birding and guided by expert naturalists, these excellent half-day tours ($130; transport included) explore Ulva Island. Book at the **Stewart Island Gift Shop** (03-219 1453; www.facebook.com/StewartIsland GiftShop; 20 Main Rd, Oban; 10.30am-5pm, reduced hours in winter). If you're a mad-keen twitcher, look for the Birding Bonanza trip ($480) on Ulva's website.

Aihe Eco Charters & Water Taxi BOATING
(03-219 1066, 027 478 4433; www.aihe.co.nz) Scenic and nature-spotting cruises with in-depth commentary. Options include wildlife-spotting cruises around Paterson Inlet ($75 per person for an hour or $130 for 2½ hours), or cruise and walk packages to the old Norwegian Whalers' Base ($95 per person for two hours, or $140 for three hours). Minimum group numbers apply, usually two to four people depending on the tour.

Aihe also offers water-taxi services.

Ruggedy Range Wilderness Experience ECOTOUR
(03-219 1066, 0274 784 433; www.ruggedyrange.com; 14 Main Rd, Oban) Nature-guide Furhana runs small-group guided walks, including 'bird and forest' trips to Ulva Island (half/full day $135/255); overnight trips to see kiwi in the wild (adult/child from $825/695); and a three-day guided wilderness walk where your packs are ferried to huts along the route ($1050).

Rakiura Charters & Water Taxi BOATING
(0800 725 487, 03-219 1487; www.rakiuracharters.co.nz; 10 Main Rd, Oban; adult/child from $100/70) The most popular outing on the *Rakiura Suzy* is the half-day cruise that stops in at the historic Whalers' Base. Trips can be tailored to suit timing and interests, such as wildlife-spotting and tramping.

Phil's Sea Kayak KAYAKING
(027 444 2323; www.observationrocklodge.co.nz; trips from $90; mid-Sep–May) Stewart Island/Rakiura's only kayaking guide, Phil runs trips on Paterson Inlet tailored for all abilities, with sightings of wildlife along the way.

Stewart Island Experience TOURS
(0800 000 511, 03-212 7660; www.stewartisland experience.co.nz; 12 Elgin Tce) Runs 2½-hour Paterson Inlet cruises (adult/child $95/22), including a 45-minute guided walk on Ulva Island; and 1½-hour minibus tours of Oban and the surrounding bays ($45/22). Also offers tours in search of the Southern brown kiwi between September and May ($199).

Sleeping

Finding accommodation can be difficult, especially in the low season when many places shut down. Booking ahead is highly recommended. The island has many holiday homes, which are often good value and offer the benefit of self-catering, which is especially handy if you do a spot of fishing. (Note that many impose a two-night minimum stay or charge a surcharge for one night.)

Invercargill i-SITE (p626) and the Red Shed Oban Visitor Centre (p638) can help you book holiday-home rentals on the island. See also www.stewartisland.co.nz.

Jo & Andy's B&B B&B $
(03-219 1230; jriksem@gmail.com; 22 Main Rd, Oban; s $65, d & tw $95;) A great option for budget travellers, this cosy blue home squeezes in twin, double and single rooms that share bathroom facilities. A big breakfast of muesli, fruit and eggs prepares you for the most active of days. Jo is splendid company and there's hundreds of books if the weather packs up. Two-night minimum stay.

Bunkers Backpackers HOSTEL $
(027 738 1796; www.bunkersbackpackers.co.nz; 15 Argyle St, Oban; dm/d $34/80; closed mid-Apr–mid-Oct;) A converted wooden villa houses Stewart Island/Rakiura's best hostel option, which is somewhat squeezed but offers the benefits of a cosy lounge, sunny garden, inner-village location and friendly vibe. Perks include a barbecue area, hammocks and board games.

Bay Motel MOTEL $$
(03-219 1119; www.baymotel.co.nz; 9 Dundee St, Oban; units from $180;) This hillside motel offers spacious, comfortable units with lots of light and views over the harbour. Some rooms have spa baths, all have kitchens and two are wheelchair-accessible. When

Oban

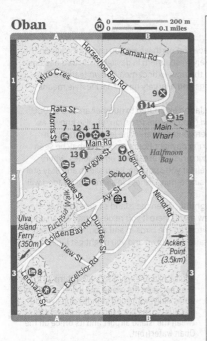

Oban

◎ Sights
1 Rakiura Museum B2

⊕ Activities, Courses & Tours
2 Observation Rock A3
3 Rakiura Charters & Water Taxi B2
4 Ruggedy Range Wilderness
   Experience A2
Stewart Island Experience ....(see 14)

⊟ Sleeping
5 Bay Motel A2
6 Bunkers Backpackers A2
7 Jo & Andy's B&B A2
8 Observation Rock Lodge................... A3

⊗ Eating
9 Church Hill Restaurant &
   Oyster Bar B1

⊙ Drinking & Nightlife
10 South Sea Hotel B2

⊕ Entertainment
11 Bunkhouse Theatre A2

⊙ Shopping
12 Stewart Island Gift Shop A2

⊕ Information
13 Rakiura National Park Visitor
   Centre... A2
14 Red Shed Oban Visitor Centre B1

⊕ Transport
15 Stewart Island Experience B1

you've exhausted the island's bustling after-dark scene, Sky TV's on hand for on-tap entertainment.

★ **Observation Rock Lodge** B&B $$$
(☑ 03-219 1444; www.observationrocklodge.co.nz; 7 Leonard St, Oban; r with/without bathroom $395/195; ☏) Secluded in bird-filled bush and angled for sea, sunset and aurora views, Annett and Phil's lodge has three stylish, luxurious rooms with private decks and a shared lounge. Guided activities, a sauna, a hot tub and Annett's gourmet dinners are included in the deluxe package ($780) or by arrangement as additions to the standard B&B rate.

✗ Eating & Drinking

**Church Hill Restaurant
& Oyster Bar** MODERN NZ $$$
(☑ 03-219 1123; www.churchhill.co.nz; 36 Kama-hi Rd, Oban; mains $38-40; ☺5.30pm-late daily Sep-May) During summer this heritage villa's sunny deck provides hilltop views, and in cooler months you can get cosy inside beside the open fire. Big on local seafood, highlights include oysters, crayfish and salmon, prepared in refined modern style, followed by excellent desserts. Bookings advisable.

South Sea Hotel PUB
(☑ 03-219 1059; www.stewart-island.co.nz; 26 Elgin Tce, Oban; ☺7am-9pm; ☏) Welcome to one of NZ's classic pubs, complete with stellar cod and chips, beer by the quart, a reliable cafe (mains $15 to $33) and plenty of friendly banter in the public bar. Great at any time of day (or night), and the Sunday-night quiz offers an unforgettable slice of island life. Basic rooms are available, too.

☆ Entertainment

Bunkhouse Theatre CINEMA
(☑ 027 867 9381; www.bunkhousetheatre.co.nz; 10 Main Rd, Oban; tickets $10; ☺screenings 11am, 2pm & 4pm) Oban's comfy little theatre screens the quirky, cute 40-minute film *A Local's Tail*, which provides an entertaining overview of Stewart Island/Rakiura history and culture. Jaffas and DIY popcorn.

SPOTTING A KIWI

Stewart Island/Rakiura is one of the few places on earth where you can spot a kiwi in the wild – and certainly the only place you're likely to see them in daylight. The bird has been around for 70 million years and is related to the now-extinct moa. Brown feathers camouflage the kiwi against its bush surroundings and a largely nocturnal lifestyle means spying one in the wild is a challenge.

As big as a barnyard chicken, with a population estimated to number around 13,000 birds, the Stewart Island/Rakiura brown kiwi (*Apteryx australis lawryi,* also known as the tokoeka) is larger in size, longer in the beak and thicker in the legs than its northern cousins. It is also the only kiwi active during daylight hours, and birds may be seen around sunrise and sunset foraging for food in grassed areas and on beaches, where they mine sandhoppers under washed-up kelp. If you spot one, keep silent, and stay still and well away. The birds' poor eyesight and single-mindedness in searching for food will often lead them to bump right into you.

Organised tours are your best bet for a sighting. Given the island's fickle weather – with tours sometimes cancelled – allow a few nights here if you're desperate for an encounter. Otherwise, it's sometimes possible to spot the birds in and around Oban itself. Head to the bushy fringes of the rugby field after sundown and you might get lucky.

ⓘ Information

The best place for information is the Invercargill i-SITE (p626) back on the mainland.

Rakiura National Park Visitor Centre (☑03-219 0009; www.doc.govt.nz; 15 Main Rd, Oban; ⊗8am-5pm Dec-Mar, 8.30am-4.30pm Mon-Fri, 9am-4pm Apr-May & Oct-Nov, 8.30am-4.30pm Mon-Fri, 10am-2pm Sat & Sun Jun-Sep) Stop in to obtain information on walking tracks, as well as hut bookings and passes, topographical maps, locator beacons, books and a few tramping essentials, such as insect repellent and wool socks. Information displays introduce Stewart Island/Rakiura's flora and fauna, while a video library provides entertainment and education (a good rainy-day Plan B). Register your intentions here via AdventureSmart (www.adventuresmart. org.nz), so there is a record of your tramping plans if you get into trouble along the way.

Red Shed Oban Visitor Centre (☑0800 000 511, 03-219 0056; www.stewartislandexperience. co.nz; 12 Elgin Tce, Oban; ⊗7.30am-6.30pm Oct-Apr, 8am-5pm May-Sep) Conveniently located next to the wharf, this Stewart Island Experience booking office can hook you up with nearly everything on and around the island, including accommodation, guided tours, boat trips, bikes, scooters and rental cars.

Stewart Island/Rakiura has no banks. In the Four Square supermarket there's an ATM, which has a mind of its own; credit cards are accepted for most activities.

ⓘ Getting There & Away

AIR

Stewart Island Flights (☑03-218 9129; www. stewartislandflights.co.nz; Elgin Tce, Oban; adult/child one way $125/80, return $215/130) Flies between the island and Invercargill three times daily, with good standby and over-60 discounts. The price includes transfers between the island airport and its office on the Oban waterfront.

BOAT

Stewart Island Experience (☑0800 000 511, 03-212 7660; www.stewartislandexperience. co.nz; Main Wharf, Oban; adult/child one way $79/40, return $139/40) The passenger-only ferry runs between Bluff and Oban up to four times daily (reduced in winter, June to August). Book a few days ahead in summer (December to February). The crossing takes one hour and can be a rough ride. The company also runs a shuttle between Bluff and Invercargill (adult/child $24/12), with pick-ups and drop-offs in Invercargill at the i-SITE, Tuatara Backpackers and Invercargill Airport.

Vehicles can be stored in a secure car park at Bluff for an additional cost.

ⓘ Getting Around

Roads on the island are limited to Oban and the bays surrounding it. Stewart Island Experience rents cars and scooters from the Red Shed.

Water taxis offer pick-ups and drop-offs to Ulva Island and to remote parts of the main island – a handy service for trampers. Operators include Aihe Eco Charters & Water Taxi (p636), **Ulva Island Ferry** (☑03-219 1013; return adult/child $20/10; ⊗departs 9am, noon, 4pm, returns 12.15pm, 2.15pm, 4.15pm, 6pm) and Rakiura Charters & Water Taxi (p636).

Understand New Zealand

New Zealand Today

Despite a decade marred by disasters, including devastating earthquakes and mining and helicopter tragedies, New Zealand never loses its nerve. The country remains a titan on both the silver screen and the sports field, and change is coming in the world of politics...

Best on Film

Lord of the Rings trilogy (2001–03) Hobbits, dragons and magical rings – Tolkien's vision comes to life.

The Piano (1993) A piano and its owners arrive on a mid-19th-century West Coast beach.

Whale Rider (2002) Magical tale of family and heritage on the East Coast.

Once Were Warriors (1994) Brutal relationship dysfunction in South Auckland.

Boy (2010) Taika Waititi's bitter-sweet coming-of-age drama set in the Bay of Plenty.

Best in Print

The Luminaries (Eleanor Catton; 2013) Man Booker Prize winner: crime and intrigue on West Coast goldfields.

Mister Pip (Lloyd Jones; 2006) Tumult on Bougainville Island, intertwined with Dickens' *Great Expectations*.

Live Bodies (Maurice Gee; 1998) Post-WWII loss and redemption in NZ.

The 10pm Question (Kate de Goldi; 2009) Twelve-year-old Frankie grapples with life's big anxieties.

The Collected Stories of Katherine Mansfield (2006) Kathy's greatest hits.

The Wish Child (Catherine Chidgey; 2016) Harrowing, heartbreaking WWII novel; NZ Book Awards winner.

Jacinda-Mania

In 2010 she was NZ's youngest sitting MP, by 2017 she was running the country. The swift rise of Jacinda Ardern has been touted as part of a global political shift. Ardern became the youngest ever Labour Party leader in 2017, only a few weeks ahead of the election that propelled her to the role of prime minister at the age of 37 – making her NZ's youngest PM for 150 years. Passionate about climate change, unabashedly feminist and an ardent supporter of gay rights, Ardern's ability to win support with her energetic style was dubbed 'Jacinda-mania'. The final polls gave Labour a less-than-maniacal 37% of the vote, but resulted in a coalition government led by Labour.

Ardern's articulacy and verve have seen her aligned with other youthful, socially progressive world leaders like Justin Trudeau and Emmanuel Macron, part of a youth-powered political sea change. But Ardern's style remains quintessentially Kiwi: unpretentious and accessible.

Cultural and Sporting Colossus

Cementing NZ's reputation as a primo movie set, movie director James Cameron has been working out of Wellington on his long-awaited four *Avatar* sequels. They're slated for staggered release between 2020 and 2025. Meanwhile, director Taika Waititi has been enjoying a wave of global adulation. His works *Boy* (2010) and *Hunt for the Wilderpeople* (2016) broke records in NZ, and vampire flat-sharing mockumentary *What We Do in the Shadows* (2014) ensnared a cult following. But Waititi went stratospheric as the director of *Thor: Ragnarok* (2017), injecting distinctly Kiwi humour into a Marvel franchise that had lost its zest.

In the world of sport, NZ remains a force to be reckoned with. Following the All Blacks' success at the 2011

Rugby World Cup at home, the beloved national team beat arch-rivals Australia in 2015, becoming the first country ever to win back-to-back Rugby World Cups. The pressure is on for the 2019 World Cup. After the Black Caps made the final of the Cricket World Cup for the first time in 2015, they were deprived of glory in a stinging loss to their trans-Tasman rivals Australia. The 2019 World Cup is their chance to seize victory. Out on the water, Emirates Team New Zealand scored a victory in 2017 at venerable sailing race the America's Cup. Auckland 2021, anyone?

Big Issues

Being a dream destination isn't all it's cracked up to be, especially when tourist numbers boom and property investors swoop in. Aussie and Asian buyers are increasingly wise to NZ property: cue a spiralling housing crisis, and the IMF ranking NZ's housing as the most unaffordable in the OECD in 2016. With Auckland's population expected to increase by one million in the next 30 years, the fixes can't come swiftly enough.

The issue of managing NZ's increasing number of visitors – now an annual 3.54 million – is also high on the agenda. In response to the enormous popularity of the Tongariro Alpine Crossing, the DOC has placed a time limit at the car park at the beginning of the track, forcing tourists to use traffic-reducing shuttle services. Meanwhile tourism hubs like Te Anau, gateway to world-famous Milford Sound, are seeing their peak season start ever earlier. A country beloved for being wild, green and beautiful faces the challenge of keeping it that way, in the face of a tourism stampede.

Never Forget

Kiwi battler spirit has been repeatedly pushed to its limits over the past decade. Christchurch's recovery from the 2010 and 2011 earthquakes suffered a setback when another quake hit in 2016, while earthquakes in Kaikoura in November 2016 rattled road and rail access until repairs were finished at the end of 2017. But NZ doesn't just rebuild, it reinvents: pop-up cafes and restaurants and a shipping-container mall showed how fast Christchurch could dust itself off after disaster. Ensuing years have allowed the bigger post-earthquake projects to take shape, including the Canterbury Earthquake National Memorial, unveiled in 2017.

Another notable memorial remembers the Pike River Disaster in 2010, in which a methane explosion claimed 29 lives – the country's worst mining accident in more than a century. By the wishes of the families of the men killed in the accident, the site of the mine has been folded into Paparoa National Park and their memorial will be a new 'Great Walk', opening in 2018.

POPULATION: **4.83 MILLION**

AREA: **268,021 SQ KM**

GDP: **$268.1 BILLION**

INFLATION: **1.9% (2017)**

UNEMPLOYMENT: **4.8% (2017)**

if New Zealand were 100 people

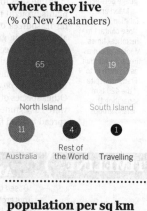

65 would be European
15 would be Maori
12 would be Asian
7 would be Pacific Islanders
1 would be Other

where they live
(% of New Zealanders)

65 North Island
19 South Island
11 Australia
4 Rest of the World
1 Travelling

population per sq km

NEW ZEALAND   AUSTRALIA   USA

≈ 3 people

History

Historians continue to unravel New Zealand's early history...with much of what they discover confirming traditional Māori narratives. In less than a thousand years NZ produced two new peoples: the Polynesian Māori and European New Zealanders (also known by their Māori name, 'Pākehā'). New Zealand shares some of its history with the rest of Polynesia, and with other European settler societies. This cultural intermingling has created unique features along the way.

Māori Settlement

The Ministry for Culture & Heritage's history website (www. nzhistory.net.nz) is an excellent source of info on NZ history.

The first settlers of NZ were the Polynesian forebears of today's Māori. Archaeologists and anthropologists continue to search for the details, but the most widely accepted evidence suggests they arrived in the 13th century. The DNA of Polynesian rat bones, dated to centuries earlier, has been written off as unreliable (and certainly not conclusive evidence of earlier settlement). Most historians now agree on 1280 as the Māori's likeliest arrival date. Scientists have sequenced the DNA of settlers buried at the Wairau Bar archaeological site on the South Island, and confirmed the settlers as originating from east Polynesia (though work is ongoing to pinpoint their origins more precisely). The genetic diversity of the buried settlers suggests a fairly large-scale settlement – a finding consistent with Māori narratives about numerous vessels reaching the islands.

Similarities in language between Māori and Tahitian indicate close contact in historical times. Māori is about as similar to Tahitian as Spanish is to French, despite the 4294km separating these island groups.

Prime sites for first settlement were warm coastal gardens for the food plants brought from Polynesia (kumara or sweet potato, gourd, yam and taro); sources of workable stone for knives and adzes; and areas with abundant big game. New Zealand has no native land mammals apart from a few species of bat, but 'big game' is no exaggeration: the islands were home to a dozen species of moa (a large flightless bird), the largest of which weighed up to 240kg, about twice the size of an ostrich...preyed upon by *Harpagornis moorei*, a whopping 15kg eagle that is now extinct. Other species of flightless birds and large sea mammals, such as fur seals, were easy game for hunters from small Pacific islands. The first settlers spread far and fast, from the top of the North Island to the bottom of the

TIMELINE

AD 1280	1500–1642	1642
Based on evidence from archaeological digs, the most likely arrival date of east Polynesians in NZ, now known as Māori.	The 'classic period' of Māori culture, where weapon-making and artistic techniques were refined. Many remain cultural hallmarks to this day.	First European contact: Abel Tasman arrives on an expedition from the Dutch East Indies (Indonesia) but leaves in a hurry after a sea skirmish with Māori.

THE MYTHICAL MORIORI

One of NZ's most persistent legends is that Māori found mainland NZ already occupied by a more peaceful and racially distinct Melanesian people, known as the Moriori, whom they exterminated. This myth has been regularly debunked by scholars since the 1920s, but somehow hangs on.

To complicate matters, there were real 'Moriori', and Māori did treat them badly. The real Moriori were the people of the Chatham Islands, a windswept group about 900km east of the mainland. They were, however, fully Polynesian, and descended from Māori – 'Moriori' was their version of the same word. Mainland Māori arrived in the Chathams in 1835, as a spin-off of the Musket Wars, killing some Moriori and enslaving the rest, but they did not exterminate them.

South Island within the first 100 years. High-protein diets are likely to have boosted population growth.

By about 1400, however, with big-game supply dwindling, Māori economics turned from big game to small game – forest birds and rats – and from hunting to farming and fishing. A good living could still be made, but it required detailed local knowledge, steady effort and complex communal organisation, hence the rise of the Māori tribes. Competition for resources increased, conflict did likewise, and this led to the building of increasingly sophisticated *pā* (fortified villages), complete with wells and food storage pits. Vestiges of *pā* earthworks can still be seen around the country (on the hilltops of Auckland, for example).

Around 1500 is considered the dawn of the 'classic period', when Māori developed a social structure and aesthetic that was truly distinct, rather than an offshoot of the parent Polynesian culture. Māori had no metals and no written language (and no alcoholic drinks or drugs). Traditional Māori culture from these times endures, including performance art like *kapa haka* (cultural dance) and unmistakeable visual art, notably woodcarving, weaponry and *pounamu* (greenstone).

Spiritual life was similarly distinctive. Below Ranginui (sky father) and Papatūānuku (earth mother) were various gods of land, forest and sea, joined by deified ancestors over time. The mischievous demigod Māui was particularly important. In legend, he vanquished the sun and fished up the North Island before meeting his death between the thighs of the goddess Hine-nui-te-pō in an attempt to bring immortality to humankind.

Rumours of late survivals of the giant moa bird abound, but none has been authenticated. In recent years there has been enthusiasm around attempting to 'de-extinct' the moa using DNA samples, though scientists see conserving existing species as the bigger priority. Spoilsports.

1769	1772	1790s	1818–36
European contact recommences with visits by James Cook and Jean de Surville. Despite violence, both manage to communicate with Māori. This time NZ's link with the outside world proves permanent.	Marion du Fresne's French expedition arrives; it stays for some weeks at the Bay of Islands. Relations with Māori start well, but a breach of Māori *tapu* (sacred law) leads to violence.	Whaling ships and sealing gangs arrive in the country. Relations are established with Māori, with Europeans depending on the contact for essentials, such as food, water and protection.	Intertribal Māori 'Musket Wars' take place: tribes acquire muskets and win bloody victories against tribes without them. The wars taper off, probably due to the equal distribution of weapons.

Enter Europe

The first authenticated contact between Māori and European explorers took place in 1642. Seafarer Abel Tasman had just claimed Van Diemen's Land (Tasmania) for the Dutch when rough winds steered his ships east, where he sighted New Zealand. Tasman's two ships were searching for southern land and anything valuable it might contain. Tasman was instructed to pretend to any natives he might meet 'that you are by no means eager for precious metals, so as to leave them ignorant of the value of the same'.

When Tasman's ships anchored in the bay, local Māori came out in their canoes to make the traditional challenge: friends or foes? The Dutch blew their trumpets, unwittingly challenging back. When a boat was lowered to take a party between the two ships, it was attacked and four crewmen were killed. Having not even set foot on the land, Tasman sailed away and didn't return; nor did any other European for 127 years. But the Dutch did leave a name: initially 'Statenland', later changed to 'Nova Zeelandia' by cartographers.

Contact between Māori and Europeans was renewed in 1769, when English and French explorers arrived, under James Cook and Jean de Surville – Cook narrowly pipped the latter to the post, naming Doubtless Bay before the French party dropped anchor there. The first French exploration ended sourly, with mistrust between the ailing French seamen and Māori, one of whom they took prisoner (he died at sea). Bloody skirmishes took place during a second French expedition, led by Marc-Joseph Marion du Fresne, when cultural misunderstandings led to violent reprisals; later expeditions were more fruitful. Meanwhile Cook made two more visits between 1773 and 1777. Exploration continued, motivated by science, profit and political rivalry.

Unofficial visits, by whaling ships in the north and seal-hunting gangs in the south, began in the 1790s (though Māori living in New Zealand's interior remained largely unaffected). The first Christian missionaries established themselves in the Bay of Islands in 1814, followed by dozens of others – Anglican, Methodist and Catholic. Europe brought such things as pigs and potatoes, which benefited Māori and were even used as currency. Trade in flax and timber generated small European–Māori settlements by the 1820s. Surprisingly, the most numerous category of 'European' visitor was probably American. New England whaling ships favoured the Bay of Islands for rest and recreation, which meant sex and drink. Their favourite haunt, the little town of Kororāreka (now Russell), was known as 'Gomorrah, the scourge of the Pacific'. As a result, New England visitors today might well have distant relatives among the local Māori.

Abel Tasman named NZ 'Statenland', assuming it was connected to Staten Island near Argentina. It was subsequently named after the province of Zeeland in Tasman's native Holland.

One of the first European women to settle in New Zealand was Charlotte Badger, a convict mutineer who fled to the Bay of Islands in 1806 and refused to return to European society.

1837	1840	1844	1858
European settlers introduce possums from Australia to NZ, creating a possum population boom that comes to threaten native flora and bird life.	Starting at Waitangi in the Bay of Islands on 6 February, around 500 chiefs countrywide sign the Treaty of Waitangi to 'settle' sovereignty once and for all. NZ becomes a nominal British colony.	Young Ngāpuhi chief Hone Heke challenges British sovereignty, first by cutting down the British flag at Kororāreka (now Russell), then by sacking the town itself. The ensuing Northland war continues until 1846.	The Waikato chief Te Wherowhero is installed as the first Māori King.

One or two dozen bloody clashes dot the history of Māori–European contact before 1840 but, given the number of visits, interracial conflict was modest. Europeans needed Māori protection, food and labour, and Māori came to need European articles, especially muskets. Whaling stations and mission stations were linked to local Māori groups by intermarriage, which helped keep the peace. Most warfare was between

CAPTAIN JAMES COOK

Countless obelisks, faded plaques and graffiti-covered statues remember the renowned navigator James Cook (1728–79). It's impossible to travel the Pacific without encountering the captain's image and his controversial legacy in the lands he opened to the West.

Cook came from an extremely pinched and provincial background. The son of a day labourer in rural Yorkshire, he was born in a mud cottage, had little schooling and seemed destined for farm work. Instead, Cook went to sea as a teenager, worked his way up from coal-ship servant to naval officer, and attracted notice for his exceptional charts of Canada. But Cook remained a little-known second lieutenant until, in 1768, the Royal Navy chose him to command a daring voyage to the South Seas.

In a converted coal ship called *Endeavour*, Cook sailed to Tahiti and then became the first European to land in New Zealand and the east coast of Australia. While he was there Cook sailed and mapped NZ's coastline in full – with impressive accuracy. The ship almost sank after striking the Great Barrier Reef, and 40% of the crew died from disease and accidents, but somehow the *Endeavour* arrived home in 1771. On a return voyage (1772–75), Cook became the first navigator to pierce the Antarctic Circle and circled the globe near its southernmost latitude, demolishing the ancient myth that a vast, populous and fertile continent surrounded the South Pole.

Cook's travels made an enormous contribution to world thought. During his voyages, Cook and his crew took astronomical measurements. Botanists accompanied him on his voyages, diligently recording and studying the flora they encountered. Cook was also remarkable for completing a round-the-world voyage without any of his crew dying of scurvy – adding 'nutrition' to his impressive roster of specialist subjects.

But these achievements exist beneath a long shadow. Cook's travels spurred colonisation of the Pacific, and within a few decades of his death, missionaries, whalers, traders and settlers began transforming (and often devastating) island cultures. As a result, many indigenous people now revile Cook as an imperialist villain who introduced disease, dispossession and other ills to the region (hence the frequent vandalising of Cook monuments). However, as islanders revive traditional crafts and practices, from tattooing to *tapa* (traditional barkcloth), they have turned to the art and writing of Cook and his men as a resource for cultural renewal. Significant geographical features in NZ bear his name, including Aoraki/Mt Cook, Cook Strait and Cook River, along with countless streets and hotels.

For good and ill, a Yorkshire farm boy remains one of the single most significant figures in shaping the modern Pacific.

1860–69	1861	1863–64	1867
The Taranaki wars, starting with the controversial swindling of Māori land by the government at Waitara, and continuing with outrage over the confiscation of more land as a result.	Gold discovered in Otago by Gabriel Read, an Australian prospector. As a result, the population of Otago climbs from less than 13,000 to over 30,000 in six months.	Waikato Land War. Up to 5000 Māori resist an invasion mounted by 20,000 imperial, colonial and 'friendly' Māori troops. Despite surprising successes, Māori are defeated and much land is confiscated.	All Māori men (rather than individual landowners) are granted the right to vote.

Māori and Māori: the terrible intertribal 'Musket Wars' of 1818–36. Because Northland had the majority of early contact with Europe, its Ngāpuhi tribe acquired muskets first. Under their great general Hongi Hika, Ngāpuhi then raided south, winning bloody victories against tribes without muskets. Once they acquired muskets, these tribes then saw off Ngāpuhi, but also raided further south in their turn. The domino effect continued to the far south of the South Island in 1836. The missionaries claimed that the Musket Wars then tapered off through their influence, but the restoration of the balance of power through the equal distribution of muskets was probably more important.

The Māori population for 1769 has been estimated at between 85,000 and 110,000. The Musket Wars killed perhaps 20,000, and new diseases (including typhoid, tuberculosis and venereal disease) did considerable damage, too. Fortunately NZ had the natural quarantine of distance: infected Europeans often recovered or died during the long voyage, and smallpox, for example, which devastated indigenous North Americans, never arrived. By 1840 Māori had been reduced to about 70,000, a decline of at least 20%. Māori bent under the weight of European contact, but they certainly did not break.

'I believe we were all glad to leave New Zealand. It is not a pleasant place. Amongst the natives there is absent that charming simplicity...and the greater part of the English are the very refuse of society.' Charles Darwin, writing about his 1835 visit to Kororāreka (Russell).

Growing Pains

Māori tribes valued the profit and prestige brought by the Pākehā and wanted both, along with protection from foreign powers. Accepting nominal British authority was the way to get them. New Zealand was appointed its first British Resident, James Busby, in 1833, though his powers were largely symbolic. Busby selected the country's first official flag and established the Declaration of the Independence of New Zealand. But Busby was too ineffectual to curb rampant colonisation.

By 1840 the British government was overcoming its reluctance to undertake potentially expensive intervention in NZ. The British were eager to secure their commercial interests and they also believed, wrongly but sincerely, that Māori could not handle the increasing scale of unofficial European contact. In 1840 the two peoples struck a deal, symbolised by the treaty first signed at Waitangi on 6 February that year. The Treaty of Waitangi now has a standing not dissimilar to that of the Constitution in the US, but is even more contested. The original problem was a discrepancy between British and Māori understandings of it. The English version promised Māori full equality as British subjects in return for complete rights of government. The Māori version also promised that Māori would retain their chieftainship, which implied local rights of government. The problem was not great at first, because the Māori version applied outside the small European settlements. But as those settlements grew, conflict brewed.

The Waitangi Treaty Grounds, where the Treaty of Waitangi was first signed in 1840, is now a tourist attraction for Kiwis and non-Kiwis alike. Each year on 6 February, Waitangi hosts treaty commemorations and protests.

1868–72	1886–87	1893	1901
East Coast war. Te Kooti, having led an escape from his prison on the Chatham Islands, leads a holy guerrilla war in the Urewera region. He finally retreats to establish the Ringatū Church.	Tuwharetoa tribe gifts the mountains of Ruapehu, Ngauruhoe and Tongariro to the government to establish NZ's first national park.	NZ becomes the first country in the world to grant the vote to women, following a campaign led by Kate Sheppard, who petitioned the government for years.	NZ politely declines the invitation to join the new Commonwealth of Australia, but thanks for asking.

LAND WARS

Starting in Northland and moving throughout the North Island, the New Zealand Wars had many complex causes, but *whenua* (land) was the one common factor. In these conflicts, also referred to as the Land Wars or Māori Wars, Māori fought both for and against the NZ government, on whose side stood the Imperial British Army, Australians and NZ's own Armed Constabulary. Land confiscations imposed on the Māori as punishment for involvement in these wars are still the source of conflict today, with the government struggling to finance compensation for what are now acknowledged to have been illegal seizures.

In 1840 there were only about 2000 Europeans in NZ, with the shanty town of Kororāreka as the capital and biggest settlement. By 1850 six new settlements had been formed, with 22,000 settlers between them. About half of these had arrived under the auspices of the New Zealand Company and its associates. The company was the brainchild of Edward Gibbon Wakefield, who also influenced the settlement of South Australia. Wakefield hoped to short-circuit the barbarous frontier phase of settlement with 'instant civilisation', but his success was limited. From the 1850s his settlers, who included a high proportion of upper-middle-class gentlefolk, were swamped by succeeding waves of immigrants that continued to wash in until the 1880s. These people were part of the great British and Irish diaspora that also populated Australia and much of North America, but the NZ mix was distinctive. Lowland Scots settlers were more prominent in NZ than elsewhere, for example, with the possible exception of parts of Canada. New Zealand's Irish, even the Catholics, tended to come from the north of Ireland. New Zealand's English tended to come from the counties close to London. Small groups of Germans, Scandinavians and Chinese made their way in, though the last faced increasing racial prejudice from the 1880s, when the Pākehā population reached half a million.

Much of the mass immigration from the 1850s to the 1870s was assisted by the provincial and central governments, which also mounted large-scale public works schemes, especially in the 1870s under Julius Vogel. In 1876 Vogel abolished the provinces on the grounds that they were hampering his development efforts. The last imperial governor with substantial power was the talented but machiavellian George Grey, who ended his second governorship in 1868. Thereafter, the governors (governors-general from 1917) were largely just nominal heads of state; the head of government, the premier or prime minister, had more power. The central government, originally weaker than the provincial governments, the imperial governor and the Māori tribes, eventually exceeded the power of all three.

'Kaore e mau te rongo – ake, ake!' (Peace never shall be made – never, never!) War chief Rewi Maniapoto in response to government troops at the battle of Orakau, 1864

1908	1914–18	1931	1935–49
NZ physicist Ernest Rutherford is awarded the Nobel Prize in chemistry for 'splitting the atom', investigating the disintegration of elements and the chemistry of radioactive substances.	NZ's contribution to WWI is staggering: for a country of just over one million people, about 100,000 NZ men serve overseas. Some 60,000 become casualties, mostly on the Western Front in France.	A massive earthquake in Napier and Hastings kills at least 256 people.	First Labour government in power, under Michael Savage. This government creates NZ's pioneering version of the welfare state, and also takes some independent initiatives in foreign policy.

The Māori tribes did not go down without a fight. Indeed, their resistance was one of the most formidable ever mounted against European expansion. The first clash took place in 1843 in the Wairau Valley, now a wine-growing district. A posse of settlers set out to enforce the myth of British control, but encountered the reality of Māori control. Twenty-two settlers were killed, including Wakefield's brother, Arthur, along with about six Māori. In 1845 more serious fighting broke out in the Bay of Islands, when Hōne Heke sacked a British settlement. Heke and his ally Kawiti baffled three British punitive expeditions, using a modern variant of the traditional *pā* fortification. Vestiges of these innovative earthworks can still be seen at Ruapekapeka (south of Kawakawa). Governor Grey claimed victory in the north, but few were convinced at the time. Grey had more success in the south, where he arrested the formidable Ngāti Toa chief Te Rauparaha, who until then wielded great influence on both sides of Cook Strait. Pākehā were able to swamp the few Māori living in the South Island, but the fighting of the 1840s confirmed that the North Island at that time comprised a European fringe around an independent Māori heartland.

In the 1850s settler population and aspirations grew, and fighting broke out again in 1860. The wars burned on sporadically until 1872 over much of the North Island. In the early years the King Movement, seeking to establish a monarchy that would allow Māori to assume a more equal footing with the European settlers, was the backbone of resistance. In later years some remarkable prophet-generals, notably Titokowaru and Te Kooti, took over. Most wars were small-scale, but the Waikato war of 1863-64 was not. This conflict, fought at the same time as the American Civil War, involved armoured steamships, ultra-modern heavy artillery, and 10 proud British regular regiments. Despite the odds, Māori forces won several battles, such as that at Gate Pā, near Tauranga, in 1864. But in the end they were ground down by European numbers and resources. Māori political, though not cultural, independence ebbed away in the last decades of the 19th century. It finally expired when police invaded its last sanctuary, the Urewera Mountains, in 1916.

From Gold Rush to Welfare State

From the 1850s to the 1880s, despite conflict with Māori, the Pākehā economy boomed. A gold rush on the South Island made Dunedin NZ's biggest town, and a young, mostly male population chased their fortunes along the West Coast. Fretting over the imbalance in this frontier society, the British government tried to entice women to settle in NZ. Huge amounts of wool were exported and there were unwise levels of overseas borrowing for development of railways and roads. By 1886 the popula-

Maurice Shadbolt's *Season of the Jew* (1987) is a semi-fictionalised story of bloody campaigns led by warrior Te Kooti against the British in Poverty Bay in the 1860s. Te Kooti and his followers compared themselves to the Israelites cast out of Egypt. For more about the NZ Wars, visit www.newzealandwars.co.nz.

Former NZ Prime Minister Julius Vogel (1835–99) wrote a science fiction novel *Anno Domini 2000* (1889) in which he imagines a utopian society led by women. Very prescient, considering NZ was the first country to give women the vote...

1936	1939–45	1930s	1953
NZ aviatrix Jean Batten becomes the first aviator to fly solo directly from Britain to NZ.	NZ troops back Britain and the Allied war effort during WWII; from 1942 as many as 45,000 American soldiers camp in NZ to guard against Japanese attack.	Maurice Schlesinger begins producing the Buzzy Bee, NZ's most famous children's toy.	New Zealander Edmund Hillary, with Tenzing Norgay, 'knocks the bastard off': the pair become the first men to reach the summit of Mt Everest.

tion reached a tipping point: the population of non-Māori people were mostly born in NZ. Many still considered Britain their distant home, but a new identity was taking shape.

Depression followed in 1879, when wool prices slipped and gold production thinned out. Unemployment pushed some of the working population to Australia, and many of those who stayed suffered miserable working conditions. There was still cause for optimism: NZ successfully exported frozen meat in 1882, raising hopes of a new backbone for the economy. Forests were enthusiastically cleared to make way for farmland.

In 1890 the Liberals, NZ's first organised political party, came to power. They stayed there until 1912, helped by a recovering economy. For decades, social reform movements such as the Woman's Christian Temperance Union (WCTU) had lobbied for women's freedom, and NZ became the first country in the world to give women the vote in 1893. (Another major WCTU push, for countrywide prohibition, didn't take off.) Old-age pensions were introduced in 1898 but these social leaps forward didn't bring universal good news. Pensions only applied for those falling within a very particular definition of 'good character', and the pension reforms deliberately excluded the population of Chinese settlers who had arrived to labour in the goldfields. Meanwhile, the Liberals were obtaining more and more Māori land for settlement. By now, the non-Māori population outnumbered the Māori by 17 to one.

Nation-Building

New Zealand had backed Britain in the Boer War (1899–1902) and WWI (1914–18), with dramatic losses in WWI. However, the bravery of AN-ZAC (Australian and New Zealander Army Corps) forces in the failed Gallipoli campaign endures as a nation-building moment for NZ. In the 1930s NZ's experience of the Great Depression was as grim as any. The derelict farmhouses still seen in rural areas often date from this era. In 1935 a second reforming government took office, campaigning on a platform of social justice: the First Labour government, led by Australian-born Michael Joseph Savage. In WWII NZ formally declared war on Germany: 140,000 or so New Zealanders fought in Europe and the Middle East, while at home, women took on increasing roles in the labour force.

By the 1930s giant ships were regularly carrying frozen meat, cheese and butter, as well as wool, on regular voyages from NZ to Britain. As the NZ economy adapted to the feeding of London, cultural links were also enhanced. New Zealand children studied British history and literature, not their own. New Zealand's leading scientists and writers, such as Ernest Rutherford and Katherine Mansfield, gravitated to Britain. Average

Revered NZ Prime Minister (1893–1906) Richard 'King Dick' Seddon popularised the country's self-proclaimed nickname 'Godzone' with his famous final telegraph: 'Just leaving for God's own country'.

Wellington-born Nancy Wake (codenamed 'The White Mouse') led a guerrilla attack against the Nazis with a 7000-strong army. Her honours included being the Gestapo's most wanted person and a highly decorated Allied servicewoman, and she was memorialised as 'the socialite who killed a Nazi with her bare hands'.

1974	1981	1985	1992
Pacific Island migrants who have outstayed visas are subjected to Dawn Raids (crackdowns by immigration police) under Robert Muldoon and the National government. Raids continue until the early 1980s.	Springbok rugby tour divides the nation. Many New Zealanders show a strong anti-apartheid stance by protesting the games. Other Kiwis feel that sport and politics should not mix and support the tour.	*Rainbow Warrior* sunk in Auckland Harbour by French government agents, preventing the Greenpeace protest ship from sailing to Moruroa, where the French government is conducting nuclear testing.	Government begins reparations for land confiscated in the Land Wars, confirming Māori fishing rights in the 'Sealord deal'. Major reparations follow, including those for the Waikato land confiscations.

living standards in NZ were normally better than in Britain, as were the welfare and lower-level education systems. New Zealanders had access to British markets and culture, and they contributed their share to the latter as equals. The list of 'British' writers, academics, scientists, military leaders, publishers and the like who were actually New Zealanders is long.

New Zealand prided itself on its affluence, equality and social harmony. But it was also conformist, even puritanical. The 1953 Marlon Brando movie, *The Wild One,* was banned until 1977. Full Sunday trading was not allowed until 1989. Licensed restaurants hardly existed in 1960, nor did supermarkets or TV. Notoriously, from 1917 to 1967, pubs were obliged to shut at 6pm (which, ironically, paved the way for a culture of fast, heavy drinking before closing time). Yet puritanism was never the whole story. Opposition to Sunday trading stemmed not so much from belief in the sanctity of the sabbath, but from the belief that workers should have weekends, too. Six o'clock closing was a standing joke in rural areas. There was always something of a Kiwi counterculture, even before imported countercultures took root from the 1960s onward.

In 1973 'Mother England' ran off and joined the budding EU. New Zealand was beginning to develop alternative markets to Britain, and alternative exports to wool, meat and dairy products. Wide-bodied jet aircraft were allowing the world and NZ to visit each other on an increasing scale. Women were beginning to penetrate first the upper reaches of the workforce and then the political sphere. Gay people came out of the closet, despite vigorous efforts by moral conservatives to push them back in. University-educated youths were becoming more numerous and more assertive.

New Zealand's staunch anti-nuclear stance earned it the nickname 'The Mouse that Roared'.

Scottish influence can still be felt in NZ, particularly in the south of the South Island. New Zealand has more Scottish pipe bands per capita than Scotland itself.

The Modern Age

From the 1930s, Māori experienced both a population explosion and massive urbanisation. Life expectancy was lengthening, the birth rate was high, and Māori were moving to cities for occupations formerly filled by Pākehā servicemen. Almost 80% of Māori were urban dwellers by 1986, a staggering reversal of the status quo that brought cultural displacement but simultaneously triggered a movement to strengthen pride in Māori identity. Immigration was broadening, too, first allowing in Pacific Islanders for their labour, and then (East) Asians for their money.

1995	2004	2010	2011
Peter Blake and Russell Coutts win the America's Cup for NZ, sailing *Black Magic;* red socks become a matter of national pride.	Māori TV begins broadcasting – for the first time a channel committed to NZ content and the revitalisation of Māori language and culture hits the small screen.	A cave-in at Pike River coalmine on the South Island's West Coast kills 29 miners.	A severe earthquake strikes Christchurch, killing 185 people and badly damaging the central business district.

Then, in 1984, NZ's next great reforming government was elected – the Fourth Labour government, led nominally by David Lange, and in fact by Roger Douglas, the Minister of Finance. This government adopted a more-market economic policy (dubbed 'Rogernomics'), delighting the right, and an anti-nuclear foreign policy, delighting the left. New Zealand's numerous economic controls were dismantled with breakneck speed. Middle NZ was uneasy about the anti-nuclear policy, which threatened NZ's ANZUS alliance with Australia and the US. But in 1985 French spies sank the anti-nuclear protest ship *Rainbow Warrior* in Auckland Harbour, killing one crewman. The lukewarm American condemnation of the French act brought middle NZ in behind the anti-nuclear policy, which became associated with national independence. Other New Zealanders were uneasy about the more-market economic policy, but failed to come up with a convincing alternative. Revelling in their new freedom, NZ investors engaged in a frenzy of speculation, and suffered even more than the rest of the world from the economic crash of 1987.

From the 1990s, a change to points-based immigration was weaving an increasingly multicultural tapestry in NZ. Numbers of incoming Brits fell but new arrivals increased, particularly from Asia but also from North Africa, the Middle East and various European countries. By 2006 more than 9% of the population was Asian.

By 2017 NZ had a new face to the world. Helmed by Jacinda Ardern, a coalition government was formed by Labour and NZ First, with support from the Green Party. New Zealand's third woman prime minister is faced with a balancing act between her governing parties while tackling the housing crisis and effecting bigger investment in education and health. It's no wonder that Ardern's ascendancy has been touted as the dawn of a new period of major reform.

In 2015 there was a public referendum to decide between five proposed designs for a new national flag, and the winner was a black- and blue-backed silver fern. During a second referendum in 2016, Kiwis decided that on reflection, they preferred the original flag – if it ain't broke...

2011	2013	2013	2015
NZ hosts and wins the Rugby World Cup for just the second time; brave France succumbs 8–7 in the final.	New Zealand becomes one of just 15 countries in the world to legally recognise same-sex marriage.	Auckland teenager Ella Yelich-O'Connor, aka Lorde, hits No 1 on the US music charts with her mesmeric, chant-like tune 'Royals'.	New Zealand's beloved All Blacks win back-to-back Rugby World Cups in England, defeating arch-rivals Australia 34–17 in the final.

Environment

New Zealand's landforms have a diversity that you would expect to find across an entire continent: snow-dusted mountains, drowned glacial valleys, rainforests, dunelands and an otherworldly volcanic plateau. Straddling the boundary of two great colliding slabs of the earth's crust – the Pacific plate and the Indian/Australian plate – NZ is a plaything for nature's strongest forces.

The Land

New Zealand is a young country – its present shape is less than 10,000 years old. Having broken away from the supercontinent of Gondwanaland (which included Africa, Australia, Antarctica and South America) some 85 million years ago, it endured continual uplift and erosion, buckling and tearing, and the slow fall and rise of the sea as ice ages came and went.

Evidence of NZ's tumultuous past is everywhere. The South Island's mountainous spine – the 650km-long ranges of the Southern Alps – grew from the clash between plates at a rate of 20km over three million years... in geological terms, that's a sprint. Despite NZ's highest peak, Aoraki/Mt Cook, losing 10m from its summit overnight in a 1991 landslide (and a couple of dozen more metres to erosion), the Alps are overall believed to be some of the fastest-growing mountains in the world.

Volcanic New Zealand

The North Island's most impressive landscapes have been wrought by volcanoes. Auckland is built on an isthmus peppered by some 48 scoria cones (cinder cones, or volcanic vents). The city's biggest and most recently formed volcano, 600-year-old Rangitoto Island, is a short ferry ride from the downtown wharves. Some 300km further south, the classically shaped cone of snowcapped Mt Taranaki overlooks tranquil dairy pastures.

But the real volcanic heartland runs through the centre of the North Island, from the restless bulk of Mt Ruapehu in Tongariro National Park, northeast through the Rotorua lake district out to NZ's most active volcano, White Island, in the Bay of Plenty. Called the Taupo Volcanic Zone, this great 350km-long rift valley – part of a volcano chain known as the 'Pacific Ring of Fire' – has been the seat of massive eruptions that have left their mark on the country physically and culturally. The volcano that created Lake Taupo last erupted 1800 years ago in a display that was the most violent anywhere on the planet within the past 5000 years.

You can experience the aftermath of volcanic destruction on a smaller scale at Te Wairoa (the Buried Village) (p309), near Rotorua on the shores of Lake Tarawera. Here, partly excavated and open to the public, lie the remains of a 19th-century Māori village overwhelmed when nearby Mt Tarawera erupted without warning. The famous Pink and White Terraces, spectacular naturally formed pools (and one of several claimants to the title 'eighth wonder of the world'), were destroyed overnight by the same upheaval.

New Zealand is one of the most spectacular places in the world to see geysers. Rotorua's short-lived Waimangu geyser, formed after the 1886 Mt Tarawera eruption, was once the world's largest, often gushing to a dizzying height of 400m.

Born of geothermal violence, Waimangu Volcanic Valley (p307) is the place to go to experience hot earth up close and personal amid geysers, silica pans, bubbling mud pools and the world's biggest hot spring. Alternatively, wander around Rotorua's Whakarewarewa village (p296), where descendants of Māori displaced by the eruption live in the middle of steaming vents and prepare food for visitors in boiling pools.

The South Island can also see some evidence of volcanism – if the remains of the old volcanoes of Banks Peninsula weren't there to repel the sea, the vast Canterbury Plains, built from alpine sediment washed down the rivers from the Alps, would have eroded long ago.

Earthquakes

Not for nothing has New Zealand been called 'the Shaky Isles'. Earthquakes are common, but most only rattle the glassware. A few have wrecked major towns. In 1931 an earthquake measuring 7.9 on the Richter scale levelled the Hawke's Bay city of Napier, causing huge damage and loss of life. Napier was rebuilt almost entirely in then-fashionable art-deco architectural style.

Over on the South Island, in September 2010 Christchurch was rocked by a magnitude 7.1 earthquake. Less than six months later, in February 2011, a magnitude 6.3 quake destroyed much of the city's historic heart and claimed 185 lives, making it the country's second-deadliest natural disaster. Then in November 2016 an earthquake measuring 7.8 on the Richter scale struck Kaikoura – further up the coast – resulting in two deaths and widespread damage to local infrastructure.

Native Fauna

New Zealand's long isolation has allowed it to become a veritable warehouse of unique and varied plants. Separation of NZ's landmass occurred before mammals appeared on the scene, leaving birds and insects to evolve in spectacular ways. As one of the last places on earth to be colonised by humans, NZ was for millennia a safe laboratory for risky evolutionary strategies. But the arrival of Māori, and later Europeans, brought new threats and sometimes extinction.

The now-extinct flightless moa, the largest of which grew to 3.5m tall and weighed more than 200kg, browsed open grasslands much as cattle do today (skeletons can be seen at Auckland Museum), while the smaller kiwi still ekes out a nocturnal living rummaging among forest leaf litter for insects and worms. One of the country's most ferocious-looking insects, the mouse-sized giant weta, meanwhile, has taken on a scavenging role elsewhere filled by rodents.

Many endemic creatures, including moa and the huia, an exquisite songbird, were driven to extinction, and the vast forests were cleared for timber and to make way for agriculture. Destruction of habitat and the introduction of exotic animals and plants have taken a terrible environmental toll – and New Zealanders are now fighting a rearguard battle to save what remains.

Birds & Bats

Pause in any NZ forest and listen: this country is aflutter with melodious, feathered creatures. The country's first Polynesian settlers found little in the way of land mammals – just two species of bat – and most of NZ's present mammals are introduced species. New Zealand's birds generally aren't flashy, but they have an understated beauty that reveals itself in more delicate details: the lacy plumage of rare white heron (kōtuku), the bespectacled appearance of a silvereye or the golden frowns of Fiordland penguins.

Travellers seeking sustainable tourism operators should look for businesses accredited with Qualmark (www.qualmark.co.nz) or those listed at Organic Explorer (www.organicexplorer.co.nz).

The most beautiful songbird is the tui, a nectar-eater with an inventive repertoire that includes clicks, grunts and chuckles. Notable for the white throat feathers that stand out against its dark plumage, the tui often feeds on flax flowers in suburban gardens but is most at home in densely tangled forest ('bush' to New Zealanders). The bellbird (korimako) is also musical; it's common in both native and exotic forests every-

ENVIRONMENTAL ISSUES IN NEW ZEALAND

New Zealand's reputation as an Eden, replete with pristine wilderness and eco-friendly practices, has been repeatedly placed under the microscope. The industry most visible to visitors, tourism, appears studded in green accolades, with environmental best practices employed in areas as broad as heating insulation in hotels to minimum-impact wildlife-watching. But mining, offshore oil and gas exploration, pollution, biodiversity loss, conservation funding cuts and questionable urban planning have provided endless hooks for bad-news stories.

Water quality is arguably the most serious environmental issue faced by New Zealanders. More than a quarter of the country's lakes and rivers have been deemed unsafe for swimming, and research from diverse sources confirms that the health of waterways is in decline. The primary culprit is 'dirty dairying' – cow effluent leaching into freshwater ecosystems, carrying with it high levels of nitrates, as well as bacteria and parasites such as E. coli and giardia. A 2017 report by the Ministry for the Environment and Statistics showed that nitrate levels in water were worsening at 55% of monitored river sites, and that urban waterways were in an especially dire state – with levels of harmful bacteria more than 20 times higher than in forest areas. A government push to make 90% of rivers and lakes swimmable by 2040 was met with initial scepticism about the metrics involved, but it's hoped that it will provide an impetus to make NZ's waterways worthy of the country's eco-conscious reputation.

Another ambitious initiative is Predator Free 2050, which aims to rid NZ of introduced animals that prey on native flora and fauna. The worst offenders are possums, stoats and rats, which eat swaths of forest and kill wildlife, particularly birds. Controversy rages at the Department of Conservation's (DOC) use of 1080 poison (sodium fluoroacetate) to control these pests, despite it being sanctioned by prominent environmental groups, such as Forest & Bird, as well as the Parliamentary Commissioner for the Environment. Vehement opposition to 1080 is expressed by such diverse camps as hunters and animal-rights activists, who cite detriments such as by-kill and the potential for poison passing into waterways. Proponents of its use argue that it's biodegradable and that aerial distribution of 1080 is the only cost-effective way to target predators across vast, inaccessible parts of NZ. Still, 'Ban 1080' signs remain common in rural communities and the controversy is likely to continue.

As well as its damaging impact on NZ waterways, the $12 billion dairy industry – NZ's biggest export earner – generates 48% of NZ's greenhouse gas emissions. Some farmers are cleaning up their act, lowering emissions through improved management of fertilisers and higher-quality feed, and major players DairyNZ and Fonterra have pledged support. But when it comes to contributing to climate change, the dairy industry isn't NZ's only dirty habit. New Zealand might be a nation of avid recyclers and solar-panel enthusiasts, but it also has the world's fourth-highest ratio of motor vehicles to people.

There have been fears about safeguarding the principal legislation governing the NZ environment, the 1991 Resource Management Act, in the face of proposed amendments. NGOs and community groups – ever-vigilant and already making major contributions to the welfare of NZ's environment – will find plenty to keep them occupied in coming years. But with eco-conscious Jacinda Ardern leading a coalition government from 2017, New Zealanders have reason to be hopeful of a greener future – Ardern has pledged an ambitious goal of reducing net greenhouse gas emissions to zero by 2050. More trains, 100% renewable energy sources and planting 100 million trees per year...goals worthy of NZ's clean, green reputation.

where except Northland (though it is more likely to be heard than seen). Its call is a series of liquid bell notes, most often sounded at dawn or dusk. Fantails (pīwakawaka) are also common on forest trails, swooping and jinking to catch insects stirred up by passing hikers

At ground level, the most famous native bird is of course the kiwi, NZ's national emblem, with a rounded body and a long, distinctive bill with nostrils at the tip for sniffing out food. Sightings in the wild require patience and luck but numerous sanctuaries allow a peep of this iconic bird. Look out for other land birds like pukeko, elegant swamphens with blue plumage and bright-red beaks. They're readily seen along wetland margins and even on the sides of roads nearby – be warned, they have little road sense. Far rarer (though not dissimilar in appearance) is the takahe, a flightless bird thought extinct until a small colony was discovered in 1948. It's worth seeking them out at Te Anau's **bird sanctuary** (Te Anau Bird Sanctuary; www.doc.govt.nz; Te Anau–Manapouri Rd; ☺dawn-dusk) **FREE**.

If you spend any time in the South Island high country, you are likely to spot the kea (unless it finds you first). A dark-green parrot with red underwings and a sense of mischief, the antics of this bold bird are a source of frustration and delight to New Zealanders, who crowned the kea 'Bird of the Year' in 2017. Kea are particularly common in car parks along the Milford Hwy, and in the West Coast's glacier country, where they hang out for food scraps or tear rubber from car windscreens (we've also seen them nibbling at ski bindings in winter sports resorts around Queenstown...consider yourself warned). Resist the urge to feed them, as it's hugely damaging to their health.

And what of the native bats? Populations of both short-tailed and long-tailed bats are declining at frightening speed, though Kahurangi National Park and Nelson are believed to be home to small populations. DOC is hard at work to protect bats, including ambitious plans to resettle them on predator-free islands. If you spot a bat, count yourself lucky – and consider telling DOC.

New Zealand's Ancient Lizard

The largest native reptile in NZ is the tuatara, a crested lizard that can grow up to 50cm long. Thought to be unchanged for more than 220 million years, these endearing creatures can live for up to a century. Meet them at Auckland Zoo (p88), Invercargill's Southland Museum (p625), Hokitika's National Kiwi Centre (p463), and other zoos and sanctuaries around NZ.

Marine Mammal–Watching

Kaikoura, on the northeast coast of the South Island, is NZ's nexus of marine mammal–watching. The main attraction here is whale-watching. The sperm whale, a toothed whale that can grow up to 18m long, is pretty much a year-round resident here. Depending on the season you may also see migrating humpback whales, pilot whales, blue whales and southern right whales. Other mammals – including fur seals and dusky dolphins – are seen year-round.

Kaikoura is also a hotspot for swimming with dolphins, with pods of up to 500 dusky dolphins commonly seen. Dolphin swimming is common elsewhere in NZ, with the animals gathering off the North Island near Whakatane, Paihia, Tauranga and in the Hauraki Gulf, and off Akaroa on the South Island's Banks Peninsula. Seal swimming also happens in Kaikoura and in Abel Tasman National Park.

But these kinds of wildlife encounters are controversial. Whale populations around the world have declined rapidly over the past 200 years: the same predictable migration habits that once made the giants easy

B Heather and H Robertson's *Field Guide to the Birds of New Zealand* is a comprehensive guide for bird-watchers and a model of helpfulness for anyone even casually interested in the country's remarkable bird life. Another good guide is *Birds of New Zealand: Locality Guide* by Stuart Chambers.

Nature Guide to the New Zealand Forest by J Dawson and R Lucas is a beautifully photographed foray into NZ's forests, home to ancient species dating from the time of the dinosaurs.

ENVIRONMENT NATIVE FAUNA

prey for whalers nowadays make them easy targets for whale-watchers. As NZ's whale-watching industry has grown, so has concern over its impact. At the centre of the debate is the practice of swimming with whales and dolphins. While it's undoubtedly one of the more unusual experiences you can have on the planet, many observers suggest that human interaction with these marine mammals has a disruptive effect on behaviours and breeding patterns. Taking a longer view, others say that

National Parks & Forest Parks

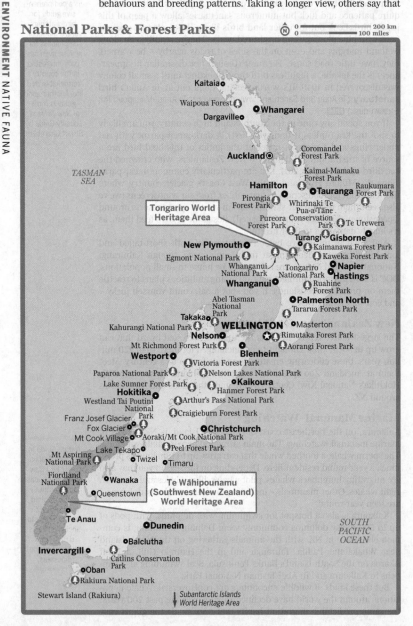

0 ___ 200 km
0 ___ 100 miles

Kaitaia

Waipoua Forest
Whangarei
Dargaville

Coromandel Forest Park
Auckland

TASMAN SEA

Kaimai-Mamaku Forest Park
Hamilton
Pirongia Forest Park
Tauranga
Raukumara Forest Park

Whirinaki Te Pua-a-Tāne
Pureora Conservation Forest Park
Te Urewera

Tongariro World Heritage Area

Turangi
Gisborne
Kaimanawa Forest Park

New Plymouth
Egmont National Park
Kaweka Forest Park

Whanganui National Park
Tongariro National Park
Napier
Hastings

Whanganui
Ruahine Forest Park

Abel Tasman National Park
Palmerston North
Tararua Forest Park

Takaka
Kahurangi National Park
WELLINGTON
Masterton

Nelson
Rimutaka Forest Park
Aorangi Forest Park

Mt Richmond Forest Park
Blenheim

Westport
Victoria Forest Park

Nelson Lakes National Park
Paparoa National Park
Kaikoura
Lake Sumner Forest Park
Hanmer Forest Park
Hokitika
Arthur's Pass National Park
Westland Tai Poutini National Park
Craigieburn Forest Park
Franz Josef Glacier
Fox Glacier
Christchurch
Mt Cook Village
Aoraki/Mt Cook National Park
Mt Aspiring National Park
Lake Tekapo
Peel Forest Park
Twizel
Timaru
Fiordland National Park

Te Wāhipounamu (Southwest New Zealand) World Heritage Area

Wanaka
Queenstown

Te Anau

Dunedin

SOUTH PACIFIC OCEAN

Balclutha
Invercargill
Catlins Conservation Park

Oban
Rakiura National Park

Stewart Island (Rakiura)

Subantarctic Islands World Heritage Area

given humanity's historic propensity for slaughtering whales by the tens of thousands, it's time we gave them a little peace and quiet.

The Department of Conservation's guidelines and protocols ensure that all operators are licensed and monitored, and forbids swimming with dolphin pods that have vulnerable young calves. If it's truly a bucket-list essential for you, give yourself a few days to do it so that there is no pressure on the operator to 'chase' marine mammals to keep you happy. And if you feel your whale-, dolphin- or seal-swim operator has 'hassled' the animals or breached the boundaries in any way (like loud noises, feeding them or circling them), report them to DOC immediately.

National Parks

More than 85,000 sq km of NZ – almost one-third of the country – is protected and managed within parks and reserves. Almost every conceivable landscape is present: from mangrove-fringed inlets in the north to the snow-topped volcanoes of the Central Plateau, and from the forested fastness of the Urewera ranges in the east to the Southern Alps' majestic mountains, glaciers and fiords. The 13 national parks and more than 30 marine reserves and parks, along with numerous forest parks, offer huge scope for wilderness experiences, ranging from climbing, skiing and mountain biking to tramping, kayaking and trout fishing.

Three places are World Heritage Areas: NZ's Subantarctic Islands, Tongariro National Park and Te Wāhipounamu (Southwest New Zealand), an amalgam of several national parks in southwest NZ that boast the world's finest surviving Gondwanaland plants and animals in their natural habitats.

Access to the country's wild places is relatively straightforward, though huts on walking tracks require passes and may need to be booked in advance. In practical terms, there is little difference for travellers between a national park and a forest park, though pets are generally not allowed in national parks without a permit. Disability-assist dogs can be taken into dog-controlled areas without a permit. Camping is possible in all parks, but may be restricted to dedicated camping grounds – check with DOC first.

The Department of Conservation website (www.doc.govt.nz) has useful information on the country's national parks, tracks and walkways. It also lists back-country huts and campsites.

ENVIRONMENT NATIONAL PARKS

Māori Culture

'Māori' once just meant 'common' or 'everyday', but Māori today are a diverse people. Some are engaged with traditional cultural networks and pursuits; others are occupied with adapting tradition and placing it into a dialogue with globalising culture.

Māori are New Zealand's *tangata whenua* (people of the land), and the Māori relationship with the land has developed over hundreds of years of occupation. Once a predominantly rural people, many Māori now live in urban centres, away from their traditional home base. But it's still common practice in formal settings to introduce oneself by referring to home: an ancestral mountain, river, sea or lake, or an ancestor.

The Māori concept of *whanaungatanga* – family relationships – is central to the culture: families spread out from the *whānau* (extended family) to the *hapū* (subtribe) and *iwi* (tribe) and even, in a sense, beyond the human world and into the natural and spiritual worlds.

If you're looking for a Māori experience in NZ you'll find it – in performance, in conversation, in an art gallery, on a tour...

Māori Then

Some three millennia ago people began moving eastward into the Pacific, sailing against the prevailing winds and currents (hard to go out, easier to return safely). Some stopped at Tonga and Samoa, and others settled the small central East Polynesian tropical islands.

The Māori colonisation of Aotearoa began from an original homeland known to Māori as Hawaiki. Skilled navigators and sailors travelled across the Pacific, using many navigational tools – currents, winds, stars, birds and wave patterns – to guide their large, double-hulled ocean-going craft to a new land. The first of many was the great navigator Kupe, who arrived, the story goes, chasing a giant octopus named Muturangi. But the distinction of giving NZ its well-known Māori name – Aotearoa – goes to his wife, Kuramarotini, who cried out, '*He ao, he ao tea, he ao tea roa!*' (A cloud, a white cloud, a long white cloud!).

Kupe and his crew journeyed around the land, and many places around Cook Strait (between the North and South Islands) and the Hokianga in Northland still bear the names that the crew gave them and the marks of their passage. Kupe returned to Hawaiki, leaving from (and naming) Northland's Hokianga. He gave other seafarers valuable navigational information. And then the great *waka* (ocean-going craft) began to arrive.

The *waka* that the first settlers arrived on, and their landing places, are immortalised in tribal histories. Well-known *waka* include *Tākitimu, Kurahaupō, Te Arawa, Mataatua, Tainui, Aotea* and *Tokomaru*. There are many others. Māori trace their genealogies back to those who arrived on the *waka* (and further back as well).

Kupe's passage is marked around NZ: he left his sails (Nga Ra o Kupe) near Cape Palliser as triangular landforms; he named the two islands in Wellington Harbour Matiu and Makoro after his daughters; his blood stains the red rocks of Wellington's south coast.

Māori legends are all around you as you tour NZ: Maui's *waka* became today's Southern Alps; a *taniwha* (legendary water being) formed Lake Waikaremoana in its death throes; and a rejected Mt Taranaki walked into exile from the central North Island mountain group, carving the Whanganui River.

HOW THE WORLD BEGAN

In the Māori story of creation, first there was the void, then the night, then Ranginui (sky father) and Papatūānuku (earth mother) came into being, embracing with their children nurtured between them. But nurturing became something else. Their children were stifled in the darkness of their embrace. Unable to stretch out to their full dimensions and struggling to see clearly in the darkness, their children tried to separate them. Tāwhirimātea, the god of winds, raged against them; Tūmatauenga, the god of war, assaulted them. Each god child in turn tried to separate them, but still Rangi and Papa pressed against each other. And then Tāne Mahuta, god of the great forests and of humanity, placed his feet against his father and his back against his mother and slowly, inexorably, began to move them apart. Then came the world of light, of demigods and humanity.

In this world of light Māui, the demigod ancestor, was cast out to sea at birth and was found floating in his mother's topknot. He was a shape-shifter, becoming a pigeon or a dog or an eel if it suited his purposes. He stole fire from the gods. Using his grandmother's jawbone, he bashed the sun so that it could only limp slowly across the sky, so that people would have enough time during the day to get things done (if only he would do it again!). Using the South Island as a canoe, he used the jawbone as a hook to fish up Te Ika-a-Māui (the fish of Māui) – the North Island. And, finally, he met his end trying to defeat death itself. The goddess of death, Hine-nui-te-pō, had obsidian teeth in her vagina (obsidian is a volcanic glass that takes a razor edge when chipped). Māui attempted to reverse birth (and hence defeat death) by crawling into her birth canal to reach her heart as she slept. A small bird – a fantail – laughed at the absurd sight. Hine-nui-te-pō awoke, and crushed Māui to death between her thighs. Death one, humanity nil.

What would it have been like making the transition from small tropical islands to a much larger, cooler land mass? Goodbye breadfruit, coconuts, paper mulberry; hello moa, fernroot, flax – and immense space (relatively speaking). New Zealand has more than 15,000km of coastline. Rarotonga, by way of contrast, has a little over 30km. There was land, lots of it, and a flora and fauna that had developed more or less separately from the rest of the world for 80 million years. There was an untouched, massive fishery. There were great seaside mammalian convenience stores – seals and sea lions – as well as a fabulous array of birds.

The early settlers went on the move, pulled by love, trade opportunities and greater resources; pushed by disputes and threats to security. When they settled, Māori established *mana whenua* (regional authority), whether by military campaigns, or by the peaceful methods of intermarriage and diplomacy. Looking over tribal history it's possible to see the many alliances, absorptions and extinctions that went on.

Histories were carried by the voice, in stories, songs and chants. Great stress was placed on accurate learning – after all, in an oral culture where people are the libraries, the past is always a generation or two away from oblivion.

Māori lived in *kainga* (small villages), which often had associated gardens. Housing was quite cosy by modern standards – often it was hard to stand upright while inside. From time to time people would leave their home base and go to harvest seasonal foods. When peaceful life was interrupted by conflict, the people would withdraw to *pā* (fortified dwelling places).

And then Europeans began to arrive.

The best way to learn about the relationship between the land and the *tangata whenua* (people of the land) is to get out there and start talking with Māori.

Māori Today

Today's culture is marked by new developments in the arts, business, sport and politics. Many historical grievances still stand, but some *iwi* (Ngāi Tahu and Tainui, for example) have settled major historical grievances and are significant forces in the NZ economy. Māori have also addressed the decline in Māori language use by establishing *kōhanga reo, kura kaupapa Māori* and *wānanga* (Māori-language preschools, schools and universities). There is now a generation of people who speak Māori as a first language. There is a network of Māori radio stations, and Māori TV attracts a committed viewership. A recently revived Māori event is becoming more and more prominent – Matariki (Māori New Year). The constellation Matariki is also known as the Pleiades. It begins to rise above the horizon in late May or early June and its appearance traditionally signals a time for learning, planning and preparing as well as singing, dancing and celebrating. Watch out for talks and lectures, concerts, dinners and even formal balls.

Arriving for the first time in NZ, two crew members of *Tainui* saw the red flowers of the pohutukawa tree, and they cast away their prized red feather ornaments, thinking that there were plenty to be had on shore.

Religion

Christian churches and denominations are prominent in the Māori world, including televangelists, mainstream churches for regular and occasional worship, and two major Māori churches (Ringatū and Rātana). But in the (non-Judeo-Christian) beginning there were the *atua Māori,* the Māori gods, and for many Māori the gods are a vital and relevant force still. It is common to greet the earth mother and sky father when speaking formally at a *marae* (meeting house). The gods are represented in art and carving, sung of in *waiata* (songs), invoked through *karakia* (prayer and incantation) when a meeting house is opened, when a *waka* is launched, even (more simply) when a meal is served. They are spoken of in the *marae* and in wider Māori contexts. The traditional Māori creation story is well known and widely celebrated.

The Arts

There are many collections of Māori *taonga* (treasures) around the country. Some of the largest and most comprehensive are at Wellington's Te Papa museum (p368) and the Auckland Museum (p86). Canterbury Museum (p487) in Christchurch also has a good collection, while Te Hikoi Southern Journey (p624) in Riverton has riveting displays on early interactions between Māori and Pākehā.

Wikipedia has a good list of *iwi* websites and a map showing *iwi* distribution (www.wikipedia .org/wiki/ list_of_iwi).

You can stay up to date with what's happening in the Māori arts by listening to *iwi* stations (www.irirangi.net) or tuning into Māori TV (www. maoritelevision.com) for regular features on the Māori arts. Māori TV went to air in 2004, an emotional time for many Māori who could at last see their culture, their concerns and their language in a mass medium. Over 90% of content is NZ made, and programs are in both Māori and English: they're subtitled and accessible to everyone. If you want to really get a feel for the rhythm and meter of spoken Māori from the comfort of your own chair, switch to Te Reo (www.maoritelevision.com/tv/te-reo -channel), a Māori-language-only channel.

At the time of research, production of Māori lifestyle magazine *Mana* (www.manaonline.co.nz) had stopped, but there were hopes of a relaunch down the line.

Tā Moko

Tā moko is the Māori art of tattoo, traditionally worn by men on their faces, thighs and buttocks, and by women on their chins and lips. *Moko* were permanent grooves tapped into the skin using pigment (made from burnt caterpillar or kauri gum soot) and bone chisels (fine, sharp combs for broad work, and straight blades for detailed work). Museums in the major centres – Auckland Museum (p86), Te Papa (Wellington; p368) and Canterbury Museum (Christchurch; p487) – all display traditional implements for *tā moko*.

The modern tattooist's gun is common now, but bone chisels are coming back into use for Māori who want to reconnect with tradition. Since the general renaissance in Māori culture in the 1960s, many artists have taken up *tā moko* and now many Māori wear *moko* with quiet pride and humility.

Can visitors get some work done? The art of *tā moko* is learned by, and inked upon, Māori people – but the term *kirituhi* (skin inscriptions) has arisen to describe Māori-motif-inspired modern tattoos that non-Māori can wear. *Kirituhi* can be profoundly meaningful and designed to fit the wearer's personal story, but there's an important line in the sand between *kirituhi* and *tā moko*.

Carving

Traditional Māori carving, with its intricate detailing and curved lines, can transport the viewer. It's quite amazing to consider that it was done with stone tools, themselves painstakingly made, until the advent of iron (nails suddenly became very popular).

Some major traditional forms are *waka* (canoes), *pātaka* (storage buildings) and *wharenui* (meeting houses). Along the greenstone-rich West Coast, numerous workshop-boutiques double as galleries that showcase fine examples of modern *pounamu* carving (particularly in Hokitika). You can see sublime examples of traditional carving at Te Papa (p368) in Wellington, and at the following:

Auckland Museum (p86) Māori Court

Hell's Gate (p307) Workshop where you can try your hand at woodcarving; near Rotorua

Otago Museum (p554) Impressive *waka taua* (war canoe); Dunedin

Putiki Church (p248) Interior covered in carvings and *tukutuku* (wall panels); Whanganui

Taupō Museum (p269) Carved meeting house

Te Manawa (p259) Museum with a Māori focus; Palmerston North

Waikato Museum (p184) Beautifully carved *waka taua*; Hamilton

Wairakei Terraces (p268) Carved meeting house; Taupo

Waitangi Treaty Grounds (p158) *Whare Rūnanga* and *waka taua*

Whakarewarewa (p296) The 'living village' – carving, other arts, meeting house and performance; Rotorua

Whanganui Regional Museum (p248) Wonderful carved *waka*

The apex of carving today is the *whare whakairo* (carved meeting house). A commissioning group relates its history and ancestral stories to a carver, who then draws (sometimes quite loosely) on traditional motifs to interpret or embody the stories and ancestors in wood or composite fibreboard.

Rongomaraeroa Marae at Te Papa in Wellington, carved by pioneering artist Cliff Whiting, is a colourful example of a contemporary reimagining of a traditional art form. The biggest change in carving (as with most traditional arts) has been in the use of new mediums and tools. Rangi Kipa uses a high-density plastic to make his *hei tiki* (traditional pendants). You can check out his gallery at www.rangikipa.com.

Read Hirini Moko Mead's *Tikanga Māori*, Pat and Hiwi Tauroa's *Te Marae*, and Anne Salmond's *Hui* for detailed information on Māori customs.

For information on Māori arts today, check out Toi Māori at www.maoriart.org.nz.

Weaving

Weaving was an essential art that provided clothing, nets and cordage, footwear for rough country travel, mats to cover earthen floors, and *kete* (bags) to carry stuff in. Many woven items are beautiful as well as practical. Some were major works – *korowai* (cloaks) could take years to finish.

VISITING MARAE

As you travel around NZ, you will see many *marae* complexes. Often *marae* are owned by a descent group. They are also owned by urban Māori groups, schools, universities and church groups, and they should only be visited by arrangement with the owners. Some *marae* that may be visited with an invitation include: **Koriniti Marae** (p255) on the Whanganui River Rd; **Mataatua** (p323) in Whakatane; and the *marae* at **Te Papa museum** (p368) in Wellington.

Marae complexes include a *wharenui* (meeting house), which often embodies an ancestor. Its ridge is the backbone, the rafters are ribs, and it shelters the descendants. There is a clear space in front of the *wharenui*, the *marae ātea*. Sometimes there are other buildings: a *wharekai* (dining hall); a toilet and shower block; perhaps even classrooms, play equipment and the like.

Hui (gatherings) are held at *marae*. Issues are discussed, classes conducted, milestones celebrated and the dead farewelled. Te reo Māori (the Māori language) is prominent, and sometimes the only language used.

Visitors sleep in the meeting house if a *hui* goes on for longer than a day. Mattresses are placed on the floor, someone may bring a guitar, and stories and jokes always go down well as the evening stretches out...

The Pōwhiri

If you visit a *marae* as part of an organised group, you'll be welcomed in a *pōwhiri*.

Outside the *marae*, there may be a *wero* (challenge). Using *taiaha* (quarter-staff) moves, a warrior will approach the visitors and place a baton on the ground for a visitor to pick up, to demonstrate their peaceful intent.

There is a *karanga* (ceremonial call). A woman from the host group calls to the visitors and a woman from the visitors responds. Their long, high, falling calls begin to overlap and interweave and the visiting group walks on to the *marae ātea* (meeting house courtyard). It is then time for *whaikōrero* (speechmaking). The hosts welcome the visitors, the visitors respond. Speeches are capped off by a *waiata* (song), and the visitors' speakers present a *koha* (gift, usually an envelope of cash). The hosts then invite the visitors to *hariru* (shake hands) and *hongi*. Visitors and hosts are now united and will share light refreshments or a meal.

The Hongi

Press forehead and nose together firmly, shake hands, and perhaps offer a greeting such as *'Kia ora'* or *'Tēnā koe'*. Some prefer one press (for two or three seconds, or longer), others prefer two shorter (press, release, press). Men and women sometimes kiss on one cheek. Some people mistakenly think the *hongi* is a pressing of noses only (awkward to aim!) or the rubbing of noses (even more awkward).

Tapu

Tapu (spiritual restrictions) and *mana* (power and prestige) are taken seriously in the Māori world. Sit on chairs or seating provided (never on tables), and walk around people, not over them. The *pōwhiri* is *tapu*, and mixing food and *tapu* is right up there on the offence-o-meter. Do eat and drink when invited to do so by your hosts. You needn't worry about starvation: an important Māori value is *manaakitanga* (kindness).

Depending on area, the *pōwhiri* has gender roles: women *karanga* (call), men *whaikōrero* (orate); women lead the way on to the *marae*, men sit on the *paepae* (the speakers' bench at the front). In a modern context, the debate around these roles continues.

Woven predominantly with flax and feathers, they are worn now on ceremonial occasions – a stunning sight.

Today, tradition is greatly respected, but not all traditions are necessarily followed. Flax was (and still is) the preferred medium for weaving. To get a strong fibre from flax leaves, weavers scraped away the leaves' flesh with a mussel shell, then pounded until it was soft, dyed it, then dried it. But contemporary weavers are using everything in their work: raffia, copper wire, rubber – even polar fleece and garden hoses!

The best way to experience weaving is to contact one of the many weavers running workshops. By learning the art, you'll appreciate the examples of weaving in museums even more. And if you want your own? Woven *kete* and backpacks have become fashion accessories and are on sale in most cities. Weaving is also found in dealer art galleries around the country.

See Ngahuia Te Awekotuku's book *Mau Moko: The World of Māori Tattoo* (2007) for a close-up of Māori body art, including powerful, beautiful images and an incisive commentary.

Haka

Haka can be adrenaline-pumping, awe-inspiring and uplifting. The *haka* is not only a war dance – it is used to welcome visitors, honour achievement, express identity and to put forth very strong opinions.

Haka involve chanted words, vigorous body movements and *pūkana* (when performers distort their faces, eyes bulging with the whites showing, perhaps with tongue extended).

The well-known *haka* 'Ka Mate', performed by the All Blacks before rugby test matches, is credited to the cunning fighting chief Te Rauparaha. It celebrates his escape from death. Chased by enemies, he hid himself in a food pit. After they had left, a friendly chief named Te Whareangi (the 'hairy man' referred to in the *haka*) let him out; he climbed out into the sunshine and performed 'Ka Mate'.

You can experience *haka* at various cultural performances, including at Mitai Māori Village (p305), Tamaki Māori Village (p305), Te Puia (p295) and Whakarewarewa (p296) in Rotorua; Ko Tane (p491) at Willowbank in Christchurch; and Kiwi Haka (p588) in Queenstown.

But the best displays of *haka* are at the national Te Matatini National Kapa Haka Festival (p32), when NZ's top groups compete. It's held every two years (and heads to Wellington in 2019).

A conversation starter for your next New Zealand barbecue: would NZ's 2011 and 2015 Rugby World Cup–winning All Blacks teams have been as unstoppable without key Māori players such as Dan Carter, Piri Weepu, Nehe Milner-Skudder and Aaron Smith?

Contemporary Theatre

Powered by a wave of political activism, the 1970s saw the emergence of many Māori playwrights and plays, and theatre remains a prominent area of the Māori arts today. Māori theatre drew heavily on the traditions of the *marae*. Instead of dimming the lights and immediately beginning the performance, many Māori theatre groups began with a stylised *pōwhiri*, had space for audience members to respond to the play, and ended with a *karakia* (prayer or incantation), or a farewell.

Taki Rua is an independent producer of Māori work for both children and adults and has been in existence for more than 30 years. As well as staging its shows in the major centres, it tours most of its work – check out its website (www.takirua.co.nz) for the current offerings. Māori drama is also often showcased at the professional theatres in the main centres as well as the biennial New Zealand Festival (p377). Look out for work by Hone Kouka, Briar Grace-Smith and Mitch Tawhi Thomas.

Contemporary Dance

Contemporary Māori dance often takes its inspiration from *kapa haka* (cultural dance) and traditional Māori imagery. The exploration of pre-European life also provides inspiration.

New Zealand's leading specifically Māori dance company is the Atamira Dance Collective (www.atamiradance.co.nz), which has been producing critically acclaimed, beautiful and challenging work since 2000. If that sounds too earnest, get acquainted with the work of musician and visual artist Mika Torotoro, who happily blends *kapa haka*, drag, opera, ballet and disco. You can check out clips of his work at www.mika.co.nz.

The first NZ hip-hop song to become a hit was Dalvanius Prime's 'Poi E', which was sung entirely in Māori by the Patea Māori Club. It was the highest-selling single of 1984 in NZ.

Māori Film-Making

Although there had already been successful Māori documentaries (*Patu!* and the *Tangata Whenua* series are brilliant), it wasn't until 1987 that NZ had its first fictional feature-length movie by a Māori writer and director, with Barry Barclay's *Ngati*. Mereta Mita was the first Māori woman to direct a fiction feature, with *Mauri* (1988). Both Mita and Barclay had highly political aims and ways of working, which involved a lengthy pre-production phase, during which they would consult with and seek direction from their *kaumātua* (elders). Films with significant Māori participation or control include the harrowing *Once Were Warriors* and the uplifting *Whale Rider*. Oscar-nominated Taika Waititi, of Te Whānau-ā-Apanui descent, wrote and directed *Eagle vs Shark* and *Boy*.

Ngā Taonga Sound & Vision (www.ngataonga.org.nz) is a great place to experience Māori film, with most showings being either free or relatively inexpensive. It has locations in Auckland and Wellington.

Māori Writing

There are many novels and collections of short stories by Māori writers, and personal taste will govern your choices. How about approaching Māori writing regionally? Read Patricia Grace *(Potiki, Cousins, Dogside Story, Tu)* around Wellington, and maybe Witi Ihimaera *(Pounamu, Pounamu; The Matriarch; Bulibasha; The Whale Rider)* on the North Island's East Coast. Keri Hulme *(The Bone People, Stonefish)* and the South Island go together like a mass of whitebait bound in a frying pan by a single egg (ie very well). Read Alan Duff *(Once Were Warriors)* anywhere, but only if you want to be saddened, even shocked. Definitely take James George *(Hummingbird, Ocean Roads)* with you to Auckland's west-coast beaches and Northland's Ninety Mile Beach. Paula Morris *(Queen of Beauty, Hibiscus Coast, Trendy but Casual)* and Kelly Ana Morey *(Bloom, Grace Is Gone)* – hmm, Auckland and beyond? If poetry appeals, you can't go past the giant of Māori poetry in English, the late, lamented Hone Tuwhare *(Deep River Talk: Collected Poems)*. Famously sounding like he's at church and in the pub at the same time, you *can* take him anywhere.

Could heavy metal be the newest form of expressing Māori identity? Singing (and screaming) in Te Reo Māori, Waipu guitar trio Alien Weaponry thrash out songs that narrate the battles of their ancestors.

Contemporary Visual Art

A distinctive feature of Māori visual art is the tension between traditional Māori ideas and modern artistic mediums and trends. Shane Cotton produced a series of works that conversed with 19th-century painted meeting houses, which themselves departed from Māori carved houses. Kelcy Taratoa uses sci-fi, superheroes and pop-art imagery.

Of course, Māori motifs aren't necessarily the dominant features of work by Māori artists. Major NZ artist Ralph Hotere was wary about being assigned any cultural, ethnic or genre label and his work confronted a broad range of political and social issues.

Contemporary Māori art is by no means only about painting. Many other artists use installations or digital formats – look out for work by Jacqueline Fraser, Peter Robinson and Lisa Reihana.

There are some great permanent exhibitions of Māori visual arts in the major centres. Both the Auckland Art Gallery (p82) and Christchurch Art Gallery (p482) hold strong collections, as does Wellington's Te Papa (p368).

Arts & Music

Māori music and art extends back to New Zealand's early, unrecorded history, but its motifs endure today in diverse forms. European settlers imported artistic styles from back home, but it took a century for postcolonial NZ to hone its distinctive artistic identity. In the first half of the 20th century it was writers and visual artists who led the charge, but in the decades that followed, music and movies catapulted the nation's creativity into the world's consciousness.

Literature

In 2013 New Zealanders rejoiced to hear that 28-year-old Eleanor Catton had become only the second NZ writer to ever win the Man Booker Prize, arguably the world's most prestigious award for literature, for her epic historical novel *The Luminaries* set on the West Coast. Lloyd Jones had come close in 2007 when his novel *Mister Pip* was shortlisted, but it had been a long wait between drinks since Keri Hulme took the prize in 1985 for her haunting novel *The Bone People*.

The TV show *Popstars* originated in New Zealand, though the resulting group, TrueBliss, was short-lived. The series concept was then picked up in Australia, the UK and the US, inspiring the *Idols* series.

Catton and Hulme continue in a proud line of NZ women writers, starting in the early 20th century with Katherine Mansfield. Mansfield's work began a Kiwi tradition in short fiction, and for years the standard was carried by novelist Janet Frame, whose dramatic life was depicted in Jane Campion's film of her autobiography, *An Angel at My Table*. Frame's novel *The Carpathians* won the Commonwealth Writers' Prize in 1989. A new author on New Zealanders' must-read lists is Catherine Chidgey, whose heart-rending novel *The Wish Child* (2016) won the country's top fiction prize at 2017's NZ Book Awards.

Less recognised internationally, Maurice Gee has gained the nation's annual top fiction gong six times, most recently with *Blindsight* in 2006. His much-loved children's novel *Under the Mountain* (1979) was made into a seminal NZ TV series in 1981, and then a major motion picture in 2009. In 2004 the adaptation of another of his novels, *In My Father's Den* (1972), won major awards at international film festivals.

The late Maurice Shadbolt also achieved much acclaim for his many novels, particularly those set during the New Zealand Wars. Try *Season of the Jew* (1987) or *The House of Strife* (1993).

MĀORI VOICES IN PRINT

Some of the most interesting and enjoyable NZ fiction voices belong to Māori writers, with Booker-winner Keri Hulme leading the way. Witi Ihimaera's novels give a wonderful insight into small-town Māori life on the East Coast – especially *Bulibasha* (1994) and *The Whale Rider* (1987), which was made into an acclaimed film. Patricia Grace's work is similarly filled with exquisitely told stories of rural *marae*-centred life: try *Mutuwhenua* (1978), *Potiki* (1986), *Dogside Story* (2001) or *Tu* (2004). *Chappy* (2015) is Grace's expansive tale of a prodigal son returning to NZ to untangle his cross-cultural heritage.

MIDDLE-EARTH TOURISM

Did the scenery of the epic film trilogy *Lord of the Rings (LOTR)* lure you to Aotearoa? The North Island has most of the big-ticket filming locations but both islands have knowledgeable operators that can take you set-jetting on foot, horseback or by 4WD. Dedicated enthusiasts can buy a copy of Ian Brodie's *The Lord of the Rings: Location Guidebook* for detail on filming locations and their GPS coordinates. Online, DOC has a useful primer (www.doc.govt.nz/lordoftherings).

North Island

Matamata, aka Hobbiton Peter Jackson's epic film trilogy *LOTR* put this town on the map and after the filming of *The Hobbit,* the town wholeheartedly embraced its Middle-earth credentials. **Hobbiton Movie Set Tours** (p198) allows you to pose by hobbit holes and enjoy a drink at the Green Dragon Inn.

Mt Ngauruhoe, aka Mt Doom Turns out the one ring to rule them all was forged in Tongariro National Park, in the North Island's youngest **volcano** (p281). Stickler for detail? A few Mt Doom scenes were filmed at Mt Ruapehu (best take a look at both).

Putangirua Pinnacles, aka Paths of the Dead An eerie landscape resembling giant organ pipes, the **pinnacles** (p399) were an obvious fit to portray the spooky passage through the White Mountains in *Lord of the Rings: Return of the King*.

Rover Rings (p377) and **Wellington Movie Tours** (p377) both offer half- to full-day tours of *LOTR* locations in and around Wellington.

South Island

Southern Alps, aka Misty Mountains Peter Jackson made the most of this untamed landscape, choosing Mt Cook Village as the setting for Minas Tirith.

Nomad Safaris (p582) and **Private Discovery Tours** (p594) offer a range of 4WD tours out of Queenstown, complete with Middle-earth movie locations. Glenorchy-based **Dart Stables** (p592) runs horse treks along a *LOTR* theme.

Cinema & TV

If you first became interested in New Zealand when watching it on the silver screen, you're in good company. Sir Peter Jackson's NZ-made *The Lord of the Rings* and *The Hobbit* trilogies were the best thing to happen to NZ tourism since Captain Cook.

Yet NZ cinema is hardly ever easygoing. In his BBC-funded documentary, *Cinema of Unease,* NZ actor Sam Neill described the country's film industry as producing bleak, haunted work. One need only watch Lee Tamahori's harrowing *Once Were Warriors* (1994) to see what he means.

The uniting factor in NZ film and TV is the landscape, which provides a haunting backdrop – arguably as much of a presence as the characters themselves. Jane Campion's *The Piano* (1993) and *Top of the Lake* (2013), Brad McGann's *In My Father's Den* (2004) and Jackson's *Heavenly Creatures* (1994) all use magically lush scenery to couch disturbing violence. It's a land-mysticism constantly bordering on the creepy.

Even when Kiwis do humour it's as resolutely black as their rugby jerseys; check out Jackson's early splatter-fests and Taika Waititi's *Boy* (2010). Exporting NZ comedy hasn't been easy, yet the HBO-produced TV musical parody *Flight of the Conchords* – featuring a mumbling, bumbling Kiwi folk-singing duo trying to get a break in New York – found surprising international success. It's the Polynesian giggle-factor that seems likeliest to break down the bleak house of NZ cinema, with feel-good-through-and-through *Sione's Wedding* (2006) enjoying the biggest opening weekend of any NZ film at the time.

Jane Campion was the first Kiwi nominated as Best Director and Peter Jackson the first to win it. *The Return of the King* won a mighty 11 Oscars in 2004.

Also packaging offbeat NZ humour for an international audience, *Hunt for the Wilderpeople* (2016) and *What We Do in the Shadows* (2014) have propelled scriptwriter and director Taika Waititi to critical acclaim, while *Thor: Ragnarok* (2017) made him a household name – though many argue that the director's star turn as a softly spoken rock creature is the movie's highlight.

New Zealanders have gone from never seeing themselves in international cinema to having whole cloned armies of Temuera Morrisons invading the universe in *Star Wars*. Familiar faces such as Cliff Curtis and Karl Urban seem to constantly pop up playing Mexican or Russian gangsters in action movies. Many of them got their start in long-running soap opera *Shortland Street*.

The only Kiwi actors to have won an Oscar are Anna Paquin (for *The Piano*) and Russell Crowe (for *Gladiator*). Paquin was born in Canada but moved to NZ when she was four, while Crowe moved from NZ to Australia at the same age.

Visual Arts

The NZ 'can do' attitude extends to the visual arts. If you're visiting a local's home, don't be surprised to find one of the owner's paintings on the wall or one of their mate's sculptures in the back garden, pieced together out of bits of shell, driftwood and a length of the magical 'number 8 wire'.

This is symptomatic of a flourishing local art and crafts scene cultivated by lively tertiary courses churning out traditional carvers and weavers, jewellery-makers, and moulders of metal and glass. The larger cities have excellent dealer galleries representing interesting local artists working across all media.

Traditional Māori art has a distinctive visual style with well-developed motifs that have been embraced by NZ artists of every race. In the painting medium, these include the cool modernism of Gordon Walters and the more controversial pop-art approach of Dick Frizzell's *Tiki* series. Likewise, Pacific Island themes are common, particularly in Auckland; look out for the intricate, collage-like paintings of Niuean-born, Auckland-raised John Pule.

Charles Frederick Goldie painted a series of compelling, realist portraits of Māori, who were feared to be a dying race. Debate over the political propriety of Goldie's work raged for years, but its value is widely accepted now: not least because Māori themselves generally acknowledge and value them as ancestral representations. In 2016 Goldie's last work became the first NZ painting to be sold for more than $1 million.

A wide range of cultural events are listed on www.eventfinda.co.nz. This is a good place to find out about concerts, classical music recitals and *kapa haka* performances. For more specific information on the NZ classical music scene, see www.sounz.org.nz.

Recalibrating the ways in which Pacific Islander and Māori people are depicted in art, Lisa Reihana wowed the Venice Biennale in 2017 with her multimedia work *In Pursuit of Venus*.

Depicting the Land

It's no surprise that in a nation so defined by its natural environment, landscape painting constituted the first post-European body of art. In the late 19th century, John Gully and Petrus van der Velden were among those to arrive and capture the drama of the land in paintings.

Colin McCahon is widely regarded to have been NZ's most important artist. Even where McCahon lurched into Catholic mysticism, his spirituality was rooted in geography. His brooding landscapes evoke the land's power but also its vulnerability. McCahon is widely quoted as describing his work as a depiction of NZ before its seas become cluttered with debris and the sky turns dark with soot.

Landscape photographers also capture the fierceness and fragility of NZ's terrain. It's worth detouring to a few of the country's resident photographers, many of whom have their own gallery (sometimes within, or adjoining their own home). Westland is home to the gallery of exceptionally gifted photographer **Andris Apse** (☎021 884 618, 03-753 4241; www.andrisapse.com; 109 The Strand; ⊙hours vary) and to the

Petr Hlavacek Gallery (☏03-753 4199; www.nzicescapes.com; 2811b SH6; ⊙9am-7pm Mon-Fri) FREE, which showcases some of NZ's finest landscape photography.

Music

New Zealand music began with the *waiata* (singing) developed by Māori following their arrival in the country. The main musical instruments were wind instruments made of bone or wood, the most well known of which is the *nguru* (also known as the 'nose flute'), while percussion was provided by chest- and thigh-slapping. These days, the liveliest place to see Māori music being performed is at *kapa haka* competitions in which groups compete with their own routines of traditional song and dance.

Tickets for most events can be bought at www. ticketek.co.nz, www.ticket master.co.nz or, for smaller gigs, www.underthe radar.co.nz.

Classical & Opera

Early European immigrants brought their own styles of music and gave birth to local variants during the early 1900s. In the 1950s Douglas Lilburn became one of the first internationally recognised NZ classical composers. More recently the country has produced a number of world-renowned musicians in this field, including legendary opera singer Dame Kiri Te Kanawa, million-selling classic-to-pop singer Hayley Westenra, composer John Psathas (who created music for the 2004 Olympic Games) and composer/percussionist Gareth Farr (who also performs in drag under the name Lilith LaCroix).

Rock & Metal

New Zealand's most acclaimed rock exports are the revered indie label Flying Nun and the music of the Finn Brothers.

Started in 1981 by Christchurch record-store owner Roger Shepherd, many of Flying Nun's early groups came from Dunedin, where local musicians took the DIY attitude of punk but used it to produce a lo-fi indie-pop that received rave reviews from the likes of *NME* in the UK and *Rolling Stone* in the US. Many of the musicians from the Flying Nun scene still perform live to this day, including David Kilgour (from the Clean) and Shayne Carter (from the Straitjacket Fits, and subsequently Dimmer and the Adults).

Want something heavier? Hamilton heavy-metal act Devilskin's 2014 debut album hit the top spot on NZ's charts, as did their punchy 2016 follow-up *Be Like the River*. Beastwars, a rasping, trance-inducing sludge metal band from Wellington, is another stalwart of NZ's heavy-metal

---

THE BROTHERS FINN

There are certain tunes that all Kiwis can sing along to, given a beer and the opportunity. A surprising proportion of these were written by Tim and Neil Finn, many of which have been international hits. Tim Finn first came to prominence in the 1970s group Split Enz, who amassed a solid following in Australia, NZ and Canada before disbanding in 1985. Neil then formed Crowded House with two Australian musicians (Paul Hester and Nick Seymour) and one of their early singles, 'Don't Dream It's Over', hit number two on the US charts. Tim later did a brief spell in the band, during which the brothers wrote 'Weather with You' – a song that reached number seven on the UK charts, pushing their album *Woodface* to gold sales. Neil has also remained busy, organising a set of shows/releases under the name 7 Worlds Collide – a collaboration with well-known overseas musicians. Tim and Neil have both released a number of solo albums, as well as releasing material together as the Finn Brothers.

In April 2018 Fleetwood Mac announced that Neil Finn would be joining the band, following the unexpected departure of Lindsay Buckingham. Finn, along with Mike Campbell (guitarist with Tom Petty and the Heartbreakers) will replace Buckingham on the band's 2018 tour.

GOOD LORDE!

The biggest name in Kiwi music is Lorde, a singer-songwriter from Devonport on Auckland's North Shore. Known less regally to her friends as Ella Yelich-O'Connor, Lorde was 16 years old when she cracked the number-one spot on the US Billboard charts in 2013 with her magical, schoolyard-chant-evoking hit 'Royals' – the first NZ solo artist to top the American charts. 'Royals' then went on to win the Song of the Year Grammy in 2014. Her debut album *Pure Heroine* spawned a string of hits and sold millions of copies worldwide, while moody follow-up *Melodrama* instantly topped charts in NZ and the US upon its release in 2017.

scene. Meanwhile, hitting the big leagues during tours of North America and Europe, technical death-metal band Ulcerate have risen to prominence as NZ's best-known extreme metal act. We're not worthy.

Reggae, Hip-Hop & Dance

The genres of music that have been adopted most enthusiastically by Māori and Polynesian New Zealanders have been reggae (in the 1970s) and hip-hop (in the 1980s), which has led to distinct local forms. In Wellington, a thriving jazz scene took on a reggae influence to create a host of groups that blended dub, roots and funky jazz – most notably Fat Freddy's Drop.

The local hip-hop scene has its heart in the suburbs of South Auckland, which have a high concentration of Māori and Pacific Island residents. This area is home to one of New Zealand's foremost hip-hop labels, Dawn Raid, which takes its name from the infamous 1970s early-morning house raids that police performed on Pacific Islanders suspected of outstaying their visas. Dawn Raid's most successful artist is Savage, who sold a million copies of his single 'Swing' after it was featured in the movie *Knocked Up*. Within New Zealand, the most well-known hip-hop acts are Scribe, Che Fu and Smashproof (whose song 'Brother' held number one on the NZ singles charts for 11 weeks).

For more on local hip-hop, pop and rock, check out www.thecorner. co.nz and the long-running www.muzic. net.nz.

Dance music gained a foothold in Christchurch in the 1990s, spawning dub/electronica outfit Salmonella Dub and its offshoot act, Tiki Taane. Drum 'n' bass remains popular locally and has spawned internationally renowned acts such as Concord Dawn and Shapeshifter.

Movers & Shakers

Since 2000, the NZ music scene has developed new vitality after the government convinced commercial radio stations to adopt a voluntary quota of 20% local music. This enabled commercially oriented musicians to develop solid careers. Rock groups such as Shihad, the Feelers and Opshop thrived in this environment, as have a set of soulful female solo artists: Bic Runga, Anika Moa and Brooke Fraser (daughter of All Black Bernie Fraser). New Zealand also produced two internationally acclaimed garage rock acts over this time: the Datsuns and the D4.

Current Kiwis garnering international recognition include the incredibly gifted songstress Kimbra (who sang on Gotye's global smash 'Somebody That I Used To Know'); indie electro-rockers the Naked and Famous; multitalented singer-songwriter Ladyhawke; the arty Lawrence Arabia; and the semipsychedelic Unknown Mortal Orchestra.

R&B singer Aaradhna made a splash with her album *Treble & Reverb*, which won Album of the Year at the 2013 New Zealand Music Awards. When the title track of her album *Brown Girl* was awarded a gong for 'best hip-hop' in 2016, she turned it down saying she'd been placed in the wrong musical category because of the colour of her skin.

Survival Guide

Directory A–Z

Accommodation

B&Bs

➡ Bed and breakfast (B&B) accommodation in NZ pops up in the middle of cities, in rural hamlets and on stretches of isolated coastline, with rooms on offer in everything from suburban bungalows to stately manors.

Breakfast may be 'continental' (a standard offering of cereal, toast and tea or coffee, or a heartier version with yoghurt, fruit, home-baked bread or muffins), or a stomach-loading cooked meal (eggs, bacon, sausages...though with notice, vegetarians are increasingly being well catered for). Some B&B hosts may also cook dinner for guests and advertise dinner, bed and breakfast (DB&B) packages.

B&B tariffs are typically in the $120 to $200 bracket (per double), though some places cost upwards of $300 per double. Some hosts charge cheeky prices for what is, in essence, a bedroom in their home. Off-street parking is often a bonus in the big cities.

BOOK YOUR STAY ONLINE

For more accommodation reviews by Lonely Planet authors, check out http://lonelyplanet.com/new-zealand/hotels/. You'll find independent reviews, as well as recommendations on the best places to stay. Best of all, you can book online.

Booking Services

Local visitor information centres around NZ provide reams of local accommodation information, sometimes in the form of folders detailing facilities and up-to-date prices; many can also make bookings on your behalf.

Lonely Planet (www.lonelyplanet.com/new-zealand/hotels) The full range of NZ accommodation, from hostels to hotels.

Automobile Association (www.aa.co.nz/travel) Online accommodation bookings (especially good for motels, B&Bs and holiday parks).

Jasons (www.jasons.co.nz) Long-running travel service with myriad online booking options.

New Zealand Bed & Breakfast (www.bnb.co.nz) The name says it all.

Bed & Breakfast New Zealand (www.bed-and-breakfast.co.nz) B&B and self-contained accommodation directory.

Rural Holidays NZ (www.ruralholidays.co.nz) Farm and homestay listings across NZ.

Book a Bach (www.bookabach.co.nz) Apartment and holiday-house bookings (and maybe even a bach or two!).

Holiday Houses (www.holidayhouses.co.nz) Holiday-house rentals NZ-wide.

New Zealand Apartments (www.nzapartments.co.nz) Rental listings for upmarket apartments of all sizes.

Camping & Holiday Parks

Campers and campervan drivers converge on NZ's hugely popular 'holiday parks', slumbering in powered and unpowered sites, cheap bunk rooms (dorm rooms), cabins (shared bathroom facilities) and self-contained units (often called motels or tourist flats). Well-equipped communal kitchens, dining areas, games and TV rooms, and playgrounds often feature. In cities, holiday parks are usually a fair way from the action, but in smaller towns they can be impressively central or near lakes, beaches, rivers and forests.

The nightly cost of holiday-park tent sites is usually $15 to $20 per adult, with children charged half price; powered campervan sites can be anything from a couple of dollars more to around the $40 mark. Cabin/unit accommodation normally ranges from $70 to $120 per double. Unless noted otherwise, Lonely Planet lists campsite, campervan site, hut and cabin prices for two people.

DOC & FREEDOM CAMPING

A fantastic option for those in campervans is the 250-plus

vehicle-accessible 'Conservation Campsites' run by the Department of Conservation (DOC; www.doc.govt.nz), with fees ranging from free (basic toilets and fresh water) to $21 per adult (flush toilets and showers). DOC publishes free brochures with detailed descriptions and instructions to find every campsite (even GPS coordinates). Pick up copies from DOC offices before you hit the road, or visit the website.

The DOC also looks after hundreds of 'Backcountry Huts' and 'Backcountry Campsites', which can only be reached on foot. 'Great Walk' huts and campsites are also managed by DOC.

New Zealand is so photogenic, it's tempting to just pull off the road at a gorgeous viewpoint and camp the night. But never assume it's OK to camp somewhere: always ask a local or check with the local i-SITE visitor centre, DOC office or commercial campground. If you are 'freedom camping', treat the area with respect. If your chosen campsite doesn't have toilet facilities and neither does your campervan, it's illegal for you to sleep there (your campervan must also have an on-board grey-water storage system). Legislation allows for $200 instant fines for camping in prohibited areas or improper disposal of waste (in cases where dumping waste could damage the environment, fees are up to $10,000).

See www.camping.org.nz for more freedom-camping tips and consider downloading the free Campermate App (www.campermate.co.nz), which flags drinking-water sources, public toilets, freedom-camping spots and locals happy to rent their driveway to campervans.

Farmstays

Farmstays open the door to the agricultural side of NZ life, with visitors encouraged to get some dirt beneath their fingernails at orchards, and dairy, sheep and cattle farms. Costs can vary widely, with bed and breakfast generally costing $80 to $140. Some farms have separate cottages where you can fix your own food; others offer low-cost, shared, backpacker-style accommodation.

Farm Helpers in NZ (www.fhinz.co.nz) produces a booklet ($25) that lists around 350 NZ farms providing lodging in exchange for four to six hours' work per day.

Hostels

New Zealand is packed to the rafters with backpacker hostels, both independent and part of large chains, ranging from small, homestay-style affairs with a handful of beds, to refurbished hotels and towering modern structures in the big cities. Hostel bed prices listed by Lonely Planet are nonmember rates, usually $25 to $35 per night.

WWOOFING

If you don't mind getting your hands dirty, an economical way of travelling around NZ involves doing some voluntary work as a member of the international **Willing Workers On Organic Farms** (WWOOF; ☑03-544 9890; www.wwoof.co.nz; ⊙9am-3pm Mon-Fri) scheme. Down on the farm, in exchange for a hard day's work, owners provide food, accommodation and some hands-on organic farming experience. Contact farm owners a week or two beforehand to arrange your stay, as you would for a hotel or hostel – don't turn up unannounced!

A one-year online membership costs $40 for an individual or a couple. A farm-listing book, which is mailed to you, costs an extra $10 to $30, depending on where in the world your mailbox is. You should have a Working Holiday Visa when you visit NZ, as the immigration department considers WWOOFers to be working.

HOSTEL ORGANISATIONS

Budget Backpacker Hostels (www.bbh.co.nz) A network of more than 160 hostels. Membership costs $45 for 12 months and entitles you to stay at member hostels at rates listed in the annual (free) BBH Backpacker Accommodation booklet. Nonmembers pay an extra $4 per night. Pick up a membership card from any member hostel or order one online ($50).

YHA New Zealand (www.yha.co.nz) Around 40 hostels in prime NZ locations. The YHA is part of the Hostelling International network (www.hihostels.com), so if you're already an HI member in your own country, membership entitles you to use NZ hostels. If you don't already have a home membership, you can join at major NZ YHA hostels or online for $25, valid for 12 months (it's free for under 18s). Nonmembers pay an extra $3 or more per night. Membership has other perks, such as discounts on some

SLEEPING PRICE RANGES

The following price ranges refer to a double room with bathroom during high season. Price ranges generally increase by 20% to 25% in Auckland, Wellington and Christchurch. Here you can still find budget accommodation at up to $120 per double, but midrange stretches from $120 to $250, with top-end rooms more than $250.

$ less than $120

$$ $120–$200

$$$ more than $200

car-hire providers, travel insurers, DOC hut passes and more.

Base Backpackers (www.stayatbase.com) Chain with nine-plus hostels around NZ: Bay of Islands, Auckland, Rotorua, Taupo, Wellington, Wanaka, Queenstown, Dunedin and Christchurch. Expect clean dorms, women-only areas and party opportunities aplenty. Offers a flexible 10-night 'Base Jumping' accommodation package for $289, bookable online.

VIP Backpackers (www.vip backpackers.com) International organisation affiliated with around 20 NZ hostels (not BBH or YHA), mainly in the cities and tourist hotspots. For around $61 (including postage), you'll receive a 12-month membership entitling you to a $1 discount off nightly accommodation and discounts with affiliated activity and tour providers. Join online or at VIP hostels.

Haka Lodge (www.hakalodge.com) A local chain on the way up, with snazzy hostels in Auckland, Queenstown, Christchurch, Taupo and Paihia. Rates are comparable to other hostels around NZ, and quality is high. Tours are also available.

Pubs, Hotels & Motels

The least expensive form of NZ hotel accommodation is the humble pub. Some are full of character (and characters); others are grotty, ramshackle places that are best avoided (especially by women travelling solo). Check whether there's a band playing the night you're staying – you could be in for a sleepless night. In the cheapest pubs, singles/doubles might cost as little as $45/70 (with a shared bathroom down the hall); $70/90 is more common.

At the top end of the hotel scale are five-star international chains, resort complexes and architecturally splendorous boutique hotels, all of which charge a hefty premium for their mod cons, snappy service and/or historic opulence. We quote 'rack rates' (official advertised rates) for such places, but discounts and special deals often apply.

New Zealand's towns have a glut of nondescript, low-rise motels and 'motor lodges', charging $90 to $200 for double rooms. These tend to be squat structures skulking by highways on the edges of towns. Most are modernish (though decor is often mired in the early 2000s or earlier) and have basic facilities, namely tea- and coffee-making equipment, fridge and TV. Prices vary with standard.

Rental Accommodation

The basic Kiwi holiday home is called a 'bach' (short for 'bachelor', as they were historically used by single men as hunting and fishing hideouts); in Otago and Southland they're known as 'cribs'. These are simple self-contained cottages that can be rented in rural and coastal areas, often in isolated locations, and sometimes include surf, fishing or other outdoor gear rental in the cost. Prices are typically $90 to $180 per night, which isn't bad for a whole house or self-contained bungalow. For more upmarket holiday houses, expect to pay anything from $180 to $400 per double.

Customs Regulations

For the low-down on what you can and can't bring into NZ, see the New Zealand Customs Service website (www.customs.govt.nz). Per-person duty-free allowances:

➡ Three 1125mL (max) bottles of spirits or liqueur

➡ 4.5L of wine or beer

➡ 50 cigarettes, or 50g of tobacco or cigars

➡ Dutiable goods up to the value of $700

It's a good idea to declare any unusual medicines. Tramping gear (boots, tents etc) will be checked and may need to be cleaned before being allowed in. You must declare any plant or animal products (including anything made of wood), and food of any kind. Weapons and firearms are either prohibited or require a permit and safety testing. Don't take these rules lightly – noncompliance penalties will really hurt your hip pocket.

Discount Cards

The internationally recognised **International Student Identity Card** is produced by the ISIC Association (www.isic.org), and issued to full-

---

PRACTICALITIES

Newspapers Check out Auckland's *New Zealand Herald* (www.nzherald.co.nz), Wellington's *Dominion Post* (www.stuff.co.nz/dominion-post) or Christchurch's *The Press* (www.stuff.co.nz/the-press).

TV Watch one of the national government-owned TV stations – including TVNZ 1, TVNZ 2, Māori TV or the 100% Māori-language Te Reo.

Radio Tune in to Radio New Zealand (www.radionz.co.nz) for news, current affairs, classical and jazz. Radio Hauraki (www.hauraki.co.nz) cranks out rock.

DVDs Kiwi DVDs are encoded for Region 4, which includes Australia, the Pacific, Mexico, Central America, the Caribbean and South America.

Smoking Smoking on public transport and in restaurants, cafes, bars and pubs is banned.

Weights & measures NZ uses the metric system.

Climate

Auckland

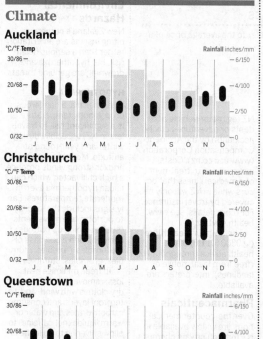

°C/°F Temp — Rainfall inches/mm

30/86 — — 6/150
20/68 — — 4/100
10/50 — — 2/50
0/32 — — 0
J F M A M J J A S O N D

Christchurch

°C/°F Temp — Rainfall inches/mm

30/86 — — 6/150
20/68 — — 4/100
10/50 — — 2/50
0/32 — — 0
J F M A M J J A S O N D

Queenstown

°C/°F Temp — Rainfall inches/mm

30/86 — — 6/150
20/68 — — 4/100
10/50 — — 2/50
0/32 — — 0
J F M A M J J A S O N D

Electricity

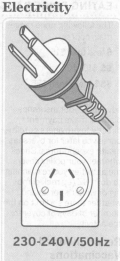

230-240V/50Hz

time students aged 12 and over. It provides discounts on accommodation, transport and admission to attractions. The same folks also produce the **International Youth Travel Card**, available to travellers aged under 31 who are not full-time students, with equivalent benefits to the ISIC. Also similar is the **International Teacher Identity Card**, available to teaching professionals. All three cards ($30 each) are available online at www.isiccard.co.nz, or from student travel companies like STA Travel.

The **New Zealand Card** (www.newzealandcard.com) is a $35 discount pass that'll score you between 5% and 50% off a range of accommodation, tours, sights and activities. Browse participating businesses before you buy. A **Budget Backpacker Hostels** (www.bbh.co.nz) membership card costs $45 and entitles you to discounts at BBH member hostels, usually snipping $4 off the price per night.

Travellers aged over 60 with some form of identification, the emphasis is card from your home country) are often eligible for concession prices.

Food

New Zealand is a mighty fine place to wine and dine (p64). From country pubs to chic restaurants, the emphasis is on home-grown ingredients like lamb, seafood and venison, with a thriving vegetarian and vegan food scene to cleanse the palate. Dining choices depend on destination: you'll be spoilt for choice in Auckland while little seaside towns might have just a bakery and pub to pick from.

Health

New Zealand poses minimal health risks to travellers. Diseases such as malaria and typhoid are unheard of, poisonous snakes and other dangerous animals are absent, and there are currently no dangerous insect-borne diseases. The biggest risks to travellers involve exploring the great outdoors: trampers must be clued in on rapid-changing weather and diligent about sharing any plans to visit remote areas, meanwhile drivers must exert extreme caution on NZ's notoriously winding roads.

Health Insurance

Health insurance is essential for all travellers. While health care in NZ is of a high quality and not overly expensive by international standards, considerable costs can be built up and repatriation is pricey.

If you don't have a health insurance plan that covers you for medical expenses incurred overseas, buy a travel insurance policy – see www.lonelyplanet.com/travel-insurance. Find out in advance if your insurance plan will make payments directly to providers or reimburse you later for overseas health expenditures. Check whether your policy covers the activities you're planning to do in NZ (eg rock climbing or winter sports) and whether there's a limit on the number of days of cover for the activity.

Recommended Vaccinations

New Zealand has no vaccination requirements for any traveller, but the World Health Organization recommends that all travellers should be covered for chickenpox, diphtheria, hepatitis B, measles, mumps, pertussis (whooping cough), polio, rubella, seasonal flu, tetanus and tuberculosis, regardless of their destination. Ask your doctor for an *International Certificate of Vaccination* (or 'the yellow booklet') in which they will list all the vaccinations you've received.

Medications

Bring any prescribed medications for your trip in their original, clearly labelled containers. It is also wise to bring a signed and dated letter from your physician describing your medical conditions and medications (including generic names), and any requisite syringes or needles.

Availability & Cost of Health Care

New Zealand's public hospitals offer a high standard of care (free for residents). All travellers are covered for medical care resulting from accidents that occur while in NZ (eg motor-vehicle accidents or adventure-activity accidents) by the Accident Compensation Corporation (www.acc.co.nz). Costs incurred due to treatment of a medical illness that occurs while in NZ will only be covered by travel insurance. For more details, see www.health.govt.nz.

The 24-hour **Healthline** (☑ 0800 611 116) offers health advice throughout NZ (free from local mobile or landlines). Interpreters are available.

Pharmaceuticals

Over-the-counter medications are widely available in NZ through private chemists (pharmacies). These include painkillers, antihistamines, skincare products and sunscreen. Some medications, such as antibiotics, are only available via a prescription obtained from a general practitioner. Some varieties of the contraceptive pill can be bought at pharmacies without a prescription (provided the woman has been prescribed the pill within the last three years). If you take regular medications, bring an adequate supply and details of the generic name, as brand names differ country to country.

Tap Water

Tap water throughout New Zealand is generally safe to drink, and public taps with nondrinkable water tend to be labelled as such. However, water quality has faced pollution challenges in some places. Very occasionally, a warning may be issued that tap water must be boiled – your accommodation should inform you if this happens.

Environmental Hazards

New Zealand's numerous biting insects are an irritation rather than a serious health risk, but hypothermia and drowning are genuine threats.

HYPOTHERMIA

Hypothermia, a dangerous drop in body temperature, is a significant risk to travellers in NZ, especially during winter and year-round at altitude. Mountain ranges and/or strong winds produce a high chill factor, which can cause hypothermia even in moderate temperatures. Early signs include the inability to perform fine movements (such as doing up buttons), shivering and a bad case of the 'umbles' (fumbles, mumbles, grumbles, stumbles).

To treat, minimise heat loss: remove wet clothing, add dry clothes with wind- and waterproof layers, and consume carbohydrates and water or warm liquids (not caffeine) to allow shivering to build the internal temperature. In severe hypothermia cases, shivering actually stops; this is a medical emergency requiring rapid evacuation in addition to the above measures.

SURF BEACHES

New Zealand has exceptional surf beaches. The power of the surf can fluctuate as a result of the varying slope of the seabed: rips and undertows are common, and drownings do happen. Check with local surf lifesaving organisations before jumping in the sea, always heed warning signs at beaches, and be realistic about your own limitations and expertise.

BITING INSECTS

Wear long, loose clothing and use an insect repellent containing 20% or more DEET to ward off sandflies and mosquitoes, which are particularly common in lake areas and tree-lined clearings on the South Island. Bites are intensely itchy, but fortunately don't spread disease.

Infectious Diseases

Aside from the same sexually transferred infections that are found worldwide (take normal precautions), giardiasis is the main infectious disease to be aware of when travelling in NZ.

GIARDIASIS

The giardia parasite is widespread in NZ waterways: drinking untreated water from streams and lakes is not recommended. Using water filters and boiling or treating water with iodine are effective ways of preventing the disease. The parasite can also latch on to swimmers in rivers and lakes (try not to swallow water), or through contact with infected animals. Symptoms consist of diarrhoea, vomiting, stomach cramps, abdominal bloating and wind. Effective treatment is available (tinidazole or metronidazole).

Insurance

A watertight travel-insurance policy covering theft, loss and medical problems is essential. Some policies specifically exclude designated 'dangerous activities', such as scuba diving, bungy jumping, white-water rafting, skiing and even tramping. If you plan on doing any of these things (a distinct possibility in NZ!), make sure your policy covers you fully.

It's worth mentioning that under NZ law, you cannot sue for personal injury (other than exemplary damages). Instead, the country's Accident Compensation Corporation (www.acc.co.nz) administers an accident compensation scheme that provides accident insurance for NZ residents and visitors to the country, regardless of fault. This scheme, however, does not negate the necessity for your own comprehensive travel-insurance policy, as it doesn't cover you for such things as income loss, treatment at home or ongoing illness.

Consider a policy that pays doctors or hospitals directly, rather than you paying on the spot and claiming later. If you have to claim later, keep all documentation. Some policies ask you to call (reverse charges) to a centre in your home country where an immediate assessment of your problem is made. Check that the policy covers ambulances and emergency medical evacuations by air.

Worldwide travel insurance is available at www.lonelyplanet.com/travel-insurance. You can buy, extend and claim online anytime – even if you're already on the road.

Internet Access

Getting online in NZ is easy in all but remote locales. Expect abundant wi-fi in cafes and accommodation in big towns and cities, but thrifty download limits elsewhere.

Wi-fi Access

Wi-fi You'll be able to find wi-fi access around the country, from hotel rooms to pub beer gardens to hostel dorms. Usually you have to be a guest or customer to log in; you'll be issued with an access code. Sometimes it's free, sometimes there's a charge, often there's a limit on time or data.

Hotspots The country's main telecommunications company is Spark New Zealand (www.spark.co.nz), which has more than 1000 wireless hotspots around the country. You can purchase prepaid access cards or a prepaid number from the login page at any wireless hotspot using your credit card. See Spark's website for hotspot listings.

Equipment & ISPs If you've brought your tablet or laptop, consider buying a prepay USB modem (aka a 'dongle') with a local SIM card: both Spark and Vodafone (www.vodafone.co.nz) sell these from around $50.

Internet Cafes

There are fewer internet cafes around these days than there were five years ago, but you'll still find them in the bigger cities (frequented more by gamers than tourists). Access costs anywhere from $3 to $6 per hour.

Similarly, most hostels and holiday parks have done away with actual computers in favour of wi-fi. Most hotels, motels, B&Bs and holiday parks also offer wi-fi, sometimes for free, but usually for a small charge.

Legal Matters

If you are questioned or arrested by police, it's your right to ask why, to refrain from making a statement, and to consult a lawyer in private.

Plans are brewing for a referendum on whether personal use of cannabis should be decriminalised, but at the time of writing it was still illegal. Anyone caught carrying this or other illicit drugs will have the book thrown at them.

Drink-driving is a serious offence and remains a significant problem in NZ. The legal blood alcohol limit is 0.05% for drivers aged 20 years and over, and zero for those under 20.

LGBTIQ+ Travellers

The gay tourism industry in NZ isn't as high profile as it is in some other developed nations, but LGBT communities are prominent in Auckland and Wellington, with myriad support organisations across both islands. New Zealand has progressive laws protecting human rights: same-sex marriage and adoption by same-sex couples were legalised in 2013, while the legal minimum age for sex between consenting persons is 16. Generally speaking, Kiwis are fairly relaxed and accepting about gender fluidity, but that's not to say that homophobia doesn't exist. Rural communities tend to be more conservative; here public displays of affection should probably be avoided.

Resources

There are loads of websites dedicated to gay and lesbian travel in NZ. Gay Tourism New Zealand (www.gaytourismnewzealand.com) is a starting point, with links to various sites. Other worthwhile websites include the following:

➡ www.gaynz.net.nz

➡ www.lesbian.net.nz

➡ www.gaystay.co.nz

Check out the nationwide monthly magazine *express* (www.gayexpress.co.nz) for the latest happenings, reviews and listings on the NZ gay scene. New Zealand Awaits (www.newzealandawaits.com) is a local operator specialising in tours serving LGBT travellers.

Festivals & Events

Auckland Pride Festival (www.aucklandpridefestival.org.nz) Two-and-a-bit weeks of rainbow-hued celebrations in February.

Big Gay Out (www.biggayout.co.nz) Part of the Auckland Pride Festival in February, this flagship day features live music and 'Mr Gay New Zealand'.

Gay Ski Week (www.gayskiweekqt.com) Annual Queenstown snow-fest in August/September.

Maps

New Zealand's **Automobile Association** (AA; ☑0800 500 444; www.aa.co.nz/travel) produces excellent city, town, regional, island and highway maps, available from its local offices. The AA also produces a detailed *New Zealand Road Atlas*. Other reliable countrywide atlases, available from visitor information centres and bookshops, are published by Hema and KiwiMaps.

Land Information New Zealand (www.linz.govt.nz) publishes several exhaustive map series, including street, country and holiday maps, national park and forest park maps, and topographical trampers' maps. Scan the larger bookshops, or try the nearest DOC office or visitor information centre for topo maps.

Online, log onto AA Maps (www.aamaps.co.nz) or Wises (www.wises.co.nz) to pinpoint exact NZ addresses.

Money

ATMs & Eftpos

Branches of the country's major banks across both islands have ATMs, but you won't find them everywhere (eg not in small towns).

Many NZ businesses use Eftpos (electronic funds transfer at point of sale), allowing you to use your bank card (credit or debit) to make direct purchases and often withdraw cash as well. Eftpos is available practically everywhere: just like at an ATM, you'll need a PIN number.

Bank Accounts

You'll need to open a bank account if you want to work in NZ in any capacity (including working holiday scenarios) and it's best to do your homework before you arrive. Some banks, such as ANZ, allow you to apply before you arrive and activate the account at a branch when you get here (armed with the requisite ID, usually a passport, certified translation if applicable, and proof of NZ residence). Proof of address might involve using an identity verification service.

Credit Cards & Debit Cards

CREDIT CARDS

Credit cards (Visa, Master-Card) are widely accepted for everything from a hostel bed to a bungy jump, and are pretty much essential for car hire. Credit cards can also be used for over-the-counter cash advances at banks and from ATMs, but be aware that such transactions incur charges. Diners Club and American Express cards are not as widely accepted.

DEBIT CARDS

Debit cards enable you to draw money directly from your home bank account using ATMs, banks or Eftpos facilities. Any card connected to the international banking network (Cirrus, Maestro, Visa Plus and Eurocard) should work with your PIN. Fees will vary depending on your home bank; check before you leave. Alternatively, companies such as Travelex offer debit cards with set withdrawal fees and a balance you can top up from your personal bank account while on the road.

Currency

New Zealand's currency is the NZ dollar, comprising 100 cents. There are 10c, 20c, 50c, $1 and $2 coins, and $5, $10, $20, $50 and $100 notes. Prices are often still marked in single cents and then rounded to the nearest 10c when you hand over your money.

Money Changers

Changing foreign currency (and to a lesser extent old-fashioned travellers cheques) is usually no problem at NZ banks or at licensed money changers (eg Travelex) in major tourist areas, cities and airports.

Taxes & Refunds

The Goods and Services Tax (GST) is a flat 15% tax on all domestic goods and services. New Zealand prices listed by Lonely Planet include GST. There's no GST refund available when you leave NZ.

Tipping

Tipping is completely optional in NZ; see First Time (p25) for more information.

Travellers Cheques

Amex, Travelex and other international brands of travellers cheques are a bit old hat these days, but they're still easily exchanged at banks and money changers. Present your passport for identification when cashing them; shop around for the best rates.

Opening Hours

Opening hours vary seasonally depending on where you are. Most places close on Christmas Day and Good Friday.

Banks 9am–4.30pm Monday to Friday, some also 9am–noon Saturday

Cafes 7am–4pm

Post Offices 8.30am–5pm Monday to Friday; larger branches also 9.30am–noon Saturday

Pubs & Bars noon–late ('late' varies by region, and by day)

Restaurants noon–2.30pm and 6.30pm–9pm

Shops & Businesses 9am–5.30pm Monday to Friday and 9am to noon or 5pm Saturday

Supermarkets 8am–7pm, often 9pm or later in cities

Post

The services offered by **New Zealand Post** (☎0800 501 501; www.nzpost.co.nz) are reliable and reasonably inexpensive. See the website for info on national and international zones and rates, plus post office (or 'post shop') locations.

Public Holidays

New Zealand's main public holidays:

New Year 1 and 2 January

Waitangi Day 6 February

Easter Good Friday and Easter Monday; March/April

Anzac Day 25 April

Queen's Birthday First Monday in June

Labour Day Fourth Monday in October

Christmas Day 25 December

Boxing Day 26 December

In addition, each NZ province has its own anniversary-day holiday. The dates of these provincial holidays vary: when they fall on Friday to Sunday, they're usually observed the following Monday; if they fall on Tuesday to Thursday, they're held on the preceding Monday. To see an up-to-date list of provincial anniversaries during the year you travel, see www.govt.nz/browse/work/public-holidays-and-work/public-holidays-and-anniversary-dates.

School Holidays

The Christmas holiday season, from mid-December to late January, is part of the summer school vacation: expect transport and accommodation to book out in advance, and queues at tourist attractions. There are three shorter school-holiday periods during the year: from mid- to late April, early to mid-July, and late September to mid-October. For exact dates, see the Ministry of Education website (www.education.govt.nz).

Safe Travel

➡ Kiwi roads are often made hazardous by map-distracted tourists, wide-cornering campervans and traffic-ignorant sheep.

➡ Major fault lines run the length of NZ, causing occasional earthquakes.

➡ Avoid leaving valuables in vehicles: theft is a problem, even in remote areas.

➡ New Zealand's climate is unpredictable: hypothermia is a risk in high-altitude areas.

➡ At the beach, beware of rips and undertows, which can drag swimmers out to sea.

➡ New Zealand's sandflies are an itchy annoyance. Use repellent in coastal and lakeside areas.

Telephone

New Zealand uses regional two-digit area codes for long-distance calls, which can be made from any payphone. If you're making a local call (ie to someone else in the same town), you don't need to dial the area code. But if you're dialling within a region (even if it's to a nearby town with the same area code) you do have to dial the area code.

To make international calls from NZ (which is possible on payphones), you need to dial the international access code 00, then the country code and the area code (without the initial '0'). So for a London number, for example, you'd dial 00-44-20, then the number. If dialling NZ from overseas, the country code is 64, followed by the appropriate area code minus the initial '0'.

GOVERNMENT TRAVEL ADVICE

The following government websites offer travel advisories and information on current hotspots:

Australian Department of Foreign Affairs & Trade (www.smarttraveller.gov.au)

British Foreign & Commonwealth Office (www.gov.uk/fco)

Dutch Ministry of Foreign Affairs (www.government.nl/ministries/ministry-of-foreign-affairs)

Foreign Affairs, Trade & Development Canada (www.international.gc.ca)

German Federal Foreign Office (www.auswaertiges-amt.de)

Japanese Ministry of Foreign Affairs (www.mofa.go.jp)

US Department of State (www.travel.state.gov)

Mobile Phones

Most NZ mobile phone numbers begin with the prefix 021, 022 or 027. Mobile phone coverage is good in cities and towns and most parts of the North Island, but can be patchy away from urban centres on the South Island.

If you want to bring your own phone and use a prepaid service with a local SIM card (rather than pay for expensive global roaming on your home network), Vodafone (www.vodafone.co.nz) is a practical option. Any Vodafone shop (in most major towns) will set you up with a NZ Travel SIM (from around $30; valid for 30, 60 or 90 days). Top-ups can be purchased at newsagents, post offices and petrol stations all over the country.

Phone Hire New Zealand (www.phonehirenz.com) rents out mobiles, modems and GPS systems (from $3/10/7 per day).

Pay Phones

Local calls from payphones cost $1 for the first 15 minutes, and $0.20 per minute thereafter, though coin-operated payphones are scarce (and if you do find one, chances are the coin slot will be gummed up); you'll generally need a phonecard. Calls to mobile phones attract higher rates.

Premium-Rate & Toll-Free Calls

Numbers starting with 0900 charge upwards of $1 per minute (more from mobiles). These numbers cannot be dialled from payphones, and sometimes not from prepaid mobile phones.

Toll-free numbers in NZ have the prefix 0800 or 0508, and can be called from anywhere in the country, though they may not be accessible from certain areas or from mobile phones. Numbers beginning with 0508, 0800 or 0900 cannot be dialled from outside NZ.

Phonecards

New Zealand has a wide range of phonecards available, which can be bought at hostels, newsagents and post offices for a fixed-dollar value (usually $5, $10, $20 and $50). These can be used with any public or private phone by dialling a toll-free access number and then the PIN number on the card. Shop around – rates vary from company to company.

Time

New Zealand is 12 hours ahead of GMT/UTC and two hours ahead of Australian Eastern Standard Time. The Chathams are 45 minutes ahead of NZ's main islands.

In summer, NZ observes daylight saving time, where clocks are wound forward by one hour on the last Sunday in September; clocks are wound back on the first Sunday of the following April.

Toilets

Toilets in NZ are sit-down Western style. Public toilets are plentiful, and are usually reasonably clean with working locks and plenty of toilet paper.

See www.toiletmap.co.nz for public-toilet locations around the country.

Tourist Information

The website for the official national tourism body, Tourism New Zealand (www.newzealand.com), is an excellent place for pre-trip research. The site has information in several languages, including German, Spanish, French, Chinese and Japanese.

Princes Wharf i-SITE (☑09-365 9914; www.aucklandnz.com; Princes Wharf; ⊗9am-5pm) Auckland's main official information centre.

Auckland International Airport i-SITE (Map p78; ☑09-365

9925; www.aucklandnz.com; International Arrivals Hall; ⊗6.30am-10.30pm)

Christchurch i-SITE (Map p484; ☑03-379 9629; www.christchurchnz.com; Arts Centre, 28 Worcester Blvd; ⊗8.30am-5pm)

Christchurch Airport i-SITE (☑03-741 3980; www.christchurchnz.com; International Arrivals Hall; ⊗8am-6pm)

Queenstown i-SITE (Map p578; ☑03-442 4100; www.queenstownsite.co.nz; cnr Shotover & Camp Sts; ⊗8.30am-8pm)

Local Tourist Offices

Almost every Kiwi city or town seems to have a visitor information centre. The bigger centres stand united within the outstanding i-SITE network (www.newzealand.com/travel/i-sites) – more than 80 info centres affiliated with Tourism New Zealand. The i-SITE centres have trained staff, information on local activities and attractions, and free brochures and maps. Staff can also book activities, transport and accommodation.

Bear in mind that some information centres only promote accommodation and tour operators who are paying members of the local tourist association, and that sometimes staff aren't supposed to recommend one activity or accommodation provider over another.

There's also a network of Department of Conservation (DOC; www.doc.govt.nz) visitor centres to help you plan outdoor activities and make bookings (particularly for tramping trails and huts). The DOC visitor centres – in national parks, regional centres and major cities – usually also have displays on local flora and fauna.

Travellers with Disabilities

Kiwi accommodation generally caters fairly well for travellers with disabilities, with most hostels, hotels and motels equipped with one or two wheelchair-accessible rooms. (B&Bs aren't required to have accessible rooms.) Many tourist attractions similarly provide wheelchair access, with wheelchairs often available. Most i-SITE visitor centres can advise on suitable attractions in the locality.

Tour operators with accessible vehicles operate from most major centres. Key cities are also serviced by 'kneeling' buses (buses that hydraulically stoop down to kerb level to allow easy access), and many taxi companies offer wheelchair-accessible vans. Large car-hire firms (Avis, Hertz etc) provide cars with hand controls at no extra charge (but advance notice is required). Air New Zealand is also very well equipped to accommodate travellers in wheelchairs.

Download Lonely Planet's free Accessible Travel guides from http://lptravel.to/AccessibleTravel.

Activities

Out and about, the DOC has been hard at work improving access to short walking trails (and some of the longer ones). Tracks that are wheelchair accessible are categorised as 'easy access short walks': the Cape Reinga Lighthouse Walk and Milford Foreshore Walk are two prime examples.

If cold-weather activity is more your thing, see Snow Sports NZ's page on adaptive winter sports: www.snowsports.co.nz/get-involved/adaptive-snow-sports.

Resources

Access4All (www.access4all.co.nz) Listings of accessible accommodation and activities around New Zealand.

Firstport (http://firstport.co.nz) Includes a high-level overview on transport in NZ, including mobility taxis and accessible public transport.

Mobility Parking (www.mobilityparking.org.nz) Apply for an overseas visitor mobility parking permit ($35 for 12 months) and have it posted to you before you even reach NZ.

Visas

Visa application forms are available from NZ diplomatic missions overseas, travel agents and **Immigration New Zealand** (☑ 09-914 4100, 0508 558 855; www.immigration.govt.nz). Immigration New Zealand has more than 25 offices overseas, including the US, UK and Australia; consult the website.

Visitor Visa

Citizens of Australia don't need a visa to visit NZ and can stay indefinitely (provided they have no criminal convictions). UK citizens don't need a visa either and can stay in the country for up to six months.

Citizens of another 58 countries that have visa-waiver agreements with NZ don't need a visa for stays of up to three months per visit, for no more than six months within any 12-month period, provided they have an onward ticket and sufficient funds to support their stay: see the website for details. Nations in this group include Canada, France, Germany, Ireland, Japan, the Netherlands, South Africa and the USA.

Citizens of other countries must obtain a visa before entering NZ. Visitor visas allow stays of up to nine months within an 18-month period, and cost $170 to $220, depending on where in the world the application is processed.

A visitor's visa can be extended from nine to 12 months, but if you get this extension you'll have to leave NZ after your 12-month stay has expired and wait another 12 months before you can come back. Applications are assessed on a case-by-case basis; you may need to provide proof of adequate funds to sustain you during your visit ($1000 per month) plus an onward ticket establishing your intent to leave. Apply for extensions at any Immigration New Zealand office – see the website (www.immigration.govt.nz) for locations.

Work Visa

It's illegal for foreign nationals to work in NZ on a visitor visa, except for Australian citizens or permanent residents, who can legally gain work without a visa or permit. If you're visiting NZ to find work, or you already have an employment offer, you'll need to apply for a work visa, which can be valid for up to three years, depending on your circumstance. You can apply for a work permit after you're in NZ, but its validity will be backdated to when you entered the country. The fee for a work visa can be anything upwards of $190, depending on where and how it's processed (paper or online) and the type of application.

Working Holiday Scheme

Eligible travellers who are only interested in short-term employment to supplement their travels can take part in one of NZ's working holiday schemes (WHS). Under these schemes citizens aged 18 to 30 (occasionally 35) years from 44 countries – including France, Germany, Ireland, Japan, Malaysia, the Netherlands, Scandinavian countries and the USA – can apply for a visa. For most nationalities the visa is valid for 12 months but citizens of Canada and the UK can work for up to 23 months. It's only issued to those seeking a genuine working holiday, not permanent work, so you're not supposed to work for one employer for more than three months.

Eligible nationals must apply for a WHS visa from within their own country. Applicants must have an onward ticket, a passport valid for at least three months from the date they will leave NZ and evidence of at least $350 in accessible funds for each month of their stay. The application fee is $165 and isn't refunded if your application is declined.

The rules vary for different nationalities, so make sure

you read up on the specifics of your country's agreement with NZ at www.immigration.govt.nz.

Volunteering

New Zealand presents an array of active, outdoorsy volunteer opportunities for travellers to get some dirt under their fingernails and participate in conservation programs. These programs can include anything from tree planting and weed removal to track construction, habitat conservation and fencing. Ask about local opportunities at any regional i-SITE visitor information centre, join one of the programs run by DOC (www.doc.govt.nz/getting-involved), or check out these online resources:

➡ www.conservation volunteers.org.nz

➡ www.helpx.net

➡ www.nature.org.nz

➡ www.volunteeringnz.org.nz

➡ www.wwf.org.nz

Women Travellers

New Zealand is generally a very safe place for female travellers, although the usual sensible precautions apply (for both sexes): avoid walking alone at night; never hitchhike alone; and if you're out on the town, have a plan on how to get back to your accommodation safely. Sexual harassment is not a widely reported problem in NZ, but of course that doesn't mean it doesn't happen. See www.womentravel.co.nz for tours aimed at solo women.

Work

If you have been approved for a working holiday scheme (WHS) visa, there are a number of possibilities for temporary employment in NZ. Pay rates start at the minimum wage ($16.50 per hour, at the time of writing), but depend on the work. There's

plenty of casual work around, mainly in agriculture (fruit picking, farming, wineries), hospitality (bar work, waiting tables) or at ski resorts. Office-based work can be found in IT, banking, finance and telemarketing. Register with a local office-work agency to get started.

Seasonal fruit picking, pruning and harvesting is prime short-term work for visitors. Kiwifruit and other fruit and veg are harvested from December to May (and other farming work is available outside that season). Fruit picking is physically taxing toil, working in the dirt under the hot sun – turnover of workers is high. You're usually paid by how much you pick (per bin, bucket or kilogram): if you stick with it for a while, you'll get faster and fitter and can actually make some reasonable cash. Prime North Island picking locations include the Bay of Islands (Kerikeri and Paihia), rural Auckland, Tauranga and the Bay of Plenty, Gisborne and Hawke's Bay (Napier and Hastings); on the South Island try Nelson (Golden Bay), Marlborough (around Blenheim) and Central Otago (Alexandra and Roxburgh).

Winter work at ski resorts and their service towns includes bartending, waiting, cleaning, ski-tow operation and, if you're properly qualified, ski or snowboard instructing.

Resources

Backpacker publications, hostel managers and other travellers are often good sources of info on local work possibilities. Base Backpackers (www.stayatbase.com/work) runs an employment service via its website, while the Notice Boards page on the Budget Backpacker Hostels website (www.bbh.co.nz) lists job vacancies in BBH hostels and a few other possibilities.

Kiwi Careers (www.careers.govt.nz) lists professional opportunities in various fields (agriculture, crea-

tive, health, teaching, volunteer work and recruitment), while Seek (www.seek.co.nz) is one of the biggest NZ job-search networks, with thousands of jobs listed.

Try the following websites for seasonal work:

➡ www.backpackerboard.co.nz

➡ www.seasonalwork.co.nz

➡ www.seasonaljobs.co.nz

➡ www.picknz.co.nz

➡ www.pickingjobs.com

➡ www.picktheworld.org

Income Tax

Death and taxes – no escape! For most travellers, Kiwi dollars earned in NZ will be subject to income tax, which is deducted from payments by employers – a process called Pay As You Earn (PAYE).

Income tax rates are 10.5% for annual salaries up to $14,000, then 17.5% up to $48,000, 30% up to $70,000, then 33% for higher incomes. A NZ Accident Compensation Corporation (ACC) scheme levy (around 1.5%) will also be deducted from your pay packet. Note that these rates tend to change slightly year to year.

If you visit NZ and work for a short time (eg on a working holiday scheme), you may qualify for a tax refund when you leave. Lodging a tax return before you leave NZ is the best way of securing a refund. For more info, see the Inland Revenue Department website (www.ird.govt.nz), or call 03-951 2020.

IRD Number

Travellers undertaking paid work in NZ (including working holiday scenarios) must first open a New Zealand bank account, then obtain an Inland Revenue Department (IRD) number. Download the *IRD number application - non-resident/offshore individual IR742* form from the Inland Revenue Department website (www.ird.govt.nz). IRD numbers normally take eight to 10 working days to be issued.

Transport

GETTING THERE & AWAY

New Zealand is a long way from almost everywhere – most travellers jet in from afar. Flights, cars and tours can be booked online at lonelyplanet.com/bookings.

Entering the Country

Disembarkation in New Zealand is generally a straightforward affair, with only the usual customs declarations and luggage-carousel scramble to endure. Under the Orwellian title of 'Advance Passenger Screening', documents that used to be checked after you touched down in NZ (passport, visa etc) are now checked before you board your flight – make sure all your documentation is in order so that your check-in is stress-free.

Passport

There are no restrictions when it comes to foreign citizens entering NZ. If you have a current passport and visa (or don't require one), you should be fine.

Air

New Zealand's abundance of year-round activities means that airports here are busy most of the time: if you want to fly at a particularly popular time of year (eg over the Christmas period), book well in advance.

The high season for flights into NZ is during summer (December to February), with slightly less of a premium on fares over the shoulder months (October/November and March/April). The low season generally tallies with the winter months (June to August), though this is still a busy time for airlines ferrying ski bunnies and powder hounds.

Airports & Airlines

A number of NZ airports handle international flights, with Auckland receiving the most traffic:

Auckland Airport (AKL; Map p78; ☑09-275 0789; www.aucklandairport.co.nz; Ray Emery Dr, Mangere)

Christchurch Airport (CHC; ☑03-358 5029; www.christchurchairport.co.nz; 30 Durey Rd)

Dunedin Airport (DUD; ☑03-486 2879; www.dnairport.co.nz; 25 Miller Rd, Momona; ☎)

Queenstown Airport (ZQN; Map p591; ☑03-450 9031; www.queenstownairport.co.nz; Sir Henry Wrigley Dr, Frankton)

Wellington Airport (WLG; ☑04-385 5100; www.wellingtonairport.co.nz; Stewart Duff Dr, Rongotai)

Note that Hamilton, Rotorua and Palmerston North airports are capable of handling direct international arrivals and departures, but are not currently doing so.

CLIMATE CHANGE & TRAVEL

Every form of transport that relies on carbon-based fuel generates CO_2, the main cause of human-induced climate change. Modern travel is dependent on aeroplanes, which might use less fuel per kilometre per person than most cars but travel much greater distances. The altitude at which aircraft emit gases (including CO_2) and particles also contributes to their climate change impact. Many websites offer 'carbon calculators' that allow people to estimate the carbon emissions generated by their journey and, for those who wish to do so, to offset the impact of the greenhouse gases emitted with contributions to portfolios of climate-friendly initiatives throughout the world. Lonely Planet offsets the carbon footprint of all staff and author travel.

AIRLINES FLYING TO & FROM NEW ZEALAND

New Zealand's international carrier is Air New Zealand (www.airnewzealand.co.nz), which flies to runways across Europe, North America, eastern Asia, Australia and the Pacific, and has an extensive network across NZ.

Winging in with direct flights from Australia, Virgin Australia (www.virginaustralia. com), Qantas (www.qantas. com.au), Jetstar (www.jetstar. com) and Air New Zealand are the key players.

Joining Air New Zealand from North America, other operators include Air Canada (www.aircanada.com) and American Airlines (www. aa.com) – the latter has direct flights from Los Angeles to Auckland.

From Europe, the options are a little broader, with British Airways (www.britishair-ways.com), Lufthansa (www. lufthansa.com) and Virgin Atlantic (www.virginatlantic. com) entering the fray. Flights go via major Middle Eastern or Asian airports. Several other airlines stop in NZ on broader round-the-world routes.

From Asia and the Pacific there are myriad options, with direct flights from China, Japan, Singapore, Malaysia, Thailand and Pacific Island nations.

Sea

Cruise Ship If you're travelling from Australia and content with a slow pace, try P&O (www. pocruises.com.au) and Princess (www.princess.com) for cruises to New Zealand.

Cargo Ship If you don't need luxury, a berth on a cargo ship or freighter to/from New Zealand is a quirky way to go. Freighter Expeditions (www.freighterex-peditions.com.au) offers cruises

to New Zealand from Singapore (49 days return) and Antwerp in Belgium (32 days one way).

Yacht It is possible (though by no means straightforward) to make your way between NZ, Australia and the Pacific Islands by crewing on a yacht. Try asking around at harbours, marinas, and yacht and sailing clubs. Popular yachting harbours in NZ include the Bay of Islands and Whangarei (both in Northland), Auckland and Wellington. March and April are the best months to look for boats heading to Australia. From Fiji, October to November is a peak departure season to beat the cyclones that soon follow in that neck of the woods.

GETTING AROUND

Air

Those who have limited time to get between NZ's attractions can make the most of a widespread (and very reliable and safe) network of intra- and inter-island flights.

Airlines in New Zealand

The country's major domestic carrier, Air New Zealand, has an aerial network covering most of the country, often operating under the Air New Zealand Link moniker on less popular routes. Australia-based Jetstar also flies between main urban areas. Between them, these two airlines carry the vast majority of domestic passengers in NZ. Beyond this, several small-scale regional operators provide essential transport services to outlying islands, such as Great Barrier Island in the Hauraki Gulf, to Stewart Island and the Chathams. There are also plenty of scenic- and charter-flight operators around NZ, not listed here. Operators include the following:

Air Chathams (0800 580 127; www.airchathams.co.nz) Services to the remote Chatham Islands from Wellington, Christchurch

and Auckland. Auckland–Whakatane flights also available.

Air New Zealand (0800 737 000; www.airnewzealand.co.nz) Offers flights between 20-plus domestic destinations, plus myriad overseas hubs.

Air2there.com (0800 777 000; www.air2there.com) Connects destinations across Cook Strait, including Paraparaumu, Wellington, Nelson and Blenheim.

Barrier Air (0800 900 600; www.barrierair.kiwi) Flies the skies over Great Barrier Island, Auckland and Kaitaia (and seasonally, Tauranga and Whitianga).

FlyMySky (0800 222 123; www.flymysky.co.nz) At least three flights daily from Auckland to Great Barrier Island.

Golden Bay Air (0800 588 885; www.goldenbayair.co.nz) Flies regularly to Takaka in Golden Bay from Wellington and Nelson. Also connects to Karamea for Heaphy Track trampers.

Jetstar (0800 800 995; www.jet star.com) Joins the dots between key tourism centres: Auckland, Wellington, Christchurch, Dunedin, Queenstown, Nelson, Napier, New Plymouth and Palmerston North.

Soundsair (0800 505 005; www.soundsair.co.nz) Numerous flights daily between Picton and Wellington, plus flights from Wellington to Blenheim, Nelson, Westport and Taupo. Also flies Blenheim to Christchurch, Kaikoura, Paraparaumu and Napier, and Nelson to Paraparaumu.

Stewart Island Flights (03-218 9129; www.stewartislandflights. co.nz) Flies between Invercargill and Stewart Island three times daily.

Sunair (0800 786 247; www. sunair.co.nz) Flies to Whitianga from Ardmore (near Auckland), Great Barrier Island and Tauranga, plus numerous other North Island connections between Hamilton, Rotorua, Gisborne and Whakatane.

Air Passes

Available exclusively to travellers from the USA or Canada who have bought an Air New Zealand fare to NZ from the USA or Canada, Australia or the Pacific Islands, Air New

Zealand offers the good-value New Zealand Explorer Pass (www.airnewzealand.com/explorer-pass). The pass lets you fly between up to 37 destinations in New Zealand, Australia and the South Pacific islands (including Norfolk Island, Tonga, New Caledonia, Samoa, Vanuatu, Tahiti, Fiji, Niue and the Cook Islands). Fares are broken down into four discounted, distance-based zones: zone one flights start at US$99 (eg Auckland to Wellington); zone two from US$129 (eg Auckland to Queenstown); zone three from US$214 (eg Wellington to Sydney); and zone four from US$295 (eg Tahiti to Auckland). You can buy the pass before you travel, or after you arrive in NZ.

Bicycle

Touring cyclists proliferate in NZ, particularly over summer. The country is clean, green and relatively uncrowded, and has lots of cheap accommodation (including camping) and abundant fresh water. The roads are generally in good nick, and the climate is usually not too hot or cold. Road traffic is the biggest danger: trucks overtaking too close to cyclists are a particular threat. Bikes and cycling gear are readily available to rent or buy in the main centres, and bicycle-repair shops are common.

By law all cyclists must wear an approved safety helmet (or risk a fine); it's also vital to have good reflective safety clothing. Cyclists who use public transport will find that major bus lines and trains only take bicycles on a 'space available' basis (in cities, usually outside rush hour) and may charge up to $10. Some of the smaller shuttle bus companies, on the other hand, make sure they have storage space for bikes, which they carry for a surcharge.

If importing your own bike or transporting it by plane within NZ, check with the relevant airline for costs and the degree of dismantling and packing required.

See www.nzta.govt.nz/walking-cycling-and-public-transport for more bike safety and legal tips, and the New Zealand Cycle Trail (Nga Haerenga; p60) – a network of 22 'Great Rides' across NZ.

Hire

Rates offered by most outfits for renting road or mountain bikes are usually around $20 per hour to $60 per day. Longer-term rentals may be available by negotiation. You can often hire bikes from your accommodation (hostels, holiday parks etc), or rent more reputable machines from bike shops in the larger towns.

Buying a Bike

Bicycles can be readily bought in NZ's larger cities, but prices for newer models are high. For a decent hybrid bike or rigid mountain bike you'll pay anywhere from $800 to $1800, though you can get a cheap one for around $500 (but you still then need to buy panniers, helmet, lock etc, and the cost quickly climbs). Other options include the post-Christmas sales and midyear stocktakes, when newish cycles can be heavily discounted.

Boat

New Zealand may be an island nation but there's virtually no long-distance water transport around the country. Obvious exceptions include the boat services between Auckland and various islands in the Hauraki Gulf, the inter-island ferries that cross the Cook Strait between Wellington and Picton, and the passenger ferry that negotiates Foveaux Strait between Bluff and the town of Oban on Stewart Island.

If you're cashed-up, consider the cruise liners that chug around the NZ coastline as part of broader South Pacific itineraries: P&O Cruises (www.pocruises.com.au) is a major player.

Bus

Bus travel in NZ is easygoing and well organised, with services transporting you to the far reaches of both islands (including the start/end of various walking tracks)...but it can be expensive, tedious and time-consuming.

New Zealand's main bus company is **InterCity** (www.intercity.co.nz), which can drive you to just about anywhere on the North and South Islands. **Naked Bus** (☑09-979 1616; https://nakedbus.com) has similar routes and remains the main competition. Both bus lines offer fares as low as $1(!). InterCity also has a South Island sightseeing arm called **Newmans Coach Lines** (www.newmanscoach.co.nz), travelling between Queenstown, Christchurch and the West Coast glaciers.

Privately run shuttle buses can transport travellers to some trailheads or collect them from the end point of a tramp; advance booking essential.

Seat Classes & Smoking

There are no allocated economy or luxury classes on NZ buses (very democratic), and smoking on the bus is a definite no-no.

Naked Bus has a sleeper class on overnight services between Auckland and Wellington (stopping at Hamilton and Palmerston North) where you can lie flat in a 1.8m-long bed (bring a sleeping bag, pillowcase and maybe earplugs). See http://nakedbus.com/nz/home/sleeper-bus for details.

Reservations

Over summer (December to February), school holidays and public holidays, book well in advance on popular routes (a week or two ahead if possible). At other times, a day or two ahead is usually fine. The best prices are generally available online, booked a few weeks in advance.

Bus Passes

If you're covering a lot of ground, both InterCity and Naked Bus offer bus passes (respectively, priced by hours and number of trips). This can be cheaper than paying as you go, but do the maths before buying and note that you'll be locked into using one network. Passes are usually valid for 12 months.

On fares other than bus passes, InterCity offers a discount of around 10% for YHA, ISIC, HI, Nomads, BBH or VIP backpacker card holders. Senior discounts only apply for NZ citizens.

NATIONWIDE PASSES

Flexipass A hop-on/hop-off InterCity pass, allowing travel to pretty much anywhere in NZ, in any direction, including the Interislander ferry across Cook Strait. The pass is purchased in blocks of travel time: minimum 15 hours ($125), maximum 60 hours ($459). The average cost of each block becomes cheaper the more hours you buy. You can top up the pass if you need more time.

Aotearoa Explorer, Tiki Tour & Island Loop Hop-on/hop-off, fixed-itinerary nationwide passes offered by InterCity. These passes link up tourist hotspots and cost $775 to $1140. Passes with a narrower scope (eg West Coast or Southern Alps) are also offered. See www.intercity.co.nz/bus-pass/travelpass for details.

Naked Passport (www.naked passport.com) A Naked Bus pass that allows you to buy trips in blocks of five, which you can add to any time, and book each trip as needed. Five/15/20 trips cost $159/269/439.

NORTH ISLAND PASSES

InterCity offers six hop-on/hop-off, fixed-itinerary North Island bus passes, from short $125 runs between Auckland and Paihia, to $405 trips from Auckland to Wellington via the big sights in between. See www.intercity.co.nz/bus-pass/travelpass for details.

SOUTH ISLAND PASSES

On the South Island, InterCity offers six hop-on/hop-off, fixed-itinerary passes, from $125 runs along the West Coast between Picton and Queenstown, to a $549 loop via Christchurch, Queenstown and the West Coast glaciers. See www.intercity.co.nz/bus-pass/travelpass for details.

Shuttle Buses

As well as InterCity and Naked Bus, regional shuttle buses fill in the gaps between the smaller towns. Operators include the following (see www.tourism.net.nz/transport/bus-and-coach-services for a complete list), offering regular scheduled services and/or bus tours and charters:

Abel Tasman Travel (www.abeltasmantravel.co.nz) Traverses the roads between Nelson, Motueka, Golden Bay and Abel Tasman National Park.

Atomic Shuttles (www.atomic travel.co.nz) Has services throughout the South Island, including to Christchurch, Dunedin, Invercargill, Picton, Nelson, Greymouth, Hokitika, Queenstown and Wanaka.

Catch-a-Bus South (www.catch abussouth.co.nz) Invercargill and Bluff to Dunedin and Queenstown.

Cook Connection (www.cookcon nect.co.nz) Triangulates between Mt Cook, Twizel and Lake Tekapo.

East West Coaches (www.eastwestcoaches.co.nz) Offers a service between Christchurch and Westport via Lewis Pass.

Go Kiwi Shuttles (www.go-kiwi.co.nz) Links Auckland with Whitianga on the Coromandel Peninsula daily.

Hanmer Connection (www.hanmerconnection.co.nz) Daily services between Hanmer Springs and Christchurch.

Headfirst Travel (www.travel headfirst.com) Does a loop from Rotorua to Waitomo (with an option to finish in Auckland).

Manabus (www.manabus.com) Runs in both directions daily between Auckland and Wellington via Hamilton, Rotorua, Taupo and Palmerston North. Also runs to Tauranga, Paihia and Napier. Some services operated by Naked Bus.

Tracknet (www.tracknet.net) Summer track transport (Milford, Hollyford, Routeburn, Kepler) with Queenstown, Te Anau and Invercargill connections.

Trek Express (www.trekexpress.co.nz) Shuttle services to all tramping tracks in the top half of the South Island (eg Heaphy, Abel Tasman, Old Ghost Road).

West Coast Shuttle (www.westcoastshuttle.co.nz) Daily bus from Greymouth to Christchurch and back.

Bus Tours

Clock up some kilometres with like-minded fellow travellers. The following operators run fixed-itinerary bus tours, nationwide or on the North or South Islands. Accommodation, meals and hop-on/hop-off flexibility are often included. Styles vary from activity-focused itineraries through to hangover-mandatory backpacker buses.

Adventure Tours New Zealand (www.adventuretours.com.au/new-zealand) Four 11- to 22-day NZ tours of North or South Island, or both.

Bottom Bus (www.travel headfirst.com/local-legends/bottom-bus) South Island nether-region tours ex-Dunedin, Invercargill and Queenstown.

Flying Kiwi (www.flyingkiwi.com) Good-fun, activity-based trips around NZ with camping and cabin accommodation from a few days to a few weeks.

Haka Tours (www.hakatours.com) Three- to 24-day tours with adventure, snow or mountain-biking themes.

Kirra Tours (www.kirratours.co.nz) Upmarket coach tours (graded 'Classic' or 'Platinum' by price) from an operator with 50 years in the business.

Kiwi Experience (www.kiwi experience.com) A major hop-on/hop-off player with eco-friendly credentials. Myriad tours cover the length and breadth of NZ.

Stray Travel (www.straytravel.com) A wide range of flexible hop-on/hop-off passes and tours.

Car & Motorcycle

The best way to explore NZ in depth is to have your own wheels. It's easy to hire cars and campervans, though it's worth noting that fuel costs can be eye-watering. Alternatively, if you're in NZ for a few months, you might consider buying your own vehicle.

Automobile Association (AA)

New Zealand's **Automobile Association** (AA; ☑0800 500 444; www.aa.co.nz/travel) provides emergency breakdown services, distance calculators and accommodation guides (from holiday parks to motels and B&Bs).

Members of overseas automobile associations should bring their membership cards – many of these bodies have reciprocal agreements with the AA.

Driving Licences

International visitors to NZ can use their home-country driving licence – if your licence isn't in English, it's a good idea to carry a certified translation with you. Alternatively, use an International Driving Permit (IDP), which will usually be issued on the spot (valid for 12 months) by your home country's automobile association.

Fuel

Fuel (petrol, aka gasoline) is available from service stations across NZ: unless you're cruising around in something from the 1970s, you'll be filling up with 'unleaded', or LPG (gas). LPG is not always stocked by rural suppliers; if you're on gas, it's safer to have dual-fuel capability. Aside from remote locations like Milford Sound and Mt Cook, petrol prices don't vary much from place to place: per-litre costs at the time of research were hovering above $2.

Hire

CAMPERVAN

Check your rear-view mirror on any far-flung NZ road and you'll probably see a shiny white campervan (aka mobile home, motor home, RV) packed with liberated travellers, mountain bikes and portable barbecues cruising along behind you.

Most towns of any size have a campground or holiday park with powered sites (where you can plug your vehicle in) for around $35 per night. There are also 250-plus vehicle-accessible Department of Conservation (DOC; www.doc.govt.nz) campsites around NZ, priced up to $21 per adult. Weekly campsite passes for rental campervans slice up to 50% off the price of stays in DOC campgrounds; check the website for info.

You can hire campervans from dozens of companies. Prices vary with season, vehicle size and length of rental, and it pays to book months in advance.

A small van for two people typically has a minikitchen and foldout dining table, the latter transforming into a double bed when dinner is done and dusted. Larger, 'superior' two-berth vans include shower and toilet. Four- to six-berth campervans are the size of trucks (and similarly sluggish) and, besides the extra space, usually contain a toilet and shower.

Over summer, rates offered by the main rental firms for two-/four-/six-berth vans booked three months in advance start at around $120/150/230 per day (though they rise much higher, depending on model) for a rental of two weeks or more. Rates drop to $60/75/100 per day during winter.

Major operators include the following:

Apollo (☑0800 113 131, 09-889 2976; www.apollocamper.co.nz)

Britz (☑09-255 3910, 0800 081 032; www.britz.co.nz) Also does 'Britz Bikes' (add a mountain or city bike from $12 per day).

Maui (☑09-255 3910, 0800 688 558; www.maui-rentals.com)

Wilderness Motorhomes (☑09-282 3606; www.wilderness.co.nz)

Budget players in the campervan industry offer slick deals and funky (often gregariously spray-painted), well-kitted-out vehicles for backpackers. Rates are competitive (from $30/60 per day for a two-/four-berth van from May to September; from $90/170 per day from December to February). Operators include the following:

Escape Campervans (☑0800 216 171; www.escaperentals.co.nz)

Hippie Camper (☑0800 113 131; www.hippiecamper.co.nz)

Jucy (☑09-374 4360, 0800 399 736; www.jucy.co.nz)

Mighty Cars & Campers (☑0800 422 505; www.mightycampers.co.nz)

Spaceships (☑09-526 2130, 0800 772 237; www.spaceshipsrentals.co.nz)

Tui Sleeper Vans (☑03-359 4731; www.sleepervans.co.nz)

CAR

Competition between car-hire companies in NZ is torrid, particularly in the big cities and Picton. Remember that if you want to travel far, you need unlimited kilometres. Some (but not all) companies require drivers to be at least 21 years old – ask around.

International car-hire firms don't generally allow you to take their vehicles between islands on the Cook Strait ferries. Instead, you leave your car at either Wellington or Picton terminal and pick up another car once you've crossed the strait. This saves you paying to transport a vehicle on the ferries, and is a pain-free exercise. However, some local car-hire firms (such as Apex) are fine with you taking your rental vehicle on the ferry and will even book your ferry ticket for you.

The big multinational companies have offices in most major cities, towns and airports. Firms sometimes offer one-way rentals (eg collect a car in Auckland, leave it in Wellington), but there are usually restrictions and fees.

The major companies offer a choice of either unlimited kilometres, or 100km (or so) per day free, plus so many cents for subsequent kilometre. Daily rates in main cities typically start at around $40 per day for a compact, late-model, Japanese car, and from $70 for medium-sized cars (including GST, unlimited kilometres and insurance).

Avis (☎0800 655 111, 09-526 2847; www.avis.co.nz)

Budget (☎09-529 7788, 0800 283 438; www.budget.co.nz)

Europcar (☎0800 800 115; www.europcar.co.nz)

Hertz (☎0800 654 321; www.hertz.co.nz)

Thrifty (☎03-359 2721, 0800 737 070; www.thrifty.co.nz)

Local rental firms proliferate. These are almost always cheaper than the big boys – sometimes half the price – but the cheap rates may come with serious restrictions: vehicles are often older, depots might be further away from airports/city centres, and with less formality sometimes comes a less protective legal structure for renters.

Rentals from local firms start at around $30 or $40 per day for the smallest option. It's cheaper if you rent for a week or more, and there are often low-season and weekend discounts.

Affordable, independent operators with national networks include the following:

a2b Car Rentals (☎0800 545 000, 09-254 4397; www.a2b -car-rental.co.nz)

Ace Rental Cars (☎0800 502 277, 09-303 3112; www.ace rentalcars.co.nz)

Apex Rentals (☎03-595 2315, 0800 500 660; www.apex rentals.co.nz)

Ezi Car Rental (☎0800 545 000, 09-254 4397; www.ezicar rental.co.nz)

Go Rentals (☎0800 467 368, 09-974 1598; www.gorentals. co.nz)

Omega Rental Cars (☎09-377 5573, 0800 525 210; www. omegarentalcars.com)

Pegasus Rental Cars (☎0800 803 580; www.rentalcars.co.nz)

Transfercar (☎09-630 7533; www.transfercar.co.nz) Relocation specialists with massive money-saving deals on one-way car rental.

MOTORCYCLE

Born to be wild? New Zealand has great terrain for motorcycle touring, despite the fickle weather in some regions. Most of the country's motorcycle-hire shops are in Auckland and Christchurch, where you can hire anything from a little 50cc moped (aka nifty-fifty) to a throbbing 750cc touring motorcycle and beyond. Recommended operators (who also run guided tours) offer rates around $100 per day:

New Zealand Motorcycle Rentals & Tours (☎09-486 2472; www.nzbike.com)

Te Waipounamu Motorcycle Tours (☎03-372 3537; www. motorcycle-hire.co.nz)

Insurance

Rather than risk paying out wads of cash if you have an accident, you can take out your own comprehensive insurance policy, or (the usual option) pay an additional fee per day to the rental company to reduce your excess. This brings the amount you must pay in the event of an accident down from around $1500 or $2000 to around $200 or $300. Smaller operators offering cheap rates often have a compulsory insurance excess, taken as a credit-card bond, of around $900.

Many insurance agreements won't cover the cost of damage to glass (including the windscreen) or tyres, and insurance coverage is often invalidated on beaches and certain rough (4WD) unsealed roads – read the fine print.

See www.acc.co.nz for info on NZ's Accident Compensation Corporation insurance scheme (fault-free personal injury insurance).

Purchase

Planning a long trip? Buying a car then selling it at the end of your travels can be one of the cheapest and best ways to see NZ. Auckland is the easiest place to buy a car, followed by Christchurch: scour the hostel noticeboards. Turners Auctions (www.turners.co.nz) is NZ's biggest car-auction operator, with 11 locations.

LEGALITIES

Make sure your prospective vehicle has a Warrant of Fitness (WoF) and registration valid for a reasonable period: see the New Zealand Transport Agency website (www.nzta.govt.nz) for details.

Buyers should also take out third-party insurance, covering the cost of repairs to another vehicle in an accident that is your fault: try the **Automobile Association** (AA; ☎0800 500 444; www.aa.co. nz/travel). New Zealand's no-fault Accident Compensation Corporation (www.acc.co.nz) scheme covers personal injury, but make sure you have travel insurance, too.

If you're considering buying a car and want someone to check it out for you, various companies inspect cars for around $150; find them at car auctions, or they will come to you. Try Vehicle Inspection New Zealand (09-573 3230, 0800 468 469; www.vinz.co.nz) or the AA.

Before you buy it's wise to confirm ownership of the vehicle, and find out if there's anything dodgy about the car (eg stolen, or outstanding debts). The AA's LemonCheck (09-420 3090; www.lemoncheck.co.nz) offers this service.

BUY-BACK DEALS

You can avoid the hassle of buying/selling a vehicle privately by entering into a buy-back arrangement with a dealer. Predictably, dealers often find sneaky ways of knocking down the return-sale price, which may be 50% less than what you paid, so hiring or buying and selling a vehicle yourself (if you have the time) is usually a better bet.

Road Hazards

There's an unusually high percentage of international drivers involved in road accidents in NZ – something like 30% of accidents involve a nonlocal driver. Kiwi traffic is usually pretty light, but it's easy to get stuck behind a slow-moving truck or campervan – pack plenty of patience, and know your road rules before you get behind the wheel. There are also lots of slow wiggly roads, one-way bridges and plenty of gravel roads, all of which require a more cautious driving approach. And watch out for sheep!

To check road conditions, call 0800 444 449 or see www.nzta.govt.nz/traffic.

Road Rules

➡ Kiwis drive on the left-hand side of the road; cars are right-hand drive. Give way to the right at intersections.

➡ All vehicle occupants must wear a seatbelt or risk a fine. Small children must be belted into approved safety seats.

➡ Always carry your licence when driving. Drink-driving is a serious offence and remains a significant problem in NZ, despite widespread campaigns and severe penalties. The legal blood-alcohol limit is 0.05% for drivers aged over 20, and 0% (zero) for those under 20.

➡ At single-lane bridges (of which there are a surprisingly large number), a smaller red arrow pointing in your direction of travel means that you give way.

➡ Speed limits on the open road are generally 100km/h; in built-up areas the limit

is usually 50km/h. Speed cameras and radars are used extensively.

➡ Be aware that not all rail crossings have barriers or alarms. Approach slowly and look both ways.

➡ Don't pass other cars when the centre line is yellow.

➡ It's illegal to drive while using a mobile phone.

Hitching & Ride-Sharing

Hitching is never entirely safe, and we don't recommend it. Travellers who hitch should understand that they are taking a small but potentially serious risk. That said, it's not unusual to see hitchhikers along NZ country roads.

Alternatively, check hostel noticeboards for ride-share opportunities.

Local Transport

Bus, Train & Tram

New Zealand's larger cities have extensive bus services but, with a few honourable exceptions, they are mainly daytime, weekday operations; weekend services can be infrequent or nonexistent. Negotiating inner-city Auckland is made easier by Link buses; Hamilton has a free city-centre loop bus; Christchurch has city buses and the historic tramway. Most main cities have late-night buses for boozy Friday and Saturday nights. Don't expect local bus services in more remote areas.

The only cities with decent local train services are Auckland and Wellington, with four and five suburban routes respectively.

Taxi

The main cities have plenty of taxis and even small towns may have a local service. Taxis are metered, and are generally reliable and trustworthy.

Train

New Zealand train travel is all about the journey, not about getting anywhere in a hurry. **Great Journeys of New Zealand** (☏ 0800 872 467, 04-495 0775; www.great journeysofnz.co.nz) operates four routes, listed below. It's best to reserve online or by phone; reservations can be made directly through Great Journeys of New Zealand (operated by KiwiRail), or at most train stations, travel agents and visitor information centres. Cheaper fares appear if you book online within NZ. All services are for day travel (no sleeper services).

Capital Connection Weekday commuter service between Palmerston North and Wellington.

Coastal Pacific Track damage during the 2016 earthquakes put this scenic Christchurch–Picton route out of action, but when we went to press it was estimated to return in 2018.

Northern Explorer Between Auckland and Wellington: southbound on Mondays, Thursdays and Saturdays; northbound on Tuesdays, Fridays and Sundays.

TranzAlpine Over the Southern Alps between Christchurch and Greymouth – one of the world's most famous train rides.

Train Passes

A Scenic Journeys Rail Pass allows unlimited travel on all of its rail services, including passage on the Wellington–Picton Interislander ferry. There are two types of pass, both requiring you to book your seats a minimum of 24 hours before you want to travel. Both have discounts for kids.

Fixed Pass Limited-duration fares for one/two/three weeks, costing $629/729/829 per adult.

Freedom Pass Affords you travel on a certain number of days over a 12-month period; a three-/seven-/10-day pass costs $439/969/1299.

Behind the Scenes

SEND US YOUR FEEDBACK

We love to hear from travellers – your comments keep us on our toes and help make our books better. Our well-travelled team reads every word on what you loved or loathed about this book. Although we cannot reply individually to your submissions, we always guarantee that your feedback goes straight to the appropriate authors, in time for the next edition. Each person who sends us information is thanked in the next edition – the most useful submissions are rewarded with a selection of digital PDF chapters.

Visit **lonelyplanet.com/contact** to submit your updates and suggestions or to ask for help. Our award-winning website also features inspirational travel stories, news and discussions.

Note: We may edit, reproduce and incorporate your comments in Lonely Planet products such as guidebooks, websites and digital products, so let us know if you don't want your comments reproduced or your name acknowledged. For a copy of our privacy policy visit lonelyplanet.com/privacy.

OUR READERS

Many thanks to the travellers who used the last edition and wrote to us with helpful hints, useful advice and interesting anecdotes:

Amanda Wee, Beverley Homel, Bordiec Karine, Carol Henshaw, Dana Emanuel, Daniel Brown, Dermot Gatenby, Diana Draper, Dominique Hudson, Ewan Starkey, Gabriella Wortmann, Jean-Pierre Melon, Jenny Reeve, Jo Austin, Joshua Hoe, Julie Woods, Karen Cumming, Leanne Flynn, Lindsey Pointer, Lyndon Moore, Mateusz Kmiecinski, Melissa Bowles, Michael Batt, Ruth Emerson, Sarah Duff-Dobson, Scott Menzies, Shenali Kalawana, Stacey Marr, Steve Sherman, Susan Murray, Tadeo Hernandez Kelly, Wenneke van Weelden.

WRITER THANKS

Brett Atkinson

Thanks to all of the i-SITE, DOC and information centre staff who helped on the road, especially Glenn Ormsby and Mariet van Vierzen in Kaikoura. Cheers to the innovative chefs and inspired craft brewers of New Zealand for surprises and sustenance, and to Carol for support on occasional beach, island and city getaways. Thanks to my fellow authors and to Tasmin Waby at Lonely Planet for the opportunity to once again explore my Kiwi backyard.

Andrew Bain

Thanks primarily to Jason and Megan Hopper, who took me to the heights of the mountains and let me take them to the depths of Queenstown's basement bars. Gracias to Robyn Columbus Pester for a host of information, and the myriad business operators who answered my many queries along the journey. To my greatest gifts – Kiri and Cooper – a big thanks for rolling with it as ever as I wandered in and out of NZ and our other life.

Peter Dragicevich

Hitting the road in my home country is always a special treat, especially as it provides the opportunity to spend time with family and friends. Special thanks are due to Christine Henderson for her hospitality in the Far North, Richard King in Wellington and the extended Erceg and Wilson clans in Whakatane, especially Manda and Les Wilson. Thanks too to my sister Joanne Cole for her expert appraisal of the standard of cappuccino in the Bay of Plenty.

Samantha Forge

Thank you to the many wonderful Kiwis I met throughout the South Island for giving so freely of your time, knowledge and kindness. Thanks to Karyn, my travelling companion in Central Otago, for the cake and companionship. And finally, huge thanks to the other Team NZ authors for their friendship and generosity, and to everyone at LP responsible for piecing this puzzle together, especially the lovely Tasmin Waby.

Anita Isalska

Huge thanks to Tasmin Waby for bringing me aboard Team NZ, and to my fellow writers for being wonderful to work with – especially the above-and-beyond input from Andrew Bain, Brett Atkinson and Peter Dragicevich. Thanks for helpful suggestions from Nathan Watson and the Mountain Safety Council, patient counsel from numerous i-SITEs, blunt input from Tamara Goodwin, and Jane Atkin's great wisdom. Thank you Normal Matt, not for accidental acrobatics in Cardrona but for energetic driving, cruising and pub-hopping in Fiordland.

Sofia Levin

Thank you to my supportive and loving husband, who was left twiddling his thumbs just days after our wedding when I took off for this project; my dear friend Katherine Cameron for constantly checking in on me on the road, you are a fountain of encouragement; and to my two biggest fans – Mum and Dad.

ACKNOWLEDGEMENTS

Climate map data adapted from Peel MC, Finlayson BL & McMahon TA (2007) 'Updated World Map of the Köppen-Geiger Climate Classification', Hydrology and Earth System Sciences, 11, 163344.

Cover photograph: Te Puia, Rotorua, North Island, Ruth Black/Shutterstock ©

THIS BOOK

This 19th edition of Lonely Planet's *New Zealand* guidebook was curated by Charles Rawlings-Way, and researched and written by Brett Atkinson, Andrew Bain, Peter Dragicevich, Samantha Forge, Anita Isalska and Sofia Levin. The previous three editions were written by Charles Rawlings-Way, Brett Atkinson, Sarah Bennett, Peter Dragicevich and Lee Slater.

This guidebook was produced by the following:

Destination Editor
Tasmin Waby

Product Editors Will Allen, Kate Chapman, Tracy Whitmey

Senior Cartographer
Diana Von Holdt

Book Designer
Michael Weldon

Assisting Editors Janet Austin, Michelle Bennett, Michelle Coxall, Andrea Dobbin, Victoria Harrison, Jennifer Hattam,
Jodie Martire, Lou McGregor, Kristin Odijk, Monique Perrin, Simon Williamson

Assisting Cartographers
Julie Dodkins, James Leversha

Cover Researcher
Naomi Parker

Thanks to Jennifer Carey, Heather Champion, Daniel Corbett, Mazzy Du Plessis, Jane Grisman, Liz Heynes, Claire Naylor, Karyn Noble, Kathryn Rowan, Jessica Ryan, Victoria Smith, Sam Wheeler

Index

Map Pages **000**
Photo Pages **000**

Map Legend

Sights
- Beach
- Bird Sanctuary
- Buddhist
- Castle/Palace
- Christian
- Confucian
- Hindu
- Islamic
- Jain
- Jewish
- Monument
- Museum/Gallery/Historic Building
- Ruin
- Shinto
- Sikh
- Taoist
- Winery/Vineyard
- Zoo/Wildlife Sanctuary
- Other Sight

Activities, Courses & Tours
- Bodysurfing
- Diving
- Canoeing/Kayaking
- Course/Tour
- Sento Hot Baths/Onsen
- Skiing
- Snorkelling
- Surfing
- Swimming/Pool
- Walking
- Windsurfing
- Other Activity

Sleeping
- Sleeping
- Camping
- Hut/Shelter

Eating
- Eating

Drinking & Nightlife
- Drinking & Nightlife
- Cafe

Entertainment
- Entertainment

Shopping
- Shopping

Information
- Bank
- Embassy/Consulate
- Hospital/Medical
- Internet
- Police
- Post Office
- Telephone
- Toilet
- Tourist Information
- Other Information

Geographic
- Beach
- Gate
- Hut/Shelter
- Lighthouse
- Lookout
- Mountain/Volcano
- Oasis
- Park
- Pass
- Picnic Area
- Waterfall

Population
- Capital (National)
- Capital (State/Province)
- City/Large Town
- Town/Village

Transport
- Airport
- Border crossing
- Bus
- Cable car/Funicular
- Cycling
- Ferry
- Metro station
- Monorail
- Parking
- Petrol station
- Subway station
- Taxi
- Train station/Railway
- Tram
- Underground station
- Other Transport

Routes
- Tollway
- Freeway
- Primary
- Secondary
- Tertiary
- Lane
- Unsealed road
- Road under construction
- Plaza/Mall
- Steps
- Tunnel
- Pedestrian overpass
- Walking Tour
- Walking Tour detour
- Path/Walking Trail

Boundaries
- International
- State/Province
- Disputed
- Regional/Suburb
- Marine Park
- Cliff
- Wall

Hydrography
- River, Creek
- Intermittent River
- Canal
- Water
- Dry/Salt/Intermittent Lake
- Reef

Areas
- Airport/Runway
- Beach/Desert
- Cemetery (Christian)
- Cemetery (Other)
- Glacier
- Mudflat
- Park/Forest
- Sight (Building)
- Sportsground
- Swamp/Mangrove

Note: Not all symbols displayed above appear on the maps in this book

Samantha Forge
Christchurch & Canterbury, Dunedin & Otago Samantha became hooked on travel at the age of 17, when she arrived in London with an overstuffed backpack and a copy of LP's *Europe on a Shoestring*. After a stint in Paris, she moved back to Australia to work as an editor in LP's Melbourne office. Eventually, however, her wanderlust got the better of her, and she now works as a freelance writer and editor.

Anita Isalska
Fiordland & Southland, West Coast (South Island) Anita is a travel journalist, editor and copywriter whose work for Lonely Planet has taken her from Greek beach towns to Malaysian jungles. After several merry years as an in-house editor and writer – with a few of them in Lonely Planet's London office – Anita now works freelance between the UK, Australia and any Balkan guesthouse with a good wi-fi connection. Anita writes about travel, food and culture for a host of websites and magazines. Read her stuff on www.anitaisalska.com.

Sofia Levin
Taranaki & Whanganui, Taupo & the Ruapehu Region Sofia is a Melbourne-based journalist with an insatiable appetite for food and travel. A regular contributor to Lonely Planet, Fairfax newspapers and a range of magazines, she has been referred to as "one of Melbourne's most influential and creative social media personalities" by Tourism Victoria. When she's not travelling, Sofia runs Word Salad – a social media and copywriting business established in 2012 – and spreads smiles with her Insta-famous toy poodle, @lifeofjinkee. Follow her adventures at @sofiaklevin.

OUR STORY

A beat-up old car, a few dollars in the pocket and a sense of adventure. In 1972 that's all Tony and Maureen Wheeler needed for the trip of a lifetime – across Europe and Asia overland to Australia. It took several months, and at the end – broke but inspired – they sat at their kitchen table writing and stapling together their first travel guide, *Across Asia on the Cheap*. Within a week they'd sold 1500 copies. Lonely Planet was born.

Today, Lonely Planet has offices in Franklin, London, Melbourne, Oakland, Dublin, Beijing and Delhi, with more than 600 staff and writers. We share Tony's belief that 'a great guidebook should do three things: inform, educate and amuse'.

OUR WRITERS

Charles Rawlings-Way

Charles is a veteran travel, food and music writer who has penned 30-something titles for Lonely Planet – including guides to Singapore, Tonga, Toronto, Sydney, Tasmania, New Zealand, the South Pacific and Australia – and numerous articles. After dabbling in the dark arts of architecture, cartography, project management and busking for some years, Charles hit the road for LP in 2005 and hasn't stopped travelling since.

Brett Atkinson

Auckland, Waikato & the Coromandel Peninsula, East Coast (North Island), Marlborough & Nelson Brett is based in Auckland but frequently on the road for Lonely Planet. He's a full-time travel and food writer and is featured regularly on the Lonely Planet website, and in newspapers, magazines and websites across New Zealand and Australia. Craft beer and street food are Brett's favourite reasons to explore places. Since becoming a Lonely Planet author in 2005, Brett has covered areas as diverse as Vietnam, Sri Lanka, the Czech Republic, Morocco, California and the South Pacific.

Andrew Bain

Queenstown & Wanaka Andrew's writing and photography feature in magazines and newspapers around the world, and his writing has won multiple awards, including best adventure story and best Australian story (three times) from the Australian Society of Travel Writers. He was formerly commissioning editor of Lonely Planet's outdoor adventure series of titles, and is the author of *Headwinds*, the story of his 20,000-kilometre cycling journey around Australia, and Lonely Planet's *A Year of Adventures*. His musings can be found at www.adventurebeforeavarice.com.

Peter Dragicevich

Bay of Islands & Northland, Rotorua & the Bay of Plenty, Wellington Region After a successful career in niche newspaper and magazine publishing, both in his native New Zealand and in Australia, Peter finally gave into Kiwi wanderlust, giving up staff jobs to chase his diverse roots around much of Europe. Over the last decade he's written dozens of guidebooks for Lonely Planet on an oddly disparate collection of countries, all of which he's come to love. He once again calls Auckland his home – although his current nomadic existence means he's often elsewhere.

OVER PAGE MORE WRITERS

Published by Lonely Planet Global Limited
CRN 554153
19th edition – Sep 2018
ISBN 978 1 78657 079 6
© Lonely Planet 2018   Photographs © as indicated 2018
10 9 8 7 6 5 4 3 2 1
Printed in Singapore

Although the authors and Lonely Planet have taken all reasonable care in preparing this book, we make no warranty about the accuracy or completeness of its content and, to the maximum extent permitted, disclaim all liability arising from its use.